Encyclopedia of
Nordic Crime Fiction

*Works and Authors of Denmark,
Finland, Iceland, Norway and
Sweden Since 1967*

Mitzi M. Brunsdale

McFarland & Company, Inc., Publishers
Jefferson, North Carolina

ISBN (print) 978-0-7864-7536-0
ISBN (ebook) 978-1-4766-2277-4

LIBRARY OF CONGRESS CATALOGUING-IN-PUBLICATION DATA

BRITISH LIBRARY CATALOGUING DATA ARE AVAILABLE

Front cover images © iStock/Thinkstock

Printed in the United States of America

McFarland & Company, Inc., Publishers
Box 611, Jefferson, North Carolina 28640
www.mcfarlandpub.com

In loving memory of Drake,
my constant companion through this work,
and my dear, dear friend.

TABLE OF CONTENTS

ACKNOWLEDGMENTS

My thanks to Dale Nelson for his appreciation of Nordic literature and his contributions of research materials; to Dr. Hiram Drache and Dr. Verlyn Anderson for their encouragement and suggestions; to Anne Jones, yet again for her blessedly sound sense; to Ann Zavoral for generously promoting the cause of Nordic crime literature; to my Fargo friends Monica and Betty and Judie, and Mecca Chapter, O.E.S., for their caring support; to my family for their understanding and help, especially Margaret and Norbert, and Jean and Maureen; and most of all, with love, to John, who provided me such an exquisite working environment for this large project.

PREFACE

As a long-time American book critic, several years ago I was struck by the scope, quality, and diversity of the crime fiction emerging since 1967 from the Nordic countries—Sweden, Norway, Denmark, Iceland, and Finland. I also saw a pattern beginning to emerge, an ominous foreshadowing of totalitarianism reborn. The native Nordic populations are aging and leaving the labor market while immigration soars, encouraged by bureaucratic policies, often tainted by corruption, that have promoted substantial increases in immigration-related bureaucracy that until recently has seemed unable or unwilling to undertake effective integration programs. As a result, both skilled and unskilled adult asylum-seekers from the former Soviet bloc countries and the Moslem Third World and their children who grow up in the Nordic countries often do not successfully assimilate or join the work force. Taxes, crime rates, and racial tensions are adversely affecting the native Nordic populations, increasing the appeal of neo–Nazi groups, rapidly growing in political influence in the Nordic nations as well as across Europe. Because I believe Nordic crime fiction, which largely deals with the serious societal problems resulting from originally well-intentioned Nordic welfare state policies now proving problematic, has enormous relevance to today's dangerous world, I undertook this project to bring the magnitude and importance of Nordic crime literature to English-speaking readers.

At first I had little idea of the impressive amount of crime fiction involved and of the intricate historical-cultural relationships underlying it in each country, though professionally as a comparatist I have always been fascinated by the literature of the North. My first published scholarly article treated Ibsen's *Rosmersholm;* my first national conference paper dealt with correspondences between Ibsen's *Vikings at Helgeland* and *Hedda Gabler* and D.H. Lawrence's use of the Northern myth of Brynhild; and I have written extensively on Sigrid Undset, Norway's only female Nobel Prize winner, including a book-length literary biography, *Sigrid Undset: Chronicler of Norway.*

I am personally acquainted with Nordic culture, too. Though I have not one drop of Scandinavian blood, I have lived almost all of my life in eastern North Dakota, home to many descendants of the Norwegian "newcomers" who began arriving in the late 1800s. I know Icelandic descendants who boast that their women are the most beautiful in the world, because their ancient ancestors stole only the loveliest Irish women to bring home. Many Swedish descendents live in nearby Minnesota, where Finns celebrate St. Urho's Day and Danish smorgasbords and pastries abound. Just across the Red River from our Fargo home a new museum houses the *Hjemkomst,* a replica Viking longship that sailed to Norway a few years ago; my Labrador retriever came from Sweden; two of our daughters attended St. Olaf College in Northfield, Minnesota, and devoutly make *lefse* every winter; my husband is a six-foot-three spiritual son of the Vikings; and his father's family taught me to bake *sandbakkelse* and *Berliner kranser* and *krumkake* (in Traill County called *strul*), like the treats provided every *Syttende Mai* (Norwegian Independence Day) in certain small-town banks, served by women wearing the authentic *bunad* and *sølje* (dress and jewelry) of their forefathers' Norwegian home regions. I draw the line at *lutefisk,* lye-soaked cod that a Swedish friend claimed forced her to leave Scandinavia.

1

All those colorful experiences, however, reflect the Scandinavia of old, not today's Nordic countries, whose serene surfaces often place them at the top of "world's happiest countries" lists but conceal roiling swells of threatening social, economic, and political issues that animate the plots of their contemporary crime fiction. Today's torrent of Nordic crime novels, even in translation, with many being made into movies and television series, demonstrates the dramatic extent and significance of this literary phenomenon. I strongly believe Americans need to pay attention to these ill tidings from the North.

INTRODUCTION

You hold a mirror to crime to see what's happening in society.
—Henning Mankell

We do not know enough, and we should know far more about Nordic crime fiction, which for a long time was dismissed in their home countries as popular entertainment not worthy of the attention that mainstream works received. Today the achievements of Nordic crime fiction authors deserve as much, if not more, attention as "serious" novels do, not only by native-speaker scholars but by general readers in translation, to ponder the profound social, political, economic, and cultural issues they present. Each Nordic country's crime fiction is presented here separately, headed by an epigraph from its earliest literature: for Sweden, Norway, Denmark, and Iceland, the *Hávamál;* and for Finland, the *Kalevala.* Each country's section contains an introductory essay placing the development of its crime fiction in its historical-cultural context; lists of that country's major awards for crime fiction; a parallel chronology of the country's major literary-cultural events and those of the world; an alphabetical listing of authors whose crime fiction mainly appears after 1967 with brief essays analyzing their major crime fiction; lists of selected works set in that country by non-native authors, where applicable; and a Works Cited listing. The 1967 publication in English translation of the first Sjöwall-Wahlöö Martin Beck novel *Rosanna* marks the beginning of the contemporary explosion of "Nordic *noir*" fiction.

Today the term "Nordic" is used to indicate the five north European countries collectively, while "Scandinavian" generally refers to Norway, Sweden, and Denmark, and usually includes Iceland. Finland's Finno-Ugric language and the nation's complicated historical relationship with Russia set it apart from its neighbors which share the Germanic roots of their languages and traditions. In the discussion below, however, "Nordic" and "Scandinavian" may be used interchangeably, especially in quoted material, as is still done in general non-professional usage.

With an eye to the needs of today's general non–Nordic readers, I have assembled historical and cultural material germane to the development of crime fiction for each country in each introductory essay, placing its crime fiction in its historical-cultural context and presenting the main social, cultural, historical, political and economic issues being explored by today's crime fiction writers. While every Nordic author may not directly attach praise or blame to societal institutions in his or her fiction, many do, especially with regard to the implementation, development, and functioning of the *Folkhemmet* (welfare state) concept in their countries and its impact on and/or relationship to racism and immigration-related issues; crime and terrorism; domestic violence; drug and alcohol abuse; human trafficking; local and international gang activity; and the alarming rise of neo–Nazism, apparently fueled by the individual welfare states' immigration policies dating chiefly from the previous century and the relation of present-day immigration to sharp increases in criminal activity.

The ramifications of a central traumatic national event or chain of events in each country are also explored where relevant to the works of individual authors, both in each introductory essay and in his or her specific entry. These "loss of innocence" historical events include for Sweden, the 1986 assassination of Prime Minister Olof Palme ; for Norway, the 2011 terrorist massacre carried out by Anders Breivik; for Denmark, the immigration crisis leading to the 2014 terrorist attacks in Copenhagen; for Iceland the near-disastrous 2008 financial "Crash"; and for Finland, its costly 20th century wars and its complex relationship with Russia and Russians.

In the alphabetical lists of each country's crime fiction authors publishing mainly from 1967 to 2014, each author's entry contains available basic biographical information, including his or her birth date (and death date where applicable), residence(s), and occupation(s). An analytical essay with coverage appropriate to the significance of each author's work includes when possible his or her own descriptions of personal literary aims and working method(s) as well as critical opinions from reliable Nordic and worldwide sources. Also provided are lists of each author's crime fiction, selected where appropriate; major awards received; and a website if available. English renditions of titles of works which have not yet been translated appear in quotation marks and may not reflect later published English titles. English titles of translated published works appear in italics, with names of translators and dates of published translations. A separate Works Cited list supports each country's section.

Beginning in the late 1960s, Swedish Marxist authors Maj Sjöwall and Per Wahlöö in their Martin Beck police detective series. *The Story of a Crime,* denounced their Swedish welfare state government as too capitalistic and thus failing to provide an adequate state-supported environment for its citizens. Most Nordic crime fiction since has addressed sociopolitical issues through the crime fiction subgenre of the police procedural, inspired for many authors by American Ed McBain's 87th Precinct series and European Georges Simenon's Inspector Maigret novels. The resulting mode of crime fiction is often described by literary critics as "Nordic *noir*," exhibiting a wide range of opinions vis-à-vis the welfare state principle, ranging from extreme leftist Marxist and Trotskyite stances to conservative far-rightist views. Other Nordic authors choose simply to present observations of societal and emotional tensions and like Ibsen, require readers to make up their own minds. The Nordic police procedural mode remains popular, although in the new century Nordic writers are beginning to explore vital issues through the vehicle of the psychological thriller and even more experimental forms.

Foreign language–challenged American readers should remember, too, that they are not reading exactly the same works as their Nordic authors originally wrote. Many translators are highly skilled, but some are producing pedestrian work from Nordic texts, whose problems in translation, as British critic Barry Forshaw points out in *Death in a Cold Climate,* differ subtly from those of other languages. For readers chiefly looking for plot-driven crime novels, however, the difference may not matter, since according to translator Sarah Death, "the appeal remains the same ... the lure of the (slightly) exotic, plus a vague sense of schadenfreude [no italics in original] that the wheels are coming off the utopian welfare-state bus" (quoted in *Death in a Cold Climate* 8).

In confronting painful human issues in their crime fiction, most Nordic protagonists, both male and female, display qualities handed down to them from their nations' earliest literary art, for Iceland, Norway, Sweden, and Denmark the pagan Germanic mythic tales appearing in the *Poetic Edda*; especially for Iceland, the Sagas of the Icelanders and the *Prose Edda*; and for Finland the collection of native narrative poems known as the *Kalevala,* which harks back to pre–Christian times.

Modern Nordic crime fiction heroes, like their mythic literary ancestors, often are trapped in the crushing coils of societal strictures attempting, like the World Serpent that gnaws at the roots of the World Tree Yggdrasil, to choke off the demands of the heroes' consciences. The villains those heroes battle often are vicious giants wielding powerful near-superhuman weapons conferred on them by superior and often corrupt governmental, financial, or industrial forces; or malignant trolls rising up out of the heroes' own fears and compulsions. In a world apparently abandoning Christian belief and possibly approaching a flaming Ragnarok where gods and men alike will perish, men and women heroes of today's Nordic crime fiction, seeking like their ancient heroes to conquer evil and restore justice, almost always fear and often know, "this is a battle we can't win, but ... we have to fight to the end" (Edwardson 134). All that can matter, all that is proving fascinating to so many readers around the world, is the courage with which they face their fates.

Most of today's Nordic *noir* fiction thus conveys the stern traditions of the people of the north who live much of their lives in cold and darkness, their bleak themes swooping into our modern lives through Thought and Memory, the raven-messengers of the old god Odin, who could confer both poetic inspiration and *berserker* madness. These stories, forcing us to consider whether doing evil to ostensibly produce good—and what is "good"?—is ever defensible, will definitively be analyzed by future literary historians possessing the essential perspective of years, not by this contemporary snapshot of a time when Nordic *noir* crime authors are still writing and developing. I hope, though, I have provided scholars to come a useful springboard and, more important, that I have given today's readers matter for reflection, perhaps even helping them question the potentially lethal societal and political paths we, following our northern cousins, are treading.

An abbreviated version of the above Introduction was published in the winter 2014–2015 issue of Mystery Readers Journal, *with all rights reserved.*

DENMARK

A guest thinks him witty who mocks at a guest
and runs from his wrath away;
but none can be sure who jests at a meal
that he makes not fun among foes.
—*Hávamál*, The Words of Odin the High One,
Wisdom for Wanderers and Counsel to Guests, 31

The Cultural Context of Danish Crime Fiction

Denmark, the southernmost of the Nordic countries, is also considered the most cosmopolitan nation of Scandinavia. Its five and a half million people occupy about sixteen and a half thousand square miles of low-lying basically agricultural land, although since the end of World War II Denmark has been rapidly expanding its industrial base. Denmark has a long tradition of cosmopolitanism; to a greater extent than in any other of its Nordic neighbors, French, German, English and Italian literary fashions "have in varying degrees regularly made their way to Denmark" (Mitchell 9), and though slower than the other Nordic nations to produce contemporary crime fiction, Denmark now is beginning to realize its own special variations of the genre, including "more outward-looking, Le Carré–like spy fiction, à la Leif Davidsen" as well as intricate psychological thrillers by Jussi Adler-Olsen and others, and Peter Høeg's remarkable and difficult to classify *Smilla's Sense of Snow*, "an important American breakthrough" (Kachka). The special flavors of Danish crime fiction have developed through the Danish literary heritage, which reflects the nation's domination in the late Middle Ages of extensive areas of northern Europe, the achievements of internationally recognized Danish authors and thinkers during Denmark's Golden Age, 1800 to 1850, and the nation's contemporary prosperity and societal satisfaction.

Often described by non–Danes as the happiest people in the world, Danes today "coolly regard themselves as blessed" (Forshaw 157), an opinion apparently bolstered by the low Danish homicide rate, between 2006 and 2008 only 12.2 murders per million people (Kachka). That fact, coupled with the Danes' acknowledged personal satisfaction with their lives, may have slowed the development of Denmark's contemporary crime fiction, as compared to the production of crime fiction in the other Nordic countries, particularly Sweden, but the Danish version of the genre is currently gathering momentum. One of the most evident special characteristics that have grown out of Denmark's historical and cultural heritage is the Danish "unlikely combination of dark fiction and fairy tales … both *Hamlet* and *The Little Mermaid*" (Kachka). The dark side seems to prevail in the *CNN Travel* listing of the Danes' capital city as second in their 2013 "9 Top Cities for 'Detective Travel,'" primarily because of "three twisty seasons of [the] TV drama *The Killing*, where Copenhagen appears as 'dark, cold, perpetually overhung with rain clouds, riddled with corruption and littered with corpses,' where Detective Inspector Sarah Lund, 'an obsessive near-psychopath'" wearing $370 Faroe Island sweaters, relentlessly pursues suspects with an occasional spot of relief at the Holberg No. 19 Café on Holbergsgade, also a favorite stop for *The Killing's* star, Sophie Gråbøl (Neild).

Denmark dominated northern Europe during the Middle Ages, even ruling England by 1016. Three and a half centuries later the Kalmar Union brought Sweden and Norway under the rule of Denmark's Queen Margaret I, and while Sweden broke away from that union in 1523, Denmark ruled Norway until 1814, imposing Danish standards and conventions on the Norwegian culture and language. Denmark's reversals because of the Thirty Years' War, 1618–1648, and its conflict with Sweden, 1657–1660, diminished Danish prestige in Europe, which further deteriorated with the loss of Norway to Sweden in 1814 and the loss of Schleswig-Holstein in 1864, due to Denmark's defeat by Prussia and Austria.

The earliest Danish literature was the work of Denmark's pagan Vikings who savaged Europe from the ninth to eleventh centuries. It consisted of Germanic poems that celebrated the exploits of kings and warriors on runestones chiseled from ca. AD 200 until the Danes were Christianized in the tenth century. Saxo Grammaticus' eleventh-century *Gesta Danorum*, the keystone of medieval Danish literature, offers significant information on Scandinavian myths and legends, the author's reflections on his times, and the tragic murder-filled tale of Prince Amlietus, the model for Shakespeare's Hamlet. Danish medieval literature also included popular ballads, recorded in the sixteenth century by aristocratic ladies. During the subsequent Lutheran Reformation, religious texts, especially the Danish translation of the Bible, dominated Danish literary efforts. The Old Testament translation by Hans Tausen, the "Danish Luther," was published in Magdeburg, Germany, in 1535, and though Tausen was not the prolific author Martin Luther was, Tausen and his contemporaries did help mold a secular language beyond the influence of the Church, "a prerequisite for the growth of popular literature" (Mitchell 51).

For over a century after Tausen, with the exception of its folklore, "Danish literature had little independent national existence" because Danish literary works drew heavily on French and English, and later German, models until the mid–1800s, when the new vernacular European literatures began to appear, born of a secular culture that had been breaking away from ecclesiastical domination since the Reformation (Mitchell 75). Denmark's new literature reflected trends from the outside world, since Danish readers and authors were becoming familiar with works like Montesquieu's *Lettres Persanes*, Defoe's *Robinson Crusoe*, and Swift's *Gulliver's Travels*. This "transfusion of newer French and English currents" (Mitchell 77) came to Denmark chiefly through the highly versatile and prolific "founding father" of Danish literature, Ludwig Holberg, 1684–1754. Holberg wrote philosophical treatises and historical works, but he is best known for initiating Denmark's professional drama. Holberg's twenty-five satiric comedies rank him in the history of European comedy below only Aristophanes, Plautus, Shakespeare, and Molière (Mitchell 80). Holberg incorporated a kind of humor recognized today as typically Danish into his plays, all written between 1722 and 1728 during the Enlightenment, a period of revolutionary achievements in science, philosophy, politics, and culture that swept away the medieval worldview and ushered in the modern Western world. After new scientific discoveries began to explain the workings of the natural world, "philosophy" abandoned its role as a "handmaiden of theology" and became "an independent force with the power and authority to challenge the old and construct the new," fostering the age's expectation that "philosophy (in this broad sense) would dramatically improve human life" (*Stanford Encyclopedia of Philosophy*).

Holberg's international perspective flowered in philosophical works like his *Epistles*, which like Montaigne's *Essays* display both skepticism and ironic humor. Holberg was then invited to write comedies for the new Danish national theatre, which opened on September 23, 1722, with

Molière's *The Miser*, followed two days later by Holberg's *The Political Thinker*. Holberg shared Molière's implicit belief in the power of common sense, so like Molière, Holberg created characters who each exhibit an obsessive trait carried out into absurdity, a technique discernible in a modern adaptation in Danish crime author Jussi Adler-Olsen's novels. Holberg also added elements of desperation or even momentary insanity to his characters' personalities, developed from broad comic types he had seen in Italian *commedia dell'arte* troupes performing in Paris. He added characteristics from Danish persons he had observed in Copenhagen to stereotypical characters like the foolish old man, the scheming servant, the callow young lovers, and so forth.

For all the comic foibles he portrayed on stage, Holberg also consistently maintained a strong moral purpose. His comedies unveil human folly and make audiences laugh at it and themselves, like the antics of a farmer's son in Holberg's *Erasmus Montanus*, who after graduating from college pompously forces his newly "educated" status on his family and neighbors. Holberg's social-satire comedies both appealed to and reinforced the peculiarly quirky Danish sense of humor, so much a part of the national character that Holberg's fellow Dane Georg Brandes later declared, "He who does not understand a joke ... does not understand Danish," an observation that holds true in reading Denmark's contemporary crime fiction.

As non–Danes are still discovering, however, Danish jokes can be dark and even twisted, recalling the ominous element of madness Holberg often incorporated into his comedies. Today a reader observes in the "cranky flier" website, "It's cold and dark, for much of the time [in Denmark]. So you know it has to be their sense of humor that gets them through until summer." That Danish humor can often be disturbingly *noir*. The "cranky flier" website also notes that a Danish media conglomerate created a popular internet game, "Dash 'n' Crash," named for the Scandinavian airline SAS's short-hop Dash 8 Q400 aircraft, reputedly almost impossible to land without its nose gear either collapsing or falling off (crankyflier.com). An American Fulbright scholar who studied at the University of Esbjerg went further, explaining he had discovered that Danes easily can make sensitive subjects, like one's death, into something funny: during an outing interrupted by a ferocious wind storm, his Danish friends roared with laughter when he was almost impaled by a flying patio umbrella stake (Brunson). Danish humor even produced an international shock wave at the 2012 Cannes film festival when at a news conference the famous Danish film director Lars von Trier informed assembled journalists that he was a Nazi. Though in the past von Trier had won many awards at Cannes, officials there immediately declared him *persona non grata*. Von Trier later tried to explain to the Israeli publication *Haaretz* that he had been joking, claiming he had been misunderstood because of the "untranslatable nature of Danish humor" and declaring that he would never make public comments again (Harrison).

Full of such Danish humor, Ludwig Holberg's comedies are still widely taught in Danish schools and their quirky spirit pervades much modern Danish literature, including Danish crime fiction. Maja Heid, writing for Denmark's official website, called her country's humor "cozy racism," claiming that its "dark and twisted" nature is intrinsic to Danish culture: "Danes relay heavily on sarcasm and irony.... [with] sensibilities ... [that] are indispensable to our daily life." She observed that Danes "push things to the limit," and while they can tone down this tendency in the presence of non–Danes, "The truly cruel, dark jokes are reserved ... for fellow countrymen," so that among Danish friends, "no subject is taboo" (Heid, quoted in Garrison). Holberg's social satire echoes down the years into the work of contemporary Danish crime authors, giving their fiction a distinctive dark dimension which the English-speaking world is now discovering, notably in Jussi Adler-Olsen's Department Q crime novel series and even in the Danish television series *The Killing*, currently popular in the United Kingdom.

The Golden Age

The importation of German Romanticism into Denmark, linking nature, history, and humankind, produced Denmark's Golden Age of Literature, roughly 1800 to 1850. The period formally opened in 1803 with the _Poems_ of Adam Oehlenschläger, 1779–1850, quickly followed by the fairy tales of Hans Christian Andersen, 1805–1875; the educational reforms and hymns of Nikolai Grundtvig, 1783–1872; and the existentialist philosophy of Søren Kierkegaard, 1813–1855. In 1800, the University of Copenhagen foreshadowed the future course of Danish literature by posing a thought-provoking question as the subject of an essay competition: Should Old Norse mythology be introduced into literature rather than the traditional classical mythology? A proponent of classicism won first place in the contest, but young Oehlenschläger, pleading eloquently for the use of Old Norse mythology, took second place (Mitchell 103). Using the Old Norse myths, Oehlenschläger's _Poems_ soon reinvigorated Danish poetic language, at the same time investing it with Romantic heightened emotion and elevation of the senses above the intellect.

According to Johan de Mylius in the _Gyldendal Leksikon_, Oehlenschläger's 1807 _Nordic Poems_ turned Old Norse myth and legend into "a living source of inspiration" for a broad range of Danish literature and culture in both historical dramas and psychological plays. That ancient pagan mythology, much of which is described in Saxo Grammaticus' _Gesta Danorum_, centered on the concept of Yggdrasil, the ash tree of the universe; gods and goddesses inhabited its branches, constantly warring with monsters and giants who threatened the world, while human beings lived on its trunk, visited by the deities and preyed upon by evil beings from below, and a monstrous serpent and a host of lesser snakes gnawed continuously at its roots. In this pagan belief system, eventually the serpents gnawing at its roots would cause Yggdrasil to fall, all once-fettered monsters would break loose, gods and men alike would perish, and fire would consume the earth. In the face of that inevitable doom, men of the pagan North held "a firm sense of values and certain intense loyalties" (Davidson 27). The northern myths that Oehlenschläger revitalized and made a vital component of Danish culture thus celebrated "a spirit of heroic resignation" that taught despite life's slings and arrows, "courage, adventure, and the wonders of life are matters for thankfulness" to be savored while life lasts. The "great gifts" of those pagan Germanic gods "were readiness to face the world as it was, the luck that sustains men in tight places, and the opportunity to win that glory which alone can outlive death" (Davidson 218). Today's Danish fictional detectives face a life in a country proving not to be the ideal society Danes who created their celebrated welfare state had hoped. These detectives need all the luck they can get in the tight spots caused by organized crime, drug-related issues, and political and cultural corruption; and too often they fail to receive any recognition, let alone thanks or glory to allow them to be remembered.

As Oehlenschläger was reshaping Danish poetry, Hans Christian Andersen was becoming internationally famous for his 156 fairy tales. A dozen of them derive from folk tales and legends he heard as a child, like "The Wild Swans," while some contain elements of Danish history and still others themes from foreign literature, like "The Elf of the Rose," which he borrowed from one of Boccaccio's novels, but most sprang from Andersen's own fertile imagination (Booss xx). After his father's death and his mother's remarriage, Andersen experienced an unhappy poverty-stricken youth; he later claimed that his years at school were the darkest and bitterest of his whole life because his classmates bullied him and his teachers sent him into depression by discouraging him from writing. He then tried and failed at acting and singing and playwriting, and only later, having often experienced the pangs of unrequited love, he began to produce his fairy tales. His first short story appeared in 1829, and in 1833 a small travel grant allowed him to spend time in various European cities, providing cosmopolitan experiences that give his fiction universality.

The first volume of Andersen's *Fairy Tales*, some based on stories he had heard as a child, appeared in 1835, 1836, and 1837 installments, but it did not sell well because of difficulties in translating his unique combination of humor and dark pathos (http://www.hcandersen-homepage.dk). Four more of Andersen's stories appeared in 1838 in *Fairy Tales Told for Children*, and at last in 1845 four different columns of translations brought him international acclaim. The British periodical *Athenaeum* for February 1846 trumpeted, "This is a book full of life and fancy, a book for grandfathers no less than grandchildren, not a word of which will be skipped by those who have it once in hand." Andersen continued to write fairy stories until 1872, when he began to suffer from the liver cancer that took his life in 1875.

In Andersen's old age, though he had achieved enormous fame with his fairy tales which he often read aloud to Denmark's king, he poignantly remarked, "I have imagined so much and had so little" (quoted in Booss xxi). Andersen's tendency to identify himself with his leading characters, portraying in them his own fears and anguish, often appears in his letters and autobiographical writings, where, thirsting lifelong for praise and fame, he created a myth of himself as "the ugly duckling," a self-portrait that seems to have been popularly accepted as his own symbol for his life, despite the popularity of his fairy tales and the generous support he received from various patrons, including the Danish royal family (Mitchell 154).

Later authors of children's stories like Beatrix Potter and A.A. Milne further developed Andersen's gentle technique of bringing toys to life and allowing animals to display charming human traits, but even more important, the darker elements and pathos of Andersen's stories like "The Snow Queen," "The Little Mermaid," and "The Little Match Girl" have inspired both mainstream and science fiction and fantasy authors of other countries, like Joan D. Vinge's "The Snow Queen," Jane Gardam's "The Pangs of Love," and Joyce Carol Oates's "You, Little Match Girl." Fictional Danish detectives, especially female protagonists like Sara Blædel's Detective Inspector Louise Rick, often possess these chiaroscuro character traits seemingly to a greater extent than their counterparts in the other Nordic crime literatures do.

The pathos that Andersen drew from his own experience of poverty and from his observation of the plight of Denmark's poor, echoes today in fictional female figures like Louise Rick and inveterate do-gooder Red Cross nurse Nina Borg, who debuted in *The Boy in the Suitcase* by Lene Kaaberbøl and Agnete Friis. Such social tensions helped to inspire the Danish nineteenth-century internal reforms that transformed Denmark's impoverished peasantry into the most prosperous small farmers in Europe. Nikolai Grundtvik, a wide-ranging church leader and educator, played a significant role in those reforms. Grundtvik contributed significantly to the reawakening of interest in Scandinavian antiquity, to the Danish hymnbook, and to Denmark's constitution, its educational system, and its historiography. While Grundtvik's contemporary Søren Kierkegaard is better known abroad, "Grundtvik exceeds Kierkegaard as an influence on daily life and thought in Denmark" (Mitchell 126). Grundtvik bolstered Danish nationalism by retelling the pagan Scandinavian myths in his *Northern Mythology*, 1808, and his 1809 drama *The Fall of the Heroic Life of the North*. Grundtvik also wrote or translated about 1,500 hymns which dramatically transformed Danish Lutheran church services by substituting the hymns of national poets for the more somber orthodox Lutheran church music of the time. As an educator, Grundtvik's most significant achievement was the founding of the Danish folk high school movement, creating adult educational institutions which brought increased religious dedication and patriotism to young Danish adults, allowing them "to appreciate their country's culture, its history and its literature." Grundtvik thus substantially contributed to making Denmark "the highly literary country it is today" (Mitchell 134).

While Oehlenschläger, Andersen, and Grundtvik remain the towering figures of Denmark's literary Golden Age, "an unsuccessful clergyman, a hapless husband, and an incompetent business man" but an incomparable storyteller (Mitchell 120) distantly related to Martin Luther, Steen Steensen Blicher, 1782–1848, created the first Danish crime story and possibly the first crime novel (technically a novella) in European literature, *The Parson of Vejlby* (*Proesten i Vejlby*). Blicher based the work on the actual 1625 case of Soren Jensen Quist, a Danish clergyman executed for a murder he did not commit. *The Parson of Vejlby* was published in 1829, two years before Norway's Mauritz Hansen's *The Murder of Engineer Roolfsen* and four years before Edgar Allan Poe's *The Murders in the Rue Morgue*. *The Parson of Vejlby* also pioneered the device of the unreliable first-person narrator. In 2006, *The Parson of Vejlby* was placed in the Danish *Kulturkanon*, making it one of only ten Order of Merit novels in Danish literature, and it has also been made into a modern film.

Denmark's most famous philosopher, Søren Kierkegaard, not well known beyond Denmark until the twentieth century, is considered the father of religious existentialism, which has exerted enormous influence on Protestant theology and the literary culture of Europe and the United States. As an intense critic of idealist thinkers like Goethe, Schlegel, and Hans Christian Andersen, Kierkegaard addressed the issue of how one lives one's life by prioritizing concrete human reality over abstract thinking and highlighting the importance of personal choice and absolute adherence to one's commitment. Kierkegaard's religious writings, especially *Works of Love*, 1817, and *Training in Christianity*, 1850, and his better known philosophical works *Either/Or*, 1843, and *Stages on Life's Way*, 1845, emphasize faith over reason. Kierkegaard's opposition to the concept of Christianity as a state religion with respect to the established Church of Denmark helped bring about changes in its administration by 1855. One such change, dramatic at that time, allowed church members to attend the ministry of any clergyman, not just the clergyman whose parishioners they were. In 1857, debates arose regarding the possibility of adopting a constitution for the Church of Denmark (Grundtvik opposed having any written rules for the church at all), and again in response to Kierkegaard's criticism, the Danish church officially admitted that problems and corruption did exist.

In his philosophical works, too, Kierkegaard broke new ground, exploring the emotions of individuals when faced with serious life choices (Hong 131). Kierkegaard saw the stages of human existence as an "existential dialectic" progressing from the aesthetic, first through the ethical, and then the religious, in the process becoming increasingly aware of one's relationship to God. Kierkegaard believed that such awareness would lead to despair when the individual realized the antithesis between temporal existence and eternal truth. Therefore human reason could not bring one to the final "religious" stage; only a willing "leap of faith" beyond rational thought could do so. The existential approach increases one's awareness of God, but if one cannot make the "leap of faith" that inability intensifies despair at not being able to achieve eternal truth. Such despair often imposes the inner conflicts in which today's protagonists of Danish crime fiction find themselves.

Kierkegaard's fellow Dane Georg Brandes was the first academic to draw attention to Kierkegaard's works; Brandes lectured on them in Copenhagen and published the first book on Kierkegaard's life and theories in 1879. In an 1888 letter to the German philosopher Friedrich Nietzsche, Brandes hailed Kierkegaard as "one of the profoundest psychologists to be met with anywhere" (Brandes, *Reminiscences* 108). Western thinkers soon began to agree. By 1900, Kierkegaard's publications on existentialism had been translated into the major European languages, and a half century later they were powerfully influencing Western culture through the works of many world-famous authors, theologians, and philosophers who drew their fundamental concepts from Kierkegaard, including Simone de Beauvoir, Niels Bohr, Albert Camus, Reinhold

Niebuhr, Jean-Paul Sartre, Thomas Merton, and Miguel de Unamuno. Karl Popper even claimed that Kierkegaard was "the great reformer of Christian ethics, who exposed the official Christian morality of his day as un–Christian and anti-humanitarian hypocrisy" (Popper 131).

Increasing attention is currently being paid to Kierkegaard's work as inspiration for the contemporary "*Scandikrim*" wave of *noir* crime writing. This does not appear only in Scandinavia; Taylor University's Writer-in-Residence Thom Satterlee's debut crime novel *The Stages*, 2013, centers upon the mysterious fictional disappearance of a Kierkegaard manuscript and the death of the head of Copenhagen's Søren Kierkegaard Research Center. In a February 28, 2013, interview, Satterlee noted that his hero Daniel Peters, who has Asperger's Syndrome, is "both the mouthpiece for Kierkegaard and a contemporary likeness to him. Both men were loners, cared deeply about word-work, never married … and were considered off—outsiders—by others" (quoted in Bowman).

May 5, 2013, saw the bicentenary of Kierkegaard's birth celebrated with a public symposium, "Kierkegaard, the Uncanny and Nordic Noir," at University College London, which recently announced a new fully funded three-year Ph.D. fellowship sponsored by *Statens Kunstråds Litteraturudvalg* (the Danish Arts Council), beginning in October 2013. The fellowship's focus is a literary-sociological analysis of the reception and marketing of Danish crime literature in the context of the current popular and media interest in Danish culture. The May 5 symposium superimposed Kierkegaard's writings with the "contemporary and notoriously unsettling representation" of Copenhagen seen through the television series *The Killing*, "which won over the hearts and minds of the UK media and public." As a special feature of their Kierkegaard symposium, UCL's Centre for Advanced Spatial Analysis also provided a virtual tour of Copenhagen's fictional crime scenes on May 11, 2013 (Stougaard).

The Modern Breakthrough

Besides the influence of Kierkegaard's Christian existentialism, seen in the despair at human inability to achieve absolute truth that is today often reflected in Danish as well as other contemporary Nordic crime literature, the Scandinavian literary movement known as "The Modern Breakthrough" has strongly contributed realistic and naturalistic elements to "Nordic *noir*." Between 1865 and 1870, Georg Brandes, 1842–1927, generally considered the father of this movement, had encountered liberal European thinkers on visits to Italy, France, and England. He brought their ideas back to Denmark, where his 1871 lectures on "Main Currents in 19th Century Literature" marked the beginning of his lifelong crusade to modernize Danish literature by vigorously assaulting the Danish reluctance to accept new and foreign social and literary theories, especially realism and naturalism. "Brandes projected these issues on the Danish cultural landscape and aroused his countrymen to a new consciousness of foreign literature and to the European demand for a new literature" (Mitchell 173).

Brandes left Denmark in 1899 and settled in Berlin, where he became recognized as one of the leading literary critics of the time, but his radicalism eventually made living in Prussia unacceptable for him. Upon returning to Denmark in 1883, Brandes proclaimed, "'My ideals are the ideas of the intelligent in Europe,'" and insisted that literature should "'make problems a matter of debate'" (quoted in Mitchell 177). With these controversial statements, Brandes electrified a group of like-minded thinkers called "The Men of the Modern Breakthrough," which included notable Danish authors and poets as well as the Norwegian dramatist Henrik Ibsen. Brandes himself had coined the term "modern breakthrough," publicly criticizing romanticism, rigid sexual regulation, and the institution of marriage and the family. He also published penetrating critiques of contemporary poets and initiated radical reforms in both criticism and politics, shaping "a literary and spiritual renewal in Danish cultural life" (http://www.danmarkshistorien.dk) which emphasized a broad international outlook, a freer concept of sexuality and religion, and interest in such then-controversial scientific theories as Darwinism. Further, Brandes insisted that literature should bring problems into debate, paving the way for twentieth century (and later) Danish authors to address social issues through their dramas and fiction.

Brandes was highly acclaimed internationally for his 1887–1898 study of Shakespeare, translated into English by William Archer, which like all of Brandes' critical works was written in a distinctively brilliant, lucid, and approachable style. The American historian Will Durant placed Brandes' six-volume *Main Currents in Nineteenth-Century Literature*, 1906, among the hundred best books Durant recommended for education. In Brandes' later life he was a passionate proponent of the "great individual" as "the source of culture." He himself became one of the most influential figures in Danish culture, both celebrated by liberals as liberating Danish thought from repressive norms and hypocrisy and reviled by conservatives for his alleged immorality, lack of patriotism, and the kind of blasphemy demonstrated in a humorous but penetrating statement Brandes made in a 1888 letter to Friedrich Nietzsche: "It would be as impossible for me to attack Christianity as it would be impossible for me to attack werewolves."

In her Introduction to *Twentieth Century Danish Writers* (*DLB*, vol. 214), editor Marianne Stecher-Hansen observed that 1900 marked the arrival in Europe of a "distinctly modern worldview –incorporating artistic, intellectual, cultural, and scientific influences" that shaped Danish literature for nearly the whole twentieth century (xv). That worldview began the transformation of Danish society from a rural agrarian culture into a modern industrialized welfare state that since the 1980s has begun to change yet again, into a technological information society (xxi). In the first two decades of the twentieth century, this process manifested itself in Danish literature as democratization, with working-class and women writers entering the previously elitist Danish literary establishment.

During the early twentieth century, too, just when Kierkegaard's star was rising in the philosophical world, Brandes encouraged a little-known author who established crime novels as a separate Danish literary genre. Palle Rosenkrantz, 1867–1941, was a baron who after an impecunious youth became a lawyer with expensive house-building habits and a reputation for unauthorized use of public funds, an arrest record, and a bankruptcy. Rosenkrantz turned to journalism and editing, translation, play- and scriptwriting, and producing novels—overall some eighty books— to support his family. Georg Brandes wrote the foreword to Rosenkrantz's first novel, "The Mistress of Havre Holm," a mainstream work written in the spirit of the modern breakthrough. Many of Rosenkrantz's subsequent novels were frankly commercial potboilers, but *Mordet i Vestermarie* ("Murder at Vestermarie"), Rosenkrantz's first crime novel, 1902, about an 1833 financial theft, has since been celebrated as Denmark's first crime novel. As the only one of Rosenkrantz's crime novels to be translated into English so far, it appeared as *The Magistrate's Own Case* in 2012. Rosenkrantz also wrote successful short crime fiction, one story of which was included in Hugh Greene's *Rivals of Sherlock Holmes* anthologies and was later made into a teleplay in Greene's 1970s *Rivals of Sherlock Holmes* television series.

Around 1900, too, the influence of Norwegian writers, especially Ibsen, Bjørnson, and Jonas Lie, who had played important roles in the development of nineteenth century Danish literature, generally waned in Denmark. Though Norway and Denmark had separated in 1814, the two countries' use of the Dano-Norwegian language represented a literary union which for a long time survived political separation and increasing cultural differences. By the early years of the twentieth century, however, that literary union was dissolving, and even "The proud imprint of the Gyldendal publishing company, 'Kjobenhavn og Kristiania' came to mean less and less" (Mitchell 231). One contributing factor was Norway's *Nynorsk* (*Landsmal*) movement, begun in 1848, which founders based on Norwegian dialects to be independent of Danish. *Nynorsk* today is used by a minority of Norwegians, since most use the form of the language called *bokmal*. Norwegian books are often translated into Danish and vice versa.

Considered the father of Danish modernism and the first great Danish writer of the twentieth century, Johannes Vilhelm Jensen, who won the Nobel Prize for Literature in 1944, is best known for *The Fall of the King* (*Kongens Fald*), written in 1900–1901, a historical novel about eighteenth century King Christian II that in 1999 was named the best twentieth century Danish novel. Martin Seymour-Smith has described *The Fall of the King* as "an indictment of Danish indecision and lack of vitality, which Jensen saw as a national disease" (Seymour-Smith 1101), helping to nudge Danish writers out of their comfort zones and into new experiments in fiction which took place after World War I.

As happened in the other European countries and the United States, that war shattered Danish idealism and belief in progress, since technological advances not only failed to improve human life as so many had hoped, but the new inventions instead enabled armed conflict of a monstrous new kind and scope. Denmark's neutrality in the war, possibly a symptom of the "national disease" Jensen had decried, provided the nation commercial benefits, but Danish literature took conflicting new paths. Intense radicalism appeared in the works of a group of young postwar "so-called Americanized, whiskey-drinking writers ... a disillusioned generation of intellectual revolt" (Mitchell 255). One typical example was Tom Kristensen, born in 1893, who promoted the fiction of William Faulkner, Ernest Hemingway, and Erskine Caldwell in Denmark. Kristensen declared in his 1920 poem "Atlantis": "as beautiful as a bombarded railway station/is our youth, our force, our wild ideas" (quoted in Mitchell 235). Representing the other extreme in Danish literature of the 1920s and 1930s, Jacob Paludan, a Social Rightist critic, adhered to the humanistic tradition by disliking everything he knew of the New World and sympathizing with belief in the supernatural.

In this period, a few Danish authors maintained Brandes' social radicalism, but generally Denmark's literary and social pendulum reacted against naturalism and swung back toward nationalism and social realism, exploring the problems of the working class. Martin Andersen Nexo's *Pelle Erobreren* ("Pelle the Conqueror") opened a whole new area of social concern by presenting working women sympathetically. Regional literature like the novels of Marie Bregendahl began to appear with similar concerns. Like Bregendahl's contemporaries Norway's Sigrid Undset and Sweden's Selma Lagerlöf, each of whom won a Nobel Prize for Literature, Bregendahl set her stories in the Scandinavian countryside of her youth, but she concentrated more than Undset and Lagerlöf did on the transition of the peasant culture "from isolation to involvement in modern European politics ... in a style of tragic realism" (Mathiasen 5).

Denmark's best-selling novel of all time, Hans Kirk's *The Fishermen* (1928), relates the collective story of fishermen new to a northern Jutland village who as members of a puritanical revivalist movement, the "Inner Mission," call themselves "The Pious," accepting all of life's trials as "God's will." In their pietism they contrast with the more tolerant Grundtvigian local inhabitants as they all struggle with economic hardship. Kirk was a lifelong member of the Danish Communist Party and during the Nazi occupation of Denmark he was interned by the Gestapo, who destroyed the projected continuation of a never-completed trilogy Kirk had begun with *The Day Laborers* and *The New Times*, chronicling the 1920s industrialization of Denmark's agrarian society.

As the storm clouds of another world war began to gather during the 1930s, Danish writers pursued several diverging literary directions. Authors of fiction who had heretofore concentrated on social problems began to interpret psychological issues: for some, "Freud was becoming more important than Marx as a prophet" (Mitchell 258). Others replaced their pacifism with activist agendas opposing the wave of fascism which first established itself in Italy, then in Germany, and soon after in Spain. As a reaction against Ibsen's realistic dramas, Danish dramatists began to synthesize naturalism and symbolism, reinvigorating the Danish stage and raising issues that burgeoned during the Nazi occupation. Danish poets began to demonstrate profound worries about the future, and toward the end of the 1930s many shifted from anxiety to outright defiance of Germany's National Socialism.

The most important Danish author to begin writing in the 1930s, Karen Blixen, 1885–1962, who wrote as "Isak Dinesen" in both English and Danish, is well known for both the fairy-tale style she used in *Seven Gothic Tales*, 1934, and *Winter's Tales*, 1942, and her autobiographical *Out of Africa*, 1937. At twenty-two, Blixen had pseudonymously published her first two short stories later collected in *Osceola*, 1962, youthful fiction which displays perseverant elements in her mature work: "a concern for identity, a sympathy with nature, and a reverence for the story as art" (Danielson and Stecher-Hansen 43). Blixen's writing ceased when on the rebound she married the twin brother of the man who had jilted her for a woman eight years younger. Blixen would much later allegorically represent "This rash determination to reach the object of her desire through a substitute in stories that deal with the issue of vicarious achievement" (Danielson and Stecher-Hansen 44). Karen Blixen and Bror Blixen were married in Mombasa, British East Africa, on January 14, 1914, with grand plans for a pioneering coffee plantation there.

A year later, Karen Blixen learned that her husband had infected her with syphilis; she left him and attempted suicide, then endured mercury treatments and arsenic intravenous injections. Though afterward she displayed no further evidence of the disease, she believed for the rest of her life that she would never recover. She reconciled briefly with Bror Blixen, but in 1918 she began a new friendship with the charismatic English aristocrat Denis Finch-Hatton, whom she described as "my ideal realized in him" (quoted in Donelson and Stecher-Hansen 44).

Shortly after the close of World War I, Karen Blixen separated permanently from Bror Blixen and operated two 4,500-acre Kenyan coffee plantations by herself. The Karen Coffee Corporation never made a profit, and so, as she explained in her autobiography *Out of Africa*, "I had to collect my energy on something…. I began in evenings to write stories, fairy tales and romances that would take my mind off [the situation]" (quoted in Donelson and Stecher-Hansen 44–45). After seventeen years of mounting financial reverses, drought, locusts, two miscarriages resulting from her relationship with Finch-Hatton, and the 1929 stock market collapse, Karen Blixen had to sell her plantations in 1931. A few weeks later Finch-Hatton died in an air crash. During the aftermath of these disasters, Karen Blixen wrote stories in English, sending them out to publishers while she endured a trying readjustment to living with her mother back in Denmark. Published in the United States in 1934 when she was forty-nine, *Seven Gothic Tales*, selected by the American Book of the Month Club, launched her new career as "Isak Dinesen"; "Isak" in Hebrew means "one who laughs." *Seven Gothic Tales* laid the foundation for her subsequent literary success, summed up by Ernest Hemingway. who when he won the Nobel Prize for Literature in 1954, declared that it should instead have been given to Isak Dinesen.

Dinesen described her writing style ironically as "old fashioned": "In Denmark my young author friends say that I am three thousand years old" (quoted in Donelson and Stecher-Hansen 45). She called her stories "gothic" because they contain supernatural and tragic elements which convey positions she considered profound, but they also exhibit the Danish sense of humor: "Their gothic nature arises from the author's sense of whimsy; even in her most tragic story, Dinesen wanted the reader to discover a joke" (Donelson and Stecher-Hansen 46). In both her fantasies and her autobiography Dinesen reveals intense observation, a passion for adventure, and a concern with the past, all "rarely surpassed in patience and precision" (Mitchell 276–7). The characters of her fantasies also often seem propelled by a perverse fate into situations verging on madness (Mitchell 276), elements frequently recognizable in the villains of contemporary Danish crime novels, especially those dealing with psychopathic personalities beset by long repressed sexual urges which explode into homicide.

Isak Dinesen's unique contribution to Danish literature remains "her vision of the ... collective memory of the wisdom bequeathed to humans through the centuries," manifested by manner and style, made concrete by Dinesen through the symbol of the mask, which she felt allowed its wearer "to live up to his or her own highest ideal ... the answer to the fundamental question in the existentialist canon, 'Who am I?'" (Donelson and Stecher-Hensen 58). Often in contemporary Danish crime fiction, the masks of detectives, villains, and bystanders often drop or shatter, leaving their wearers fatally frustrated by their consequent inability to live up to the ideals they themselves, their loved ones, or their society imposes on them, often expressed in Danish crime fiction in the context of dark, even tragic, jokes. Dinesen took the symbol of the mask to a philosophical, even theological, level. She claimed that except for God, she believed in nothing whatever; her God was "closer to the deities of Asgard than to God the Father"; and for her, Christ "almost becomes the Divine Joker, even at the Crucifixion playing a masked role," because being really God, His sacrifice "was no sacrifice at all." In consequence Dinesen might have consoled herself by pursuing "the only true fun in all the world ... with a joke, a mocking echo of the laughter of the Gods" ("In Love with Destiny").

Denmark and Its Literature During World War II

Isak Dinesen was producing her fiction during some of the most traumatic years of Denmark's modern history. Prior to the outbreak of World War II in 1939, the Depression and the threat of Fascism had radicalized the theory that the arts, and especially literature, should foster the transformation or reformation of society. The socialist sympathies of some Danish authors and their rebellion against what they considered the misdirection of the bourgeois Danish society led them to Marxism and Communism, notably Hans Scherfig, 1905–1979, who produced an ironic detective novel *The Dead Man*, 1937, and *Scorpio*, 1953, an attack on corruption in the Danish police structure, media, judiciary, and administration. Several of Scherfig's anti-bourgeois works were filmed in the 1990s.

Social realism became the dominant literary trend in 1930s Denmark, but almost immediately with the Nazis' April 1940 Operation *Weserübung*, their occupation of Denmark made Danes more aware of their national identity and more desirous of "symbols which could grant a kind of security in the face of material and political exigency" (Mitchell 279). Poetry, some of it relatively obscure, seemed to answer these needs for Danes at that time, and very little Danish literature of any kind addressed the wartime tensions directly. Denmark's experience of occupation differed markedly from similar situations in other countries the Nazis overpowered, too, primarily because of the "occupation policy" that the Danish "Protectoral Government" held from 1940 to 1943. That year, after Allied victories began to turn the tide of the war and Denmark saw an upsurge in anti–Nazi sabotage and labor strikes, the Germans dissolved the Danish "Protectoral Government."

Denmark's occupation policy (*Samarbejdspolitik*) which some postwar Danish historians refer to as the country's "collaboration policy," derived in some measure from the country's special brand of romantic nationalism which had been evolving since the mid-nineteenth century. It emphasized the importance of "smallness," close-knit communities, and traditions. Over time, this national attitude probably resulted from Denmark/s wartime losses in the 1800s which prevented the nation from asserting itself as a major European power. Historian Leni Yahil, in *The Rescue of Danish Jewry: Test of a Democracy*, 1969, claimed that Denmark's non-aggressive nationalism, influenced by Nikolai Grundtvig's spiritual leadership, even led the Danes to identify with the Jewish plight under the Nazis, although "small-scale anti–Semitism had been present in Denmark long before the German invasion" (quoted in Buckser 347).

The Nazis originally intended to occupy Denmark to facilitate their invasion of Norway and to preclude British interference with the invasion by pretending to "protect" Denmark from British incursion. The Nazis broke their 1939 non-aggression pact with Denmark on April 9, 1940, moving ground troops across the border and landing others from ships docked at Copenhagen. In 2010, decades after sixteen Danish soldiers armed with obsolete equipment died in the two hours before their government capitulated, questions were raised about the fact that the Germans had evidently not expected resistance, since they arrived in unarmored ships and vehicles (Østergaard).

The Danes had had long-standing dealings with Germany, especially regarding the northern part of Schleswig, which had been returned to Denmark in 1920. Initially Danish authorities cooperated with the Nazis, who in turn announced they would respect Danish sovereignty, territorial integrity, and neutrality (Hæstrup 9), but as the war proceeded Danish resistance to the Nazis mounted.

Hitler, considering the Danes "fellow Nordic Aryans," had originally wanted to make Denmark a "model protectorate" to show the world what a future Nazi-controlled Europe might become (Poulsen 10). The pre-war Danish Prime Minister, a Social Democrat, strongly opposed the Nazi takeover, but his party, feeling that cooperation would best maintain Danish democracy and Danish control of their country, joined all the other Danish mainstream democratic political entities to form a coalition government satisfying the Nazis, compromising fundamental Danish governmental positions. The Danish government thus created in direct contradiction of the Danish constitution had to follow the Nazis' orders to outlaw all newspaper articles which might jeopardize German-Danish relations; to demand the arrest of all Danish Communists on June 22, 1941, and to ban the Danish Communist Party; to sever all normal relations with the Allied countries; to redirect Danish industrial production and trade toward Germany; and to demobilize the Danish army to about 2,300 men and 1,100 auxiliary troops. In 1943, the Nazis dissolved the entire Danish army.

By terms of the occupation policy, the Danish coalition government was able to reject certain German demands, among them anti–Jewish legislation; the introduction of a national death penalty; the transfer of Danish army units to German military use; and German jurisdiction over Danish citizens. The Danes also kept National Socialists out of their government, and in the middle of the war the Danes even held a relatively free election, only 2.1 percent voting for the Nazi party (Voorhis 183).

The occupation policy did allow Denmark to avoid much of the harsh treatment Norway suffered under the Nazis, outrages which provided motivations and background motifs for some of Norway's prominent contemporary crime fiction authors like Jo Nesbø. So far Denmark's crime fiction authors have not addressed their occupation experiences as widely or as brutally as Norway's have done, possibly because Denmark's resistance took an entirely different path from Norway's.

"The Danes challenged the most barbaric regime of the modern period not with troops or tanks but with singing, striking, going home to garden, and standing in public squares" (Ackerman and DuVall 14). During the Nazi occupation, Danes seem to have abandoned the national indecision that Johannes Vikhelm Jensen had so deplored. Eventually tens of thousands of them refused the Nazis' terms, and instead created a substantial underground movement. In the end, the nonviolent Danish resistance refused to grant the Nazis what Hitler wanted most from Denmark: the shining example of what Nazi domination could bring to Europe.

Though the Danish government pursued its occupation policy to avoid as much Nazi interference in their country's affairs as they could, and while the Danish population generally opposed the idea of sabotage, small but aggressive Danish Resistance groups who believed Denmark should have opposed the German invasion much more forcefully than they had began to form in 1942. By that fall, Danish sabotage against the Nazis had increased to such a degree that Germany declared Denmark "enemy territory" (Voorhis 181). In August of 1943, the Nazis imposed martial law on Denmark, now exerting the full weight of German oppression on the Danes. In response, Danish resistance fighters increased their efforts, which included one of World War II's best known operations to save Jews from deportation and the death camps. Alerted by the Nazis' deportation of Norway's Jews in 1942, the Danes had taken clandestine measures to save their Jewish population, mobilizing fishing boats and private motorcraft to ferry over 1400 Danish Jews to asylum in Sweden. In all, the Germans captured only 472 out of over 7200 Danish Jews, although the famous story about King Christian X's announcement that he would wear the Star of David if the Nazis forced Danish Jews to do so has since been proved apocryphal (see http://www.snopes.com/history/govern/denmark, a site created by the National Denmark-America Association) (Vilhjálmsson, "The King and the Star").

One of the larger groups of the Danish Resistance was Holger Danske, named for Denmark's national hero, one of Charlemagne's knights first mentioned in the eleventh-century *Song of Roland*, then chronicled in the late 1200s' Icelandic *Karlemagnùssaga* as "*Oddgeir danski*." Hans Christian Andersen immortalized Holger Danske in 1845 as magically slumbering deep in the bowels of Kronberg Castle, ready to awaken when needed to defend Denmark against its foreign enemies.

Danish volunteers who had fought with the Finns against the Soviet Union in the Winter War founded the Holger Danske resistance group in Copenhagen in 1942. One of its members, Gunnar Dyrberg, who later published his autobiography *De ensomme Ulve* ("The Lonely Wolves"), recalled that the sight of Danes in friendly conversation with the Nazis just after the invasion had inspired him to join Holger Danske as "Bob Herman." Dyrberg became one of the group's chief liquidators of Nazi personnel. By the end of the war, Holger Danske consisted of about 350 volunteers responsible for about a hundred sabotage operations, including assisting with the Jewish rescue operations, blowing up the Forum Arena in 1943, and attacking Burmeister & Wain in 1944. The group executed about 200 Danish informers responsible for the deaths of over 60 resistance members at the hands of the Gestapo, which infiltrated Holger Danske twice.

Immediately after the liberation of Denmark, considerable popular hero worship grew up around two of Holger Danske's most effective operatives, who died a week apart in 1944, trapped by the Gestapo. Jorgen Haagen Schmith and Bent Faurschou-Hviid, under their respective aliases "Citronen" (the Lemon) and "Flammen" (the Flame), carried out effective sabotage and assassination operations on Nazis and Danish collaborators. The Lemon, born in 1910, worked for Copenhagen's Citroen car company, where he sabotaged German cars and trucks. The Flame, ten years younger with hair that had turned a violent copper shade after an unsuccessful attempt to dye it blond, was an ice water-veined marksman who during 1943–1944 was the Gestapo's most wanted Dane.

Both the Norwegian film *Max Manus: Man of War* and the Danish film *Flammen og Citronen*

("Flame and Lemon") appeared in 2008, indications of the growing re-evaluation of their wartime activities now taking place in Norway and Denmark. *Flammen og Citronen* was co-written and directed by Ole Christian Madsen, filmed in Potsdam-Babelsberg, Germany, Prague; and Copenhagen, and budgeted at 6.16 million euros, making it one of the most expensive Danish-language films in history. It has received high praise from both film critics and the Danish public, and it was nominated for several international cinema awards. Often compared to *Max Manus: Man of War* and generally considered less action-oriented and more moral in approach, *Flammen og Citronen* not only follows its protagonists through their assassinations of Nazis and collaborators but also reveals their clashes with deceitful handlers, competing resistance groups, and a possibly duplicitous *femme fatale*; in the end, Flame and Lemon could trust only one another. Director Ole Christian Madsen has admitted that in making *Flammen og Citronen* he was influenced by Jean-Pierre Melville's French film *Army of Shadows*, which unsparingly depicts everyday tensions and betrayals among French Resistance groups.

Denmark's Postwar Welfare State and Its Literature

Liberated in May 1945 by British forces, Denmark has been described as having suffered least of the other Nazi-occupied countries, with fewer than 5,000 casualties attributed to the war. Direct Danish participation in the Nazi war machine was minuscule; according to historian Bo Lidegaard, in 1941 6,000 Danes, of whom 1,500 belonged to the German minority in Denmark, had signed up for the Nazi-sponsored Free Corps Denmark to fight against the Soviet Union (Lidegaard 462). (Other estimates place the size of the Free Corps Denmark at 12,000 [Osborn].) Immediately after the war, 40,000 Danes were arrested as suspected collaborators; 13,500 received punishment, and of those 46 were executed.

Analyzing postwar Danish literary trends, Marianne Stecher-Hansen observed that the war "created a deep sense of pessimism and, among writers, a generation of skeptics" (DLB, vol. 214, xviii) and eventually contributed to the New Radicalism of the 1960s, a political movement tied to the 1930s' Cultural Radicalism, which had embraced the sexual revolution and demanded educational reforms (DLB vol. 214, xix). Danish postwar poetry emphasized "the isolated condition of the modern individual" (Stecher-Hansen, DLA vol. 214, xx). This isolation and a consequent yearning for community, led to a 1960s–1970s generation of Danish "*saere fortaellere*" ("strange storytellers") who abandoned realism to follow a fantasy-like logic in a symbolic world often reminiscent of the tales of Hans Christian Andersen and ancient myths "which demonstrate a heightened psychological sense, the plot often driven by the repressed desires or irrational urges of the subconscious" with existential overtones (Stecher-Hansen, DLB vol. 214, xx). The "strange stories" also may have inspired "magical narratives," products of the late twentieth century "magic realism" literary movement, suspending "the strictures of realism in order to merge elements of myth, fairy tale, ghost story, or murder mystery into the plot." Peter Høeg's immensely popular *Smilla's Sense of Snow*, 1992, an example of this trend, creatively merged "science fiction, the crime thriller, and the fantastic narrative" (Stecher-Hensen DLB vol. 214, xxii) and has inspired later experimenters in the Danish crime fiction genre.

The "strange story" trend temporarily gave way in the mid–1970s to "*Virkeligheden der voksede*" ("The Reality That Grew"), reflecting a renewed politicization of literature, also contributing to the relative drought of popular Danish crime fiction in the period. In the spirit of "new reality," the Danish government's occupation policy during World War II has become a hotly controversial issue in Denmark (Haarder), so that a darker view of that policy is currently emerging. In 2002, Claus Bryld, professor of modern history at Roskilde University, called for the opening of a sealed national archive which may hold the names of up to 300,000 Danish Nazis or Nazi sympathizers, mainly motivated by financial gain. According to Bryld, "Big business figures may be compromised by its release and there may be revealing information in the files on the royal family." Bryld claim very intimate relations existed between higher ranking German officials and their Danish counterparts, who "traded with the Germans as if they were normal people. A moral perspective was totally absent" (Bryld, quoted in Osborn).

Potentially more damaging to Denmark's World War II legacy are other archives, opened in the 1990s, which reveal that some postwar Danish historians had glorified the occupation policy as "a necessity," "even arguing that other European nations should have adopted the same approach" (Vilhjálmsson and Blüdnikjow).These archives indicate that since 1935 Denmark had been turning Jewish refugees away from their borders and in 1940–1943 had sent twenty-one of them to probable death in German concentration camps. In addition, when many non–Danish Jews who had been evacuated to Sweden in 1943 tried later to return to Denmark, Danish authorities gave them short notice to leave the country. The archives also show that certain Danish firms had used Jewish slave labor, and that most of Denmark's agricultural products had helped to supply the *Wehrmacht:* "The profits streamed back to the Danish industries but were of little benefit to the [Danish] citizens" (Vilhjálmsson and Blüdnikjow). Currently Claus Bryld and other Danish scholars who are studying the effects of the Nazi occupation in the collective Danish memory are openly deploring other academics who "specialize in wrenching events and conditions from their historical context and thus display a glaring lack of historical consciousness which entails the risk of sliding into the world of propaganda" (Bryld).

Immediately after the war, very little Danish fiction dealt directly with the 1940–1945 Danish experience under the Nazis. In the 1950s, lyric poetry replaced social novels and drama as the predominant Danish literary genre (Mitchell 279), since poetry seemed to allow a camouflaged venting of feelings in ways prose could not. During the turbulent 1960s, according to Danish critic Torben Brostrøm, a wave of "modernism" struck Denmark as "an effort to penetrate that which is human, and above all in those areas which have not previously been treated consciously by older writers" (quoted in Mitchell 303), with syntactical and grammatical experimentation, imagery often exhibiting sexual experiences, and dependence on word associations (Mitchell 310). This took literary form in the fiction of Villy Sørensen (1929–), a student of German fiction and philosophy and an author of fantastic, even grotesque, tales; and the versatile Klaus Rifbjerg (1931–), who often displayed a preoccupation with sexuality in his poems and fiction. As editors of *Vindrosen*, a leading Danish critical and literary journal, Sørensen and Rifbjerg not only published the work of new Danish writers but also presented the imaginative prose of Samuel Beckett, Brendan Behan, and Alain Robbe-Grillet as well as articles by progressive French and German critics to Danish readers (Mitchell 309), increasingly emphasizing political issues by the end of the 1960s.

One Danish writer did manage to keep crime fiction alive from the 1950s through the early 1970s, though crime fiction readers' interest seemed to focus then on non–Danish authors' work. Tage la Cour, 1915–1993, a hotel manager, was fascinated by crime literature and wrote crime fiction himself as well as editing several crime fiction anthologies. His three most notable works, all published in Swedish, were "Murder in the Library," 1953, "Journey to the Moon," 1961; and "Myths of Mysteries," 1973. He also co-edited *The Murder Book*, subtitled *An Illustrated History of the Detective Story*, 1971, with Harald Mogensen. It contains photographs, paintings, movie stills, cartoons, sketches, cover art, and illustrations with limited amounts of text, to provide "a broad overview of the genre's development" rather than an in-depth examination (Ergang). La

Cour's personal crime fiction library contained several thousand volumes, now contained in the Tage La Cour Collection of Popular Fiction at the University of Tulsa. He and Mogensen, the literary editor of the Danish periodical *Politiken*, were "in the forefront of an immensely well-informed Scandinavian group of writers and critics who are interested not just in reading the latest books, but in discussing the background and history of the crime story" (Ergang). La Cour was an honorary member of the Baker Street Irregulars and was awarded the Norwegian Riverton Club Honorary Prize in 1990.

While post–World War II Danish fiction seemed to languish and original Danish crime fiction was nearly nonexistent, significant changes were beginning to appear in Danish political structures. The Danish Constitution, proposed by a right-of-center government and proclaimed on June 5, 1953, essentially brought its text into line with the political practices that the Danish government had been following for the past thirty years. Except for the land-use laws of 1963 and the 1970s' petroleum concessions, the fear of state takeovers of business that had been prevalent among the nonsocialist parties just after the war was not "a significant issue in the past forty years" (Einhorn and Logue 59–60). With no strong unified opposition, the Danish Social Democrat government had easily assumed power in 1929, and as their counterparts in the other Scandinavian countries had done, the Danish Social Democrats, allied with the Liberals and the Agrarians, laid the foundation of the modern Danish welfare state. They governed Denmark until 1968, with only two intervals of nonsocialist government, from 1945 to 1947 and from 1950 to 1953 (Einhorn and Logue 18).

The late 1960s ushered in turmoil in Denmark as elsewhere. In 1968 both the "Easter Marches" against nuclear weaponry and a student revolt at the University of Copenhagen erupted. The students demanded privileges hitherto reserved only for senior faculty, and within a year the situation in Copenhagen sparked similar outrages at every Scandinavian university. In 1973, the Danish political party system, like Norway's, fragmented, and the Social Democrats experienced their lowest level of support since 1906. The early focus the Social Democrats had maintained on economic growth, distribution, and redistribution became fractured by "new issues—moral, cultural, and environmental ... an explosive growth in voter volatility ... [so that] the extraordinary stability that characterized Scandinavian politics and policy in the postwar period is gone" (Einhorn and Logue 31).

The 1971 European Community referendum campaigns in Denmark and Norway became the "most bitter political conflict" in Scandinavia since the Nazi occupation (Einhorn and Logue 22), and in the subsequent referenda the gulf between Danish advocates of economic growth and their opponents, primarily the Socialists, continued to widen. Danes voted down the Maastricht Treaty in 1992 and opposed full acceptance of the euro in 2000. As in the rest of Scandinavia, new issues, especially "internally generated strains" like swelling bureaucracy and high taxes have since shaken the outwardly idyllic Danish welfare state.

Both as a sociological ideal and as a practical system, the welfare state concept was based on two assumptions: first, the Western idea, dating from ancient Rome, that the government has the duty of ensuring its subjects' material and spiritual well-being; and second, the late nineteenth-century socialist workers' claims that market capitalism was socially and morally inadequate, and that the state had the duty to correct it (Gress 34). As Ritt Bjerregaard, then Danish Minister for Social Services, announced in 1982, the welfare states assume that market capitalism must be corrected through state action, economic planning, redistribution by taxation, and increasing the influence of workers' organizations. These precepts together represent a socialist theory of economics and government resulting from the Great Depression of the 1930s (Gress 34).

During the 1930s the original Danish welfare programs took about 8 percent of the national budget and were considered "emergency measures" to deal with grave needs the Depression had forced on individuals. By the 1970s, however, postwar affluence driven by technical and scientific breakthroughs and increased productivity allowed Danish health and educational services to expand greatly, resurrecting neo-Marxism and other forms of radical socialism which insisted that "Private consumption and market choice must wherever possible be replaced by the morally superior instruments of public consumption and public-sector choice" (Gress 36). Danish social services ballooned from 19 percent to 28 percent of the national income, creating "a vast voting population of 'public-sector employees' larger than the number of workers employed by private industry, informing the ruling political party that it must satisfy not private workers' claims but those of public sector employees" (Gress 37).

By 1982, welfare programs were consuming almost 45 percent of Denmark's national budget (Gress 35). Costs of these programs have continued to rise, and in order to fund even more services higher taxation has become necessary. In the 1990s, Denmark began attempting to restructure its welfare system from a Keynesian welfare state to a Schumpeterian workfare post national regime (Torfing 369). This did result in a temporary drop in unemployment, but to date those efforts have not dramatically altered the effects of Danish welfare policies.

Today the Scandinavian welfare systems attempt to achieve equality of their citizenries through higher taxation of the highest earners, based on the principle that all citizens have the right to social security. In practice, this means citizens receive generous unemployment insurance, health care, maternity and paternity leave, pensions, support for the disabled, and education at all levels, everything free of charge and funded by taxation. According to Denmark's Finance Ministry, the nation now has the most evenly distributed standard of living in the world, ranking first in Europe's 2007 pension barometer survey. Members of Denmark's lowest income group before age 65 retirement now receive 120 percent of their pre-retirement income in pensions and various subsidies. The Danish cradle-to-grave safety net includes even for the wealthiest citizens free child care and maid service for the elderly, in addition to a de facto minimum wage of $20 per hour. Denmark's flexible work culture and its affordable and extensive childcare policies have returned a large proportion of mothers to the Danish workforce, making Denmark fifth for female employment among the 34 countries in the Organization for Economic Cooperation and Development (OECD) (Rock). Because of flexible working hours, fathers can take about three months' paternity leave. Families pay about 25 percent of day care costs, with sibling discounts, and the government picks up the rest of the bill, which amounts to an average of one-third of parents' net household income. Danes, however, are recently finding that cuts in government day care spending are forcing a drop in standards of care and reducing numbers of child care staff (Rock).

Social and Cultural Tensions

The current Danish welfare system is expensive. Denmark levies the world's highest taxes: a 25 percent value-added tax on most goods and services, including groceries, and an income tax ranging progressively from 37.5 percent to 63 percent on 4 out of 10 full time employees. Up to December 2008, 44 percent of all full time Danish employees paid a marginal income tax of 63 percent and a combined marginal tax of 70.9 percent (OECD Economic Survey of Denmark 2008; see http://www.oecd.org/document/44/0). In 2013 the Danish tax bracket of 56.5 percent was levied on incomes over $80,000.

According to David Gress who lived most of his life in Denmark, some Danes call their welfare system "the provident state" (*Daseinsvororgestaat*) (Gress 33). Among the Nordic countries,

Denmark is unique in combining its generous welfare benefits with a flexible and theoretically easy hiring and firing system: "... in Denmark it is now easier to lose one's job but at the same time employers are more willing to hire new staff" and unemployment benefits are combined with free education programs. The system relies heavily on the notion that "Those who are unwilling to participate or accept suitable positions can find their benefits withdrawn" (Medicoline). About 100,000 Danes change their jobs frequently by choice each year, making the Danish labor market one of the world's most flexible. The Danish welfare system is also becoming one of the world's most high-tech governmental entities. Officials are hoping to save 12 billion kroner by 2020 through digital and technological welfare solutions rolled out in 2013. These include electronic smart boards in schools, robots to help the handicapped to cook and eat, and equipment to allow medical tests to be done at home rather than in a hospital, according to Economy and Interior Minister Margrethe Vestager ("High-Tech Welfare State").

Recently, however, substantial cracks are appearing in the surface of the generous Danish welfare system. Social tensions, cultural conflicts, and crime provide subject matter for Denmark's growing numbers of crime fiction authors. Economists and sociologists are beginning to point out what Gress already in 1982 had recognized as "important—and disturbing" effects on "social attitudes toward assistance, work, business, and even privacy" (Gress 33). Danish Finance Minister Bjarne Corydon stated in an August 20, 2003, interview that Denmark, as Scandinavia's weakest nation, can no longer afford the entitlements that its citizens have grown up enjoying. Denmark's economy flatlined in 2009 due to a burst housing bubble, and Corydon believes that in the current global competition for jobs, the welfare state must be modernized, because if left unchanged its welfare habits will not allow it to compete with populations that will work harder at a lower cost. Most Danes today leave work at 4 p.m., and between 2000 and 2012, the average hours worked in Denmark fell by 8 percent. This may have made Danes feel and/or appear "happier," but it left their work force less productive. In 2012, the nation's $320 billion economy shrank by 0.5 percent. Even more ominous, the Danish unemployed can claim up to 80 percent of their previous salary for two years after losing their jobs. While working Danes earn more and work less on average than their rich-world peers, "out-of-work Danes in some cases earn even more than those in low-skilled jobs," so that about 250,000 Danes have no incentive to give up their unemployment benefits and go to work. Corydon concluded that the modern welfare state will have to prioritize "things in a new way" to make the Danish welfare system viable in the future (quoted in Levring).

Right-wing commentators claim that the generous Danish welfare policies are making Danes too complacent, a polite way of describing the general reaction to a 2012 appearance on a Danish television talk show by one Robert Nielsen, nicknamed "Lazy Robert," who now sells self-branded shirts proclaiming "Keep your crappy job" and "Gimme, gimme." Nielsen admitted "he would rather live on social benefits [which give him more money than his current clothing sales do] than take a job he didn't find meaningful ("Denmark's Lazy Robert"). The "welfare state mentality" enjoys a symbiotic relationship with "top heavy and unresponsive bureaucracy" that tends to transform its people from citizens with rights and duties to recipients of aid and services who wait to be told what to do: "the split between those who take action individually, and those who demand that the authorities assist them" (Gress 41) is evidently producing more and more "Lazy Roberts."

In a June 2013 study by CEPOS, a libertarian Danish think tank, Casper Hunnerup concluded that a large welfare state negatively impacts not only a person's willingness to work but also diminishes an individual's performance when or if he or she takes a job: "The more generous the welfare state, the lower the work ethic of the individual citizen." Hunnerup also insisted that unless Denmark's social benefits system is radically overhauled, the nation risks raising a generation that prefers "working as little as possible" (quoted in "Denmark's 'Lazy Robert'").

The unemployed supported by government subsidies also experience an increased risk of interpersonal violence in Denmark, where alcohol consumption is both a subject of national pride and a national problem. Danish children generally begin drinking at 15 or 16, often even younger (Foote), and according to a 2010 study by the University of Southern Denmark, 57 percent of boys and 50 percent of girls aged 16 had been drunk at least once (quoted in Foote), promoting interpersonal violence. Cases of assault with violence in Denmark where victims are young men show that the incidence of fights and assaults rises during after-hours drinking around bars and restaurants. In the home, where women account for 64 percent of assault victims, alcohol was involved in 43 percent of the cases and fists were the most frequent assault agent (Hedeboe et al.) Since 1985 such statistics have increased sharply, resulting in the recent adoption of a Danish zero tolerance policy toward violence against women and girls, although a 2012 study by the Danish Institute of Public Health which shows that 7.4 percent of young Danish women have been exposed to "physical, psychological, or sexual violence by their partner" shows that zero tolerance of such acts has not yet been achieved ("Zero Tolerance").

While attempts to revamp the Danish welfare system and prod Danes into working more or longer or both are continuing, the aging Danish population and the increase in the numbers of the unemployed—whom some describe as "dawdling university students, young pensioners or welfare recipients" like single parents—may spell trouble ahead (Daley), a breeding ground for crime. A hefty 18 percent of Denmark's population now is over 65, compared to the United States' 13 percent (Daley), and a projection by the Danish municipal policy research group Kora recently found that only 3 of the 98 Danish municipalities will have a majority of residents working in 2013 (Daley). Some Dales are alarmed by this situation. Comparing Denmark's welfare expenditures to Sweden's, Joachim B. Olsen, a Danish Liberal Alliance politician, noted that if Denmark used Sweden's policies on government benefits, Denmark would have about 250,000 fewer citizens living on welfare (quoted in Daley).

Observers like George Blecher, however, who divides his time between Denmark and the United States, take a more sanguine view, feeling that the "myth of the welfare state fostering a lazy citizenry just doesn't hold water," because "besides brilliant architects" and "innovative designers," Denmark is producing well-written television shows and mystery novels" (Blecher). Danish television shows like the popular *The Killing* and a growing number of distinguished Danish crime novels are now exposing social issues like immigration-related tensions, drug usage, organized crime, human trafficking, and disruptions of family life, all symptoms of social disorder which even the ultra-generous Danish welfare system has proved inadequate to prevent or stamp out and may even be promoting.

In another area of Danish life proving a fertile breeding ground for crime, Denmark's "most generous" immigration policies at first offered "the best welcome in Europe" to new immigrants: "generous welfare payments from first arrival plus additional perks in transportation, housing and education" were deliberately designed "to set a world example for inclusiveness and multiculturalism" (MacAllan) for the many Muslim immigrants who arrived in the 1970s from Turkey, Pakistan and Morocco to work in Denmark. In the 1980s and 1990s these were followed by Muslim refugees and asylum seekers from Bosnia, Lebanon, Iraq, and Somalia. Following the 9/11 attacks and bombings in London and Madrid, however, this idealistic vision about immigration collapsed. In 2005, a series of Danish political newspaper cartoons featuring the Prophet Mohammed set off an intense reaction: a Somali man attempted to murder the cartoonist Kurt Westergaard, riots left dozens dead in Danish streets, and Danish neo–Nazi groups promulgated new racist slogans like "Denmark for Danes."

Already by the 1990s, most of the growing urban Muslim population in Denmark had shown itself unwilling to integrate into Danish society, and according to a *New York Post* article by Daniel Pipes and Lars Hedegaard, tensions between Muslim immigrants and Danes were sharply escalating: at around 5 percent of the Danish population, Muslim immigrants who were consuming "upwards of 40 percent of the welfare spending" comprised a majority of Denmark's rapists, "an especially combustible issue given that practically all of the female victims are non–Muslim. Similar, if lesser, disproportions are found in other crimes" (quoted in MacAllan). In the ensuing years, press coverage of stresses between Danes and Muslim immigrants steadily increased, as have reports of Muslim criminal activity.

Many Danes are beginning to see Islam as "incompatible with their long-standing values: belief in personal liberty and free speech, equality for women, tolerance for other ethnic groups, and a deep pride in Danish heritage and history" (MacAllan). In 2001, Denmark's most conservative government in 70 years has produced the strictest immigration policies in Europe: immigrants had to attend three years of classes in Danish and pass tests in Danish history, culture, and language. Immigrants also had to have a job waiting in Denmark and live there for seven years before applying for citizenship, and Muslims could not build mosques in Copenhagen. In an evident reprisal by Muslims, Rikke Hvilshoj, the Conservative Minister of Immigration and Integration, who refused to question "democracy, equal rights, and freedom of speech," had her house torched while she and her husband and children slept. They escaped unharmed, but they have since moved to a secret location where they, like other members of the Danish government, live under the care of bodyguards for the first time in Danish history. *BBC News* reported in 2011 that critics of Denmark's new immigration rules, especially regulations on marrying foreigners, claim that Denmark is violating European human rights legislation and the European Union's legal protection of "the right to family life," but Naser Khader, the Palestinian-Syrian immigration spokesman for the Conservatives, insisted that Denmark should not admit "people who don't want to contribute." Denmark's populist Danish People's Party (*Dansk Folkeparti*—DFP) won 13 percent of the vote in the 2011 parliamentary elections, making this alleged neo–Nazi party the third largest political party in Denmark, headed by Pia Kjaersgaard, often voted the nation's most powerful woman. The ruling parties under the current coalition government have had to depend on the DFP to pass legislation. In return, the DFP received the other parties' agreement "to even stricter rules on immigration and integration" (Bowlby). Although Danish film director Nick Donato has observed that the problem in Denmark with neo–Nazis is that Danes have them in their midst, but don't see or hear about them, the DFP is becoming substantially more influential in Danish government and life.

Soeran Kern, a Senior Fellow at New York's Gatestone Institute, reported in November 2012 that a controversy over Muslim immigrants who forced the cancellation of a traditional Christmas display near Copenhagen costing $1200 while spending $10,000 on the Islamic Eid festivity marking the end of Ramadan has sparked a national scandal, "an angry nationwide debate over the role of Islam in post–Christian Denmark" (Kern). Kern also denounced the proliferation in Denmark of immigrant gangs—ethnic Arabs, Bosnians, Turks, Somalians, Iraqis, Moroccans, Palestinians, and Pakistanis, who are involved in "countless criminal activities, including drug trafficking, illegal weapons smuggling, extortion, human trafficking, robbery, prostitution, automobile theft, racketeering and murder."

Danish right-wing politicians continue to appear impervious to complaints like journalist Ralf Christensen's about the Danish Immigration Services' lengthy wait times he and his Turkish wife faced for her family reunification application, before it was eventually denied (Cremer), or to a 2013 report in *The Copenhagen Post* from the Organisation for Economic Cooperation and Development (OECD) that attempts to allay fears of Danish "naysayers who say 'welfare tourism' by immigrants flocking to the country to suck on the state is draining the society dry" ("Immigrants Are Good). This report claims that money spent on immigrants and taxes paid by immigrants outpace the public services they use, resulting in a net gain of over a billion kroner per year for the Danish economy, but Mads Rørvig, spokesman for the rightist Venstre party, declared that the thousands of students who are coming to Denmark from other EU countries to get an education and student aid, are "a bomb under the entire SU system." Pia Adelsteen of the Danske Folkeparti (DF) suggests that "We are not saying that the welfare system will collapse tomorrow, but little by little every system is being eroded. Unemployment, child allowances ... what's next?" (quoted in "Immigrants Are Good").

The problems associated with Muslim immigration to Denmark continue to increase, while viable solutions seem few. The 2005 publication of cartoons depicting the prophet Mohammed in Copenhagen's *Jyllands-Posten* newspaper stirred Muslim rage worldwide, and the Danish anti-immigrant right-wing political party is steadily growing. Denmark's public education system is deteriorating because most children of Arabic descent are severely disruptive, and more and more Danes are sending their children to private schools where discipline can be maintained because those schools have fewer "double-linguistic" (Muslim) students. At the same time, an estimated 40 percent of Muslim students are leaving Danish public schools functionally illiterate, again because of their lack of discipline. The Pew Research Center estimates that Denmark's 2010 Muslim population of 226,000, 5.7 percent of the total Danish population, will rise in 2030 to 317,000, or 5.6 percent of the total Danish population (Pew Research Center, "Region: Europe"). Denmark currently is offering immigrants from "non–Western" countries $20,000 apiece if they give up their legal residency in Denmark and go "home," but so far the Danish government has not calculated how many people might accept that offer ("Bare Naked Islam").

Economically, according to a 2013 Danish government report, the tightened immigration laws over the past ten years saved Denmark 6.7 billion euros. Migrants from non–Western countries had cost Denmark 2.3 billion euros and those from the West had contributed 295 million euros to the Danish government coffers, so DPP finance spokesman Kristian Thulesen Dahl concluded that "restrictions [on immigrants] pay off" (quoted in Reimann). The new Danish Social Democratic government which took office in 2013 pledging to ease the tight Venstre-Conservative regulations on immigration, however, on May 15, 2013, produced new guidelines on the hot-button issue of family reunification for immigrants and loosened rules for permanent residence cases on the following June 1, but even with these changes, "Denmark will continue to have some of the most harsh immigration laws in Europe" (Wenande).

Overall, the number of asylum seekers and relatives of immigrants wishing to reside in Denmark dropped more than two-thirds within nine years up to the 2013 election because of the nation's toughened immigration laws, which seem to have met with public approval. Driven by right-wing Danish populists, the approval ratings of the Social Democrats who favor looser immigration regulations, fell after the 2013 election. Immigration, especially in cases involving Muslim minorities, seems to be a perennially troubling concern in Denmark, where currently 10 percent of the nation's population of 5.5 million are migrants (Reimann). The immigration issue alone provides a growing amount of raw material for crime novelists who are fictionalizing immigration-related cultural and social problems that Denmark's police and other crime-solvers encounter, as notably shown in Jussi Adler-Olson's Department Q novels (see below).

As a sidelight to the problem of Muslim immigrants in Denmark, the *New York Times* reported in April 2014 that eighteen-year-old Danish Palestinian Yahya Hassan "emblazoned himself on Denmark's consciousness" with a collection of poetry that had a print run of 800 in the fall of 2013 and since has sold over 100,000 copies. Hassan's poems criticize the Danish welfare state, his family, and Danish Muslims at large. "for hypocrisy, cheating, and failure to adapt." He has received questionable praise from right-wing politicians as well as death threats. At the 2014 Leipzig Book Fair, Hassan recited his poems, which the German publisher Ullstein had rushed out in German translation, selling 9,000 copies in its first week. Hassan's background seems murky; He arrived in Denmark at 13 and caused so much trouble to his family and society that he was removed from their home in Aarhus and placed in a series of Danish state institutions, which he seems to believe has increased "his contempt for the state and its actions toward him." The *New York Times* article concluded, "The question now is whether he is just anther teenage flash in the pan" (Smale).

Denmark also continues to experience major tensions because of one of Europe's most pervasive drug cultures. In 2004, Copenhagen's police chief Kai Vittrup, just back from service in Iraq, launched a "spectacular crackdown" on drug dealers in Christiania, a notorious hippie enclave about five minutes from the center of Copenhagen that "has functioned as an autonomous 'state within a state' for some 30 years" (Arun). The raid smashed a local cannabis economy estimated at an annual $80 million, but Christiania residents blamed the then conservative Danish government for an "urban counter-terrorism" operation against leftist residents living on real estate which in overcrowded Copenhagen is highly desirable property. The sale of cannabis, illegal in Denmark, has been controlled by biker gangs who act as "enforcers" for the resident hippies and political idealists (Arun).

The cannabis trade in Denmark at large seems to continue unabated. In 2010, Denmark's Health and Medicines Authority (*Sundhedsstryrelsen*), formerly the National Board of Health, reported an estimated 33,000 drug users among Denmark's population of 5.5 million; 11,000 of these drug users used cannabis alone. In 2006, over 7,000 used only cannabis. These statistics were based on the number of individuals estimated to use drugs on a constant basis, "leading to physical, mental and/or social injuries." An estimated 13,000 drug users inject the drugs, risking serious injuries, diseases, and death. Cannabis is the most often used drug in Denmark, followed by amphetamine, cocaine, and ecstasy (DrugWarFacts.org).

The same report reveals that the Danish drug problem substantially affects its youth. In Denmark's school population, minor but significant increases in the experimental use of cannabis, ecstasy, and cocaine appeared beginning in 2003 although the current use of cannabis seems to have stabilized by 2010 (DrugWarFacts.org). According to the register of Denmark's National Commissioner of Police, drug-related mortality in Denmark increased 13 percent between 2008 and 2009, and it reached an all-time high in 2011, when. 24 percent of drug-related deaths were caused by heroin/morphine or those drugs in combination with others, and 52 percent were caused by methadone or methadone in combination with another drug. Almost 16,200 Danish drug users were admitted to treatment in 2011, "the second highest number registered [of] drug abusers since the opening of the register" (DrugWarFacts.org).

Attempts to deal with the soaring drug problem in Denmark have included proposals for involuntary treatment, shown by scientific evidence to be as effective as voluntary treatment, according to Social Minister Benedikte Kjaer, "only if it serves a good purpose" ("Drug Use Soars"). A 19-point policy launched in 2009 included supply-reduction, prevention, treatment and rehabilitation, with outreach programs, prison treatment programs, and a focus on mental health issues. The government allows syringe exchange plans in Danish municipalities, where "clean" syringes and needles are handed out in treatment centers, pharmacies, drop-in centers, and even vending machines.

Perhaps most controversial is Denmark's new "injection room" strategy. Despite objections such as Minister of Justice Lars Barfoed's denunciation of the "injection room" strategy as "immoral," in June 2012, Denmark's government allowed municipalities to establish drug consumption rooms for those over age 18 and those with "long-term and persistent abuse of psychoactive substances" to use Class A drugs like heroin and cocaine free of prosecution. In Copenhagen's Vesterbro area, the city's former meat-packing district, beginning at 8:30 a.m. daily, the city's 8,000 addicts, about 75 percent of them male and two-thirds between 31 and 50 (Boffey), can "shoot up" in a clean supervised facility with impunity. The "injection room" seems to have had a calming effect on the vicinity: burglaries are down by 3 percent, theft and violence are down about 5 percent. Nearly 10,000 syringes used to be picked up on Vesterbro streets weekly before the room opened; now very few are found. The relevant Danish governmental act specifies that the drug consumption rooms must be monitored by qualified personnel who will also monitor drug intake, under the assumption that "Harm reduction will therefore continue to be a fundamental pillar in drugs policy in Denmark." Reactions to this strategy of preventing death from drug abuse, not preventing or curing drug abuse in the first place, have been predictably mixed. Proponents believe that by providing safe havens for drug users, crime has decreased and Danish streets are safer; even in Britain, a movement advocates a similar facility for the south coast of England. Danish opponents insist that the injection rooms make drug abuse simpler and send the public the wrong message. Only five people using the Copenhagen room have been put on treatment for addiction since October 2013. Administrators of a high school across the road from the Vesterbro injection room, understandably concerned about its effect on their students, insist, "We can't live with it so close" (quoted in Boffey).

During the past decade, Danish governmental attempts to deal with Denmark's drug issues have seemed contradictory. After refusing to legalize cannabis in 2005, the government launched a program to treat heroin addicts with prescription heroin in March 2010, at a cost of 8.5 million euros (DrugWarFacts.org). The current Danish government policy correlates Denmark's drug abuse and problematic social and economic living conditions, seeing abusers as socially marginalized, with minimal educational backgrounds. They are also "more frequently provided for through cash benefits and pensions," though while the Danish Prison and Probation Service provides medical substitution treatment for drug addicted offenders, they do not provide them with free syringes and needles (DrugWarFacts.org). The most dangerous result of the ever-increasing abuse of illegal drugs in Denmark seems to be the related upsurge in organized crime Denmark is also experiencing.

A comprehensive 2005 report produced by Denmark's Civil and Police Department concluded that "organised crime is continuously committed in Denmark," particularly by the biker groups and by other criminal groups and networks consisting primarily of non–Danish young men, though "it was … committed at a relatively low level compared to other countries" ("Organised Crime in Denmark" 1). The biker movement is "massively involved" in crimes involving violence, robberies, drug crimes, smuggling, and intimidation of various kinds. Biker groups are also affiliated with "certain companies and associations" to commit organized financial crimes. Non–Danish ethnic criminal activity includes drug smuggling and trafficking, producing an upsurge in the dissemination of drugs in small towns. A drop in drug prices indicates that the supply of cannabis, heroin, cocaine, and synthetic controlled drugs like ecstasy is rising. Credit card crime also is increasing, while the incidence of violent robberies has decreased and no signs of undue influence by organized crime on public administration seem to have appeared. The report predicts a rising threat to Denmark by international organized crime ("Organised Crime in Denmark" 23–4).

Despite the claim made in Denmark's 2013 Crime and Safety Report that "Denmark remains a relatively safe and secure country" with homicide and assault rates occurring "less frequently than in the U.S." ("2013 Crime and Safety Report"), other recent studies bear out the 2005 Civil and Police Department predictions. Gang activity is overwhelmingly the major concern of Denmark's police and public. The Danish Security and Intelligence Service (*Politiets Efterretningstjeneste*, or PET) in cooperation with the Danish National Police investigates criminal gangs and networks operating in Denmark with international affiliations that have committed "extremely serious" drug and weapons violations as well as "crimes resulting in serious bodily harm." As one example of the extent of the drug smuggling problem, in 2010, PET broke a massive smuggling ring related to the Danish gang movement which was responsible for smuggling cannabis from Spain into Denmark in German-registered Mercedes passenger cars, loaded with drugs in Spain and driven into Denmark by Eastern European personnel. As an offshoot of this operation, they also arrested a fortyish Danish businessman caught with 20 kilos of cannabis, revolvers and machine guns, 5,000 rounds of ammunition, and 400,000 Danish kroner—a sizeable strike at a major criminal network in Denmark ("International Cannabis and Weapons League").

Internally, 2010 also saw outbreaks of long-simmering feuds between native Danish biker groups like the Hell's Angels and non–Danish ethnic minorities. Kim Kliver, head of the National Investigation Centre in Copenhagen, attributes the clashes to conflict over the control of criminal markets in narcotics and human trafficking, but journalist Khaled Ramadan believes it is due to frustrations felt by immigrants over the strict Danish immigration rules that have become "a cornerstone of government policy" ("Denmark's Gang War"). In 2010 the rightist Danish government sought tougher measures against "the obtuseness and brutality of the gang environment." According to Brian Mikkelsen, a former Danish Minister of Justice, "If you are a criminal with a foreign background then there is only one way. That is out of Denmark and back to the country where you came from" (quoted in "Denmark's Gang War"), but opposition leaders of the government that took over in 2013 feel that such measures will only intensify the problem by alienating ethnic minority youth. Journalist Khaled Ramadan cautions: "Radicalism usually comes out of [an] economic crisis or [a] social political crisis. And in the 1930s we have seen that the formation of Nazism was very much related to economy…. It is scary" (quoted in "Denmark's Gang War").

Ramadan's warning has proven prophetic. In 2012, Soeren Kern reported that "immigrant gangs have proliferated geographically across all of Denmark" (Kern), with escalating turf wars between rival Muslim gangs for control of "drug trafficking, illegal weapons smuggling, extortion, human trafficking, robbery, prostitution, auto theft, racketeering, and murder" (Kern). An estimated 700 immigrants between 18 and 25 join the over 100 Danish criminal gangs yearly. One of the largest such gangs in Denmark is the "Black Cobra" Muslim group founded in 2000 by Palestinian immigrants in Roskilde, near Copenhagen, which now has branches in all Danish cities and has spread to Sweden, primarily in the Islamized Tensta and Rinkeby suburbs of Stockholm and the Rosengård district of Malmö. The Danish Black Cobra group also controls a youth gang, the "Black Scorpions."

Attempted crackdowns on gangs by Danish police, such as the arrest of 350 lower-ranking gang members in 2011 and the government's commitment of $9 million in 2012 to a project aimed at preventing gang recruitment in certain areas, according to Kern have been half-hearted at best. Releasing 135 or 140 Muslims only a few hours after arresting them for an assault on a Glastrup courthouse on March 6, 2012, resulted in a rampage in nearby Vaerebroparken, where the perpetrators set fires and attacked police. Kern attributes a large part of the problem to fear, because immigrant gangs often operate in "no-go" zones in suburbs of Copenhagen and other cities where police are afraid to venture, a model adapted from Muslim enclaves in Britain. Kern quotes an Asian Muslim gangster named Amir: "'…with Islam comes fear, and with fear comes power … if you [oppose] … a Muslim gang you'd better be able to run fast or hide well, because they will come back at you in numbers" (quoted in Kern).

Gang activity in 2013 reached such a level in Denmark that Professor Michael Hvild Jacobsen of Aalborg University indicated, "There have never been more gang members on the streets than now. The recruitment of new immigrant gang members ... is higher than the number of gang members we manage to put in jail." Police Inspector Michael Ash, head of Denmark's National Police Research Centre, agrees; following an epidemic of arson attacks in West Copenhagen, the possibility of calling out the Danish army and the National Guard is being discussed, because as police officer Morten Rasmussen, who answers calls from citizens to Copenhagen's central police station, city police are so involved with Muslim gang-related violence that they cannot answer calls for assistance from the public (quoted in "Police Hemorrhaging"). In particular, police are trying to quell battles between Danish biker gangs like the Hell's Angels and the Muslim gangs which have involved a substantial increase in drive-by shootings and stabbings since 2008.

Gang activity also often includes human trafficking, on the rise in Denmark as in the rest of the world. The Danish Anti-Trafficking Center finds that women trafficked for sexual exploitation constitute the largest group, with between 4,000 and 6,000 women working in Denmark as prostitutes, about half of whom are foreigners (Espersen and Vasquez). The numbers of boys and men trafficked for similar purposes is also increasing. (While procurement of a prostitute is not illegal in Denmark, pimping and participating in the recruitment process are banned by law) (Espersen and Vasquez). Trafficking victims also may find themselves virtually enslaved in cleaning rackets or in selling drugs. Most victims, which include an increasing number of minors, come to Denmark from West Africa, West Europe, and Thailand. In Denmark, re-trafficking also occurs when authorities deport victims of trafficking, who then are victimized by traffickers again, using psychological duress, abuse and intimidation, including death threats, to prevent the victims from seeking help from authorities, according to Anne Brandt Christensen, chairman of HopeNow, a Copenhagen organization assisting women victims of trafficking (quoted in Espersen and Vasquez). In 2002, the Danish government began planning action to help fight human trafficking and assist victims of this crime (HopeNow). This process has since continued through the 2007 Action Plan to Combat Trafficking in Human Beings, which allows victims to remain in Denmark for up to 100 days, and in 2008, Denmark's Ministry of Immigration opened a pilot program to fund safe repatriation of victims to their home countries if and only if the possibility of rehabilitation can be assured (Espersen and Vasquez). To date, these attempts are proving ineffective because of corruption in victims' home countries and victims' fears that lead them to cooperate with criminals rather than with Danish authorities. Christensen, speaking for HopeNow, believes that at least some of the trafficked women should receive asylum in Denmark.

Denmark participates in the apprehension of international criminals, which includes those involved in human trafficking. Interpol maintains a branch in Copenhagen, which is a part of Denmark's National Centre of Investigation (NCI), with about 30 staff members. In 2013, this group helped snare a U.S. school volunteer suspected of child abuse and helped rescue another child from an abuser in Georgia. The Danish Interpol unit has also participated in hunts for international fugitives and for operations involving online supplies of counterfeit and illegal medicines.

Denmark has also made an unusual contributions to real-life high-financial crime exposure via the film *Carbon Crooks*, a documentary by Danish filmmaker Tom Heinemann aired on Danish television in September 2013 which exposes the theft, fraud, and money laundering in Europe's carbon market that since its beginning in 2005 had cost European companies and taxpayers more than $29.9 billion. Criminals targeted the world's largest carbon market, the EU Emissions Trading Scheme (ETS), between 2008 and 2011 in what some observers call "the crime of the century," where criminals tied to worldwide organized crime syndicates used the Internet to exploit illegal schemes. The crooks used false identities to open accounts at Denmark's national emissions registry to commit international tax fraud amounting to over 5 billion euros. The film's allegation, that "the Danish registry was mismanaged by Denmark's Energy Agency," was substantiated by independent auditors in March 2012, showing conclusively that the registry had also impacted the scope of VAT (value-added tax) fraud in other EU member states. Both the Clean Development Mechanism, a carbon offset scheme designed under the 1997 Kyoto Protocol climate pact, and a voluntary carbon offsetting scheme in Kenya were also exposed in the film as fraudulent (Szabo).

The current increase in various forms of criminal activity in Denmark furnishes substantial material for Danish crime writers, who for their sources are drawing not only upon this criminal activity but upon Denmark's unique combination of cosmopolitanism, its proclivity for "strange stories" often involving supernatural or mythic elements, the quirky Danish brand of humor combined with dark intimations of existentialism, the unrelenting realism and naturalism of the Modern Breakthrough shown in their unflinching treatment of today's crimes, and the postwar pessimism currently being revivified by the opening of once-secret government archives. Adding impetus to these is Denmark's distinguished record of filmmaking, especially the dynamic contributions since the 1970s of original Danish television series to Danish popular culture (see below).

Denmark's authors of crime fiction, though less numerous than their counterparts in Sweden and Norway, are addressing universal themes with characteristic Danish acumen, humor, and style. Nearly all of Denmark's crime fiction authors today are pursuing issues involved with what the "acclaimed godmother of Nordic noir" Sweden's Maj Sjöwall lamented at the 2013 Edinburgh International Book Festival as "love relationships" and family, rather than just "police work and crime" and dismissed as "girls' books" (quoted in Maxted). While Sjöwall deplored Danish crime fiction's focus on women's issues, nevertheless Danish fictional explorations of those problems seem to constitute a major element in their appeal: the problems and tensions of Danish protagonists, both male and female, drive their personal stories, for without fascinating protagonists, "an author has no tale to tell, regardless of what fantastic action, shocking twists and eviscerated bodies litter his or her pages" (Maxted). From their earliest writings, the old sagas full of the passion that so often brings on violence and the wry humor that leavens the killings, the Danes have realized that "Desire is why crime occurs ... as without passion ... there would be no crime fiction" (Maxted). Today's Danish crime authors and scriptwriters are dramatically proving so yet again.

Award-Winning Danish Crime Fiction

Titles in quotation marks are unpublished English versions of the original Danish titles. Titles of published English translations appear in italics.

The Golden Laurel

With a few notable exceptions, Danish crime novels and thrillers generally have not been well represented in lists of "best Danish novels." Denmark's premier literary award, The Golden Laurel (*De Gylden Laurbær*, originally *Boghandlernes Gyldne Laurbær*), established in 1949, is presented annually in February or March by the *Committee De Gyldne Laurbær* (previously *Boghandlerklubben*, or "the Bookshop's Club") to the best Danish book published in the previous year, as voted by all Danish bookstores. The Award itself consists of a laurel wreath, a framed certificate, and a 2,500 DKK book gift. To date, only seven Danish crime novelists have received the Golden Laurel:

1962: Poul Ørum, for *Scapegoat* ("Nothing but the Truth")
1968: Anders Bodelsen, for *Tænk på et tal* ("Think of a Number")
1991: Leif Davidsen, for *Den sidste spion* ("The Sixth Spy")
1993: Peter Høeg, for *De måske egnede* (*Borderliners*)
2002: Jakob Ejersbo, for *Nordkraft*
2004: Christian Jungersen, for *Undtagelsen* ("The Exception")
2010: Jussi Adler-Olsen, for *Journal 64* (*The Purity of Vengeance*)

Jyllands-Posten *15 Best Danish Contemporary Novel Book Awards*

In 2013, one of Denmark's largest newspapers, *Morgenavisen Jyllands-Posten* (usually shortened to *Jyllands-Posten* or *JP*), listed the *Jyllands-Posten* 15 Best Danish Contemporary Novel Book Awards. The Danish crime novels listed are:

Die måske egnede (*Borderliners*), by Peter Høeg
Forestilling om det tyvende århundrede (*The History of Danish Dreams*), by Peter Høeg
Kvinden og aben (*The Woman and the Ape*), by Peter Høeg
Kongens Fald (*The Fall of the King*) by Johannes V. Jensen
ABC ("ABC"), by Ida Jessen
Fasandræberne (*The Absent One*), by Jussi Adler-Olsen

Palle Rosenkrantz Prize

Beginning in 1987, the *Danske Kriminalakademi* (Danish Crime Academy) has annually awarded the Palle Rosenkrantz Prize, named after the generally accepted first Danish crime writer, for the best crime fiction novel published in Danish (not necessarily by a Danish author) the previous year. Danish winners of this prize include:

1989: Leif Davidsen, for *Den russiske sangerinde* ("The Russian Singer")
1993: Peter Høeg, for *Frøken Smillas fornemmelse for sne* (*Smilla's Sense of Snow*)
2005: Henning Mortensen, for *Den femte årstid* ("The Fifth Season")

Harald Modensen Prize

Since 2007, the Danish Crime Academy has also annually awarded the Harald Modensen Prize for the previous year's best Danish thriller:

2007: *Sin brors vogter* (*His Brother's Keeper*), by Kirsten Holst
2008: *Drager over Kabul* (*Dragons of Kabul*), by Morten Hesseldahl
2009: *Drengen i kufferten* (*The Boy in the Suitcase*), by Lene Kaaberbøl and Agnete Friis
2010: *Flaskepost fra P* (*A Conspiracy of Faith*), by Jussi Adler-Olsen
2011: *Doderummet* (*Dead Space*), by Susanne Staun
2012: *Det syvende barn* (*The Seventh Child*), by Erik Valeur
2013: *Sort sne falder* (*Black Snow Falling*), by Michael Katz Krefeld

The Glass Key Award

The Glass Key Award (Swedish *Glasnyckeln*), named for Dashiell Hammett's novel *The Glass Key*, is a real glass key given yearly by the Crime Writers of Scandinavia (*Skandinaviska Kriminalsällskapet*) to a crime novel by a Danish, Finnish, Icelandic, Norwegian, or Swedish author. The short list for this award is made up of one novel from each country, chosen by each nation's members of the organization. Since the award's inception in 1992, Danish Glass Key winners have included:

1993: Peter Høeg, for *Frøken Smillas fornemmelse for sne* (*Smilla's Sense of Snow*)
1995: Erik Otto Larsen, for *Masken i spejlet* ("Mask in the Mirror")
1999: Leif Davidsen, for *Limes billede* (*Lime's Photograph*)
2010: Jussi Adler-Olsen, for *Flaskepost fra P* (*A Conspiracy of Faith*)
2012: Erik Valeur, for *Det syvende barn* (*The Seventh Child*)

A Parallel Chronology of Danish Literature and World Events

Danish literature and events are listed in Roman type with world literature and events interspersed in italics.

1188–1201: Life of Saxo Grammaticus, first Danish writer (historian) who wrote *Gesta Danorum* (16 vols.)

1397: Queen Margaret I achieves the Kalmar Union of Denmark, Norway, and Sweden

1523: Sweden leaves Kalmar Union

1684–1754: Life of Ludvig Holberg, famous for comic drama

1779–1850: Life of Adam Oehlenschläger, Denmark's national poet

1783–1871: Life of Nikolai Grundtvig, author and founder of Danish folk schools and a new form of non-aggressive nationalism

19th century: Reforms make Denmark's poor peasantry the most prosperous in Europe

1805–1875: Life of Hans Christian Andersen. writer of fairy tales

1811: François Vidocq, former criminal, heads Paris Sûreté

1813: Denmark-Norway goes bankrupt

1813–1855: Life of Søren Kierkegaard, philosopher, originator of Christian existentialism

1814: Denmark's union with Norway dissolves; Denmark keeps Iceland, Greenland, and the Faroe Islands

1814: Norway unites with Sweden

1828–29: Vidocq's Memoirs *are published*

1829: Steen Steensen Blicher's *The Priest of Vildby*, crime suspense novella

1830s: Danish liberal and national movement gains momentum

1839: Mauritz Hansen (Norway) writes murder novel, Mordet på Maskinbygger Roolfsen

1841: Poe's "The Murders in "The Rue Morgue"

1842–1927: Life of George Brandes, literary critic

1843: First appearance of the word "detective" in English

1847–1885: Life of Jens Peter Jacobsen, novelist and poet

June 5, 1849: Denmark becomes a constitutional monarchy

1857–1943: Life of Henrik Pontoppidan, novelist and Nobel Prize winner; opponent of materialism

c. 1859: Cheap detective books appear in U.S. and Britain

1864: Denmark cedes Schleswig and Holstein to Prussia

1868: Wilkie Collins' The Moonstone, *first full-length detective novel in English*

1869: Emile Gaboriau's Monsieur Lecoq, *first police procedural*

1869–1954: Life of Martin Andersen Nexo, novelist

1873–1950: Life of Johannes Vilhelm Jensen, essayist and Nobel Prize winner

1879–1880s: "The Modern Breakthrough" led by Georg Brandes

1885–1962: Life of Isak Dinesen (Karen Blixen), novelist and short story author

1887: Arthur Conan Doyle's "A Study in Scarlet," first Sherlock Holmes story

1889–1968: Life of Carl Dreyer, cinema director

1897: Beginning of Danish cinema

1900–1930: First Danish Golden Age of crime fiction

1902: Palle Rosenkrantz's *Mordet i Vestermarie* ("Murder in Vester-Marie"). First Danish crime novel

1905–1979: Life of Hans Scherfig, Naivist author, critic and artist

1906–1910: Andersen Nexo's proletarian novel *Pelle the Conqueror* inspires social reforms

1914–1918: World War I (Denmark neutral)

1920: Northern Schleswig returned to Denmark; celebration of first "Reunion Day" (*Valdemarsdag*), 15 June

1920: Agatha Christie's first detective novel, The Mysterious Affair at Styles

1920s–1930s: Britain's Golden Age of crime fiction

1929: Dashiell Hammett's The Maltese Falcon

1930–c. 1939: The Great Depression

1931: Life of Klaus Rifbjerg, author and film producer; first true modernist in Danish cultural history

1939: Denmark signs 10-year nonaggression Pact with Nazi Germany

1939–1945: World War II

April 9, 1940: Nazis break pact and invade and occupy Denmark

1940–1943: Denmark officially cooperates with Germany

1940–1945: Denmark occupied by Nazis; Danish volunteers (*Frikorps Danmark*) fight USSR with Nazis; Danish resistance post 1943 helps rescue Jews and carries out anti–Nazi sabotage

1943: Denmark sinks most of its navy and sends majority of its naval officers to Sweden

1944: Iceland becomes independent

1946–1993: Life of Dan Turèll, popular crime fiction author

1946–c. 1989: Cold War

1947: Mickey Spillane's I, the Jury

1948: Faroe Islands get home rule

1949: Denmark joins NATO

1949: First Dragnet *radio show*

1951: First Dragnet *television episode*

1953: Denmark changes to one-house Parliament; Social Democrats assume leadership and maintain it for most of the 20th century

1953: First James Bond novel, Casino Royale

1963: John Le Carré's The Spy Who Came in from the Cold

1967: Maj Sjöwall and Per Wahlöö publish first Martin Beck detective novel, Roseanna *(Swedish)*

1972: Denmark joins European Common Market

1972: The Riverton Club founded (Norway)

1973: Denmark joins European Economic Community

1973: Faroe Islands reject EEC membership

1976: Matti Joensuu (Finland) publishes first Finnish police procedural

1977: Debut of Marcia Muller's (U.S.) Sharon McCone (first female P.I.) novels; debut of Gunnar Staalesen (Norway) Varg Veum novels

1978–1981: Airing of television series Matador

1979: Greenland gets Home Rule

1980s: State-supported Danish Film Institute promotes Danish film industry, noted for realism, sexual frankness, and technical innovation

1982–1993: Conservative People's Party leads right-wing coalition government

1982: Debuts of female PI fiction: V.I. Warshawski (by Sara Paretsky) and Kinsey Milhone (by Sue Grafton)

1986: Greenland rejects EEC membership

1990s: Denmark deregulates labor market

1993: Denmark accepts Maastricht Treaty (further European integration) with opt-out concessions

1993: Peter Høeg's *Smilla's Sense of Snow* becomes top U.S. seller of 1990s; Sara Blædel founds "Sara B" mystery publishing house

1993: Debut procedurals from Anne Holt and K.O. Dahl (Norway)

1994: Lars von Trier's *The Kingdom* television series

1995: Danish film industry burgeons

1995: Debut of Karin Fossum's (Norway) Inspector Sejer series

1996: Michael Larsen's *Uncertainty*

1997: Henning Mankell's (Sweden) first Wallander novel, Faceless Killers, *translated to English; Jo Nesbø's first Harry Hole novel* The Bat *(Norway)*

2000: Danes reject the euro as national currency

2001: New center-right coalition government promises tighter immigration control

2002: *Unit One* television series

2003: *Forn Siðr* (revival of Old Norse paganism) receives state recognition

2004: Sara Blædel's novel "Green Door" debuts Detective Louise Rick; start of Danish *femikrimi*

2005: *Code Name: Eagle* television series

2005: Stieg Larsson (Sweden) dies just before The Girl with the Dragon Tattoo *is published in Sweden*

2006: Leicester University (UK) declares Danish population has highest life satisfaction in the world

2007: Jussi Adler-Olsen's *Keeper of Lost Causes*; Leif Davidsen's *The Serbian Dane*; *The Killing* aired on Danish television and continues; *Anna Pihl* television series appears

2008: Kaaberbøl and Friis co-author *The Boy in the Suitcase*; *The Protectors* television series; *Flame and Lemon* (feature film)

2009: Right-wing populist People's Party leads Gov-

ernment; more debate on immigration and integration problems' *The Protectors* television series
2010: *Borgen* (television series) opens
2010: *Liza Marklund is second Swedish author to top
Times (UK) bestseller list; Jo Nesbø sells four novels
to Knopf (U.S.)*

2010: Danish unemployment rises to 7.4 percent
October 3, 2011: Helle Thorning-Schmidt leads
newly- elected Social Democrat coalition government as first woman Danish Prime Minister
2012: David Hewson publishes first fictionalization
of *The Killing*

Contemporary Danish
Authors of Crime Fiction

An asterisk (*) indicates some or all of the author's work is available in English.

**Jussi Adler-Olsen*

b. August 2, 1950, Copenhagen, Denmark; *Residence:* Hald Hovdegaard (Danish Centre for Writers
and Translators), near Viborg, Jutland, Denmark; *Occupations:* editor, publisher, author

Denmark's leading crime fiction author, Jussi Adler-Olsen, grew up near various Danish mental
institutions where his father was a head psychiatrist. After that, according to Jussi Adler-Olsen's
official autobiographical statement, he had an extremely wide variety of educational and avocational
experiences. As a teenager, he played lead guitar with pop bands like the Dirty Drummer Trousers,
and in 1969 he became a medical science collaborator on the *Nordic Encyclopedia*. Since then, he
has worked in nearly every aspect of publishing. Between 1980 and 1982, he wrote his first novel,
Russisk Kabale ("Russian Cabal"), as yet unpublished. Before he began writing his three psychological thrillers in 1995, he studied university-level medicine and cinematography, ran a secondhand
bookstore, wrote Walter Lantz cartoons and Disney scripts, edited magazines and comics, produced
the "bible" of Danish comic books, *Komiklex*, still in use, composed music for the film *Valhalla*,
wrote and published two books on Groucho Marx (as whom he dressed 50 TV audience members
for a live show in 1985), and authored *Fred på tryk* (*Peace in Print*), the only wide-spectrum bibliography of literature dealing with the Danish peace- and security policy.

Between 1997 and 2006, Adler-Olsen produced three highly successful popular international
suspense novels, *Alfabethuset* (*The Alphabet House*), 1997; *Firmaknuseren* ("The Company
Basher"), 2003; and *Washington Dekretet* ("The Washington Decree"), 2006. (In a 2013 interview
at Minneapolis' Once Upon a Crime bookstore, Adler-Olsen noted that in 2000, a year prior to
the terrorist attack on New York's World Trade Center, he was writing about an airplane falling
into a high tower and anthrax letters being sent through the mail.) From 2004 to 2007, while
writing the first volume of his Department Q series, he served as chairman of the Board of Directors of DK Technologies A/S, a world leader in advanced sound and image measuring television
and film equipment. Since 2007, Adler-Olsen has written full time, drawing on his unusual background and interests. Subsequent installments in the series, which Adler-Olsen intends to comprise "the longest story ever made in the world," about 5,000 pages (quoted in the *Once Upon a
Crime* interview), have been appearing annually. Adler-Olsen does not know why Penguin, his
British publisher, gives these novels one-word titles, like *Mercy*, their title for the first volume in
the series, titled in Danish *Kvinden i buret* ("The Woman in the Cage") and in the U.S. titled *The
Keeper of Lost Causes*. He admits he has trouble remembering which title represents which novel
(*Once Upon a Crime* interview).

Adler-Olsen prides himself on answering his e mail and generously provides numerous interviews, many of which appear on his official website. He frequently points to his childhood experiences in mental hospitals as being the "most important in relation to what I do today" (quoted in Andersen) because they taught him empathy. When he was five, his father, a compassionate physician, told him that the forcibly restrained, caged, and shock-therapy treated patients who screamed and spat at him were "like you—once." A year later, young Jussi befriended a wife-murderer named Mørck (the Danish word means "dark") who had been psychopharmically treated for ten years: "I could see good and evil very well combined [in him], and I see that, in fact, in every person" (quoted in *Once Upon a Crime* interview). Intrigued by mental illness, "Adler-Olsen subsequently and tellingly named the detective protagonist of the Department Q series "Carl Mørck," Carl being his own first baptismal name. Adler-Olsen has also claimed that while he may be "a Copenhagener on the surface" he is "a Vendelbo (a native of the Vendsyssel region of northern Jutland) inside," and growing up "north of the fjord" made him one of the "folks [who] can say everything without saying it at all" (*Jyllenposten* interview), a key to his psychological insights and literary style.

While completing his third psychological thriller, Adler-Olsen was asked by Danish film producer Rumle Hammerich, who disliked working with Swedes, to do a follow up series to the Swedish Sjöwall-Wahlöö Martin Beck series. Adler-Olsen initially refused, because he said he preferred to write stories about preventing crime rather than stories about solving it, but his thrillers, while selling well in the Netherlands and Germany, did not have much success in Denmark. His first, *Alfabethuset* (*The Alphabet House*), 1997, tr. 2014, tells a horrifying story: two World War II British airmen are shot down and confined in a mental hospital for SS officers, where they are subjected to all the harrowing medical treatments of the time. Three decades later a day of reckoning ensues at the 1972 Munich Olympics. Adler-Olsen's second novel, "The Company Basher," was filled with "terror, superstition, strange traditions, erotic situations and exotic environments" (Lauridsen) and it appeared on Dutch bestseller lists for three weeks, but Adler-Olsen was virtually unknown at home. He suspected that because "Danes take things as they come," international thrillers with political themes were not "the Danes' cup of tea" (quoted in Lauridsen). He followed "The Company Basher" with "The Washington Decree," dealing with the 2011 World Trade Center attack, but he gradually became intrigued by the possibility of writing the world's longest story. In his 2013 Minneapolis interview, he described each of his Department Q books as being a chapter in the overarching tale of deeply flawed Copenhagen police detective Carl Mørck, Mørck's peculiar secretary Rose Knudsen, and his enigmatic Arabic-speaking assistant with the potentially explosive name of Hafez al-Assad. In a *Politiken* interview, Adler-Olsen revealed that he knew Carl Mørck's story immediately and could have written it in one long novel, but when he conceived Rose and Assad, he had a leitmotif that he says will run through all the novels, at least ten of which he has currently planned (Andersen). Adler-Olsen has safely stored their outlines and other materials for a successor in case of his death (*Once Upon a Crime* interview).

Adler-Olsen called the first of the Department Q novels "the platform," a very simple case. He described the second as "how violent you can be"; the third, "a little up" and the fourth "a little down." He did not mention the fifth, which has been called a version of *Oliver Twist*, but he said that the sixth begins the end of the overall narrative; the seventh is Rose's story; the eighth, Assad's; the ninth, Carl's; and "number ten is fireworks" (quoted in *Once Upon a Crime* interview). Each Department Q novel currently in print has appeared in editions of 60,000 to 80,000 copies and has immediately reached best seller lists.

Adler-Olsen claims he is a thriller writer, not a crime writer. In *The Keeper of Lost Causes* Deputy Detective Superintendent Carl Mørck, an unusual protagonist who has no routine restrictions, either in geography or the types of cold cases he investigates, allows Adler-Olsen free rein for his satiric talent. Carl Mørck is lazy and not well liked by most of his associates, but he was once one of Copenhagen's most effective detectives, respected for his intuition and skill (Amazon interview). After a shattering case-gone-wrong in which one of his police partners was killed and the other paralyzed, Mørck, physically debilitated and emotionally damaged, has been "promoted" (i.e., marginalized) to run the newly created "Department Q" from a musty police headquarters basement. Charged with investigating "special focus" cold cases, he now has as his only staff Rose Knudsen, a "kohl-faced beanstalk" (*The Purity of Vengeance* 20), a superb researcher and an abrasive washout from the police academy, as his secretary and Hafez al-Assad, an eccentric and enigmatic Middle Eastern assistant who speaks riotously imperfect Danish, drives like a pig, and provides both near-constant comic relief and sympathetic insight into the Muslim immigrant's life in Copenhagen.

   In *The Keeper of Lost Causes*, a novel of second chances highly praised by reviewers, Mørck awakens from his post-traumatic funk to probe the disappearance of rising young progressive politician Merete Lynggaard, who five years earlier had been kidnapped and sealed into a pitch black cell by an unhinged vindictive man from her past. Since then, imprisoned and desperate, Merete has struggled ever since to maintain her sanity and plan her escape.

   Barry Forshaw has pointed out that while Denmark prides itself on being "the cultural nexus of Scandinavia, boasting a cornucopia of modern design, tolerance, and innovation," Copenhagen, Carl Mørck's home base, today suffers badly from crime, so that "the good and the bad" constantly informs Adler-Olsen's fictional world of "corrupt individuals, social outsiders and manipulative psychopaths…. The spectacle of the abuse of power in the 'perfect' social democracy … has a lacerating force" (Forshaw, Review of *Mercy*, the British title of *The Keeper of Lost Causes*).

   Publishers Weekly found that Adler-Olsen's second Department Q novel, *Fasandræberne*, 2008 (*The Absent One*, tr. 2012). "outdoes his outstanding debut" (*Publishers Weekly* review of *The Absent One*). The plot opens in 1987, when a teenaged brother and sister were brutally murdered in a summer cottage. Their six boarding-school "friends" were prime suspects, but their involvement could not be proved. Mørck and his peculiar assistants take on the case, confronting the ruthless six, now all powerful millionaires who, "seduced by violence," delight in torturing animals, fearing only a homeless woman who was once part of their group. The novel indicts societal corruption that parallels Mørck's mounting guilt over the role he played in the earlier case which left his old partner Hardy so despondent over his near-total paralysis that early in the series he asks Carl to help him die; Carl instead takes Hardy into his own chaotic home and cares for him there.

   Adler-Olsen consistently produces poignant insights into social ills through outcasts and the unwanted in today's Denmark, ironically famed for the "happiness" of its population. Adler-Olsen often voices these through Assad, an outsider himself, who sadly tells Mørck, "'They say he [Hardy] cries so very often…. Even though they give him a lot of pills and all, he still cries" (*The Absent One* 42). The pathetic character Kimmie, homeless, drunken, and addicted, reflects bitterly, "… thanks to the so-called health-conscious government, alcohol costs next to nothing…. What a terrific society Denmark had become" (*The Absent One* 38). Adler-Olsen cannily balances such pain with Rose's gravelly laughter and custard pastries, Assad's inspired malapropisms, and the romantic machinations of Mørck's psychiatrist Mona Ibsen, whose "backside and bouncing breasts" drive him to agonizing distraction (*The Absent One* 108) in this shocking and complex case.

   Third in the Department Q series, *Flaskepost fra P*, 2009 (*A Conspiracy of Faith*, tr. 2013), opens with another harrowing scene, two desperate boys chained and gagged in a boathouse. The older manages to write a message in his own blood and inserts it into a bottle, which he tosses into the sea. After it has languished for years on a windowsill in a Scottish police station, it ends up in Mørck's hands just as he is displaced from his basement lair by absurd Health and Safety officialdom hellbent on asbestos mitigation. Morck, Assad, and Rose's bizarre sister Yrsa, Rose's temporary replacement, piece together an unsettling case involving nonconformist religious groups whose children are being kidnapped for ransom, but Adler-Olsen invests this grim tale with unshakable faith in humanity's goodness.

In *Journal 64*, 2010 (The *Purity of Vengeance*, tr. 2013), Adler-Olsen creates a darker view of humanity, unveiling one of Denmark's darkest violations of human rights. A missing-person case dating from 1987 opens up the lamentable historical account of the Danish island of Sprogø, where from 1922 to 1961 young women considered social liabilities were housed: well into the 1960s in the much-praised Danish welfare state, many of such women were being forcibly sterilized. Adler-Olsen's fictionalization focuses on the character he calls Dr. Curt Wad, long associated with this national disgrace. Wad founded the Purity Party, a neo–Nazi political party whose aim is to promote "healthy Danishness" by aborting fetuses from parents considered unfit for "normal" Danish life. A woman whose life Wad thus wrecked is taking a gruesome revenge on those she feels were responsible, while Mørck faces a complicated mix of personal Angsts. In a libido-blasting "surprise," his psychiatrist lover Mona asks him to dinner with her surly daughter and the daughter's monstrous son-god child, just when Mørck is coming down with a vicious stomach virus. He is also facing accusations of responsibility for the debacle that landed him in Department Q; his ex-wife Vigga is threatening him with financial ruin; and he's suspected of culpability in his own uncle's death. Only Assad's relentless cheeriness and apparently honest concern lightens Mørck's burdens, making this novel a *tour de force* that could have been written only by an author capable of turning stomach flu diarrhea into a redemptive belly laugh—in other words, a Dane.

In *Marco effekten*, 2012 (*The Marco Effect*, tr. 2014), the fifth Department Q novel, Adler-Olsen takes a more cosmopolitan stance, shifting far afield into the African jungle and up to the cabinet minister level in Denmark and centering on another underdog, Marco, a gypsy child victimized by his cruel Uncle Zola and the rest of their clan into pickpocketing, panhandling, and burglary. When Marco learns his family plans to cripple him to amplify his appeal as a beggar, he flees as far as he can from Zola, only to see a missing person poster months later and deduce that his family has brutally murdered the missing man and hidden his corpse. His family targets Marco as a mortal threat, but Carl Mørck, Rose, and Assad are already working another angle of the case, which involves financial corruption in a Danish third-world development group. They learn that the murdered man had been a potential whistle-blower killed by gypsies, leading them to Marco. Dumped by Mona and beset by the unpredictability of Rose and Assad, Mørck now contemplates returning to street beats until Adler-Olsen brings his various story lines into a hilarious and heart-breaking conclusion.

Adler-Olsen, who sees Danish Scandinavian heritage as vital to crime fiction. claims, "I would like to be the band-aid, being pulled off [his country's wounds] slowly" (quoted in *Jyllen-posten* interview). Connecting to his Minneapolis audience, many of whom share Scandinavian ancestry, he observed, "You know, this is Viking blood [pointing to himself]; this is a Dane. The Swedes? Phht. The Norwegians? [shakes his head]. It's us! ... that's why we are such good story-tellers. Because we have nothing to do…. The Vikings, they're good at murders, they killed people just to keep warm." He also emphasized, "We are funny in Denmark," and "That's not the same with Swedes. You read Henning Mankell, that's funny? And the Norwegians, they're just crazy." He notes that he is "a big success in Europe, most of all in Germany." Beneath the cool Teutonic exterior, Adler-Olsen discovered the Germans "were like Danes in disguise," not like Swedes and Norwegians. In his Minneapolis interview, he traced his popularity in Germany to the similarity of the modern German and Danish languages, especially their "sinister sibilants" (quoted in *Once Upon a Crime* interview).

Adler-Olsen attributes his success in mixing humor and darkness in the Department Q novels to the first goal he sets for an author: to respect his readers, which he says he learned from his extensive experience in nearly every facet of the publishing business. He revises constantly, first in WordPerfect 5.1, then converts to Word and throws out "a lot"; then he converts to PDF and tries to keep his imaginary reader from falling asleep in bed by alternating fright with humor: "I can so clearly see what is necessary when I'm reading it in PDF" (quoted in *Once Upon a Crime* interview). For his writing to satisfy himself, Adler-Olsen makes his research as thorough as possible, devoting time to detail so the reader realizes that Adler-Olsen has taken immense care with every sentence of his long novels (Lauridsen).

To avoid falling into the Great-Detective-Sidekick stereotype in the Department Q novels, Adler-Olsen made sure to give each of his three main characters deeply hidden secrets, so that the different aspects of the personalities of Carl, Rose, and Assad are unique to each one. Adler-Olsen claims the part of himself, "Carl Waldemar Jussi Adler-Olsen," in Carl Mørck is humorous and frank and disregards authority. He invented Assad as a humorous Syrian immigrant whose outward eagerness to please masks impressive intelligence and physical prowess, which allows Adler-Olsen to use comedy to help bridge the gap between many Danes and the country's Muslim immigrants. He calls Rose, on the other hand, "pure anarchy." These characters provide Adler-Olsen "an endless possibility of actions between them" (*Once Upon a Crime* interview).

Adler-Olsen wants his readers to hunger for each new volume: "... the reader shouldn't want it [the next story in the series] to end, either. But just when the reader wants to know more, something new has to happen. This too, is humour" (quoted in Andersen). In an interview with Jeppe Bangsgaard for *Berlingske Tidende* made when Adler-Olsen was working on *The Purity of Vengeance*, Adler-Olsen denied that he takes his readers too seriously, as he says many of his fellow authors do. Instead, Adler-Olsen insists that "There has to be an accordance between my interpretation of the book and the reader's" (quoted in Bangsgaard). He also feels that readers must be able to create their own images from his descriptions, which he calls "the missing voice" in the story. If he constantly tries to challenge the individual psychological experiences of his readers, Adler-Olsen feels "we will all end up with not only a good reading but also a better understanding of of the life and individuals around us. And THAT'S powerful" (quoted in *ShotsMag* interview). His readers around the world apparently agree.

The Department Q novels are being adapted by the Danish film company Zentropa for television. *The Keeper of Lost Causes*, written by screenwriter Nikolaj Arcel, directed by Mikkel Norgaard, and starring Nikolaj Lie Kaas as the young Carl Mørck, appeared on Danish television in the fall of 2013. Plans are for one novel to appear as a five-episode television series each year (Adler-Olsen, quoted in Andersen).

Adler-Olsen claims his stand-alone thriller *Alfabethuset* (*The Alphabet House*, tr. 2014) is "not a war novel," but an exploration of breaches in personal relationships, set during World War II and based upon his childhood experiences with physicians, nursing staff members, and patients in the mental institutions where his progressive psychiatrist father worked. Adler-Olsen needed eight years to write this story, which he first outlined to his wife in 1987 (*The Alphabet House* v–vi).

Thrillers:

1997: *Alfabethuset* (*The Alphabet House*, tr. Steve Schein, 2014)
2003: *Firmaknuseren/Og hun takkede guderne* ("The Company Basher")
2006: *Washington Dekretet* ("The Washington Decree")

The Department Q Series:

2007: *Kvinden i buret* (*The Keeper of Lost Causes*, tr. Lisa Hartford, U.S., 2011; also published as *Mercy* [UK, 2011])

2008: *Fasandræberne* (*The Absent One*, tr. K.E. Semmel, U.S. 2012; also published as *Disgrace* [UK, 2012])

2009: *Flaskepost fra P* (*A Conspiracy of Faith*, tr. Martin Aitken, U.S. 2013; also published as *Redemption* [UK 2013])

2010: *Journal 64* (*The Purity of Vengeance*, tr. Martin Aitken, U.S. 2013, also published in the UK, 2013)

2012: *Marco Effekten* (*The Marco Effect*, tr. Martin Aitken, 2014)

Major Awards:

2009: The Glass Key Award, for *Flaskepost fra P* (*A Conspiracy of Faith*)
2010: The Golden Laurel, for *Journal 64* (*The Purity of Vengeance*)
2011: Danish Reader's Book Award and Danish Thriller of the Year, for *Kvinden i buret* (*The Keeper of Lost Causes*)

Website: http://www.jussiadlerolsen.com

*Naja Marie Aidt

b. December 24, 1963, Aasiaat, Greenland; *Residence:* Brooklyn, New York, USA; *Occupations:* poet, fiction author

In a 2014 interview in Minneapolis, Naja Marie Aidt, who describes herself as primarily a poet, revealed that spending her first eight years in Greenland had influenced her writing: "I grew up with all the fairy tales…. There's a strong oral storytelling tradition, and it's a rough and harsh place." Most of Aidt's nearly twenty books are collections of poetry, but she has also published five collections of short fiction, one of which, *Bavian* (*Baboon*), 2006, tr. 2014, won the Nordic Council Literature Prize in 2008, praised for its passion and lack of sentimentality (Wilson).

Baboon contains fifteen realistic stories covering a wide range of crimes—"infidelity to assault to grocery-store theft to child abuse"—with "novel perspectives" and distinctive humor (*Publishers Weekly* review August 15, 2014). Aidt describes her method as "trying to force the reader to react in a certain way instead of doing psychological realism" (quoted in Wilson).

Short Fiction Collection:

2006: *Bavian* (*Baboon*, tr. Denise Newman, 2014)

Major Awards:

2006: Danish *Kritikerprisen*, for *Bavian* (*Baboon*)
2008: Nordic Council Literature Prize, for *Bavian* (*Baboon*)

Website: N/A

Erik Amdrup

b. February 21, 1923, Visby, Tonder, Denmark; d. February 22, 1998; *Residence:* Copenhagen; later Århus, Denmark; *Occupations:* physician, professor of surgery, author

Before he began to write crime fiction at age 56, Amdrup held prominent positions in Denmark's medical community, as Deputy Chief of Copenhagen's Municipal Hospital, as head of gastrointestinal surgery at Århus General Hospital, and as professor of surgery at the University of Århus, where he attained international recognition in the surgical treatment of ulcers. He also helped found and headed Århus University's Institute of Experimental Clinical Research and wrote several surgical essays.

Amdrup made his crime fiction debut in 1979 with *Hilsen fra Hans* ("Greetings from Hans") and continued to produce many popular crime novels, historical novels, short fiction, and young adult books until his death in 1998. Not surprisingly, some of his crime novels utilize medical and biological research settings.

In 1984, Amdrup published a revealing essay, "To Write Crime Novels," in which he explained his attraction to writing fiction. Seeing fiction as an outlet for his pleasure in storytelling, he felt that while a scientific article must be "short and concise," the crime novel gives "room for digressions" as well as the opportunity to develop one's creativity to a "significantly greater extent" than scientific articles do. He insisted that "preparatory work" was "extremely essential," praising Agatha Christie's plotting and the enormous preparation—years of study of English bell-ringing—that went into Dorothy L. Sayers' *The Nine Tailors*. In discussing the elements he felt essential to quality crime fiction, Amdrup also considered the victim's personality as "vitally important" as the analysis of abnormal character that he felt must go into the creation of a convincing murderer, whom he preferred to introduce in his novels' first pages. Amdrup also discussed several successful fictional detectives from Sherlock Holmes to Sayers' "noble Peter Wimsey" and loners like those created by Hammett, Chandler, and Simenon, concluding that his own work was a hobby that allowed him to experience "something fun" (all quoted material from Amdrup's "To Write Crime Novels").

When Amdrup received the Palle Rosenkrantz Award from the Danish Police Academy in 1990. Birgit Brown humorously singled out "clues" buried in his past that might have foreshadowed his "petty criminal career." Brown recounted a request from Amdrup's wife that probably helped him begin writing fiction: she said she had nothing "decent" to read, and could he write a great book? According to Brown, after writing some early novels with professional settings, Amdrup began "pushing boundaries" by examining "people's dark sides" (Rosenkrantz Award Citation).

Several of Amdrup's crime novels were named as their year's best, and his Rosenkrantz Award-winning novel *Renters rente* ("Compound Interest"), 1989, was filmed as a Danish television series in 1996. To date none of Amdrup's crime novels has appeared in English translation.

Selected Crime Novels:

1979: *Hilsen fra Hans* ("Greetings from Hans")
1981: *Den næste* ("The Next")
1983: *Muldvarpen* ("Mole")
1985: *Arme riddere* ("French Toast")
1985: *Hvem førte kniven?* ("Who Led the Knife?")
1986: *Skybrud* ("Torrential Rain")
1988: *Lucifers lov* ("Lucifer's Law")
1989: *Rentes rente* ("Compound Interest")
1992: *Virtuosen* ("Virtuosi")
1993: *Tro, håb og nederlag* ("Oh, to Control!")
1997: *Den andens brød* ("The Other's Bread")
1998: *I skygge* ("In the Shadow")

Major Awards:

1984: The Golden Handcuffs (*De gyldne handjern*), by the Poe Club of Denmark, for the novel *Hvem førte kniven?* ("Who Led the Knife?")

1985: The Golden Handcuffs for *Uansøgt afsked* ("Compulsory Retirement")

1990: The Palle Rosenkrantz Prize, for *Rentes rente* ("Compound Interest")

Website: N/A

Jonas T. Bengtsson

b. 1976, Brønshøj, Denmark; *Residence:* Northwest District of Copenhagen, Denmark; *Occupation:* author

Jonas T. Bengtsson sets his fiction in Copenhagen's Northwest District where he lives, one of the city's areas least scrutinized by contemporary crime authors. He claims his "hobby" is writing about society's outcasts, those he says others do not want to write about.

In Bengtsson's fiction debut, *Aminas breve* ("Amina's Letters"), 2005, he traced the misfortunes of one of those outcasts, 24-year-old Janus, who suffers from paranoid schizophrenia. In this harrowing first-person narrative, Janus has just been released from four years in a mental institution where his only lifeline was letters from Amina, a Turkish immigrant girl. The letters have stopped, and deeply afraid for her safety, he desperately searches for her in his old pre-illness Copenhagen drug- and crime-infested haunts, finally arriving in the city's Muslim community. Denmark's *Weekendavisen* found this *noir* debut novel "raw and angry," with "a classic love story and social sympathy," while Germany's *Deutschlandfunk* described it as a "furious" exploration of the real world "underneath the normal," framed in "vivid, minute, precise" language "of great elegance."

Again evoking "the murky backwaters of humanity and society" in today's Copenhagen, *Submarino*, 2007, bears a menacing title, the term referring to a form of torture where the victim is held under water just to the limit of choking to death. Bengtsson's novel thrusts two brothers, men alienated from one another by a traumatic childhood and devoid of any shred of hope, "under water," tortured by societal forces they cannot escape, sinking into Copenhagen's underworld. Each of the brothers, one a heroin addict and dealer trying to care for his six-year-old son, the other a hard-drinking bodybuilder battling his own violent and self-destructive personality, tells his story in his own half of the novel, so that Bengtsson builds sympathy for them both, while, as a critic for France's *Le Monde* observed, he makes his readers feel the same vertigo that torments his protagonists. *Submarino* was made into a brutal 2010 Danish social realism film directed by Thomas Vinterberg and financed by TV 2 on condition that for authenticity half of the cast and crew had to be novices. It won the 2010 Nordic Council Film Prize and was nominated for 15 Robert Awards, but according to *Berlingske Tidende* it failed to reach a large audience in Denmark, selling only 46,000 admissions.

Bengtsson's third novel, *Et eventyr* (*A Fairy Tale*), 2011, is his first to appear in English. Bengtsson set this coming-of-age novel in 1986, in both Denmark and Sweden, when in a borderless Europe social norms have become fragile. A boy living on the fringes of society is forced to confront the sins of his loving father and his grandfather, "fleeing like his father, fleeing because of his father" (*Le Monde*) in a tale of love and legacy that *Weekendavisen* (Denmark) called "highly moving, symbolic, psychological, and realistic."

Crime Novels:

> 2005: *Aminas breve* ("Amina's Letters")
> 2007: *Submarino* ("Submarino")
> 2011: *Et eventyr* (*A Fairy Tale*, translated by Charlotte Berglund, 2014)

Major Awards:

> 2005: BG Bank Debut Prize, for *Aminas breve*
> 2010: P.O. Inquest Literary Prize, for *Submarino*

Website: N/A

Steen Bille and Lisbeth A. Bille

> (Biographical information unavailable)

Steen Bille: Former host at DR1; Film Commissioner at the Danish Film Institute; co-author of the films *The Dream*, 2006, and *Two Worlds*, 2008. Lisbeth A. Bille: Science reporter at *Magisterbladet*.

The husband and wife writing team of Steen and Lisbeth A. Bille, who met during a course on narrative journalism, opened their contemporary crime fiction series featuring science journalist Thea Wind with *Gudindens sidste offer* ("The Goddess's Last Victim"), 2012. Lisbeth Bille, who has studied anthropology and the history of religions, observed in *litteratursiden.dk* that they build their narratives on a foundation of "fidelity to facts," out of respect for their readers and because both enjoy researching to broaden their horizons ("Lisbeth A. Bille").

In "The Goddess's Last Victim" Thea Wind, interviewing a famous archaeologist at the Carsten Niebuhr Institute of the University of Copenhagen, glimpses an ancient-appearing statue in his office and mentions it in her article. The day after the interview is published, the archaeologist is found murdered in his office and the statue is missing, setting off a fast-paced combination of antiquities-trafficking, ruthless archaeological rivalry, and sinister religious cultism. As Thea pursues the mystery of the goddess's statue to Syria, the authors use multiple cliffhangers, scenes of gruesome torture, and a wealth of Babylonian and Assyrian mythology to bolster their Indiana-Jones-type adventure plot.

For their second novel, *Nattens gerning* ("Night Deed"), Lisbeth Bille has indicated that for primary sources, she interviewed several astrophysicists from the Space Technical University of Denmark and visited the Nordic Optical Telescope on La Palma. In a March 2013 interview with Daniel Øhrstrøm, she declared, "You rarely see what you see. And certainly not when you look up at the stars, where the delay of the light means that you can see the stars, perhaps long dead. The reality ... always surprises." Such surprises permeate "Night Deed," set in the rarefied community of astrophysicists. Traumatized by her experiences in Syria, Thea Wind accepts an invitation from her friend Charlotte, the director of an optical telescope research station in the Canary Islands and plunges into a dangerous story involving the abuse of power and intense professional jealousy. Reviewer Lise Majgaard found that in this "average Femina crime" the Billes tried to merge academic research with superficial action and concluded that their "combination of science and over-ambitious researchers and abhor[rent] Ph.D. students" who are "willing and hysterical enough to kill for their research" was "quite comical and interesting ... a parody of academia" (Majgaard).

Crime Novels:

2012: *Gudindens sidste offer* ("The Goddess's Last Victim")
2013: *Nattens gerning* ("Night Deed")

Website: http://www.billebille.dk

*Mikkel Birkegaard

b. 1968, Denmark; *Residence:* Copenhagen, Denmark; *Occupations:* IT developer, author

Interviewed for the British website http://authorsplace.co.uk in 2009, Mikkel Birkegaard admitted that though since childhood, when he accompanied his mother to the libraries where she worked, he has always loved books and their stories, he didn't recall consciously deciding to become a writer: "When I started to write it was because I couldn't help it." Authorship had always mystified him, because he had observed that in Denmark only a few people can make a living by writing full time, but he discovered that being a computer systems developer wasn't quite "the creative endeavor" he had expected, and in 1999 he began writing short stories for the internal newsletter of the IT company where he then worked. Eventually, because he felt he was not good at reading aloud for others, he became intrigued with the notion that those good at reading aloud might be able to manipulate the feelings of others, and perhaps even influence their thoughts, the genesis of his first novel, *Libri di Luca*, 2007 (*The Library of Shadows*, tr. 2009), which was one of the most successful of Danish debut novels, having since been translated into 25 languages (Nurnberg).

Birkegaard plans his novels thoroughly before writing: "I don't write the first sentence until I know the last, and I have a pretty good idea of what goes on in between." After the notes and ideas reach "a critical mass," he's "pouring down everything on paper" or into his computer, and then the rewriting—never ending, for him, he says—begins (quoted in *AuthorsPlace* interview). He produced the first draft of *The Library of Shadows* in six months, but then in a two-year "massacre" rewrote it completely: "only ten pages or so" from the first draft made it into the second (quoted in *AuthorsPlace* interview). Rejection by Danish publishers resulted in a third version that the fifth publishing house he contacted accepted —a total of nearly six years from start to publication in Denmark.

In *Libri di Luca*, 2007 (*The Library of Shadows*, 2009), a supernatural mystery thriller, Birkegaard wanted to convey the special atmosphere that books bring to a room (*AuthorsPlace* interview). His inspiration was Michael Ende's *The Neverending Story*, which he said felt "glued to the palms of my hands for years" because it involves the power of books to carry their readers into other universes, the foundation of *The Library of Shadows*, in which John Campelli, a young attorney, upon his father's mysterious death returns to Copenhagen, his home town, and his father's elegant bookshop, *Libri di Luca*, where he is drawn into a circle of "Lectors" with magical powers to affect people's lives through reading. John's latent powerful Lector power awakens, and he and the "good" Lectors of the Libri di Luca, primarily Katharina and Iversen, two of the shop's remaining employees, must battle an evil ancient cult of Lectors whose members intend to use John to help them control the world's leaders. A plot element involving anti–Islamic racism in Denmark brings the story a contemporary sociological dimension, fortifying Birkegaard's Copenhagen setting, in which most of the places he describes are actual locations. He feels that tension is magnified "when the surroundings are familiar but just beneath the surface something else and more sinister is going on" (quoted in *AuthorsPlace* interview).

Birkegaard's second novel, *Over mit lig*, 2009 (*Death Sentence*, tr. 2011), equally well received, features horror writer Frank Føns, who lives in a secluded house on the remote Danish coast of Zealand. While waiting for his own new novel, *In the Red Zone*, to be published, Føns has a call from his Copenhagen police contact, informing him that the body of a young woman, Føns' former lover, has been found chained and mutilated in a small fishing village near his home—an exact copy of the horrifying murder he described in his forthcoming novel. More murders follow, each mirroring one of Frank Føns' grisly horror novels. Føns has to admit that somehow he must have inspired the killer, so Føns plays detective to trap him. According to reviewer Rich Westwood, Føns' life and his art have been inextricably bound together, damaging both beyond repair and forcing him to confront "the time-honoured question—when life imitates art, does the artist have to shoulder the responsibility?" (Westwood), or as Birkegaard himself put it, "Does your imagination have any real-life consequences?" which is, according to Birkegaard, "quite a scary question" (quoted in AuthorsPlace interview).

Birkegaard's 2012 novel, *Fra drømmenes bog* ("From the Book of Dreams") is set in 1846 Copenhagen. After his father mysteriously drowns, seventeen-year-old Arthur is apprenticed to Mortimer Welles, a strange book antiquarian, pawnshop owner, and amateur detective. Arthur accompanies Welles on his investigations of citizens who have vanished in Copenhagen's noisome outskirts, including Welles' own wife, at a time when the despotic Danish king is suppressing all literary and artistic dissent. Despite that crackdown, a "Library of Dreams" is supposed to exist, housing everything the king's Ministry of Books has attempted to smother. Welles would like to open the Library of Dreams to all as an instrument of overthrowing the king. According to Birkegaard's literary agency, the Library does hold the key to solving the disappearances, "but the search for eternal wisdom comes at a price, a price terrible beyond all imagination," in an adventure tale inspired by Jules Verne and Arthur Conan Doyle (Nurnberg). Birkegaard himself observed that reading the work of other writers is "a great inspiration" for him, and he insists, "Sometimes you may even think 'I can do better than that!'" (quoted in AuthorsPlace interview).

Crime Novels:

2007: *Libri di Luca* (*The Library of Shadows*, tr. Tiina Nunnally, 2009)
2009: *Over mit lig* (*Death Sentence*, tr. Charlotte Barslund, 2011)
2012: *Fra drømmenes bog* ("From the Book of Dreams")

Website: N/A

*Sara Blædel

b. August 6, 1964, Copenhagen, Denmark; grew up in Havalsø, Denmark; *Residence:* Copenhagen, Denmark; *Occupations:* Graphic artist, television director, journalist, author

In 1993 Sara Blædel founded "Sara B," the first dedicated crime fiction publishing house in Denmark, which published Danish translations of American crime novels. Her own police procedural series stars Detective Sergeant Louise Rick of the Copenhagen Police Homicide Unit A and journalist Camilla Lind, linking police investigative procedure with contemporary women's issues. Blædel's books, which launched the "*femikrim*" subgenre of detective fiction in Denmark, have been published in seventeen countries, and in 2011 she was voted Denmark's most popular novelist for the third time.

As the "half urban and half rural" (Wegner) only child of a famous Danish journalist and a well known Danish actress who often read Agatha Christie's novels to Sara in her childhood, Sara

Blædel grew up in two worlds, one surrounded by professional writers and performers, the other private and bookish. She was dyslexic, but mystery novels like Christie's allowed her to escape daily life: "As a child I found peace in crime novels, and it is with them that I find peace today" (quoted in http://sarablaedel.com/sara/). In her other, rural, world, she was a passionate equestrienne, as a child riding her fjord horses Lady and Tulle, and later competing in dressage. At eighteen she became an apprentice waiter at Copenhagen's Hotel Plaza, later moving into graphic design and television research and editorial directing.

Blædel describes her books as "made up of a bit of everything … but most importantly, they are good stories about extraordinarily ordinary people, and the kinds of problems and challenges that we all meet up with in our lives" (Blædel, "Unboxing Books" 25). She dates her conception of the Louise Rick series from a ski trip to Norway she took while a journalist, later contacting Copenhagen's homicide police chief Ove Dahl to research investigative work. In the summer of 2003, while picking her bicycle up from a shed behind the Royal Hotel where she was working on a television program, she was struck by the thought, "What if they found a corpse in the bicycle shed, and imagine if it turned out to be a journalist!" (quoted in Wegner). Louise Rick herself sprang into Blædel's mind around the same time, when the author wondered "What if I could write a crime novel myself?" Blædel based both Louise Rick and Camilla Lind on television colleagues, because she wanted to put distance between herself and her protagonists ("Man of the Book Q and A"). Blædel's debut novel and first of the series, Grønt støv ("Green Dust"), 2004, where Louise Rick simultaneously faces the murder of a young girl and the murders of two crime reporters, earned her the Danish Crime Academy's debut novel award in 2004.

"What if" has become Blædel's usual springboard for beginning a novel. Besides Agatha Christie's detectives, Blædel's literary inspirations include the Martin Beck series by Maj Sjöwall and Per Wahlöö, Ed McBain's 87th Precinct novels with hero Steve Carella, and "of course" P.D. James' Adam Dalgleish of Scotland Yard (Wegner). Blædel consistently devotes considerable time and energy to researching her books, using real-life locations, like her own old Copenhagen apartment on the fourth floor of a building in Hollaendervej, which she calls a "lovely historical neighborhood," near the Frederiksberg Garden where Louise generally runs, for Louise Rick's home, and her own favorite cafés for Louise's. Blædel sketches her stories' developments on a large whiteboard she calls her "killing wall," because she says she needs visual stimulation to ignite her creativity, and she frequently calls on experts for background material: "I am so fortunate to have good helpers in those areas where I really need factual knowledge—whether in the Homicide Division, Forensics or Forensic Psychology" (quoted in http://sarablaedel.com/sara/).

Blædel admits that while writing, "I am absolutely not fun to be with. And therefore everyone is happiest if I get it over with somewhere else" (quoted in http://sarablaedel.com/sara/), meaning the calm summer house where she creates brutal crime novels that paradoxically bring her the kind of peace that Hercule Poirot and Miss Marple gave her as a child.

The Louise Rick series typically addresses crimes severely impacting women, like honor killings, drug-related crimes, online dating scams, human trafficking, and biker-related homicides. In "Meet Louise" on Blædel's home page, the author describes her protagonist as tall, slim, and athletic, not much given to makeup except for mascara, with green eyes and long dark curly hair usually worn in a ponytail. She customarily wears jeans, long sleeved tee shirts, and sneakers, but she'd occasionally like to appear a bit more "lady-like." She prefers male company and avoids all-girl social gatherings that "involve dinner conversations all about stupid husbands" or cocktail parties that facilitate one-night stands. Blædel gave Louise Rick her own primary school at Hvalsö, 35 miles west of Copenhagen and a younger brother, Mikkel, who lives with his wife and two children a few miles from their parents.

Louise had an eight-year relationship with Peter, who then left for Scotland, fruitlessly hoping Louise would follow; they briefly lived together after he returned, but it didn't work, so Louise now lives alone, relishing her freedom and her "aunt and nephew" relationship with Marcus, the son of her close long-time friend Camilla Lind. After graduating from Denmark's National Police College with honors at 26, Louise began working at the national police headquarters in Copenhagen, where she became a homicide detective as described in *Kald mig prinsesse*, 2005, Blædel's second novel in the series, titled *Call Me Princess* in her American debut, 2011. Louise and Camilla, "one another's families by choice," develop together throughout the series, navigating both through Copenhagen and into the countryside "with large forests, fjords, and villages. A region with an ancient history and a thousand year-old mythology" (Blædel, "Unboxing Books" 25).

Blædel's novels all treat violence against women. Opening with a brutal rape scene, *Kald mig prinsesse,* 2008 (*Call Me Princess,* tr. 2011), traces the horrifying consequences of an extremely popular online dating website. The victim, Susanne Hansen, barely survives, but soon another victim is found, this time dead, and Louise plunges herself into the online dating world of "nightwatch.dk" to catch the killer.

Louise Rick later joins PET, the *Politiets Efterretningstjeneste,* the Danish Security and Intelligence Service. Her training at the U.S. FBI Academy in hostage negotiation equipped her to work in PET's Negotiator Group, and she also assisted the Serious Crime Squad in *Kun ét liv,* 2007 (*Only One Life,* tr. 2012), which treats honor killings in the Muslim immigrant community. *Aldrig mere fri,* 2008 (*Farewell to Freedom,* tr. 2012), addresses human trafficking, Eastern European young women enslaved by gangsters and forced into prostitution on Copenhagen streets. Most tourists never see this aspect of Copenhagen, "a city constantly battling an influx of Eastern European gangsters without regard for human life" (Cogdill). This novel also reveals the inner workings of Danish police procedures and "how internal politics and sexism are universal problems with which female cops, no matter their ethnicity, must deal" (Cogdill). Blædel's eighth Louise Rick novel, *Dødesporet,* 2013 ("Dead Track") has received strong reviews in Europe, earning Blædel her third nomination for the Martha Prize, given since 1989 by booksellers Bog & Ide to "The Favorite Danish Author." *De glemte piger* (*The Forgotten Girls*), the fourth Louise Rick novel published in English, 2014, places Rick at the head of the new Special Search Agency, but its initial case also "plunges her back into a nightmare she has spent decades struggling to forget," a tragedy she suffered as an adolescent that shaped her life. (*Publishers Weekly* review November 17, 2014). This case involves a mentally handicapped murdered woman that Louise identifies as having been sent to the Eliselund mental institution-cum-orphanage at three, "a special kind of hell where parents were discouraged from visiting their children and most were abandoned" (O'Brien, Review of *The Forgotten Girls* 48).

The entire Louise Rick series deals with ordinary people faced with "small joys and great sorrows," living unfulfilled lives "robbed of any potential for happiness" (Fourouklas)—"Copenhagen's downtrodden," who are often overlooked or forgotten by many who prefer to see only the sunny surface of Denmark's welfare state. Blædel unflinchingly portrays its "immigrants, failures, and the chronically unlucky" in a "tough narrative voice that curbs sentiment" (*Publishers Weekly* review October 29, 2012).

In all of Louise Rick's cases, critic Lakis Fourouklas observes that Blædel produces multilayered stories in which the first layer presents facts; the second, hidden truths; the third, the characters' lies; and the fourth, social commentary. "Blædel is more interested in exploring the tortured psyches of her subjects than providing the reader with a fast-paced narrative," telling "the story behind the story, to see where people are coming from and where they dream of going … to make us think" (Fourouklas). Blædel herself knows how hard it is to write fiction like this:

she says she "can easily remember how the feeling was when I sat in front of the [blank computer] screen ... and thought: Will there ever be a book out of it?" (quoted in Wegner).

Sara Blædel has also participated in collaborative writing projects. She co-authored *I skyggen af Sadd* ("In the Shadow of Sadd") with fellow Danish crime writers Grete Lise Holm, Lars Kjædegaard, and Steen Langstrup (see **Steen Langstrup,** below), from Langstrup's concept of a mob boss in an unnamed European city, involved with homicide, dirty money, and striped aquarium fish. Blædel also contributed to *Dødelig alvor* ("Deadly Earnest"), 2012, a nine-author Scandinavian crime fiction anthology benefiting Doctors Without Borders.

Crime Novels:

Detective Louise Rick Series:

2004: *Grønt støv* ("Green Dust")
2005: *Kald mig prinsesse* (*Call Me Princess,* tr. Erik J. Macki and Tara F. Chace, 2011; also published as *Blue Blood,* 2012)
2007: *Kun ét liv* (*Only One Life,* tr. Erik J. Macki and Tara F. Chace, 2012)
2008: *Aldrig mere fri* (*Farewell to Freedom,* tr. Erik J. Macki and Tara F. Chace, 2012)
2009: *Hævnens gudinde* ("Goddess of Revenge")
2010: *Dødsengelen* ("Angel of Death")
2014: *De glemte piger* (*The Forgotten Girls,* tr. Signe Rød Golly, 2014)

Collaborative Crime Novels:

2005: *I skyggen af Sadd* ("In the Shadow of Sadd") co-authored with Grete Lise Holm, Lars Kjædegaard, and Steen Langstrup, from a concept, plot, and characters by Steen Langstrup

Crime Fiction Anthology:

2012: *Dødelig alvor* ("Deadly Earnest"), with eight other Scandinavian crime authors

Major Awards:

2004: Danish Crime Academy Award for *Grønt støv*
2010: Author of the Year Award (Denmark)
2014: The Martha Prize (Denmark's Most Popular Novelist, for fourth time)

Website: http://sarablaedel.com/louise

*Anders Bodelsen

b. February 11, 1937, Frederiksberg, Denmark; *Residence:* N/A; *Occupations:* journalist, author

Writing in the 1960s' neo-realistic tradition, Anders Bodelsen has earned an international reputation with his extensive body of thrillers, crime fiction, science fiction, and adventure, many adapted for films and television. After studying law, economics, and literature at the University of Copenhagen in 1959–1960, Bodelsen wrote freelance film criticism, and in 1967 he began to review books and television dramas for *Politiken.* According to *The Great Danish Encyclopedia,* his 1973 novel *Bevisets stilling* (*Consider the Verdict,* tr. 1976) presents a taxi driver accused of murdering a young woman but who is subsequently and belatedly acquitted because of insufficient evidence, allowing Bodelsen to place an individual in an extreme situation in order to clarify the downside of competition and the negative social values of consumerism that too often clash with basic human values. In most of his socialist-oriented thrillers he also explores the conflicts ordinary individuals face when tempted by crime, much as authors who inspired him, like Patricia Highsmith and Georges Simenon, had done. His most famous crime novel was *Tænk på et tal*, 1968 (*Think of a Number,* tr. 1978), filmed as *The Silent Partner* in 1978.

In both his fiction and his films, which expand upon Alfred Hitchcock's techniques, Bodelsen tended to criticize Danish society from his socialist political position, which seems to have made him a target for more extreme Marxist ideologues.

A case in point is Bodelsen's 1988 historical crime novel *Mørklægning* ("Blackout"), from which Bodelsen wrote the script for Palle Kjaerulff-Schmidt's two-part television miniseries produced by Danish Television in 1992. As Bodelsen's treatment of police activity and existential conditions during World War II, one of Denmark's darkest moments in modern history, "Blackout" treats the moral dilemmas of Danish police officers in Copenhagen's Criminal Investigation Division, faced with more murders than they can possibly solve, especially with German authorities watching their every move. In the narrative, Otto Baumann, a producer who has covertly produced a German propaganda film, is murdered coming from a party, by means of weapons from the Danish Resistance. Danish police detectives Nielsen and Andersen become suspicious, however, when they learn that all photographs of Baumann vanished before the murder occurred, which leads them to believe that Baumann's secrets went beyond a simple film job for the Nazis.

Bodelsen used the term "blackout," the wartime term for curfews and windows darkened in case of air attacks, as a metaphor for assassinations during the war as well as the sinister mood prevalent in occupied Denmark, where discoveries a half-century later are indicating the nature and the extent of things immorally "blacked out" of the national consciousness and temporarily at least expunged from its history. On the personal level, Bodelsen also used "blackout" to denote Baumann's past sins which after his death are coming to light during the police investigation, which Detective Nielsen pursues secretly after the Nazi crackdown and takeover of the Danish police in 1944. Calling the television version of "Blackout" a minor classic of Danish TV drama history, film critic Kim Toft Hansen believes that the miniseries "Blackout" displays a "ratio between dark and light in the detection process," since "Crime fiction is a genre of enlightenment" that works toward the "light" or "clarity" of the solution to a crime. "The blackout is thus an obscuration" of the process of crime solution, "which is what the [Danish] police suffer through war" (Hansen).

After about a six year hiatus, Bodelsen returned to crime stories with *Den åbne dør* ("The Open Door"), 1997, a psychological thriller about a girl who has gone missing, originally a magazine serial. Bodelsen has also written thrillers for children, notably *Guldregn* ("Golden Shower"), 1986, filmed with Bodelsen's cooperation by Danish National Television.

Crime Novels:

1968: *Hændeligt uheld* (*One Down,* tr. Carolyn Bly [UK 1970], also published as *Hit and Run* [U.S. 1970])

1968: *Tænk på et tal* (*The Silent Partner,* tr. David Hohnen [UK 1969], also published as *Think of a Number* [U.S. 1978])

1969: *Frysepunktet* (*Freezing Down,* tr. Joan Tate, 1971)

1971: *Straus* (*Straus,* tr. Nadia Christensen and Alexander Taylor, 1974)

1973: *Bevisets stilling* (*Consider the Verdict,* tr. Nadia Christensen, 1976)

1975: *Operation Cobra* (*Operation Cobra,* tr. Joan Tate, UK 1976, U.S. 1979)

1988: *Mørklægning* ("Blackout")

1997: *Den åbne dør* ("The Open Door")

Major Awards:

1988: The Martin Beck Award, for *Mørklægning* ("Blackout")

Website: N/A

Benni Bødker and Karen Vad Bruun

Benni Bødker: b. 1975; *Residence:* Copenhagen, Denmark; *Occupation:* young adult author and crime fiction co-author

Karen Vad Bruun: b. 1977; *Residence:* Copenhagen, Denmark; *Occupation:* literary agent

The writing team of Benni Bødker and Karen Vad Bruun debuted in 2011 with *Blod vil have blod* ("Blood Will Have Blood"), the first novel they wrote together as well as their first thriller, written in the tradition of Scandinavian contemporary realism and according to the Nordin Agency, providing "rare insight" into legal anthropology, the scientific specialty of its heroine Linnea Kirkegaard, who uses her expertise to restore "human dignity to the victims with tragic fates" ("Benni Bødker and Karen Vad Bruun").

The Bødker-Bruun team addresses international crises in their crime novels, beginning with the discovery of the bones of an Iraqi interpreter, buried with a 4,000-year-old clay tablet in "Blood Will Have Blood," followed a few days later by a savage murder in Copenhagen, where Linnea Kirkegaard has returned to work at the Institute of Forensic Medicine after her father's funeral. The novel touches on the psychological consequences for Danish soldiers who served in Iraq and Afghanistan. In *Før døden lukker mine øjne* ("Before Death Closes My Eyes") Linnea and Police Assistant Commissioner Thor M. Dinesen investigate a case involving the hijacking of a Danish ship by Somali pirates off the Horn of Africa and an arms-smuggling ring, while in *Når solen forsvinder* ("When the Sun Disappears"), Linnea probes the dangerous activities of a gangster ring in Spain. Danish critics have praised the authors' "unusually varied characterizations and their skillfully constructed plots, "Brilliant research and exciting highlights" (*Politiken*, quoted in the Nordin Agency's website).

Crime Novels:

2011: *Blod vil have blod* ("Blood Will Be Blood")
2012: *Før døden lukker mine øjne* ("Before Death Closes My Eyes")
2013: *Når solen forsvinder* ("When the Sun Disappears")

Website: N/A

Jonas Bruun

b. 1968; *Residence:* N/A; *Occupations:* Poet, author

After publishing two collections of poetry, Bruun turned to crime fiction. He compares himself to writers like Raymond Chandler, Dan Turèll, and "especially Christian Dorph," all of whom had a love for poetry that Bruun believes led them to write one or more novels; he also enigmatically stated, "in any case, it seems that poets like criminals" (quoted in Pedersen, litteratursiden.dk interview).

In Bruun's debut novel, *Drivjagt* ("Driven"), 2006, alcoholic village clergyman Knud Thorm, who. gifted with an uncanny ability to see into the darkest recesses of the soul, has lost his faith in God and man, is accused of killing his abrasive neighbor Peter Kowalski during a hunting trip, Thorm is arrested, but he is released because of lack of evidence, and another killing, this time of Thorm's only friend, follows. Attempting to clear his name, Thorm begins to investigate the murder, in the process uncovering the dark secrets of incest, jealousy, and greed that underlie the Zealand village's apparently serene surface. Reviewer Tonny Hornbaek praised Bruun's "flair for languages" and his use of unusual personality types in this traditional village crime framework (Hornbaek).

Danish critic Kim Toft Hansen found "Driven" "immersive and linguistically seductive." He found Bruun's second crime novel, *Morelli-metoden* ("The Morelli Method"), 2008, greatly different from "Driven," but "in its own way [it] is just as—if not more captivating." Using a Philip Marlowe–like Copenhagen private investigator protagonist unusual in Danish and even Nordic crime literature, Bruun takes his PI Slavek Lorentzen afield to Sweden in search of Annika Olafsdottir, recently missing. He finds her, sleeps with her, and awakens the next morning to find her murdered and himself the prime suspect in her death. As Slavek, now on the run, returns to Copenhagen and probes into the rarefied world of art and its sometimes shady dealers, Bruun "presses the relationship between art and exploration" (Hansen). Kim Toft Hansen summed up "The Morelli Method" as "a fresh breeze from crime fiction['s] vast sea [which] could do with rebellion now and then" (Hansen).

Crime Novels:

2006: *Drivjagt* ("Driven")
2008: *Morelli-metoden* ("The Morelli Method")

Major Awards:

2007: The Danish Crime Academy Debut Prize, for *Drivjagt* ("Driven")

Website: N/A

Robert Zola Christensen

b. July 15, 1964, in Copenhagen; lived as a child in Amager and Frederiksværk in North Zealand, Denmark; *Residence:* North Bjert, outside Kolding, Denmark; *Occupations:* professor (Danish language), University of Southern Denmark, Kolding, freelance film concept developer, author

From his childhood, Christensen has been writing, first poems pasted up in his bedroom and later articles for his school magazine. His adult fiction, influenced, he said, by Milan Kundera, Albert Moravia, and James Ellroy among others, has frequently combined science and crime, as in his diaristic debut novel, *Kristinas tavshed* ("Kristina's Silence"), 1997, a study of a mentally ill woman seduced by her institution's director. In 1999, he published *Good Luck, Mr. Gorsky* (title in English only), a story collection he intended to show that people's narratives intersect arbitrarily, even transoceanically. Christensen turned to science for *Biologen der tabte hovedet* ("The Biologist Who Lost His Head"), 2000, featuring molecular biologist Pelle Beck, who has glimpsed the rapist and murderer of a dead child found near his mistress's home and is drawn into a case involving the organized sexual abuse of children. The short stories in Christensen's collection *Fancy og andre dyr* ("Fancy and Other Animals"), 2003, involve peculiar crimes, as does *Jysk Fitness* ("Jysk Fitness"), 2004, in which thirtyish Kenneth Kirkholm, new to Jutland from Copenhagen, shuts his archenemy Uffe in a sauna, not knowing Uffe is already dead, a situation which involves Kenneth in sinister Jutland family relationships.

Christensen moved away from crime with *Tennis* ("Tennis"), 2006, a study of a family in crisis, and *Aldrig så jeg så dejligt et bjerg* ("I Never Saw So Great a Mountain"), 2009, a stream of consciousness coming-of-age novel told by a burnt-out alcoholic high school teacher. Christensen published his first real scientific thriller, *Is i blodet* ("Ice in the Blood"), 2013, first of a planned series of science-centered crime novels, in which Theis, a researcher at the Niels Bohr Institute, goes to the Greenland ice cap only to find all but one of his colleagues naked and dead on the ice. The missing one is Vibe, a former environmental activist and Theis' girlfriend, and during Theis' search for her, he learns that the mystery extends back into the 1960s, when Americans lost nuclear bombs on the ice cap. This novel has met with mixed reviews because of its heavy use of scientific background and terminology, but it is Christensen's first attempt at allowing a true criminal plot to control his narrative (Ravn).

Selected Crime Novels:

1997: *Kristinas tavshed* ("Kristina's Silence")
2000: *Biologen der tabte hovedet* ("The Biologist Who Lost His Head")
2004: *Jysk Fitness* ("Jysk Fitness")
2013: *Is i blodet* ("Ice in the Blood")
2013: *Hævn* ("Revenge")

Major Awards: N/A

Website: http://www.forfatterweb.dk

Leif Davidsen

b. July 25, 1950, Otterup, Funen, Denmark; *Residences:* After Spain and Moscow, Copenhagen, Denmark; *Occupations:* journalist, television editor, author

Davidsen says that he has never regretted his more than twenty years working as a foreign journalist for the Danish Broadcasting Corporation. His juvenilia includes lyrics, modernist short stories, and radio drama, but on a 1980 trip to Moscow, relatively late in his life, he discovered the possibilities of the thriller genre and began *Unhellige alliancer* (*Unholy Alliances*), 1984, tr. 1988, his first effort at writing about political, historical, and social issues that concerned him (quoted in http://www.litteratursiden.dk). Davidsen retired from journalism at the end of 1998 to write fiction full-time and since has produced several short story collections and twenty-three novels, as well as *Østfronten* ("Eastern Front"), 1999, a study of the 12,000 Danish volunteers who fought for Germany in World War II, including 6,000 who served with the Waffen-SS on the Eastern Front; *Danske øjeblik* ("Danish Moments"), a description with press photographs of Danish work, social, and cultural life through the twentieth century; and *Dostojevskiis sidste rejse* ("Dostoevsky's Last Journey"), 2000, Davidsen's diary of a two-week river trip from Moscow to Perm in 2000.

Davidsen's political thrillers fall into three categories, not necessarily written in chronological order: two novels about Spain; the "Balkan trilogy"; and the "Russian tetralogy." He often set them outside of Denmark, treating individual protagonists, usually Danes, caught up in a dangerously changing world. His first, *Uhellige alliance,* 1984 (*Unholy Alliances,* tr. 1986), also published as *The Sardine Deception*), 1984, involves political intrigue in Spain's Basque region just after Franco's death in 1975, followed by *Den russiske sangerinde,* 1988 (*The Russian Singer,* tr. 1991) set in the chaotic period after the fall of Soviet Communism in Russia, with a Danish diplomat who falls in love with a Moscow nightclub singer. *The Russian Singer* was made into a 1993 film directed by Morten Arnfred. *Den sidste spion* ("The Last Spy"), 1991, traces the hunt for a top-level Soviet mole in Denmark's government just after the destruction of the Berlin Wall.

Davidsen's award-winning *Den serbiske dansker*, 1996 (*The Serbian Dane*, tr. 2004), follows Vuk, a young Bosnian Serb hit man who grew up in Denmark. He wanders through Copenhagen, amazed at how the city has changed since he left, and through Vuk's contacts with a childhood friend, Davidsen reveals the traumatic experiences in the former Yugoslavia that turned Vuk into a hired killer now contracted to kill Iranian dissident author Sara Santanda, invited by Danish PEN to speak in Copenhagen, with a four million dollar *fatwa* price on her head offered by Iranian mullahs. Vuk is tracked by tough Danish Detective Inspector Per Toftlund, assigned to protect Santanda in this thriller that reveals the cracks in Denmark's welfare state system and the corruption of its double-dealing politicians.

The protagonist of *Lime's billede*, 1998 (*Lime's Photograph*, tr. 2001), shortlisted for the 2002 Ian Fleming Steel Dagger Award, Peter Lime, is a handsome alcoholic loner, a *paparazzo* making his living from "today's narcissism and insatiable appetite for gossip" (*Lime's Photograph* 43). He intends to make a lot of money from his shot of a Spanish government minister *in flagrante* with a young Italian actress, but before he can sell it, he is arrested and his home is bombed. In pursuit of his antagonists, he flashes back to the 1960s, the 1970s, the fall of the Berlin Wall at the end of the 1980s, and the riotous 1990s in Europe. Lime concludes, "If you live by the media, you die by the media. Either abruptly, or that slow, painful death, when no one points the viewfinder at you any more. When you're no longer a story, just a memory" (*Lime's Photograph* 302).

Davidsen wrote and set *De gode søstre* (*The Woman from Bratislava*) in 2000, but it did not appear in English until 2009. His Danish perspective assesses the Yugoslavian conflict in the light of World War II and the 1989 fall of the Berlin Wall, with a strong moral message helping to make sense of a conflict that has seemed "confusing and obscure" to outsiders, in particular how NATO bombing against Milosevic devastated the country, sending thousands of refugees into poverty-stricken Albania, which could not care for them. This turned "individuals, families and local communities against each other" (Clarke, May 2010). Maxine Clarke has observed that Davidsen unflinchingly exposed Denmark's "enthusiastic embrace of Nazism" at the start of World War II, and how Denmark then "turned on its former military heroes, branding them as traitors and attacking or ostracizing their families" and rewrote history to show the Danes as heroically resisting Nazi evil and to suppress information about Danes who supported the Nazis. Davidsen reveals these cover-up actions, which still affect his own country and Europe as a whole, through the story of a family fatally disrupted by those historical events. "Nazism's shadow has cast a pall that has lasted until the present-day, aided by the smug hypocrisy of countries like Denmark, which would prefer to brush their support for fascism under the carpet rather than openly examine it" (Clarke, May 2010).

Davidsen's *Patriarkens hændelige død* ("The Accidental Death of the Patriarch"), 2013, has been hailed as his finest novel to date, dealing with what his literary agency Leonhardt & Høier calls "the unholy alliances between religion and politics and between love and revenge." Gabriel Lassen, a Danish employee of the Russian Orthodox hierarchy, is found beaten to death in a Moscow alley the very night the patriarch of Russia dies peacefully in his sleep; When Gabriel's brother Adam, a meteorologist, sets out to solve Gabriel's murder, Adam probes his parents' Danish-Russian love affair in the 1970s Soviet Union as well as economic and religious machinations in today's Russia with a renamed and still-thriving KGB operating a political game with Greenland's rich natural resources as its major prize. In awarding this novel five stars, *Politiken* compared its enigmatic fascination to "the famous Russian wooden dolls that always hide a new surprise," and praised it as Davidsen's "best political thriller yet." Davidsen himself notes the most telling endorsement for this novel is that this book cannot be published in Russia. Fear has prevented its publication in Japan as well (*Politiken March* 13, 2013 and February 4, 2013 respectively).

Crime Novels:

1984: *Uhellige alliancer* (*The Sardine Deception*, tr. Tiina Nunnally and Steve Murray, 1986; also published in 1988 as *The Unholy Alliances*)

1988: *Den russiske sangerinde* (*The Russian Singer*, tr. Jørgen Schiøtt, 1991)

1991: *Den sidste spion* ("The Last Spy")

1996: *Den serbiske dansker* (*The Serbian Dane*, tr. Gaye Kynoch, UK 2007; tr. Barbara J. Haveland, U.S. 2014)

1998: *Lime's billede* (*Lime's Photograph*, tr. Gaye Kynoch, 2001)

2001: *De gode søstre* (*The Woman from Bratislava*, tr. Barbara J. Haveland, 2009)

2004: *Fjenden i spejlet* ("The Enemy in the Mirror")

2006: *Den ukendte husfru* ("The Unknown Wife")

2008: *På udkig efter Hemingway* ("Looking for Hemingway")

2010: *Min broders vogter* ("My Brother's Keeper")

2013: *Patriarkens hændelige død* ("The Accidental Death of the Patriarch")

Short Story Collection:

2011: *Utahs bjerge og andre historier* ("Utah's Mountains and Other Stories")

Major Awards:

1997: Best Fiction Book Award from *De 12 bøger* book club

1988: Palle Rosenkrantz Prize, for *Den russiske sangerinde* (*The Russian Singer*)

1991: The Golden Laurel Award, for *Den sidste spion* ("The Last Spy")

1999: The Glass Key Award, for *Lime's billede* (*Lime's Photograph*)

2007: Danish Favorite Author Prize

Website: N/A

Literary Biography:

"But It Always Starts with a Protagonist: The Leif Davidsen Writings," by Lars Ole Sauer Berg, 2006; as yet untranslated.

Christian Dorph

b. August 27, 1966, Odense, Denmark; *Residence:* N/A; *Occupations:* poet, teacher, author

After studying Danish literature at Aarhus University, Dorph has been teaching creative writing at Christian Testrup Højskole. After publishing two volumes of poems in 1992 and 1995 respectively, Dorph wrote crime novels *Øjet og øret* ("Eye and Ear"), 1999 and *Hylster* ("Holster"), 2003. Sharing their leftist convictions, Dorph cites the work of Swedish crime authors Maj Sjöwall and Per Wahlöö and American James Ellroy, along with "the old hard-boiled" classic writers Raymond Chandler and Dashiell Hammett (Lisbeth Larsen) as inspirations for his detective novels, though he also is "just as inspired" by Hemingway, Kerouac, and William S. Burroughs, "because they mastered a more literary prose, while they are also very hard-boiled" (quoted in Libseth Larsen). Both "Eye and Ear" and "Holster" feature private detective Frank Harder, who in "Eye and Ear" investigates a woman's murder in Odense. In "Holster," Harder works on a case of anti–Semitic graffiti placed on a wealthy Jewish doctor's home. Since 2003 Dorph has collaborated with Simon Pasternak on historical crime novels dealing with Danish history of the past quarter century. (See "Christian Dorph and Simon Pasternak," and "Simon Pasternak," both below.)

Crime Novels:

1999: *Øjet og øret* ("Eye and Ear")
2003: *Hyslter* ("Holster")

Major Awards: N/A

Website: N/A

Christian Dorph and Simon Pasternak

In a 2005 interview with *Politiken*, Dorph observed, "I like to seduce the reader, so I am very interested in the plot of the thriller.... I like to ... discuss my plots, for example, with my editor" (quoted in Lisbeth Larsen). Dorph's editor Simon Pasternak also liked to discuss plots with Dorph, so they combined their efforts to produce a series of crime novels set in the previous three decades. Their first collaboration, *Om et øjeblik i himlen* ("In a Moment in Heaven"), 2005, opens with the triple homicide of fashion house director Stones Bang, his wife Ellen, and their young daughter, just after the 1975 bloody "Red Army" faction hostage case. Copenhagen police detectives Ole Larsen and his sexually ambivalent colleague Erik Rohde soldier through the case while facing their own intimate problems. Set in October 1979 on the day when Danish Finance Minister Knud Heinesen resigned his position, *Afgrundens rand* ("Edge of the Abyss"), 2007, has Rohde struggling with personal issues related to the AIDS epidemic, while Larsen has to save Rohde from being the prime suspect in the death of a prominent businessman found with his belly slashed open, Greenland ritual-style, in a sauna frequented by Copenhagen's gay community. The novel also refers to the Nazi artist circle in Denmark, the 1979 oil crisis, the Cold War, and missile threats. *Jeg er ikke her* ("I'm Not Here"), 2010, features policewoman Anita Jensen, introduced in "Edge of the Abyss," who competes against Rohde and Larsen for the reader's attention as they work a complicated 1980s case involving mysterious Arab immigrants and terrorists in the death of a sexually abused young Copenhagen woman. *Dagbladet* critic Niels Vestergaard has praised the three Dorph-Pasternak collaborations, noting that like their protagonists, the authors are "children of a time when terrorism, nuclear bomb[s] and the Cold War ... created a spectacle about living on borrowed time." While noting that Dorph and Pasternak make the turbulent seventies and eighties seem like yesterday, Vestergaard observes that they also look behind "the ambiguous slogans and myths of the fundamental forces of the twentieth century's great political, cultural and scientific trends" (Vestergaard).

Collaborative Crime Novels:

2005: *Om et øjeblik i himlen* ("In a Moment in Heaven")
2007: *Afgrundens rand* ("Edge of the Abyss")
2010: *Jeg er ikke her* ("I'm Not Here")

Major Awards: N/A

Website: http://www.dorphpasternak.dk

*Elsebeth Egholm

b. September 17, 1960, Nyborg, Denmark; Residence: Aarhus (also spelled Ärhus), Denmark; Occupations: pianist, journalist, author

Elsebeth Egholm first studied piano at the University of Aarhus and the Danish Royal Academy of Music, but in 1989 she graduated from the Danish School of Journalism, also in Aarhus, and then worked for the *Berlinske Tidende* as a backing editor. In 1992, she moved to Malta and worked as a freelance journalist and married British thriller writer Philip Nicholson; until his death in 2005 they resided half the year in Aarhus and the other half on the small Maltese island of Gozo. She now lives mainly in the countryside at Kasted near Aarhus, but she also spends time at Gozo, where according to her website she writes and finds "strength in sunshine with good friends," so that her life is permanently split "between Denmark and Gozo, and between reality and fiction" (see http://www.elsebethegholm.dk).

Egholm's debut novel, *De frie kvinders klub* ("The Free Women's Club"), 1999, and the two which followed, *Sirocco* ("Sirocco"), 2000; and *Opium* ("Opium"), 2001, met with some success as "typical women's literature," but in 2006 she turned to *femikrimi* with *Nærmest pårørende* (*Next of Kin*, tr. 2013), the first of her novels to appear in English, starring journalist and amateur detective Benedicte ("Dicte") Svendsen. Egholm has since continued the Benedicte Svendsen series in print and extended the concept into television with the ten-part *Benedicte* series for Denmark's TV2. The series premiered on January 7, 2013, starring Iben Golden Plover as Dicte and Lars Brygman as investigator John Wagner.

Prior to presenting the "Benedicte" series, in 2012 TV2 had shown *Those Who Kill*, a six-part crime series based on an original universe created by Elsebeth Egholm, with protagonists Detective Inspector Katrine Ries Jensen and forensic psychiatrist Thomas Schaeffer working together in Copenhagen's Special Crimes Unit to solve serial murder cases with bizarre psychological ramifications. The director of the popular two television series *Wallander* and *The Killing* also directed *Those Who Kill*, which was the basis for *Shadow of the Past*, a full-length movie premiering in 2012 (Hunt).

In "My Two Worlds," a statement available on Egholm's website (http://www.elsebeth egholm.dk), Egholm declares she always knew that she would write, and that her favored genre was crime fiction. While studying at the music conservatory, she even wrote a story about a student who was found dead at his Steinway grand piano. Egholm maintains in her website that crime fiction offers not just grisly crimes but "the great human emotions: jealousy, revenge, hatred, love." As a journalist, too, Egholm is fascinated by both human nature and human society. She claims not to be Benedicte Svendsen; although they share a house in Aarhus, a dog, and a background in journalism. Egholm says that Benedicte was raised a Jehovah's Witness and gave up a son for adoption, and "she is also much more brave and stubborn than I am."

Egholm spends months planning a novel before she begins to write, working two to three hours each morning and then taking a long walk to plan beyond the chapter at hand. She calls herself "a bit of a control freak." Her Benedicte Svendsen series involves broad social problems like immigration and terrorism, but she leaves conclusions on these issues to her readers. Often topics from the daily news or from her journalist friends spark her ideas for a future novel; getting chills when she hears such an item, she says, is "a good sign." Though the events that appear in her novels are very close to reality, Egholm insists her characters are important, though entirely fictional, "but plot is the engine that drives them forward and also develops them" (Egholm website).

The plots Egholm has used in her Benedicte Svendsen series all involve large-scale events which severely impact Benedicte's personal life. They range from the discovery by Benedicte and two friends, all about 40 years old, of the body of a newborn baby in *Skjulte fejl og mangler* ("Hidden Defects") to arson and murder in a neighbor's stable in *Selvrisiko* ("At Your Own Risk"); the murder of a young Eastern European immigrant in *Personskade* ("Personal Injury"); a CD of an apparent ritual Muslim beheading sent to Benedicte in *Nærmiest pårørende* (*Next of Kin*); an approach to Dicte by a prisoner under sentence for murder in *Liv og legeme* (*Life and Limb*); and in *Vold og magt* ("Violence and Power") a bombing in Aarhus which now brings to the forefront Peter Boutrup, just released from prison, who is the son Benedicte had had adopted. His past catches up with him in *Tre hundes nat*, 2011 (*Three Dog Night*, tr. 2013) and *De dødes sjæles nat*, 2012 (*Dead Souls*, tr. 2014), the latter involving a murdered nun found in a moat. Peter was last to see her alive in this plot rooted in the Nazi Occupation. In *Eget ansvar* ("At Your Own Risk"), 2013, Benedicte and Peter reluctantly team up, risking their lives to solve another particularly violent murder. Egholm intends to continue writing about Benedicte Svendsen as long as the character evolves while hiding her secrets (see Egholm's website).

Crime Novels:

2002: *Skjulte fejl og mangler* ("Hidden Defects")
2004: *Selvrisiko* ("At Your Own Risk")
2005: *Personskade* ("Personal Injury")

Selected Novels of the Benedikte Svendsen Series:

2006: *Nærmest pårørende* (*Next of Kin*, tr. Don Bartlett and Charlotte Barslund, 2011)
2008: *Liv og legeme* (*Life and Limb*, tr. Don Bartlett and Charlotte Barslund, 2010)
2009: *Vald og magt* ("Violence and Power")
2011: *Tre hundes nat* (*Three Dog Night*, tr. Don Bartlett and Charlotte Barslund, 2013)
2012: *De dødes sjæles nat* (*Dead Souls*, tr. Don Bartlett and Charlotte Barslund, 2014)
2013: *Eget ansvar* ("At Your Own Risk")
2014: *Kød og blod* ("Flesh and Blood")

Major Awards:

2000: "12 Permanent" Literature Prize (shared with Carsten Jensen)

Website: http://www.elsebethegholm.dk

Jakob Ejersbo

b. April 6, 1968, Rødovre, Denmark; d. July 10, 2008, Aalborg, Denmark; Residence: Aalborg, Denmark; Occupations: journalist, author

Before his death at forty from esophageal cancer, Jakob Ejersbo, a modernist and neorealist Danish author, wrote four novels, a volume of short fiction, and a short story collection co-authored with Morten Alsinger. Ejersbo's first three novels formed a trilogy based on his youth in Tanzania. Ejersbo is best known for his fourth novel, *Nordkraft* ("Northern Force"), 2003, a powerful treatment of three youths caught up in the early 1990s drug scene in Aalborg, Denmark. *Nordkraft* sold over 100,000 copies and was made into a 2005 film directed by Ole Christian Madsen. Comparing *Nordkraft* to Irving Welsh's *Trainspotting, Litteratursiden* critic Michael Høyer has described *Nordkraft* as "a powerful testimony" not only against the crime-ridden drug culture of the 1990s but also "against Denmark in 2002, when designer drugs flow[ed] to a younger audience, while well-meaning parents, politicians, and naïve journalists grop[ed] in the dark for answers" (Høyer).

Crime Novels:

2003: *Nordkraft* ("Northern Force")

Major Awards:

2003: The Golden Laurel, for *Nordkraft*

Website: N/A

Agnete Friis see *Lene Kaaberbøl,* below

> b. 1974; Residence: N/A; Occupations: journalist, children's book author, co-author with Lene Kaaberbøl of the Nina Borg detective series

Ole Frøslev

> b. 1943; Residence: N/A; Occupation: teacher, author

Between his literary debut in 1989 and 2002, Ole Frøslev, who was also a teacher for thirty years, produced twelve crime novels, mostly contemporary police stories in his Detective Benny Rasmussen series. After a six-year break from writing fiction, he published the "Polar Night" historical police procedural series, set during the Nazi occupation of Denmark and featuring young Danish police detective Paul Bjørner and drawing on Frøslev's contacts with former policemen who had served during the Nazi occupation.

Frøslev told *litteratursiden.dk* in 2002, "The real excitement" of reading comes when a book's "people and surroundings [are] so credible that even the most unlikely plot becomes terrifying[ly] likely" ("Ole Frøslev"). His award-winning debut novel, *Tornen i øjet* ("Thorn in the Eye"), 1989, starred Detective Benny Rasmussen and his team from Nørrebro's Police Station 3, and continued their crime-fighting activities in six more procedurals. Between 1993 and 1999, Frøslev tried his hand at mainstream novels—among them marital woes in "The Danish Ladies," 1995, satire in "Lykkeland: An Edifying Story," a medical novel, "Deadline," 1998; what he calls "a rune thriller," the archaeological thriller "The Haraldinske Snake," 2000, where researchers collide with racist neo–Nazi cultists; and "Special Exhibition," a family saga with an ethnologist as hero, in 2003. Since 2005, he has completed his seven-novel World War II historical crime series using interviews with former policemen who had served under the Nazi occupation. He feels that to experience Denmark's five years under Nazi occupation, "it's a good idea to read the books in order" (Krimifan). Frøslev presently now is working on a new project, a stand-alone historical novel set in a big farmhouse on Amager around 1900.

As several other Danish crime fiction writers do, Frøslev cites Sjöwall and Wahlöö and Ed McBain as favorite authors, as well as Arthur Conan Doyle, Georges Simenon and Dorothy L. Sayers (though not Agatha Christie) ("Ole Frøslev," *litteratursiden*.dk). He also likes "good story-tellers"—Graham Greene, Maugham, le Carré, Ian Rankin, and Kate Atkinson, as well as Magnus Mills, who never wrote crime novels but still beat "quite a few people to death"(quoted in "Ole Frøslev," *litteratursiden.dk*). Frøslev also listens to jazz while he writes because it alone reminds him that one has to live in the present, "indispensable to life" (quoted in "Ole Frøslev," *litteratursiden.dk*).

Crime Novels:

Detective Benny Rasmussen Crime Novels:

1989: *Tornen i øjet* ("A Thorn in the Eye")
1990: *Symbion-affæren* ("The Symbion Affair")
1991: *To mand frem—* ("Two Men Forward—")
1992: *Culotte-tyven* ("Culotte-thief")
1993: *Virus* ("Virus")
1999: *Frosne sjæle* ("Frozen Souls")
2002: *Nedrivning* ("Demolition")

The Mørkstid ("Polar Night") Historical Procedural Series:

2005: *Den grønne bar* ("The Green Bar")
2006: *Hestetyven* ("Horse Thief")
2007: *Slagteren fra Ryesgade* ("The Butcher of Ryesgade")
2008: *Profeten* ("The Prophet")
2009: *Dragerkuskens brudenat* ("Dragerkusken's Bridal Night")
2010: *Gangsterpigen* ("Gangster Girl")
2012: *Haltefanden* ("The Lame Devil")

Archaeological Thriller:

2000: *Den haraldinske slange* ("The Haraldinske Snake")

Major Awards:

1990: The Danish Crime Academy Debut Prize, for *Tornen i øjet* ("Thorn in the Eye")
2006: The Danish Crime Academy Diploma, for *Den grønne bar* ("The Green Bar")

Website: N/A

Sissel-Jo Gazan (S.J. Gazan)

> b. 1973, Aarhus, Denmark; Residence: Berlin, Germany; Occupations: biologist, cultural journalist for the magazine Femina, author

In her *litteratursiden.dk* autobiographical statement, Sissel-Jo Gazan attributes her earliest interest in writing to her three-year journey at age five with her mother around the Mediterranean in a sailboat, when the child sent letters and stories home to friends. Gazan's many travels probably awakened both her sense of rootlessness and her love for biology, which she studied at the University of Copenhagen, graduating in 2004 with a specialty in dinosaurs. Starting in 1995, she wrote three early books during lengthy stays away from Copenhagen, "women's novels" addressing "the big issues of life: lies, cruelty, identity, freedom, and grief," and an interview collection, "Say yes—what priests know about love," ten conversations with pastors about the nature of love and faith in love ("Svalen graph," *litteratursiden.dk*).

Gazan's widely praised breakthrough novel *Dinosaurens fjer*, 2008 (*The Dinosaur Feather*, tr. 2013), centered on the scientific problem of whether birds descended from dinosaurs, opens in typical Nordic noir/*femikrim* fashion: heroine Anna Bella Nor, a beleaguered single mother, is two weeks from defending her Ph.D. dissertation on the saurian origin of birds when her professionally respected but generally detested academic advisor Dr. Lars Helland is discovered horribly slain in his office, his severed tongue on his bloody shirtfront and her thesis in his lap. Police

Superintendent Søren Marhauge is faced with untangling the Gordian knots of rivalries and hatreds that boil up in the scientific community.

In a 2013 interview with *Publishers Weekly*, Gazan indicated that she incorporated part of herself in Anna; Gazan's husband had just left her and she was alone with a one-year-old child, "frustrated and angry": with a working environment at the university that was "a bit scary": "I was all alone and there were dead creatures under glass everywhere and even the night guard seemed scared" (quoted in Lambert). Explaining the irritability that readers often perceive in Anna, Gazan explains that while writing *The Dinosaur Feather*, she saw herself in Anna, "hurt and frustrated and challenged," and she "wanted people to think, 'What a bitch'—and still really like her" (quoted in Lambert). Commenting on whether the toxic effects of lies and the parents-children theme are central to the novel, Gazan also noted that she is fascinated with lies in families, because they take up so much energy in individuals' lives (Lambert, "The Passion of Anna").

Crime critic Maxine Clarke saw *The Dinosaur Feather* as not a "typical" crime novel but a novel principally dealing with the individual interpersonal relationships of Anna, of Søren Marhauge, and of Clive Freeman, a Canadian evolutionary biologist, in a huge "back story" that occupies the first 300 pages of the novel, which Clarke found excessive. Clarke felt that *The Dinosaur Feather* was "far too long and discursive," so that a "firmer edit (for length and style) would have made it a much better focused, smoother read, and allowed it to fulfill its potential" (Clarke, June 2011).

Gazan's second crime novel, 2013's *Svalens graf* (*The Arc of the Swallow*, tr. 2014) combines passionate relationships with scientific crime, using characters familiar from *The Dinosaur Feather*. Gazan's new heroine Marie Skov cannot believe that her former research supervisor, professor of immunology Kristian Storm, has committed suicide, and neither does Superintendent Søren Marhauge, now romantically involved with Anna Nor. While Marie was working with him, Storm had discovered that a widely endorsed and used DTP vaccine was actually increasing child mortality around the world, but he was accused of academic dishonesty by the vested-interest pharmaceutical industry as well as by other researchers promoting their own unethical agendas. Line Hoffgaard, writing in *litteratursiden.dk*, concludes that by emphasizing Marie's struggles with breast cancer and Søren's suspicions that Anna may be unfaithful to him because of the scientific conflicts in this plot make *The Arc of the Swallow* more a family drama than a crime story (Hoffgaard).

Crime Novels:

2008: *Dinosaurens fjer* (*The Dinosaur Feather*, tr. Charlotte Barslund, 2013)
2013: *Svalens graf* (*The Arc of the Swallow*, tr. Charlotte Barslund, 2014)

Major Awards (all for *The Dinosaur Feather*):

2008: Denmark Radio Literature Prize for Best Novel of the Year
2009: Danish Broadcasting Corporation Award for Crime Novel of the Decade
2013: The Literature Prize of the Ambassadors of the French-Speaking Countries

*Lotte and Søren Hammer

Lotte Hammer: b. 1955; Residence: Frederiksvaerk, Denmark; Occupations: nursing and nursing administration, politician, author

Søren Hammer: b. 1952; Residence: Frederiksvaerk, Denmark; Occupations: computer programmer and lecturer at Copenhagen University's College of Engineering, author

Siblings Lotte and Søren Hammer have been writing together since 2004, when Søren moved into the first floor of the house where Lotte and her family live. Prior to that time, Lotte frequently worked abroad in health care, including stints on North Sea oil rigs and American Air Force bases in Greenland. She headed Public Eldercare in Halsnaes, Denmark, from 1995 to 2010, and as a Social Democrat, she was elected to the Halsnaes City Council in 2007. Søren shares her interest in politics and left his position at Copenhagen University in 2010 to write full time. In reading other Scandinavian crime writers, Lotte prefers the work of Henning Mankell, while Søren says he loves the Martin Beck series by Maj Sjöwall and Per Wahlöö.

After six years of writing together that they say was mostly for amusement, Lotte and Søren Hammer published *Svinehunde* (lit. "Pig Dogs," tr. as *The Hanging*, 2013) in 2010. Gyldendal sold pre-publication rights to the novel to an unprecedented sixteen foreign countries, and almost immediately upon publication the novel sold 60,000 copies, soon doubling that figure in Denmark alone.

The Hammers have now published five of the six planned books in their Konrad Simonsen series. As many authors of police procedurals do, the Hammers use an ensemble cast and a plot structure common to all the novels. Their central figure, middle- aged and overweight Detective Chief Inspector Konrad Simonsen of the Copenhagen Police's Homicide Division, is frequently criticized by his superiors for being too loyal to his team. Simonsen solves his cases on moral principles, but he often finds himself unable to act speedily in crisis situations. He has a complicated relationship with his adult daughter Anna Mia, in part because of his developing relationship with one of his team, the Countess, a wealthy aristocratic woman who fears commitment because she has recently lost a son. She shares her home with Simonsen, but after the heart attack he suffers between the second and third installments of the series and his subsequent rehabilitation, tensions develop between them. Simonsen's team originally included martially challenged Arne Pedersen who has an on-again, off-again affair with ambitious young policewoman Pauline Berg; computer expert Malthe Borup, and officer Poul Troulsen, who is on the verge of retirement and doesn't mind using excessive force. The Hammers wrote Troulsen out after the second book in the series.

The Hammers use the omniscient point of view to explore the complicated relationships among their characters and the individual methods of investigation each prefers. They also treat the pressures exerted by political figures and the media to influence police investigations, which in *The Hanging* involve a particularly revolting crime: one morning two Turkish immigrant school children discover the bodies of five naked and horribly mutilated men hanging execution-style in their school's gymnasium. Delayed by a racially prejudiced policeman's tardiness in answering the crime report and the necessity of bringing Simonsen back from a vacation, the investigation develops slowly, but eventually all the victims are shown to be pedophiles, arousing pro-vigilantistic public opinion that the victims received what they deserved. Public and media pressure in favor of harsh anti-pedophilia punishment mounts, much of it engineered by the "avenging" killers, themselves all survivors of sexual abuse. The plot allows the Hammers to lay bare the ramifications of Denmark's relatively mild sentencing of pedophiles in what they themselves call "a tale of manipulation and demagoguery" (quoted in http://hammerhammer.com).

According to the Hammers' website, the other novels in the Konrad Simonsen series all begin with mysterious deaths, followed by tortuous investigations which involve both the Hammers' implicit commentaries on Denmark's contemporary social and political vicissitudes; and flashbacks to crucial episodes in the police team members' lives. *Alting har sin pris* ("Everything Has Its Price"), 2010, second in the series, opens with the German Chancellor's discovery of a young woman's corpse while on a fact-finding trip to the Greenland ice cap. Sent there to investigate, Simonsen learns the victim had been killed decades earlier, and the mode of death proves that Simonsen's prime suspect in that earlier case, one he would rather forget, was actually an innocent man who has since killed himself. That discovery contributes strongly to Simonsen's heart attack.

Ensomme hjerters klub ("The Lonely Hearts Club"), 2011, brings Simonsen back to work in Copenhagen after cardiac surgery. His first case after his return initially appears to be an apparently simple 2008 accident, the death of postman Jørgen Kramer Nielsen, but it turns out to be a homicide with connections leading back to 1969. The investigation causes Simonsen to flash back to his youthful love for Rita, a hippie he met during the 1970s, which in turn adversely affects his relationship with the Countess and carries over into *Pigen i Satans mose* ("The Girl in the Lake"), 2012, when the body of a young African prostitute is found in a lake north of Copenhagen, involving Simonsen and his team with Denmark's murky world of human trafficking and prostitution. Some of Denmark's wealthiest and most and powerful citizens are connected with this racket, allowing the Hammers to denounce what they call their society's "ice-cold cynicism and contempt of human life" (http://hammerhammer.com). *Den sindssyge polak* ("The Night Ferry"), 2014, hit hard at the core of Simonsen's team. A Copenhagen canal tour boat strikes a boat from Oslo in Copenhagen's harbor, and when the bodies are recovered, four of the victims appear to have been murdered. This crime has roots linked to a case Pauline Berg had tried to solve years earlier, as well as to a 1995 secret mission to Berlin where Danish UN troops were involved, so Simonsen has to go to Bosnia to find a solution (see http://hammerhammer.com).

Each case exacts a heavy price from Simonsen. At the end of each one, he collapses, as he did at the close of *The Hanging* "…they [Anna Mia and the Countess] didn't talk about the case. The case was closed. Simonsen was placed in an armchair…. If they spoke to him he answered politely but in monosyllables, as if he was not one-hundred-percent clear on what was happening around him" (*The Hanging* 297)—the price, according to the Hammers, that decent Danes like Simonsen pay for bringing the "pig dogs" they hunt to justice.

Crime Novels:

The Konrad Simonsen Series:

2010: *Svinehunde* (lit. "Pig Dogs"; *The Hanging*, tr. Ebba Segerberg, 2013)
2010: *Alting har sin pris* ("Everything Has Its Price")
2011: *Ensomme hjerters klub* ("Lonely Hearts Club")
2012: *Pigen i Satans mose* ("The Girl in the Lake")
2014: *Den sindssyge polak* ("The Night Ferry")

Major Awards: N/A

Website: http://www.hammerhammer.com

Morten Hesseldahl

b. December 11, 1964, Odense, Denmark; Residence: Humlebæk, North Zealand, Denmark; Occupations: comic book author, publishing director, broadcasting executive, author of thrillers

Morten Hesseldahl has successfully lived and prospered in two professional worlds generally considered diametric opposites. After an interdisciplinary academic education in philosophy and economics at the University of Copenhagen, he began his literary career by writing comics and later produced an acclaimed comic book series on Denmark's experiences in World War II. Hesseldahl studied business management at New York University and received an MBA in 2009 from the Copenhagen School of Business. As a business executive, he co-founded CEPOS, a civic think tank; he became a board member of Danish PEN; he has chaired the Danish Film Institute; and in 2007 he became the CEO of *Dagbladet Information.* He is currently the Director of Culture of the Danish Broadcasting Corporation and a member of its executive board. In the literary world, Hesseldahl is best known for his international political thrillers, in particular *Drager over Kabul* ("Dragons of Kabul"), 2007.

Hesseldahl believes that his background in philosophy, which began, he says, when he was a young man lying in a hammock near the Amazon River, reading *Zen and the Art of Motorcycle Maintenance,* has made him better at his executive positions (*Kubulus Alumni*). Education, Hesseldahl believes, "give[s] one a different perspective on the world" (quoted in *Kubulus Alumni*).

Hesseldahl's perspective differs markedly from that of many of Denmark's leftist crime authors who address social issues in their police procedurals. When Hesseldahl was named Director of Culture for the Danish Broadcasting Corporation, *Dagbladene* critic Per Knudsen wondered if a person could "become CEO on the left wing newspaper Information if you were one of the founders of the bourgeois think tank CEPOS?" (Knudsen). Morten Hesseldahl has not only done that, he has produced political thrillers that address burning international topical issues. In *Drager over Kabul* ("Dragons of Kabul"), 2007, the action involving Islam, terrorism, and fanaticism takes place mostly in Denmark, when Matthias, a young Danish artist, searches for Alice, a girl he met on a vacation to Norway. Two Islamic terrorists pursue him, but they are also planning an attack when Afghan President Karzai and Mona Tariq, a character based on the real-life critic of Islam Hirsi Ali, meet in Denmark during a visit arranged by the Danish Foreign Minister (Steen). In his next novels Hesseldahl created similarly compelling plots basic on current events, like *En tid til at dø* ("A Time to Die"), 2013, which involves a scandal-stricken Danish clergyman and a central African nation rich in raw materials whose aging dictator foresees a devastating power struggle to come upon his demise. In *litteratursiden.dk* Anne Klara Baehr pointed out that Hesseldahl leavens even such a stark tale with humor, warmth, and empathy—the likely result of his ability to function successfully with both worlds, international economics and the humanities.

Selected Thrillers:

1986: *Et spørgsmål om Wagner* ("A Question of Wagner")
1987: *Tågernes dal* ("The Clouds Valley")
1988: *Panik!* ("Panic")
1991: *Den skjulte protokol* ("The Hidden Protocol")
1991: *Sørøver Skummelskraeks skat* ("Pirate Skummelskraeks' Tax")
1992: *Arkivaren* ("The Keeper of the Archives")
1995: *Svanesang: Danmark befriet* ("Swansong")
1996: *Næste år i Jerusalem* ("Next Year in Jerusalem")
2007: *Drager over Kabul* ("Dragons of Kabut")
2009: *Natten er lige begyndt* ("The Night Has Just Begun")
2011: *Blodet fra Solsortesletten* ("The Blood of Blackbirds")
2013: *En tid til at dø* ("A Time to Die")

The World War II Series:

1990: *1940—Opbrud* ("1940—Breakup")
1990: *1941–42 Bristepunktet* ("1941–42—The Breaking Point")
1990: *1943—Swingtime* ("1943—Swing Time")

1991: *1944—Skumring* ("1944—Twilight")
1994: *1945—Hjemsøgt* ("1945—Seeking Home")

Major Awards:

2008: The Year's Best Danish thriller, from the Danish Crime Academy, for "The Dragons of Kabul"

Website: http://danskedagbladet.dk/nyhed/portrait-morten-hesseldahl

Peter Høeg

> b. May 17, 1957, Copenhagen, Denmark; Residence: Nørre Snede, Jutland, Denmark; Occupations: Ballet dancer, fencer, actor, sailor, mountaineer, author

Elusive in both authorship and personal life, Peter Høeg has incorporated many of his own experiences in his multifaceted fiction, including various genres and styles, such as post-modernism, magical realism, and the gothic. In 2007, however, Christian Egesholm observed that a "red thread" of theme runs throughout all of Høeg's fiction, his view of the consequences of the progress of civilization (Egesholm). For much of his work, that view was negative, although Høeg's most recent life events and work seem sunnier.

Høeg cherishes his privacy, so between publications he seems to vanish from public view. He told interviewer Christian House in 2012, "I felt from the first book, *The History of Danish Dreams*, that there was a danger, some possible dilemma between my natural wish for a drawn-back life and the larger audience and the media," so from then on he has been "placing filters: protecting my life, having a secret address and having a secret phone number" (quoted in House).

Reaction to Høeg's work has been mixed. His 1988 debut, *Forestilling om det tyvende århundrede* (*The History of Danish Dreams*), tr. 1995, enjoyed considerable acclaim, and *De måske egnede* (*Borderliners*), 1993, tr. 1994, won international awards. His best known novel and the only one which can be called a crime novel, *Frøken Smillas fornernmelse for sne* (*Smilla's Sense of Snow*), 1992, tr. 1993, was a enormous global success, followed by a well-received Hollywood film version. Between 1996's *Kvinden og aben* (*The Woman and the Ape*) and *Den stille pige* (*The Quiet Girl*), 2006, tr. 2007, however, Høeg published nothing, experiencing a divorce and a self-imposed exile from Copenhagen. *The Quiet Girl*, a difficult "multilayered philosophical thriller about a gambling clown with a Bach obsession" (House) was coldly received, though Danish literary critic Poul Behrendt insisted most commentators did not understand the novel's complexity and scope. Høeg's most recent work, *Elefantpassernes børn*, 2010 (*The Elephant Keeper's Children*, tr. 2012), is "a thriller of sorts, more humorous than frightening, and more of a coming-of-age story than a suspense yarn" (*Publishers Weekly August* 13, 2012). Høeg himself seems pleased with this more positive story. He says, "There's more tolerance ... and ... more humour and maybe a little more warmth.... That is, in a way, where I would like my life to move" (quoted in House).

Under the happier surface of *The Elephant Keeper's Children*, though, Høeg still addresses problems he sees brought to Denmark today by "progress": "serious issues about neglected children, venal church officials, and the paths to intellectual and spiritual freedom" (*Publishers Weekly August* 13, 2012). Høeg's official biography published by the Royal Danish Embassy, Washington, D.C., indicates that *Smilla's Sense of Snow*, *Borderliners*, and *The Woman and the Ape* share a theme also apparent in *The Elephant Keeper's Children*; that those who live beyond society's norms—and their children—must pay a price. In the case of *Smilla's Sense of Snow*, Høeg's heroine Smilla Qaaviqaaq Jaspersen, whose deceased mother was a Greenland Inuit hunter and her father a wealthy Danish physician, allows Høeg to explore Denmark's post-colonial history as well as the individual's relationship to his or her society and the prices paid for doing so. Her mixed heritage makes Smilla an outsider in Copenhagen, often misunderstood and usually ignored or treated with hostility by authorities.

Opening with the death of a six-year-old Inuit boy who falls from a Copenhagen apartment building, *Smilla's Sense of Snow* follows a cold and angry-appearing young woman, tough, intelligent, clever, and sometimes compared in her exoticism and obsessive, even violent, pursuit of justice to Stieg Larsson's Lisbeth Salander. Smilla's uncanny knowledge of snow convinces her that the boy was murdered, though the police dismiss the death as accidental. Smilla hunts for the boy's killer with Peter, her neighbor and lover, eventually risking her life by sailing to the glacial island of Gela Alta off Greenland with a crew intending to kill her. As gradually a strange archaeological conspiracy unfolds, Peter turns out to be a person other than the ordinary mechanic he let Smilla believe he was, and the secret connection to the boy's death proves to be a meteorite containing a deadly parasite which had infected the child. Smilla identifies the killer as the expedition's leader Dr. Andreas Tork, whom she pursues out onto the Greenland ice pack in the novel's indeterminate ending. Social inequality and injustice, focused here on the plight of the Greenland Inuits, and a huge-scale conspiracy based on corporate greed thus form the backdrop for Smilla's quest for justice, but many critics feel the science fiction-like conclusion detracts from the novel's impact.

The same criticism arose over the American 1997 movie version of *Smilla's Sense of Snow*, directed by Bille August with Julia Ormond as Smilla, Gabriel Byrne as Peter, Richard Harris as Tork, and Vanessa Redgrave as a retired mining company secretary pivotal to the plot. The film closes as Tork vanishes into the freezing water off the island and Smilla gazes out over the frozen land of her childhood—an implausible ending, according to Roger Ebert and most other film critics. Ebert would have preferred the film (and by implication the novel) to concentrate on Smilla's life as an outsider in Copenhagen, omitting its science fiction conclusion. Giving it a three-star rating out of five, Ebert declared, "Here is a movie so absorbing, so atmospheric, so suspenseful and so dumb, that it proves my point: The subject matter doesn't matter in a movie nearly as much as mood, tone and style" (Ebert).

Høeg's most recent novel, *Effeketen af Susan* ("The Susan Effect"), 2014, like *Smilla's Sense of Snow* is highly original and difficult to classify, though it strongly displays thriller elements. The special talent of its protagonist, fortyish physicist Susan Svendsen, is that people easily confide in her, a quality she has often put to use as a police consultant. Around Susan and her family swirls an unsettling image of a western civilization near total economic collapse, while environmental disaster looms and the world seems on the brink of an apocalyptic war unless Susan can locate members of a shadowy commission founded in the 1970s. *Liiteratursiden.dk* predicts that this novel will become a new international sensation ("The Effect of Susan").

Looking back in 2010 over his literary career, Peter Høeg concluded that his books, which differ so much in style and genre, are "playgrounds where everything is permitted" (bookblog). If so, *Smilla's Sense of Snow*, his major novel of crime and punishment, illustrates the self realization Høeg permits himself and his heroine and his readers: "Under certain circumstances the fateful decision in life, sometimes even in matters of life and death, are made with an almost indifferent ease. While the little things—for instance, the way people hang on to what is over—seem so important" (*Smilla's Sense of Snow* 276).

Novels:

1988: *Forestilling om det tyvende århundrede* (*The History of Danish Dreams*, tr. Barbara Haveland, 1995)

1990: *Fortællinger om natten* (*Tales of the Night*, tr. Barbara Haveland, 1998)

1992: *Frøken Smillas fornemmelse for sne* (*Smilla's Sense of Snow*, also published as *Miss Smilla's Feeling for Snow*, tr. Tiina Nunnally, 1993)

1993: *De måske egnede* (*Borderliners*, tr. Barbara Haveland, 1994)

1996: *Kvinden og aben* (*The Woman and the Ape*, tr. Barbara Haveland, 1996)

2006: *Den stille pige* (*The Quiet Girl*, tr. Nadia Christensen, 2007)

2010: *Elefantpassernes børn* (*The Elephant Keepers' Children*, tr. Martin Aitkin, 2012)

2014: *Effekten af Susan* ("The Susan Effect")

Major Awards:

1992: Crime Writers Association Silver Dagger, for *Smilla's Sense of Snow*

1993: The Golden Laurel Award and the Danish Critics Prize, both for *Borderliners*

Website: N/A

Gretelise Holm

> b. March 22, 1946, Tonder, Jutland, Denmark; Residence: From 1993 to 1998, Zimbabwe; Copenhagen and Praesto, Zealand, Denmark; Occupations: journalist, university professor, social critic, author

In her long career, Gretelise Holm, whose first name is often spelled "Grete Lise," has written more than thirty books ranging from textbooks and children's and young adult fiction to thrillers, but she is best known for her Karin Sommer crime series. She has based most of her writing on her own experiences, beginning with a childhood she describes in *Jesus, pengene og livet* ("Jesus, Money and Life"), the first volume of her autobiography, a squalid and abusive youth. She was second oldest of ten children (eight survived), and her fundamentalist and nearly illiterate father often beat his children mercilessly with the blessing of her mother, a Salvation Army devotee. The family moved constantly around the Kolding area of Denmark and lived in grinding poverty; one child died at fifteen days from malnourishment and tetanus because the midwife cut his umbilical cord with poultry scissors found in the bedroom, where the family also raised chickens (*Avisen* interview February 8, 2013). Four of Holm's five brothers have received disability pensions and three died from abuse and mental disorders. Despite it all, Holm maintains that because of their religious convictions, her parents could not have acted otherwise (Kardel).

As a tough foul-mouthed seventeen-year-old with twenty-three dental cavities because her father did not allow tooth brushing, Holm set out to make her own living, working first as an apprentice reporter for the *Kolding Folkeblad*, then for the *Berlingske Tidende* and finally Copenhagen's *Politiken*. Holm joined the Danish School of Journalism in Aarhus as an associate professor in 1983, and she became its vice rector in 1985. She and her husband, a clinical immunologist, then spent four years in Zimbabwe, the basis for her textbooks for the relief organization Danida and her first crime novel, *Mercedes Benz-syndromet* ("The Mercedes Benz Syndrome"), 1998, which treats African women's conditions and rights (Eeg) from a special perspective: Holm saw parallels between the poor Africans' lifestyle and her own sordid upbringing, just as she did with the plight of the Mideastern immigrants in Denmark (Syberg). In "The Mercedes Benz Syndrome" Holm focuses on Western aid and the effects it has had on African women through the eyes of her main character, a female Danish lawyer who observes deaths related to corruption abounding in Zimbabwe's cultural and its political system, while she herself is contemplating divorce (Chest).

As a frankly feminist author, Holm often stresses that in her fiction as in her life she aims to inform readers and generate debate about women's issues, with particular emphasis on gender equity. She firmly backs attempts to impose quotas to balance male and female hiring and prevent the "glass ceiling" phenomenon. Her support for abortion, pay equity, and sexual liberation, and her opposition to marijuana, poverty, romance, violent parenting, and "hypocrisy about [Danish] cooperation during World War II" springs from her own experiences (Syberg), in the context of the strong Scandinavian tradition of community involvement and criticism of capitalism. Because her stories always revolve around current affairs and sometimes contain harsh social criticism, Holm has frequently been criticized for sketching some of her characters too closely to actual political figures.

In Karin Sommer, the heroine of the *femikrimi* series upon which Holm's literary reputation today chiefly rests, Holm has always emphasized both the neglect of older women in modern society and the difficulties of aging, like debilitation and disease. Karin Sommer is a dynamic middle-aged woman journalist working for the South Zealand *Post* and fighting a long battle with depression. In her first case, *Paranoia*, 2002, strangers disrupt Sommer's quiet life, threatening her at night and hanging her dead cat on her apartment door while she is covering a peculiar case of a father who has killed all the members of his own family. When she complains to the police about harassment, she is considered "paranoid" and has to seek psychiatric hospitalization again, where she continues to probe into the strange family murders with support from her brother, a city official, and Andrea, a younger lawyer. As Karin unravels the crime, Holm also fleshes out her theme, that only the thinnest line divides self-interest and psychopathy.

Robinsonmordene ("The Robinson Murders"), 2003, takes Sommer to the small Danish island of Skejo on a three-month working vacation from the *Post* to write her next book, allowing Holm a scathing look at small town life. When a homicide occurs in a local nursing home and both the imported staff and local Satanists, outcasts as far as the town is concerned, are handy scapegoats, Karin finds that "there was one big lie beyond all the little lies. One big lie, there was [like] a fog bank over Skejo" (*Robinsonmordene* 63). Holm deepens this detective narrative by paralleling Karin Sommer's research into medieval witch burnings with the islanders' proclivity for blaming people unlike themselves for heinous crimes.

In *Under fuld bedøvelse* ("Under General Anesthesia"), 2005, Karin is hoping to settle down with her new lover George, a physician she met in "The Robinson Murders," but when a colleague is killed, police think Karin was really the target. This novel reaches back into Karin's childhood and out into Danish involvement in the Iraq war, allowing Holm to compare Denmark's policies regarding its Mideastern refugees to the harsh Danish treatment of German refugees who arrived in Denmark after World War II, concluding that the Danes' treatment of refugees today is just as inhuman as conditions were in the postwar Danish refugee camps. Holm's title refers to "the numbing indifference" with which Danes at the time Holm was writing this novel ignored the whole Iraq war and its consequences for refugees: how will the world look, Holm implicitly asks, if we insist on isolating ourselves from countries and people who possess world views different from our own? (Eeg).

Holm used her most sophisticated plot structure in the Karin Sommer series in *Nedtælling til mord* ("Countdown to Murder"), 2007, developing multiple story lines involving political assassinations that eventually merge into a compelling conclusion. Karin Sommer, in Lithuania to write an anniversary piece for a large company, soon encounters the organized crime and exploitation of the poor that has scourged Eastern Europe since the collapse of the Soviet Union and that today increasingly spreads illegal labor, human trafficking, and political corruption into the Nordic countries. Heightening the tension of the novel, Karin's husband George is suffering from cancer, but her reluctance to care for him reflects her own fear of growing old; in this novel Karin's personal life, however, is secondary to Holm's political reflections (Eeg).

Holm's fifth installment of the Karin Sommer series, *Møgkællinger* ("Women Who Hate Themselves"), a title possibly playing off Stieg Larsson's original Swedish title "Men Who Hate Women" for *The Girl with the Dragon Tattoo*, combines detection with political feminism. Grisly homicide occurs at a Halloween party where college student Rebecca Madsen, dressed as a skeleton, is found strangled and her lover and teacher Jonas Kampers, dressed as Death, discovered with a green bathrobe belt around his neck. Kampers is speedily jailed, but his faithful wife asks Karin Sommer, now widowed and retired, to help prove his innocence. At the same time, a mysterious "Cat Woman" is assaulting men, carrying out her self-assumed mission of castrating one man for every rape taking place in Denmark, and there are many—about 2,000 to 3,000 reported annually. By creating Cat Woman and her crusade, Holm insists that the Danish judiciary virtually ignores rape by doling out light sentences for it; while as Karen Syberg has noted, Holm also insists that when the victims are men, "there must merely be a few scratches in the groin before horror will ever end" (Syberg) Holm here attacks the prejudiced Danish society that closes its eyes to inequality and injustice, in a novel "that is indignant without being holy" (Syberg).

In a 2008 interview with Gitte Fangel, Gretelise Holm described her motivation for dissecting evil in her crime novels: "I want to examine the individual psychological, social, cultural or political mechanisms which form the basis for the ultimate evil, murder. I am looking in other words after the evil enigma" that is also the puzzle of the human mind (quoted in Eeg). In doing so via Karin Sommer, Holm updates Christie's Miss Marple by incorporating today's worldwide women's issues with Karin's unbending stance on gender equality, a combination that dominates the plots of Holm's popular crime series.

Besides her Karin Sommer series, Gretelise Holm also wrote several non-series crime novels, young adult crime novels, and feminist works, and participated in the four-author collaborative novel *I skyggen af Sadd* (*In the Shadow of Sadd*) (see **Steen Langstrup**, below), 2005, with Sara Blædel, Lars Kjædegaard, and Steen Langstrup. Her memoirs have appeared in two volumes: *Jesus pengene og livet* ("Jesus, Money and Life"), 2012; and *Kærligheden, kampen og kloden* ("The Love, Fight and Globe"), 2014.

Selected Crime Novels:

1998: *Mercedes Benz-syndromet* ("The Mercedes-Benz Syndrome")
2009: *Forhærdede tidselgemytter* ("Shriveled Tidselkgeemytter")
2011: *Firmaets bedste mænd og kvinder* ("The Company's Best Men and Women")

The Karin Sommer Series:

2002: *Paranoia* ("Paranoia")
2003: *Robinsonmordene* ("The Robinson Murders")
2005: *Under fuld bedøvelse* ("Under General Anesthesia")
2007: *Nedtælling til mord* ("Countdown to Murder")
2010: *Møgkællinger* ("Women Who Hate Themselves")

Collaborative Novel:

2005: *I skyggen af Sadd* ("In the Shadow of Sadd") with Sara Blædel, Lars Kjædegaard, and Steen Langstrup

Selected Young Adult Crime Novel:

1989: *Kniven i hjertet* ("The Knife in the Heart")

Major Awards:

1998: The Danish Crime Academy Prize, for *Mercedes Benz-syndromet* ("The Mercedes Benz Syndrome")

2000: The Danish Crime Academy Prize, for *Møglællinger* ("Women Who Hate Themselves")

Website: http://www.gretelisehom.dk

Hanne-Vibeke Holst

b. February 21, 1959, Hjørring, Denmark; Residence: N/A; Occupations: journalist, author

Hanne-Vibeke Holst, the daughter of two well-known Danish mainstream novelists and herself a journalist, fictionalizes Danish politics and combines the vicissitudes inherent in politics with her emphasis on women's issues. Three of her recent novels utilize the image of hereditary royalty as a metaphor for contemporary Danish political struggles. *Kronprinsessen* ("The Crown Princess"), 2002, displays an insider's viewpoint on political party intrigue, carried through in *Kongemordet* ("The Regicide"), 2005, in which following a general election the deputy leader of the losing party plots to unseat his leader. The deputy leader succeeds but is forcibly unseated himself by his own wife in revenge for years of subjection. Another character in this novel, a young upwardly mobile Muslim woman, experiences her Turkish family's vicious reaction to her "Danification," illustrating Holst's message that "domestic violence is classless and universal" (Paterson 46). In *Dronningeofret* ("The Queen's Sacrifice"), 2008, the fictitious Danish president Elizabeth Meyer fights an incipient mental problem and racist terrorist threats in an attempt to return her party to power and dominate Crown Princess Charlotte.

Crime Novels:

2002: *Kronprinsessen* ("The Crown Princess")

2005: *Kongemordet* ("The Regicide")

2008: *Dronningeofret* ("The Queen's Sacrifice")

Major Awards:

2003: The Søren Glydendal Prize

2008: The Golden Laurel, for *Dronningeofret* ("The Queen's Sacrifice")

Website: http://www.hannevibekeholst.dk

Kirsten Holst (Johanne Kirsten Holst Høybye)

b. March 18, 1936, Lemvig, Denmark; d. September 22, 2008, Vajle, Denmark; Occupations: teacher, editor, author of popular children's books and adult crime novels

In his *Politiken* obituary for Kirsten Holst, Danish crime critic Bo Tao Michaelis called her "Our crime queen whose kingdom was perhaps smaller than the English or Swedish, but whose regime was milder" (Michaelis, *Politiken* obituary). Kirsten Holst, the daughter of a police officer, grew up in Jutland and was a teacher before she married the writer Knud Holst Andersen. She worked for the Danish Broadcasting Corporation (DR) as an editor of children's programming and later reviewed children's literature for *Berlingske Tidende*. As her three children grew, she wrote many children's and young people's novels, which include the "Safty" series and "the kids" series, both featuring young detectives. In 1976, Holst opened her adult crime series, 1976–1998, with *De unge, de rigt og de smukke* ("The Young, Rich and Beautiful"), set in provincial Jutland, using as central figures the rural police detectives Hoyer and Terkelsen, poles apart from the hard-boiled urban detectives who have since captured so much attention both at home in Denmark and abroad. Holst's detectives inhabit a gentler world, one focused on human relationships and problems. Holst became president of *Skandinaviska Kriminalsälskapet* (Crime Writers of Scandinavia), and in 2006, after a long break from writing fiction, Holst returned to the "Detective Bea" series she had published between 1977 and 1983 with *Sin brors vogter* ("His Brother's Keeper") which according to Michaelis proved "she could still hold the scepter [of Danish crime fiction] in [her] right hand" (Michaelis).

Crime Novels:

The Hoyer and Terkelsen Series:

1976: *De unge, de rige og de smukke* ("The Young, Rich, and Beautiful")
1981: *De lange skygger* ("The Long Shadows")
1982: *Det tomme hus* ("The Empty House")
1983: *Når det regner på praesten* ("When It Rains on the Priest")
1984: *Se, døden på dig venter* ("See, Death Awaits You")
1985: *Damen i gråt* ("The Lady in Gray")
1988: *Dødens dunkle veje* ("Death's Dark Roads")
1989: *Sov dukke Lise* ("Sleep, Doll Lise")
1991: *Som ringe i vandet* ("The Ripple")
1994: *I al sin glans og herlighed* (also called *Murder på Gran Canaria*) ("All Its Splendor and Glory")
1998: *Mord i Skagen* ("Murder in Skagen")

Detective Bea Series:

1977: *Dødens rejser med i* ("*Death Traveling Along*")
1978: *Syv til alters* ("Seven to Communion")
1982: *Fabriks-hemmeligheden* ("Factory Secret")
1983: *Puslespil* ("Puzzle")
2006: *Sin brors vogter* ("His Brother's Keeper")

Major Awards:

1981: The Poe Prize ("The Golden Handcuffs"), for *De lange skygger* ("The Long Shadows")
1982: The Danish Ministry of Culture's Book Prize

Website: N/A

Steffen Jacobsen

> b. November 27, 1956, Rødovre, Denmark; Residence: Birkeroed, North Zealand, Denmark; Occupations: orthopedic surgeon, author

A successful orthopedic surgeon whose four crime novels who has become a recent addition to Denmark's crime best seller lists, Steffen Jacobsen revealed in a lengthy 2013 interview with Rikke Struck Westersø that the death of his cherished cat during his neglected childhood in "godforsaken" Gellerupparken, a huge and dismal concrete housing development near Aarhus that today he calls "a Kafkaesque hell," was the pivotal point in his life: he had to decide whether to give in to the intergenerational violence of his environment or pull himself together and work toward a better life. At fifteen he chose the latter (Westersø).

After going to eight different schools as the child of divorced parents, losing his mother to cancer as a teenager and struggling on his own all the way through a university degree and then medical school and defense of his doctoral thesis, Jacobsen felt let down, but he took up another challenge. For some time he had been thinking about issues in the lives of middle-aged men—their self-understanding, vanity, and concern for their image (Andreasen)—and about what might happen to such individuals in severe crises, like an accident in the North Sea, with a young woman who showed them real strength and heroism These thoughts coalesced into his debut crime novel, *Passageren* ("The Passenger"), 2008 (Andreasen), featuring a young woman protagonist, Robin Hansen, a Danish corrections commissioner who also appears in his second novel, *Den gode datter* ("The Good Daughter"). 2010, Jacobsen, having tasted literary success with "The Passenger," continues to write: "...although I often have been wanting to quit, I know because it [is] also fun—and interesting to let the subconscious speak" (quoted in Andreasen).

Jacobsen's literary models are John le Carré, Philip Kerr, Kate Atkinson, Eric Ambler, and Martin Cruz Smith. He likes to read Agatha Christie–type puzzlers, but he says he would never write that way (Andreasen). Jacobsen's writing is the part of his adult life most closely associated with his own past (Westersø), though he never experienced crime or police procedures directly. His criminals are known from the outset in his stories, and he puts his characters into a large-scale contemporary social and historical context, like a terrorist attack. His crime novel *Trofæ* ("Trophy"), published in 2013, is based on his 2008 doctoral thesis, which inspired him to begin writing crime fiction.

For his third novel, which he hoped to make a "classic Hitchcock-esque thriller" (Thorhauge), Jacobsen was influenced by *Gomorrah*, Roberto Saviano's non-fiction study of the Neapolitan Camorra, Naples' mafia. Jacobsen needed the kind of "serious criminals" that seemed to be lacking in Denmark, so he sent his heroine, Sabrina D'Avalos, a deputy district attorney whose father was murdered by the Mafia, to Naples. In *Når de døde vågner*, 2011 (*When the Dead Awaken*, tr. 2014), one of only two of Jacobsen's novels currently available in English, Jacobsen made Sabrina a strong female protagonist comparable to Stieg Larsson's Lisbeth Salander, using an approachable literary style. Tough heroines fighting as underdogs against entrenched male-dominated societal forces likely arise from the difficult past Jacobsen himself overcame, so that today the impatience he displays with both the underprivileged and the elite of Denmark fuel much of the power of his fiction: "I [am] not only indignant that the upper class get everything donated, I will also [be] indignant when the underclass can not get its act together" (quoted in "Elite kids").

Crime Novels:

   2008: *Passageren* ("The Passenger")
   2010: *Den gode datter* ("The Good Daughter")
   2011: *Når de døde vågner* (*When the Dead Awaken*, tr. Charlotte Barslund, 2014)
   2013: *Trofæ* (*Trophy*, tr. Charlotte Barslund, 2014)

Major Awards: N/A

Website: N/A

*Sander Jakobsen (pseudonym of *Dagmar Winther and Kenneth Degnbol)*

Dagmar Winther: b. December 4, 1980; Residence: Thorsager, Jutland, Denmark; Occupations: journalist, teacher, singer, author

Kenneth Degnbol: b. 1972; Residence: Horhalet, Jutland, Denmark; Occupations: musician, teacher, author

When fellow teachers at the Roende College, Roende, Denmark, Dagmar Winther and Kenneth Degnbol led a school trip to Romania in 2010, on that "long, boring bus ride" they discussed how to go about writing collaborative crime fiction, and when they returned to Denmark, they decided to enter the newspaper *Politiken*'s crime writing competition. After six months of "frenetic writing," they won second place with *Forkynden* (*The Preacher*), which Winther translated into English. The manuscript was sold to Little Brown in 2013, and in English it was published as a paperback in 2014, to enthusiastic critical praise (Davies) and has subsequently been published in Denmark and Japan.

The Preacher, a powerful psychological thriller about two murders that occur in a small Danish town, involves the love and guilt of normal people under abnormal pressures in the "real Denmark" where the authors live with what Degnbol calls "a creepy plot" and "a multi-faceted gallery of characters," all connected to the homicides (NTN Interview) and an intriguing protagonist, Thea Krogh, lonely, empathic, very rational, and living in a long-term relationship with a married man. The authors are at work on their second Thea Krogh novel prompted by Anders Breivik's 2011 massacre of 69 youths on a Norwegian Labour Party camp.

Crime Novels:

2013: *Forkynderen* (*The Preacher*, tr. Dagmar Winther, 2014)

Major Awards: N/A

Website: http://www.sanderjakobsen.dk

Martin Jensen

b. 1946; Residence: Haarby, Denmark; Occupations: teacher and headmaster in Sweden and Denmark, author

Martin Jensen began writing historical fiction in 1996 and today has twenty-one novels in print. His best known work in Denmark is his seven-novel Eske Litle series, which features a stubborn medieval bailiff, but he has also produced stand-alone mainstream historical novels, contemporary literary novels, a travel book, and his King Cnut series of historical mysteries, now beginning to appear in English translation.

Jensen's King Cnut series, set in the early eleventh century when Denmark ruled a sizeable portion of Britain called the Danelaw, has been favorably compared to Bernard Cornwell's Viking Trilogy. Upon conquering England, King Cnut laid down new laws conflicting with England's old Germanic code of personal honor and causing considerable tension in the land. Jensen's sleuthing pair are Winston, a former novice monk now an illuminator of medieval manuscripts, and Halfdan, as his name implies, a charming half-Danish, half-English rogue with a sly sense of humor, once a Saxon nobleman made a pauper by the Danish takeover. In 1018, Cnut has commanded Winston to paint his portrait, and on the way to Oxford where Cnut holds court, Halfdan rescues Winston from robbers and narrates *Kongens hunde* 2010 (*The King's Hounds*, tr. 2013). In this novel Cnut commissions Winston not only to paint a portrait of Cnut, but to solve the killing of Osfrid, a Saxon whose widow is accusing Cnut of causing Osfrid's death. Cnut is thus hoping that the diverse backgrounds of Winston and Halfdan as investigators can help maintain peace in the English lands chafing under Danish domination.

In their second case, *Edbryder*, 2011 (*Oathbreaker*, tr. 2014), Halfdan and Winston are asked to solve the murder of a monk, slain at prayer in the church of the monastery where Halfdan and Winston are staying the night. Starting with the monk's severed right hand, their first clue, the pair tread a slippery path between bitter monastic rivals in a shaky political structure where pleasing the Danish king is crucial to their survival. Reviewing *The King's Hounds* in 2013, *Publishers Weekly* predicted that fans of historicals "will find much to savor" in Jensen's King Cnut series.

Crime Novels:

The King's Hounds Series:

2010: *Konges hunde* (*The King's Hounds*, tr. Tara Chace, 2013)
2011: *Edbryder* (*Oathbreaker*, tr. Tara Chace, 2014)
2011: *En bondes ord* (*The Word of a Peasant*, tr. Tara Chace, scheduled for 2015)
2012: *Den tredje mønt* ("The Third Coin")
2013: *Sværdets bid* ("Sword Edge")

Major Awards:

Royal Library Prize, for *Soldaterhoren* ("Soldier's Whore"), not a crime novel

Website: https://twitter.com/kimartinjensen

*Christian Jungersen

b. July 10, 1962, Copenhagen, Denmark; Residences: Dublin, Ireland; Malta; and New York City, New York; Occupations: script consultant, screenwriter, and film teacher, author

Christian Jungersen's novels have to date been translated into eighteen languages. His debut novel *Krat* ("Undergrowth"), written after several unsold screenplays (Bartholdy), took him four years to write. It gradually reveals the deterioration of a seventy-year relationship between two men who first became friends growing up in a well-to-do Copenhagen suburb in the 1920s, and who after not speaking to one another for decades end up as mortal enemies.

Jungersen's second novel, *Undtagelsen,* 2004 (*The Exception,* tr. 2006), remained on the Danish bestseller list for eighteen months, in 2008 winning the Golden Laurel award and in 2009 voted the second best Danish novel of the past twenty-five years (http://www.vortidsdankse roman.dk) by readers of *Jyyllans-Posten,* Denmark's largest newspaper. This psychological thriller, related by four women at one another's throats in the small office of the Danish Center for Information on Genocide, maintains that the impulse toward genocide is common to all human beings: "When push comes to shove, most people will acquiesce in harming their fellow citizens. Very often, what is truly exceptional is not cruelty, but the person who resists it" (Theroux). In Jungersen's novel, two of the women receive e mail death threats which at first appear to be from a deranged neo–Nazi escaping from justice, but shortly their office becomes "a paranoid cockpit of shifting antagonisms, and finally … a crucible" where readers receive "a profound and unsettling examination of evil" (Theroux). In a 2004 interview, Jungersen commented that he had long pondered the problem of how apparently "congenial, charming, and nice" people can become "virtual demons." He concluded, "evil is most often committed by people like you and me," and he wanted to portray the self-delusion that makes people become evil and think they are really not (Bartholdy).

Du forsvinder, 2012 (*You Disappear*, tr. Misha Hoekstra, 2014), poses a troubling moral question: a headmaster of a private Copenhagen school has embezzled 12 million krone, and the following year he is diagnosed with a brain tumor that causes dramatic personality changes. The novel poses the eternal problem of free will: is the headmaster guilty of the crime, or was the tumor already affecting his behavior and thus making him innocent by reason of mental illness?

In discussing the fiction which arises from his Spartan lifestyle (Bartholdy) and his own brain, Jungersen told interviewer Stine Charlotte Hansen in April 2013 that he had begun writing to feel "he was coming closer to the world," and he claims he must open his characters up: "Experience life more richly by living your way into them." In his explorations of some of the most troubling moral issues, Jungersen sees the complexities of life that vex most human beings as being for him "fine, beautiful, special": "We should ask questions about everything. And part of literature's job is to take that certainty from us" (quoted in Stine Charlotte Hansen).

Crime Novels:

1999: *Krat* ("Undergrowth")
2004: *Undtagelsen* (*The Exception*, tr. Anna Paterson, 2006)
2012: *Du forsvinder* (*You Disappear*, tr. Misha Hoekstra, 2014)

Major Awards:

2008: The Golden Laurel, for *Undtagelsen* (*The Exception*)
2012: Leif and Inger Sjoberg Prize from the American-Scandinavian Foundation, to Misha Hoekstra for the English translation of *You Disappear*

Website: http://www.christianjungerson.com

Pia Juul

b. 1962, Korsør, Denmark; Residence: near Praestø, Denmark; Occupations: poet, translator, author

Best known for her poetry and short fiction, Pia Juul has written one short book which might be called a crime novel, *Mordet på Halland* ("The Murder of Halland"), 2009. Juul herself passionately reads crime fiction and several of her previous works deal with murder. She curiously told Peter Nielsen in 2009, "If you look at the books I have written, … there are many who die, murder, and in my drama people who shoot each other. I did not choose the crime genre to write this book" (quoted in Nielsen). She concentrates on characters' relations to one another, not conveying political messages or exploring social problems. Instead, "The Murder of Halland" presents "a series of life choices" (Nielsen).

Juul opens this short novel with a shocking scene: Bess, her heroine, who in some respects might be a dark side of herself (Nielsen), awakens one morning when her lover Halland is shot just outside their house, in the main square of a little rural village, forcing Bess to confront grief and loss and to reassess her friends, her family, and ultimately herself. Bess, who like Juul enjoys crime stories, gradually emerges from the dazed state the murder had swept over her, reliving in monologues her painful divorce from her husband Troels, whom she had left to be with Halland, and her loss of her daughter Abby. Juul raises far more questions than answers in this novel, where "Nothing can be taken at face value…. What is fraud? What is a lie? And what is the truth of the individual? This circle of truth and the different stories and versions of the truth … is a recurring theme in several of Pia Juul's works" (Hundahl).

Crime Novel:

2009: *Mordet på Halland* ("The Murder of Halland")

Major Awards:

1999: Danish Arts Foundation Production Prize
2009: Danish Bank Prize for Literature

Website: www.forfatterarweb.dk/oversigt/juul00

Lene Kaaberbøl (see also *Lene Kaaberbøl and Agnete Friis,* below)

> b. 1960, Copenhagen, Denmark; Residence: The Island of Sark; Occupations: translator, author of young adult fantasy fiction, co-author of adult crime fiction with Agnete Friis

Lene Kaaberbøl says, "When I write solo, without Agnete to ensure a solid social conscience, I tend to go a little wild" (Kaaberbøl, "Will There Be Snow?" 29). She sets her "Cadaver Doctor" historical crime novels in a small village in 1890s France, with a strong and determined heroine, Madeleine Karno, who refuses to accept the restrictions women faced at that time. Madeleine is the daughter of Dr. Albert Karno, the village's "Doctor of Death," its unofficial chief pathologist. Having taken up her father's profession, she herself would be called a coroner today, and as a protagonist of crime fiction, she can be compared with Patricia Cornwell's Dr. Kay Scarpetta. Her first case involves, according to its author, "wolves, nuns, and mysterious mites issuing from the nostrils of a dead young girl … [the novel is] my flirt with the werewolf myth" requiring Madeleine "to take a long look at what it really means to be human" (Kaaberbøl, "Will There Be Snow?" 29). Appearing in a praised English translation in 2014, this novel explores such themes as "the struggles between mind and body, science and spirit—without detracting from a gripping plot" (Review of *Doctor Death*).

Crime Novels:

Cadaver Doctor series (projected trilogy):

2010: *Kadaverdoktoren* (*Doctor Death,* tr. Elisabeth Dyssegaard, 2014)
2012: *Levende kød* ("Living Flesh")

Major Awards:

2004: Nordic Children's Book Prize

Website: http://www.kaaberboel/dk/uk-cv.htm

Lene Kaaberbøl and Agnete Friis

In a 2011 interview with *Publishers Weekly,* Lene Kaaberbøl and Agnete Friis announced that as writers for children and young adults, they had "both learned a lot from 13-year-olds." That age group craves action in their reading, and in the collaborative *femikrimi* Nina Borg series, Kaaberbøl and Friis aim for "old-fashioned storytelling," "the grab-you-by-the-throat style of writing … the kind that drags you [readers] through hellfire and damnation," and causes people to miss their buses (quoted in Foster). In a 2015 article, Kaaberbøl observed that the majority of

Nordic crime fiction shares a common "insistence on explaining *why* [italics in original] a crime happens. Brought up as we are in societies brimming with affordable childcare, free education, free health care, and a penal system emphasizing rehabilitation, ... we are still entranced by those who, on the page at least, take a switchblade to the welfare state cocoon" (Kaaberbøl, "Will There Be Snow?" 28).

The authors do their own slashing to the Danish welfare system by making their protagonist Nina Borg a Danish Red Cross nurse whose compassion (some might say her bleeding heart) causes her to risk her own life by volunteering in the world's trouble spots and in the less-than-wholesome areas tourists rarely visit in Denmark. They also differentiate Danish crime writers from their Scandinavian counterparts by calling on Danish humor, incorporating "a little bit" of humor in their weather-related Nordic- moody fictional atmospheres (Foster).

As Kaaberbøl and Friis point out on their official website, a *noir*-ish and occasionally humorous discrepancy exists between Nina Borg's professional ability to cope efficiently with "arterial bleeding or a gunshot wound," and her tendency to fall apart at home, unable to manage mundane domestic chores like cooking or the laundry. Her husband Morten wonders why she's so concerned with other people's children, often to the point of ignoring her own, and eventually their relationship flounders.

Drengen i kufferten, 2008 (*The Boy in the Suitcase,* tr. 2011) was inspired by learning that in the seven years before they wrote their novel, "more than 600 so-called unaccompanied minors had vanished from the refugee centers run by the Danish Red Cross" (Kaaberbøl, "Will There Be Snow?" 28). Nina is working at a Copenhagen refugee center for undocumented women and children. After her friend Karin asks Nina to pick up a bag from a railway station locker, Nina finds a three-year-old boy in that suitcase, drugged but alive. Pursuing his identity leads Nina "to the edges of Danish society where the ultrarich take whatever they want from the poorest of the poor, including their children" (Ryan), in this case children smuggled into Denmark by a human trafficking ring. This is a "very simple story of a woman who's lost a child and a woman who's found it, and how are they ever going to meet" (Kaaberbøl, quoted in House, "Nordic Crime Writers"), In their first novel, they keep most of the violence, sexual abuse, and teen prostitution offstage, concentrating instead on the causes of these crimes, making their readers empathize with the tragedy of wasted lives (Ryan).

In *Et stille umærkeligt,* 2010 (*Invisible Murder,* tr. 2012), Nina again takes on an errand for a friend, this time visiting a sordid hiding place for undocumented Hungarian Roma (gypsies) in an old machine shop in a Copenhagen suburb and uncovering their criminal mistreatment, overlooked by Danish policies and officialdom. Although she has promised Morten she'll not so get involved in such cases that she puts aside her own family's needs, Nina cares for the sick Roma children, made ill by a stolen radioactive device. For *New York Times* crime critic Marilyn Stasio, the multiplicity of plot threads and numbers of characters in this novel "might just cause readers to bail out" before Nina takes control of the story; she's "a compassionate heroine who deserves a better chance to shine her light on the terrible things she sees" (Stasio).

The third installment of the Nina Borg series, *Nattergalens død* (*Death of a Nightingale*), 2013, tr. 2013, involves Nina not only in "today's liberal-minded Denmark" but also the "mobbed-up Ukraine" and "the starvation-racked Soviet Union of the Stalinist '30s" (Powers). Nina has bonded with Natasha Doroshenko, a Ukrainian mail-order bride sexually abused by her Danish fiancé in *The Boy in the Suitcase.* Now Natasha has been convicted and imprisoned for involvement in his murder. Kaaberbøl and Friis deepened Natasha's psychological complexity, showcasing Denmark's immigration problem in a "fresh, feminist-inflected direction" by focusing on " the powerless, and thus the most endangered of migrant newcomers: women and especially, children"

(Powers). Because she routinely leaves her own children to help other people's, Nina and Morten are now estranged; he complains with reason that she's carrying on a one-woman world-saving crusade, but for her part, Nina, though she knows she's going too far, even risking her own life, can't control her involvement with society's victims. "For Nina, compassion fatigue isn't a real syndrome. It's merely an excuse" (Powers). Kaaberbøl observed that "Nina's psychologically wired so that the only way that she can feel competent and in control is ... if she is the person saving lives or at least attempting to do so" (Lambert, "Through the Looking Glass"). While this results in Nina's marital breakup, Friis intends to try in upcoming novels to move Nina to "a better place," not because she and Kaaberbøl want her to lose her urge to care for others, but because she needs to care about herself, too (Lambert, "Through the Looking Glass").

Kaaberbøl has noted that Nina, like other Scandinavian female detectives, battles "stereo-typed expectations," because when men leave their families to fight injustice, they are hailed as heroes, but when a woman does the same, she is generally called a "bad mother." Kaaberbøl and Friis "have had more than a few readers tell her [Nina] to 'go home to her husband and her children'" (Kaaberbøl, "Will There Be Snow?" 28). For all the exasperation Nina Borg's unbridled altruism evokes, however, she remains a witness to the feminist social consciousness of her creators. "'Like most people,' says Kaaberbøl of herself and Friis, 'we just pay a certain amount to charity organizations and hope other people do the dirty work'" (quoted in Ryan). With her series' continuing "looking-glass theme" of comfortable and safe reality on one side and on the other the harsh world of the suffering outcasts (Lambert, "Through the Looking Glass"), Nina Borg's compulsion to do society's dirty work makes her readers aware, at least, that it exists.

Crime Novels:

2008: *Drengen i kufferten* (*The Boy in the Suitcase*, tr. Lene Kaaberbøl, 2011)
2010: *Et stille umærkeligt drab* (*Invisible Murder*, tr. Tara Chace, 2012)
2013: *Nattergalens død* (*Death of a Nightingale*, tr. Elisabeth Dyssegaard, 2013)

Major Awards:

2008: The Harald Mogensen Award for *Drengen i kufferten* (*The Boy in the Suitcase*)

Website: http://kaaberbol-friis.dk

A.J. Kazinski (pseudonym of filmmakers Anders Rønnow Klarlund and Jacob Weinreich)

Anders Rønnow Klarlund: b. 1971; Residence: Copenhagen, Denmark; Occupations: film director, screenwriter, novelist, co-author with Jacob Weinreich

After an award-winning career in film, Rønnow Klarlund published his first novel, *De hengivne*, in 2009.

Jacob Weinreich: b. April 1972, Haslemere, Denmark; Residence: Copenhagen, Denmark; Occupations: screenwriter, filmmaker, author

After training at the Danish Film School as a screenwriter from 1995 to 2001, Weinreich produced two mainstream novels, short fiction, and twenty-plus children's and young adult books, including the ten-volume "Monster Hunter" series. He also wrote the screenplay for the young adult film *Koma*, directed by Kasper Bisgaard.

In 1999 Jacob Weinreich was so impressed by Anders Rønnow Klarlund's film *The Possessed* he proposed to Klarlund that they work together on a film project which became their collaborative novel *Den sidste gode mand* (*The Last Good Man*) published in 2011 and since translated into fifteen languages including English (2012). The novel's title derives from the Jewish legend that there are thirty-six righteous "good" people on earth. When "good people" worldwide begin to be killed, all marked with the same tattoo, an Interpol advisory arrives on the desk of veteran Copenhagen detective Niels Bentzon, who with the help of Hannah Lund, a bright young astrophysicist, predicts the last two murders, which will take place in Venice and Copenhagen, and they race against the clock to prevent them. In a conversation printed in Simon & Schuster's Reading Group Guide for *The Last Good Man*, Weinreich and Klarlund declared they researched everything in the book "to the smallest detail, turning the search for evil which animates crime fiction upside down to focus on "goodness," which the pair say they cannot define, though the novel treats the concept on several levels because the authors want readers to define it for themselves. They also address the moral question of whether those in the Western world still can believe in something larger than themselves. In the novel, which has had remarkable success, the authors remind readers, "You're only two handshakes away from evil…. Maybe it's the same thing with goodness…. Just remember that all of the upheavals in world history, both good and bad, were initiated by individuals" (Reading Book Guide).

As A.J. Kazinski, Weinreich and Klarlund plan a sequel they call "The Sleep and the Death," "a thriller dealing with near-death experiences. Very dark and scary. And it will make you cry" (Reading Book Guide).

Collaborative Crime Novel:

2010: *Den sidste gode mand* (*The Last Good Man*, tr. Tiina Nunnally, U.S., 2012)

Major Awards:

2011: Danish Crime Academy Debut Award, for *Den sidste gode mand* (*The Last Good Man*)

Website: http://www.jacobweinreich.dk

Lars Kjædegaard

b. 1955, Scotland; Residence: Elsinore, Denmark; Occupation: author (also writes under pseudonym "Grethe Lange")

Since his literary debut in 1981, popular "pulp" crime author Lars Kjædegaard has produced many conventional suspense novels and short stories set mostly in Elsinore, Denmark. According to *littatursiden.dk* these stories "take place at the inter-personal level," without branching out into espionage, international intrigue, or politics, being "simple stories about how quickly life can be difficult and confusing for ordinary people." Kjædegaard's popular fiction allows readers to identify comfortably with characters because as Kjædegaard says, he writes as "a completely spontaneous activity. I do not mean anything by it, I do not mean … the world['s] state has [any] bearing on what I write" (quoted in *litteratursiden.dk*). He also produced one mainstream historical novel, "Something Strange," 2004, set in Elsinore in the 1860s, dealing with the 1864 Battle of Dybboel, a Prussian victory over Denmark, and its aftermath.

Lars Kjædegaard also participated in the four-author collaborative novel *In the Shadow of Sadd*, 2005, based on a concept and characters created by Steen Langstrup, with Sara Blædel and Gretelise Holm (see **Steen Langstrup,** below).

Crime Novels:

1981: *Sidste år* ("Last Year")
1994: *Ringelheim* ("Ringelheim")
1995: *Et helvedes hus* ("A Hell House")
1996: *Hvor hunden ligger begravet* ("Where the Dog Is Buried")
1997: *Et slag på tasken* ("A Guesstimate")
1998: *Herren giver* ("The Lord Giveth")
1999: *Som man råber* ("As You Yell")
2001: *Nekrolog* ("Obituary")
2002: *Det store sus* ("The Big Rush")
2003: *Israel Falk* ("Israel Falk")
2006: *Thelma* ("Thelma")
2006: *Montebello* ("Montebello")
2007: *Solsorten* ("Blackbird")
2009: *Illinois* ("Illinois")
2011: *Den sidste dommer* ("The Last Judge")

The Anita White-Thor Belling Series:

2011: *Smukke Jan* ("Beautiful Jan")
2012: *Den røde labyrint* ("The Red Maze")
2012: *Goyas hund* ("Goya's Dog")
2013: *Sorte sø* ("Black Sun")

Collaborative Novel:

2005: *I skyggen af Sadd* ("In the Shadow of Sadd" with Sara Blædel, Gretelise Holm, and Steen Langstrup)

Major Award:

2004: Elsinore Municipality Culture Award

Website: N/A

Michael Katz Krefeld

> b. 1966, Holte, Denmark; raised in Hvidovre, a suburb of Copenhagen, Denmark; Residences: Copenhagen and Berlin; Occupations: film and television producer and screenwriter, advertising writer, author

Michael Katz Krefeld, the grandson of detective novelist Herman Krefeld, originally directed short films, but he soon began to write screenplays and worked on popular Danish television series, including the Emmy-winning *Nikolaj & Julie*. At the same time he began work on his first novel, *Før stormen* ("Before the Storm"), which took him four years to complete (CrimeHouse interview). Plot-driven crime fiction and films have always fascinated him. He lists Brian de Palma, Alfred Hitchcock, Martin Scorsese, and Orson Welles as his film idols, and he admires crime novelists Cormac McCarthy, Michael Connolly, Elmore Leonard, and "of course" James Ellroy (CrimeHouse interview).

For his debut novel, which led off his Dr. Maja Holm series, *Før stormen* ("Before the Storm"), 2006, Krefeld created Dr. Maja Holm, noting that as a male writer, he can see detail about a female character that a woman would not notice, due to "the fascination of the differences between the sexes" (CrimeHouse interview). Maja's romantic relationship has just failed, and she is working in provincial Norway when one of her patients fatally overdoses. As she investigates the death with the help of a television reporter, Maja becomes the target of powerful forces bent on destroying her. In *Pans hemmelighed* ("Pan's Secret"), 2009, Maja returns to Copenhagen, where a serial killer is preying on little boys, their sexually abused bodies found with Peter Pan photos in their hands. Maja joins forces with Deputy Crime Commissioner Katrine Bergman and undergoes such traumatic experiences that Krefeld gave Maja a vacation from detecting in his third novel and made Katrine Bergman his protagonist for *Protokollen* ("Protocols"), 2010 (CrimeHouse interview), which addresses Muslim terrorism in Copenhagen, opposed by a private security company composed of former Afghan soldiers and a secret brotherhood called "Protocol." Bergman, suspended after violently attacking a suspect, and PET (Danish National Police) Chief of Operations Nicholas Storm investigate a fatal bombing in a Copenhagen restaurant, with Bergman undercover in her own neighborhood. They soon realize, however, that evidence points away from the young Muslims who have confessed to a Copenhagen bombing. Krefeld's website notes that this novel causes Storm and Bergman to explore Denmark's dark side as a nation for the first time in over a century fighting not a foreign enemy but one at home, "very close to its own heart" (quoted on Krefeld's website).

In Krefeld's fourth novel, *Sort sne falder* ("Black Snow Falls"), 2012, Bergman, now Crime Commissioner, and Storm probe an assassination attempt on Peter Levin, a Danish politician of dubious reputation, and they tackle a touchy case involved with a secret lodge of which Storm's late father, a prominent architect, was a member. *Afsporet* ("Derailed"), 2013, departs from the female protagonist structure of Krefeld's earlier novels and instead focuses on detective Thomas Ravnsholdt, called "Raven" by his friends, who is on leave, guiltridden over the murder of his lover Eva. He lives on his old houseboat in a welter of booze and guilt with his only companion, his aging overweight English bulldog Møffe. Raven reluctantly accepts a missing person job, which leads him into Copenhagen's underworld and its Eastern European gangs who are running drug and prostitution rackets. Krefeld's complicated narrative combines three story lines: serial killings that began in 1979; a missing girl's 2010 case; and Raven's life from 2013. This makes for a "frightening and sobering" novel, tempered only by a few passages of quiet humor involving the bulldog Møffe and Krefeld's dismissal of Sweden as a home only for moose and neo–Nazis (Arne Larsen).

Krefeld devotes up to ten or twelve hours a day to his literary work. He sums up his approach to fiction by distinguishing sharply between bad and good crime writers: "If it is not personal for your protagonist it will not work …. The good writers believe their main character and drama to be found in psychology, not in how many bodies there are on the table," and he defends the bulldoggish tenacity of his heroines, which makes them occasionally hard to like: "Maybe I just like troublesome characters who challenge me and that it takes an effort for me as a writer to understand" (CrimeHouse interview).

Crime Novels:

Dr. Maja Holm Series:

2006: *Før stormen* (lit. "Before the Storm," also called "The Anatomy of Death")
2009: *Pans hemmelighed* ("Pan's Secret")

Katrine Bergman Series:

2010: *Protokollen* (lit. "Protocols," also called "The Real Enemy")
2012: *Sort sne falder* ("Black Snow Falls")

Stand-Alone Novels:

2013: *Afsporet* ("Derailed")
2013: *Sekten* ("Sects")
2014: *Savnet* ("Missing")

Major Awards:

2006: Danish Crime Academy Debut of the Year Award, for *Før stormen* ("Before the Storm")
2012: The Harald Mogensen Prize, for *Sort sne falder* ("Black Snow Falls")

Website: http://www.michaelkatzkrefeld.dk

*Steen Langstrup

b. September 13, 1968, Anisse North, Zealand, Denmark; Residence: Copenhagen, Denmark; Occupations: cartoonist: comic book author, publisher, author (short stories, nonfiction, fiction)

According to his autobiographical statement in *littetursiden.dk*, when Steen Langstrup
decided he could not make a living as a cartoonist and after his comic book about a devil who
lost his home in hell and had to live on earth failed, he began writing his first novel, a horror tale
called *Kat* ("Cat"), published in 1995 to considerable success. Since then, Langstrup has mainly
produced pulp-type horror fiction dealing with what he calls on his official website "the darker
sides of human nature," which he feels are "most clearly spotted in time of war."

Langstrup's most important fiction may be his two historical Sabotage Group BB novels,
based on Denmark's experiences during the last years of Nazi Occupation. They are his first novels
published in English, by his own publishing house, 2 Feet Entertainment. Langstrup says that in
1944 Copenhagen, the earlier German term for Denmark, "The Whipped Cream Frontier," gave
way to the Nazis' "pure killing spree in broad daylight. No one could feel safe anywhere … as
good fought evil, the criminals took over. And this is where my novel, *The Informer*, begins"
(quoted on Langstrup's website). Langstrup created the fictional Danish Sabotage Group BB for
his first novel in the series, *The Informer*, which poses the life-and-death dilemma all such groups
face: Who can be trusted? In a conversation with radio drama director Ole Kroll when Langstrup
was working out the plot of *The Informer*'s sequel, *Codename Panzer*, Kroll told Langstrup that
his ideas for this novel strongly resembled an old tale, possibly apocryphal, that toward the end
of the war certain Resistance members had supposedly met with German leaders in Copenhagen's
Hotel d'Angleterre to discuss joining forces to fight Communists within the Resistance, in case
Denmark should be "liberated" by the Soviets. "Some still believe this myth to be true, others
reject it fiercely. Me, I don't know," said Langstrup; in actuality the British liberated Denmark.
Langstrup fiercely denounces Danish politicians who had cooperated with the Germans; and he
observes that about 2,000 young Danes, encouraged to volunteer for the *Wehrmacht*, died fighting
on the Eastern Front. Danish politicians also urged Danes to denounce Resistance members,
"then [the politicians] returned to power after the war"; "They reintroduced the death penalty
and adopted retroactive laws to punish the traitors serving the Germans. The smaller perpetrators
got the worst punishment, the bigger got less, and some seemed too big for justice." Langstrup
concludes, "This made my story plausible" (see Langstrup's website).

While working on his World War II novels, Langstrup also conceived the plot and sketched
the characters for *I skyggen af Sadd*, 2005 ("In the Shadow of Sadd"), a humorous *noir* collaborative
gangster novel set in Anywhere, Europe, with mob boss Sadd running a Grand Theft Auto ring
involving a body found in an old Chevy van, plenty of shady money, the unstable wife of a wealthy

lawyer, and tanks of striped tropical fish. For a long time, Langstrup had contemplated "a crazy dream" of a novel made up of four related short stories by four different authors, but he thought that publishers would not be willing to try to market it. Finally in 2002 he left Gyldendal, Denmark's premier publishing company, to found his own house, 2 Feet Entertainment, and convinced "three of the most talented Danish crime writers around," Sara Blædel, Grete Lise Holm, and Lars Kjædegaard, to join him in fitting their contributions together "like a jigsaw puzzle." The result became one of Langstrup's bestselling novels and received the 2006 Danish Crime Academy award.

In "When Crime was Reborn," a short essay available on his website, Langstrup indicates that in the 1990s, something happened to crime fiction: the core of storytelling "flipped around," and a new sub-genre was born that challenged its audience's intellect and political correctness. Taking Quentin Tarantino's film *Pulp Fiction* as his inspiration, Langstrup says that the characters in this new kind of crime novel are "strangely unique" psychopaths that exist in a subculture that sees crime and murder as "everyday business," and feel no pangs of conscience or guilt. As in *Pulp Fiction*, their stories are told non-chronologically, forcing the audience to connect the chapters correctly, a technique Langstrup emulated in his 2013 crime novel *Russian Dope*, set in the late 1990s, when the Russian mafia was taking over organized crime in Denmark. Langstrup indicates he feels closer to black humored and explicit crime novels than to the later wave of Scandinavian mysteries (for all quotes see Langstrup's website).

Horror Novels:

> 1995: *Kat* ("Cat")
> 1995: *Blodets nætter* ("Blood Nights")
> 1996: *Pyromania* ("Pyromania")
> 1997: *Forvandling* ("Transformation")
> 1998: *Dope* ("Dope")
> 1999: *Fluernes hvisken* ("Visken Flies")
> 2002: *Fra ryggen* ("Castor Oil")
> 2003: *Stikker* ("Sticks")
> 2004: *Måne måne* ("Moon Moon")
> 2010: *Plantagen 1* and *Plantagen 2* ("Plantation 1" and "Plantation 2")
> 2011: *Plantagen 3* ("Plantation 3")
> 2011: *Alt det hun ville ønske hun ikke forstod* ("All That She Wished She Did Not Understand")

Crime Novels:

> 2013: *Russian Dope* (published in English)

The Sabotage Group BB Series:

> 2005: *The Informer*
> 2006: *Codename Panzer*

Collaborative Novels:

> 2005: *I skyggen af Sadd* ("In the Shadow of Sadd"), with Sara Blædel, Gretelise Holm, and Lars Kjædegaard
> 2007: "In the Shadow of Horsens," conceived and planned by Steen Langstrup and written by amateurs

Major Awards:

> 2004: Danish Crime Academy Diploma
> 2006: Danish Crime Academy Diploma, for "In the Shadow of Sadd"

Website: http://www.langstrup.com

Erik Otto Larsen

> b. November 26, 1931, Hvodovre, Denmark; d. January 2008; Residence: N/A; Occupations: visual
> artist, author

Before he turned to writing crime novels, Erik Otto Larsen was a well-known visual artist who had first exhibited his work—paintings, photographs, and graphic prints—at the 1965 Artists' Exhibition. In 1994 *Danmarks Radio* (DR) filmed Larsen's novel *Manden der holdt op med at smile* ("The Man who Stopped to Smile") as a four-part television series. The citation for the Glass Key Award Larsen received from the Scandinavian Crime Society in 1995 for *Masken i spejlet* ("The Mask in the Mirror") praised Larsen's relatively small literary output, police procedurals featuring Detective Inspector George Birch of Denmark's National Police (PET) and Detective Erik Swan of the Copenhagen Police in cases involving psychologically traumatized killers. Larsen's novels are not "whodunits"; "The exciting thing is instead *whether* [italics in original] the police will solve" [the crimes]" (Glass Key Citation). Larsen sympathizes with his psychotic murderers, but he has no compassion for those who profit from "helping" them. Larsen also provided notable cover art for his novels.

Crime Novels:

> 1988: *Pondus sidste sag* ("Pondus' Last Case")
> 1989: *Så længe jeg lever* ("As Long as I Live")
> 1990: *Manden der holdt op med at smile* ("The Man Who Stopped to Smile")
> 1994: *Masken i spejlet* ("The Mask in the Mirror")
> 1996: *En kat fortræd* ("A Cat Mischief")

Major Awards:

> 1988: Danish Crime Academy Debut Prize, for *Pondus sidste sag* ("Pondus' Last Case")
> 1995: Glass Key Award, for *Masken i spejlet* ("The Mask in the Mirror")

Website: http://www.litteratursiden.dk/forfattere/erik-otto-larsen

Jesper Stein Larsen

> b. February 28, 1965; Residence: Copenhagen, Denmark; Occupations: journalist, author

In his biographical statement for the Danish Crime Academy, Jesper Stein Larsen, a veteran journalist and food critic, says that his father brought him up with a combination of "two-thirds Ed McBain and a third Danish poetry." He also names fellow Nordic crime writers Jo Nesbø, Leif G.W. Persson, and Arnaldur Indriðason among his favorite crime writers, many of whom he has interviewed across the globe, but he admits he has "really never gotten over his first encounter with Michael Connelly's debut novel *The Black Echo*, 1992, the first appearance of Connolly's protagonist Harry Bosch, who likes to steep himself in alcohol and music.

Larsen sets his highly realistic crime novels in Nørrebro, a section of Copenhagen, with Deputy Police Commissioner Axel Steen as his popular protagonist. He writes in intense spurts of up to sixteen hours at a time, addressing social problems like rape and the victimization of women in Denmark in *Bye Bye Blackbird* and the drug abuse in *Akrash*. In a 2014 interview, Larsen noted, "it is clear that our [Scandinavia's] reputation for being happy countries with high welfare and equal rights for men and women etc. is a good background to write really nasty novels. The Nordic Noir wave breaks down the illusion [that] the Scandinavian countries are a happy safe-haven.... Denmark is a very peaceful country ... but there is still something rotten ... you know the saying" (quoted in Surgey).

Crime Novels:

Deputy Police Commissioner Axel Steen Series:

2012: *Uro* ("Turmoil")
2013: *Bye Bye Blackbird* ("Bye Bye Blackbird")
2014: *Akrash* ("Akrash")

Major Awards:

2012: Danish Crime Academy Debut Prize, for *Bye Bye Blackbird* ("Bye Bye Blackbird")

Website: N/A

*Michael Larsen

b. November 28, 1961, Vaerløse, Denmark; Residence: North Zealand, Denmark; Occupation: journalist, film scriptwriter, author

After covering films as a journalist for some time, Michael Larsen debuted as a novelist in 1992 with a humorous work, *Med livet i hælene* ("With Life on the Heels"), but since he turned to writing full time in 1994, he has become best known for two thrillers, *Uden sikker viden*, 1994 (*Uncertainty*, tr. 1996), and *Slangen i Sydney*, 1997 (*The Snake in Sydney*, tr. 2000), using cinematic techniques like detailed action sequences that he learned in his film journalism career.

Following in the technothriller footsteps of Peter Høeg's *Smilla's Sense of Snow*, Larsen's fast-paced *Uncertainty* has tabloid journalist Michael Molberg, riddled with alcohol and pills and sus-pected of killing his fiancée Monique, exploring his own psyche and sexuality as he attempts to find the real murderer. *The Snake in Sydney* became an immediate success in Denmark, remaining on Danish bestseller lists for seven months. It features Danish physician and snake specialist Annika Niebuhr, a distant and less sympathetic literary relative of Høeg's Smilla Jespersen (Corn-well). With its wealth of herpetological lore like the unsettling fact that the Australian taipan is 850 times more poisonous than the American rattlesnake, *The Snake in Sydney* also involves dark government secrets as well as the conventional crime novel elements of "an apparent suicide, a sympathetic policeman, mysterious photographs, an attempt on Annika's life" (Cornwell), but as in *Smilla's Sense of Snow*, the complex plot seems to flounder toward the end, frustrating some readers and critics.

Larsen followed *The Snake in Sydney* with another thriller, *Femte sol brænder* ("The Fifth Sun Burns"), 2000, and *Den store tid* ("The Big Time"), 2004, a two-volume historical novel set in nineteenth-century Denmark.

Crime Novels:

1994: _Uden sikker viden_ (_Uncertainty_, tr. Lone Thygesen Blecher and George Blecher, 1996)
1997: _Slangen i Sydney_ (_The Snake in Sydney_, tr. Anne Born, 2000)
2000: _Femte sol brænder_ ("The Fifth Sun Burns")

Major Award: N/A

Website: N/A

Anita Lillevang

> b. 1959, North Zealand, Denmark; Residence: Old Sole, between Vejle and Horsens, Allerød, Denmark; Occupations: journalist, teacher, author

Anita Lillevang, one of the most recent Danish _femikrimi_ novelists, has been called "Denmark's Agatha Christie." Lillevang draws heavily on her own experiences as a freelance journalist like Carla, her thirtyish freelance journalist protagonist, introduced in _Trappen og tågen_ ("The Stairs and the Fog"), 2007. Carla has fallen on tough times because of the severe unemployment in her small provincial town in Jutland. She has been psychologically injured by a relationship gone badly wrong, and she tends to isolate herself, living on her freelance writing assignments and whatever other honest odd jobs she can find, like housecleaning. Drugs are a major problem in her town, and when sudden deaths occur there while Carla is working on an article on the town's leading trucking company, she uncovers some unpleasant information about the town's richest family. In _Vreden og varmen_ ("The Anger and the Heat"), 2008, the unexpected death of Carla's landlord upsets her growing affection for a local policeman and throws her into another dangerous investigation, the same type of situation found in _Længere ud på landet_ ("Farther out in the Country"), 2011. In 2014's _Den gale mand fra Arnstad_ ("The Mad Man from Arnstad"), Lillevang created a new amateur-detective heroine, Nina Klostergaard, who investigates the disappearance of a citizen no one else seemed to miss. Although these plots do not open up much new territory in today's Nordic crime landscape, Lillevang seems to handle her material with realism and intensity (Lidegaard).

Crime Novels:

The "Carla" Series:

2007: _Trappen og tågen_ ("The Stairs and the Fog")
2007: _Vreden og varmen_ ("The Anger and the Heat")
2011: _Længere ud på landet_ ("Farther Out in the Countryside")

A Nina Klostergaard Novel:

2014: _Den gale mand fra Arnsted_ ("The Mad Man from Arnsted")

Major Awards: N/A

Website: http://www.anitalillevang.dk

*Jakob Melander

> b. February 15, 1965, Copenhagen, Denmark; Residence: Copenhagen, Denmark; Occupations: rock band director and guitarist, author

Jakob Melander's 2013 debut crime novel *Øjesten* (*The House That Jack Built*, tr. 2014), shifts between past and present: during World War II, a young girl falls in love with the wounded English pilot she is tending in a Copenhagen cellar, but the relationship has tragic consequences a half-century later, when a young prostitute is found murdered on Amager Common with her eyes surgically removed. When another murder soon follows, the press begins to call them "the Sandman murders." Lars Winkler, a loner and former squatter addicted to rock music and the occasional line of speed and now one of Copenhagen's best police detectives assigned to the Serious Crime Department, takes on the case, the first in Melander's projected police procedural trilogy, written when his rock band didn't get the break he had hoped for (Surgey, "Jakob Melander"). After Winkler's wife left him for his former boss and best friend, Winkler is trying to get his life back in order, living in a rundown apartment with his sixteen year old daughter Maria and battling his marginalization by his police superiors, while his own checkered past catches up with him. Early reviews praise Melander's elegant use of language, his evocative portrait of Copenhagen scenes, and his special touch, his involvement of the contemporary rock music world. He also often draws on the experiences of his father-in-law, a real-life retired police officer (Surgey, "Jakob Melander").

In *Serafine*, 2014 (*The Scream of the Butterfly*, tr. 2015), the second volume in the series, the murdered body of Copenhagen's Lord Mayor is discovered in his luxury Frederiksberg apartment in the presence of a young foreign prostitute who will say nothing but her name, "Serafine." The novel shifts between 1999 and 2013, unveiling the international trafficking ring that brought Serafine to Denmark from Kosovo via Hamburg and Sandholm, and also treating child prostitution and political corruption. This novel concentrates less on Winkler's troubled past and present life than on governmental corruption, tracing the machinations of his mortal enemy, a PET agent who obstructs Winkler's work under the direction of the victim's mother, a leader of a radical political party and Denmark's Minister of Economy. In a reference to the notion that when a butterfly flaps its wings in one part of the world, a storm comes up elsewhere, this novel is scheduled for publication in English translation in 2015, under the title, "The Scream of the Butterfly." Melander's third novel in the series, *De berusedes veje* ("The Berusedes Way") was published in Denmark in February 2015, and he is at work on his fourth.

Melander believes that since Scandinavia is "a dark and cold place for most of the year," the climate fuels his stories, especially the intrinsic Scandinavian melancholia, which he claims to "like a lot." He also likes popular fiction genres, especially horror and comic books, and for *The House That Jack Built* he combined a serial killing thriller with a story of how to be a good father. In noting that he has always been fascinated by the dark side, Melander insists he wants to engage all the reader's senses in his fiction in order to share the characters' experiences as fully as possible (Surgey, "Jakob Melander").

Crime Novels:

Lars Winkler Series:

2013: *Øjesten* (*The House That Jack Built*, tr. Paul Russell Garrett, 2014; the translated title of this novel is also referred to as "Darling")

2014: *Serafine* (*The Scream of the Butterfly*, tr. Paul Russell Garrett, 2015)

2015: *De berusedes veje* ("The Berusedes Way")

Major Awards: N/A

Website: N/A

Henning Mortensen

> b. July 12, 1939, Esbjerg, Denmark; Residence: Horsens, Denmark; Occupations: teacher, publisher, author

Henning Mortensen has published almost a hundred books in many different styles and genres of literature since his debut with a poetry collection in 1966. His oeuvre falls into three distinct periods. Like many poets of his generation, Mortensen first experimented with language in avant-garde surrealistic poetry. He then turned to novels, first writing dark social realistic stories, then a series of 1980s thrillers dealing with crimes in various levels of the Danish social spectrum; and after that two series of autobiographical *Bildungsroman*, one a ten-volume series featuring a boy with a strong ear for language, covering 1993 to 2000, and the other a five-volume group that Anders Olling in *The Great Danish Encyclopedia* describes as "psychologically penetrating," composed in changing styles and narrative modes. Mortensen has now returned to crime fiction with *Den femte årstid* ("The Fifth Season"), 2004, and the Sondrup trilogy, 2005 to 2007, which according to Olling combines "light and dark elements" from Mortensen's previous work (Olling). *Det blanke vand* ("The Glossy Water") 2009, and its sequel, *Slottet ved Det Liguriskie Hav* ("The Castle by the Ligurian Sea"), 2011, are psychological thrillers.

In nearly all of his work, Mortensen, whose literary idols include Shakespeare, Rabelais, and James Joyce, dissects the "comfortable and cozy" veneer of Danish life, which he sees as "a sham": outwardly serene houses hide "sad red wine drunks and cruelties so vile" they must be hidden away. Uncovering those lies and that misery "often in Mortensen's universe requires a detective to unravel the truth" (Olling). As in Mortensen's Sondrup trilogy, crime novels built around the stabbing of local architect René Monkholm also treats the social and psychological interactions of small-town life between lower-class racists, psychopathic members of the elite, refugees, and the self-satisfied bourgeoisie. Danish critic Tue Andersen Nexø points out that each of the three novels contains "a murder, an attempted murder, and detective work," but Mortensen uses those elements only as "a framework" for "his linguistic spirals" and "his tingling, lively pictures of Danish provincial life…. Henning Mortensen does not write crime novels meant to be read for a thrill" (Nexø).

Psychological Thrillers:

2004: *Den femte årstid* ("The Fifth Season")
2009: *Det blanke vand* ("The Bright Water")
2011: *Slottet ved Det Liguriske Hav* ("The Castle by the Ligurian Sea")

The Sondrup Trilogy:

2005: *Næb og kløer* ("Tooth and Nail")
2006: *Ræven går derude* ("The Fox Is Out There")
2007: *Rita Korsika* ("Rita Corsica")

Major Awards:

2005: Palle Rosenkrantz Award, the Danish Crime Academy, for *Den femte årstid* ("The Fifth Season")

Website: N/A

*Torben Nielsen

> b. 1918; Residence: N/A; Occupation: author

Little is known today about Torben Nielsen's crime novels, though two were published in English translation. *Galgesangen*, 1973 (*An Unsuccessful Man*, tr. 1976), puts Maigret-like patient and tenacious Detective Superintendent Archer on the trail of a killer who made a young man's death by hanging appear a suicide over an unrequited love. A reviewer in the May 1977 issue of *The Mystery Fancier* found that the novel's conclusion was not "wholly satisfactory." *Nitten røde roser*, 1974, published in England as *19 Red Roses*, 1978, was made into a 1988 film starring Henning Jensen and Bendt Rothe. Nielsen's story line involved the hit and run death of an architect's girl-friend. In a grisly revenge, he tracks down and kills not the four drunken roisterers who were responsible, but a loved one of each of them, to inflict the same kind of grief and inner torment he himself feels. *AMG Movie Guide* called this thriller "uncomfortably close to American novelist Cornell Woolrich's classic *The Bride Wore Black*, the basis for a memorable 1967 film version directed by Francois Truffaut and starring Jeanne Moreau, but nevertheless, *Nitten røde roser* was the biggest Danish box office hit of its time."

Crime Novels:

1973: *Galgesangen* (*An Unsuccessful Man*, also published as *A Gallowsbird's Song*, tr. Marianne Helweg, 1976)

1974: *Nitten røde roser* (*Nineteen Red Roses*, UK, 1978)

*Poul Ørum (Poul Erik Norholm Ørum)

> b. December 23, 1919, Nykobing, Denmark; d. December 27, 1997; Residence: Fano, Denmark; Occupations: journalist, poet, author

Very little is known today about Poul Ørum or his work. Andrew Nestingen notes that Ørum, like Torben Nielsen, was inspired by the socially critical Sjöwall-Wahlöö Martin Beck procedural series to write crime fiction in that mode during the late 1970s (Nestingen and Arvas 64).

Crime Novels:

1972: *Syndebuk* (*Scapegoat*, also published as *The Whipping Boy*, tr. Kenneth Barclay, 1975)
1974: *Kun sandheden* (*Nothing but the Truth*, tr. Kenneth Barclay, 1976)

Major Awards:

The Danish Authors Association Award, for *Syndebuk* [*The Whipping Boy*]).

Website: N/A

Rie Osted

> b. November 3, 1940; Residence: Camps, in a rural area of Denmark; Occupations: journalist, free-lance editor, author

At 69, journalist and freelance editor Rie Osted published her first crime novel, *Dag & nat* ("Day and Night"), 2010, followed by *Den røde dame* ("The Red Lady"), 2012, and *Huset på skræn-ten* ("The House on the Cliff"), 2013, all "cozies" featuring former lawyer Andrea de Lima, now a private investigator.

Beginning in 1969, Rie Osted worked mostly as a freelance journalist and in the 1990s she was a columnist for *Berlingske Tidende*. She also wrote school books and young adult novels as well as mainstream women's novels before turning to crime fiction. Her detective novels deal with current Danish social problems, using an approach quite different from other contemporary Danish women crime writers, who tend to write relentlessly realistic works. In a sympathetic and perceptive review for *Politiken*, Bo Tao Michaelis compares Osted's crime fiction to "sedate and classic crime novels," that according to longtime mystery reviewer Harald Mogensen "cuddle you with creepy." He also compares Osted's genteel sleuth Andrea de Lima to Precious Ramotswe of Alexander McCall Smith's fictional Number One Ladies Detective Agency series, set in Botswana. "My old late mother," Michaelis claims, would have been amused by Osted's novels, "about nice people who speak nicely to each other, go to bed nicely with each other, and beat each other nicely to death." Michaelis feels that Osted pleases her readers by offering "tea with biscuits," not brass-knuckle bludgeoning (Michaelis, "Soft-boiled")

Crime Novels:

2010: *Dag & nat* ("Day and Night")
2011: *Den røde dame* ("The Red Lady")
2012: *Huset på skrænten* ("The House on the Cliff")

Major Awards: N/A

Website: http://www.rieosted.dk

Simon Pasternak (see also *Christian Dorph* and *Christian Dorph and Simon Pasternak*)

b. 1971; Residence: N/A; Occupations: Editor, publisher, author

Since collaborating on three crime novels with Christian Dorph, Simon Pasternak revealed in an autobiographical note for his publisher Gyldendal that he shares Dorph's admiration for the work of James Ellroy. Pasternak also likes American true crime authors Truman Capote and Norman Mailer, and "all the living great Danish writers." Besides co-writing the script for the movie *Spies & Glistrup*, 2013, with Christoffer Boe, Pasternak has written *Dødszoner* ("The Death Zones"), 2013, a powerful 900-page historical novel about the horrors of the front lines in chaotic German-occupied Belarus during World War II. Its hero *Polizei Oberleutnant* Heinrich Hoffmann, who uses excessive force only when compelled to do so, relates the story, centered on the death of SS General Steiner, found fatally mutilated in a barn in the summer of 1943. Manfred Schlosser, a stereotypical SS officer and Steiner's protégé, orders Hoffmann, who is engaged to his friend Manfred's sister, to find Steiner's killer, which happens midway through the novel, allowing Pasternak to definitively explore the ravages of war in Belarus, site of his own Jewish roots. Literatursiden.dk reviewer Bettina Schnegelsberg-Larsen found this novel a welcome addition to World War II fiction, since few novels have treated Belarus during that period. In litteratursiden.dk, Niels Torben Herrig finds Pasternak's description of "the unimaginable cruelty and senselessness that characterized the so-called *Einsatzgruppen*" "excellent," agreeing with *Dagbladet*'s Moritz Schramm that "The Death Zones" "will not be surpassed for many years" (Schramm). An English translation of the novel is scheduled for 2015 publication.

Crime Novels:

2013: *Dødszoner* ("The Death Zones")

Major Awards: N/A

Website: See above: Christian Dorph and Simon Pasternak

Lotte Petri

b. 1968, Hvalsey, Denmark; Residence: Hillerød, Denmark; Occupations: businesswoman, author

Drawing on scientific research into bioterrorism and biological warfare, Lotte Petri, whose father was a chief psychiatrist at a Danish mental institution, writes crime novels involving medical-scientific and psychological content, eschewing a formal outline for an intuitive approach with surprises even for her as the author, since she feels otherwise she would find writing fiction boring ("Mail Interview"). After ten years as a marketing manager, she found herself needing a new challenge, so she left her job and plunged into a project based on her fascination with the anxiety that followed the 2001 terrorist attack on New York's World Trade Center. The result was her first thriller, *Den 5. plage* ("The Fifth Plague"), 2009, featuring Selma Eliassen, head of the Danish Epidemiological Surveillance Service and dealing with a suspected bioterrorist attack in Copenhagen. Selma's friend Lisa Brodersen, victimized by her mentally unstable and violent former husband, allows Petri to simultaneously treat the issues of Muslim terrorism and domestic violence. In its sequel, *Vand til blod* ("Water for Blood"), 2011, Selma and Lisa again deal with a Muslim attempt at bioterrorism, while *Sort død* ("Black Death"), 2014, involves both the Nazi experiments on identical twins and contemporary bioengineered plague bacteria in the context of right-wing terrorism like the deadly 2011 Breivik rampage in Norway. Petri's fourth novel, *Hvidt snit* ("White Cut") is scheduled for 2015.

Crime Novels:

The Selma Eliassen Series:

2009: *Den 5. plage* ("The Fifth Plague")
2011: *Vand til blod* ("Water for Blood")
2014: *Sort død* ("Black Death")
2015: *Hvidt snit* ("White Cut")

Major Awards: N/A

Website: http://lotte.petri.dk

*Morten Ramsland

b. 1971, Næsby on Funen, Denmark; Residence: N/A; Occupations: poet, author of children's literature, author

Morten Ramsland, also recognized as a successful author of six children's picture books, produced one remarkable novel that tangentially treats crime in Denmark. His generational novel *Hundehoved*, 2005, translated as *Doghead*, 2010, took Ramsland five years to write, tracing a dysfunctional Norwegian family and its vicissitudes through the 20th century. The multiple award-winning novel, actually a series of colorful though generally sordid vignettes, has been translated into thirteen languages and is scheduled to appear as a twelve-episode Norwegian television series. Ramsland's most recent novel is the autobiographical *Sumo brødre* (*Sumo Brothers*, tr. 2010).

Like several other major Danish novelists, Ramsland takes his inspiration for the family troubles in *Doghead* from the moral issues raised during the Second World War. Grandfather Askild, first hailed as a hero for hitting a German soldier over the head with a stick, turns out to be a petty war profiteer who stole lumber from the Nazis and then sold it back to them; worse, he betrayed a friend in order to survive a concentration camp. All this causes "a pile of skeletons to clatter in rapid succession from the Erikssons' overstuffed closet" (Clare Clark).

Ramsland describes his writing process as "a journey of discovery into new landscapes" (litteratursiden.dk), and calls his style "grotesque realism" (quoted in Clare Clark). He cites the "colorful maximalism" of Gabriel Garcia Marquez and Salman Rushdie as his literary inspiration (*Dagbladet* Information), while he uses shocking languages and situations to convey the horrors—"adultery, duplicity and casual violence"—which ordinary families endure to survive. "While enthusiastically engaging with the coarser aspects of life, [Ramsland] displays a grimly pessimistic view of human nature" (Clare Clark).

Crime Novels:

2005: *Hundehoved* (*Doghead*, tr. Tiina Nunnally, 2010)

Major Awards:

2006: The Golden Laurel, for *Hundehoved* (*Doghead*)
2006: Readers' Book Award, for *Hundehoved* (*Doghead*)

Website: N/A

*Ole Sarvig

b. 1921, Copenhagen, Denmark; d. 1981, Copenhagen, Denmark; Residence: Copenhagen, Denmark; Occupations: poet, editor, author

According to *The Great Danish Encyclopedia*, modernist literary editor, poet, and author Ole Sarvig was convinced that modern culture suffers from a crisis of values that had to be overcome through a quasi-religious human conversion, identifiable by a redemptive option via symbolic language that can transform sensual reality into spirituality. His one crime novel, *Havet under mit vindue* (*The Sea Beneath My Window*) 1960, combines that metaphysical symbolic interpretation with criminal intrigue: Miriam, an amnesiac young woman, awakens alone in a strange room, and when a man is found dead nearby, she appears to be the protagonist of the ensuing events, whose James Bond–like dimensions lead "into the realms of [East-West] world politics" (Rossel 608). Comparing Miriam's uncertainties to those of Kafka's Josef K., critic Jakob Mikkelsen Kousgaard observed in 2006 that such uncertainties arise "from a modern sense of crisis about not belong[ing] anywhere, but being a stranger everywhere" (Kousgaard).

Crime Novels:

1960: *Havet under mit vindue* (*The Sea Beneath My Window*, tr. Anni Whissen, 2003)

Major Awards:

1967: The Grand Prize of the Danish Academy

Website: N/A

Susanne Staun

b. December 31, 1957, Frederiksberg, Denmark; Residence: Frederolssund, Denmark; Occupations: freelance journalist, editor, scriptwriter, author of children's detective fiction, crime novelist

The *Berlingske Tidende* literary critic Lars Bukdahl praised Susanne Staun, one of Denmark's most humorous crime writers, once called "Tarantino on estrogen" (*Gyldendal* publicity), in 2004 as "a counter-image to the general misery on the bestseller lists" (Staun's website), probably because, as she admits in her official website biography, Staun describes her departure from *femikrimi* tradition in her most popular crime novels. Her Dr. Fanny Fiske series has been called "the exact goth/noir equivalent of chick lit" (Holst). While many Nordic women crime authors share the same serious social concerns, particularly human trafficking and exploitation of women, Staun has given *femikrimi* the facelift that feminist critic Hanne-Vibeke Holst believes will save these novels from dying a natural death (Holst).

Staun's Dr. Fanny Fiske is a refreshing middle-aged behavioral psychologist living in a "slightly dystopian" near-future university town south of London (Staun website). As a profiler specializing in serial killings, she assists police by exposing "the social and psychological DNA of criminals" who lack the usual motives (Staun website). During her five novels which lead up to her early retirement brought on by her professional stresses, Fanny takes heroic measures to remain looking thirty-something: four face lifts, more laser resurfacing than she can recall, and twice-yearly Restylane (like Botox) injections; declaring that it's bad enough that all humans die, but it's absolutely unacceptable to endure such a short period as a desirable woman (Staun website). She devours young lovers, she "has an appetite like a horse" for French cuisine, and her wardrobe costs a fortune. In short, Dr. Fanny Fiske surges through her cases with panache that riotously uplifts her female readers, even when in *Mit smukke lig* ("My Beautiful Corpse") she learns from her plastic surgeon that she has passed beyond repair.

Staun often likes to shock her readers, as when she says that Maria Krause, the heroine of Staun's second series, "needs to be raped every now and then" (Staun website). For the lead-off novel in this series, the award-winning *Døderummet* ("Dead Space"), 2010, set in Odense, Staun constructed a more traditional thriller than the Fiske novels are. In presenting a psychopathic serial killer through diary segments, Staun uses serious background research without overwhelming her readers with forensic detail, so that critics hailed the Maria Krause series, her departure from "the dirty Fanny books," as a solid traditional crime success (Staun website).

Crime Novels:

Dr. Fanny Fiske Series:

1999: *Som arvesynden* ("An Original Sin")
2000: *Mord som forløser* (*Liebe*) ("Murder as the Redeemer")
2008: *Mine piger* ("My Girls")
2009: *Mit smukke lig* ("My Beautiful Corpse")
2009: *Før jeg dør* ("Before I Die")

Maria Krause Series:

2010: *Døderummet* ("Dead Space")
2011: *Hilsen fra Rexville* ("Greetings from Rexville")
2012: *Helt til grænsen* ("Quite to the Limit")

Major Awards:

2010: Harald Mogensen Prize, for *Døderummet* ("Dead Space")

Website: http://www.susannestaun.com

Dan Turèll

> b. March 19, 1946, Vangede (suburb of Copenhagen), Denmark; d. October 15, 1993, Copenhagen, Denmark; Residence: Copenhagen, Denmark; Occupation: author

Dan Turèll, who died at 47 from esophageal cancer, in Danish letters is known affectionately as "Onkel Danny" because of his influence on many younger Danish authors. He wrote in both Danish and English and explored a wide variety of forms: poetry in the vein of American Beat poet Alan Ginsburg, short stories, an autobiographical novel, essays, articles, film studies, photobooks of the Copenhagen Jazz festival, and a study of the teachings of Donald Duck. Both the Café Dan Turèll, one of the first cafés in Copenhagen, and a "Plat" (plaza) commemorate him as one of Denmark's most popular authors.

When Turèll was a boy, his father gave him a copy of Dostoevsky's *Crime and Punishment*, awakening his taste for serious literature and setting the stage for Turèll's interest in the crime genre. Turèll's hard-boiled *"Mord-serie"* ("Murder Series"), directly inspired by American authors like Raymond Chandler, includes twelve novels and one short fiction collection, published between 1981 and 1989, set in a fictionalized and somewhat sanitized version of the Copenhagen borough of Vesterbro. The protagonist is a nameless freelance reporter who works for the *Bladet*, Turèll's fictitious Copenhagen newspaper. The series has no fixed chronology, although as it proceeded, Turèll seems to have deepened both its characters, especially Copenhagen Police Inspector Ehlers, and its setting. Turèll's 1981 novels *Mord i mørket* (*Murder in the Dark*) and *Mord i Paradis* ("Murder in Paradise") were made into films in 1986 and 1988 respectively.

Turèll's work is beginning to receive renewed interest. In a 2009 EuroCrime interview, Don Bartlett, the translator of many Scandinavian crime novels including several by Norway's Jo Nesbø, thinks that Turèll's work definitely merits translation, declaring that he had "always been a big fan of Dan Turèll. A larger than life Danish writer ... [who] wrote ... with great style, wit and warmth" (EuroCrime interview with Don Bartlett). With the permission of Turèll's widow Chili and support from the Danish Arts Council, William Kennedy began translating Turèll's poetic "The Big City Trilogy" in 2009, and the first English translation of Turèll's first crime novel, *Mord i mørket* (*Murder in the Dark*), was published in 2013 by Norvik Press, translated by Mark Mussari with an afterword by Barry Forshaw. *Murder in the Dark* combines a traditional crime story with what Norvik Press's publicity calls "a cool, unsentimental appraisal of Scandinavian society ... through the eyes of its shabby, unconventional anti-hero ...The descriptions of Copenhagen channel [Turèll's] poetic sensibility: 'Copenhagen is at its most beautiful when seen out of a taxi at midnight, right at that magical moment when one day dies and another is born, and the printing presses are buzzing with the morning newspapers.'"

Crime Novels:

The "Murder Series":

1981: *Mord i mørket* (*Murder in the Dark*, tr. Mark Mussari, 2013)
1981: *Mord i Rodby* ("Murder in Rodby")
1983: *Mord ved runddelen* ("Murder by the Circle")

1983: *Mord på Malta* ("Murder in Malta")

1984: *Mord i marts* ("Murder in March")

1984: *Mord i september* ("Murder in September)

1985: *Mord i myldretiden* ("Murder during Rush Hour")

1986: *Mord på møntvaskeriet og andre kriminalhistorier* ("Murder in the Launderette and Other Crime Stories"), short fiction collection

1987: *Mord i rendestenen* ("Murder in the Gutter")

1988: *Mord i Paradis* ("Murder in Paradise")

1988: *Mord på medierne* ("Murder on the Media")

1989: *Mord på markedet* ("Murder on the Market")

1989: *Mord i San Francisco* ("Murder in San Francisco")

Major Awards: N/A

Website: N/A

Sanne Udsen

b. 1953; Residence: Copenhagen; Occupations: business consultant, etiquette adviser, lecturer; author

Besides producing a handbook for career women and a guide to good manners at work, and two studies of corporate bosses, nonfiction books with considerable popularity in Europe, *Psykopater i jakkesæt* ("Psychopaths in Suits"), 2006, and *Parasitter i habitter* ("Parasites in Suits"), 2013, Sanne Udsen has published one crime novel, *Alle guds børn* ("All God's Children"), 2008, featuring young defense attorney Sarah Berthelsen, newly employed by a law firm. In her first case, Sarah defends a young man accused of slashing an elderly woman's throat. Sarah solves the crime in a typical *femikrimi* manner that seems to telegraph the novel's conclusion too soon. The novel has been damned with faint praise as "chicklit with a touch of suspense," a "story about life down among the women, cluttered with cinnamon buns, baby poo and menstruation blood, garnished with a spot of crime (chicklit with a murder in it)" (DJs krimiblog).

Crime Novels:

2008: *Alle guds børn* ("All God's Children")

Website: http://www.udsen.dk

*Erik Valeur

b. September 2, 1955, Copenhagen, Denmark; Residence: Copenhagen, Denmark; Occupations: journalist, author

Erik Valeur's distinguished award-winning journalistic career began with in the late 1970s with several years at *Berlingske Tidende*. He and two colleagues founded *Monthly Magazine Press* in 1985, and subsequently he headed DR's (Danish Radio) Documentary Group PI. He presently writes for *Politiken* and *Jyllands-Posten*. He also co-edited *The Book of Power*, an exposé of political scandals.

Valeur's 2011 crime novel *Det syvende barn* (*The Seventh Child*) presents seven adopted children caught in a web of secrets and lies. They are being cared for at the Kongslund Orphanage on September 11, 2001, when the body of an unidentified woman is found on a lonely beach in the outskirts of Copenhagen, surrounded by a strange collection of objects that includes a photograph of that orphanage. The 2001 terrorist attack on the World Trade Center, however, overshadows the homicide, and that photograph, a small link to the orphanage, is forgotten until the disgraced journalist Knud Taasing begins to probe the institution's history, suspecting that the orphanage has covered up the secrets of some of Denmark's most powerful leaders who will do anything to hide them. *Litteratursiden* critic Arne Larsen calls *The Seventh Child* "an enigmatic, soulful and exciting novel" with "precise and sharply drawn psychological ... descriptions" (Arne Larsen, "The Seventh Child").

Crime Novels:

2011: *Det syvende barn* (*The Seventh Child*, tr. K.E. Semmel, 2011)

Major Awards:

2012: The Glass Key Award, for *Det syvende barn* (*The Seventh Child*)
Website: N/A

Inger Wolf

b. 1971, Herning, Denmark; Residences: Århus, Denmark; southern Spain; Occupations: translator, novelist

Inger Wolf should not be confused with "Inger Ash Wolfe," the pseudonym under which a Canadian literary mainstream author published *The Calling*.

Inger Wolf's award-winning debut crime novel *Sort sensommer* ("Black Indian Summer"), 2006, introduced her sleuth, police Chief Inspector Daniel Trokic, and his team, opening a police procedural series praised for its professionalism and marked by terrifying atmospherics. After a divorce and subsequent struggles with intermittent depression, Wolf returned to her home town of Århus, where she says the lovely local land- and seascapes inspired her first Chief Inspector Daniel Trokic novel (see Wolf's website).

Ondt vand ("Evil Water"), 2012, opens with a gruesome discovery by an Århus area farmer: the bodies of two women who had been missing for weeks stuffed into suitcases under a pile of stones. Filled with "macabre scenery and rituals," this novel involves an African tribe, religious insanity, and a horrific scene with leeches that has made some readers feel that the very life is being sucked out of them as they read.

Wolf hopes to have her Trokic novels translated into English, and she also intends to widen her detective's experiences. Accordingly, her sixth novel in the series, *Under en sort himmel* ("Under a Black Sky"), 2013, marks a departure from the Århus locale where Trokic and his team usually operate. Wolf felt a need for a new setting, and during what she calls an "intense and fantastic" week in Alaska focusing on the Anchorage Volcano Observatory and the Anchorage Police Station and a tour of the University of Alaska campus and the surrounding glaciers and mountains, Wolf worked on "Evil Water" in which a Danish volcano scientist, his wife, and his son are found slain and their nine-year-old daughter is missing. This precipitates the involvement of Daniel Trokic, who because of the victims' Danish nationality arrives to investigate the case with the help of an Alaskan female detective (see Wolf website). Trokic's seventh case, *Det perfekte sted at dø* ("The Perfect Place to Die"), 2014, takes him to Japan to investigate the death of a Danish biologist in a remote forest.

Overall, Wolf scrupulously researches her novels and follows her own advice for authors: "read a hell of a lot of books, and learn from the masters" (quoted on Wolf website).

Crime Novels:

The Inspector Daniel Trokic Series:

2006: *Sort sensommer* ("Black Indian Summer")
2008: *Frost og aske* ("Frost and Ashes")
2009: *Sangfuglen* ("Songbird")
2011: *Hvepsereden* ("Wasp's Nest")
2012: *Ondt vand* ("Evil Water")
2013: *Under en sort himmel* ("Under a Black Sky")
2014: *Det perfekte sted at dø* ("The Perfect Place to Die")

Major Award:

2006: Danish Crime Academy Debut Award, for *Sort sensommer* ("Black Indian Summer")

Website: http://www.ingerwolf.com

Anthology of Danish Short Crime Fiction

Copenhagen Noir, ed. Bo Tao Michaëlis, trans. from the Danish by Mark Kline, 2011

Editor Bo Tao Michaëlis prefaced this collection of fourteen crime stories thus: "All the short stories in *Copenhagen Noir* are about meaninglessness, violence, and murder in various districts of the city." They focus on "alienated people who recognize they're wandering in a moral void," according to a November 29, 2010 *Publishers Weekly* review (pp. 32–33), which claims the collection has "grim, uncomfortable power." Blogger Lisa Hayden Espenschade (http://lisasother books.clogspot.com/2011) found that its "stories melded together for me into an uneasy Copenhagen populated by sex traffickers, willing and hesitant murderers, and kind people."

Danish Television Crime Series

While Danish crime fiction authors came later into the contemporary field than their Swedish and Norwegian counterparts, since 2000 Danish television crime series have dominated European television crime show viewing with no signs of decreasing interest. The Danish crime series concentrate on sociopolitical issues seen through the police procedural model familiar in Scandinavian crime literature since the Sjöwall-Wahlöö Martin Beck series of novels began appearing in 1967. Often the television series, as in most of current Scandinavian crime fiction, implicitly or explicitly holds failures of the welfare state system and/or political or economic corruption responsible for the crimes that overworked, underpaid, and usually emotionally or psychologically flawed but essentially principled detectives must solve.

About a decade after the publication of the first Martin Beck novel, *Rosanna*, Denmark began experiencing what Danish critics call "The Matador Effect," named for the Danish television crime series *Matador* which aired from 1978 to 1981, acknowledged as "one of the most significant series in the history of Danish television" (Eurochannel) because of its realistic characters and its accurate descriptions of family life in an imaginary Danish province during the 1930s depression and the Nazi Occupation. The enormously successful Matador Effect set off a generation of related television drama series.

Despite Denmark's accepted reputation as a "happy" country, its television musicals, comedies, and mainstream drama programs have not achieved much success, while its television crime and thriller series have become internationally famous. In the 1980s, lighter television shows temporarily captured Danish viewers' attention, but in 1994 Danish director Lars von Trier set a new series, *The Kingdom*, in a hospital built on a former marsh where patients believe they encounter ghosts. This series paved the way for subsequent popular Danish police procedural television series and inspired an American remake, Stephen King's *Ghosts*, 2011. A succession of highly popular Danish crime television series then erupted, greatly encouraged by the Danish government, which provides its film and television industries with stable and continuous funding through the annual fee all Danes with television sets must pay, allowing a firm structure for nurturing productions (Enker).

Rejseholdet *(international title* Unit One*)*, 2000–2004

Rejseholdet, produced by Danish Radio (DR, Denmark's public broadcaster), aired in 32 television episodes between 2000 and 2004. Its ensemble cast included Charlotte Fich as detective Ingrid Dahl, who at the beginning of the series has just been placed in command of "Unit One," an elite mobile national police task force that helps local Danish police solve sensational crimes based on actual events. Filmed mostly in Denmark, each episode treats a particular social issue, such as political and press influence on the Danish judiciary, balancing the investigative process and the back story of relationships among Unit One members, like volatile leading man DI Allan Fischer, played by Mads Mikkelsen; their families; and other police functionaries, using Danish settings but also including wider Scandinavian locales. Each episode closed with a "Ten Most Wanted"-type appeal for public assistance.

Rejseholdet was televised in Denmark, Sweden, Iceland, Germany, and Australia. DVDs of the first and second series were released in the United Kingdom in 2013 as part of Arrow Films' Nordic Noir releases. As *Unit One*, the series received the Emmy Award for Best Drama Series from the International Academy of Television Arts and Sciences.

The Eagle: A Crime Odyssey *(Danish* Ørnen: En krimi-odysse*)*, 2004–2006

The Eagle, produced by Danish Radio (DR), aired in 24 episodes, each named for a character from Greek mythology, between October 2004 and November 2006. Its lead character Halgrim Ørn Hallgrimsson ("Eagle"), played by Jens Albinus, is a half-Icelandic, half-Danish policemen heading a special unit of experts who investigate international biker gang crimes, terrorist threats, international fraud, and former Soviet KGB atrocities. The series was filmed in various northern European locales, including Iceland. English subtitled DVDs are available in Australia. *The Eagle* won an International Award for 2005's best non–American television drama series from the International Academy of Television Arts and Sciences.

Anna Pihl, 2006–2008

Danish TV2's production of the *Anna Pihl* series aired from 2006 to 2008 in three seasons of ten episodes each. It starred Charlotte Munck as policewoman Anna Pihl, with Peter Mygind and Iben Hjele as Anna's police colleagues. In the *femikrimi* tradition, the series realistically explores both Anna's work and her personal life in a flat she shares with her son and a gay male housemate. The series was aired in Denmark, Iceland, Sweden, Norway, and Finland, but in Germany low ratings caused its cancellation after nine episodes of its first season. It has also been seen in Australia on SBS and in the United States on Eurochannel.

The Killing (*Danish* Forbrydelsen), 2007–2013

The biggest hit among the distinguished contemporary Danish television crime series, *The Killing*, created by Søren Sveistrup and produced by the Danish Broadcasting Corporation, features near-sociopathic Detective Inspector Sarah Lund of Copenhagen's main police department, played by Sofie Gråbøl. Series One, 2007, consisted of 20 one-hour weekly episodes each covering one day of the investigation of the murder of a young woman, a case that continued through the whole season. Besides intricate plot twists in the main investigation, the series with its impressively photographed dark, menacing Copenhagen setting emphasizes the story of the murder victim's family equally with the investigation of the central homicide. Series Two, 2009, aired in ten episodes between September and November 2009, and Series Three premiered on Danish television in September 2012.

The Killing has become a worldwide cult phenomenon, especially in the United Kingdom, where the BBC beginning in 2007 broadcast a subtitled version that *The Guardian's* Vicky Frost said prepared the way for more subtitled European crime dramas (Frost). Even the expensive black and white Nordic designed Faroe Island sweaters worn by Sarah Lund have become sensations; after asking to visit the series' television set, Prince Charles' wife Camilla received a similar sweater, to her considerable delight (Albrechtsen).

The Killing set off a hunt by purchasers interested in older Danish series (Albrechtsen), and in 2011, the American cable channel AMC remade *The Killing*. When she heard about this version, Sofie Gråbøl, possibly channeling her character Sarah Lund, commented in a 2011 BBC interview that Americans either can't read subtitles or don't want to.

The Killing and its stars have won seven international television awards and thirteen nominations. Jan De Clercq, who had considerable difficulty selling the TV rights to *The Killing*, commented on the series' success in DVD: "They thought that they could sell 3,000 copies, but they ended up selling more than 10,000 box sets…. I think people are a bit tired of clichéd American and British crime thriller fiction" (quoted in Albrechtsen).

British crime fiction author David Hewson, whose Detective Nic Costa series is set in Italy, has published novelizations of Søren Sveistrup's *The Killing: The Killing: Book One* and *The Killing: Book Two*, 2012 and 2013 respectively.

The Protectors (*Danish* Livvagterne), 2009–2010

The Protectors, set in Copenhagen and based on Denmark's PET. (*Politiets Efterretningstjeneste*), a governmental unit charged with protecting Danish royalty and politicians somewhat resembling the U.S. Secret Service, aired in two ten-episode seasons in 2009 and 2010. Created and written by Peter Thorsboe and Mai Brostrøm, *The Protectors* featured three PET recruits: Jasmina El-Murad, an Egyptian Muslim woman, played by Cecilie Stenspil; Jonas Goldschmidt, played by Søren Vejby; and Rasmus Poulsen, played by André Babikian. They begin as trainees and advance in the series to full-fledged bodyguards. *The Protectors* won an International Emmy Award for the 2009 Best Non-American Television Drama Series from the International Academy of Television Arts and Sciences.

The Protectors has been aired in Australia on SBS and is available on DVD with English subtitles.

Borgen *("The Government"), 2010–2013*

The Danish noun "borgen" means "the castle," and "The Castle" is the Danish nickname for "the government," since Christiansborg Palace in Copenhagen houses all three governmental branches—the Danish Parliament, the Prime Minister's Office, and the Danish Supreme Court. Created and written by Adam Price and co-writers Jeppe Gjervig Gram and Tobias Lindholm and produced by DR, *Borgen* centers on Birgitte Nyberg, the fictional politician who becomes Denmark's first female Prime Minister, played by Sidse Babett Knudsen, with Pilou Asbaek as spin doctor Kasper Juul and Birgitte Hjort Sørensen as news anchor Katrine Fønsmark. The fictional Prime Minister, Birgitte Nyborg, assumes power after her predecessor Lars Hesselboe, played by Soren Spanning, is caught in a political scandal involving a credit card statement and his unstable wife's shopping binge. The series begins with the forming of the center-left coalition government and Nyborg's position as its leader, showing her developing from a political ingénue to a "steely ruler": this drama deals with both political and domestic concerns "as Nyborg inevitably succumbs personally to the demands of ruling the state" (Blundell). *Borgen* aired in two sets of ten episodes each in 2010 and 2011, followed by a third ten-episode season in 2013, which Adam Price stated would be its last.

Adam Price has observed that he was shocked at *Borgen's* success. "We were told at the outset by management that this would not travel…. The Swedes and the Norwegians might buy it out of politeness, as we do in Scandinavia, but that would be it" (quoted in Enker). Local relevance and international appeal, however, proved Price's management opinion was dead wrong. (Enker). As a politically-oriented series, *Borgen's* political parties and characters have certain real-life analogues. According to *The Radio Times*, Birgitte Nyborg's centre-left party, *De Moderate* (the Moderates) resembles the Danish Social Liberal Party (*Radikale Venstre*), and the New Right (*Ny Højre*) resembles the right-wing Conservative People's Party (*Konservative Folkeparti*). In real life, after the 2011 parliamentary election, a leftist coalition headed Denmark's government, with Helle Thorning-Schmidt becoming Denmark's first female Prime Minister. Both British and American critics have praised *Borgen*, which the *New York Times* called "a bleaker, Nordic version of *The West Wing*," with political drama involving such social issues as pension plans, prostitution, and pig farming (quoted in "Cover-Ups").

Borgen's star Sidse Babett Knudsen received a 2011 International Emmy Award for Outstanding Actress in a Drama Series from the International Academy of Television Arts and Sciences. *Borgen* won the British Academy International Prize Award in 2012. A U.S. remake of *Borgen* announced in 2012 did not materialize, but Adam Price confirmed in 2013 that HBO and BBC Worldwide were beginning production on a U.S. *Borgen* remake.

Those Who Kill *(Danish* Den som dræber*), 2011*

Those Who Kill, created and written by Elsebeth Egholm and Stefan Jaworski with numerous other writers working on individual episodes, is a Danish-German-Swedish-Norwegian production. It aired in five two-part stories in Denmark in 2011, when diminishing viewer response caused

TV2 to announce its cancellation. Featuring a fictitious unit of the Copenhagen police force devoted to investigating serial homicides, *Those Who Kill* starred Laura Bach and Jakob Mikkelsen and aired as five feature length episodes in nine other countries, with a separate 2013 feature film shown in Denmark in 2012. This film is being aired as a concluding episode of the series in Germany and on the UK's commercial channel ITV 3. In the U.S., A&E began filming a pilot episode in December 2012, starring Chloe Sevigny as Detective Catherine Jensen and James D'Arcy as profiler Thomas Scheffer. A&E announced in 2013 that they would premiere a ten-episode first season of *Those Who Kill* in 2014.

Issues raised by series like *The Killing, Borgen,* and *Those Who Kill,* such as immigration and the treatment of asylum seekers, are resonating around the world (Ecker). *Borgen's* success also illustrates the "particular insight" that "Denmark and the rest of Scandinavia have developed ... concerning the sexes, careers and society matters," according to Helene Aurø, head of the Danish Broadcasting Corporation's international sales. Nadia Kløvdal Reich, chief of Danish Broadcasting's fiction division, believes that such successes "help us to tell stories which have both a political dimension and relate to the dilemmas that exist between family and society," as when the prime minister in *Borgen* has to cope simultaneously with an international conflict and her daughter's mental illness (Aurø and Reich, quoted in Albrechtsen). The worldwide popularity of these Danish television crime series, seen in such far-flung venues as the Republic of Korea and Brazil, also indicates to Gunhild Agger of Denmark's Aalborg University that these series exhibit "particular skill at focusing on universal themes which extend interest in them beyond the country's borders ... [and are] responsive to the problems of our time—not only in Denmark but also abroad" (quoted in Albrechtsen).

FINLAND

Many runes the cold has taught me,
Many lays the rain has brought me,
Other songs the winds have sung me.
...
Music from the whole creation,
Oft has been my guide and master.
—*Kalevala*, line 65

The Cultural Context of Finnish Crime Fiction

Finnish crime fiction reflects the contradictions implicit in its country's name: Suomi, the Land of the Midnight Sun. Finland's laconic people boast the creation of Nokia and the playful charm of Tove Jansson's popular Moomins cartoon characters arose from Finland's harsh climate and violent twentieth century history. For many non–Scandinavians, "Finland remains something of a closed book," and few of the conventional observations about the other Nordic countries seem to apply to it (Forshaw 144). Books play an enormous role in Finnish life, however. Finns rightly pride themselves on literacy. leading world lists in newspaper reading and library use, and Finnish children are said to be better readers than any other country's youngsters (Papinnirmi, "Letter").

Finland has a long-standing history of popular detective fiction, but not many non–Finnish detective novel readers know much about it. Few Finnish crime novels have been translated into English, possibly because of the difficulty of the Finnish language and because Finnish mysteries may be too bleak for American and British readers (see Sequelswww). Since the 1970s much Finnish crime literature has shared the neoliberal stance of its Nordic neighbors' crime literature, but many Finnish authors now also delve more deeply into the psychological roots of crimes of passion (Kachka), often concentrating on the complex relationship between Finland and Russia, a relationship responsible for the significant numbers of Russian characters presented either as victims or, more often, villains in their plots (Kachka; Nestingen and Arvas 115).

Today a 118,000 square mile republic bounded on the west by branches of the Baltic Sea, in the northwest by Norway and Sweden, and in the north by a 1300-kilometer border with Russia, Finland is a small, sparsely populated, geographically isolated country with a population of about 5.5 million. Their median age in 2010 was 42.7, making Finns one of the oldest national groups in Europe; half their voters are estimated to be over fifty. In 2011, Finland experienced 23.4 homicides per million people, the highest rate among the Nordic countries, but about half of the United States' 56.3 murders per million of population (Kachka). Finnish, a Finno-Ugric language, is one of only four official European languages not of Indo-European origin, linguistically completely different from the Germanic languages of its Nordic neighbors. Swedish, Finland's second official language, is currently used by about 5.4 percent of the Finnish population. Though Finland has historically been mostly agricultural, only about 9 percent of its land is arable because thousands of interconnected lakes and heavy forests cover about 70 percent of the country.

Originally inhabited by primitive hunters, Finland saw its indigenous Sami people driven to the far north by ethnic Finns in the first millennium AD. During the Middle Ages, with the exception of one birch bark letter from Novgorod, almost no literature existed in Finnish. Until the Reformation, Christian texts were available to Finns in Latin and Swedish, with a few texts in French and German. Under Swedish rule from the 12th century, Finland was a Christianized Swedish grand duchy with Swedish as its official language. Finnish was used by the peasantry, the clergy, and some local courts until Protestant Bishop Mikael Agricola (1510–1557) translated the New Testament in 1548, establishing written Finnish literature concurrently with the Finns' conversion to Lutheranism.

Widespread economic and political disasters during the following two centuries brought significant changes to Finland. By the 17th century, Sweden's King Gustavus Adolphus and his successors had made Sweden a major military power that had conquered immense territory around the Baltic Sea, but at a heavy price. More than twenty years of war with Russia fought mainly on Finnish soil impoverished and devastated Sweden and finally lost the Swedes their recently conquered Baltic provinces. Russia occupied Finland, which lost a third of its population in the famine of 1696–1697, and then experienced a severe outbreak of plague. Finns were faced with what they call "The Greater Wrath," 1714–1721, a Swedish conflict with Russia when Finnish homes, farms, and Helsinki itself were burned and nearly an entire generation of young Finnish men perished. In making peace with Russia in 1721, Sweden took Finland back but lost Karelia, a province between Finland and the White Sea fought over by the three countries for centuries (Ahokas 23).

Finland's turbulent 18th century saw "The Lesser Wrath," 1742–1743, a briefer but no less violent Russian occupation. Virtually no Finnish literature appeared during that century, though some intellectuals and members of the Finnish nobility were beginning to dream of separation from Sweden, which had brought the Finns so much misery. After Sweden's King Gustav III's 1788–1790 Russo-Swedish War, the Finns' desire for independence grew, although no genuine Finnish independence movement existed until the early 20th century. Yet another conflict between Sweden and Russia ended in 1809 when Tsar Alexander I's armies occupied Finland. Sweden at last ceded Finland to Russia in 1809, leaving Finland as an autonomous Russian grand duchy until the 1917 Bolshevik Revolution. These successive changes in foreign domination left deep impressions on the Finns' national psyche and their literature.

The Finns' association with the Russian Empire in the 19th century at first proved generally beneficial for the Finns. Even though their long union with Sweden had made most of Finland spiritually and socially a Scandinavian country, and although for most Finns Russia was "alien in spirit, tradition, and social structure, as well as overwhelmingly powerful" (Ahokas 35), Finland's ruling class felt their new semi-independent position in the Russian Empire was advantageous (Ahokas 35). At the same time, a small group of young Finnish progressives began advocating for Finnish as the official language of law, government, education, and the Finnish church, fennophile demands that were not realized until 1861. The Russian government initially supported the Finns' growing desire to establish the Finnish language as official because Russia felt the predominant use of Finnish would preclude any Finnish desire for reunification with Sweden. In the same spirit, Russian authorities moved the Finnish capital in 1812 from Turku to Helsinki, which lay closer than Turku to the Russian capital of St. Petersburg. They also moved the University of Turku to Helsinki in 1828, where the university soon became the focus of Finnish nationalism.

In the early 19th century, the Finns' resentment toward the predominance of the Swedish language paralleled the fennophile Finnish intellectual activity that had begun to bloom under the relatively permissive Russian authorities. Johann Vilhelm Snellmann began to compose treatises on Hegel's philosophy, governmental theory, and nationalism; M.A. Costrén initiated the scientific study of the Finno-Ugric languages, and by 1815, the philologist, poet, physician, and folklorist Elias Lönnrot who practiced medicine along the eastern Finnish border was collecting folk songs and other folk material which became the raw material for the *Kalevala*, Finland's national epic (Ahokas 38). These early works, especially Lönnrot's collections, provided significant momentum to the Finns' desire for the primacy of their language.

The *Kalevala*, or *Poems of the Kaleva District*, is not a heroic epic in the sense of Greece's *Iliad* and *Odyssey* or England's *Beowulf*. The *Kalevala* is "essentially a conflation and concatenation of a considerable number and variety of traditional songs, narratives, lyrics, and magic, sung by unlettered singers, male and female," most living in northern Karelia, around Archangel (Magoun's Foreword to *The Kalevala* xiii). Because of the amount of folk material it has contributed to Finnish culture, Karelia has become an icon of Finnish identity, even though it was taken over by the Soviet Union during World War II and became an autonomous republic of the U.S.S.R.

Elias Lönnrot was one of a group of early Finnish-language proponents who felt their folk songs could form the basis for a Finnish national epic like the German *Nibelungenlied*, and he collected about half the material contained in *The Kalevala*. Although for years *The Kalevala* was considered a simple "collection," today scholars generally believe that Lönnrot amalgamated his source material and shaped it into a loosely connected whole that he published in 1835 ("The Old Kalevala"). David E.D. Europaeus' additions to Lönnrot's collection created the 1849 edition ("The New Kalevala"), containing fifty poems comprising 22,795 lines. Composed in the ancient Indo-European oral poetry formulaic tradition and sung to the accompaniment of a *kantele*, a small harp-like instrument, the idiosyncratic style of *The Kalevala* songs derives from the quantitative Finnish language, with an effect similar to the trochaic four-beat line American poet Henry Wadsworth Longfellow, himself influenced by a German translation of *The Kalevala*, used in *Hiawatha* (Magounn xvi). The Finnish language, akin to Hungarian and Estonian and little known even among Europeans, makes access to the original text of *The Kalevala* difficult, but available to English-speaking readers in Francis Peabody Magoun, Jr.'s 1963 translation, the work confirms the essential cultural individuality that in the mid–19th century Finns were beginning to celebrate.

Widely considered the single literary work which has had the greatest effect on Finnish art, *The Kalevala* contains many songs that probably date from AD 700 to 1000. Many celebrate the exploits of three gigantic semi-divine brothers, now thought to have originally been historical heroic personages who lived during the Viking Age. These songs also exhibit Biblical themes and saints' legends (Salminen and Tarkiainen, in *The Kalevala* 355).

Passages from *The Kalevala* inspired many 19th century Finnish lyric poets and numerous Finnish and Swedish sculptors, illustrators, painters, and composers, including Finland's towering Jean Sibelius. In terms of aesthetic and moral significance, Elias Lönnrot pointed out in his 1834 "Preface to the Old Kalevala" that the character Väinämöinen, almost always described in the songs as old, steadfast, wise, and prophetic, apparently represents Finland's prototypic hero, a "man of great knowledge" and an accomplished musician, providing values that future Finnish generations would most need. The character Lemminkäinen, a powerful light-hearted, boastful and arrogant young champion, gave "little thought" to the future (Lönnrot, in an appendix to *The Kalevala* 371). Another figure, Ilmarinen, is a tireless worker. These iconic figures seem to lay down psychological patterns seen in the behavior of modern Finnish fictional detectives and their criminal opponents, as noted below. Finnish scholars Väinö W. Salminen and Vikjo Tarkiainen writing in 1933 also indicated that since the characterizations of these three brother-characters who are principal figures in *The Kalevala* remain constant throughout the work, and "Certain typical fundamentals of the Finnish national character are outlined in them ... in Väinämöinen one sees meditative stability and wisdom, in Ilmarinen workaday industry, in Lenninkäinen sportive recklessness." The secondary characters Kullervo and Aino respectively seem to represent "dark defiance" and "tender dreaminess." These characterizations make *The Kalevala* the earliest symbol of Finnish nationalism and identity representing "a more primitive stage of spiritual development than the old epics of the Western peoples" (Salminen and Tarkinaimen, in *The Kalevala* 159).

Thousands of examples of Finnish folk poems were also collected in the 33-volume *Kansan vanhat runot* ("The Ancient Poems of the Finnish People"), which like *The Kalevala* reveal significant national qualities of the hardy, stubborn, originally pastoral Finnish people: "individualism, endurance, and love of liberty" (Booss, Introduction to *Scandinavian Folk and Fairy Tales* xix). James Cloyd Bowman, co-editor of *Tales from a Finnish Tupa* [peasant's cottage], 1936, claimed:

> The heart of Finnish folklore is magic ... the magic of words ... [of] a strange people [who] loved ... peace, and hated violence. They approved of strength and courage and right doing, and liked nothing better than to trip up the heels of the oppressor and the deceiver.
> On the surface they were cold and inexpressive, and seemed as frozen over as their lakes in winter. But beneath their fur coats their hearts were warm and deep within their hearts, when least expected, there was a droll laughter, and a keen sense of human values [quoted in Booss' Introduction to *Scandinavian Folk and Fairy Tales* xix–xx.

These national qualities survive in much contemporary Finnish detective literature and even seem to dominate many Finnish crime novels' leading characters. Interviewed in connection with Nordic Cool, a four-week festival of the arts held at Kennedy Center in Washington, D.C., in February–March 2013 with participants from all the Nordic countries, three prominent crime writers emphasized these typically Finnish characteristics as prevailing in current Finnish detective fiction. Finns Leena Lehtolainen and Tapani Bagge and American James Thompson, who lived in Finland for over fifteen years, insisted that "books from Finland are different" (Cord). Lehtolainen stressed that the Finns' connection with Russia is a major factor in the Finnish national character: "We have our common history and a long border with Russia, and it [is] impossible to forget it." She finds the temperament of Eastern Finns closer to the typical Russian than to the typical Swedish disposition, and she also claims, "We are part of the Nordic countries, but we used to be part of Russia, so we and our books are a link between the two worlds" (quoted in Cord). Comparing Finnish detective fiction to that of the other Nordic countries, Bagge feels "We have more humour and a certain Finnish craziness," with more Finnish crime fiction written from the criminal's point of view than the detective's. Bagge also thinks "Finns aren't talkative," so the dialogue in Finnish crime novels is "realistic, simple and particularly important." Thompson emphasized Finland's special quality as "an eccentric and quirky country ... unique and exotic.... Stories set in Finland can take you to new realms and expose the work to you in a way you never before envisioned" (quoted in Cord).

Lehtolainen, Bagge, and Thompson agreed that the Finnish climate plays a central role in their fiction. Laitolainen saw Finland's extreme weather conditions and seasons as having "special meaning ... more than a backdrop," because she feels Finns behave differently in the different seasons, especially during the long winters which make them melancholic. Bagge concurred: "Long, dark periods bring dark ideas," and Thompson felt the winter environment in Finnish fiction becomes "almost a character ... part of us, an antagonist and source of conflict. In ways, it shapes us." After Bagge observed that "In winter, you can hide bodies under icy lakes, or under snow drifts in the forest," Thompson completed the thought with a typically Finnish twist: "And the spring thaw turns up many or most of the people reported missing during the winter" (quoted in Cord).

The uniquely Finnish approach to literature began in the country's early 19th century upsurge of nationalism and its emphasis on folklore. "The Finnish national character includes a penchant for the incessant questioning of one's own identity" (Papinniemi, "Letter") which began in earnest with the Fennoman movement, a political movement that emerged from the fennophile sentiment of the 18th and early 19th centuries. The Fennomans advocated the establishment of Finnish as the national language and became the most powerful political force in 19th century Finland (*Country Studies*). Members of the Saturday Society and the Finnish Literary Society, established in 1830 and 1831 respectively, devoted themselves to Finnish language and literature and fervently opposed the Svecomans, who insisted on the primacy of Swedish in Finland and the maintenance of Finland's ties with the Germanic countries. Ending the connection with Sweden forced the Finns to begin defining themselves; although many first-generation Fennomans spoke Swedish, they learned Finnish and even Finnicized their family names in the spirit of the Fennoman motto, attributed to Adolf Ivar Arvidsson: We are no longer Swedes, we cannot become Russians, so we must be Finns (paraphrased from a quotation in Ahokas 35). At this time, the Swedish-language poet Johan Ludvig Runeberg authored a popular nationalistic poetry collection, *The Tales of Ensign St. Al*, whose first poem, "Our Land," set to music, became Finland's national anthem.

Especially during the reign of Tsar Alexander II, 1855–1881, a liberal reformer who abolished Russian serfdom in 1861, the Russian government was somewhat sympathetic to the Fennoman movement and the Finnish Party that the Fennomans created shortly after the close of the Crimean War in 1856. Because Finland remained peaceful during the 1863 Polish revolt against Russia, an Imperial Russian edict allowed Finland to summon its own Diet (parliament) for the first time since 1809 and permitted the Diet to establish a separate Finnish monetary system and a separate Finnish army. At the urging of Fennoman leader Johan Vilhelm Snellman, another 1863 Imperial Russian edict established the Language Ordinance, and although Swedish speakers blocked some of the Ordinance's provisions, over the next two decades it provided Finnish a status equaling the position of Swedish in official business and enabled a vast expansion of the Finnish language school system, which ultimately "led to the creation of an educated class of Finnish speakers, who provided articulate mass support for the nationalist cause" (*Country Studies*). Alexander II also ordered that by 1883 Finnish should gain governmental and judicial parity with Swedish. In part to counter effects of the famine of 1866–1868, one of the worst in European history, killing nearly 15 percent of Finland's population, the Russian government also relaxed financial regulations, allowing a rapid development of the Finnish economy and the Finns' political self-awareness. In the 1860s, the Fennoman movement formed the Finnish Party to advance their cause, but in the 1890s it split into the Old Finnish and the Young Finnish Parties over constitutional issues.

In 1870, not long after the formation of the Finnish Party, Aleksis Kivi (1834–1872) published the first novel to appear in Finnish, *Seven Brothers*, since 1927 available in English translation and still widely viewed as one of the greatest works of Finnish literature. "Many Finns would claim…. Kivi, the 'father' of both modern Finnish literature and of Finnish theatre, as the distinguished precursor of the crime novel also" (Forshaw 145). The theme of *Seven Brothers*, one that still appears in many Finnish novels, treats the survival struggles of uneducated peasants in the nation's developing urban civilization. *Seven Brothers* initiated the Finnish trend, predominant at the time in Europe and the United States, of novels dealing with the problems that industrialization caused for the middle class and the peasantry. Kivi himself described *Seven Brothers* as "a merry tale" (quoted in Ahokas 83), but it also contains unadorned scenes of violence, terror, and brutality: "The Finns have been accused occasionally of lengthy brooding over real or imaginary wrongs ending in sudden eruptions of destructive violence. Kivi describes this temperament in his characters" (Ahokas 83), a technique frequently used by contemporary Finnish crime writers. Barry Forshaw contends that *Seven Brothers* foreshadows today's Finnish crime fiction, because the novel's closing chapters contain the solution of a classic locked-room mystery (Forshaw 145, and Demko). Like many sunlight-deprived persons, Kivi probably suffered from SAD (Seasonal Affective Disorder) and depression. His personal life also illustrates the problems with alcoholism that bedevil Finnish society: "... he often found that the only source of mirth in life's difficulties was alcohol, which hastened his death [at thirty-eight]" (Ahokas 73).

After the assassination of Tsar Alexander II in 1881, Finland's relationship with Russia soured under his fanatic and reactionary son Alexander III who forcibly Russified minorities, persecuted Jews, and began to limit Finnish autonomy. He made Finland's 1906 adoption of universal suffrage nearly meaningless because as an absolutist tsar, he did not have to allow any law passed by the Finnish parliament, causing Finnish radical liberals and socialists to dramatically increase their demands for independence.

The first two decades of the 20th century saw profound changes in all areas of Finnish life. In mainstream literature, Swedish-language modernism became one of the most praised literary movements in Finland's history, but resentment toward Swedish was rising. Two new political parties, the Young Finnish Party, founded in 1894, and the Finnish Workers Party which shortly after its founding in 1899 changed its name to the Social Democrat Party, began to openly attack Finland's autonomous position in the Russian Empire. This coincided with a shift in literary emphasis that Finland shared with the rest of Europe, away from realism and naturalism and toward romanticism and symbolism, ushering in Finland's period of nationalist romanticism, expressed in the Finnish language (Ahokas 146–7). Despite the prevalence of romanticism at that time, however, Finland's first recognized mystery, Harald Selmer-Geeth's *Min första brogd* ("My First Case"), written in Swedish, appeared in 1904.

Detective fiction began to flourish in Finland at the opening of the 20th century, at first through translations of English and American stories which soon inspired Finnish authors to write their own. Almost all of those early Finnish efforts had Sherlock Holmes stories as their model (Kukkola 208). In 1910 the acknowledged "father" of the Finnish mystery, Rudolf Richard Ruth, as "Rikhard Hornanlinna" pseudonymously produced two short mystery novels, drawn from his background as a private investigator who himself had served jail time for blackmail. Showing the influence of both Arthur Conan Doyle and Edgar Allan Poe, *Kellon salaisuus* ("The Secret of the Clock") and *Lähellä kuolemaa* ("A Close Run with Death") feature a gentlemanly amateur detective, Max Rudolf, who foreshadows British Golden Age sleuths like Dorothy L. Sayers' Lord Peter Wimsey and Margery Allingham's Albert Campion, with "a Holmesian flair for disguises and deduction" (Demko). In 1939, Ruth published *Yhä murhat jatkuivat* ("And the Murders Went On") under the name "H.R. Halli," adopted as a feature film, *Viimeinen vieras* ("The Last Guest") in 1941.

The 1916 novel *Guldgruvan* ("The Gold Mine"), subtitled "A Detective and Adventure Story," by Henning Söderhjelm (pen name "Lennart Wikström"), a Finn who wrote in Swedish, displays two distinct parts, the first involving the mysterious disappearance of the heroine, which follows the detective story conventions of the time, and the second dealing with a search for her kidnapper and a battle with him, in the mode of the American Nick Carter tales then being translated and published in Finland. The novel furnishes a portrait of Finland's "lost generation" of depressed and decadent young Swedish-speaking Finns and "poses questions about the author's class identity," since Finland's aristocratic Swedish speakers lost power and status in this period of modernization of Finnish society and culture (Malmio 456). The novel's hero Olle, an upper-class alcoholic with diminished financial prospects, often comments on Sherlock Holmes' deductive method, which Olle uses to trace his sweetheart's disappearance. Olle also disparages detective fiction, dismissing it as having low cultural and social connotations (Malmio 465). Söderhjelm himself insisted on using a pen name and told his publishers that he did not want his detective fiction identified with him because he felt it would damage his academic reputation.

An interesting sidelight to Finnish crime fiction is the story of a real-life 1918 crime, the 1920 lynching of Olli Kinkkonen, a Finnish immigrant, in Duluth, Minnesota. Like many of his countrymen Kinkkonen had come to the United States in the early 1900s and worked in northern Minnesota as a logger and a Duluth dockworker. Because he vociferously opposed compulsory military service during World War I, he was abducted from a Duluth boarding house in September 1918 for his "un–American views" and vanished; his body was found three weeks later hanging from a birch tree in Duluth's Lester Park and ruled a suicide with the perpetrators never apprehended. Kinkkonen's story is chronicled in *Suomalaiset: People of the Marsh*, a 2010 novel about Finns in Minnesota by Cloquet, Minnesota, author Mark Munger.

During the 1920s and 1930s, detective fiction helped Finns deal with wartime and postwar tensions. Two months after Russia's October 1917 Bolshevik revolution erupted, Finland's rightist nationalistic government (the "Whites," or the "White Guards") declared Finland's independence. The Social Democrat Party (the "Reds," or the "Red Guards," supported by the Soviets) staged a coup and held the southern part of Finland and Helsinki, while the Whites continued in exile from Vaasa. The conflict ignited the Finnish Civil War, which lasted through the winter of 1917 and the spring of 1918. In April a German division requested by the Whites landed in Finland seeking a potential satellite for Kaiser Wilhelm's Reich. Led by Baron Carl Gustav Mannerheim, the Whites prevailed with the aid of young Finns who had secretly received military training in Imperial Germany. The Whites briefly flirted with installing a German prince, the Kaiser's brother-in-law, as Finland's king, but he never ruled, and Mannerheim, Finland's national hero, became regent in 1919, until the Social Democrats assumed power in the new presidential republic.

Finland's Civil War left a deep social and political gulf between Reds and Whites, because after the war ended, the Whites had interned tens of thousands of Reds and suspected Communist sympathizers who perished in the thousands from malnutrition, disease, and execution. The Treaty of Tartu established the Finnish-Russian border according to historical tradition and granted the Barents Sea harbor of Pechenga to Finland, but the war and Finnish activists' expeditions into Soviet territory seriously strained relations between the Soviet Union and Finland. At home the new Finnish government engineered land reforms that made 90 percent of Finnish farmers independent.

Finnish authors generally have treated the Civil War indirectly. "Finnish literature … deals with individuals rather than types or social classes and is remarkably free from political and social propaganda" (Ahokas 183). Early mystery novelist Rudolf Richard Ruth seemed to ignore most aspects of the war in his 1920 Poe-esque horror and romance novel *Musta tohtori* ("The Black Doctor"). His subsequent classic mystery *Yhä murhat jatkuivat* ("And the Murders Went On") treated Helsinki's rampant postwar black markets, and his last novel, *Viides ja viimeinen uhri* ("The Fifth and Final Victim") incorporated elements of the fantastic. None of Ruth's fiction is available in English. Ruth's contemporary, theater director and manager Jalmari Finne, also seemed to downplay the war in his 1928 mystery novel *Verinen lyhty* ("Blood on the Lantern"), set in rural Finland and featuring a female sleuth resembling Agatha Christie's Miss Marple. Finne followed that novel with a gothic thriller, *Kohtalan käsi* ("The Hand of Fate").

Wounds from a civil war and its bitter aftermath heal slowly. In Finland's case, the war fostered an ambivalent approach to the portrayal of Russians in Finnish crime fiction. The rightist Finnish elite who had called the 1917–1918 conflict not a civil war (*sisellissota*) but "Finland's War of Independence" (*valaussota*), blamed it on the Bolsheviks, and during the conflict and for a long time afterward they successfully promulgated russophobia (*ryssavilia*). This buttressed the Finns' general belief that communism threatened their drive for independence, so Russophobia and anticommunism together sank deeply into Finland's political and cultural climate. During the 1930s, a period of vicious purges within the Soviet Union, popular Finnish crime authors portrayed their Russian characters as "cruel, beastly, and barbaric Bolsheviks" (Arvas 115).

During World War II, popular Finnish crime authors depicted Russians differently, now viewing them as criminals and spies (Arvas 116), While much of the rest of the world was battling Hitler's Nazi Germany, Mussolini's Fascist Italy, and Imperial Japan, Finland suffered the most tumultuous period of its brief history as a modern independent nation, torn between Nazi Germany and the Soviet Union. According to historian Paul Johnson, "… the Hitler phenomenon cannot be seen except in conjunction with the phenomenon of Soviet Russia," since the fear of Communism had both put Hitler in power and kept him there. By the end of 1938, British weakness at the Munich Conference had resulted in diplomatic surrender and military disaster. The carving up of Czechoslovakia ensured moral collapse in eastern Europe, so that without firing a shot Hitler seemed "to have restored all the splendor of Wilhelmine Germany" (Johnson 353). In 1939, to fulfill his world expansionist dreams with a German war machine that could not as yet sustain a protracted conflict, Hitler had to wage a *blitzkrieg* ("lightning war"), "short, ferocious campaigns of overwhelming power and intensity but very limited duration" similar to Bismarck's 19th century campaigns. Hitler intended that his last and decisive *blitzkrieg* would be waged against the Soviet Union (Johnson 358), so he made what he called "a pact with Satan to drive out the devil" (quoted in Johnson 358), a supposed nonaggression pact with Stalin.

Nazi Germany's invasion of Poland in 1939 forced Britain and France to declare war on Nazi Germany. After the Soviet Union demanded that the Finns demilitarize their Mannerheim Line, defensive fortifications across the Karelian Isthmus, Soviet troops marched into Finland. Commanded by Mannerheim, the Finns heroically resisted but were defeated in 1940 in the conflict called the Finnish-Russian War, or the Winter War. Then wanting to recover territories lost to the Soviets, Finland joined Nazi Germany when Hitler broke his pact with Stalin and attacked the Soviet Union in 1941. In this Continuation War, the Finns fought the Soviets from 1941 to 1944, achieving a stalemate. The 1944 armistice required Finland to expel German forces from its territory in a conflict called the Lapland War of 1944–1945, which devastated northern Finland. Between 1940 and 1944, the Finns lost 93,000 men. In the 1947 and 1948 peace treaties Finland signed with the Soviet Union, the Finns also lost two important seaports, 20 percent of their industrial capacity, and 10 percent of their prewar land area, most of Finnish Karelia, Salla and Petsamo. Most of the population of these areas, about 400,000 people, fled into what remained of Finland.

Crime literature helped Finns survive the sacrifices and tensions of the post–World War II period, when "anything Anglo American was a plus" in all areas of Finnish culture. One of the most prolific writers in the mystery genre, Kaarlo Nuorvala, 1910–1967, wrote novels, children's literature, and twenty film scripts at a staggering pace. With new publishers sprouting up in 1945, Nuorvala produced 28 books for twenty publishers—in one remarkable burst, 250 pages in three days. Nuorvala liked to set his stories in newspaper offices, often in America ("A Book a Month").

The postwar population shift presaged a major transformation of Finland from an agrarian society to an industrial one. By1950, only 46 percent of Finnish workers were engaged in agriculture. About a third of the Finnish population now were living in urban centers, attracted by new employment opportunities in trade, services, and manufacturing. According to official Finnish government statistics, the baby boom that peaked at 3.5 children per family in 1947 could not be accommodated when these children entered the labor market, and hundreds of thousands of Finns emigrated to far more industrialized Sweden between 1967 and 1979. Finns who stayed hungered for relief from their postwar stresses, and many found it in popular detective novels.

During World War II, rightist Finnish politician Vilho Helanen, 1899–1952, used his personal anti–Communist activities as background for his crime fiction. As a youth during the Finnish Civil War, Helanen had joined the White Guards and participated in underground activity against the Reds, and in the 1930s he belonged to the Lapua Movement, dedicated to rooting all vestiges of Marxism out of Finland, even vocally supporting Adolf Hitler. (The Germans, however, considered Helanen a fanatical chauvinist.) Helanen had already expressed his ultra-nationalistic views strongly in the detective novels he began writing in the late 1930s. After he lost the 1939 Nordic novel Glass Key competition to Mika Waltari, he began to publish his Kaarlo Rauta detective series in 1941 under a pen name. In the first novel, Rauta, a lawyer, saves a friend from murder accusations by uncovering the real culprit, the female leader of a anarchic Communist spy ring ("Vilho Helanen," in *Books and Authors*). After World War II, when Helonen had headed the Finnish Civil Service, he was sentenced to prison in 1948 for treasonous activities but was later pardoned. Upon his release he wrote more popular detective novels to support his family, some reminiscent of S.S. Van Dine's Philo Vance mysteries, which Helanen admired. Most of the villains of Helanen's postwar novels were no longer evil Communists but wicked female schemers. At the time of his fatal heart attack in 1952, Helanen was planning to meet with popular Swedish mystery novelist Maria Lang, hoping to have his books published in Sweden. For a long time after his death, Helanen was marginalized because of his extreme rightist views, but recently Finnish scholars have revived interest in his work, notably Paula Arvas, whose book-length study "Rauta and Ristilukki: Vilho Helanen['s] Detective Novels" appeared in Finnish in 2009.

Many other popular Finnish authors were creating detective series between the 1930s and the 1960s, when police procedurals became the Finnish public's most popular reading material. One of the best known authors of police procedurals in Finland was Viktor Aarne Haapakoski (Arne Viktor Laitinen, also known as "Outsider"), 1904–1961, whose history parallels Europe's trials during the first half of the 20th century (Bujalance). He wrote many novels and radio plays under a dozen pseudonyms. His first novel, a non-procedural mystery, was a finalist in the 1938 Glass Key competition, and between 1941 and 1948 he produced an 18-novel series starring detective and architect Klaus Karma, who battled the Nazis while carrying on a love affair with a Gestapo spy who was trying to dismantle a Finnish anti–Nazi organization. Laitenen also wrote science fiction and horror novels. After 1945 he created his most popular work, a series featuring an odd couple of adventurers. It became highly popular in 1950s radio and film versions (Bujalance). He also created a series of science fiction novels starring the robot Atorox whose name has been given to the awards presented by the Turku Science Fiction Society. Laitinen's work today is kept alive by the Aarne Haapakoski Society, established in 2011 (see http://www.aarnehaapakoski-seura.fi).

Laitinen's good friend Martti Löfberg who wrote as "Marton Taiga," 1907–1969, shunned publicity, but he wrote around sixty books and was one of the most popular Finnish "pulp" authors during the 1930s and 1940s. Beginning in 1938, he adopted the pseudonym "M. Levik" to publish a procedural series whose protagonist is obese and crafty Inspector William J. Kairala, a character who influenced the creation of Mika Waltari's popular Komisario Palmu, possibly the best-known fictional policeman in Finland (see below). Löfberg also published a time-travel novel based in ancient Egypt, *Osiriksen Sormus*, in 1934, a precursor of Waltari's best known historical fiction.

Löfberg also wrote apocalyptic science fiction and an adventure comic book series that was reprinted in the 1970s.

Lesser-known detective authors of this period include Tauno Yliruusi, 1927–1994, who enjoyed an international reputation as a playwright and radio and television scriptwriter as well as a novelist and author of humorous satiric short fiction. . His plays were translated into fifteen languages including English and have been presented in twenty-five countries. His radio plays include a late 1950s series called "Murder for Fun" (Demko) as well as procedurals featuring Inspector Suominen, including *Murder Game*, 1951, and *Detective's Holiday*, 1962. Publisher Tauno Karilas, 1900–1980, became a popular boys' adventure series author who wrote police procedurals after World War II and a stand-alone novel, *Nokinen jälki* ("Soot Marks"), inspired by Poe's "The Murders in the Rue Morgue" (Demko).

One of the first (and still today very few) female Finnish crime authors was Kirsti Hellin Fogelholm. She wrote stage and radio plays under the pen names Kirsti Porras, Gretel Nieme, and Cathelyn Steve, and in 1942, 1944, and 1945 she published three procedural detective novels featuring Helsinki Police Inspector Kanerba, assisted by a crime author.

Mika Waltari, 1908–1979, a major 20th century author and Finland's best internationally known novelist, wrote nineteen novels, numerous short stories, six poetry collections, and 26 plays as well as screenplays, nonfiction, and translations. His works have been translated into over forty languages. Waltari's large-scale historical works like *The Egyptian*, *The Roman*, and *The Etruscan*, all available in English and voicing his perseverant theme of humanistic values' tragic fate in a materialistic world, are today his best known works outside of Finland, but long before he wrote them he authored a popular detective series, representing what he called his "secondary side" as a writer. The series began with *Kuka murhasi rouva Skrofin?* ("Who Killed Mrs. Skrof?"), 1939, which won that year's Glass Key competition. Its protagonist is aging and irascible Helsinki Inspector Frans J. Palmu, a bowler-hatted and cigar-puffing hero whose cases are narrated in the classic Holmesian manner by a Dr. Watson figure. During World War II while Waltari was working for the Finnish Information Service he followed his first and immensely popular Palmu novel with two more, *Komisario Palmun erehdys* (""Inspector Palmu's Mistake") and *Tähdet kertovat, komisario Palmu!* ("The Stars Will Tell, Inspector Palmu!"). None of Waltari's Palmu novels have been translated into English.

Beginning in 1960 with "Inspector Palmu's Mistake," Finnish director Matti Kassila filmed Waltari's three Palmu novels. These instant movie hits made the humorous character of Inspector Palmu "instantly recognizable by most Finns" (Demko). Between 1961 and 1963, Kassila and Waltari worked on another Palmu script, this one set in Helsinki's theater world, but it was never published. In 1969 Kassila and Georg Korkman wrote a screenplay for another Palmu film, not based on Waltari's original text (Liukkonen).

For his first detective novel, Waltari drew on three crime fiction sources, Poe's 1840s stories starring M. Auguste Dupin, considered the first amateur genius detective in fiction; the Sherlock Holmes stories; and the British Golden Age whodunit tradition popular between the two world wars for his stolid sidekick narrator, the puzzle-like plot, and a now familiar cast of character types (Pyrhönen 23, 35). The announcement for the Glass Key competition had specified that authors should use variations from the traditional detective story format to express "a nationally specific inflection of the genre" (Pyrhönen 24), so Waltari "imbued these models with markedly Finnish characteristics, thus producing a humorously playful version of the whodunit" (Pyrhönen 23–24).

Heta Pyrhönen's analysis of "Who Murdered Mrs. Skrof?" highlights several typically Finnish elements that allowed Waltari to infuse the detective genre with a uniquely Finnish flavor. The victim is a stingy, irritable old woman who has tried to make her stepdaughter marry her nephew so that the stepmother's wealth would be kept in the family. Waltari used "the wavering finger of suspicion" mystery technique with a cast of conventional characters: the tyrannical parent figure, the eligible girl, an endearing rascal, and a decadent artist-villain. All of them except the stepdaughter Kirsti are of aristocratic Finnish-Swedish descent, allowing Waltari to explore the degeneracy of that class (Pyrhönen 26, 28). Kirsti, the only purely Finnish character, "reinforces a Finnish prejudice" as the means by which Finnish blood could restore "vigour and moral rectitude" to the aristocracy. Palmu, a street-smart, commonsensical self-educated pure Finn, contrasts dramatically with his inane youthful sidekick's upper class arrogant "superiority." By using such national clichés and stereotypes, Waltari's detective story relies on a fundamental departure from the whodunit world of Christie and other conventional mystery authors who were committed to the support of aristocratic social systems, principally because Waltari's criminal scapegoat allows Waltari to deride the very kind of hierarchy the other writers support. "Finns strive toward social sameness, not social difference" (Pyrhönen 30).

Pyrhönen also observes that Waltari believed that since his adolescence he had felt split in two by having two personalities, and throughout his life he attempted to contain his decadent impulses through hard work and disciplined habits. In his detective fiction, he could don the criminal's mask to draw on his "irrational, creative impulses," while curbing them with the detective's mask which represented his rational, form-giving impulses (Pyrhönen 31). In "Who Murdered Mrs. Skrof?" Waltari demonstrated his understanding of the whodunit author's role by giving the novel a triangular structure, with a narrator recounting the actions of both a rational, paternalistic figure (Palmu) and a decadently romantic adolescent one (the villain). Pyrhönen concludes that Waltari's crime fiction, written when he was a relatively young man, characterizes him as a boyish detective story writer who produced playful self-reflexive fiction. On the contrary, Pyrhönen suggests, most of today's Finnish detective novels follow the examples of Sjöwall and Wahlöö and Georges Simenon by reflecting their nation's reality and the causes and effects of its crime, much of it due to lapses of the welfare state government. Most contemporary Finnish detective fiction dwells not on mafia-style professional killings but on individual offenses like wife-beating and drunken manslaughter. In Finland's crime literature, such crimes arise from social problems, usually solved by world-weary policemen or hard-boiled American-style private eyes (Pyrhönen 35).

Immediately after World War II, Mika Waltari's large-scale historical novels dominated mainstream Finnish fiction. According to Finnish literary historian Jaako Ahokas, those novels which made Waltari the best known and wealthiest Finnish author of all time also reflect the prevailing postwar mood of the Finnish middle class. *The Egyptian*, 1945, is usually considered at least a partial allegory of World War II. No other book has sold so quickly in Finland. It also topped the U.S. bestseller lists for many weeks, possibly also as a symptom of postwar disillusionment.

During the Cold War, Finland in deference to Soviet wishes refused offers of U.S. Marshall Plan aid, though secretly the Finns' Social Democrat Party received American development funds intended to bolster the country's independence. In 1950, 46 percent of Finnish workers were engaged in agriculture, but new international trade relations with the West and reparations to the Soviet Union encouraged Finland to continue its transformation into an industrialized nation. Finland also benefited from liberalized international trade policies established by the World Bank and the International Monetary Fund.

During the modern period, discussions about the nature of Finland's relationships with East and West, always "an integral part of Finnishness" (Papinnirmi, "Letter"), became even more evident in Finland's culture, especially its popular literature. In tracing the lasting effect of the complex

World War II period Russian-Finnish relations on Finnish crime literature, Paula Arvas has observed that the Finnish government refused to take rigid policy positions vis-à-vis their powerful eastern neighbor, and instead "sought a pragmatic relationship with the Soviet Union by currying favor with her leaders" to maintain Finnish independence . [so that] during that period "Russian villains vanished from Finnish crime fiction" (Arvas 16).

Mauri Sariola, 1924–1985, a controversial author who also wrote as "Esko Laukko," produced more than 80 novels translated into ten languages in twenty countries, about half of them dealing with crime. He also wrote numerous magazine articles, short fiction, radio plays, and television scripts, besides translating the mystery novels of twelve English-language authors. Sariola's books have sold over two million copies in Finland. In 2006, the Finnish detective publication *Ruumiin kulttuuri* acknowledged that in the mid–1950s, Finnish crime fiction seemed "dormant" until Sariola introduced "new blood" with his first novel, *Laukausten hinta* ("The Price of Shots"), 1956.

Because of his lifelong adherence to pronounced right-wing views, Sariola has been called the successor of Vilho Helanen, 1899–1952, a fervent rightist-nationalist politician and crime fiction author. Sariola became internationally famous for his thirty Inspector Susikoski novels, which began to appear in 1956 and continued throughout his career. He received the French Prix du Roman d'Aventures for his most popular novel, *Lavean tien laki* (*The Helsinki Affair*), 1961, translated to English by Alan Blair in 1970, which sold 100,000 copies in Finland alone. Sariola patterned his young lawyer hero Matti Vilma after Perry Mason, Erle Stanley Gardner's lawyer-sleuth, probably because Sariola as a young man had translated Perry Mason novels into Finnish. As Counsel for the Defence at Helsinki's Criminal Court, Vilma, in a dramatic courtroom finale, unmasks the perpetrators of a blackmailing and homicide plot—his client's friend and Vilma's own attractive secretary. Sariola followed *The Helsinki Affair* with four more Matti Vilma novels, but only one, *Punainen kukon laulu* (The Torvik Affair), 1963 has been translated into English. Starting in 1959 Sariola's novels featuring Inspector Leo Olavi Susikoski, who after Waltari's Inspector Palmu is likely the best known police figure in Finnish literature, were adapted for film and television. Sariola had his two most popular characters, police detective Suskoski and lawyer Matti Vilma, meet in *Pyykki on pantu ja pysyy* ("Washing Has Been and Will Remain"), 1965.

Sariola, who detested the liberalism of the 1960s and 1970s, accurately portrayed Finnish life between the 1950s and 1980s, but he wrote very quickly and usually did not edit his work, feeling that a book is best written in one fell swoop. He was accused of plagiarism in the 1950s, and later critics often found his work overly conservative and somewhat sloppy. He also wrote a military fiction trilogy about three Finnish soldiers, each of whom respectively received the Mannerheim Cross for heroism in the Winter War, the Continuation War, and the postwar reconstruction period. He followed these with a novel treating the fate of Finnish prisoners of war. In the early 1990s, several Susikoski novels appeared under the name of Sariola's second wife Tuula Kerpela Sariola, but in June 2006 these novels as well as the rest of her sixteen books were proved to have been ghost written by her journalist friend Ritva Sarkola ("Mauri Sariola," in *Books and Writers*).

During the Cold War period, Finland, officially neutral, had to find a way to maintain its independence in the face of threats from the Soviet Union. The Finns' solution was "Finlandization," a negative term originating in West Germany to describe a small nation's loss of sovereignty to a powerful neighbor. Even the most politically conservative Finns, however, saw Finlandization as key to survival of their independence. Ramifications of the Finnish-Russian Agreement of Friendship, Cooperation, and Mutual Assistance, known in Finland as the "YVA Treaty," in effect between 1948 and the collapse of the Soviet Union around 1992, peaked between 1968 and 1982, a period that also saw a dramatic change taking place in Nordic crime fiction.

As the explosive 1960s were drawing to a close, readers encountered a new trend in Nordic crime fiction, until then dominated by the police procedural. Swedish Marxist authors Maj Sjöwall and Per Wahlöö published *Rosanna* in 1967, the first of their ten Martin Beck novels, a series they called collectively "The Story of a Crime," in which they hoped "to use the crime novel as a scalpel cutting open the belly of the pauperized and morally debatable so-called welfare state" (quoted in Murphy 33). The "crime" they wanted to expose was in their opinion Sweden's societal failure in becoming a capitalistic country masked by a socialistic façade, a country that they felt hypo-critically encouraged or drove individuals to commit crimes, so that they made the detective story a Marxist critique of capitalism (Murphy 456). Sjöwall and Wahlöö gradually built a cast of con-vincing police detectives around Martin Beck, caught in a job that pitted his conscience against the bureaucracy that entrapped him (Murphy 43).

After the Martin Beck novels captured the mystery-reading public's imagination, crime authors in the other Nordic countries began to explore the impact, which they frequently con-sidered negative, of welfare state policies on their fiction, especially the fictional detectives and the villains they created. Three major positions developed. The two extremes were represented by the leftists like Sjöwall and Wahlöö who used their procedurals to critique political systems they felt did not sufficiently espouse or even betrayed Marxist goals, and the capitalist-oriented rightist authors who used their crime stories to show that the welfare state's socialistic policies were doomed to failure, In positions ranging between these two extremes, other Nordic crime authors felt that their principal reason for writing their stories was to produce fully realized fictional worlds for their readers, "rather than social or political proselytizing," though most insisted on incorporating "pithy undercurrents of social and political criticism into their work" (Forshaw 146).

From the 1970s until the Soviet Union collapsed in 1992, Finnish crime novels generally took the middle road, though they differed from their Nordic neighbors' work in several important respects, notably in their attitude and practices regarding Soviet characters. Between 1968 and 1992, largely because of their country's fragile relationship with the Soviet Union, Finnish crime writers largely kept Russian characters out of their fiction, instead, like Mauri Sariola, providing homegrown villains and *femmes fatales*. Barry Forshaw also argues that Finnish crime fiction is singular because it "has something of a playful relationship" with the traditional conventions of crime writing. Such conventions allow readers to hold certain expectations when they open a new British, European, or American detective story. The Finns, however, set up those conventions only to shred them, an "audacious strategy because it forces readers of these highly personal books to commit to constantly exercising mental acuity, to constantly monitor the text's density, and to keep themselves open to the allusions and subtleties that underlie the conventional-seeming sur-face of the story" (Forshaw 147).

The concept and implementation of the welfare state concept that has played so important a role in the shaping and execution of most Nordic *noir* crime literature took an individual path in Finland largely because of the highly charged factionalism resulting from the Finnish Civil War which affected the political-economic forces that shaped Finland's own welfare state policies. These forces varied materially from those of the other Nordic countries. Until the 1950s, Finland's economy continued as it had always been, based on agriculture in a land whose acidic soil and a problematic climate of severe winters and ambivalent summers capable of both frosts and droughts made profitable agriculture challenging at best. Forestry, somewhat less dependent on weather but demanding hard outdoor labor, also has been a major economic factor in Finland and today still anchors Finland's wood processing industries.

In the late 19th century, Finland's industrialization and consequent population shift from the countryside to the cities favored the construction of a welfare state that has resulted in one of the world's most extensive welfare systems, supported by governmental policies produced mainly through coalition efforts among Finland's several political parties. Since 1906 three parties have been especially influential in the Finnish Parliament: the Centre Party (originally the Agrarian Union); the National Coalition Party (traditionally the conservatives); and the leftist Social Democrats; with the Communists occupying a strong fourth place until the 1990s. According to the International Monetary Fund, Finland today enjoys widespread prosperity and one of the world's highest per capita incomes, with high rankings in education, economic competitiveness, civil liberties, quality of life, and human development, making Finland *Newsweek's* 2010 choice for "the best country in the world" (Morten).

Even "the best country in the world," however, today faces serious tensions that are frequently being aired in its crime fiction. One of the most potentially destructive political trends in Finland is the rise in influence of the extreme rightist nationalistic Finns Party, which had earlier called itself the "True Finns," and the apparent decline in influence of the other major parties. In the April 2011 parliamentary election, two parties led in number of delegates elected to Finland's 200-member parliament: the National Coalition Party (Finnish *kokoomus*) won 44 seats with the Social Democrats close behind at 42. All parties in 2011 lost seats except the Finns Party, which dramatically increased its parliamentary representation from 5 seats in the previous election to 39 in 2011. Today, as they always have been, Finnish cabinets are multi-party coalitions. In general the Finnish Prime Minister is the leader of the largest party in the parliament, and the Minister of Finance is the leader of the second largest party. Until 2011, the Finnish government directing the nation's welfare state policies has balanced the leftist Social Democrats' aims with those of the conservative National Coalition Party, but since 2011 a change rooted in Finland's turbulent 20th century history seems to be looming.

According to its 2013 official home page (http://www.kokoomus.fi), Finland's National Coalition Party was founded in 1918 from the majority of the members of the monarchist Finnish Party and a minority of the Young Finnish Party with the aim of strengthening "the forces that maintain society" (*Kansallisen* 1918 [Archives of the National Coalition Party]). Acknowledging, too, that "constructive reform" was necessary, the National Coalition Party, which had originally favored a constitutional monarchy like those of Norway, Denmark, and Sweden, soon after its founding advocated reforms that included compulsory education, universal health care, and progressive income and property taxation (*Konsallisen* 1919 [Archives of the National Coalition Party]). Between the world wars, the party's major support derived from large farms and businesses in southern Finland, favoring stability over reform. During the 1930s, it maintained contact with radical right-wing movements that for a time threatened Finnish democracy ("Country Studies").

From the late 1920s, the conservative National Coalition Party, then the most right-wing political party in Finland, strongly favored the use of Finnish over Swedish and opposed Finnish Communism, picturing itself as the defender of democracy against various Communist organizations chiefly made up of youthful Finns. After the Christian Democrats split from the National Coalition Party in the late 1950s, a time of ideological reform, voters considered the National Coalition Party too rightist and shut them out of the Finnish government from 1966 to 1987, the period in which Finland felt it had to maintain rapport with the Soviet Union. When the Soviet Union collapsed, National Coalition membership grew steadily. In 1987 a National Coalition Prime Minister led Finland for the first time since 1950, pledging his government to preserve Finland's welfare state while maintaining a free market economy able to compete abroad and safeguard Finnish prosperity ("Country Studies"). The National Coalition Party was out of power again from 2003 to 2007, but today it is Finland's largest political party.

According to the National Coalition Party's 2014 official website (http://www.kokoomus. fi/en), the party today "uses responsible politics to develop the Finnish state. In Parliament we push for laws that promote a positive, civilized, caring and tolerant society," requiring "a new, active and entrepreneurial spirit." The party's official platform stresses that the party's ideology "combines freedom with responsibility, democracy, and quality." From 2004 to 2013 Finland's Prime Minister was National Coalition Party leader Jyrki Katainen, who retired to take a position with the European Union. Alexander Stubb was elected as leader of the National Coalition Party and Prime Minister in June 2013. Katainen had led the shift in the National Coalition Party's orientation from its former upper class-dominated socially conservative neoliberal stance to its current center-right, mostly urban and moderately liberal reformist position, which favors such progressive concepts as multiculturalism and same-sex marriage. Stubb, however, stated in 2010 that under Katainen the party had become "unambiguously liberal ... [and had taken] a positive attitude toward immigration and toward internationalism in general" (Karlsson). In the electoral term 2011–2013, the National Coalition-led government has cut Finnish taxes by over 4 billion euros, claiming that spending 150 million euros to improve both earnings-related and basic unemployment allowances was too expensive (Alaja).

The chief political opponent to Finland's National Coalition Party has been the Social Democrat Party (since 1903 the _Suomen Sosialide Mokrorrinwn Puolue_ or SDP), founded in 1899 as the Finnish Labor Party, born out of the nation's trade union movement and since the 1920s fostered by Soviet Communists. As a leading force in Finnish politics for decades, the SDP achieved major welfare state reforms beginning in the 1960s.

In Finland as in the other Nordic countries, trade unions have exerted a strong influence on governmental policies, and Finnish workers had had a long association with leftist and Communist factions. In 1905 the unions created Red Guard units which heavily influenced the new parliament that resulted from the Finnish General Strike that year, elected by universal suffrage for the first time in Europe with women winning a surprising 10 percent of the parliamentary seats (Einhorn and Logue 269). Between 1904 and 1906, the Social Democrats quadrupled their party membership, and in the 1916 general election, they won slightly more than an absolute majority, the last time any Finnish political party has done so ("Country Studies"). Acrimony between conservatives and labor unionists increased dramatically after the 1917–1918 Civil War, which devastated Finland's labor movement. The unionists, who had had 157,000 members at the end of 1917, lost about 25,000 members in the war and thousands of others fled to Russia. The winning Whites executed 8,000 Reds and incarcerated another 80,000 is concentration camps where 12,000 perished from starvation and disease (Einhorn and Logue 174). Starting in 1937, the SDP began to demand the right to collective bargaining, but between 1919 and 1938, Finnish unionization, dominated by the Communists, had averaged only 8 percent, compared to Sweden's 30 percent (Einhorn and Logue 275). The Finnish labor union movement was revitalized in 1940 at the outbreak of the Winter War against the Soviet Union, when employers accepted labor's right to organize and bargain collectively. Just after 1945, the SDP fragmented over the question of how closely its relationship with the Soviet Union should be maintained, and following the Finnish Communists' 1948 election defeat, the SDP suffered from continued internal strife regarding its relations with the Soviet Union, weakening labor politically until 1996, when Finns elected a joint Social Democrat and Communist coalition government, allowing movement toward the more general Scandinavian welfare model.

In the 1960s, the SDP, together with its "popular front" allies, the agrarian Centre Party and the Finnish People's Democratic League, began to implement significant welfare state policies. In the next decade they introduced comprehensive school and health care reforms and achieved income policy agreements with the labor unions, balancing agreements on wage increases with "wide agreements on the improvement of the social security system, pensions, unemployment benefits and work protection" (Alaja). In the process, the SDP began becoming increasingly moderate, eventually in the 1990s approaching the center of Finnish politics.

After 1983, the SDP had difficulty attracting new voters from the post-industrial service sector, and their traditional base of blue-collar workers was declining. In the early 1990s, the collapse of trade with the disintegrating Soviet Union caused a deep economic crisis in Finland, exacerbated by "badly managed liberalization of the financial sector and monetary and fiscal policies" (Alaja). Finnish unemployment approached 20 percent and the GDP fell 14 percent in three years. White-collar workers threatened with loss of their jobs demanded unemployment compensation, contributing to a 13 percent jump in Finnish union membership and a feminization of the union movement. The SDP abandoned its 1991–1995 opposition position to join in the 1995 Rainbow Coalition, comprised of the SDP, the National Coalition Party, the Left Alliance and Greens League, and the Swedish People's Party, adopting a pro–European line and promoting Finland's membership in the European Union.

The Rainbow Coalition ushered in a new era in Finland that some researchers have called "the post-expansionist welfare state" (Alaja). To maintain its education and research and development funding, the government had to make major cuts in welfare spending. Led by the Social Democrats under SDP Prime Minister Paavo Lipponen, the government reached income policy agreements with labor, but in this new economic and political context, they exchanged wage moderation for tax cuts. Finland eagerly fulfilled the Maastricht criteria and in 2002 it became one of the first nations to adopt the new euro currency (Alaja).

In the process, the SDP retained its connection with organized labor, but other areas of their support declined. Finnish unionization rates of the gainfully employed rose from 33.1 percent to 95.6 percent in 1996, compared to the United States' rate of 14.5 percent in the same year. Finnish women in 1999 comprised 51 percent of union membership and occupied greater roles in union leadership than ever before (Einhorn and Logue 177). Today the SDP calls itself "a modern, centre left party" with "progressive ideas," and states its key values as: first, "a fair society" with success, opportunity, and freedom open to all, where "The measure of people should be their respect for others, not their wealth and background or characteristics such as race, sexuality or gender." The second value is "a supportive state," that gives people the power to make their own choices and provides a solid base on which they can build their dreams. Third is "a sustainable future," dealing with threats such as environmental damage, reckless economic activity, and the "weakening of social care" (see the SDP website, http://www.sdp.fi/en).

During the 1990s, the SDP fostered policies that brought Finland unprecedented prosperity, transforming Finnish society and dissolving old voting blocs (Country Studies), but their very achievements seem to have caused their political waterloo. The Rainbow Coalition era made the SDP membership look like oldsters (the SDP average age is now well over 60), establishment supporters, and baby boomers, a party image unattractive to younger people. Since the 1990s, new progressive activists have been joining further-left entities, principally the green, redgreen, and alter-globalization movements. The redgreens in particular behave offensively, squatting in empty houses, demanding basic incomes, and demonstrating in favor of far-left causes and environmental issues. The present criticism in Finland of the SDP seems to pertain to its association with the trade unions, so that the party now appears to be defending only the interests of organized labor. A single sign of hope for the SDP seems to be the Finnish public's recognition that "The sharp rise of income inequality has now become a significant policy problem" (Alaja).

Laura Saarikoski and Saska Saarikoski have recently argued that the 2012 presidential election marked "the end of the 30-year social democrat]sic] tenure" [no capitals in original], because the SDP's ideas had worked too well: Finland topped international charts for "a system of free schools and universities, state-funded health care [and] benefits for the poorest," but today young Finns have become disillusioned with the aging SDP, because the party has proved unable to reconcile the conflicting claims of a national labor force and international markets. Finnish industries now are moving operations to countries with cheap labor, so that "1960s radicals turned into advocates of vested interests." Economically, Finland is one of only four remaining triple-A countries in the Eurozone, but Finns are facing tax increases and cuts in government spending, and many of them "are tired of picking up the bill for what they see as tax-dodging free-riding south Europeans" like the Greeks (Saarikoski and Saarikoski), one reason many Finns today doubt the merits and value of European Union membership.

In the 2012 Finnish presidential election, the former finance minister, conservative National Coalition candidate Sauli Niinistö, ran against the Green Party's Pekka Haavisto, the nation's first openly gay presidential candidate, whose partner is an Ecuadorian hairdresser. The first conservative to become Finland's president in fifty years, Niinistö leads a prosperous Finland that nevertheless faces both external and internal challenges, one of the most problematic being the rapid rise of the Finns Party.

Saarikoski and Saarikoski also observe that in the 2011 parliamentary election, "many embittered blue-collar workers turned to the nationalistic, anti-migration True Finn party," which by winning 19.1 percent of the votes cast became the Finnish Parliament's third largest party, its largest opposition party, and potentially one of the most divisive elements in modern Finnish politics. Now calling themselves the "Finns Party," the "True Finns" (Finnish *perussuomalaiset* or PS) was founded in 1995 after the dissolution of the Finnish Rural Party. According to its official website (http://www.perusuomalaiset.fi/in-english), the Finns Party combines left-wing economic policies with conservative social values, socio-cultural authoritarianism, and ethnic nationalism, drawing support from both the right and the left while firmly supporting Finnish welfare state policies. In the fall of 2010, debates over immigration and gay rights polarized many Finns, "in some ways reinforce[ing] conservative sentiments in Finland" (Alaja, "True Finns ...") and thus strengthened the appeal of the Finns Party.

Before the founding of the Finns Party, populist Veikko Vennamo had split with the Agrarian League to found the predecessor of the Finns Party, the Finnish Rural Party, in the late 1960s. Vennamo sharply criticized the ruling Social Democrats for widespread corruption and his party's influence rose for the next twenty years, but it filed for bankruptcy in 1995. Some of its former members then formed the "True Finns" Party, later the Finns Party which today describes itself as centrist. It has 8,000 members united by patriotism and social conservatism. Its support among blue collar workers and voters earning between 35,000 and 50,000 euros a year is rising, with about 50,000 of them earning over 50,000 euros annually (Mars). The Finns Party today denies accusations that its roots lie in neo–Nazi political views.

In its short history, the Finns Party has grown dramatically. In 2005 its members numbered only about 1000, rising rapidly to 8000 in 2013. Its youth organization grew from about 800 before the 2011 election to over 2200 in 2013. The Finns Party's success in the 2011 parliamentary election, garnering 39 seats to the National Coalition's 44 and the Social Democrats 42, paralleled the triumph of its firebrand leader Timo Soini, whose personal votes exceeded Finance Minister Alexander Stubb's in his election district. The Finns Party refused to compromise its principles to join a coalition government, especially because of their opposition to membership in the European Union and NATO. The Finns Party advocates nationalism and preaches populism as an ideology that seeks to empower the people (*Vaalohjelmien*). Its policies include progressive taxation to support the welfare state, achieving energy self-sufficiency, and a pro-industry environmental stance. They also advocate teaching "healthy national pride" in schools, removal of the obligatory second language status in education (Swedish in Finnish-speaking areas and vice versa), and promotion of activities stressing Finnish identity as well as the traditional family model. Regarding the volatile issue of immigration, the Finns Party supports limiting humanitarian immigration strictly to refugee quotas, deporting criminal immigrants, and requiring immigrants to accept Finnish cultural norms (Karvonen). The Finns Party program for 2011 read in part, "Finnish immigration policy should be based on the fact that the Finns should always be able to decide for themselves the conditions under which a foreigner can come to our country and reside in our country" (p. 40).

Ugly anti-black, racist anti–Muslim and anti-gay statements have been attributed to Finns Party politicians and members (see http://truefinns.tumbler.com). While Finns Party leaders publicly deny that they hold such views, several have been accused and even fined for doing so, episodes Swedish *Expo* journalist Lisa Bjurwald aired in *Europe's Shame: Right-Wing Extremism on the Rise*, 2012. A Finns Party member of parliament even declined an invitation to the presidential Independence Day ball because he openly declared he did not care to see same-sex couples dancing together. The 2011 international press coverage of the Finns Party's dramatic election success described the party as "far right, xenophobic, populist, anti–EU, anti–Islam, and racist" (quoted in Karvonen). According to journalist Kyösti Karvonen who has covered the Finns Party and its predecessors since the early 1980s, those terms are valid, but he also believes that the party has struck a chord in the "deeper currents in the Finnish psyche…. Being a Finn ultimately entails suspicion of, or even detest for, the powers-that-be." Issues that Karvonen feels especially aroused voters' ire and turned them toward the Finns Party include resentment of EU bailouts, election financing scandals, and "an extremely unpopular law that forces the Finns to build expensive sewage systems for their beloved summer cottages" (Karvonen).

Official Finnish broadcasting coverage (*YLE News*) amassed by Bob Pitt (see http://www.islamophobiawatch.co.uk/category/finland), shows that while the Finns Party officially denies it holds racist views, certain of its members do. In 2009, Freddy van Wonterghem, the Finns Party councilor in the southeastern city of Kotka, proposed a ban on buildings "harmful to the cultural identity of the city," referring to a Muslim request to build a mosque there. The same year, a Finns Party candidate running in the Kotka municipal election called for Muslims to be "cooked alive." *YLE News* reported on May 10, 2012 that Finns Party member of parliament Olli Immonen announced, "Islamisation is one of the most significant challenges facing western culture." Also in 2012 the Finnish Parliament took formal action against outspoken Finns Party member Jussi Halla-aho, forcing him to resign from an influential parliamentary committee for publicly linking Islam to pedophilia and Somalis with theft. Finns Party MP James Hirvisaari was convicted and fined by both the Kuovala District Court and Finland's Supreme Court for "inciting hatred against an ethnic group," and in October 2013 the Finns Party voted unanimously to expel him after he admitted he photographed a friend posing in a Nazi salute at the Finnish Parliament and posted the photograph online. Hirvisaari's parliamentary assistant Helena Eronen even suggested on the *Uusi Suomi* website that immigrants, homosexuals and Swedish Finns should all wear distinctive armbands to "make policing significantly easier" (Pitt).

The 2011 Finnish parliamentary election marked a significant eurosceptic change in the country's political landscape that reflects right-wing political movements gaining momentum across Europe. In the UK, two anti-immigration politicians previously convicted for inciting ethnic-related tensions were admitted in June 2013 to David Cameron's eurosceptic alliance in the European Parliament, a result of Tory MPs' earlier overwhelming vote to join forces with the

Danish People's Party and the True Finns (Pitt). Professor Jan Sundberg of the University of Helsinki feels that the Finns Party members' resentment of immigrants and EU bailouts for Greece and Portugal is rubbing off on some of Finland's more established political parties ("Euroskeptic Finns Party").

Fred Weir of the *Christian Science Monitor* agrees, calling the Finns Party's election success "a political earthquake" that brought euroscepticism "roaring into the political mainstream" with the potential of shaking Finland out of the European Union. Weir cites the party leaders' statement that belonging to the EU for ten years "has allowed Brussels bureaucrats to usurp Finnish sovereignty." Weir compares the Finns Party's identification with Christianity as a hallmark of Finnishness and its fervent opposition to "free immigration, easy abortion, same-sex marriage, and the 'Islamization' of Europe" to the United States' Tea Party's positions. On the other hand, Weir also observes that U.S. conservatives would "recoil" at the Finns Party's demands for a strong social safety net and government regulations to equalize incomes, differing from rising European eurosceptic parties that generally "combine a xenophobic message with contempt for the welfare state."

In an extensive 2011 analysis, "The Rise of Right-Wing Populism in Finland: The True Finns," Carl Mars sees the 2011 election as indicating that the Finns Party shares views with other rightist populist anti-immigration parties like France's National Front, Austria's Freedom Party, Norway's Progress Party and Denmark's People's Party in combining "rightwing market ideology, political authoritarianism, and anti-foreigner attitudes" (Mars). Mars also believes a new class of the working poor has emerged in Finland since the end of the 1980s, which with the failure of many Finns to achieve financial well being commensurate with the nation's economic growth has caused Finns to be "mobilized by fear—fear of immigrants, criminals, and licentiousness, a public sector that is becoming a burden or an ecological catastrophe." Moreover, in an atmosphere currently fraught with the fear of terrorism, to many Finns the world has become divided into friends and foes, and fear makes a morally righteous "we" a homogenous group that magnifies anti–"Them" views (Mars, citing Mudde 89). In such a fearful atmosphere, a slide toward extreme far-right positions, in Finland as in other European nations, could be envisioned, as Nordic anti-neo–Nazi journalists and crime novelists like Sweden's Stieg Larsson have demonstrated.

Set amid Finland's politically complicated political backdrop, the portraiture of Russians in popular Finnish crime fiction has shifted with the prevailing economic-political winds from the East. Russian villains disappeared from the popular Finnish crime novels of the Cold War period, since Finns and Russians were then official, if uneasy, comrades, bound together by political and economic exigencies. During that period, many Finnish authors censored themselves, refusing to allow negative portrayals of Russians in their fiction and criticizing anything thought negative about the Soviet Union, because many Finns then saw finlandization as necessary to their survival as an independent nation.

When the Cold War ended. Russian characters returned to Finnish crime fiction. Paula Arvas divides them not as pro– or anti–Russian factions, seeing instead three groups: Red Army–trained killers or "agents of death"; "beautiful, powerless, and abused" Russian women, typically exploited prostitutes trafficked to the West; and Russian "middle men" whom Arvas feels exhibit positive Russian cultural elements that tend to humanize Russians in the eyes of Finnish readers (Arvas 116–117). These character types suggest socioeconomic problems in modern Finland that contribute to a uniquely Finnish treatment of the crime novel, where according to author Tapani Bagge, "Good does not always win in the end" (quoted in Cord). Comparing Finnish crime writing to works produced in the other Nordic countries, Bagge believes the Finns' crime novels are "more hard-boiled." James Thompson concurs, as an American author whose wife is Finnish and who lived more than fifteen years in Finland, producing several police procedurals convincingly set in Finland. Thompson calls Finnish thrillers *noir*, not "Crime writing": "Noir [no italics in original] embraces a darker, sometimes even dystopian worldview ... the world may be in balance at the beginning of the story, but the balance is grim. The crime usually gets solved, but the world isn't left a better place ... and the protagonist isn't changed, at least not for the better" (quoted in Cord). Not all Finnish crime fiction adheres strictly to these views, but Finland, supposedly. "the best country in the world," is dealing with serious sociopolitical problems that lend its crime fiction its own deeply chiaroscuro flavor.

Finland may enjoy an enviable international reputation as a model socialist workers paradise, but deficiencies in its welfare state's operation have begun to surface. *The Washington Post's* Robert G. Kaiser noted in 2005 that the Finns' per capita income is around 30 percent lower than Americans' per capita income. Finns pay almost half their national income in taxes compared to the average 30 percent that Americans pay to their federal, state, and local governments. Finland is the only European country that has never had a king or a native aristocracy, and Finns consider their egalitarian free educational system the key to their nation's successes (Kaiser), but in 2010, Kaj Grüssner spoke for many reputable economists in presenting a bleaker analysis of Finland's present and future, focusing on its educational system. He pointed out that Finland's high per capita number of twenty universities and 27 polytechnic institutes is a result of politicians who buy votes by creating institutions that maintain government jobs in depressed areas, bringing the overall level of education down because not enough qualified personnel are available there to staff them. Consequently unemployment among educated Finns who graduate with valueless degrees has become a chronic problem. Grüssner also argues that Finland's much-praised municipal health care system is "bad," even by universal health care standards, because only those patients registered in a given district can be treated there. (See James Thompson's first-person experiences of the Finnish state health system, below.) The individual municipalities also breed bureaucracy, so that while medical personnel are often "made redundant" to meet budgets, no administrator is ever laid off: "Finland has some of the best private hospitals in the world, but ... very few Finnish citizens ever get to benefit from them" (Grüssner).

Grüssner, a tax consultant, also feels the Finnish retirement system is close to collapse, and the high taxes and legal and financial risks of employing workers have made 8 percent unemployment in Finland considered "normal." He claims that Finnish tax authorities, which he compares to the United States' Internal Revenue Service, "don't care about the law," because "The state enacts vague legislation and then makes the taxpayer pay for its interpretation." Grüssner sees the Finnish welfare state facing grim reality today and even more negative future prospects because of increasing deficits and national debts, incurred through government spending that rose from 52.7 billion euros in 1994 to 85 billion euros in 2010 without corresponding rises in tax revenues. He concludes that Finland's welfare state "comes at a price we can't afford" (Grüssner).

In Finland's 2011 general election, tax reform was a major issue. The conservative National Coalition Party's slim victory over the Social Democrats produced a coalition government that slightly reduced the corporate tax rate but raised the capital gains tax and the estate tax and made both progressive for the first time in Finnish history, as well as increasing the VAT rates by one percent. Grüssner commented in a September 2012 blog that with public debt and the deficit "ballooning and the high cost of labor ... penalizing companies, the outlook in rather grim" (see http://www.libera.fi/en/author/kaiGrüssner).

To put cold economic realities into the context of Finland's crime literature, folklorists point out that the "twin plagues of the peasant farmer," hunger and poverty, often figure in the traditional tales of an agrarian people, with characters who are "either good and generous" or "stingy and selfish," the latter usually deserving and receiving punishment. "In these struggles between good and evil, the power of darkness often figures." In traditional Finnish literature, *noir* villains usually battle protagonists who reflect the traditional Finnish values of "individualism, endurance, and love of liberty" (Booss xvii–xiv). In modern Finnish crime fiction, the socio-economic-political problems apparent in today's Finnish welfare state often provide the causes or precipitating events for the crimes that the detectives, often scarred by the same problems, have to solve. Such problems include the rise of far-right political groups; immigration issues and racism, especially involving Muslim incomers; drug and alcohol abuse; gender issues; organized international crime; and Finland's complex relationship with Russia.

With its high standard of living, Finland might seem an attractive destination for immigrants, but "many regard Finland as a remote, cold, taciturn country displaying passive reluctance toward immigrants." Further, "the integration problem is not yet solved. Humanitarian related immigration does not yet convert to a productive labor force, and the majority of the Finnish population does not support further immigration" (Tanner). Against that position, Finland's Non-Discrimination Act "prohibits discrimination based on ethnic or national origin, nationality, language, religion, beliefs, opinion, medical condition, disability, sexual orientation or other reason connected to a person." The Act prohibits "creating a threatening, hostile, disparaging or humiliating atmosphere" and opposes racism as manifested in "violence, defamation, discrimination, threats, harassment or vandalism" (quoted in "Discrimination and Racism"). Both discrimination and racism, however, seem to be increasing in Finland today. In 2007, a "Migrant Tales website" (http://www.migrant tales.net) claimed that "In a country like Finland, racism happens through exclusion," noting that Finland's immigrant unemployment rate at that time was triple the national average, one of the highest in the European Union. Already in 1990, too, a group of "skinheads," popularly considered neo–Nazis, had launched a wave of attacks against Somali refugees, culminating with a firebomb assault (Argon).

At least one political organization farther to the extreme right than the Finns Party exists in Finland. Though small as yet, the militant and increasingly violent Finnish Resistance Movement (Finnish *Suomen vastarintaliike* or SVL) espouses openly neo–Nazi themes of anti–Semitism and white supremacy and opposes multiculturalism, homosexuality, miscegenation, and the European Union. In April 2013, the Finnish Interior Ministry issued its first ever review of extremism and violence in Finland. Mentioning the SVL by name, the report stated that although the Ministry believes that "the risk of extremist broad-based violence in Finland is low and cases of extremist violence are local and isolated," the ministry considers the SVL "potentially dangerous because its members are organised , it is anti-democracy and has a combative spirit" ("Ministry Report"). The Ministry also found that the SVL seeks to establish a more visible presence in Finland through violence directed at targeted individuals and groups. SVL members sell Nazi propaganda online and publish a magazine promoting their neo–Nazi ideology.

In July 2010, several SVL members attacked a Helsinki Gay Pride event with tear gas and pepper spray, resulting in 87 counts of assault; in 2012, a similar SVL assault on gay rights occurred in Oulu; and in January 2013, three SVL members stabbed an organizer of a library discussion event featuring a book claiming that racism was becoming more acceptable in Finland. Two months later, Finnish police discovered a list of 300 Jews in one neo–Nazi's home (see http://yle. fi/uutiset). One recent indication of the Finns' increasing attention to neo–Nazism is *Heart of a Lion*, a "dramedy" shown at the 2013 Toronto Film Festival. Directed by Dome Karukoski, a rising Finnish filmmaker, it has "taken on the country's neo–Nazi issues and brought them very close to home" by portraying a Finnish skinhead who falls in love with a Finnish woman who has a half–Muslim son. The play treats the situation in a provocative mixture of "hatred with humor" (Sharkey).

One of the chief targets of Finnish neo–Nazism is the social tension engendered by the nation's swelling Muslim immigrant population. According to the U.S. State Department, the Muslim population in Finland, around 1,000 in 1990 and 15,000 in 1999, rose to approximately 40,000 by 2009, primarily due to the high birth rate of immigrants. As of 2009, an estimated 20,000 such immigrants were Sunni and around 10,000 were Shiite Muslims, with Somalians as the largest ethnic group. Researcher Tuomas Martikainen estimates that Finland's 2014 Muslim population will reach 60,000 ("CNN: Finland Tops…"). Finland's changing demographics are reflected in the unprecedented exodus of members from the Finnish Evangelical Lutheran Church, attributed to a October 12, 2009 Finnish Broadcasting Company (YLE) televised debate on gay rights and gender-neutral marriage. The same report cited Finland's official defense of religious freedom and its antidiscrimination policy, while noting that Finland's Police Academy reported in 2009 that 8.2 percent of all hate crimes were related to ethnic or foreign national background (referenced in "Finland," U.S. Department of State; see http://www.state.gov/documents/finland).

While considering the terrorist threat from radical Islam "minimal" in Finland, the 2013 Finnish Interior Ministry report also warns that "committed and disciplined" extremists could pose a "significant security risk" both locally and nationally. Finland's immigration policy has been one of the most liberal in Europe. The Finnish government pays immigrants 8 euros per day to attend free Finnish language classes, but Muslim immigrants generally refuse to learn the language and largely fail to integrate into Finland's culture, despite encouragement from Mideast countries promoting emigration to Finland. In 2009, an *Egypt Today* article promoting Muslim immigration stated that the Finnish government was providing immigrants with free homes, health care for the entire family, free education for their children through the university level, and a monthly stipend of 367 euros per adult until they could begin earning their own living. At the time, these benefits were funded by Finland's progressive income tax that could exceed 50 percent of personal income. The Finnish Ministry of Foreign Affairs officially insists that Finland needs immigrants and that "in the long run, they [the immigrants] are not a burden on society."

A substantial number of the Muslim immigrants who have come to Finland are proving to cause problems. By 2010, the number of immigrants from Somalia, most of whom were illiterate, had doubled, according to *Helsingin Sanomat*, Finland's premier newspaper. In the same year, Finnish authorities admitted that many of the Somalis were facilitating human trafficking by abusing the Finnish family unification procedure (Kern). A disturbing 2010 report from the Swedish newspaper *Vasabladet* revealed that Finnish Muslim immigrants were being trained in Pakistan and Somalia as jihadists, and *Helsingin Sanomat* reported that year that al-Shabab, the Somali terrorist group, was recruiting young Somalis living in Finland. In response, Finland's Interior Minister Anne Homland announced in December 2010 that training persons to commit terrorist acts would be considered a criminal offense in Finland. No statistics are available on the results of that announcement.

The Finnish Ministry's 2013 report also reflects concern that second- and third-generation immigrants may become radicalized by being self-marginalized from Finnish society, at the same time losing their identification with their parents' society: "International experience shows that the alienation of immigrants from an Islamic background increases the risk that individuals may subscribe to a violent religious worldview" ("Ministry Report"). The Finnish Broadcasting Company (YLE) and CNN both reported on September 2, 2014, that most of the foreign Muslims fighting in Syria were coming from Finland, a report confirmed by SUPO, the Finnish security police. The Finnish Broadcasting Company journalist Tom Kankkonen, author of *Islam Europassa* (*Islam in Europe*), estimates that as of 2014 several hundred hard line Wahhabi Muslim fundamentalists were living in Finland (Kern).

At least one Muslim cleric and a YLE Muslim freelance journalist have recently attempted to salve tensions between the native Finnish public and radical Muslim immigrants. In his 2014 online article "Islam Question and Answer: Advice to the Moslems in Finland," General Supervisor Shaykh Muhammad Saalih al-Munajjid, who estimates the 2014 Muslim population of Finland at 100,000, advised them to "be aware that you are living in a Christian ... country, whose flag bears the cross!" He warns that Sunni Muslims in Finland in 2009 had formed the Finnish Islamic Party (Finnish: *Suomen Islamilainen Puolue*), which demands strict Islamic measures including the establishment of *sharia* law and a ban on all alcohol sales in Finland [possibly an unworkable proposal; see below] (al-Munajjid). The Finnish Islamic Party's extensive "'green program" also advocates Finland's withdrawal from the European Union and the European Monetary Union. It calls for reinforcement of all Muslim rights, such as male circumcision and ritual slaughter of animals; the total rebuilding of immigrant education, "freeing" Muslim children from music classes in state-supported Finnish schools; and dropping the enforced study of Swedish. The Finnish Islamic Party also demands "a full employment situation"; income support including a free apartment for each family; and interest-free loans for buying houses (see the party's website, http://www.suomenislamilainenpuolueEN.html).

Shaykh al-Munajid states that the Sunni Muslim immigrants also want Finland to allow all Muslim practices, especially the wearing of the *hijab* by Muslim women, practices which are currently against Finnish government policy (al-Munajid). The issue is becoming problematic in Finland. In March 2014 the Helsinki municipal court fined a clothing store manager for discriminating against a veiled Muslim employee. The next month a 38-year-old Muslim woman wanted to join the Helsinki police force where Finnish hijab regulations would have banned her from wearing a head scarf on duty. She said she spoke for Muslim women who wanted "police to be more diverse," urging the Finnish government to allow the hijab "to encourage integration of the minority in society" (France in 2004 banned the wearing of the hijab, but Sweden does allow veiled Muslim women to join their police force.) ("Finnish Muslims Want Police Hijab").

Al-Munaijid also urges that "every Muslim should try to return to his homeland." If that is impossible, he declares that the Finnish Islamic Party, which he does not mention by name, should "invest their efforts in establishing Islamic institutions, schools, Muslim graveyards" in those non–Muslim countries where Muslims reside and "stop thinking about establishing an Islamic state ... a farfetched idea, the consequences of which will be bad for you" (Al-Munajjid). This apparently moderate statement, however, is being publicly defied by other Muslim leaders in Finland. They arouse the ire of Finnish non–Muslims with such demands as Imam Anas Hajjar's insistence that non–Muslims cannot teach Muslims about religious issues in Finnish schools, where religion is taught. Imam Anas Hajjar also demands that four paid public holidays be mandated for Muslims only ("Muslims in Finland..."). The controversial Muslim cleric Bilal Philips in a 2014 two-day visit to Finland denied that he has extremist ties or promotes radical views, rather insisting that "these [Muslim] true teachings do not allow terrorism." He attributed Muslim terrorist activity to the refusal of certain other countries to allow him entry because of his alleged call for the death penalty for homosexuals ("Controversial Cleric").

In an attempt at moderation, journalist Wali Hashi has recently requested the Finnish Muslim community to examine itself regarding the issue of young Muslim immigrants who answer the call of radical Islam to fight as jihadists with ISIS in Syria. Hashi, who produced a television program examining recruitment practices by extremist organizations in Finland, Sweden, and Denmark, believes "It's precisely the Muslim community that should be looking to find out how our young people are being radicalized.... Our religious leaders in particular, our imams, should take better care of our youth" (Hashi).

The native Finnish response to escalating Muslim demands varies from mild to outraged. A few pushbacks like the City of Helsinki's 2011 opening of swimming facilities time slots to all women, not only to Muslim women as earlier had been done, has been relatively minor (Kern), but some Finns Party members are voicing more vociferous anti–Muslim opinions and even carrying them out in action. Charges were brought in March 2009 against Finns Party politician and rightwing commentator Jussi Halla-aho, and he was fined for "disturbing public [Muslim] worship." Halla-aho, who was amply quoted in the manifesto published by Norwegian Anders Breivik who massacred over 70 persons in Oslo in 2011, has received death threats for his popular blog *Scripta* criticizing the number of immigrants entering Finland. He contends that Muslims cannot be integrated into Finnish society, and in 2014 he demanded that the costs of immigration to Finnish taxpayers be made public, which set off an uproar among Somalis at a town hall meeting in Lieksa. To counter Halla-aho's popularity, the Finnish Ministry of the Interior has initiated a politically correct Internet site on immigration, intended, it says, "to get away from an 'us and them' position as well as from preaching and guilt attitudes," but the site does not have a discussion forum. Polling data from a *Suomen* [Finnish] Gallup poll commissioned in 2011 by the *Helsingen Sanomat* newspaper, however, shows that almost 60 percent of Finns then opposed integration, up considerably from 36 percent in 2007 and 44 percent in 2009 (Kern). Since 2009, Finland has had the Assisted Voluntary Return program (AVR) of the International Organisation for Migration, which pays immigrants to return to their native countries, but by 2011, according to YLE, only about 45 immigrants had returned voluntarily to countries outside the European Union ("One Way"). Such factors as the Finnish government's proposals to provide public health services for illegal aliens; the fact that Swedish has been overtaken by immigrant languages; and the dramatic statistic that 70 percent of Finland's population growth is due to immigration make for an increasingly tense atmosphere regarding immigration issues in Finland which are increasingly reflected in the country's contemporary crime literature (Kern).

The problems of Muslim immigrants in Finland seem especially taxing to Somali Muslim women. Activist Maryan Abdulkarim, who has lived in Finland for over twenty years, observed in a 2013 interview with *Helsingen Sanomat* that "Finland is a very racist country, has always been." Inspired by news of U.S. anti-discrimination activists like Malcolm X, Abdulkarim insists that "People from immigrant backgrounds are targeted in violent attacks" in Finland that she says are reported as mental health or substance abuse problems, not hate crimes. She also believes that immigrant women "are presently deemed suitable for manual work. Foreign qualifications are not recognised and even highly educated people are retrained for the service and care sectors." She believes that activism is necessary for "a genuinely equal society" (quoted in Huhtainen and Teivainen).

Aside from the difficulties immigrant women may face, on the surface, the situation of women in Finland in general appears progressive. Since 1906, Finland has guaranteed women the right to vote, the first country in the world to do so, but reliable internal and external sources indicate that Finnish women still face serious problems in contemporary Finnish society, as often demonstrated in Finnish crime fiction. The 2004 "Overview of Gender Equality Issues in Finland" prepared by the Finnish Institute of Occupational Health showed that Finland's 1987 Act on Equality between Women and Men had three major goals: the prevention of sex discrimination; the promotion of equality between women and men; and the improvement of women's status, especially in working life. In 1992, discrimination on grounds of pregnancy and family responsibilities was prohibited in Finland, and since 1995, employers must provide equality in staff, training, and labor protection programs.

For years, however, domestic violence has plagued Finland (Huuhtanen). The 1987 Equality

Act did not apply to activities involved with religious observances and practices or to private family or individual affairs, so a new Equality Act was developed beginning in 2004, supplanting its predecessor with European Union legislation and directives and providing an Ombudsman for Equality to supervise compliance with the Act and to monitor its implementation. This officer currently handles about 200 discrimination cases annually. The new Equality Act also requires a five-person Equality Board to receive cases of noncompliance with the Act submitted by the Equality Ombudsman, and it can use administrative coercive means in settling such issues. The Council on Equality, a subordinate unit of the Ministry of Social Affairs and Health, includes a Subcommittee on Men's Issues, calling for men's participation in child care and other gender-related issues. Earlier the Council had had a Subcommittee against Violence that attempted to deal with removing and preventing violence ("Overview"). In the light of Finland's prevailing problem of violence against women (see below), it is not clear why this Subcommittee was discontinued.

According to the 2004 Overview, progress in women's issues in Finland has been made in several areas since the 1980s. Women's studies were established in Finnish universities and research institutes, and organizations for minority and disabled women were formed, as well as men's anti-violence groups. Challenges still remain, however, including overcoming obstacles to women's entrepreneurship; establishing more flexible family leave policies; improving women's employment; and reducing the wage differential between women and men. Some progress has been made in these areas; notably four years after the 2004 Overview, Finland had both its first female President and its first female Prime Minister. The report submitted to the United Nations' Women's Anti-Discrimination Committee by Arto Kosonen, Director of Finland's Foreign Affairs Ministry revealed that his government had also made progress in promoting women's issues by establishing a National Plan of Action against Human Trafficking and improving facilities and benefits for asylum seekers. By 2008 women held 43 seats in the Finnish Parliament and 60 percent of the ministerial posts, and the government had reached its goal of filling 40 percent of all seats of administrative boards of fully and partially state-owned businesses with women. Kosonen admitted, however, that Finnish women were still earning 20 percent less than their male counterparts and "carried less weight in the political arena and corporate boardrooms than men," though he cited a 2007 study by the Finnish Business and Policy Forum which indicated that businesses run by Finnish women were financially more successful than those run by men, and that those businesses preserved women's self-esteem ("Finland's New Gender Equality Plan").

Despite those advances, the U.N. Committee on Elimination of Discrimination against Women found several major areas of concern in Kosonen's report: Finland still was exhibiting significant instances of offenses against women, especially domestic violence; discrimination against immigrant women; marginalization of Roma (Gypsy) and Sami women; and female genital mutilation. The Finnish government had cut the national budget for gender equality over the previous three years by one-third, and the 20 percent pay gap between men's and women's earnings remained; perpetrators of sexual harassment in the workplace received only weak penalties; and the Finnish rate of suicide among young girls was the second highest in the world ("Finland's New Gender Equality Plan"). Reporting in 2014 on suicide as a "big problem" for Finland, which also has the sixth highest overall suicide rate in the world, *Helsingen Sanomat* did report a sharp decline in the suicide rate of Finnish men aged 25 to 44 who are apparently now more willing than earlier to seek help ("Sharp Decline"). On the other hand, the high rate of suicide among young Finnish girls may be a paradoxical result of Finland's increasing perceived happiness, because of its welfare state policies of "reducing economic inequality" so that "comparisons with others of relative happiness … rather than status may play a role…. Both happiness and crime rates tend to be tied to rankings of economic inequality" (Szalavitz).

Cases of domestic violence that appear frequently in Finnish crime fiction reflect real-life infringements of gender equality and abuse of women and children which persist in Finland. Disturbing discrepancies exist between Finland's official policies on gender equality and the actual evidence of violent abuse there. Finnish Minister for International Development Pekka Haavisto voiced his government's position on women's issues in a December 2013 interview with the UN Entity for Gender Equality and the Empowerment of Women: "In all countries, including my own, there is room for improvement in the area of gender equality ... [which is a] cornerstone of Finland's development policy" ("Interview with Finnish Minister"). Despite such statements, for deep-seated cultural reasons the prevention of violence toward women, often linked with heavy alcohol consumption by men (Bell), has been and possibly will be a long time coming in Finland ("Interview with Finnish Minister"), where today nearly one-quarter of police house calls deal with domestic violence (Bruno).

In 1998, Matti Huuhtanen reported from Helsinki to the *Los Angeles Times* that Finland's "vision of beauty and calm hides a grim fact ... the highest rate of deaths from violent crimes in Western Europe.... Finnish newspapers are a chronicle of domestic bloodshed: a 39-year-old man repeatedly stabs his wife and three children to death; a 22-year-old drunken woman hacks her lover to death with an ax" (Huuhtanen). Markku Heiskanen of the Finnish statistics agency estimates 200,000 unreported cases of violence occur per year in Finland, 90 percent being domestic violence (cited in Huuhtanen). Huuhtanen also cites the opinion of Finnish crisis center worker Petteri Sveins that "Finnish men resort to violence because they cannot talk about their problems." Huuhtanen claims that neither can the Finnish government, because the prevailing general attitude remains that what happens in a Finnish person's home is no one else's affair: "You wash your own dirty linen." Sveins insisted, too, that alcohol is the catalyst for violence, not the cause. He feels that men drink because they are depressed, and violence then results (quoted in Huuhtanen). In addition, social isolation contributes to the problem, creating violent loners, generally male, often portrayed in Finnish literature starting with *The Kalevala*, which is full of knife-wielding men bent on revenge. Huuhtanen also indicated that in 1995, 20 percent of Finland's homicide victims were women, a trend on the increase. He cites the opinion of sociologist Elina Haavio-Mannila, who theorizes that violence so often occurs today because women are having more affairs than heretofore, so "The men become jealous." Finnish women, too, are becoming more violent, beginning at school, where bullying is becoming increasingly common among girls (Huuhtanen).

Finland's "paradox of equality: professional excellence, domestic abuse" (Hopkins), often the tragic staple of Finnish fiction, shows no signs of abating, though many theories about its causes exist. With economic austerity currently in place, the Finnish government does not seem to provide adequate funds to address the domestic violence situation (Bruno). Finnish sociologists observed in 2005 that 43.5 percent of Finnish women had been subjected to physical or sexual violence or threat of violence at least once after age fifteen in intimate relationships at home and in their workplaces. Such violence has had a long history in Finland. Until 1994, being raped by one's husband had not been considered a crime in Finland (Bruno). In 2008 *Guardian* journalist Edward Dutton, who has lived in Finland for several years, commented that "Stereotypically, Finland is either portrayed as a forest paradise or a dark wilderness teeming with alcoholic suicides. Both portrayals are absurd. But what is statistically true is that Finnish men are relatively violent." Dutton cites Anthony Upton, a specialist in Finnish cultural history, who believes that even in the 19th century Finland was considered "two to three times more violent than Western countries."

Causes of Finnish male violence are complicated. Both Finland's high male suicide rate and the equally high rate of men's violence toward women have been attributed to the inability of

Finnish men to express their emotions. A male teacher from Helsinki claims, "If a man talks a lot he is considered effeminate," and a northern security guard points to "the violent, passionate side that they [Finnish men] are keeping down all the time" (both quoted in Dutton). Lack of self-esteem may also drive some men to "being unemotional and tough," just as low national self-esteem due to Finland's long periods of domination by Sweden and Russia and Finland's 20th century wars may also contribute to the problem (Dutton). Finland's geography and its forbidding winters that necessitate close contact in restricted interiors for extended periods of time probably also incubate domestic violence.

With a rate of domestic violence nearly twice the European average in 2013, Finland is "not an appealing place to be in a committed relationship" (Hopkins). Valerie Hopkins pointed out in 2013 that the notoriously difficult Finnish language has gender-neutral pronouns that everyone uses, but that linguistic indication of gender equality does not seem to carry over into human activity. Hopkins notes that in 2013 domestic violence cases were responsible for 43.55 percent of all reported crimes in Finland, according to *Naisten Linja*, a Finnish hotline for victims of family violence, while the entire country has only 21 shelters for battered women. Finnish sociologists substantiate Hopkins' findings. Professor Suvi Ronkainen of the University of Lapland attributes Finnish domestic violence to "the paradox of gender equality…. Our welfare state wasn't an open feminist project … it was part of national building." The Finnish welfare state gives labor market rights to women, "not equality in private life," according to Päivi Naskali, professor of gender studies also at the University of Lapland. In Finland, mediation, not the judicial system, is considered "the best means of coping with domestic violence." This approach is sharply criticized by Amnesty International, not least because mediation usually leads to re-victimization of women. Amnesty lawyer Kevät Nousiainen feels the reliance on mediation may be the reason so few Finnish rapes—2 percent to 10 percent, compared to Denmark's 25 percent of reported crimes—are reported. One of the biggest strengths of the Finnish personality, respect for women, may paradoxically harm more than help the domestic violence situation, Hopkins also maintains, "because women are so respected in Finnish culture … violence toward them almost seems unthinkable" and thus should not be reported, so that while 43 percent of Finns deplore domestic violence, they tend to think it does not require punishment or even revelation (Hopkins).

The alcoholism of so many Finnish men seems to be integral to Finnish history and culture. Each Finn drinks 10.4 liters (approximately 2.74 gallons) of alcohol per year, the highest rate in the Nordic countries ("Nordic Alcohol"). In *Desire and Craving: A Cultural Theory of Alcoholism*, Finnish sociologist Pertti Alasuutari of the University of Tampere concludes that the "logic of freedom" governs the drinking behavior of many Finnish blue collar workers, wherein only men enslaved by alcohol can achieve complete freedom from the world (Bryan M. Johnstone, quoted on the back cover of *Desire and Craving*). Alasuutari sees the rejection of Finland's 19th century temperance movement as a component of the nation's cultural slide from asceticism to hedonism (Alasuutari 20). By studying the case histories and taciturn behavior of Finnish working class men, he observed that their drinking habits were "a symbolic way of dealing with the tensions and contradictions between work, family life, and their own preferences," to maintain "control over their life and preserve their self-esteem" (Alasuutari 160). Heavy drinking thus expresses the man's dissatisfaction with his life, his perceived lack of freedom, and his pursuit of personal freedom, away from the wife whom he must respect as caregiver but whom he resents as the enforcer of sobriety. This pattern is repeated continuously in Finnish crime fiction: "He wants to relax … [so] he violates the rules of a decent life … and insults the wife." When she tries to limit his drinking, "the spouses battle over power and the man's independence. The vicious circle is completed" (Alasuutari 79–80), and domestic violence too often ensues.

One consequence of the worldwide popularity of Nordic crime fiction today is that international attention is being paid to the Nordic countries' reputation for violence. BBC journalist Bethany Bell reported in March 2014 that "the highest number of incidences of physical and sexual violence were seen in Denmark (52 percent), Finland (47 percent), and Sweden (40 percent), states that are often commended for gender equality" (Bell), paralleling a major study of 42,000 European Union women by the European Union's Fundamental Rights Agency that showed levels of such abuse in Finland approximately 50 percent higher than the European average of 20 percent, confirming that "Finland is one of Europe's most violent places for women" (Milla Aaltonen, from the Finnish League for Human Rights, quoted in "Finland Is EU's Secondmost Violent Country for Women" [after Denmark]), a statistic that substantiates the appearance of so many abused and murdered women as victims in Finnish crime literature.

Whether the abuse of alcohol and drugs is a cause or a catalyst for violence in Finnish society, alcohol and drugs play a major role in Finland's overall crime rate, the backdrop for Finnish police procedural fiction. Alcoholic perpetrators are responsible for most crimes in Finland: 61 to 75 percent of homicides, 71 to 78 percent of attempted homicides, 71 to 73 percent of assaults, and about 50 percent of thefts. Criminal offenses in Finland have risen from 480,000 in 1980 to 787,964 in 2004 (see http://www.stat.fi). Although Finns have the fourth highest per capita number of firearms in the world, homicides by gun comprise only 14 percent of the total homicides in Finland ("Finland Moves"). As for perpetrators, Finnish sources classify Finnish homicides into four groups: 50 percent are committed by unemployed, undereducated, or drug-or alcohol-addicted men; 35 percent are committed by family members; and 10 percent are committed by youths. These groups seem to inspire the creation of many of the perpetrators in Finnish crime fiction. To deal with such real-life criminals, Finland in 2009 had about 150 police officers per 100,000 people, compared to the United States' 240-plus (Smolej and Kivivuori).

The 2012 report of the U.S. Overseas Security Authority (OSAC) of the Department of State warns that "Alcohol is the major social ill that contributes to criminal activity in Finland," and since intoxicated individuals are often found on public transportation and in tourist venues, especially after dark, visitors should avoid direct contact "so as to minimize the possibility of becoming victimized." Currently the incidence of alcohol-related crime in Finland remains a larger challenge for local law enforcement than hard drug use does, since Finland seems to be a transit point rather than an end-use destination for drug dealers, although drug use and trafficking in Finland itself are rising and will be substantial by 2020, according to Finland's National Police College. In 2012 drug use by young Finnish women increased from 25 percent to 40 percent (Thomas).

The incidence of nonviolent crimes committed by Finns, especially the so-called "white-collar crimes" seems to be low both in real life and in Finnish crime fiction. Sentences for insider trading and tax evasion in particular are much lower than international averages, considering the high potential returns from those criminal activities. Political corruption in Finland is also lower than the murder rate; between 2002 and 2007, no corporations were fined and no businesses received prohibitions for bribery (Smolej and Kivivuori).

Crime engineered by outsiders, however, seems to be rising in Finland and is accordingly reflected in current Finnish crime novels and thrillers. Even though the threat of terrorism in Finland appears low, "since 2001 Arabs and terrorism have entered Finnish crime fiction" (Arvas, "Contemporary Finnish Crime Fiction" 8). Organized crime involving drugs, smuggling, human trafficking, and prostitution caused Finland to tighten its borders in 2012, especially with respect to human trafficking (OSAC 2012). Several motorcycle gangs operate in Finland, supporting themselves through the drug trade, including the international Bandidos and Hell's Angels as well as the Finnish Rogues Gallery. Most gang members are recruited in prison, often through contact with Estonian prisoners. The *Obtshak*, a consortium of the Estonian mafia, operates in Finland, as does the Russian mafia, traditionally deeply involved in prostitution. Both of these groups employ Finnish gangsters as enforcers.

Finland's National Bureau of Investigation indicates that the number of organized crime groups operating in Finland has decreased from 78 groups in 2008 to 66 in 2009 with 948 members, but the reason for the decrease is not known. The members of these groups are mostly Finns, but non–Finns supply them with illegal goods and services, especially with respect to drug crimes. Property crimes like robberies often are committed in Finland by organized crime figures who flee to their own countries to escape capture, and credit card fraud, currently increasing, is being operated by Bulgarian and Romanian groups. Cyber crime in Finland, directed by non–Finnish criminals, is also growing (Elonheimo et al. 913).

The involvement of Russian organized crime in Finland has a complicated history, because "unlike the normal situation in civilized societies, there is no clear distinction in Russia between criminal enterprises and the government" (Burton and Burges). Shifts in Finnish government policies have influenced Finnish attitudes and affected reportage about Russian criminal involvement in Finland to a considerable extent over the years. Finnish newspapers began to take note of Russian organized crime shortly after the breakup of the Soviet Union in the early 1990s, when Russian prostitutes began appearing in Finnish cities. In 2007, Stratfor Global Intelligence reports that Russian organized crime (the "Russian Mafia") has been "an intricate network throughout Russian society" running "extortion, fraud, cargo theft, prostitution, drug- and arms-trafficking and more." It "has penetrated business and state-run enterprises to a degree unheard of anywhere in the Western world" (Burton and Burges). In the 1990s. the UK Conflict Studies Research Center blamed the 50,000 Russians living permanently in Finland for crimes including car theft and smuggling of controlled substances, weaponry, and precious metals, as well as human trafficking, prostitution, and the entire hashish and marijuana trade. A conflicting report from Britain's Exeter University, however, found "little evidence" for that opinion, claiming that homegrown Finnish criminals dominated their country's drug and prostitution rings ("Organised Crime in Finland"). Often the bosses of those crimes prove difficult to pin down. Such crimes reflect economic downturns; people suffering financial hardship and trying to improve their circumstances are easy prey for traffickers, as in prostitution enterprises, where operators control women with fines, debt bondage, threats of physical violence and psychological pressure (Viuhko and Jokanen 129–130, 133).

The Exeter report indicates that the major threat Russian organized crime posed to Finland in the 1990s was the distortion of the Finnish market economy through money laundering and the attempted corruption of government officials ("Organised Crime in Finland"). A decade later, when Finland's National Criminal Justice Reference Service attempted in 2000 to identify pressures on Finland from organized crime in northwestern Russia and to determine Finland's potential for becoming victimized by Russian organized crime, the Service found that contract cheating between businesses, a new form of organized crime, emerged at the same time the Finnish government was exerting stricter controls on other forms of crime. The Service also stated that illegal traffic in drugs and arms had become the "most important form of organized crime in northwestern Russia, especially in St. Petersburg. The article concludes that effective Russian and Finnish crime prevention had "hindered the activity of Russian crime in Finland" (Backman).

Even if Russian organized crime activity in Finland may have diminished, for a long time Finnish crime fiction has often taken advantage of the special connections between Russian and Finnish crime operations. "At the moment [2007] many crime writers comment on the real life operations of Russian criminals in Finland" (Arvas, "Contemporary Finnish Crime Fiction"). According to Paula Arvas' classification of Russian figures appearing in contemporary Finnish crime fiction, Finnish crime novelists typically portray former Red Army professional killers ("agents of death") as mercenaries selling their services on the black market, "usually linked to the historical relationship between Finland and Russia, often embodying "an incomprehensible, existential threat…. An allegory for the relationship between Russia and Finland." Arvas describes "beautiful, powerless, and abused Russian women" who appear typically as the helpless trafficked prostitutes working the Finnish streets, "abject figures" not only representing "the legal failings of the post–Soviet states, but also the failures of the Scandinavian welfare states to enforce the rule of law " and fulfill "their commitments to gender equality." Arvas' third category, the Russian "middle men" fictional characters underscore "the positive elements of Russian culture and its complicated relationship to Finland and the Scandinavian world [and] … which work[s] to humanize Russians" (Arvas 117).

In the face of such problems as societal violence, alcohol abuse, and organized crime, international research indicated in 2008 that Finns have a very high level of public trust in their police, more than do other Europeans. Juha Kääriäinen of the Police College of Finland at Tampere has determined that " broader social factors than the effectiveness of police work, the proximity of the police, or the quality of police work" are responsible for the Finns' trust in their police. Finland has the lowest number of police officers per capita of all the Nordic countries, all of which enjoy a strong reputation for safety. Kääriäinen concludes that public trust in their police relates to the Nordic governments' welfare state policies and the lack of corruption in the respective governments: "citizens trust public services most of all in countries that had invested the most in public social welfare and health services as well as in income transfer," but as many Finnish crime authors implicitly do in their fictional portrayals of the relationship between the police and the public they serve, Kääriäinen calls for more research on his final rhetorical question, "Could it be so, that people trust in the police in countries like Finland as a consequence of well functioning public social, health, and school services?" (Kääriäinen 157). In Finnish crime fiction, at least, some doubt exists about that.

Despite the long, complex, and intriguingly individual development of crime fiction in Finland, Finnish detective novels and thrillers are probably the least well known of the crime fiction output of the five Nordic nations because relatively few Finnish novels have been translated into English, though at home they enjoy a rich history and long-lasting popularity. Besides their extensive crime fiction readership, Finland's Whodunnit Society (*Suomen Dekkariseura*), founded in 1984, displays what Barry Forshaw calls "a playful relationship" (148) with the conventions of crime fiction, a distinguishing characteristic of Finnish crime writing. The Society relishes its status as what it calls a "cover organization" for all friends of detective stories and crime fiction, promotes the genre, and frequently arranges events concentrating on fictional murder and mayhem. Their organizational emblem celebrates Mika Waltari's famous Inspector Palmu, today known better through the highly popular 1960s film versions than through Waltari's novels.

In 1985, the Whodunnit Society inaugurated their Clew (also "Clue") of the Year Award, its annual prize for the best crime production in any medium. The Society's traveling trophy is a foot-high wooden relief carving of Inspector Palmu. The winner also receives an engraved ceramic plate and a diploma thumbprinted in the presence of a police officer. The Whodunnit Society also makes special awards to foreign authors for outstanding works in the genre. It publishes a quarterly journal, *Ruumiin kulttuuri* ("Body Culture"), with a review column titled "*Kirjakarajay*" ("Capital Sentences"), as well as a series of centenary celebrations of "cornerstone: figures" of the genre like Agatha Christie. The Society's other publications include collections of essays, a study of American pulp fiction published in Finnish between 1939 and 1989, and its first serial thriller, *Kultainen peura* ("The Golden Reindeer"), about a heist-gone-wrong and a chase from Lapland to Helsinki (see the Society's website, http://www.dekkariseura.fi/en_aula.html).

Even though to American readers much Finnish crime fiction may seem bleak and pessimistic, American interest in Finnish crime fiction seems to be awakening. Ice Cold Crime, LLC, was founded in 2009 in Minneapolis–St. Paul, Minnesota, "to originate, translate, publish, and promote Finnish fiction in the United States and other English-speaking countries" (see http://icecoldcrime.com). Ice Cold Crime currently publishes four of Jarkko Sipilä's Helsinki Homicide novels; two installments of Harri Nykänen's *Raid* series starring "a hard-nosed but compassionate hit man"; and novels by Seppo Jokinen and Anja Snellman. In 2013, the firm also published Jari Tervo's novel *Among the Saints*, a story of a murder told from 35 different perspectives. In another manifestation of upper Midwest America's interest in Finnish crime writing, FinnFest USA, August 7–10, 2014, commemorated St. Urho's Day (celebrating a fictional Finnish saint), with an appearance by Finnish authors Antti Tuomainen, Jarkkio Sipilä, and Jari Tervo at the Minneapolis Once Upon a Crime bookstore in connection with a conference on "Finland and Public Education in the 21st century: A Dialogue with Minnesota" (see http://wwww.finnfestusa2014.org/finnfest-2014).

Crime fiction historian G.J. Demko calls contemporary Finland "a hotbed of mystery fans and writers" of a genre that was initially strongly influenced by American and British writers, but which has since achieved a genuinely Finnish spirit running to police procedurals and thematic mysteries that reflect social and economic issues (Demko). Several Finnish crime authors are now challenging the conventional tradition with increasingly popular psychological thrillers, some incorporating experimental literary techniques. Like Finland's mainstream fiction, Finnish crime fiction still today exhibits trademark paradoxes shaped by the nation's geography, history, culture, and especially its climate. Exemplifying the individual character of Finnish crime fiction along with its satiric and humorous undercurrents, the forty to fifty Finnish *noir* crime novels being published annually "routinely suggest that a real engagement with the reader is *de rigueur.*" Barry Forshaw believes that Finnish crime novels, "often written in a taciturn style typical of this independent and laconic people," are "notably more personal" than the work of other nationalities, demanding that their readers commit to them with "finely tuned intelligence" open to "allusions and subtleties" (Forshaw 147). Like Finnish mainstream novelists, the crime authors of Finland also often poignantly counterpoint their crimes stories with lament for a lost less consumption-driven culture, as voiced in this analysis of the central paradox of Finnish life and fiction by contemporary Finnish novelist Petter Sairanen:

> For thousands of years, the Finns have struggled against the cold. The enemy was huge and perpetual, but we grew fond of it…. But the modern world has conquered the weather … and Finns do not know how to live because they are not allowed to wrestle with their darling enemy, the cold. We live in rooms where the temperature is always the same, wondering what has gone wrong. We feel empty. This predicament also manifests itself in our fiction. The characters in our novels … are often hollow, unable to fathom the cause of their emptiness [Sairanen].

Finnish Crime Fiction Awards

The Clew of the Year Award (Vuoden Johtolanka)

This is awarded by the Finnish Whodunnit Society.

1985: *Harjunpää ja heimolaiset* ("Harjunpää and the Tribesmen"), by Matti Yrjänä Joensuu

1986: *Sulevi Manner* ("Sulevi Manner"), by Juha Numminen and Eero J. Tikka

1987: *Sinivalkoiset jäähyväiset* ("Blue and White Farewell"), by Pentti Kirstilä

1988: *Häkkilinnut* ("Cage Birds"), by Paul-Erik Haataja

1989: Radio theater production: *Karkeatasoisesta dekkarikuunnelmatuotannosta*

1990: *Takapiru* ("Blue Devil") by Harri Nykänen

1991: *Suomenkielisen rikoskirjallisuuden ja sen reuna-alueiden bibliografia 1857–1989* ("A Bibliography of Finnish Crime Literature, 1857–1989"), by Simo Sjöblom

1992: *Kuolemanuni*, by Markku Ropponen

1993: *Imelda*, by Pentti Kirstilä

1994: *Harjunpää ja rakkauden nälkä* (*To Steal Her Love*, tr. David Hackson, 2008), by Matti Yrjänä Joensuu

1995: Award to Best Finnish Publisher, Book Studio, Ltd., for promotion of crime fiction

1996: *Nyman*, by Hannu Vuorio

1997: *Lumminainen* ("Snow Woman"), by Leena Laitolainen

1998: *Murha pukee naista Artikkelikokoelma* ("Murder Places a Woman: Female Detective Novels and Detective Stories about Women"), ed. Ritva Hapuli and Johanna Matero

1999: *Karjalan lunnaat* ("Ransom of Karelia"), by Ilkka Remes

2000: *Minun sukuno tarina* ("My Family Chronicle"), by Jari Tervo

2001: *Raid-sarjan* (Television series *Raid*), by Harri Nykänen

2002: *Hukan enkelit* (*Wolves and Angels*, tr. Owen Witesman, 2012), by Seppo Jokinen

2003: *Koston Komissio* ("Revenge: The Commission"), by Taavi Soininvaara

2004: *Harjunpää ja pahan pappi* (*The Priest of Evil*, tr. David Hackston, 2006), by Matti Yrjänä Joensuu

2005: *Vaimoni* ("My Wife"), by Tuula-Liina Varis

2006: *Ystävät kaukana* ("Faraway Friends") by Matti Rönkä

2007: *Musta taivas* ("Black Sky"), by Tapani Bagge

2008: *Jäätyneitä ruusuja* ("Frozen Roses"), by Marko Kilpi

2009: *Seinää vasten* (*Against the Wall*, tr. Peter Ylitalo Leppa, 2010), by Jarkko Sipilä

2010: *Ansa* ("Home Peace"), by Marko Leino

2011: *Parantaja* ("Healer"), by Antti Tuomainen

2012: *Vilpittömästii sinun* ("Sincerely Yours"), by Pekka Hiltunen

2013: *Sheriffi* ("The Sheriff"), by Reijo Mäki

2014: *Mustamäki* ("Black Hill"), by Timo Sandberg

The Glass Key Award

The Glass Key Award, given yearly to a crime author from the Nordic countries by the crime writers of Scandinavia, has been awarded only once to a Finnish author, Matti Rönkä, for *Ystävät kaukana* ("Far Away Friends"), in 2007. Several Finnish crime authors (see below) have been nominated for both the Glass Key Award and for the Finlandia Prize, the most prestigious literary award in Finland, awarded by the Finnish Book Foundation. This award as of 2010 carried a prize of 30,000 euros.

A Parallel Chronology of Finnish Literary and World Events

Finnish events and literature are listed in Roman type with world literature and events interspersed in italics.

c. 8500 BC: Stone Age hunters in Finland

c. AD 300: Agricultural development; Finnish spoken in southern Finland; Sami tribes driven to far north

1100–1249: the Northern Crusade: Swedish kings establish Christianity and rule Finland; Swedish becomes dominant language in Finland

11th–14th Centuries: Crusades against Muslims by Christians

1517–c. 1600: Finland gradually converts to Lutheranism

1517: Luther posts 95 Theses, initiating Lutheranism

1581: Finland becomes a Swedish grand duchy

1733: earliest knowledge of *Kalevala* by scholars

1803–1815: Napoleonic Wars; Russia invades Finland

1809: Sweden cedes Finland to Russia; Russia makes Finland a grand duchy; Finnish begins to be re-established

1828–1829: Vidocq's Memoirs

1835: Publication of the *Kalevala*

1841: Poe's "Murders in the Rue Morgue"

1843: First use of the word detective" in English

1860s: Growth of Fennoman nationalistic movement

1853–1856: Crimean War

1866–1868: Famine kills 15 percent of Finnish population; Russia eases financial regulation and Finnish economy and politics develop rapidly

1866: Dostoevsky's Crime and Punishment

1869: First police procedural, Emile Gaboriau's Monsieur Lecoq

1870: Aleksis Kivi's *Seven Brothers*, first novel to appear in Finnish

1889: First Sherlock Holmes story, "A Study in Scarlet"

1890–c. 1914: approx. 1 million Finns emigrate, about half to North America

1892: Finnish achieves equal legal status with Swedish in Finland

1899: Social Democrat Party founded

c. 1900: Baltic Tatars arrive in Finland

1906: Elected Finnish parliament established; universal suffrage established in Finland

1910: Rudolf Richard Ruth publishes first Finnish mystery novel

1914–1918: World War I

1917: Finnish rightist government proclaims Finnish independence; 90 percent of Finnish farmers become independent

1917: Russian revolutions in February and October

1917–1918: Finnish Civil War between Reds and Whites; Whites win with German help; take severe measures against Reds

1917–1920: Russian Civil War

1918: National Coalition Party founded

1919: Finnish republic established

1920: First Agatha Christie novel, The Mysterious Affair at Styles

1920s–1930s: Golden Age of British detective fiction

1920s–1951 U.S. Black Mask *magazine popularizes hard-boiled PI fiction*

1921: USSR established

1925: Finnish Islamic Association founded

1929: Dashiell Hammett's The Maltese Falcon

1930s: Vilho Helanen writes popular mysteries

1930: First three Nancy Drew detective novels

1930–c. 1938: The Great Depression

1930s: Stalinist purges within USSR

1931: Georges Simenon's first Inspector Maigret novel

1934: First Perry Mason novel; first Nero Wolfe novel

1939: USSR demands demilitarization of Mannerheim Line; Finland refuses and USSR invades Finland in November 1939

1939–1945: World War II

1939: First international spy thriller. Eric Ambler's A Coffin for Demetrius; *Raymond Chandler's* The Big Sleep

1939–1940: The Winter War; USSR defeats Finland; Finland loses border territories

1939: Mika Waltari's "Who Killed Mrs. Skrof?" initiating Inspector Palmu novels; Finnish vogue for police procedurals begins

1941–1948: "Outsider" publishes Klaus Karma detective series

1941–1944: The Continuation War: Finland joins Nazi Germany's attack on USSR to obtain lost territories

1941: Japan attacks Pearl Harbor, USA enters World War II

June–July 1944: Finland fights USSR offensive to a standstill; armistice with USSR

1944–1945: The Lapland War; Finns force Germans out of northern Lapland

1945: USA drops atomic bombs on Japan, ending World War II

1945: Mika Waltari's *The Egyptian*

1947–1947: Peace treaties Finland signs with Allies give 10 percent of Finnish territory to USSR and 40,000 Finns flee that area; Finns lost 93,000 casualties in war, 3rd highest rate of World War II

1947: *Mickey Spillane's* I, the Jury

1948–1950s: Finnish Social Democrats dominate government; economy shifts from agriculture to industrialization

c. 1946–c. 1980s: *Cold War period*

c. 1946–c. 1990s: Russian villains largely vanish from Finnish crime literature

1948: Period of YVA Treaty with USSR begins

1949: *First radio* Dragnet *episode*

1951: *First* Dragnet *telecast*

1953: *First James Bond novel,* Casino Royale

1955: Finland joins United Nations

Mid–1950s: Mauri Sariola revitalizes Finnish crime fiction with Inspector Susikoski novels

1956–1970: Finnish government implements welfare state policies

1960: Inspector Palmu films begin to appear

1961: Finland joins European Free Trade Association

1962: *First James Bond film*

1966: Communists included in Finnish coalition cabinet for first time since 1948

1967: *First Martin Beck novel by Marxist Swedes Sjöwall and Wahlöö 1968–c. 1982: Trend toward social criticism in Nordic detective fiction*

1971: *First* Dirty Harry *film, starring Clint Eastwood*

1976: Matti Joensuu begins writing police procedurals

1977: *Debut of Marcia Muller's U.S. first female private detective, Sharon McCone*

1984: Finnish Whodunnit Society founded

1985: Clew of the Year Award initiated

1987: Islamic Society of Finland founded; Finland passes Act on Equality between men and women

1990: Estimated 1000 Muslims in Finland; dramatic rise in that population begins

c. 1992: *Collapse of Soviet Union*

1995: True Finns Party founded (now Finns Party)

1997: *Henning Mankell's first Inspector Wallander novel appears in English*

1997: Leena Lehtolainen is first woman author to win Clew of the Year Award

1999: Estimated 15,000–20,000 Muslims in Finland

2001: *Muslim terrorist attack on U.S. World Trade Center and Pentagon*

2005: *Stieg Larsson's* The Girl with the Dragon Tattoo (tr. 2008; Larsson dies just before its publication)

2006: *Larsson's* The Girl Who Played with Fire, *tr. 2009*

2007: Matti Rönkä becomes first Finn to win Glass Key Award

2007: *Larsson's* The Girl Who Kicked the Hornet's Nest, *tr. 2009*

2008: Finnish Resistance Movement (militant neo–Nazi movement) founded

2010: *Newsweek* names Finland "Best Country in the World"

2011: Presidential election chooses first National Coalition president in 50 years; impressive rise of Finns Party

2012: Finland begins Assisted Voluntary Return program to encourage immigrants to leave the country (not successful)

2013: Estimated 64,000 Muslims in Finland

Contemporary Finnish Authors of Crime Fiction

An asterisk (*) indicates some or all of the author's work is available in English.

Jonni Aho

b. 1965, Helsinki, Finland; Residence: Helsinki, Finland; Occupations: journalist, copy writer, author

After spending a decade in California, Jonni Aho returned to Finland, wrote a biography of Tony Halme, Finland's answer to Jesse Ventura, an American professional wrestler turned politician, and debuted with the hard-hitting crime novel *Musta sade* ("Black Rain"). Described in Aho's publication publicity as "rougher than Remes (a Finnish author)—tougher than Vares" (another Finnish author), "Black Rain" opens a series which Aho hopes will reinvigorate the traditional hard-boiled private detective story for the Finnish public. Drawing on both his reading of classic American crime authors like Dashiell Hammett, Raymond Chandler, and James M. Cain and his own background as a journalist in California and Las Vegas, Aho created his Helsinki-based private eye Riku "Rocky" Laine, who knows much he shouldn't and like Aho returns to his native Finland to accomplish great things—in Laine's case, to revitalize his country, not just its literature. "Black Rain" opens when the lovely blonde wife of a member of the Finnish parliament enters Laine's office, fearing for her life. The novel proceeds to lay bare Helsinki's night life, described in the novel's publicity as "soft and sweet" as a "first kiss," and as "raw and naked" as a just-slaughtered calf. The "Black Rain" musical theme has become a gold-record seller in Finland.

Crime Novels:

2002: *Musta sade* ("Black Rain")

Major Awards: N/A

Website: N/A

Tapani Bagge

> b. October 2, 1962, Kerava, Finland; Residence: Hämeenlinna, Finland; Occupations: radio and television scriptwriter, editor, translator, author

Tapani Bagge wrote his first story at age seven and became a full-time writer in 1983. Bagge has since produced more than 70 books: almost sixty Jerry Cotton pulps, three crime novel series and numerous short stories, plays, radio and television scripts, and children's books. He has translated more than forty books from English to Finnish and produced scripts for the popular Moomin comics. Finnish crime literature critic Paula Arvas considers Bagge the Finnish writer "closest to the American hard-boiled tradition" (Arvas, "Contemporary Finnish Crime Fiction" 6).

Bagge served his thriller apprenticeship in the 1970s by writing 110-page Jerry Cotton pulps, the Finnish version of Germany's popular series about an American FBI Special Agent. From there Bagge moved to translating foreign authors' work and then by writing his own crime novels, which he feels have been influenced by Elmore Leonard and Donald E. Westlake, writers who Bagge says "can both be funny and touching in the same sentence." He also praises Joe R. Lansdale's "dark sense of humour," as well as his favorite American crime authors Paul Cain and James M. Cain and Chester Himes and science fiction author Fredric Brown (quoted in Lefran).

Bagge began his crime novel career with *Puhaltaja* ("The Jack"), 2002, opening his *Hämeenlinna noir* series, set in his home town and showing the dark comedy and violence of its equally human crooks and cops. Bagge notes this series has no protagonist, "no good guys or bad guys, just people who make wrong choices." One of its central figures, Detective Leila Pohjanen, and one of the crooks, snitch and former burglar Allu Nygren, even have a child together (Bagge). The fifth installment of the series, *Musta taivas* ("Black Sky"), 2006, which won the 2007 Clew of the Year Award and was shortlisted for the Glass Key Award in 2008, finds Ernesto, a gangster, in deep trouble with both the police and his bosses when a tornado blows away his loot from an armored car heist, so he escapes to Hämeenlinna where he has criminal contacts, allowing Bagge to illustrate his belief that "In real life most criminals are sad cases" (Bagge).

Bagge started his four-novel historical mystery series in 2009, using as his protagonist Detective Sergeant Väinö Mujunen of Valpo, the Finnish State Police, to trace the effects of Finland's 20th century wars. *Valkoinen hehku* ("White Heat"), a title taken from Raoul Walsh's classic film), set in 1938 when the scars of the Civil War were still fresh, deals with a murder, a missing-person case, and an assassination plot targets then Minister of Internal Affairs Urho Kekkonen, later Finland's president for over a quarter century. Bagge's *Sininen aave* ("The Blue Phantom"), set in 1949, just following the Winter War, shows Finland's bitter choice between what Bagge calls "the plague and the cholera" meaning Nazi Germany and the Soviet Union. Bagge's Detective Mujunen, recently widowed, simultaneously pursues criminals and an affair with a Lithuanian dancer who has dubious intentions. In *Musta pyörre* ("Black Whirlpool"), Bagge treats Finland's 1942 support of the Nazis against the Soviets, with Mujunen assigned as bodyguard to visiting SS chief Heinrich Himmler while Mujunen himself is involved with two *femmes fatales*. In *Punainen varjo* ("Red Shadow"), set in the harrowing days of 1944 just after the punitive peace treaty which caused the Finns to fight against the Germans in the Lapland War, Mujunen must investigate the murder of a Russian officer, which the Soviets may be using as an excuse to occupy Finland. Bagge calls Mujunen "a man of principle," often caught between his own conscience and the demands of the state for which he is a reliable workhorse: "Drinking doesn't help, so he takes action. And if the law is wrong, you have to break it. Or at least bend it a little" (Bagge). In both his *Hämeenlinna noir* novels and his Mujunen series, Bagge feels his central topic is betrayal: "Cheating in family, between friends, between business associates and lovers … through the whole society. You cannot really trust anybody. Not even yourself" (quoted in Lefran).

Bagge's darkly satiric side as an author emerged with his Onni Syrjänen short stories and novels about a disreputable alcoholic lawyer too poor to afford a private detective, so he does his own investigations. Onni's clients are his old school pals and his drinking buddies, who are all as incompetent as Onni himself is. Two of the Syrjänen short stories have appeared in English translation, "The Face in the Concrete" and "One More Shot," in the Summer 2005 and Spring 2008 issues respectively of *The Thrilling Detective* website. Bagge's short story "Hard Rain," translated by Kristian London, appears in *Helsinki Noir*, 2014.

Bagge describes his "take on life" as "mostly black and sometimes absurd" (Bagge). He says that reading Raymond Chandler's *The Lady in the Lake* at age ten began his "never-ending love story with tough guys and dangerous dames." He now writes his fiction at about one five-page chapter per day. He also claims that the best part of his writing comes when the characters take over and run with the story: "the most high I've ever gotten, and it leaves no hangover whatsoever" (quoted in Lefran).

Crime Novels:

The Hämeenlinna Noir Series:

2002: *Puhaltaja* ("The Jack")
2003: *Paha kuu* ("Bad Moon")
2004: *Kohtalon tähti* ("The Fate of a Star")
2005: *Julma maa* ("The Cruel Land")
2006: *Musta taivas* ("Black Sky"), opening passages tr. Minna K. Haapio
2008: *Kummisedän hautajaiset* ("Godfather's Funeral")
2014: *Havannan kuu* ("Havana Moon")
2015: *Pieni talvisota* ("A Little Winter War")

The Detective Sergeant Väinö Mujunen Series (Historical Mysteries):

2009: *Valkoinen hehku* ("White Heat")
2011: *Sininen aave* ("The Blue Phantom")
2012: *Musta pyörre* ("Black Whirlpool")
2013: *Punainen varjo* ("Red Shadow")

Selected Onni Syrjänen Fiction:

2005: "Kasvot betonissa" ("The Face in the Concrete"), short story adopted as radio play, 2006; tr. Minna K. Haapio

2010: *Kasvot tuulilasissa* ("The Face in the Windshield"), novel

2011: *Kasvot katuojassa* ("The Face in the Gutter")

Major Awards:

2007: The Clew of the Year Award, for *Musta taivas* ("Black Sky")

Website: http://tapanibagge.com; Blog: http://www.tapanibagge.blogspot.fi

*Monika Fagerholm

b. February 26, 1961, Helsinki, Finland; Residence: Ekenäs, Finland; Occupation: author

Monika Fagerholm, a Finnish author who writes in Swedish, believes writing is an exploration, "the attempt ... to throw light on something on what we do not see ... what cannot be explained by psychology, human existence" (quoted in Hildenheimo). Fagerholm's first two novels, *Underbara kvinnor vid vatten* ("Wonderful Women by the Water"), 1994, nominated for the Finlandia Prize, and *Diva* ("Diva") both explore the development of young women's selves. Fagerholm continued that theme through her highly praised two-part novel *Den amerikanska flickan* (The American Girl), 2005, and its sequel, *Glitterscenen* ("The Glitter Scene"), 2009, and her recent *Lola uppochner* ("Lola Upsidedown"), 2012. These novels are all stylistically experimental with murders as the catalysts for their intricate plots.

Reviewing for *O Magazine*, April 2010, Karen Holt observed that "Nothing is obvious" in *The American Girl*, Fagerholm's only novel to have been translated into English, "part literary mystery and part sexual coming-of-age story" (Holt). In 1969, a girl from America drowns in a Finnish marsh; her Finnish lover hangs himself; and their grief-stricken best friend loses the ability to speak. Years later two local girls, Doris and Sandra, become obsessed with the tragedy, role-playing it over and over, until Doris begins to suspect Sandra may be hiding a terrible secret. Doris finally commits suicide, whereupon Sandra tries to solve Doris's mystery within the old enigma of the American girl's death. The narrative travels back and forth in time and becomes increasingly fragmented, as does "The Glitter Scene," which features another pair of young girls years after the original tragedies. This time, sad and silent Suzette and curious and outgoing Maj-Gun are bound together by the local myths about the dead teenagers, and the girls dream themselves into a state of mind where the gap between fantasy and reality is blurred. An omniscient narrator links events told through several other narrators, until finally a shocking dénouement is reached, allowing "a myriad of possible interpretations" and many levels of readings (Lykkegaard).

Fagerholm's latest novel, *Lola uppochner* ("Lola Upsidedown"), 2012, is a strange novel written in a paradoxical style, "severe and accessible ... playful, at the same time very serious" in a context inspired by the enigmatic American television series *Twin Peaks*, which mixed "comedy and dark drama" (Rabe). "Lola" is a nasty rag doll that serves as a "kind of omen" in the nontraditional murder tale that entangles three women, wheelchair bound Anita Brooks, social climber Minnie Backlund, and former pastor Eva Anderberg. Fagerholm herself calls each of her works a mystery, citing the work of film director John Cassavetes as one of her major inspirations because she finds his work almost improvisational, a technique she herself espouses. She also works with a completely original Swedish syntax mixing colloquial language with digressive poetic passages, and achieving a fragmented effect that nonetheless analyzes "the paradoxical relationships between surface and depth, between emptiness and content" (Rabe).

Literary Crime Novels:

2005: *Den amerikanska flickan* (*The American Girl*, tr. Katarina E. Tucker, 2010)
2009: *Glitterscenen* ("The Glitter Scene")
2012: *Lola uppochner* ("Lola Upsidedown")

Major Awards:

2007: The August Prize (Sweden), for *Den amerikanska flickan* (*The American Girl*)
2005: The Swedish Literature Society Award (Sweden's most prestigious literary prize), for *Den amerikanska flickan* (*The American Girl*)

Website: N/A

Paul-Erik Haataja

b. December 12, 1944; Residence: Helsinki, Finland; Occupations: photographer, author

In awarding his 1987 novel *Häkkilinnut* ("Cage Birds") the Clew of the Year Award, the Who-dunnit Society's jury commended Haataja, a professional photographer who did not begin writing detective novels until he was forty, for his ability to construct dramatic scenes in comic situations and dialogue. Haataja's procedural fiction, often compared to Georges Simenon's Maigret novels, consistently involves the same police team headed by Lieutenant Armas Tammelin, a cantankerous sixtyish cop physically debilitated by illness, who strongly dislikes children. Each of his team members, highly competent in his own sphere, finds it difficult to talk to the others, something that critic Ritva Sorvati indicates is always difficult for Finnish men (Sorvati), which in Haataja's books often makes team members irritated with each other. The team members—sloppy Olle Strömberg with a perennially dripping nose and dreams of Rio de Janeiro; ugly Sulo Miettinen, shy but gentle with women; small gum-chomping Aulis, a brutal interrogator; young playful Lap-lander Niilo Pitkävuoma, the only team member with children—talk constantly about women, their prevailing topic of conversation. As they solve crimes involving racism, drug trafficking, ecoterrorism, and money laundering, they deal gingerly with their terrifyingly efficient female supervisor Helena Rantanen (Sorvali). This team always functions as more than the sum of its parts.

Selected Crime Novels:

1984: *Nuori, kaunis ja kuollut* ("Young, Beautiful and Dead")
1985: *Lähto ilman jäähyväisiä* ("Check-air Goodbyes")
1987: *Häkkilinnut* ("Cage Birds"), made into both a radio play and a television drama
1991: *Jenkki* ("Yankee")
1996: *Rosvo ja poliisi* ("Cops and Robbers")
2000: *Vaarojen mailla* ("The Hazard Lands")
2005: *Urakan loppu* ("The Contract Is Finished")

Major Awards:

1987: The Clew of the Year Award, for *Häkkilinnut* ("Cage Birds")

Website: N/A

Erkki Hämäläinen

> b. 1934; Residence: Helsinki, Finland; Occupations: translator, author

Erkki Hämäläinen produced one parodic Finnish detective novel in 1966. It features the Finnish private eye Ylermi K. Tammi, a native of Helsinki, who in a James Bond fashion collects weapons and cars and leaves a trail of mayhem and beautiful women behind him.

Crime Novel Parody:

1966: *Ei verta karvalankamatolle* ("No Blood on the Carpet")

Major Awards: N/A

Website: N/A

Karo Hämäläinen

> b. 11 June 1976, Mikkeli, Finland; Residence: Tampere, Finland; Occupations: economics journalist, editor, literary critic, author

A veteran critic and executive producer of *Parnasson*, Finland's best-known literary journal, with passions for literature and the stock market, Karo Hämäläinen has also written numerous young adult novels and a fictionalized biography of Finnish president Urho Kekkonen which treats globalization, market-driven unification and social development. His high-crime financial thrillers are based on actual events like the 2008 crash of the Icelandic Glitner Bank, explored in his 2011 breakthrough thriller *Erottaja* ("The Buyout"), where he dissects the deadly consequences of fear and greed in the world of big money and its capital-money intrigue. *Kolmikulma* ("The Bailout"), 2012, reveals countries and people behaving like the stock market by pretending to be what they are not, risking both billions of dollars and human lives. For *Ilta on julma* ("Cruel Is the Night"), 2013, his literary agency announced "Agatha Christie meets Quentin Tarantino by way of Alfred Hitchcock." In the Golden Age "locked room" mode it contains four first-person narratives that chronologically report a dinner given by Robert, a successful unscrupulous banker with his young trophy girlfriend Elise, for his oldest friend Mikko, an idealistic reporter who's been plotting Robert's murder, and Mikko's wife Veera, Robert's former lover. Weapons and motives for homicide abound in this literary *tour de force*, optioned in 2013 for publication in English translation by Soho Press.

Crime Novels:

2011: *Erottaja* ("The Buyout")
2012: *Kolmikulma* ("The Bailout")
2013: *Ilta on julima* ("Cruel Is the Night")

Major Awards:

2012: The Tampere Literary Prize, for *Erottaja* ("The Buyout")

Website: http://karohamalainen.wordpress.com

Marja-Liisa Heino

b. 1969; Residence: Tampere, Finland; Occupations: librarian, writer for Nokia, author

When Marja-Liisa Heino's first crime novel *Enkelimies* ("Angel Man") appeared, a Finnish newspaper reviewer called it "a kindly girl's harsh crime novel." The novel studies the dehumanizing effect a prison sentence wreaks upon its young male convict-narrator, unsparingly presenting prison violence, homosexuality, and drug use. It also explores his life after release, full of the trouble he attracts like a magnet ("Brick Bite"). "Angel Man" was nominated for the *Helsingen Sanomat* Literature Prize in 2006, and since then Heino has developed as one of the most original Finnish crime writers, one whose books differ widely from each other (Nummelin).

Heino continued her treatments of social demarcation as a focus for her next three domestic criminal novels. Her second, the Kalevi Jäntti Prizewinning novel *Suomen suuntaan* ("In the Direction of Finland"), 2008, features a middle-aged former KGB officer living in St. Petersburg whom Heino treats with dry humor. Her third, *Niemisen tyttövainaan tapaus* ("The Niemisen Case"). 2011, set in December 1941, has a Russian as prime suspect in a village homicide. One commentator considers Heino's fourth novel, *Astuit väärään autoon* ("You Stepped on the Wrong Train"), 2013, also set in 1941, "an absurd Dostoyevskyian study of guilt, written in prose that's both diffuse and clear at the same time" (Nummelin). It "traces the activities of Russian prisoners of war in the Tampere region as well as young Red vandals, in the context of a village homicide," including a peculiar subplot in which a rapist released from prison moves in with one of his victims and acts as her handyman. In all her work, Heino combines insight into the social causes of criminality with "parodic and comical overtones" in language that fits her stories "like a knife between the ribs" ("Brick Bite").

Crime Novels:

2006: *Enkelimies* ("Angel Man")
2008: *Suomen suuntaan* ("In the Direction of Finland")
2011: *Niemisen tyttövainaan tapaus* ("The Niemisen Case")
2013: *Astuit väärään autoon* ("You Stepped on the Wrong Train")

Major Awards:

2009: Kalevi Jäntti Award, for *Suomen suuntaan* ("In the Direction of Finland")

Website: N/A

Kati Hiekkapelto

b. 1970, Oulu, Finland; Residence: Island of Hailuoto, Finland; Occupations: Special education teacher, author

As a special education teacher, Kati Hiekkapelto has worked extensively with immigrants to Finland. She incorporated her experiences into crime fiction, beginning with *Kolibri*, 2013 (*The Hummingbird*, tr. 2014), where she addresses thorny issues of immigration, multiculturalism, xenophobia, and small-town tensions. Her protagonist, Anna Fekete, ethnically Hungarian, escaped as a child with her family from the vicious war in Serbia and grew up in Finland. In her debut novel, Anna is a thirtyish detective working in a small north Finland coastal town with a surly racist and misogynist police partner. While Anna is investigating a serial murder case, she is also attempting to save a young Muslim Kurdish immigrant girl from her family's "honor violence" while battling her own addictive demons—alcohol, tobacco, and casual sex. The second novel in the series, *Suojattomat* ("Vulnerable") was published in Finland in 2014.

From the viewpoint of Bihar, the teenager Anna tries to help, Hiekkapelto sums up the plight of asylum seekers entering Finland. Relegated sometimes for years to refugee centers, families are inevitably split apart; the children go out to school, so they quickly learn the Finnish language and customs, but the adults wait and wait for the wonderful new life that never comes, eventually becoming enraged at their children, who fail to succeed at anything, and at themselves, who sacrificed everything to come to the new country, a lethal breeding ground for racial tensions. Through Bihar, Hiekkapelto suggests only one solution: make the adults go to work, sink or swim: " of course this would mean less funding for integration projects, fewer jobs and meetings for all those experts" (*The Hummingbird* 130–131). In the bleak Finland of Hiekkapelto's fiction, there's virtually no hope for either refugees or for the Finnish society's attempt to assimilate them.

Crime Novels (Anna Fekete series):

> 2013: *Kolibri* (*The Hummingbird*, tr. David Hackston, 2014)
> 2014: *Suojattomat* ("Vulnerable")

Major Awards:

> 2014: Clew of the Year Award, for *Kolibri* (*The Hummingbird*)

Website: http://www.katihiekkapelto.com (Finnish)

Harri V. Hietikko

> b. February 21, 1970, Vaasa, Finland; Residence: Tampere, Finland; Occupations: theater director, author

The key to the world view implicit in Harri Hietikko's crime novels is myth, specifically the myth of J.R.R. Tolkien's Sauron, the Eternal Enemy of Good. Hietikko used Sauron as the central metaphor for his 2008 dissertation in Administrative Sciences for the University of Tampere, "Management by Sauron: Power, Leadership, Destruction and Hope in the Work of J.R.R. Tolkien's *Lord of the Rings*." Hietikko saw today's world-of-work management themes—power, leadership, destruction and hope—played out through Tolkien's pairs of opposing mythical characters. Gandalf the Good, in charge of the nine Ring-seekers, represents a wise and patient leader who often holds development discussions, even considering the opinions of the lowliest team member, Frodo, as important. Sauron represents the dominant leader who inculcates fear and despair among his subordinates, forcing them to obey unquestioningly in a linear fashion ("The Crime Writer").

Sauron-type management overwhelms the dark, brutal world of Hietikko's hard-boiled crime fiction, where "goodness, beauty and truth" are criticized and ridiculed, revealing the "general emptiness and decadence of Western life" ("The Crime Writer"). Hietikko's 2013 novel, *Lausukaa Paranoid* ("Recite Paranoid"), centered on an unnamed protagonist and exhibiting "social hostility, profanity, and sado-masochistic elements," shows the breakdown of the social contract in today's society, as Hietikko develops this dismaying theme through social criticism and the use of mythological elements ("Amman Reading Time"). Hietikko himself is said to have called this novel "an update of Sergio Leone with Harley Davidsons" (quoted in Nummelin).

Crime Novels:

Roger Repo Series:

1999: *Kadonnut Hamlet* ("Lost Hamlet")
2001: *Lävistetty kevät* ("Pierced Spring")
2005: *Roger Repo ja tuonen väki* ("Roger Northern and the Tuonen Crowd")
2013: *Lausukaa Paranoid* ("Recite Paranoid")
2014: *Näkemiin Shosanna* ("Goodbye, Shosanna")

Major Awards: N/A

Website: N/A

*Pekka Hiltunen

b. 1966, Oulu, Finland; Residence: Helsinki, Finland; Occupations: journalist, editor, author

In 2011 with the publication of his first crime novel, the psychological thriller *Vilpittömästi sinun* (*Cold Courage*), twenty-year journalist Pekka Hiltunen became the "new trendsetter" in Nordic crime fiction by adding "global political and societal topics to a modern, urban setting" (Allen). Hiltunen, currently managing editor of *Mondo* magazine, set his *Studio* novels in London, his favorite city, because he felt that his readers would find it "refreshing to see the slightly dark and deep Nordic characteristics in a different setting" (quoted in Allen).

Hiltunen claims that one of his literary role models is Danish author Peter Høeg, author of *Smilla's Sense of Snow*, whose half–Danish, half–Greenlander heroine becomes involved in solving a crime in a city not her own. In a subtle parallel, *Cold Courage*'s Finnish expatriates Lia and Mari, who want to make the world a better place, unconventionally wage war on the operators of horrifying human trafficking, in the process addressing political populism and the tough working-class culture of the times. *Cold Courage* received both the Clew of the Year Award and the Kaarle (Charles) Prize in 2012, as well as nominations for the 2013 Glass Key Award and the *Helsingen Sanomat* debut novel award. *Sysipimeä* (*Black Noise*, tr. 2014), second in the *Studio* series, was chosen for the 2012 *Helsingen Sanomat* "In the Books" list. Hiltunen's publisher calls *ISO*, 2013, third in the series, "burningly topical," dealing with obesity and the embarrassment, shame, and prejudice it often involves. By his innovative combination of painful societal issues with his non–Nordic setting, Hiltunen seems to have "kick-started a new phase in Finnish crime literature" (Allen).

Crime Novels:

The Studio Series:

2011: *Vilpittömästi sinun* (*Cold Courage*, tr. Owen F. Witesman, 2013)
2012: *Sysipimeä* (*Black Noise*, tr. Owen F. Witesman, 2014)
2013: *ISO* ("ISO")

Major Awards:

2012: The Clew of the Year Award, for *Vilpittömästi* (*Cold Courage*)
2012: The Kaarle Award, for *Vilpittömästi* (Cold Courage)

Website: N/A

Johanna Holmström

b. 1981, Sipoo, Finland; Residence: Helsinki, Finland; Occupation: journalist, author

Johanna Holmström, a Finnish-Swedish author writing in Swedish, first known for prizewinning short fiction, made her novel debut in 2007 with the mainstream book *Ur din längtan* ("Out of Your Longing"). She has since produced her third short-story collection *Camera obscura*, a prize-winning series of related stories which explore the lives of young Helsinki eco-terrorists. Her 2013 young adult novel *Asfaltsänglar* ("Asphalt Angels") explores the problem of multiculturalism in Finland through two sisters, Leila and Samira, whose mother, an ethnic Finn, has converted to Islam and through her fanaticism has driven the girls' North African father out of the family. The girls' suffering in this situation is compounded by racist bullying at school, which Holmström treats with skill, understanding, and a "finely-tuned sense of humour," while she poses the question bedeviling many societies today: "Who poses the greater danger to a young dark-skinned woman, the racist skinheads on the street or the members of the Islamic religious community, who ... lock them up in arranged marriages, and possibly even kill a daughter who brings 'shame' on the family?" (Söderling).

Connected Crime Short Story Collection:

2009: *Camera obscura* ("Camera Obscura")

Young Adult Thriller/Psychological Novel:

2013: *Asfaltsänglar* ("Asphalt Angels")

Major Awards:

2009: *Svenska Dagbladet* Literature Prize, for *Camera obscura* ("Camera Obscura")

Website: N/A

Jari Järvelä

b. November 21, 1966, Helsinki, Finland; Residence: Kotka, Finland; Occupations: elementary school teacher, author

Until the 2014 publication of *Tyttö ja pommi* ("The Girl and the Bomb"), the first volume of a projected crime trilogy, Jari Järvelä was recognized for distinguished mainstream novels, two of which, *Lentäjän poika* ("The Way to the Stars"). 1999, and *Romeo ja Julia* ("Romeo and Juliet"), 2007, were nominated for the prestigious Finlandia Prize.

According to his March 2014, *Crime Time* statement, Järvelä indicated that when Harri Nykänen of Crime Time, Finland's crime publishing cooperative, contacted Järvelä in the fall of 2012 proposing that Järvelä try his hand at a crime novel, Jarvela had already had an idea in mind: the graffiti and graffiti makers in the rough port town of Kotka, a subject that he felt had been largely ignored in fiction, and one that Järvelä believed opened up the larger question of who controls public space, with what right to do so. "As soon as we step out of the door, we are sensitive to continuous advertising ... held in the modern world for granted and legitimate," Järvelä said, pondering the mushrooming number of CC-TV cameras on city streets: "We are ... continually TV stars, without knowing it, [whether] we want it or not" ("Jari Järvelä"). In *Tyttö ja pommi* ("The Girl and the Bomb"), the first volume of a crime trilogy, Järvelä declared his intention to explore "new, unfamiliar, frightening things and landscapes." The English rights to this novel have been sold, and the second volume of the trilogy, *Tyttö ja rotta* ("The Girl and the Rat"), was scheduled to appear in 2015.

Crime Novels (projected trilogy):

2014: *Tyttö ja pommi* ("The Girl and the Bomb")
2015: *Tyttö ja rotta* ("The Girl and the Rat")

Major Awards (for mainstream novels and short fiction):

1996: The Finnish Writers' Debut Prize
2002: The Kalevi Jäntti Prize
2007: The Finland State Prize for Literature

Website: N/A

Matti Yrjänä Joensuu

> b. October 31, 1948, Helsinki, Finland; d. December 4, 2011, Valjeakoski, Finland; Residence: Helsinki, Finland; Occupations: policeman, author

One of Finland's bestselling crime authors, Matti Joensuu worked as a full-time police officer for more than thirty years until he retired in 2006, most recently in the Arson and Explosives Unit of the Helsinki Police. His novels have been translated into twenty foreign languages and made into radio and television plays and movies. Joensuu was the first writer to win the Finnish State Award for Literature with a crime novel (1982). He is the only author to have won the Clew of the Year Award three times; two of his novels have been shortlisted for the Finlandia Prize, Finland's highest literary honor, and *The Priest of Evil* was nominated in 2004 for the Glass Key Award.

Because he wrote while working full time as a policeman, Joensuu's output was not large, but according to his publisher, it has been praised for its skillful combination of police procedure with insights into the psychology of ordinary people who feel that disruptive changes in society have driven their world out of control; the often ominous significance of dreams, and individual attempts to function proactively in the modern world. In a perceptive essay defending thrillers as "haute cuisine in the genre of crime," Pia Ingström observes that Joensuu's work has modulated from "sensibly treated" formulaic procedurals avoiding "Sweden's monstrosities," which she says unite violence as entertainment with "claims to social relevance," into novels as "meditations over various kinds of major deprivation," either specifically pertaining to the family or "more generally and existentially," presented in "muffled, melancholy prose" not usually used in the crime genre (Ingström).

Joensuu's protagonist, Detective Sergeant (later Inspector and finally Chief Superintendent) Timo Jukani Harjunpää of the Helsinki Police Department's CID unit is one of Finland's best known fictional policemen, a conscientious ordinary man solving ordinary crimes committed by ordinary people, exposing "the darker sides of society and the day-to-day misery and suffering which gives rise to crime," sharing with Joensuu "a strong social conscience and a tendency toward melancholy" (Papinniemi). These appear in *Harjunpää ja rakkauden nälka*, 2003 (*To Steal Her Love*, tr. 2008), where Harjunpää is suffering from conflicts in both his work and his life, because although he is married with children, due to a midlife crisis he has fallen in love with his police colleague Onerva.

During the 1980s, police colleagues criticized Joensuu for exposing "prejudice, greed and abuse of power" in the police force, whose superior officers at that time tended to be what Joensuu called "stern old dictators." Subsequent superintendents," Joensuu later said, are "a world apart," highly trained and competent (quoted in Papinnniemi). Beginning in 1993, Joensuu struggled with a divorce and other painful personal problems and could not write until he produced *Harjunpää ja pahan pappi*, 2003 (*The Priest of Evil*, tr. 2006) possibly the darkest of his novels. "You just can't force creativity," Joensuu admitted, explaining his decade of writer's block. He felt that "ordered chaos" made writing flow properly, "and my chaos was out of control" (quoted in Papinniemi).

Joensuu finally ordered his chaos. Using his earlier research into the 300-kilometer maze of underground tunnels beneath Helsinki, he focused on the terrifying Brocken, the congruence of several railway tracks where he placed a deranged figure calling himself the Earth Spirit, brainwashing teenagers into carrying explosive-laden backpacks and worshipping a goddess to whom he sacrifices human victims. Detective Sergeant Timo Harjunpää of Helsinki's Violent Crime Unit, even more fatalistic than Henning Mankell's Kurt Wallander ("Finnish Mystery Series"), faced with an apparent witnessless suicide in a Helsinki subway station, concludes that an exceptionally dangerous serial killer is at work (*Scandinavian Books*). In a 2006 interview, Joensuu described *The Priest of Evil* as differing from his earlier work, because there he had tried to explain " what contributed to making someone a criminal," but "In this book, that is left unexplained, an absolute inexplicable evil" (quoted in Cornwell).

Joensuu, who claimed the work of Georges Simenon had influenced his own work most, fundamentally attributed criminality to depriving children of love, a trend that he saw growing everywhere in today's societies: "It's the way that children are treated and brought up that makes them emotionally damaged…. So criminals are made" (quoted in Cornwell). Drawing on his own police experience, Joensuu also believed that the themes he treated in his novels years later became subjects of media discourse, like the violence against women he explores in one of his books, and the crimes committed by children which appear in 1983's *Harjunpää and the Stone Murders*, echoed in a real-life double murder committed by Finnish teenagers.

Joensuu's last novel, *Harjunpää ja rautahuone* ("Harjunpää and the Iron Room"), 2007, plunges Timo Harjunpää, struggling with his own marital difficulties, into the investigation of another serial homicide case, with wealthy women victims linked by their purchases of sex from a masseur-gigolo. "Nearly every scene is shot through with themes of lovelessness, exploitation and the connection between malice and sex" (Paavolainen). At the time of his death, Joensuu was working on a new Harjunpää novel.

Pia Ingström believes that Joensuu's "concern with the requirements of the crime genre has diminished in inverse proportion to the growth of his obsession with affliction and deprivation … [an] innovative method of using trivial criminal material as a basis for heavily loaded symbols" (Ingström), producing "dark fairytales, with rich atmospheric and psychologically penetrating mysteries" ("Scandinavian Books").

Crime Novels:

Timo Harjunpää Series:

1976: *Väkivallan virkamies* ("Official Violence")

1978: *Harjunpää ja pyromaani* ("Harjunpää and the Pyromaniac")

1981: *Harjunpää ja kapteeni Karhu* ("Harjunpää and Captain Bear")

1982: *Harjunpää ja ahdistelija* ("Harjunpää and the Molester")

1983: *Harjunpää ja poliisin poika* (*Harjunpää and the Stone Murders*, tr. Raili Taylor, 1986)

1984: *Harjunpää ja heimolaiset* ("Harjunpää and the Tribesmen")

1985: *Harjunpaa ja rakkauden lait* ("Harjunpää and the Laws of Love")
1986: *Harjunpää ja kiusantekijät* (Harjunpää and the Bully")
1993: *Harjunpää ja rakkauden nälkä* (*To Steal Her Love*, tr. David Hackston, 2008)
2003: *Harjunpää ja pahan pappi* (*The Priest of Evil*, tr. David Hackston, 2006)
2007: *Harjunpää ja rautahuone* ("Harjunpää and the Iron Room")

Major Awards:

1982: The Finnish State Award for Literature
1985: The Clew of the Year Award, for *Harjunpääja heimolaiset* ("Harjunpää and the Tribes-men")
1987: The Martin Beck Award
1994: The Clew of the Year Award, for *Harjunpää ja rakkauden nälkä* (*To Steal Her Love*)
2004: The Clew of the Year Award, for *Harjunpää ja pahan pappi* (*The Priest of Evil*)

Website: N/A

Seppo Jokinen

b. April 13, 1949, Tampere, Finland; Residence: Tempere, Finland; Occupations: chief IT specialist for the City of Tampere, author

Fictional Detective Lieutenant Sakai Koskinen, sometimes compared in Finland to George Simenon's Inspector Maigret, like his creator, former computer specialist Seppo Jokinen, lives and works in Tampere, Finland's third largest city. In 2001's *Hakan enkelit* (*Wolves and Angels*, tr. 2012), Jokinen's only novel to have appeared in English thus far, Jokinen is newly divorced and throwing himself with extreme *sisu*, the special Finnish quality of dogged determination and per-severance, into a strenuous regime of bodybuilding, at which he does better than at dating. The case he's working starts with the murder of a disabled man who has been a member of the "Fallen Angels," wheelchair-bound motorcyclists now living in a community center for the disabled. Attacks on other residents follow, allowing Jokinen to explore the physical and emotional problems of the disabled and their underpaid caregivers.

In addition to the full-time writing he has pursued since 2006, Jokinen has been instrumental in efforts to publish Finnish crime novels in English, beginning with the publication of *Wolves and Angels* by the Minnesota publishing house Ice Cold Crime in 2012.

Selected Crime Novels:

Inspector Sakari Koskinen Series:

1996: *Koskinen ja siimamies* ("Koskinen and Siimamies")
2001: *Hukan enkelit* (*Wolves and Angels*, tr. Owen Witesman, 2012)
2004: *Suurta pahaa* ("Great Evil")
2009: *Lyöty mies* ("The Beaten Man")
2013: *Vihan sukua* ("The Wrath of Kin")
2013: *Mustat sydämet* ("Black Hearts")

Major Awards:

2002: The Clew of the Year Award, for *Hakan enkelit* (*Wolves and Angels*)
2003: Great Finnish Book Club Award

Website: N/A

Totti Karpela

b. November 5, 1940, Turku, Finland; Residence: Turku, Finland; Occupations: prison director, police officer, public prosecutor, author

Totti Karpela bases his conventional police procedurals on his law enforcement experience in Turku. His son, Matti Mikael Karpela, is a Finnish safety specialist.

Selected Crime Novels:

2004: *Kiimakorttelin keltainen kaisa* ("Horny Black Yellow Kaisa")
2006: *Juhli ja kuole* ("Celebrate and Die")
2008: *Sudet, lampaat ja paimenet* ("Wolves, Sheep and Shepherds")

Major Awards: N/A

Website: N/A

Teemu Kaskinen

b. August 12, 1976, Joutseno, Finland; Residence: N/A; Occupations: playwright, translator, author

After his 2009 literary debut with an award-nominated near-future science fiction novel set on the Norway-Finland border, Teemu Kaskinen has co-authored two detective novels with Heikki Heiskanen. Both show police detectives as corrupt and evil as the criminals they pursue (Thompson, *Helsinki noir* endnotes).

Crime Novels Written with Heikki Heiskanen:

2010: *Norsun vuosi* ("Year of the Elephant")
2011: *Norsu tulee!* ("Elephant Coming!")

Major Awards: N/A

Website: N/A

Marko Kilpi

b. 1969, Rovaniemi, Finland; Residence: Kuopio, Finland; Occupations: police officer, documentary filmmaker, author

In learning to write books, Marko Kilpi, a senior Kuopio police officer, says he sent a huge amount of material "straight to the trash" (quoted in Salvén). His persistence has been well rewarded. He made his crime fiction debut in 2007 with the award-winning *Jäätyneitä ruusuja* ("Frozen Roses"), starring Olli Repo, a former highly paid ad man who now as a senior detective mentors young policemen. Kilpi's second novel *Kadotetut* ("Lost") was nominated for the Finlandia Prize, and he received the Savonia Literature Prize in 2012. Before turning to crime writing, Kilpi made several documentary films presented on Finnish television, and he has also written a children's book, *Konstaapeli Kontio* ("Officer Kontio"), 2010.

The Finlandia Prize jury praised "Lost" highly, declaring it "blows away the accepted conventions of the detective genre" (quoted in Kilpi's web page). In this novel, Repo, faced with a series of violent crimes while he is working with Heikki, a prospective policeman, must also deal with Heikki's own disturbing violent outbursts. Kilpi wrote this novel in response to shooting rampages in Finnish schools and the media frenzy that ensued. The Finlandia jury also commented, "The crime is looked at as a serious social phenomenon with psychological, human and moral undertones," involving a criminal impelled by the contemporary media society, police under psychological stress, and a "rescued " victim left with permanent psychological damage. The novel thus "takes issue with the malaise of the youth and our harsh life values" (website). In both "Lost" and *Elavien kirjoihin* ("Living Books") where Kilpi pairs Olli Repo with a maverick detective to investigate the local drug trade, once run by a woman who after giving birth to her son in prison now wants to go straight, Kilpi invites his readers to ponder tough ethical questions, rethink familiar values, and "tackle some of the most acute problems of our society" (quoted in website).

Crime Novels:

2007: *Jäätyneitä ruusuja* ("Frozen Roses")
2009: *Kadotetut* ("Lost")
2012: *Elävien kirjoihin* ("Living Books")
2011: *Tykki-kirja* ("8-Ball")
2013: *Kuolematon* ("Immortal")

Major Awards:

2008: The Clew of the Year Award, for *Jäätyneitä ruusuja* ("Frozen Roses")
2012: The Savonia Literature Prize

Website: http://en.markokilpi.kotisivukone.com

Pentti Kirstilä

b. May 26, 1948, Turku, Finland; Residence: Tampere, Finland; Occupations: journalist, translator, author

In 2009, Finland's Whodunnit Club declared that its two-time winner Pentti Kirstilä had been "at the cutting edge of Finnish crime writing for more than 30 years," using various narrative techniques and structures including the puzzle mystery, the hard-boiled novel, the thriller, and psychological suspense, all combining meticulous attention to procedural detail with piquant humor. In addition, in 2005–2007, Kirstilä and his wife Anya Angel wrote three puzzle-type detective novels with various sleuths and set in exotic locales—Malta, a small French town, and a Belgian farm—under the pen name "Ursula Auer," a collaborative effort which Kirstilä has described as "fun to start with, but then it turned into hard work," selling as badly as poetry collections: "Not much of an incentive to continue" (quoted in "English Summary," *Ruumiin kulttuuri* 3/2009). By himself, Kirstilä has also written three collections of short fiction, articles, and radio, theater and television plays. Kerstilä's Hanhivaara detective stories have been made into three Finnish television series and four television dramas.

Kirstilä's first and best known detective protagonist, influenced by Raymond Chandler's Philip Marlowe and Dashiell Hammett's Sam Spade, is Sergeant Lauri Hanhivaara, originally of the Tampere police but later working with the Helsinki police. Hanhivaara, whose sharp-tongued wit evolves over his ten-novel career, is initially bland, disillusioned, and reclusive. From his first appearance, *Jäähyväiset rakkaimmalle* ("Farewell, Dearest"),1977, when Hanhivaara investigates the murder of a beautiful woman in Tampere, to his 2002 outing, *Hanhivaara ja mies joka murhasi vaimonsa* ("Hanhivaara and the Man Who Murdered His Wife"), this laconic policeman slogs his way through horrific crimes. By the time he works in Helsinki, he has honed his appealing dry sense of humor and his perspective of Finnish crime has broadened from the homegrown to the international.

Selected Crime Novels:

Lauri Hanhuivaara Series:

1977: *Jäähyväiset rakkaimmalle* ("Farewell, Dearest")
1986: *Sinivalkoiset jäähyväiset* ("Blue and White Farewell")
1996: *Jäähyväiset unelmille* ("Farewell to Dreams")
2002: *Hanhivaara ja mies joka murhasi vaimonsa* ("Hanhivaara and the Man Who Murdered His Wife")

Experimental Psychological Detective Novels:

1992: *Imelda* ("Imelda")
1993: *Elektra* ("Electra")

Narcotics Officer Sergeant Kaistila Novels:

1982: *Jumalia ei uhmata* ("Shock Vein")
1984: *Munthe* ("Munthe")

Novels Written as "Ursula Auer," with Anja Angel:

2005: *Murhia Maltalla* ("Murders in Malta")
2006: *Murhia Maintenonissa* ("Murders in Maintenon")
2007: *Murhia Mankalassa* ("Murders in Mankala")

Short Fiction:

2003: *Varo, kulta, varo* ("Be Careful, Honey")

Translated Short Story:

"Brown Eyes and Green Hair," tr. Michael Garner, in *The Oxford Book of Detective Stories*

Major Awards:

1986: The Clew of the Year Award, for *Sinivalkoiset jäähyväiset* ("Blue and White Farewell")
1992: The Clew of the Year Award, for *Imelda* ("Imelda")

Website: N/A

Matti Kokkonen

> b. February 24, 1932, Rautalampi, Finland; d. October 13, 1992, Rautalampi, Finland; Residence: Rautalampi, Finland; Occupations: radio executive, translator, author

After spending most of his writing career from 1955 to the early 1970s producing seven young adult adventure novels, Matti Kokkonen published three adult thriller-type crime novels with strong adventure content.

Crime Novels:

1970: *Ei taivahalla kuolon vaaraa* ("There Is a Danger of Death as Heavens Rage in Storms")
1971: *Tuonen tuutunen parempi* ("Tuonen … Better")
1974: *Kenen kynsi kylmeni* ("Who Put the Nail in the Freezer?")

Major Awards: N/A

Website: N/A

Wexi Korhonen

b. October 9, 1949; Residence: Tampere, Finland; Occupations: journalist, amateur skydiver, author

According to Wexi Korhonen's "Author Presentation" on the *Kirjasampo.fi* website, he never wanted to become a detective author. An avid amateur skydiver, he wrote his first two books, "Sky Divers: Killers in the Sky," 1984, about paratroopers, and "The Last Dive," 1989, about his favorite sport. Fifteen years later, he published the first of his seven crime novels featuring a scruffy alcoholic anti-hero named Kari Salo, who after getting himself fired from his police job became one of relatively few private investigators in Finnish crime fiction. Working in Tampere, he contemplates suicide after being diagnosed with cancer, but he pulls himself together, goes into remission, and, unscrupulous and computer-savvy, he earns a meager living by solving cases replete with Kerhonen's intimate knowledge of Tampere and its local color—bars, the city center, and its market.

Korhonen, said to be "Tampere's Ross McDonald," in 2009 compared his writing method to a scientist's research; he says he "collects data from which then eventually I edit the book," gleaning background information from forensics, weaponry, and telecommunications sources (quoted in Niemelä, "Wexi Korhonen"). In 2011, after a five-year hiatus, Kerhonen, a long-time admirer of Ernest Hemingway's African fiction, revived his detective Salo and sent him to Africa in a new novel, which Tampere critic Jari Niemelä found not a traditional detective story but an adventure tale with a mystery in the background (Niemela, "Wexi Korhonen").

Crime Novels:

Kari Salo Series:

1999: *Kiusaksi keuiskattu murha* ("To Annoy Whispered Murder")
2000: *Kuka peikää kuolemaa* ("Who Is Afraid of Death")
2001: *Pahempi kuin murha* ("Worse Than Murder")
2002: *Tunnustus tai kuolema* ("Confession or Death")
2003: *Perintönä murha* ("A Legacy of Murder")
2004: *Kuoleman kuva* ("The Death of the Image")
2006: *Murhakoodi* ("Murder Code")
2011: *Kujanjuoksu Keniassa* ("Alley Running in Kenya")

Major Awards: N/A

Website: N/A

*Leena Lehtolainen

b. March 11, 1964, Vesanta, Finland; Residence: Degerby, Finland; Occupations: literary researcher, columnist, literary critic, author

Leena Lehtolainen, Finland's bestselling female crime fiction author, published her first novel at twelve years old and as a teenager followed it with another novel in 1981. Prior to 1991 she earned a degree in literature from the University of Helsinki and studied vocal performance and music at two Finnish conservatories. A full-time author since 1993, she has become most popular for her Maria Kallio series, twelve novels to date, She has sold more than 2 million books and sold rights to twenty-nine countries. The novels have been adapted for MTV3 as the *Detective Maria Kallio* series. In addition to her second crime series, the Bodyguard Trilogy, which also features a tough female protagonist, Lehtolainen has written mainstream stand-alone literary novels, most recently *Kuusi kohtausta Sadusta* ("A Life in Six Scenes"), 2014. With Kaisa Viitanen, editor-in-chief of Finland's professional figure skating journal, Lehtolainen co-authored *Taitoluistelun lumo* ("The Enchantment of Figure Skating"), voted 2010 Sports Book of the Year in Finland.

In a 2011 self-interview for *Sea Minor*, Leena Lehtolainen, herself a voracious and wide-ranging reader, declared she would create her stories even if no one would publish them, because they serve as both her entertainment and her therapy ("Dancing with Myself"). She draws the atmosphere of her novels from their settings, while her events and characters, whose names are often symbolic, are almost always the products of her imagination, especially her most famous character Maria Kallio, a "purely imaginary" figure who Lehtolainen says has been living in her mind for two decades ("Dancing with Myself"). Maria has been sharing Lehtolainen's own taste in music, whisky, and men ("Leena Lehtolainen"), ever since Lehtolainen was researching the work of earlier female Finnish crime author Eeva Tehunen and realized how few women had written in the male-dominated Finnish crime fiction genre. According to Lehtolainen, "Maria knows how to fix cars and shoot, but I'm a better cook than she is" ("Questions and Answers," on http://www.leenalehtolainen.fi/faq)

In *Ensimmäinen murhani*, 1993 (*My First Murder*, tr. 2012), 23-year-old Sergeant Maria Kallio of the Helsinki Police handles "the jealous grumbling among the boys" she works with by being "tough" and making "far and away the most callous wisecracks in the police cafeteria" after inspecting evidence like "the rotting, vomit-sodden, eviscerated corpse" of a wino who had drunk a mixture of water and sulfuric acid (*My First Murder* 8–9)."Real policewomen" have told Lehtolainen that they can see themselves in Maria Kallio, confirming Lehtolainen's intention of convincingly presenting a policewoman who can question suspects and make arrests, but who has to work within the law ("Dancing with Myself") and deal with often chauvinistic male attitudes toward women in their profession.

Lehtolainen especially likes the clear structure of crime novels: a crime happens, and it has to be solved. She says an author can build almost anything into that framework. In a 2004 interview, Lehtolainen commented, "It [the detective story] can be full of joy and pain, of suspense and atmosphere, it can annoy readers and even reduce them to tears. Whenever any boundaries are set, I try to push them back through my writing" ("Leena Lehtolainen"). Through her series, Kallio rises from an entry-level police position to a high administrative post, but she "never hesitates to get involved in the nitty-gritty" ("Finnish Mystery Series"). Besides pushing the traditional boundaries that had kept Finnish women out of police work, throughout her series Maria Kallio unconventionally and mostly successfully balances the demands of her work and her personal needs and duties as lover, wife, and mother, making the series as a whole a "growing-up story" seen through "a new kind of protagonist" in the Finnish detective story tradition ("Leena Lehtolainen"), one who never falls victim to the fatigue and depression that afflict many of her fictional male counterparts.

"Kallio," literally "the rock," the pen name of an early 19th century Finnish nationalist poet, also suggests that Maria Kallio represents the indomitable spirit of Finnish women as she addresses modern social problems: child abuse and domestic violence, prostitution, gender equality, alcoholism, drugs, business and industrial-business corruption and environmental crimes. From the beginning, Maria never gives up easily, either in her work or her personal relationships (*Her Enemy* 105); for example, in *Her Enemy* Maria faces down an older and respected male gynecologist who jeers that Maria "has the calves of a feminist." In that episode she thus earns an accolade from her new boss, who "can't stand women who knuckle under" (*Her Enemy* 16). To illustrate the plight of women who do give in to economic and social pressures, even criminal ones, in *Rivo Satakieli* ("The Dirty Nightingale"). 2005, Lehtolainen uses both the motif of the professional Russian killer as "agent of death" and the motif of the exploited and denigrated Russian woman in a subplot about Russian human trafficking and exploitation of young former Soviet-bloc women, which Lehtolainen also specifically addresses in *Veren vimma* ("Rage"), 2003, making these crimes integral to her realistic police procedurals (Arvas, *Scandinavian Crime Fiction* 122).

Lehtolainen deliberately made her other series heroine Hilja Ilveskero, protagonist of Lehtolainen's Bodyguard Trilogy, very different from Maria Kallio. Often brooding over her tragic past (her father killed her mother when Hilja was four), Hilja is a politically incorrect danger junkie, as instinctively lethal as her favorite animal, the lynx.

Paula Arvas, who writes extensively on contemporary Finnish crime fiction, sees Lehtolainen's crime novels as combining elements of the police procedural, the classical puzzle mystery, and "hard-boiled feminist crime fiction." Arvas also finds it surprising that Lehtolainen "remains alone as a writer of this subgenre [feminist crime fiction] today, even though her books are very popular in Finland" (Arvas, "Contemporary Finnish Crime Fiction" 5).

Crime Novels:

Maria Kallio Series:

1993: *Ensimmäinen murhani* (*My First Murder*, tr. Owen F. Witesman, 2012)
1994: *Harmin paikka* (*Her Enemy*, tr. Owen F. Witesman, 2012)
1995: *Kurarisydän* ("Copper Heart")
1996: *Luminainen* (*Snow Woman*, tr. Owen F. Witesman, 2014)
1997: *Kuolemanspiraali* ("Death Spiral")
1998: *Tuulen puolella* (Unwind")
2000: *Ennen lähtöä* ("Before I Go")
2003: *Veren vimma* ("Rage")
2005: *Rivo Satakieli* ("The Dirty Nightingale")
2008: *Väärän jäljillä* ("On the Wrong Track")
2010: *Minne tytöt kadonneet* ("Where Have All the Young Girls Gone")
2013: *Rautakolmio* ("The Iron Triangle")

The Bodyguard Trilogy:

2009: *Henkivartija* (*The Bodyguard*, tr. Jenni Salmi, 2014)
2011: *Oikeuden jalopeura* ("The Lion of Justice")
2012: *Paholaisen pennut* ("The Devil's Cubs)

Major Awards:

1997: The Clew of the Year Award, for *Luminainen* ("Snow Woman")
1998: The Clew of the Year Award, for *Kuolemanspiraali* ("Death Spiral")

Websites: http://www.leena-lehtolainen.de; http://www.leenalehtolainen.net

Marko Leino

b. September 8, 1967, Helsinki, Finland; Residence: Helsinki, Finland; Occupations: screenwriter, author

Marko Leino, a highly regarded Finnish screenwriter whose movie *Miracle of a Winter Night*, 2007, remains the largest Finnish box office hit of all time, is also a versatile and prolific author of children's mysteries, short stories, plays, novels, poetry, and a highly regarded thriller trilogy.

In "My Life as a Crime Fiction Author," a statement prepared for his literary agency, Leino attributed his reluctance to make public appearances to his desire that his books speak for themselves because he feels "publicity can be a prison." His crime trilogy dwells "primarily on our darkest secrets," hinted at through their titles: *Epäilys* ("Suspicion"), 2004; *Ansa* ("Trap"), 2009; and *Saasta* ("Filth"), 2013. Leino found writing them draining. Dealing with that "merciless and pitch black landscape" forced him, he said, to address other projects between each installment of the trilogy "to maintain my own sanity" ("My Life").

According to its 2010 Clew of the Year citation, "Trap," which was nominated for the Glass Key Award, employs fast cinematic cuts between scenes and uses the form of a traditional tragedy, set in a world of double-dealing drug trafficking Eastern European, Baltic, and Finnish gangsters. It features Detective Inspector Juka Viitasalo, who has sent drug trafficker Reino Sundström to prison where Sundström continues to direct his criminal operations. Sundström holds secret information over Viitasalo, whose finances are in ruins and whose wife is unemployed and suffering from postpartum depression, so that disaster increasingly looms for the policeman, who finds the line of demarcation between good and evil becoming increasingly indistinct: "The characters' choices are weighed up by the standards of the underworld" (quoted in Leino's "My Life as a Crime Writer"). Upon the 2014 publication of "Trap" in its Danish translation, Marko Leino was hailed as presenting a new generation of Finnish crime writers dealing with their contemporary society (see http://www.litteratursiden.dk).

Crime Trilogy:

2004: *Epäilys* ("Suspicion")
2009: *Ansa* ("Trap")
2013: *Saasta* ("Filth")

Major Awards:

2010: The Clew of the Year Award, for *Ansa* ("Trap")

Website: N/A

Glory Leppänen

b. November 28, 1901, Paris, France; d. October 26, 1979, Helsinki, Finland; Residence: From 1949, Helsinki, Finland; Occupations: actress, theater and film director, author

After an impressive career in theater and film as both actress and director, Glory Leppänen, the first Finnish woman to direct a film, wrote murder mysteries and became "the leading figure" of female Finnish crime writing in the 1960s. According to Veikko Lindroos, Leppänen's narrative style was "dazzlingly dramatic," revealing glimpses of the lives of the rich and famous. "Hate, greed, envy, revenge, and passion lurk in the midst of glamour and success" (Lindroos).

Crime Novels:

1963: *Punainen Fiat BA 777* ("Red Fiat 777 BA")
1964: *Kärpät saalistavat* ("Weasels' Prey")
1966: *Eski on kuollut* ("Eski Is Dead")
1967: *Pääosassa kuolema* ("Starring Death")

Major Awards: N/A

Website: N/A

Minna Lindgren (*Minna-Liisa Gabriela Lindgren*)

b. January 22, 1963, Helsinki, Finland; Residence: Helsinki, Finland; Occupations: musicologist, journalist, author

Minna Lindgren worked as a journalist, editor, producer, and manager for YLE, the Finnish Broadcasting Company, from 1986 until 2008, when she became a full-time freelance writer. She received the 2009 Bonnier Prize in journalism for her widely praised article "Death of a Father," subsequently dramatized as a Finnish Television documentary. It explored end-of-life issues connected with the death of her father Kaj Lindgren, whose wishes to pass away peacefully without extreme medical intervention conflicted with nursing home and hospital bureaucratic policies.

Minna Lindgren incorporated her experiences of eldercare into her trilogy of cozy mysteries set in a retirement home aptly called "Twilight Grove," with well-to-do nonagenarians Siiri and Irma sleuthing out nefarious events in their assisted-living facility. The second novel of the trilogy, *Ehtoolehdon pakolaiset* ("Escape from Twilight Grove"), 2014, scored fifth on Finnish bestseller lists and was nominated for the 2015 Runeberg Literature Prize. Pan Macmillan will be bringing out English editions of the trilogy beginning in 2016 with "Death in Twilight Grove," with a bow to Alexander McCall Smith's popular Botswana series by titling Lindgren's series "The Lavender Ladies Detective Agency" and also describing its protagonists Siiri and Irma as "the Finnish Miss Marple[s]." Pan Macmillan's Natasha Harding observes, "The central characters are both funny and endearing and they make for an interesting detective duo" (quoted in "Pan Macmillan").

Crime Novels:

The Twilight Grove Trilogy; also called The Lavender Ladies Detective Agency Series:

2013: *Kuolema Ehtoolehdossa* ("Death in Twilight Grove")
2014: *Ehtooiehdon pakolaiset* ("Escape from Twilight Grove")
2015: *Ehtoolehdon tuho* ("The End of Twilight Grove")

Major Awards:

2009: The Bonnier Prize (for journalism)
2014: Signature Award of the Aleksis Kivi Society

Website: http://www.ahlbackagency.com/aba_authors/lindgren-minna

Tuomas Lius

b. May 8, 1976, Joensuu, Finland; Residence: Rural north Karelia; Occupation: journalist, cartoonist, author

According to James Thompson in an endnote for *Helsinki Noir*, Tuomas Lius began his publishing career at nine years old, with short detective stories published in a provincial paper. He has since gone on to produce crime novels that have received "both critical and commercial success with [a] unique blend of suspense, action, and pitch-black humor" (Thompson, *Helsinki Noir*). Lius' Detective Agency trilogy, set mostly in North Karelia, features police sergeant Julia Noussairen, who solves crimes with an amateur sleuth, Marko Pippurisen. In 2012, *What's Up Finland* reported that Lius and film director Markku Pölönen were preparing a script for a three-part adventure movie based on the mythology of the *Kalevala*, wrapping myths and historical events into contemporary events (Benedek).

Selected Crime Novels:

Detective Agency Trilogy:

2009: *Haka* ("Haka")
2010: *Laittomat* ("Illegal")
2011: *Härkäjuoksu* ("Taurus Running")

Major Awards: N/A

Website: N/A

Reijo Mäki

b. October 12, 1958, Siikainen, Finland; Residence: Turku, Finland; Occupations: banker author

Each year after his crime fiction debut in 1985, Reijo Mäki, one of Finland's most popular crime authors, has produced a slightly parodic thriller starring Jussi Vares, a hard-boiled, hard-drinking, love 'em and leave 'em, people-hating, frequently beaten-up private investigator addicted to questionable one-liners. Vares lives and works in Mäki's home town of Turku, where the author has become a local celebrity, often seen frequenting his favorite Turku bar, Apteekki (*Thrilling Detective* website) . Mäki's fiction generally doesn't address "the large sociological and political questions, not to mention questions regarding gender and minorities, that characterize most of Scandinavian crime fiction" (Nummelin), but though critically dismissed as chauvinistic, sexist, racist, and promoting drunkenness, the Vares novels have sold almost two million copies in Finland alone. Several have been made into popular films; *Vares—Private Investigator*, adapted from Mäki's 1999 novel *Keltainen leski* ("Yellow Widow"), became Finland's most watched movie of 2004, and seven more Vares films followed. Television and DVD versions aired as *Vares—Private Eye* in the 2011 and 2012 seasons. When questioned about the financing for these films, Mäki satirically "revealed" that Solar Films had "outsourced" the financial backing for the Vares films: "the capital required would probably have left even St. Petersburg's shady circle out of pocket," so "other participants included the Sicilian Cosa Nostra and some very helpful gentlemen from Naples and 'Ndrangheta…. The Medellin family would have liked to join in,' but they demanded 'powdery placement'" so the whole thing, Mäki said, had to be called off (quoted in Yü-Juonikas).

Since 2008, stage versions of several Vares novels have also appeared, with wide general appeal. Maki has also written ten non–Vares thrillers, one, *Kruunun vasikka* ("The Crown's Calf"), 1994, featuring Sakari Roivas, an undercover cop with the Swedish police.

Mäki's style, as shown in his tongue-in-cheek description of the Vares film financing scheme, has been described as "Henning Mankell meets Hasse Alfredsson" ("Reijo Mäki," Bazar Publishing). Alfredsson, born in 1931, was a Swedish film director and comedian often called a humorous humanist known for his ability to extemporize wildly absurd comic situations.

Mäki grew up on a farm near a small village with only one road and has become wealthy from his writing, which has negatively impacted his lifestyle. Since to gather background material for his hard-hitting books, Mäki often met with hard core criminals, some imprisoned, who wanted to tell their stories, he occasionally gets not only letters and postcards from inmates, but starting about ten years ago, he began to receive death threats as well. Mäki says he has not let the threats affect his writing or behavior, claiming he has not built a panic room, but he does have a permit to carry a gun and installed a security system in his home. Religious groups have also assured him that if he does not accept Jesus in his heart "He will burn in the fire of hell" (Jauhiainen).

Criticism fails to bother Mäki, who thinks of himself as "an old man of the people's pulps." He doesn't care for e books, but for practical reasons, twenty of his Vares novels appear in that format (Törmänen). Mäki brushed off the negative review from *Helsingen Sanomat*, the capital's largest newspaper, which negatively discussed his 2012 Clew of the Year Award for *Sheriffi* ("The Sheriff"), observing that such opinions could not affect him in the "sunset colors " of his career, adding coolly, "My audience is able to deal with such criticism" (quoted in Gustafsson).

Selected Crime Novels:

Jussi Vares Series:

1986: *Moukanpeli* ("Moukanpeli")
1987: *Satakieli lauloi yöllä* ("The Nightingale Sang at Night")
1989: *Marraskuu on musta hauta* ("Garter Snake")
1990: *Jäätynyt enkeli* ("Dead Angel")
1995: *Enkelit kanssasi* ("Angels with You")
1999: *Keltainen leski* ("Yellow Widow")
2002: *Tukholman keikka* ("The Stockholm Case")
2009: *Valkovenäläinen* ("White Russian")
2012: *Sheriffi* ("The Sheriff")
2013: *Intiaani* ("Indian")

Selected Other Books:

2003: *Jussi Vareksen drinkkiopas* ("The Jussi Vares Drink Guide")
2009: *Vares Turku* ("Jussi Vares' Turku")

Major Awards:

1996: Great Finnish Book Club Award
2013: The Clew of the Year Award, for *Sheriffi* ("The Sheriff")

Website: N/A

Max Manner

b. September 2, 1965, Turku, Finland; Residence: Luxembourg; Occupations: businessman, author

Finnish author Max Manner, who has lived in Luxembourg for more than a decade, names Henning Mankell's *The Dogs of Riga* as the novel which impelled him to write his own traditional thrillers. One of very few male Finnish crime authors who use female protagonists, Manner featured Superintendent Anna Mäki of the Turku police in his first two novels, and next created a trilogy starring Annika Malm, a Finnish-born Chinese woman who is a member of Stockholm's narcotics police unit. In 2012, Manner opened a new series with *Vapautttaja* ("Liberator"), 2012, and a male protagonist, Sten Storensensitä, a Norwegian police sergeant, including Anna Mäki in a plot involving criminal gambling operations and women's issues. Storensen (the Norwegian spelling of the name) settles in Turku for his 2013 case, *Räsynukke* ("Rag Doll," which combines a police investigation with Storensen's problematic relationship with his daughter Nina and his own midlife crisis over the old philosophical conundrum of the existence of evil). Still in Turku for *Banditti* ("Bandits"), in 2014, Storensen, again backed up by Anna Mäki, infiltrates a gang of Spanish mobsters trying to establish their criminal operations in Finland.

Crime Novels:

Superintendent Anna Mäki Series:

2007: *Revanssi* ("Revenge")
2008: *Demi-sec* ("Demi-Sec")

Annika Malm Series:

2009: *K18* ("K18")
2010: *72 h* ("72 Hours")
2011: *13. huone* ("Room 13")

Stein Storensen Series:

2012: *Vapauttaja* ("Liberator")
2013: *Räsynukke* ("Rag Doll")
2014: *Banditti* ("Bandits")

Major Awards: N/A

Website: http://www.maxmanner.com

"Sulevi Manner" (pseudonym of *Juha Numminen and Eero J. Tika*)

Journalist and crime author Juha Numminen (see below) and screenwriter Eero J. Tikka co-authored four detective novels, after which Numminen wrote crime fiction alone.

Crime Novels:

1983: *Isä, mitä tapahtui?* ("Dad, What Happened?")
1984: *Ristilukki* ("Cross Spider")
1985: *Susi* ("Wolf")
1986: *Tervetuloa tuomiolle* ("Welcome to the Judgment")

Major Awards:

1987: The Clew of the Year Award, for *Susi* ("Wolf")

Jorma Napola

b. February 4, 1914, Helsinki, Finland; d. April 25, 2000, Espoo, Finland; Residence: Espoo, Finland; Occupations: artist, sculptor, author

Fewer than a dozen private eyes prowl Finland's fictional mean streets. *Thrilling Detective* theorizes that the private eye is "a product of a culture that believes heavily in individualization and the right to take the law into one's hands if necessary. But Finland is ... a culture that relies on authority and on letting someone else take care of things" ("Jaakko Piira"). One outstanding exception in Finnish crime literature is Jorma Napola's protagonist Jaakko Piira, apparently a close relative of Philip Marlowe, a fatigued, disillusioned, depressed, and near-alcoholic rundown wisecracking Helsinki investigator who's hired by a mysterious woman in his first case and becomes entangled in deceit, blackmail, and multiple murders.

Ruuvikierre ("The Turn of the Screw"), 1962, Napola's second detective novel, beat 129 other detective novels for the 1962 Best Detective Novel competition sponsored by WSOY, a Helsinki publishing house founded in 1878. Napola also entered his first crime novel, *Ministeri on murhattu* ("The Minister Has Murdered"). That novel, a traditional domestic mystery plot lacking the saving grace of humor, won second place in the same competition. The protagonists of both novels recall the bleaker aspects of Georges Simenon's Inspector Maigret. Napola, who was a painter and sculptor, fell into depression after winning the WSOY prizes; his first place award. a million Finnish marks, ironically brought him the loss of his literary creativity (Arvas, "Best Murder Rewarded").

Crime Novels:

   1962: *Ruuvikierre* ("Turn of the Screw")
   1981: *Ministeri on murhattu* ("The Minister Has Murdered")

Major Awards:

   1962: WSOY Big Detective Novel Competition, for *Ruuvikierre* ("The Turn of the Screw")
   1981: WSOY Detective Story Competition, for *Ministeri on murhattu* ("The Minister Has Murdered")

Website: N/A

Juha Numminen

b. September 10, 1938; Residences: Rauma and Helsinki, Finland; Occupations: journalist, author

After co-authoring four crime novels with screenwriter Eero J. Tikan, respected journalist Juha Numminen walked the fictional mean streets by himself and became one of the big names in Finnish suspense fiction (*Ruumiin kelttuuri* 3/2007). Numminen also co-founded the Finnish-English Literary Translation Cooperative in 2012. Its purpose is to showcase the work of leading translators from Finnish to English and to introduce Anglophone readers to significant emerging and established Finnish literary voices (see http://feltcooperative.org).

In a 2011 statement for *Crime Time*, Numminen declared that writing his fast-paced action-filled novels has become an ambivalent obsession for him, "a pleasure and reward,": but also "an invisible cage" controlling his life. Numminen's fiction is highly realistic, addressing the themes of the exercise of power in Finnish society, the scientific aspects of crime solving, and the role of the media vis-à-vis police procedures. He deplores the current sensationalist media: "You can write about anything.... But what is the effect on people? When all public morals and any feeling of shame are forgotten, the lurid headlines brutalize us. We lose respect, we condemn a public person without a trial" (quoted in *Ruumiin kelttuuri* 3/2007).

Selected Crime Novels:

1987: *Viimeiseen pisaraan* ("The Last Drop")
1990: *Sininen rotta* ("Blue Rat")
1995: *Se huutaa joka pelkää* ("It Screams to Fear")
2004: *Täydessä ymmärryksessä* ("In Full Agreement")
2008: *Kyyhkynen* ("Dove")
2013: *Arvokas elämä* ("Valuable Life")

Major Awards: N/A (see above, "Sulevi Manner")

Website: N/A

Eppu Nuotio

> b. February 13, 1962, Iisalmi, Finland; Residences: Hiittinen (an island in the southwestern Finnish archipelago), Finland; later Berlin, Germany; Occupations: actress, translator, lyricist, stage and film director, author

Multi-talented Eppu Nuotio has produced five crime novels featuring an unusual protagonist, Pii Marin, the fictional first black African television news anchor in Finland. Feeling she is an outsider in Finnish society, Marin quits her television job and moves to a small town in Finland, where she becomes involved in the gruesome crimes of her novel series. Nuotio probably drew elements of Marin's personality from experiences Nuotio had as a UNICEF Goodwill Ambassador, visiting Africa for the first time in 2008. Besides solving crimes, Marin attempts to sort out her own identity as well as the events of her father's life. Nuotio's crime fiction has been compared to the works of Finland's Leena Lehtolainen and Sweden's Liza Marklund.

In 2011 Nuotio ended the Pii Marin series with *Loppu* ("The Last") and turned to other endeavors. *Musta* ("The Black"), 2006, first of the series, has recently been made into a feature film. Nuotio has also written over twenty children's books, translated stage plays into Finnish from English and Swedish, and between 2003 and 2005 published a mainstream novel trilogy about the life of a Finnish woman born on the day of Marilyn Monroe's death.

Crime Novels:

Pii Marin Series:

2006: *Musta* ("The Black")
2007: *Kosto* ("Revenge")
2008: *Maksu* ("Payment")
2009: *Varjo* ("Shadow")
2010: *Paine* ("Pressure")
2011: *Loppu* ("The Last")

Major Awards: N/A

Website: http://www.eppunuotio.com

*Harri Nykänen

b. June 20, 1953, Helsinki, Finland; Residence: Helsinki, Finland; Occupations: journalist, author

Harri Nykänen is one of Finland's most prolific crime authors. For 22 years he covered real life crime stories for *Helsingen Sanomat*, and in 2001 he turned to full time writing, both crime fiction and true crime books. Nykänen has produced four crime fiction series, plus several stand-alone novels, true crime studies, and many articles. His *Raid* series, his most popular work, was adapted as a twelve-part Finnish television series also aired in a few U.S. markets, and a *Raid* feature film was shown throughout Finland. Nykänen's *Raid* novels are being published in English by Ice Cold Crime of Minneapolis–St. Paul, USA. With Jouni Tervo, Nykänen heads Pulitzer, Ltd., a Finnish publishing company.

In the *Raid* novels, Nykänen fictionalizes his intimate knowledge of the Helsinki underworld through the eyes of his unusual protagonist Raid, a taciturn young hit man with a heart. In *Raid ja mustempi lammas* (*Raid and the Blackest Sheep*), 2000, the first *Raid* novel to appear in English, Raid is accompanying Nygren, an elderly ex-con who is hunting down those who bilked him out of ill-gotten gains before he was sent to prison. As they travel across Finland, Raid uses increasingly ruthless methods to restore Nygren's lost money, while between "jobs" Nygren tells Raid stories about his checkered past. Overweight, middle-aged Helsinki detective Janssen tracks this odd couple, bent on discovering why his workaholic superior Kempas is so determined to find Nygren guilty again. Maxine Clarke found this novel "an unusual mix of themes—police procedural, epic journey, "mysterious hard man," and ironic humor "that allows readers to appreciate the [Finnish] national sport of cracking jokes at the expense of the Swedes" (Clarke, "Book Review: Raid and the Blackest Sheep by Harri Nykänen").

In *Raid ja poika*, 2003 (*Raid and the Kid*, tr. 2011), the mysterious Raid is holed up in the farm house he inherited from Nygren, when a local boy arrives with two Bolivian drug traffickers hot on his heels. Raid kills them to save the boy but becomes the target of the Bolivians' bosses, while back in Helsinki, Detective Jannsen and his team are closing in on the Bolivian cartel. Here as he does throughout the series, Nykänen uses understated narrative and quiet humor to illustrate his combination of the police procedural and hard-boiled conventions. Raid is a new kind of crime novel protagonist; as a quasi-retired underworld figure who left Finland and returned hoping to detach himself from his former underworld associates with whom he still has economic and social ties, Raid represents a new fictional breed of "entrepreneurial investigators," experts at their work and how to market it, but the bone-weariness from his previous jobs "gives credibility to his moral stance." His alter ego Janssen, struggling to carry out his work despite crippling budget cuts, also uncovers governmental corruption. In this startling reversal, "The moral code shared by Raid and Janssen, not the symbolic function of the state or the police, offers reassurance" (Nestigen, "Unnecessary Officers" 175–176).

Nykänen created an altogether different protagonist in Ariel Kafka of the Helsinki Violent Crimes Unit, one of just two Jewish policemen in Finland. *Ariel*, 2004 (*Nights of Awe*, tr. 2012), Kafka's first case, involves two murdered Arabs and the official visit to Finland of a high Israeli governmental official. Nykänen, not Jewish (though he says some of his ancestors came from near the Russian border), told the *Times of Israel* he was interested in "the conflicts of everyday life and the traditions of the Jewish religion" (quoted in Burstein). He knew a Jewish policeman in Finland whom he used as a resource, and he researched Jewish history and culture, especially praising Finland's relationship with Israel and the contributions of the small but active Jewish community in Finland. Nykänen's Ariel Kafka series frequently refers to Finnish neo–Nazis and skinheads, but unlike other Scandinavian novelists, Nykänen doesn't see such groups as particularly dangerous. "It's strange, but neo–Nazis don't think that Jews are the enemy. They think that Finnish Jews are Finnish citizens. They fight instead against Arab immigrants, black people and all Muslims, except for the Finnish Tatars [who have lived for 150 years in Finland]" (quoted in Burstein).

Ariel Kafka, a tough, experienced Helsinki cop who is also a Jew, cannot forget "Auschwitz and Treblinka," but he also knows that the Holocaust's aftermath, "an incomprehensible amount of agony, rage and fear" sometimes makes anti–Semitism "detected where it doesn't exist" (*Nights of Awe* 235). Kafka's first case involves equally villainous Arab terrorists and drug traffickers and the Israeli Mossad between Yom Kippur, the Jewish Day of Atonement, and Rosh Hashanah, the beginning of the new year, forcing Kafka to confront not only the crimes he 's investigating but his own sins. Nykänen sums up this unusual character by admitting Ariel is always a little bit of an outsider and a little bit of a melancholic character, "Like Finnish men often are" (quoted in Frazer).

The second Ariel Kafka novel to be published in English, *Jumalan selän takana*, 2009 (*Beyond God's Back*, tr. 2014), has the detective investigating the murder of a Jewish businessman whose daughter Kafka had once dated. The complicated plot also involves business dealings engineered by Kafka's brother Eli's law firm and the Kafkas' second cousin, with entanglements leading to the Russian mafia. "The sympathetic Kafka manages to perform a delicate balancing act" as he resolves this touchy familial and Jewish-community crime (Review of *Behind God's Back*).

Crime Novels:

The Raid Series:

1992: *Raid* ("Raid")
1994: *Raid ja paperiansa* ("Raid and His Paper")
1997: *Raid ja lihava mies* ("Raid and the Fat Man")
2000: *Raid ja mustempi lammas* (*Raid and the Blackest Sheep*, tr. Peter Ylitalo Leppa, 2010)
2001: *Raid ja pelkääjät* ("Raid and the Shotgun")
2002: *Raid ja legioonalainen* ("Raid and a Legionary")
2003: *Raid ja poika* (*Raid and the Kid*, tr. Peter Ylitalo Leppa, 2011)
2006: *Raid ja tappajat* ("Raid and the Killers")
2010: *Paha paha tyttö* ("Bad Bad Girl")
2012: *Susiraja* ("The Wolf Limit")

The Inspector Ariel Kafka Series:

2004: *Ariel* (*Nights of Awe*, tr. Kristian London, 2012)
2005: *Ariel ja hämähäkkinainen* ("Ariel and the Spider")
2009: *Jumalan selän takana* (*Behind God's Back*, tr. Kristian London, 2014)
2011: *Pyhä toimitus* ("Holy Delivery")
2013: *Leijonakuningas: komisario Ariel Kafkan tutkimuksia* ("The Lion King: Inspector Ariel Kafka Studies")

The Johnny & Bantzo Series:

2005: *Johnny & Bantzo* ("Johnny & Bantzo")
2008: *Johnny & Bantzo osa 2: Operaatio Banana Split* ("Johnny & Bantzo 2: Operation Banana Split")
2009: *Johnny & Bantzo osa 3: Viimeinen hippi* ("Johnny & Bontzo 3: The Last Part of the Hippie")
2011: *Pamalaton jumaus* (tr. N/A)

The Arctic Noir Series:

2014: *Mullasta maan* ("The Soil")

Major Awards:

1990: The Clew of the Year Award, for *Paha paimen* ("Back Devil")
2001: The Clew of the Year Award, for *Raid ja mustempi lammas* ("Raid and the Blacker Sheep")

Website: N/A

Outi Pakkanen

> b. January 27, 1946, Kokkola, Finland; Residence: Helsinki, Finland; Occupations: marketing and advertising, editor, author

Although Helsinki author Outi Pakkanen's first novel featured Inspector Antti Viitala investigating a strangling related to Helsinki's advertising world with the assistance of ad woman Katja Kivinen, Pakkanen decided she did not know enough about police operations to write procedurals, so she then produced over twenty traditional "cozy" detective novels, often opening with a murder at an upper-middle-class gathering like a family reunion and set in Helsinki's luxurious venues and the advertising and art worlds in which she grew up and lives (Arvas, "Contemporary Finnish Fiction" 6). Pakkanen also says she admires the detective fiction of Maria Lang, Georges Simenon, Hanning Mankell, and Patricia Cornwell ("Outi Pakkanen").

Pakkanen's best known series stars graphic designer Anna Laine, who like the popular American fictional amateur sleuth Jessica Fletcher of *Murder She Wrote* solves murders as an inquisitive amateur. Anna is a tall, model-slim woman who always wears black, devotes herself to gourmet cooking, and lives with a fat elderly dachshund named Justus. A few of her books contain gourmet recipe sections. Several Anna Laine novels have been adapted for a popular TV2 series premiering in 1989 and set not in Helsinki but Tampere. Pekkanen also has written numerous other traditional mysteries, biographies of prominent Finns Emmi Jurkasta and Aino Acktésta, as well as *Porosta parmesaaniin* ("Reindeer Parmesan: The Anna Laine Cookbook"), 2003. Pakkanen was editor in-chief of *New Books* from 1987 to 2004 and belongs to the Finnish Crime Time Cooperative.

Crime Novels:

Anna Laine Series:

1994: *Rakkaudesta kuolemaan* ("The Love of Death")
1999: *Macbeth on kuollut* ("Macbeth Is Dead")
2001: *Pelistä pois* ("Out of the Game")
2004: *Yön yli* ("Overnight")
2005: *Hinnalla millä hyvänsä* ("At Any Price")
2007: *Talvimies* ("Winter Man")
2010: *Seuralainen* ("Companion")
2012: *Toinen kerros* ("Second Floor")
2013: *Rakastaja* ("Lover")

Selected Crime Novels:

1973: *Murhan jälkeen mainoskatko* ("After the Murder of a Commercial Break")
1990: *Kissa kuussa* ("Cat of the Month")
2004: *Punainen pallotuoli* ("The Red Ball Chair")

2012: *Julma kuu* ("Second Floor")
2014: *Marius* ("Marius")

Major Awards:

2014: The Whodunnit Club Special Award, for her long-time work in the Finnish detective story genre

Website: http://www.outipakkanen.com

Ilkka Remes (Petri Pykälŏ)

> b. December 13, 1962, Luumäki, Finland; Residences: Porvoo, Finland, and Hastings, England; Occupations: teacher, businessman, author

The publicity-shunning author who writes as "Ilkka Remes" is Finland's best-selling crime author, selling over a million books by 2006. Currently with fifteen adult thrillers and eight young people's books in print, he also is the "Great Unknown" of Finnish crime literature. Little is known about his personal life, beyond the observation of his WSOY publisher Leena Majander that he is extremely cooperative and pleasant, with a keen sense of humor, though he does not want to be identified or featured as a person (Rytkonen).

Since 1997, Remes has been producing one high-octane thriller a year set in an international venue, works comparable to the novels of Tom Clancy and Ken Follett. A few of Remes' characters repeat their appearances in his fiction, primarily Antii Keopi, a policeman assigned to anti-terrorism; a female police psychologist, Johanna Vahtera; and a narcotics officer, Riku Tanner. Remes' young adult novels recount the adventures of Aaro Korpi, Antti Korpi's son. The prevailing theory about Remes' desire to avoid publicity suggests that he may wish to write future books in other genres.

Remes' narrative technique combines meticulous attention to detail with breathless action. Early in his writing career, Remes revealed that crime is not an absolute value to him, it just happens to fuel the high drama of his stories (Rytkonen). His general topic is Finland, but he unflinchingly treats specific touchy international issues like environmentalism, immigration, chemical warfare, and weapons trafficking. His 2013 *Omertan liitto* ("Omerta Association") addresses the European Union as what Remes called in a blog "A world that's teeming with more covert operations, fraud, illegal searches and seizures, the struggle for power, corruption, mafia-type activity, unexplained deaths and intrigue than I had never been able to imagine" (from Remes' blog September 25, 2013, quoted in "Success[ful] Author).

In reviewing Remes' 2005 thriller *Nimessä ja veressä* ("In the Name and the Blood"), which treats religious fundamentalism, Pia Ingström found that his books reflect "polished anonymity," using plots teeming with super-powerful international secret agents and "competently researched local colour" and somewhat shallow characterizations, but considering Remes' high sales, she suggests, "who cares if his books don't exactly lead the field in psychological insight?" (Ingström).

Remes also sees Finland as politically and geographically a hub of intelligence gathering. His villains are almost always Russian killers to be overcome by Finnish heroes, since the "tense relationship" between Russian and Finland central to his books assumes Russia's nuclear and biological weaponry pose "an acute physical threat." He also depicts Russia as so "lawless" that illicit weapons-dealing can be easily accomplished there. When *Ruttokellot* ("The Bells of Plague") appeared in 2000, assuming Russian complicity in biological weapons trafficking, then Finnish Foreign Minister Erkki Tuomioja deplored in his blog what he termed Remes' attribution of "all

evil" to Russia and Russians. Remes countered by insisting that he was not intentionally denigrating Russia (Arvas 119). In his thrillers Remes does encourage Finns "to try to understand and
respect Russians, instead of fearing and hating them" (Arvas, "Contemporary Finnish Crime Fiction" 7).

Selected Thrillers:

1997: *Pääkallokehrääjä* ("The Death's Head Moth")
1998: *Karjalan lunnaat* ("The Ransom of Karelia")
2000: *Ruttokellot* ("The Bells of Plague")
2002: *Itäveri* ("Eastern Blood")
2005: *Nimessä ja veressä* ("In the Name and Blood")
2008: *Pyörre* ("Vortex")
2012: *Ylösnousemus* ("Resurrection")
2013: *Omertan liitto* ("Omerta Association")

Major Awards:

1997: *Kalevi Jäntti* Literature Award, for *Pääkallokehrääjä* ("The Death's Head Moth")
1999: The Clew of the Year Award, for *Karjalan lunnaat* ("Ransom of Karelia")
1999: The Olvi Foundation Literature Award, for *Karjalan lunnaat* ("Ransom of Karelia")

Website: http://www.ilkkaremes.com

Markku Ropponen

> b. February 12, 1955, Lappeenranta, Finland; Residence: Jyväskylä, Finland; Occupations: librarian,
> author

Veteran librarian Markku Ropponen published three anthologies of poetry in the 1980s,
then turned to detective fiction in 1990 with *Pronssijuhlat* ("Bronze Festival"), the first of seven
stand-alone crime novels he set in an unnamed small town resembling his own home town,
Jyväskyla. In 2002, he began a series featuring a western Lapland private investigator, aging whisky-
loving Otto Kuhala with his dog Hippu, stories which have brought him the title of "Finland's
Raymond Chandler." In writing his Kuhala novels, Ropponen eliminated some of the social criticism he had used in his earlier crime novels. Here his western Lapland setting could be compared
to Hollywood's Wild West (Novak and Puttonen). Ropponen's poetic gifts, praised in his citation
for the 1991 Clew of the Year Award, animate his descriptions of Lapland countryside, while he
deplores the region's economic malaise seen in its frequent business bankruptcies, the decay of
traditional small town life, and the problems associated with immigrants flooding the town centers.
Several of Ropponen's novels have been adapted as radio plays. In 2012 he introduced a new
detective called "Pimento." Markku Ropponen is one of the co-founders of the Finnish Crime
Time Cooperative.

Selected Otto Kuhala Novels:

2002: *Puhelu kiusaajalta* ("Call Tempt Period")
2005: *Linnut vaikenevat* ("The Birds Are Silent")
2009: *Kuhala ja hautausmaan risteys* ("Kuhala and the Cemetery Intersection")
2012: *Kuhala & yöjuna* ("Kuhala & the Night Train")
2014: *Kuhala ja tuomitut* ("Kuhala and the Sentenced")
2015: *Kuhala ja vapaa pudotus* ("Kuhala and Free-Fall")

Selected Stand-Alone Crime Novels:

1990: *Pronssijuhlat* ("Bronze Festival")
1991: *Kuolemanuni* ("Kuolemanuni")
1993: *Paholaisen kiireet* ("The Devil's Worries")
2000: *Lavastus* ("Sets")
2012: *Pimento* ("Pimento")

Major Awards:

1991: The Clew of the Year Award, for *Kuolemanuni* ("Kuolemanuni")

Website: N/A

Matti Rönkä

b. September 9, 1959, Kuusjärvi, Karelia, Finland; Residence: Helsinki, Finland; Occupations: radio, magazine, and television journalist, news anchor for YLE Television 1, author

Matti Rönkä, known familiarly since 2003 as "the Voice of Finland," the anchor of YLE's *8:30 National Report*, began writing crime novels in 2002 and is the only Finn to have won the Glass Key Award. Considering Raymond Chandler the greatest detective story writer, Rönkä wanted to achieve "A combination of [the] Scandinavian social detective story with the American hard-boiled noir tradition, [with] a morally clear private character [who] solves crimes ... at least by working on problems and help[ing] those in need or abused" ("Matti Rönkä," *Crime Time Writers*). Rönkä grew up in northern Karelia, near the Russian border. He gave many of his experiences there to his protagonist Viktor Kärppä, whom he made what Finns call a "returning emigrant by grace of Koivisto, a former Soviet citizen of some Finnish ancestry ... granted Finnish citizenship after the collapse of the Soviet Union and the right to 'return' to a homeland where they had never lived and whose language they couldn't speak" (Ingström 2012). (Mauno Koivisto was Finland's president from 1982 to 1994.)

The Finnish-Russian border is one of the most dramatic "frontiers between prosperity and poverty in Europe," for long "a setting for undercover transactions" (Ingström 2012). Kärppä's father was a Finnish defector who moved to the USSR in the 1920s, and Kärppä himself was trained in the Red Army's special forces. The name "Kärppä" means "ermine," a slick little weasel who is fast and fluid (Arvas 123). On arriving in Finland. Kärppä, both an "outsider" because of his Russian background and an "insider" because of his name and his "pitch-perfect Finnish" (Arvas 123), begins to build a successful construction company for himself. He uses some shady connections involving unregistered workers and questionably-sourced building materials, but he refuses to engage in trafficking and abuse; Paula Arvas considers him a "middle man" Russian figure because while his Red Army training equipped him with "lethal skills" he refuses to use them, instead functioning symbolically as "a hybrid of Finnish and Russian culture and history" as he negotiates between the two nationalities. "Kärppä may recall the dilapidated condition of brutalist Leningrad housing estates, but he also remembers the cozy conviviality of sitting in such apartments with friends and relatives eating, drinking and talking" (Arvas 124).

Rönkä insists that as a novelist, "I'm not interested in taking pictures of evil and I do not indulge in violence" (quoted in "Matti Rönkä," *Crime Time Writers*). Because of his Karelian background, Kärppä knows many people, including Russians, who need help, and he also strikes up a grudging friendship with a Finnish policeman, Teppo Korhonen, giving Rönkä opportunities for exploring a convincing petty Helsinki underworld from an unusual dual perspective as Kärppä, almost Finnish but still part Russian, gradually adapts to Finnish society.

In June 2013, Rönkä, who believes that loneliness is the hardest part of writing, announced that *Levantin kyy* ("The Viper from Levante") would be his last Kärppä novel, declaring he had "just felt like crying" when he wrote its final scene (quoted in "Detective Series"). Rönkä believes a writer can tell different kinds of stories, and he has indicated he may turn to mainstream fiction (he admires the work of Annie Proulx and John Irving). A Swiss critic has called Rönkä's Viktor Kärppä "a great invention" and a German reviewer cited Rönkä's "fascinating characters from a part of the world we know all too little about." The 2007 Glass Key jury praised Ronka for possessing the writer's "most important tool," "A voice of his own.... The Soviet Union of the protagonist's youth, and the Finland and Russia of his present, provide an opportunity to observe society with a critical eye" (quoted from the Stilton Literary Agency's website, http://www.stilton. fi/authors).

Crime Novels:

The Viktor Kärppä Series:

2002: *Tappajan näköinen mies* ("A Man with a Killer's Face")
2003: *Hyvä veli, paha veli* ("Good Brother, Bad Brother")
2005: *Ystävät kaukana* ("Far Away Friends")
2008: *Isä, poika ja paha henki* ("The Father, the Son, and the Unholy Ghost")
2009: *Tuliaiset Moskovasta* ("Souvenir from Moscow")
2011: *Väärän maan vainaja* ("Dead in a Foreign Country")
2013: *Levantin kyy* ("The Viper from Levante")

Short Fiction Collection:

2007: *Mies rajan takaa* ("The Man from Beyond the Border")

Major Awards:

2006: The Clew of the Year Award, for *Ystävät kaukana* ("Far Away Friends")
2007: The Glass Key Award, for *Ystävät kaukana* ("Far Away Friends")
2008: The *Deutscher Krimi Preis* (Germany, third place, for *Tappajan näköinen mies* "A Man with a Killer's Face")

Website: N/A

Timo Sandberg

b. 1946, Lahti, Finland; Residence: Nastola, Finland; Occupations: forestry, metal working, artist, author

Since Timo Sandberg debuted as a published author in 1990 with the novel *Unta ei voi tunnustaa* ("Sleep Can Not Recognize"), he has produced fourteen adult novels, four young adult books, and several histories of metal workers' union branches. He has also co-authored one novel with Mari Sandberg Kaviopolkka, under the joint pen name "Mary Timonen."

Sandberg's protagonist Inspector Erkki Heittola faces a growing drug-related crime problems in *Kihokki* ("Sundew"), 2002; a threat to his own daughter through a satanic cult in the small town of Järvenpää in *Pahan morsian* ("Evil Bride"), 2006; and Russian agent-of-death villains in *Pöllön huuto* ("Owl's Cry"), 2007. Starting with *Pirunpesä* ("The Devil's Den"), 2009, Heittola's colleague and lover Female Sergeant Lord allows Sandberg to explore the role of women in a traditionally male workplace. Lord gradually takes a larger role in the investigation which deals with marginalized and troubled youths. In the next Heittola novels, Sandberg humanely treats the struggles of Finland's "little people," as they encounter societal changes which threaten their daily lives.

Sandberg's award-winning 2013 stand-alone historical crime novel *Mustamäki* ("Black Hill"), set in the turbulent 1920s, marks a substantial shift in his literary career, presenting a new hero, Detective Constable Otso Kekkiä, who probes cases involving villainous Russians in a Finland still divided by those who perpetuate bitter memories of Finland's civil war between Whites and Reds and its violent aftermath.

Stand-Alone Crime Novel:

2013: *Mustamäki* ("Black Hill")

Inspector Erkki Heittola Series:

2002: *Kihokki* ("Sundew")
2006: *Pahan morsian* ("Evil Bride")
2007: *Pöllön huuto* ("Owl's Cry")
2009: *Pirunpesä* ("The Devil's Den")
2010: *Dobermanni* ("Doberman Pinscher")
2011: *Kalmankokko* ("Kalmankokko")
2012: *Vainooja* ("The Persecutor")
2014: *Kärpäsvaara* ("Kärpäsvaara")

Major Awards:

2014: The Clew of the Year Award, for *Mustamäki* ("Black Hill")

Website: See http://www.saunalahti.fi/tsand/

Salla Simukka

> b. June 16, 1981. Tampere. Finland; Residence: Tampere, Finland; Occupations: literary critic, translator, author

Salla Simukka has created a Young Adult version of Lisbeth Salander in the seventeen-year-old heroine of her 2013–2014 Snow White Trilogy. Earlier the Topelius Prize jury described Simukka's major themes as an individual's struggle to be him- or herself against society's pressures to succeed and the tendency today of the virtual world to become too real. These themes also appear in the trilogy through Lumikki Andersson, a student at a school of performing arts, who in *Punainen kuin veri*, 2013 (*As Red as Blood,* tr. 2015), finds herself enmeshed in the international drug trade and pursued by Estonian and Russian criminals in the coldest Tampere winter in years. In *Valkea kuin lumi*, 2013 (*As White as Snow,* tr. 2015), Lumikki is backpacking in a sultry Prague summer when a girl who claims to be her half-sister persuades her to join a religious cult; Lumikki runs for her life when she learns the cult leaders are planning a mass suicide. Back in the Tampere performing arts school, Lumikki, chosen to lead the primary role in an updated version of the Snow White tale, is stalked by a dangerous secret admirer. Having learned how to defend herself and to trust no one, Lumikki prevails through all her trials.

Young Adult Crime Novels:

The Snow White Trilogy:

2013: *Punainen kuin veri* (*As Red as Blood*, tr. Owen Witesman, 2015)
2013: *Valkea kuin lumi* (*As White as Snow*, tr. Owen Witesman, 2015)
2014: *Musta kuin eebenpuu* (*As Black as Ebony*, tr. Owen Witesman, forthcoming)

Major Awards:

2013: The Topelius Prize, for Best Finnish Young Novel, for *Jäljellä* ("Without a Trace") and *Toisaalla* ("Elsewhere")
2013: The Finland Prize, for "a promising breakthrough"

Website: https://snowwhitetrilogy.wordpress

Jarkko Sipilä

b. 1964, Helsinki, Finland; Residence: Espoo, Finland; Occupations: Crime/legal journalist; author

Jarkko Sipilä told a *Finpop* interviewer in 2006 that he wrote *Koukku* ("Hook"), 1996, at the suggestion of his friend, crime writer Harri Nykänen, and to see if he, Sipilä, could write a book ("Interview: Jarkko Sipilä). Since the publication of *Kosketuslaukaus* ("Touch Shot"), 2001, the initial appearance of his series protagonist Detective Lieutenant Kari Takamäki of the Helsinki Police Violent Crimes Unit, Sipilä has produced a police procedural in his Helsinki Homicide series nearly every year. He has also written radio dramas, which he said helped him learn to create convincing dialogue. He works full time as the head of the Crime News Link of the nationwide Finnish Channel 3 News. He and his friend Jouni Molsa wrote the scripts for *Detectives Don't Sing*, a television series based on Sipilä's Helsinki Homicide novels, so popular that nearly a million Finns watched its 2006 premiere. From an idea Sipilä and his brother Jouko, then a Wall Street banker, first discussed in 2006, Jouko Sipilä left banking and founded Ice Cold Crime in 2009, a Minneapolis, Minnesota, publishing house dedicated to presenting Finnish crime fiction in English translation. Ice Cold Crime has published five of Jarkko Sipilä's crime novels in English to date.

Sipilä, who lived in Cleveland, Ohio, as a boy, makes his style "as realistic as possible." His police and his criminals appear equally unhappy in a "dark and cold" world—"like it really is" (quoted in "Interview: Jarkko Sipilä"). Writing at night and on weekends, he outlines his work first, then incorporates action into plots involving current issues he lists on his website: "racism, immigration, witness protection, and legality/morality of police activity" as well as the stresses under which dedicated policemen and women work. Sipilä says that Lieutenant Kari Takamäki, the central figure of Sipilä's fictional police crime team, differs from most Finnish police characters because he is "not a boozing wildcat, but the ultimate professional ... [and] a family man who strives to spend any extra time with his family," even though his job often makes it impossible (see http://www.jarkkosipila.com).

In "Thus Was Born Takamäki," a statement for *Crime Time*, Sipilä noted that around 2000, the main characters of foreign mystery novels were brilliant detectives with topical problems like drug abuse in the background. Sipilä said that though he had met many police officers in his journalistic work, he had never met a detective like that in real life, so he decided his policemen should be "real cops." In his first Helsinki Homicide novel, Takamäki is forty-something, and his family life is not particularly important. In the next books, Sipila added additional main characters:

Suhonen, an undercover policeman; Suhonen's ex-con friend Salmela; and crime reporter Rompotti. Anna Joutsama also appears, a thirty-something single woman police officer whom Takamäki often chooses to lead an investigation.

Sipilä told interviewer J.N. Duncan in 2014 that following real crime stories as a journalist had helped him make the Helsinki Homicide stories fiction that "could really happen" (quoted in Duncan). Sipilä also sees that the desire of policemen and women to get the "bad guys" behind bars makes them willing to do almost anything to achieve it. "This is a strength, but [it] also becomes a weakness at times" (quoted in Duncan). He also observes that Finnish crime fiction doesn't need excessively violent criminals or serial killers, because Finland hasn't had many of them; he says that Finnish fictional crimes are in a way "smaller," but he hopes that therefore "you get 'closer' to the reader" (quoted in Duncan). His own favorite crime fiction authors are Americans Ed McBain and John Grisham.

The five Helsinki Homicide novels currently available in English bring familiar crimes close to American readers, with Sipilä focusing on the crimes and the perpetrators rather than the home lives of the police team. . In *Seinää vasten*, 2008 (*Against the Wall*, tr. 2009), nominated for the Glass Key Award, Takamäki and Suhonen, who gets dangerously involved in his undercover role, tackle a gang-related homicide. In *Vengeance*, 2009, tr. 2010, a newly-released boss of the Skulls gang sets his sights on Suhonen, who sent him to prison, while Suhonen is tracking a Russian gangster who seems to be infiltrating Finnish crime circles. *Nothing but the Truth*, 2006, tr. 2011, follows the plight of a witness to a shooting who refuses police protection for herself and her twelve-year-old daughter. In *Kylmä jälki*, 2007 (*Cold Trail*, tr. 2013), when a convicted murderer escapes from prison, Takamäki at first takes the case lightly, but soon the chase intensifies as the police delve into the killer's background, finding he might have been unjustly imprisoned and is now seeking revenge. *Muru*, 2011 (*Darling*, tr. 2014), opens with a straightforward-appearing case of a murdered young woman that soon proves to Takamäki's team that they have violated their own motto, "Never assume." All of the Takamäki novels demonstrate Sipilä's belief that crime should be neither glorified nor discredited, since he feels it is "a black, magnifying mirror that reflects the bad things like greed and wickedness of the current society" (quoted in Walkley).

Selected Crime Novels:

Helsinki Homicide Series:

 2001: *Kosketuslaukaus* ("Touch Shot")
 2002: *Tappokäsky* ("Kill Command")
 2003: *Karu keikka* ("The Rugged Gig")
 2005: *Likainen kaupunki* ("Dirty City")
 2006: *Mitään salaamatta* (*Nothing but the Truth*, tr. Peter Ylitalo Leppa, 2011)
 2007: *Kylmä jälki* (*Cold Trail*, tr. Kristian London, 2013)
 2008: *Seinää vasten* (*Against the Wall*, tr. Peter Ylitalo Leppa, 2009)
 2009: *Prikaatin kosto* (*Vengeance*, tr. Kristian London, 2010)
 2011: *Muru* (*Darling*, tr. Katriina Kitchens, 2014)
 2013: *Valepoliisi* ("Vale Police")
 2014: *Luupuisto* ("Luupuisto")

Short Fiction:

 1998: *Kulmapubin koktaili* ("Corner Pub Cocktail")

Major Awards:

2004: Cross of Merit, from the Finnish Ministry of the Interior Police Department
2006: The Kaarle Prize
2009: The Clew of the Year Award, for *Seinää vasten* (*Against the Wall*)

Website: http://www.jarkosipila.com

Anja Snellman

b. May 23, 1954, Helsinki, Finland; Residence: Helsinki, Finland, and Crete; Occupations: journalist, author

Since her literary debut in 1981 with the critically acclaimed novel *Sonja O. kävi täällä* ("Sonja O. Was Here"), still Finland's best-selling first novel, Anja Snellman, today one of Finland's premier mainstream authors, has published over twenty novels, two poetry collections, and numerous magazine and newspaper articles and columns. She has studied solution focused psychotherapy for four years and has hosted popular Finnish television programs, including MTV3's Thursday morning *Good Morning Finland* from 2008 to 2012.

Snellman's fiction, which has been translated into over twenty languages, chiefly deals with women's positions on the central issues she lists on her website, especially female sexuality, mother-daughter relationships, fear, aggression, and power. Her award-winning "Sonja O. Was Here," still a cult favorite in Finland and elsewhere, treated the 1970s' bohemian subculture, with a female narrator who like Snellman had appropriated freedoms traditionally reserved for men (Schoolfield 178). In *Lemmikkikaupan tytöt,* 2007 (*Pet Shop Girls*), tr. 2013, Snellman's only novel to have been published in English, she explores the contemporary social ills of pornography, human trafficking, child prostitution, and pedophilia, using multiple perspectives to tell the painful story of a girl who has disappeared and the mother who will not give up searching for her from multiple perspectives, exhibiting Snellman's trademark command of language and psychological insight.

Crime Novel:

2007: *Lemmikkikaupan tytö* (*Pet Shop Girls*, tr. Scott Kaukonen and Helena Halmari, 2013)

Major Awards:

2007: The Pro Finlandia Medal

Website: http://www.anjasnellman.info

Taavi Soininvaara

b. July 11, 1966, Imatra, Finland; Residence: Tornio, Finland; Occupations: attorney, author

In a 2005 interview, Taavi Soininvaara, who worked ten years as a corporate attorney before deciding to write fiction full time, declared he had wanted to write ever since his student days. He also admitted that he writes what he himself likes, choosing primarily political topics without preaching or favoring one political position over another. He conceived of his first protagonist Arto Ratamo, a former scientist working for the Finnish Security Police, as "an ordinary guy," neither a superhero nor a divorced, alcoholic, middle-aged American-style PI, but Soininvaara has indicated that he himself prefers his second central figure, Leo Kara, a United Nations Special

Adviser who investigates international conflicts and threats. Several of Soininvaara's crime novels have been made into Finnish films.

Some, though not all, of Arto Ratamo's cases portray Russians as villains. His debut thriller *Ebola-Helsinki* ("Ebola-Helsinki") involves the Russian mafia as Finnish military intelligence seeks to uncover a biological weapon, and his second shows the Russian mafia with its tentacles extending into the Finnish information industry. The award-winning *Koston komissio* ("Man on the Commission"), however, uses dissention over Finland's entry into the European Union as its platform for Ratamo's investigation of crimes across Europe. The most recent Ratamo thriller, *Toinen peto* ("Steel Coffin"), 2013, finds him probing assassinations related to the Middle East nuclear arms race.

Leo Kara's first case, *Krittinen tiheys* ("Critical Density"), 2009, shows Russians in the "middle man" position described by Paula Arvas, who also considers Soininvaara's fictional focus in both series as the conflicts between large organizations, not the traditional thriller recipe of a heroic individual battling an entire malignant organization (Arvas, "Contemporary Finnish Crime Fiction" 7). In the later Kara novels, Soininvaara pursues global criminals menacing entire continents and even outer space.

Selected Inspector General Arto Ratamo Novels:

2000: *Ebola-Helsinki* ("Ebola-Helsinki")
2002: *Koston komissio* ("Man on the Commission")
2005: *Pimeyden ydin* ("Marshal of the Sword")
2008: *Rikollisen kaunis* ("Criminal Beautiful")
2013: *Toinen peto* ("Steel Coffin")

The U.N. Special Advisor Leo Kara Series:

2009: *Krittinen tiheys* ("Critical Density")
2010: *Pakonopeus* ("Escape Velocity")
2011: *Punainen jättiläinen* ("Red Giant")
2012: *Valkoinen kääpiö* ("White Dwarf")

Major Awards:

2003: The Clew of the Year Award, for *Koston komissio* ("Man on the Commission")

Website: See http://www.tornio.fi/soininvaara

Sirpa Tabet

b. September 18, 1943, Riihimäki, Finland; Residence: Karjalohja, Finland; Occupations: business-woman, author

At eleven, Sirpa Tabet read her first detective novel, one by Agatha Christie, and thirty years later published one of her own, a historical mystery, followed by books in which Tabet mingled elements unusual to the crime/detective genres. Her protagonists are neither police figures nor gifted and inquisitive amateurs but ordinary women who find themselves in the middle of strange, even supernatural, events. Paula Arvas ranks Tabet among the best female Finnish crime writers, most of whom, Arvas says, have preserved the classical clue-puzzle subgenre, which Tabet, as other women crime writers often do, links to the psychological crime novel, showing natural explanations for even the oddest twists in her carefully constructed plots. Her plots always contain a surprise ending, a technique which makes readers view the narrative from an entirely new angle. According to Arvas, Tabet's perseverant theme is that "one cannot escape one's past" (Arvas, "Contemporary Finnish Crime Fiction" 6).

Selected Crime Novels:

1989: *Punainen metsä* ("Red Forest")
1990: *Ovi* ("The Door")
1995: *Kissan vuosi* ("Cat Year")
1998: *Äidin tyttö* ("Mother of the Girl")
2001: *Varjomies* ("Shadow Man")
2003: *Syyttäjä, poliisi ja tuomari* ("The Prosecutor, the Police, and the Judge")
2006: *Onnen kauppaa* ("Lucky Trade")

Major Awards: N/A

Website: N/A

Eeva Tenhunen

b. January 2, 1937, Sortavala, Finland; Residences: Kitee Puhos and Pielavesi, Finland; Occupations: teacher, author

In 2013, Finland's Whodunnit Society presented Eeva Tenhunen with its Hornanlinna Award, named for Finland's first detective, for her lifetime achievements in crime fiction: "At the time when Tenhunen started writing, Finnish crime fiction was almost completely dominated by male authors. For many female crime writers, she has been a forerunner and an inspiration" (quoted in *Ruumiin kulttuuri* 3/2010).

Eeva Tenhunen's debut novel *Mustat kalat* ("Black Fish"), 1964, one of Finland's best-known detective novels, is the first of her humorous Inspector Martin Halla classic puzzle mystery series. Tenhunen often incorporated her own background and experiences into her fiction, especially her Savonia settings and her work as a teacher. In "Black Fish," still a popular novel in Finland, Halla investigates the murder of a young woman serving as a guide at Olaf's Castle, a historic site in Savonia where Tenhunen herself had worked as a guide for five summers during her student days. Alice Rautasalo, another guide and friend of the murdered girl, helps Halla with his detection and eventually becomes his wife.

Tenhunen, who wrote "Black Fish" on a 1930s Remington typewriter hoping to "earn a little money to study," retired from teaching in 1976 to write full time, publishing five novels in the next decade, but she has said that her husband's death in 1986 drained the light touch from her writing, so much so that it "dried up" (quoted in "Readers Loved Eve Tenhunen"). Tenhunen's influence on female Finnish crime writers, however, has been strong. Leena Lehtolainen wrote her dissertation "Old, New, Borrowed and Blue," on Tenhunen's three novels, "Black Fish," "Sleep Well, Little Red Riding Hood," and "Death in the Family Tree," works which provided a major impetus for Lehtolainen's own career in detective fiction.

Crime Novels (Inspector Martin Halla novels indicated by *):

1964: *Mustat kalat** ("Black Fish")
1971: *Keisari seisoo palatsissaan* ("The Emperor's Palace Stands")
1973: *Nuku hyvin, Punahilkka* ("Sleep Well, Little Red Riding Hood")

1976: *Kuolema savolaiseen tapaan** ("Death the Savo Way")
1978: *Hyvän tytön hautajaiset** ("A Good Girl's Funeral")
1980: *Viimeinen pari** ("The Last Pair")
1985: *Kuolema sukupuussa* ("Death in the Family Tree")
1987: *Joka uniinsa uskoo** ("Every Unliinsa Believes")

Major Awards:

2013: The Hornanlinna Award (named for the first Finnish detective, documented in 1910), by The Whodunnit Club, for lifetime service to the Finnish detective story

Website: N/A

*Jari Tervo

b. February 2, 1959, Rovaniemi, Finland; Residence: Espoo, Finland; Occupations: journalist, author

One of Finland's constantly bestselling authors and a familiar personality on a Finnish TV quiz show, Jari Tervo, who grew up in Lapland near the Arctic Circle, has published over a dozen novels, most of them dealing with the seamy world of petty criminals he reported on as a journalist; three collections of poetry, and the scripts for television series aired in 2006 and 2011. In Minneapolis, Minnesota, to appear with Jarkko Sipilä and Antti Tuomainen as the featured Finnish crime authors at the August 2014, FinnFest, Tervo indicated that he wants his fiction to portray life in the northernmost area of Finland where he grew up, and he added that the northerners feel his work "truly captures their highly individual experience," characterized by "a certain amount of craziness," which Tervo attributes to Laplanders "living in darkness in the winter and constant light in summer" ("Finns in Minnesota").

Tervo seems to incorporate zany Lapland humor into most of his work, of which only one novel has been translated into English thus far. His American publisher, Ice Cold Crime, describes Tervo's style as "Quentin Tarantino meets William Faulkner," but Tervo himself said he prefers the description "brilliant yet cheap" (quoted in "Finns in Minnesota"). *Pyhiesi yhteyteen* (*Among the Saints*), 1996, tr. 2014, starts with the murder of Marzipan Raikkonen, a small-time Lapland crook, close to his home. Tervo then tells the story of the killing in thirty-five chapters from the points of view of no less than thirty-five first-person narrators, ranging from near-normal to outright crazy. Reader responses to the English translation have found this unusual treatment "wonderfully insightful," "odd and quirky," and "capturing the rhythms of different voices, from a young female witness to cops, nurses, and low- life criminals" (see Amazon.com: Books entry for Jari Tervo).

Besides homicide, Tervo has addressed other painful aspects of Finnish life and culture in his fiction. His historical trilogy *Myyrä*, *Ohrana*, and *Troikka* ("The Mole," "Ohrana," and "The Troika," 2004, 2006, and 2008 respectively) deals with the politics of the Finnish struggle for independence. In *Koljatti* ("Goliath"), he satirized contemporary Finnish politics by apparently modeling his fictional "isolated and beleaguered" Prime Minister almost too closely for comfort on then Prime Minister Matti Vanhanen, though Tervo's "critical barbs" were aimed not at politics, but at the media's pursuit of sensationalism at the cost of any substantive information (Papinniemi October 23, 2009). *Layla* ("Layla"), 2011, explores human trafficking, immigration, prostitution and economic inequality through the story of a young Kurdish girl who escapes a harsh fate in Turkey only to become a prostitute in Finland. Here Tervo takes a feminist position by showing male characters as "cold tyrants" who see women as merchandise in a novel that critic Jarmo Pap-inniemi found "tragic and defiant, but also amusing and lively" (Papinniemi October 28, 2011). According to Ice Cold Crime, critics see Tervo's "inimitable style and voice" as original and as satis-fying as do the Finnish readers who consistently place his books at the top of their best seller lists.

Novels (with varying degrees of criminal involvement):

1992: *Pohjan hovi* ("The Court of the North")
1993: *Poliisin poika* ("Policeman's Son")
1995: *Pyhiesi yhteyteen* (*Among the Saints*, tr. Daniel H. Karvonen, 2014)
1997: *Tuulikaappimaa* ("Windswept Expanse")
1999: *Minun sukuni tarina* ("My Family Chronicle")
2000: *Kallellaan* ("Tilted: Father's Diary")
2001: *Suomemme heimo* ("We Translated the Tribe")
2002: *Rautapää* ("Rautapää)
2004: *Myyrä* ("The Mole")
2006: *Ohrana* ("Ohrana")
2008: *Troikka* ("The Troika")
2009: *Kohljatti* ("Goliath")
2011: *Layla* ("Layla")
2013: *Jarrusukka* ("Brake Sock")
2013: *Esikoinen* ("Firstborn")
2014: *Revontultentie* ("The Northern Lights")

Major Awards:

2000: The Clew of the Year Award, for *Minun sukuni tarina* ("My Family Chronicle")
2005: WSOY's Literature Foundation Award

Website: N/A

*Antti Tuomainen

> b. 1971; Residence: Helsinki, Finland; Occupations: journalist, copywriter, author

The Salomonsson Literary Agency claims that Antti Tuomainen is one of the first authors to challenge the Scandinavian crime genre formula. For a long time, the police procedural couched in as realistic though laconic language as possible has been the dominant subgenre of crime fiction in the Nordic countries, but already in his first thriller, *Tappaja, toivoakseni* ("The Killer, I Hope"), 2006, a study of revenge and justice written with linguistic brilliance from the protagonist's point of view and revealing Helsinki's harsh realities, Tuomainen struck out into new literary territory. Tuomainen's website describes *Veljeni vartija* ("My Brother's Keeper"), 2009, as "an intense yet poetic crime novel about fathers and sons," who all drift into lives of crime. The novel begins in the 1940s, shifting through successive eras to a present-day solution of a decades-old crime.

Tuomainen's critically acclaimed and award-winning *Parantaja*, 2010 (*The Healer*), tr. 2013), combines poetic language with dense *noir* realism in a bleak near-future dystopian Helsinki setting. Poet Tapani Lehtinen's wife Johanna, a journalist, has disappeared while covering serial killings by "the Healer" in a soggy, dismal climate-changed Helsinki teeming with criminals, victims of an Ebola pandemic, and desperate refugees from wars to the south. The beleaguered Helsinki police cannot help him, so Tapani himself tries to find Johanna by tracking the Healer, an "avenger" who strikes down CEOs of companies he blames for causing climate change as well as their families, the catalyst for Tapani's real quest, which transforms him from a dreamy ineffectual artist figure into a man of action (PW review). The UK *Metro* glowingly summed up the English translation of *The Healer:* "… the murders and their culprit take a backseat in this fraught thriller as Tuomainen conjures up in spare, softly poetic prose the collapse of social order and human decency in the face of environmental havoc" ("New Crime Fiction").

Harvill Secker, the UK publisher of *The Healer*, announced the acquisition of Commonwealth rights to Tuomainen's fourth novel, *Synkkä niin sydämeni* ("Dark as My Heart"), 2013, in early November 2013, with its English translation to appear in 2015. Described by Alison Hennessey, Harvill Secker's Senior Crime Editor, as "a fantastic psychological thriller," this novel's narrator Aleksi, whose mother vanished when he was a child, sets out to find her by taking a job as the caretaker of her former employer's seaside estate. Hennessey predicts it will appeal strongly to fans of Patricia Highsmith, Karin Fossum, and Alfred Hitchcock.

Crime Novels:

> 2006: *Tappaja, toivoakseni* ("The Killer, I Hope")
> 2009: *Veljeni vartija* ("My Brother's Keeper")
> 2010: *Parantaja* (*The Healer*, tr. Lola Rogers, 2013)
> 2013: *Synkkä niin kuin sydämeni* ("Dark as My Heart")

Major Awards:

> 2011: The Clew of the Year Award, for *Parantaja* (*The Healer*)

Website: http://www.anttituomainen.com

Tuula-Liina Varis

> b. June 30, 1942, Loimaa, Finland; Residence: Joensuu, Finland; Occupations: journalist, editor, television personality, author

Tuula-Liina Varis, a freelance author since 1979, a journalist, editor, and Chair of the Finnish Writers from 2009 to 2014, has written novels, short story collections, and more than a thousand columns for a variety of Finnish newspapers. She also hosted TV1's literary program *Books A & O* from 1999 to 2005.

When Tuula-Liina Varis' novel *Vaimoni* ("My Wife") won the Clew of the Year Award for 2005, reviewer Ritva Sorvali commented that it was not a traditional detective story but a hybrid, "a kind of psychological detective story." A man's wife inexplicably disappears from their home, leaving everything behind—even her purse. While the police search for her goes on, he narrates the back story: years ago, they lost a disabled child. His work outside the home as a newspaperman helped him cope with his grief and shame, but since his wife had no such outlet, her extreme grief caused her to gain so much weight that he's ashamed of her appearance and cannot be seen with her. He concocts a fictitious identity for her, telling it to his associates while she remains hidden at home; their marriage has become two individuals living in different worlds. Sorvali feels that "My Wife" strengthens the domestic psychological detective story genre by exploring the destruction the lack of love can cause.

Varis' most recent novel *Naisen paras ystävä* ("A Woman's Best Friend"), 2014, follows the same psychological thriller tradition, opening with a crime in which both the victim and the killer are immediately known and gradually revealing the series of seemingly random events which led to it. The psychopathic killer, son of an unwed alcoholic mother, was the object of a good deed—his aunt tried to save him—which goes horribly wrong, allowing Varis to reinforce a theme that she has illustrated in many of her columns: that both technology and the idealization of youth are false idols whose worship can and does destroy. Varis' psychological detective narrative unveils the price that a web of lies exacts from the tale-teller whom these falsehoods entrap.

Selected Psychological Thrillers:

2004: *Vaimoni* ("My Wife")
2014: *Naisen paras ystävä* ("A Woman's Best Friend")

Major Awards:

2005: The Clew of the Year Award, for *Valimoni* ("My Wife")
2011: WSOY's Literature Foundation Award

Website: N/A

Hannu Vuorio

b. March 16, 1941, Helsinki, Finland; Residence: Helsinki, Finland; Occupations: journalist, critic, author

After a career in journalism, Hannu Vuorio published his first detective novel, *Nyman* ("Nyman") in 1995 which received the Clew of the Year Award and a nomination for the *Helsingin Sanomat* debut novel award. He has maintained that he is less interested in the technological aspects of crime fiction than in its social and psychological aspects, and throughout his detective novels he has integrated his hard-boiled crime novels with his social criticism in a highly individual humorous style, creating a variety of Finnish crime literature very different from the traditional police procedural subgenre. Each of Vuorio's crime novels has a different cast of characters and the police play a relatively minor role, since he prefers to concentrate on male characters who often are drawn into crime by social ills: "unemployment, poverty, marital problems, drugs, neo–Nazis, the integration of prisoners, alcoholism, corruption, tax evasion, prostitution, terrorism, racism, immigrant integration, and burnout," as in *Heil!* ("Heil!," 2001), which treats neo–Nazi activities, terrorism, and police corruption (Järvinen). Vuorio also uses the rich Helsinki dialect to bring his city setting to life, often portraying his downtrodden individual characters with a light humorous touch. His favorite authors are Raymond Chandler, Dashiell Hammett, Matti Joensuu and Swedish authors Sjöwall and Wahlöö ("Hannu Vuorio," *Dekkari Netti*).

Vuorio often handles his criminals sympathetically. His first crime novel, *Nyman* ("Nyman"), 1995, focuses on one Nyman, convicted but innocent of a brutal shotgun slaying. Upon his release from years in prison, he intends to find and bring the actual killers to justice, but changes he had not foreseen in the world prevent him from doing so and he finds himself incarcerated again. Vuorio's 2012 novel *Isän poika*, produced after a hiatus in his writing, attributes commonplace racism against Somali immigrants to a genetic tendency toward violence in Finland, a country where, according to *Dekkari Netti*, if someone is born elsewhere, that person inescapably becomes the target of social exclusion and crime. (*Dekkari Netti* ["Detective Story Online"] is a City of Tornio, Finland, website focused on Finnish and international mystery fiction since 1998, maintained by Terttu Uusimaa of the Tornio City Library. Tornio is in Lapland. See http://www.tornio.fi/Dekkari Netti.) That position that illustrates Vuorio's unique contribution to Finnish detective literature ("Hannu Vuorio," *Dettari Netti*).

Crime Novels:

1995: *Nyman* ("Nyman")
1997: *Friman* ("Friman")
1998: *Hagman* ("Hagman")
1999: *Sjöman & Co.*("Sjöman & Co.")
2000: *Bäng!* ("Bang!")
2001: *Heil!* ("Heil!")
2003: *Miami* ("Miami")
2007: *Syvä matala* ("A Deep Low")
2009: *Hyvästi, Monika* ("Goodbye, Monika")
2012: *Isän poika* ("Father's Son")

Major Awards:

1996: The Clew of the Year Award, for *Nyman* ("Nyman")

Website: N/A

Kjell Westö

b. August 6, 1961, Helsinki, Finland; Residences: Stockholm, Sweden, and Helsinki, Finland; Occupations: journalist, poet, author

Kjell Westö, a Finland-Swede who writes in Swedish, won the prestigious Finlandia Prize for his meticulously researched mainstream historical novels set in Helsinki. In *Books in Finland* 2000. Westö's alter ego, a discontented poet named Anders Hed, conducted an unusual self-interview with Westö, in which Westö described his childhood experience of being "different," "bullied and beaten up" because he spoke Swedish, his mother tongue. It made him "a convinced anti-racist," who could "understand and accept the differences between others and their ways," the key to the major theme of his fiction. Westö also revealed the bipolarity that growing up in his times had internalized in him. Both his grandfathers were killed, one in the Winter War and the other in the Continuation War, and as he said, "Wounds like that are not healed in one generation." He sees himself as a "pitiful relic" of the Sputnik–Cold War period who "had to take all those brezhnevs and reagans and all those long-distance missiles" seriously, and then were confronted with the dizzying changes of the 1980s. Westö thus insisted he specialized "in being the wrong man in the wrong place at the wrong time," an incongruity whose black humor he now recognizes as the reason he feels compelled to "write myself into wholeness. I look for stories where there's a world that has a place for me in it" (Westö, "Compelled to Write").

Westö's 2002 classic psychological thriller *Lang* (*Lang*), 2002, tr. 2005, illustrates that intention by probing the precipitating crime's involved background and motives (Dickens). Critic Eric Dickens points out that Westö used the Swedish name Helsingfors for the officially bilingual Helsinki, a symbol of the city's subliminal role in the novel, which also involves a classic love triangle between Lang, an upper-middle-class Swedish-speaking television personality; Sarita, a Finnish-speaking working class woman; and Sarita's ex-husband Marko. "This is not a Maigret, more one of Simenon's studies in psychology" (Dickens). *Lang* was nominated for the Finlandia Prize in 2002, one of Westö's five such nominations. He also has been nominated for the 2013 August Prize and the 2014 Nordic Council Literature Prize. His Finlandia Prize–winning novel *Dar vi en gäng gätt* ("Where We Once Passed") was adapted for a drama presented at the Helsinki City Theatre in April 2008.

Selected Thriller:

2002: *Lang* (*Lang*, tr. Ebba Segerberg, 2005):

Major Awards (for mainstream novels):

1990: State Prize for Literature
2006: The Finlandia Prize, for *Dar vi en gäng gätt* ("Where We Once Passed")

Website: N/A

Tauno Yliruusi

> b. May 4, 1927, Tampere, Finland; d. June 17, 1994, Espoo, Finland; Residence: Espoo, Finland;
> Occupations: dramatist, journalist, radio and television scriptwriter, author

In his time, playwright and author Tauno Yliruusi was considered one of the most internationally-known Finnish writers. His novel *Yllätysmurha* (*Murder for Fun*), 1959, tr. 1960, became a popular radio play throughout Europe, translated into nine languages, including an English version by Dorothy ("Kitty") Black, a well known prolific London dramatic agent and translator. *Rikosetsivien vapaapäivä* ("A Detective's Holiday"), 1963, stars Superintendent Manki in a plot resembling Agatha Christie's *Ten Little Indians*; Manki and seven husbands spend a weekend locked into a deserted villa on an island near Helsinki, where one after another is killed and each body disappears. In 1963, Yliruusi wrote two mystery novels for the P.C. Rettig tobacco company and a novel which appeared in the international Lightning Series with works by Maria Lang, Ellery Queen, and Erle Stanley Gardner ("Tauno Yliruusi").

Starting in the 1960s, Yliruusi began to produce polemical works opposing "Finlandization," Finnish President Kekkonen's version of neutrality during the Cold War, which favored accommodation with the Soviet Union. Yliruusi also strongly criticized Marxist ideology. In 1969. Yliruusi published *Dead End*, a political pamphlet denouncing the Soviet Union's suppression of Czech leader Alexander Dubcek's "socialism with a human face," and in 1974, following Aleksandr Solzhenitsyn's expulsion from the Soviet Union, Yliruusi wrote a play defending the Russian dissident author. With the change in Finland's political climate in the 1990s after the collapse of the Soviet Union, Yliruusi produced autobiographical essays and short story collections.

Selected Crime Novels:

1959: *Yllätysmurha* (*Murder for Fun*, tr. Dorothy ["Kitty"] Black, 1960)
1960: *Sitä ei satu kaikille* ("Surprise Murder")
1962: *Kuolema kertoo vitsin* ("Death Tells a Joke")
1963: *"Hermosavut": Kassakaappimurrot* ("Nerve Smoke: Safe Burglary")
1963: *Rikosetsivien vapaapäivä* ("A Detective's Holiday")
1963: *Joulu Toijalan takana* ("Christmas at the Rear of the DBS")
1964: *Savuverho* ("Smoke Curtain")

Major Awards: N/A

Website: N/A

Anthology of Short Finnish Crime Fiction

Helsinki Noir, ed. James Thompson. Brooklyn, New York: Akashic Books, 2014. This anthology contains fourteen short stories, one contributed by Thompson himself and the rest by contemporary Finnish crime writers. In his Introduction, "A Parallel Universe," Thompson describes the vast differences which underlie Finland's seemingly normal surface: "Finns live internal lives full of dreams…. And they hide their frustrations and anger—until they don't" (*Helsinki Noir* 12).

Selected Non-Finnish Authors of Crime Novels Set in Finland

Simon Boswell

> b. October 16, 1956, Kingston, Surrey, UK; Residence: Helsinki, Finland; Occupations: musician, conductor, producer, film score composer, teacher, author

According to his official website, British-born musician and composer Simon Boswell has lived in Finland more than half his life, working as an English teacher. He studied composition at Helsinki's Sibelius Academy and currently holds a permanent full-time lectureship in English there. In 2006, he debuted as a crime author with *The Seven Symphonies*, which became a Number 4 bestseller in Finland. With a backdrop of the Finnish musical world, *The Seven Symphonies* presents serial murders of musicians starting with a young woman found dead in Helsinki's Sibelius Park, the first of grisly mementos removed from her body. Each successive homicide is connected with one of the symphonies composed by Finland's towering Jean Sibelius. According to Boswell's website, " the story unfolds as a disturbing exploration of sexual obsession and the more sinister aspects of human sexuality" (also see http://www.SevenSymphonies.com).

Crime Novel Set in Finland:

2006: *The Seven Symphonies: A Finnish Murder Mystery*

Major Awards: N/A

Website: http://www.simonboswell.com

James Thompson

> b. October 16, 1964, Kentucky, USA: d. August 2, 2014, Lahti, Finland; Residence: Lahti, Finland; Occupation: Author

In an interview following publication of his second novel, *Lucifer's Tears*, American author James Thompson revealed that after being accepted to the University of Helsinki he had come to Finland with a Finnish girl, but "The relationship didn't last…. I didn't really have anything in the States to go back to, so I just stayed…. Now, culturally, I'm more comfortable here than anywhere else and have no desire to leave" ("Interview," 2011) Thompson was so comfortable in Finland that he authored two novels published in Finnish as well as his four Inspector Kari Vaara novels in English, written, he said, to acquaint American readers with Finland, so in them he used expository material about Finland that he cut out for Finnish audiences. Responding to complaints that his work shows Finland as a country "where everyone is drunk or crazy," Thompson claimed he wrote "dark, noir fiction," not material for the Finnish Board of Tourism ("Interview," 2011).

Snow Angels, Thompson's first novel published in English, is set in Kittilä, Finnish Lapland, a hundred miles into the Arctic Circle, during the two-week period of absolute dark called *kaamos*, just before Christmas. Inspector Kari Vaara, a laconic policeman, suffers from intense migraines, as Thompson himself did, an ailment which some medical authorities attribute to *kommos*, which causes chemical changes in the brain that inflict depression in much of the Finnish population ("My Life"). Some try to fend off its effects through quantities of .cheap Russian alcohol. In this novel Inspector Vaara, who has a much younger American wife, investigates the murder of a young Somali actress, a very different crime from what Vaara, Thompson's narrator, describes as Finland's typical homicide: "We kill the people we love, our husbands and wives, brothers and sisters, parents and friends, almost Always in drunken rages" (*Snow Angels* 9–10). *Snow Angels* received the Booklist Best Crime Debut Award and nominations for the U.S. Edgar and Anthony Awards.

In a scalding 2011 web posting, "My Life Just Isn't Anybody Else's Business," Thompson described his own battle with persistent migraines, "suicide headaches" beginning around 2004, when through "the miraculous Finnish public health care system" he was misdiagnosed. In pain, with constant vomiting and seizures, he wrote *Lucifer's Tears* in Spain, where he and his Finnish wife had gone to try to alleviate his condition (it didn't); the novel brings Vaara to Helsinki, where despite his agony, he faces two cases, one the violent homicide of a Russian businessman's wife and the other a *sub rosa* probe of an aged Finnish hero of World War II, Finland's "crowning moment." Thompson defended his disparaging portrayal of Finnish wartime and postwar leaders in this novel, which he accurately suspected would anger many people, by insisting his research bore out the issue of collaboration with the Nazis that he raised in this novel ("Interview," 2011).

"Writers just sit alone and bleed into the keyboard," Thompson noted in 2013, after publication of Vaara's third case, *Helsinki Blood*, which involves the problem of addiction. Thompson believed that Finns are the "top abusers of any mind-altering substance ... their suicide rate is sky-high. It seems Finns have an innate desire for oblivion," or, he added, they may just keep better statistics than other Europeans do (Godwin). In this novel, Vaara has become more isolated than heretofore, which Thompson said Vaara himself considers simply "a normal sense of privacy " (quoted in Godwin), a manifestation of the typical Finnish male's reticence.

"My entire vision of writing books set in Finland," Thompson stated, "was to demonstrate what the world is like moment to moment in the mind of an average Finnish man" in " the land of sad songs" (quoted in MacDougall). Jukka Petaja, a *Helsingin Sanomat* critic, felt that "Having some distance from Finland, Jim Thompson [could] also see some phenomen[a] even clearer than many Finns [do]" (quoted in MacDougall).

Crime Novels:

Inspector Kari Vaara Series:

2009: *Snow Angels*
2011: *Lucifer's Tears*
2012: *Helsinki White*
2013: *Helsinki Blood*
2014: *Helsinki Dead*

Short Fiction Anthology (James Thompson, editor and contributor):

2014: *Helsinki Noir*

Major Awards:

2010: The *Booklist* Best Crime Debut Award, for *Snow Angels*

Websites: http://jamesthompsonauthor.com; http://www.akashicbooks.com/author/james-thompson

Jan Costin Wagner

> b. October 13, 1972, Langen, Hessen, Germany; Residences: Germany and Finland; Occupations: journalist, author

Jan Costin Wagner, a German author who for almost two decades has spent half his time in Finland with his Finnish wife, writes crime novels in German about Turku, Finland, police detective Kimmo Joentaa. Wagner is building a solid international reputation with his Kimmo Joentaa novels, several of which are available in English translation.

Wagner said in 2008 that "The thing that started me writing was the desire to put something down in language that cannot be expressed any other way, to exemplify extreme situations, and murder and manslaughter are particularly extreme situations" (quoted in Fritzsche). He does not like classical crime novels or regional thrillers, aiming instead "to encapsulate a moment of comprehension—through leaving things out" and providing no black and white or good and evil solutions, "because life itself offers no solutions" (quoted in Fritzsche).

Wagner's first Joentaa novel, *Eismond* (*Ice Moon*), 2003, tr. 2005, opens with tragedy: Joentaa's lovely young wife has just died of cancer. He goes back to work but his life is now appallingly empty just when he has to investigate serial killings in Turku, Finland's oldest city. In a subplot, Joentaa's middle-aged superior Ketola, in the midst of a farcical search for the attempted assassin of a local politician seems to be becoming unhinged, leavening Joentaa's personal tragedy with the saving grace of humor. In the award-winning *Das Schweigen* (*Silence*), 2007, tr. 2010, Wagner is less interested in the solution to the precipitating murder involved with child pornography than how guilt afflicts the persons left behind.

Crime Novels (written in German):

2002: *Nachtfahrt* ("Night Journey")

Detective Kimmo Joentaa Series:

2003: *Eismond* (*Ice Moon*, tr. John Brownjohn, 2005)
2005: *Schattentag* ("Shadow Day")
2007: *Das Schweigen* (*Silence*, tr. Anthea Bell, 2010)
2009: *Im Winter der Löwen* (*The Winter of the Lions*, tr. Anthea Bell, 2011)
2013: *Das Licht in einem dunklen Haus* (*Light in a Dark House*, tr. Anthea Bell, 2013)

Major Awards:

2002: The Marlowe Prize for Best Crime Novel, for *Nachtfahrt* ("Night Journey")
2008: *Krimipreis* (Germany), for *Das Schweigen* (*Silence*)
2014: The Petrona Award, for *Das Licht in einem dunklen Haus* (*Light in a Dark House*)

Website: http://www.jan-costin-wagner.de

ICELAND

Wise he is deemed who can question well,
And also answer back:
The sons of men can no secret make
Of the tidings told in their midst.
—*Hávamál*, The Words of Odin the High One,
Wisdom for Wanderers and Counsel to Guests, 28

The Cultural Context of
Icelandic Crime Fiction

In Icelandic usage, generally only the first name denotes a person. In the following discussion, Icelandic individuals are referred to by given name(s) plus patronymic (ending in *–son* for men and *–dóttir* for women; in rare cases by matronymic); or by family name if used by the individual.

The distinguishing characteristic of Iceland's crime fiction, its "obsession with national identity" (Kachka), paradoxically springs from its combination of opposing elements in nearly every facet of its existence. Tiny Iceland, "the Land of Fire and Ice," contains immense contrasts and contradictions in geography, geology, climate, ethnicity, politics, economy, demographics, history, and culture. Iceland also produces more published authors than anywhere else on earth, about 1000 titles a year (Medley), because, according to prize-winning Icelandic mainstream author Ólafur Gunnarsson, there is some truth in the joke that "every Icelander is a writer"; he feels that "The urge for creative writing is almost a national mania" ("Ólafur Gunnarsson Interview"). All these elements contribute to the development of Iceland's contemporary crime literature, providing significant themes and enriching its growth and impact in the early twenty-first century, when, according to Quentin Bates, "Iceland is awash with crime these days [2015] ... crime fiction. After years of languishing in the shadows as being something that proper writers didn't do, crime has come into its own" (Bates, "Icelandic noir").

The small island nation of Iceland, about 40,000 square miles, lies west of Norway on the Mid-Atlantic Range between Europe and the New World. Iceland is the most sparsely populated country in Europe, its 320,000 people currently living at about 7.5 persons per square mile. Approximately 93 percent of them are called " Icelandic," 3 percent are Polish, and 4 percent other nationalities, but the term "Icelandic" itself involves two distinct cultural heritages. The "dominant social elite" of the settlers coming to Iceland between 870 and 930 A.D. "was Norse in language and culture." Archaeological evidence, the 12th-century Icelandic *Landnámabók* ("The Book of Settlement"), the *Islendabók*, and the *Liber de Mensura Orbis Terrae* written by the Irish monk Dicuil in 825, all agree that Celtic monks resided in Iceland in the late 8th century. According to Dicuil, the monks left because of Viking raids before the first permanent settler of Iceland, Ingólfr Arnarson, exiled from Norway for starting a blood feud, arrived in 874, joined by other Norse

Viking chieftains who fled to Iceland with their families and retainers because they opposed the ruthless unification of Norway by the Norwegian king Harold Fairhair (b. 850) in 872. Historical and genetic evidence, however, has shown that "a substantial percentage" of Iceland's original settlers were of Celtic origin. (Ólason 1). Recent DNA examinations, including a 2009 study of the teeth of 95 early medieval Icelandic skeletons (Ramirez 3), prove that the country's ethnic Icelanders have nearly as much Scottish and Irish genetic material in their heritage as they do Norse. The same current research finds that an estimated 75 percent of male Icelandic settlers were Norse, while 63 percent of the women settlers were of Irish or Scottish origin (Ramirez 3). According to Barry Forshaw, "This all [the Celtic heritage in Iceland] comes through the female line—a legacy of Vikings raping and pillaging" (Forshaw 133). Whether the long-maintained legend that the Norwegian raiders stole Irish women because Norwegian women were "not compliant" is true or not, common belief insists that "the majority of the male settlers were Nordic but the majority of the women were Gaelic" (Forshaw 130). Descendants of Icelandic settlers in North Dakota still insist that their women are the most beautiful in the world because after their raids the Icelandic Vikings returned with only the best-looking ones.

The Vikings did bring their pagan Germanic religion with them to Iceland. In Old Norse belief, the worship of Thor, who was originally the chief god of Norwegian life, representing truth-telling and oath-keeping, gave way to the cult of the imported Saxon god Wotan, known in Scandinavia as Odin, who conferred battle-frenzy on his chosen *berserker* warriors and poetic inspiration on his warrior *skalds*. In that basically pessimistic pagan Germanic belief, the universe-tree Yggdrasil and both gods and men would eventually perish in flames, so that humans could win everlasting life only by deeds that ensured their heroism would live on in songs and stories. Even after Iceland formally accepted Christianity in AD 1000, remnants of the old paganism lingered throughout Iceland.

The Celts, mostly women, taken to Iceland by the Vikings brought as strong a storytelling tradition as the Norse one, but the Celts drew upon a completely different religion and culture. Pagan Celtic belief in a parallel twilight dimension of life involving "little people" like fairies, elves, and gnomes remained in Ireland even after St. Patrick's completion of the country's Christian conversion in the 5th century. Conversion to Christianity introduced the Irish Golden Age, marked by remarkable achievements in literature and art lasting until the Viking raids of the 8th century. Irish Christianity markedly diverged from Roman Christian dogma and practices, especially in the Irish acceptance of women in the priesthood and in other prominent societal roles, like the brehon law judiciary. Irish Christianity also favored the Gospel of John over the three synoptic Gospels, a theological position which the Irish fought hard to retain until, due to the decisions made at the Synod of Whitby in 663, the Irish were forced to yield to Roman Catholicism.

The Celtic Irish and Scots held a long tradition of storytelling as an integral and respected part of life. The pagan *fili* (bards) were highly trained and favored members of Celtic society who over twelve years orally learned hundreds of stories, poems, genealogies, and histories by heart. Since the Irish Celts believed the spoken word "held the power of breath," and was a gift from the great goddess Brigid, patroness of poetry and divination, they also believed that the spoken word could make magic. After Ireland became Christian, the *seanchaithe* (storytellers) carried on the folk traditions as did their counterparts, the *seanchaidh* in Scotland. Those traditions were such integral elements of their societies that the Celts whom the Vikings brought to distant Iceland clung to the importance of the storytellers' words and influenced the development of Iceland's crowning literary achievement, the Icelandic sagas.

In post-conversion Iceland, the Old Norse and the Celtic cultural strains, including their pagan elements, met and mingled. Most medievalists concur that possibly "the combination of male heroic minstrels [the Norse skalds] and female [Irish] storytellers contributed to Iceland's distinctive literary tradition" (Ramirez 2) that now exhibits an idiosyncratic mixture of old and new, high tech and superstition. "Everyone in Iceland seems to be on Facebook, yet everyone's granny has spoken to elves…. The architecture is modern … but the landscape is suffused with myth and legend. Trolls frozen to stone on mountain tops, hidden people slinking out of rocks and stones to meddle in the affairs of men" (Forshaw 133). This unusual combination of the real and the fantastic prevails in Iceland's literature, where even today the spirit of the medieval Icelandic sagas permeates almost all Icelandic imaginative writing (Forshaw 133).

The land where the Vikings brought their Celtic captives in the 9th century is the world's 18th largest island, circumnavigated in 870 by the Swedish explorer Garðar Svavarsson in 870. Just south of the Arctic Circle, about two-thirds of Iceland is tundra, with another 14 percent covered by lakes and glaciers. Many fjords move inland from its coastline, where most of the population is concentrated. Only about 23 percent of Iceland is vegetated because the interior of the island is uninhabitable, comprised of sand, mountains, and lava fields from Iceland's hundreds of volcanoes. About a third of the volcanoes are active, responsible for historical disasters like the Laki eruption of 1784–5, which caused the "Mist Hardships" (Móduharðinden), a "New Ice Age" period of famine in which over half the country's livestock and about a quarter of the Icelandic population died. In modern times, the Eyjafjallajökull eruption of 2010 forced hundreds of Icelanders to leave their homes, and the following year the more powerful Grímsvötn eruption disrupted air travel across Europe. On the other hand, Iceland's plentiful geothermal and hydroelectric power supply inexpensive hot water, heating and electricity, and the warm North Atlantic current provides annual temperatures comfortably higher than those of areas in similar latitude. Iceland's coasts remain ice free throughout the winters, a substantial boon to Iceland's fishing industry, which is a major factor in the nation's economy. Farming and forestry are declining, however. Iceland's first settlers saw forests "from mountains to sea shore," but human needs for shelter and warmth have largely deforested the country, and sheep overgrazing has led to so much loss of topsoil and soil erosion that many farms have been abandoned.

The first generations of Icelandic settlers "seem to have influenced profoundly the country's sense of national identity" and largely forged Iceland's desire for independence and the country's social and political fabric (Ramirez 2). In the 9th century the ferocious practices of Norway's first king Harald Fairhair and his son and heir Erik Bloodax drove many chieftains and their followers out of Norway to Iceland and fortified their resistance to monarchy. In 930 Icelanders formed the Althing, a legislative and judicial assembly considered the world's oldest existing parliament, to regulate their Icelandic Commonwealth, which lasted in its independent form for only about 200 years. Originally Icelandic chieftains (goðorðsmenn or goðar) from the various regions of the island would travel to an impressive assembly field called the Þingvellir on the shore of Iceland's largest lake, surrounded with rocks bearing enormous clefts. At the Althing the chieftains made political and legal decisions according to laws memorized, not written down, by the elected lögsögumaður (law speaker). Because the Althing had no law enforcement power, individuals had to enforce the laws through a system of payment for crimes. The blood feuds that often resulted could keep cycles of retaliation going for years, providing a wealth of material for the Icelandic authors who later produced the Sagas of Icelanders (Ramirez 2).

The Althing functioned reasonably well during Iceland's Commonwealth Era, roughly 930 to. 1130, but rivalries among Icelandic chieftains eventually caused the independent Althing to fail. The term "Age of the Sturlings," 1200 to 1260, refers to the powerful western Icelandic family whose member Snorri Sturluson, author of the Prose Edda, one of the most important Old Norse literary works, swore allegiance to Haakon IV of Norway, setting off a civil war against other Icelandic families. Power became concentrated in fewer and fewer groups, bringing Iceland to virtual civil war. Finally the Althing established a union with Norway, which itself later became a dependency of Denmark in the Kalmar Union of 1415, bringing Iceland as a part of Norway, Norway itself, and Sweden under Danish rule. Until World War II, Icelanders willy-nilly remained a "colonial backwater" of Denmark (Forshaw 128), an extended unpopular experience that bolstered Icelanders' national consciousness and their desire to maintain a national identity. After the Kalmar Union floundered in 1523, Iceland remained a Norwegian dependency under Denmark for about four hundred years, but Icelanders had not forgotten the fierce desire for independence that had brought the original settlers to their country and impelled them to form the Althing, the world's first parliamentary assembly.

Economic and political events eventually enhanced the Icelandic thrust toward regaining independence. During the 19th century Iceland's climate became colder, and approximately 15,000 Icelanders out of a population of 70,000 emigrated to Canada, especially Manitoba, and to a lesser extent the north central United States. During the 1850s when nationalism was rising in many parts of Europe, a growing national consciousness fueled the Icelandic independence movement, inspired by Icelandic intellectuals and led by Jón Sigurðsson. In 1874 Denmark granted Iceland limited home rule under its own constitution, and in the Danish-Icelandic Act of Union signed on December 1, 1918, Iceland became a fully sovereign state as the Kingdom of Iceland, in a "personal union" with Denmark under the Danish monarch.

After Nazi forces occupied Denmark in April 1940, the Althing declared Iceland's neutrality and announced that the Icelandic government would operate separately from Denmark's. A month later, fearing that Nazi Germany would occupy Iceland, Britain invaded and occupied Iceland for a year. The United States then assumed occupation of Iceland, freeing the British garrison for service elsewhere, until 1946. Meanwhile, Iceland's Act of Union with Denmark had expired and 97 percent of Icelanders voted to abolish the monarchy and establish a republic effective June 17, 1944. Despite considerable public uproar, Iceland joined NATO in 1949 and in 1951 signed a defense agreement with the United States, allowing American troops to return to Iceland where they remained through the Cold War period, not completely withdrawn until 2006. As well as exerting a considerable cultural influence on Iceland, the American presence greatly improved Iceland's economy during the postwar period. Through the Marshall Plan Icelanders received the most per capita American aid of any European nation, $209 per Icelander, as compared to the distant second $109 per citizen in the war-ravaged Netherlands (Müller and Myllyntaus 385).

Throughout those long years of Danish domination, Iceland's literary heritage provided a major impetus toward preserving the nation's national identity that most Icelanders considered vital, as they still do: in a 2005 European Commission study, over 85 percent of Icelanders considered independence "very important," compared to 47 percent Norwegians and 49 percent Danes who believed thus (*Social Values Analysis* 35). Geography and language have materially contributed to the primacy of Icelandic saga literature in maintaining the Icelanders' cherished national identity. As an island nation, Iceland was both physically and culturally isolated prior to e-mail and the Internet, keeping the modern Icelandic language so close to Old Norse that Icelandic schools still teach 800-year-old literature in a language used in the late Middle Ages, instilling the sagas' techniques and values in most of the Icelandic population. Ólafur Gunnarsson, one of Iceland's most lauded mainstream novelists, notes that a "great surge" of creative writing has erupted there in the last thirty-five years, with its roots firmly planted in Iceland's medieval sagas (quoted in "Ólafur Gunnarsson Interview").

Besides receiving elements from the oral traditions of the earliest pagan Norse settlers, medieval Icelandic literature, including primarily the Eddas, skaldic poetry, and the sagas, was strongly affected by the two centuries of native Icelandic history known as the Commonwealth Era and Iceland's harsh native environment as well as the poetry and legends imported from other parts of Europe through trade (Neijmann 2–3), full of ferocious battles and family rivalries. Even though their early literature was written and probably shaped to some extent by Christian scribes, Old Icelandic poetry remains "by far the richest source preserving the pre–Christian mythology of the Germanic peoples as well as their heroic legends" (Ólason and Tómasson in Neijmann 3). It thus effectively transmitted Germanic cultural values, reinforced by the Celtic proclivity for storytelling, accompanied by theological principles inculcated by the early Icelandic church.

Having no king or central authority that could exert executive power, medieval Iceland soon became "an unstable federation of chieftaincies accepting a common law and a common system of courts." This meant that medieval Icelanders held themselves to a "stringent code of heroic conduct," making them responsible for their own safety and obliged to defend their individual honor, their families, and their chieftains to the death (Neijmann 2). At the same time they accepted Christian teaching, because in Iceland the church did not try to stamp out the older traditional culture, instead cooperating with it. The *Poetic (Elder) Edda*, dated roughly from the first half of the 13th century, is an anonymously authored collection of Old Icelandic poems dating from the late 10th century, celebrating the exploits of Dark Age kings like Attila the Hun (d. 453), and illustrating the Old Germanic code of conduct and the tragic consequences when it was violated. The *Poetic Edda* also preserves pagan Germanic myths as well as the *Voluspá* ("Sayings of the Wise One") in which a seeress outlines matters normally hidden by the Germanic gods from men (Davidson 119). The *Prose (Younger) Edda*, composed by the Icelandic skald (poet)-warrior, chieftain, politician, historian, and saga-writer Snorri Sturluson around 1220, was assembled somewhat earlier than the *Poetic Edda*. In the *Prose Edda*, Snorri preserved the old tales of the gods "with wit, irony, and a lively delight in their imaginative beauty" (Davidson 24). He wrote from a Christian standpoint, but he did so with tolerance for the old values, refusing to categorize the pagan gods who embodied them as demons, as was done by Christian scribes in other European literatures (Davidson 25).

Snorri also intended his *Prose Edda* to serve as a poetic manual for the Icelandic skalds, mostly professional warrior-poets obligated to celebrate the deeds of kings and nobles and to commemorate or satirize current events. Norway's Saint and King Olaf II, for example, at the Battle of Stiklestad in 1030 where he died defending Christianity against pagan Russians, placed his skalds at the center of his sworn warriors, so that the skalds might survive to endow his exploits with poetic immortality. Icelandic skalds participated in societal poetic meetings, composed religious poems, and without risk of personal censure could produce anonymous poetic commentaries, some even critical, upon events and leaders in their society.

The Icelandic sagas which still strongly influence Icelandic literature were composed by unknown authors somewhat later than the majority of the skaldic poems. Most of the sagas contain accounts of Scandinavian history between the 9th and 13th centuries, the period when the old religion was being set aside and Christianity was taking its place. Written in Old Icelandic prose, the sagas fall into three categories. The historical sagas recount the migration of northern peoples to Iceland and the Viking explorations of the New World; the legendary or "heroic" sagas like the *Völsunga Saga*, analogous to the German *Nibelungenlied*, contain material relating to the Dark Age migrations of the Germanic peoples and their pagan beliefs; and the Sagas of Icelanders deal with actual personages and events. Though they also contain mythological and folklore motifs, all of the sagas celebrate values typical of Old Icelandic culture: fidelity to a sworn oath, courage even in the face of certain doom, and regard for one's future reputation as witnessing truth to one's beliefs. Alma Gudmundsdóttir, curator of the Icelandic Saga Center in Hvolsvöllur, a village in southern Iceland, insists, "The sagas of Icelanders, being renowned as outstanding masterpieces of literature, rank with the world's greatest literary treasures.... The epics of Homer, the Greek tragedy, and the plays of Shakespeare" (quoted in Lovgren). Echoes of the sagas continue to resound through modern Icelandic literature.

The *Völsunga Saga*, probably composed between 1270 and 1275 at the close of the skaldic era, is a heroic saga tracing the legendary deeds of the dragon-slaying hero Sigurd (analogous to the German Siegfried, hero of the *Nibelungenlied*); and his fatal relationship with Brynhild, a warrior maiden Odin had magically entranced and placed in a ring of fire for her disobedience. In Chapter 5 of the *Völsunga Saga*, Sigurd's ancestor King Volsung announces the code by which the traditional Icelandic hero was to live and die:

> All men can say in their own words that I gave my word, as an unborn child, and made this vow, that I would flee from neither fire nor iron because of fear, and so I have done even until now.... It is my counsel that we flee not at all, but do with our hands as bravely as we can.... I have always had victory, and it shall never be said that I would flee or sue for peace [quoted in Anderson 15].

In Chapter 20 of the *Völsunga Saga*, Sigurd breaks through the magic fire, releases Brynhild, and is as enthralled by her wisdom as by her beauty. He, the primordial Germanic hero, asks her to teach him, an example of the high regard for women in the primitive Germanic societies probably reinforced in Iceland by the Celtic tradition of women's equality with (and in some cases, superiority to) men. She agrees, on condition that they first drink together, a symbol of equals pledging fidelity to each other. The knowledge she teaches him appears in runes, magic preliterate Norse symbols incised on weapons and trees and ship prows and heroes' hands, primarily victory-runes, "cut on sword's hilt"; surf-runes, "to come safe from the sea"; speech-runes, "That no man may hatefully pay you back harm ... at the Thing,/When the folk shall fare unto full judgment" (quoted in Anderson 91). After she teaches him these and other runes, Sigurd replies: "I would not flee, though you knew me doomed;/ I have not been born with fear," and they bind one another with oaths. Later through witchcraft Sigurd breaks his oath to Brynhild, causing her to destroy him and then join him on his funeral pyre.

Scholars have suggested that after the writing of the heroic 13th–14th century sagas of kings and heroes, Icelanders realized that the original settlers from Norway were just as remarkable. Between the 13th and the 15th centuries they authored some forty of these stories in "prose transformations of certain Eddic motifs: of heroism, moral duties, and ideals," a literary period reaching its Golden Age between 1250 and the mid–1300s. Unlike the heroes of epics of other lands, however, the main characters of the Icelandic sagas are more realistic: they "are not consistently heroic" (Ólason and Tómasson in Neijmann 122), and often they suffer and even perish for their acts.

The Sagas of Icelanders reflect this people's intense interest in the settlement period and an equally powerful desire to preserve it in writing. Gisli Sigurðsson has cited two primary reasons for this literary phenomenon: first, settlement societies tend to be conservative in customs and traditions, but secondly and probably more pertinent in this case, "Iceland was not, originally at least, a purely Scandinavian country but had, at the time of the settlements, been a cultural and ethnic melting pot of people from both Norway and the Gaelic British Isles" (Hermann 287). The Icelanders who created the family sagas realized that memory alone could be an imperfect repository for their cultural values and that writing could save what might otherwise could be forgotten (Hermann 289). Their solution was unique in choosing special techniques to save memories from oblivion: "their recording of memories also involved a dynamic and creative dimension that not only saved memories from oblivion but also organized memories according to present needs" (Hermann 293). Danish scholar Pernille Hermann argues that the society in which the saga authors lived had experienced dramatic changes in a relatively short time—the settlement itself in the late 800s, then the acceptance of Christianity in 1000, and then the takeover by Norway in the mid–1200s. The Icelandic sagamen considered their work as "cultural memory" with "an interplay between present and past" enabling their society to survive changes and permit it to endure (Hermann 302).

In the "Old Icelandic Prose" section of *A History of Icelandic Literature*, Sverrir Tómasson outlines various techniques used by the authors of the Sagas of Icelanders, techniques preserved over many centuries that today provide a powerful and unique flavor to contemporary Icelandic crime fiction (see discussions of individual 21st century authors and their works below). According to Tómasson, the Sagas of Icelanders are mostly fictional, written in a narrative style close to actual spoken language that like the religious texts of the same historical period allows maximum comprehension. They are unusually objective, with relatively few dependent clauses or rhetorical devices like alliteration or metonymy but frequent instances of understatement and often illustrative proverbs. The vocabulary stresses action verbs and nouns demoting everyday objects, and when the anonymous narrator rarely intrudes, the first person plural pronoun "we" is used (Tómasson in Neijmann 86). Most of these stylistic traits are still observable in contemporary Icelandic crime fiction, even in translation of these works.

Today's authors of Icelandic crime fiction also frequently utilize the six-part structure that Tómasson cites as basic to most of the Sagas of Icelanders (again, see individual analyses below): an introduction, which in the Sagas usually includes genealogies; a generally brutal conflict leading to a climax; revenge; reconciliation; and the aftermath of these events. The individual events of the sagas often appear in chronological order, but many years may pass between them, and the narration generally reveals information in a restrained manner from a limited point of view. Frequent scene changes also slow down the approach of the climax (Tómasson in Neijmann 130–131).

Saga dialogues are "more reminiscent of refined spoken language in realistic plays ... than colloquial language" (Dasent 1), the kind of realistic verbal fireworks Ibsen brought to the stage and that now often animates conversations between contemporary Icelandic fictional detectives and their associates or the villains they interrogate, as with Arnaldur Indriðason's middle-aged, depressed, and laconic Erlendur or Yrsa Sigurðardóttir's Thora, a canny lawyer who usually cannot bring herself to answer the gibes of her irritating assistant Bella. One of the most accomplished of the Sagas of Icelanders, the *Njáls saga* (also called the *Njála*), illustrates the technique of foreshadowing favored by these authors and their literary descendants. At the beginning of this saga, the tale of the destruction of a respected family through a woman's infamy, the author shows that woman as a pretty little girl playing on the floor; her proud father asks his brother what he thinks of her, and finally his brother reluctantly replies, "Fair enough is this maid, and many will smart for it, but this I know not, whence thief's eyes have come into our race" (Dasent 1–2)—a stinging but realistic observation that presages the fatal family feud.

The authors of the Sagas of Icelanders, probably well-traveled in Europe and England, generally develop their characters from the outside, showing characters' thoughts through actions and events, usually highlighting some physical characteristic like the child's eyes in the *Njals saga*. Presenting such a physical feature upon the first introduction of the person gives an important clue to that person's behavior in the story like the physical appearance of the main revenge figure in the *Njáls saga*, Skarpéðinn, very much a warrior; the clash between his fine eyes and his ugly mouth indicates the warrior's dual role in this society: to nobly avenge his family's honor using as brutal means as he can.

Some saga characters also possess traits drawn from Norse mythological figures, though the characters are never exact avatars of those figures. Other characters may exhibit animal traits or relate to real life individuals, and some characters' names may refer to their roles in the narratives (Tómasson in Neijmann 135–7). The villains in the Sagas of Icelanders often exhibit supernatural characteristics, particularly the Icelandic *Draugr*, undead beings generally categorized as either ghosts or vampires. The sort of ghosts Icelanders call *trylla* (trolls) do not drain the actual blood of their victims, but like Tolkien's Nazgûl, their literary offspring, or Harry Potter's Dementors, themselves inspired by the Nazgûl, the Icelandic ghosts leave their victims drained of a vital force, like energy, mental faculties, or spirit. "Troll" can also denote a witch who "rides" her victims, which wicked Icelandic women often would be accused of doing.

In the medieval *Grettis saga*, Glámr, an Icelander with strange wide grey eyes, is hired to fight a monster that is haunting a valley so fearsomely that no one will tend the sheep there. Glámr boasts he does not fear evil spirits, but when he is found dead the evil spirit disappears and Glámr takes over its malignant operations in the valley. After the hero Grettir fights and defeats him, Grettir becomes feared and shunned in his own society. Medieval Icelanders seem to have accepted the notion that the German philosopher Nietzsche much later defined: "Whoever fights monsters should see to it that in the process he does not become a monster. And when you look long into an abyss, the abyss also looks into you" (quoted in Jakobsson 313). The principal danger for monster hunters in today's crime fiction is that the detective risks turning into a monster himself, a victim of the depression, the *Weltschmertz*, the emotional insecurity troubling many Icelandic detectives, notably Arnaldur Indriðason's moody Inspector Erlendur.

In presenting the respective roles of men and women, most of the Sagas of Icelanders show that "good" housewives rarely figure in the plots, but anonymous (or nearly so) itinerant women and servants can and do influence the plot, usually bringing about some negative development (Tómasson in Neijmann 135–7). The *Svarfdale Saga*, one of the lesser Sagas of the Icelanders, follows the intertwined fortunes of two male characters and unites elements of historical fact and fairy tale. It stands out from the other Sagas of Icelanders because of its treatment of a central female figure (Bachman and Erlingsson 4) and foreshadows the feminist themes apparent in 21st century Scandinavian crime fiction, especially novels by Icelandic women authors. Throughout the *Svarfdale Saga*, no female character is treated with much sympathy; this fact demonstrates misogyny and contempt for the erotic, shown through vicious attacks, both by humiliating language and by physical torture of the central female character Yngvildr, who because of a territorial conflict is caught between her lover and his sworn enemy, a monstrous-looking *berserker* eight feet tall, with a twisted body, two teeth protruding from his skull, and a gaping mouth, suggesting legendary trolls and demons. As her family's bargaining chip, Yngvildr is eventually forced to marry him. During peace negotiations, she dares speak out against what she considers the vast injustice of this forced marriage and thereby incurs severe torments lasting over many years. Yngvildr loses almost everything, and eventually filled with remorse and shame, she "accepts that she is 'entirely responsible' for the causes of her grief and resigns herself to the idea that her life cannot exist without men…. Some say she killed herself out of unhappiness" (Waugh 177). By speaking out she threatened her society and the social repercussions of doing so cause her prolonged and unjust suffering. The *Svarfdale Saga* thus illustrates "a deep prejudice against this woman's abilities: expressiveness, directness, intelligence, discernment, leadership, self-promotion, and originality" (Waugh 151). Yngvildr's fate illustrates the repercussions of an attitude responsible for many of the crimes against women that appear in contemporary Scandinavian crime fiction.

As a group the Sagas of Icelanders present a world view marked by the struggle to survive in an unforgiving environment, "which determines the way people in the sagas view themselves, their existence, and their families" (Barraclough 365). Other major themes also appear: the sagas often show cases where an individual has to take power, establish himself as a family chieftain, and establish control over the family, a process which he initiates by traveling abroad to observe successful rulers. In these sagas, the concept of honor covers the entire family, and it never can be compromised without retaliation upon the offenders. Luck or fate also plays an important part in the sagas, with success or failure of a family occurring arbitrarily. Discussing the motif of outlawry, the ultimate punishment in Germanic society for major offenses such as breaking one's oath, scholars have found that features of the physical Icelandic saga landscape and its climate act as literary devices the author uses to direct the action (Barraclough 365), as for example the snowstorm which operates so importantly in the psychological portrait Arnaldur Indriðason created for his detective protagonist Erlendur. Finally, the supernatural, through magicians and sorcerers, also often figures in the sagas, an echo of the old pagan culture that still resounds in superstition motifs of contemporary Icelandic crime novels, in particular Yrsa Sigurðardóttir's fiction.

The genre of the Sagas of Icelanders peaked "when antiheroes who mocked the old ideals and values started to appear" (Tómasson). Saga writing decreased markedly after the 14th century, when the old sagas began to be copied and sometimes emended. Imitations of the old sagas were still being produced in the 17th century and even well into the 19th century, with new stories set in districts of Iceland not represented in earlier sagas (Tómasson in Neijmann 139). The continued popularity of the saga genre in Iceland is probably due to its development during the medieval saga period, when Icelandic writers had exhibited "remarkable obstinacy" in not adopting the Latin narrative modes popular in Europe, instead using conflicting elements of two cultures, the native oral tradition and the learned rhetorical process. Tómasson believes that Iceland's medieval masterpieces, like the *Njáls saga*, used the best from "native artistic skill" and "a critical attitude toward foreign learning" (Tómasson in Neijmann 173).

The Sagas of the Icelanders provide the most important source of Icelandic historical and cultural material as well as a significant genre of national literature that has transmitted many techniques, themes, and ideals to modern Icelandic letters, including crime fiction. The Middle Icelandic literature that followed between the 15th and the 19th centuries was comprised mostly of religious works, especially after the Reformation, when Iceland was still a part of Denmark. After Christian III came to the Danish throne in 1536, he immediately adopted Lutheran Protestantism, seized Roman Catholic church property, and in 1550 executed the last Roman Catholic bishop in Iceland, effectively destroying that denomination's political power and influence in the country. The Lutheran Church owned and controlled all the printing in Iceland for the next two centuries, though the new Icelandic Lutheran bishops maintained their enthusiasm for Old Icelandic literature. Often ordained Lutheran clergymen copied medieval sagas, usually on paper, not vellum (Stevens xviii). Oddur Gottskálksson's full Icelandic translation of the Bible appeared in 1540, the oldest book printed in Icelandic, as did Jón Þorláksson á Baegisá's *Paradisarmissir*, a translation of John Milton's *Paradise Lost*, a powerful example of the new ideas entering Iceland from abroad and profoundly affecting its society, while the new church was strictly regulating literature and culture (Eggertsdóttir in Neijmann 194). One of those ideas was Milton's portrait of a powerful and charismatic Satan in Book I of *Paradise Lost*, prefiguring many later magnetic fictional criminals.

In the 17th century, Icelanders, then about 55,000, suffered under severe trade restrictions imposed by the Danish monarchy that limited Icelandic commerce to certain Danish citizens and thus turned Iceland into "a zone of fisheries and a source of income only the Danes could exploit" (Eggertsdóttir in Neijmann 195). About a quarter of Icelanders were literate, however, and because of the Icelandic *kvoldvaka* tradition of at-home evening entertainments with music and stories, all Icelanders had access to some literature, preferably romances, folktales, and of course the sagas. In 1688 the printing press at Skálholt in southern Iceland published the first work of secular Old

Icelandic literature in the island nation, the *Landnámabök* (The Book of Settlements), one of the earliest accounts of the first settlers in Iceland.

According to Icelandic literary historian Margrét Eggertsdóttir, the optimistic and reformational 18th century Enlightenment, that renewal of classicism and awakening of rationalism so significant in the literary history of England and Germany, did not take a firm hold in Iceland, mostly because Icelandic society at that time was largely static and agrarian. The country also had no emergent bourgeois class hungering for novels, as European society was then doing (Eggertsdóttir in Neijmann 226). Romances and folktales instead maintained their popularity in Iceland and substantially influenced the development of the novel there. Other factors peculiar to Iceland severely limited the Enlightenment's influence as well; at the start of the 18th century, Iceland experienced extensive crop failures and famine, and the 1706–1709 smallpox epidemic reduced the population to under 40,000, its all-time low. The worst volcanic eruptions in Iceland's history exacerbated Iceland's misery, beginning with the Katla eruption in 1755 and peaking with the Skaftá eruption in 1783–84, its lava flows and lethal ash producing the "Famine of the Mist," followed by earthquakes, widespread starvation, and yet another smallpox epidemic. Iceland's literature exhibited a striking contradiction: during the Enlightenment, the Icelandic language began to reject the Danish linguistic influence and return to the style of the Saga Age, while at the same time Icelandic translations from world literature fostered an incipient nationalism and produced a spirit of cosmopolitanism by infusing new ideas from Europe (Stevens xx).

Despite all of Iceland's 18th century hardships, Old Icelandic was "alive and understandable" in the 18th century (Eggertsdóttir in Neijmann 230). Scholarly opinion differs on when the novel first appeared in Icelandic literature, though an experiment in storytelling, Eirikur Laxdal's romance, *Saga Ólafs Þórhallasonar* ("The Saga of Ölafur Þórhallason") appeared in the latter half of the 18th century, combining a language very close to the Old Norse of the sagas in both grammar and syntax with some elements of the modern novel. Laxdal had spent considerable time in Copenhagen and was familiar with the works of the important Danish author and playwright Ludwig Holberg, especially Holberg's adventure story *Niels Klim*, an episodic coming-of-age tale. Laxdal's young hero Ölafur has many adventures, too, with a peculiarly Icelandic supernatural twist: some of them involve female elves who control Ölafur's subsequent destiny as he overcomes obstacles and learns through adversity that self-knowledge is the path to maturity. Eggertsdóttir concludes that Ölafur resembles characters in modern or postmodern literature, because his personality is "divided and inconsistent" and "the truth is fluid, things are not always as they seem" (quoted in Óskarsson, in Neijmann 250), a major motif in Icelandic crime fiction.

At the opening of the 19th century, Iceland experienced a linguistic and literary revival. Not only did Romantic poetry captivate Icelandic poets and readers in the 1830s, but exciting new forms of literature also became popular. Matthias Jochumsson, 1835–1920, initiated modern Icelandic drama. Jónas Hallgrimsson, a poet and natural scientist who produced the first modern Icelandic short stories, influenced Jón Thoroddsen, 1818–68, who authored the long narrative *Piltur og stúlka* ("Lad and Lass"), making him generally accepted as the father of the modern Icelandic novel. The supposedly new literary forms, however, drew upon staples of Icelandic storytelling, like Icelandic patriotism, which Hallgrimsson defended by honing the contrast between the nation's golden age of sagas and its subsequent "downfall and humiliation." Throroddsen's novels, which became models frequently used by Icelandic 19th and 20th century novelists, followed one basic pattern, the struggles of virtuous young lovers whose wicked parents or relatives have other marital plans for them. According to Þórir Óskarsson, Throroddsen's "comic and grotesque 'antiheroes'" (Óskarsson in Neijmann 296–7), recall the monstrous saga villains who personified human flaws. Such characters represent Throroddsen's major contribution to revitalizing Icelandic prose. Because of the rise of nationalism in the mid–1800s, around 1860 Icelandic collectors began to publish folk and fairy tales, always "the mainstay of Icelandic narrative art," stories about "outlaws, trolls, elves, ghosts, and magic," linking their traditional material and style to the rising nationalistic spirit (Óskarsson in Neijmann 297, 299). Benedikt Gröndal, another innovative author of the times, broke with tradition by creating boisterous comic stories in the 1860s, parodying the style of Icelandic chivalric narratives. Óskarsson feels that no other author influenced Icelandic comic and parodic writing so strongly, especially influencing þórgergur Þórdarson, 1888–1974, and Halldór Laxness, 1902–1998, two of Iceland's major 20th century novelists. Finally, a proliferation of translations brought more new literary ideas into Iceland, especially Hallgrímsson's translations of German Romantic poet Heinrich Heine's works, which critics have suggested left the most lasting impression of any foreign author on Icelandic literature. In addition, the second Icelandic printing press, set up in 1852 in Akureyri, allowed more Icelandic authors to see their work in print.

Toward the end of the 19th century, the progress and innovation that Europe was enjoying seemed to have passed Iceland by; according to Árni Pálsson, "the idea that Iceland was in fact a doomed country—doomed to huddle outside European culture, the nation, like an outlaw, incapable of taking part in the work of progress of other nations—had taken root like a poison in the minds of most Icelanders" (Á víð og dreif 333–34, quoted by Elísson in Neijmann 309). Pálsson even suggested that Denmark might have been happy to be rid of Iceland when Christian IX granted the Althing legislative authority and issued a new Icelandic constitution, granting the nation Home Rule (Elísson in Neijmann 309). More volcanic eruptions, grueling winters, and a series of earthquakes intensified the nation's collective pessimism, causing about 15,000 Icelanders, over 80 percent of them under thirty, to emigrate to North America, most of them settling in Manitoba between 1870 and 1914 (Elísson in Neijmann 310). The general sense of hopelessness that beset the Icelanders who stayed home only gradually lifted in the early 20th century, when telegraph communication between Iceland and other nations broke Iceland's long isolation. The shift in Iceland's fisheries from open rowboats to motorized trawlers revolutionized the country's fishing industry, so that farmers flocked to coastal towns. Romantic fiction gave way to realistic and naturalistic stories and novels which addressed Iceland's social problems, embodying powerful social criticism in the most objective descriptive writing possible.

In the late 19th century Danish critic Georg Brandes, 1842–1927, had provided the major impetus for the development of Scandinavian literary realism. Many Icelanders sent to Copenhagen for their higher education became acquainted with his theory that literature in his time lived "because it puts problems under debate" (quoted in Elísson in Neijmann 312). Brandes felt that Scandinavian authors should become society's healers, and his opinions, published in the journal Verðandi in 1882, mark the beginning of Iceland's realist movement. Gestur Pálsson, one of the journal's founders, issued a manifesto for the movement the next year that insisted nothing could be beautiful unless it was true, and that writers should "look into the hearts and souls of men, learn to know them, write about them," so that literature could be "truly useful to human society" (quoted in Elísson in Neijmann 313).

Starting with Denmark's granting of home rule to Iceland in 1874, Iceland's independence movement progressed in slow but steady peaceful stages: in 1918 the country received independent status under the Danish king, and the Republic of Iceland was declared on June 17, 1944. During the twentieth century Iceland transitioned from a virtually medieval agrarian society to a modern affluent and chiefly urban society based on its newly motorized fishing industry. In 1900, Reykjavik's population was less than 7000, but by 2000 it had swelled to 283,000. This transition from a basically rural to a basically urban society "with the fundamental contrasts that mark off a rural and frugal past from the modern, metropolitan materialism of Europe and North America, is one of the great tensions that Icelandic literature, particularly fiction, portrays" (Stevens xxii), a contradictory tension embodied in the literary genre of the realistic novel, in which authors portray and dissect both the ills and the benefits of a newly affluent society. Iceland's realistic novels rely on Icelandic history and "the ethos of Icelandic country living," functioning in turbulent modern times just as the medieval Sagas of Icelanders did during their socially volatile time. Both the Icelandic realistic novels and the Sagas of Icelanders depict "not only difficult, often tragic, personal circumstances but also the backdrop of insidious societal changes" (Stevens xxiii). This is particularly true of Icelandic crime fiction, though it did not achieve widespread popularity until early in the new millennium.

Halldór Laxness, 1902–1998, Iceland's national icon and its only recipient of the Nobel Prize for Literature (1955), was a prolific and versatile author of poetry, fiction, drama, and autobiography recognized as both thoroughly Icelandic and international in scope (Kress 127). Writing in the realist tradition, "he believed he understood social issues better than anyone else," and according to his Nobel citation, in his long life, which nearly spanned the 20th century, Laxness renewed "the great narrative art of Iceland through the epic power of his work" (Kress 128). Laxness's first volume of short fiction, 1923, announced his decades-long preoccupation with the typical Iceland farmer's struggles against inimical nature. In one story, his protagonist lives by the old saga code and believes in the pagan gods, and when competing for the love of a local girl against a young cosmopolitan artist who has come to paint in the area, the farmer wins her by acting courageously during a volcanic eruption, while the artist flees in terror, an illustration of Laxness's abiding theme: an Icelander can simultaneously belong to his own country and the world through maintaining his unique cultural values, like courage and fortitude in the face of extreme adversity.

Two of Laxness's literary descendants in the mainstream Icelandic realist tradition, Einar Már Guðmundsson, b. 1954, and Einar Kárason, b. 1955, both maintain literary affinities with the saga tradition while using realistic, even naturalistic, techniques. Einar Már Guðmundsson, a poet and screenwriter, also experiments with "magic realism" in the mode of Gabriel Garcia Márquez and Salman Rushdie, using "tones and modulations ... at once international and cosmopolitan as well as deeply traditional," often melding poems with stories in a coherent narrative, "a technique as old as the sagas" (Allard 52). Einar Kárason, another dramatist and screenwriter, writes novels which mythologize urban life among the underprivileged. His best-known work is the *Island* ("Iceland") trilogy on life in postwar Reykjavik, realistically tracing three generations through a transitional phase in Icelandic culture, "when industrialization, urban living, American influences, increasing wealth, and a newly independent Republic of Iceland ... came of age in the 1950s ... an almost mythical period" in a narrative form "reminiscent of folktales" (Guðmundsdóttir 44). The first volume of the *Island* trilogy appeared as a play in 1987, and volumes one and two were made into films in 1996 and 2002.

Deriving both from the sagas and the modern realist movement, crime fiction, most often focusing on social issues, burgeoned much earlier in the other Nordic countries than it did in Iceland. Norway's crime fiction experienced its first golden age between 1910 and 1930, largely through the stories of Sven Elvestad, and its second golden age during the Nazi occupation, 1940–1945. Denmark saw a rise in its crime fiction just prior to World War II, Finland's crime fiction flourished while the nation was fighting wars with the Soviet Union between 1939 and 1944, and Sweden's began slowly in the 1930s, grew steadily in the 1950s, and began to explode after the 1967 publication of *Roseanna*, the first novel of the Martin Beck series by Sjöwall and Wahlöö, which ignited the contemporary phenomenon of *Scandikrimi*.

Although almost all of the medieval Icelandic sagas involve crime and punishment, the Iceland's modern crime fiction tradition grew slowly. Katrín Jakobsdóttir, in "Meaningless Icelanders: Icelandic Crime Fiction and Nationality" (Jakobsdóttir in Nestingen and Arvas 46–61), considers nationality a theme in "what was probably the first Icelandic crime story" (46), "An Icelandic Sherlock Holmes," written in the early 20th century in Canada by Jóhann Magnus Bjarnason and featuring a young Icelandic emigrant to Canada who investigates criminal activity. Bjarnason, born in Iceland in 1866, had himself immigrated to Canada in 1875. According to *The Canadian Encyclopedia*, Bjarnason, considered the greatest and most prolific of Icelandic-Canadian novelists, wrote three novels, poetry, articles, and at least twenty plays, all firmly rooted in the Icelandic-Canadian emigrant experience, while teaching in small communities in Manitoba and North Dakota. Jakobsdóttir feels that "An Icelandic Sherlock Holmes" confirmed the need Icelanders felt to have their own Great Detective "in order to be equal with other nations." The story "excited Icelanders back in Iceland and appealed to their idea of nationality" (Jakobsdóttir in Nestigen and Arvas 46–47).

Between 1916 and 1922 the popular Icelandic novelist Einar H. Kvaran wrote well received novels involving crime, books which advanced his bourgeois Protestant orientation as well as his interest in spiritualism. *Sambýli* ("Neighbors"), 1918, and *Sálin vaknar* ("The Soul Awakens"), 1916, both contain characters who for moral reasons commit crimes, and through Christian repentance they receive material rewards. The protagonist of "The Soul Awakens," a clairvoyant, solves a crime and then chooses a jail sentence for smuggling the murderer out of the country, but he is rewarded for his charitable though unlawful action by a bright future in politics.

For a long time, according to Quentin Bates, a British author who sets his own crime novels in Iceland, Icelanders did not consider crime stories as "literature," one major reason for the relative lack of Icelandic crime fiction prior to 2000. Bates has researched a short list of Icelandic crime fiction authors writing prior to 1967, including "Einar Skálaglamm," the pseudonym of Guðbrandur Jónsson, author of *Húsið við Norðurá* ("The House by the North River"), 1926, which Bates says may be the first homegrown Icelandic crime novel. Bates believes the "first true Icelandic crime story" was *Allt i lagi i Reykjavik* ("All's Well in Reykjavik"), 1939 (Bates, "Icelandic noir"), but other literary historians give that title to historical novelist Gunnar Gunnarsson's *Svartfugl*, 1929 (*The Black Cliffs*, tr. 1967), although it is not a detective or suspense story. Gunnarsson based it on an actual early 19th century Icelandic murder case, using official documents from the trials of Bjarni Bjarnason and Steinunn Sveinsdóttir, sentenced to death for murdering their spouses on the small western Iceland farm where they all lived. Gunnarsson probes the issue of human responsibility through his narrator, the parish pastor who witnessed the trials, forced the accused into confessing their crimes, and later pondered his responsibility for their fates (Jóhannsson in Neijmann 378). Bates lists but does not discuss three 1932 crime novels by "Valentinus," the pen name of Steindór Sigurðsson: *Sonur Hefndarinnar* ("The Son of Vengeance"); *Týnda flugvélin* ("The Lost Aircraft"); and *Leyndardómar Reykjavikur* ("Reykjavik Secrets"); and a series of post–World War II crime novels Steingrímur Sigfússon wrote under the name "Valur Vestan." Bates also notes that at least three other Icelandic authors published crime fiction under pseudonyms (Bates, "Legacy").

Andrew Nestigen and Paula Arvas state that Iceland experienced a golden age of crime fiction during the 1930s and 1940s (Nestingen and Arvas 4), but the only author and work they specify from this period is Ólafur Friðriksson, a leftist political figure whose *Allt i lagi i Reykjavik* ("All's Well in Reykjavik," 1939), criticized Iceland's ruling elite and the system that supported them (Nestigen and Arvas 4). Much later Viktor Arnar Ingólfsson produced two youthful crime novels in 1978 and 1982 respectively, but he did not return to the genre until 1998, when he published

Engin Spor ("No Trace"), followed by several other crime novels. In "Icelandic Prose Literature, 1940–2000," in *A History of Icelandic Literature*, literary historians Ástráður Eysteinsson and Úlfhildur Dagsdóttir maintain that "Popular genres such as crime fiction have no tradition in Iceland," but they note that Birgitta H. Halldórsdóttir, b. 1959, began publishing romance-thriller-crime-story novels in 1983. After that, she published approximately one novel per year, eventually contributing to the "sudden surge" in Icelandic crime fiction that began in 1997 when Arnaldur Indriðason and "Stella Blómkvist" (a pseudonym) published their first crime novels, *Synir duftsins* ("Sons of Earth") and *Morðið í Stjórnarráðinu* ("Murder at Government Hall") respectively. A newly respectful critical attitude toward Icelandic crime fiction thus seems to be emerging recently. Eysteinsson and Dagsdóttir concur with Katrín Jakobsdóttir that since crime novels allow social analysis and commentary about current issues (Jakobsdóttir in Nestigen and Avras 48), they are now a "welcome addition" to contemporary Icelandic literature, which they feel has tended to focus on the past and "not attended to the nuances of modern society" (Eysteinsson and Dagsdóttir in Neijmann 459).

Another reason for the dearth of original Icelandic crime fiction in the 1940s and 1950s may have been the boom in translated fiction that comprised most Icelandic book production during that period. During the World War II American occupation of Iceland, Icelandic publishers issued over 700 translated novels and short story collections, three times as many as they had during the 1930s (Eysteinsson and Dagsdóttir in Neijmann 409). Much of it was popular literature, and much of that was American hard-boiled detective fiction. Eysteinsson and Dagsdóttir conclude that translations for a long time predominantly filled the needs for popular, as opposed to literary, fiction for contemporary Icelandic readers: "Until late into the twentieth century it was an exception to see … a thriller or a detective novel written by a native author" (Eysteinsson and Dagsdóttir in Neijmann 409). For Icelanders the most popular mainstream translated authors were Americans John Steinbeck, Ernest Hemingway, Pearl Buck, and Jack London, all writing in the realist tradition, and major early 20th century Scandinavian authors like Sigrid Undset and Knut Hamsun of Norway, Selma Lagerlöf of Sweden, and Martin Andersen Nexo of Denmark (Eysteinsson and Dagsdóttir in Neijmann 409–410). Moreover, even today Icelandic publishers bringing out new home-grown fiction must compete hard for the attention of readers who are as comfortable with English as they are with their own language (Bates, "Iceland noir").

Until recently, Iceland's relatively homogeneous and highly literate population and its low crime rate have contributed to its late development of native crime fiction, also affected by the nation's concentration on "serious" literature. Iceland, boasting a 99 percent literacy rate, publishes more books per capita—3.5 books published for every 1000 Icelanders—than any other country in the world, a number double that of Norway, Sweden, Finland and Denmark combined (Medley). Sjón, one of the foremost Icelandic mainstream authors today, claims that since Iceland was a very poor country until well into the 20th century, "We have no cathedrals … no paintings … no symphonies …. Literature is the only constant cultural activity that has been going on throughout the centuries" (quoted in Medley). Iceland's capital Reykjavik became one of only seven UNESCO Cities of Literature in 2011.

Largely due to the work of the first two highly popular Icelandic crime authors Arnaldur Indriðason and Yrsa Sigurðardóttir, however, Icelandic crime fiction has now become "mainstream [and] respectable … even Iceland's current education minister, Katrín Jakobsdóttir, completed a university thesis that focused on crime fiction" (Bates, "Iceland noir"). Recently Iceland has been hosting increased numbers of tourists interested in its literary culture, including crime fiction, highlighted in the initial Iceland Noir festival held on November 20–23, 2014, with prominent internationally known crime writers David Hewson (Britain), Johan Theorin (Sweden), Vidar

Sundstøl (Norway), and Antti Tuomainen (Finland) as featured guest speakers (see entry for Ragnar Jónasson, below),

Most new Icelandic novels first appear in the *Jolabokaflod*, the "Christmas Book Flood" (Teicher), a tradition dating from World War II. Kristján B. Jónasson, president of the Iceland Publishers Association, notes that gift books, mostly hardcovers, are given on Christmas Eve "and people spend the night reading ... it's the backbone of the publishing sector here in Iceland" (quoted in Teicher). Most of the 1.2 million books loaned to a city population of 200,000 by the Reykjavik City Library in 2009 were general fiction and biographies, though Icelanders have shown some other surprising reading tastes. In 2007 one unusual bestseller was a pictorial history of tractors in Iceland, and another was Gudmundur Kristinsson's self-published *Summerland*, an account of the octogenarian author's purported dialogues with the dead, which sold out completely before Christmas 2010 and again in a February 2011 reprint edition (Teicher). Crime fiction is also making inroads in that holiday publishing flood. The growing success of translated Scandinavian crime fiction has recently introduced a new trend by bringing more paperbacks into the Icelandic book market. "The book in Iceland is such an enormous gift, you give a physical book. You don't give e-books here" (quoted in Teicher).

When it did begin appearing, Iceland's crime fiction addressed the same social problems that preoccupied other Nordic crime authors. The severe Icelandic financial crisis that began in 2008 ("The Crash") may well be the most significant event that has affected both Iceland's problems and the Icelandic crime fiction that deals with them. Before the crash, Iceland had already experienced an extreme economic transformation: prior to 1900, it was one of the poorest countries in Western Europe with an income derived mainly from fishing, but only a century later, in 2007 Iceland ranked seventh among the most productive countries in the world, with a per capita income of $54,858 and such a strong economic growth that it ranked first on the United Nations' Human Development Index. With a "Scandinavian-type social-market economy [that] combines a capitalist structure and free-market principles with an extensive welfare system .... Iceland had achieved high growth, low unemployment, and a remarkably even distribution of income" (*Index Mundi*). Since the economy still depended heavily on the fishing industry and fishing stocks began to decline around 2000, Iceland diversified into manufacturing and service industries, primarily fueled by the nation's abundant geothermal and hydroelectric power sources which attracted substantial foreign investment in the aluminum sector.

Before the crash, "everything had been more or less exaggerated: salaries, the value of the Icelandic crown, housing prices, the standard of living" (Kennedy). Households had taken on huge debts equivalent to 213 percent of their disposable income, leading to inflation which dramatically increased when the Central Bank of Iceland issued liquidity loans to banks on the basis of newly-issued uncovered bonds—in essence printing money on demand ("Kreppanomics"). After the privatization of the Icelandic banking sector in 2001, banks ballooned, backing risky ventures by "Icelandic Finance Vikings" (Sigfússon), and the country's financial sector aggressively expanded in foreign markets, with both consumers and businesses borrowing heavily. Consumption and the real estate market also rose markedly, swelling the economy and causing even more massive borrowing. As a result, the world recession that began in December 2007 devastated Iceland's economy. When the access to easy loans halted, three of the nation's largest banks, almost the nation's whole financial system, failed within a week of each other. Their foreign exposure was unsustainable: loans and other assets totaled more than ten times the country's Gross Domestic Product of $19 billion, and their combined debt exceeded approximately six times that figure. Taxes on companies and capital had also been lowered, further overheating the economy (Sigfússon) and economic collapse ensued. Iceland's unemployment peaked at 9.4 percent in February

2009, and the same year the nation's Gross Domestic Product fell 6.8 percent (*Index mundi*). On October 9, 2008, the government froze all trading on the OMX Iceland Nordic Exchange for two days; the crash also effectively shut down the foreign exchange market, the Icelandic *krona* was devalued by nearly 50 percent, the assets of pension funds were expected to shrink by 15 to 25 percent, and unprecedented riots broke out in Reykjavik. Reflecting on his October 2008 visit to Reykjavik to offer assistance from the International Monetary Fund, Poul M. Thomsen commented, "The sense of fear and shock were palpable—few, if any, countries had ever experienced such a catastrophic economic crash" (Thomsen).

Iceland staggered under the crash. In 2008 no one knew how large the losses would be and how they would be shared between foreigners and Icelanders. Fears that deposit runs would cripple what was left of the financial system were rampant (Thomsen). By late November 2008, the economic indicators of the Central Bank of Iceland revealed that unemployment had more than tripled; 24 percent of the workforce had experienced pay cuts, and inflation was predicted to climb as high as 75 percent. Some analysts predicted mass emigration, double dip recession, and sovereign default (Sigfússon). The bank accounts of all Icelanders plummeted, and a political crisis loomed when President Ólafur Grímsson refused to sign a bill to repay Britain and the Netherlands more than $5 billion, calling for a referendum (Quinn, January 6, 2010). That controversy arose because of the collapse of Icesave, a subsidiary of the Icelandic bank *Landsbanki* which operated in Britain and the Netherlands only. Tens of thousands of British and Dutch customers, lured by high interest rates, had lost the savings they had invested there, and since the British and Dutch governments had compensated them for their losses, those governments now expected to have Iceland repay them over $5 billion—an estimated cost to Icelandic taxpayers of up to $18,000 per citizen, including interest payments. At this point, Iceland was relying on a $2.1 billion loan from the International Monetary Fund and a $2.5 billion loan from the Scandinavian countries to cover their obligations (Quinn, January 6, 2010). Voters, however, rejected the debt repayment plan as "an unfair result of their own government's failure to curtail the recklessness of a handful of bank executives," particularly those who grew their operations to attract British and Dutch customers with promised high returns from online savings (Quinn, March 7, 2010).

Disgusted with the policies and persons they blamed for the crash, Icelanders took to the streets in January 2009 in "collective rage against elites who trashed a once thriving country and thought they could get away with it" (Klein). For the first time since the anti–NATO protests in 1949, the government had to use tear gas to disperse the rioters in front of the Althing building. Guðrun Jónsdóttir, a 36-year-old office worker, summed up the prevailing public mood bluntly: "I don't trust the government, I don't trust the banks, I don't trust the political parties and I don't trust the IMF. We had a good country, and they ruined it" (quoted in Klein). Responding to this bitterness in a 2009 interview with *ForbesWoman*, newly elected Prime Minister Jóhanna Sigurðardóttir promoted several solutions: seeking Iceland's entrance into the European Union and adopting the euro; and balancing the country's 12 percent of GDP deficit by 2012 through deep expenditure cuts and tax increases. She declared, "Purchasing power and standard of living will therefore have to contract sharply," and she also insisted that cuts to Iceland's welfare system, around 70 percent of government expenditure, "will be unavoidable" (quoted in Serafin).

Criminal investigations into the causes of the crash began in April 2009 under special consultant Eva Joly, who predicted that building evidence for securing prosecutions would take two to three years. Her investigation was expected to focus on Icelandic banks' questionable financial practices, such as making nearly half their loans to holding companies connected to their own banks. Another of the banks' questionable procedures involved loaning money to their own employees to buy shares in the same banks while using the same shares as collateral for the loans. Interest payments were deferred until the end of the period, and the loans were then allegedly written off a few days before the banks collapsed. Kaupthing, the largest bank in Iceland, allowed a Qatari investor to "buy" 5 percent of its shares using a loan from Kaupthing itself and a holding company that was associated with one of Kaupthing's associates, so that the bank was actually buying its own shares (Mason). Iceland's former Prime Minister Davíð Oddson insisted that the investigation should also include "unusual and unconventional loans banks gave to senior politicians prior to the Crash" (Mason). Björn Bjarnason, Iceland's former Minister for Justice and Ecclesiastical Affairs, in a blog compared some aspects of the causes of the crash to the U.S. Enron situation. He also claimed, "Here companies have been playing a game, using the media and publishing to make themselves look good. We only hope that the foreign media will soon begin to understand what has been going on" (quoted in Mason).

Since 2009, three major strategies in emergency legislation passed in October 2008 seem to be putting Iceland's finances back on a sustainable path (Thomsen). First, the national Financial Supervisory Authority would take over the domestic operations of the three largest banks; second, the IMF Stand-By-Arrangement, in effect since November 2008, would mandate tax raises and painful austerity, a downsized domestic banking system, and capital controls; and third, the government would apply for European Union membership, which would enhance Iceland's credibility on international financial markets (Jonsson). Currently Icelandic unemployment is decreasing and banks are now fully recapitalized (Thomsen), but unanswered questions and public outrage remain. Both pundits and the public hold the right-wing Independence Party, which had led most Icelandic coalition governments for the three decades prior to the 2009 election, responsible for political and economic policies causing the crash. Many Icelandic business leaders have received negative public scrutiny for their roles in the crash; some have fled the country, three have become subjects of YouTube satire set to the movie "Godfather" musical theme, and Jón Ásgeir Jóhannesson, who co-owned the huge Baugur Group retail empire that included a large part of Iceland's media, was found guilty at trial for false accounting (Mason).

During her 2011 lecture visit to Iceland, Margrit Kennedy, author of *Interest and Inflation Free Money*, gathered anecdotal evidence about Icelanders' perceptions of the effects of the crash. She had gone to Iceland to discover whether the new popularly elected 25-member Constitutional Council, whose responsibility was the formulation of proposals for a new Icelandic constitution, had issued any statements about the nation's financial system, because Kennedy had been unable to find any such material. Kennedy heard several differing views. An ethics professor from Reykjavik University told Kennedy that the Council was occupied with "laying new groundwork" for their democracy, environmental protection, and protection of the commons, more transparency in governmental affairs and thereby better regulatory capacities, but they had not studied the "systemic monetary roots of the crash." An Icelandic economist told Kennedy that Iceland was now catching up to the rules other European democracies had long been following, such as transparency of public budgets; earlier monetary matters had not been discussed by government leaders, except that an index was applied to loans to reduce excessive credit demands. A young singer Kennedy met told her that people had been furious at becoming poorer, but he had not seen any new values being adopted. Such anecdotal evidence apparently reflects lingering public discontent with governmental financial policies.

Barry Forshaw has recently noted "a widespread perception that Icelandic politics are markedly corrupt," promoting an endemic "culture of cronyism" there (Forshaw 129). He also sees a "grim specter" in the rise of the far right in Iceland, citing Quentin Bates, who lived in Iceland for over ten years and writes respected crime novels with Icelandic settings and characters.

Bates believes that the growing far right movement with possible neo–Nazi roots unsettles older Icelanders who have "numerous skeletons rattling in closets" (quoted in Forshaw 129). Besides political and economic corruption and neo–Nazism, other symptoms of societal tensions that the crash and its bitter aftermath intensified include immigration and racism; drug problems; and women's issues, particularly those related to Iceland's welfare system. All provide raw material and strong themes and motifs for Iceland's growing number of crime fiction authors.

Compared to other countries, modern Iceland has experienced very little crime, which may also provide a reason for the late development of contemporary Icelandic crime fiction. According to Yrsa Sigurðardóttir, Iceland's current "Queen of Crime," Iceland's lack of crime is "extremely depressing for a crime writer," especially since those few crimes are "excruciatingly boring" (Sigurðardóttir 61), though probably not so for the victims. Currently Iceland boasts the lowest homicide rate in Scandinavia: in 2011 2.2 murders per 1 million people, compared to Norway's 6.9 per 1 million, Sweden's 10.6, Denmark's 12.2, Finland's 23.4, and the United States' 56.3 (Kachka). Comparisons between Iceland's crime rates in 1997–1998 and in 2011–2012, however, show that the incidence of crimes other than murder is rising in Iceland. Interpol data indicate that between 1997 and 1998, the murder rate in Iceland decreased by 100 percent, the incidence of rape decreased by 11.1 percent and burglary decreased by 15.7 percent, but aggravated assaults increased by 31.6 percent, robbery by 100 percent, and larceny increased an astonishing 4,661 percent, The same report noted that violence against women in 1997–1998 continued to be a concern, because while the incidence of rapes and sexual assaults appeared low, the numbers of women seeking help from various agencies and hospitals indicated that many such incidents were going unreported, despite strong governmental directives against violence directed at women and children. In the same period, too, human trafficking rose with Eastern and Central European women either brought to Iceland and coerced to work in striptease clubs and/or prostitution or temporarily situated in Iceland as a transit point between Europe and North America. The Interpol report also cited growing concern that with the 1990s trend of increased narcotics use, even in Iceland, mainly amphetamines, cocaine and ecstasy, in the future Iceland could not only see increased local drug sales but it could also become a transit point for drug trafficking (Interpol data cited from "Crime and Society").

According to the 2012 "Overall Crime and Safety Report" for Iceland published on the OCS website by the U.S. Bureau of Diplomatic Security of the Department of State, drawn from local news sources and from the Icelandic National Police records for 2001–2010, Iceland's Crash caused "a relatively minor up-tick in general crime." The report also found that no significant political demonstrations had occurred since 2009, though when the Althing opened in October 2011, Icelanders still disturbed by the crash pelted the parliament building with eggs, paint, and garbage. Icelandic police have identified minor organized crime groups from Eastern Europe and from the other Nordic countries, like the Icelandic extension approved by the Norwegian Hell's Angels, though the National Security Union closed off Iceland's borders to prevent the Norwegian group from joining the Icelandic Hell's Angels inaugural celebration. Since then Iceland's Hell's Angels have concerned themselves with extortion, narcotics, and violent crime. Marijuana cultivation for domestic consumption is increasing, and so is the smuggling of narcotics from Europe into the U.S. and Canada via Iceland.

Icelanders often attribute the low incidence of violent crime in their country to the egalitarian culture promoted by the country's social welfare system and an education system in which "the tycoon's children go to school with everyone else" (quoted in Clark). When crimes do occur in Iceland, they usually do not involve firearms, though the 300,000 Icelanders own about 90,000 guns, mostly hunting rifles and shotguns, since their culture has always involved hunting wild animals, and in any case gun ownership demands a medical examination and a written test. Yrsa Sigurðardóttir describes the typical Icelandic murder as taking place in a kitchen between two drunken men, with one happening to stab the other with a butcher knife and when the police arrive ten minutes later, the assailant wondering "what the hell possessed him to do such a thing." She concludes, "An Icelandic murder lacks motive and the murderer is never egged on by any evil impulses, merely stupidity and impaired judgment" (Sigurðardóttir 62).

Iceland's police are unarmed, except for the SWAT-type Viking Squad. "The few times they are in the media," Sigurðardóttir notes, "it is usually because of some fiasco," as when they were photographed ramrod straight in bullet proof vests "trying to coax out a dangerous criminal that had been observed wielding a particularly menacing shotgun which turned out to be a vacuum cleaner nozzle held by an old lady cleaning her curtains" (Sigurðardóttir 63). On December 3, 2013, the Viking Squad did shoot and kill a criminal for the first time, and then apologized to the man's family (Edwards). Icelandic police try to pre-empt crime issues before they arise or defuse them before they become worse. They presently are attempting to crack down on organized crime.

Despite the relatively low incidence of crime in Iceland, Icelanders and foreign observers alike predict three trends will affect Iceland and the other Nordic countries for the next decades. Immigration and multiculturalism tend to cause major polarization, especially in times of economic downturns; materialist values, which pursue economic growth and technological innovation; and postmaterialist values, which stress human and iconological goals, all forcefully divide social groups. State decision making often conflicts with market choice, too, since modern managerial theory encourages greater competition and private choice (Einhorn and Logue 32–33). Because these trends are currently affecting Iceland and its popular culture, Icelanders' reactions to them have become increasingly apparent in the country's current crime fiction.

Yrsa Sigurðardóttir has remarked, "The more of a mess the state of our nation, the gloomier I feel and write" (quoted in Forshaw 138). Even if some of the miseries left by the crash seem to be diminishing, many tensions remain, some of them contributing to the increase, however modest, in the incidence of both crime and crime fiction in Iceland. Like their Nordic crime-writing counterparts, today's Icelandic crime authors are addressing societal issues that often contribute to criminal activity: immigration/racism, crimes against women and children, and drug-related problems, all currently increasing in Iceland.

In 2005, the Icelandic Liberal Party opened a Pandora's box with debate in the Althing about immigration, which had begun in Iceland around 1991, somewhat later than in other European countries. The RÚV (Ríkisútvarpið, the Icelandic National Broadcasting Corporation) reported in September 2002 that the number of immigrants in Iceland was increasing faster than in the other Nordic countries and "twice as fast as in Denmark" (quoted in Guðmundsson). Hjörtur J. Guðmundsson, a conservative commentator for *The Brussels Journal*, observed in 2006 that persons "of foreign origin" made up a large proportion of Icelandic welfare beneficiaries, "in some cases more than one third" (Guðmundsson). Between 1991 and 2006, official records showed that an estimated 20,000 foreigners, about 6.6 percent of the total population of 300,000 were living legally in Iceland, so that "Iceland has reached a level of immigration comparable to Norway, Denmark, and Sweden, in a much shorter time" (Guðmundsson). Several thousands of the immigrants in 2006 were Eastern Europeans, mostly Poles, who came to Iceland as "guest workers" in the fishing industry and stayed, so that foreigners had become a large percentage of many small Icelandic towns, especially in the Westfjords, sometimes one-third or more of their populations. At that time little effort was devoted to assimilating them into Icelandic society, though in 2004–2005, the government required foreigners who had been granted work and residence permits to attend classes in Icelandic; no examinations, however, were given. At the United Nations' request,

Iceland also accepted hundreds of refugees from the former Yugoslavia. In addition, in 2006 an estimated several hundred illegal immigrants were living in Iceland. Ghettos sprang up in Reykjavik, spawning conflicts between foreign and native youths, "but the authorities still insist this has nothing to do with race" (Guðmundsson).

Sunni Muslim immigration, a growing concern in the other Nordic countries, has also increased rapidly in Iceland. According to *Statistic Iceland*, numbers of Muslim immigrants have risen from 78 in 1997 to 1,200 in 2013 and now comprise about 0.4 percent of the total Icelandic population and about 1 percent of Reykjavik's population (*Iconoclast*), a number roughly proportionate to 180,000 in the UK. The Muslim community in Iceland, small by comparison with such communities in other European countries, has thus grown exponentially. For years Muslims demanded that the first mosque in Iceland be built in Reykjavik (Guðmundsson), and in January 2013, Reykjavik's environment and planning board granted the Association of Muslims a plot of land in the center of the city for that purpose. The situation has ludicrous elements: the Reykjavik city council is led by the semi-serious far left Best Party that swept into power as a backlash against the establishment parties widely blamed for the crash. Opponents have suggested that the grant to the Muslim group is a move by the Best Party's leader Jón Gnarr, a professional stand-up comedian, to fulfill his stated political aim of upsetting the established order in Reykjavik (*Iconoclast*). The 800-square meter mosque project, estimated at $3.3 million, has serious ramifications, however. Suggesting that Mideast financing for the mosque might "increase the influence of Islam in Iceland," the former mayor of Reykjavik, Ólafur F. Magnússon, opposes the project and instead suggests "a temple of the Nordic gods.... Such a cultural gem would bring joy to the majority of the city's residents, as well as other Icelanders, and wouldn't be as out of place as a mosque would" (quoted in Zakalwe). More seriously, Magnússon also has publicly asked whether political movements and feminist groups can tolerate a religion that he says degrades women.

In 2006, Toshiki Toma, who is an Asian immigrant to Iceland, a pastor to foreign immigrants, and a political scientist, illustrated liberal positions on *innflytjendavandamá* (immigration problems) being then debated in the Althing. Toma found the term "immigrants" "too vague for constructive talk" because he said that it included a wide range of foreign persons: recently arrived guest workers, wives from Asia or Africa with Icelandic husbands, refugees who settled in Iceland and their families, and foreigners who had recently attained citizenship. Toma observed that many guest workers came to Iceland because of its industrial projects, and he asked, "If Icelanders think they see too many guest workers here, shouldn't they stop these huge projects?" Toma also placed the responsibility for having guest workers in the first place to Iceland's decision to belong to the EEA (European Economic Area), and he maintained that immigrants cannot "steal" Icelanders' jobs when unemployment is only 1 percent, as it was in 2006. As for other objections to immigration, Toma insisted that the immigrants pay taxes to help support their lessons in Icelandic; that negative opinions of educational possibilities "in one's mother tongue is nothing but ignorance"; that organized crime in Iceland was "a sort of 'cooperation' between Icelandic and foreign criminals; and that as for Moslems, 'why is this potentially part of a problem?'" (Toma). Toma optimistically insisted Icelanders and immigrants "have to start working together" (Toma).

A 2009 working paper, "Immigration and the Economic Crisis: The Case of Iceland," with preliminary results from a then ongoing governmental project, traces Iceland's transformation from a culturally homogenous society to a multicultural one as "a recent phenomenon" (Eydal and Ottósdóttir 6). Almost half of Icelanders felt this was a negative development. In 2008, Gallup Iceland found that 45 percent of Icelanders believed regulations on immigration were too loose. The Icelandic government that year tightened those restrictions to reduce the flow of unskilled labor while making room for more skilled workers (Eydal and Ottósdóttir 9). After the October

2008 crash, however, the 9.5 percent unemployment rate caused many immigrants to leave Iceland, primarily because salaries had fallen to half their pre-crash rates. The 2009 working paper also found that under immediate post-crash conditions, issues involving abuse of the system by asylum seekers by far dominated the Icelandic mass media and aroused negative public opinion toward asylum seekers. Defending a 2008 raid on the residence of some supposed asylum seekers, Haukur Gudmundsson, Director of the Immigration Office, said, "it is not well when persons, who are not really refugees, view their situation as a matter of a free hotel and send their wages back home to their relatives" (quoted in Eydal and Ottósdóttir 20), but the media treated the situation as a human rights issue. The following year the Human Rights Office of Iceland launched a "Thank You" campaign to raise citizens' awareness about the positive impact of multiculturalism on Icelandic society and "to eradicate prejudism and negative attitudes toward immigrants" (quoted in Eydal and Ottósdóttir 22), acknowledging that negative attitudes toward foreigners did indeed exist in Iceland, as they do in the other Nordic countries, even lending impetus to neo–Nazi movements.

With the improvement of economic conditions since 2009, Iceland's *fjölmenningarsetur* (The Multicultural and Information Center) indicates that immigration to Iceland has rebounded to 25,936 foreign nationals living in Iceland, most of them in Reykjavik. The numbers of men and women foreigners are now approximately equal, whereas at the beginning of 2008 foreign men outnumbered foreign women in Iceland by 5000. Immigrants to Iceland now total 29,130 if their children who were born in Iceland are included, indicating that 9.1 percent of the Icelandic population now are either immigrants or second generation immigrants.

Societal stresses related to immigration are beginning to appear in Iceland: 44 percent of the immigrants are from Poland and have a 15 percent unemployment rate, compared to 2013's four percent unemployment among native Icelanders. A total 6 percent of all primary school children in Iceland have a foreign mother tongue. Fewer immigrants complete secondary education than the native Icelanders do; and the number of foreign nationals receiving student loans has increased about 1,167 percent since 2002. A disturbing one-third of women who sought the services of the Women's Shelter last year were foreigners. Because of financial restructuring, however, Iceland has substantially decreased its budget for immigration issues since 2008. That year the government spent ISK 21,000 on each foreign national, which decreased to ISK 9,000 by 2013.

Prior to the crash Iceland enjoyed an enviable reputation for equality between the sexes, an echo of the Celtic respect for women's capabilities among the nation's original settlers. Iceland voted into office the world's first democratically elected female head of state, Vigdis Finnbogadóttir, who served from 1980 to 1996. The Icelandic all-female Women's Alliance political party formed in 1983 has successfully fought for better wages for women and helped pass legislation to protect women and children. Ingibjörg Gísladóttir served as mayor of Reykjavik from 1994 to 2003, and in 2009, Jóhanna Sigurðardóttir, openly lesbian, became Iceland's first female prime minister. In 2011, Iceland was named for the consecutive second year the most feminist nation in the world, scoring at the top of the World Economic Forum's 2010 Global Gender Gap Rankings, beating out Norway, Finland, and Sweden. The same year, after a survey on health, education, economics, politics, and justice, *Newsweek* named Iceland "the best place in the world for women" (Cochrane). Sigurðardóttir felt *Newsweek*'s praise was "not only for women … we know that gender equality is one of the best indicators for the overall quality of societies" (quoted in Cochrane).

Not all Icelandic women, however, felt that reality matched those rosy descriptions. Guðrun Jónsdóttir, a feminist counselor for victims of sexual violence, notes that by 2011 the rape crisis unit at Reykjavik hospital assisted around 150 women annually, "but we can count the annual rape sentences on one women's fingers" (quoted in Cochrane). Women's wages, too, were still about 10 percent less than men's, and sexual crimes against women and children often went unreported or never prosecuted. Icelandic women held "women's day off" walkouts in 1975 and in 2005, and on October 24, 2011, activists from *Stigamot*, Reykjavik's rape crisis center, presented the Justice Minister with "black boxer briefs with the words I AM RESPONSBILE written down the crotch." The next day some 50,000 women and their supporters, about one-sixth of Iceland's population, staged a walkout called "Women Strike Back," calling for "women's freedom from male violence and the closing of the gender pay gap" (Johnson).

The crash intensified attention to women's issues. By 2011, it had become clear that the crash had been driven by a masculine enterprise called The Locomotive Group, enthusiastic proponents of Milton Friedman's version of neoliberalism. One of the group's leaders, Davíð Oddsson, became head of the center-right Independence Party and then prime minister between 1991 and 2003 and chair of Iceland's Central Bank from 2005 to 2009. The overwhelmingly male Locomotive Group's network of financiers and policy-makers "lived it up in fast cars, fancy suits, bars, and [according to the spokeswoman of the Feminist Society of Iceland] strip clubs." The Locomotive Group argued that only men, not women, "have what it takes, the bravado to take enormous risks" and considered themselves "daring adventurous Vikings" (Johnson). Janet Elise Johnson, a political science professor at the City University of New York, discovered on a visit to Iceland in 2011 that the average woman and man on Reykjavik's streets casually refer to the "daring, adventurous Viking" Locomotive Group and its colluders as "the men who stole all our money" (quoted in Johnson).

After the crash, "a testosterone-fueled boom and bust, the women of Iceland took charge" (Johnson). The new government in 2009 under Jóhanna Sigurðardóttir aimed "to get a better understanding of the role of gender in relation to the crisis, and to ensure the inclusion of women in initiatives to restore the economy" (quoted in Olsen) by presenting the Iceland 2020 policy statement, all of the provisions of which incorporate gender perspectives. In a 2012 interview, however, a member of the United Nations' Human Rights Committee still identified the two principal human rights problems in Iceland as "inequality between women and men ... especially in the labor market and the :sexual abuse of children" (Human Rights Committee). The Nordic Center for Spatial Development also cites concerns about establishing initiatives to solve issues of gender equity and rape and abuse. Women, especially young women, are increasingly moving from rural areas of Iceland to Reykjavik because they cannot find jobs that match their education, suggesting that rural communities may begin to collapse from within. As remedies, the Regional Development Institute of Iceland supports distance learning to promote women's entrepreneurship and tourism, an area in which many women currently work. Although the government is making efforts in these areas, "There is a need for a better match between the education of women and job opportunities in the rural areas" (Olsen). Contemporary Icelandic crime fiction, especially the novels of both Yrsa Sigurðardóttir and Quentin Bates, treat the problematic ramifications of women's outmigration from rural areas.

Substance abuse also poses a potentially troublesome issue in Icelandic society today, one with an obvious connection to the issue of the abuse of women and children. Historically the Icelandic government has tried various means of controlling drug abuse. To address adolescents' social and medical problems caused by the use of intoxicating drugs, in 1990 Iceland introduced a Skills for Adolescence (SFA) program, which, however, showed "no significant difference in the level of drug use of teenagers who had participated in SFA and those in the control group" (Gislason et al. 244). The official report on the project also indicated that 44.4 percent of the 15–16-year- olds studied had imbibed alcohol four times or more and 5 percent had a history of repeated drug abuse. The use of one type of drug also supported the use of other drugs, leading to low academic grades, less self-confidence, and the tendency to be more easily influenced (Gislason et al. 244).

A more recent initiative, the Icelandic Model of Adolescent Substance Use Prevention, seems to be having a more positive effect on 14 to 16-year-olds, because it "focuses on reducing known risk factors for substance abuse, while strengthening a broad range of parental, school and community protective factors" (Sigfussdóttir et al.). Under this model, between 1997 and 2007, incidences of these teenagers being drunk in the previous month, smoking cigarettes and trying hashish had declined steadily, indicating that the Icelandic Model promoted adolescent well-being "by capitalizing on opportunities at several community levels to reduce substance abuse nationally" (Sigfussdóttir et al.) Alcohol has long been Iceland's drug of choice. A 2005 Gallup poll showed that despite Iceland's high alcohol tax, almost 86 percent of all Icelanders admitted having had some kind of alcohol in the previous year, and the police generally overlook fully displayed open containers (Fontaine-Nikolov).

Since 2000 Iceland has been enacting stricter laws against drug and alcohol abuse, but despite longer sentences and stiffer penalties, "drug use in Iceland continues to grow" (Fontaine-Nikolov). In 2005 The *Reykjavik Grapevine*, Iceland's only English-language newspaper, collected interviews with anonymous addicts who insisted that methamphetamines, cocaine, and ecstasy are apparently the currently preferred intoxicating drugs, confirmed by a 2004 Gallup Poll of Icelandic drug users. One addict commented, "On any given weekend night in downtown Reykjavik, these three drugs can often be found being flagrantly used," and "patrons of upscale establishments had been seen cutting lines of cocaine in plain sight on tables" (Fontaine-Nikolov). Another addict claimed that intravenous drug use in Iceland is growing because of the easy access to "coke, speed and ecstasy," and she continued, "most abusers start their drug use in grade school" (Fontaine-Nikolov).

According to a October 28, 2013 article titled "Drug Abuse Not a Great Problem in Iceland," an RÚV survey conducted by criminologist Helgi Gunnlaugsson showed one-fourth of Icelanders had experimented with drugs and about 10,000, mostly young people, use cannabis regularly (Björnsdóttir). The prevailing view is that most Icelanders who tried drugs "grew out of it," although Gunnlaugsson admitted that Iceland's "few hundred" injection drug addicts posed "a very profound problem, a sociological problem"; addicts generally lack even elementary education, some have health problems, and some exhibit suicidal tendencies. In an apparent contradiction of the article's title, Gunnlaugsson also stated that "drug abuse is seen as a serious threat to society" (quoted in Björnsdóttir). The suffering brought about by drug abuse is graphically portrayed in the painful relationship between Arnaldur Indriðason's world-weary Inspector Erlendur and his addict daughter, a continuing plot line throughout Indriðason's Erlendur crime series.

Coping with social ills like drug abuse and crime as well as providing economic and social security requires heavy investments from welfare state governments. Prime Minister Jóhanna Sigurðardóttir stated upon taking office in 2009 that after the crash, Iceland would have to make difficult choices about limiting welfare expenditures. Iceland's welfare state policies had developed more slowly than those of the other Nordic countries, beginning with the comprehensive social insurance legislation in 1934 and extended state-provided health care in 1936. By the end of World War II, both Europe and the United States had reached a consensus that "society had to guarantee minimum living standards and employment opportunities not only to minimize individual hardship but also to protect society itself from political extremism" (Einhorn and Logue 18). After 1945, the Icelandic Social Security Act of 1946 made the central government of Iceland the primary source of welfare provisions. The Act combined all social insurances under one system, the first comprehensive legislation on social insurance in the Nordic countries to do so. It included an old-age pension for all people over 67 and introduced occupational accident insurance for all wage earners, disability benefits, and death benefits, ensuring greater coverage than in most European countries at that time, to about 80 percent of the population (G. Jonsson 260). On the other hand, the Icelandic tradition of self-financing and even self-construction of housing persisted well into the 1980s, but "by the end of that decade, the State Housing Agency was furnishing about 85 percent of all residential housing credit" (G. Jonsson 262). The dip in the Icelandic economy, however, between 1988 and 1995 with unemployment zooming from 0.5 percent to over 5 percent necessitated cuts in the welfare system. The once free National Health Service now had to impose charges and restrictions, and medication costs rose from 18 percent to about 32 percent between 1991 and 1996, with overall social expenditure's proportion of the GDP remaining between 17 and 19 percent. These cutbacks were gradually lifted in the late 1990s (Jonsson 164).

Though in many respects Iceland's history and culture strongly resemble those of the other Nordic countries, Iceland's system of welfare had lagged behind theirs except for a brief period after World War II. Iceland's late industrialization made it less immediately committed to social equality. Icelanders instead "emphasized market solutions and self-reliance (with a great deal of family support), not [reliance] on a socially defined minimum level of living based on a social right" (Jonsson 265). Iceland also had a weaker political Left than the other Nordic countries did, which allowed the rightist Independence Party to shape postwar social policy at a time when the Icelandic culture extolled a strong work ethic "more reminiscent of American-style individualism than the pro-welfare attitudes prevailing in the Nordic countries" (Jonsson 267).

Around 2000, the Icelandic welfare system substantially changed. According to statistics provided by the Central Bank of Iceland, by 2006, Iceland's spending on health, education, social security, welfare, and other social matters had risen to over 30 percent of the GDP. Most health care became free. Public education was also free or at a nominal charge, including primary education from 6 to 16; secondary education; and higher education at several universities. In 2005, 30.6 percent of the Icelandic population held a university degree.

After the crash and the collapse of the neoliberalist right-wing Independence Party–dominated coalition government, Icelanders had to decide how to fund these liberal welfare policies: they had either to raise taxes or cut public expenditures. The Minister of Finance in the new government, Steingrimur Sigfússon, advocated bringing the state's deficit down to zero in three to five years principally by raising taxes (quoted in Holm). As has been frequently pointed out, the Scandinavian crime novel genre has been "one of the great popularizers of criticisms of neoliberalism" (Nestingen and Arvas 9), but it remains to be seen how crime authors will respond to the leftist emphasis on raising taxes to fund the universal welfare state to provide universal health care, education, retirement and child support (Nestingen and Arvas 8), Iceland's tradition of self-reliance, which makes its implementation of welfare policies somewhat different from those of its Nordic neighbors, seems to argue for different approaches, which seem to be appearing in the crime fiction now being produced there.

Iceland's centuries-long "obsession with national identity" (Kachka), specifically its powerfully self-reliant Norse-Celtic heritage, its history of coping with contradictions in nearly every facet of its national life, and the recent crash and all its concomitant pressures together have shaped the peculiarly Icelandic twenty-first century crime fiction. The most recent and the smallest of the Nordic crime fiction genres, Icelandic crime fiction, anchored solidly in the nation's saga tradition which permeates everything Icelandic (Forshaw 133), blends the old and the new, the realistic and the magical, the dead-serious and the wickedly funny; it combines "elements of Norwegian, Danish, British and American societies" and "its own turbulent geology and its terrible weather to create a uniquely fascinating setting for a crime story" (Ridpath, quoted in Forshaw 134).

Awards for Icelandic Crime Fiction Novels

The Blóðdropinn ("Drop of Blood" or "Blood Drop") Award

Since 2007 the Reykjavik City Library has awarded the *Blóðdropinn* ("Drop of Blood") annually to the best Icelandic crime novel of the previous year. The author of that novel goes on to represent Iceland in the Glass Key competition for the best Nordic crime novel of the year, awarded by the Crime Writers of Scandinavia.

2007: *Skipið* ("The Ship"), by Stefán Máni
2008: *Harðskafi* (*Hypothermia*, tr. 2009), by Arnaldur Indriðason
2009: *Land tækifæranna* ("Land of Opportunities"), by Ævar Örn Jósepsson
2010: *Þegar kóngur kom* ("When the King Came"), by Helgi Ingólfsson
2011: *Ég man þig* (*I Remember You*, tr. 2012), by Yrsa Sigurðardóttir
2012: *Klækir* ("Monkey Business"), by Sigurjón Pálsson
2013: *Húsið* (*The House*, tr. 2013), by Stefán Máni
2014: Grimmd ("Cruelty"), by Stefán Máni

The Glass Key Award

The Crime Writers of Scandinavia (*Skandinaviska Kriminalsällskapet*) since 1992 annually present the Glass Key Award to a crime novel by an author from Denmark, Finland, Iceland, Norway, or Sweden. The short list for the award consists of a candidate novel chosen by each country's members of the organization. To date, Arnaldur Indriðason is the only Icelander to have received this award:

2002: *Myrin* (*Jar City*, tr. 2004)
2003: *Grafarþögn* (*Silence of the Grave*, tr. 2006)

A Parallel Chronology of Icelandic Literature and World Events

Icelandic literature and events are listed in Roman type with world literature and events interspersed in italics.

453: *Death of Attila the Hun (mentioned in* Poetic Edda *["Elder Edda"])*
8th century [?]: Irish monks visit Iceland
c. 850–870: Norse settlers arrive in Iceland
874: Arrival of Ingólfr Arnarson, first permanent settler in Iceland
9th–11th century: The Viking Age
930: The Althing is established
930–c. 1130: The Commonwealth Period
c. 1000: Christianity is introduced
11th–13th centuries: The Saga Age
11th–14th centuries: The Crusades
12th century: *The Book of Settlement*

c. 1220: *The Prose Edda*
1179–1241: Life of Snorri Sturluson
1200–1260: Age of the Sturlings
13th century: Peak of Old Norse (Icelandic) literature
Prior to 1250: Assemblage of *Poetic Edda*
1261–64: Haakon IV of Norway claims Iceland; decline of Icelandic literature
1380: Norway and Iceland pass under Danish crown
1397: Iceland becomes a Danish colony
1517: Luther launches Protestant Reformation
1536: Ruled by Denmark, Iceland accepts Lutheranism

1315: The Kalmar Union joins Norway, Sweden, Iceland under Danish rule

1602: Danish private trade monopoly ruins Iceland's economy

1730–1855: The Enlightenment

1775–1783: The American Revolution

1784–1785: Epidemics and volcanic eruptions in Iceland cause widespread death and famine.

1787: U.S. Constitution established

1799: The Althing is suspended 19th C.: Rebirth of national culture; independence movement led by Jón Sigurðsson

1828–1829 Vidocq's Memoirs

1830s: Romantic revival stresses Icelandic nationalism

1841: Poe's "The Murders in the Rue Morgue"

1843: First use of word "detective" in English

1845: The Althing is re-established

1850: *Piltur og stúlka* ("Lad and Lass") by Jón Thoroddsen, first Icelandic novel

1866: Dostoevsky's Crime and Punishment

1869: Gaboriau's Monsieur Lecoq, first police procedural novel

1870–1914: 15,000 Icelanders emigrate to North America

1874: Home Rule for Iceland; Christian IX grants the Althing legislative power and gives Iceland a new constitution

1882: Brandes publishes theory of literary realism in Denmark

1887: First Sherlock Holmes story, "A Study in Scarlet"

19th–20th centuries: Development of classic Icelandic style

1904: Iceland's national government established

1914–1918: World War I

1915–1999: Armann Einarsson's children's detective novels

1916: "An Icelandic Sherlock Holmes" (first Icelandic crime story)

1916–1922: Einar H. Kvaren's novels combining crimes and spiritualism

1918: Iceland has "personal union" with Denmark under Danish king (Iceland a sovereign state)

1920s–1930s: Golden Age of Mystery Fiction (Britain)

1920s–1951: Black Mask magazine: American hardboiled detective fiction

1920: First Agatha Christie novel, The Mysterious Affair at Styles

1928: Guðbrandur Jónsson's *Húsið við Norðurá* "The House by the North River" (possibly the first homegrown Icelandic crime novel)

1929: Gunnar Gunnarsson's *Svartfugl:* first Icelandic crime novel (based on true crime)

1930–c. 1938: The Great Depression

1932: Three novels by Steindór Sigurðsson with crime characteristics

1939: Ólafur Friðriksson's "All's Well in Reykjavik": use of crime to criticize Iceland's ruling elite: first true Icelandic crime story

1939–1945: World War II

May 10, 1940: British occupy Iceland

1941: Americans replace British occupying force

1943–1946: Haldor Laxness' *Iceland's Bell*

June 17, 1944: Iceland declared independent republic

Post–1945: Novels by Steingrímur Sigfússon

1949: Iceland joins NATO

1955: Halldóra B. Björnsson: *"Faðmlag dauðans"* ("Death's Embrace")—detective short story

1967: First Martin Beck novel, Roseanna, by Sjöwall and Wahlöö

1973: Thorgeir Thorgeirson, "The Authorities"

1976: Matti Joensuu crafts Finnish police procedural, focused on the evil side of human nature

Late 1970s: Viktor Arnar Ingólfsson's early crime novels; new wave of translated novels come into Iceland

1977: Debut of first female PI, Marcia Muller's Sharon McCone

1980: Vigdís Finnbogadóttir elected president; world's first directly elected female head of state

1983: Birgitta Halldórsdóttir's romance/crime thrillers; Women's Alliance formed, first political party in the world formed and led entirely by women

1986: Thor Vilhjalmsson's *Justice Undone*

1987: Svava Jakobsdóttir's "Odin's Theft"

1993: Peter Høeg's Smilla's Sense of Snow

1996: Vigdís Finnbogadóttir retires from presidency

1997: First Wallander novel (Faceless Killers) by Henning Mankell translated to English

1999: Women's Alliance disbands and joins with Social Democrats

2000: Arnaldur Indriðason's first novel, *Jar City*; *Blóðdropinn* Award established for best Icelandic crime novel of the year, by the Icelandic Crime Writers Association

2002: Ævar Örn Jósepsson's first crime novel, *Skíiadjobb*

2005: Stieg Larsson's The Girl with the Dragon Tattoo, outsells any other Scandinavian crime novel to date

2007: Yrsa Sigurðardóttir's first novel, *Last Rituals*

2008: The Crash devastates Iceland's economy

2009: Jóhanna Sigurðardóttir becomes world's first openly gay head of government as prime minister; Iceland applies for EU membership

2010: Major volcanic eruption
2010: *Liza Marklund co-writing with James Patterson*
tops New York Times' *bestseller list; Knopf buys four*
Nesbø novels

2014: November 2013: Iceland's first festival of crime
fiction, "Iceland Noir"

Contemporary Icelandic Authors of Crime Fiction

*An asterisk (*) indicates some or all of the author's work is available in English. Dates of English
translations refer to United States publication unless otherwise noted.*

Thrainn Bertelsson (Þráinn Bertelsson)

b. November 30, 1944; Residence: Reykjavik, Iceland; Occupations: film director, journalist,
teacher, newspaper editor, politician, author

Þráinn Bertelsson received a degree in film directing and cinematography at the *Dramatiska
Institutet*, Stockholm. He has written, directed and produced seven feature films, including *Magnús*,
nominated for two European Film Awards and winner of Iceland's 1990 DV Cultural Prize. Ber-
telsson has also had a long career in journalism, editing the newspaper *Þjóðviljinn* from 1987 to
1988 and editing the magazine *Hesturinn okka* in 1990. His autobiography *Einhvers konar ég*
("Myself and Me"), which introspectively concentrates on his childhood and "unusual family life"
(Dagsdóttir), sold more than 20,000 copies in Iceland and appeared in English in 2004. Currently
Bertelsson writes a regular column for *Fréttablaðið*, Iceland's largest newspaper. Just after the 2008
Crash, Bertelsson entered politics and was elected to the Althing in 2009 as a member for the
Citizens' Movement, but he soon became an independent member of the Icelandic parliament
before joining the Left-Green Movement, which he now represents.

Prior to writing *noir* comic crime novels in 2004, Bertelsson had translated into Icelandic
some of the Martin Beck police procedural series by Swedish authors Maj Sjöwall and Per Wahlöö.
Úlfhildur Dagsdóttir thought Bertelsson's own crime novels might be the start of a similar series,
which she said has become "highly popular" in Iceland. Dagsdóttir also traces "a kind of suspense
theme" which ran throughout Bertelsson's several early existentialist novels written in the 1980s.
The first, *Sunnudagur*, contains a murder, and the second, *Stefnumót í Dublin*, also an existentialist
work, deals with IRA terrorism. Crimes occur in the rest of Bertelsson's early novels as well. Dagsdóttir feels the last of that group is "a kind of forerunner of the new crime fiction," featuring a
journalist who receives and then publishes information about the criminal activities of important
political figures and foreshadowing Bertelsson's first two mature crime novels, *Dauðans óvissi tími*
("Death's Uncertain Hour") and *Valkyrjur* ("Valkyries").

"Death's Uncertain Hour," 2004, involves a bank robbery that turns into murder and a brutal
homicide. The character Víkingur Gunnarsson of Reykjavik's Criminal Investigation Division, a
"depressed theologian" (Dagsdóttir), leads the investigations of both cases amid conflicts with
the Icelandic Police's National Commissioner and two governmental ministers. The bank robbery
at first seems a straightforward crime, but soon an important clue arises. The homicide victim
had a business partner who supplies an important bit of insight: the partner describes his own
best friend, newly wealthy entrepreneurs Haraldur Rúriksson, as "a modern Viking" bent on
fortune-hunting in Russia: "Our forefathers got to experience such periods here in Iceland around
1000 years ago, [...] the most fertile period of all for this nation," when no executive power could
limit the individual's creativity and freedom. "The fittest, that is the chieftains, rose above the
masses" (translated by Dagsdóttir from *Dauðans óvissi tími* 316–17). Dagsdóttir notes that Ber-

telsson frequently refers to the medieval sagas, to Shakespeare's *Macbeth*, and to the BBC television series *Yes, Minister* in order to discuss the volatile mixture of "freedom and capital, business and crime," concluding that Icelandic business leaders were guilty of large-scale bank robbery in their lust for financial gain.

In *Valkyrjur* ("Valkyries"), 2005, Víkingur and his team are investigating the murder of Freya Hilmarsdóttir, a radical feminist journalist and a parliamentary deputy of the Icelandic Women's Party, found dead in her car outside Reykjavik and at first presumed a suicide. In the course of writing a book called "Valkyries" about the low status of Icelandic women due to male obsessions with beauty and pornography, Freya had included two controversial interviews with the ex-wives of powerful men, a supermarket magnate and a former Finance Minister, who had each divorced his spouse for a younger "trophy" wife. Both men had received blackmailing e mails offering to stop the book's publication for hefty payments, and now Freya's book is missing, causing the investigators to conclude her death is a homicide. A German reviewer, Sabine Reiss, observes that Bertelsson exceeds the by now conventional Scandinavian social criticism crime novel by unveiling "the political scene with all its hypocrisy, the power games and the lust for power" and by addressing the U.S. policy toward Iceland as well as the issue of secret intelligence gathering in Iceland and its accompanying deterioration of civil rights. Reiss notes that Bertelsson's style is "very fluid" and spiced with "a good sense of humor," especially satirical and exaggerated" when representing politicians.

Bertelsson's third Víkingur procedural, *Englar dauðans* ("Angels of Death"), 2007, involves high-visibility crimes bearing runic inscriptions: the explosion of an amphetamine factory in Estonia, with runic characters found in the debris; three brutally tortured victims are found in an Icelandic summer house, their bodies inscribed with similar runic signs; and the torso of Víkingur's missing stepson Magnús is then found in a travel bag in Rotterdam also with runes incised on the chest, causing Víkingur's wife, Magnús' mother, to fatally overdose a few days later. This grim novel combines personal and professional tragedies, allowing Bertelsson to probe the personal conflict between duty and family concerns.

Crime Novels:

> 2004: *Dauðans óvissi tími* ("Death's Uncertain Hour")
> 2005: *Valkyrjur* ("Valkyries")
> 2007: *Englar dauðans* ("Angels of Death")

Major Awards:

> 1984: Children's Literature Prize of Reykjavik Board of Education, for *Hundrað ára afmaelið*

Website: http://www.imdb.com/name/nm0077881/

Stella Blomkvist (pseudonym of an anonymous prominent Icelandic public figure)

> b. ?; Residence: ?; Occupation: ?

According to "Stella Blomkvist"'s publisher, a well-known Icelandic public figure has written mystery fiction under that pseudonym and kept the true identity secret to the present time. Beginning as a lark in 1997, six Stella Blomkvist novels have sold well in Iceland, and starting in 2003, they have enjoyed "outstanding success" in Germany, but so far except for two novels translated into Czech, no other Blomkvist translations have been made (Hammett, *Krimibuchhandlung*).

Since the author displays considerable experience of Iceland's political scene, its media, and its judiciary as well as thorough knowledge of the varied settings for the novels, guesses as to his/her identity have included well known Icelanders like author Arni Þorarinsson and even former Prime Minister Davíð Oddsson, who left office in the wake of the 2008 crash. "Stella Blomkvist" has promised to reveal the identity behind the pseudonym when the seventh novel in the series appears, but though *Morðið á Bessastöðum* ("Murder in Bessastöðum") was announced in 2007 and published in 2012, no definitive identification of the author has yet been made.

The young, savvy, good-looking heroine and narrator of the Blomkvist novels is also named "Stella Blomkvist" and described as "Iceland's pugnacious defense lawyer," who successfully tackles controversial criminal cases in the far north. These range from 1997's *Morðið í Stjórnarráðinu* ("The Bronze Statue") in which Stella defends the former lover of an aspiring female government official found dead of a blow to the head in the Althing's main chamber. In *Morðið í sjónvarpinu* ("The Perfect Crime"), 2000, Stella deals with the death of an Icelandic television personality who drops dead after a live on-camera sip of water. *Morðið í hæstarétti* ("The False Killer"), 2001, takes Stella into the theatre world after an actress is compromisingly found dead in a respectable judge's office. In *Morðið í alþingishúsinu* ("The False Witness"), 2002, Stella defends a right-wing individual involved in the death of a journalist working on neo–Nazi riots, and in *Morðið í drekkingarhyl* ("Murder at Thingvellir"), 2005, she becomes involved with what appears to be a Muslim father's honor killing of his pregnant daughter. *Morðið í Rockville* ("The Last Meeting"), 2006, takes Stella to Keflavik and "Rockville," a former U.S. radar station on Iceland's southwest coast, to defend a wealthy businessman accused of a vicious mutilation-murder. Author Stella Blomkvist explained in a 2005 interview that he/she reveals more details about the character Stella's past as the series proceeds, especially the "nightmarish childhood" which has shaped her as "so angry, independent, resourceful" and isolated (Ruckh 2005).

When first creating Stella, the author says he/she decided to make "The Bronze Statue" Stella's book and Stella's alone, noting in doing so, the tradition of Icelandic detective fiction being written during the first half of the 20th century to appear under pseudonyms was followed (Ruckh 2005). The author also stressed that in 1997, crime stories had not been published in Iceland for years, only translations of Agatha Christie, Alistair McLean, and other foreign authors. The name "Stella Blomkvist" arose during a shopping trip to Brussels, when the author spotted a person drinking a cold Stella Artois beer at a neighboring table. He/she thought "Stella" ("Star") seemed a "great first name," and produced "a delicious irony" when "my naughty heroine" connected with the last name of "Kalle Blomkvist," the "sweet and innocent Swedish boy" who is the hero of Astrid Lindgren's children's mystery series: "Stella Blomkvist? Eureka!" (quoted in Ruckh 2005)— the name of a heroine ferociously determined to succeed in a male-dominated world,

"Stella Blomkvist" sees his/her novels as "part fun and games. Part social commentary," with fast paced plots viewing "unpleasant aspects" of modern Icelandic society, like financial scheming and corrupt politicians, through its protagonist's clever eyes. Stella the character looks at human trafficking, prostitution, the dramatic increase she sees in drug abuse, the tensions associated with immigration, economic globalization, right-wing extremism, and American mass culture, and finds them all "completely unacceptable." Stella the character is also bisexual from the beginning, and gradually she develops a mostly long-distance relationship with Ludmilla, a "real tigress" from Eastern Europe. The author also made all the murder victims in her books women, because he/she wanted to emphasize "the brutal fate" that young women often face in trying to succeed in a man's world. The author deliberately conceived of Stella the character as a "little sister to Philip Marlowe," a female version of the hard-boiled, hard-drinking, smart-mouthed American male private eye, to demonstrate that women can play successful leading roles in crime fiction today (Ruckh 2005).

In a 2005 *Schwedenkrimi* interview, Elena Teuffer, the German translator for the Stella Blomkvist novels, observed that they contain "a lot of direct speech, with word jokes, sarcasm, taunts." Teuffer stressed that conveying witty material effectively must first of all preserve accuracy, a challenge with the Stella novels. In a 2007 interview Stella Blomkvist noted that as the series progressed, Stella the character pursued new paths in battling the government's legislative and executive branches while coming to terms in "Murder in Thingvellir" with her father's death and dark secrets revealed about their stormy relationship that had influenced her own personality. No matter what Stella the character's personal tribulations might be, the author insists, Stella the character will continue "her battle against the political establishment, the power junkies to the end" (Ruckh 2007).

Stella Blomkvist the author indicated in a 2011 interview with Hildur Knútsdóttir that Stella the character, despite her clear feminist orientation, "seems to be for both sexes," both "for the super [male] hero of the Saga" and for the typical "hairy wife" heroine of Icelandic literature. The author deliberately made Stella the character "the alpha and omega" of her books, "alive and militant. Free and independent" (quoted in Knútsdóttir). The most telling point to date about both Stella Blomkvist the author and Stella the protagonist is their favorite author, Sylvia Plath, whose spirit, Stella the author claims, lives on:

> Out of the ash
> I rise with my red hair
> And I eat men like air.

Says "Stella Blomkvist," "Wonderful!" (quoted in Knútsdóttir).

Crime Novels:

1997: *Morðið í Stjórnarráðinu* ("The Bronze Statue")
2000: *Morðið í sjónvarpinu* ("The Perfect Crime")
2001: *Morðið í haestarétti* ("The False Killer")
2002: *Morðið í alþingishúsinu* ("The False Witness")
2005: *Morðið í drekkingarhyl* ("Murder in Thingvellir")
2006: *Morðið í Rockville* ("The Last Meeting")
2012: *Morðið á Bessastöðum* ("Murder in Bessastöðum")

Major Awards: N/A

Website: N/A

Steinar Bragi (Guðmundsson) (publishes under the first two names only)

b. August 15, 1975, Reykjavik, Iceland; Residence: Reykjavik, Iceland; Occupations: poet, author

After studying literature and philosophy at the University of Iceland, Steinar Bragi began his literary career in 1998, with *Svarthol* (*Black Hole*), a book of poetry, and over the next ten years he produced ten books—poetry, short stories and novels—most featuring the brutal theme of the loneliness of humanity on earth. Steinar Bragi used an old-fashioned pastiche style for his one detective novel, *Hið stórfenglega leyndarmál Heimsins* ("The Magnificent Secret of the World"), 2006. The name of the protagonist Stein Steinar probably refers to the author's own name and that of a nationally famous poet. Beneath the quasi-humorous surface of the novel, Steinar Bragi shows hideous atrocities carried out on a huge ship called "World."

Steinar Bragi's literary world is full of dark humor, often incorporating supernatural elements. In November 2013 he commented about "Belt Games," his recently published collection of interviews about ghost stories with contemporary Icelanders, infused with historical material, that "My faith in ghosts is wide open and humble" (quoted in "Steinar Bragi: My Faith"). He also takes Iceland's contemporary literary critics to task for their timidity, asking in a 2012 interview whether any current critics are willing to make literary breakthroughs: "Critics who do not take themselves [seriously] wither and die; such examination requires conflict" ("Steinar Bragi... Hard Words").

Crime Novels:

2006: *Hið stórfenglega leyndarmál Heimsins* ("The Magnificent Secret of the World")

Major Awards: N/A

Website: N/A

Sigrún Daviðsdóttir

b. 1955, Reykjavik, Iceland; Residence: London, UK; Occupations: journalist, broadcaster, author

Sigrún Daviðsdóttir, since 2000 a respected London correspondent for RÚV (Icelandic State Broadcasting), regularly comments on Icelandic current affairs, but she originally studied Icelandic literature, and in 1979 she published a respected study of Old Norse court poetry. In 1978 she published her first of several cookbooks, and she received the Reykjavik City Literary Award in 1989 for her children's book *Silfur Egils* ("Silver Egils"). Her first novel, *Uchronia* ("Uchronia"), 2006, a love story set in the Icelandic countryside, opens with a fairy tale the narrator's aunt told her. A notable passage from "Uchronia" offers a telling comment on Icelanders' typical reverence for their traditional fairy tales: "those who grow up with the tales live in fairy tales for the rest of their lives. Invariably sad, the tales are about longing ... not sadness that should be cured" (quoted in Fontaine-Nikolov). She has been nominated as RÚV's Reporter of the Year and has earned her colleagues' respect for her thorough research into various worldwide tax havens used by Icelanders. She has also probed deeply into Icelandic cronyism and its possible political and economic repercussions if it is not halted.

In 2012, Daviðsdóttir published her first crime novel, *Samhengi hlutanna* ("Not a Single Word"), which arose from her investigative reporting about the 2008 crash (*kreppa*) because she felt a novel could tell a story that might not yet have appeared as fact in the newspapers (Valgardson). In her second in a series of lectures on Iceland sponsored by the Richard and Margaret Beck Trust on February 29, 2012, she addressed her combination of international finance reporting and the writing of fiction, relating that she had wanted to write a novel about 18th century Venice, but the crash intervened. She noted that although she had been inspired by several contemporary novelists like Denmark's Leif Davidsen and the U.S.'s John Grisham, she felt they didn't allow their readers to understand financial information or tax evasion schemes completely. She chose Peter Høeg's *Smilla's Sense of Snow* as the chief influence on her own fiction, primarily because she wants to balance reality and imagination. Daviðsdóttir focused on the "mental landscape" of the crash, because she felt strongly that although the crash might have been created by a relatively few individuals (the "Viking" entrepreneurs), many others either went along with them or turned a blind eye to their unethical financial manipulations. In both her lecture and her novel, she asked discomfiting questions: "Who wanted the banks privatized? Who worked together to get it done? Who set up a system of loans without collateral? ... how did they think, what were their morals, motives?" (quoted in Valgardson). She addressed all of these questions and more on March 2, 2012, her third Beck lecture. She exposed the reasons for the crash powerfully through her 2010 crime novel, *Samhengi hlutanna* ("Not a Single Word").

In "Not a Single Word" Hilda, an Icelandic journalist living in London in 2010, dies in an apparent hit and run bicycle accident, and Raggi, a fellow journalist and Hilda's old friend from Iceland, believes her death was a homicide connected to Hilda's scathing exposé of the roles in the crash played by Icelandic bankers and businessmen and their contacts in the UK, Russia, and Latvia. After Raggi convinces Arnar, Hilda's Icelandic fiancé, to join him in investigating Hilda's death, the two men receive a crash course in Icelandic banking and international finance from Mara, a Finnish-Chinese private detective. As a grim result, after being marooned in Iceland because of the Eyjafjakkjokull eruption, Arnar must reassess his own family to understand Hilda's fate and his country's in the aftermath of the financial crisis that so nearly brought Iceland to ruin.

Crime Novels:

2010: *Samhengi hlutanna* ("Not a Single Word")

Major Awards: N/A

Website: N/A

Ólafur Gunnarsson

> b. July 18, 1948, Reykjavik, Iceland; Residence: A small farm near Reykjavik, Iceland; Occupations: ambulance driver, poet, translator, author

Since his literary debut in 1978 with *Milljon prósent menn* (*Million-Percent Men*, tr. 1996), Ólafur Gunnarsson, one of Iceland's most important contemporary realist storytellers, has published poetry, children's literature, translations, short fiction and novels. Besides *Million-Percent Men*, English translations of several others of his nineteen books are beginning to appear: *Gaga*, published in 1988 by Penumbra Press (Canada); *Tröllakirkja* (*Troll's Cathedral*, tr. 1996) and *Potter's Field*, both published in 1996 by Mare's Nest (UK); and *The Thaw and Other Stories*, published in 2013 by New American Press. An adaptation of *Troll's Cathedral* premiered by the Icelandic National Theatre in 1996, and film rights for *Troll's Cathedral* and television rights for *Blood Field* have been sold. Ólafur Gunnarsson has also published translations of Jack Kerouac's *On the Road* and Dashiell Hammett's *The Maltese Falcon*.

The first of Ólafur Gunnarsson's full-length works, his only psychological crime novel, to appear in English and his best-known book, *Troll's Cathedral* is set in Reykjavik in 1952. The title refers to an actual high mountain on Iceland's Holtavorduheidi Moorland, where Icelandic legend recounts that during the Age of Settlement, Iceland's ogres and trolls, most of them peaceful, met to discuss their reaction to the influx of humans to the island. Almost all the trolls have left the area, but one remained, wreaking devastation on a nearby human church and all the people of its village. In Gunnarsson's novel, ambitious architect Sigurbjörn is building Iceland's first department store, but shortly before it is ready to open, a neighborhood pedophile lures Sigurbjörn's twelve-year-old son inside and brutally beats and sexually assaults him, a devastating crime that destroys nearly all the lives it touches. Sigurbjörn loses everything, his business, his friends, his marriage, his faith, even his mental equilibrium. Ólafur Gunnarsson "often juxtaposes materialism, with its idealization of the individual, with faith in God and Jesus' message of forgiveness and love for our fellow humans," especially in the trilogy opened by *Troll's Cathedral*, which also includes *Pot-*

ter's Field, 1996, and *Vetrarferðin* ("Winter Journey," 1999), described by critic Einar Mar Jonsson as "a triptych, each novel set in a different time with different characters but linked thematically by the conflict between Christianity and materialism" (Vogler).

In an interview with France's *Levure littéraire* conducted by Rodica Draghincescu, Ólafur Gunnarsson named Shakespeare and Dostoevsky as his favorite authors, "who both surprise and shock me." He feels the best things about writing is "the work itself," recalling the German poet Rilke's observation that if one locks himself in a room and asks whether he or she can live without writing, and answers "yes," then that person should go into another field. One day, Ólafur Gunnarsson recalled, something about the movement of a tree's leaves told him he was a writer, "and everything else came second So I sold the [export-import] firm and began writing in earnest and everyone thought I had gone insane." He also revealed his greatest wish: "to write something Dostoevsky might nod his head and say, not bad. Not bad at all" (quoted in Draghincescu).

Crime Novels:

1992: *Tröllakirkja* (*Troll's Cathedral*, tr. David McDuff, 1996)

Major Awards:

2003: The Icelandic Booksellers Prize and the Icelandic Literature Prize for *Öxin og jörðin* ("The Axe and the Earth")

Website: N/A

Birgitta Hrönn Halldórsdóttir

b. 1959; Residence: Southern-Löngunmyri, Iceland; Occupations: farmer, Reiki master, author

"Popular genres such as crime fiction have no tradition in Iceland" (Neijmann 458), but one tradition may be currently developing. Since 1983, Birgitta Halldórsdóttir, who from her childhood wanted to write stories, has produced almost one romance-cum-thriller-crime novel per year, almost entirely neglected by literary critics in Iceland and elsewhere (Eisteinsson and Dagsdóttir in Neijmann 458). She consistently features a Scandinavian updated Nancy Drew as her heroines—slightly older, relentlessly independent, sexually savvy and even aggressive, with an eye for handsome young men. She also often includes gothic elements in her stories.

Cultural studies researcher Úlfhildur Dagsdóttir has analyzed Halldórsdóttir's writing with respect to the negative attitudes that often face women writing popular fiction. Dagsdóttir finds that although Halldórsdóttir writes in the traditional style and structure that characterize popular fiction, using the Icelandic country romance tradition found in works by Guðrun frá Lundi, Ingibjörg Sigurðardóttir, and later Snjólaug Bragadóttir, although Birgitta Halldórsdóttir adds "strong elements of crime and suspense fiction," allowing her novels to be classified as both thrillers and romances (Dagsdóttir, "Heroines"). In addition, she adds a contemporary reversal of male-female roles; her heroines are sexually active, often openly admiring and desiring men and taking the initiative in relationships. Threats that her heroines face are also often sexual, allowing these novels to be categorized as horror stories and/or gothic tales. Dagsdóttir concludes her discussion of Birgitta Halldórsdóttir's crime fiction by observing that in 1960s Iceland, "female imagery was used to describe and condemn popular writings by both women and men. In this way the woman was made responsible for the degradation of good taste, 'sentimentalising' culture and diluting it" (Dagsdóttir, "Heroines"), Halldórsdóttir seems to have reacted against that view current in her youth, to produce new and progressive models of women in crime literature ranging over a large number of narrative styles (see listing below, with classifications from Dagsdóttir's "Heroines in Distress").

Selected Novels with Crime Components:

1983: *Inga* ("Inga"): traditional love story, with a crime

1984: *Háski á Hveravöllum* ("Danger at Hveravellir"): expanded crime element

1985: *Gættu þín Helga* ("Watch out, Helga"): kidnapping crime with amateur sleuth

1989: *Sekur flýr þó enginn elti* ("The Guilty [One] Runs Though None Pursues"): expanded crime element

1990: *Myrkraverk í miðbænum* ("*Dark Deeds Downtown*"): determined, sexually aggressive heroine with supernatural element

1993: *Örlagadansinn* ("Dance of Destiny"): crime novel with romance

1995: *Andlit öfundar* ("Face of Envy"): supernatural thriller

1998: *Renus í hjarta* ("Renus at Heart"): pure thriller

2000: *Fótspor hins illa* ("Footprints of Evil"): horror story

2002: *Óþekkta konan* ("Table for Four"): thriller

2010: *þar som hjartað slær* ("Where the Heart Beats"): romantic thriller

Major Awards: N/A

Website: http://birgittahh.123/is

Hallur Hallsson

> b. 1951, Reykjavik, Iceland; Residence: Reykjavik, Iceland; Occupations: journalist, television commentator, author

In 1975, Hallur Hallsson, today one of Iceland's top journalists, founded the daily *Dagbladið*, now the second largest newspaper in Iceland. He was also a leading journalist with *Morgenbladið* and has been an anchor at Iceland's Channel 2 and State Television. Currently he is a commentator for the television station INN.TV, Iceland's leading independent television station.

Hallur Hallsson's debut novel *Vulture's Lair*, a near-future political dystopian thriller, was published in English in 2012. Its setting is the European Union, which has become a completely federalized superstate with an uncontrollable political elite led by "the Vulture," an Orwellian Big Brother figure who uses holographic police to control the populace. The protagonist who with other protestors fights the regime by slapping its members with wet fish becomes predictably involved with intrigue, mayhem, and murder. An Amazon reviewer has observed, "If this book was written by an English author about English heroics against a European Superstate it would be banned and branded Rascist and Fascist ... as a book that should never have been allowed to be published."

Crime Novels:

2012: *Vulture's Lair* (published in English)

Major Awards: N/A

Website: N/A

*Hallgrímur Helgason

b. February 18, 1959, Reykjavik, Iceland; Residence: Reykjavik, Iceland; Occupations: painter, translator, columnist, novelist

Offbeat author Hallgrímur Helgason claims that being a writer is like being a killer: "You are killing people all the time ... you have to be mean and vicious. Sometimes the people you write about get hurt ... you can't write my types of books without hurting someone" (quoted in Weinman). Helgason is not only cruel to his fictional people, he treats Iceland mercilessly, with "a history of tearing his native country apart" (Weinman), a sadistic streak that encourages him to balance heavy drama with black humor. His crime novel, *The Hitman's Guide to House Cleaning*, written first in English, then published in Icelandic in 2008, was published in English in 2012, when it immediately knocked Stieg Larsson's *The Girl with the Dragon Tattoo* from its first place on Amazon's Kindle Best Sellers list for thrillers (Weinman).

The central figure of *The Hitman's Guide to House Cleaning* is Tomislav Bokšić, nicknamed "Toxic," a Croatian professional killer with 60-plus "jobs" on his résumé. After killing an FBI agent in New York, Toxic has to flee the country for his home town of Split, but instead he finds himself flying to Iceland and posing as a televangelist, "Father Friendly." Iceland is alien ground for him: the police can't carry guns, he can't pronounce the language, and occasionally there's not even one murder in a given year. Toxic, now known as Tommy, has to reform in a hurry, but his past soon catches up with him: "Can a hitman find forgiveness ... can a hitman find love?" (caite).

By writing this novel in English, Hallgrímur Helgason became "a foreigner in his own country." Seeing and conveying its society's pitfalls through a foreigner's eyes is a "rough and incomparable use of English [that is] the perfect voice for a Croatian hitman whose mother tongue is not English" (Weinman). Helgason also attributes his violent narrative to his attempt to balance Scandinavia's low violent-crime rate with its thriving crime literature: "In the Nordic countries, there are hardly any societal problems, but we writers are bloodthirsty people like anyone else so we have to quench this thirst with literature" (quoted in Weinman).

Crime Novels:

2012: *The Hitman's Guide to Housecleaning*, written first in English; the Icelandic version is titled *10 ráð til að hætta að drepa fólk og byrja að vaska upp*, 2008

Major Awards:

2001: The Icelandic Prize for Literature

Website: http://hallgrimurhelgason.com

*Arnaldur Indriðason

b. January 28, 1961, Reykjavik, Iceland; Residence: Reykjavik, Iceland; Occupations: journalist, film critic, author

A 1997 eruption of detective novels in Iceland "seemed to confirm that Icelandic crime fiction was here to stay" (Eysteinsson and Dagsdóttir in Neijmann 458). Arnaldur Indriðason has emerged as the Icelandic crime genre's "king" by celebrating its national identity in his fiction at home and abroad. In 2004, his award-winning novels amounted to seven of the ten most popular titles loaned by the Reykjavik City Library. Each pre–Christmas book-buying season sees Icelanders waiting anxiously for "the next Erlendur"; worldwide his Inspector Erlendur series has been published in 26 countries and translated into more than twenty languages, including Chinese, Croatian, and Catalan.

After studying history at the University of Iceland and working from 1986 to 2001 as a film critic for *Morgunblaðið*, Iceland's largest daily newspaper, Arnaldur Indriðason turned to detective fiction with *Synir duftsins* ("Sons of Dust"), 1997, and *Dauðarósir* ("Silent Kill"), 1998, both of which probably will not be translated into English. He believes that he learned "many things about characters and structure and visual storytelling" from working as a film critic, even from bad movies, which he says taught him what not to do (Spencer-Fleming). A far more important influence, however, on Arnaldur Indriðason's work is Iceland's medieval saga literature, "bloody songs of ice and fire." As he explained in a 2013 interview, one can read them over and over and "always find something new, and we writers in Iceland are lucky to have this huge bank of stories to go to. They are priceless, absolutely priceless" (quoted in Kerridge).

The Sagas of Icelanders have influenced almost every facet of Arnaldur Indriðason's fiction. He says their themes—"revenge, honour, family loyalty"—have been "a huge influence," and he has consciously adopted their laconic, direct style: "I try to use as few words as I possibly can," he insists, claiming he would find writing a five- or six- hundred-page novel "unimaginable" (quoted in Kerridge). Instead, he produces novels in the social realism tradition, framed in a style and a structure closely related to the Icelandic sagas to which he is uncompromisingly devoted.

Beginning with the late Bernard Scudder, expert translators have rendered Arnaldur Indriðason's novels into successful English versions. In the saga tradition, the diction and syntax of Indriðason's fiction strongly resemble actual speech. Like the sagas, too, his novels are highly objective, using few dependent clauses or rhetorical flourishes. Often in English the style employs verbs of action and nouns denoting everyday objects, thus creating powerfully understated narration, as in this passage from *Grafarþögn*, 2000 (*Silence of the Grave*, tr. 2004): "He [Erlendur] avoided thinking about what was really haunting him that night and morning, and managed to keep it at bay. More or less" (168). For only one example, *Silence of the Grave*, like most of Arnaldur Indriðason's fiction, exhibits most of the elements of saga structure. As scholars of the medieval sagas have observed, those writings generally employ limited points of view. Arnaldur Indriðason likes to shift frequently from Erlendur's point of view to that of a victim of decades-earlier crime, showing his characters' thoughts and motivations chiefly through actions and events. As the sagas and other novels in the Inspector Erlender series do, *Silence of the Grave* centers on a brutal relationship between criminal and victim leading to a horrifying climax of revenge; the conclusion of the novel reveals a convincing reconciliation. The aftermath, Erlendur's solution of the crime, supplies a satisfying coda to the work, brought about through a small physical detail. In *Silence of the Grave* the red current bushes near the spot where a skeleton was unearthed furnish that crucial detail, which Erlendur had observed immediately at the outset. Arnaldur Indriðason also maintains that crime must entail punishment. He views the concept of nemesis as "the retribution that is inevitably visited on the criminal," even though violence and justice in his novels appear in many shapes and forms: what is justice, he asks through his fiction; is it meted out by law, or "is it something that you give yourself"? (quoted in Kerridge).

Each of the Inspector Erlendur novels contains intertwining plots: the immediate crime for Erlendur and his team to solve, and the continuing struggle Erlendur wages with himself and his own past, specifically the traumatic childhood event that shaped the rest of his life. Throughout the series, Erlendur blames himself for losing his little brother in a terrifying blizzard, and each year he makes a guilt-ridden pilgrimage to the severe hills of his boyhood, looking for his brother's body. Arnaldur Indriðason notes that Erlendur, born in 1946, has lived through Iceland's enormous transformation from an impoverished peasant society to "a very, very rich modern society" fraught with simmering societal tensions. With all change, some people are left behind, "and Erlendur was one of them. He is rooted in the past." He obsessively reads about people lost in Iceland's rugged terrain, and he prefers to eat sheep's head, turnip mash, and blood pudding, peasant's food he ate as a poor farm boy (quoted in Kerridge). Erlendur is not the only lost soul in these stark novels, either; years ago he left his wife and two small children without knowing exactly why. His former wife loathes him for it and tries to make his children hate him as well. Erlendur's alienated son Sindri Snaer seems to be lost to alcoholism; through most of the series his daughter Eva Lind is a drug addict that he cannot seem to help.

Members of Erlendur's police team have their own inner demons to battle. Elinborg, a capable fortyish woman detective coping with her own family tensions, tries to solve crimes as she would compose a new recipe with harmonious ingredients; Sigurdur Óli, Erlendur's skeptical young subordinate, selfishly unable to establish a stable relationship with his lover, continually struggles with his own irresponsibility. When in the series Erlendur goes on an extended leave to haunt the scenes of his rural childhood, Arnaldur Indriðason makes Elinborg and Sigurdur Óli each a central character of a novel in the Inspector Erlendur series.

In a 2006 interview, German critic Jürgen Ruckh observed that "Erlendur" means "stranger" in Icelandic. He asked Arnaldur Indriðason whether his protagonist is a stranger in time, or in his society, or to the author himself: "Erlendur is a part of you?" Arnaldur Indriðason replied, "Maybe he is." Indriðason also noted that in several respects Erlendur is a stranger throughout the series. Coming from a farm, he is a stranger to Reykjavik; he proves a stranger to his wife and his children; and sometimes he feels alien even to himself. "But you have to feel sympathy for him," the author says, because Erlendur, like everyone, constantly tries to do the right things and to be "a decent man" (quoted in Ruckh 2006), the identifying characteristic of the Old Norse hero.

Neither of the first two Erlendur novels has been translated into English. *Synir duftsins* ("Sons of Dust"), 1997, introduces Reykjavik police inspector Erlendur Sveinsson, about 50, long divorced and beset by his family problems, especially Eva Lind's drug addiction, concerns which continue in *Dauðarósir* ("Silent Kill"), 1998. They counterpoint the violent deaths Erlendur has to investigate. *Jar City*, 2000, introduces Erlender's superior Marion Briem, Elinborg, and Sigurdur Óli, working on the murder of an old man eventually connected to several individuals throughout Iceland and even a high-tech laboratory ("jar city"). The novel was made into a 2006 film with the top Icelandic talents in their fields, director Baltasar Kormákur and leading man Ingvar E. Sigurðsson as a world-weary Erlendur. The film received the Crystal Globe Grand Prix at the 2007 Karlovy Vary International Film Festival and the Breaking Waves Award at the 15th Titanic International Film Festival, Budapest, and it has been released on DVD in Europe. In 2008, Overture Films bought remake rights to *Jar City*, with Kormákur again as producer for the new film, to be set in a small Louisiana town.

Silence of the Grave, 2001, was the second Erlendur novel to appear in English (2006). Here Erlendur's investigation of a skeleton gradually unearthed at a Reykjavik construction site parallels his efforts to save Eva Lind, who lies near death from a miscarriage. The present-day plot lines alternate with flashbacks to a vivid depiction of domestic violence, "hard to read but it's even harder to write," Arnaldur Indriðason told Barbara Fister, showing a crime which he believes is the most despicable of all crimes. In this novel, he incorporated echoes of one of the most famous of the Icelandic sagas, the *Njáls saga*, to raise the moral question of whether violent revenge, even murder, can be condoned if committed for reasons that may be justifiable, given unspeakable provocation. To suggest this issue, he gave a minor character, an archaeologist, the name Skarphédinn, the name of a key revengeful character in the *Njáls saga*. He also gave the archaeologist an ugly deformed mouth like the saga character's, which denotes the capacity of both characters for deadly action. *Silence of the Grave* set off an international literary controversy when it won the British 2005 Crime Writers Association Gold Dagger Award because the CWA then decided to exclude fiction in translation from subsequent Gold Dagger competition. The award increased Arnaldur Indriðason's sales in Iceland, but the CWA's decision caused hot debate; some participants wanted to make awards to only British crime writers, while others felt that excluding translated novels was "like all the European countries ganging together and deciding to exclude Brazil from the World Cup" (quoted in Rushton).

As a series, the Inspector Erlendur novels treat contemporary Icelandic social issues in parallel with horrific old crimes often dating back to World War II, crimes that affect the present-day investigations. Arnaldur Indriðason deepened his original major characterizations and themes in *Röddin* (*Voices*), 2002, tr. 2007, and in *Kleifarvatn* (*The Draining Lake*), 2004, tr. 2008. Erlendur, a "champion of those who disappear and comforter of those who still wait for them" (Stasio), experiences a love interest with Valgurdur, a biotechnician. Erlendur's son Sindri Snaer abruptly reenters his life, as Arnaldur Indriðason probes Icelandic history during the Cold War period. *Vetrarborgin* (*Arctic Chill*), 2005, tr. 2009, involves the murder of a young Thai boy and Sigurdur Óli's unyielding xenophobia. both reflecting an unpleasant underside of Iceland's liberal surface with respect to immigration; and in *Harðskafi* (*Hypothermia*), 2007, tr. 2009, Erlendur begins to rebuild his relationship with his children and attends the deathbed of his old mentor Marion Briem in a nursing home.

With Erlendur absent on one of his mysterious excursions to the Icelandic hinterland, *Myrká* (*Outrage*), 2008, tr. 2011, features Elinborg as she investigates the murder of a date rape predator, and eventually her life at home with her family and her gourmet cookery play important roles in solving the crime. In *Svörtuloft* (*Black Skies*), 2009, tr. 2012, a denunciation of Iceland's greedy industrialists and their cynical bankers, those chiefly responsible for the crash, Sigurdur Óli, who was trained in criminology in the United States and who plays fast and loose with other people's feelings, investigates a homicide under especially trying circumstances. He has to keep himself professionally uninvolved from the death of a blackmailer a friend asked him to look into informally, but he is also beset by the failure of his own marriage and harried by a domineering mother, who provides one of the rare flashes of *noir* humor in the Inspector Erlendur novels.

Furðustrandir (*Strange Shores*), 2010, tr. 2012, possibly the last case of Erlendur's career, finds him at his ruined old family farm home in the East Fjords, brooding on his memories and his emotions in a final effort to find out what happened to his brother. Camping out in his parents' old home, now in ruins, he discovers an old missing person case from the World War II British occupation of Iceland, when a group of British soldiers actually perished in one of Iceland's lethal mountain storms. Erlendur learns that Matildur, a young local woman, vanished in a monstrous January storm on the same day his little brother perished in a blizzard, and as near hallucinating he searches for his brother's bones, he untangles the woman's sad story, a saga itself of love, betrayal, and revenge, mourning himself for the old traditional Iceland he feels slipping away in the whirlwind of Iceland's industrialization, new technology, and imported foreign ideologies. Arnaldur Indriðason deliberately left the ending of *Strange Shores* inconclusive, but he has followed it with novels relating to Erlendur's youth.

Einvígið (*The Duel*), 2011, set during the famous 1970s chess match between Bobby Fisher and Boris Spassky, with Erlendur's superior and mentor Marion Briem as protagonist, investigating the assault of an adolescent boy at the time the historic chess match is taking place. Also published during Iceland's 2011 Christmas book sale season (*jólabókaflóð*) was Ottar M. Norðfjörð's novel *Lygarinn: Sönn saga* ("The Liar: True Story"), set like *The Duel* against the famous chess match. Norðfjörð, whose work has not yet been translated into English, has been called the "crown prince" to Indriðason's "king" of Icelandic crime fiction, and he called the coincidence "a little nuts," but he felt it would make for one of the most interesting Christmas sale seasons he had experienced ("Two Crime Authors").

The action of *Reykjavikurnætur*, 2012 (*Reykjavik Nights*, tr. 2014), takes place prior to *The Duel*, showing Erlendur at the beginning of his police career, when he meets his future wife, establishes his working relationships with his colleagues, and becomes obsessed with solving the drowning of a homeless man no one else seems to care about. Arnaldur Indriðason says that as a writer he found going back to the vanished pre–Internet, pre-cell phone era "highly enjoyable" (quoted in Dead Good Books interview).

Barbara Fister believed that Erlendur's cases "are based on human failings that are recognizable everywhere," and Erlendur's "moody, crotchety approach to his work is based on deep empathy for its victims." Each of his cases is "a pathetic Icelandic murder," in Sigurdur Oli's words, "Squalid, pointless and committed without any attempt to hide it, change the clues or conceal the evidence" (*Jar City* 7), but by imbuing those sordid murders with the spirit of the sagas, Arnaldur Indriðason gives them, their victims, and their suffering detectives life beyond the printed page. His crowning achievement, Detective Erlendur Sveinsson who struggles with the contradictory demands of a completely messed-up family life and a brilliant professional one, remains like every great fictional character "a bit of an enigma" to both his creator and his reader, so that Erlendur strikes "a common chord while introducing readers to a small, cold country with a long and powerful storytelling tradition" (Fister). About his own reading preferences, Arnaldur Indriðason admits to admiring the Swedish Martin Beck novels of Maj Sjöwall and Per Wahlöö and American Ed McBain's fiction; he loves poetry and believes that "every crime writer should read at least one poem a day, " and in 2013 he was again re-reading a saga, this one about Grettir, a great outlaw from the time of Iceland's settlement.

Arnaldur Indriðason's stand-alone novels also display his keen interest in history. *Operation Napoleon* is a historical mystery about a Nazi German bomber that crash landed in an Icelandic blizzard in 1945. Indriðason describes *Bettý* ("Betty") as his "femme fatale" novel. He delved deeply into Iceland's national history in "The King's Book." Another stand alone novel, *Skuggasund* ("Shadow Channel"), was published in Icelandic and Spanish in November 2013.

Crime Novels:

> 1999: *Napóleonsskjölin* (*Operation Napoleon*, tr. Victoria Cribb, 2010)
> 2003: *Bettý* ("Betty")
> 2006: *Konungsbók* ("The King's Book")
> 2013: *Skuggasund* ("Shadow Channel")

> *Inspector Erlendur Sveinsson Series:*

> 1997: *Synir duftsins* ("Sons of Dust," as yet not translated to English)
> 1998: *Dauðarósir* ("Silent Kill," as yet not translated to English)
> 2000: *Myrin* (*Jar City*, tr. Bernard Scudder, 2004; published in UK as *Tainted Blood*)
> 2001: *Grafarþögn* (*Silence of the Grave*, tr. Bernard Scudder, 2006)
> 2002: *Röddin* (*Voices*, tr. Bernard Scudder, 2007)
> 2004: *Kleifarvatn* (*The Draining Lake*, tr. Bernard Scudder, 2008)
> 2005: *Vetrarborgin* (*Arctic Chill*, tr. Bernard Scudder, 2009)
> 2007: *Harðskafi* (*Hypothermia*, tr. Victoria Cribb, 2009)
> 2008: *Myrká* (*Outrage*, tr. Anna Yates, 2011)
> 2009: *Svörtuloft* (*Black Skies*, tr. Victoria Cribb, 2012)

2010: *Furðustrandir* (*Strange Shores*, tr. Victoria Cribb, 2012)
2011: *Einvígið* (*The Duel*, tr. Victoria Cribb, 2013; not strictly a part of the Erlendur series, but it features his mentor, Detective Marion Briem)
2012: *Reykjavíkurnætur* (*Reykjavik Nights*, tr. Victoria Cribb, 2014)
2014: *Kamp Knox* (*Into Oblivion*, tr. Victoria Cribb, 2015)

Major Awards:

2001: The Glass Key Award for *Myrin* (*Jar City*)
2002: The Glass Key Award for *Grafarþögn* (*Silence of the Grave*)
2003: The Glass Key Award for *Röddin* (*Voices*)
2005: The Crime Writers' Association Gold Dagger Award for *Grafarþögn* (*Silence of the Grave*)
2008: The Blóðdropinn for *Harðskafi* (*Hypothermia*)
2013: The RBA International Prize for Crime Writing, the world's most lucrative crime fiction award, for *Skuggasund* (*Shadow Channel*)

Website: By choice, Arnaldur Indriðason does not have a website.

Helgi Ingólfsson

b. July 18, 1957, Reykjavik, Iceland; Residence: Reykjavik, Iceland; Occupations: teacher, author

Helgi Ingólfsson has taught ancient history and art history as well as writing poetry, scholarly articles, teaching materials, short fiction, and novels. After two novels set in the ancient Roman Empire, he turned to humorous contemporary Icelandic fiction. His award-winning historical crime novel *þegar kóngur kom* ("When the King Came"), 2010, sets a murder within a royal visit during Iceland's 19th century struggle for sovereignty, a crucial point in Icelandic history. Critics praised Helgi Ingólfsson's originality and his reconstruction of a vital historical era, and fellow Icelandic author Hallgrímur Helgason found that "The Reykjavik of 1874 springs to life, complete with colorful personalities from all walks of life—each and everyone awaiting the king's arrival. [...] it's like stepping into a time-machine, impossible to abandon without profound regret" (quoted in "When the King Came": Interview").

In the novel "When the King Came," Helgi Ingólfsson achieved historical verisimilitude by refusing to use any detail that was not verifiable, even making sure the colors of the historical figures' eyes are accurate. The novel, which provides what its author calls "another look" at Iceland's struggle for independence, begins with the murder of a young mother, bludgeoned while she is nursing her baby at the very moment the Danish King Christian IX arrives in Reykjavik to celebrate Iceland's thousand-year anniversary of settlement. The royal visit to Denmark's Icelandic territory conceals the homicide, which is hushed up and investigated discreetly to avoid scandal. Helgi Ingólfsson maintains that placing national heroes "on a saintly pedestal is no good to anyone," so he made "When the King Came" a reminder that heroes are also fallible human beings. He maintains that nine out of ten readers who approached him about the book told him they were happy with it and that it made 19th century Reykjavik come to life for them; and he found their encouragement "exhilarating and liberating" (quoted in "When the King Came": Interview").

Crime Novels:

2010: *Þegar kóngur kom* ("When the King Came")

Major Awards:

2010: Blóðdropinn, for *Þegar kóngur kom* ("When the King Came")

Website: N/A

*Viktor Arnar Ingólfsson

b. April 12, 1955, Akureyri, Iceland; Residence: Reykjavik, Iceland; Occupations: civil engineer, author

While writing crime novels, Viktor Arnar Ingólfsson continues to work full time as a civil engineer for Iceland's Public Roads Administration. He has been the Icelandic nominee twice for the Scandinavian Glass Key Award.

According to Úlfhildur Dagsdóttir, Viktor Arnar Ingólfsson's crime fiction career falls into two stages. His first short crime novels, *Dauðasök* ("Capital Punishment"), 1978, and *Heitur snjór* ("Hot Snow"), 1982, appeared at a time when only a few Icelandic authors were attempting to introduce crime fiction to Icelandic readers. Both novels combine elements of the police procedural with those of the contemporary thriller. In "Capital Punishment" a German policeman on an anti-terrorism task force trails a young woman to Iceland, where he is arrested twice himself because he has no papers. "Hot Snow" addresses drug smuggling and addiction, focusing on the career of an Icelandic drug dealer. Dagsdóttir implies these novels are pop fiction that resemble Birgitta Halldórsdóttir's popular novels, describing the work of both authors as "ripples of pulp in the literary landscape" (Dagsdóttir, "Mystery").

After a sixteen-year break during which he wrote only one short crime story, Viktor Arnar Ingólfsson developed a different approach to crime fiction. *Engin spor* (tr. as *House of Evidence*, 2012) was refused by several publishers before he published it himself in 1998, the year after Arnaldur Indriðason and Stella Blomkvist had published their first detective novels. Due to enthusiastic reader reaction, one of the publishers who had originally turned down *Engin spor* reissued it as a paperback. Viktor Ingólfsson set both *Engin spor* and *Flateyjargáta*, 2002 (*The Flatey Enigma*, tr. 2012), in the relatively recent past of the 1960s–1970s, evidently a more effective approach for him than his earlier contemporary thrillers had been (Dagsdóttir). Both novels were nominated for Glass Key Awards in 2001 and 2004 respectively.

In *House of Evidence*, available in English only since 2012, the various perspectives of police detectives investigating the 1973 murder of an engineer, Jacob Kieler, shot in his museum-like home in Reykjavik, alternate with diary entries kept from 1910 to 1946 by Kieler's father, also an engineer, shot to death in 1946 by an unknown assailant in the same living room as his son. Kieler senior's lifelong ambition to bring the railroad to Iceland was disrupted by the events leading to and during World War II, illustrating the late arrival of industrialization in Iceland. The lead detective Jóhann Pálsson, trained in then new forensic science, and his team unravel a deadly combination of family secrets with a powerful historical dimension.

Viktor Arnar Ingólfsson prefers to call his novels "mysteries" rather than "crime stories" (Dagsdóttir). In his fourth novel, *Flateyjargáta*, 2002 (*The Flatey Enigma*, tr. 2012), set in 1960, seal hunters from Flatey, a tiny poverty-stricken island off the west coast of Iceland, find the decomposing body of a man on an uninhabited islet in the Breiðafjörður fjord. Kjartan, the magistrate's assistant sent against his own will to oversee the transport of the body and determine its identity, soon discovers a connection to the Book of Flatey, an actual historical artifact containing manuscripts of the Sagas of the Kings of Norway, Tales of Icelanders, the Saga of the Greenlanders, and other medieval writings (Dagsdóttir). Viktor Ingólfsson adds a fictional riddle (the "Flatey Enigma") to real information about the Book of Flatey, and brings in Dagbjartur Arnason, a Reykjavik policeman, to add his perspective on the dead man to Kjartan's thoughts. The victim turns out to have been a Danish professor researching the Book of Flatey and trying to solve the puzzle, questions from which serve as chapter-closing counterpoints to the murder investigation. After another body is found, this time mutilated in the Saga Age's stomach-churning fashion called the Blood Eagle in which the living victim's back cut open to expose the lungs to be eaten by shoreline crabs, the murders all turn out to be perverse copies of deaths related in the sagas (Dagsdóttir).

With 2006's *Afturelding* (*Daybreak*, tr. 2013), Viktor Ingólfsson launched a procedural series with a new kind of detective, Birkir Li Hinriksson, a naturalized Icelander whose parents were Vietnamese boat people who died in a refugee camp. Birkir came to Iceland with foster parents, also Vietnamese, who then left him with an elderly Icelandic couple, so that he grew up "as culturally Icelandic as anyone," learning the complicated Icelandic language, speaking it well, and being familiar with all of the major works of Icelandic authors, but Asian in appearance (Katrín Jakobsdóttir in Nestigen and Arvas 48). The cultural contradiction that Birkir represents immediately strikes those who meet him and allows Viktor Ingólfsson to simultaneously address two heated issues for Icelanders, ethnic prejudice and the status of the Icelandic language, the latter such an important concern in Iceland that "a special public committee shapes Icelandic policy and language concerns are commonly aired in the Icelandic media" (Katrín Jakobsdóttir in Nestigen and Arvas 49). Both Birkir, who is sometimes taken for a Greenlander (as such, also a target of some prejudice in Iceland), and his older, overweight and possibly alcoholic police partner in the Violent Crimes Unit and best friend Gunnar Maríuson, whose vanished father was German. Gunnar goes by his mother's matronymic rather than his father's patronymic. Both are thus marginalized outsiders in Icelandic society but because Birkir is so much more visibly so, he is subject to much greater prejudice from native Icelanders, allowing the author to comment on the growing social problems of immigration and assimilation (or the failure thereof) in Iceland today. In *Daybreak*, first one, then another, and then a third goose hunter is shot, each at the break of dawn, and Birkir and Gunnar track a serial killer across the Icelandic countryside. *Daybreak* was the basis for the popular 2008 Icelandic television four-episode series *Mannaveiðar* ("I Hunt Men") with an odd-couple pair of detectives. Since the series appeared in March 2008 prior to the crash, its portrayal of an arrogant and slippery banker "so perfectly hits the mark that it's enough to induce a wince from an Icelandic viewer" ("I Hunt Translators").

The second novel in this series, 2009's *Sólstjakar* (*Sun on Fire*, tr. 2014) opens with another gruesome homicide, a dead Icelandic tycoon found nearly eviscerated in the office of the Icelandic embassy to Germany. Birkir Li Hinriksson, his partner Gunnar Maríuson and Anna Þorðardóttir undertake the investigation which proves complex, with roots in the distant past. In commenting on the gap between Ingólfsson's first two thrillers and his police procedurals written after a two-decade-long hiatus, Úlfhildur Dagsdóttir observes that Ingólfsson's literary career reveals "a lesson … about the attitudes of Icelanders toward popular culture" (Dagsdóttir, "Mystery").

Crime Novels:

    1978: *Dauðasök* ("Capital Punishment")
    1982: *Heitur snjór* ("Hot Snow")
    1998: *Engin spor* (*House of Evidence*, tr. Andrew Cauthery, 2013, also called "Without a Trace")
    2002: *Flateyjargáta* (*The Flatey Enigma*, tr. Brian FitzGibbon, 2012)
    2006: *Afturelding* (*Daybreak*, tr. Björg Arnadóttir and Andrew Cauthery, 2013)
    2009: *Sólstjakar* (*Sun on Fire*, tr. Björg Arnadóttir and Andrew Cauthery, 2014)

Major Awards: N/A

Website: N/A

Ragnar Jónasson

b. 1976, Reykjavik, Iceland; Residence: Reykjavik, Iceland; Occupations: lawyer, journalist, editor, author

Trained as a lawyer, Ragnar Jónasson has worked as a television news reporter for the Icelandic National Broadcasting Service and now teaches copyright law at Reykjavik University. He is also a member of the UK Crime Writers' Association. Between 1994 and 2009 he translated fourteen of Agatha Christie's novels and edits an Icelandic website devoted to her fiction. He co-founded *Iceland Noir*, the first festival of crime fiction in Iceland, held in October 2013, which was selected by *The Guardian* as one of the world's best crime-writing festivals.

Ragnar Jónasson told interviewer Bob Cornwell that he hoped he had picked up "quite a few tricks" from Dame Agatha for writing his own mystery novels, none as yet translated into English, like her trademark final plot twists, plenty of red herrings, and "mysterious characters." He combined those Christie-inspired elements in his first crime novel *Fölsk nota* ("Past Tense"), 2009, with a coming of age theme in which his young protagonist searches for his missing father (Cornwell).

Ragnar Jónasson set his Dark Iceland series, not yet translated into English, in Siglufjord, the northernmost town in Iceland and once the center of the nation's herring fishing industry. Siglufjord, though dark and virtually snowbound during the long far north winters, is roughly analogous to Miss Marple's St. Mary Mead, a little village where at a glance nothing seems to happen, yet where dark secrets and deeds seethe beneath the deceptively idyllic surface. In *Snjóblinda* ("Snowblind"), 2010, newly assigned village policeman Ari Thor Arnason has to investigate two peculiar deaths during the claustrophobic winter, uncovering hidden crimes while disturbingly aware he cannot trust anyone in this tightly-knit little community. According to Ragnar Jónasson's website, Ari ("eagle") Thor (a reference to the Old Norse god of justice and oath-keeping), who as an orphan was raised by his grandmother, first studied philosophy, then theology, then became a policeman. Recently transferred from Reykjavik, he resents his losses, is prone to jealousy, has few friends and only a sporadic relationship with his girlfriend, and is convinced justice is only an illusion. In *Myrknaetti* ("Dark Night"), 2011, set in the summer, he struggles with his personal difficulties while investigating the death of a woman and her old secrets, accompanied by Isrún, a young female reporter from Reykjavik, representing a new interest in his life. Isrún also shares Ari Thor's next case, *Rof* ("Erosion"), 2012, another instance of an decades-old crime rising up to spawn new ones, as happens again in *Andkof* ("Breathless"), 2013, on the day before Christmas in this bleak, gloomy far northern village.

Since the Dark Iceland novels convey a gentler tone or flavor than other Scandinavian crime authors do with their violent urban and countryside crime scenes, Ragnar Jónasson is adding something "new to Icelandic crime fiction, suggesting a successful marriage of skills old and new" (Cornwell). The television rights to the Dark Iceland series were purchased in 2012 by a leading Icelandic production company and their screenwriting began in 2013.

Ragnar Jónasson's only work available in English to date, the short story "Death of a Sunflower," appeared in the January 2013 issue of *Ellery Queen's Mystery Magazine*, the first story by an Icelandic author to appear there. *Snjóblinda* is scheduled for UK publication in English translation as *Snowblind* in 2015, with *Myrknaetti* to appear there as *Nightblind* in 2016. Jonasson's Dark Iceland crime series is also being developed for television.

Crime Novels:

2009: *Fölsk nota* ("Past Tense")

The Dark Iceland Series:

2010: *Snjóblinda* ("Snowblind"; see above)
2011: *Myrknaetti* ("Nightblind Night"; see above)
2012: *Rof* ("Erosion")
2013: *Andköf* ("Breathless")

Major Awards: N/A

Website: http://www.ragnarjonasson.com

Ævar Örn Jósepsson

> b. August 25, 1963, Hafnarfirði, Iceland; Residence: Mosfellsbaer, near Reykjavik, Iceland; Occupations: journalist, translator, author

In 2002, when he was around forty years old, Ævar Örn Jósepsson began publishing crime fiction, opening a police procedural series that is popular in Iceland, Germany, and the Netherlands but is relatively unknown in the English speaking world (Forshaw 127). *Black Angels*, a translation of *Svartir englar*, 2004, by Frank Workman, was published in 2006 by Signature, but it seems to be no longer available. *Svartir englar* was nominated for the Glass Key Award in 2004.

The title of Ævar Örn Jósepsson's first crime novel, *Skítadjobb*, 2002, politely translated as "A Dirty Job," indicates the tacky opinion that overworked and underappreciated policemen and women of Reykjavik's crime investigation unit and many non-police Icelanders in this series hold of their duties. The series features an "odd couple" of male detectives, but instead of the now near-cliché of an "old guard" superior officer who is grumpy and bitter over health and marital problems and a brash young techie colleague, Ævar Örn Jósepsson reversed their images, making Stefan, the boss, gentle, calm, warm, and happily married for over thirty years, and Arni, his thirty-something assistant a "wishy-washy" police academy dropout who wound up in the detective unit by coincidence (Dagsdóttir). The developing relationship between Stefan and Arni provides humorous scenes in the series, which lighten the author's preoccupation with political issues, which he illustrates through the various attitudes his cast of characters are constantly voicing as reflections of the diverse positions evident in Iceland's society today (Jakobsdóttir in Nestingen and Arvas 50).

By "Black Angels," third in the series, the two men have become good friends, supported by two traditional figures, Guðni, a traditional tough-guy detective, and Katrin, the token female on the team, whose temporary appointment as its leader when Stefan is on leave irks Guðni, allowing the author to explore gender issues in the police force. "Black Angels" also involves the issue of electronic surveillance by "the Authorities." *Blóðberg* ("Blood Mountain"), 2005, similarly illustrates how the crime fiction genre some Icelandic commentators believe is inferior to mainstream fiction "can throw a new and fresh light onto a very worn-out political issue" (Dagsdóttir). This homicide occurs at the controversial Kárahnjúkar power plant, one of the biggest political issues in Iceland from 2002 to 2008 (Jakobsdóttir in Nestingen and Arvas 50–51), "where any rational discussion has drowned in heated arguments between ... suited industrialist right-wing politicians, and dread-locked over-romantic left-wing environmentalists" (Dagsdóttir). Ævar Örn Jósepsson manages to show both sides of the debate fairly, but through skilled descriptions he stresses the national pride Icelanders take in overcoming even the most challenging aspects of their environment. Here, too, Guðni exhibits "the essence of bankrupt masculinity" rebelling against women and concerns about Iceland's environment, while Katrín "represents feminine values, including nature and Icelandic nationality" (Jakobsdóttir in Newstigen and Arvas 51).

Katrín Jakobsdóttir suggests that the detectives' opposition to one another's positions "may reflect a change in how the Icelandic national identity is defined. Earlier Icelandic identity was "associated with masculine Viking-warrior values," but "'the Icelander' is now becoming a nostalgic woman in touch with nature" (Jakobsdóttir in Nestingen and Arvas 51). These themes seem to be continuing in later installments of Josepsson's series, like *Sá yðar sem syndlaus er* ("He Who Is Without Sin"), 2006, nominated for the Blóðdropinn Award in 2007. This novel involves the case of a religious fanatic linked to the sect of The Holy Truth found in his armchair over a year after his murder. With Guðni sidelined after a heart attack, the rest of the team uncovers connections to the Baltic underworld as well as Reykjavik's own hardened criminals. Jósepsson's *Land tæki-færanna* ("Land of Opportunities"), 2008, nominated for the Glass Key Award, relentlessly exposes the construction and real estate machinations that led to the 2008 Crash that nearly devastated Iceland's economy. *Önnur líf* ("Other Life"), 2010, continues that theme with two serious assault cases related to protests against the crash.

The Icelandic production company Sagafilm premiered an adaptation of "Black Angels" written by Sigurjón Kjartansson and Óskar Jónasson as a highly popular Icelandic State Television six-part series in the fall of 2008, where it received viewing ratings still listed among the highest ever recorded for original programming. The four detectives in the series present "conflicting approaches to police methodology," societal changes due to globalization, and the internationalization of criminal activity. "Moral certitude is presented as being either weak or nonexistent," with opening visual images of social realism grounding "the central thesis that Icelandic society is increasingly becoming fractured, possibly even dysfunctional" ("Euro but Not Trash"). The second nine-episode series, "Black Angels 2," based on "He Who Is Without Sin," "Land of Opportunities," and "Life Lies Bleeding," was announced in September 2013 ("Sagafilm Readies New Drama Series").

Crime Novels:

   2002: *Skítadjobb* ("A Dirty Job")
   2003: *Svartir englar* ("Black Angels")
   2005: *Blóðberg* ("Blood Mountain")
   2006: *Sá yðar sem syndlaus er* ("He Who Is Without Sin")
   2008: *Land tækifæranna* ("Land of Opportunities")
   2008: *Tabú* (Taboo")
   2010: *Önnur líf* ("Other Life")

Major Awards:

   2009: The Blóðdropinn, for *Land tækifæranna* ("Land of Opportunities")

Website: N/A

Stefán Máni (Stefán Máni Sigþórsson)

b. June 3, 1970, Reykjavik, Iceland; Residence: Reykjavik, Iceland; Occupation: author

Since his literary debut in 1996 with a self-published crime novel, Stefán Máni has combined thriller elements with horror in the Stephen King mode. *Svartur á leik* ("Black Curse"), 2004, spins a young man into a deadly maelstrom of theft, extortion, prostitution, and drug-dealing based on actual recent crimes in Iceland. This novel set off a scandal in Iceland upon its publication, because of events the author based closely on an extensive investigation he had conducted into Reykjavik's seedy underworld. In *Feigð* ("Spendthrift") Stefán Máni focuses on a one-eyed crime boss named Odin, a specialist in drug dealing and arson with connections to high-level businessmen.

Stefán Máni reached into magical realism for his best-known novel, *Skipið* (*The Ship*), 2006, tr. 2012, which like *Húsið* ("The House"), 2013, was nominated for the Glass Key Award. "The Ship," a freighter, takes its readers with its nine-man crew, all hiding sinister secrets, from Grundartangi, its Icelandic port, toward far off Surinam, a journey of sabotage and mutiny, piracy, and satanic ritual that a reviewer for *Der Spiegel* called "a reliable companion for nights of fever and chills."

Selected Crime Novels:

1996: *Dyrnar á Svörtufjöllum*
2001: *Hótel Kalifornía* ("Hotel California")
2002: *Ísrael* ("Israel")
2004: *Svartur á leik* ("Black Curse")
2005: *Túristi* ("Tourist")
2006: *Skipið* (*The Ship*, tr. W. Jöhansdóttir, 2012)
2008: *Ödáðahraun* ("Memento Mori")
2009: *Hyldýpi* ("Abyss")
2012: *Feigð* ("Spendthrift," or "God of Emptiness")
2013: *Húsið* ("The House")
2014: *Litlu dauðarnir* ("Small Deaths")

Major Awards:

2007: Blóðdropinn, for *Skipið* ("The Ship")
2013: Blóðdropinn, for *Húsið* ("The House")

Website: N/A

Óttar Norðfjörð

b. 1980, Reykjavik, Iceland; Residences: Iceland and Spain; Occupations: poet, editor, painter, author

Besides philosophy, his major field, Óttar Norðfjörð's wide academic background includes Arabic, medicine, history, and the arts. His literary career began in 2002 with the first of six volumes of poetry, and he published his first of three mainstream novels, *Barnagaelur* ("Child's Play") in 2005. Norðfjörð's website provides brief descriptions of his four crime novels, all of which exhibit extensive historical research and clever presentations of radical theories about ancient peoples, including non–Westerners, and their cultures through juxtapositions of contemporary events and ancient riddles.

In *Hnífur Abrahams* ("Abraham's Knife"), 2007, Norðfjörð's hero James Donnelly, an Irish writer, and his Icelandic assistant pursue an ancient secret through the streets of post–9/11 New York, a riddle about their common ancestor Abraham that can disrupt the beliefs of Jews, Christians, and Muslims. After extensive historical research, Norðfjörð produced not only a fictionalized account, faithful to historical fact, of the fundamental conflicts that have torn the Holy Land since time immemorial, but also a possibility of peace among them, based on a "secret" about Abraham and his sacrifice that is familiar to the Islamic world but not to the West. This novel immediately became a bestseller in Iceland, it was nominated for the Blóðdropinn Award, and it was sold to the ZikZak film production company,

For his second thriller, *Sólkross* ("Sun Cross"), 2008, Norðfjörð turned to Iceland's Viking heritage, taking Adam Swift, a character from "Abraham's Knife," and his Icelandic girlfriend Embla Þöll first to Reykjavik and then to Iceland's south, the settings of the Icelandic Sagas, to investigate a radical theory about Iceland's settlement that involves pagan temples and Nordic mythology, sacred geometry, and a mysterious Nazi visit to Iceland in 1938.

Attablaðarósin ("The Eight Pointed Rose"), 2010, combines Anglo-American and Scandinavian crime novel conventions with three plots connected through the titular symbol, an eight-pointed rose quilt motif dating from the medieval Vikings that suggests a hidden message about an old crime to feminist scholar Árára Axelsdóttir. Her story intertwines with the problems of a troubled boy and the struggle of an Icelandic businessman to save Iceland's largest geothermal company from a foreign takeover. Norðfjörð here explores the relationship between post–Crash Iceland and the international firms who are demonstrating substantial interest in Iceland's geothermal resources.

Flashing back to the 1972 World Chess Championship match between Bobby Fischer and Boris Spassky at the height of the Cold War, *Lygarinn* ("The Liar"), 2013, a political thriller, also treats contemporary issues like WikiLeaks, privatization of national goods, and the dealings behind the crash, all in the context of a dark secret about the controversial Icelandic group *Eimreiðarhópurinn*, whose members include three previous prime ministers.

Coincidentally, both "The Liar" and Arnaldur Indriðason's *Einvígid* ("The Duel"), his 15th novel, were released for the 2011 Christmas season (*jólabókaflóð*), and Norðfjörð had even considered the title *Einvígid* for "The Liar." Calling the coincidence "ridiculous," Norðfjörð commented, "It's a question of whether Arnaldur ad I should play a game of chess. I challenge him!" ("Two Crime Authors").

Crime Novels:

> 2007: *Hnífur Abrohams* ("Abraham's Knife")
> 2008: *Sólkross* ("Sun Cross")
> 2010: *Áttablaðarósin* ("The Eight Pointed Rose")
> 2013: *Lygarinn* ("The Liar")

Major Awards:

2014: The *Tindabikkjan* Award from *Glaepafelag Vestfjorda* (Crime Literature Organization of Western Fjords of Iceland) for Best Icelandic Crime Novel of 2013; award includes two kilos of rayfish, a traditional food of the area

Website: http://www.ottarnordfjord.com

Olaf Olafsson (Ólafur Jóhann Ólafsson)

> b. September 26, 1962, Reykjavik, Iceland; Residence: New York City, U.S.A.; Occupations: business executive, author

The son of the noted Icelandic author who first won the Nordic Council's Literature Prize, Olaf Olafsson, author of four widely respected novels and a short story collection, in 1991 founded

Sony Interactive Entertainment, building and managing its businesses in the United States and Europe as president and CEO for six years, where he introduced the famous Sony PlayStation. Today he is the Executive Vice President for International and Corporate Strategy of Time Warner.

Olafsson's novels, written since 2000 and published in over twenty languages, are "each built around tortured expatriate protagonists who leave their native Iceland but continue to be haunted by past crimes or tragedies." His short fiction collection, *Valentines*, 2007, present "failed romantic relationships and lovers broken and defeated by poor judgment, selfishness, and past mistakes" (Sullivan). He has lived in the United States after taking a degree in physics from Brandeis University but wrote his fiction, all based on meticulous historical research, first in Icelandic and later others, like *Restoration*, 2012, first in English, with consultation with Victoria Cribb, one of the most skilled translators of Icelandic literature.

Olafsson based *Restoration* on "a dark mystery taking place in the sunlit vistas of Tuscany" (Carr) during the closing days of World War II, with Allied and Axis armies closing in on a decaying villa where the two central women protagonists are living. Olafsson had come across the diaries of Iris Origo, who had restored the Tuscan estate where during the war she sheltered refugee children, and he used her as the model for one of the protagonists of a novel that *Library Journal* called "beautifully realized."

Olafsson's 2000 novel *Slóð fiðrildanna* (*The Journey Home*) is under consideration for film adaptation by Palomar Pictures.

Novels (titles given in English for Olafsson's English versions):

1994: *Absolution*
2000: *Slóð fiðrildanna* (*The Journey Home*)
2003: *Walking into the Night*
2012: *Restoration*

Short Fiction:

2006: *Valentines*

Major Awards:

2006: Icelandic Literary Prize for Fiction, for *Valentines*

Website: http://olafolafsson.author

Sólveig Pálsdóttir

b. 1959; Residence: Reykjavik, Iceland ;Occupations: actor, teacher, author

Sólveig Pálsdóttir launched a light formulaic police procedural series in 2012 with *Leikarinn* ("The Actor"), based on her experiences in drama. The collapse and death of a leading man on a stage set sets off a conventional investigation by detectives Gudgeir and Andres, who also feature in her second installment in the series, *Hinir réttlátu* ("The Righteous Ones"), 2013, where a businessman dies on a golf course at the same time an explosion rocks a whaling vessel off Reykjavik and protesters demonstrate against Reykjavik restaurants that serve whale meat. In a 2011 statement for the Icelandic Visual Art Organization, Pálsdóttir described the basis for her approach to popular crime fiction as the "need for creativity [which] is rooted deep in our nature and is a defence mechanism against constant visual stimulation."

Crime Novels:

2012: *Leikarinn* ("The Actor")

2013: *Hinir réttlátu* ("The Righteous Ones")

Major Awards: N/A

Website: http://www.solveigpalsdottir.is

Páll Kristinn Pálsson (see also Arni Thorarinsson and Pall Kristin Palsson)

b. April 22, 1956, Reykjavik, Iceland; Residence: Reykjavik, Iceland ; Occupation: journalist, editor, film producer, author

With Arni Thorarinsson, Páll Kristinn Pálsson has co-authored two crime novels and has co-written several successful television crime series (see below).

Sigurjón Pálsson

b. 1950, Húsavik, Iceland; Residence: Reykjavik, Iceland ; Occupations: designer, author

Sigurjón Pálsson is a graduate of the Danish Academy of Fine Arts and a designer of elegantly simple *objets d'art*, notably his "Shorebirds" collection of decorative wooden birds, a product of his guiding principle that optimum design should be a inseparable unity of function, form and aesthetics, a unity "which cannot be meddled with, without being destroyed" (quoted in "Interview with Sigurjón Pálsson"). He has also authored two well-received thrillers. The first, *Klaekir* ("Monkey Business"), 2011, received the 2012 Drop of Blood Award and was nominated for the Glass Key Prize. The action of "Monkey Business" takes place first in Afghanistan, where its central figure, a woman employee of a prosthetics manufacturer, has come to help victims of landmines. During an attack on a visiting U.S. Senator and his entourage in a Herat bazaar she helps to save the senator, becoming wounded herself. Two years later, after he has been elected President of the United States, two young Afghanis arrive in Iceland and the woman again becomes involved in one dangerous plot twist after another. Both this novel and *Blekking* ("Deception"), 2012, set in the author's home town of Húsavik, juxtapose the remote past and the investigative present in the context of Biblical lore and archeological discoveries.

Crime Novels:

2011: *Klaekir* ("Monkey Business")

2012: *Blekking* ("Deception")

Major Awards:

2012: The Blóðdropinn, for *Klaekir* ("Monkey Business")

Website: N/A

Lilja Sigurðardóttir

b. 1972; Residence: Reykjavik; Occupation: author

Lilja Sigurðardóttir's first crime novel, *Spor* ("Steps") won the publisher Bjartur's competition to find the next Dan Brown. Her conventional procedural series, set in Reykjavik, features writer and romance translator Magni Thorsson and his ex-wife police detective Idunn Baldursdóttir. Each of their cases involves a series of homicides that turn out to be linked and uses a combination of alcoholism, religious problems, cooking, and personal relationships as secondary themes.

Crime Novels:

Magni Thorsson and Idunn Baldursdóttir Series:

2009: *Spor* ("Steps")
2010: *Fyrirgefning* ("Forgiveness")

Major Awards: N/A
Website: N/A

Yrsa Sigurðardóttir

b. August 24, 1963, Reykjavik, Iceland; Residence: Seltjarnarnes, a suburb of Reykjavik, Iceland; Occupations: civil engineer, author

Trained as a civil engineer at the University of Iceland and Concordia University in Montreal, Yrsa Sigurðardóttir, one of Iceland's best selling authors, is also a senior partner in Fjarhitun, one of the largest engineering firms in Iceland. She was the technical manager for the Karahnjukar dam project, the largest of its kind in Europe, and she is now a project manager for two geothermal power plants in northern Iceland. She began her writing career in 1998 with children's fiction and turned to crime novels in 2005, with *Þriðja táknið* (*Last Rituals*), the debut of her Thora Guð-mundsdóttir series, which has been translated into more than thirty languages and sold for English-language television production. She has also written two stand-alone horror novels which have both been acquired for filming in the United States.

In a 2010 interview for *The Scotsman*, Yrsa Sigurðardóttir observed that real-life Icelandic murders, on average only 1.3 per year, have always exhibited "a depressing stupidity." She illustrates her point by harking back to the medieval *Egilssaga*, which relates events from the year 914: "Egil is forced to explain to his father why, aged four, he has just killed a man. He says he couldn't help himself; the man was just so well positioned for a bludgeoning…. Things haven't changed much" (quoted in "Interview with Yrsa Sigurðardóttir"). Sigurðardóttir feels that her daytime engineering job and her evening writing are so different that juggling two professions doesn't seem arduous, because she can both make up and solve the problems in her books, making the plots plausible and bringing the characters to life. Originally she wrote humorous children's books because she says she noticed the books her son was reading were "lousy," but since she found it hard to be funny all the time, she started writing crime fiction. Humor steadily creeps into her lawyer Thora's romantic and domestic crises (Kerridge 2010), because Sigurðardóttir finds peaceful Iceland's few criminals ludicrous. Recently she cited as an example the years-long attempt of a Icelandic motorcycle gang to affiliate with the international Hell's Angels. The locals were arrested and taken to court for having attempted to torture a woman who had offended them, but Sigurðardóttir gleefully recounts that instead of carrying out their original intention of cutting off one of the woman's fingers, they had "chickened out" and cut out her hair extensions instead, for which they were duly sentenced (Yrsa Sigurðardóttir, "Murderous Greetings").

Though Sigurðardóttir provides impressive descriptions of the Icelandic landscape in her adult books, she concentrates on realistically gruesome details she feels necessary to make the story convincing. When she was in Greenland to research *Auðnin* (*The Day Is Dark*), natives wanted to show her the land's stern beauties, but she asked instead, "'... what would happen if you put a dead body in front of the sleigh dogs? Would they eat it?'" (quoted in Kerridge 2010).

The subtitle of Sigurðardóttir's *Þriðja táknið* (*Last Rituals*), "A Tale of Secret Symbols, Medieval Witchcraft, and Modern Murder," describes the eerie world that Thora Gudmondsdóttir, a lawyer and divorced single mother, enters in her first case, where a German student in Iceland is found ritually disfigured and murdered. Thora has to exert considerable intuition and rigorous logic to cut through the misinformation everyone in the victim's circle tosses at her, a device used in all of her novels. Sigurðardóttir also incorporates trademark spooky supernatural-seeming elements into all her plots, like the legendary malign Arctic spirit Tupilak which haunts *The Day Is Dark*, as well as peculiarly Icelandic geological and meteorological features like the volcanic eruption that dominates *Aska* (*Ashes to Dust*), the menacing Greenland winter storms in *The Day Is Dark*, and the personal horror of being stranded on a boat in the middle of the ocean, unable to trust anyone else, in *Brakið* (*The Silence of the Sea*"). In Thora's fifth mystery, *Horfðu á mig* (*Someone to Watch Over Me*, tr. 2014), she accepts a client who insists he wants his friend Jakob, a Down's Syndrome case, cleared of arson charges in a fire at his residential facility a year and a half earlier. Thora receives mysterious text messages that lead her into a welter of rape evidence, financial irregularities, and ethical violations, while she fends off her client's increasingly manipulative tactics. In this novel, Sigurðardóttir combines the depressing fallout of Iceland's devastating Crash "while poignantly showing the despair permeating working-class families and the devastating impacts on society's most vulnerable members" (Review of *Someone to Watch Over Me*).

Yrsa Sigurðardóttir gave Thora a temporary leave of absence with her first stand-alone horror tale, 2010's *Ég man þig* (*I Remember You*, tr. 2012), a hair-raising ghost story with all the familiar trappings of its genre, encouraging crime critics to compare her work with Stephen King's. This novel won her the Icelandic Blóðdropinn Award as well as a nomination for the all–Scandinavia Glass Key Award. *I Remember You* became one of Iceland's top bestsellers, and the German translation alone sold over 60,000 copies. In this eerie novel, she draws on ancient Icelandic folklore and ghost stories, playing them off against one of her favorite targets, Iceland's financial Crash which is "indirectly feeding the novel's dark strategies" (Forshaw, *I Remember...*).

On receiving the Blóðdropinn Award, Yrsa Sigurðardóttir happily commented, "'I really love making people's flesh creep!'" (quoted in Forshaw, *I Remember...*). British critic Barry Forshaw agreed: "Ms. Sigurðardóttir is clearly relishing the business of scaring our collective pants off" (Forshaw, *I Remember...*). Summing up the contributions to Nordic crime fiction made by Icelandic authors despite the dearth of actual crime scene material, Sigurðardóttir notes that Icelanders nonetheless add life to their works by using "the all-encompassing Icelandic nature and wilderness," the tightly-knit rural life and "harsh history," and "the long, dark winters." "As our ancestors used to say: If your sword is too short, take a step forward" (Yrsa Sigurðardóttir, "Murderous Greetings" 37).

Crime Novels:

Thora Guðmundsdóttir Series:

2005: *Þriðja táknið* (*Last Rituals*, tr. Bernard Scudder, 2007)
2006: *Sér grefur gröf* (*My Soul to Take*, tr. Bernard Scudder and Anna Yates, 2009)
2007: *Aska* (*Ashes to Dust*, tr. Philip Roughton, 2010)
2008: *Auðnin* (*The Day is Dark*, tr. Philip Roughton, 2011)
2009: *Horfðu á mig* (*Someone to Watch Over Me*, tr. Philip Roughton, 2013)
2011: *Brakið* (*The Silence of the Sea*, tr. Philip Roughton, 2014)

2013: *Lygi* ("The Exchange")
2014: *DNA* ("DNA")

Other Crime Novels:

2010: *Ég man þig* (*I Remember You*, tr. Philip Roughton, 2012; also called *Blessed Are the Children*)
2012: *Kuldi* ("Colds")

Major Awards:

2011: The Blóðdropinn Award for *Ég man þig* (*I Remember You*)
2015: The Petrona Award, for *Brakið* (*The Silence of the Sea*)

Website: N/A

Jón Hallur Stefánsson

> b. 1959, Iceland; Residence: Reykjavik, Iceland; Occupations: Literary editor; radio producer; musician; poet; translator; author

Jon Hallur Stefánsson worked as a radio journalist in Ríkisútvarpið from 1993 to 2003. His Detective Inspector Valdimar series of Reykjavik police procedurals debuted in 2005 with *Krosstré* ("Ice-Cold Silence"), set during endless summer nights in Reykjavik, treating a bleak world with violent everyday life where Inspector Valdimar is no less depressed than his surroundings. *Vargurinn* ("Arsonists"), 2008, is set in the small fishing village of Seydisfjord where a series of fires affects three families—the pastor's, a fishing captain's, and the fishing company director's, all related. In the course of his investigation, Valdimar has to sort through a torrent of village gossip and untangle old rivalries and relationships full of hatred, jealousy, and passion.

Crime Novels:

Inspector Valdimar Eggertson Series:
2005: *Krosstré* ("Ice-Cold Silence"), Norwegian tr. Eric Boury
2008: *Kvinden der forsvandt* ("The Woman Who Disappeared")
2008: *Vargurinn* ("Arsonists")

Major Awards:

2004: Icelandic Thriller Short Story Competition, for *"Enginn engill"* ("Far from Being an Angel")

Website: N/A

*Arni Thorarinsson (Árni Þórarinsson)

> b. August 1, 1950; Residence: N/A; Occupations: journalist, media personality, author

Einar, the hero of Arni Thorarinsson's popular crime series, is an irritable journalist with a talent for becoming personally involved in solving violent crimes, the platform for the author's analysis of Icelandic society through the perspective of Iceland's history and various geographical settings. Einar's creator likes to title his novels after popular song titles as a means of announcing his themes. In Einar's first outing, *Nóttin hefur þúsund augu* ("The Night Has a Thousand Eyes"), 1999, excruciatingly hung over, he covers a vicious murder at the Airport Hotel; in *Hvíta kanínan* ("The White Rabbit"), 2000, he and his daughter vacation in Spain, where they discover a chain of horrible events; and in *Blátt tungl* ("Blue Moon"), 2001, a mysterious Christmas disappearance threatens Einar's reputation and his mind. *Tími nornarinnar* (*Season of the Witch*), 2006, tr. 2012, was nominated for the Icelandic Literature Prize. It transfers an unwilling Einar to the small town of Akureiri, also the setting of *Dauði trúðsins* ("Death of a Clown").2007. Einar leaves for the remote West Fjords in *Sjöundi sonurinn* ("The Seventh Son"), 2008, and *Morgunengill* ("Angel of the Morning"), 2010, returns him to Reykjavik. *Ár kattarins* ("The Year of the Cat"), 2012, maintains Einar's reputation for professional and rigorous probing into societal evils and sustains Arni Thorinsson's popularity as a sensitive and ironic observer of contemporary Icelandic society.

"Season of the Witch" was adapted for television and aired to mixed reviews in 2011.

Crime Novels:

Einar Series:

1998: *Nóttin hefur þúsund augu* ("The Night Has a Thousand Eyes")
2000: *Hvíta kanínan* ("The White Rabbit")
2001: *Blátt tungl* ("Blue Moon")
2006: *Tími nornarinnar* (*Season of the Witch*, tr. Anna Yates, 2012)
2007: *Dauði trúðsins* ("Death of a Clown")
2008: *Sjöundi sonurinn* ("The Seventh Son")
2010: *Morgunengill* ("Angel of the Morning")
2012: *Ár kattarins* ("The Year of the Cat")
2013: *Glæpurinn* ("Full Tilt Poker")

Major Awards: N/A

Website: N/A

Arni Thorarinsson and Páll Kristin Pálsson

The two novel collaborations between Arni Thorarinsson and Páll Kristin Pálsson have been categorized as psychological thrillers, with amateur detectives plunged into violent crimes that involve painful re-evaluations of their own lives.

Arni Thorarinsson and Páll Kristin Pálsson are also among famous Icelandic crime authors who have written episodes of the 2008 six-part SagaFilm television series *Pressa* ("The Press"). The lead character, Lara, is a thirtyish single mother and reporter for a Reykjavik tabloid. She investigates one case per episode, all of which are connected in an overarching story line about a missing person who may have been a victim of foul play.

Crime Novels:

2002: *Í upphafi var morðið* ("And God Created Murder")
2006: *Farþeginn* ("The Passenger")

Óskar Hrafn Thorvaldsson

b. N/A; Residence: Reykjavik, Iceland; Occupations: news director, author

Oskar Hrafn Thorvaldsson resigned in May 2010 from his position as news director for Iceland's Channel Two television and the Internet news website *Vísir* over issues connected with his investigation of corporate raiding in Iceland. On his experiences, he based the first novel of a projected police procedural series with Detective Gunnar Finnbjörnsson as his lead character. In *Martröð millanna* ("Millionaires"), he used the brutal murder of Reynir Sveinn Reynisson, a wealthy notorious corporate raider, snob, and womanizer found dead in his lavish hot tub, to open this hardboiled exposé of Reykjavik's underworld, Russian mafia infiltration into Iceland, the corruption rampant in Icelandic banking, and the decadence of the country's corporate raiders.

Crime Novels:

2012: *Martröð millanna* ("Millionaires")

Major Awards: N/A

Website: N/A

Eyrún Ýr Tryggvadóttir

b. 1978; Residence: Husavik, Iceland; Occupations: library director, author

Eyrún Ýr Tryggvadóttir, director of the Library of Husavik, Iceland, writes romance- thrillers about young adults that appeal to general audiences. Her first novel, "Second Chance," 2004, was not initially in general circulation, but it was republished in 2013. *Hvar er systir min?* ("Where Is My Sister?") has a conventional plot about Andrea, an intrepid young heroine entangled in evil, love, and excitement. *Fimmta barnið* ("The Fifth Child") follows Andrea as she begins working as a reporter with a predictable involvement in a mysterious homeless child, a case reaching far into the past. In *Ómynd* she probes into a child's disappearance. "Where Is My Sister?" and "Omynd" were both nominated for the Blóðdropinn Award. Eyrún Ýr Tryggvadóttir also co-authored the romance-thriller "Carpe Diem."

Crime Novels:

2008: *Hvar er systir mín?* ("Where Is My Sister?")
2009: *Fimmta barnið* ("The Fifth Child")
2011: *Ómynd* ("Omynd ")
2013 (originally published in 2004): "Second Chance"

Major Awards: N/A

Website: N/A

Thorunn Erlu Valdimarsdóttir (Þorunn Valdimarsdóttir)

b. August 25, 1954, Reykjavik, Iceland; Residence: Reykjavik, Iceland; Occupations: historian, poet, author

Nominated for the Icelandic Literary Prize, the Nordic Council Literary Prize, and the Blóð-dropinn Award, Thorunn Valdimarsdóttir since 1983 has produced over twenty books, including two volumes of poetry, six historical studies, four biographies, several academic publications, radio and television material, and nine novels.

In "Lines Drawn in Snow," a 2010 speech delivered at the Sylvia Kekkonen Symposium in Finland, Thorunn Valdimarsdóttir described a strange dream her mother had while she was pregnant with Thorunn: the Mountain Lady, the romantic nationally dressed female symbol of Iceland, handed her a newborn baby, but Thorunn's mother felt disappointed that the baby was a girl, since she had thought that in Iceland's male-dominated society, the baby given her by the national symbol would be a boy. To salve that disappointment, Thorunn Valdimarsdóttir says she has addressed themes involving women throughout her fiction.

Thorunn Valdimarsdóttir's two crime novels blend contemporary narratives with the Sagas of Icelanders. Like most of her other stories, they feature independent young heroines in a patriarchal society. She loves to mix literary genres, and so she used two of the most important medieval sagas as models for her two crime novels, both nominated for the Icelandic Literary Prize: the *Njáls saga* for the first, *Kalt er annars blóð* ("Cold Blood"), 2007, and the *Laxdaela saga* for the second, *Mörg eru ljónins eyru* ("The Lion Has Many Eyes"), 2010.

Thorunn Valdimarsdóttir called the writing of these novels "a very satisfying intellectual game for me as a historian to see how medieval themes and psychological patterns played out in contemporary society" ("Lines Drawn in Snow"). Her detective hero and his team solve crimes in the tradition of the modern genre, but her saga prototypes provide an Icelandic traditional perspective into the crime of murder, which in the sagas is often instigated by women and involved with feuds which maintained "respectability and honour," reflecting the saga age's position that when a killing's basis was the maintenance of one's honor, it was not considered murder. In "Cold Blood," a raven, in Norse myth the messenger of the chief god Odin, circles over Reykjavik, watching crimes usually hidden from human sight: graft, arson, senseless killings of animals and humans and a body accidentally discovered outside the city. This device allows the author to explore various human motives for crime. As an example of her authorial method, Thorunn Valdimarsdóttir cites the passage from the *Njáls saga* in which Hallgerður, one of the most notorious women in Icelandic sagas, refuses to give her lover Gunnar a lock of her hair for the bowstrings that would save his life, because he had abused her verbally and physically. In "Cold Blood," the character Gunnar asks Halla to hand him her mobile phone, but she refuses because he had struck her n a fit of anger. With no phone, he cannot call for help and dies.

Thorunn Valdimarsdóttir had previously used the *Laxdaela saga* ("The Saga of the Laxdaelir") as a blueprint for the modern settings of both her mainstream novels *Alveg nóg* ("Quite Enough"), 1997, and *Stúlka með fingur* ("Girl with a Finger"), 1999; the latter, which won the 1999 DV Newspaper Cultural Award, is widely considered to be her most fascinating novel to date (Eysteinsson and Dagsdóttir in Neijmann 465). She also used the *Laxdaela Saga* as the foundation for her second crime novel, *Mörg eru ljónsins eyru* ("The Lion Has Many Eyes"), 2010. The *Laxdaela saga* appeals strongly to women readers and authors, because it involves a powerful female antagonist and emphasizes women's activities. "A curious female perspective runs through the entire story, frequently suppressed by the genre's demand for masculine adventures and exploits" (Kress in Neijmann 510). Helga Kress points out that this saga is a "symbolic narrative" centered on the Irish princess Melkorka, now a slave in Iceland, who rebels against her captivity by pretending she cannot speak, though her master one day overhears her talking to her son in Celtic and realizes she can indeed speak. The image of a mother secretly passing on her native language to her child, according to Kress, illustrates the power of women's cultural influence to shape a nation's literary tradition: "Because women held a strong position in the native [Icelandic] oral tradition ... passed on to their learned sons, the [Icelandic] literature was written in the vernacular rather than in Latin, Europe's then official language" (Kress in Neijmann 510).

To the Icelandic literary world which for a long time considered crime literature less important than mainstream fiction, Thorunn Valdimarsdóttir justified her combination of crime fiction and saga lore: "I hate literature snobbery.... Thus I planned to write a crime novel with originality and use so called *fine* [italics in original] literary style. To have fun on more levels I modeled my crime novels on medieval sagas ... [which have] low key very intricate psychology, love and passion ... [producing] double reading fun, enjoying a crime novel through the medieval mirror." She concluded that she has always maintained the purpose she had had since she was a child, "wanting to expand human consciousness to help make a better world" ("Lines Drawn in Snow").

Crime Novels:

> 2007: *Kalt er annars blóð* ("Cold Blood")
> 2010: *Mörg eru ljónsins eyru* ("The Lion Has Many Eyes")

Major Awards:

> 1999: DV Newspaper Cultural Award for *Stúlka með fingur* ("Girl With a Finger")

Website: N/A

Jökull Valsson

> b. June 6, 1981; Residence: Ársta, Iceland; Occupation: author

Jökull Valsson's first book, a Young Adult horror novel called *Börnin í Húmdölum* ("Children of Húmdölum") appeared in 2004, followed by *Skuldadagar* ("Days of Reckoning"), 2006, an adult horror novel nominated for the Blóðdropinn Award. It presents the tribulations of a youth who hopes to make enough quick drug-dealing profits to achieve the good life in contemporary Reykjavik. Instead, he falls into the lethal grasp of the underworld, which Valsson portrays with chilling realism.

Crime Novels:

> 2006: *Skuldadagar* ("Days of Reckoning")

Major Awards: N/A

Website: N/A

*Thor Vilhjálmsson

> b. August 12, 1926, Edinburgh, Scotland; d. March 2, 2011, Reykjavik, Iceland; Residence: Reykjavik, Iceland; Occupations: poet, playwright, translator, novelist

One of Iceland's most respected literary figures, Thor Vilhjálmsson was a modernist who produced novels, short stories, essays, translations, and poetry. His acclaimed 1986 novel *Grámosinn glóir* (*Justice Undone*, tr. 1997) received the 1992 Nordic Prize (the "Nordic Booker Prize"). Based on an actual historical trial for incest and infanticide committed by half-siblings in a remote rural area of 19th-century Iceland, the novel follows an idealistic young magistrate conducting the first case of his career, which leads him into a surreal dreamscape mingled with the saga world. Poet Ted Hughes observed, "Vilhjálmsson's hallucinatory imagination creates an eerily beautiful vision of things, Icelandic in far-seeing clarity, precision, strangeness. Unique and unforgettable" (quoted in *goodreads*).

Crime Novels:

> 1986: *Grámosinn glóir* (*Justice Undone*, tr. Bernard Scudder, 1997)

Major Awards:

1992: Swedish Academy Nordic Prize, known as "The Little Nobel Prize," for *Justice Undone*

Website: N/A

Non-Icelandic Authors of Novels
with Icelandic Settings

Quentin Bates

After writing non-fiction for some time, including *Life on the Edge,* a travelogue featuring the UK fishing industry, English journalist and author Quentin Bates moved to Iceland in the late 1970s, when the country was "remote," with no e mail or faxes and international phone calls were major undertakings. He lived there until 1990 and found the culture fascinating: "There's a strange blend of worldview and small-town attitudes that sit uncomfortably together" (quoted in "Quentin Bates: An Interview"). In the 1970s, Bates had discovered a "small and informal" Iceland, "very close to being a very equal society," with no one "obscenely rich" and "no abject poverty either." Bates then found watching the subsequent changes in Iceland's economy and culture "an intriguing process" (quoted in "Quentin Bates: An Interview"), and he made Iceland's 2008 financial crisis (the crash) the background for his crime fiction series.

Bates used Iceland's 2008 financial crisis ("the crash") with environmental issues as the backdrop for *Frozen Assets*, the first volume of a planned multi-volume detective series with a female detective, Gunnhildur Gisladóttir (Gunna) as its protagonist: "a middle-aged, fairly sensible uniformed female rural police officer" (Bates, "Joining" 22), who "just jumped off the screen, fully formed, demanding attention" ("Quentin Bates: An Interview"). Bates also wanted to show the rural Iceland he preferred to Reykjavik. In the villages, he says, "People talk differently, they don't think in the same way, and they have a bone-dry humor that often flies right over the heads of many locals" (Bates, "Joining" 22). At his publisher's request, he cut ten years from Gunna's age and has steadily moved closer to Iceland's capital for his settings, but he likes to take his heroine out into the country when possible.

Bates followed *Frozen Assets* with two more novels, seeing Gunna as "heroic," because she demands answers to "questions that others don't think or want to ask" (quoted in "Quentin Bates: An Interview"). In *Cold Comfort*, Bates poses plenty of questions about the crash, creating a particularly complex combination of three plot lines all reflecting the continuing chaos of an Iceland struggling to recover after half the value of its currency disappeared, ordinary citizens faced new and heavy taxes, government services were cut dramatically, and those responsible for the disaster still profited from it all.

Bates is "particularly fond" of the Swedish crime writers Sjöwall and Wahlöö and Henning Mankell, the Finnish author Matti Joensuu, and Icelander Arnaldur Indriðason, whose latest Erlendur novel Bates, like many Icelanders, eagerly awaits as each November 1 approaches (" ... there's a lot of discussion of 'the new Erlendur': 'Is it as good as the last one?'"), but the fictional detective Bates continually returns to, "who never goes stale is Maigret" (quoted in "Quentin Bates: An Interview"), a clue to Bates' own crime novel techniques. In addition to the Gunna novels listed below, Bates has produced *Cold Steal* in e book format only, a Kindle-only novella, *Winterlude*, and an e-novella *Summerchill*. A new full- length Gunna novel, *Thin Ice*, is scheduled for early 2016 publication (Bates, "Joining" 24).

Crime Novels:

The Gunnhildur Gisladóttir Series:

2011: *Frozen Assets* (titled *Frozen Out* in the UK)
2012: *Cold Comfort*
2013: *Chilled to the Bone*

Website: http://graskeggur.com

Hannah Kent

Australian author Hannah Kent co-founded the Australian literary journal *Kill Your Darlings*, for which she serves as deputy editor. Her debut novel, *Burial Rites*, 2011, fictionalizes the true story of a servant named Agnes Magnúsdóttir ambiguously implicated in a double murder. Agnes was Iceland's last individual to be executed, and Kent learned her story as a seventeen-year-old exchange student to Iceland. In a 2013 interview, Kent revealed that she had expected to stay in Reykjavik but instead was assigned to a dark, snowy fishing village not even on her map: "it felt like oblivion, like the edge of the world," where her host family told her Agnes's story and frequently drove her past the site of Agnes' beheading. Kent became "desperately curious" to probe into Agnes' personality, which was never described in the information Kent could discover that time because she herself felt so homesick, but Kent felt "some kind of kinship with this woman that was 'completely irrational'" (quoted in Cummins).

In *Burial Rites*, Agnes tells her own story while she awaits execution on the farm of District Officer Jon Jonsson, where Jonsson and his family at first refuse even to speak to her. The young pastor appointed as Agnes' spiritual adviser gradually helps Agnes reveal her tale against the stark backdrop of the grueling struggle for life in rural Iceland, leaving readers to decide Agnes' guilt or innocence. Kent maintains that her major interest in writing historical crime novels is her love of research; she doesn't consider *Burial Rites* primarily a crime novel, or even a historical novel, because she says the latter term reminds her of bodice-rippers. (Cummins).

Crime Novel:

2011: *Burial Rites*

Major Awards:

2011: Writing Australia Unpublished Manuscript Award (inaugural award), for *Burial Rites*

Website: http://hannahkentauthor.com

Michael Ridpath

Former British bond trader and author Michael Ridpath went to Iceland on a book tour to promote the first of his eight financial thrillers, and there he encountered businessmen who believed in elves (Jones). His fascination with the apparent contradictions of Icelandic culture grew, and thirteen years later, he began his *Fire and Ice* mystery series with *Where the Shadows Lie*, 2010. He has since produced three more books in the *Fire and Ice* series starring Magnus Jonson, a detective born in Iceland who grew up in the United States where his father had accepted a position as a mathematics professor. As an Icelandic teenager who was an outsider in a U.S. high school, young Magnus comforts himself by reading the Icelandic sagas . He later had to abandon his plans for law school when his father was murdered and police could not find the killer. Twelve years later Magnus was a Boston homicide detective caught up in a police corruption scandal and forced to leave Boston for his own safety. He takes an advertised position in Reykjavik, training policemen there in U.S. methods of dealing with big-city crime, "an Icelandic speaking cop who sees his country through the eyes of an American detective" (Jones).

Ridpath indicates that in this series he wants to "explain why Icelanders behave the way they do, to get under the skin of the people" and to convey what he sees as Iceland's overwhelming theme: "the clash of the old and the new" (Jones). In reviewing *Where the Shadows Lie*, *Publishers Weekly* found that "Ridpath smoothly melds history, legend, and a police procedural" (quoted in Jones), probably because Ridpath finds Iceland "fascinating," and its people "a hard-working, manic lot with a highly developed sense of humour, big on irony." He sees several conflicts there, citing Iceland's rise from 1940s poverty and its post–World War II technological advancement, the ancient-appearing landscape of glaciers and lava fields that is really geologically very young but still "full of myths and legends, trolls and elves, and the sites of the great medieval sagas" (quoted in Jones). Because his stated desire is to show what Iceland and its people are like and how the country works, Ridpath makes Iceland "part of each of my characters in different ways," and picks symbolic landmarks for each novel to familiarize readers, providing bizarre or counterintuitive details, since he feels "there are loads of these in Iceland" (quoted in Jones).

When he began his *Fire and Ice* series, Ridpath researched contemporary English and American crime writers who used foreign detectives in foreign settings, like Donna Leon, David Hewson, Martin Walker, and Craig Russell. He found Scottish author Craig Russell his major inspiration in "how to write about a foreign country convincingly" (quoted in Jones).

Crime Novels:

The Fire and Ice Series:

2010 (UK); 2011 (USA): *Where the Shadows Lie*
2011 (UK); 2012 (USA): *66 Degrees North*
2012 (UK); 2013 (USA): *Meltwater*
2014 (UK); 2014 (USA): *Sea of Stone*

Major Awards: N/A

Website: N/A

Betty Webb

b. N/A; Residence: Scottsdale, Arizona; Occupations: journalist, author

After several installments of her Scottsdale-based PI series starring former policewoman Lena Jones, who investigates cases involving controversial feminist issues like polygamy, genital mutilation, human trafficking, and swindling connected with the U.S. welfare system, Betty Webb launched a cozy series in 2008 that features Theodora ("Teddy") Bentley, a Monterey Bay, California, zookeeper and amateur sleuth, enlivening the strong animal stories of her Gunn Zoo series with non-cloying unsentimental humor. Webb moved Teddy off her home turf and to Iceland for *The Puffin of Death*, 2015, She had intended that novel "to take place at the puffin breeding ground in Vik í Mýrdal, and the American victim would be murdered by one of those perverse Icelanders, chopped up, and saved in a jar to snack on later," but when Icelanders in person on their home ground proved to Webb that they committed very little homicide and usually just apologized for non-lethal assaults when they sobered up, she revamped her earlier concept of "an Icelandic cannibal serial killer" and did "what a writer has to do" (Webb 42–43).

Crime Novel:

The Gunn Zoo Series:

2015: *The Puffin of Death*

Major Awards: N/A

Website: http://www.bettywebb-zoomystery.com

NORWAY

At every door-way,
as one enters,
one should spy round,
one should pry round
for uncertain is the witting
that there be no foeman sitting,
within, before one on the floor.

> —*Hávamál*, The Words of Odin the High One,
> Wisdom for Wanderers and Counsel to Guests, 1

The Cultural Context of Norwegian Crime Fiction

In 2007, Nils Nordberg, one of Norway's foremost crime fiction critics and for over twenty years editor of *Rivertonklubben*, the Norwegian Crime Writers' Association, estimated that approximately 1,300 Norwegian crime novels and short story collections had been published in the genre's 180-year history. About half have appeared in the past 30 years, which Nordberg feels may be the genre's most recent "Golden Age" in Norway. Despite the current popularity of Norwegian crime fiction, however, the country actually has a very low incidence of homicides—between 2006 and 2008 only 6.9 murders per 1,000,000 people (Kachka).

Many critics and authors, both Norwegian and non–Norwegian, concur that Norway's crime fiction has always exhibited its own special characteristics. In 1971, Einar Øklund declared that Norwegian literature did not follow either Continental or even Scandinavian trends, instead fostering storytellers who preferred to use conventional sentence structure as writers of "themes and things rather than of structures, theories or philosophies" (Øklund 1078). *New York Magazine*'s Boris Kachka concluded in 2011 that Norwegian crime fiction has "More landscape, less action and adrenaline than its Swedish counterparts," and UCLA professor Claus Elholm Andersen agreed that Norwegian crime stories are "Much more calm, local, focused on the subtleties in the puzzle" than other Scandinavian work in the genre (quoted in Kachka). Jo Nesbø, Norway's most popular crime author today, also insists that while cultural, demographic, and geographical similarities do exist in Scandinavian crime fiction, "the voices [of Norwegian and Swedish authors] are very different" (Foster 94). Norway, "God's country, especially if God happens to be a Lutheran" (Mogk 21), has become the scene of *noir* crime fiction that is less Continental than Danish or Swedish crime literature and more provincial, almost always "driven by greed or jealousy or sex" (Audun Engelstad, quoted in Forshaw 97). Most Norwegian crime fiction presently uses police procedural conventions as its springboard, with fictional crimes ranging from Nesbø's chilling urban serial killings to Karin Fossum's rural homicides, which occur in deceptively placid but actually ominous settings, like much too still pools with rotting somethings in their depths (Mogk

22). Between these extremes, Norwegian crime authors produce subtle shades of deeply hidden horror.

Today Norway is the second least densely populated country in Europe. Living in Norway's 138,747 square miles of "intimidating vastnesses" (Forshaw 96) has always demanded that its relatively small population—currently about 5 million, or 35 persons per square mile—contend strenuously with nature for their daily bread. For a long time, too, Norwegians have had to live with "a nearly hopeless attempt to annihilate the realities of distance" (Beyer 1). Norway's mountains and fjords force its people to live in widely separated habitable spots, making physical contacts even today possible only by skis, airplane, boat, or hair-raising road trips (Beyer 1). Henrik Ibsen, Norway's greatest dramatist, declared, "The spectacular but severe landscape ... and the lonely shut-off life ... force them [the Norwegians] not to bother about other people, but only their own concerns, so that they become reflective and serious, they brood and doubt and often despair" (from Feliz Philippi's October 1902 conversation with Ibsen, quoted as an epigraph to Michael Meyer's *Ibsen*).

While modern technology now provides near-instantaneous communication, the Norwegian qualities of reserve, repression and suspicion of emotion, and outward impassiveness fostered by geographic separation and isolation persist in their literature. Norwegian crime authors often see these qualities as engendering and concealing powerful psychological drives responsible for horrendous crimes that can lie long hidden as easily in crowded city apartment buildings as in remote forests, a circumstance illustrated by a peculiar fact of Norwegian publishing and readership. Most of the Christian world rejoices and celebrates at Easter, but in Norway, Easter is the prime season for launching literary *påskekrim* ("Easter crime"). Norwegian families and friends typically load up on new crime novels, oranges, and the popular KitKat-like *KvikkLunsj* chocolate bars in March and April (Swift), then gather at their *hytte* (cabins) deep in the woods during the Easter vacation, relishing fiction where often characters are similarly "far away from other people" when one of them is mysteriously killed ("The Norwegian 'Easter-Crime' Phenomena") in a sinister setting the pagan *Hávamal* ("Sayings of the Wise One") of the Viking Age called "frost-cold mountains" and "wolf valleys," "flood-wet fells" and "dismal slopes" (quoted in Beyer 10). Today the Norwegian milk company Tine even decorates its milk cartons with crime-related comic strips written and illustrated by some of Norway's finest authors and commercial artists (Swift).

Two psychological types usually oppose each other in today's Norwegian crime fiction: the person of good will, most often a flawed male police detective, but sometimes a private investigator or even a woman sleuth, each plagued with some debilitating problem, must face a monstrous criminal and bring him/her to justice. These types descend from Norway's oldest literature, the myths of the pagan Germanic gods, where Thor, the honest native–Norwegian deity of oath-keeping and defender of humanity, represents the human desire to right the wrongs that society, or at least its misguided, warped, or corrupted members, forces upon individuals. (Thor was later supplanted by Odin, the All-Father Wotan imported from northern Germany, who endowed his warrior-poet skalds with poetic gifts and openheartedness.) In pagan Norse mythology, Thor battled the monsters devouring the roots of the World Tree Yggdrasil, monsters frequently revived by modern Norwegian crime fiction in human form as self-appointed shaman figures considering themselves divinely chosen instruments of evil powers.

While Christianity attempted to stamp out those pagan beliefs, for a long time Norwegian national consciousness seemed subordinated to other Scandinavian cultures, principally that of Denmark, which ruled Norway from 1397 until ceding Norway to Sweden in 1814. Norway's national consciousness reawakened in the mid-nineteenth century, when the nation's authors broke away from the formal Dano-Norwegian tradition. They found their inspiration in Norway's ancient myths, folklore, history, culture, and folk literature, expressing their themes in a more natural style considered "more Norwegian" than previous Norwegian literary works which had been heavily influenced by Swedish and Danish writings (Beyer 141). Camilla Collett's anonymously published *The Governor's Daughters*, 1854–1855, the first salvo of the Norwegian women's rights movement, strongly impressed Henrik Ibsen, who mercilessly dissected both society and the individual psyche in the latter half of the nineteenth century. Driven by his absolutist demand to "Be Thyself!," Ibsen's plays probed the secrets of the human heart and the depths of the human unconscious, "where strange fish slowly circle" (Meyer 659), many of them spawned by a powerful sense of guilt, as Ibsen expressed it in *A Comedy of Love:* "There is a retribution that runs through life" (quoted in Beyer 216). Almost all of the plays with which Ibsen rocked the world deal with serious crimes, even murder, and consequent retribution.

One of Ibsen's early dramas, *The Vikings at Helgeland*, illustrates the impact the ancient Norse myths had made upon him. Ibsen worked from the pre–Christian *Volsungasaga*, a twelfth-century Icelandic prose saga related by a common ancestor to the German *Nibelungenlied*. In *The Vikings at Helgeland*, Ibsen echoed the hero Sigurd's death, engineered by his rejected lover Brynhild in the pre–Christian *Volsungasaga*, by creating a fierce heroine, Hjørdis, a fourteenth-century pagan priestess, who slays her lover Sigurd because he has married a Christian woman and adopted her new religion of peace and love. Decades later, Ibsen reworked that ancient theme of thwarted love, the frustrated will-to-power, and consequent death into one of his most powerful plays, *Hedda Gabler*, whose gifted heroine, fatally frustrated by society's restrictions on women, drives her former admirer Eilert Løvberg to suicide, then destroys herself and her unborn child.

Transgression, guilt, and retribution—the stuff of crime fiction— have become Norwegian crime authors' major preoccupations, from Norway's pioneering crime authors in the 1800s through three national "Golden Ages" of the genre: the first, from 1910 to 1925, beginning just after Norway separated from Sweden in 1905; the second, 1940 to 1947, the bitter years of Norway's Nazi Occupation and its aftermath; and the third, the renaissance or "contemporary" period of Norwegian crime fiction beginning in the early 1970s and continuing into the new millennium, today showing few signs of decline.

The Pioneers

Probably because of the relative obscurity of the Norwegian language, the earliest Norwegian contributions to the development of crime fiction have largely been overlooked. The first known Norwegian experimenter with the genre was Maurits Hansen (1794–1842), a teacher, short story writer, and author of a major Norwegian grammar text. He published arguably the world's first crime novel, *The Assassination of Engineer Roolfsen. A Correctional Anecdote from Kongsberg*, in 1839, two years before Edgar Allan Poe published his short story "The Murders in the Rue Morgue," the first appearance of private detective C. Auguste Dupin, the prototype for hordes of both conscious and unconscious fictional imitations (Murphy 154). Most Norwegian literary historians believe Hansen also inspired Henrik Ibsen's retrospective narrative technique, a narrative device that has since been used frequently by Norwegian mystery authors. *The Assassination of Engineer Roolfsen* was reissued in translation in 2004.

Another Norwegian crime fiction pioneer was Hanna Winsnes (1789–1872), who crime historian and critic Nils Nordberg feels could likely have been the world's first woman mystery writer. A parson's wife who became a household name with a cookbook that was a standby in Norwegian kitchens for generations, Winsnes, writing as "Hugo Schwarz," produced two thrillers possibly inspired by Maurits Hansen in the early 1840s, involving murders, abductions, and illicit love, substantially predating mystery novels written by two American women. Winsnes's thrillers were not widely known, again probably because so few people then as now were able to read Norwegian. Early American women crime writers, writing in English, have thus been hailed as important pioneers in the genre. *The Dead Letter*, 1867, by Seeley Regester (Metta Victoria Fuller Victor), is now recognized as the first American detective novel written by a woman, preceding Anna Katherine Green's *The Leavenworth Case*, 1878, which for a long time received that distinction. *The Leavenworth Case*, featuring New York policeman Ebenezer Gryce and employing a romantic subplot, was one of the most successful novels of the nineteenth century, selling 750,000 copies in fifteen years and paving the way for women crime authors to come. Á propos the fact that about a century later it took contemporary Norwegian women crime authors like Anne Holt and Karin Fossum ten years after their British and American cousins to produce their psychologically penetrating mystery novels, Nordberg remarked, "The only comfort is that the Swedes and Danes were even slower," since they had to move into another millennium before Swede Liza Marklund and her Danish sisters-in-crime began to publish their crime fiction.

Norwegians famous in other fields also experimented with early crime fiction. Realist and naturalist author Jonas Lie (1833–1908), one of the "Four Greats" of 19th century Norwegian literature who claimed it was his need and passion to depict all of Norway in his fiction (Beyer 233), explored crime in five detective short stories featuring DCI Ove Bjelke in mysterious cases somewhat resembling Poe's stories involving the supernatural. Inspired by Arthur Conan Doyle's Sherlock Holmes stories, Christian Sparre, a Norwegian member of the 1900–1901 Council of State Division (a body advocating the separation of Norway from Sweden) had already published *The Adventures of Karl Monk*, a popular thriller, in 1897. Lie and Sparre probably were influenced by Conan Doyle's Great Detective, who still enjoys considerable popularity throughout Scandinavia, according to Bjarne Nielsen's *Scandinavia and Sherlock Holmes*, a 2006 English-language collection of "the best Holmesian writings of Denmark, Sweden, and Norway," containing essays dating from the 1950s to the present that deal with Holmesian scholarship and minutiae, illustrated by sixty Sherlockian drawings by Henry Loritzen.

The First Golden Age of Norwegian Crime Fiction

Crime and mystery fiction took firm hold among Norwegian readers accustomed not only to respecting the law and condemning lawbreakers, but also to concealing their own feelings and suspecting their neighbors of hiding heinous vicissitudes. Real-life crime journalism often launched careers in fiction for Norwegian novelists and short story writers who supplied crime fiction fans with popular reading material. Journalist and editor Øvre Richter Frich (Gjert Øvre Richter Frich), 1872–1945, worked from 1895 to 1910 as a reporter for Oslo's *Aftenposten*, covering vital events like the dissolution of Norway's union with Sweden in 1905 so competently that he is considered to have revitalized Norwegian newspaper reporting. Frich then traveled widely before spending his last fifteen years in Sweden, writing about seventy books that sold at least two million copies, including twenty-one novels about the crime-solving doctor and adventurer Jonas Fjeld, who debuted with great popular success in 1911.

Another journalist, Stein Riverton (pseudonym of Sven Elvestad, born Kristoffer Elvestad Svendsen), 1884–1934, became the most famous author of the first Golden Age of Norwegian crime fiction. Having changed his name in his youth after being caught embezzling from his employer, Riverton/Elvestad began a new career as a journalist in Oslo (then called Christiania).

As a young sensationalism-prone reporter, Riverton once spent a day in a cage with a circus lion, but his greatest coup was the first interview of Adolf Hitler by a foreign reporter; despite his own fascist leanings, Riverton presciently described Hitler as "a dangerous man."

Riverton initiated Norwegian police procedural fiction, today the dominant form of the genre in all the Scandinavian countries. He began by writing semi-documentary reports and then, working from his acquaintance with actual policemen, he created a fictional retired police detective, "Asbjørn Krag," and developed Krag into a classical middle-aged goateed private detective with strong police connections. In 1908, under a different pen name, Riverton also created Knut Gribb, a tough, clean-shaven police detective later taken over by other authors. Riverton's total crime fiction output, some ninety stories, includes both short fiction and full-length novels. Confusingly, some Gribb mysteries have appeared as Asbjørn Krag books authored by "Stein Riverton."

In 1909, Riverton published *Jernvognen* (*The Iron Chariot*), considered his masterpiece, a thriller ranked second in *Dagbladet's* 2009 "25 Best Norwegian Crime Novels." The novel is set on a resort island off Norway's southern coast, where a legendary iron wagon that leaves no tracks haunts the island's moors. Its ghostly sounds are heard the night the body of Forestry Agent Blinde, the head bashed in, is discovered, and later, after master sleuth Asbjørn Krag arrives to investigate, the wagon is heard again when the body of Blinde's fiancée's old grandfather is found in virtually the same spot, with a similar fatal wound. Riverton employed a complex neo-romantic narrative style and a narrative point of view that according to J. Randolph Cox's foreword to James P. Jensen's 2005 paperback English translation of the novel may have been inspired by Arthur Conan Doyle's spooky *The Hound of the Baskervilles*, 1902. According to Cox, too, Riverton also invented a clever plot twist, unveiling the least-likely person as the killer. Much later Agatha Christie used the same device in *The Murder of Roger Ackroyd*, 1926, sparking critical debate on whether Christie might have violated mystery fiction's "fair play" rules because she both presented and hid the key to the crime's solution. "Few readers in 1926 realized that a Norwegian named Stein Riverton had anticipated her illusion some 16 years earlier" (from Cox's Foreword to James Jensen's translation of *The Iron Chariot*), a point that was first made definitively in a May 1982 article on the "Christie Connection" in *Ellery Queen's Mystery Magazine*.

Continuing his innovations in crime fiction, Riverton incorporated Freudian theories of the subconscious into his later thrillers, eventually adopting a more realistic modern style. Riverton's achievements as the founding father of modern Norwegian crime fiction are commemorated in Norway's Riverton Prize for each year's best Norwegian detective novel. His notable novels available in English translation include:

1909: *Jernvognen* (*The Iron Chariot*, bilingual edition, tr. James P. Jensen, 2005)
1915: *Manden som vilde plyndre Kristiania* (*The Man Who Plundered the City*, tr. Frederick H. Martens, 1924).
1923: *Fenomenet Robert Robertson* (*The Case of Robert Robertson*, tr. Agnes Platt, 1930).

One of the most notable authors who took over the character of Riverton's fictional detective Knut Gribb was Øyulv Gran, 1902–1972, whose Gribb stories appeared in *Detektiv-Magasinet*. Gran's stories were also published in book form: *Svindler-syndikatet*, 1972; *Mannen bak masken*, 1976; and *Nattens konge*, 1985, and since that time, according to the *Store norsk leksikon*, they have shaped the Norwegian public's perception of Detective Knut Gribb. During Norway's Nazi Occupation, Gran was an active Nazi, and his anti–Semitic, anti–Communist, and anti–"Yellow Peril" views pervade his writings, though Professor Willy Dahl does not believe that Gran went so far as to produce Nazi propaganda (Birkeland et al. 85).

Riverton's contemporary Olaf Bull, 1883–1933, not to be confused with the renowned Norwegian violinist Ole Bull, was known as "the Oslo poet" although he lived for long stretches in France and Italy. There he possibly was working on his only novel, the detective story *Min navn er Knoph* ("My Name Is Knopf") as early as 1909. It was first printed as a serial in 1913–1914 and later under the pen name "Olaf Breda" it became the first Norwegian book to be translated into Danish. *The Norwegian Biographical Encyclopedia* notes that recently this novel has been hailed as "innovative," and it was ranked fifteenth by *Dagbladet* in their 2009 listing of Norway's twenty-five greatest crime novels. Bull began but never finished a second crime novel about a police investigator named Bleng.

In an intriguing episode of literary history, Bull, an anti-authoritarian who suffered from financial woes and depression so severe he attempted suicide in 1925, moved to Paris the next year and met Irish expatriate James Joyce at Sylvia Beach's Shakespeare and Company bookstore. Bull became the first of Joyce's five tutors in Norwegian while Joyce was writing *Finnegans Wake*, a linguistic/literary assemblage of puzzles that Joyce himself called "this spider's web of words." Bull signed a letter of protest against the U.S. pirating of Joyce's *Ulysses* in 1926, and in *Finnegans Wake* Joyce immortalized Bull as "Olaph the Oxman," a pun on Bull's surname.

The British Golden Age of mystery fiction, the 1920s through the 1930s, dominated by Agatha Christie, Dorothy L. Sayers, Josephine Tey, and Ngaio Marsh, inspired Norwegian crime authors who wrote between the first and second Golden Ages of their own crime fiction. A singular Norwegian literary event occurred in 1923, when "Jonathan Jerv," a pseudonym for two impecunious Norwegian university students, produced *Bergenstoget plyndret i natt* ("The Bergen Train Robbed Tonight") a novel about a Holy Saturday train robbery that became the most popular Easter book in Norwegian history (Swift). The head of Norway's largest publishing house at that time happened to be the brother of one of those enterprising students and agreed to print a few copies of their novel. The students then produced a screaming ad headline for *Aftenposten's* April 1, 1923, edition, "The Train to Bergen Robbed Tonight," causing a national uproar and initiating that singularly Norwegian custom of "Easter crime," celebrating Christ's redemptive victory over sin with a few days off from work and taking to the woods, the more remote the better, to devour grisly fictional crimes in grimly isolated settings (Singh and Normann 30–1).

Popular early "Easter crime" included works by Alf Bonnevie Bryn (1889–1949), a patent engineer, who produced four crime novels between 1924 and 1938 with a millionaire playboy amateur detective, Peter Van Heeren, who resembles gentlemanly British crime solvers like Dorothy L. Sayers's Lord Peter Wimsey. Bryn's first Van Heeren novel was the basis for the highly popular Norwegian film *Peter van Heeren.*

Arthur Omre, 1887–1967, pursued careers as a journalist, sailor, construction worker in the United States, Oslo engineer, and entrepreneur. After going bankrupt in 1922, he became a bootlegger, swindler, and thief and spent considerable time in prison. He then drew on his criminal experiences for his hardboiled debut crime novel *Smuglere* ("Smugglers"), 1935, followed by *Flukten* ("Escapes"), 1936, which ranked fifth in the 2009 list of twenty-five best Norwegian crime novels published by *Dagbladet*. More wrote much of "Escapes" in a small rented loft in Oslo's Rosenkrantzgata district, claiming he liked the noise of the heavy street traffic and the docks, but his royalties from "Escapes" allowed him to move into a stylish villa on Hanko. The protagonist of "Escapes," running from both the police and the underworld, establishes himself in a small town where he lives a normal bourgeois life as a fishmonger, amid characters who like him conceal terrible secrets. The plot of "Escapes" presents a key to Omre's theme: the more civilized the surface of bourgeois existence appears, the harder the secrets below it are to hide. He followed "Escapes" with two more detective novels in 1937 and 1938 respectively.

Yet another crime reporter, Fridtjof Knutsen, 1894–1961, and his wife Lalli adapted about thirty crime novels from popular English-language novels by authors like "Carolyn Keene," the pseudonym for various writers who created installments of the long-running American "Nancy Drew" young adult mystery series. Since the series opened in 1929 with *The Secret of the Old Clock*, Nancy Drew novels have been widely translated and have sold more than 200 million copies worldwide. Intrepid Nancy Drew, an Americanized watered-down version of the Scandinavian warrior-goddess Valkyries, has sparked the aspirations of independent-minded young women worldwide by being so accomplished and fearless "that she can lie bound and gagged in a dank basement or snowed-in cabin for as much as twenty-four hours without wetting her pants" (Mason 52). Through the Knutsen translations, highly popular in Norway, Nancy's indefatigable "ball-busting" ability "to reduce her villains to broken old men" (Zacharias 1038) may well have encouraged Norwegian women authors to create credibly unconventional female detective protagonists like Anne Holt's lesbian detective Hanne Wilhelmsen and insightful psychologist Inger Vik, Pernille Rygg's rule-breaking Igi Heitmann, and Kjersti Scheen's tough PI Margaret Moss.

The Second Golden Age of Norwegian Crime Fiction

Norwegian crime fiction blossomed again during modern Norway's most traumatic years, its World War II Nazi occupation. This period produced two significant lasting effects on the development of the country's crime fiction. Crime fiction and its then-standard assumption that right and justice, struggling against immense odds, would eventually triumph over monstrous evil supplied badly needed distraction from the country's woes under the Nazis, reinforcing the genre's traditional popularity. The Occupation and its bitter aftermath also provided thematically important flashback material crucial to the plots of a number of Norwegian crime authors writing today. New perspectives and material regarding Norway's experiences during the war and its recovery continue to surface through historical research and in the country's contemporary crime fiction.

The Munich Pact, the futile attempt Britain and France made in 1938 to appease Nazi Germany, lasted only a few months. After the Nazi *blitzkrieg* quickly crushed Polish resistance in early September 1939, Britain and France declared war, and during the following winter's "Phony War" their Allied forces huddled behind the supposedly impregnable Maginot Line. On April 9, 1940, Germany's land, sea, and air forces invaded Denmark and Norway. Denmark surrendered almost immediately, while Norway, with an underequipped and largely untrained military, managed to delay the Nazi takeover for 62 days. The Allies, mainly Britain, attacked German naval forces and landed British and French ground troops in Norway within a week of the invasion, but the Axis takeover of the Low Countries in May 1940 provided the Luftwaffe the air bases they needed to bomb Norway, and after fierce fighting, especially at Narvik on Norway's north coast, the Allied troops had to be withdrawn for the futile defense of France. Before Norway was forced to capitulate in June of 1940, the Norwegian government had contracted all of the country's substantial merchant marine to Britain for the duration of the war under the auspices of the Nortraship organization, at that time the world's biggest shipping company, a significant factor in Britain's wartime maritime activity. Norway's strategic location also played a crucial role in Nazi strategy which providentially aided the Allies. Fearing that the Allies might try to recapture Norway and thus deny Germany access to the North Atlantic, the Nazi leadership held thousands of troops in Norway that might have seen action elsewhere, their absence perhaps even tipping the balance of major battles elsewhere.

Since World War II, popular opinion has generally assumed that the great majority of Norwegians fervently resisted the Nazi Occupation, a view promoted in the United States by one of Norway's most distinguished authors, Sigrid Undset, Norway's 1928 Nobel laureate, who was the first major European author to denounce Adolf Hitler.

Today Undset, a prolific novelist, short story writer, essayist, and Christian apologist whose consistent focus was the necessity for humanity to recognize and atone for its sins is best known for her historical trilogy *Kristin Lavransdatter*, 1920–1922, set in the turbulent fourteenth century when Norway was experiencing intense political ferment and the old pagan religion had not yet completely died out. The novel's protagonist, caught up in a passionate youthful affair with a married man that results in the suspicious death of his wife, atones for her sins throughout a guilt-wracked life of trial and suffering. Though *Kristin Lavransdatter* achieved enormous popularity, especially in Scandinavia and Germany, and won the Nobel Prize for Literature in 1928, Undset herself preferred her historical tetralogy *The Master of Hestviken*, 1925–1927, a product of her 1924 conversion to Roman Catholicism and a searing fictional exploration of crime and punishment. Its hero Olav Audunsson pays for the murder of an itinerant Icelander who raped Olaf's wife with a lifetime of successive hard-won free spiritual choices marking stages on his road to Christian reconciliation.

Having worked for arrogant Prussians at Oslo's German Electric Company as a young woman, Undset had suspected German motives for a long time, and she reacted powerfully against Adolf Hitler's savage new incarnation of the Saxon god Wotan, known in Norway as Odin. In ancient times, Norwegians had feared and distrusted the magical runes and *berserker* rage of Odin's warrior cult that arose among Norway's nobility, and its Nazi revival proved no less deadly. In the early 1930s, Hitler had begun preaching his contrived white-supremacist religion, a seductive mixture of anti–Semitism and pseudo–Germanic mythology that ominously appealed to Germans chafing under economic hardship caused by World War I reparations and eager for relief, if not outright revenge. Appointed Germany's Chancellor in 1933, Hitler the following year purged his Nazi party, enacted anti–Semitic laws, and set up the first concentration camps, announcing his intention of "eradicating Christianity in Germany down to the last root-fibre" and opposing the Christian doctrine of the eternal worth of the individual with "the immortality of the nation in this world" (Vermeil 218). Undset, a devout Roman Catholic convert, struck back. Her writing had become well known in Germany, and in her essay "*Fortschritt, Rasse, Religion*" ("Progress, Race, Religion"), 1935, she addressed the German people in their own language, comparing "modern graven images like technological progress, racial superiority and 'self-created' religion" to the fatal pride of Lucifer (Undset 43). In 1938, when Hitler was wooing Britain's Neville Chamberlain into the Munich Pact, Undset warned the world that whether the absence of good that men call evil is implemented by a Cromwell or a Hitler, the hatred that such tyranny engenders is a "uniform and rallying emotion" (*Men, Women and Places* 163).

Sigrid Undset paid a heavy price for her opposition to Nazism. Almost immediately on their arrival in Norway, the Nazis shot and killed her oldest son Anders, a resistance fighter, close to their home at Lillehammer. As the President of the Norwegian Authors' Guild, Undset was advised that she might have to make Nazi propaganda broadcasts—or worse. She abandoned Lillehammer on April 20, 1940, and made a tortuous journey on foot and skis over the mountains into Sweden, then across the Soviet Union by train, on to Japan, and finally by ship to the United States, where she spent the war years as what she liked to call "a soldier with a typewriter" raising funds for the Norwegian resistance. She died in Norway in 1949.

Many Norwegians, though not all, shared Undset's hatred of the Nazis and their cause, and they undertook bold efforts to subvert Nazi operations both within Norway and beyond. Disturbed by the growing international tensions in the 1930s, Oscar Torp, Norway's Minister of Finance, initiated measures to protect the National Treasury, 53 tons of gold worth approximately $670 million in today's U.S. dollars. At the outbreak of World War II, laborers packed the gold into crates and barrels, and on April 9, 1940, civilian trucks carried it from storage at Norges Bank's Oslo vault to Lillehammer, mere hours before elements of the *Wehrmacht* arrived in the capital. At the same time, Norway's royal family, the entire *Storting* (Parliament), and the cabinet fled from Oslo to Hamar and then to Elverum. While Allied and Norwegian soldiers were fighting in the north, a small Norwegian coastal battery defending the Narrows at Oslofjord sank the German heavy cruiser *Blücher* at Drøbak Sound, delaying the German invasion for a crucial few hours and buying time for the *Storting* to pass the Elverum Authorization, a measure giving King Haakon VII and the government constitutional authority to reject the German surrender ultimatum to "accept the protection of the Reich."

With the Nazis in close pursuit, the gold, the royal family, and governmental officials left by train, arriving at a station near Åndalsnes, the staging area for the British expeditionary troops, on April 20. Nazi bombers were leveling the town, so the Norwegians requested the Royal Navy to transport the gold by ship to Britain and possibly later to the United States. Carrying part of the gold, the British cruiser *Galatea* left Åndalsnes on April 25. Well-equipped Nazi troops were approaching rapidly from Gudbrandsdalen while Norwegians again loaded the rest of the gold onto civilian trucks. They struck out for Molde on Norway's west coast, intending H.M.S. *Glasgow* to take it and the Norwegian dignitaries to Britain. Nazi parachute troops and the Luftwaffe bombing attack on Molde, however, forced the dignitaries to take cover in the woods, and only 23 tons of the gold were shipped on *Glasgow*, which left Norway on April 29 with King Haakon, Crown Prince Olav, and others. The King asked to be taken to remote northern Norway where he intended to oppose the Nazis, and *Glasgow* proceeded to the Clyde.

By trucks, coastal steamer, and small fishing boats, the thirty remaining crates of gold arrived in Tromsø on May 24, from where H.M.S. *Enterprise*, unescorted, transported it to Britain. At first the gold was stored in the vault of the Bank of England and later shipped in installments to Canada and then the United States, some to be sold to finance the Norwegian resistance effort. Ten tons of coins finally returned to Norway in 1987. Of the original fifty tons of gold that left Oslo, only 297 coins were missing, a testament to Norwegian determination and ingenuity.

A little-known controversy regarding the gold's shipment to Britain illustrates the perils associated with naval transport in 1940 and the price of preserving Norway's royal family. On June 7, King Haakon decided not to remain in Norway, and he and Crown Prince Olav left on the British heavy cruiser H.M.S. *Devonshire* to lead their people from exile in England. Rumors still continue to circulate that *Devonshire* also carried either a small amount of gold or possibly the Norwegian crown jewels. While en route, *Devonshire* received an SOS from the British aircraft carrier *Glorious* that *Glorious* and her two destroyer escorts were under attack, but *Devonshire* did not go to their aid, instead increasing speed to 30 knots for Scotland. Only 41 of the 1156 British sailors from *Glorious* and her destroyers survived the icy North Atlantic. No mention of this episode exists in Britain's National Archives and the official British position maintains that *Devonshire*'s prime responsibility was to convey Norway's royalty and "some valuables" to safety (Pearson, "Royal Navy Memories").

During the Occupation, the Norwegian resistance's primary goals were sabotage and intelligence gathering, involving various segments of the Norwegian population as well as outside forces. The Norwegian Communist Oswald Group led by Asbjørn Sunde formed a leading homegrown sabotage organization, and the United States loaned OSS personnel, including William Colby, who later became the director of the CIA, to support Norway's sabotage activities.

Clandestine Swedish cooperation allowed camps camouflaged as police training installations along the Norwegian border to secretly train about 8000 Norwegian men by 1944. In "Operation Archery," about 600 British commandos, supported by elements of the Royal Navy and Royal Air Force with information supplied by the Norwegian resistance, raided German positions on Vaagso on December 27, 1941, forcing the Nazis, who suspected the Allies might use Norwegian bases to influence Sweden and Finland, to increase their troops in Norway.

Many of Norway's youth formed secret organizations to help gather intelligence for the Allies. "XU," established by Arvid Storsveen, recruited young men and women like Anne-Sofie Østvedt, who became one of the group's four leaders, from the University of Oslo, where starting in 1940 many students wore apparently innocuous paper clips in their lapels, signifying "we are bound together," to represent unity against the invaders and collaborators. In response, the Nazis outlawed symbols like the paper clips, red clothing items, and the popular crowned H7 monogram of King Haakon VII on pain of arrest and punishment.

Besides harsh reprisals on civilians who performed acts of civil disobedience, the Nazis maintained their policy of taking no prisoners from Norwegian raiding parties, making such activities virtual suicide missions. Despite the dangers, Norwegians, both at home and in exile, participated in the disabling of the Nazi heavy water facilities in Telemark, one of the most dramatic sabotage actions of the war. In 1934, Norsk Hydro had built a plant at Vemork in Telemark that could produce twelve tons of "heavy water" (deuterium oxide) per year, the world's largest facility for producing that key component in the development of nuclear weaponry. After the Nazis occupied Norway, the Allies, with Norwegian assistance, made several attempts to destroy that plant in order to prevent Nazi development of the atomic bomb.

In 1942, the first such attempt, Halifax bombers towed gliders with thirty-four commandos to Telemark; all were killed or captured by the Gestapo. In a 1943 operation planned in London by Norwegian Leif Tronstad, six British-trained Norwegian saboteurs skied down a supposedly unclimbable gorge, entered Norsk Hydro through ducts, set explosives, and escaped without firing a shot. Though the plant was not completely crippled, that operation has been called World War II's most successful sabotage act, inspiring the 1965 Hollywood film *The Heroes of Telemark*, starring Kirk Douglas.

After subsequent Allied bombing raids ensured that no new amounts of heavy water could be produced at Norsk Hydro, the Nazis attempted to ship the remaining heavy water and critical machinery to Germany, but on February 20, 1944, Norwegian resistance fighters used preplanted bombs to sink the ferry carrying this cargo to the bottom of Lake Tinnsjø, successfully ending the threat of Nazi creation of atomic devices which potentially could have changed the outcome of the war.

Many ordinary Norwegians also did what they could to oppose the Nazis, defying Nazi paramilitary groups that terrorized Norwegians who so much as drew or created the crowned H7 symbol. The Nazi puppet government in Norway even ordered Norwegian police not to respond to calls from citizens thus intimidated (Voksø 94). Since radios, like the symbolic paper clips, were *verboten*, citizens distributed illegal newspapers and kept up an "ice front" against the German soldiers, never speaking to them if at all possible (although German was widely spoken in Norway at that time) and refusing to sit beside them on buses and trains. This provoked the Germans into decreeing that standing on a bus was illegal if seats were available, one of many Nazi intrusions on Norwegian personal freedom recorded in the Norwegian Resistance Museum located in the Akershus Fortress in Oslo.

The Occupation taught Norwegians some brutal lessons that later would resurface in popular Norwegian crime fiction. According to Norwegian historian Jacob Worm-Muller, in the late 1930s

"The great majority of Norwegian people really could not believe that the Germans would ever attack and suppress the Nordic people who desired to live in peace…. We failed to realize, therefore, that this new war vitally concerned us" (quoted in Kurzman 63). Norwegian naiveté proved lethal: "with no military traditions, when they were thrust into war for the first time in 126 years and faced defeat, they were 'bewildered and paralyzed,' as Worm-Muller would say." As British historian William Warbey also observed, the modern descendants of the Vikings who had ravaged England and northern Europe now "had a certain squeamishness about taking a man's life…. They would have to learn to be cunning, secretive, deceitful, two-faced, ruthless toward their friends and comrades as well as toward their enemies … [to learn] the art of lying brazenly, of suspecting all strangers, of concealing their thoughts even from their wives and their mothers" (Kurzman 63). All those lessons, echoes of Norway's wartime Occupation and the hatred it spawned, provide significant plot elements in many of today's Norwegian crime novels, like Jo Nesbø's bestseller *The Redbreast*, set in contemporary Oslo. *The Rebreast* deals powerfully with both neo–Nazism in Norway and serial murders of old Norwegians who had chosen to fight beside the Nazis against the Russians on the Eastern Front of World War II. Echoes of the Occupation awakened by Nazi memorabilia also play significant roles in Norwegian crime novels like K.O. Dahl's *The Man in the Window*, 2008.

While crime fiction, like other Norwegian literary forms, could not flourish during the bitter Nazi Occupation of Norway, a few writers managed to produce notable examples of the genre during the early 1940s. Norwegian author and garden enthusiast Harald Thaulow, 1887–1971, provided a clear picture of Norwegian political life during the Occupation in *Til Herr Politimesteren* ("To Mister Commissioner"), 1940, which *Dagbladet* placed fourteenth in their 2009 roster of the twenty-five best Norwegian crime novels of all time.

A contemporary response to the Occupation, *Det vil helst gå dogt* ("It Usually Ends Well") and *Det blir alwar* ("It Gets Serious"), the memoirs of Norwegian resistance hero Max Manus, 1914–1996, a brilliant saboteur, provided the basis for *Max Manus: Man of War*, a large-scale 2008 Norwegian biographical war film that sparked intense debate in Norway over questionable Resistance activities during the Occupation. Manus had fought as a volunteer for Finland in the Soviet-Finnish Winter War of 1939–1940 and returned to Norway to pioneer its resistance movement. The Gestapo arrested Manus in 1941, but though injured he escaped to England, and after training as a marine saboteur he joined Norway's *Lingekompaniet* (Independent Company 1), working undercover, and eventually he used homemade limpet mines and even "swimmer-assisted torpedoes" to sink *Kriegsmarine* ships, including the SS *Donau*, a major coup, on January 16, 1945. For his efforts, Manus twice received Norway's highest military decoration, the War Cross with two swords, as well as the British Military Cross and Bar.

Max Manus: Man of War, supported by the Norwegian Film Fund with a budget of over NOK 50 million, required 1800 extras, most costumed in *Wehrmacht* uniforms and shown marching down Oslo's streets with the Nazi flag flying from the roof of the Norwegian Parliament for the first time in sixty years. The film's screenwriter Thomas Nordseth-Tiller and directors Espen Sandberg and Joachim Rønning maintained considerable historical accuracy, but even prior to its premiere the film stirred up controversy. In an *Aftenposten* article, writer Erling Fossen decried the role of the Norwegian resistance as "inefficient, irresponsible, and in some cases directly counter-productive." While many academics retorted that Fossen's analysis was "largely based on ignorance," historian Lars Borgersrud also actively criticized several of the film's departures from historical fact.

Upon its 2008 release, the ambivalent reactions of Norwegian film critics toward *Max Manus: Man of War* suggested two very different views drawn from Norwegian memories of the

Occupation and its aftermath. The Oslo *Aftenposten*'s Per Haddal praised the film's star Aksel Hennie's acting but found its format traditional and Hollywood-like lacking in originality, as did the Oslo *Dagbladet*'s Eirik Alver. In Norway at large, critics tended to compare the film unfavorably to the Danish wartime resistance film *Flammen og Citronen* (*Flame and Citron*), also released in 2008, considering the Danish film more complex because it addressed moral issues. Critic Terje Eidsvag of the Trondheim *Adressavisa* dismissed Hennie as "a Norwegian Rambo," and said the film exhibited "no moral issues," while *Stavanger Aftenblad*'s film critic Kristin Ålen insisted that Norway needed a film that questioned the savage liquidations carried out by Norwegian resistance fighters. The opening weekend box office attendance for *Max Manus: Man of War* in Norway set a national record—149,500—for a Norwegian film, and by December 2009, it had sold 1,161,855 tickets. Two weeks after its release, a pirated copy appeared on file sharing networks.

Perhaps Norwegian critics were still too close to the Occupation to see the merits of *Max Manus: Man of War* as clearly as many ordinary Norwegian moviegoers evidently had. Outside Norway, too, it enjoyed critical acclaim. Released in 2009 in Britain and shown beginning on September 3, 2010, in the United States, *Max Manus: Man of War* received considerably more critical praise than it had in Norway. The British *Daily Mail*'s Chris Tookey described it as "an old-fashioned, full-blooded, non-ironic World War II movie" which established Manus as "a flawed, uneducated, but extremely interesting human being" whose wartime experiences "scarred his soul … a stirring, uplifting story." Tookey found Aksel Hennie's acting "tremendous," contrasting his intelligence and restraint with "the absurd, macho posturing" of the actors in the U.S. made block-buster *Terminator: Salvation*, and concluded that *Max Manus: Man of War* was "the most successful Norwegian film ever." After its international premiere in Toronto in 2009, *Max Manus: Man of War* won seven Amanda Awards at the 2009 Norwegian International Film Festival, the most Amandas given to one film in a given year to that date. It was released on DVD on June 28, 2011.

As Norwegian critical reaction to this film suggests, anti–Nazi sentiment was not universal in Norway during the Occupation, a painful national issue that contemporary authors like Jo Nesbø are exploring in their crime fiction. Even prior to April of 1940, one significant Norwegian political party had been sympathetic toward Nazi Germany. When Hitler came to power in 1933 in Germany, Norwegian politician Vidkun Quisling, whose surname later became a synonym for "traitor," had founded Norway's *Nasjonal Samling* ("NS," or "National Union"), patterned after Hitler's National Socialist party. About 45,000 Norwegian collaborators eventually joined the Norwegian National Union.

The NS included several Nazi-type sub-organizations. The most influential of these, the *Rikshird*, was Occupied Norway's version of the German SA (Storm Troopers). (Since *hird* was the Old Norse term for "the sworn warriors of a king," the term *Rikshird* represents "warriors of the state" [*feldgrau*]). Formed in 1933 from men 18 to 45 who usually served in it part-time, the *Rikshird* initially involved only about 500 members. By 1940, encouraged by both Quisling and Josef Terboven, Hitler's *Reichscommissar* for Norway, it had swelled to 6000, and in 1943, when it became part of the official Nazi-dominated Norwegian Armed Forces, the *Rikshird*'s tentacles eventually extended into nearly every segment of the Norwegian citizenry, with approximately 50,000 members in seven regiments throughout Norway and independent units abroad composed of Norwegian students in German schools. Other Nazi-style organizations enjoyed significant membership, like the *Foregarden*, Quisling's personal bodyguard.

From 1941 on, all able-bodied Norwegian males from 10 to 18 were expected to join the *Unghird*, the Norwegian version of the Hitler Youth. *Hirdmarinen*, the naval NS organization, pro-vided training for Norwegian recruits into the German *Kriegsmarine*; the *Hirdens Flykorpset* sim-ilarly trained young Norwegian men for entrance into the Nazi *Luftwaffe*; the *Kvinnehird* provided the female counterpart of the *Ungehird*; and the *Kvinne-Organisasjonen* included mature Norwegian women. In addition, the *Arbeids-tjensten*, organized in 1940, paralleled the German State Labor Service, a paramilitary organization providing labor for both civilian and military projects.

As head of the pro–Nazi National Union, Quisling immediately upon the invasion announced himself as dictator of Occupied Norway, a puppet state. According to feldgrau.com, a nonpolitical German military history website, opinion currently is divided on whether the National Union actively aided the Nazi invasion. Most Norwegians, however, refused to accept Quisling, and after only a week Hitler asked him to relinquish his "dictatorship," though Quisling remained head of the National Union, the only Norwegian political party the Nazis allowed. In February 1942, Hitler appointed Quisling as Norway's "Minister President," an ambiguous title, since the real power in Norway was wielded by Nazi official Josef Terboven. Terboven had two German deputies who directed all the SS and Gestapo activities in the country under the supervision of Heinrich Himmler, an arrangement which left Quisling and Terboven each constantly trying to undermine the other's authority. Quisling did support the Nazis by encouraging volunteers to join the Waffen-SS, championing the deportation of Norwegian Jews, and ruthlessly executing Norwegians who resisted the Occupation. Once the war was over, the Norwegians speedily executed Quisling.

Prior to the war's turning point in 1942–1943, the expression "Look to Norway!" had become popular among opponents of Nazism abroad, and by 1944 Norwegians were reputedly largely spurning Quisling. By the time the Nazis surrendered Oslo's Akershus Fortress on May 11, 1945, the originally small Norwegian sabotage group "Milorg" had become a full military force. "Company Linge," a special operations unit, was carrying out coastal insertions and was engaged in actual combat, and Norwegian spotters had helped destroy German warships, notably the pocket battleship *Bismarck* and the heavy cruiser *Tirpitz*. The Norwegian resistance also smuggled groups and individuals to and from Norway through Sweden or at sea by "the Shetland bus." These actions did not go unpunished by the Nazis. From the beginning of the Occupation, after every Resistance operation the Germans brutalized and executed many innocent Norwegian men, women, and children. Out of her maternal grief and her exile's outrage Sigrid Undset sounded a fervent alarm in 1942 for her country's soul: "How in God's name will it be possible to neutralize that hate which consumes all the victims of Germany's lying and faithlessness, German sadism, German rapaciousness and greed ... so that it does not completely paralyze all constructive forces in the peoples?" (*Return to the Future* 211). Undset saw literature as a "constructive force," because the strictures of wartime life naturally affected the production of any kind of art, especially fiction.

Many Norwegian authors suffered for their anti–Nazi positions. During the Occupation, the influential Leftist journalist and author Anton Beinset, 1894–1927, was forced to abandon the position as a political commentator at *Dagbladet* he had held since 1936 and make his living as a farmer and fisherman near his boyhood home at Aukra. With Stein Ståle (pen name of Trygve von Hirsch) Beinset published one crime novel, *Döden går påbedehus* ("Death Goes to Worship") in 1945.

Other Norwegian authors chose exile during the Nazi occupation, including Christopher Brogger, 1911–1991, who escaped from the Gestapo and fled to Sweden in 1942. While there he wrote a crime novel in Swedish on the murder of a Gestapo officer in Stockholm which was later filmed by Ingmar Bergman. Brogger's novel *Den osynliga fronten* ("The Invisible Front"), 1943, published in German in Switzerland, analyzed the Norwegian resistance movement and became controversial because the Nazis used it to identify and capture Norwegian resistance fighters. The Norwegian Authors' Union sharply criticized Brogger for this novel and formally accused him of serious crimes in writing it, but he was acquitted during Norway's postwar legal proceedings.

A postwar upsurge in Norwegian crime fiction did provide an imaginative outlet for readers whose physical existence was severely restricted by Nazi policies, shortages, and rationing. Nils Nordberg indicates that in the dismal Occupation years between 1940 and 1945 and into the immediate postwar period, Norwegian authors produced about 140 new crime novels—the genre's second Golden Age. Nordberg cites as one notable example Stein Ståle's *The Spirit Mask*, with a realistic police detective investigating an occultist homicide, inspired by the crime novels American author John Dickson Carr often provided with supernatural elements.

Anker Rogstad (1923–1994), another notable Norwegian crime author of this period, during the war was involved in petty theft and illegal resistance activity before fleeing to Sweden in 1942. He killed a Norwegian Nazi policeman in a border skirmish, but in 1948 charges against him for that murder were dropped. In the mid–1950s, he spent eight years in prison for safecracking and there began to write fiction based on his criminal background, strongly accusing the Norwegian judicial system of unwarranted harshness, especially in his autobiographical novel *Solicitors*, 1969. His fiction was highly praised by *Dagbladet* reviewer Sonja Hagemann, who compared him to Arthur More and Aksel Sandemose, and in 1974 Rogstad received the Riverton Prize for *Lansen* ("The Lance").

After the liberation on May 8, 1945, the restored Norwegian government sentenced to death and executed 37 Norwegian collaborators. Norwegians who had volunteered for military service with the Nazis and Norwegian members of the Gestapo and the Nazi-run Norwegian police force were subject to criminal prosecution for war crimes that included torture, executions, and mistreatment of prisoners. Individuals who had economically supported the Nazis were also considered criminals. Norwegians who served with the Waffen-SS on the Eastern Front, however, were charged and tried for treason, not war crimes. In all, 28,750 Norwegians received fines or prison sentences for treasonous collaboration with the Nazis, which included membership in the pro–Nazi National Union. A controversial measure called *tap av almenn tillit* ("loss of public confidence") also removed various civil privileges from those convicted as collaborators. During the summer of 1945, a sharp debate arose in Norwegian newspapers between the "silk front," those who opposed the death penalty for collaborators, and the "ice front," who demanded harsh retaliation. Since subsequent historical research questions the degree of justice administered, the collaboration issue remains highly sensitive in Norway today.

Postwar living conditions in Norway were extremely harsh because the Labor Party elected to lead the government in 1945 mandated strict policies directed at reconstructing Norway's heavy industry in five years, prioritizing industrialization over the production of consumer goods. As a result, while the Norwegian population lacked many creature comforts and even certain necessities in the postwar period, Norway's economy experienced rapid growth and progress. According to the official Norwegian web site *Norway*, by 1946 both Norway's GDP and its industrial production exceeded 1938 figures, and by 1948–49 the country's real capital had substantially exceeded its pre-war level. Much of the profit of this economic expansion was devoted to building the Norwegian welfare state, aimed at the creation of an egalitarian society.

The Norwegian Welfare State and Norway's Third Golden Age of Crime Fiction

In the high-growth years following World War II, the Scandinavian nations each implemented a social support system generally referred to as the "welfare state" (Beardsley), funded chiefly through taxation. Shortly after 1945, the Norwegian government nationalized all German business interests in Norway, including acquiring 44 percent of Norsk Hydro's shares. This move began the Norwegian practice of controlling business through shares rather than regulation, a policy which the nation has perpetuated. According to the Norwegian Business School's Torger Reve, "We invented the Chinese way of doing things before the Chinese" (quoted in *The Economist*, February 2, 2013).

Norway's largest "constructive force" in the modern era has been the creation of a welfare model in which public authorities carry out the production and financing of welfare, providing universal social rights and rejecting means testing entirely. Long prior to the outbreak of World War II, most of Norway's political thinkers, like those in the other Nordic countries, had been contemplating a theory of government in which the state protects and promotes the economic and social well-being of its citizens. According to sociologist T.H. Marshall, the modern "welfare state" combines democracy, welfare, and capitalism through the redistribution of wealth via a progressive tax that seeks to at least moderate the income inequalities between the wealthy and the poor. Modern welfare states typically provide cash benefits for old-age pensions, unemployment benefits, and welfare services like health care and child care, thus affecting their citizens' well being and personal autonomy and influencing their consumerism and their leisure pursuits (Rice et al.).

Norway had operated as a "social state" between 1890 and 1945, attempting to ameliorate the country's grinding poverty which in the 1880s had forced more than 1 percent of the population, mainly young adults, to emigrate annually (Einhorn and Logue 8). After Norway separated from Sweden in 1905 and became the first of the Scandinavian countries to attain parliamentary government, its government launched a series of reforms which over decades halted the emigration problem and made Norway a successful welfare state. During the Great Depression of the 1930s, Norway's Social Democrats began to concentrate on social security as a public obligation, maintaining that position through the Nazi Occupation.

Emerging from Norway's trying prewar and Occupation years, Aksel Sandemose's 1944 crime novel *Det svunde er en drøm* ("It's a Dream Gone By") was ranked twenty-fourth in the 2009 *Dagbladet* list of Norway's twenty-five best crime novels of all time. Sandemose (1899–1965), half–Norwegian and half–Danish, drew on his experiences as a sailor, teacher, journalist, and lumberjack in Newfoundland. In the 1920s he had produced a series of articles, short stories, and three novels based on his years in Canada, translated into English in 1929. After returning to Norway in 1930, he wrote the novel *A Fugitive Crosses His Tracks*, translated in the same year, which announced his major theme: that people inflict evil on others through narrowmindedness and limited imagination.

Sandemose placed an unreliable narrator, John Torson, at the heart of "It's a Dream Gone By," a ferocious revenge saga. In a letter to his son, Torson, living in the United States, describes a visit he made to Norway just before the war, trying to solve an old murder which his brother had been blamed for committing. Because its detective Torson's apparently rational appearance conceals irrational and destructive motives, critic Cecelie Naperville, writing in *Dagbladet* for July 2, 2009, compared Sandemose's novel to both Riverton's *Jernvonen* and Agatha Christie's *The Murder of Roger Ackroyd*, foreshadowing the trend toward psychologically penetrating mystery fiction later popular in Norway. Naperville also observed that Sandemose's use of a detective who embodies "irrational and destructive powers under the seemingly rational surface" points to the influence of both Poe's groundbreaking detective Auguste Dupin and Arthur Conan Doyle's Sherlock Holmes. Intriguing parallels also exist between this novel and Vidar Sundstøl's contemporary Minnesota Trilogy, discussed below.

During the Second World War, Sandemose had worked with the Norwegian Resistance until he was forced to flee to Sweden. At the time, he bitterly commented, "We don't want to live if the

Germans win this war!" and later he exclaimed, "The worst thing the Germans did was to let stupidity loose in the land." Sandemose's writings are dominated by his credo, "Stupidity will never die. It is simply too stupid to die." His novel *The Werewolf*, 1958, translated in 2002, an illustration of that position, highlights a murder caused because a too-strictly raised young girl cannot accept unconventional generosity.

Another precursor of today's Norwegian crime fiction, "Death Is a Caress" by Arve Moen (1912–1976), ranked seventeenth in *Dagbladet's* 2009 list of the twenty-five best Norwegian crime novels of all time. It was re-released in 2012, the centennial of Moen's birth, with an afterword by Geir Vestad. When "Death Is a Caress" was made into a 1949 film by director Edith Carlmar it aroused both critical acclaim and popular ire. Moen, a judge, based his plot on an actual case in which an auto mechanic and his employer's wife entangled themselves in a sexually obsessive relationship that descended from passion into rampant violence, jealousy, and madness. For its alleged visual and verbal eroticism, the Carlmar film version was banned in Kristiansand, Norway, and at its Oslo premiere an outraged traditionalist viewer even threatened to shoot Carlmar.

Through the postwar Norwegian government's efforts to rebuild the nation and recuperate from the stresses of the Occupation, the Norwegian welfare state began to mushroom. In 1946 the government established the first National Housing Bank, housing cooperatives, "social homes," and family allowances, and established a new university at Bergen, followed by a public banking system for students in 1947. In the 1950s, Norwegian health insurance became obligatory and universal, and a universal old age pension did away with means testing. A universal unemployment benefit was established in 1959, and public comprehensive schooling was extended to nine years. All of these implementations of Norwegian welfare state policies were greatly aided by the 1959 discovery of the North Sea oil fields. In 1963 the Norwegian government proclaimed sovereignty over the Norwegian continental shelf, which immediately began to transform the Norwegian economy.

While the Norwegian government was putting large-scale welfare programs into place, authors were exploring new approaches to crime fiction. The most notable Norwegian examples of the postwar period display a strong interest in the supernatural, not only including eerie motifs like those that John Dickson Carr had incorporated into his crime fiction, but using the psychological, the supernatural, and even the extrasensory as integral plot elements of mystery novels. Norway's national fascination with the paranormal stems from their earliest folk tales of "fairies, elves, ghosts, goblins, dwarfs, giants, trolls, and spirits of the house and barnyard, such as nisses and tomts" (Booss xiv). Beginning with *Norwegian Folk and Fairy Tales*, 1842, the folk tale collections assembled by Peter Christian Asbjörnsen, a zoologist, and the lyric poet Jorgen Moe, familiar ever since to almost every Norwegian, celebrate "the quaint wit, the savage pathos, the intimate and tender sympathy with all that is wild and solitary" (quoted in Booss xvii) in Norway, which gives much Norwegian literature that involves strange supernatural beings, both good and evil, its remarkable individual flavor.

Two immensely popular crime novels centered on the supernatural were authored by André Bjerke, 1918–1985, who wrote as "Bernard Borge." Borge, a chess player, a poet, a translator of works ranging from Shakespeare's plays to *My Fair Lady*, was also a founder of the Norwegian Academy for Language and Literature. He drew heavily upon the fascination with psychoanalysis that was already widespread in Norway during the 1930s and 1940s for his debut crime novel, *Night People*, 1941. His most famous crime novel, "Lake of the Dead" (*De dødes tjern*, also known as "Lake of the Damned"), 1942, was the basis for a widely praised 1958 film directed by Kåre Bergstrøm, with Borge himself playing magazine editor Gabriel Mork, a complex character involved with the supernatural.

Set in August 1958, the black and white film version of "The Lake of the Dead" takes six Oslo individuals—Gabriel Mork; Bernhard Borge, a crime author, and his wife Sonja; Harald Gran, a lawyer, and his fiancée Liljan Werner; and psychoanalyst Kai Bugge—to visit Liljan's brother Bjørn, who lives in a hunting cabin with an eerie history, deep in the Østerdal woods. The cabin had belonged to a man who had killed his sister and her lover and then drowned himself in the lake, and a legend sprang up that anyone staying in the cabin would also be compelled to drown him- or herself there. The visitors find Werner's dog dead at the edge of the water and discover that Werner himself has disappeared. Each of the visitors then has his or her own theory about the mystery, but the lake's dark powers obsess them all.

The film version of "The Lake of the Dead" was virtually unknown outside of Scandinavia until 1998, when 101 Norwegian cinema critics nominated it as the fourth best Norwegian film of all time, and it since has competed strongly for the title of best Norwegian horror movie in cinema history. An English-subtitled DVD version was released in 2009.

Borge's later crime novels also dealt with occult phenomena. *Døde menn går i land* ("Dead Men Disembark"), 1942, as yet not translated into English, placed seventh in the 2009 *Dagbladet* list of twenty-five best Norwegian crime novels of all time. Reviewing for *Dagbladet*'s list, Nils Nordberg praised Borge as "the regular supplier to all backpacks at Easter holiday," and the first Norwegian author to master the classic British mystery novel that Christie and Sayers had perfected, at the same time using psychoanalysis as a primary crime solving method. Nordberg also noted that the detectives of "Dead Men Disembark" solve the mystery more conventionally than his other sleuths do, here sending married investigators Rancred and Ebba to Kapergärden, a Gothic city in an impoverished section of Norway's southern Bible Belt, where a haunted mansion provides the eerie legend of a Norwegian "Flying Dutchman" who conveys souls to Hell. Later in "Hidden Pattern," 1950, and "Breaking Dawn," 1963, Borge returned to his earlier psychoanalytical themes. He received the Riverton Prize in 1973.

Borge's notable crime fiction includes:

1941: *"Night People"*
1942: *De dødes tjern,* *"Lake of the Dead"*
1947: *Døde menn går i land* (*"Dead Men Disembark"*)
1950: "Hidden Patterns"
1963: "Unicorn" (filmed in 1964 as *"Clocks in the Moonlight"*)
1970 "Uncle Oscar Starts Up" (detective short stories, with Harald Tusberg)
1970: "Uncle Oscar Is Running On" (detective short stories, with Harald Tusberg)
1971: "Detective Hobby: Stories of Klaus Vangli" (crime short fiction)

Recently critic Anna Westerstahl Stenport has called attention to another Norwegian novel with innovative psychological treatments of crime tinged with the supernatural. Tarjei Vesaas' enigmatic *The Ice Palace* (*Is-slottet*), 1963, is considered a classic of Norwegian literature, a "critical part" of the Norwegian reworking of crime fiction that critic Lee Horsley claims had begun some years earlier (see Horsley 66–104). Vesaas wrote this novel, which won the Nordic Council's 1964 Literature Prize, in *nynorsk*, one of Norway's two official written languages, created in the mid–19th century by Ivar Aasen as an alternative to the Dano-Norwegian then used in Norway. Today about 12 percent of Norwegians, mainly in the western part of the country, use *nynorsk*.

In *The Ice Palace*, Unn and Siss, two preteen girls, meet and become friends in a tiny rural Norwegian town one frigid winter in the 1950s. One day they undress together for "fun," and Unn claims she has a secret that will prevent her from going to heaven. She tries to reveal it to Siss, but after Siss rejects Unn's confidences the girls dress again. Siss leaves, confused, and runs home alone through the dark forest. The next day, all alone Unn explores an "ice castle" that formed near a waterfall, but she cannot find her way out and freezes to death with Siss's name on her lips. Siss, traumatized by people's suspicions of her, struggles her way out of her own emotional "ice castle," and by the next spring she at last achieves the beginning of her adult life.

Vesaas, often compared to Kafka and Beckett, has been hailed as one of the "foremost innovators in Norwegian literary modernism" (Stenport). *The Ice Palace* won the illustrious Nordic Council literary prize in 1964 and appeared in English translation in 1966. The novel, which contains no explicit crime, no clues, no perpetrator, no resolution, no clear moral universe, and a setting constantly shifting from realism to lyricism and back again, has been generally considered "high-modernist narrative," though Stenport believes its importance lies more in "its sophisticated manipulation of the postmodern crime genre and its reconstruction of detective fiction as a significant subset of literary modernism." She also feels it foreshadows successful Scandinavian crime novels of the first decade of the 21st century "as a reworking of fairy-tale tropes that link landscape depiction with trauma suppression," implicitly commenting on "the social reconstruction of Norway's collective response" to the Nazi Occupation (Stenport). Filmed in 1987, the movie version of *The Ice Palace* won the Grand Prix at the Flanders International Film Festival the following year and was released on VHS in 1991, circulating since in bootleg DVDs and downloads.

Stenport believes *The Ice Palace* exhibits "key components" of metaphysical detective fiction: a missing person, a *doppelgänger* motif, and several locked rooms, labyrinths, and mazes, elements familiar as fairy-tale tropes. Stenport reads the novel's veiled hints at Unn's possible sexual abuse by her father and its suggestion that her mother had been a "*tyskertoes*," a woman who had a sexual relationship with a Nazi occupier, as social commentary on the Norwegian community's ability "to sweep over traces of traumas." She correlates this Norwegian social tendency with general Scandinavian welfare state principles that stress collective consensus over an individual's viewpoint (Stenport). Stenport concludes that *The Ice Palace* foreshadows not only the literary innovations of later Scandinavian crime authors, but also it helps readers to understand the origins of international postmodern crime fiction, which in its Scandinavian mode coincides with the maturation of their welfare state structures in the 1960s.

The peak period of the Norwegian welfare state that began concurrently with the oil boom led in 1960 to the establishment of Norway's Regional Development Bank and the 1961 implementation of disability and rehabilitation allowances. In 1965, the government mandated subsidies for widows and single mothers (extended to single fathers in 1981), and in 1968 created two more new universities at Tromsø and Trondheim. Nursing homes for the aged remain run mostly by Norwegian municipalities, and in 1969, the government enacted a new hospital law financing hospitals mainly through the state budget but requiring them to be run by the individual counties. These steps in redistribution of wealth and implementation of social safety nets accompanied a popular-literature craze for American Westerns in fiction and film.

Nils Nordberg feels that the Norwegian absorption with the American Wild West's blazing-saddle cowboys caused a general precipitous decline in Norwegian crime writing between its postwar Second Golden Age and its revitalization in the 1970s, though three Norwegian women authors did attempt to keep the classic crime genre alive. Gerd Nyquist, 1913–1984, wrote several novels and short stories, including the crime novels "The Deceased Did Not Want Flowers," 1960, and "Silent as the Grave," 1966, which earned Nyquist the title of "The Queen of [Norwegian] Crime." Blind author Edith Ranum, 1922–2001, according to Nordberg was at that time the only Norwegian practitioner of P.D. James's contemporary psychological detective-puzzle novel approach. Beginning in 1979, Ranum authored popular radio serials starring fictional crime writer and amateur detective Julia Tinnberg. Ella Griffeths, 1923–1990, a prolific author of both children's fiction and adult crime novels, over three decades wrote nearly twenty popular novels and hundreds of short stories, one of which was televised in Roald Dahl's *Tales of the Unexpected*. "Greeting Lucifer," 1970, has been described as Griffeths' best novel.

Ella Griffeths' crime novels include (nonitalicized titles below are not available in English):

1960: "She Met a Stranger"; "'The Night Is My Enemy"; "Echoes of Lost Steps"
1962: "In the Shadow of Doubt"
1969: "One of Your Dearest Friends"
1970: "Greeting Lucifer"
1971: "Sunk into the Earth"
1977: *Vann enken* (*The Water Widow*, tr. J. Basil Cowlishaw, 1986)
1978: "Unknown Worms"
1979: "Ace of Spades"
1981: "Wet Grave"
1983: *Mord på side 3* (*Murder on Page 3*, tr. J. Basil Cowlishaw, 1984)
1984: "General Agent"
1985: "Five of Twelve"
1986: "Nude Virgin"
1988: "Toxic Friendships"; "Operation Gemini" (UNL)

While Norway's social welfare system grew and became entrenched during the 1960s, a new kind of crime literature debuted in Sweden. *Rosanna*, 1967, by Swedish Marxist authors Maj Sjöwall and Per Wahlöö, marked the beginning of Scandinavian emphasis on the police procedural as a vehicle for social criticism. Each Nordic country has since produced procedurals exhibiting their own individual themes, characterizations, and flavors.

By the 1970s in Norway, a new well-educated, politically radicalized, and internationally focused generation had assumed leadership of the nation's literary community, and Marxist and Maoist authors began to openly criticize Norwegian society in major political debates. The women's movement also caused Norwegians to rethink traditional gender roles, and the two-income family became the norm (*Dictionary of Literary Biography* 297, p. xxi). Two main emphases subsequently took root in contemporary Norwegian crime literature: the individual's response, usually painful, to his or her homeland's societal and political pressures, many of them springing from the Occupation and its aftermath; and the Norwegian welfare state's role in causing or exacerbating many of those pressures.

Sigrun Krokvik's 1972 thriller *Bortreist på ubestemt tid* (*Gone Until Further Notice*, alternatively titled *Away Indefinitely* in English, filmed in 1974), is a pivotal work often credited with revitalizing Norwegian crime fiction, ranking tenth on *Dagbladet*'s 2009 list of the twenty-five best Norwegian crime novels of all time. Krokvik (the pen name of Sigrun Karin Christiansen, born in 1932) centered this psychological thriller on the inner torments of Alex, a painter who has just murdered his wife and placed the body in their freezer, when a new lover, Christina, arrives at his door. In 1973 the novel won the Riverton Prize for Norway's best crime novel of the year. Since then, many of Norway's most popular crime fiction heroes like Jo Nesbø's alcoholic police detective Harry Hole also battle internal demons, the kind of destructive impulses Krokvik dramatically delineated. Such traumatic inner conflicts are often forced upon the protagonists of Norwegian crime novels by political and social vicissitudes which their authors explore with as ruthless realism as Ibsen used in exposing hypocrisy and invidious compromise, often accompanied by the personal conflicts he incorporated into the suffering characters of his social problem dramas (Beyer 204).

Selecting the twenty-five best Norwegian crime novels of all time in 2008–2009, *Dagbladet's* formidable jury included Nils Nordberg, then CEO of Norwegian Radio Theatre's crime section; *Dagbladet's* literary director Fredrik Wandrup and its crime reviewers Terje Thorsen and Kurt Hansen; Willy Dahl, professor emeritus of Scandinavian literature; *Dagbladet* associate Cecelie Naperville; translator Rune Larsstuvold; Gyldendal editor Else Barrett-Due; editor and publisher Irene Engelstad; Cis-Doris Andreassen; and Cappelen Damm editor Mariann Fugelsø Nilssen. These authorities on Norwegian crime fiction agreed that important changes in the genre began to take place in the 1970s. In particular, Wandrup observed that Norwegian interest in crime fiction "really took off' in 1976 when the literary magazine *Bazaar* published Kjarten Fløgstad's classic essay "The Dialectic Detective," linking crime fiction with social issues.

When *Dagbladet* also asked fifteen Norwegian authors to name their five favorite detective fiction writers, most included Sherlock Holmes' creator Arthur Conan Doyle; American hard-boiled fiction authors Raymond Chandler and Dashiell Hammett; Swedes Maj Sjöwall and Per Wahlöö; and Belgian Georges Simenon. Norwegian author George Johannesen, however, placed "world history" first on his list of favorite crime authors, followed in order by the Book of Genesis, "King Oedipus," the American Declaration of Independence, and "the evening news"—a revealing list that speaks to Norway's contemporary socio-political atmosphere. Johannesen's list with its emphasis on both external and internal dangers may also reflect the pagan *Weltbild* of ancient Scandinavia, in which since the world would perish in flames, all that really mattered was how bravely a hero, in spite of his flaws, met his inevitable death. Over and over, today's fictional Norwegian detectives, typically exemplified by Nesbø's Harry Hole, beset by demons within and without themselves, endure having their hearts ripped out and subside with grim Viking smiles upon their lips.

Commenting upon another dominant feature of Norwegian crime fiction that began to appear in its 1970s renaissance, Nils Nordberg observes that when the criminal is identified at the close of many Norwegian crime novels, a larger cultural "message of social, moral, or political content" appears, which he believes may reflect Norwegians' "old puritanical worry that whatever is purely for pleasure must be, somehow, sinful. Or at least fattening." Sinful or fattening pleasures notwithstanding, many observers agree with crime fiction authority Willy Dahl, whom Nordberg cites as believing that Norway's crime fiction serves a socially critical function in a Norwegian society that now finds itself "more vulnerable and complex than before" (Per Laegrid, quoted in "Rethinking Societal Security").

Today Norway's surface appears affluent and happy, with "low unemployment, one of the world's highest standards of living, and strong prospects for more economic growth" (Berglund). In 2005, the United Nations ranked Norway as the most prosperous country in the world for the fifth year, though BBC journalist Lars Bevanger noted a "downside to paradise": medical doctors then earned about $3,500 a month, the same as factory workers and bus drivers did, but prices of consumer goods, like beer at nearly $8 a pint and a $7.69 Big Mac that then sold for $4.37 in the United States, were high. Norwegians over 80 today seem to be remarkably healthy, mothers enjoy their 10-month full-pay maternity leave (Bevanger), and the Norwegian population has become one of the tallest in the world, overtaking Americans in both height and longevity, suggesting that the Nordic welfare states "translate income quite effectively" into the whole population's biological well being (Sunder). The Norwegian welfare state has also eliminated much of the difference between the incomes of divorced spouses by subsidizing single parents with lower tax rates and additional child benefits, reduced schooling rates, and up to three years of "transitional [cash] allowances" for low-income single parents raising children alone. In 2012, 15 to 20 thousand Norwegian single parents were receiving those benefits (Ladegaard).

A joint interview of four Norwegian business leaders on January 2, 2011, indicated that even wealthy and powerful individuals praise the "Norwegian model" which refused to invest too heavily in "unhealthy" real estate booms and thus spared the nation the financial woes suffered by the other Scandinavian nations, especially Iceland. They also cited Norway's recent pension reforms, its *handlingsregel* policy which limits use of oil revenue and in consideration of a post-oil future put aside about $189 billion in 2005 for coming generations (Bevanger), as well as the nation's support for industries other than oil, especially shipping. The sovereign-wealth fund these business leaders cite, known officially as Norway's Government Pension Fund Global, established in 1990, accounts for 1 percent of all the world's stocks. This fund blacklists offending companies and is notoriously slow to take action, but it enjoys its reputation as one of the best-run such funds in the world. It features a clear division between Norway's Finance Ministry as owner and the Norwegian central bank as manager and consistently strives to improve returns and diversify risks (*The Economist*, February 2, 2013). Overall, most business leaders strongly praise Norway's *omstille*, the national capacity for renewal and reorganization (Berglund).

Norway's sparse population—13 people per square kilometer—depends on its government to manage the country's natural resources and provide their comfortable social benefits. As a result of the oil boom, public spending since 1970 has doubled the number of Norwegians involved in education and quadrupled the number of those in health and social services. Today the public sector accounts for 52 percent of the Norwegian GDP. The North Sea oil which since 1969 has transformed the country's economy today accounts for 30 percent of the government's revenues (*The Economist*, February 2, 2013) and remains the basis for Norway's attraction to state capitalism.

Norway's present ability to spend more of its national wealth on welfare-related programs than it ever has before (Haugen and Lie) derives in large part from the nation's position as the world's eighth largest oil exporter, providing a per-person GDP of $52,000, second behind Luxembourg among industrial democracies (Thomas). According to *The Economist*'s special report for February 2, 2013, at a time when the other Nordic countries are flirting with free markets, "Norway is embracing state capitalism." Its Statoil petroleum company is the largest in Scandinavia, and the Norwegian state also owns large stakes in most of its important businesses and industries: Telenor, Norway's biggest telephone company; Norsk Hydro, its largest aluminum producer; Yara, the largest Norwegian fertilizer producer; and DnBNor, the country's largest bank; as well as 37 percent of the Oslo stock market.

Because of its economic successes, Norway shows the world a placid, thrifty, and financially secure exterior: "the air is clear, work is plentiful and the government's helping hand is omnipresent" (Thomas). Norway has successfully weathered substantial economic crises in the last half of the twentieth century, especially the 1987 Norwegian Financial Crisis, the first systemic crisis in a major industrialized country since the 1930s, a boom-bust event that economist Kristin Gulbransen calls "a deadly cocktail" of deregulation and liberalization, exceptionally strong lending growth, reduced supervisory regulation, and relaxed capital regulation. She concludes that Norway's government escaped a financial hangover by refusing to bail out speculators and by refusing to provide blanket guarantees or to use asset management companies, thus avoiding the subprime debacle that the United States faced (Gulbransen).

During the 2008 world financial meltdown, Norway again avoided calamity. Its economy actually grew by 2.2 percent, making it the only Western industrialized nation to emerge relatively unscathed. According to then Norwegian Prime Minister Jens Stoltenberg in an April 21, 2010, interview with *Newsweek*'s Jerry Guo, the Norwegian government held unemployment to 3.3 percent, the lowest in Europe, by reducing the interest rate from 5.75 percent to 1.25 percent and increasing market demand by expanding fiscal stimuli. Stoltenberg also praised Norway's "strong and responsible" labor unions and a large pension reform estimated eventually to reduce pension spending by 3 percent of the GDP, emphasizing that the Norwegian government avoids "the Dutch disease" by keeping spending as low as possible, with a goal of replacing oil and gas income with equity and bonds in the international market ("The Rescue That Really Worked").

As the world financial crisis continued into 2009, investment in Norwegian industry declined substantially, Norway's Government Pension Fund Global sovereign wealth fund (unofficially called "the oil fund"), continued to lose value, Norsk Hydro planned cost cuts and layoffs, and in August 2011 the Oslo Stock Exchange's main index fell to a new low for the year. Norway's Socialist Finance Minister Kristin Halvorsen took an unorthodox step by authorizing the $300 billion oil fund to expand its stock buying program by $60 billion, 23 percent of Norway's economic output, causing the *New York Times'* Landon Thomas, Jr., to observe that Norway survived by "going its own way. When others splurged, it saved. When others sought to limit the role of government, Norway strengthened its cradle-to-grave welfare state." Norway emerged from that financial crisis with a budget surplus of 11 percent.

Several economists attribute Norway's financial success to factors in its national character. Anders Aslund of the Peterson Institute for International Economics, Washington, notes that "The U.S. and the UK have no sense of guilt. But in Norway, there is instead a sense of virtue. If you are given a lot, you have a responsibility." Norwegian economist and crime novelist Eirik Wekre feels, "We cannot spend the money now; it would be stealing from future generations," and he quotes Ibsen: "'The strongest man is he who stands alone in the world'" (Aslund and Wekre, quoted in Thomas). Finn Jebsen, chairman of the Konsberg Group, observes that Norway's manual workers, some of the world's best paid, earn three times as much as their British counterparts. Norway also has some of the world's lowest-paid CEOs; Statoil's CEO earns about $2 million per year (*The Economist*, February 2, 2013). Such circumstances reflect the prudent lending policies of Norway's banks, policies which successfully avoided the risks that brought down financial institutions in Iceland and several other countries.

A darker facet of Norway's financial success exists, however. Many observers, both Norwegians and those from other countries, feel the "oil wealth and state largesse" have made Norwegians dangerously complacent. According to Knut Alton Mork of Oslo's Handelsbanken, Norwegians now work fewer hours than citizens of any other industrialized democracy. Norwegian workers have more holidays, and they enjoy "extremely generous benefits and sick leave policies." Mork concludes flatly, "Some day the dream will end" (quoted in Thomas). In August 2012, Steven Desmyter of the British investment firm Man Investments also declared that Norway was not immune to an economic crisis. Desmyter noted that the higher value of the Norwegian *kroner* is due to investors seeking shelter from the world's financial storms affecting the export industry. Jens Stoltenberg, Norway's previous Prime Minister, expressed concern over the euro's future and warned that it would be naïve to believe that oil could keep Norway safe forever (quoted in Lindsey Smith).

Contributing to these negative predictions, Norway's ever-increasing welfare programs are exerting heavy and growing pressures on Norway's economy. Funding the country's comprehensive welfare initiatives—state-fostered social equality; free and equal services to every citizen regardless of private means, produced and paid for by public authorities; and equality among Norway's various regions—demands constant and considerable economic growth and almost full employment.

Norway's ever-growing welfare programs also require a demographic pattern containing enough young working people to pay the pensions of retirees (Søvik). Beginning in the late 1970s, new challenges and pressures against established welfare institutions begin to arise, which many Norwegian crime fiction authors have uncovered in powerfully realistic works that chronicle the cracks in the country's social welfare structure and the venality of public officials who profit from it.

Eventually in the 1990s and into the beginning of the 21st century, Norway, due to a shift in political ideology, began to modernize its welfare state, moving like some other European countries from welfare to work. The Norwegian Labor Government enacted "an overall strengthening of the emphasis on employment in the Norwegian Insurance System" (Syltevik 78) through the 1991 revised Social Assistance Act stating that benefits could be conditional on the claimant's willingness to do municipal work required by local authorities.

These reforms have dramatically affected two segments of the Norwegian population: the elderly and the disabled, and single parents, most of whom are women. Since the 1990s, de-institutionalization programs for the elderly and the handicapped have mandated home care for the mentally handicapped and for chronic psychiatric patients, but since funding these facilities rests with municipalities whose financial resources are dwindling, the effectiveness of such programs varies widely. Portrayals of such facilities in contemporary crime fiction display conditions ranging from borderline acceptable to deplorable, due to lack of trained personnel and financial support.

Other changes in Norwegian social programs include an increase in the basic non-earning segment of the old-age pension and the extension of parental leave from 28 to 42 weeks with a 100 percent wage compensation; and the Family Cash Benefit plan, introduced in 1998. The reforms strengthened patients' rights, the right to work, and the right to participate in community affairs despite mental and/or physical handicaps, but "the general increase in prosperity and the accompanying ideal of 'freedom of choice' will probably contribute to a stronger 'public-private' welfare mix, while ... an increasing number of people face new risks and new uncertainty concerning private welfare institutions such as the market, family, and civil society" (Botten et al. 83).

For single parents, the Norwegian welfare reform also significantly impacted a lifestyle that had been steadily declining prior to 1990, the traditional Western lifestyle where a parent, usually a mother, stayed at home and lengthily interrupted a working career to raise children. For Norwegians, that way of life "was no longer an option that could expect support from the public purse." The majority of parliament members debating the issue felt that "employment [w]as synonymous with activity and independence, whereas the receipt of childcare benefits was associated with passivity and dependence," [and] caring for children older than four or so was "something one is expected to do in one's time off from paid work" (Syltevik 78).

Globalization also seems to increasingly influence attitudes toward and implementation of welfare programs. Norway's local governments, principally its 435 municipalities, are responsible for implementing the central government's welfare policies: "Provision of health care, social welfare, and education," as well as "water supply, municipal roads, sewage, garbage collection and disposal, and the organization of land within the municipality," employ 25 percent of the working Norwegian population, accounting for 80 percent of all public sector employees (Edigheji 213). Some economists suggest that globalization today "is corroding the welfare state" by undermining both the municipalities' capacity to fulfill these services and the Norwegian central government's capacity to provide basic service to its population, because "new managerialism" is becoming a dominant central-governmental theme, and a "'beggar-thy-neighbor" competition for industrial location is adversely affecting local governments (Edigheji 216).

The social challenges and pressures which since the 1970s have faced Norway, like the rest of Scandinavia, not only involve the internal imbalance of high costs for Norway's health-related benefits in relation to its unemployment benefits but also the dramatic increase in immigration to Norway from Third World countries and the countries formerly belonging to the now-collapsed Soviet bloc. The Pew Research Center estimated in 2011 that Norway's 2010 Muslim population of 144,000 would grow to 359,000 in 2030, a projected 6.5 percent of the total Norwegian population ("Region: Europe"). On Oslo's major streets today the *nouveaux riches* flash their wealth, East European wait staff and swarthy Muslim prayer bead-wielding taxi drivers abound, and indigent drug addicts and dropouts beg for money. Presently 11 percent of Norway's residents are foreign-born (*The Economist*, February 2, 2013), accounting for troubling symptoms of societal malaise that lurk on the side streets and back alleys beneath Norway's placid surface, and Norwegian crime authors are increasingly exposing societal ills most Norwegian politicians refuse publicly to acknowledge. Other symptoms of societal malaise include the "oil-for-leisure" thinking which debilitates Norway's traditionally strong work ethic and the consequent moral decline that encourages citizens to defraud the welfare system; the stresses produced by a swelling immigrant population from Eastern Europe and the Third World; the drug problem, escalating through the powerful foreign cartels expanding into Norway; and potentially most devastating, the destruction of the traditional family and its values that a sobering number of sociologists feel has been caused by welfare state policies.

A significant influence on the Norwegian welfare state is the "massive shift of power" which left-wing labor movement historian Asbjørn Wahl, writing in *The Rise and Fall of the Welfare State*, 2011, attributes to globalization and the neoliberal offensive (quoted in Dufour). Wahl sees the trade union movement in Norway, as in the other Scandinavian countries, now "de-ideologized and suffering under its social partnership ideology" and "badly prepared to meet the renewal of the class struggle" being implemented by "the economic and political elites ... in the process of reconquering privileges." Wahl also feels that the weakened labor unions, "ridden by bureaucracy" and "influenced by the social partnership ideology," have been pushed toward radicalization by world financial crises (quoted in Dufour). These ominous symptoms of the developing split between Norwegian haves and havenots can often be found in contemporary Norwegian crime fiction, generally more strongly presented by leftists than by middle-of-the-road or rightist crime authors.

Senior Researcher Aksel Hetland at NOVA–Norwegian Social Research, writing under the auspices of the Research Council of Norway, believes the Norwegian welfare state is not being dismantled but rather restructured, and he feels at least one area of that restructuring merits serious concern. In Norway as elsewhere, unemployment benefits are usually considered temporary, while illness and disability benefits are generally permanent. According to Hetland, "In 2007 expenditures for disability and sickness benefits in Norway were 24 times higher than expenditures for unemployment benefits." Hetland claims that the jobless prefer to receive sickness or disability benefits because the jobless believe that individuals in those programs have more rights and fewer obligations than those declaring unemployment status do. "Statistics show that practically no one returns to working life once they have been granted disability benefits" so that a large part of Norway's health service funding actually goes to people whose only problem is unemployment (Hetland). Besides the obvious moral and ethical ramifications of encouraging the falsification this abuse of public funds encourages, Hetland predicts that the trend of providing more services and fewer cash benefits to children, the elderly, and the sick will divide those who can understand the complex welfare schemes from those who can't. The growing well-educated segment of Norway's population will "manage just fine," he concludes, but those who can't avail themselves of the welfare programs "will lose out," becoming an increasingly challenging societal issue (quoted in Haugen and Lie).

The swelling influx of immigrants from former Soviet bloc and Third World countries, many of them Islamic, into Norway also is not only challenging the nation's welfare system and its economic foundation but it is affecting the Norwegian population's feelings of solidarity toward that system (Nilsen). The first significant numbers of labor migrants arrived in Norway in the late 1960s. Norway, like other European countries, established an "immigration stop" in 1975 to halt the influx of third-world labor immigration (Hagelund 670). After that, however, specialists from western countries continued to arrive, as well as people attracted by Norway's family reunification schemes, refugees, and asylum-seekers. By 2004, Norway's immigrant population had reached 7.6 percent of the nation's total population of approximately 5 million, about a third of the immigrants with unskilled refugee backgrounds. Their overall employment rate that year was 48 percent, compared to the native Norwegians' 70 percent, resulting in lower incomes and higher dependence on social programs for most immigrants. This situation polarizes many Norwegians, especially in connection with cultural issues like Muslim enforced marriages, genital mutilation of young women, and "honor killings," that make women both "heroes and victims" in conflicts of "tradition vs. modernity, force vs. freedom, family vs. individual, and foreign ways—particularly Islamic—vs. core Norwegian values" (Hagelund 672). An even more troubling issue, one treated prominently and compassionately in such Norwegian crime novels as Karin Fossum's *The Indian Bride*, is that the Norwegian state has failed to protect women's rights, in particular neglecting to demand higher standards in the immigrants' attitude toward those rights, and thus has not satisfactorily integrated immigrants into Norwegian society (Hagelund 671–2).

In 2005, after earlier attempts at assimilating immigrants had largely proven ineffective, Norwegian authorities established a compulsory two-year program for immigrants with new financial and educational components. Out-payments depended upon participation in a full time training program aimed at making immigrants self-sufficient members of Norwegian society (Hagelund 669). This program strongly emphasizes learning both the Norwegian language and skills necessary to succeed in Norway; and according to Anniken Hagelund, it is "a far cry from multicultural celebrations of diversity or complex attempts at forging increased levels of tolerance toward foreign practices" (Hagelund 680).

Stresses between native Norwegians and newly arrived immigrants continue to impact Norway's political and economic well-being. Sylvi I. Nilsen warns in her 2008 master's thesis for Oslo University College, "Immigration and the Welfare State in a Norwegian Context: a Literature Review," that in the predicted extensive imbalance between Norway's increasing elderly generation and the working generation, the immigrants' statuses as workers and tax-contributors and as welfare recipients will deeply affect the welfare state's future (Nilsen 22).

After 1975, immigrants to Norway were mostly arriving through either a desire for family reunification or a desire to find political refuge. By the 1990s, it had become apparent that despite Norway's generous support in facilitating immigrant integration, like state-funded language classroom instruction, new arrivals continued to lack adequate Norwegian-language skills and participated to such a low degree in the labor market that they were heavily dependent on welfare. Norway now tries to direct most immigrants into the labor force, labeling them as "work migrants." Nilsen cites scholarly opinions, however, that indicate increasing immigration, even of potential work force members, may lower the degree of societal trust necessarily for the successful functioning of the welfare state—the expectancy that others will not do given individuals any harm (32). This situation is complicated by the continually growing immigrant population, which now involves numerous nationalities and variations in culture and background both within and between groups (Nilsen 45).

A 2013 study by Mette Wiggen of the University of Leeds indicates that xenophobia is now strong in Norway and visible in Norwegian mainstream media, debates, everyday life, and social media, where young people commonly leave comments like "'I'm not racist, but if they can't behave the way we want them to they should just pack it up and go home'" (quoted in Ladegaard, "Norway's Problem"). Norway's anti-immigrant and populist Progress Party won more than 22 percent of the votes in the two general elections prior to 2013 and was predicted in that year to become part of a coalition government with the Conservative Party, which headed Norway's government in 2014.

Although according to Wiggen, immigrants in Norway have a 69.1 percent labor market participation as compared to the OECD average of 62.8, those coming to Norway from European countries far outstrip African and Mideastern immigrants in education and employment (Ladegaard "Norway's Problem"). Other current scholarship reveals the Norwegian general public's view that even in "high-trust" countries like Norway, immigrants "take out more than they give in" (Nilsen 33), causing resentment and prejudicial activity that often spirals downward into crime both by and against immigrants. Nilsen concludes as well that the mass media's role in the Norwegian debate on immigration's effect on the welfare state has not been widely investigated, though the "reality" that the media presents deeply affects society at large and people's attitudes in particular. Currently, Nilsen feels, the Norwegian population's "actual knowledge on immigration, integration and the welfare state is undetermined" (Nilsen 37) by social scientists, but it is being substantially reflected in and affected by current Norwegian crime fiction. The Islamic extremist problem in particular shows no signs of diminishing, if anything becoming more volatile. In 2014 Muslims demanded that the Gronland section of Oslo be made a separate Muslim *sharia*-law state within Norway. Ansar al–Sunna, a Muslim living in Norway, threatened, "Do not confuse the Moslems' silence with weakness … do not force us to do something that cannot be avoided … the consequences can be fatal … a 9/11 on Norwegian ground…. We do not want to be a part of Norwegian society. And we do not consider it necessary either to move away from Norway. Bar this city quarter and let us control it the way we wish to do it…. We do not wish to live together with dirty beasts like you" (quoted in "Norway's Islamic Extremism Problem").

Another critical social problem, illegal drug use, also pervades both Norwegian society and Norwegian crime fiction. A 2010 European Monitoring Centre for Drugs and Drug Addiction study reveals the magnitude of Norwegian drug abuse: 29 percent of Norwegians aged 18 to 30 had tried cannabis, and about 17 percent of them eventually turned to injected amphetamines. The same report indicated that Oslo has an average of approximately 1800 problem cocaine users per year and 10,200 others who use this drug less frequently (recreationally). Heroin addiction is an even greater concern. According to Europe's narcotics-monitoring Pompidou Group, since 2000 Oslo, with a population of about 640,000, has averaged about 7000 heroin addicts per year and held the regrettable title of first among 42 European cities in seizures and deaths caused mostly by heroin (Hoge). In 2013 an estimated 14,000 Norwegian addicts injected rather than smoked heroin, smoking the drug being the prevalent usage in other European countries (Hoge). Two hundred ninety-four injecting Norwegian addicts died from overdoses in 2011, compared to 170 Norwegians killed that year in traffic accidents (Norwegian Institute for Alcohol and Drug Abuse, quoted in Berglund). Many of Norway's thousands of narcotics addicts also concoct an injectable witches' brew of heroin, alcohol and the "date rape" drug Rohypnol, which depresses the nervous system (Hoge).

According to sociologist Sveinung Sandberg of the University of Bergen, ethnic minorities are responsible for two of the three "ideal-typical" trajectories in Norwegian street drug dealing: "the first … emerges from migration and early experiences in war-inflicted countries," and the second "from an increasing drug habit and early socialization in established criminal networks."

These trajectories dominate among refugees from Russia and the former Soviet bloc countries and southeast Asians. Between 2002 and 2004, the war in Afghanistan did temporarily interrupt the production and distribution of heroin, causing drug deaths to decline temporarily in Norway, but since then the number of fatal overdoses has risen again. Serbian and Albanian gangs are smuggling heroin produced from Afghan opium through Bulgaria and Romania and distributing it across Central and Northern Europe, already in 2004 a $2.8 billion enterprise (Fleishman). That year Oslo police removed addicts from a park near the city's main railway station, which to the dismay of shopkeepers only dispersed the addicts throughout the city. Norway's failure to widely distribute methadone until the late 1990s and the low number of addicts seeking rehabilitation also have seemed to exacerbate the problem.

The third trajectory of illegal drug use in Norway that Sandberg cites, the "alternative search for identity," may be traced to the Norwegian custom of heavy drinking. The effects of Norway's 1920s prohibition period, which created the widespread Norwegian habit "of drinking the strongest liquor possible—and plenty of it—the moment one got hold of it" (Hoge) that has lingered for nearly a century despite efforts to control it. Today in Norway liquor sales are still restricted. Urinating, if performed in a public place, carries a 10,000 kronor fine, and drinking on a private balcony if observable by others are also illegal ("Drinking and Drug Safety Issues in Norway"), but the Norwegian "binge mentality" has contributed to a preference for the bigger rush, suggesting that intravenous injected use of heroin seems to be preferable to smoking it among Norwegian addicts (Hoge). On March 1, 2013, Norway's Health Minister Jonas Gahr Støre announced a government-backed proposal claimed by some to be an "historic liberalization" allowing addicts to smoke heroin under controlled circumstances as an attempt to curb overdose deaths. The proposal called for municipalities to provide "smoking rooms," an initiative that seems ironic in light of Norway's strict laws against smoking tobacco (Bergland, "Heroine Smoking"). "What began as a druggy counterculture movement of 'flower power hippies' ... evolved into a population of medical and psychological outcasts that is testing Norway's sympathy for the downtrodden" (Fleishman) and providing material for many contemporary Norwegian crime authors like Jo Nesbø, in whose novel *Phantom* popular detective Harry Hole, himself an alcoholic, dramatically battles the Oslo drug scene and the international drug cartels which supply and fund it.

In Norway, as everywhere, alcoholism and drug abuse wreak havoc upon family life. Circumstances peculiar to the Norwegian version of the welfare state, however, also materially contribute to societal problems addressed by crime authors, particularly the single-mother family disasters that Karin Fossum often chillingly presents in her crime fiction. The Norwegian government's radical 1990s revision of its system of benefits for single mothers had radically changed the Norwegian "conception of the interrelations between gender, the labour market, and the welfare state" (Syltevik 75). Formerly single mothers could stay at home as housewives until their youngest children were about ten years old, but unlike the situation in the other Scandinavian countries, Norway's new policy intends to empower single parents by diminishing the time a lone mother can remain at home to raise her children, assuming that her earlier return to the work force will provide her more independence, a higher income and self-realization (Syltevik 75). Work or educational activity for single parents is now mandatory when children are three years old. The new policy also limits the time a single parent can take education while receiving a transitional allowance. Slightly increased childcare benefits and mandatory part-time employment or education, with coverage of books and travel expenses, are now limited to three years (Syltevik 76–7). The changes' main thrust "was to ensure that the greatest possible number of lone mothers should be able to support themselves and their children through participation in the labour market" (Syltevik 77–78).

However grounded by a governmental emphasis on employment, in practice these changes are being questioned. In her 2006 assessment of the current single-parent welfare situation in Norway, sociologist Liv Syltevik concluded that these gender-neutral changes paradoxically mean that in Norwegian everyday life, "gender-specific responsibilities and bonds dominate," so that "what was meant to be a means of achieving a better life ... has become a source of greater oppression of those who cannot cope." Syltevik also predicted that negotiating the labor market will soon involve increased risks for single mothers, making them "even more vulnerable" (90), citing the "demeaning" feeling of failure women experience when they find themselves unable to perform work responsibilities adequately and are forced to abandon jobs and go back to being welfare mothers (91).

A February 2013 working paper from the University of Linz's Department of Economics, "Does the Welfare State Destroy the Family?," notes a broader ramification of welfare policies on Norwegian family life: "the welfare state decouples marriage and fertility, and therefore, alters the organization of the family" (1). This report finds that while the welfare state may support the formation of families by raising overall fertility and increasing the turnover in the marriage market, the welfare state may concurrently crowd out the traditional organization of the family (15). Many of today's Scandinavian crime authors seem to find plentiful source material for their fiction in the family tensions owing to the abandonment of traditional family life, the establishment of new "blended" families because of divorces and remarriages or changed relationships, and the rigors of single-parent child-rearing, all of which can increase domestic violence, which generally is directed at women. A 2004 comparison of Norwegian and Australian abuse of women by their partners indicated that Norway provides a more woman-friendly welfare state than Australia does, but in Norway women who seek refuge from abusive relationships "are more likely to be of foreign birth than women living in couples generally" (Hutchinson and Weeks 404). In Norway, the prevailing welfare policy is aimed at assisting such women into full-time employment. Their public assistance provides a living standard slightly above the poverty level, but "Until the welfare states recognize the burden of being both primary care provider and primary earner," women will too often reassume their relationships with violent partners (Hutchinson and Weeks 405).

Norwegian politicians are increasingly voicing concerns about the influence that immigration from countries with different religions and values may be exerting upon Norway's culture (Madslien). Besides the stresses arising from differences in cultural areas like marriage and interactions between cultures, anti-immigration sentiment is fueling one of the most disturbing elements of present day Norwegian society and one that has recently proven to make that society frighteningly vulnerable: the Norwegian neo–Nazi movement. In the past, Norway's formal neo–Nazi groups have been much smaller than similar groups in the other Scandinavian countries, but they currently seem to be rising. One of the oldest such groups, the National Socialist Movement of Norway, based at Eidsvoll and estimated by the Stephen Roth Institute in 2009 at 40 to 50 members (http://www.tau.ac.il/Anti-Semitism/asw2008/norway.html) denies the Holocaust and opposes globalization. Its original members were probably Norwegian Nazis left over from World War II, but younger members seem to have become involved with neo–Nazism through the 1970s *Norsk Front* organization.

Possibly the most widely recognized European neo–Nazi group, the Skinheads, so far seems to have only about 150 members in Norway, led by Ole Krogstad. Though they claim that not all Skinheads are neo–Nazis, in 1991 a few of them were allowed to join the Swedish Nazi terrorist network, and in 1994 the first Norwegian Skinhead rock band, the Rinnan band, named for the most hated and feared Gestapo torturer in Occupied Norway, surfaced. Although almost all Norwegians consider the Norwegian Skinheads as "madmen," other neo–Nazi groups use them as "foot soldiers," and their numbers seem to be slowly growing.

Other Norwegian neo–Nazi groups have appeared in recent years. The *Norsk Hedensk Front* (Norwegian Heathen Front or NHF), an offshoot of the international anti–Semitic, xenophobic, and ecofascistic *Allgermanische Heidenische Front* (AHF) which promulgated an "odinist" pagan ideology, was founded in 1993, with rumored linkage to the Norwegian black metal musician Varg Vikernes. Vikernes denies that linkage, though he maintained an affiliation with the group during his prison term. The NHF apparently became defunct in 2006 (http://heathenfront.org/ehf/faq.html).

Vigrid, founded by Tore W. Tvedt in 1999 to combine racial ideology with Norse mythology, is a neo–Nazi Norwegian group registered as a political party. Its members deny the Holocaust, which they call "HoloCa$h," and they consider Adolf Hitler Europe's "savior," claiming that non–Aryan races have caused most, if not all, of the world's problems. Despite *Vigrid*'s claim to be a non-violent organization, the Norwegian Police Security Service describes the group's ideology as violent, and some members have been involved in aggravated assaults (*"Ekstremt rasistisk og voldelig,"* *Ostlandets Blad*, January 26, 2009).

Vigrid uses the historical Viking Age mound burial site at Borre, Norway, for their initiation ceremonies, an activity bitterly opposed by Labour Party politician Nils Henning Hontvedt in the light of the July 22, 2011, racially-inspired massacre by Anders Behring Breivik. The 32-year-old Breivik carried out a lethal bombing in downtown Oslo followed by a premeditated massacre of 77 individuals, many of them youngsters, at an island Labour Party camp about twenty miles from the capital.

Breivik's brutal Nazi-style killings reignited the Norwegian hatred for Nazi Germany that Sigrid Undset had described so vividly in 1942. The day after the massacre, the BBC reported that Norwegian police had indicated that Breivik had referred to himself as a "nationalist," but according to the Norwegian newspaper *Aftenposten*, Breivik was a right-wing extremist of the kind that police authorities in the West have feared for some time. That fear has been heightened by "the potentially explosive mix of economic recession and unemployment, strengthening racism and an ever stronger anti–Muslim sentiment" (Madslien). In the mid–1990s, Swedish crime writer and fervent opponent of the neo–Nazis Stieg Larsson characterized the Norwegian neo–Nazi movement as far smaller than their Swedish counterparts, describing the Norwegian neo–Nazis as "shabby," "incoherent," "disorganized and chaotic," but more recently the Norwegian far-right extremists have been re-imaging themselves as well-intentioned traditional citizens and linking themselves strongly with other similar groups abroad, as well as with organized criminal communities.

The case of neo–Nazi Anders Behring Breivik illustrates those ominous connections. Breivik, who allegedly had connections to the far-right racist English Defence League, planned for almost a decade to bomb a Norwegian government building in Oslo and the Labour Party youth camp on Utoeya Island. Breivik, a diplomat's son who had been alienated from his father since adolescence, had been a member since 2009 of the *Forum Nordisk*, whose 22,000 members, according to Stieg Larsson's anti–Nazi magazine *Expo*, range "from high-ranking members of the Sweden Democrats, a nationalist party with seats in the Swedish parliament, to leading members of the Nazi movement and to unhinged psychopaths. What unites the whole lot is a hatred of immigration and immigrants" (quoted in Ridgeway). Breivik also belonged to the Norwegian anti-immigration Progress Party, now the second largest party in Norway's government and was a gun club member. As a farm owner, he was able to purchase six tons of fertilizer for the car bomb he exploded on July 22, 2011, outside then–Norwegian Prime Minister Jens Stoltenburg's Oslo office, killing seven people there.

Breivik urged the slaughter of many European leaders in a 1,518-page English-language manifesto, "2083: A European Declaration of Independence," based in part on the manifesto of U.S. Unabomber Ted Kaczynski. Breivik published his manifesto online just prior to his 2011 bombing and massacre, accompanying it with pictures of himself in an elaborate black uniform that according to psychologist Don Foster demonstrated Breivik's delusion of personal grandeur as a "protector of the nation" (Nixdorf). CNN reported that in the manifesto, Breivik identified himself as a "Justiciar Knight Commander for Knights Templar Europe and one of several leaders of the National and pan–European Patriotic Resistance Movement," calling for "a European civil war over the next 70 years, the deportation of Moslems from Europe, and the execution of 'cultural Marxists'" (quoted in Hodapp).

Breivik twisted the term "Knights Templar," which refers to the 12th–14th century Christian monastic military order formed to protect pilgrims to the Holy Land during the Crusades. Today the term also denotes certain degrees of Freemasonry. Besides his manifesto, Breivik also posted online a picture of himself in Norwegian Masonic regalia, sparking anti–Masonic furor from Britain's *Daily Mail* and others "naming Breivik as a foot soldier in some worldwide Masonic revolution" (Hodapp). On July 23, 2011, the day after the massacre, Ivar A. Skaar, Grand Master of the Grand Lodge of Norway, which requires affirmation of a prospective member's Christian belief, issued an unequivocal denunciation of Breivik, who had had "minimal contact" with the St. Olaus T.D. Tre Solier No. 8 Lodge where he was a member. Grand Master Skaar firmly declared Breivik possessed values "completely incompatible with what we stand for" and immediately expelled him from the Masonic Order (quoted in Hodapp). Breivik was sentenced to 21 years in prison, Norway's maximum penalty for murder, though his release can be delayed indefinitely if the Norwegian justice system deems him a threat to society.

Matthew Goodwin, an expert on British fascist movements, observed in *The Guardian* that before Breivik's rampage, European democracies had dismissed rightist extremists "and their more violent affiliates" as "disorganized, fragmented and irrelevant," but the massacre Breivik engineered, Goodwin felt, might prove "to be a watershed moment in terms of how we approach far-right followers, groups and their ideology" (quoted in Ridgeway). A number of Norwegian crime novelists, through the monstrous evildoers they created and incorporated into their fiction, had already been warning about such criminals for years.

Breivik's crime may also have sparked at least one "copycat" rampage. On February 18, 2013, Peter Finocchiaro of Reuters quoted a CBS News report of the same date which claimed that Adam Lanza, who killed twenty children and four adults in Newtown, Connecticut, on December 14, 2012, wanted to kill more people than Breivik had. Though Connecticut State Police have denied that this information is official, CBS cited two officials briefed on the Connecticut case as believing that Lanza saw the elementary school as the "easiest target" with the "largest number of people," an indication that he wanted to compete with Breivik.

Almost immediately after Breivik committed his 2011 bombing and massacre, questions began to arise about the Norwegian government's failure to recognize the threat posed by ultra-right extremists, a threat "clearly described by some of the country's leading crime writers" that tore the civilized veneer from "one of the most generous welfare systems ... and revealed the existence of a tormented and divided society beneath the surface" (Poggioli). Crime author Anne Holt, a former Norwegian police official and justice minister whose novel *Fear Not* unveiled what Holt terms "the relation between spoken violence on one hand and actual violence on the other" (quoted in Poggioli), believes that crime fiction, which in Norway burgeoned after the still unsolved 1986 murder of Swedish Prime Minister Olof Palme, is "the best genre to reflect society" because it mirrors society's fears. She feels the social changes that Norway, even with its current low crime rate, is experiencing—growing racism, discrimination against new immigrants, rising anti–Semitism, and homophobia—are causing Norwegians to fear hate crimes and deranged killers far more than other types of crime. From varying points of view, Holt and other influential Norwegian crime writers are continuing to address these threats to Norwegian law and order in their fiction.

British commentator Andrew Anthony, interviewing several prominent Norwegian crime authors for a November 2011 *Guardian* article, contends that Norway, which he called "the most benign of the Nordic nations in practice and the most malevolent in prose," seems to have taken the advice of two of its literary giants too literally: Ibsen's admonition to "Wake the people up and make them think big!" and Knut Hamsun's declaration that writers ought to describe "the whisper of blood, and the pleading of bone marrow." Anthony concludes that the Norwegian crime fiction that has appeared since the Breivik massacre has been "as vivid and incongruous as spilled guts on virgin snow." Norwegian crime author Kjell Ola Dahl, however, views the aftermath of the killings somewhat differently. Dahl's young niece was on the island when Breivik rampaged there; she survived unhurt, but Dahl, badly shaken upon hearing the news, intuitively saw the attack as confirmation that "the Nazis are still there and still active." Later Dahl told Anthony, however, that he now feels Norwegians have tired of the media's fixation on Breivik.

According to Anthony, Jo Nesbø refused to comment directly on the massacre itself, but Nesbø nonetheless believed Breivik's killing spree cost Norway its innocence, insisting, "There is no road back to the way it was before." Nesbø, like Dahl, believes his writing will change because of Breivik's crimes, a reflection of Norway's need to "understand" why Breivik acted as he did, a position Anne Holt also strongly espouses. Anthony attributes these authors' convictions in part to what he feels is the overly deterministic "Scandinavian analysis of errant behaviour, which invariably ascribes criminality to society's faults." He also believes that Breivik's crimes affected nearly all of Norway's 5 million people.

Anthony also interviewed Jan Kjaerstad, a theology graduate and prize-winning literary novelist, whose *Homo Falsus*, 1984, explored a television personality's "perfect murder" of his wife, "a revealing portrait of Norwegian preoccupations and insecurities." Kjaerstad does not believe the present search for societal answers to Breivik's crime will prove fruitful. He compares neo–Nazi ideology to a "particularly uncompromising vision of Marxism-Leninism" that existed in Norway in the 1970s. Kjaerstad told Anthony that many of those would-be revolutionaries who had been close, Kjaerstad said, "to making lists of people who they were going to kill when the Soviets took over," and who now hold high newspaper and television positions, providing "a faint whiff," Anthony says, "of socialist realism" in the didactic tone evident in some Norwegian crime novels. Overall, he concludes, Norway's crime fiction is attempting to celebrate Norwegian traditions and unique character, while it attributes the crimes it presents to "isolationist, nationalist, or inward-looking thinking," issue-producing factors which U.S. political scientists Eric Einhorn and John Logue believe will continue to shape the politics of Scandinavia for the next several decades. They feel immigration and multiculturalism have "the potential to produce major polarization, especially in an economic downturn." They see a sharp division between materialist values which pursue economic growth and technological innovation, and postmaterialist values which emphasize human and ecological goals, and. finally they perceive "a conflict between state decision making vs. market choice, especially in light of modern managerial theory, which encourages greater competition and private choice" (Einhorn and Logue 17).

Working on an even larger scale, *The Norwegian Study of Power and Democracy*, a massive political self-examination published in 2004 and available at http://www.sv.uio.no/mutr/english/index.html, mobilized nearly all of Norway's "formidable social-science community as well as strong forces in law, history, the humanities and other disciplines ... to diagnose the health of an advanced democratic system" when democracy had achieved its "final victory" in the twentieth century's ideological wars" (Ringen 3). The study ominously concluded that "the very fabric of rule by popular consent is disintegrating [in Norway] before our eyes" (Ringen 3). The symptoms are clear: voter participation is declining; political parties are becoming "professional political machines"; local democracy is dwindling, "driven in part by irrationalities in the welfare state" (Ringen 4); business has acquired veto power in economic policy by the threat of moving capital out of the country; supranational law can now bind and limit national legislation (Ringen 4–5). These weaknesses in the chain of command from voters to political decisions can be found individualized through the protagonists and the antagonists of contemporary Norwegian crime fiction, in fictional conflicts which, as some of today's most influential Norwegian crime authors have implicitly theorized, may accentuate or even provoke aberrant destructive behavior.

The development of Norway's crime fiction over the past three decades seems to be paralleling the shifting focus of Norwegian crime films during that period. According to a 2011 study by Audun Engelstad, the typical 1980s Norwegian crime film showed the detective as an outsider left behind by the changing times and invidious changes which involved the destabilization of the family, increased immigration from the Mideast, and the rise of the yuppie culture with its attendant drug and sexual problems, so dismaying that the detective seemed incapable of meeting the new age's demands. The Norwegian crime films of the new millennium, however, seem to show the investigator, either an amateur or a police officer, while still an outsider, more at ease with himself or herself in dealing with the now often experienced and analyzed results of those societal shifts. Engelstad concluded that "Norwegian crime films no longer seem to impart any implicit politically charged critique" (Engelstad 205). Norwegian crime fiction in the new millennium also seems to exhibit less political positioning that it had done twenty years ago, especially by comparison with the highly political themes apparent in Swedish crime fiction today.

The 2013 election of Conservative Prime Minister Erna Solberg (popularly known as "Iron Erna"), whose party won an impressive 25-seat majority in the 169-seat Norwegian Storting (Parliament) apparently reflects a substantial "right turn" in Norwegian readers' views toward their country and themselves. Solberg and the Conservatives had reached out strongly to both youthful and blue-collar voters, promising hope that the Conservatives could do much better for the Norwegian people than the left had (Hipp, quoting Conservative party activist Knut Fangberget), the optimistic appeal Margaret Thatcher and Ronald Reagan represented.

The term "conservative," however, does not carry the same political connotations to Norwegians that it does to Americans. Prime Minister Solberg's election slogan was "People, not Billions," the title of her book on Norway's needs. Often praised for the courage to speak clearly and forcefully even on sensitive issues, Solberg enjoys a $80 billion surplus in her country of 4.5 million people, and she intends to spend more on social services, especially expanded government-run health care, while maintaining Norway's progressive tax system, keeping high earners in their present tax rate and decreasing the tax rate for middle and low income earners.

Solberg's Conservative Party operates in a coalition government with the populist Progress Party, also headed by a woman, economist Siv Jensen, now Norway's Finance Minister. The Progress Party supports low taxes and stricter limits on immigration and has significant worries about Muslim extremism (Fund). The Progress Party carried about 16 percent of the 2013 vote, which may "help the Conservatives demonstrate that it is possible to reform the welfare state" (Fund).

One indication of the new government's tightening of Norway's formerly liberal immigration policy is a 2013 study that showed Norway losing "4.3 million kroner ($713,740.30) for each non-western immigrant coming into the country," and immigration as a whole costing Norway "70 billion kroner ($412,185,810) in [the past] seven years. Including social benefits and course fees, the state has spent a total of 56 billion kroner ($9,747,080,000) on training of 56,000 immigrants from 2004 to 2010. Norway has spent ... as much on getting 33,000 non-western immigrants into work or studies within six years as it has on its total spending for day care, school, education, and research for the whole Norwegian population's budget for 2013" (Greenfield).

The new government has implemented a new program focused on attempting to halt the increase of immigrant-related crime in Norway, authorizing increased staff and resources, and ruling that in 2014, 7,100 immigrants who had committed crimes or violated Norwegian immigration policy, such as asylum seekers who had been rejected for continued asylum, would be deported, along with their families, mostly to Afghanistan and Nigeria. The National Police Immigration Service Norway (*Politiets Utlendingsenhet—PU*) is setting new deportation records, in October 2014 deporting a record 824 persons. Kristin Kvine, head of PU, stresses that these deportations should be seen in the context of falling crime rates across Norway (quoted in "Norway deports...").

Despite current developments in Norway's political and cultural climate, however, individual *angst* and social issues and a less overt though still present political content still intertwine like the coils of the Midgard serpent in contemporary Norwegian crime fiction, where detective protagonists and villains alike tend to share Ibsen's reasons for his own reticence: "You must never tell everything to people .... To keep things to oneself is the most valuable thing in life" (quoted in Meyer 659). Like Ibsen's dramas, too, contemporary Norwegian crime fiction discomfits readers by making them think hard, sometimes even painfully, to unravel somber mysteries. Norway's "cold, dark climate, where doors are bolted and curtains drawn, provides a perfect setting.... The nights are long, the liquor hard, the people, according to ... [Jo] Nesbø, 'brought up to hide their feelings' and hold on to their secrets. If you are driving through Norway at dusk and see a farmhouse with its lights on and its doors open, do not stop.... You are as likely to be greeted by a crime scene as a warm welcome" ("Inspector Norse" 86).

Award-Winning Norwegian Crime Fiction

Titles in quotation marks are English versions of original Norwegian titles as yet untranslated into English; these may not resemble eventual English titles. Titles of published English translations appear in italics.

The Riverton Prize

The Riverton Prize, the leading Norwegian prize for crime fiction, also called the Golden Gun, has been awarded annually since 1972 to feature films, television dramas, and radio plays as well as crime novels. The award was named after the early Norwegian mystery author Stein Riverton and is the collaborative effort of the Riverton Club, the Norwegian Publishers Association, and the Norwegian Book Club, to promote the quantity and quality of Norwegian crime fiction. The physical prize itself is actually a "golden gun," a *Nagantrevolver*, a Belgian-made handgun with a gold stock, inspired by the two gold dueling pistols owned by author Stein Riverton's fictional detective Asbjørn Krag. Norwegian police used the *Nagantrevolver* at the time Krag was working as a detective. Two other awards, the Riverton Club Award and the Riverton Club International Award, are also "Golden Guns," given to individuals who according to Nils Nordberg, 'have made a special effort [for] Norwegian crime fiction, at home or abroad (Nordberg, "Murderers' Cheerful Siblings").

Riverton Prize Winners:

1972: *Bortreist på ubestemt tid* ("Away for an Indefinite Time"), by Sigrun Krokvik

1973: *Etterforskning pågår* ("The Investigation Is Ongoing"), by David Torjussen (pseudonym of Tor Edvin Dahl)

1974: *Lansen* ("Lansen") by Anker Rogstad

1975: *Rygg i rand, to i spann* ("Back to the Border, Two in the Bucket"), by Gunnar Staalesen

1976: *Den hvite kineser* ("The White Chinese"), by Pio Larsen

1977: No prize awarded

1978: *Blindpassasjer* (television series by Jon Bing and Tor Åge Bringsvaerd)

1979: *Operasjon* ("The Operation"), by Helge Riisøen

1980: *Kortslutning* ("Short Circuit"), by Fredrik Skagen

1981: *Hvit som snø* ("White as Snow"), by Jon Michelet

1982: *Thomas Pihls annem lov* ("Thomas Pihl's Other Law"), by Torolf Elster

1983: *Nattdykk* ("Night Dive") by Kim Småge

1984: No prize awarded

1985: *Spionen som lengtet hjem* ("The Spy Who Longed for Home"), by Michael Grundt Spang

1986: *Ringer i mørkt vann* (radio series by Edith Ranum)

1987: *Sneglene* ("The Snails"), by Lars Saabye Christensen

1988: *Kharg* ("Kharg"), by Alf R. Jacobsen

1989: *13 Takters blues* ("13 Bar Blues"), by Idar Lind

1990: *Den mekaniske kvinnen* ("The Mechanical Woman"), by Ingvar Ambjørnsen

1991: *Valsekongens fall* ("The Waltz King Case"), by Audun Sjøstrand

1992: *Orakel* ("Oracle"), by Arild Rypdal

1993: *Begjaerets pris* ("The Price of Desire"), by Morten Harry Olsen

1994: *Salige er de som tørster* ("Blessed Are Those Who Thirst"), by Anne Holt

1995: *Død mann i boks* ("A Dead Man in a Box"), by Kolbjørn Hauge

1996: *Se deg ikke tilbake* (*Don't Look Back*), by Karin Fossum

1997: *Flaggermusmannen* (*The Bat*), by Jo Nesbø

1998: *Kalde hender* ("Cold Hands"), by Jan Mehlum

1999: *Drømmefangeren* ("The Dream Catcher"), by Unni Lindell

2000: *En liten gyllen ring* ("The Last Fix"), by Kjell Ola Dahl

2001: *Den frosne kvinnen* ("The Frozen Woman") by Jon Michelet

2002: *Som i et speil* ("Reflections in a Mirror"), by Gunnar Staalesen

2003: *Hjemsøkt* ("Haunted"), by Kurt Aust (pseudonym of Kurt Østergaard)

2004: *Svarte penger: hvite løgner*, television series by Ulf Breistrand and Jarl Emsell Larsen

2005: *Flytande bjørn* (*The Shadow in the River*), by Frode Grytten

2006: *Dødsriket* ("Realm of the Dead"), by Tom Kristensen

2007: *Høstjakt* ("Autumn Hunt"), by Jørgen Gunnersud

2008: *Drømmenes land* (*The Land of Dreams*) by Vidar Sundstøl

2009: *Lucifers evangelium* ("The Gospel of Lucifer"), by Tom Egeland

2010: *Dødens sirkel* ("Circle of Death"), by Chris Tvedt

2011: *Ildmannen* ("The Arsonist"), by Torkil Damhaug

2012: *Jakthundene* ("The Hunting Dogs"), by Jørn Lier Horst

2013: *Drømmenes land* (*The Land of Dreams*), by Vidar Sundstøl

Riverton Club Award Winners:

1973: André Bjerke
1976: Bjørn Carling
1978: Gerd Nyquist
1990: Tage LaCour
1992: Nils Nordberg
1997: Willy Dahl, Sigurd B. Hennumgården, and Torolf Elster
2012: Varg Veum (Gunnar Staalesen's fictional detective)

Riverton Club International Award Winners

1991: Ruth Rendell
1993: P.D. James
1997: Ed McBain
2006: Maj Sjöwall
2012: Henning Mankell

The Glass Key Award

Six Norwegian crime authors have won the Glass Key Award, given yearly by the Crime Writers of Scandinavia for the best crime novel by a Danish, Finnish, Icelandic, Norwegian, or Swedish author. The short list for the prize is made up of one novel from each country, chosen by the members of the Crime Writers of Scandinavia from that country.

Norwegian Glass Key Winners:

1994: *Sub Rosa* ("Sub Rosa"), by Kim Småge
1996: *Nattsug* ("Night Swoon"), by Fredrik Skagen
1997: *Se dig ikke tilbake!* (*Don't Look Back*), by Karin Fossum
1998: *Flaggermusmannen* (*The Bat*), by Jo Nesbø
2004: *Hjemsøkt* ("Haunted"), by Kurt Aust (pseudonym of Kurt Østergaard)
2013: *Jakthundene* ("The Hunting Dogs"), by Jørn Lier Horst

The Petrona Award

The Petrona Award was established in memory of British crime fiction critic Maxine Clarke and awarded since 2013 for the best Scandinavian crime novel of the year. Norwegian author Thomas Enger received the Petrona Award for 2013 for *Fantomsmerte* (*Pierced*). Norwegian author Jorn Lier Horst's *Jakthundene* ("The Hunting Dogs") was nominated for the 2014 award.

A Parallel Chronology of Landmark Norwegian Crime Fiction and Events and World Crime Fiction and Events

Norwegian crime fiction and events are listed in Roman type with world crime fiction and events interspersed in italics.

c. 900: Harold I Fairhair briefly unites Norway

9th to 11th centuries: Viking raids on British Isles and Europe

1015–1028: Reign of Olaf II (St. Olaf); Christianity established in 994 but not universally practiced in Norway

12th–13th centuries: consolidation of royal power

1397: Kalmar Union unites Norway, Sweden, and Denmark

1523: Sweden breaks from Kalmar Union

1811: François Vidocq, former criminal, becomes head of Paris Sûreté

1814: Denmark cedes Norway to Sweden; Norwegian nationalism arises

1821: First "crime story," "The Mad Christian," by Mauritz Christopher Hansen

1828: Henrik Ibsen born

1828–29: Vidocq's Memoirs published

1835: First portions of Gjest Baardsen's "Autobiography" published (written in Akershus Prison)

1839: Hansen's "The Murder of Engineer Roolfsen," first "detective story"

Early 1840s: Hanna Winsnes' two thrillers, possibly first crime novels by a woman

1841: Poe's "The Murders in the Rue Morgue"

1843: First appearance of the word "detective" in English

c. 1850: Cheap books about sleuths appear in Britain and the United States

1866: Dostoevsky's Crime and Punishment

1868: Wilkie Collins' The Moonstone, considered first full-length detective novel

1869: Emile Gaboriau's Monsieur Lecoq, first police procedural

1882: Sigrid Undset, Norway's "Christian realist," born

1887: Arthur Conan Doyle's "A Study in Scarlet," first Sherlock Holmes story

1890: Ibsen's *Hedda Gabler*

1897: Christian Sparre's "The Adventures of Karl Monk"

1904: Sven Elvestad's stories about "Asbjørn Krag," former police investigator and action hero begin to appear

May 17, 1905: Norway attains independence from Sweden

1906: Ibsen's death

1909: "The Iron Chariot"; author Sven Elvestad takes the pseudonym "Stein Riverton"

1910–1925: "The first Golden Age of Norwegian crime Fiction" (Nordberg)—Elvestad's 90 stories, from short fiction to full length novels

1911: Riverton's "The Fear" (novel), centered on guilt and anxiety; *The Money Spider*, by William Le Queux, set in Trondheim

1914–1918: World War I (Norway neutral)

1920: The Mysterious Affair at Styles, Agatha Christie's first detective novel

1923: Jonathan Jerv's "The Bergen Train Robbed Tonight!" probably started the Norwegian tradition of linking crime fiction to Easter (A.B. Christiansen)

1920s–1930s: Golden Age of Mystery Fiction (Britain)

1920–1951: Publication of Black Mask, U.S. magazine developing American hard-boiled detective fiction

1924–1938: Alf B. Bryn's four crime novels starring millionaire playboy Peter Van Heeren, amateur sleuth

1928: Undset receives Nobel Prize for Literature for *Kristin lavransdatter*; publication of *The Master of Hestviken* follows

1929: Dashiell Hammett's The Maltese Falcon, starring Sam Spade

1930: First three "Nancy Drew" novels published

1930–c. 1938: The Great Depression

1931: Debut of Georges Simenon's Inspector Maigret

1934: Arthur Omre's "Smugglers," followed by a straight police procedural novel

1934: First Perry Mason novel, by Erle Stanley Gardner; first Nero Wolfe novel, by Rex Stout

1936: Torolf Elster's "The Wall," revealing Nazi tactics before their takeover of Germany

1939: Eric Ambler's A Coffin for Demetrios, novel of international intrigue; debut of Raymond Chandler's Philip Marlowe in The Big Sleep

1939–1945: World War II; Norway occupied by Nazi Germany beginning on April 9, 1940.

1930s: About 30 criminal novels by respected Oslo crime reporter Fridtjof Knutsen, many in collaboration with his wife Lalli Knutsen; several of them were adapted from "Carolyn Keene"'s Nancy Drew novels

April 9, 1940: German invasion of Norway; publishing houses under Nazi control

1940–1947: "Second Golden Age of Norwegian Crime Fiction" (Nordberg):140 new crime novels produced

1941: André Bjerke's *Night Man*, with psycho-analyst Kai Bugge as detective

1942: Bjerke's masterpiece crime novel *Lake of the Dead*, filmed in 1958

1942: "The Spirit Mask," inspired by John Dickson Carr's work, by Stein Ståle; a realistic policeman investigates an occultist homicide

c. 1946–c. 1989: Cold War period

1947: Precipitous decline in Norwegian crime fiction under influence of American Westerns (Nordberg)

1947: Mickey Spillane's I, the Jury becomes bestseller

1949: Death of Sigrid Undset

1949: *Debut of Lew Archer in Ross Macdonald's* The Moving Target; *first radio* Dragnet *show*

1950: *Patricia Highsmith's* Strangers on a Train

1951: *First telecast of* Dragnet

1950s–early 1960s: Nordberg: Norwegian crime fiction very limited

1953: *First James Bond novel,* Casino Royale, *published*

1957: Waldemar Brøgger's *The Murderer Picks Fly Agaric,* first of four thrillers

1958: *Blake Edwards'* Peter Gunn *television series begins*

1960: Regular television broadcasting begins in Norway (state monopoly); North Sea oil development brings new revenue to Norway

1960 and 1966: Gerd Nyquist's two detective novels make her the then "Queen of Crime" in Norway

1962: *James Bond film,* The Spy Who Loved Me, *starring Sean Connery; P.D. James' first Adam Dalgleish novel,* Cover Her Face

1963: *John Le Carré's* The Spy Who Came in from the Cold

1965: *Maj Sjöwall and Per Wahlöö, Communists, decide to expose Swedish capitalism by pioneering the Nordic procedural (Kachka, "Winter")*

1967: Rosanna, *first Martin Beck novel by Sjöwall and Wahlöö:*

1968: *First* Columbo *television appearance by Peter Falk*

1970s: Renaissance of Norwegian crime fiction; politically radicalized leadership takes over Norwegian literary community; women's movement becomes radicalized

1971: Knut Faldbakken's *The Sleeping Prince*

1971: *First* Dirty Harry *film starring Clint Eastwood*

1972: The Riverton Club founded (The Norwegian Society of Crime Fiction), establishing the Golden Gun Prize for the year's best piece of crime writing, the first to Sigrun Krokvik; Gerd Nyquist becomes the club's first president.

September 25, 1972: Norway rejects EEC member-ship

1972: Sigrun Krokvik's "Away for an Indefinite Time" revitalizes Norwegian crime fiction

1972–1976: Annual number of Norwegian crime titles rises from three or four to over twenty, the present number (Nordberg), concurrent with Norway's oil-based economic and social changes, introducing the recurrent theme of the loss of innocence

1973: Tor Edvin Dahl ("David Torjussen") first new Norwegian writer in Gyldendal's Black Series *Investigations in Progress*

1974: Krokvik's "Away for an Indefinite Time" filmed

1976: Debut of Marxist-Leninist Jon Michelet's "red" cop Vilhelm Thygesen, in "The Iron Cross"

1976: *Finnish author Matti Joensuu initiates his noir procedurals*

1977: Debut of Varg Veum, first idealistic alcoholic Norwegian PI, by Gunnar Staalesen

1977: *Debut of Marcia Muller's Sharon McCone, first female PI*

1978: First Morten Martens novel by Fredrik Skagen, "The Wolves"

1980s: Beginning of influx of immigrants and refugees into Norway

1981: Dissolution of Norwegian state broadcasting monopoly

1982: *Debuts of Sara Paretsky's V.I. Warshawski and Sue Grafton's Kinsey Malone, female PIs*

1984: *First telecast of* Murder, She Wrote *(U.S.)*

1988: *Debut of Elizabeth George's Inspector Lynley series*

1990: *Debut of Patricia Cornwell's Kay Scarpetta series*

1993: K.O. Dahl's *Lethal Investments*; Anne Holt's first Hanne Wilhelmsen novel, *Blind Goddess*

1993: *Peter Høeg (Danish) publishes* Smilla's Sense of Snow

1995: Karin Fossum's first Inspector Sejer novel, *In the Darkness*; Pernille Rygg's first Igi Heitmann (female) novel, *The Butterfly Effect*

1997: Jo Nesbø's first Harry Hole novel, "*The Bat*"

1997: Faceless Killers, *Henning Mankell's first Wallander novel, is translated from Swedish to English*

1984: Kim Småge's first Hilke Torhus (female) novel, "Night Dive" begins use of female detective in Norwegian crime fiction

1998: Kjersti Scheen's first Margaret Moss detective novel, *Final Curtain,* tr. 2002

Late 1990s: Gunnar Staalesen's 1900 trilogy, world's longest detective novel (Nordberg)

2001: Tom Egeland's *Relic*; Anne Holt's first Vik/Stubo novel, *Punishment,* tr. 2006

2001: *Terrorist attack on U.S. World Trade Center and Pentagon*

2005: *Stieg Larsson's* The Girl with the Dragon Tattoo, *tr. 2008; Larsson dies just before its Swedish publication*

2006: *Larsson's* The Girl Who Played with Fire, *tr. 2009*

2007: *Larsson's* The Girl Who Kicked the Hornet's Nest, *tr. 2009*

2010: Thomas Enger's *Burned*; Alfred A. Knopf buys four of Nesbø's novels for publication in the USA, promoting Nesbø as Norway's "King of Crime"

2010: Liza Marklund (with James Patterson) becomes second Swedish author to top New York Times' bestseller list

October 16, 2013: Conservative government under Prime Minister Erna Solberg replaces Social Democrats

Dagbladet's Twenty-Five Best Norwegian Crime Novels of All Time (2009)

1. *Elskede Poona*, by Karin Fossum (tr. as *The Indian Bride*, 2007; also titled *Calling Out for You*)
2. *Jernvognen* (tr. as *The Iron Chariot*, 2005), by Stein Riverton, 1909
3. *Hvit som snø* ("White as Snow,") by Jon Michelet, 1980
4. *Historien om Gottlob* ("The History of Gottlob"), by Torolf Elster, 1941
5. *Fluten* ("Escape"), by Arthur More, 1936
6. *Falne engler* ("Fallen Angels"), by Gunnar Staalesen, 1989
7. *Døde menn går i land* ("Dead Men Disembark"), by André Bjerke, 1947
8. *Siste skygge av tvil* ("Recent Shadow of a Doubt"), by Kjell Ola Dahl, 1998
9. *Rødstrupe* (tr. as *The Redbreast*, 2006), by Jo Nesbø, 2000
10. *Bortreist på ubestemt tid* ("Absent Indefinitely"), by Sigrun Krokvik, 1932
11. *Drømmenes land* (tr. as *The Land of Dreams*, 2013), by Vidar Sundstøl, 2008
12. *Raymond Isaksens utgang* ("Raymond Isaksen's Exit"), by Jørgen Gunnerud, 1994
13. *Perdido, Perdido* ("Perdido, Perdido"), by Olav Angell, 1975
14. *Til Herr Politimesteren* ("To Mr. Commissioner"), by Harald Thaulow (as Jon Hell), 1940
15. *Mitt navn er Knoph* ("My Name Is Knoph"), by Olav Bull, 1914
16. *Kainan* ("Canaan"), by Kim Småge, 2006
17. *Døden er et kjaertegn* ("Death Is a Caress"), by Arve Moen, 1948
18. *Nattsug* ("Night Pain"), by Fredrik Skagen, 2003
19. *Mississippi* ("Mississippi"), by Morten Harry Olsen, 1990
20. *Stalins øyne* ("Stalin's Eyes"), by Ingvar Ambjørnsen, 1985
21. *Nattens joker* ("Night Joker"), by Frank Tandberg, 1995
22. *Renhetens pris* ("Purity Prize"), by Bergljot Hobaek Haff, 1992
23. *Snuff* ("Snuff"), by Jan H. Jensen, 1982
24. *Den svunde er en drøm* ("It's a Dream Gone By"), by Aksel Sandemose, 1944
24. *Salige er de som tørster* (tr. as *Blessed Are Those Who Thirst*, 2012), by Anne Holt, 1994

Contemporary Norwegian Authors of Crime Fiction

Authors marked with an asterisk (*) have crime novels currently available in English translation. References to standard reference sources such as *The Norwegian Biographical Encyclopedia* and to dated reviews in major Norwegian newspapers, primarily *Dagbladet* and *Aftenposten*, appear in the text.

Ingvar Ambjørnsen

b. 1956, Tønsberg, Norway; Residence: Oslo, Norway; Occupation: novelist

According to critic Øystein Rottem in *The Norwegian Biographical Encyclopedia*, Ambjørnsen recalls that when he was a child, his family often sacrificed their food budget to buy books. He himself dropped out of school very early and worked at various jobs, including low-level positions in psychiatric institutions, before the publication of his first novel, *23-salen* ("Room 23"), a semi-autobiographical documentary sharply critical of Norwegian policies in the treatment of the mentally ill, written while he was a conscientious objector serving at the Salvation Army facility in Oslo. Using a hard-boiled style, Ambjørnsen continues to depict depressed individuals on the fringes of Norwegian society, leavening his fiction with flashes of black humor.

Since his breakthrough novel *Hvite Niggers* ("White Niggers"), 1986, Ambjørnsen has drawn his edgy novels from the Norwegian "drugs and despair" scene, championing the cause of society's outsiders and mercilessly describing the dark corners of Norwegian life that they inhabit. His crime novel *Stalins oyne* ("Stalin's Eyes"), 1985, features Ronny and Laila Olsen, a down-at-heels married private detective team who operate in a seedy section of Oslo. Ambjørnsen echoes elements of the American stereotypical hardboiled detective genre, especially Dashiell Hammett's popular Nick and Nora Charles, protagonists of *The Thin Man*. Ambjørnsen also shifts scenes between eastern Oslo and the harbor at Hamburg, using tragic near-forgotten World War II figures in his plots. *Dagbladet* placed "Stalin's Eyes" twentieth in their 2009 list of Norway's twenty-five best crime novels of all time.

Ambjørnsen writes quickly in several genres. For his second adult crime novel, *Heksenes kors* ("The Witches' Cross"), 1987, he created a different protagonist, Harry Kramer, a widowed sailor who lived in Edinburgh. For *Den mekaniske kvinnen* ("The Mechanical Woman"), 1990, he created private eye Victor Van Valk, who works in Hamburg's tough St. George District (Nordberg). Ambjørnsen continued with a shorter Van Valk piece which to date has appeared only in Germany.

Inspired by the English-language Hardy Boys novels, Ambjørnsen also has produced the *Pelle og Proffen* young adult crime series, featuring a pair of teen detectives who deal with crimes involving drugs, pollution, and neo–Nazism, two of which have been made into successful Norwegian movies. He also authored another young adult crime novel, *Drapene i Barkvik* ("The Murders in Brakvik"), about Philip Moberg, an adolescent detective solving an axe murder in a small Norwegian village.

Adult Crime Novels:

1985: *Stalins øyne* ("Stalin's Eyes")
1987: *Heksenes kors* ("The Witches' Game")
1990: *Den mekaniske kvinnen* ("The Mechanical Woman")

The "Pelle and Proffen" Young Adult Crime Series (translated titles):

1987: "Giants Fall"
1988: "Death at Oslo Central Station"
1989: "Toxic Falsehoods"
1990: "Truth for Sale"
1991: "The Blue Wolves"
1992: "Flames in the Snow"
1993: "After the Hurricane"
1994: "Vengeance from Heaven"
1995: "Large Village Voice"
1996: "The Assassination of Aker Brygge"

Stand-Alone Young Adult Crime Novel:

2005: "The Murders at Branvik"

Major Awards:

1991: The Riverton Prize, for "The Mechanical Woman"

Website: http://www.kjenfolk.no/forfattere/ambjørnsen

Olav Angell

> b. August 4, 1932, Trondheim, Norway; grew up in Oslo, Norway; Residence: Oslo; Occupations: poet, novelist, translator, jazz musician

As well as his crime novel *Perdido, Perdido*, 1975, which ranked thirteenth in *Dagbladet's* list of the twenty-five best Norwegian crime novels of all time, Angell has written poetry, science fiction, and memoirs. He also received the Norwegian Arts Council's Translator's Award for his translation of James Joyce's *Ulysses*, 1992. Angell translated Raymond Chandler's *The Big Sleep* and Jack Kerouac's *On the Road* as well as works by other American beat poets, all of which influenced *Perdido, Perdido*, a portrait of a new generation lost to unthinking protests, drugs, alcohol, and sexual excess. Specifically, the novel traces an individual's dissolution under the combined influence of his brother's death, the breakup of the individual's marriage, and a mysterious death he may have caused—in short, the stuff of contemporary tragedy.

Crime Novel:

1975: *Perdido, Perdido* ("Perdido, Perdido")

Website: N/A

Kurt Aust (pseudonym of Kurt Østergaard)

> b. December 6, 1955, Ikast, Denmark; Residence: Horten, Norway, since 1982; Occupation: author

Aust, best known as an author of historical crime novels, also has written a cartoon script, contemporary thrillers, and a children's book, the last with his wife and co-illustrator Kin Wessel. Aust set his four historical mysteries in the 18th century, when Norway was ruled by Denmark. His series characters are Professor Thomas of Boueberg of Copenhagen University and his assistant and "Dr. Watson," the Norwegian student Petter Hortten, who narrates the stories. Aust's third historical detective novel, "Afflicted: Next to God," won the 2003 Glass Key Award and was praised for its readability and verisimilitude. *Dagbladet* critic Torbjørn Ekelund described Aust's fifth novel in this series, "When the Dead Whisper" as "perfect for dark autumn evenings," a tale of the search that Thomas and Petter are assigned to make in 1705 for a bailiff, Moritz Gledde, who mysteriously vanished on the lonely island of Anhol between Denmark and Sweden, a place long suspected of harboring wreckers, criminals who lure ships to their destruction and plunder the resulting debris. Jon Terje Grønli of *Gjengangeren* found that "When the Dead Whisper," like Aust's other novels, possesses "an intimacy of its own and a level of reality that you rarely find in this genre."

Aust's contemporary thriller *De usynlige brødre* ("The Invisible Brothers"), 2006, has been translated into eight languages, though not as yet into English. It has often been compared to Dan

Brown's *The Da Vinci Code*, because both novels feature mysterious brotherhoods, religion-related conspiracies, esoteric codes, and alchemy. Aust also has written two plays, one a historical drama titled "Legends, Fanaticism, and Black Art at Olavskilden."

Historical Crime Novels:

1999: *Vredens dag* ("Day of Wrath")
2001: *Den tredje sannhet* ("The Third Truth")
2003: *Hjemsøkt, next etter Gud* ("Afflicted, Next to God"; also translated as "Haunted")
2004: *Kongefrykt* ("A King's Fear")
2011: *Nar døde hvisker* ("When the Dead Whisper")

Contemporary Crime Novels/Thrillers:

2006: *De usynlige brødre* ("The Invisible Brothers")
2008: *Kaos og øyeblikkets renhet* ("Chaos and the Purity of the Moment")
2009: *Hevnens alkymi* ("The Alchemy of Revenge")

Major Awards:

1999: Aschehoug's Debut Endowment, for "Day of Wrath"
2003: The Riverton Prize, for "Afflicted, Next to God"
2004: The Glass Key Award, for "Afflicted, Next to God"

Website: http://www.kurtaust.dk

Anita Berglund

b. 1963, Fagernes, Norway; Residence: Beechwood at Larvik, Norway; Occupations: computer programmer, financial analyst, novelist

Berglund has moved 27 times at home and abroad, spending eleven years in the United States. Her debut novel *I fritt fall* ("In Free Fall"), 2009, was the first Norwegian crime novel to feature a profiler, Didrik Claussen, as protagonist, whom Berglund portrays as having worked for the FBI for a long time before visiting Norway for the first time in fifteen years. There he investigates the murder of his childhood sweetheart, Hege Furuset, who now is a famous lawyer. Just before her death, Hege had received a threatening letter and a note containing the names of four Greek gods, clues which Claussen must unravel to solve her murder. A *Dagbladet* reviewer found this novel a "lifeless crime debut" (April 30, 2010), but Berglund's second crime novel, *Midvintermørke* ("Midwinter Dark"), 2011, received a better appraisal. This time Claussen probes a brutal attack on pregnant Rebecca Tangen at her home in Stornoway, where almost simultaneously a murder occurs in a quiet local street. The town's police believe the crimes are connected to an Eastern European crime mob, but Claussen suspects a domestic motive, making for a complex, if somewhat predictable plot.

Crime Novels:

2009: *I fritt fall* ("In Free Fall")
2011: *Midvintermørke* ("Midwinter Darkness")

Major Awards: N/A

Website: N/A

Bjørn Bottolvs

b. March 5, 1946; Residence: Baerum, Norway; Occupations: former Oslo Chief of Police, novelist and author of children's books

Bottolvs began his literary career by writing children's books, but he also writes realistic police procedurals centered on policeman Jo Kaasa, who works out of the Majorstua ("Anytown") police station. Bottolvs' novels are short, usually around 200 pages, developing true-to-life plots based on his over thirty years' experience as a policeman and couching them in a laconic, almost Dragnet-style prose. *Dagbladet* crime critic Torbjørn Ekelund and others compare Bottolvs' writing to the work of Jørgen Gunnerud, who like Bottolvs writes for Colon Publishers.

Crime Novels:

1999: *Kometen* ("Comet")
2002: *Is* ("Ice")
2004: *Mairegn* ("May Rain")
2006: *Når natta er som svartest* ("When the Night Is Darkest")
2007: *Døde vitner lyver ikke* ("Dead Witnesses Don't Lie")
2009: *Granaten* ("Shell")
2010: *Drapet på Taparud gård* ("The Murder at Taparud Farm")
2012: *Etter den søte kløe* ("After the Sweet Itch")

Major Awards: N/A

Website: N/A

*Jørgen Brekke

b. April 26, 1968, Horten, Norway; Residence: Trondheim, Norway; Occupations: teacher, freelance journalist, author

Jørgen Brekke's debut crime novel, *Nådens omkrets*, 2011 (*Where Monsters Dwell*, tr. 2014), was on Norway's bestseller lists for four months and has been sold in twelve countries. A grisly thriller spanning two continents and five centuries, it opens with the brutal murder of the curator of the Edgar Allan Poe Museum in Richmond, Virginia, paralleled by a similar killing of an official at Trondheim's Gunnerus Library, both victims flayed alive and decapitated. Alternating the two crime venues, Brekke's two police detectives, Richmond homicide squad member Felicia Stone and Trondheim's Chief Inspector Odd Singsaker, gradually learn that the cases are related, while flashbacks reveal information about the creation of the Johannes Book (the Book of John), a handwritten 17th century medical text bound in human skin, an item central to both murders. Although a Kirkus reviewer (February 11, 2014) found far more red herrings than Agatha Christie would have approved and reviewer Anna Creer cautioned that it is "not for the faint-hearted," *Where Monsters Dwell* has received major crime debut awards in Norway.

Brekke's next three novels promise to be equally shocking. Rights to the sequel to *Where Monsters Dwell. Drømmeløs*, 2012 (*Dreamless*, tr. 2015), have been sold to eight countries. It opens on a shocking murder scene in which a promising young singer's body is discovered in a forest during a snowstorm, with her larynx removed and an antique music box that plays an unusual unidentifiable tune placed on her body. Odd Singsaker, now married to Felicia Stone but struggling with personal issues that leave his inner life in turmoil, investigates both this murder and a missing person case that follows, discovering that they are connected by the music box's obscure 17th century lullaby. These killings are the work of a psychotic killer able to combine his everyday job with the accomplishment of his dark desires. Singsaker's physician concludes, "we're never going to find any scientific explanation for evil" (*Dreamless* 300), but Brekke's novels come close to providing an emotional description of human beings who have chosen to become monsters.

Menneskets natur ("The Nature of Man"), 2013, praised by *Adresseavisen* as Brekke's best novel to date, takes Odd Singsaker to the island of Hitra after his wife Felicia Stone has left him. Singsaker finds himself in a horrifying situation, with a corpse next to him while he is aiming a shotgun at a person lying in a charred sofa. Brekke's fourth novel in as many years, *Doktor Fredriks kabinett* ("Doctor Fredrik's Closet"), 2014, set in 1769 Trondheim, interrupts the Odd Singsaker series to explore the activities of testy but canny 18th century police chief Nils Bayer, who appeared in *Dreamless* and now investigates a case involving a physician's mysterious cabinet and a sleepwalker with the gift of prophecy.

Crime Novels:

Odd Singsaker Series:

2011: *Nådens omkrets* (U.S. title *Where Monsters Dwell*, tr. Steven T. Murray, 2014, titled in the UK *Where Evil Lies* and also referred to as "Realm of Grace")
2012: *Drømmeløs* (*Dreamless*, tr. Steven T. Murray, 2015)
2013: *Menneskets natur* ("Human Nature" or "The Nature of Man")

Stand-Alone Historical Crime Novel:

2014: *Doktor Fredriks kabinett* ("Doctor Fredrik's Cabinet")

Major Awards:

2011: Norlis Debut Prize for *Nådens omkrets* (*Where Monsters Dwell*)
2012: Mauritz Hansen Debut Prize for *Nådens omkrets* (*Where Monsters Dwell*)

Website: N/A

Magnhild Bruheim

b. September 17, 1951, Skjåk, Norway; Residence: Lillehammer, Norway; Occupations: novelist, author of children's literature, and radio and television journalist

Best known for producing "rural crime" novels, Bruheim writes in *nynorsk* ("New Norwegian"), one of the two official versions of the Norwegian language. *Bokmål*, more heavily influenced by Danish, is the written form of the language used by many Norwegians, primarily in the eastern part of southern Norway, but most Norwegians speak various dialects rather than the "Standard Østnorsk." *Nynorsk* was created in the mid–19th century by Ivar Aasen as an alternative to Danish, then used widely in Norway; *nynorsk* is therefore closer in grammar to Old West Norse than *bokmål* is. Currently approximately 27 percent of Norway's municipalities have adopted *nynorsk* as their official form of the written language, totaling about 12 percent of the nation's population, chiefly in Western Norway.

Bruheim invariably creates exciting and credible plots set in rural areas and small villages, strongly adhering to the literary dictum, "Show, don't tell." Her first of six adult crime novels, *Varselet* ("Forecast"), 1997, introduces her series protagonist, Oslo detective Morton Strand, a "lovesick, awkward policeman" (Skjonsberg) plunged into village narrow-mindedness and spiteful reluctance to abandon old feuds. In *Maskerade* ("Masquerade"), 1999, Strand temporarily leaves off his investigation into the murder of a ordinary woman, Oddny Wangen, at a 1970 New Year's Eve masquerade party to crawl "into bed with a key witness," an ill-advised lapse in professional conduct that creates serious consequences for him (Skjonsberg). Critic Harald Skjonsberg praises Bruheim's re-creation of the overheated and rebellious 1970s atmosphere, while he questions whether Bruheim's portrayals of modern Norway as "stuffy, cramped, and provincial" are denunciations of today's Norwegian society or simply reflections of it.

In her young adult crime novels to date, Bruheim also addresses contemporary societal problems in Norway through teenaged female central figures, Kami and Bente, who like America's perennial teen heroine Nancy Drew appeal to their contemporaries by investigating questionable activities that land them in dangerous predicaments which they always survive with zeal. In Bruheim's first young adult novel, *Ny melding* ("A New Message"), 2003, Kami disappears while walking home from a bus stop with an unknown boy, and Bente has to find her. In *Venneringen* ("No Friends"), 2007, a vicious crime disrupts the girls' vacation at a summer cottage; in *På flukt* ("On the Run"), 2010, Bruheim tackles honor killings and forced marriages, problems that Muslim immigrant girls face in Norway as well as other countries; and *Blod på hendene* ("Blood on Their Hands"), 2011, explores fur farming, animal rights, and bullying.

Crime Novels:

> 1997: *Varselet* ("Forecast")
> 1999: *Maskerade* ("Masquerade")
> 2000: *Utan englevakt* ("Without an Angel's Care")
> 2001: *Svart arv* ("Black Heritage") (produced for radio, 2008)
> 2002: *Dragsug* ("Undertow")
> 2010: *Det som ein gong var* ("What Once Was")

Selected Young Adult Crime Novels:

> 2003: *Ny melding* ("A New Message")
> 2007: *Venneringen* ("No Friends")
> 2008: *Nattskrik* ("Night Screams")
> 2010: *På flukt* ("On the Run")
> 2011: *Blod på hendene* ("Blood on Their Hands")

Major Awards: N/A

Website: http://www.magnhildbruheim.no.wordpress/om-meg3

Bjørn Carling

> b. July 7, 1919; d. May 17, 2005; Residence: Oslo, Norway; Occupations: journalist, writer, and translator

In 1976, Bjørn Carling produced *Norsk kriminallitteratur gjennom 150 år* ("Norwegian Crime Fiction: 150 Years"), the first history of Norwegian crime literature, covering the period from 1825 to 1975. As one of the founders of the Riverton Club, he suggested that the Riverton Award should be a "golden gun," a revolver with gold ornamentation that refers to Stein Riverton's 1914 novel "The Finger of Death," where Riverton's detective Asbjørn Krug possesses a black case containing two dueling revolvers with gold chasing. Besides producing two crime novels of his own written under the pseudonym "Erik Vendel," Carling co-authored *Døde menn går i land* ("Dead Men Come Ashore" or "Dead Men Disembark"), 1947, with André Bjerke, who used the pen name "Bernhard Borge." Carling also adapted three of Stein Riverton's novels for Norwegian *Radioteateret:* "The Killer Without a Face," in four episodes, 1983; "The Grand Duchess of Speil-salen," in five episodes, 1984; and "Red Widow," in four episodes, 1996. Carling's notable trans-lations include John Dickson Carr's *The Cave Man,* tr. 1973, and Bram Stoker's *Dracula,* tr. 1974.

Crime Novels:

1947: *Døde menn går i land* ("Dead Men Come Ashore"), as Erik Vendel, with Bernhard Borge (André Bjerke)
1952: *Tornerose er våken i natt* ("Sleeping Beauty Is Awake at Night"), as Erik Vendel
1989: *Den tålmodige tinnsoldat* ("The Patient Tin Soldier"), as Erik Vendel

Major Awards: N/A

Website: N/A

Lars Saabye Christensen

> b. September 21, 1953, Oslo, Norway (holds Danish citizenship); Residence: Earlier, Sortland, Nor-way; currently Blindern, Oslo's university district; Occupations: poet, screenwriter, author

Christensen began publishing in 1972 as a poet and has since produced poetry, film scripts, and children's books, but he is best known for his novels. Only one, *Jokeren,* 1981 (*The Joker,* tr. 1991), is considered a thriller. He is a member of the Norwegian Academy for Language and Literature.

According to *The Complete Review, The Joker*'s opening "promises dark fun": on February 18, 1978, a former jailbird and loner Hans Georg Windelband reads his own obituary in the news-paper. Upon investigating, Windelband learns that the corpse resembles him and in fact had briefly lived under Windelband's name. Windelband's major crime has been a bank heist that provided him an easy living, but as he delves further into the mystery of the mistaken obituary, he stumbles into drug smuggling, family secrets, and organized gambling. A convincing supporting cast includes Windelband's only friend, the Butcher, who constantly complains that his children are being corrupted by the state educational system.

Crime Novels:

1981: *Jokeren* (*The Joker,* tr. Stephen Michael Nordby, 1991)
1988: *Sneglene* ("The Snails")

Major Awards:

1988: The Riverton Prize, for *Sneglene* ("The Snails")
2006: Commander of the Royal Norwegian Order of St. Olaf
2008: *Chevalier dans L'ordre des Arts et Lettres* (France)

Website: http://www.cappelendamm.no

K.O. (Kjell Ola) Dahl

> b. February 4, 1958; Residence: Oslo, Norway; Occupation: author

Since 1993 when he first treated white-collar crime in *Dødens investeringer* (*Lethal Investments,* not translated until 2011, though it puts all the rest of Dahl's novels in context), Dahl's police procedurals have featured two Oslo detectives, grouchy Inspector Gunnarstranda, a small, bald, first-nameless widower with false teeth, and his beefy assistant, ladies' man Frank Frølich. In a November 7, 2012, presentation at the Singapore Writers Festival, Dahl, who has worked extensively with people suffering from drug-related problems, said that he began his literary career because he wanted to write a book with "a morbid plot" about those problems. Since then Dahl's detective plots have maintained that gruesome intention.

Since Dahl's development of the relationship between the two detectives is central to the series, non–Scandinavian readers of Dahl's Gunnarstranda and Frølich novels do well to begin with *Lethal Investments* and read the other novels in the order Dahl wrote them, not in the reverse order they have been published in English translation, a strange publishing procedure that has befallen other Nordic authors. In *Lethal Investments*, Gunnarstranda initially seems unimpressive to both Frølich and Dahl's readers. To develop the professional and personal relationships between his detectives in *Lethal Investments*, Dahl painstakingly works through not only their interviews with witnesses and suspects, but more importantly their interactions with each other following the discovery of the body of Reidun Rosendal, a pretty salesgirl at Software Partners, a firm seething with potentially fatal rivalries. Shortly before her death, Reidun had picked up Sigurd, a young laborer, for a one-night stand, which at first makes him the prime suspect in her murder, but soon Sigurd himself is found slain. Gunnarstranda, who devotes his leisure time to caring for his dead wife's garden, and Frølich, who is carrying on an affair with a girl from a local commune, exchange cynicisms that allow Dahl to make pungent comments on contemporary Norwegian society as they untangle the leads and motives of repellent characters.

Frølich appears to be better educated than Gunnarstranda, but Frølich gradually learns to appreciate his senior partner's experience and insight. Most of *Lethal Investments* moves slowly, but after two more killings Gunnarstranda makes an intuitive leap which leads to a speedy conclusion. British reviewer Laura Root sees "more characterisation [sic] and social satire" than plot in *Lethal Investments*, and she praises Dahl's "sharp and dry wit" as well as his "rather brutally accurate observations about character and appearance ... [and] the less pleasant aspects of sex," features that frequently recur in Dahl's subsequent fiction.

En liten gyllen ring, 2000 (*The Last Fix*, tr. 2009), which won the Riverton Prize, synthesizes classic police procedure and social criticism (Forshaw 119), the latter through some "caustic observation" by the detectives about "the absurdities and irritations of Norwegian society" (Forshaw 120). Dahl continues to portray Gunnarstranda and Frølich as unarmed and uncorrupted police officers, honest, ordinary fellows who simply want to do their jobs. By again killing off a main character at the beginning of this novel, Dahl emphasizes the tragically wasted lives of drug addicts. Threatened by a creepy intruder at the travel agency where she now works, his central figure Katrine, who is completing a drug rehabilitation program at a commune for youthful addicts, leaves her skinhead boyfriend at a boozy drug-ridden party the commune ironically sponsors to celebrate Katrine's new sobriety. Disturbed by the hypocrisy of the situation, Katrine leaves the party and walks alone near a lake, where a naked man approaches her, the last sight she sees. Gunnarstranda and Frølich again patiently interview the obvious suspects, mostly addicts Katrine knew while she was addicted herself, but soon the detectives begin to interrogate the commune's staff, most of whom are concealing disturbing sexual secrets. Dahl's grim humor intermittently surfaces in his characters' incongruous activities, as when inmates at the drug rehabilitation center pelt Gunnarstranda with tomatoes and when Frølich's mother throws him out of his own apartment so she can clean it. Overall, as Mary Whipple observed in "Seeing the World through Books," Dahl relies on dialogue rather than action to advance his plot, which tends to limit both excitement and involvement with the novel.

Third in this series, *Mannen i vinduet*, 2000 (*The Man in the Window*, tr. 2008), like other current Norwegian crime novels harks back to the traumatic Nazi occupation of Norway. Dahl begins the novel by piling up a sordid roster of homicide motives: on a gloomy Friday, January 13, in Oslo, seventy-nine-year-old grouchy antique dealer Reidar Folke Jespersen watches his much younger wife Ingrid enter her lover's apartment. A little later Jespersen argues viciously with his two brothers, who intend to sell the family antique business. Jespersen then interrupts Ingrid's tryst with a vituperative phone call and rearranges his own assignation with a lovely actress who at his direction enacts events from his past. Then Jespersen quarrels with a seedy business associate before dining with his unappealing son, daughter-in-law, and two grandchildren. The next morning, Jespersen's corpse is found naked in an armchair in his own shop window, a red ligature around his neck and three crosses and the number 195 incised across his bare chest. A Nazi uniform, bayonet, and medal play important roles in this homicide case, causing Gunnarstranda and Frølich to carry out their investigation in the far-reaching shadow of the Nazi Occupation.

In this distasteful case, love, loyalty, revenge, and guilt intertwine, paralleling issues in the detectives' own lives. Gunnarstranda is tentatively exploring the possibility of a new romantic relationship while Frølich exploits his male magnetism with a succession of willing women. Dahl makes his detectives wade through so many red herrings, that hoary old detective fiction device drawn from the British custom of training foxhounds by dragging smoked herrings through the fields, that critic Norman Price, writing in *Euro Crime* for May 2008, observed tongue in cheek that perhaps the Scandinavians' extensive exposure to herrings makes them "so good at writing crime fiction" (Price).

Dahl's *Den fjerde raneren*, 2005 (*The Fourth Man*, tr. 2007), opens with an obsessive and passionate affair between Frølich and Elisabeth Faremo, the sister of an Oslo gangster implicated in a recent larceny. When she disappears, Frølich plunges into a reassessment of their relationship, questioning everything he thought he knew about her. Frølich's attachment to Elisabeth also makes Gunnarstranda believe that Elisabeth has victimized him. Sensing that Frølich cannot work the case objectively, Gunnarstranda puts Frølich, now a prime murder suspect, on an extended leave which Frølich uses to unofficially investigate Elisabeth's disappearance, delving into a sordid combination of arson, theft, and killings which makes *The Fourth Man* arguably Dahl's most complex procedural.

Dahl made Gunnarstranda's colleague Lena Stigersand the main character of his eighth Gunnarstranda-Frølich novel, *Isbaderen* ("The Ice Swimmer"), 2011. Lena is youthful, red haired, and volatile; despite her natural inclination to guard her heart, she becomes involved with a charming but deceitful reporter while investigating a case loaded with immoral politicians, violent security contractors. She is even warned to leave it alone by the National Security Service, but in one of the most trying fictional situations for a female detective, she prevails despite a diagnosed breast cancer. Norway's NRK 2 reviewer observed that in this novel Dahl again demonstrated an outstanding ability to depict social issues convincingly in the mode of the police procedural.

Acknowledging that Dahl's "lean" and "brilliant" style is "rather different" from "the probing psychological novels of Karins [sic] Fossum or Alvtegen … the richness of Jo Nesbø's big thrillers … the detailed police-work of Åke Edwardson or Henning Mankell … or the elegant stylishness of Håkan Nesser or Arnaldur Indriðason," Fiona Walker, reviewing for *EuroCrime* in 2007, noted Dahl's stylistic similarity to American hard-boiled detective novels.

Dahl's 1998 stand alone *noir* thriller *Siste skygge av tvil* ("Last Shadow of Doubt"), placed eighth on *Dagbladet*'s 2009 list of the twenty-five all-time best Norwegian crime novels. Its protagonist John Hammersten, just released from prison, is determined to discover the truth behind the crime for which he believes he was wrongly convicted. That truth lies in the dark past he shares with his old friend Abel and Abel's former lover Grethe Lindeman, but gradually other figures reappear from Hammersten's pre-prison life, several with every reason to keep the truth buried in this miasma of erotic and psychological obsession. "Last Shadow of Doubt" was dramatized in 2003 as a four-part series for Norwegian Radio Theatre.

Despite Dahl's emphasis on often stomach-wrenching crimes and twisted psychological motivations, Dahl insisted in the website *Moments in Crime* that he feels Scandinavian crime fiction protagonists are often very stable, exhibiting the positive impact of the Scandinavian welfare states. Summing up her reaction to Dahl's fictional combination of sharply realistic crimes with the decent and hardworking detectives who have to solve them, fellow Norwegian crime author Karin Fossum deplores detective fiction that fails to depict real life. She praises Dahl's convincing portrayal of both the good and the evil in today's Norwegian culture. Fossum concludes, "If I don't believe in them [crime novels], they don't impress me. But when K.O. Dahl tells his stories, I believe every single word" (Fossum).

Crime Novels:

Gunnarstranda and Frølich Series:

1993: *Dødens investeringer* (*Lethal Investments*, tr. Don Bartlett, 2011)
2000: *En liten gyllen ring* (*The Last Fix*, tr. Don Bartlett, 2009)
2001: *Mannen i vinduet* (*The Man in the Window*, tr. Don Bartlett, 2008)
2003: *Lille tambur* ("Little Drummer Boy," set partly in Africa)
2005: *Den fjerde raneren* (*The Fourth Man*, tr. Don Bartlett)
2007: *Svart engel* ("Dark Angel")
2010: *Kvinnen i plast* ("The Faithful Friend")
2011: *Isbaderen* ("The Ice Swimmer")

Stand Alone Novel:

1998: *Siste skygge av tvil* ("Last Shadow of Doubt")

Major Awards:

2000: The Riverton Prize, for *En liten gyllen ring* (*The Last Fix*)

Website: http://www.kodahl.com; see also English miniblog: http://www.momentsincrime.com

Tor Edvin Dahl (David Torjussen)

> b. September 10, 1943, Oslo, Norway; Residence: Oslo, Norway; Occupations: translator, author of children's books (some of them are children's mysteries), short fiction, radio and television scripts, dramas and music, documentaries and textbooks, and crime fiction.

One of the most prolific authors in modern Norwegian publishing history, Tor Edvin Dahl has produced two police procedural series, one written between 1970 and 1985 under the pseudonym "David Torjussen" and the other from 1997 to the present under his own name.

Dahl's Norwegian publisher Gyldendal, inspired by Marcel Duhamel's famous French *La serie noire*, revolutionized the Norwegian book market in the 1960s by publishing The Black Series, quality paperback versions of classic detective fiction by Arthur Conan Doyle, Sjöwall and Wahlöö, Patricia Highsmith, Len Deighton, Dick Francis, and other widely read crime fiction authors (Nordberg). As "David Torjussen," Tor Edvin Dahl was the first Norwegian author to appear in The Black Series.

Since 1985 Dahl's new and unusual crime series has appeared under his own name, with a young female Oslo East End clergyperson named Pernille as his detective protagonist. Pernille's assistant and her "Dr. Watson" is a transvestite named Roger. Nils Nordberg finds Dahl's unusual detectives are symptomatic of the progressive development of the detective character in Norwegian crime fiction since the 1970s. Pernille's character in particular draws on Dahl's own childhood in a Pentecostal family, allowing Dahl to explore contemporary social conflicts, as in *Ett skritt fra døden* ("One Step from Death"), 2009, which is set in Namibia and dissects Norway's role vis-à-vis the development of Third World countries.

Dahl has also written two detective series for children, "Grorud Valley Vultures," 1975–1977, and "Kenneth Books," 1986–1986.

Crime Novels (as David Torjussen):

1973: *Etterforskning pågår* ("Investigation Is Ongoing")

1974: *Kriminalpolitiet etterlyser* ("Crime Police Calls")

1974: *Liket i skogen* ("The Corpse in the Woods")

1974: *En kiste for Thomas Ryer* ("A Coffin for Thomas Ryer" [a Knut Gribb novel])

1975: *Ung pike funnet død* ("Young Girl Found Dead")

1975: *Sist sett søndag ettermiddag* ("Last Seen on Sunday Afternoon")

1976: *Beleiring* ("Siege")

1981: *Morderens ansikt* ("Murder's Face")

1983: *Jakt på skygger* ("Hunting the Shadows")

1984: *Døden i telefonen* ("Death in the Phone")

1985: *Gjemt i mur* ("Hidden in the Walls")

Crime Novels (as Tor Edvin Dahl):

1985: *Skjult mørke* ("Hidden Dark")

1985: *Mine skip dør aldri* ("My Ship Never Dies," with John Olav Egeland)

1997: *Døden skal vaere deres hyrde* ("Death Will Be Their Shepherd")

1999: *Døden gir tilbake* ("Death Gives Back")

2001: *Skyldig til døden* ("Owed to Death")

2009: *Ett skritt fra døden* ("One Step from Death")

2010: *Hodet ved døra* ("The Head at the Door")

Major Awards:

1973: The Nordic Council Literature Prize for mainstream novel "The Servant of God"

1973: The Riverton Prize for *Etterforskning* ("Investigation in Progress")

Website: see http://www.snl.no/Tor_Edvin_Dahl

Torkil Damhaug

b. November 8, 1958, Lillehammer, Norway; Residence: Lofoten, Norway; Occupations: itinerant construction worker, psychiatrist, author

Damhaug studied comparative literature and anthropology at the University of Bergen, and after receiving a medical degree from the University of Oslo, he worked as a psychiatric consultant at Akershus. Damhaug's writing often explores "sick minded and damaged souls" (*Modtryk*).

German reviewer Jörg Kijanski praises *Se meg, Medusa*, 2008 ("See Me, Medusa"; its 2010

German edition carries a title that translates to English as "The Bear Claw"), for Damhaug's masterful use of red herrings to complicate his unusual plot. In this novel, Oslo's Police Commissioner Viken faces the near-simultaneous killings of three women in central Oslo, apparently clawed to death by a bear—but since the closest bear park is 150 kilometers away at Hemsedal, one of Viken's beleaguered detectives wryly suggests that perhaps the bear took the bus. Because the famous physician Alex Glenne knew all the victims, he appears to be the prime suspect and tries to flee from the police, while his wife Bie believes Glenne thinks the killer is his identical twin brother, whom Glenne has not seen in over twenty years. This novel was nominated for the best Norwegian thriller of 2007.

A shocking and horrific opening of *Døden ved vann* ("Death by Water"), 2009, a psychological thriller, introduces the story of Liss Bjerke, a protagonist eerily resembling Stieg Larsson's Lisbeth Salander. At first, Liss inhabits the superficially glamorous Amsterdam "modeling" scene, rife with cocaine and quasi-pornographic photo shoots. When her sister Mailin, a psychologist, goes missing in Oslo, Liss, who herself has a touchy relationship with the police, leaves her clingy girlfriend and returns to that city, spiraling into a nightmarish world of unscrupulous psychiatrists and their troubled clients, making for a haunting novel that several Norwegian critics found hard to put down.

When Damhaug won the 2011 Riverton Prize for his psychological thriller *Ildmannen* ("Arsonist"), the awards committee observed that this complicated novel's universe is "excruciatingly painful, strong, and not least, current," because its theme parallels Anders Behring Breivik's real-life massacre in Norway. This novel first presents the 1970s story of a young Pakistani immigrant who works on an Oslo-vicinity horse farm and falls in love with the owner's daughter. Then Damhaug explores the obsession of an arsonist in Lillestrøm at Easter 2003, a man who sees flames as cleansing agents to erase everything that recalls his own troubled youth. At the same time, teenaged Karsten falls in love with Jasmeen, his classmate; and her Muslim family explodes, setting off a violent cultural clash. For protection from the Muslims, Karsten joins a dangerous secret nationalistic group, then disappears and never returns. Seven years later, his younger sister Synne, the novel's major protagonist, attempts to uncover Karsten's fate, rousing sinister consequences by re-igniting the arsonist's dormant pyromaniac activities at a time when many Norwegians are feeling increased resentment toward non–Scandinavian immigrants. The vengeful serial arsonist burns the farm and many of its horses.

Danish crime critic Bo Tao Michaelis finds *Ildmannen* "eerily realistic" and deplores the "completely insane" forces in Norway who he feels will stop at nothing to achieve neo–Nazi goals, "an intolerant monocultural sublimation, dressed from top to toe in a chauvinistic national costume." Michaelis also lauds *Ildmannen* as evidence that probably "Norway is the most innovative and original country of Nordic crime literature." The novel's citation for the 2011 Riverton Prize praises Damhaug's ability to convey the pain suffered by those of non–Scandinavian ethnicity who grow up in Norway, and the exploitation of the young, the neglected, and those who accept responsibility and its often concomitant stresses.

Interest in Damhaug's fiction appears to be spreading beyond Scandinavia. In April 2013, the British publishing firm Headline signed four of Damhaug's novels. Headline's publishing director Imogen Taylor and editor Flora Rees bought world English-language rights, with release of translations of these crime thrillers scheduled for 2014 and 2015.

Crime Novels:

    1996: *Flykt, måne* ("Flight")
    1999: *Syk rose* ("The Sick Rose")

2006: *Overlord* ("Overlord")
2008: *Se meg, Medusa* ("See Me, Medusa"; the English translation of its 2009 German title is "The Bear Claw")
2009: *Døden ved vann* ("Death by Water")
2011: *Ildmannen* ("The Arsonist")

Major Awards:

2011: Riverton Prize for *Ildmannen* ("Arsonist")

Website: http://www.pluto/no/doogie/volapuk/mk.kveld/Damhaug_Torkil.htm

Tom Egeland

> b. July 8, 1959, Oslo, Norway; Residence: N/A; Occupations: television journalist and producer, novelist

Tom Egeland likes to pose well-presented contemporary problems against ancient riddles in exotic settings. He introduced an unusual detective pair in *Trollspeilet* ("Troll Mirror," 1997), youthful TV personality Kristin Bye and much older Gunnar Borg, a retired journalist, who share a father-daughter type of relationship neither consciously recognizes. They also feature in Egeland's *Åndebrettet* ("The Ouija Board," 2004), a classic murder mystery in which Bye, Borg, and a psychic, Victoria Underhaug, go to Juvdal in Telemark so that they can solve a twenty-five-year-old double murder case before it is permanently closed. *Ulvenatten* ("The Night of the Wolf," 2005), deals with Chechen terrorists who take a television studio hostage. This novel premiered in Norway as a feature movie in 2009 and became a three-episode television miniseries there in 2010. Egeland also appeared as an extra in *Star Wars V*, playing a rebel soldier fighting in the Battle of Hoth.

Beyond Norway, Egeland is probably better known for his "ancient riddle" novels. The publication of Egeland's fourth novel *Sirkelens ende*, 2001 (*Relic*, tr. 2010), preceded Dan Brown's *The Da Vinci Code* by two years, and critics have observed many similarities in the two novels. Egeland acknowledges this, noting in particular that both novels employ an hypothetical last living descendent of Jesus and Mary Magdalene as each novel's female protagonist, a result of the two authors using similar sources, in particular the controversial nonfiction study *Holy Blood, Holy Grail.*

Relic and *Paktens voktere*, 2007 (*The Guardians of the Covenant*, tr. 2009), share the same main character, the albino modern-day archaeologist Bjørn Beltø, who pursues cryptic clues in his hunt for ancient manuscripts and an Egyptian mummy. From a prologue briefly presenting a fatally poisoned unknown Egyptian personage, the plot abruptly shifts to an old Viking, nearly blind, laboriously writing his memoirs about his service to his king by flickering candlelight in an eerie monastery. Though Egeland frequently shifts between time frames, he mainly focuses on Beltø, who journeys to strange locales like remote Icelandic churches and caves, Roman ruins, and sites of Egyptian antiquities, where he meets enigmatic characters bent on murdering him to keep him from finding the mummy's secret. Writing in *EuroCrime* for September 2009, Amanda Gillies found *Guardians of the Covenant* "fascinating," because "it tantalizingly drip-feeds you tasty morsels of information" that take considerable time to piece together (Gillies).

Egeland's *Lucifers evangelium* ("The Gospel of Lucifer"), 2009, which won the Riverton Prize, according to Egeland's official website explores theories of creation, centering on how the human myths of heaven and hell were created and bringing together such disparate elements as the Dead Sea Scrolls, the Viking king Harald Hardrade, and ET. Egeland's three major characters, archaeologist Bjørn Beltø, Italian demonologist Giovanni Nobile, and American scientist Carl Collins work toward an unusual explanation of the identity of Satan and the nature of evil through a search of the ruins of the legendary Tower of Babel, Egeland's metaphor for human civilization. Egeland continued his Beltø series of historical secrets and modern intrigue with *Den 13. Disippel* ("The Thirteenth Disciple"), 2014, in which an Israeli archaeologist finds a hitherto unexplored tomb holding a tantalizing secret, but the scientist is soon killed and the Israeli military re-seals the tomb, an irresistible situation for Bjørn Beltø.

Egeland also approached the young adult audience and extended his absorption with history and the occult in his YA thriller *Katakombens hemmelighet* ("The Secret of the Catacombs"), 2013, which combines Roman myths with Viking raids. The novel's teenage Norwegian protagonist Robert faces some lethal consequences of archaeology when he discovers footprints not his own as he seeks to escape from an eerie catacomb far beneath the streets of Rome, allowing Egeland again to pose issues of religion and fanaticism in an exotic setting.

Crime Novels and Thrillers:

   1988: *Stien mot fortiden* ("Ragnarok")
   1993: *Skyggelandet* ("Shadowland")
   1997: *Trollspeilet* ("Troll Mirror")
   2001: *Sirkelens ende* (*Relic: The Quest for the Golden Shrine*, tr. Tara Chace, 2010)
   2004: *Åndebrettet* ("The Ouija Board")
   2005: *Ulvenatten* ("Night of the Wolf")
   2007: *Paktens voktere* (*The Guardians of the Covenant*, tr. Kari Dickson, 2009)
   2009: *Lucifers evangelium* ("The Gospel of Lucifer")
   2010: *Fedrenes løgner* ("The Lies of the Fathers")
   2012: *Nostradamus testamente* ("The Testament of Nostradamus")
   2014: *Den 13. disippel* ("The Thirteenth Disciple")

Young Adult Thriller:

   2013: *Katakombens hemmelighet* ("The Secret of the Catacombs")

Major Awards:

   2009: The Riverton Prize, for *Lucifers evangelium* ("The Gospel of Lucifer")

Websites: http://www.tomegeland.com; http://www2/aschehaug.no/lf/aschehougagency/innhold.php?artlD=53

Torolf Elster

   b. May 27, 1911 in Oslo, Norway; d. November 4, 2006, Oslo; Residences: Various; Occupations: newspaper and radio journalist, editor; Director-General of the Norwegian Broadcasting Corporation, 1972–1981.

Elster, a member of the Norwegian Communist movement *Mot Dag*, fled from Norway to Sweden during Norway's Nazi occupation. While in Stockholm, he edited the underground newspaper *Håndslag* with Eivind Johnson and Willy Brandt. During the Nazi occupation *Håndslag* was distributed illegally in Norway, by 1945 appearing to be about 20,000 copies.

Elster's *Historien om Gottlob*, 1941 ("The Story of Gottlob"), a strongly anti-fascist novel, placed fourth on *Dagbladet*'s 25 Best Norwegian Crime Novels, 2009. *Dagbladet* considers *Historien om Gottlob* is one of very few Norwegian psychological thrillers to attain international stature. Its protagonist is one Johan Gottlob, an indecisive banker in the fearful world of 1939. In a lifeboat in the North Sea after the ship on which he is escaping from Norway has struck a mine are seven despairing, angst-ridden characters each with a dramatic story to tell, like Gottlob himself, who has embezzled from his bank. In this restricted setting, a little world of its own, truth is evasive and reality is constantly shifting its appearance. As a series of 1969 radio plays, "The Story of Gottlob" enjoyed considerable success.

Elster's 42 other published books include his first novel, a crime story called "*Wall*," 1936, published under the pen name "Hans Brückenberg," treating "the Nazi hell." Critic Johan Borgen has called it the best political thriller written in the Nordic region and one of the most driven psychoanalytical novels of its time (Borgen). Elster also wrote "Adam's Journey"; a series about one Charles Johansen, a retired Chief of Detectives; and a final crime novel, "There Were Three Things," written when Elster was 86. From 1954 to 1963 Elster wrote for *Arbeiderbladet* and produced several nonfiction political works. His adventure novel *Thomas Pihls annen lov* ("Thomas Pihl's Other Law"), 1996, focused on intelligence gathering. Elster began his employment with the Norwegian Broadcasting Corporation in 1963 and served as its Director General from 1972 to 1981.

Selected Crime Novels:

1941: *Historien om Gottlob* ("The Story of Gottlob").
1981: *Thomas Pihls annen lov* ("Thomas Pihl's Other Law")

Major Awards:

1982: The Riverton Prize, for *Thomas Pihls annen lov* ("Thomas Pihl's Other Law").

Website: N/A

Thomas Enger

b. 1973, Oslo, Norway; Residence: Oslo, Norway; Occupations: journalist, composer, author

Enger claimed to Barry Forshaw that both he himself and his hero Henning Juul are products of their environment, introverted men who possess a powerful quintessentially Norwegian sense of "responsibility and injustice" (Forshaw 99). Like many of his fellow Norwegian crime and thriller authors, Enger is as concerned with his country's societal problems as he is with its crimes. His Norwegian publisher Gyldendal described his first novel, *Skinndød,* 2010 (*Burned,* tr. 2011), as probably "the best crime novel manuscript we've ever received from a new author" (quoted in Scandinoir.com).

Enger's Henning Juul series arose from his own literary disappointments. In "How Did I Become an Author," a revealing blog statement posted in July 2012, Enger addressed the fascination with words that he has felt since childhood. He confessed something was "ignited" for him in eighth or ninth grade when he set down on paper his dream of starring with Michael Jackson in *Moonwalker,* feeling a "rush of emotions" as he wrote. A little later he picked up a crime novel and devoured it in three or four days. After that, he says, he "was hooked."

After two unpublished attempts at a novel and a degree in journalism earned at the University of Stavanger, Enger returned to Oslo in 1997, first studying history at the university and then working as a journalist. During the Easter holiday of 2005, an idea popped into his head and he couldn't let go of it; he "wrote like crazy, day and night," ten pages a day, in addition to his job and the family responsibilities he had by now acquired. He quit working to finish this novel, but after Aschehaug, a leading Oslo publishing firm, rejected it, Enger was for a while convinced he "simply wasn't good enough" (quoted in "How Did I Become an Author").

Enger then developed a new idea involving a savagely wounded character named Henning Juul. Soul-searching, Enger says, taught him that he had been making mistakes that had doomed his earlier attempts: he now would write about characters he knew intimately and cities he knew well, and plan carefully before writing. Dedicated to these goals, in the summer of 2009, encouraged by two other Oslo publishers, Enger received a contract from Gyldendal for a crime series featuring Henning Juul, a crime reporter who was devastatingly damaged in both mind and body by a fire which destroyed his home and killed his son. Juul cannot remember the events which led up to the disaster, but he is convinced it was arson, and once back at work, though still shaky, he pursues lead after lead to find those responsible.

After fifteen years of trying, Enger thus became a published novelist, and now he believes he is living his boyhood dream. By 2012 his first Juul novel, *Skinndød*, 2010 (*Burned*, tr. 2011) was being sold in 21 countries, allowing Enger to travel abroad talking about Henning Juul's fictitious world, stressing an overwhelmingly optimistic message: "Don't give up. Don't you ever give up." By continuing the Henning Juul series, he is carrying out his intention of making "the same narrative impact as the popular Nordic TV series, like *The Killing* and *The Bridge*" (Creer). Enger plans a series of at least six novels featuring Henning Juul, and the film rights for the first six have been purchased by the Norwegian film company 4½.

Inspired by the fiction of Henning Mankell and Harlan Coben, *Burned* involves an apparent *sharia* honor killing of a young woman in Norway, allowing Enger to explore religious fundamentalism and interracial tensions. Enger observed in a 2012 interview with Adrian Magson that Juul, scarred badly both physically and emotionally, returned to his job as a crime reporter two years after that fatal fire. That same day a young woman was found in a solitary tent, half-buried and stoned to death, with whiplashes across her back. One of her hands had been cut off. The police made an early arrest of a Muslim man, but Juul does not believe they apprehended the right person. In the face of discouragement and derision from his old journalist colleagues, the police, and his ex-wife, who is now in a relationship with the reporter Juul is assigned to work with on the story, Juul pursues the story, whizzing around Oslo on his Vespa to probe a case that puts his own life at risk. Enger says he finds himself "fascinated and impressed" by people like Henning Juul "who manage to keep things going, to pick up the pieces of their lives, even after experiencing the worst things imaginable" (quoted in Magson).

Fantomsmerte, 2011 (*Pierced*, tr. 2012), second in the Juul series, treats organized crime in Norway. Convinced that the fire that scarred him for life and killed his son was a case of arson, Juul is contacted by Tore Pulli, a gang enforcer now in jail for killing a rival gangster boss, though he insists he is innocent of that crime. Pulli offers Juul a deal he can't refuse: find out who murdered the boss and free Pulli, and Pulli will tell Juul everything he knows about the fatal fire—but shortly thereafter, Pulli is killed in prison. Plunging into the sordid Oslo criminal underworld of bodybuilding gyms and professional killers to solve both murders, Juul observes, "Norway is an attractive country for criminal gangs because we're an affluent nation … with a chronically understaffed police force" (quoted in Creer).

The Norwegian media responded just as enthusiastically to Enger's third novel, *Blodtåke*, 2013 ("Mist of Blood"), released as *Scarred* in the United States in 2014. Norway's *Bokklubben* hailed it as "well crafted" and "multilayered," and *Tronder-Avisa* claimed that Enger "cuts through the chase in credible everyday life in Oslo." In this thriller, Henning Juul is caught up simultaneously in two high profile cases. In one brutal homicide, a vengeful killer slays an elderly woman in an Oslo nursing home while at the same time Juul's sister Trine Juul-Osmundsen, Norway's

Secretary of State, is accused of sexually harassing a young male politician; as a result she receives anonymous threats demanding that she resign. The two cases eventually intersect, allowing Enger to denounce what he feels is Norway's shoddy treatment of its elderly as he continues Juul's search for those responsible for his own tragedy. In all three of these novels, suffering Henning Juul's appeal remains simply this: despite all of his challenges and adversities, like his creator Thomas Enger, Juul never gives up.

According to Enger's website, his plans for filming the Henning Juul series came to fruition in 2013, when the famous Danish screenwriter Stefan Jaworski, whose successes included the crime series *Anna Pihl*, adapted *Burned* for film, with Kristoffer Jonas starring as the tormented Henning Juul.

Earlier Enger had announced on his website that his new young adult stand-alone novel *Den onde arven* ("The Evil Legacy") would appear in Norwegian bookstores in September 2013. Enger intended this novel for an audience he described as children from 12 to 100, with a sixteen-year-old heroine Julie, bullied at school and befriended by only her cat—until when she begins to probe her family's sinister secrets her cat becomes afraid of her and thirteen ravens began to spy on Julie's every move. Enger described this novel as 10 percent fantasy, 70 percent thriller, and 20 percent crime—therefore, he claimed, it was 100 percent suspense.

Crime Novels:

2010: *Skinndød* (*Burned*, tr. Charlotte Barslund, 2011)
2011: *Fantomsmerte* (*Pierced*, tr. Charlotte Barslund, 2012; also titled "Phantom Pain")
2012: *Blodtåke* (*Scarred*, tr. Charlotte Barslund, 2014)

Planned Novels in the Series (tentative titles):

2013: *Den onde arven* ("Killer Ants")
2014: *Våpenskjold* ("Quick and Dead")
2015: *Banesår* ("Revelation")

Stand Alone Young Adult Novel:

2013: *Den onde arven* ("The Evil Legacy")

Major Awards:

2013: Petrona Award for *Fantomsmerte* (*Pierced*)
2014: The Riverton Prize (Best Crime Novel of the Year), for *Blodtåke* (*Scarred*)

Website: http://www.thomasenger.net

Jon Ewo (Jon Tore Halvorsen)

b. June 29, 1957, Oslo, Norway; Residence: Oslo, Norway; Occupations: author of adult and children's literature, librarian

Ewo's *oeuvre* includes mostly children's books and young adult books, but he also has produced three near-future crime novels set in Oslo and featuring Alex Hoel, an underworld hitman.

On his website, Ewo claims he has read several thousand crime novels. Between 1991 and 1994 he wrote eight crime stories with Robert Wood for magazines like *All Men* and *Criminal Records*. When an editor asked Ewo to write a book-length thriller, Ewo says he refused to write about private detectives because they gave him "a rash." Instead, he spent the next year or so producing *Torpedo* ("Torpedo"), 1996, which views Oslo's criminal underworld "from the inside out," a gangster culture that *Crime Forum* for February 9, 2013, noted "one would never guess [exists] in a country like Norway." In this novel, Ewo's protagonist Alex Hoel shuttles between the Russian mafia and the Yugoslav gang in a laconic, fast-paced narrative that Ewo describes as all about "a manhunt, power, and big money." Because he was concentrating on portraying the Oslo underworld as realistically as possible, Ewo interviewed several real-life "torpedoes," whom he unexpectedly found were "not real bullies" but smart, well-spoken, and discriminating men. Though Ewo does not celebrate them as heroes, he refuses to treat them as brutal monsters, either in "Torpedo" or in his two novels which followed it. In *Hevn. Torpedo II* ("Revenge. Torpedo II"), 1997, Alex Hoel, attempting now to go straight as a bar owner, finds himself entangled in the case of a serial killer who preys on motorcyclists. In *Gissel* ("Hostage"), 1998, the last of Ewo's Torpedo series, Hoel has to rescue his friend Jamil Rahman, kidnapped and held hostage by a neo–Nazi group. Ewo's fictional Oslo has become a hub for drugs, alcohol, and power, a Norwegian criminal reality that he claims will only get larger as former Eastern European mobs increase their numbers in Scandinavia.

Crime Novels:

> 1996: *Torpedo* ("Torpedo")
> 1997: *Hevn. Torpedo II* ("Revenge")
> 1998: *Gissel* ("Hostage")

Young Adult Crime Fiction:

> 2007: *Fortellingen om et mulig drap* ("The Story of a Possible Murder")

Major Awards:

> 2007: The Brage Prize for *Fortellingen om et mulig drap* ("The Story of a Possible Murder")

Website: N/A

Knut Faldbakken

> b. August 31, 1941, Oslo, Norway; grew up in Hamar, Norway; Residence: N/A; Occupation: journalist and author, studied psychology at the University of Oslo and worked at various occupations in Europe

Faldbakken, a highly prolific and popular novelist, also edited the literary journal *Vinduet* (*The Window*) from 1975 to 1979. Although often criticized as a sensationalist and an opportunist, Faldbakken combines sexually shocking subject matter with powerful ethical earnestness (DLB 297, 74). As a prominent male author who espouses feminist issues and examines men's changing gender roles (DLB 297, xxi), Faldbakken also makes his fiction reflect the Norwegian realist tradition that began in the 1870s, which he extrapolated into unusually frank portrayals of unconventional sexual relationships such as incest. Faldbakken's novels often use crime as a springboard for, counterpoint of, or result of unconventional sexuality, as in *Maude danser*, 1971 (*The Sleeping Prince*, tr. 1988), and his two-volume near-future novel *Famine*, nominated for the Norwegian Literary Prize and comprised of *Uår: Aftenlandet,* 1974 (*Twilight Country,* tr. 1993) and *Uår: Sweetwater*, 1976 (*Sweetwater*, tr. 1994). His trilogy *Når jeg ser deg* ("When I See You"), 1996; *Eksil* ("Exile"), 1997; and *Alt hva hjertet begjærer* ("All That the Heart Desires"), 1999, centers on the ramifications of the murder of a wife's young lover by her husband, a former homicide detective. Faldbakken's books, published in 21 countries and translated into 18 languages, have sold over two million copies worldwide.

Though maintaining his interest in abnormal psychology, Faldbakken significantly shifted literary genres with his debut crime novel *Alle elsker en hodeløs kvinne* ("Everyone Loves a Headless Woman"), 2002. He then produced a police procedural series featuring fortyish Superintendent Jonfinn Valmann of the Hamar police force. According to Gyldendal, Faldbakken's Norwegian publisher, this series follows Valmann's progress after losing his wife three years earlier, to falling in love again and moving in with Anita Hegg, a policewoman. In each novel of this series, Valmann has to solve crimes involving abnormal psychology while coping with serious sexual and emotional problems in his personal life. In *Turneren* ("The Gymnast"), 2004, Valmann experiences sexual frustration while investigating a savage rape-homicide. In *Grensen* ("The Border"), 2005, he exhibits the loneliness of middle-aged widowerhood as he probes a case involving an East European prostitute. In *Nattefrost* ("Night Frost"), 2006, he struggles with tensions between himself and his police superior Gertrude Moen; and in *Tyvene* ("The Thieves"), 2007, Valmann strives to learn how to build a new relationship between himself and Anita Hegg. *Senskade* ("Late Damage"), 2008, explores intense jealousy; *Totem* ("Totem"), 2009, treats the stresses of single motherhood; and *Natthagen* ("The Night Garden"), 2011, deals with severe psychological aberrations. The jury which awarded Faldbakken the Brage Prize in 2012 concluded, "Faldbakken researches the darkest sides of mankind. He does so with great insight and an uncanny boldness."

Novels with Strongest Crime Elements:

1971: *Maude danser* (*The Sleeping Prince*, tr. Janet Garton, 1988)
1974: *Uår: Aftenlandet* (*Twilight Country*, tr. Joan Tate, 1993).
1976: *Uår: Sweetwater* (*Sweetwater*, tr. Joan Tate, 1994)
1980: *E 18* ("Highway 18")
1996: *Når jeg ser deg* ("When I See You")
1997: *Eksil* ("Exile")
1999: *Alt hva hjertet begjærer* ("All That the Heart Desires")
2002: *Alle elsker en hodeløs kvinne* ("Everyone Loves a Headless Woman")

The Jonfinn Valmann Novels:

2004: *Turneren* ("The Gymnast")
2005: *Grensen* ("The Border")
2006: *Nattefrost* ("Night Frost")
2007: *Tyvene* ("The Thieves")
2008: *Senskade* ("Late Damage")
2009: *Totem* ("Totem")
2011: *Natthagen* ("The Night Garden")

Major Awards:

2012: The Brage Prize

Website: See http://www.gyldendal.no/Forfattere/Faldbakken-Knut

Kjartan Fløgstad

b. June 7, 1944, Sauda, Norway; Residence: Various; Occupations: poet and novelist

After studying literature and linguistics at the University of Bergen, Fløgstad worked in industry and as a sailor before publishing *Valfart* ("Pilgrimage"), a volume of poems, in 1968, the first of his more than thirty books. His lifelong Marxist orientation appeared in his first published prose work, *Fangliner* ("Ropes"), 1970. His subsequent novels, satirical socialist critiques of Norway's contemporary society (*Dictionary of Literary Biography* 297: 94), traced Norway's economic and social changes in its transition from an agricultural culture to an industrialized one, later becoming a post-industrial society. Because of Fløgstad's conviction that the use of English endangers his beloved Norwegian dialects, he fervently championed the use of *nynorsk*, Norway's minority language form which its proponents consider more expressive than *bokmål*, the majority form of the language. Flogstad's prose style involves allusion, plays on words, and magic realism, where he combines fantasy elements with realistic plots. He is highly critical of capitalism and the mass media, which he believes have transformed serious social commentary into mere entertainment (*Dictionary of Literary Biography* 297: 90).

Many critics consider Fløgstad one of Norway's most influential authors and "a mordant social critic ... [with] a strong sense of solidarity with the oppressed." His most celebrated mainstream novel, *Dalen Portland*, 1978 (*Dollar Road*, tr. 1978), severely indicts Mobil Oil's exploitation of Norway's petroleum resources (Norseng), and his widely praised mainstream novel *Grense Jakobselv* ("Crossing the River Jacob"), 2009, treats worldwide ideological power struggles, focusing on what World War II changed and left unchanged (*World Literature Today*). Fløgstad wrote two crime novels, generally considered of lesser quality than his mainstream work, publishing them under pseudonyms.

Crime Novels (written under the names "K. Villun" and "K. Villum"):

1975: *Døden ikke heller* ("Death Without End"), as "K. Villum"
1976: *Ein for alle* ("One for All"), as "K. Villun"

Major Awards (all for non-crime novels):

1978: The Nordic Council Literature Prize, for *Dalen Portland* (*Dollar Road*, tr. Nadia M. Christensen, 1978)
1983: Nynorsk Literature Prize, for *U3* ("U3")
1986: Nynorsk Literature Prize, for *Det 7, klima* ("The Seventh Climate")

Website: N/A

*Karin Fossum

b. November 6, 1954, Sandefjord, Norway; Residence: Southeastern Norway; Occupation: novelist

Karin Fossum, hailed by London's *Times* as one of the "50 Greatest Crime Writers" and Norway's latest "Queen of Crime," according to Nils Nordberg is one of the greatest stylists of today's Norwegian crime fiction, producing soul-shattering psychological mysteries (Nordberg). Fossum began writing as a teenager, inspired by the procedural novels of Sjöwall and Wahlöö and her long-time favorite English author Ruth Rendell (quoted in Forshaw 111), and since then she has drawn upon varied adult work experiences, including those as a psychiatric ward aide and a taxi driver. Fossum herself has lived in a small Norwegian village of about 2,000 and sets her fiction in similar small Norwegian towns and rural areas. She claims that she could never write a novel set in a big city, because she doesn't know what it would be like (quoted in Forshaw 112). Fossum's small town and rural settings and her characters, often described in connection with images of familiar foods tied "to the fields and farm tables of the region," recall similar elements of Agatha

Christie's sharp-edged Miss Marple cozies (Mogk 22, 23). Like Christie, Fossum slowly reveals the horrors lurking just beneath apparently serene surfaces, like lethal bacteria swarming in a quiet rural pond, unseen by the naked eye. Fossum's plots, however, are generally more disturbing than Christie's; Fossum's English translator, Charlotte Barslund describes Fossum's plots as "slow-burning," climaxing in "a devastating emotional punch" (quoted in Forshaw 103).

Fossum's award-winning series featuring Inspector Konrad Sejer and his assistant Inspector Jakob Skarre has been published in over thirty countries (Forshaw 109). Sejer is a middle-aged widower with one adult daughter, the unusual hobby of parachute jumping, and some of Fossum's own interests, like music and whisky. She has said she deliberately made Sejer both ethical and appealing, a "kind and serious" 1950s–1960s television hero, "decent and good" (quoted in Forshaw 111). Critic Kevin O'Kelly believes Sejer's personal life itself could "make a novel," one whose ordinary but heart-wrenching daily trials are shared by many readers today. Sejer still mourns his dead wife, he worries about not visiting his aged mother more, he anguishes over the many hours each of his successive dogs has had to spend alone at home because of Sejer's police work, and he "watches helplessly as his son-in-law's [medical] career takes his daughter and grandson to another country" (O'Kelly 7).

A lonely man whose headquarters is in Drammen, south of Oslo, Sejer somewhat resembles Martin Beck, the "serious and self-lacerating" homicide detective created by Sjöwall and Wahlöö (Murphy 32). Sejer even named the dog who appears in his earlier novels "Kollberg," a playful reference to Lennert Kollberg, the self-isolated Beck's closest friend on the police force, an uncomplicated, sensual fellow (Nordberg). The highly intelligent and melancholy Sejer's emotional reserve and his capacity for deep and passionate feeling reflects "Fossum's Norwegian landscape itself" (Mogk 24).

Fossum's novels often involve helpless victims. Sometimes they are children, either innocents victimized by predators, or adolescents stripped of morality by societal shortcomings, or young single mothers whom society has oppressed. Her first Sejer novel, *Evas øye*, 1995 (*Eva's Eye*, tr. 2012), centers on Eva Magnus, a young divorced mother raising her seven-year-old daughter Emma. On a walk one wintry day they glimpse a body floating in the icy river, and Eva, though she pretends to call the police, actually phones her father. Although Fossum's Inspector Sejer has by now become familiar to her readers, in this early novel he takes second place to Eva, who develops from a struggling artist and single mother into a new and unpredictable personality who becomes Sejer's prime suspect in an involved murder investigation. The Norwegian film adaptation of *Eva's Eye* starring Bjørn Sundquist as Sejer was released in 2013.

In her subsequent Sejer novels, Fossum broadens her protagonist's character and deepens his appeal. Sejer acquires a female friend, a psychologist, in *Den som frykter ulven*, 1997 (*He Who Fears the Wolf*, tr. 2005), where Sejer witnesses a broad-daylight bank robbery that turns into a volatile hostage situation. Sejer initially blames himself for not having acted earlier even though he had suspected Errka Johrma, a severely troubled schizophrenic, of being a serial killer, but in one of Fossum's eerie twists of fictional fate, Johrma turns out to be one of the hostages.

Fossum's 1998 novel *Djevelen holder lyset* (*When the Devil Holds the Candle*, tr. 2004), expands her trademark technique of pitting Sejer's decency and intelligence against mindless violence, in this case carried out by bored and vicious adolescents that society by default allows to prey upon the helpless. The novel opens on an all-too-possible police mistake made by Sejer's assistant Jacob Skarre: he fails to understand sixtyish recluse Irma Funder when she attempts to relate the whereabouts of Andreas, a narcissistic dissolute teenager who has recently gone missing. From that apparently simple official error, Fossum develops a brutal crescendo of crime with an unexpected and gruesome finale. A few days earlier, Andreas and Zipp, his only friend, had first harassed a

Somali boy, who they don't know is Inspector Sejer's adopted grandson. The teenagers then decide to mug someone defenseless and choose a young mother pushing a baby carriage with her purse over the handle. In the ensuing scuffle for the purse, the baby disastrously falls out of the carriage and Andreas and Zipp run off to drink up their ill-gotten gains. They then stalk Irma, who was walking back from the theater. The boys split up when they reach her house, with Zipp staying outside. Andreas enters and tries to rob Irma, but she shoves him down the cellar steps. A peculiar relationship develops between Andreas, now a paralyzed captive, and his captor, the disturbed Irma. Finally Sejer unravels Irma's deadly secrets in the novel's last harrowing pages. Though several critics feel Fossum unaccountably telegraphs Andreas' fate "much too early," Fossum nevertheless chillingly illustrates how seemingly random acts of violence can force "so many lives to intersect in so many horrifying ways" (Stasio 2006, 23).

Entertainment Weekly called *Elskede Poona*, 2000 (*The Indian Bride*, tr. 2007, also titled in English *Calling Out for You*), "a Nordic Sherlock Holmes story, with characters by Bergman and blood by Tarantino," conveying heartbreaking compassion for both lonesome Norwegian men, isolated by circumstance and culture, and South Asian women caught in the ambivalent position of being strangers in a land that legally must accept them but then psychologically and sometimes even physically destroys them. Fossum personalizes Norway's increasing unease with its immigrant population through her protagonist Gunder Jomann, a bachelor tractor dealer, who shocks "the good people" of the small town of Elvestad by traveling to India and returning a married man. After two weeks, on the day his bride is supposed to arrive, the gruesomely murdered body of an Indian woman is discovered in the outskirts of the town. Sejer handles the case with his usual sympathetic aplomb, allowing Fossum to tacitly deplore the treatment of immigrants in today's Norway. *The Indian Bride* was ranked first on *Dagbladet*'s 2009 list of best Norwegian crime novels of all time.

Fossum's *Svarte sekunder*, 2002 (*Black Seconds*, tr. 2005), is considered one of her finest works. Fiona Walker observed, "sad simplicity adds to the strange power of her novels, with their achingly realistic crimes and their achingly realistic victims, their relatives and neighbors" (Fiona Walker, in *EuroCrime*, http://www.eurocrime.co.uk/, July 2007). Fossum's somewhat predictable plot focuses on Ida Joner, a sweet ten-year-old, who disappears one day while riding her new yellow bicycle to a store for candy. A few days after a desperate search fails to locate her, her body is found next to a well-traveled road. Fossum describes the child's disappearance as a net that draws all the villagers together in suffering. She depicts Ida's depressed mother Helga as distraught over losing her idolized daughter; Ruth, Helga's sister, as herself agonizing over her sullen and antisocial son Tomme; and embittered Else Marie Mork, as fearing the worst for Emil, her sadly retarded fifty-year-old son. Sejer patiently unravels the crime against a convincing backdrop of pain-filled village characters, using his innate compassion to break through their protective secrets and lies (Stasio 2008, 25).

Drapet på Harriet Krohn, 2004 (*The Murder of Harriet Krohn*, tr. 2014), Fossum's seventh Sejer novel, uses the unusual plot device of a first-person narrator who is a murderer known to readers as such from the start. He is Charles Olav Torp, a former car salesman, a compulsive gambler owing an enormous sum of money to a former friend. Torp inveigles his way into the life and home of an elderly woman, with a subsequent brutal homicide that shakes even Sejer and Skarre.

The unsavory subject of pedophilia makes *Den som elsker noe annet*, 2007 (*The Water's Edge*, tr. 2009), Fossum's eighth Sejer novel, one of her less palatable works. On a walk in the forest one day, Kristine and Reinhardt, who have been married long enough not to hold hands any more, find the body of Jonas August Løwe, eight years old and apparently sexually abused. As Sejer and Skarre investigate the crime, first interviewing known local pedophiles, Kristine's marriage begins to crumble, finally disintegrating completely. Amid escalating small-town jealousies and tensions,

Sejer patiently unravels the crime, using his innate compassion to break through the villagers' protective secrets and lies (Stasio 2008, 25).

Fossum intensifies this police procedural by dissecting the motivations that draw decent men like Sejer and Skarre into police work. She makes Sejer, who had never been morbidly attracted to death or "seduced by sensation" (*The Water's Edge* 47), and Skarre, who admits to being a little jealous of criminals because they simply take what they want as a kind of protest against society (*The Water's Edge* 47), explore why "nothing sells better than murder and the worse it is, the more interested people are" (*The Water's Edge* 48). She also reveals her own opinions about the popularity of crime fiction through Sejer when he attributes the Norwegians' fascination with literary homicide to their image of their old Nazi enemy. During the Occupation, Sejer tells Skarre in *The Water's Edge*, anti–Nazi sentiment unified Norwegians and allowed them to easily discern the good from the bad; but now, Sejer claims, "in our wealthy western world where race and democracy reign," criminals have assumed the Nazis' role as enemies, so that in the midst of their vaunted societal peace and quiet, Norwegians now can feel alive through learning about heinous fictitious crimes and congratulate themselves that they, not being wrongdoers, are both morally good and lucky not to have been victimized (*The Water's Edge* 48). Then, too, Sejer wryly admits another dimension: "some criminals acquire a heroic status." He acknowledges with Fossum that Norwegians by and large are "terribly law-abiding," but "this slavish obedience in every aspect of our lives can lead to self-loathing" (*The Water's Edge* 48).

In *Den onde viljen*, 2008 (*Bad Intentions*, tr. 2010), Fossum again probes the fatal consequences of young adults' thoughtless actions in a story "of a friendship gone wrong, [and] the weight of guilt" (Simon). Three young men who have known one another since boyhood make a weekend trip to a forest cabin near a lake. The charming but sinister Axel Frimann and the "slow, meek" and fecklessly drug-addicted Philip Reilly take Jon Moreno on an overnight stay from the mental hospital where he is recovering from a guilt-induced breakdown. After Jon drowns in an ill-advised nighttime boating excursion on the lake, Axel and Reilly claim he took his own life. Sejer, now feeling his age and still hurting from memories of his own lost love, still remains sensitive to people's motivations and is as always skilled at penetrating their social masks (Simon) as he investigates Jon's apparent drowning suicide. Sejer patiently strips away the defenses of Moreno's friends Axel and Reilly, who are not so much hiding secrets as refusing to face the truth about their relationships with Moreno and the Vietnamese immigrant boy Kim Van Chau whose year-dead body was found shortly after Moreno's death. "Loyalties are tested, trust disintegrates, and off-kilter behavior takes over." Sejer, greyer now and "leaner and more lined" (*Bad Intentions* 152), fulfills his promise to Kim's mother that he would learn the truth about her son's death, while a healing friendship between Kim's mother and Jon's as they plan their own revenge "leavens this shattering tale of crime and punishment. When Sejer finally untangles the mystery, we are stunned at how possible it all seems" (Simon).

Varsleren, 2009 (*The Caller*, tr. 2010), Fossum's tenth Sejer novel, initially confronts Sejer, now fighting bouts of dizziness that he fears may presage a stroke, with cruel hoaxes that descend into wickedness he and Skarre have never seen before. A horrible event shakes the methods each detective has developed to remain calm in the face of terrifying tragedies: the tangled remains of a child found on a rural trail brutally torn to bits, Sejer discovers, by dogs. This kind and decent detective, sickened by the crime, now even sees in Frank Robert, his own pet Shar-pei, from a Chinese fighting breed, a "potential for brutality" that sickeningly shifts his imagination, Fossum relentlessly insists, "To what was raw and brutal at the heart of every living creature" (*The Caller* 211), encapsulating the message at the heart of all her novels: that the human goodness and responsibility Konrad Sejer represents eternally struggles against monstrous evil that lurks always and everywhere beneath benign-looking fairy-tale surfaces, aided and abetted by social pressures to maintain the community's appearance of normalcy and happiness.

After several years, the ultra-humane Inspector Sejer returned in *Carmen Zita og døden* ("Carmen Zita and Death") 2013, often communing with his beloved and departed wife Elise, and enjoying his one whiskey and single cigarette before he falls asleep, the faithful Frank Robert by his side. To open this case, Sejer's associate Skarre appears on the scene of a young child's drowning, which at first seems accidental. Skarre, however, finds something unsettlingly shallow about the child's mother Carmen, and in the ensuing investigation he and Sejer uncover unexpected and disquieting truths. Fossum's 2014 Sejer novel *Helvetesilden* ("Hellfire") again treats mother-child relationships, this time through two single mothers, Mass and Bonnie, and their sons from December 2004 to July of 2005. From a horrifying opening scene of a young mother and her little son stabbed to death in a tawdry old camper, Fossum steadily explores shocking grotesqueries of unnatural drives and pathological rage.

Most of Fossum's Inspector Sejer novels have been adapted as Norwegian television series, and several have been made into feature films in Scandinavia.

Fossum's 2006 stand-alone crime novel *Brudd* (*Broken*, tr. 2008), a haunting psychological suspense thriller, employs the unusual narrative device of alternating chapters told by Fossum herself as the first-person narrator, with third-person-narrated chapters in which her main character, an eccentric and isolated middle aged art gallery worker, Alvar Eide, pleased with Fossum's understanding of him. Alvar, who has never been in love, pities a teenaged heroin addict who uses and abuses him because, in trying to be "a good person," he "was taken with her frailty" (*Broken* 76). The key to Alvar's tragedy is the metaphor Fossum incorporates through Alvar's long-time yearning to buy a painting of a broken bridge. "The novel's title alludes to 'the kinds of broken lives that Karin Fossum evokes so brilliantly in her Inspector Sejer series and now in this odd, memorable book" (Lipez).

EuroCrime critic Maxine Clarke observed that in *Broken*, where Alvar and Fossum-as-narrator "are very similar in character," Fossum provides "tantalizing glimpses into the creative process as well as ... insights into the character of the author herself," who at the start of *Broken* calls herself "a tired middle-aged woman trying to keep going" (*Broken* 1) and at its close admits, "My dissatisfaction [with this novel] drives me to act, to write another book" (*Broken* 264).

Fossum's other stand-alone suspense novel, *Jeg kan se i mørket* (*I Can See in the Dark*, tr. 2014), is narrated by Riktor, an unpleasant orderly in a small Norwegian town's nursing home whose restricted life revolves around persons he sees at a local park. Fossum begins Riktor's descent into madness when he witnesses the death of a cross-country skier who falls through ice and drowns in a nearby lake. Riktor becomes obsessed by rage over the event and feeling that his world has become a wasteland, he begins to abuse his elderly patients, eventually being arrested for the murder of one of them, allowing Fossum to turn her plot inside out in one of her trademark revelations of human nature.

Crime Novels:

The Inspector Konrad Sejer Series:

1995: *Evas øye* (*In the Darkness*, tr. James Anderson, 2012)

1996: *Se deg ikke tillbake!* (*Don't Look Back*, tr. Felicity David, 2002)

1997: *Den som frykter ulven* (*He Who Fears the Wolf*, tr. Felicity David, 2005)

1998: *Djevelen holder lyset* (*When the Devil Holds the Candle*, tr. Felicity David, 2006)

2000: *Elskede Poona* (*The Indian Bride*, tr. Charlotte Barslund, 2007; previously published in the UK as *Calling Out for You*)

2002: *Svarte sekunder* (*Black Seconds*, tr. Charlotte Barslund, 2007)

2004: *Drapet på Harriet Krohn* (*The Murder of Harriet Krohn*, tr. Charlotte Barslund, 2014)

2007: *Den som elsker noe annet* (*The Water's Edge*, tr. Charlotte Barslund, 2009)

2008: *Den onde viljen* (*Bad Intentions*, tr. Charlotte Barslund, 2010)

2009: *Varsleren* (*The Caller*, tr. K.E. Semmel, 2011)

2013: *Carmen Zita og døden* ("Carmen Zita and Death")

2014: *Helvetesilden* ("Hellfire")

Stand-Alone Crime/Suspense Novels:

2006: *Brudd* (*Broken*, tr. Charlotte Barslund, 2008)

2011: *Jeg kan se i mørket* (*I Can See in the Dark*, tr. James Anderson, 2014)

Major Awards:

1996: Glass Key Award, for *Se deg ikke tillbake!* (*Don't Look Back*)

1996: Riverton Prize for *Se deg ikke tillbake!* (*Don't Look Back*)

2002: Martin Beck Award for *Svarte sekunder* (*Black Seconds*)

2007: Gumshoe Award for *Djevelen holden lyset* (*When the Devil Holds the Candle*)

2008: *Los Angeles Times* Book Prize for *Elskede Poona* (*The Indian Bride*), also shortlisted for the Crime Writers of America Golden Dagger Award in 2005.

Website: N/A

*Frode Grytten

> b. December 11, 1960, Bergen, Norway; Residence: Bergen, Norway; Occupations: journalist for *Bergens Tidende*, Bergen's local newspaper, and *Dagbladet*, Oslo-based national newspaper, poet, author of poems and children's books, adult short stories (some written in response to Edward Hopper's paintings), and novels.

Grytten addresses Norway's sociopolitical issues with globalization and immigration in his novel *Flytande bjørn* (*The Shadow in the River*, tr. 2007). According to British crime fiction critic Maxine Clarke, this is an unconventional crime story, primarily because Grytten refuses to tie its loose ends up into a tidy solution to the problems he presents. In the dying xenophobic industrial town of Odda, where Grytten grew up and which he later made the setting for several of his other works, cynical journalist Robert Bell has chosen the role of an outsider, working as a stringer for a large newspaper that regularly rejects his serious investigative feature stories. His unflappable woman editor assigns Bell to follow the case of a local teenager who is thought to have fatally driven into the local river. Though the body has not been found, Serbians living in a nearby hostel are widely suspected of murdering the boy. As Bell struggles to maintain his professional objectivity, his own problems mount, including incipient alcoholism and the tension between Bell and his brother Frank, the local police chief, caused by Robert's affair with Frank's wife Irene.

Through Robert Bell, Grytten describes his departure from traditional detective films and fiction, which he says often "start in darkness and slowly emerge into light." In reality, he feels, things at first seem "clear and comprehensible, before they descend into the murk and the mud. As the end approaches you lose all track of the plot and have no idea how it's going to end" (quoted in Clarke).

Crime Novels:

2005: *Flytande bjørn* (*The Shadow in the River*, tr. Robert Ferguson, UK, 2007)
2009: *Det norske huset* ("The Norse House")
2011: *Saganatt. Lundetrilogien* (a trilogy released as one book)

Major Awards:

2005: The Riverton Prize, for *Flytande bjørn* (*The Shadow in the River*)

Website: N/A

Jørgen Gunnerud

b. June 2, 1948, Oslo, Norway; Residence: Oslo, Norway; Occupation: author

According to *Dagbladet* critic Kurt Hansson, Jørgen Gunnerud, an active participant in the Norwegian Marxist-Leninist movement as a youth, has developed into one of Norway's most capable and most overlooked crime authors. Gunnerud's debut police procedural *Raymond Isaksens utgang*, 1994 ("Raymond Isaksen's Exit"), introduced his series protagonist, NCIS detective Kurt Moen, a competent and basically solid policeman.

Moen initially believes most Norwegian village murders occur within a group of people well known to one another, producing humdrum cases that are usually easy to solve, but his first investigation demands lengthy and complex police work which Gunnerud conveys realistically. *Raymond Isaksens utgang* placed twelfth in *Dagbladet*'s 2009 list of twenty-five best Norwegian crime novels of all time. Gunnerud's seventh crime novel, *Høstjakt* ("Autumn Hunt"), 2007, received the Riverton Prize; the jury praised Gunnerud's solid literary craftsmanship and his precise and convincing linguistic detail. Gunnerud has also published a historical novel set in the ancient Saga Age of Scandinavia, *Håvard den halte* ("Havard the Lame"), 2004.

Crime Novels:

1994: *Raymond Isaksens utgang* ("Raymond Isaksen's Exit")
1996: *Kvinnen fra Olaf Ryes plass* ("The Women from Olaf Rye's Place")
1998: *Gjerningsmann: Ukjent* ("A Criminal: Unknown")
2000: *Selvtekt* ("Taking the Law into One's Hands")
2003: *Til odel og eie* ("To the Inheritance")
2004: *Håvard den halte* ("Havard the Lame")
2006: *Djelvelen er en løgner* (The Devils Are Liars")
2007: *Høstjakt* ("Autumn Hunt")
2009: *Byen med det store hjertet* ("The City with a Big Heart")
2010: *Skje din vilje* ("Thy Will Be Done")
2012: *Mistanken* ("Suspicious")

Major Awards:

2007: The Riverton Prize, for *Høstjakt* ("Autumn Hunt")

Website: N/A

Bergljot Hobæk Haff

> b. May 1, 1925, Holmestrand, Norway; Residence: Oslo, Norway, after teaching in Denmark for 24 years; Occupations: teacher, author

In the course of her long literary career, Bergljot Hobæk Haff has received several important literary awards as one of Norway's most important storytellers. In her sixteen novels, Haff experimented with various narrative forms while concentrating on women in their roles as mothers, prostitutes, and witches. Her first novel, *Raset* ("The Landslide"), a realistic psychological study of the dilemma in which gifted women must choose between motherhood and their potential as individuals, features a talented woman pianist who realizes that her pregnancy by her power-hungry and destructive husband will doom her musical career. The husband also recognizes her tragedy: as she performs the debut recital in which she will die, he significantly comments on her "wild and completely inhuman beauty.... She looked like a witch who had mounted the pyre to be burnt" (quoted in Knudsen).

The topic of delusion and its consequences dominates Haff's 1992 crime novel *Renhetens pris* ("The Price of Purity"), which ranked twenty-second in the 2009 *Dagbladet* list of twenty-five best Norwegian crime novels of all time. According to the *Norwegian Encyclopedia*, this historical novel, based on the 16th-century Spanish Inquisition, treats the psychological conflict between pride and purity through the thoughts of Desiderius, a dying inquisitor who reminiscences about his youth, when, driven by fanatic zeal to stamp out sin in the name of God, he investigated the case of Beatriz Mendoza, a young nun who mysteriously bore a child with horns on its head, a mark of dedication to the Devil. Inger Merete Hobbeland notes in her 2009 *Dagbladet* review of this novel that it is not a traditional crime novel but a "gothic and saturated narrative" approaching melodrama, with "smoldering intensity" achieved by Haff's tracing "the rare battle that boils under the skin of the protagonists of repressed trauma, longing, lust and revenge" in a society forbidding anything but "absolute innocence and purity" to appear on its surface. Haff thus demonstrates how paranoid and hypocritical persecution by those who sit in judgment over the lives and deaths of others engenders worse crimes than do many other human failings.

Crime Novel:

1992: *Renhetens pris* ("The Price of Purity")

Major Awards:

1992 and 1996: Norwegian Critics Prize for Literature
1988: Norwegian Academy Prize

Website: N/A

Kolbjørn Hauge

> b. April 2, 1926, Kyrkjoy, Norway; d. August 15, 2007; Residence: Western Norway; Occupations: teacher, author

Hauge, one of relatively few Norwegian crime authors to write in *nynorsk*, Norway's second official language, published his first novel at age 65. He initiated an important trend in Norwegian crime fiction which helped revitalize the genre in the 1990s by setting his novels in the Western Norwegian countryside where he was born, exposing the changing lifestyle of those rural areas (Nordberg). With Magnhild Bruheim, Hauge has been among the foremost exponents of the

Norwegian literary subgenre of *bygdekrim*, regional/rural crime fiction, and *Dagbladet* critic Fredrik Vandrup has praised Hauge's "deep knowledge of the West Norwegian folk temperament." Hauge's rural police detective protagonist Petter Eliassen is a pietistic Christian, an unusual religious orientation for a modern crime investigator. Hauge himself has wryly noted that Eliassen is probably the only detective in crime fiction who says Grace before his meals.

Crime Novels:

1991: *Kofferten* ("Suitcases")
1993: *Heit juice* ("Hot Juice")
1995: *Død mann i boks* ("A Dead Man in a Box")
1997: *Til jord skal du bli* ("In Earth You Shall Remain")
1999: *Over mitt lik* ("Over with the Corpse")
2003: *Nord og ned* ("North and Down")
2004: *To perfekte mord og andre kriminelle historier* ("The Perfect Murder and Other Crime Stories")

Major Awards:

1993: Sunnmørs Prize (for the year's best *nynorsk* crime novel), for *Heit juice* ("Hot Juice")
1995: The Riverton Prize, for *Død mann i boks* ("A Dead Man in a Box")

Website: N/A

*Gaute Heivoll

b. March 13, 1978, Finsland, Norway; Residence: Various; Occupations: teacher, author

Gaute Heivoll has written in a wide range of genres, including poetry, short fiction, essays, literary criticism, lyrics for dance performances, and children's fiction. His genre-crossing semi-autobiographical crime novel *Før jeg brenner ned*, 2010 (*Before I Burn*, tr. 2013), has been translated into more than twenty languages. Heivoll was born and christened in a small Norwegian village shortly after the last of ten highly destructive fires set by an arsonist in one month, and for this novel, a gripping first-person narrative, he returned thirty years later, interviewing villagers about the arson that had terrorized them so brutally. National Public Radio critic Rosecrans Baldwin commented on January 2, 2014, that "the mystery we have to solve [in *Before I Burn*] is less about who did it than why," but since the chapters about the arsonist interweave with those about Heivoll's evolution as an author, the book is "a portrait of two young men, one an arsonist, the other an artist" (Baldwin).

Since publishing *Before I Burn*, Heivoll has continued to produce unusual fiction mixing literary genres and distinguished by "terrifically sensory" prose (Baldwin). In 2008 and 2010, Heivoll published two children's books, "Heaven Behind the House" and "The Boat Between the Stars," both dealing with death and the departed, nontraditional topics for children's literature. Heivoll's 2012 children's novel *Svalene under isen* ("Swallows Under the Ice"), shows two youngsters sharing a serious magical event. His 2013 adult historical mainstream novel *Over det kinesiske hav* ("Over the Chinese Sea"), set just after World War II and based on actual events, treats the existential issue of "otherness" by examining the period in Norway when "mentally retarded" individuals were disempowered and subjected to forced hospitalization and sterilization. In the novel, a married couple, a deacon and his wife, a nurse, take five neglected siblings into their home, which by 1945 already housed three adults who needed care and the couple's own two children, one of whom retrospectively narrates the story many years later. Even though a tragic event occurs, Heivoll's comedic touches effectively lighten this tale of grief. In 2013 Adrian Broch Jensen of *Sudvest Bergen* praised Heivoll's ability to combine real events with artistic freedom in a manner he felt few other contemporary Norwegian authors have achieved (Jensen).

Crime Novels:

2010: *Før jeg brenner ned* (*Before I Burn*, tr. Don Bartlett, 2013)

Major Awards:

2011: Sørlandets Literature Prize for *Før jeg brenner ned* (*Before I Burn*)

Website: http://www.gauteheivoll.no/forside/index.php

*Anne Holt

> b. November 16, 1958, Larvik, Norway; she grew up in Lillestrøm and Tromsø; Residence: Oslo, Norway; Occupations: lawyer, television anchor, journalist, author, Norwegian Minister of Justice, 1996–1997 (a serious illness forced Holt to step down)

Bestselling Norwegian crime novelist Anne Holt insists she writes about people, not about Scandinavia (quoted in Forshaw 114). Holt's work as a public prosecutor forced her into a traumatic confrontation with organized crime, profoundly affecting her approach to mystery fiction; she has observed, "What people are afraid of can tell us a lot about society" (quoted in Forshaw 114). In 2010, Holt pointed out differences between her style of crime writing, "more typically Scandinavian," and Stieg Larsson's: "He wrote in more of an American style; very tough, brutal stories. The rest of us who have been translated into English—Henning Mankell, Jo Nesbø, and myself— write in more of a social realistic/political way, in the [Maj] Sjöwall and [Per] Wahlöö tradition" (quoted in Davies 23). Holt has also noted that the contemporary Scandinavian crime novel involves mostly dynamic protagonists who grow older and develop as the series proceeds, as opposed to fictional British and American sleuths like Christie's Miss Marple who remain the same in all their books (quoted in DeMarco). Holt believes that the current Scandinavian literary environment considers crime writing as valid a concern for authors as serious mainstream work, which ensures "both breadth and quality" in Norwegian and Swedish crime fiction (quoted in DeMarco).

Holt's own fiction exhibits a clear-eyed view of Norway and Norwegians. In her 2007 novel, *1222* (*1222*, tr. 2011), her heroine Hanne Wilhemsen forthrightly describes the characteristic attitude of her fellow passengers, stranded by a train wreck during a ferocious snowstorm, toward the staff of a remote hotel, who are trying hard to make their unexpected guests comfortable: "We [the passengers] really were an ungrateful lot. We really were Norwegians, the majority of us" (*1222*, 155), but when another character insists that in the last ten years Norway has gone to "rack and ruin, with corruption everywhere and the theft of public resources as an everyday occurrence," Hanne then wryly declares that at least today such things are being exposed (*1222*, 244), exactly what Holt accomplishes in her novels.

Both of Holt's two successful crime series, which together have sold over 4 million copies worldwide, present personal fears and societal tensions. The protagonists of both series are women, because in a 2010 article, Holt stressed her conviction that "If the great male detectives are archetypically loners, female detectives are doubly so. They are alienated both by entrenched male hierarchies at work and the Janus-like disjunction between their formidable professional personas and their vulnerable private lives." Holt also believes that women's special sensitivity toward victims and their repressed compassion "fuels their zeal to see justice done," and that because women detectives lack the physical strength of their male counterparts, women have to be "more resourceful, intelligent and tactical" than men are to solve difficult cases (Anne Holt, "Anne Holt's Top 10 Female Detectives").

Holt's beautiful, intelligent, and competent police officer Hanne Wilhelmsen, initially a closeted lesbian, is professionally hampered almost continuously by Norway's severe legal restrictions on police investigations. Holt's second series pairs Inspector (later Police Commissioner) Yngvar Stubo with Oslo psychology professor and profiler Inger Johanne Vik, whom he marries during the series. In 2012, Holt told Laura DeMarco, a *Cleveland Plain Dealer* journalist, that Holt's publishers made the decision to translate Holt's books out of the order in which they were written. Holt indicated that she is published in "around 30 languages," and that she trusts her publishers to know best how to launch her two series (quoted in DeMarco).

In *Blind gudinne*, 1993 (*Blind Goddess*, tr. 2012), the first book of the Hanne Wilhelmsen series and Holt's second novel to appear in English, Detective Hanne Wilhelmsen is only one of three protagonists (the others are Karen Borg, a successful lawyer, and Håkon Sand, a less successful public prosecutor) probing homicides related to a drug-smuggling ring organized by highly placed persons to finance the operations of Norwegian Military Intelligence. *Blind Goddess* was filmed for television in 1997.

By popular demand, Wilhelmsen became the focus of *Salige er de som tørster*, 1994 (*Blessed Are Those Who Thirst*, tr. 2013), the second novel in the series. Holt addresses the moral question of the relation between justice and revenge (Nordberg), while sympathetically treating Hanne's desire to keep her lifestyle and her female lover secret, which causes a serious conflict in their relationship. With Håkon Sand, Hanne tracks an apparent serial rapist and killer who each Saturday night leaves a room with cryptic numbers inscribed in blood on its walls, though no bodies are found there. Sand discovers that the numbers correspond to the filing numbers of missing female foreign immigrants, while a rape victim and her father pursue vigilante justice. A *Publishers Weekly* reviewer praised Holt's evocative prose in this novel, citing as especially effective the passage, "the intense hue only a Scandinavian sky in springtime is blessed with—royal blue on the horizon and lighter toward the meridian, before dissolving into a pink eiderdown where the sun was still lying lazily in the east" (*Publishers Weekly*, November 26, 2012, 33). *Blessed Are Those Who Thirst* was filmed for theatrical release in 1997 and ranked twenty-fifth in the 2009 *Dagbladet* list of twenty-five all-time best Norwegian crime novels.

Initial sales of *Demonens død*, 1995 (*Death of the Demon*), tr. 2013, Holt's third book in the series, reached 120,000 hard cover copies, an "unheard of" success, Nordberg noted in 2005, before or since for a crime novel in Norway. In *Death of the Demon*, a murder occurs in a well-run children's home, where a social service intervention has placed 12-year-old Olav, the repulsive and hyperactive son of an alcoholic single mother. This situation allows Holt to present another troubling modern dilemma: "how can it be that all our social investment is of no help in confronting the seemingly radical evil present in this little boy? The welfare society and the *folkhemmet* ideology provides [sic] no answer to this question" (Saarinen 132). Neither does Holt. In this searing exposure of a failing governmental system, Holt takes Hanne Wilhelmsen, recently promoted to Chief Inspector but chafing at the position's dull managerial routine and the professional intrigue it involves, into the grisly killing of the administrator of the foster children's group home where Olav has been placed. Holt also exposes troubling internal demons in Hanne's personal life, because her close working friendship with her flamboyant assistant, detective Billy T., causes her to question her relationship with Cecelie, the partner with whom Hanne has shared her life and love since they were in their teens. Cecelie's longing for a child which Hanne has denied for seventeen years is reaching a tipping point just when Olav's case forces Hanne to confront the tragic ironies of a society that prides itself on cradle-to-grave welfare yet condemns its neediest citizens, like Olav and his mother, to inevitable disaster.

Holt co-authored her fourth and sixth Hanne Wilhelmsen novels, *Løvens gap* ("The Lion's Mouth"), 1997, and *Uten ekko* ("Without an Echo"), 2000, with Berit Reiss-Andersen, who was the under-secretary for the Minister of Justice and Police during Anne Holt's term in that office from 1996 to 1997. Reiss-Andersen currently serves as President of the Norwegian Bar Association and until 2017 is a member of the Norwegian Nobel Committee which awards the Nobel Peace Prize. "The Lion's Mouth" deals with large-scale political machinations, opening with a fictional Norwegian Prime Minister found shot to death in her office. The ensuing investigation involves neo–Nazis and governmental corruption. "Without an Echo" concentrates on the psychological ramifications of betrayal and broken relationships, with Hanne Wilhelmsen returning to Norway from a self-imposed exile in an Italian monastery following the death of her partner Cecelie. At first relegated to paper-shuffling, Hanne investigates the murder of a famous chef, and with Billy T. she untangles the involved psychological relationships underlying the case.

Holt considers her eighth Wilhelmsen novel, *1222*, first of this series to appear in English (2010), a traditional "locked room" mystery and a homage to Agatha Christie. It has received mixed reviews at home and abroad, because the investigation is "purely tactical," without access to technology (Derbyshire). Holt says she tried "to write a very old-fashioned story, but with a tempo that was more contemporary" (Davies 23). *1222*, which sprang from Holt's experience of being stuck in the remote Norwegian village of Finse for two days because of a winter storm, finds Hanne wheelchair-bound from a deadly criminal incident. Now retired from the police force and as an amateur detective more sharp-tongued than ever, she is stranded in an old picturesque Finse hotel by a storm-related train derailment. Holt complicates Hanne's frustration by adding an unexplained fellow passenger who is under armed guard and two homicides that occur rapidly after the derailment, keeping Hanne busy investigating and waspishly haranguing her fellow passengers, the hotel staff, and even the policemen who struggle through the raging wind and heavy snow to untangle the situation. Arguably one of the least powerful novels in this series, Hanne's first-person narration of *1222* does reveal her more human side. She is beginning to move out of the self-imposed shell she has built around herself since she became partially paralyzed in a police operation, and she even contemplates inviting a sympathetic fellow passenger, psychologist Magnus Streng, into the home she now shares with Nefis, her Turkish lover, and their daughter.

Besides its concentration on government-involved crimes, Holt's Hanne Wilhelmsen series as a whole treats Hanne's ongoing struggle to accept her sexual orientation, a factor which Holt considers somehow "subversive" (Forshaw 112); and to deal with both the loss of Cecelie, her first partner, from cancer; and the partial loss of her own independence through being partially paralyzed and wheelchair-bound. While readers might be tempted to draw parallels between Holt and Hanne, Holt insists, "The only thing we have in common is that we both live with women.... [Hanne] is beautiful, I'm not. She is highly intelligent and intuitive, but also very unsociable and hiding from everyone—everything that is not me" (quoted in Davies 31). In Hanne Wilhelmsen, Holt has created such a convincing character that one reader, certain Hanne was a real person, sent Holt a letter recommending psychiatrists that Hanne should consult (Davies 23). The out-of-chronological-order English publication of this series unfortunately makes following Holt's development of her intriguing protagonist at present an unwieldy task for non–Scandinavian readers.

Holt's Vik and Stubo police procedural series teams edgy, guilt-ridden Johanne Vik, a former

FBI profiler and now an Oslo University professor, with jovial police inspector Yngvar Stubo. *Det some er mitt*, 2001 (*Punishment*, also titled *What Is Mine*, tr. 2006), presents a case based on a real-life Norwegian homicide. Holt's novel involves Aksel Seier, a man sentenced for child molestation, though Johanne suspects he is innocent. Seier now lives in exile on Cape Cod, Massachusetts, where Johanne visits him to try to understand his situation. In addition she herself is facing an even more harrowing case, in which after a series of child abductions back in Norway, two dead children have been delivered to their respective parents with notes that read chillingly, "You got what you deserved." Both Johanne and Stubo are also coping with difficult personal situations. Johanne, recently divorced, is raising a possibly autistic six-year-old, and Stubo's wife and young child have recently died. In the course of this savage investigation, tensions mount between Johanne and Stubo, in part because the Aksel Seier case continues to prey on Johanne's mind. A *Kirkus Reviews* writer commented about this novel on May 15, 2006, "Holt's work is cerebral, complicated and immensely rewarding."

In *Det som aldri skjer*, 2004 (*What Never Happens*, tr. 2008), Holt explores issues that upset Johanne's personal life; now married to Stubo, she is at home with their newborn child and her young daughter, who is showing developing symptoms of autism. Stubo is investigating a new series of grisly homicides of celebrities: a talk-show host is found slain with his tongue slashed down the middle, and the body of a well-known literary critic is discovered with a pen plunged through one eye. Stubo asks Johanne to help him unravel the case, and in reluctantly doing so, she gradually realizes that these murders remind her of something that occurred when she was a profiler at Quantico, an experience that she has kept hidden even from her husband. She also realizes that if this killer maintains his pattern, the next victim will be a policeman, which puts her husband's life and her own at risk. *What Is Mine*, Holt's first crime novel in this series to be released in the United States, and *What Never Happens* have both received critical acclaim for their perceptive portrayals of her lead characters' family lives. Holt continued to explore that theme in *Presidentens valg*, 2005 (*Madame President*, also titled *Death in Oslo*, tr. 2010), in which America's first female president is kidnapped during a state visit to Norway. Holt uses the same theme in *Pengemannen*, 2009 (*Fear Not*, tr. 2012), which puts Johanne and her husband and daughter into grave jeopardy. Fifth and last in the series, *Skyggedød*, 2012 (*What Dark Clouds Hide*, tr. 2013), centers on the mysterious death at home of eight-year-old Sander Mohr. The death comes to light on July 22, 2011, the day of the real-life massacre carried out by Norwegian white supremacist Anders Breivik. When nearly everyone, including Vik, believes the death is a terrible accident, rookie detective Henrik Holme manages to convince Vik to join him in suspecting homicide. In the shadow of Breivik's monstrous crime, Vik and Holme unravel sinister family secrets and system failures that contributed to Sander's death.

In addition to her Hanne Wilhelmsen series and the Vik-Stubo series, Anne Holt has written several powerful stand-alone novels with sociopolitical themes, notably *Flimmer*, 2010 ("Arrhythmia"), co-authored with Even [sic] Holt, which deals with a sophisticated pacemaker device suspected in the deaths of several heart patients. Anne Holt also is authoring a children's series featuring two eight-year-old girls, lonely little May-Britt, who has a eccentric mother and a irritating little sister, and May-Britt's friend March-Britt.

Typically Holt writes the last ten pages of a novel first, which she uses as a guide to the rest of the book, a preoccupation with producing exceptionally strong endings that greatly reinforces the impact of her stories (Davies). Holt's novels also exemplify her recommendation that a reader going to visit a country new to him or her should read one of its crime novels or one of its home decorating magazines, because she feels in each case, "You will learn more than any travel guide can tell you" (quoted in Forshaw 115).

Through her two crime series, Holt, who published seventeen novels in as many years, hopes to raise significant political issues, uncover governmental corruption, and address social ills (DeMarco), but she never presents facile solutions, believing readers should work these out for themselves. She prefers "to provide insight into the human condition" (quoted in Forshaw 115), and so she considers her fourth Vik/Stubo novel, *Pengemannen*, 2009 (*Fear Not*, tr. 2011), the most important book that she has written (quoted in Forshaw 116), because it draws not only the two major figures but their autistic daughter into a dangerous investigation.

The British publisher Corvus began publication of both Holt's Vik/Stubo series and books one through seven of the Hanne Wilhelmsen series in 2011. Holt's U.S. publisher is following suit as well as re-releasing the Vik/Stubo series, so that now English-speaking readers will be more easily able to judge whether, as Scottish crime author Val McDermid claims, "Anne Holt is the latest crime writer to reveal how truly dark it gets in Scandinavia" (see http://www.salomonsson agency.com/authors).

Crime Novels:

The Hanne Wilhelmsen Series:

1993: *Blind gudinne* (*Blind Goddess*, tr. Tom Geddes, 2012)

1994: *Salige er de som tørster* (*Blessed Are Those Who Thirst*, tr. Anne Bruce, 2013).

1995: *Demonens død* (*Death of the Demon*, tr. Anne Bruce, 2013).

1997: *Løvens gap* (*The Lion's Mouth*," co-authored with Berit Reiss-Andersen, tr. Anne Bruce, 2014)

1999: *Død joker* ("Dead Joker")

2000: *Uten ekko* ("Without an Echo," co-authored with Berit Reiss-Andersen)

2003: *Sannheten bortenfor* ("The Truth Beyond")

2007: *1222* (*1222*, tr. Marlaine Delargy, 2011)

The Vik/Stubø Series:

2001: *Det some er mitt* (*Punishment*, tr. Kari Dickson, 2006; also known as *What Is Mine*)

2004: *Det som aldri skjer* (*What Never Happens*, tr. Kari Dickson, also known as *The Final Murder*, 2008)

2005: *Presidentens valg* (*Madam President*, tr. Kari Dickson, 2010, also known as *Death in Oslo*)

2009: *Pengemannen* (*Fear Not*, tr. Marlaine Delargy, 2011)

2012: *Skyggedød* ("What Dark Clouds Hide")

Stand-Alone Crime Novel:

2010: *Flimmer* ("Arrhythmia"), co-authored with Even [sic] Holt

Major Awards:

1994: The Riverton Prize, for *Salige er de som tørster* (*Blessed Are Those Who Thirst*)

Website: N/A

Jørn Lier Horst

> b. February 27, 1970, Bamble, Telemark, Norway; Residence: Larvik, Norway; Occupations: policeman and police chief, novelist

Jørn Lier Horst draws on his twenty-plus-year career as a police officer in Larvik for his scrupulously credible and complex police procedurals, which contain significant social and political subtexts and focus on Horst's methodical protagonist Chief Inspector William Wisting. According to the biography supplied for the fictional Wisting on Horst's website, Wisting grew up west of Stavern, Norway. He and his wife Ingrid, who died in 2006, were parents of twins born in 1983. Horst made Wisting the great-grandson of the real-life polar explorer Oscar Wisting who accompanied Roald Amundsen as the first explorers to reach both the North and South Poles.

Horst's first William Wisting novel, and his literary debut, was *Nøkkelvitnet* ("Key Witness"), 2004, based on a true homicide. *Bunnfall*, 2010 (*Dregs*, tr. 2011), sixth in the series, is set near Larvik in Stavern, a quiet little town on Norway's southeast coast. In one week, four severed left feet float onto different parts of the shoreline; they prove to be parts of four different murder victims, one a mentally ill woman with no known connection to the others, and three elderly men who knew one another during World War II. Horst keeps his macabre plot moving rapidly, accompanied by sociological and philosophical insights into crime and police work.

Vinterstengt, 2011 (*Closed for Winter*, tr. 2014), Horst's complex seventh William Wisting procedural, brings Wisting to a resort area in coastal Vestfold County where a battered body has been discovered in a broken-into and robbed cottage belonging to a popular television interviewer. Wisting traces the theft to a gang of Lithuanian criminals, but the body disappears en route to the police morgue. Personal complications arise for the inspector because Tommy Kvantner, the Danish lover of Wisting's reporter daughter, appears to be involved.

Even more intimate trauma afflicts Chief Inspector Wisting in the prizewinning *Jakthundene*, 2012 (*The Hunting Dogs*, tr. 2014), the third Wisting novel to appear in English. Horst considers *The Hunting Dogs* his best work yet. In the first case he solved, Wisting had led a well-publicized investigation into the death of young Cecelia Linde who had gone missing and was found dead twelve days later, but now seventeen years later, the media accuse Wisting of having planted DNA at the scene of her murder and of failing to take evidence from an important witness, and so the convicted killer, Rudolf Haglund, is granted parole as possibly innocent. Wisting falls under grave suspicion and is suspended from duty pending an administrative review, causing the press to pillory him and forcing him to reassess his entire life. Wisting's journalist daughter Line helps him uncover the person who tempered with the evidence and to ascertain whether Haglund is indeed guilty. Despite the lack in this novel of elements now familiar from the work of other popular Scandinavian crime writers—a self-destructive hero, overt brutality, lurid family secrets—most reviewers and readers found *The Hunting Dogs* impossible to put down. Horst followed *The Hunting Dogs* with *Hulemannen* (*The Caveman*), 2013, tr. 2015, involving Wisting in an international investigation that explores the questions of loneliness in the modern world and whether Norwegian society has lost its sense of continuity.

In addition to the William Wisting series, Horst is writing two young adult detective series, the Clue Series, beginning in 2012; and the Detective Agency No. 2 series, beginning in 2013. Horst also frequently lectures to schoolchildren on crime prevention and police work.

Crime Novels:

The Inspector William Wisting Series:

2004: *Nøkkelvitnet* ("Key Witness")
2005: *Felicia forsvant* ("The Disappearance of Felicia")
2006: *Når havet stilner* ("When the Sea Calms")
2007: *Den eneste ene* ("The Only One")
2009: *Nattmannen* ("Nocturnal Man")
2010: *Bunnfall* (*Dregs*, tr. Anne Bruce, 2011)
2011: *Vinterstengt* (*Closed for Winter*, tr. Anne Bruce, 2014)

2012: *Jakthundene* (*The Hunting Dogs*, tr. Anne Bruce, 2014)
2013: *Hulemannen* (*The Caveman*, tr. Anne Bruce, 2015)

The Hunter Series:

2008: "Codename Hunter"

Major Awards:

2012: Norway's Bookseller's Prize for *Vinterstengt* (*Closed for Winter*)
2012: The Riverton Prize, for *Jakthundene* (*The Hunting Dogs*)
2013: The Glass Key Award, for *Jakthundene* (*The Hunting Dogs*)

Website: http://www.jlhorst.com

Alf R. Jacobsen

b. February 21, 1950, Hammerfest, Norway; Residence: N/A; Occupations: journalist and author

A highly prolific author of books and radio and television scripts, Jacobsen has produced mainly adventure tales, espionage thrillers, and documentaries of naval warfare, especially World War II naval action in the North, including "Sharnhorst Mortally Wounded," 2001; "Tirpitz and the Pursuit of X5," 2003; "Nickel, Iron and Blood," 2006, and "The Cruiser Blücher," about the sinking of the German cruiser by Norwegians in Drøbaksundet on April 9, 1940. Jacobsen's crime novel *Kharg*, 1988 ("Kharg"), also set during World War II, following protagonist Norwegian journalist Jonathan Brink from a ship disaster to India, received the Riverton Prize in 1988. *Tango bacalao* ("Tango Bacalao"), 2000, was made into the 2000 film *Passing Darkness*, directed by Knut Erik Jensen.

Crime Novels:

1982: *Stalins gull* ("Stalin's Gold")
1986: *Osiris* ("Osiris")
1988: *Kharg* ("Kharg")
1994: *Rødt som kirsebær* ("Red as Cherries")
1998: *Kameleon* ("Chameleon"), with Ingvald Thuen
1999: *Typhoon* ("Typhoon"), with Ingvald Thuen
2000: *Tango bacalao* ("Tango Bacalao")

Major Awards:

1988: The Riverton Prize for *Kharg* ("Kharg")

Website: N/A

*Roy Jacobsen

b. December 26, 1954, Oslo suburb in the Groruddalen valley, Norway; Residence: 1979–1986: Solfjellsjøen in northern Norway; Oslo, Norway; Occupation: full-time author since 1990

Jacobson, a member of the Norwegian Academy for Language and Literature, is not primarily a crime fiction author. His distinguished and influential literary works are famous for tracing "the great class journey," the rapid societal changes experienced by most of the Norwegian population as Norway's previously rigid agrarian and proletarian society became a post-industrial and technological education-and-welfare society, providing Norwegians with both opportunities and challenges. Against the backdrop of Norway's history and national transformation, Jacobsen has explored themes and pressures involving criminal activity.

Jacobsen writes from his personal experiences with the working lives of people in small northern Norwegian communities as well as the lives of academics and psychological therapists in Oslo. His breakthrough novel *Seierherrene* ("The Conquerors"), 1991, explored national and private identity. Jacobsen's epic historical novel *Frost* ("Frost"), 2003, traces the career of Gest, a 10th century Icelander outlawed at age 13 for killing one of Iceland's most powerful rulers in revenge for Gest's father's murder. Gest eventually participates in the Viking conquest of parts of England in 1016. *Hoggerne* (*The Burnt-Out Town of Miracles*), 2005, tr. 2008, takes place during the Winter War in 1939, when badly outnumbered, around 2000 Finns fought about 50,000 Russians to a standstill. In Jacobsen's novel, based on an actual event, a simple woodcutter refuses to leave his native village even though the Russians are advancing, allowing Jacobsen to explore the lives of ordinary folk caught up in conflicts they neither started nor understand.

Major Works:

1987: *Det nye vannet* (*The New Water*, tr. William H. Halverson, 1997)
1991: *Seierherrene* ("The Conquerors")
1995: *Trygve Brattell: En Fortelling* (biography of Trygve Brattell, former Norwegian Labour Party Prime Minister)
2003: *Frost* ("Frost")
2005: *Hoggerne* (*The Burnt-Out Town of Miracles*, tr. Don Bartlett and Don Shaw, 2008)

Major Awards:

1989: Norwegian Critics' Prize for Literature, for *Det kan komme noen* (short stories, 1989)
1991 and 2004: Nordic Council Literature Prize nominations, for *Seierherrene* ("The Conquerors") and *Frost* ("Frost") respectively

Website: N/A

Jørgen Jaeger

b. July 29, 1946, Bergen, Norway; Residence: The Hop, Bergen, Norway; Occupations: originally a sales manager, advertising consultant, author of novels and short stories

Jaeger, presently an advertising consultant for the Norwegian newspaper *Fanposten* and an inveterate dog lover, lives with his wife and Border Collie Aic in Bergen, where he composes his detective series featuring the strong-willed police chief Ole Vik. Jaeger's previous dog, a Border Collie named Birk who died in 2011 lives on in all of Jaeger's novels, appearing as the only real-life character. Jaeger generally uses a light touch in treating serious issues facing today's Norway: mental illness, white-collar crime, police corruption, and cultural discrimination.

Jaeger's 2007 novel *Blodskrift* ("Blood Scripture") illustrates his tendency toward exaggeration, though in his afterword he indicates that he based this plot on a true story and dedicated the novel to the doctor-patient relationship. This novel takes place in the once- peaceful little west coast Norwegian town of Fjellberghavn, where after receiving death threats a respected dentist, Joakim Sørensen, is found shot dead. Then the *Lensmannhof*, the local police station where Chief Ole Vik both works and lives, is torched, depriving Vik of both home and office, and a crate of dynamite placed somewhere in Fjellberg Harbor poses a substantial bomb threat to the whole area. Jaeger goes so far as to make flames talk, and as German critic Wolfgang Franssen has pragmatically observed, this tendency often presses Jaeger's points home with undue force and ferocious platitudes: "That the words of an enclosed flame [are] able to reassure people is doubtful" (Franssen). Jaeger sends Ole Vik to solve this complicated set of disasters, aided by what Franssen calls the "unsung hero" of the novel, Birk the Border Collie, who has been kept from his rest so long by the investigation he foams at the mouth from boredom, only getting to play as a reward for helping to solve the crimes (Franssen).

In *Karma* ("Karma"), 2010, subtitled "The Missing Hiker from Bergen," a hiker initially prevents a man from killing himself, but by the time the police arrive, the hiker has vanished and the man, an IT employee named Sebastian Maddox, is found dead behind a house. Some details discovered in the crime scene investigation indicate that this is not a suicide, and Ole Vik, now a Bergen police commissioner, is summoned to take over the case as a homicide. Vik discovers that a shadowy serial killer calling himself "Karma" lurks behind this killing and in his usual forceful fashion, Vik, again with Birk's help, solves the case in only a few hours. Kjell Einar Oren of the *Haugesunds Avis* uses a canine metaphor in concluding that "Karma" is "a straight piece of fireworks ... that "makes your hackles stand on end ... his [Jaeger's] best thriller so far," advancing Jaeger to the ranks of internationally recognized Norwegian crime authors (Oren).

Crime Novels:

> 2003: *Skyggejakten* ("Ghost Hunt")
> 2004: *Kameleonene* ("Chameleons")
> 2005: *Dødssymfoni* ("Death Symphony")
> 2007: *Blodskrift* ("Blood Scripture")
> 2010: *Karma* ("Karma")
> 2012: *Stemmen* ("The Voice")

Major Awards: N/A

Website: http://www.krimjager.com

Jan Henrik Jensen

b. 1944, Oslo, Norway; Residence: Trondheim, Norway; Occupation: author

Jan Henrik Jensen began writing fiction at sixteen. He has worked as a sailor, factory worker, and security guard, and became a copywriter for humorous radio sketches broadcast by Knut Lystad and Lars Mjoen. Jensen has published as a lyricist as well as producing one novel, *Snuff* ("Snuff"), 1982, often cited as a prime example of "Norwegian *noir*" and ranked twenty-third in the 2013 *Dagbladet* list of twenty-five best Norwegian crime novels. *Dagbladet* crime critic Fredrik Wandrup called "Snuff" "a novel that moves in the darkest corners of human activity" (Wandrup). The novel has been published in several editions, but it remains little known to Norwegian readers.

In "Snuff," Jensen's alcoholic antihero Bjørn Glenne, a journalist whose career is floundering, is living on the brink of despair. Hired to write a series of articles about "snuff" films, pornography which closes with an actual murder, Glenne guides Jensen's readers through a brutal world of sexual exploitation. According to Wandrup, in this novel Jensen claims that the limits of human depravity extend as far as the human imagination can reach, and that through the ages, there have always been individuals who have carried out all the demonic thoughts that have obsessed human beings (Wandrup).

Crime Novels:

   1982: *Snuff* ("Snuff")

Website: N/A

Merete Junker (Merete Junker Gundersen)

   b. 1959, Skien, Norway; Residence: Skien, Norway; Occupations: radio journalist with NFK Telemark, teacher, author

Fortified by a lavish blurb praising Junker's "fantastic characters and finely tuned suspense" from Camilla Läckberg, Sweden's current "Queen of Crime," Junker's debut novel *Jenta med ballongen* ("The Girl with the Balloon"), 2008, features Mette Minde, a radio journalist like Junker herself. On the outskirts of Skien, the small town where Ibsen grew up, a woman calls the area's emergency number, claiming she'd fallen, but when rescuers arrive, they find her strangled to death with a dog leash, with a punctured red balloon on her chest. The little girl and small dog who had accompanied the woman are missing. When Mette discovers through her husband Peter, an ambulance driver, that the victim's sister was Mette's childhood friend, she begins to investigate the crime, proving as Ibsen did that lethal secrets built on guilt and jealousy often underlie the placid surface of a small Norwegian town.

Junker told NRK reporter Ken Willy Wilhelmsen that the inspiration for her first novel came from a fall she took while walking with her dog in the woods on a "dark and nasty autumn evening" in 2005. Unable to shake the eerie mood the experience evoked, she quit her teaching job to write, producing not only her first crime novel, but "a kind of homage," she said, to her "exciting and educational" seven years at NRK in Telemark (quoted in Wilhelmsen). The subplot of "The Girl with the Balloon" involves ten-year-old Lotte, the daughter of the strangled woman who had died on Lotte's birthday. Danish reviewer Anne Clare Baehr places Junker's perceptive handling of child psychology on a par with fellow Scandinavian crime authors Karin Fossum's and Liza Marklund's, though Baehr also feels that Mette herself is "quite unique," especially as shown in humorous passages (rare in Norwegian crime fiction) involving the La Sylphide fitness club and Mette's attempts at Nordic walking (Baehr).

Junker put her own experiences as the mother of twin boys into *Tvillingen* ("Twins"), 2010, with techniques that critics compare to the work of her sisters in crime Karin Fossum and Unni Lindell. Per-Magne Midjo of *Tronder-Avisa* praised Junker's plot as "crammed with all the goodies a crime enthusiast could wish" (Midjo): a suicide, a homicide, and the disappearance of a young girl, all bound up in the lives of people tormented by powerful needs they cannot control (Berit Kobro, in Gyldendal's selection of reviews for "Twins"). This novel questions whether the twin relationship is an amazing cohesion or a destructive influence in which an "evil twin" dominates the other with sometimes deadly results. Mette Minde, assigned to cover the suicide of a young man in a swimming pool, discovers his sinister secret: just before shooting himself he had chained up a young girl, Idun. Soon after, Mette learns that Idun's twin sister Ylva has gone missing, and Mette realizes that by investigating these events she herself is in danger. Critic Merete Trap commented in *Crime Fair* for February 21, 2011, that twins have never seemed so eerie and mysterious as Merete Junker shows them in this novel (Trap).

Junker had a hard two years writing her novel *Pumasommer* ("Puma Summer"), 2012, whose title came to her in a nightmare, but she believes it turned into her best novel yet. Because Junker thinks of her books as entertainment, she tries not to inflict any specific morality on her readers, but with "Puma Summer," she explored the mind of a psychotic serial killer who calls himself "Felis" and stalks the lawyer Torkel Vaa through the environs of Porsgrunn. Junker claims that to write crime fiction, an author, even if he or she is "basically normal," must know "ugly feelings" (Sorknes). Norwegian readers' enthusiastic reception of Junker's novels seems to indicate they approve her techniques.

Crime Novels:

   2008: *Jenta med ballongen* ("The Girl With the Balloon")
   2010: *Tvillingen* ("Twins")
   2012: *Pumasommer* ("Puma Summer")
   2014: *Venuspassasjen* ("Transit of Venus")

Major Awards:

   2009: Maurits Hansen Award for Best Norwegian Crime Debut, for *Jenta med ballongen* ("The Girl with the Balloon")

Website: N/A

Jan Knudsen (Jan-Erik James Knudsen)

   b. 1957, Drammen, Norway; grew up in Asker, Norway; Residence: Asker, Norway; Occupations: teacher, novelist

Jan Knudsen, who has composed a number of popular songs, writes crime fiction that blends elements of the psychological thriller with the structure of the police procedural. According to *Aftenposten* critic Terje Sternland, Knudsen did his homework well for his 2008 fiction debut, *En fiende å frykte* ("A Foe to Fear"), which takes place in Oslo only a few weeks after the terrorist attack on New York's World Trade Center in September 2001 (Sternland). On the verge of a visit from high ranking politicians, all tied to the bloody Balkan civil wars of the 1990s, Norwegian police are investigating homicides related to organized crime, with Knudsen's Inspector Eddie Samson, independent and headstrong, and his surprisingly witty partner Bernhardt Fiske keeping their eyes on the influx of Balkan refugees entering Oslo's underworld. When the CIA sends their agent William Meyer to Oslo to pick up a Balkan defector, a professional killer prepares to strike, and when he does, Samson and Fiske encounter enough discouragement and outright lack of support from their colleagues to make the pair suspect police corruption, throwing both their own lives and the lives of others into jeopardy.

In their second case, *Memo fra en morder* ("Memo from a Killer"), 2010, Samson and Fiske confront the Russian mafia when two foreign prostitutes are slain a week apart in Oslo. The detectives uncover enough clues to realize they are faced with a criminally insane killer who then pursues Samson himself. Writing in 2010 for *Aftenposten*, Sternland predicted that if Knudsen is able to maintain the pace of his plots, "he will quietly put himself in the top echelon of Norwegian crime writers" (Sternland).

Crime Novels:

   2008: *En fiende å frykte* ("An Enemy to Fear")
   2010: *Memo fra en morder* ("Memo from a Killer")

Major Awards: N/A

Website: http://www.janerikknudsen.com

Sverre Knudsen

> b. November 22, 1955, Oslo, Norway; Residence: Oslo, Norway; Occupations: rock musician, carpenter, teacher, salesman, advertising copywriter, translator, and author of children's, young adult, and adult fiction

Known for his musical endeavors (as "Freddi Fiord"), television scripts, and over 35 translations of English-language adventure authors including Douglas Adams, Edgar Rice Burroughs, and Rudyard Kipling, Knudsen has also written three non-series *noir* thrillers which display his intimate knowledge of Oslo's underground culture.

Crime Novels:

2000: *De aller nærmeste* ("The Kins")
2002: *Død hånd* ("Dead Hand")
2004: *Fare, fare krigsmann* ("Danger, Danger, Soldier")

Major Awards:

2011: Riksmåls Prize, for *Aarons Maskin* ("Aaron's Machine," a young adult novel)

Website: http://www.knudsen.net

Tom Kristensen

> b. 1955; Residence: N/A; Occupation: banker, industrial manager, international financial consultant, author

Drawing on his experiences as a banker and consultant in the world of international finance, Kristensen has produced thrillers enthusiastically received by critics and general readers alike, making him currently one of Norway's best selling authors. Kristensen's debut novel, *En kule* ("A Killing"), 2001, showcases protagonist Mads Hammer, a twenty-eight-year-old stockbroker at his first job. He has signed on with Kinansparten, a fictional Oslo brokerage whose three owners are so desperate to recoup severe losses that they are engaging in stock market fraud and entangling Hammer in a nightmarish combination of swindling and murder.

In *Dødskriket* ("Realm of the Dead"), 2006, Kristensen explored the cultural problems that the Scandinavian countries are experiencing because of increasing Muslim immigration. For this novel, Kristensen created two fictional failed terrorist attacks: an assassination attempt on a Saudi prince in Jeddah and a suicide bombing set off accidentally in Oslo, plot elements that according to a *Dagens Naeringsliv* critic combine "the inevitable and the surprising" couched in a hard-boiled economical style similar to literary styles used by Americans Dashiell Hammet and Ernest Hemingway.

Anne Holt found Kristensen's 2010 novel *Dypet* ("The Deep") particularly "provocative" (Forshaw 118), flashing back to divers' working conditions in 1981 during the Cold War, when North Sea oil exploration was burgeoning. In "The Deep," Norway's Oil and Industry Minister receives a threatening letter: unless drilling development of the Troll area ceases, an oil rig will sink—and one shortly thereafter does. Later, during a fierce North Sea storm, two divers are down 266 feet, cutting wires that connect a rig with the wellhead. A horrible accident kills one diver; the other survives, but the rig sinks and more mysterious demands ensue. The narrative jumps ahead to 2010: the day after a frightened old diver tells a confused story about the diver lost in 1981, the old diver is himself found dead. The surviving diver's son begins to probe his own father's past, unraveling discoveries that make this novel "the perfect thriller," according to a reviewer for *Oppland arbeiderblad*.

Kristensen ratchets up tension in his 2012 thriller, *Korsbæreren* ("The Cross Bearer"), 2012, praised by Turid Larsen of *Dagsavisen* for its solid plot and literary craftsmanship. In "The Cross Bearer," one of Oslo bank manager Elvira Elton Eikenes's major clients, an oil company, faces the threat of defaulting on an enormous loan, while Elvira's boss suspects her of incompetence and drug abuse. In San Francisco, her secret lover and former employer David Nomura, himself the target of Japanese mafia creditors, has to come up with forty million dollars in the next three weeks, so he flies to Oslo to utilize Elvira's bank connections, not knowing that a "Cross Bearer" is on his way there to exploit them both. Another *Dagsavisen* reviewer has remarked that Kristensen's books are perfect for killing time on a bus; the only problem is that a reader might forget to get off the bus in time.

Selected Crime Novels:

2001: *En kule* ("A Killing")
2002: *Hvitvasking* ("Laundering")
2003: *Freshwater* ("Freshwater")
2005: *Profitaeren* ("The Profiteer")
2006: *Dødskriket* ("Realm of the Dead")
2008: *Dragen* ("The Dragon")
2010: *Dypet* ("The Deep")
2012: *Korsbæreren* ("The Cross Bearer")
2014: *Dødspakten* ("The Death Pact")

Major Awards:

2006: The Riverton Prize, for *Dødskriket* ("Realm of the Dead")

Website: N/A

*Hans Olav Lahlum

b. September 12, 1973, Mo i Rana, Norway; grew up in Rødoy, Norway; Residence: Lillehammer, Norway; Occupations: historian, chess player, politician, crime author

Lahlum described his youth in the small Norwegian town of Rødoy as "gloomy." Later he became a county leader of the Socialist Left Party. After taking his Master's degree in history from the University of Oslo, Lahlum produced biographies of politicians: a 560-page book on Norway's former prime minister Oscar Torp in 2007; a 2008 study of the U.S. presidents that included both personal and "tabloid" material; and a large-scale 2009 biography of Norway's former Labour Party secretary Haakon Lie, debunking rumors that Lie was an undercover U.S. CIA agent (Strand). Lahlum also wrote a 2013 biography of Håvard Vederhus, a Norwegian Workers' League member killed during the Breivik massacre in 2011.

Recently Lahlum, an eccentric author with a flair for the unconventional (Jørvell), has turned to writing classic police procedural crime novels set in the late 1960s: *Menneskefluene*, 2010 (*The*

Human Flies, tr. 2015); *Satelittmenneskene*, 2011 (*Satellite People*, tr. 2015); *Katalysatormordet* ("The Catalyst Killing"), 2012; and a 2012 collection of three murder mysteries set at Christmas 1971, *De fem fyrstikkene* ("The Five Matches: Three Murder Stories").

The Daily Mail literary critic Barry Turner praised Lahlum in 2015 as the latest Scandinavian crime author to appear in the English market and as an admirer of Agatha Christie. In *The Human Flies*, Lahlum recalls the Nazi Occupation with a revenge subplot beneath Inspector Kolbjørn Kristiansen's 1968 investigation of a former Resistance leader slain in his downtown Oslo apartment (Turner). Also appearing in English translation in 2015, *Satellite People*, a Christie-type closed circle mystery, also featured Kristiansen (called "K2") and is set in 1969, when wealthy businessman Magdalon Schelderup dies suspiciously while entertaining dinner guests, ten "satellite people" each of whom may have wanted Schelderup dead. Kristiansen again traces clues back to the Occupation, while his unofficial partner Patricia, who is wheelchair bound, carries out the "Poirotesque deduction" (Wilson, "Best Recent Crime Novels").

Regarding Lahlum's short fiction, Norwegian critic Torbjørn Ekeland discussed "The Five Matches" in *Dagbladet* on December 18, 2012, finding Lahlum's detective fiction of "consistently high quality" and calling him "a fresh addition to the Norwegian crime fauna, a new species, almost," although Ekelund also found that Lahlum's "old fashioned language" did not seem as effective in "The Five Matches," as it had been in Lahlum's earlier novels (Ekeland). In "The Five Matches," an old resistance fighter is found dead in the snow at a time when Norway's war veterans were still active and "nothing," Ekelund says, about the war had been forgotten, a familiar motif used by several Norwegian crime authors. Because Ekeland finds the longest of the three stories in "The Five Matches" most effective, he feels Lahlum should "stick to the novel format" for his crime fiction (Ekeland).

Crime Novels:

> 2010: *Menneskefluene* (*The Human Flies*, tr. 2015, by Kari Dickson)
> 2011: *Satelittmenneskene* (*Satellite People*, tr. 2015, by Kari Dickson)
> 2012: *Katalysatormordet* ("The Catalyst Killing")
> 2012: *De fem fyrstikkene* ("The Five Matches") (short stories)

Major Awards: N/A

Website: N/A

Pio Larsen (Oddvar Johan Larsen)

> b. January 11, 1928, d. 1982; Residence: N/A; Occupations: journalist, translator, editor, author

Larsen used several pseudonyms for his literary work, which included journalism and humor as well as two original crime novels. He began his writing career in 1959 as "John Pio," and also wrote six Knut Cribb pulp-type novels as "Pierre Pio."

Crime Novels:

> 1959: *Amandus og de tre døde* ("Amandus and the Three Dead"), by "John Pio"
> 1976: *Den hvite kineser* ("The White Chinese")

Major Awards:

> 1976: The Riverton Prize for *Den hvite kineser* ("The White Chinese")

Website: N/A

Stein Morten Lier

b. June 3, 1967; Residence: Various; Occupation: author

The son of Norwegian police chief Leif A. Lier, Stein Lier has published three documentary books on organized crime as well as a fiction series dealing with Eastern European gangsters operating in Scandinavia. In reviewing Lier's nonfiction study *Mafia in Norway: The New Criminal Landscape*, 2013, for *Bokklubben*, Bente Eriksen Einan finds Lier's analysis effective, showing how beginning in the 1990s "a naïve Norway" has given up the fight against organized crime by bootleggers, motorcyclist gangs, ethic minorities, smugglers, prostitution rings, and drug traffickers (Eriksen), all of which seem to be contributing to Norway's increased violence, subversion of the economy, and multiple murders. Lier believes that the biggest criminal threat in Norway today comes from criminal West Africa, especially Nigeria, but he also feels that little doubt exists that cybercrime is the future of organized crime worldwide. Øystein Dahl Johansen in *Akersposten* for April 3, 2013, notes that Lier calls for "drastic changes," principally tightening Norway's borders, introducing passport control, and strengthening the country's penal system, if any hope for effectively fighting organized crime exists (Johansen). Lier's concerns are paramount in much of the crime fiction being produced in Norway today, including his own crime novels and his first Young Adult thriller, "The Rookie."

Crime Novels:

2004: *Catch* ("Catch")
2005: *Mafiya* ("Mafia")
2006: *Bizniz* ("Bizniz")
2008: *Øye for øye* ("An Eye for an Eye")
2009: *Haukene* ("Hawks")
2011: *Bunnen av himmelen* ("The Bottom of Heaven")

Young Adult Thriller:

2012: "The Rookie"

Major Awards: N/A

Website: http://www.sn.no/Stein_Morten_Lier

Idar Lind

b. 1954, island of Otterøya, Nord-Trøndelag, Norway; Residence: Trondheim, Norway; Occupations: author, crime writer, lyricist, playwright

Lind specializes in hard-boiled crime novels that treat inflammatory topics in contemporary Norwegian culture, such as the 1970s rock and folk music movement. Lind's original series protagonist was António Steen, a Caribbean-Norwegian night watchman for a seedy Trondheim hotel. Lind has also used the name "Antonio Steen" as a pseudonym. Lind, who frequently puts other writers' characters into his books, gave Steen a female private detective partner, Telma B.S. Hansen, and placed her name as sole author or as Steen's co-author on some of Lind's own novels (Nordberg). Lind generally uses the Trondheim area from about 1980 to 2000 as the setting of his fiction, as do several other Norwegian crime fiction authors, including Fredrik Skagen, Kim Småge, and Anne Birkefeldt Ragde.

Lind exposed the widespread use of electronic means such as credit cards and telephone cards to create alibis and trace individuals in *Usynlige spor* ("Invisible Tracks"), 1994, the first Norwegian novel of its genre to be published on the Internet. His 1996 novel *Hysj!* ("Hush") treated the 1996 scandal in which a Norwegian government commission aired a strong connection between the Police Special Branch and the Labor Party, which had conducted extensive secret political surveillance of Norwegian citizens. Lind has also published *Drakeblod* ("Dragon's Blood") in a Young Adult series, and the reference work *Norse Mythology from A to Z*.

Crime Novels:

> 1985: *Hotell Tordenskjold* ("Hotel Tordenskjold")
> 1986: *Ormens gift* ("The Worm Married")
> 1989: *13 takters blues* ("13 Bar Blues")
> 1993; *Som to dråper blod* ("Like Two Drops of Blood"), as "Telma B.S. Hansen"
> 1994: *Usynlige spor* ("Invisible Tracks"), as "Telma B.S. Hansen"
> 1996: *Hysj!* ("Hush"), as "Telma B.S. Hansen" and "Antonio Steen"

Major Awards:

> 1985: Aschehaug Competition Prize for *Hotell Tordenskjold* ("Hotel Tordenskjold")
> 1989: The Riverton Prize for *13 takters blues* ("13 Bar Blues")

Website: http://snl.no/Idar_Lind

Unni Lindell

> b. April 3, 1957, Oslo, Norway; Residence: Oslo, Norway; Occupations: journalist, children's author, novelist

Lindell, a prolific popular author, has published poems and short fiction as well as children's and young adult literature, but she is best known for her crime novels, which have often been praised for psychological insights and unusually perceptive language. Lindell's series protagonist is middle-aged and methodical Detective Cato Isaksen, an inveterate womanizer with a turbulent private life, troubled by his on-and-off marriage and his fears for his children. In *Honningfellen* ("The Honey Trap"), 2007, her sixth Isaksen novel, Lindell complicated Isaksen's professional life by giving him Marian Dahle, a young and tough-minded female detective colleague.

Lindell admits that she herself is a very frightened person, and for her fiction she incorporates her own apprehensions into peaceful ordinary suburban settings (Nordberg). Her crime fiction, especially her more recent work, often begins with ordinary realistic settings that quickly segue into surrealistic and even nightmarish vistas. She often also opens a crime story with a ghastly lie that sets everything else in motion.

"The Honey Trap" revolves around two grim events, the missing person case of a seven-year-old boy last seen in an area said to be frequented by pedophiles and a hit and run killing of a Latvian woman which seems to be connected to the boy's disappearance. This combination of crimes brings out Detective Isaksen's aggressive tendency, reinforced by the introduction of Marian Dahle into the case, to whom Isaksen responds ambivalently.

Sukkerdøden ("Sugar Death"), 2010, opens with an obese woman named Kari Bieler abruptly recalling the death of her little brother sixteen years earlier. The secrecy that surrounded the baby's death has permitted a psychopath to live a free double life ever since, until Kari's memory triggers a string of brutal murders, including the killing of Police Chief Martin Egge. Because Detective Marian Dahle's past is involved with the case, her relationship with Isaksen and the entire police department is jeopardized, leading to a horrific conclusion which sets the stage for the subsequent and continuing edgy love-hate working relationship (Melia) between Marian and Cato Isaksen. Isaksen and Dahle come to share a warm friendship, although in *Mørkemannen* ("The Dark Man," also translated as "The Ogre"), 2008, Lindell reveals some of Marian Dahle's "dark past" (Melia), while downplaying Isaksen's marital troubles, which come to light more fully in "Sugar Death." By that time, even the sight of Marian and her boxer dog Birka that she insists on bringing along to work sets Isaksen's teeth on edge, but he cannot get rid of either Marian or Birka.

Lindell continues the peculiar relationship between Dahle and Isaksen, allowing it to counterpoint their most recent investigation. Lindell's breathlessly paced 2010 novel *Djevelkysset* ("The Devil's Kiss") has been widely praised for its tight construction, which according to *Dagsavidsen* critic Turid Larsen, like all of Lindell's crime fiction, this novel treats "sinister close family relations, neighborliness, and [twisted] dark secrets."

Lindell commented in her 2012 *Uncategorized* blog that prior to the 1990s, Nordic detective novels were categorized as pulp fiction, but she feels that when women authors took up the genre, they added "something new," a female approach to psychological realism. She also believes that "The buildup of intrigue is basically a bit like being in the kitchen, mess up [sic] and rattle the pots and then clean up and put everything back" (*Uncategorized*, 8/20/2012). According to Lindell, Nordic crime fiction writers generally do not write "the American way" with "bad guys" and "good guys," instead concentrating on ordinary folk, where the most dangerous villains can still have good attributes (*Uncategorized*). In addition, she praises crime fiction for its concentration on plot and theme, insisting that "Books are not automatically Art because they do not have a plot!" Lindell finds it "amazing" to be gestating a new book and "fantastic" to be translated and published in countries other than Norway, even if, she says, foreign agents receive 25 percent of Norwegian authors' income (*Uncategorized*, 1/11/2012 and 8/20/2012).

To date, two of Lindell's Cato Isaksen novels have been aired as successful television series. Despite the popularity of her work, Lindell fears failure: "Writing for me is 85 percent work and discomfort and 15 percent joy and happiness" (quoted in Melia).

Crime Novels:

Cato Isaksen Series:

1993: *En grusom kvinnes bekjennelser* ("The Confessions of a Cruel Woman")
1996: *Slangebæreren* ("The Thirteenth Constellation") (filmed)
1999: *Drømmefangeren* ("The Dream Catcher") (filmed)
2000: *Sørgekåpen* ("The Mourning Cloak") (being filmed)
2002: *Nattsøsteren* ("The Night Nurse")
2005: *Orkestergraven* ("The Orchestra Pit")
2007: *Honningfellen* ("The Honey Trap"), filmed, starring Per Olav Sørensen, 2008
2008: *Mørkemannen* ("The Ogre," or "The Dark Man")
2010: *Sukkerdøden* ("Sugar Death")
2012: *Djevelkysset* ("The Devil's Kiss")

Stand-Alone Crime Novel:

2004: *Rødhette* ("Little Red Riding Hood")

Major Awards:

1998: The Mads Wiel Nygaards Endowment

1999: The Riverton Prize for *Drømmefangeren* ("The Dream Catcher")

Website: http://www.unnilindell.no

Richard Macker (crime fiction pseudonym of *Reidar Thomassen*)

b. 1936, Harstad, Norway; Residence: Baerum, Norway; Occupations: teacher, editor, author

After writing several successful mainstream novels beginning in 1969, Reidar Thomassen, writing as "Richard Macker," published his first crime novel, *Mange om liket* ("Much of the Body") in 1974. He has since become better known for his short crime stories than for his novels. As its first Norwegian contributor, he published four of his many short crime stories in English translation in issues of *Ellery Queen's Mystery Magazine*. His second story published there, "*Dødelig spøk*" ("A Deadly Joke"), August 2005, is the title story of a collection published in Norway in 1986 by Aschehoug, the Norwegian publishing house, in honor of Macker's fiftieth birthday. That year "A Deadly Joke" was filmed by NRK, Norway's premier television station and shown during the Easter holidays. Two more of Macker's short crime stories followed in *Ellery Queen's Mystery Magazine*, "The Killer Who Disappeared," 2006, and "The Live Weapon," 2007 (*Mystery Readers Journal*, Fall 2007, 82).

"A Deadly Joke," probably the best known of Macker's hundreds of short crime stories, opens with a verbal fencing match between two men one stormy evening on a Easter vacation hiking trip in the Norwegian wilderness. Karl Rynndal, a self-described elitist, verbally jabs away at Olav Morvik, once his friend and now the butt of a cruel joke by Rynndal that backfires tragically. Macker's ability to evoke crescendoing tensions amid grisly and shocking twists of plot makes this story a standout in its genre.

Crime Fiction:

1974: *Mange om liket* ("Much of the Body"); novel

1975: *Sekretærene som forsvant* ("Secretaries Who Disappeared"); novel

1979: *Ztaib-mysteriet og andre kriminalnoveller* ("The Ztaih Mystery and Other Short Stories"); short fiction collection

1982: *Liket som smilte* ("The Body Smiling"); novel

1986: *Saken mot Anny Brem* ("The Case Against Anny Brem"); novel

1986: *Dødelig spøk* ("A Deadly Joke"), short fiction collection

1989: *Mord i grevens tid og andre kriminalhistorier* ("Murders in the Nick of Time and Other Crime Stories"); short fiction collection

1997: *I sakens anledning* ("In this Context"); short fiction collection

2013: *Fjellro-mysterienie* ("Fjeliro Mysteries); short fiction collection

Major Awards: N/A

Website: N/A

Jan Mehlum

b. January 1, 1945, Tønsberg, Norway; Residence: N/A; Occupations: sociologist, teacher, author

A writer with a varied background that includes an associate professorship in sociology, work in cinema and leadership development, and teaching early childhood education, Mehlum made his popular detective fiction debut in 1998 with the novel *Gylne tider* ("Golden Times"). His series hero is cynical Svend Foyn, a divorced, middle-aged, Jaguar-driving lawyer in the Raymond Chandler tradition with overtones of fictional Swedish detectives Martin Beck and Kurt Wallander. Foyn practices in Tønsberg, and like Karin Fossum's Inspector Sejer, Foyn has a daughter; a dog; a friend, Wilhelm Moerck, who is also a police officer; and a heart of gold. Despite his accountant's objections, he often takes on *pro bono* cases at his own expense. Foyn makes bad choices in women and spends more of his time investigating homicides than he does in court.

Mehlum consistently looks behind society's exterior to seek out his characters' hidden agendas, and he often expands plots which open in the small town setting of Tønsberg and swell into international scope, uncovering commonalities in criminal motivations. Mehlum's second Foyn novel, *Kalde hender* ("Cold Hands"), 1998, which won the Riverton Prize for that year, involves neo–Nazism. A fifteen-year-old skinhead approaches Foyn's office but leaves without a word and later is fatally run over by a train. Mehlum's tenth Foyn novel, *Madrugada* ("Madrugada"), 2009, tackles the hotly debated issue of asylum-seeking refugees when Jasmin Alavi, a Muslim woman, hires Foyn to help her get a Norwegian residence permit. This allows Mehlum to explore human trafficking and the abuse of women, taking Foyn from Tønsberg to Iran.

Each of Mehlum's novels opens with a mysterious precipitating incident that sets Foyn on the trail of miscreants coming from organized crime or possessing pathological personality disorders. The strangely titled *Bake kake søte* ("Bake Cake Sweet"), 2010, seems particularly chilling: an infant girl disappears from her carriage in Tønsberg's town square, setting in motion a huge investigation which uncovers a number of skeletons in various closets. Mehlum's readers consistently applaud his work's verisimilitude and his attention to investigational detail, and *Aftenposten* has declared that no other Norwegian author has stimulated such a desire to read.

Adaptations of Mehlum's novels *En nødvendig død* ("A Necessary Death"), 2002; *Den siste dansen* ("The Last Dance"), 2003; and *Din eneste venn* ("Your Only Friend"), 2005, have been presented by the Norwegian Radio Theatre. The film rights to all Mehlum's Svend Foyn novels have been sold to a major Scandinavian film production company.

Crime Novels:

1996: *Gylne tider* ("Golden Times")
1998: *Kalde hender* ("Cold Hands")
1999: *Det annet kinn* ("The Other Cheek")
2000: *En rettferdig dom* ("A Fair Judgment")
2002: *En nødvendig død* ("A Necessary Death")
2003: *Den siste dansen* ("The Last Dance")
2005: *Din eneste venn* ("Your Only Friend")
2007: *For Guds skyld* ("For God's Sake")
2008: *Det ingen vet* ("That No One Knows")
2009: *Madrugada* ("Madrugada")
2010: *Bake kake søte* ("Bake Cake Sweet")
2011: *Straffen* ("Penalty")

2012: *En god sak* ("A Good Case")
2014: *Ren samvittighet* ("Clear Conscience")

Stand-Alone Thriller:

2013: *Lengsel etter penger* ("Longing for Money")

Major Awards:

1998: The Riverton Prize for *Kalde hender* ("Cold Hands")
2003: The Vestfolds Litterature Prize

Website: http://www.janmehlum.no

*Jon Michelet

> b. July 14, 1944, Moss, Norway; Residence: N/A; Occupations: seaman, stevedore, journalist, television host, editor, publisher, and author

Jon Michelet has produced a wide variety of literature: children's books, plays, thrillers, and crime fiction. He also has been prominent in Norwegian left-wing politics. In 1970, Michelet occupied a central position in the Norwegian Marxist-Leninist Movement, and ever since has been considered a leader of that political group. Until 2003, police surveillance agents monitored his telephone and correspondence. Michelet was president of the Riverton Club from 2003 to 2009, attesting to his contributions to Norwegian crime fiction, which began in 1975 with politically relatively mild novels denouncing white collar crime and superpower spying, though in the late 1970s he also produced powerful anti–Nazi and anti-neo–Nazi statements. Michelet's Maoist detective series hero is the "red" policeman Wilhelm Thygesen, whose more passive than active career as what Nils Nordberg describes as a Ulysses seeking his Ithaca (Nordberg), includes fame on television, a stint as a defense attorney, and imprisonment for murder. Michelet closes Thygesen's career in fiction by portraying him as an aged man wanting nothing but to be let alone to work in his garden. Several Thygesen novels furnished the basis for a popular Norwegian Television (NRK) series.

Regarding Michelet's 1977 thriller *Orions belte* (*Orion's Belt*), probably Michelet's best known work, *Dagbladet* observed, "Jon Michelet cannot change the course of the world, but he can write. His writing makes the sparks fly. It sets off grenades and bombs!" *The London Standard* concurred, praising *Orion's Belt* as "one of the best thrillers of our time." The novel's unusual setting is Norway's remote northern Svalbard archipelago (Spitzbergen), a frigid territory with two principal assets, its coal fields and its strategic location. The territory was awarded to Norway in 1920 with a stipulation forbidding military installations and allowing claims by various nations to parts of its coal resources. The Svalbard coal mines were burned by the Allies in 1941 to keep them from falling into Nazi hands and the Norwegians expelled a German garrison in 1942. In 1944 Norway initially rejected the Soviet Union's demand for a share in the defense of the islands, but during the Cold War Norway allowed a 3000-man Soviet presence on Svalbard, as central a location to a potential Cold War theater as the belt stars are to the constellation Orion, hence Michelet's title. The popularity of this novel sprang mostly from the Norwegian public's fear of nuclear war and their negative reaction to learning that their government had allowed the Soviets to create an installation on Svalbard.

The initial central characters of *Orion's Belt* are Lars, Sverre, and Tom, three shady Norwegian sailors on the cargo ship *Sandy Hook* out to make some easy money by shooting polar bears on a deserted Svalbard island. That "inaccessible island" turns out to house a Soviet secret weapon, and the *Sandy Hook* crew has to fight off a heavily armed Soviet helicopter disguised as a civilian Aeroflot aircraft. They flee for their lives, but Lars and Sverre are killed in another helicopter attack. Tom escapes and walks across Svalbard, but after rescue he is sent to Oslo for interrogation by American military officers. To hush up the affair and maintain the delicate international status quo, the Soviets want to liquidate him and the Americans need to interrogate him, but Tom again escapes, only to be killed under mysterious circumstances. Michelet leaves open whether the Soviets or the Americans are responsible in both the novel and its 1985 film version.

The production of the film version of *Orion's Belt* broke new ground for the Norwegian movie industry. Dag Alveberg and Petter Borgli, neither of whom had ever produced a movie, each mortgaged his home to raise half a million Norwegian *krone* to begin the project, and they hired British screenwriter Richard Harris to adapt the novel for filming. Harris shortened the story but retained Michelet's left-wing political stance. Each scene was recorded twice, once for a Norwegian movie theater version and immediately thereafter with the actors speaking English for an English-language telefilm. All 60 of the cast and crew lived aboard ship for the duration of what was essentially a three-month polar expedition to produce Norway's first action film. The Norwegian Ministry of Foreign Affairs slapped down an official complaint from the Soviet Union's Embassy that charged the filming of *Orion's Belt* disguised military activity, but securing total financing proved more difficult. Norwegian film subsidies increased in the 1980s under an unusual system which increased private capital for film investments, but the total financial package, estimated at 15 million *krone*, was not worked out until 1985.

Overall reception of the film in Norway was positive; most critics praised its exciting story and its conviction that the individual is virtually unimportant in superpower politics. *Adresseavisen* even stated that the film was "too good to be Norwegian." *Orion's Belt* took three top places at Norway's premier film awards, it was nominated for best film at an International Mystery Film Festival, its composers received the 1986 Film Critics' Prize for the musical score, and in 2007, *Dagbladet* ranked *Orion's Belt* as Norway's tenth most important film. The *Svalbardtema* from the musical score, based in part by composers Geir Bøhren and Bent Åserud on whale song and Inuit native flute music, has supplied a haunting *de facto* anthem for the Svalbard archipelago.

Two versions of the original film exist. The first (and inadequate) DVD version appeared in 2004, and an improved DVD accompanied by bonus material became available in 2005. Tomas Backström announced in May 2012 that he had secured half the financing necessary for a remake of the film.

While *Orion's Belt* remains Michelet's greatest success, *Den gule djevelens by* ("The Yellow Devil City"), partly a documentary about the unsolved killing of a Norwegian sailor in New York (Nordberg), is also popular in Norway. Michelet received the Riverton Prize twice, once in 2001, for *Den frosne kvinnen* ("The Frozen Woman") and in 1981 for *Hvit som snø* ("White as Snow") which in 2009 was ranked third among *Dagbladet's* 25 best Norwegian crime novels of all time. In "White as Snow," arguably Michelet's most effective hardboiled crime novel, Wilhelm Thygesen, now both an ex-lawyer and an ex-policeman, awakens hung over one morning with no idea how blood got on his bedclothes and how an obviously murdered corpse got into his bathroom. In the course of his subsequent attempt to clear himself by finding the real killer, Thygesen encounters provocative Linda Leirgulen and probes the menacing Oslo underworld, where he comes too close to narcotics for either his own comfort or safety.

When asked to list his favorite books on crime, Jo Nesbø, who feels that mixing agendas very seldom produces good literature, recalled reading "White as Snow" in the 1980s, a period full of passionate political rhetoric in Norway. Nesbø says he was surprised at how well Michelet, then a prominent left wing political figure, could write (*The Browser*).

Crime Novels:

1975: *Den drunkner ei som henges skal* ("The Drowning One That Should Be Hanged")
1977: *Orions belte* (*Orion's Belt*, tr. Ellen Nations)
1980: *Hvit som snø* ("White as Snow")
1981: *Den gule djevelens by* ("The Yellow Devil City")
1984: *Panamaskipet* ("Panama Ship")
1985: *Mannen på motorsykkelen* ("The Man on the Motorcycle")
1989: *Thygesens terrorist* ("Thygesen, a Terrorist")
2001: *Den frosne kvinnen* ("The Frozen Woman")
2003: *Aftensang i Alma-Ata* ("Evening Song in Alma-Ata")
2005: *Thygesen-fortellinger* ("Thygesen's Stories") (short fiction)
2008: *Mordet på Woldnes* ("The Murder of Woldnes")
2010: *Døden i Baugen* ("Death in the Bow")

Major Awards:

1981: The Riverton Prize for *Hvit som snø* ("White as Snow")
2001: The Riverton Prize for *Den frosne kvinnen* ("The Frozen Woman")

Website: N/A

Jo Nesbø

> b. March 29, 1960, Oslo, Norway; Residence: Oslo, Norway; Occupations: soccer player, journalist, rock music singer, financial analyst, rock climber, children's author, novelist

Jo Nesbø has been called today's "king of Nordic crime writing" with over 24 million of his books translated into forty-seven languages (McWeeney) and as of 2013 a Nesbø title was selling somewhere in the world every 23 seconds (Clare). Jo Nesbø's fiction emerged from "a long line of Scandinavian crime fiction exposing the dark side of a seemingly ideal society" (*New York Times*, quoted in Mulcahy). Nesbø claims Henrik Ibsen as the major influence on his work, because in Ibsen's plays like *The Wild Duck* and *Hedda Gabler*, Nesbø says, "the truth is revealed bit by bit. At the beginning everything seems normal but there are always dark secrets and the hidden secrets are always about love and greed" (quoted in Mulcahy). In a 2014 interview, Nesbø at fifty-four also claimed that "if there's anything really Norwegian" about his books, "it's probably that black humor, a really Norwegian thing" (quoted in McCabe), a quality found at its extreme in the darkly ironic plots of Ibsen's dramas.

Nesbø has also noted the strong influence of Ibsen's insistence that an individual, man or woman, be himself or herself has exerted on his Doctor Proctor children's series, currently four novels. The series, which opened in 2007 with *Doktor Proktors prompepulver* (*Doctor Proctor's Fart Powder*), according to Nesbø stresses the importance of being oneself, because human creativity and imagination give individuals the courage to do so (Hesse). The same theory of fiction animates his highly praised Harry Hole (English speakers variously pronounce the name as *hurler*, *hool-eh*, or *HEU-leh*) police procedural series, which reveals "cracks in the welfare state" (Forshaw 107), allowing Nesbø to demonstrate how challenging and painful it is for a Norwegian detective today to exercise and maintain the courage to "be himself."

Nesbo's tortured protagonist Harry Hole was born on a 1996 30-hour flight from Oslo to Sydney, Australia, to take a six-month break from his day stockbroker job; at night he performed, as he still does, as lead singer with the rock band, *Di Derre* ("Those Guys"). When Nesbø returned to Oslo in 1997, he quit his day job and in a few weeks at home with his laptop, weeks that he describes as "the happiest of his life" (Mulcahy), he finalized his first Harry Hole novel, *Flaggermusmannen* (*The Bat*, literally "The Batman"). Feeling the novel might be seen as "another crap book by a pop star" (quoted in Forshaw July 8, 2011), Nesbø sent the novel to a publisher pseudonymously, but when it was published under his real name, it won several awards, including the Scandinavian Glass Key Award for the best Nordic crime novel of the year. An English translation of *The Bat* appeared in 2012.

In a 2013 interview, Nesbø confessed he still doesn't see Hole clearly, though Nesbø says he wanted "a big man—a man who took up room physically and also mentally ... a typical Norwegian male ... a hard drinker, a hard worker, a loner" (quoted in McWeeney). Unlike the typical hardboiled American fictional detective, however, Nesbø's Hole cannot function while drunk. Harry Hole is a highly contradictory figure; his mother, one of the indigenous Sami people who herd reindeer in the far north of Scandinavia, died when Harry was in his early 20s, and he and his schoolteacher father have always had a strained relationship (McWeeney). Despite his many vicissitudes, Harry has an uncanny talent for weaving the various threads of a complex investigation into a rational pattern, as well as "a fierce commitment to justice and huge sympathy for vulnerable people" (McWeeney). Harry's close friends belong to the blue-collar and immigrant communities, but he loses everyone he ever loved. He believes in the Scandinavian legal and political systems, and he eventually feels that catching a killer accomplishes a great deal (Nesbø, quoted in Fritz).

Harry Hole is also a talented FBI-trained police detective who graduated from both a Norwegian law school and his country's police academy. As "a man at war with the world, including himself" (Fister, *Scandinavian Crime Fiction*), Hole also suffers from incurable addictions, primarily alcoholism. Basing Harry Hole on a combination of himself; characters from Molde, Nesbø's home town, especially one Olav Hole, a policeman in his grandmother's village; Frank Miller's Batman (*Publishers Weekly* 94); and Ibsen's antihero Brand (Forster 94); Nesbø created a tragic, "lonely, misguided, and tormented spirit" (Meyer 264) that Nesbø's translator Don Bartlett finds one of the most credible policemen in current fiction (Bartlett, quoted in Forshaw 106). Often compared to Henning Mankell's Kurt Wallander "but closer in age and style to Åke Edwardson's Erik Winter" (Moyer 61), Hole sometimes wears 1980s band T-shirts, always wears black Doc Marten combat boots, and frequently references popular movies (Moyer 61).

Nesbø, whose own appearance is said to resemble a cross between Sting and Daniel Craig (Mulcahy), has indicated that by the time he was working on *Rødstrupe*, 2000 (*The Redbreast*, tr. 2006), his third Harry Hole novel, he realized that Hole contained "significant areas of [Nesbø's] autobiography" that "just happened without me being aware of it" (quoted in Crace). Until he wrote *The Redbreast*, Nesbø wasn't sure that he would finish the long story line he had developed for Harry Hole, but now Nesbø feels certain he'll follow Harry to the end—and he claims, "there will be an end" (quoted in Fritz).

Over the last 15 years of his fictional career, Harry Hole "has been shot, stabbed, and beaten up countless times and has the scars to prove it, a titanium finger and a slash from mouth to ear ... and at the end of Nesbø's ninth Hole novel, *Gjenferd*, 2011 (*Phantom*, tr. 2012), Harry "was left for dead in a sewer with two bullet wounds and rats gnawing at his body" (Crace). Shot in the head by his surrogate son in *Phantom*, Hole is missing and near death throughout most of *Politi*, 2013 (*Police*, tr. 2013), his tenth novel, but at its close Nesbø brings him back feeling hopeful, at least for a time (*Police* 436).

Australian critic Sue Turnbull notes that after Nesbø conceived Harry Hole on that 1996 long-haul flight to Australia, Nesbø "hunkered down in a hotel room" and wrote 18 hours a day, inspired by a volume of Australian aboriginal myths containing the legend of the Narajdam, the bat, that the aborigines consider the symbol of death. Turnbull conjectures that *The Bat* was not translated until 2012 because publishers "didn't want to take a punt on an Australian setting for a Scandinavian crime novel." Here Hole is enmeshed in his own personal and professional problems and romantically involved with a Swedish barmaid, but with the odd-couple assistance of a friendly indigenous detective, Andrew Kensington, Harry helps the Sydney police investigate the rape and murder of a young Norwegian woman, a crime which turns out to be the work of a serial killer. Turnbull finds that Nesbø presents the Australian backdrop "with the clear-sighted precision of the jet-lagged tourist for whom everything is both strange and disorienting" (Turnbull). Not the most powerful of the Harry Hole novels, *The Bat* does supply crucial elements of Hole's back story, especially his always-doomed love affairs and his incipient alcoholism, which strikes halfway through this novel. Sue Turnbull also observes that these elements precipitate a change from "the relatively upbeat and sunny into the depths of Nordic gloom" dominating Nesbø's later Hole novels.

Apparently Nesbø also intended both *The Bat* and his second Hole novel, *Kakerlakkene*, 1998 (*Cockroaches*, tr. 2012), set in Bangkok, to reflect Norwegian society at the time (Foster 94), and when it was published in a paperback English version, *Cockroaches* sold 20 million copies worldwide. The novel's epigraph claims that Norwegians living in Thailand share a rumor that one of their ambassadors who purportedly died in an auto accident was really the victim of a mysterious plot. This springboard launches Harry Hole's second investigation, one opposed by powerful forces. Harry is supposed to defuse possible scandals in this seedy Bangkok setting, but he can't avoid airing some uncomfortable secrets as well. One of the villains he pursues realizes that Harry thinks like one of the losers he usually chases, forgetting the whole picture (*Cockroaches* 349). This attribute both ensures Harry's success and inspires his tormenting self-doubt.

Nesbø then returned Hole to Oslo, Hole's home world and his own: "If I was going to be a Scandinavian writer, the prevailing notion was that the book should be set in Norway," Nesbø admits, but Harry Hole also has a tinge of American culture. Nesbø has observed that "20 percent of the country [Norway] immigrated to America," including his own grandfather. Nesbø's father grew up in Bay Ridge, Brooklyn, but eventually he and his family returned to Norway (quoted in Ermolino 28). Today, Nesbø claims, Oslo suffers from problems similar to some that urban areas of the United States are experiencing; he believes Oslo has Europe's highest number of fatal drug overdoses, reported rapes, organized crime, hardcore prostitution, and trafficking (Fister, *Scandinavian Crime Fiction*). As both a private person and a police detective, Harry Hole suffers enormously from his personal and professional dealings with these societal ills.

In a 2010 *Publishers Weekly* interview, Nesbø indicated that though he has had no direct experience as a policeman, he makes his descriptions of Oslo's *Politihuset* (police headquarters) realistic by drawing on his general experience of people's working interactions (Ermolino 23). In an interview with *The Browser*, Nesbø cited a non-fiction crime book, Kjetil Stensvik Østli's *Cops and Robbers*, which analyzes the largest robbery in Norwegian history, a $9 million holdup of a Stavanger bank, as a huge clue to his creation of Harry Hole's fictional personality. Nesbø says that Østli shows how the robber's mentality is "actually very similar" to the police mentality, which is true, Nesbø claims, for Harry Hole: "The people he feels he can most relate to are the criminals that he is hunting" (*The Browser*). Nesbø also says that to some extent, he planned the Hole books in detail "from day one," but since he feels Harry Hole's universe is "a city with broad and narrow streets, some … just names that are yet to be explored" (Foster 94), many novelistic details are surfacing as Nesbø goes along.

Initially Nesbø chose not to have his first two Hole novels translated, so *Rødstrupe*, 2000 (*The Redbreast*, tr. 2006), was the first Harry Hole novel to appear in English. Nesbø had originally wanted to write a big mainstream European novel, but he decided to try his hand at a crime novel first, as he thought that would not be as time-consuming; he'd send it off to a publisher, and then, after "a polite rejection" he would start the bigger work—but that has never happened. After his first two Hole novels, *The Redbreast* met with such resounding success that in 2004 Norwegian book clubs voted *The Redbreast* "the best Norwegian crime novel ever written" (Moyer 61), and in 2009 *Dagbladet* ranked it ninth in the newspaper's twenty-five best Norwegian crime novels of all time.

In *The Redbreast* Nesbø ingeniously counterpointed Norwegian present-day neo–Nazi activities with painful echoes of the Nazi occupation that the Norwegian national consciousness apparently has not yet completely resolved. During World War II, Jo Nesbø's father Per Nesbø had fought with the Germans against the Soviets on the Eastern Front near Leningrad, because he believed that the Soviets were a greater threat to Norway than the Nazis were (Siegel). For doing so, Per Nesbø served three years in prison after the war. Jo Nesbø used many of his father's recollections of that grueling military service in *The Redbreast*.

The novel opens when Hole, as a talented but erratic police detective, mistakenly shoots a U.S. Secret Service agent during a presidential visit to Oslo. To maintain international rapport, Oslo bureaucrats declare Hole "a hero," promote him to Inspector, and move him to a "screened operation" in the political unit of the Oslo police force, where he investigates the reviving Norwegian neo–Nazi movement. The Norwegian neo–Nazis now embrace a firmer ideology and better organization than their 1980s predecessors had exhibited, as well as enjoying a wide financial network. They not only fervently oppose the liberal immigration policy Norway has maintained for a long time, but they also decry the country's unemployment problem, largely blaming it on governmental policies. The neo–Nazis also want a government opposed to Norway's social democracy (*Redbreast* 76)—exactly the agenda espoused in real life by Norwegian white supremacist and mass murderer Anders Breivik. In *The Redbreast*, Harry Hole carries out surveillance of a neo–Nazi ex-convict who recently avoided a jail sentence on a legal technicality. Against his superior's order, Hole also "chases wartime ghosts" (*Redbreast* 244), beginning by tracing the illegal importation into Norway of a Märklin, the world's most expensive rifle.

That rifle becomes a vital clue to serial killings Harry also investigates against orders, murders related to Norway's darkest Occupation days. Drawing edgy parallels between Norwegian pro– and anti–Nazi activity in World War II and Norway's present-day neo–Nazi movement, Nesbø underscores the complexity of Norway's response to Nazism in flashbacks to the brutal 1940s infantry warfare on the Eastern Front, where young Norwegians who like Per Nesbø joined the Nazi *Wehrmacht* to battle the Soviet Union's Red Army, were convinced that the Norwegian king and crown prince had deserted their people. As Per Nesbø had, they feared the Soviet Communists more than the German Nazis.

In *The Redbreast* one of Nesbø's fictional Norwegian soldiers claims that an average 60 percent of such Norwegian infantry companies fighting with the *Wehrmacht*, some superficially trained in Germany, died each year of the war (*Redbreast* 224), but that as late as 1944, Norwegian volunteers to the Nazi forces "streamed to the Eastern Front" in the doomed belief they could save their country from the Soviets (*Redbreast* 225). Nesbø ruthlessly yet compassionately portrays the embittered survivors who returned, shamed, to Norway. They reserved their particular scorn for "latter-day saints" "who sat on their backsides during the war and suddenly rushed into the

Resistance" as the war was ending, and who today hypocritically "swell the ranks" of those who loudly celebrate "Norwegians' heroic efforts for the right side" (*Redbreast* 249). A *Washington Post* reviewer commented, "the fact that Nesbø is able to make us understand, and almost sympathize with, a crazy, homicidal old Nazi, is itself an achievement." Even more dramatic, *The Redbreast* conveys Nesbø's strong suggestion that Norway, like his Eastern Front sharpshooter character who now shares a body with an old man who convinced others he had been a loyal resistance fighter, "is suffering from a split personality—a public persona that is peaceful and tolerating, concealing a national identity that is too close to Nazism for comfort" (Fister, "Reparations" 6).

In *The Redbreast*, Nesbø also achieved an impressive literary characterization in his development of Harry Hole as a deeply flawed yet sympathetic protagonist fighting a corrupted sociopolitical system and almost always losing: he loses both his police partner Ellen Gjelten, killed in the line of duty, and Rakel, the woman he desperately loves. Whereas for Raymond Chandler's Philip Marlowe, one of Harry Hole's spiritual ancestors, the enemy is always the "filthy rich," beyond the criminals Harry Hole tracks and often brings to his own kind of justice, the ultimate monster Hole wrestles is the soulless political corruption that Nesbø scourges through his portrayal of *The Redbreast*'s Bernt Brandhaug, a politician rotten to the core, who blasts "the scope democracy will always allow for mediocrity" because he believes no one can expect "politically elected housewives and farmers" to understand the complex responsibilities they are supposed to manage. While denigrating those housewives and farmers in Norway's parliament, Brandhaug exploits Norway's social democratic system for his own self-serving and sinister purposes (*Redbreast* 353).

In *Sorgenfri*, 2002 (*Nemesis*, tr. 2008), Nesbø individualizes the role of revenge in today's society. Harry Hole awakens so badly hung over he can't remember the previous twelve hours of his life and next to him finds Anna, who'd shared his drunken evening, dead, leaving Harry the prime suspect in her murder. To clear his name, Harry, pursued by his police colleague and bitter enemy Tom Waaler, has to leave Oslo to chase down bank robbers, eventually returning to the arms of Rakel, the woman he will always love. After this novel, Nesbø narrowed the focus of the Hole novels. Reviewing Harry Hole's next adventure in *Marekors*, 2003 (*The Devil's Star*, tr. 2010), *New York Times* crime critic Marilyn Stasio concluded that this novel explored "no comparable political or ethical issues" (*New York Times Book Review* March 10, 2010: 26), instead probing Harry Hole's "morbid obsession with his own nightmares."

Those nightmares arise from the bitter reality Harry Hole endures, facing his responsibility for his own losses in a world more subject to politics than to honest police work. This causes him to drink too much in the attempt to forget what he grimly realizes as truth: "Primarily we're doing this for those sitting in positions of power ... people who could have and should have sounded the alarm before" (*Redbreast* 516). Nevertheless, like a captured ancient Viking chieftain who defeated his enemies by laughing at them while they tore his lungs open for crabs to feast on, Harry Hole soldiers on. The wonder of Nesbø's tortured hero is that he keeps on doing so.

Nesbø feels himself more related to American hard-boiled crime writers like Raymond Chandler than to practitioners of the "Scandinavian crime novel" (Foster 94), which probably accounts for traits in Harry Hole's flawed-paladin personality as well as Nesbø's rapid-fire storytelling style, but Nesbø's "keen and intelligent engagement with social issues" seems to be a major factor in making his books consistently approach market leadership in Scandinavian crime fiction (Forshaw 107), earning high praise at home and abroad.

Since the publication of *The Redbreast* in English translation, Nesbø's reputation has soared. In 2010, Knopf bought four of Nesbø's novels, including *Sorgenfri* (*Nemesis*), originally published in 2002; *Marekors*, 2003 (*The Devil's Star*, tr. 2005); *Frelseren*, 2005 (*The Redeemer*, tr. 2009), and *Snømannen*, 2007 (*The Snowman*, tr. 2010), all translated by Don Bartlett.

When asked by *Bloomberg News* editor Alec McCabe whether he begins a book with a puzzle and then builds the story around it, or whether he allows the puzzle to develop as the book proceeds, Nesbø claimed he follows no rules. He cited as an example his use of a water bed he bought as the genesis for *The Devil's Star*, where a woman in a one-night stand discovers the nude body of the man's former lover sloshing beneath her in his water bed. This novel became "sort of a love story," Nesbø thought, because on contemplating why this grisly crime had been committed, he had theorized that the man had killed his ex-lover and put her in the bed in order to keep her with him forever (quoted in McCabe). In her 2010 review of *The Devil's Star*, Hole's speeding-bullet-paced pursuit of a serial killer, Marilyn Stasio described the Hole series as "testosterone-stoked," with Hole "in the company of the renegade loners of American crime fiction" (Stasio, "Killing" 26). A *Publishers Weekly* reviewer of *Frelseren* found that that novel treats a highly important ethical issue in today's world, "redemption through violence" ("Books of Redeeming Value"). Like *The Redbreast*, *The Redeemer* parallels two crime plots several decades apart, eventually revealing them to be related. In the 1991 plot, Nesbø's featured characters Robert Karlsen and his brother Jon are Salvation Army cadets at the organization's country retreat when a fourteen-year-old girl is raped. Twenty-two years later, as Harry Hole is closing an investigation of an Oslo drug-related homicide, a Serbian criminal mistakes Robert Karlsen for Jon and shoots him on a downtown Oslo street. Nesbø's trademark gripping prose style reinforces the unusual theme of redemption through violence that dominates most of his Hole novels.

In May 2010, Knopf released the English translation of *Snømannen*, 2007 (*The Snowman*), a harrowing tale in which the villain builds a sinister snowman to signal each of his homicides. At the beginning of this seventh novel in the series, one of Nesbø's most widely acclaimed, Hole receives a peculiar anonymous note signed by "The Snowman," and soon he begins to discover parallels to older cold cases in which women each disappeared on the first day of a season's snowfall, setting Hole, bedeviled by his alcoholism and his difficulties with society, on the trail of a serial killer nobody else believes exists. As an indication of Nesbø's growing popularity in the United States, Martin Scorsese was rumored in early 2013 to be directing the American film adaptation of *The Snowman* (Risker).

In *Gjenferd*, 2011 (*Phantom*, tr. 2012), Hole returns to Oslo from Hong Kong because his estranged teenaged "son" Oleg (actually the son of a long-lost Russian and Rakel, the abiding love of Harry's life), who is pushing "violin," a new synthetic heroin, in Oslo, has been accused of murdering Gusto Hanssen, another young drug dealer. Harry's unconventional investigation, during which he continues to "let his sensory impressions, the almost imperceptible details, do their own talking before the analytical part of the brain resumed its functioning" (*Phantom* 54), unmasks both "Dubai," the mysterious leader of the Oslo drug scene, and governmental corruption so widespread that it extends into the Oslo police force that Harry had abandoned three years earlier. Harry's dedication to the truth takes precedence over his emotional attachment to Oleg, leading to a shattering conclusion where Harry heartbreakingly has to do what he must do in a life that he believes is no longer worth living (*Phantom* 458–9).

Critic Carlo Wolff who finds Nesbø's work "deeply moral" notes that in *Phantom* Nesbø introduces an unusual narrative device of italicized sections told dreamlike from Gusto's mind, alternating Harry's story with Gusto's, "casting a kind of spell even as it develops scaffolding for the increasingly serpentine plot" (Wolff). Besides that compelling mystery plot, *Phantom* is also a tender love story, as Harry and Rakel reunite after years of separation; Wolff concludes that like Stieg Larsson and Henning Mankell, Nesbø creates his female characters with "affection and understanding." On the other hand, besides being cited for the gruesome violence in his novels, Nesbø has occasionally been suspected of drawing some characters too closely to real life. Two notable examples include a prominent Norwegian publisher who feels Nesbø made him the prototype for the villain of *The Snowman*, and a prominent real-life Norwegian female public figure who suggests Nesbø seemingly sketched her as a nymphomaniac politician (Mulcahy).

For some time, filmmakers have been adapting Nesbø's work for both movies and television. Alexander Woo adapted Nesbø's dark comedic stand-alone novel *Hodejegerne*, 2008 (*Headhunters*, tr. 2011), for Yellow Bird Entertainment, the company behind the Swedish screen version of Stieg Larsson's Millennium Trilogy, which is also developing a thriller skein for HBO with Lionsgate Television. *Headhunters'* big 2011 studio film version received modest acclaim at the 2011 Cannes film festival and then became the third highest-grossing Norwegian film of all time (Keslassy).

For years Nesbø refused to consider offers to film his Harry Hole novels, but as he told *Bloomberg News* editor Alec McCabe in 2014, he always had said, "If Martin Scorsese calls, I might reconsider ... and that's why I sold the rights to *The Snowman* to him" (quoted in McCabe). Scorsese initiated plans for a film version of *The Snowman* involving both Swedish filmmaker Tomas Alfredsen and Matthew Michael Carnahan, the screenwriter of *World War Z*, but Scorsese had to back out of the project because of scheduling conflicts (Spines). The film version of *The Snowman* remains in production with Tomas Alfredsen as director. Alfredsen is working on the film script for *The Snowman* with Soren Sveistrup, who created the popular Danish procedural television series *The Killing*. In late 2012, Warner Brothers bought film rights to Nesbø's stand-alone novel *Sønnen*, 2012 (*The Son*, tr. 2014).

In October 2013, the UK publishing form of Harvill Secker announced they would publish novels Nesbø wrote under the pseudonym "Tom Johansen." Later it was decided to publish them under Nesbø's own name. The first two of these novels, provisionally titled in English "Blood on the Snow" and "More Blood on the Water," were originally scheduled for fall 2014 and spring 2015 publication, with a third, "The Kidnapping," to follow. Leonard Di Caprio has reputedly been set to produce and possibly star in the film version of "Blood on the Snow," Nesbø's story of a hit man who falls in love with his employer's wife after he has been contracted to kill her (McNary).

In 2013, Nesbø himself became a television writer. Yellow Bird, the Swedish film company founded by novelist Henning Mankell which produced the Swedish film version of Stieg Larsson's Millennium Trilogy, is developing Nesbø's concept of a ten-part series called *Occupied*, a near-future political thriller with a "not-so-far-fetched scenario": Russia invades Norway to claim Norwegian oil reserves, and the series revolves around "how the inhabitants of a modern first-world nation might respond to becoming an occupied territory" (Spines).

Interviewing Nesbø in March 2012, John Preston of *The Telegraph* observed that in spite of Nesbø's mushrooming worldwide sales, the author himself seems somewhat bemused by the success of his claustrophobic and violent thrillers starring the "brutal yet hopelessly romantic policeman" Harry Hole. Nesbø seems to share Hole's restlessness, essential gloom, and regret for Norway's lost innocence, but his own belief in himself is unshakable. He claims, "you have to believe you're one of the best writers in the world" (Preston). Nesbø has also said he has a few more plans for Harry, who despite his bleak outlook at the end of *Phantom* will have "a few happy moments" before "things ... will get worse. And finally he will go straight to hell.... But that's life, isn't it? There are no happy endings" (quoted in Crace).

In *Politi*, 2013 (*Police*, tr. 2013). brutal serial killings that seem to call for Harry Hole's detective talents pile up, but Hole is missing for most of the novel, lying badly wounded, comatose and guarded by police in an Oslo hospital. Nesbø at the end gives his readers what seems a final glimpse of Harry Hole, with what may be second thoughts about his tortured hero's ultimate fate: "listening to the church bells pealing out over Oppsal. Feeling that everything was right with the world, at rest, in harmony. Knowing this was how things should end, like this" (*Police* 436).

Nesbo's 2012 stand-alone novel *Sønnen* (*The Son*) enjoyed a 150,000 first printing of its 2014 English translation. Nesbø began this novel on Good Friday of 2012 and based it on a Biblical text. As the story of Sonny Lofthus, a thirty-year-old heroin addict imprisoned since age eighteen in Oslo for two terrible homicides, *The Son* develops its unlikely hero, offspring of a disgraced policeman who Sonny thinks committed suicide and a mother who loses both her sanity and her life, as the recipient of fearful secrets from other prisoners, whom Sonny rewards with absolution and forgiveness (McWeeney). After Sonny learns his father may have been murdered, however, he escapes from prison and embarks as "the Buddha with the sword" (Rubin 18) on a ferocious revengeful killing spree against high-ranking drug dealing and human trafficking mob bosses, while hardboiled police detective Simon Kefas, who's battling his own demons and his wife's approaching blindness, tracks Sonny to a shattering conclusion. Capable of both "supreme goodness" and brutal violence, Sonny illustrates Nesbø's absorption with the forces that drive an individual to evil (Elphick). In Simon, who is losing his devotion to police work, Nesbø reveals "the detective's curse: Inevitably, you are almost too willing to un-see what you've seen, yet resentful of those who can't see what you've seen for them" (Rubin 18).

The Son's "surprisingly complex themes" also detour into "the increasing gentrification of Oslo and how that affects the working class families who have resided there for generations" (Elphick), painting Oslo's "seamy underbelly," a world "redolent of hypocrisy and top-to-bottom corruption" (Clare) with a plethora of grey shades, "a razor-sharp dissection of how far greed can push" some human beings (Elphick). In this complicated treatment of father-son relationships, Nesbø shows his equally complex characters seeking "redemption by spanning their private Vaterland Bridge between old and new Oslo and their old and new selves" (Rubin 19).

Jo Nesbø's literary star continues to rise. As an unusual mark of critical respect, Nesbø was chosen to contribute to Penguin-Random House's Hogarth Shakespeare project reinterpreting Shakespeare's works for a 21st-century audience, to be launched in 2016, the 400th anniversary of Shakespeare's death. Other notable participants are Margaret Atwood, retelling the *Tempest*; Howard Jacobson, *The Merchant of Venice*; and Jeanette Winterson, *The Winter's Tale* (Stock). Nesbø is producing a crime *noir* version of *Macbeth* (Elphick), a story about a returning war hero who descends into corruption and insanity. Nesbø set it in the 1970s, in an unnamed city with a corrupt police force (McCabe), a situation that he says tackles topics he has dealt with since he began writing: "A main character who has the moral code and the corrupted mind, the personal strength and the emotional weakness ... the struggle for power, set both in a gloomy, stormy crime noir-like setting and in a dark, paranoid human mind" (quoted in Stock).

In 2013, Nesbø described the three novels he had written as "Tom Johansen" as simple hard-boiled novels. According to *Dagavisen* these novels are Nesbø's tribute to pulp fiction: 2015's *Blod på snø* (*Blood on the Snow*, tr. 2015) and its successors, tentatively titled "More Blood on the Snow" and "The Kidnapping." Warner Brothers has purchased the movie rights to *Blood on Snow*.

Though Nesbø has often been compared with Sweden's Stieg Larsson, Christine Spines finds that "the moral ambiguity of Nesbø's anti-heroes and sympathetic villains has more in common with the work of Dennis Lehane, shot through with a Thomas Harris–like infusion of twisted psychopaths ... and his nascent career in TV writing has the potential to offer him a promising platform for his elegantly plotted explorations of human depravity" (Spines).

Crime Novels:

The Harry Hole Series:

1997: *Flaggermusmannen* (*The Bat*, tr. Don Bartlett, 2012)
1998: *Kakerlakkene* (*The Cockroaches*, tr. Don Bartlett, 2013
2000: *Rødstrupe* (*The Redbreast*, tr. Don Bartlett, 2006)
2002: *Sorgenfri* (*Nemesis*, tr. Don Bartlett. 2008)
2003: *Marekors* (*The Devil's Star*, tr. Don Bartlett, 2005)
2005: *Frelseren* (*The Redeemer*, tr. Don Bartlett, 2009)
2007: *Snømannen* (*The Snowman*, tr. Don Bartlett, 2010)
2009: *Panserhjerte* (*The Leopard*, tr. Don Bartlett, 2011)
2011: *Gjenferd* (*Phantom*, tr. Don Bartlett, 2012)
2013: *Politi* (*Police*, tr. Don Bartlett, 2013)

Stand-Alone Novels:

2008: *Hodejegerne* (*Headhunters*, tr. Don Bartlett, 2011)
2012: *Sønnen* (*The Son*, tr. Charlotte Borslund, 2014)

Novels Originally Intended to Appear Under the Pen Name "Tom Johansen":

2015: *Blod på snø* (*Blood on the Snow*, tr. Neil Smith, 2015)
Projected: "More Blood on the Snow," for 2015; and "The Kidnapping," for 2016

Major Awards:

1997: The Riverton Prize, for *Flaggermusmannen* (*The Bat*)
1998: The Glass Key Award, for *Flaggermusmannen* (*The Bat*)
2000: The Norwegian Booksellers' Prize, for *Rødstrupe* (*The Redbreast*)
2007: The Norwegian Booksellers' Prize, for *Snømannen* (*The Snowman*)
2010: Nomination for the Edgar Award, for *Nemesis*
2013: The Norwegian Peer Gynt Prize

Websites: http://www.jonesbo.com; http://www.jonesbo.co.uk

Aslak Nore

> b. May 12, 1978, Oslo, Norway; Residence: Various, including Guatemala; Occupations: infantry-man, journalist, editor, author

From extensive military-journalistic experience, Nore has begun to create *noir* fiction that *Dagbladet* critic Torbjørn Ekelund on September 16, 2012, called "something as rare as a wise thriller." Ekelund felt Nore's debut novel, *En norsk spion* ("A Norwegian Spy") combines military expertise and experience with writing skill. "A Norwegian Spy" uses first-person narration to follow a secret Norwegian military team collectively called "the Dove of Peace" to Dubai to meet an Iranian defector who is supposed to provide them information about missiles which will shortly be used to attack Norwegian forces in Afghanistan, the novel's principal setting. Nore comments forcefully on Norway's military involvement in Afghanistan through his narrator Peter Wessel, creating a mood, according to Ekelund, that is "reminiscent of that found in … the great American crime writers and their ragtag heroes." Ekelund closes his laudatory review by quoting the words Wessel heard when an admiral recruited him: *"'You seem to possess a rare combination of brains and balls, kid. Take care of it'"* (italics in original).

Espionage Novel:

2012: *En norsk spion* ("A Norwegian Spy")

Major Awards: N/A

Website: N/A

Gert Nygårdshaug

b. March 22, 1946, Tynset, Norway; Residence: Lier, Norway; Occupation: poet and author

According to Norwegian crime critic Nils Nordberg, Nygårdshaug is "the most idiosyncratic of Norwegian mystery mongers." Nygårdshaug has wide-ranging interests, including an enormous butterfly collection: he has traveled widely, especially in South America, and his other hobbies include archaeology and anthropology, fly fishing, wine, and gastronomy. He has produced poetry, children's literature, and novels with social issues, but he is best known for his detective novels, planned as a series of ten, for which he concocted now rare "pure puzzle" mystery plots. *Dagbladet* crime critic Kurt Hanssen on October 9, 2006, called these novels Norway's most original and playful mystery series (Hanssen).

Nygårdshaug's detective hero, Fredric Drum, an Oslo gourmet chef and Michelin-starred restaurant owner, shares some of Nygårdshaug's own esoteric pursuits, especially wine lore, archaeology, and untangling ciphers and ancient scripts. Drum's detective venues stretch from France and Italy to Egypt, Mexico, and New Guinea, in a peculiar universe full of "mystical speculation and modern science" (Nordberg). After Drum is fatally shot in the fifth book of the series, the sixth opens by revealing that all the earlier ones have been the "psychotic fantasies" of Skarphedin Olsen, a police detective with KRIPOS (Norway's National Criminal Investigation Service), whose young nephew is Frederic Drum. Nordberg saw no way to predict how the series might end, but in 2013, Nygårdshaug announced a new crime novel, *Pergamentet* ("Parchment") featuring Skarphedin Olsen investigating a mysterious murder connected with "the decoding of a most mystical book" (quoted from Nygårdshaug's website). Nygårdshaug has since participated in theme tours "in the footsteps of Fredric Drum" to Saint-Emilion.

In 2013, Nygårdshaug also reprised the interest in eco-crime which he first displayed in *Mengele Zoo* ("Mengele Zoo"), 1989, with *Chimera* ("Chimera") set in the Congo rain forest where scientists are studying effects of climate change on gorillas, orchids, and pandemics, fulfilling *Chimera*'s thesis that "To understand a forest, one has to climb more than one tree."

A year earlier, Nygårdshaug had climbed a literary tree that infuriated many other Norwegian crime writers who accused him of claiming that their work had become "an orgy of torture and brutal killing methods" (Nygårdshaug, quoted in Fjellberg). Kjetil Try believed that Nygårdshaug had underestimated readers, who Try felt were discerning enough to recognize good writing when they saw it. Try cited Stieg Larsson, Henning Mankell, and Jo Nesbø as examples of Scandinavian crime authors whose techniques and style, not the gruesome murders they depict, make them best sellers (Try). Author Jørgen Brekke also took exception to Nygårdshaug's criticism: "I think this kind of criticism [Nygårdshaug's] is approaching censorship. He has decided in advance what a book can contain"; Brekke also feels that Nygårdshaug's kind of literary criticism belongs in the 1700s. (Brekke, quoted in Fjellberg).

Lithium Entertainment, a South African film company, purchased film rights to four of Nygårdshaug's mainstream novels in 2004.

Crime Novels:

1985: *Honningkrukken* ("The Honey Jar")
1987: *Jegerdukken* ("The Hunter's Puppet")
1990: *Dødens codex* ("The Codes of Death")
1992: *Det niende prinsipp* ("The Ninth Principle")
1993: *Cassandras finger* ("Cassandra's Finger")
1996: *Kiste nummer fem* ("Coffin Number Five")
2000: *Den balsamerte ulven* ("The Embalmed Wolf")
2001: *Liljer fra Jerusalem* ("Lilies from Jerusalem")
2004: *Alle orkaners mor* ("The Mother of All Hurricanes")
2006: *Rødsonen* ("The Red Zone")
2013: *Pergamentet* ("Parchment")

Eco-Crime Stand-Alone Novels:

1989: *Mengele Zoo* ("Mengele Zoo")
2011: *Chimera* ("Chimera")

Major Awards:

2007: *Mengele Zoo* was voted "The People's Favorite" at the Lillehammer Literature Festival.

Website: http://www.pvv/ntnu.no/~terjeros/gert/

Gerd Nyquist

> b. March 15, 1913, Oslo, Norway; d. November 22, 1984, Oslo, Norway; Residence: Oslo, Norway;
> Occupations: novelist and author of children's books and documentaries

Gerd Nyquist was awarded the Norwegian Defence Medal, 1940–1945, for her work in the Norwegian Resistance during World War II. After the publication of her first novel in 1958, she produced her best known works: two adult classic crime novels, *Avdøde ønsket ikke blomster* ("The Deceased Did Not Want Flowers"), 1960, and *Stille som i graven* ("Silent as the Grave"), 1966. Her academic sleuth Martin Bakke, assisted by his physician brother and a police attorney, solves crimes committed in west Oslo's traditional bourgeois society (*Norwegian Biographical Encyclopedia*).

In 1972 Nyquist co-founded the Riverton Club and served as its president for its first five years. She also wrote children's and young adult books, documentaries, and a radio play. She belonged to the Norwegian Language Council and the Norwegian Authors' Union.

In 1981 she published *Bataljon 99* (*Battalion 99*, translated in 2014 with an expanded illustration section), based on oral history accounts told by survivors of a unique U.S. Army ski commando battalion formed in Minnesota in 1942 with Norwegian-fluent American soldiers of Norwegian descent who trained in 10,000-foot Colorado winter conditions. They participated in the D-Day invasion and were later chosen to be the honor guard for King Haakon when he returned to Norway from exile.

Crime Novels:

1960: *Andøde ønsket ikke blomster* ("The Deceased Did Not Want Flowers")
1966: *Stille som i graven* ("Quiet as the Grave")
1978: *Djevelens fotspor* ("The Devil's Footsteps")

Major Awards: N/A

Website: N/A

M.H. Olsen (Morten Harry Olsen)

b. August 15, 1960, Narvik, Norway; Residence: N/A; Occupations: travel agent, taxi driver, journalist, translator, literary critic, teacher, author

Olsen, editor of the successful Norwegian Mystery and Thriller Book Club from 1992 to 1996, studied criminology at the University of Oslo. He has written novels which differ markedly from one another, beginning with *Mississippi* ("Mississippi"), 1990, a suspense novel set in America which placed nineteenth in the 2009 *Dagbladet* list of twenty-five best Norwegian crime novels of all time. Olsen continued with a hard-boiled Oslo private detective tale, *Syndenes forlatelase* ("The Remission of Sins"), 1991, and then produced *Begjærets pris* ("The Price of Desire"), 1993, a *noir* exploration of sexual obsession, greed, and abandoned values, and *Tilfeldig utvalg* ("Random Selection," or "The Murder of Osiris"), 1996, about a serial killer obsessed with re-enacting the ancient Egyptian myth of the god Seth, which according to Nils Nordberg rekindled interest in the subsequently overused topic of Egyptian mythology in mystery fiction (Nordberg).

Olsen's 2004 novel *Størst av alt* ("Greatest of All") was the basis for a six-episode Norwegian television drama series aired on BBC 1 during the winter of 2007. It involves the murder of a famous lawyer just outside his home. When his relatives find themselves suspects, their relationships undergo severe and compelling transformations.

In 2010, Olsen published *Adrian Marconis store sorg* ("Adrian Marconi's Sorrow"), a mainstream novel exploring the midlife crisis of an author who awakens from a somnolent retirement to face political and literary debates.

Crime Novels:

1990: *Mississippi* ("Mississippi")
1991: *Syndenes forlatelase* ("The Remission of Sins")
1993: *Begjærets pris* ("The Price of Desire")
1996: *Tilfeldig utvalg* ("Random Selection," also called "The Murder of Osiris")
2000: *Mord og galskap* ("The Child from the Bog")
2004: *Størst av alt* ("Greatest of All")

Major Awards:

1993: The Riverton Prize, for *Begjærets pris* ("The Price of Desire")

Websites: http://www.morten-h-olsen.net; http://www.mortenharryolsen.no

Pål Gerhard Olsen

b. November 1, 1959, Bergen, Norway; Residence: Bergen, Norway; Occupation: author

Beginning in 1985, Olsen has produced mainstream novels dealing with trends in contemporary Norwegian culture, young adult fiction, plays, and crime novels. In 1995, Olsen sparked an enormous press debate about the genre of crime fiction by castigating most of its Norwegian practitioners. His own detective hero Aaron Ash, an "expat Bergenser" and a student of Raymond

Chandler's work, operated in Oslo until Olsen made him take "early retirement" because, according to a 2012 OP-5 blog, Olsen said he had "lost interest" in crime literature and turned to analyzing "the gravitational forces" affecting police work. His 2013 thriller "Tumbling Dice" features young friends Daniel and Joachim who find themselves stranded in Nice with their luggage stolen by masked hoodlums, the start of an action-filled chase through southern Europe.

Crime Novels:

Aaron Ash Series:

1987: *Mørk april* ("Dark April")
1990: *Overspill* ("Over Game")
2002: *Rødt regn* ("Red Rain")
1995: *Isdronningen* ("Isdronningen")
1998: *Oslo-piken* ("The Oslo Girl")
2002: *Tusenårsriket* ("The Millennium")
2005: *Nattmusikk* ("Night Music")
2009: *Bakmennene* ("Backers")

Major Awards: N/A

Website: http://snl.no/Pal_Gerhard_Olsen

Anne B. Ragde (Anne Birkefeldt Ragde)

b. December 3, 1957, Odda, Norway; Residence: N/A; Occupation: author of children's and adult fiction

Anne Ragde, who began her literary career in the 1980s with children's literature, including a prizewinning biography of Sigrid Undset, is now best known for her bestselling novel *Berliner-poplene* ("Berlin Poplars"), 2004, and its sequels *Eremittkrepesene* ("Hermit Crabs"), 2005, and *Ligge i grønne enger* ("Pastures Green"), 2006, a popular family saga trilogy which entertained over a million viewers as the most watched drama series on Norwegian television since 2000. Recently Ragde has been involved in a piracy scandal; in a 2010 interview with *Dagens Naeringsliv* she claimed to have lost 500,000 *kroner* (about $72,000), perhaps more, over pirated versions of her books, but she also admitted she herself had bought a counterfeit Prada purse and her son Jo called attention to her own large pirated MP3 music collection.

Ragde also wrote early adult short fiction for magazines in the 1980s. These have been collected and published in 2014 as *Aften rød, morgen død* ("Evening Red, Morning Death"), according to critic Knut Holt of *Faedrelandsvennen* conveying a spectrum ranging from psychological thrillers to detective fiction that pokes good-natured fun at the police procedural genre.

Beginning in 1995, Ragde published thrillers, notably *Zona frigida* ("The Frigid Zone"), 1995, set in the icy Svalbard archipelago far north of the Arctic Circle, rife with dark family secrets, lies, and ecological concerns. Bea, a ferociously independent woman, startlingly travels to Svalbard one summer and soon finds herself with a few others on a boat in the midst of the icy polar sea, allowing Ragde to explore both psychological and ecological dangers in that little-known polar region. *Le Monde des lettres* commented that reading this novel is comparable to a polar bear sinking its teeth into a seal: "The soft meat, bones, and teeth, it all goes down" (http://www.aschehougagency.no, accessed 4/22/2012).

Ragde turned in 2009 to mainstream fiction with an exploration of women's reactions to encountering the unknown in *Nattønsket* ("Night Waves"), praised for distinctive characterizations and rich detail. In 2014, she published *Jeg har et teppe i tusen farger* ("I Have a Carpet in a Thousand Colors"), based on the life in Trondheim of Ragde's Danish single mother, who died in 2012.

Selected Crime Fiction:

1995: *Zona frigida* ("The Frigid Zone")
2014: *Aften rød, morgen død* ("Evening Red, Morning Death")

Major Awards:

2001: The Brage Prize, for *Ogsaa en ung pige* (a Young Adult biography of Sigrid Undset)
2004: *Riksmål* Society Literature Prize, for *Berlinerpoplene* ("Berlin Poplars")
2005: Norwegian Booksellers Prize, for *Eremittkrepesene* ("Hermit Crabs")

Website: N/A

Anker Rogstad

> b. 8 January, 1925, Oslo, Norway; d. October 5, 1994, Oslo, Norway; Residence: Oslo, Norway; Occupations: safecracker, author

As background for his crime fiction, Anker Rogstad drew on his experiences as a convicted safecracker and his eight years' imprisonment for these crimes. In his novel, *Etterlyst* ("Wanted"), 1977, Rogstad's *alter ego* Arne Rognes claimed he had deliberately chosen his path of crime and gained "experiences, bitter perhaps, but nevertheless experiences" (quoted in Hook). Rogstad used one of his most dramatic experiences, occurring when he was seventeen and chronicled in *Unforgiven Norwegians—State Police 1941–1945*, in "Wanted," recalling that he had shot a detested Norwegian Nazi border guard who had severely abused Rogstad and two of his young friends near the Swedish border. After the killing, Rostad was actively pursued by the Nazi Quisling puppet government of Norway. After being turned back into Norway several times by Swedish authorities, Rogstad finally escaped to London with the help of Norway's exiled government there and received training as a crewman of Britain's 333 Mosquito Squadron. Back in Norway during the difficult postwar period, Rogstad drifted into criminal company and became a safecracker, eventually blowing up a post office safe containing 200,000 Norwegian *kronor* a stone's throw from the Kongsvinger police station. After his imprisonment, Rogstad insisted his prosecutor had persecuted him unfairly and that he had received far too harsh a sentence for his crimes.

Crime Novels:

1969: *Jurister i kasjotten* ("Lawyers in Cells")
1974: *Lansen* ("Lances")
1975: *Hevnen* ("Revenge")
1977: *Etterlyst* ("Wanted")
1986: *Ærens pris* ("Honor Prize")

Major Awards:

1974: The Riverton Prize for *Lansen* ("Lances")

Website: N/A

*Pernille Rygg

b. June 10, 1963, Oslo, Norway; Residence: Oslo, Norway; Occupation: author

Crime critic Maxine Clarke observed that Pernille Rygg's unusual female detective protagonist Igi Heitmann debuted in *Sommerfugleffekten*, 1995 (*The Butterfly Effect*, tr. 1997), in "a tapestry of social comment" woven from many strands of Oslo society that Rygg depicts as threatening: unscrupulous business dealings, blackmail, gambling, medical malpractice, child abuse, and modern-day Satanism. Igi, deeply disturbed by her parents' divorce and married to a bisexual transvestite, takes over her dead father's private investigation agency. Starting with an old unsolved case, Igi refuses to judge even the most unsavory characters with whom she deals. Igi has a child with her husband between *The Butterfly Effect* and *Det gyldne snit*, 2000 (*The Golden Section*, tr. 2003). Rygg's only other novel to date. In this unusual marital arrangement, Igi accepts her husband's casual affairs with other men, observing, "He will make a much better mother than I" (quoted in Nordberg). In *The Golden Section*, set in the art world, Igi has become a practicing clinical psychologist. Rygg delineates her uncompromising leading character through an indirect, *noir*, poetic, and near stream-of-consciousness style, coupled with a genuinely realistic empathy for crime victims. Rygg also can be humorous, as in *The Golden Section*'s "rumble" episode between Pakistani gangbangers and gay S & M clubgoers, providing considerable contrast with Rygg's otherwise generally poetic style.

Crime Novels:

1995: *Sommerfugleffekten* (*The Butterfly Effect*, tr. Joan Tate, UK 1997).
2000: *Det gyldne snit* (*The Golden Section*, tr. Don Bartlett, UK 2003).

Major Awards: N/A

Website: N/A

Arild Rypdal (also spelled *Ripdal*)

b. September 23, 1934, Ålesund, Norway; Residence: Ålesund; later Mandal, Norway; Occupations: pilot, engineer, author

Claiming that he wrote principally to entertain readers, Rypdal authored a long series of spy novels about Britain's MI6. His father had been a Norwegian Resistance fighter until the winter of 1941, when he had to flee with his family to the Shetland Islands in a blizzard. Rypdal's father then worked for the British Secret Intelligence Service, now MI6, for the rest of the war. Rypdal claimed that he had learned more in his years in Britain than he had during the rest of his life. The Rypdal home was a refuge for secret agents and thus an inspiration for Rypdal's fiction, which he launched after retiring as Airport Manager for Central Norway, stationed at Ålesund for seventeen years.

According to Rune Larsstuvold's article on Rypdal in the *Norwegian Biographical Encyclopedia*, Rypdal spent about six months researching each of his novels, which do not have a continuing cast of characters. Each explores international tensions, world politics, governmental corruption, and intrigue. Two examples are *Djelvelens stoff* ("The Devil's Matter"), 1995, with a main plot involving plutonium smuggling from Russia and a subplot about the German intelligence service's attempt to ensure Chancellor Helmut Kohl's re-election; and *Dødens konsulent* ("Death's Consultant"), 2000, which deals with both the Cali cocaine cartel in Columbia and Russian terrorist groups: an "organizational consultant" Matteo Orsini, contracted to shadowy Central American personages, disappears, and Rypdal's protagonist Sir Reginald Sinclair of MI6 is charged with finding him.

Espionage Novels:

1991: *Hexagon* ("Hexagon")
1992: *Orakele* ("Oracle")
1993: *Grønn desember* ("Green December")
1994: *Kodene i Metrograd* ("The Codes in Metrograd")
1995: *Djevelens stoff* ("The Devil's Matter")
1996: *Drakon* ("Drakon")
1997: *Guds brødre* ("God's Brothers")
1998: *Himmelens villmenn* ("Heaven's Savages")
1999: *Intermesso i Praha* ("Intermezzo in Prague")
2000: *Dødens konsulent* ("Death's Consultant")
2001: *Triangelets herre* ("Triangelet's men")
2002: *Svarte engler* ("Black Angels")

Major Awards:

1992: The Riverton Prize for *Orakele* ("Oracle")

Website: N/A

*Kjersti Scheen

b. August 17, 1943; Residence: Oslo, Norway; Occupations: illustrator and author

In an interview with Jennie Renton, the versatile artist Kjersti Scheen indicated that she began writing crime fiction at the age of 51 as "a bit of fun." Scheen had previously been an illustrator and later an author of children's books, books for young adults, and mainstream novels. Scheen's extended family included many artists and storytellers, and her childhood home was filled with both classics (upstairs) and popular fiction (in the cellar); she grew up reading voraciously and still maintains that she loves reading every kind of literature (Renton). Since drawing was "what [her] family did," Scheen never questioned pursuing a career as an illustrator. She attended Norway's National College of Art and Design from 1960 to 1964 and illustrated her first book in 1963, afterwards working as a freelance artist until 1970, when she received the Norwegian Culture Ministry's illustration award. For the next ten years she worked as a journalist and in 1980 turned to writing full time.

After Scheen's first daughter was born in 1975, she wrote and illustrated a picture book for her, *Fie og mørket* (*Fie and the Darkness*), which won the Norwegian Ministry of Culture's illustrated book prize. The book features a little girl who overcomes her fear of the dark by learning to distinguish reality from imagination: the troll outside her window turns out to be only a familiar tree, and the monster under her bed is really only a slipper.

Scheen proceeded to write both children's and young people's books and adult mainstream novels which examined women's issues like anorexia, female liberation, teenage sexuality, and the necessity of overcoming childhood traumas, drawing on her memories of her mother's recurrent struggles with depression so severe she wept for hours on end, a circumstance that probably contributed to the claim Scheen made in an interview that all her writing is "about fear in one way or another" (quoted in Renton). In all of her thirty-plus books, Scheen has treated women and their fears and problems with special sensitivity (Renton).

After immersing herself in books by contemporary female crime authors, Scheen abandoned realism for "the good old hard-boiled private eye novel," because that type of fiction allowed her "to take shortcuts through time and leap from here to there" (quoted in Renton). *Teppefall* (*Final Curtain*, tr. 2002), Scheen's first crime novel, appeared in Norway in 1994, starring hard-boiled private detective Margaret Moss, a hard-drinking fortyish divorcée and former actress who sleeps around. She also has a regular boyfriend, a fanciable married truck driver named Roland "to help out with the rough stuff" (Forshaw 104). The novel derives far more from the original hardboiled American private investigator tradition than more recent reinvented fictional feminist detective stories do. Moss might even be seen, as Nils Nordberg suggests, as a female version of the "typical scruffy male hero" with a "mischievous smile."

Of Scheen's Margaret Moss novels, only *Final Curtain*, 1994, has been translated into English. Moss, perennially broke, lives with her retired-actress aunt and typical-teenager daughter. Moss scrapes by on odd detective jobs like tailing the wife of a banker who suspects his wife is carrying on an affair. When Rakel, a friend from Moss's own bygone acting career, disappears, Rakel's family employs Moss to find her, setting off a string of amusing adventures in which Moss encounters feckless young neo–Nazis and meets Roland, who becomes her partner in her subsequent investigations. Plots are not Scheen's forte, but Scheen and her readers have fun with Moss, a plucky, astute, self-deprecating figure (Forshaw 104) and walking disaster area (EuroCrime), who manages to best villains ranging from neo–Nazis to Russian Mafiosi.

Crime Novels:

> 1994: *Teppefall* (*Final Curtain*, tr. Louis Muinzer, UK, 2002)
> 1996: *Ingen applaus for morderen* ("No Applause for the Killer")
> 1998: *Englemakerne* ("Hovering")
> 2000: *Den syvende synd* ("The Seventh Sin")
> 2003: *Lik i lasta* ("Like the Load")

Notable Crime Short Story:

> "Moonglow," in *Ellery Queen's Mystery Magazine*, February 2006

Major Awards: N/A

Website: N/A

Anan Singh and Natalie Normann

> Natalie Normann: b. "a small town on the West coast" of Norway (no date)
>
> Anan Singh: b. Punjab, India (no date); Residence: Oslo, Norway; Occupation: journalists, interpreters, translators, authors

Singh and Normann have together written several books for adults and children. (Normann also writes under the pseudonym "Hanna Sandvik.") In a joint autobiographical article, "Against All Odds," drawn from their experiences of multiculturalism in Norway, they describe themselves at the start of their career as "starry-eyed," utterly lacking any knowledge of the publishing world. Since then they say they have learned much about Norwegian publishing, where authors submit work directly, not through agents, to publishing houses. Their first novel, *Under den hvide bro* ("Under the White Bridge"), 1996, set in post–World War II bombed-out Hamburg, was nominated as "Norway's best suspense novel." They then produced three novels featuring "Dara Singh," a former CID officer from Punjab and according to the authors, one of Norway's unappreciated south Asian immigrants, representing the 400,000 immigrants joining Norway's 2007 population of four million-plus (Singh and Normann 65).

Norwegian publishers brought out two Dara Singh novels, but Normann and Singh found it difficult to sell the third novel of the series, *Anglafisch* ("Angel Fish"), its German title, in Norway until 2001, despite the vivid local color they achieved in their street scenes of Oslo's "Little Lahore": "Foreigners from every part of Asia and Africa were crammed into run-down old blocks of flats just below Oslo's Police Plaza. A few blocks that didn't belong to Norway. Not really.... [In] Little Lahore ... it was as if he was in the bazaars in Purani Delhi, apart from the icy wind and the slush, of course" (quoted in "Against All Odds" 65).

Singh and Normann then shelved their next adult crime novel project, this one starring Nimmi Kaur, a half–Norwegian, half–Sikh woman resident of Oslo, and turned to writing a history book for children and young people's crime novels. They claim, "We do anything to be able to keep writing our books" (Singh and Normann, "Against All Odds" 65). None of their books has as yet appeared in English.

Singh and Normann's 2010 crime novel for readers aged 10 through 12 is *Parken* ("The Park"), 2010, a thriller with a particularly horrifying cover in Aschehaug's *Lesehesten* ("Reading Horse") children's series. Little Amanda, whose parents are missing in an earthquake, came from India three months ago to live with her grandmother in Norway. Amanda has spooky adventures involving eerie creatures that pursue her, causing her grandmother to bring her to a psychologist, but the amulet Amanda brought from India always saves her, the authors' commentary on the plight of immigrant children who find adjustment to chilly Norway difficult and even frightening. Cathrine Krøger of *Dagbladet* finds "The Park" "Easy to read, but not readable," because the authors seem to attempt too much information in the small size the publisher specified for volumes in this young people's series

Selected Crime Novels (English versions of titles):

 1995: "In the Swastika's Shadow"
 1996: "Under the White Bridge"
 2001: "Angel Fish"

Selected Young Adult Thrillers:

 2008: *Loftet* ("The Loft")
 2009: *Byttingen* ("The Changeling")
 2010: *Parken* ("The Park")

Major Awards: N/A

Website: N/A

Audun Sjøstrand

 b. April 11, 1950, Radøy, Norway; Residence: N/A; Occupations: teacher, journalist, author

Sjøstrand, an author and lecturer, has also been a high school teacher and a journalist for *Gula Tidend*. He received the Riverton Prize in 1991 for *Valsekongens fall* ("The Waltz King Case"). His three crime novels are traditional mystery stories.

Crime Novels:

1985: *Hundemordet* ("Dog Murder")
1987: *Ureint trav* ("The Treacherous Trot")
1991: *Valsekongens fall* ("The Waltz King Case")

Major Awards:

1991: The Riverton Prize for *Valsekongens fall* ("The Waltz King Case")

Website: N/A

Fredrik Skagen

> b. December 30, 1936, Trondheim, Norway; Residence: Trondheim, Norway; Occupations: university librarian, author

One of Norway's most prolific and most award-winning crime authors, Skagen, like fellow writers Kim Småge, Idar Lind, and Anne Ragde, sets his police procedurals in the Trondheim area of Norway. As well as the procedurals, Skagen's wide range of crime fiction includes international espionage, suspense, and thrillers, most illustrating his favorite theme, the "little man" facing overwhelming odds. In his eight Morten Martens crime novels, Skagen based his protagonist loosely on the archetypal Norwegian rascal-hero Peer Gynt, since Martens easily drifts from career role to role, lying his way through one dubious adventure after another, "a human onion ... with no core" who often works in England and Wales and at one time even officially becomes a Welshman, Iago Davies (Nordberg). Martens, initially a Trondheim book printer, turns counterfeiter and fakes his own death to surface later in Britain, where he puts his talents and his convenient lack of moral scruples in the service of British intelligence (Nordberg). Seemingly clairvoyant, Skagen published his first Martens novel, *Viktor! Viktor!* ("Victor! Victor!"), in 1982, preceding the breakup of an actual Trondheim counterfeiting ring by a decade.

Beginning in 2001, Skagen has used journalist partners as his series characters in other novels, and he often carries minor characters from one novel into another. His 1995 novel *Nattsug* ("Attraction to Night"), however, revolves around three young people who rob a bank in Heimdal, then descend into suicidal catastrophe. *Dagbladet* critic Arne Dvergsdal observed in 2009 that in this novel Skagen "elaborates the destructive [element] in human nature," also noting that probably this book should be titled "Attraction to Death" because it portrays "the conflicting emotions of hope and apprehension that rages inside three young unfinished people" fleeing toward the abyss (Dvergsdal). *Nattsug* ranked eighteenth on *Dagbladet's* 2009 list of the twenty-five best Norwegian crime novels of all time.

Crime Novels:

1978: *Ulvene* ("Wolves")
1979: *Forræderen* ("Betrayer")
1980: *Kortslutning* ("Short Circuit")
1982: *Viktor! Viktor!* ("Victor! Victor!")
1983: *Fritt fall* ("Freefall")
1984: *Tigertimen* ("Tiger Hour")
1986: *Døden i Capelulo* ("Death in Capelulo")
1988: *Menneskejegeren* ("Human Hunter")
1990: *Alte Kameraden* ("Old Comrade")

1991: *Landskap med kulehull* ("Landscape with Bullet Holes")
1993: *Nemesis* ("Nemesis")
1993: *Dødelig madonna* ("Deadly Madonna"), with Gunnar Staalesen
1994: *Skrik* ("The Scream")
1995: *Nattsug* ("Attraction to Night")
1996: *Rekyl* ("Recoil")
1998: *Blackout* ("Blackout")
2000: *Blomster og blod* ("Flowers and Blood")
2001: *Blitz* ("Blitz")
2002: *Fri som fuglen* ("Free as a Bird")
2007: *God natt, elskede* ("Good Night, Darling")

Major Awards:

1980: The Riverton Prize, for *Kortslutning* ("Short Circuit")
1986: The Palle Rosenkrantz Prize, for *Victor! Victor!*
1996: The Glass Key Award, for *Nattsug* ("Attraction to Night")

Website: N/A

Asle Skredderberget

b. 1972; Residence: N/A; Occupations: journalist, corporate executive, author

Asle Skredderberget holds graduate degrees in business and finance from the Norwegian School of Economics, Bergen, and the Universitá Bocconi, Milan. When he moved from journalism to work on his first crime novel, *Metallmyk* ("Soft Metal"), published in Norway in 2010, he combined his knowledge of business and financial crime with his deep interest in "everything that has to do with Italy," and his half–Norwegian, half–Italian protagonist Milo Cavalli, "the wealthiest police investigator in Norway," was born (Skredderberget, "'Nuff Noir" 37). Skredderberget says he loves writing about Milo Cavalli, whose unlimited resources allow him to track villains across the globe while enjoying the attention from lovely women that his good looks and kind personality bring flocking to him. Cavalli is also Roman Catholic, in a Norway that Skredderberger describes as "non-religious," enabling his creator to set up conflicts between Cavalli and his friends and co-workers. Cavalli's closest colleague, sixtyish and bulldoggish Chief Investigator Sørensen, a chain-smoking, snuff-addicted, "fatalistic policeman" (Skredderberget, "'Nuff Noir 38), is an appropriate foil to the elegant Cavalli. Together they earned *Metallmyk* ("Soft Metal"), which treats the weapons and finance industries, a nomination for the 2010 Riverton Award. St. Martin's Press has scheduled English translations of *Metallmyk* and its sequel *Smertehimmel* ("Painkiller"), about the pharmaceutical industry, to appear in 2015.

Crime Novels:

2010: *Metallmyk* ("Soft Metal," tentative English title *Future Imperfect*)
2014: *Smertehimmel* ("A Heaven of Pain," tentative English title *Painkiller*)

Major Awards: N/A

Website: http://www.italiafrik.no/websted/Hjem.html

Kim Småge

b. June 23, 1945, Trondheim, Norway; Residence: Trondheim, Norway; Occupations: diving instructor, author of crime fiction, short stories, and children's literature

In 1983, Nils Nordberg felt so overwhelmed by the proliferation of honorable but depressed, scruffy, and almost always alcoholic male detective heroes of Norwegian crime fiction that he said he prayed for "at least one plucky dame," a female crime-solving figure not unhinged emotionally by guilt and feelings of inadequacy (Nordberg). Kim Småge, Norway's first woman scuba diving instructor, published her first novel, *Nattdykk* ("Night Dive") six months later, in 1983, with a diving heroine, Hilke Torhus, like Småge herself a lone woman in a traditionally male field. Småge used a steamy, sweaty "breathless stream-of-consciousness" style to show Torhus solving a crime and surmounting gang rape, attempted murder, and assorted cliff-hangings (Nordberg). Writing in *Store norske leksikon*, critic Hans Skei pronounced *Nattdykk* the opening salvo in "A new female wave in Norwegian crime fiction."

After what Nordberg calls "a less feverish" sequel, *Origo* ("Origo"), 1984, involving small communities threatened by Cold War maneuvers, Småge abandoned Torhus for other powerful women characters overcoming male conspiracies. In her title novelette of the 1992 collection *Kvinnens lane arm* ("The Woman's Long Arm") Småge introduced Anne-kin Halvorsen, a self-sufficient thirtyish Trondheim police detective, as the heroine of Småge's novel *Sub rosa* ("Sub Rosa"), 1993. Halvorsen went on to battle drug smuggling and white slavery in *En kjernesunn død* ("A Wholesome Death"), 1995; *Containerkvinnen* ("The Container Woman"), 1997; *Solefall* ("Sunset"), 2002, and *Dobbeltmann* ("The Double Man"), 2004.

Trondheim's special atmosphere and Småge's talent for realistic character portrayals combine effectively in her Anne-kin Halvorsen series. In "Sub Rosa," Sergeant Halvorsen investigates the brutal murder of the owner of Trondheim's Galleri Saxe, which exhibited artist Henry Aar's collages made of paper fragments torn off the walls of his home. The collage titled "Sub Rosa" differs from the rest by containing pieces of old papers and scraps of a letter that leads Anne-kin to discern connections between Trondheim's elite and the city's criminal underworld.

In her next cases, Anne-kin, a former diving instructor, has a special insight into the death during training of a promising young swimmer in "A Wholesome Death." In "The Container Woman," Anne-kin tackles the problem of human trafficking when three women are found in a freight container buried under construction debris in Trondheim. One woman survives but flees from the city hospital where she was taken, posing Anne-kin and her colleague Vang a dangerous challenge. In "Sunset," Anne-kin's well-earned vacation on the west coast of Norway is disrupted by the discovery of a weirdly mutilated body followed by a series of thefts from local homes. A local drug rehabilitation institute, a flotilla of Hell's Angels, and an enigmatic suicide confront Anne-kin until she finally knits these disparate events into a tapestry of evil. In "The Double Man," Anne-kin and Vang are working a strange case involving a missing prostitute, but Småge also unveils more of her detective's private life than she had done previously; Anne-kin's younger brother, deep in gambling debts, is being threatened by gangsters, and when she has to reject the new lover who had awakened her to hitherto unexplored heights of passion, the man refuses to go quietly.

Crime critics from Oslo's *Dagbladet* and Småge's hometown Trondheim *Adresseavisen* compare her Anne-kin Halvorsen series to the novels of Americans Sara Paretsky and Sue Grafton and their Sisters in Crime who produce feminine versions of the hard-boiled crime genre. Småge's fellow Norwegian crime author Anne Holt ranks Anne-kin Halvorsen ninth (and the only Norwegian) in her list of ten favorite international female detectives: "She's empowered but also vul-

nerable, and has an action-packed private life that she struggles to balance with her police work
... the foremother of all Scandinavian female detectives" (Holt).

According to Nils Nordberg, Småge's 1986 novel *Kainen*, ranked sixteenth in *Dagbladet's*
2009 list of all-time best Norwegian crime novels, is "a brave act at several levels." He notes that
the title *Kainen* is the name of a character that Freemasons use as a distress signal. Officially Norwegian Freemasonry concentrates on personal development through Christian thought and tradition and does not engage in national or international political issues or religious or social
disputes, instead influencing the process of personal improvement and ennoblement by promoting
the virtues of humility, tolerance and compassion. In Småge's novel, the Freemasons' all-male
secret and hierarchical society demands strict allegiance, with each level or "degree" revealing
new esoteric knowledge. She portrays the brotherhood as an exclusive and protective entity with
jealously guarded secrets, functioning as the power elite in contemporary Norwegian society,
which she feels has largely abandoned religion and offers instead state-approved social values.
Småge's female protagonist is Lena, an unemployed actress who enters the Freemasons' male bastion disguised as a young man and discovers that the Masonic system in Norway has become not
a mutual protection society but in Nordberg's words, a prison of "Loyalty claims and unspeakable
secrets" (Nordberg).

Crime Novels:

1983: *Nattdykk* ("Night Dive")
1984: *Origo* ("Origo")
1986: *Kainen* ("Kainen")

Anne-kin Halvorsen Crime Fiction:

1992: *Kvinnens lange arm* ("The Long Arm of Woman," a short story collection)
1993: *Sub rosa* ("Sub Rosa")
1995: *En kjernesunn død* ("A Wholesome Death")
1997: *Containerkvinnen* ("The Container Woman")
2002: *Solefall* ("Sunset")
2004: *Dobbeltmann* ("The Double Man")

Major Awards:

1984: The Riverton Prize, for *Nattdykk* ("Night Dive")
1993: The Glass Key Award, for *Sub rosa* ("Sub Rosa")

Website: N/A

Roar Sørensen

b. April 27, 1960, Bergen, Norway; Residence: N/A; Occupations: journalist, translator, author

In his youth a speed skater and later a nationally ranked chess player, Roar Sørensen has
translated 120 books into Norwegian, including several of Robert Ludlum's thrillers. Sørensen's
own two high-voltage suspense novels feature former Norwegian policeman Stein Inge Olsen,
also known as "Stingo," now wallowing in self-pity, alcohol, and grief over personal problems he
experienced in Norway. He has settled in the Philippines, a venue well known to Sørensen, who
in 1986 won the Philippine government's People Power Medal of Honor for his reporting during
the country's 1986 revolution. *Magellans kors* ("Magellan's Cross"), 2009, opens with Stingo on

the brink of suicide, when a dying woman falls into his arms, gasping about a plot to assassinate the Philippine president. Both this novel and its sequel, *Smertens aveny* ("Pain Avenue"), 2013, nominated for the 2013 Riverton Award, delve into the tawdry Philippine underworld, powerfully portraying the corruption and human trafficking excruciatingly common there.

Crime/Suspense Novels:

2009: *Magellans kors* ("Magellan's Cross")
2013: *Smertens aveny* (*Pain Avenue*, tr. 2014)

Major Awards: N/A

Website: N/A

Michael Grundt Spang

b. June 14, 1931, Mandal, Norway; d. November 13, 2003; Residence: Oslo, Norway; Occupations: journalist and author

Beginning in 1966, crime reporter Michael Grundt Spang used his work for *Dagbladet* and *Verdens Gang* as background for his detective novels. His prizewinning 1985 novel *Spionen som lengtet hjem* (*The Spy Who Longed for Home*, tr. 1989), features Adrian Berger, a minor Norwegian diplomat who defected to the Soviet Union. Dismayed and repulsed by the Soviet debriefings and the Moscow cold, he asks Norway, the country he betrayed, for asylum. *Kirkus Reviews* for June 4, 1989, concluded that this novel was "routine," Spang's writing was "dispirited," and "the whole enterprise seem[ed] lifeless."

In addition to his detective fiction, Spang also produced several nonfiction works in which he consistently displayed his conservatism in regard to policies of the Norwegian justice system. In his most notable work in this vein, his 1973 nonfiction book *Torgersensaken* ("The Torgersen Case"), Spang rebutted Jens Bjørneboe's book defending the convicted murderer Fredrik Fasting Torgersen as a victim of a miscarriage of justice. Spang and Kjell Syversen won the *Nordvisjonens* competition for 1981's best television crime screenplay.

Crime Novels:

1966: *En morder går løs* ("A Murderer Is Loose")
1968: *Operasjon V for vanvidd* ("Operation V for Frenzy), filmed in 1970
1969: *Malkersaken* ("The Malker Case"), with Arild Feldborg
1972: *Justismordet* ("Justice Murder")
1975: *Aksjon Ullersmo* ("Reduced Ullersmo")
1980: *Du står ved stupet* ("You Are Standing at the Precipice")
1982: *Spionen* ("Spy")
1985: *Spionen som lengtet hjem* (*The Spy Who Longed for Home*, tr. Basil Cowlishaw, 1989)

Major Awards:

1985: The Riverton Prize for *Spionen som longtet hjem* (*The Spy Who Longed for Home*)

Website: N/A

*Gunnar Staalesen

b. October 19, 1947, Bergen, Norway; Residence: Bergen, Norway; Occupation: novelist

Gunnar Staalesen ranks among the most important authors of 20th century Norwegian crime fiction. Besides Sjöwall and Wahlöö, Staalesen acknowledges Raymond Chandler, Ross Macdonald, Agatha Christie and Arthur Conan Doyle as his literary inspirations. He says he also learned a great deal from classic Norwegian authors Henrik Ibsen and Amalie Skram, claiming that like Ibsen, he asks the questions and requires his readers to supply their own answers, often involving elements of political criticism, though he cautions that today's Scandinavia is less crime-ridden than it appears in popular Scandinavian fiction (quoted in Forshaw 124).

Like Chandler, Staalesen has been described as "writing like a slumming angel," using near-classic plots and exemplifying a strong left-wing critical attitude toward social institutions (Nordberg). Staalesen himself feels that Swedish and Norwegian crime fiction exhibits two characteristics, a societal focus incorporated into the mystery plot, and nature as a key narrative element (quoted in Forshaw 125). Varg Veum, Staalesen's popular hardboiled detective protagonist, was formerly a Bergen child protection officer. Veum is now a divorced and disillusioned PI who Staalesen acknowledges is a literary descendant of Raymond Chandler's Philip Marlowe. Varg Veum debuted in 1977, though he did not appear as a fully rounded character until *Din til døden*, 1979 (*Yours Until Death*, tr. 1993 and 2009). The name "Varg Veum" is a pun on the ancient Viking expression *vargr i veum*, literally "a wolf in the sanctuary," thus indicating "an outlaw," and "a man without peace" (Nordberg). *Dødens drabanter*, 2006 (*The Consorts of Death*, tr. 2009), the novel Staalesen himself cherishes most, propels Veum into a case involving a criminal who had been savagely traumatized as a child. Veum's favorite theme is that family breakdown due at least in part to warped governmental policies severely damages human lives. That theme also appears strongly in both *Yours Until Death* and *Skriften på veggen*, 1995 (*The Writing on the Wall*, tr. 2004). Throughout his cases, Varg Veum often untangles complex effects the past exerts on the present in a bleak, rainy *noir* Bergen, Norway's second largest city and the hub of its oil industry. In Norway alone the Varg Veum series, which has been translated into twelve languages, has sold over a million and a half copies. Its television adaptations have sold more than 200,000 DVDs.

In his breakthrough novel, *Yours Until Death*, Staalesen presents Varg Veum as a private investigator who's virtually clientless, smothered in unpaid bills, and nearly broke when the youngest client he's ever had appears: eight-year-old Roar, who found Veum's name in a telephone book, wants Veum to help him get his stolen bicycle back. Teenaged Bergen hoodlums have it and Roar thinks they want to use it as bait to lure Roar's attractive mother, Wenche Andresen, into the forest to rape her. Though Veum recovers the bike and saves Wenche from these villains, he's drawn into a much more sinister investigation when Roar's father is murdered, and Wenche becomes the prime suspect. Writing in 2011 for *EuroCrime*, critic Maxine Clarke found *Yours Until Death* "a particularly interesting snapshot of [Norwegian] society" in the 1970s, with Varg Veum musing through the novel about the disintegration of traditional Norwegian culture (Clarke).

Clarke also reviewed Staalesen's *The Consorts of Death*, fourteenth in the Varg Veum series, concluding that it is "the perfect introduction" to Veum, because a large part of this novel flashes back to his pre-detective days as a social worker (Clarke). Veum's experiences in that field caused him to lose hope in "the ability or even will of the state to help the abandoned and abused children" with whom he worked (Clarke). Accordingly he left social work to become a private detective, and here he is faced with a harrowing situation. "Johnny Boy," a recently released criminal, has Veum on a "death list," a circumstance stemming from the criminal's extreme youth, when he was under the care of Veum and other social workers. Tone Sutterud, writing in *The Independent* for October 19, 2009, notes that Staalesen has been credited with introducing social realism into crime fiction, in "forbidding surroundings that reinforce the false impression of Scandinavia as a very bleak place indeed" (Sutterud). Clarke observes that Staalesen is among "the very best modern exponents of the poetic yet tough detective story with strong, classic plots; a social conscience; and perfect pitch in terms of a sense of place" (Clarke).

Staalesen's Veum novel *Falne engler* ("Fallen Angels"), 1989, as yet unavailable in English, ranked sixth in *Dagbladet*'s twenty-five best Norwegian crime novels of all time. Here Veum recalls his home in Bergen in the 1950s and 1960s, when he and his friends concentrated on girls and rock bands. Staalesen then flashed forward to the funeral of a member of The Harpers, a rock group whose lead singer is Veum's boyhood best friend Jacob. Jacob had married Veum's religiously scrupulous first love Rebecca, but now Rebecca has left Jacob. The other band members seem to be dying off too rapidly, and Veum undertakes an investigation with a painfully personal dimension.

The Norwegian film production company SF Norge announced in 2005 that they would produce six Varg Veum films starring Norwegian actor Trond Espen Seim: *Bitre blomster* ("Bitter Flowers"); *Tornerose sov hundre år* ("Sleeping Beauty Slumbered for a Hundred Years"); and "Yours Until Death," as well as *Kvinnen i kjøleskapet* ("The Woman in the Fridge") and *Begravde hunder biter ikke* ("Buried Dogs Do Not Bite") have been released as DVDs. A film version of *Falne engler* ("Fallen Angels") was directed by Morten Tyldum, who later directed the 2011 film version of Jo Nesbø's *Headhunters*; "Fallen Angels" ran on the United States' MhZ Network in October 2009. Also during 2009, SF Norge began filming six more Varg Veum novels. Several Varg Veum novels have been made into radio plays, and Veum is the only Norwegian crime character to appear in Norwegian original graphic novels (Nordberg). Recently Staalesen, a prolific novelist whose style harks back to Ed McBain while incorporating a social conscience, has announced that he may continue the Varg Veum series with a younger protagonist (Nordberg).

Crime Fiction and Crime-Related Books:

1975: *Rygg i rand, to i span* ("Back in the Border, Two in the Bucket")
1977: *Bukken til havresekken* ("The Fox Takes the Goose"), the first Varg Veum novel
1979: *Din til døden* (*Yours Until Death*, tr. Margaret Amassian, 1993)
1980: *Tornerose sov hundre år* ("Sleeping Beauty Slumbered for a Hundred Years")
1981: *Kvinnen i kjøleskapet* ("The Woman in the Fridge")
1983: *I mørket er alle ulver grå* (*At Night All Wolves Are Grey*, tr. David McDuff, 1986)
1985: *Hekseringen* ("The Fairy Ring"), short fiction
1988: *Svarte får* ("Black Sheep")
1989: *Falne engler* ("Fallen Angels")
1991: *Bitre blomster* ("Bitter Flowers")
1993: *Begravde hunder biter ikke* ("Buried Dogs Do Not Bite"); *Dødelig madonna* ("Deadly Madonna"), with Fredrik Skagen; "Varg Veum's Bergen" (Bergen travel guide)
1995: *Skriften på veggen* ("The Writing on the Wall," tr. Hal Sutcliffe, 2004)
1996: *De døde har det godt* ("The Dead Are All Well," short fiction collection)
2002: *Som i et speil* ("Reflections in a Mirror")
2004: *Ansikt til ansikt* ("Face to Face")
2006: *Dødens drabanter* (*The Consorts of Death*, tr. Don Bartlett, 2009)
2008: *Kalde hjerter* (*Cold Hearts*, tr. Don Bartlett, 2012)
2010: *Vi skal arve vinden* ("We Shall Inherit the Wind")

2012: *Der hvor roser aldri dør* ("Where Roses Never Die")

2014: *Ingen er så trygg i fare* ("None Are So Confident in Danger")

Major Awards:

1975: The Riverton Prize, for *Rygg i rand, to i span* ("Back in the Border, Two in the Bucket")

2004: The Riverton Prize, for *Som i et speil* ("Reflections in a Mirror")

Website: www.vargveum.no

*Arild Stavrum

b. April 16, 1972, Kristiansund, Norway; Residence: Oslo, Norway; Occupations: soccer player and coach, author

In a 2013 interview, star professional soccer striker and author Arild Stavrum flatly stated, "The agents, the fixers, the people who contribute nothing to football and leech money out— don't like me" (quoted in Stewart). European soccer fans, however, liked his playing very much. Stavrum's playing career began at eighteen with a local Norwegian club and before his retirement in 2004, he had played not only for Norwegian league teams but also for Helsingborg, Sweden, where he was the All-Sweden top scorer in 1998. He also played for Aberdeen, Scotland, where he was the club's top scorer in the 2000–2001 season, reaching the Scottish Cup Final. He also played briefly in Turkey. He played twice on the Norwegian national team, and since 2005 he has coached well-known Norwegian league soccer teams.

Stavrum blew the whistle on racketeering in international soccer. As well as teaching part-time and appearing as a television personality, he has written for both Norwegian and Scottish newspapers and published his first novel in 2008, an exposé of big-time criminal involvement in the sports world. He feels his writing and his soccer careers complement each other: "I found myself wanting to write books, to tell stories the way I wanted ... to write about football [soccer] (quoted in Stewart). Stavrum's approach to his fiction involves what he calls "the dark areas of the game" engineered by figures the sports public usually doesn't see, like match-fixers, black-mailers, and crooked agents (Stewart).

Stavrum's debut novel, *31 år på gress* ("31 Years on the Grass"), 2008, featured Joachim, a player whose father had hung a soccer ball over his crib and started training him at age four. As a professional player, Joachim soon peaks, then sees his career begin to slide, drained by partying, drinking, and casual affairs, while his unscrupulous agent makes shady deals to throw a major game. "31 Years on the Grass" initially met with considerable criticism because Stavrum's countrymen felt such crimes could not exist in Norway, but three months after its publication a huge Norwegian match-fixing scandal erupted, making Stavrum's book a significant success (Stewart).

In 2012, Stavrum, who has admired Scandinavian crime writers Jo Nesbø and Henning Mankell since his youth, published *Golden Boys* (he used the English title for the Norwegian version, but the novel was translated as *Exposed at the Back* in 2014), scathingly unveiling what Doug Johnstone, author of *The Dead Beat* and *Gone Again*, calls "the shocking nastiness behind the façade of football." Working from personal experience of a sport in which a deal transferring 8 or 9 million British pounds can create a scenario where some 300,000 pounds can simply disappear, Stavrum insists match-fixing and interpersonal tensions exist every bit as often in Norway and Scotland as they do in the high-profile English Premier League (quoted in Stewart).

Exposed at the Back opens with the brutal murder of Arild Golden, a fictional character who is Norway's most influential soccer agent, at his office in the national soccer stadium. A central figure in the novel, Golden was notorious for his ruthlessness and his billion-*krone* secret deals, many of which involve the exploitation of talented African players as young as fourteen or fifteen by holding their passports and other official papers and then dumping them, paperless, if they didn't make the grade on Norwegian teams. Norwegian lawyer Steinar Brunsvik, himself a former soccer player for Norway's national team, defends the African prime suspect Taribo Shorunmo, who precariously lives visa-less in Norway, and as Brunsvik investigates the case, he discovers he himself is enmeshed in a life-threatening criminal scheme.

Stavrum, a featured speaker in the 2014 Bloody Scotland Crime Festival, says he is thrilled to have *Exposed at the Back* available to English-speaking readers. He also doesn't care that in his four crime novels he has provoked the "real-life equivalents" of figures he has criticized in his books: "Football doesn't belong to them, and if readers take only that one message from my books, I will be a very happy man" (quoted in Stewart).

Selected Crime Novels:

> 2008: *31 år på gress* ("31 Years on the Grass")
> 2012: *Golden Boys* (*Exposed at the Back*, tr. Guy Puzey, 2014)

Major Awards: N/A

Website: N/A

*Vidar Sundstøl

> b. 1963, Drangedal, Telemark, Norway; Residence: Bø, Telemark, Norway; lived for some time in Egypt and on the shores of Lake Superior in Minnesota; Occupations: manual laborer in forestry and road construction, author

Since graduating from the Author Program in Bø, his only formal education, Vidar Sundstøl first wrote literary novels, then *The Minnesota Trilogy*, three connected psychological thrillers drawn from his experiences as a manual laborer and his deliberately chosen long stretches outside normal working life, all of which he considers valuable preparation for his writing. In Tiina Nunnally's surehanded translation, the first volume of the trilogy, *Drømmenes Land*, 2008 (*The Land of Dreams*, tr. 2013) became the University of Minnesota Press's biggest seller of 2013. In January 2014 the Press's regional trade editor Erik Anderson noted that *The Land of Dreams* had had a "phenomenal start," with its first printing "sold out before it even left the warehouse, because the pre-orders were so high" (quoted in Gilyard). Emily Hamilton, the University of Minnesota Press's marketing director, also observed that *The Land of Dreams* in 2013 sold more than 9000 copies and over 1500 e-book editions, as compared to the Press's typical general interest title's sales of 2500 to 3000 copies (quoted in Gilyard). *The Land of Dreams* also garnered impressive reviews from the *New York Times*, *The Washington Post*, and *Publishers Weekly*, a "huge, huge break" for the novel, according to Minnesota book publicist Kevin Finley (Gilyard). English translations of *De Døde*, 2009 (*Only the Dead*) and *Ravnene*, 2011 (*The Ravens*) appeared in 2014 and 2015 respectively, also translated by Nunnally, who won the PEN–Book of the Month Club Translation Prize for her translation of *The Cross*, the third volume of Sigrid Undset's Nobel Prize–winning *Kristin Lavransdatter* trilogy.

Kulturkompasset critic Synnove North, commenting on the original Norwegian text of *The Minnesota Trilogy*, notes that it moves slowly, with Nature playing a pivotal role throughout. Upon their Scandinavian publication, all volumes of the trilogy received impressive reviews, and *Politiken* critic Henrik Palle called *Only the Dead* "the highlight of this year's crime harvest." The trilogy's middle-aged, divorced, and depressed protagonist Lance Hansen, a 46-year-old Cook County, Minnesota, forest ranger of Norwegian descent and an amateur local historian, is a victim of his own frailties and failures. *The Land of Dreams* opens ominously one summer day when Lance encounters a distraught naked man splotched with dried blood near the corpse of a young Norwegian tourist beaten to death on the shore of Lake Superior in Minnesota's north woods, an area rife with tales of French trappers, Ojibway (Chippewa) Native Americans, and Norwegian, Swedish, and Finnish emigrants who came to Minnesota in the late 1800s. Although local police arrest a young Ojibway for the murder, Lance silently suspects his brother Andy of the killing because Lance had seen Andy near the crime scene prior to the murder. Lance is caught up in a moral dilemma which he gradually learns involve complex ancestral crimes, primarily the killing years earlier of Ojibway medicine man Swamper Caribou. Lance also discovers he himself carries Ojibway blood, and he becomes obsessed with uncovering secrets and tensions that shred the emotional bonds of his family.

"Dreams" are Sundstøl's metaphor for the monsters that both the Ojibway and the ancient Vikings knew lurked at the world's core and deep in human hearts. Sundstøl, as an outsider to Minnesota like his *Land of Dreams* character, Oslo detective Eirik Nyland who comes to the North Shore to investigate the killing of the young Norwegian tourist, recognizes the deadly violence beneath the quiet surface of the rural environment that traditionally taciturn Scandinavian settlers made their American home.

The Land of Dreams earned both Norway's 2008 Riverton Prize and a nomination for the 2008 Glass Key Award. In 2013, *The Land of Dreams* ranked eleventh in *Dagbladet's* list of twenty-five best Norwegian crime novels.

De Døde (*Only the Dead*), the second volume of the trilogy, thrusts Lance and Andy into an intense psychological *pas de deux*. Several months after the murder, on their annual November deer hunting trip, each brother finds himself caught in the other's rifle crosshairs against the imposing backdrop of the deep wintry Minnesota forest and an early season ice storm. Sundstøl counterpoints the brothers' grueling physical hunt for deer and Lance's scalding psychological search for equally elusive truths with the first-person narration of their distant relative Thormod Olson, a just-arrived young Norwegian immigrant who mysteriously survived a fall into a freezing lake in 1892 while he was seeking his uncle's north woods cabin.

After the dramatic deer hunt that dominates *Only the Dead*, *The Ravens* concludes the series with Lance at first running from both his brother and himself, then reluctantly returning to explode his family's long-preserved silence about secrets they feel they cannot reveal. In fear that Andy may kill him, Lance exiled himself to Canada, but convinced of the accused Indian boy's innocence and secretly harboring suspicions of Andy's guilt, Lance returns to his icy Minnesota home to confront not only his brother with a scalding episode from their boyhood but also to face his own fearful demons. *The Ravens* also involves powerful portrayals of Lance's aging mother and Andy's wife Tammy and daughter Crissy, as well as the Ojibway medicine man Swamper Caribou who appears to Lance in a dramatic vision, each figure playing a crucial role in Sundstøl's resolution of this handsomely crafted psychological thriller.

In a 2013 interview with *The Strathspey Herald* (Scotland) while he was attending the Nairn Arts Festival as a featured speaker, Sundstol indicated that he prefers a broader geographic and cultural setting for his fiction than the "village crime" settings popularized by Agatha Christie in her Miss Marple novels and successfully used ever since by many contemporary crime fiction authors like Karin Fossum. Sundstøl noted that during the years he and his wife lived on Minnesota's North Shore, they saw more people on skis than they had in Norway, illustrating both the special connection he acknowledges between Minnesota's descendants of Scandinavian settlers and their relatives in Norway as well as the differences between the immigrants' nostalgic dreams of their "old country" and the modern Norway that has outgrown it. Commenting on the large cast of characters in *The Land of Dreams*, Sundstøl revealed that he especially enjoyed writing about Lance's niece Crissy, since she was filled with the same sort of longing for escape from her surroundings he himself had felt as a youth. He also mentioned that his first novel since the Minnesota Trilogy would be a thriller, to be released soon in Norway (Sundstøl, Interview).

Literary Novels:

> 2005: *Kommandolinjer* ("Command Lines") (short novel)
> 2006: *I Alexandria* ("In Alexandria")
> 2007: *Tingene hennes* ("Her Things")

Crime Novels:

> *The Minnesota Trilogy:*
> 2008: *Drømmenes Land* (*The Land of Dreams*, tr. Tiina Nunnally, 2013)
> 2009: *De døde* (*Only the Dead*, tr. Tiina Nunnally, 2014)
> 2011: *Ravnene* (*The Ravens*, tr. Tiina Nunnally, 2015)

Stand-Alone Novels:

> 2013: *Besettelsen* ("Obsession")
> 2014: *Djevelens giftering* ("The Devil's Wedding Ring")

Major Awards:

> 2008: The Riverton Prize for *Drømmenes Land* (*The Land of Dreams*)

Website: N/A

Gard Sveen

> b. March 8, 1969; birthplace N/A; Residence: Enebakk, Norway; Occupations: senior adviser, Norwegian Ministry of Defence, author

The only Norwegian to have won the Riverton Prize, the Glass Key Award, and the Maurits Hansen Award—New Blood, all for a debut novel, Gard Sveen also joins Jo Nesbø as the only Norwegian authors to have won both the Glass Key Award and the Riverton Prize for a debut novel. Sveen's *Den siste pilegrimen* ("The Last Pilgrim"), 2013, first of a projected series, contains two parallel plots. The contemporary plot features controversial police investigator Tommy Bergmann, who has unpleasant psychological traits: his relationship with his girlfriend has crashed because of accusations that he had beaten her. Bergmann is probing the murder of Carl Oscar Krogh, an old Norwegian resistance fighter found cruelly slaughtered in his home at Holmenkollen, at the same time the Oslo police are attempting to connect the skeletal remains of three persons found in North Marka probably dating from the World War II period, with Krogh's death. Norwegian critics praise Sveen's ability to convey the close relationships between characters facing near-impossible choices and his insight into painful episodes of Norwegian history involving wartime liquidations.

Crime Novels:

> 2013: *Den siste pilegrimen* ("The Last Pilgrim")
> 2015: *Helvete åpent* ("Hell Open")

Major Awards:

2014: The Riverton Prize, for *Den siste pilegrimen* ("The Last Pilgrim")
2014: The Glass Key Award, for *Den siste pilegrimen* ("The Last Pilgrim")
2014: The Maurits Hansen Award—New Blood, for *Den siste pilegrimen* ("The Last Pilgrim")

Website: N/A

Frank Tandberg (J.F. Johnson Tandberg)

b. 1959, Bergen, Norway; Residence: Various; Occupation: author

Frank Tandberg knows crime from personal experience. Tandberg, often referred to as "Pimp-Frank," has been convicted for violent illegal activities: in 1990, he shot the notorious criminal Espen Lie in the thigh (Lie), and in 2013 he repeatedly stabbed a girlfriend with nail scissors, broke her nose and destroyed her front teeth, for which he served 120 days in jail and had to pay the victim 46 million *krone* in reparations (Orskaug). In 2001 he savagely denounced the Norwegian Authors' Union for not backing his demand that publishers of paperbacks should pay their authors 20 percent royalties instead of the 5 percent they now pay. Geir Pollen, President of the Norwegian Authors Union, has stated that actions like Tandberg's "do not belong anywhere" (quoted in Lie).

Tandberg's fiction reflects his unpleasant behavior. His ultra-*noir* debut novel *Nattens joker* ("Night Joker") appeared in 1995, and a later reviewer concluded that after reading it, "you feel an intense desire to wash your hands" (*Dagbladet*, July 8, 2009). "Night Joker" was nevertheless ranked twenty-first on the 2009 *Dagbladet* list of twenty-five best Norwegian crime novels of all time and described as an antidote to "today's suffocating [new moralistic] Doctor Doolittle literature." Tandberg has written two more novels starring his detective hero Martin Lorentzen. According to *Dagbladet*'s hand-washing critic, relieving the discomfort from reading all three books "definitely requires power washing, not Kleenex" (quoted in *Dagbladet*, July 8, 2009). These novels depict a filthy drug-obsessed universe, specifically the underworld seething beneath the surfaces of Copenhagen and Amsterdam. Tandberg used his acquaintance with these cities' criminal venues as background for his stories of "people with weaknesses, but without scruples" (*Dagbladet*, July 8, 2009) in violently realistic prose decidedly not for readers faint of heart or stomach.

Selected Crime Novels:

1995: *Nattens joker* ("Night Joker")
1998: *Løgnerens paradis* ("Liars' Paradise")

Major Awards: N/A

Website: N/A

Kjetil Try

b. July 24, 1959, Manglerud, Oslo, Norway; Residence: Oslo, Norway; Occupations: actor, advertising agent and agency director, crime novelist

Try, a former creative director at the Norway's Scanedo, Young & Rubicam advertising agency, founded and is the CEO and co-owner of Try/Apt Oslo. Apt develops digital communications, while Try himself manages the advertising arm of the business without a management team. He produces a number of commercials each year, and in a February 2012 interview with Jan-Sverre Syvertsen, he said that despite his dependence on his MacBook Pro, his iPhone, and his iPad, he visits in person with almost all of his agency's 50-some employees each day: "When I do not have any management team, it becomes more important for me to be close [to them] … I enjoy a lot of balls in the air" (quoted in Syverstsen). In addition to his advertising career Try also juggles his crime writing, which, as he told Syvertsen, provides him "something completely different." Try says he can't write in his high-paced agency office, so he relaxes by working on his crime scripts at home or during air travel, claiming that his fiction writing is "more a hobby than a job."

As a novelist, Try is probably best known for *La de små barn komme til meg* ("Let the Little Children Come to Me"), 2008, the first installment of Try's "Happiness" crime series featuring Detective Rolf Gordon Luck, being developed as a television series. The novel opens on a December evening, just after famous actor Reidar Dahl has successfully performed a reading of the Christmas Gospel. The next morning Dahl disappears without a trace. *Freis oss fra det onde* ("Deliver Us from Evil"), 2011, the next volume in the series, deals with the perils of online dating, summed up by the impossibility of being quite sure who is addressing whom and how in cyberspace. Try says he develops his characters as he goes along, intending primarily to entertain his readers. He rates Dennis Lehane's *Mystic River* among his favorite crime novels.

Crime Novels:

   1997: *Stø kurs* ("Staying the Course")
   2002: *Pavlovs hunder* ("Pavlov's Dogs")
   2008: *La de små barn komme til meg* ("Let the Little Children Come to Me")
   2011: *Frels oss fra det onde* ("Deliver Us from Evil")

Major Awards: N/A

Website: http://www.try.no

Chris Tvedt

   b. 1954, Bergen, Norway; Residence: Bergen, Norway; Occupations: lawyer and novelist

   Tvedt studied law and literature at the University of Bergen and practiced law until 2005, when his debut crime novel *Rimelig tvil* ("Reasonable Doubt") appeared, and he then turned to writing full time. Tvedt's first five novels feature down-at-heels defense attorney Mikael Brenne, but he launched a new detective novel series in 2012 with *Av jord er du kommet* ("Ashes to Ashes"), starring puritanical and over-scrupulous KRIPOS (Norwegian national police force) investigator Edward Matre. In a 2010 *Bokelskerinnen* interview, Tvedt commented regarding his 2010 novel *Dødens sirkel* ("Circle of Death") that his experience as a defense attorney caused him to create somewhat unrealistic fiction. About Tvedt's shift to a new protagonist with "Ashes to Ashes," NRK's *Culture News* review for February 13, 2012, called Norwegian police procedurals in general "dangerously threadbare and woefully faded in color," and took Tvedt to task for creating "monolithic characters" and "a typical serial killer crime," with "inevitable" references to the FBI and criminal profiling, concluding, "We have … read [this] before."

Crime Novels:

Mikael Brenne Series:

2005: *Rimelig tvil* ("Reasonable Doubt")
2007: *Fare for gjentakelse* ("Risk of Recurrence")
2008: *Skjellig grunn til mistanke* ("Reasonable Grounds for Suspicion")
2009: *Rottejegeren* ("Rat Hunters")
2010: *Dødens sirkel* ("Circle of Death")

Edward Matre Crime Novels:

2012: *Av jord er du kommet* ("Ashes to Ashes")
2013: *Den blinde guden* ("The Blind Girl")
2014: *Djevelens barn* ("The Devil's Playground")

Major Awards:

2010: The Riverton Prize, for *Dødens sirkel* ("Circle of Death")

Website: N/A

Herbjørg Wassmo

b. December 6, 1942, Vesterålen, Norway; Residence: Harstad, Norway; Occupations: teacher, author

Prolific author Herbjørg Wassmo has produced poetry, radio plays, a prize-winning documentary novel, and widely praised novels which Rakel Christina Granaas in *The History of Nordic Women's Literature* places "at the vanguard of the 1980s' media focus and debate on the issue of incest," while also focusing on the mother-child relationship. Wassmo's 1981 breakthrough novel, *Huset med den blinde glassveranda* (*The House with the Blind Glass Windows*, tr. 1987), was the first novel of her "Tora" trilogy, taking place in 1950s Norway and featuring a child fathered during World War II by a German soldier. The mental and sexual abuse her drunken stepfather inflicts on eleven-year-old Tora causes her abnormal refusal to communicate and powerful guilt feelings that become psychotic; she tries to escape into a fantasy world in which she imagines that her real father is returning to save her. Wassmo set the novel in a small Norwegian fishing village in the bitter aftermath of the Nazi occupation, where despite the villagers' suffering, a few compassionate women help Tora survive.

In 2009, after her parents had been dead for several years, Wassmo released her historical novel *Hundre år* ("A Hundred Years") dealing with the lives of her great-grandmother, grandmother, and mother, revealing that Wassmo's father had frequently molested her when she was a child. In her recent autobiographical novel "The Moment," Wassmo's heroine Herbjorg, who became at eleven years old a victim of incest like Wassmo herself, harbored thoughts of suicide and even the desire to kill her abusive father. Wassmo has said that after keeping her father's crimes a secret for so many years, her conscience finally forced her to reveal them to the world.

The theme of abused and abandoned children also dominates Wassmo's novel *Dinas bok*, 1985 (*Dina's Book*, tr. 1996), the first novel of Wassmo's "Dina" trilogy. Dina, a murderess, dramatically contrasts with the victimized Tora. Dina grew up in the 1800s tormented by her mother's horrifying death after Dina accidentally spilled boiling lye over her. Dina imagines her mother's ghost is visiting her, causing her to become mute and manipulative despite the efforts of her father, the town's sheriff, to raise her properly. Eventually after his own remarriage, he weds Dina to a middle-aged landowner who at first is fascinated by her untamed spirit but later dies suspiciously while she is taking him to a doctor. A Kirkus reviewer on April 1, 1994, found Wassmo's portrayals of the unscrupulous and seductive Dina and her "shattered psyche" and the primitive Norwegian landscape skillful and evocative, but described the novel's plot as "formulaic" and the prose "often clichéd and melodramatic."

In her 2006 novel *Et glass melk takk* ("A Glass of Milk, Please"), Wassmo treated the painful contemporary topic of human trafficking through Dorte, an impoverished fifteen-year-old Lithuanian girl who naively accepts an offer to work in a Stockholm restaurant because she thinks it will be an exotic adventure, only to discover that the "offer" was a brutal sham. Rights to this novel, which may reawaken interest in Wassmo's fiction, have been sold in Russia, the Netherlands, France, Denmark and Lithuania.

Psychological Crime Novels:

The "Tora" Trilogy:

1981: *Huset med den blinde glassveranda* (*The House with the Blind Glass Windows*, tr. Roseann Lloyd and Allen Simpson, 1987)
1983: *Det stumme rommet* ("The Mute Room")
1986: *Hudløs himmel* ("The Raw Sky")

The Dina Trilogy:

1989: *Dinas bok* (*Dina's Book*, tr. Nadia Christensen, 1996; filmed as *I Am Dina*, 2002, starring Maria Bonnevie and Gérard Depardieu)
1992: *Lykkens sønn* (*Dina's Son*, tr. Nadia Christensen, 2001)
1997: *Karnas arv* ("Karna's Heritage")

Selected Stand-Alone Novels:

2006: *Et glass melk takk* ("A Glass of Milk, Please")
2009: *Hundre år* ("A Hundred Years")

Major Awards:

1981: *Kritikerprisen*, for *The House with the Blind Glass Windows*
1983: *Bokhandlerprisen*, for "The Mute Room"
1986: *Nordland fylkes kulturpris*
1987: Nordic Council's Literature Prize, for "The Raw Sky"
1997: *Amalie Skram-prisen*
1998: *Prix Jean Monnet* (France)
2006: *Havmannprisen*
2007: Commander of the Order of St. Olav
2010: The Brage Prize's honorary award
2011: Knight of the French Order of Arts and Letters

Website: N/A

Øystein Wiik

b. 1956, Oslo; Residence: Oslo; Occupations: actor, professional singer, songwriter, and novelist

Wiik, a singer primarily famous for his dramatic and musical performances, also appeared as an actor at Oslo's *Nye Teater*, *Det Norske Teatret*, and *Den Nationale Scene*. He has also played leading roles in musicals, including Jean Valjean in *Les Miserables* in London and Vienna in 1989–1990. His vocal albums include *Too Many Mornings*, 1991, and *Stage*, 1993. He also published a series of crime novels beginning with *Dødelig applaus* ("Deadly Applause"), 2010, described in a 2010 *Dagbladet* review as "a fresh and lively story of murder and power games on and off the opera stage."

"Deadly Applause," nominated for the Riverton Prize, opens in Oslo with a performance of *Tosca* starring fictional world-renowned tenor James Medina. Between the acts a luscious woman, hired to stimulate Medina sensually to maximize his performance, visits him in his dressing room. Later in the opera's grand finale, Medina is shot dead—for real. The novel's detective hero, Tom Hartmann, a former *Dagbladet* music critic who has launched his own magazine, continues to investigate *outré* homicides in Wiik's *Siakteren* ("The Butcher") which involves criminal activity in the south of France. In the third mystery of the series, *Hvit panter* ("The White Panther"), shipowner Herman Nordahl is found tortured with a primitive implement favored by tribal warlords. Wiik's fourth installment in the series, *Casanovasyndromet* ("The Casanova Syndrome"), set in Venice, combines the art of love with the lust for wealth, power, new and deadly weaponry, and sinister intrigue.

Crime Novels:

2010: *Dødelig applaus* ("Deadly Applause")
2011: *Slakteren* ("The Butcher")
2012: *Hvit panter* ("White Panther")
2013: *Casanovasyndromet* ("The Casanova Syndrome")
2015: *Den syvende nøkkelen* ("The Seventh Key")

Major Awards: N/A

Website: N/A

Selected Crime Fiction Set in Norway by Non-Norwegian Authors

Robert Barnard

b. November 23, 1936, Burnham-on-Crouch, Essex, England; d. September 19, 2013, Leeds, Yorkshire, England; Residence: Leeds, Yorkshire, England; Occupation: author

Set in the far north Norwegian city of Tromsø, distinguished British mystery author Robert Barnard's seventh complex whodunit, *Death in a Cold Climate*, portrays Norway through the eyes of a perceptive outsider. Barnard, who taught English in Bergen for a decade before becoming a professor of English at the University of Tromsø for eight years, knew Norway and its people well, providing "sympathetic, yet horrifying portrait[s]" of such characters as "the perfect Norwegian housewife," the conscienceless Norwegian businessman, and a "timeless old woman" of Oslo selling hot dogs and storing up information for decades, all drawn with abundant descriptive detail. Besides *Death in a Cold Climate*, a case of a murdered boy which leads Inspector Fagermo to uncover an intricate web of blackmail and espionage, Barnard also set *The Cherry Blossom Corpse* (titled *Death in Purple Prose* in the UK), 1987, starring one of his other sleuths, Perry Trethowan, in a puzzle mystery that is also a send-up of a Romance Writers Convention in Bergen.

Crime Novels:

1980: *Death in a Cold Climate*

1987: *The Cherry Blossom Corpse* (in UK, *Death in Purple Prose*)

Major Awards:

2003: Cartier Diamond Dagger, Crime Writers Association, for lifetime achievement

Website: N/A

Jeanne Matthews

b. (?) Georgia, USA; Residence: Renton, Washington, USA; Occupations: journalist, paralegal, teacher, author

Matthews' cozy series heroine, American anthropologist and amateur detective Dinah Pelerin, junkets to Norway's anything but cozy far north Svalbard (Spitzbergen) with American politicians and agribusiness leaders to deposit valuable U.S. agricultural materials in the Svalbard Global Seed Vault, sometimes called the "Doomsday Vault," which preserves millions of seed varieties in case of a worldwide holocaust. Norwegian journalist and activist Fridjoe Eftevang joins them and disrupts the visitors' undercover agendas, lending sparks to the frigid arctic atmosphere. Murders and an attempt on Dinah's life soon erupt. Matthews describes cold weather-hating Dinah as "reluctant" about the trip, though "she might be edgy, ... she's got a sense of humor" (Matthews, "Trespassing" 35). Seeing Svalbard and Eftevang through Dinah's eyes allows American readers a bone-chilling view of today's Norway and its environmentalist movement.

Crime Novel with Norwegian Setting:

Dinah Pelerin Mystery Series:

2012: *Bonereapers*

Major Awards: N/A

Website: http://www.jeannematthews.com

Derek B. Miller

b. 1970, Boston, Massachusetts; Residence: Oslo, Norway; Occupations: international affairs specialist, author

Derek B. Miller holds a Ph.D. in national security studies from Georgetown University and is a senior fellow with the United Nations Institute for Disarmamental Research. He is Jewish and lives in Oslo with his Norwegian wife and their two children, the background for his 2013 debut novel, *Norwegian by Night*, which treats the exile of 82-year-old Jewish watchmaker Sheldon Horowitz, recently widowed and uprooted from his lifetime New York home, to Oslo. Sheldon's move was the brainchild of his granddaughter Rhea, a wannabe Jewish mother who lives with her husband Lars, a husky Norwegian, in Norway, which currently has only about a thousand resident Jews. Sheldon had served as a volunteer Marine sniper in the Korean War, but a half century later, possibly slipping a little mentally, somewhat bemused but wholly compassionate, he leaves Rhea's Oslo apartment to save a Serbian immigrant neighbor's young son from the killer of the boy's mother. Sheldon perceives and Miller effectively conveys the "polite discomfort" native Norwegians feel around Sheldon, which probably stems from Norway's ambivalent wartime conduct toward Jews. This attitude ignites Sheldon's righteous anger toward the anti–Semitism that he finds still existing in Scandinavia (O'Brien), fueled today by the growing neo–Nazi movements there.

Norwegian by Night received numerous award nominations for its excellence as a debut crime novel. Most critics agreed with Laura Wilson, reviewing for *The Guardian*, who described *Norwegian by Night* as "crime fiction of the highest order," with "all the ingredients of a top-notch thriller" (Wilson). Miller's plot is also seasoned with sly insight into Norwegian gender roles, notably a shrewd analysis of why establishing relationships with taciturn Norwegian men poses problems for Norwegian women. One of Miller's Norwegian characters, a substantially-built and plain-featured Norwegian policewoman, tries to explain this to her practical father, who wants her to marry a Norwegian man:

> "They are polite. Occasionally witty. They dress like teenagers no matter what their age, and will never say anything romantic unless it's during a drunken confessional." [Her father replies], "So get them drunk.... You look for the man staring with the greatest intensity at his own shoes while in your presence" [*Norwegian by Night* 41].

Crime Novel:

2013: *Norwegian by Night*

Major Awards:

2013: Crime Writers Association John Creasy Award for a Debut Crime Novel, for *Norwegian by Night*

Website: https://twitter.com/derekmiller

Kris Tualla

b. N/A; Residence: Arizona, USA; Occupation: author of historical romance and suspense novels

Breathlessly smitten by "a new breed of hero! Big, blond, buff and beautiful, with eyes the colors of seawater; the blood of their Viking ancestors flowing through their veins," Arizona romance author Kris Tualla insists, "Norway is the NEW [capitals on website] Scotland!" (quoted from website). The hero of Tualla's *A Discreet Gentleman of Discovery* and its four sequels, Brander Hansen, is a deaf private investigator living in 1720 Oslo (then called Christiania). Brander Hansen, blessed with hazel eyes and strawberry blond hair, sprang from Tualla's 2011 trip to Norway and his descendants have appeared in Tualla's fiction ever since. Tualla says she plans to continue writing about her many historical Hansen characters for the rest of her writing career, so she spent a week at the Bemidji, Minnesota, Norsk language camp run by Concordia College, Moorhead, Minnesota, preparing for a 2015 return visit to Norway to do research for upcoming Hansen novels set in the Renaissance era: "It's all about big, blond, beautiful Norsemen," she claims, "And it's awesome" (Tualla, "Why Norway" 39–40).

Selected Historical Suspense and Romance Novels:

The Hansen Books:

2010: *A Prince of Norway* (set in 1820)
2014: *Loving the Norseman* (set in 1354)
2014: *Leaving Norway* (set in 1749)

The Discreet Gentleman Series (set in the 1720s):

2012: *A Discreet Gentleman of Discovery*
2012: *A Discreet Gentleman of Matrimony*
2012: *A Discreet Gentleman of Consequence*
2013: *A Discreet Gentleman of Mystery*
2013: *A Discreet Gentleman of Intrigue*

Major Awards: N/A

Website: http://www.KrisTualla.com

Sweden

A coward believes he will ever live
If he keep him safe from strife:
But old age leaves him not long in peace
Though spears may spare his life.
　　　　　—*Hávamál*, The Words of Odin the High One,
　　　　　　　　　　Wisdom for Wanderers and
　　　　　　　　　　Counsel to Guests, 16

The Cultural Context of Swedish Crime Fiction

Since 1967, Sweden's crime fiction has enjoyed a remarkable explosion of popularity. In 2010, Sweden, with a population of nine million-plus against the total European population of over 800 million, had three Swedish crime fiction authors on the top ten lists of the best selling novels in Europe. Revenue from sales of Swedish novels abroad rose from around $8.5 million in the 1990s to $150 million in 2011, an impressive trend launched primarily by the works of Henning Mankell and Stieg Larsson. Swedish is now one of the world's ten most translated languages, and of the more than 3,300 Swedish titles translated into fifty other languages, half belong to the "Nordic noir" Scandinavian crime fiction genre ("Modern Swedish Literature").

As the most populous Nordic country and "the dominant force in Nordic crime" Sweden also "boasts the greatest diversity" (Kachka), a diversity reflected in its crime fiction through a multitude of geographical settings, a wide range of literary variations of the mystery and thriller formats, broad ethnic and gender perspectives, various uses of Swedish historical material, and a wide spectrum of the "embed[ded] ... lefty critique of capitalism and chauvinism" (Kachka). Håkan Nesser, one of Sweden's foremost crime fiction authors, recently underscored his opinion that the label "Scandinavian noir" should be discarded: "If you read 10 Swedish crime writers, you'll see that we're all very, very different.... It's time people look at each book instead of grouping everyone from Scandinavia in a box" (quoted in Nair).

Sweden's varied geography, with strikingly differing climatic conditions in the country's various regions, strongly affects the lives of its people, both real individuals and fictional characters, but the one common denominator constant is visual severity. A vital narrative component of Swedish crime literature is "the often bleak Scandinavian landscape" that mirrors the characters' personalities. "Vast alvars, ancient stone, and dark shores inhabit these stories ... [so that] the soul of the landscape becomes an important narrative agent, even a character in itself." Sweden's diverse landscapes also foster "ancient beliefs in ghosts, changelings, and other natural spirits" (Megraw) that cloak many Swedish crimes and the villains who commit them in an ancient pagan aura.

Sweden is the third largest country in the European Union with only 54 persons per square mile, mostly concentrated in the southern half of the country. About 85 percent of the population lives in urban areas, especially Stockholm. Sweden's twenty-five provinces (*landskap* or "landscapes"), often referred to in popular fiction because they contribute strongly to characters' self-identity, are generally grouped into three sections: Norrland, with 15 percent of its land above the Arctic Circle, occupies about 60 percent of the country; Svealand in the center has a humid continental climate; Götaland, mostly agricultural, has an oceanic climate, with the highest population density in three areas, the Öresund Region, the western coast, and Stockholm, in the valley of Lake Mälaren. Length of daylight, often a factor in human personality problems both real and fictional, varies greatly, especially in the north, where in part of the summer the sun never sets and in part of the winter it never rises. In the north, temperatures often drop below freezing from September to May, but in the south and central regions some winters have almost no snow at all.

Sweden's crime authors exhibit considerable diversity in their fictional settings. Henning Mankell's Wallander novels take place mostly in Ystad, a small town at the southern tip of Sweden; Camilla Läckberg's occur in her home town of Fjällbacka on the west coast, close to the Norwegian border; and Håkan Nesser's locale, while overtly an unspecified Baltic country, bears certain resemblances to his home town of Kumla, which houses Sweden's largest prison. Even the Stockholms of Swedish crime authors vary greatly. Stieg Larsson made the major setting of his Millennium Trilogy an investigative journalist's Stockholm, focusing on its neo–Nazi movement and its governmental-industrial-financial corruption. Leif G.W. Persson, a professor of criminology at the Swedish National Police Board, built his Palme Trilogy around the 1985 assassination in Stockholm of Prime Minister Olof Palme. Jens Lapidus ties his fast-paced, glossy young Stockholm to international drug and crime syndicates; Lars Kepler dissects a frigid Stockholm where people callously ignore each other's needs; and Roslund and Hellström view Sweden's capital as a maelstrom of addiction, crime, and revenge. Farther afield, Åsa Larsson sets her psychological thrillers in her home town of Kiruna, Sweden's northernmost town and site of the world's largest underground iron mine, and Liza Marklund, who comes from the small northern village of Pålmark, integrates her early experiences into the feminist issues her heroine Annike Bengtzon faces. Swedish crime authors have used so many villages and rural settings for their fiction that their detective novels and thrillers take place in almost every "landscape" of Sweden, which in actuality experienced only 10.6 murders per one million people between 2006 and 2008 (Kachka).

Sweden's history reflects the diverse cultural elements that have also affected the development of its crime literature. Old Norse mythology includes lists of possibly legendary Swedish kings beginning with the first centuries before Christ. Prior to the 2nd century AD, a Gothic population had crossed the Baltic Sea from Götaland (southern Sweden) and arrived in Scythia on the Black Sea coast in what is now Ukraine, eventually dividing into the redoubtable Visigoths and Ostragoths who established 5th and 6th century successor-states after the fall of the Roman Empire. The Roman historian Tacitus described the Swedes (*Suiones*) in AD 98 as a powerful tribe "distinguished not merely for their arms and men, but for their powerful fleets" (*Germania* 44–45) of longships that allowed the Swedes not only to raid other lands for profit but to import the artifacts and ideas of other cultures into their northern homeland.

Recording many of their exploits and names of male heroes on rune stones carved and kept in Sweden, Sweden's Viking Age, from the 8th to the 11th centuries, saw tall, blond, and ferocious axe-wielding seafarers moving east and south, from northern Finland through the Baltic areas, moving as far south as Baghdad, on the way frequently raiding Constantinople, capital of Byzantium. The Byzantine Emperor Theophilus employed Swedish Vikings as his personal Varangian Guard, and Swedish Vikings called the "Rus" are believed to have founded Kievan Russia. The most far-ranging (and last) Swedish Viking expedition was Ingvar the Far-Travelled's voyage to the area southwest of the Caspian Sea, where all members of his expedition apparently perished from disease.

Unlike Denmark with its *Gesta Danorum* and Norway and Iceland with their rich Old Norse literary tradition, "exceedingly few" survivals of Swedish pre–Christian literature exist, "scarcely of a high literary quality" (Gustafson vii), the first Swedish literary text being the Rök Runestone, c. AD 800, which contains passages from sagas and legends, some in Old Norse alliterative verse (*fornyrdislag*). The borders of the earliest kingdom called "Sweden" are indistinct, indicating considerable contact between Swedes and other peoples. The first king thought to have ruled both "Svealand" (Sweden) and "Götaland" (Gothia) was Erik the Victorious, but the Germanic epic *Beowulf* describes 6th century wars between the Geats from Götaland and the Swedes. The Danes and the Swedes disputed the ownership of the island of Gotland, while Swedes settled in southwest Finland and along Norrland's southern coast and enthusiastically took to trading. Ystad, a flourishing trade center with a large Swedish population, belonged during the Middle Ages to the Danish province of Scania; Paviken on the Baltic had a large shipbuilding harbor, and between 800 and 1000, Gotlanders possessed more silver from trade than the rest of the Scandinavians put together (Sawyer and Sawyer 153). Such trade brought Sweden closer than the other Nordic countries to Europe.

Alrik Gustafson, a leading Swedish twentieth century literary historian, conjectures that the absorption of Swedish Vikings not only in foreign adventure, but in extensive trading ventures in Scandinavia, domestic agriculture, and establishment of the rudiments of a stable society prevented the creation of a Swedish skaldic (poetic) tradition like the Norwegians and Icelanders possessed. By 1250 the old native Scandinavian literary traditions were dead or dying. Visiting Norwegian or Icelandic skalds might appear in Swedish courts, but Viking chieftains and their henchmen no longer existed in the North, and Old Norse mythology, the stuff of skaldic tradition, no longer retained its validity as Swedish society gradually became Christian (Gustafson 20). The prevailing language of monastic writers being Latin, not much Old Swedish textual material exists, also because the Swedish Viking was probably too busy "with immediate practical tasks to indulge more than casually in the arts" (Gustafson 13). Sweden also never developed a feudal tradition, so its peasants were free farmers for most of Sweden's history. King Magnus Erikson abolished slavery in 1335.

Literature developed slowly in Sweden, and its distinguishing feature became "a sense of continuity" so closely identifiable with the Western European cultural tradition that an English-speaking reader of Swedish literature might assume that it was the product of a derivative imitative culture. In particular during the Middle Ages, contributions of northern Germany, like those of the Hanseatic city of Lübeck, "to all aspects of Swedish culture, language, and technology were significant" (Mitchell in Warme, 18). However, the very continuity observable in Swedish literature demonstrated its capability of preserving Sweden's special identity "even while willingly—at times, indeed, eagerly—exposing itself to cultural currents originating outside its own borders" (Gustafson viii) to a much greater extent than happened in the other Nordic countries.

Christianity took root gradually in Sweden after its introduction by St. Ansgar in 819. By 1050, Sweden was considered a Christian nation, but the new religion did not fully replace paganism until the 12th century. Internal strife and conflicts with the other Nordic entities continued until about 1400, and Sweden's loss of a third of its population to the mid–14th century Black Death was not replaced until the beginning of the 19th century. Sweden remained economically impoverished through most of the Middle Ages, another contributing factor in its late development of a literary tradition.

Yet another such factor was Sweden's medieval governing structure, entangled with that of Norway and Denmark from 1319, when King Magnus Erikson united Sweden and Norway. Queen Margaret I of Denmark brought Denmark, Norway, and Sweden together in the Kalmar Union, 1397, but her Danish successors could not control the Swedish nobility. Circumstances had caused the Swedish throne to be held frequently by child monarchs, always an unstable situation, which for Sweden meant the Swedish Parliament chose regents to do the actual governing, depriving the country of stable and unifying monarchial figures and promoting dissention among the noble families. When Christian II of Denmark tried to cement his domination of Sweden by ordering a massacre of Swedish noblemen in 1520 at Stockholm (the "Swedish Bloodbath"), the remaining nobility rebelled under Gustav Vasa, whose father had been murdered in that bloodbath, and on June 6 (now Sweden's Independence Day), 1523, they acclaimed him as their king.

Gustav I's Sweden, geographically on the fringes of Europe, was poor, sparsely populated, with no significant power or reputation, but he made himself the father of modern Sweden. He almost immediately rejected Catholicism and forcibly led Sweden into the Protestant Reformation, establishing the national Protestant Church in 1527, plundering Catholic monasteries, burning Catholic books and allowing Uppsala University to flounder, so that Swedes who pursued higher education had to do so abroad, usually at the Universities of Rostock and Wittenburg. Since he wanted to control publications, only the Bible and a few other religious works could be published. In 1541, the full translation of the Bible into Swedish (the Gustav Vasa Bible) provided the major impetus to standardizing the Swedish language, which in turn allowed a native Swedish literature to develop.

Gustav I's other grand achievement was the dissolution of the Hanseatic League, which since 1356, led by the northern German city of Lübeck, had been receiving civil and commercial privileges from the princes and other leaders of the Baltic states in return for using the Hanseatic navy to rid the Baltic of pirates. The Hansa demanded that only Hansa citizens, mostly Germans, could trade from ports where they were located, free of all custom fees and taxes, and they soon dominated Stockholm's economy, making it Sweden's leading commercial and industrial city, with two-thirds of its imports being textiles and one-third salt, while it exported mainly iron and copper. Gustav I led a Danish-Swedish victory over Lübeck in 1537, bringing a dramatic rise in the country's commercial revenue reinforced by a free Swedish peasantry able to benefit more from economic improvements than feudally-dominated peasants whose income from their labor mostly went to a landowning nobility. What did dominate Sweden, however, was the Lutheran stranglehold on learning and culture due to the Reformation.

After Gustav I established the Vasa family as Sweden's royalty, during the 17th century his descendants led Sweden's emergence as a great European power. His son Gustavus Adolphus (Gustav II), ruling from 1611 to 1632, achieved internal stability through concessions to the nobility and buyoffs to the Danes to end the Kalmar War in 1613. He seized territories from Russia and Poland-Lithuania during the early part of the Thirty Years' War, 1618–1648, as defender of the Protestant faith conquering almost half of the Holy Roman states, but he was killed in the Battle of Lützen, 1632, before he could realize his dream of becoming the new Holy Roman Emperor and uniting Scandinavia. He had conquered one-third of all German towns, but gradually the German provinces extricated themselves from Sweden. Gustavus Adophus' daughter Christina, whom he unconventionally for his time had educated to rule as a young man would, succeeded him, ruling with intellectual and cultural zeal until, drawn to Catholicism and refusing to marry, she was forced to abdicate in 1654. Her cousin Charles X involved Sweden in conflicts with Poland, Russia, and Denmark, and his son Charles XI and grandson Charles XII, both absolutist monarchs, engaged Sweden in European wars which debilitated the nation. Climaxing with Charles XII's disastrous Russian campaign of 1708–9 and the invasion of Norway in which he was killed, these wars "sacrificed the last remnants of a Baltic empire" and ended Sweden's role as a great European power (Gustafson 111).

During the *Stormaktstiden*, Sweden's Great Power period following the Peace of Westphalia in 1648, Sweden experienced a cultural expansion which produced "a new type of literary personality" and "new kinds of literary ideals" by bringing the country out of its long cultural isolation (Gustafson 76). Europe's most progressive countries—Germany, France, Holland, and Italy—influenced Sweden's culture, and education was improving as the grip of the Lutheran church loosened. Several Swedish authors significantly contributed to the development of the language, like Georg Stiernhielm who in the 17th century was first to write classical poetry in Swedish, and Johan Henric Kellgren who pioneered fluent Swedish prose in the 18th century.

Though fought mostly on German soil, the Thirty Years' War (1618–1648) involved armies from all over Europe, and contact with them helped melt Sweden's stern Lutheran orthodoxy. The short reign of Queen Christina brought Continental flair to her court around 1650, but relatively little literary production emerged during Sweden's brief period of military and political eminence. With the death of Charles XII in 1718 and the Swedish parliament's subsequent insistence on ending the royal absolutism that had brought about such disasters as the loss of 200,000 men and large tracts of land in the 1721 Treaty of Nystad, a new and very different intellectual atmosphere, the Enlightenment, was beginning to enter Sweden through the English liberalism that the French took up and popularized.

By the early nineteenth century, Sweden could not maintain the territories it held outside of Scandinavia. In 1809, it even lost eastern Finland to Russia, and Finland then became the mostly autonomous "Grand Principality of Finland" in the Russian Empire. During the Napoleonic Wars, Sweden forced Denmark to cede Norway to Sweden in 1814 and coerced Norway into accepting a personal union with Sweden that lasted until 1905. Since 1814, Sweden has maintained its neutrality, defined since 1907 by the Hague Convention.

During most of the nineteenth century, poetry and drama dominated Swedish literature, its native authors mostly avoiding newly imported forms like the essay and the novel. When they did create a Swedish prose late in the century, many abandoned the earlier traditional forms and ventured into "modernity," establishing characteristics that have typified much Swedish literature well into the 21st century: a willingness to experiment, emphasis on the practical, and a clear and simple modern language technically called "Modern New Swedish," or *Yngre Nysvenska*. Olof von Dalin produced the first "really readable Swedish prose," thus becoming the first Swedish author to be read and appreciated by the general public. His earthy humor informally introduced many of the Enlightenment's most productive ideas to Sweden (Gustafson 117), in particular brilliantly and satirically stressing the necessity of parliamentary control over the monarchy. Dalin brought literature "out of the study into the tavern and the parlor" (Gustafson 117), a legacy that today's Swedish crime writers almost universally embrace.

During the 18th and 19th centuries, Sweden and Norway, with their marginal agricultural economies, were "terribly poor," and eventually emigration to America seemed the only answer for Swedes to avoid famine and political unrest. During the 1880s, more than one percent of Sweden's population annually left for the United States, totaling nearly one million emigrants between 1850 and 1910 (Einhorn and Logue 9) who settled primarily in the American Midwest, portrayed in Vilhelm Moberg's novel *Utvandrarna* (*The Emigrants*), made into a popular film. Sweden's economy remained agricultural while most of Europe was industrializing, though because its peasantry had never been feudal serfs, the farming segment of Swedish society began to participate effectively in politics, eventually forming the Agrarian Party (now called the Centre Party). The

Social Democratic Party, founded in 1889, grew out of a strong Swedish labor movement concurrently with Sweden's relatively late industrialization from 1879 to 1914.

The two great Swedish scientists of the first half of the 18th century also made significant contribution to the development of Swedish literature. Emanuel Swedenborg, 1688–1772, had spent his early career in the natural sciences until a psychological crisis turned him toward religious mysticism. In April 1745, Swedenborg envisioned God speaking directly to him; he abandoned science and devoted himself to visionary revelations which his followers later turned into the Church of the New Jerusalem. The example of Swedenborg and the excesses of his devotees, some of them pietists and some theosophists, probably has inspired the religious cultist figures in contemporary Swedish crime fiction.

The popular Swedish botanist Carl von Linné, 1707–1778, known outside Sweden as Linnaeus, employed a prose style that still appeals to modern readers—direct and concrete, economical, and related to Swedish peasant speech, not the more ornate French-inspired Swedish prose of his times. His style often alternated "sly humor" with "scientific exactitude," qualities observable in contemporary detective characters like Håkan Nesser's Inspector Van Veeteren, one of many fictional Swedish disillusioned middle-aged modern policemen.

Poetry, Sweden's preeminent literary expression in the early 19th century, was the province of its New Romantics, talented young Swedish poets strongly affected by German Romanticism, who hurled themselves and their works into "the Golden Age of Swedish poetry," breaking decisively with past poetic conventions. Their work was characterized by a preoccupation with the past and the Swedish countryside, strange and mysterious folk tales and ballads influenced by Swedenborg's mysticism, weaving a modern heroic national ideal out of the Old Norse saga world (Gustafson 156), elements which some contemporary Swedish crime writers still incorporate into their novels. At the same time, as Jane Mattisson Ekstam has recently pointed out, an early Swedish novel displayed "a coherent story centering on a crime and its solution" (quoted from Kerstin Bergman and Sara Karrhölm in Ekstam 3): *Sjömans-Hustrun: Sann handelse* ("The Mariner's Wife: A True Story"), 1837, by *"F.L.R."* (not otherwise identified), was based on a true apparent suicide. Carl Jonas Love Almqvist's *Skällnora qvarn* ("The Mill of Skällnora") deals realistically with family intrigues (Ekstam 3).

The Swedish New Romantic fervor burned itself out by 1838, however, when a political crisis that had been simmering for some time reached a flashpoint. Frustrated with absolutist policies, liberals were demanding governmental reform. The leading instrument of their propaganda was the Stockholm newspaper *Aftonbladet*, founded in 1830 and fervently opposing the King's Council which had been supporting the monarch's absolutist convictions. *Aftonbladet* and its editor-publisher Lars Johan Hierta became the focus of the new middle-class politics, articulating its cause in a language easily accessible by its readers, "concrete, direct, factual, and, when necessary, sharp, invidious, even brutal" (Gustafson 200), laying down a stylistic pattern for the many journalists who in the late 20th and early 21st centuries turned to writing powerful crime novels.

In 1840–1841, after governmental attempts to censor Hierta and *Aftonbladet* failed, the Swedish parliament enacted some long delayed reforms. The newspaper also not only promoted a concise and realistic prose style but backed short fictional forms which for the first time were being seriously produced in Sweden. *Aftonbladet's* popularity and influence marked a premonitory symptom of the general realistic ferment bubbling up in Sweden, which finally erupted in 1879 with August Strindberg's powerful novel *Röda rummet* (*The Red Room*), a novel satirizing contemporary Swedish life. In the early 1870s, Strindberg, a highly controversial figure in his own time who made Sweden's most significant contribution to world literature, frequented the "Red

Room" at Bern's Restaurant in Stockholm, where young artists and intellectuals from diverse backgrounds and persuasions gathered to share "devastating nihilistic commentary" on everyone and everything around them (Gustafson 256). Furious at having his early works ignored or forgotten, Strindberg intended to affront the Swedish public with *The Red Room*, but instead they loved its "fresh and youthful satiric aplomb" (Gustafson 258) and made him famous overnight. For the first time in Swedish literature, an author lashed out at nearly everything he found abominable in Stockholm life: "political chicanery and religious humbug, bureaucratic irresponsibility and social injustice, philosophical pretentiousness and educational reaction, journalistic opportunism and theatrical intrigues" (Gustafson 158–9), targets not only of the wrath of Strindberg and the naturalistic mainstream 20th-century authors who followed him, but also the targets of many of Sweden's contemporary crime authors today.

Swedes who stayed home in the late nineteenth century were developing a taste for crime fiction, probably in response to the nation's misery: "people like to read about what's bothering them … the rise of the detective novel parallels that of the industrial revolution: heightened anonymity, social insecurity, and urban poverty are like fertilizer for criminality" (Murphy x). Looking back over the development of Swedish crime fiction, K. Arne Blom in 1973 observed that in the last quarter of the 19th century, the classic English, French, and American crime fiction writers, notably Arthur Conan Doyle, Wilkie Collins, Emile Gaboriau, and Edgar Allan Poe, were appearing in readily available Swedish translation soon after their original publication, as well as the (at least partly fictional) *Memoirs* of François Vidocq, a former criminal who became chief of the French Sûrété, and the Gothic horror stories of the German E.T.A. Hoffman, creating a large Swedish readership for the detective genre in the early 20th century (Nestigen and Arvas 4). Blom felt that in particular the controversial Swedish author Carl Jonas Love Almqvist, 1793–1866, "the father of Swedish detective fiction," had been influenced strongly by Hoffman. Almqvist has often been called a transitional figure who described himself as torn between his mother's "poetic soul" and his father's pragmatic "accountant's soul" (quoted from Steene in Warme 208). In 1834 Almqvist published *Drottningens juvelsmycke* ("The Queen's Diamond Ornament"), a crime novel/ political thriller because its main character, a ballerina, is drawn into a plot to kill the king. In 1838 Almqvist published the short story responsible for his crime-writing reputation, "*Skällnora kvarn*" ("The Mill of Skällnora"), a fast-paced tale about a poisoning which introduces psychology into the crime story. In 1851 Almqvist himself was suspected of a homicidal poisoning and fled from Sweden to the United States, remaining there for some years before returning to Europe and dying in Germany (Blom 16).

Almqvist was among late nineteenth century authors whose realistic fiction influenced the development of modern crime fiction. Almost all of Almqvist's stories attacked both marriage and the clergy, pitting him against moralistic authors like novelist Frederika Bremer, 1801–1865, who studied women's issues in the United States in the 1850s. Her fiction, though strongly defending traditional "duty over desire" in marriage, provided "the first significant impetus" to building the Swedish tradition of combining realistic fiction with a strong sense of social conscience (Gustafson 161), especially regarding women's problems, a tradition maintained and bolstered today by Swedish *femikrim* authors and their literary sisters in the other Nordic countries. Bremer's travel books and novels foreshadowed the modern realistic literature of social protest that emerged in Sweden in the 1880s, largely inspired by European authors and paralleling the industrialization which Sweden was then experiencing. Most prominent among those European influences on Swedish literature at this time were Georg Brandes in Denmark and Henrik Ibsen in Norway. Brandes' *Main Currents in Nineteenth-Century European Literature* insisted that the Scandinavian literatures had to abandon their backward-looking conservatism and open "the windows of [their] thought toward the Continent" (quoted in Gustafson 247). Ibsen was pioneering a new realistic drama which powerfully exposed social problems and demanded reforms. His *A Doll House* set off such explosions about "the woman problem" that almost all the male Swedish literati in the 1880s were pitying supposedly helpless females, while women writers were pursuing "women's rights" to the exclusion of other troubling social issues. Because of police censorship, Strindberg's naturalistic tragedy *Miss Julie*, 1888, daring for its time, was first privately produced at the radical Brandes-inspired Student Society in Copenhagen in 1889. It closed after one performance and could not be performed in Sweden until 1906.

In 1888, as a reflection of growing Swedish interest in the United States, John Moore set a crime novel in New York, *Sju dagar och sju nätter—ur en detektivens anteckningar* ("Seven Days and Nights—from the Detective's Notebook"), followed in 1889 by *Diamantstolden—ur en detektivens anteckningar* ("Diamond Theft—from a Detective's Notebook 2") (Ekstam 3). Swedish literary historians, however, generally consider Fredrik Lindholm's *Stockholms-detektiven* ("The Stockholm Detective"), 1893, Sweden's first full-length crime novel. It introduced the first detective in Swedish crime fiction, Fridolf Hammar. Although most modern readers find *Stockholms-detektiven* "almost unreadable," at the time Lindholm was writing, Norwegians were enjoying Stein Riverton's crime tales and Danes could boast Palle Rosenkrantz's "still highly enjoyable" detective fiction (Blom 17). At the turn of the century, most Swedish literary critics considered crime fiction "vulgar trash," so Lindholm, like other writers who after him experimented with the form, wrote under a pseudonym, in Lindholm's case the aristocratic-sounding "Prins Pierre" (Holmberg 5).

The one distinguished exception to Sweden's generally low-quality crime writing of the period, primarily attributable to attempts by Swedish crime authors to copy foreign detective stories, was mainstream novelist Hjalmar Söderberg's *Doktor Glas* (*Doctor Glas*), 1905, an acclaimed psychological *fin de siècle* crime novel about a young doctor who out of passion and a thirst for vengeance decides to commit a murder, "a careful and empathetic portrayal of a good man convincing himself to do evil" (Holmberg 6). In her introduction to Paul Britten Austin's 2002 translation of *Doktor Glas*, Margaret Atwood observed that this novel "occurs on the cusp of the nineteenth and the twentieth centuries, but it opens doors the novel has been opening ever since."

Around 1910 when the elderly Strindberg was vehemently criticizing the conservative values he felt were holding back Sweden's literary development, Sweden was witnessing substantial cultural and political changes. During the nineteenth century, the "economic backwardness" prevailing in Norway and Sweden "was comparable to that of many Third World countries today" (Einhorn and Logue 9), but by 1910, the influence of labor unions was evidenced through large-scale labor strikes and demands for social reforms, the stirrings of social democracy which would change Sweden into a modern parliamentary democracy. Gradual industrialization also caused population shifts from the countryside into cities, especially Stockholm (Koblik, 303–313). Early 20th century Swedish mainstream authors concerned themselves with what they considered more elevated themes and material than crime stories provided, especially emphasizing working class life and the women's suffrage movement, to which Selma Lagerlöf, Sweden's most famous woman author, was dramatically dedicated. Lagerlöf was the first woman to be elected to the Swedish Academy and the first woman to receive the Nobel Prize for Literature. Her 1909 Nobel citation read in part, "in appreciation of the lofty idealism, vivid imagination and spiritual perception that characterize her writings." Her most famous work, *The Gösta Berlings Saga*, celebrates traditional Swedish village life, Sweden's landscape, and its history. In June of 1911, Lagerlöf gave the keynote speech at the International Suffrage Congress in Stockholm and spoke again at the victory celebration of the Swedish suffrage movement after Sweden granted women the right to vote in May 1919. At the beginning of World War II, she sent her Nobel Prize medal and the gold medal she had received from the Swedish Academy to the government of Finland to help them fight the Soviet Union, but the Finnish government raised the funds elsewhere and returned her medals in gratitude for her gesture.

Given the current quality and popularity of Nordic *noir*, the history of crime fiction in Sweden has received surprisingly little critical attention in the English-speaking world. John-Henri Holmberg's short fiction anthology *A Darker Side of Sweden*, provides the first overview of Swedish crime fiction in English as a valuable historical Introduction. Barry Forshaw's Introduction to *Death in a Cold Climate*, 2012, deals primarily with contemporary Scandinavian crime writing, writers, and their translators; and *Scandinavian Crime Fiction*, 2011, edited by Andrew Nestingen and Paula Arvas, offers a brief introductory essay, "Contemporary Crime Fiction" dealing with the crime fiction of all five Nordic countries. Two issues of *The Mystery Fancier* contain short but valuable articles: Iwan Hedman's "The History and Activities of Mystery Fans in Sweden (and Scandinavia)," in *The Mystery Fancier*, volume 3, number 4 (July-August 1979); and K. Arne Blom's "The Crime Story in Sweden," in *The Mystery Fancier*, volume 7, number 5 (September-October 1983). Hedman listed several books about the crime genre in Sweden, including his own *Deckare och Thrillers på svenska* ("Detective Novels and Thrillers in Sweden"), 1864–1973, but these are unavailable in English. *Studier om Mord från Trenter till Mankell* ("Studies on Murder from Trenter to Mankell") by Bo Lundin (Stockholm: Utbildningsförlaget Brevskolan, 1998) is also available only in Swedish. Though not exhaustive in content, these materials testify to the remarkable diversity of crime fiction produced in Sweden as a legacy of the nation's extensive contacts with European and American culture.

Crime and detective stories have existed in Sweden since at least the beginning of the 20th century, but most are "entirely unknown to non–Swedish readers" (Holmberg 4), influenced by translated versions of crime novels from abroad. K. Arne Blom believed that among outside influences, Arthur Conan Doyle's Sherlock Holmes was most responsible for liberating Swedish crime writers from their low late 19th century reputation as "trash." As well as Lindholm's pioneering *Stockholms-detektiven*, neglected for decades until republished in 1993, two collections of Sherlock Holmes pastiches by "Sture Stig" (pen name of a Swedish vicar named Frans Oscar Wägman) appeared in 1908 and 1910, parodies that gently mock the Holmes canon with the Great Detective's "eternal creaking" on the violin and unwholesome characters constantly infiltrating Baker Street (Blom 17). Another Swedish author directly inspired by Sherlock Holmes was Samuel August Duse, 1873–1933, the first important writer to write only crime fiction, over a dozen novels. His first, *Stilettkappen* ("The Stiletto Cane"), featured amateur detective Leo Carring, a lawyer who became a Swedish version of the Great Detective in thirteen novels accurately reflecting life in early 20th century Sweden.

One of Stig's readers, Gunnar Serner, beset by financial collapse due to a gambling fiasco in Monte Carlo and wanted by the Stockholm police for forgery, turned to writing humorous and exciting detective fiction as "Frank Heller." From 1914 until his death in 1947, Heller produced 43 crime novels, "still readable and interesting," including eight published in the United States in the 1920s, as well as short story anthologies and travel books which made him "Sweden's internationally most successful entertainment writer of his time" (Holmberg 5–6). French crime writers influenced Serner's work more than Sherlock Holmes did, especially one of Serner's first two books, *Herr Collins affärer i London* (translated in 1924 as *The London Adventures of Mr. Collins*), with an elegant Raffles-type detective-cum-gentleman thief Philip Collins, also known as "Professor Pelotard," inspired by Maurice Leblanc's thief-detective Arsène Lupin. Heller also wrote whodunit-like novels about Joseph Zimmertur of Amsterdam, a Jewish psychoanalyst. Blom believed that Heller was the first Swedish crime writer translated into English, appearing in both

Britain and the United States, describing Heller as "a virtuoso" among his more pedestrian fellow Swedish crime authors, "a crane among sparrows" (Blom 18).

One of those sparrows was Julius Regis (Julius Petersson), 1889–1925, a newspaper proof-reader influenced by American John T. Coryell's rousing dime novels, radio programs, and films starring Nick Carter, a hybrid of superhero and genius detective. The hero of Regis's fifteen novels is Maurice Wallion, a crime reporter for Stockholm's biggest daily newspaper. His implausible exploits combine elements of the thriller and the whodunit as he battles and invariably defeats international crooks. Blom found only one author writing prior to the 1930s about typical Swedes and their lives: Fanny Alving, 1874–1955, who produced only one crime novel, *Josefssons på Drot-tninggatan* ("The Josefssons at Queen's Street"), 1918, featuring the first Swedish woman detective, Julian Eriksson. So little genuinely Swedish crime fiction was produced up to the 1930s except for Frank Heller's many novels, that "the crime story was perceived as a non–Swedish literary field" (Holmberg 6)

Sweden's domestic crime tradition began in the 1930s, when the world was suffering from the Great Depression and in many affected countries readers were seeking vicarious relief in classic detective fiction, where a chivalric detective figure could help Right triumph over Evil, as in the novels of Agatha Christie and Dorothy L. Sayers, and a little later Ellery Queen, John Dickson Carr, and Georges Simenon, all translated to Swedish and very popular there (Holmberg 9). Probably also as escapist reading, the Swedish crime fiction pulp magazines, which the Swedish intelligentsia called "dirt literature" (Holmberg 9), began to be published in the 1930s, usually in a small-sheet stapled format with one long story instead of various short pieces (Holmberg 7).

In the novel genre, according to Blom, three 1930s newspapermen and one woman fore-shadowed altogether new approaches to Swedish crime writing: Sture Appelberg; Yngve Hedvall; and Torsten Sandberg. Appelberg produced three-dimensional characters and convincing scenery, and Sandberg's four novels exhibit genuinely Swedish people and settings. Blom ranked Hedvall's *Tragedin i Villa Siola* ("The Tragedy in Villa Siola"), 1934, a clever variation on Christie's *The Murder of Roger Ackroyd*, 1926, as "one of the best dozen crime stories written in Sweden" (Blom 19). Blom also named Kjerstin Foransson-Ljungman, 1901–1971, the first "queen" of Swedish crime fiction, for her novel *27 sekundmeter snö* ("Storm and Snow"), 1939, showcasing the murder of one of ten people stranded in the Swedish Alps. Blom considered this novel "a pearl" among Swedish crime novels (Blom 19).

Sweden's neutrality during World War II has been debated ever since immediately after hostilities ceased in 1945, Britain's Prime Minister Winston Churchill accused Sweden of profiting from both sides during the conflict. Today many Swedish authors agree with Camilla Läckberg, whose work demonstrates that "The memory of the Second World War remains very vivid for the Swedes" (quoted in Cogdill). During the war, the Swedish government tried to maintain its appearance of neutrality while "it bent to the demands of the prevailing side in the struggle … this approach generated criticism at home … problems with the warring powers, ill feelings among its neighbors, and frequent criticism in the postwar period" (Nordstrom 313–19). "The Swedes needed German coal and the Germans needed Swedish iron ore…. Such equations … defined policy. Survival mattered above all…. Morality was secondary" (Cohen). One of the harshest critics of Sweden's actions in World War II actions, Swedish journalist and crime fiction author Arne Dahl, has observed, "Sweden was not neutral, Sweden was weak" (quoted in Cohen), citing documents declassified in the 1990s and Moscow archival material accessed after the breakup of the USSR. Current research into this material authenticates awakening Swedish interest in re-examining moral issues raised by the war, such as the opinion stated by French philosopher André Glucksmann: "Before the fall of the Berlin Wall, […] We glossed over the corner of neutrality in most people, the neutrality that is also the instinct to save one's skin" (quoted in Cohen). Both in Sweden and abroad, suspicion has arisen that Swedes "profited from the Nazi conquest and genocide and that … neutrality was simply a cloak for connivance" (Cohen). Early in the war the Nazis blockaded Sweden, cutting off its ties to the rest of the world, causing the Swedish government to conclude that resistance was hopeless, and for most of the war Sweden made vital concessions to the Nazis. Sweden allowed the *Wehrmacht* to use Swedish railways to convey troops and weaponry from Norway to Finland; the Swedes sold iron ore to Germany throughout the war; and the Swedish government instructed its central bank to ignore the rumors that the gold Sweden received in payment had been looted by the Nazis from their victims (Cohen). A document discovered in a Swedish finance ministry filing cabinet in 2009 has also revealed that Sweden made secret loans totaling approximately 3.5 million UK pounds in today's currency values to Nazi Germany in 1941, loans that were never entered into Swedish official records (Hall).

For the Allied cause, however, Sweden supplied military intelligence, notably through Swedish mathematics professor Arne Beurling's breaking of the Nazi *Geheimschreiber* cypher code for telegraph traffic between Germany and Norway in the early summer of 1940, enabling the transfer of information to the Allies via the Polish resistance. Sweden helped train Danish and Norwegian resistance fighters and allowed Allied use of Swedish airfields in 1944–1945. Sweden supplied steel and important machined parts to both Britain and Germany throughout the conflict; 58 percent of Germany's ball bearing needs and 31 percent of Britain's came from Sweden, with the Swedes allowing the British to deliver the bearings through the German blockade (Golson 1). Many Swedes secretly supported the Norwegian resistance, and in 1943 they helped rescue almost all of Denmark's 8000 Jews from being deported to German concentration camps. Sweden also supplied Finland in the Winter War and the Continuation War with volunteers and materiel. The Swedes also provided refuge to thousands of Jews from the Scandinavian countries and the Baltic States. The Jewish Virtual Library states that the efforts of Swedish diplomat Raoul Wallenberg and his group saved up to 100,000 Hungarian Jews (http://www.jewishvirtuallibrary. org/jsource/biography/wallenberg).

The serious moral issues arising from Sweden's role in World War II currently are supplying significant thematic material to today's Swedish crime fiction authors, as Camilla Läckberg has observed: "The war really marked us…. We need to constantly remind ourselves of the horrible consequence of human ignorance" (quoted in Cogdill). During the Second World War and its aftermath, though, Sweden's crime writers seemed to ignore the possibility of such "horrible consequences." Traditional murder mysteries dominated Swedish crime fiction's first "Golden Age," novels based largely on British and American models, like the works of Agatha Christie, Dorothy L. Sayers, and John Dickson Carr. The most prominent practitioners were Stieg Trenter, Maria Lang (Dagmar Lange), Vic Suneson, and H.K. Rönblom, who all employed Swedish character types, settings, food and music, in their classic puzzler-whodunits (Nestingen and Arvas 4) (also see entries for Stein Trenter, Lang, and Suneson below). Holmberg calls Stein Trenter, 1914–1967, "the author who made crime fiction accepted by Swedish critics" (Holmberg 7), no mean achievement, considering that those critics had been denigrating crime fiction for years. Stig Johansson, a young journalist who took his pen name "Trenter" from E.C. Bentley's classic English detective Philip Trent, created two highly convincing sleuths: amateur detective Harry Friberg, a genial and somewhat naive photographer, and CID Superintendent Vesper Johnson as Friberg's complement. The pair combines Stockholm's ambiance with satisfying psychological insight (Blom has observed that Ulla Trenter has continued to write about Harry Friberg after her husband's death, but "One wishes she would not") (Blom 21). Vic Suneson (Sune Lundquist), 1918–1975, the first Swedish writer to portray only professional policemen as detectives, wrote traditional puzzles as police procedurals, with ordinary honest cops diligently doing their jobs without amateur assistance.

While praising Trenter and Suneson, Blom dismissed Maria Lang's work, unusually erotic for her time, as "women's romances" with detective supplements (Holmberg 7), "an uninteresting hybrid of Agatha Christie and Mary Roberts Rinehart" (Blom 21). The killer in Lang's first novel was a lesbian striking out at a woman who scorned her passionate advances (Holmberg 8). Blom praised H.K. Rönblom's (1901–1965) depictions of Swedish country life, settings where teacher Paul Kennet, a calm Maigretesque figure, solves crimes intellectually by analyzing the reciprocal actions of his characters. Recently Holmberg has observed that Rönblom was "in a sense the first recognizably modern Swedish crime writer," because he saw and accurately portrayed the "seething corruption, religious intolerance, sexism, racism, narrow-mindedness, and self righteousness" beneath the outwardly serene surface of small-town Swedish life (Holmberg 8). All of these themes are still readily discernible in today's Swedish crime fiction.

According to literary historian G.J. Demko, the mystery genre in Sweden achieved enormous popularity from the early 1940s onward, exhibiting two special traits: a strong sense of place bolstered by the long tradition of realism in Swedish literature, and the use of the mystery to reflect "the political, social, and economic policies and processes in a welfare oriented state" (Demko). After the end of World War II, Swedish crime writing also began to pursue two very different directions. One followed the whodunit tradition, for a time sold only by the established publishing houses. The other emerged from the American hard-boiled school led by Raymond Chandler and Dashiell Hammett, whose novels had already invaded Sweden via translation. When in the 1950s "shocker" writers like Mickey Spillane began publishing, their novels and those of a few Swedish imitators were sold, like the pulps, only in paperback versions at newsstands and tobacco shops and never cited in reviews, scorned by literary critics since they had not been published by the "established and respectable book trade" (Holmberg 9). Major Swedish publishers did not sell pocket-sized books in bookstores until 1956, and until then hard-boiled crime fiction fans were mostly blue-collar workers and teens. Crime novels issued by the conventional publishers remained traditional puzzlers, primarily those still being produced by Jan Ekström, Gösta Unefaldt, and Kristina Appelqvist (Holmberg 10). Helena Poloni (pseudonym of Ingegerd Stadener), 1903–1968, also wrote conventional whodunits set in the small Swedish towns she loved.

Kerstin Lillemor Ekman, a distinguished Swedish author born in 1933, made her reputation as a writer of detective novels and became the third female member of the Swedish Academy. Originally a documentary film maker, she published her first crime novel *30 meter mord* ("Thirty Meter Murder") in 1959, following it with six more crime novels. She then moved on to mainstream works, including a history of Sweden written from a troll's point of view (Lawson 13). She returned to crime fiction with the award-winning *Händelser vid vatten* (*Blackwater*), 1993, recounting a murder that tears a northern Swedish community apart. *Under the Snow*, not published in the U.S. until 1998 but originally published in Sweden as *De tre små mästerna* in 1961, is set in Lapland, where the native Sami see Swedes as such violent aliens that a Sami conspiracy of silence surrounds a mysterious killing. Ekman's *Dödsklockan* ("Bell of Death"), 1963, is still considered one of Sweden's best crime novels. Ekman observed the centrality of nature in all her works, claiming through one of her characters in *Blackwater*, "Nothing exists that is not nature" (quoted in Lawson 14).

Stieg Trenter, Maria Lang, Vic Suneson, and H.K. Rönblom all continued writing traditional crime novels into the 1980s and beyond, while authors like the pseudonymous "Bo Balderson" produced politically conservative crime novels satirizing Swedish governmental figures. Ulf Durling continues to write perceptive psychological thrillers.

In the 1960s, however, political activism was increasing in Sweden and documentary novels were becoming popular and the imported American police procedural form was giving rise in Sweden to an altogether new kind of crime literature, "Nordic *noir*," that has dominated Scandinavian crime fiction from that time to the present day. This type of contemporary Scandinavian crime fiction "often articulate[s] social criticism, critiquing national institutions and gender politics in particular" all conveyed in a "gloomy, pensive and pessimistic" tone. Many contemporary literary critics feel that this constellation of factors makes contemporary Nordic crime literature unique (Nestingen and Arvas 2).

As a crime novel subgenre, the police procedural presents the actual methods of police work, stressing realism of action, though unrealistic characters may still abound in the narrative (Murphy 404). In the early 1960s, Swedish Marxists Maj Sjöwall and Per Wahlöö chose the procedural form for their ground-breaking ten-volume Martin Beck series, *The Story of a Crime*. Like many other Nordic crime writers who followed them, Sjöwall and Wahlöö were inspired by the crime novels of American Ed McBain, "the foremost of the police proceduralists" (Murphy 404). Multiple characters carry on highly detailed and often violent police work in McBain's 87th Precinct novels, investigating diverse criminal activities and settings within the precinct's geographical boundaries. This allows the author to employ intense realism, though these aspects are often accompanied by "information-poor text ... meaningless perfunctory remarks ... and facts one does not need to know" (Murphy 310). McBain also wrote in the third person, which tends to eliminate the problem of suspension of disbelief. The popularity of police procedurals in the United States and elsewhere was probably reinforced by American police television shows like *Dragnet*. At its best in both formats, "the procedural can say something about 'the way we live now'" (Murphy 404).

In 1960s Sweden, Maj Sjöwall and Per Wahlöö used the police procedural for the first time to expose the failings of the Swedish political-cultural phenomenon of *Folkhemmet* ("The People's Home"), the Swedish term for the welfare state, which the Social Democrat party leading Sweden from 1932 to 1976 had been developing since the 1930s through "piecemeal reforms" directed at a common goal: a decent standard of living for the poorest in society and an increased degree of equality among socioeconomic groups, without detracting from the market economy. The "security net" of transfer payments in all the Nordic countries now includes substantial unemployment payments, support for the disabled, and illness insurance; old age pensions, family allowances, rent subsidies, temporary assistance of various kinds, medical and dental care, home help for the sick, disabled, and elderly; and child and after school care (Einhorn and Logue 7). After the worldwide financial crisis of the 1970s, the dominance of the Social Democrats who developed the Nordic welfare states became increasingly shaky (Einhorn and Logue 9), Critics of the welfare state emerged on the right, left, and center of Swedish politics, and Swedish writers, especially crime fiction authors, made their popular literary subgenre a weapon to attack the failings of the welfare state as sources of societal malaise and decay.

Michael Tapper, a contemporary film scholar and critic at Sweden's Lund University, indicates that the Swedish term *Folkhemmet* denoted a welfare state "defined by social equality and moral decency," a concept attacked from its 1930s inception by Communists who felt it was "liberalism in disguise." In the 1960s, the Swedish Marxist-Leninist movement denounced the welfare state as "a social-democratic betrayal of socialism, concealing the inherent fascism of a capitalist society with a democratic façade with a social agenda (Tapper, in Nestingen and Arvas 22). In that spirit, Sjöwall and Wahlöö adapted the American police procedural as their tool for "'an analysis of a bourgeois welfare state in which we try to relate crime to its political and ideological doctrines" (Sjöwall and Wahlöö, "*Kriminalromanen...*" 18), hoping to make their detective fiction "a force for political analysis, education, and change" (Holmberg 11). They saw crime as "the symptom of a brutal society marked by social conflict escalating into fascism to be followed by a communist revolution" (Tapper in Nestingen and Arvas 22).

Sjöwall and Wahlöö "document[ed] the evolution of Swedish society via the behavior of the police," showing a reversal of police roles from "an orderly, right-minded organization" to one in which their society's malaise is reflected in the growing corruption and brutality of the police (Demko), so that the Martin Beck novels gradually grow darker, longer, and more densely plotted as the ten-novel series progresses (Blom 23). Beginning with *Rosanna*, 1965 (tr. 1967), and the two novels which followed, the authors showed the initial attempts by their major figure Martin Beck of Sweden's national homicide squad to understand the actions of the criminals he pursues, in relation to the Swedish welfare society in which they all live. In the next four novels of the series, Beck and his team "operate in the 87th Precinct manner," with the villains seen through the eyes of different police figures (Blom 23). The authors use the bodily ailments of each major character, like Beck's frequent nausea and stomach pains, as metaphors for the Swedish society they think is "sick and decaying" (Tapper, in Nestingen and Arvas 23). Each of the members of Beck's team suffers from at least one physical ailment, contributing to the dark gloomy mood that pervades the entire series. Finally in the last three novels of the series, the authors "found their own style," highly realistic, written from "the underdog perspective," critical of the police and the questionable connection between the legal and the political establishments, and observant of the socioeconomic factors leading to crime (Holmberg 13), gradually "unmasking idyllic Sweden as a fully fledged fascist tyranny" (Tapper, in Nestingen and Arvas 22), though Blom, writing in 1983, believed Sjöwall and Wahlöö exaggerated Swedish society (Blom 23). The Martin Beck novels were not successful in Sweden at first because critics found them "too gritty, too depressing, too dark, too brutal" (Holmberg 10), but they eventually became bestsellers and remain in print today. The publication of *Rosanna* in English translation, 1967, opening the authors' perspective to a worldwide audience, is used here as the beginning of the "Nordic *noir*" tradition. Their success coincided with the coming of age of young readers familiar with hard-boiled paperbacks that the Swedish literary establishment had called "dirt literature," a combination that suddenly "transformed Swedish crime fiction as a whole" and created a "whole new readership for original Swedish crime fiction" (Holmberg 11, 13).

Not only criticism of the centrally planned Swedish welfare state as such but its negative impact on gender politics and its relation to neo–Nazism also appeared in the Beck novels, especially through the character of Beck's police colleague Gunvald Larsson, shown in the early novels as an "outright sexist" and a brutal Gestapo-type policeman. The Sjöwall-Wahlöö characterization of Larsson has become radically transformed in the most recent film adaptations of the Beck novels, reflecting political and cultural shifts in public attitudes. Michael Tapper indicates that during the 2001–2002 Beck film series, Larsson's character begins to develop in a different direction by addressing issues that have become more important in Swedish culture than the original 1960s Marxist-Leninist positions now seem to be. The first film, *Hämndens pris* (*Revenge*), 2001, refers to the murders of two police officers by three neo–Nazis in the peaceful village of Malexander, south of Stockholm, with Larsson revealing a "proverbial heart of gold" beneath his "hard emotional armour" (Tapper, in Nestingen and Arvas 23). In the 2006–2007 film series, Larsson, not Beck, is the main character, rescuing battered women from their abusers, a dramatic change from his original misogynistic characterization in the Martin Beck novels, a shift that Tapper attributes to a reflection of the Swedish conservative party's "compassionate" makeover that triumphed in the 2006 elections (Tapper in Nestingen and Arvas, 31–32) and seems to be growing today.

John-Henri Holmberg has remarked that as soon as the last of the ten Martin Beck novels appeared, "a tide" of politically radical Swedish crime novels began to run, with authors Uno Palmström, K. Arne Blom, Olof Svedelid, and Leif G.W. Persson producing notable novels analyzing problems bedeviling the Swedish *Folkhemmet* (Holmberg 11–12), a trend that is continuing and flourishing. Persson, a distinguished criminologist and today one of Sweden's most influential crime authors, profoundly criticizes Swedish police inefficiency as well as corruption and ineptitude in the legal system and the political and bureaucratic establishment. Other crime fiction authors are addressing the "unholy alliance" of Swedish politicians and financiers; the inhumanity of big business and big government; the profiteering of medical, chemical, and energy corporations with the government's tacit cooperation; and more recently racist and anti-immigration activity (Holmberg 12–13), national and international organized crime, and the victimization of women and children. The financial crises of 2008–2010 occasioned an international interdisciplinary conference held in Reykjavik in June 2011, which addressed the programs by which welfare states might work their way out of the economic doldrums, envisioning two main paths: a social investment strategy to stimulate the economy, and plans to cut national budgets and retrench their welfare state policies. Sweden seems to have experimented with the latter, but doing so has created new and serious difficulties.

Such problems, many Swedish crime writers feel, are symptoms of the Swedish welfare state's increasing debilitation, an opinion shared by outside observers. A 2010 report by the *Wall Street Journal* concluded that "Sweden's dramatic increase in the size of government contributed to its sluggish growth" (Bergh and Henrekson). *The Economist* pointed out on February 2, 2013, that a series of financial crises ended the Nordic region's "magical thinking" about welfare: "Denmark went into free fall in the early 1980s. Finland imploded in the early 1990s when the collapse of communism killed its most reliable market," and Norway and Sweden faced substantial financial crises, forcing Sweden into stern measures to begin balancing the national budget, reducing the national debt from 84 percent of the GDP in 1996 to 49 percent in 2011 and reforming the pension system to match lifetime incomes. Sweden also now allows private companies to compete against government entities for public contracts and permits parents to use educational vouchers to send children to schools of their choice. Nonetheless, Sweden still suffers from governmental bloat and inefficiency: one observer feels that like the other Nordic countries, Sweden is run by professional politicians "who have no idea that mandating a year's maternity leave means one thing for a government department and another for a start-up" ("More for Less").

The Achilles heel of the welfare state is its unending demand for more and more tax revenue. The principle sounds simple: if everyone wants to receive benefits, everyone must pay taxes to fund the benefits, but in practice while more and more people receive more and more benefits, fewer and fewer people are working to pay the bill. After World War II, Sweden could provide for its welfare state entitlements more easily than other European countries could for several important reasons: Sweden did not face a painful postwar recovery, it did not have to support a large defense budget, it had no immigration problems at that time, and its small population shared a common culture. By the 1970s, Sweden had almost completely realized its vision of a "people's home," but to provide such benefits as 480 days of parental leave, the Swedish tax burden became one of the heaviest in the world, imposing over 80 percent marginal tax rates on Sweden's wealthy (Dickson and Scrutton), causing authors of fiction to begin to point out deficiencies in the welfare model. Mainstream author Stig Claesson described the fate of those that the welfare state "has forgotten," like the lonely old bedridden woman in his novel *På palmblad och rosor* ("On Palm Leaves and Roses"), 1975. "In the traditional agrarian culture of the past, a support network of neighbors and kin would have cared for her; today she is alone" (Wright in Warme 439–440). With almost a fifth of the Swedish population unemployed or on long-term sick leave or disability,

100,000 immigrants arriving per year even before the 2015 flood of Syrian refugees, and a crumbling industrial base (MacDougall), the Swedish tax burden became unfeasible. The conservative government under Prime Minister Fredrik Reinfeld who took office in 2006 tried to solve Sweden's financial woes by reducing taxes and cutting benefits so that the health care system was downsized radically, cutting one fifth of its total medical staff in less than five years. By 2014, this policy had reduced the Swedish public debt to around 40 percent, half of Germany's (Dickson and Scrutton), but in the process the Swedish welfare state has deteriorated. Swedish education is slipping, with fifteen-year-olds showing the greatest decline in proficiency results of any European nation; abuses in health care of the elderly are rampant; and in 2013 serious week-long riots by immigrants occurred in Stockholm with over fifty cars set on fire and schools trashed and the violence spreading to other Swedish cities. The country may face "years of rising tax burdens ... to keep its public finances in order," because according to Torbjorn Hallo, an economist at the Swedish Trade Union Confederation, Sweden will need to raise $11.02 billion, about 2 percent of its GDP, just to keep the current welfare system going (quoted in Dickson and Scrutton).

Whether Sweden can do this seems debatable. Swedish corporations, once the backbone of the Swedish economy, are leaving the country; SAAB Automobile has ceased car production completely, and Volvo's mass transit bus division is moving production to Poland, which means the layoff of a substantial number of Swedish workers. Sweden's unemployment rate in March 2013 was 8.4 percent compared to the EU's 10.9 percent as a whole, but the Swedish 15- to 24-year-old age group had a 27 percent unemployment rate, due in part to a high minimum wage. Manufacturers also cut jobs in 2009, when Sweden's economy took a major downturn, and those jobs probably will not return, since they were typically associated with lower-skilled immigrant workers and had already been declining for decades (Matthews). Commenting on the 2013 riots, economist Andreas Jobsson of Nordea believes that Sweden has "clearly not been successful" in integrating the approximately 100,000 immigrants who prior to 2015 arrived in Sweden each year (Traynor), into its workforce (quoted in Matthews).

Though Sweden has had some of the most generous immigration, asylum, and welfare policies in the world and some members of the Swedish parliament claim immigration maintains Sweden's welfare system, the nation's current immigration problems loom as large as the financial woes brought on by the welfare state's demand for higher and higher taxes. Although Sweden has experienced both the benefits and the problems associated with "incomers" throughout its history, the growing numbers and ethnic origins of immigrants have caused controversy about ethnicity, welfare benefits, jobs, voting, and the increasing incidence of violent crimes, especially against women and children, all issues increasingly being explored in the country's crime fiction.

Following World War II, Norway and Sweden recruited immigrant labor, especially from Finland, to create the tax base necessary for expanding the public sector of their welfare states. In 1967, however, Sweden limited immigration because its labor market had become saturated. Since then, immigrants, mostly asylum seekers, have been coming to Sweden as refugees primarily from the Middle East and Latin America. Since then, too, racism has steadily mounted in the Nordic countries and across Europe. A 1993 advertising poster for the Swedish daily tabloid *Espressen* declared, "Drive them out! That's what the Swedish people think about immigrants and refugees." (*Espressen*'s editor in chief was forced to resign over this placard). The *Statens offentliga utredningar 1996* (Swedish Government Official Report for 1996) flatly stated, "The conditions [prevailing for migrants and refugees] in central social arenas—such as employment, housing, and political power—is such that not even a pessimistic scenario drawn up [as recently as] the mid 1980s could have come close to describing the current situation" (quoted in Pred 3).

Even before the 2015 Syrian refugee crisis, Sweden's immigration problems dramatically worsened. In 2012, Sweden granted about 44,000 asylum applications, a 50 percent increase over the previous year (McLaughlin). Sweden does not keep records based on ethnicity, but national backgrounds are recorded, and in 2011, 2.5 million inhabitants of Sweden had full or partial foreign backgrounds—roughly 15 percent of Sweden's total population of 9.5 million. The social and psychological problems involved with ethnicity, one's roots, and the importance of language to human identity were articulated in the 2003 debut novel *Et öga rött* ("One Eye Red") by Jonas Hassen Khemiri, the Swedish-born son of Muslim immigrant parents, recounting the early life of a teenager with Moroccan parents growing up in Stockholm, using an immigrant patois ("Modern Swedish Literature").

The rise of crime rates in Sweden is closely related to the increase in the nation's immigrant population. The Swedish National Council for Crime Prevention has reported that between 1997 and 2001, 25 percent of reported crimes were committed by people born outside of Sweden; and the Council found that immigrants, mostly North Africans and Western Asians, were four times more likely than ethnic Swedes to be investigated for lethal violence and robbery, three times more likely to be investigated for violent assault, and five times more likely to be investigated for sex crimes. Currently Sweden has one of the highest rape rates in the world (http://www.thelocal.se/20051214/2683).

Again before 2015, the issue of Muslim immigration to Sweden became particularly controversial. *Statistics Sweden* reports that in 2013, 128,946 persons had come to Sweden from Iraq; 68,554 from the former Yugoslavia; 67,211 from Iran; 65,804 from Bosnia/Herzegovina; 54,221 from Somalia; and 41,748 from Syria, all countries having majority Muslim populations. According to *The Local*, one Swedish city, Södertalje, called "Little Baghdad," had taken in more Iraqi immigrants than the United States and Canada combined, about 50 percent of its population. The Pew Research Center in 2010 predicted that by 2030 the Muslim population in Sweden would reach 993,000, 9.9 percent of Sweden's total population (Pew Research Center, "Nation: Europe"), a figure confirmed by *The Economist*, which reported in 2013 that the Muslim minority in Sweden is expected to grow from 5 to 10 percent by 2030 ("Waxing Crescent").

By 2010 resentment toward the Muslim minority in Sweden was escalating. "Signs of friction and trouble [were] … not hard to find beneath the veneer of Scandinavian order, decency and prosperity" (Traynor). The Muslim immigrants do not integrate easily into Swedish society, and their general high unemployment rate exacerbates their dissatisfaction with Swedish life. Malmö in southern Sweden, the nation's third largest city, houses the Muslim "ghetto" of Rosengard, about 20,000 immigrants, roughly half of whom are jobless. Unofficial *sharia* police there check women's clothing and have established *sharia* courts, troubling local Swedes. Some Muslim immigrants are also practicing anti–Semitism. In March 2010, Fredrik Sieradzk, a member of Malmö's Jewish community, told the Austrian Internet publication *Die Presse* that Jews were being harassed and physically attacked by Mideasterners there, in 2009 causing about thirty Jewish families to leave Sweden for Israel (*Die Presse*). *The Times of Israel* has reported that on January 24, 2015, Petter Ljunggren, a Swedish reporter who walked around Malmø wearing a Jewish skullcap and a Star of David to test attitudes toward Jews "was hit and cursed at by passersby before he fled for fear of serious violence." Ljunggren's secretly recorded experience, aired on Sveriges Television as part of a 58-minute documentary, was a repeat of a similar experiment in 2013 where the reporter had received only strange looks and giggles. "Jewish-hatred in Malmö, "where first and second-generation Middle East immigrants currently comprise a third of the city's population," is evident, since the city's population also includes several hundred Jews. Fred Kahn, leader of Malmö's Jewish community, flatly attributes most anti–Semitic incidents there to "Muslims or Arabs" (JTA).

Physical manifestations of interracial tensions between native Swedes and Muslim immigrants have become increasingly serious. In 2004 Malmö's mosque, the largest in Europe, was set on fire and an imam was shot on the premises. The number of Muslims in Malmö who are extremists is claimed to be small, but their recruitment methods are aggressive (Kellogg). Serious clashes between immigrants and the Malmö police occurred in 2008 and 2010, and by 2013, "some natives [of Malmö] say they have had it with this bottomless funding pit" (Kellogg). A Swedish Malmö resident claims, "These people [Muslim immigrants] don't share our values," and another insists, "Enough is enough.... They know they can come here, get money and not need to work" (quoted in Traynor). Malmö MP Kent Ekeroth, a member of the far right Sweden Democrat party, appeals to discontented Malmö natives: "What kind of immigrants do we take in? It's people from Somalia who have done nothing but herd sheep their whole life and we expect them to benefit our society? It's ridiculous" (quoted in Kellogg).

The riots that began on May 19, 2013, in immigrant districts of Stockholm, where police fatally shot a knife-wielding 69-year-old man originally from Portugal who had been threatened by a gang, shook Sweden. Rioting spread from Stockholm to other towns, principally Örebro and Linköping, with total damages estimated at over 1.6 million UK pounds (McLaughlin). Liberals tend to blame the violence on government cutbacks in welfare spending which seem to result in rising income inequality and unemployment, factors that substantially impact immigrants, but not only in Malmö, conservatives worrying about the cost of welfare benefits to the state are turning to the far right Sweden Democrat party. In 2010, Sweden Democrat members for the first time entered the Swedish parliament. The Sweden Democrats advocate cutting back 90 percent in immigration and redirecting the money now being used on housing and caring for refugees to aid for their home countries (Kellogg). Opinion polls indicate that the Sweden Democrats' rising popularity is partly due to the indignation many native Swedes feel at being called "racists" despite having accepted so many refugees. Michael Lundh, a former Swedish police officer who for years worked with Stieg Larsson's antiracism organization, feels "Ordinary Swedes are sitting in front of their TVs and are getting very angry at pictures of immigrants throwing stones," adding that he "didn't realize so many young people hate the police.... The police are frightened, and young people are frightened.... When frightened people meet, you only get trouble" (quoted in A. Higgins).

Sweden's most traumatic modern national tragedy underscores Higgins' point. The assassination of Swedish Prime Minister Olof Palme in 1986, initially blamed on a Kurdish immigrant group, is central to both Leif G.W. Persson's crime trilogy which began with *Between Summer's Longing and Winter's End* and Henning Mankell's play *Politik*, which premiered in 2010. A still-unknown assailant shot Palme in downtown Stockholm as he walked home with his wife at 11 p.m. from a movie. The investigation which followed, led by Hans Holmér of Sweden's National Police, became a "narrow-minded pursuit of wrong suspects, of corruption, of the petty desire for fame, of witness coaching and leading, and of improper interview methods," in two years severely damaging Swedish faith in "the authorities." As each suspect or group of suspects like alleged Kurdish terrorists was let go, the Swedish public, many of whom had resented Palme's leftist policies, became increasingly distrustful of Swedish police and other government bodies ("Olaf Palme and Swedish Crime Fiction"). One of the most reliable sources of information about the Palme assassination is Jan Bondeson's *The Killing of Olof Palme* (Ithaca, NY: Cornell University Press, 2005).

Even though the accused Kurdish organization, the PKK, has been officially cleared, since the Palme assassination trouble over immigration in Sweden has escalated. Many children of immigrants do not seem to care that newcomers are vastly better off than they were in their home countries. "Here, most of them are stuck at the bottom of the social heap. Some of them are angry, and take it out on society. They stone their own firefighters and burn their own schools," and Swedish authorities do not treat these perpetrators harshly (Dickson and Scrutton). The immigration problem has not generally been discussed publicly, because any Swedish public figure mentioning it will probably be called a xenophobic racist. Starting with Henning Mankell, however, whose first crime novel appeared in 1991, Swedish crime novelists are showing how seriously the immigration problem contributes to the rise of crime in Sweden. Anthropologist Jonathan Friedman, whose wife is Swedish, lived in Sweden for years, and he blames the Swedish refusal to face the gravity of this situation on "a politics of submission by Swedish elites who hold on to absurd ideologies of immigration as enrichment" (quoted in Wente). Journalist Margaret Wente agrees: "As Swedes redistribute more and more of their wealth to people whose habits are culturally alien, and who are permanently dependent on the state, the immigration consensus is bound to crack" (Wente). Responding to Dutch reporter Maartje Somers, Nazanin Johansson, daughter of a Persian mother and a Swedish father, said she succeeded in Swedish society because she knew she had to try harder than others did, also observing that young immigrant children "want to have a job, but only if it's a cool one. They don't want to start at the bottom. It's easy to forget that it is also the[ir] mentality that is the cause" of their dissatisfaction (Somers).

Other cracks in the *Folkhemmet* ideal are spreading. Lars Trägårdh, a professor of history at Ersta Sköndal University College, relates the *Folkhemmet* ideal to Swedish national identity, resulting in the "Swedish Model" of society where individuals contract with the state. He believes the state provides social security to allow individuals to function free of the "particular 'inequalities and dependences' of civil society institutions such as 'the family ... the churches, the charity organisations'" (quoted in McLaughlin). Trägårdh believes that the Swedish Model causes difficulties for immigrants since their different racial, ethnic or religious "modes of belonging" conflict with traditional Swedish values and thus bar them from opportunities. He also believes that though the Swedish Model can liberate women, it also can arouse "resentment, confusion and anger" especially for "young men who expect to be heads of traditional families," apparently making them feel excluded from membership in the Swedish nation (quoted in McLaughlin). Therefore one major theme of contemporary Swedish *noir* crime fiction, "the failure of the welfare state to do right by its people," contributes to the other, "the failure of men to do right by women" (MacDougall).

One area of gender issues that Sweden is trying hard to adjust is parental leave. Swedish law now permits men to take up to 390 days of paternity leave, and in 2010, 85 percent of Swedish men did take at least some parental leave, though Swedish mothers still take almost four times as much time off with children as men do (Bennhold). The intended goal seems to encourage "a new kind of manly," or as a woman police officer put it, she finds her husband most attractive "when he is in the forest with his rifle over his shoulder and the baby on his back" (quoted in Bennhold). Some observers are concerned that a gender identity crisis may be looming with men and women both working and both staying at home with the children: "Manhood is being squeezed," one gender consultant claims. The Swedish taxpayer is feeling the pinch, too, with Swedish taxes at 47 percent of the GDP (the U.S. rate is 27 percent of the GDP). As a whole, family benefits cost 3.3 percent of the Swedish GDP, the highest in the world. In addition, companies forced to pay high payroll taxes and deal with the unpredictability of employees' parental leave requests, are also uneasy, primarily because the 120-day annual allowance for tending sick children is "impossible to plan and ... suspected of being widely abused" (Bennhold).

Swedish crime fiction authors in the early 1990s took differing approaches to these basic sociological themes. Håkan Nesser and Åke Edwardson broke with the social realist crime-fiction tradition Sjöwall and Wahlöö had initiated, producing high-quality psychological procedurals,

Nesser's Inspector Van Veeteren series takes place in a fictional composite north European country, and Edwardson's Erik Winter novels are set in Gothenburg, Sweden. Both authors have helped to make the Swedish crime novel accepted as both "potentially serious fiction" and a potentially significant segment of contemporary Swedish fiction (Holmberg 15). Women authors, notably Inger Frimansson, Liza Marklund, Helene Tursten, and Aino Trosell, also entered the field of crime fiction writing in 1997–1998, bringing "a much needed renewal" to Swedish crime writing through varying forms of the subgenre, creating psychological thrillers and female anti-heroes, as well as convincing women police characters. Other authors, both men and women, have continued to produce classic police procedural novels involving realistic cop shops all over Sweden (Holmberg 15–6).

Two of Sweden's major crime authors, however, pursued the Sjöwall-Wahlöö Marxist tradition and have been followed themselves by a considerable number of journalists-turned-crime-novelists, graduates of the Stockholm College of Journalism, popularly known as the "College of Communism" (Holmberg 14). In the 1990s, almost four decades after the Sjöwall-Wahlöö Martin Beck novels, Henning Mankell, a Maoist (Holmberg 14), opened the door to the international market for Swedish crime fiction when he launched his sociologically-themed Inspector Kurt Wallander novels, critiquing the "long and painful decay of the Swedish welfare state" (Slavoj Žižek, quoted in MacDougall) and addressing misogyny in The Fifth Woman (MacDougall). Mankell dramatically contrasted the serene surface of the Scandinavian countryside around Ystad with the sordid details of violent homicides, so that "The lingonberry jam on the detective's afternoon waffles looks a darker shade of red" (MacDougall). Mankell also pillories the welfare system that affects all of Swedish life through his leading character: depressed and exhausted, lonely and perpetually unable to understand a woman well enough to establish any satisfactory relationship, Kurt Wallander seems to embody the question, "If you can't trust the welfare system, what can you trust?" (MacDougall). Several of Mankell's books have been filmed three times, twice by Swedish production companies and once in an English-language series starring Kenneth Branagh. Because of his commitment to assisting African causes, Mankell himself claims metaphorically to have one foot in snow and the other in sand; his highly praised Comédia infantil, 1995, features an abandoned boy on the streets of Maputo.

After another two decades, Stieg Larsson, a Trotskyite (Holmberg 14), demolished what he felt was the myth of the Swedish welfare state in his Millennium Trilogy, its three novels appearing in English translation in 2008, 2009, and 2010 respectively. They made Larsson posthumously "the second-bestselling writer on the planet" (Armstrong) with profits of approximately $30 million by 2014 (MacDougall). Profoundly affected by witnessing a brutal gang rape in his youth, Larsson forcefully denounced the victimization of girls and women, notably exemplified by the vicious rape of dragon-tattooed Lisbeth Salander by her state-appointed guardian. In The Girl with the Dragon Tattoo, titled in Swedish "Men Who Hate Women," Salander and reporter Mikael Blomkvist investigate an old missing-person case, in the process proving that "even, or perhaps especially, in the egalitarian welfare state, money permits wealthy male woman-haters to enact their impulses in the most abhorrent and violent ways" (MacDougall). The novel's villains are neo–Nazis, members of a Swedish cultural phenomenon which Stieg Larsson had spent most of his professional life exposing and battling.

The rise of neo–Nazism, one of the most "abhorrent and violent" cultural phenomena in Sweden since World War II, provides a theme that Swedish crime authors are increasingly addressing, both male writers like Larsson and women authors like Helene Tursten in Inspector Huss and Camilla Läckberg in The Hidden Child, who exercise a strongly feminist perspective. In 2014 Läckberg claimed that extreme right-wing parties are growing not only in Sweden but all over Europe.

Swedish neo–Nazism has deep roots that extend back to anti–Semitic organizations in the 1880s. The Swedish Nazi movement itself was founded in the 1920s, and by 1934, Swedish Nazi parties had won over a hundred municipal elections. In 1938, before the Nazi *Kristallnacht*, part of the Swedish Nazi movement broke with Hitler, creating the Swedish Socialist Coalition (SSS); its splinter group, the Swedish Opposition (SO), after the war called the New Swedish Movement (NSR), helped to smuggle and conceal Nazi collaborators, Nazi soldiers, and Swedish Waffen-SS volunteers from the Allies, and in May 1945, Swedish Nazis were among the first groups to deny that the Holocaust occurred. The Swedish Nazi Party was officially dissolved in 1950, but it revived to form the Nordic Reich Party in 1956.

Feeding on racial tensions, the most visible far-right Swedish political group today, the Sweden Democrats (SD) (Swedish: *Sverigedemokraterna*), is becoming a major force in Swedish politics, with a message that reverberates among Swedes unhappy with the results of their government's immigration policies: "We don't feel at home any more, and it's their [immigrants'] fault" (quoted in Crouch). Founded in 1988 as a right-wing populist and anti-immigration party, the Sweden Democrats describe themselves as socially conservative, with a nationalist foundation (see the Sweden Democrat website, http://wwwsvd.se). The Sweden Democrats won many municipal elections in 2006, especially in the southern part of the country; in Malmö they received over 13 percent of the votes cast, and in Helsingborg, nearly 15 percent, and since then their geographic influence has progressed toward Stockholm. As is happening with other anti-immigration European parties, in 2010 the Sweden Democrats received enough votes (5.7 percent) to win 20 seats in the Swedish parliament, and in the 2014 general election, they polled 12.9 percent and now hold 14 percent of the parliamentary seats (49). Sweden's other mainstream political parties, however, consider the Sweden Democrats too radical to work with (Bevanger).

Initially the Sweden Democrat Party was primarily composed of motorcycle gang members and white power "skinheads," but today the party insists it has abandoned its racist past (Crouch). Jimmie Åkesson, its leader, claims he has forced extremists out of the party, which has become a "slick electoral machine" that has doubled its vote every four years and forced the 2014 cabinet crisis that called for a snap election. Sweden's Social Democrat Prime Minister Stefan Löfven, who describes the Sweden Democrats as "neo-fascists" (quoted in Crouch), refused in December 2014 to call the snap election because all major parties except the Sweden Democrats and the Left Party had agreed on future budget procedures. The "December Agreement" allows an absolute minority coalition to govern without needing to form a parliamentary majority, and thus it was considered "undemocratic" by 34 percent of Swedes polled, as well as by senior politicians from several other political parties. The *BBC News* concludes that Swedish politics took a "left turn" while the "far right soars" (Bevanger).

The prevailing far-right success strategy, as practiced not only in Sweden but across Europe, has changed "from boots to suits," a long-range "make-over of everything but their xenophobic agendas" (Bjurwald). In the 1990s, the skinheads of the Sweden Democrats' youth branch relied on violence to convey their anti-immigration message: they began burning refugee centers, and a serial killer, the so-called "Laser Man," hunted immigrants with a laser-sighted rifle; bank robbers executed two policemen with their own weapons; and an investigative reporter was targeted with a car bomb. Stieg Larsson, author of the now world-famous Millennium Trilogy, founded the anti-neo–Nazi magazine *Expo* and became such a target of their violence that in fear for the safety of his life partner Eva Gabrielsson, they never married and kept their home apartment address a close secret.

In 2006, only seven years after the Swedish press widely denounced violence and murders committed by neo–Nazis, the well-funded Sweden Democrats won "seats in almost half of Sweden's local governing bodies, paving the way for their entry into parliament in 2010 ... the neo–Nazis may have hung up their boots, but Swedes with racist views keep flocking to the party" (Bjurwald). The key seems to be that to enhance their electability neo–Nazi sympathizers have transformed their image from the original brutal "skinhead" look to an appearance of normalcy, and in 2006 they even changed their party emblem from a fascist flame to an innocuous anemone (Bjurwald). Sweden's wealthiest man, Ingvar Kamprad, founder of Ikea, revealed in 1994 that he had had youthful Nazi sympathies though he could not recall if he had actually joined the Nordic Youth, the Swedish equivalent of the Hitler Youth (Armstrong). Today's Sweden Democrats, some of whose members descended from the former Nationalist Socialist Front founded on the 110th birthday of Adolf Hitler, in 2011 offered Swedish children free admission to a summer camp in southern Sweden. The camp leaders didn't necessarily "see someone as Swedish just because they have a Swedish citizenship," and their announced Sunday camp debate topic was "Who is a Swede and who isn't?" (*The Local*, Sweden). The Sweden Democrats' normalcy campaign seems to enjoy rising popularity because a sizeable number of Swedish voters evidently recognize and agree with the SD's racism and their contempt for the media. In December 2013 the Sweden Democrat party was so convincing to voters that they placed about 10 percent ahead in polls that also accurately predicted they would become Sweden's third largest political party in the 2014 general election (Bjurwold).

Neo-Nazis in Sweden have not abandoned violence. Since the 1990s, neo–Nazi violence has escalated into burglaries and anti-immigration demonstrations, and even the promotion of a white supremacist rock band, accompanying their dramatic political activities. In 2010, a small avowed neo–Nazi group, the Party of Swedes, won one seat in a Swedish municipality, the first openly Nazi party to gain public office since World War II. Over the past quarter century, another neo–Nazi group, the Swedish White Supremacists, has committed 23 known murders. According to Stieg Larsson's Expo Foundation, the neo–Nazi movement reduced its active groups from 40 in 2008 to 18 in 2013, but their documented actions rose 24 percent between 2012 and 2013, to 1824 incidents (Kendall). A December 18, 2013 UPI report indicates these incidents included attacking an antiracist demonstration in suburban Stockholm with stones, bottles, and fireworks, some of the worst rioting in Sweden in years, and two teenaged skinheads committed a racist killing in Stockholm (Mezzofiore). On Women's Day, March 8, 2014, 30 knife-wielding Party of Sweden neo–Nazis slashed and beat six feminist demonstrators—four men and two women—in Malmö. In February 2013, in an action with sinister international implications, Fredrik Hagberg, a representative of the Swedish neo–Nazi group called *Nordisk Ungdom* ("Nordic Youth"), offered comradely greetings to Ukraine from Sweden from a rostrum in Kiev's City Hall to "sweaty, bruised, and exhausted Ukrainian insurrectionists." Hagberg is also trying to provoke fellow neo–Nazis into coming to Kiev "to help shape a new, fascist-friendly Ukraine," an eerie echo of the 1930s Spanish Civil War, where sympathetic European extremists headed for a Spanish trouble spot to support their ideological brethren in a serious political conflict between Fascists and Communists (Moynihan).

Besides the literary denunciation of neo–Nazism demonstrated in his Millennium Trilogy, Stieg Larsson treated his other major theme, the victimization of women, by presenting figures of corrupt women-hating men lurking in nearly every facet of Swedish society: newspaper editors, biker gangsters, policemen, physicians, lawyers, criminal overlords, all supported or sponsored by the welfare state. In the Millennium Trilogy, where he used statistics on crimes against women as section epigraphs, Larsson claimed, "The state itself is the greatest villain" in the victimization of women (MacDougall).

In the 1250s, Swedish King Birgir Jarl passed a law prohibiting rape and/or abduction of women, but Sweden has nonetheless had a long hidden history of violation of women's rights which began to come to light in the 1970s, when Sweden abolished the joint taxation of spouses, replaced maternity leave with parental leave, and enacted a new abortion law. In 1975, the state's policy of forced institutionalization and sterilization of women considered "low class or mentally slow" was finally abolished, but not until 1997 did the government admit that 60,000 of such women had been forcibly sterilized (Armstrong). The Act on Violence against Women came into effect in 1998, with a maximum six-year prison sentence for gross violation of a woman's integrity, assessed cumulatively, but several facets of the victimization of women are still appearing in Swedish society, in contrast to the nation's reputation as one of the most progressive nations in terms of women's rights. In Sweden women are considered free to approach men "to start a conversation or initiate a romantic encounter" because as part of achieving gender equality, "The whole society now expects women to be as forward with their sexual will as men" (Herrell). This approach does not seem to be preventing men's violence, domestic and otherwise, against women.

At the time *The Girl with the Dragon Tattoo* appeared in Sweden, public attention was beginning to focus on the issue of Swedish domestic violence, a "significant blot" on Sweden's long-maintained and strengthened support for women's rights and gender equality. The country's "well-guarded sense of privacy and its leadership on women's rights" muted consideration of the issue for many years, until Amnesty International issued a stinging 2005 report accusing Sweden of "spotty prosecutions, vague statistics, old-fashioned judges and unresponsive governments" (Alvarez). In 2010, Sweden had the highest incidence of reported rape in Europe, twice the rate of the U.S. and the UK, but one of the lowest rape-conviction rates in the developed world (Harrell). Sweden's high rate of rape cases is largely attributed to Muslim immigrants. The Swedish National Council for Crime Prevention, an agency of the Ministry of Justice, reported in 2012 that the Muslim 5 percent of the Swedish population committed nearly 77.6 percent of all rape crimes between 1995 and 2001. The same agency reported that the number of reported rapes of children had nearly doubled between 1995 and 2004 ("The Muslim Issue").

As for domestic violence, a 2012 study on men's violence against women by Lucas Gottzén of the Department of Social and Welfare Studies of Linköping University concludes that men who committed violent acts upon women, including domestic violence, don't consider what they do as "violence," and neither do their friends. These men instead blame their violent behavior more often than not on substances like serotonin in the brain, ADHD, drugs, and lack of control of aggression (Fjellro). Such abuse, highlighted in many Swedish crime novels by both men and women authors, is proving hard to root out; in 2012, the Icelandic *IceNews* reported that a Swedish judge was reprimanded for a second time for ruling that a man striking his wife was "quite understandable" when she refused to tell him where she had been. The judge had added that in countries "with a more patriarchal perspective," the husband's action "would have been considered both called for and appropriate" (quoted in Erlingur). Swedish women crime authors who strongly oppose those views are now widely read both at home and abroad. Beginning with the crime fiction of Liza Marklund, Swedish *femikrim* has grown dramatically; between 1991 and 1997, only two crime novels by women appeared in Sweden, but in 2012 more than twenty Swedish women were producing crime fiction ("Modern Swedish Literature").

Instances of child abuse are increasing in Sweden as well. In November 2007, U.S. State Department statistics recorded 6192 Swedish child abuse cases that year, reporting also that homophobic crime was on the rise and that "tens of thousands of rapes and domestic violence incidents" were occurring in Sweden (quoted in Armstrong). Children are being exploited through the Internet, too; in 2006, Global Monitoring reported that Sweden allows child pornography to be viewed (though not downloaded) and fails to care adequately for children involved in sex trafficking (Armstrong).

To expose and oppose such abuses, Stieg Larsson created one of the most unusual heroines in Swedish crime literature, bisexual computer hacker Lisbeth Salander, a borderline sociopath who as a teenager was declared *non compos mentis*, allowing the state to take over her affairs. This continued even after she became an adult, since Sweden's guardianship laws permit the state to control even the mentally competent. Salander's diagnosis stemmed from her earlier attempt to kill her brutal misogynistic father after he almost beat her mother to death (MacDougall). Before his death, Larsson acknowledged he based Salander on one of the most beloved characters in Swedish children's literature, Astrid Lindgren's Pippi Longstocking: "My point of departure," Larsson claimed, "was what Pippi Longstocking would be like as an adult. Would she be called a sociopath because she looked upon society in a different way and has no social competence?" (quoted in Ryan).

Born in 1907, Lindgren wrote over a hundred children's books that sold over 130 million copies worldwide, and according to Eva-Marie Metcalf in the *Dictionary of Literary Biography*, Swedes call Lindgren their premier export product. Lindgren first conceived Pippi, her most famous character, in 1941 while telling stories to amuse her seven-year-old daughter Karin while the child was recovering from pneumonia. Karin herself named the heroine of her mother's tales "Pippi Longstocking." In 1944, Astrid Lindgren sprained an ankle and while recuperating, she decided to jot down the "Pippi" stories for Karin's tenth birthday. Later she entered *Pippi Longstocking* in a prize contest for girls' books and won, and ever since Pippi Longstocking has been arousing children's delight and often parents' consternation. Lindgren's original Pippi Longstocking book is one of the twelve most translated books in the world.

Pippi Longstocking and Lisbeth Salander are both eccentrics. Pippi's mother is "an angel in heaven," while Salander's mother is a brain-damaged martyr to her woman-hating wife-beating husband and the society that allowed him to abuse her. Pippi, supernaturally strong enough to hoist her horse and fiercely independent, has carroty red-orange braids sticking out from her head and favors peculiar clothing; skinny little Salander overcomes a huge male biker villain with a kick "transformed into kinetic energy in his crotch with a pressure of about 1,700 pounds per square inch" (quoted in Ryan). She wears offbeat haircuts and clothing, tattoos, and various piercings, looking as though she "had just emerged from a weeklong orgy with a gang of hard rockers" (Ryan). Except for her horse and her monkey, Pippi lives alone, funded by gold coins hidden in her kitchen, and she refuses to go to school; Salander lives on Billy's Pan Pizza in an apartment called V. Kulla, named for Villa Villekulla, Pippi's house, working with computers when and as she pleases. Both unconventional characters are contemptuous of authority, capable of supporting themselves, free of responsibilities except for those they want to assume, and extremely loyal to their friends. Though when the Pippi books first appeared, some parents were shocked at Pippi's behavior, children living under adult rules found Pippi immensely attractive. The secret of Pippi's incredible success, *New York Times Book Review* critic Margalit Fox declared on November 8, 1962, was her books' function as "a children's safety valve against the pressure of author and daily life." Similarly, Larsson's Lisbeth Salander with her frail child-like appearance and her taser-wielding tactics can be seen as a "safety valve" against the oppression of women and children colluded to by the Swedish welfare state. The impressive sales of both the three Pippi Longstocking books and the Millennium Trilogy and their filmic incarnations testify to their nerve-touching appeal.

Lindgren herself repeatedly declared she didn't write books for children, she wrote books for the child she was herself. In another expression of "the child within" who likes to color outside the lines, she created *Mästerdetektiven Blomkvist*, published in 1952 in English as *Bill Bergson, Master Detective*. By naming the male journalist protagonist of his Millennium Trilogy "Mikael Blomkvist," whom his fellow journalists mockingly nickname "Kalle Blomkvist," the Swedish name of Lindgren's boy detective, Larsson ironically drew upon the Swedish public's knowledge of Lindgren's bumptious young would-be sleuth who often finds himself outdone and occasionally even rescued by his young female neighbor Eva-Lotta Lisander, "a female warrior" he madly loves. Through his references to Lindgren's popular child characters, Larsson drives his message home: only women "warriors," armed with fierce independence and convention-shattering motivations, can successfully destroy the women-hating men their welfare society allows and even encourages to torment them.

The often monstrous male villains Larsson and other Swedish crime authors depict usually represent invidious elements of contemporary Swedish society, members of criminal gangs and crime organizations whose connections to corrupt government officialdom these authors often expose. Since Sweden began to collect crime statistics in 1950, the number of reported assaults and sex crimes in the country has risen dramatically even though Sweden has one of the lowest homicide rates in Europe.

Organized crime is also flourishing in Sweden. *The Local* (Sweden), an English-language digital news publication launched in 2004 and nominated in 2009 as Swedish Digital Newspaper of the Year, reported in 2007 that the Hell's Angels and the Bandidos are well established in Sweden and increasing their membership. *The Local* also reported that "a new breed of organized crime has sunk its claws into Sweden": extortion doubled between 1997 and 2007, with competing criminal gangs using "deadly violence," kidnapping, fraud, and blackmail for profit. According to Thomas Servin, chief of the Skåne police intelligence unit, "The criminal networks have multiplied and in a sense the authorities can't protect the public" (quoted in "Swedish Mafia…"). In a 2012 *Dagens Nyheter* interview, the director general of Sweden's national police and the commissioner of the national crime investigation unit list specific gang activities as "drug trafficking, armed robberies and systematic fraud; well-planned, large-scale theft; extortion and reckless human trafficking … the criminals … avoid paying taxes and live as parasites on the welfare system." Both police officials insist that "The continuous growth in organized crime must come to an end."

More than fifty organized gangs currently operate in Sweden. The Hell's Angels, established in 1990 as the first international biker gang in Sweden, and the Bandidos have been operating there and continuously expanding their activities. Some of the most dangerous Swedish gangs today were founded by and are now comprised of non–Swedish individuals. The *Brodraskapet*, a prison gang active in organized crime, is made up mostly of native Swedes, but at least nine other criminal organizations with memberships comprised of non–Swedish minorities exist in Sweden. The Original Gangsters, the *Södertäljenätverketn*, and *Asir* are Assyrian/Syriacs from Turkey; the Black Cobra gang, imported from Denmark, consists in Sweden mostly of Iraqis and Iranians; *Naserligan* and *K-falangen* are comprised mostly of Albanians; and the Chosen Ones and the Werewolf Legion, mostly Somalis, are involved with drug trafficking.

Up to the early 1970s, Sweden had had relatively permissive illegal drug policies, but the dramatic increase in amphetamine, hashish, LSD and opiate usage during the 1960s brought about a more restrictive policy on the control of narcotics, reinforced by the mobilization of a public anti-drug attitude. The Narcotics Drugs Penalty Code, 1968, increased maximum penalties for the sale and smuggling of illegal drugs, and in 1970 Sweden banned hemp cultivation. Under a "no drug tolerance" policy, Swedish drug laws were modified in the 1980s and 1990s, increasing maximum sentences and introducing treatment options such as contract treatment instead of imprisonment. The 1982 Misuser Act enabled municipalities to enforce mandatory treatment for individuals with alcohol and/or serious drug problems. The Swedish Parliament's overall objective is to make Sweden a drug-free society through restrictive but not repressive legislation and education. A 2007 study indicated drug use had declined among elementary and high school students, and Sweden currently boasts levels of drug abuse and addiction considerably below the rest of Europe. Swedish alcohol abuse is increasing, however; between the late 1990s and 2007, hospitalization for alcohol-related illnesses increased 32 percent for men and 119 percent for women ("Sweden Drug Abuse").

Another serious gang activity on the rise in Sweden, as in the rest of Scandinavia, is human trafficking. Sweden is attempting to promote awareness and victim assistance programs in trafficking source countries and to uphold its 2007 policies regarding sex trafficking and labor trafficking, which both carry penalties of six to ten years in prison, though forced labor trafficking does not seem to have been addressed as stringently in Sweden as sex trafficking. Sweden also has led Europe in battling the sex trade. Its 1999 Sex Purchase Act, an anti-prostitution law, a facet of its gender-equality campaign, assumes legally that any woman selling sex has been forced to do so by circumstances or coercion, and any man buying sexual acts faces heavy fines, public exposure and possibly a maximum of 4 years' jail time. "You're a loser if you buy sex in Sweden" (Shubert), and since the law was enacted, street prostitution has been cut in half. Simon Haggstrom, a Stockholm police officer working in the anti-prostitution unit, noted that since the law was introduced, the number of prostitutes in Sweden decreased from 2500 in 1998 to about 1000 in 2013. In 2014, Swedish Prime Minister Fredrik Reinfeldt declared that the penalties for the purchase of sexual services linked to sex-trafficking should be increased, and that prison should be a minimum sentence for those convicted of exploiting minors for sexual purposes. Reinfeldt stated that while almost 5000 sex-trafficking crimes had been reported in Sweden since 1999, no one had been imprisoned, only fined (Nordström). In evaluating the Sex Purchase legislation, the Swedish government has recently concluded that while the number of foreign women in street prostitution has increased in all the Nordic countries, including Sweden, the number of such women working in Sweden is much lower than in the other Nordic countries, claiming that the Act "counteracts" the establishment of organized crime-supported human trafficking in Sweden. Opponents, however, insist that the study was based on insufficient data (Nordström). Ruth Nordström, President of the Scandinavian Human Rights Lawyers, believes that more resources need to be directed at protecting young people from exploitation. She insists, "The European Union has the highest number of sex slaves in the world" with young Eastern European girls who dreamed of a better life caught in the nightmare of "brothels, gang rapes and sexual abuse" (Nordström).

Since the 1960s Swedish crime fiction authors have realistically portrayed a sizeable range of diverse criminal activities: the immigration issue, neo–Nazism, increased organized crime and gang activity, the financial issues connected with maintaining a high-paying welfare system, governmental and industrial collusion and corruption, and the victimization of women and children, most framed in the police procedural subgenre. In the last few years, however, Swedish crime fiction "has suddenly been enriched by innovative authors experimenting with many different forms and themes, placing the subgenre of crime fiction at both an enormously exciting and a chaotic stage of its ongoing development" (Holmberg 18–19). Approximately 200 Swedes are writing and publishing crime fiction today, offering a rich panorama of responses to their country and their times. British crime fiction critic Barry Forshaw notes that one reason for the success of Scandinavian crime fiction is "its unsentimental readiness to confront the less admirable aspects of human behaviour" (Forshaw 37). In Sweden, so often idealistically portrayed abroad as a near-perfect society, many Swedish crime authors are providing what Camilla Läckberg calls "a useful corrective" (quoted in Forshaw 40) to that sunny outward appearance, a tribute to Swedish literature's long-cherished tradition of realism and diversity.

Award-Winning Swedish Crime Fiction

Titles in quotation marks are English versions of the original Swedish titles. Titles of published English translations appear in italics.

The Swedish Crime Writers' Academy (*Svenska Deckarakademin*) was organized in 1971 to promote Swedish crime fiction. At first the Academy gave awards only to books translated into Swedish, with a few awards to the Best First Novel in Swedish. Since 1982, the Academy yearly has presented two awards: the Best Swedish Crime Novel; and the "Golden Crowbar" (originally called the Martin Beck Award for the central detective in the novels by Maj Sjöwall and Per Wahlöö), awarded to writers from all countries other than Sweden. On an irregular basis, the Academy also awards other prizes such as an award for the best debut crime novel. The Martin Beck Award ("The Golden Crowbar") is not awarded to Swedish authors.

The Best Swedish Crime Novel Awards

1982: Leif G.W. Persson, for *Samhällsbärarna* (*The Pillars of Society*)
1983: Ulf Durling, for *Lugnet efter stormen* ("The Calm After the Storm")
1984: Steffan Westerlund, for *Svärtornas år* ("Svartornas Years")
1985: Jean Bolinder, for *Fär älskarns och mördarns skull* ("For the Sake of the Lover and the Murderer")
1986: Steffan Westerlund, for *Större än sanningen* ("Larger Than the Truth")
1987: Olov Svedelid, *Barnarov* ("Barnarov")
1988: Jan Guillou, for *I nationens intresse* ("In the Nation's Interest")
1989: Kjell-Olof Bornemark, for *Skyldig utan skuld* ("Guilty Without Guilt")
1990: Jean Bolinder, for *Dödisgropen* ("Dödisgropen")
1991: Henning Mankell, for *Mördare utan ansikte* (*Faceless Killers*)
1992: Gösta Unefäldt, for *Polisen och mordet i stadshuset* ("Police and Murder in Parliament")
1993: Kerstin Ekman, for *Händelser vid vatten* (*Blackwater*)
1994: Håkan Nesser, for *Borkmanns punkt* (*Borkman's Point*)
1995: Henning Mankell, for *Villospår* (*Sidetracked*)
1996: Håkan Nesser, for *Kvinna med födelsemärke* (*Woman with Birthmark*)
1997: Åke Edwardson, for *Dans med en ängel* (*Death Angels*)
1998: Inger Frimansson, for *Godnatt min älskade* (*Good Night, My Darling*)
1999: Sven Westerberg, for *Guds fruktansvärda frånvaro* ("God's Awful Absence")
2000: Aino Trosell, for *Om hjärtat ännu slår* ("If the Heart Still Beats")
2001: Åke Edwardson, for *Himlen är en plats på jorden* (*Frozen Tracks*)
2002: Kjell Eriksson, for *Prinsessan av Burundi* (*The Princess of Burundi*)
2003: Leif G.W. Persson, for *En annan tid, ett annat liv* (*Another Time, Another Life*)
2004: Åsa Larsson, *Det blod som spillts* (*The Blood Spilt*)
2005: Inger Frimansson, for *Skuggan i vattnet* (*The Shadow in the Water*)
2006: Stieg Larsson, for *Flickan som lekte med elden* (*The Girl Who Played with Fire*)
2007: Håkan Nesser, for *En helt annan historia* ("A Completely Different Story")

2008: Johan Theorin, for *Nattfåk* (*The Darkest Room*)

2009: Anders Roslund and Börge Hellström, for *Tre sekunder* (*Three Seconds*)

2010: Leif G.W. Persson, for *Den döende detektiven* (*The Dying Detective*)

2011: Arne Dahl, for *Viskleken* ("Chinese Whispers")

2012: Åsa Larsson, for *Till offer åt Molok* (*The Second Deadly Sin*)

2013: Christoffer Carlsson, for *Den osynlige mannen från Salem* ("The Invisible Man from Salem")

2014: Tove Alsterdal, for *Låt mig ta din Hand* ("Let Me Take Your Hand")

Best Swedish First Novel (Basta svenske debut) Awards

1971: Ulf Durling, for *Gammal ost* ("Old Cheese")

1974: Valter Unefäldt, for *Råttan på repet* ("The Rat on a Rope")

1976: Tomas Arvidsson, for *Enkelstöten* ("Single Impact," also "Why Me?")

1982: Kjell-Olof Bornemark, for *Legat till en trolös* ("The Messenger Must Die")

1984: Bobi Sourander, for *Ett kilo diamanter* ("A Kilo of Diamonds")

1985: Mats Tormod, for *Movie* ("Movie")

1990: Hans Lamborn, for *Den röda slöjan* ("Downwind")

1991: Olle Hager, for *Bandyspelaren som försvann i Gambia* ("The Bandy Player Who Disappeared in Gambia")

1993: Håkan Nesser, for *Det grovmaskiga nätet* (*The Mind's Eye*)

1995: Åke Edwardson, for *Till allt som varit dött* ("To All Who Have Died")

1997: Lennart Lundmark, for *Den motsträvige kommissarien* ("The Recalcitrant Commissioner")

1998: Liza Marklund, for *Sprängaren* (*The Bomber*)

1999: Kjell Eriksson, for *Den upplysta stigen* ("The Illuminated Path")

2001: Tie: Eva-Marie Liffner, for *Camera* ("Camera"), and Åke Smedberg, for *Försvinnanden* ("Disappearances")

2002: Tove Klackenberg, for *Påtaglig risk att skada* ("Substantial Risk of Injury")

2003: Åsa Larsson, for *Solstorm* (*Sun Storm*, also *The Savage Altar*)

2006: Karin Alfredsson, for *80 grader från Varmvattnet* ("Beauty, Blessing and Hope")

2007: Johan Theorin, for *Skumtimmen* (*Echoes from the Dead*)

2008: Ingrid Hedström, for *Lärarinnan i Villette* ("The Teacher in Villette")

2009: Olle Lönnaeus, for *Det som ska sonas* ("Atonement")

2010: Anders de la Motte, for *[geim]* (sic) ("Game")

2012: Lars Pettersson, for *En blodig kniv* ("A Bloody Knife")

2013: Thomas Engström, for *Väster om friheten* ("West of Freedom")

2015: Sara Lövestam, for *Sanning med modifikation* ("Truth with Modification")

The Glass Key Award

The Glass Key Award, a real glass key named for Dashiell Hammett's *The Glass Key*, is awarded yearly by the Crime Writers of Scandinavia to a crime novel written by a Danish, Finnish, Norwegian, Swedish, or Icelandic author. Up to 2015, seven Swedish authors have received this award.

1992: Henning Mankell, for *Mördare utan ansikte* (*Faceless Killers*)
2000: Håkan Nesser, for *Carambole* (*Hour of the Wolf*)
2001: Karin Alvtegen, for *Saknad* (*Missing*)
2005: Anders Roslund and Börje Hellström, for *Odjuret* (*Beast*)
2006: Stieg Larsson, for *Män som hatar kvinnor* (*The Girl with the Dragon Tattoo*)
2008: Stieg Larsson, for *Luftslottet som sprängdes* (*The Aircastle That Blew Up*)
2009: Johan Theorin, for *Nattfåk* (*The Darkest Room*)

The Sherlock Award

The Sherlock Award, named for Arthur Conan Doyle's great detective Sherlock Holmes, was presented by the Swedish newspaper *Expressen* between 1955 and 1986 for the year's best English-style detective novel. The prize was discontinued because the culture editors of *Expressen* felt that the classical detective genre had become too frail. Winners of the Sherlock Prize are noted in the individual author descriptions below.

The Flint Axe Award

The Flint Axe Award was a Swedish literary award given from 2001 to 2007 by the journal *Jury* for the year's best historical crime novel, regardless of the nationality of the author. The Swedish author Bo R. Holmberg won this award in 2002 for his novel *Liemannen* ("The Grim Reaper").

The Poloni Prize

The Poloni Prize (*Polonipriset*) was awarded in honor of Helena Poloni between 1998 and 2001 to a promising female Swedish crime novelist. "Helena Poloni" was the pseudonym of Ingegerd Stadener (1903–1968), author of Agatha Christie–type puzzle mysteries. She also used the pseudonym "Lillevi Gavell" as well as publishing detective fiction under her own name.

1998: Liza Marklund
1999: Aino Trosell
2000: Åsa Nilsson
2001: Eva-Marie Liffner

The Petrona Award for Scandinavian Crime Fiction

The Petrona Award for Scandinavian Crime Fiction was established in 2013 for the Best Scandinavian Crime Novel of the Year in honor of Maxine Clarke, a pioneering online crime fiction reviewer with a special interest in Scandinavian crime literature. The 2013 short list for the award was based on Maxine Clarke's reviews and ratings and from 2014 onward is awarded by a judging panel using Clarke's criteria for excellence in mystery fiction: quality of plot, strength of characterization, and consideration of contemporary social issues. The winner is announced at the annual international crime fiction CrimeFest held each May–June. Swedish winners of the Petrona Award include Liza Marklund, for *Nobels testamente* (*Last Will*, tr. Neil Smith), 2013; and

Leif G.W. Persson, for *Linda—som i Lindamordet* (*Linda, as in the Linda Murder Case*, tr. Neil Smith), 2014.

A Parallel Chronology of Swedish Literature and World Events

Swedish crime fiction and events are listed in Roman type with world crime fiction and events interspersed in italics.

AD 98: Swedes mentioned in Tacitus' *Germania*

6th century: The Svear, a north Germanic tribe, conquer the Gotar (Goths) in south of Sweden; *Beowulf* mentions Swedish-Geatish wars

c. 8th–11th centuries: Swedish Viking Age; Swedish Vikings found Kievan Rus

c. 800: The Rök Runestone, first Swedish literary text

829: St. Ansgar introduces Christianity to Sweden

c. 856: Viking raids in England

By 1050: Christianity fully established by Erik IX, who also conquered Finland

1066: Norman conquest of England

1096–1291: Period of Crusades

1100–1400: Internal power struggles in Scandinavia

1233: Inquisition established in Spain

c. 1250: King Birgir Jarl passes law prohibiting rape and abduction of women

1319: Sweden and Norway united by Magnus VII

1335: King Magnus abolishes slavery in Sweden

1337–1453: Hundred Years' War between France and England

Mid-14th century: Black Death in Scandinavia and throughout Europe

1397: Queen Margaret establishes Kalmar Union of Norway, Sweden, and Denmark

1453: Fall of Constantinople to Turks; end of Middle Ages

1492: Columbus reaches America

1517: Martin Luther begins Protestant Reformation

1520: Christian II (Denmark) massacres anti–Danish Swedish nobles (Stockholm Massacre), leading to June 6, 1523: Swedish uprising under Gustav Vasa (Gustavus I, 1496–1560); June 6 celebrated as Sweden's national holiday. Under Vasa dynasty Sweden becomes major European power

1527: Gustavus I establishes Lutheranism as state religion; begins to transform Sweden into a modern state.

1541: First full translation of the Bible into Swedish (Gustav Vasa Bible)

1618–1648: Thirty Years' War between Catholics and Protestants

17th century: Swedish classical period of poetry and prose

1632: Battle of Lützen, death of Gustavus Adolphus

1648: Peace of Westphalia; start of Sweden's Great Power Period

1689: Peter the Great starts modernization of Russia

1718: End of Swedish royal absolutism

1721: Treaty of Nystad, loss of extensive Swedish land

1700–1721: Great Northern War: Sweden crushed by coalition led by Russia

1757: Emanuel Swedenborg's teachings of "New Church" which led posthumously to organization of the Church of the New Jerusalem

1808: Gustavus IV loses Finland to Russia

1809: Sweden's first modern constitution

1814: Sweden establishes neutrality policy; forces Denmark to cede Norway to Sweden

1815: Congress of Vienna joins Sweden and Norway

1821: First "crime story": "The Mad Christian" by M.C. Hansen (Norway)

1830: Establishment of *Aftonbladet* newspaper

1834: Almqvist's "The Queen's Diamond Ornament," crime novel/political thriller

1838: Almqvist's "The Mill of Skallnora," psychological crime story

1838: End of Swedish New Romantic period

1839: Norwegian Maurits Hansen's detective novel "The Murder of Engineer Roolfsen"

1841: Poe's "The Murders in the Rue Morgue," usually called the first detective story

1843: First appearance of the word "detective" in English

1850s: Fredrika Bremer studies women's issues in U.S.A.

1851: Almqvist flees from Sweden to U.S.

1859: Start of Swedish emigration to America

1868: First full-length detective novel, Wilkie Collins' The Moonstone

1869: First police procedural, Emile Gaboriau's Monsieur Lecoq

c. 1870 to 1914: Sweden shapes industrialized economy

1870s: Ibsen's realistic dramas

1879: Strindberg's *The Red Room* published

Late 19th century: August Strindberg's naturalistic dramas raise gender and social justice issues

1888: Strindberg's naturalistic play *Miss Julie*

1889: Swedish Social Democrat Party founded

1893: Frederik Lindholm publishes *Stockholmsdetekiven* ("The Stockholm Detective"); first full length Swedish mystery novel; first detective figure in Scandinavian crime fiction

19th century: Sweden liberalizes government; c. 1,500,000 Swedes immigrate to USA

1905 *Doctor Glas*, psychological crime novel 1905: Swedish union with Norway dissolved by Hjalmar Soderberg

1907: Astrid Lindgren born

1908–1910: Sture Stig's Sherlock Holmes parodies

1909: Selma Lagerlöf receives Nobel Prize for Literature

1910: Swedish labor union movement holds large strikes demanding reforms

1914–1918: World War I: Sweden neutral

1914–1947: Frank Heller's detective novels

1916: Verner von Heidenstam receives Nobel Prize for Literature

1917: Sweden avoids a communist revolution and reintroduces parliamentarianism

1920s–1930s: Golden Age of Mystery Fiction (Britain)

1920–1951: Black Mask, U.S. magazine of hard-boiled crime fiction

1920: Agatha Christie's first detective novel, The Mysterious Affair at Styles

1921: Swedish women receive right to vote and run for parliament

1930: Sweden's domestic crime tradition begins

1930s: The Great Depression

1932: Social Democrats take power in Sweden; introduction of social legislation; English-influenced crime novels appear by Swedish authors

1934: Yngve Hedvall, *Tragedin i Villa Siola*

1939: Kjerstin Foransson-Ljungman, first "Queen of Swedish crime fiction"; her novel *27 sekundmeter sno* appears

1939–1945: World War II; Sweden neutral

1940: First Social Democratic parliamentary majority in Sweden

1940s: Mysteries with strong sense of place and welfare-state issues become enormously popular in Sweden; Sweden makes wartime concessions to Nazis but assist anti–Nazi humanitarian efforts

1944–late 1960s: Stig Trenter's Stockholm based novels

1945: Astrid Lindgren publishes *Pippi Longstocking*

1946: Sweden enters the United Nations

1946–c. 1976: Social Democrats govern Sweden

c. 1946–c. 1989: Cold War period

Late 1940s–late 1950s: First "Golden Age" of Swedish crime fiction: Maria Lang (Dagmar Lange) publishes racy mysteries; Vic Suneson (Sune Lundqvist) writes working class Stockholm mysteries; R.K. Rönholm publishes small town literary mysteries; Stieg Trenter stresses "Swedishness" in crime stories; Helena Poloni, an obscure female Swedish author, writes mysteries. Sweden remains outside NATO.

1949: First Muslim congregation in Sweden (Tatars from Finland)

1950: Official dissolution of Swedish Nazi Party; Hell's Angels established in Sweden

1951: First Dragnet telecast

1951: Per Lagerkvist receives Nobel Prize for Literature

1953: First James Bond novel published

1955–1986: Sherlock Prize for year's best crime novel in English awarded by *Expressen*

1956: Neo-Nazi "Nordic Reich Party" founded in Sweden

1956: Ed McBain's first 87th Precinct novel, Cop Hater; *series continues through the 1980s*

1959: Saturday Evening Post article links Swedish welfare system to alcoholism, suicide, and crime

1960s: Strong American influence on Swedish mysteries; Muslim migrants begin to enter from Balkans and Turkey

1960s–1970s: Sweden promotes liberal "sexual revolution"

1965–1973: Capstones of Scandinavian welfare systems being set

1963: Kerstin Ekman's novel *Dodsklocken*, one of Sweden's most praised crime novels

1965: *Roseanna*, first Martin Beck novel by Sjöwall and Wahlöö; series continues until 1975, exposing Swedish capitalism via police procedural; beginning of Second Golden Age of Swedish crime fiction combining police procedural form with sociological themes

1968: Sweden's first crime/mystery fiction magazine, *DAST-Magazine*, founded post–1968: Olof Palme's Social Democrats espouse more radical "economic democracy"

1968–c. 1985: Neo-Marxist Left sees welfare state as absorbing social costs of capitalistic production

1970: Sweden modernizes constitution

1970s: World financial crisis

1970s: Nils Hovenmark writes political small town mysteries

1970s: Sweden enacts gender-equality laws

Mid–1970s: Basic structures of Scandinavian welfare states complete

1970–1990: Swedish taxes rise over 10 percent (average)

1971: Swedish Crime Writers' Academy established Martin Beck Award and Best Swedish Crime Novel Award initiated

Early 1970s: World oil crisis

1973 and 1978–1979: During oil embargoes, Sweden experiences economic decline

1974: 25 percent of work force in many Swedish factories is foreign-born, with economic and social equality guaranteed by political organizations and trade unions

1974–1978: Sweden increases incentives to put wives into wage-earning jobs; recession causes labor surpluses

1975: Per Wahlöö dies; the Abortion Act gives Swedish women the legal right to abortion during First 16 weeks of pregnancy, with stipulations for later abortion procedures

1976: Social Democrats ousted from power in Sweden; their support lowest since 1932

1976: Finn Matti Joensuu writes noir Finnish police procedural novel

1977: Debut of Marcia Muller's Sharon McCone, first U.S. female P.I.

1980: Sweden makes Act of Succession gender-neutral

1980s: Restructuring of Swedish industry, slowing the expansion of the Swedish welfare state; Swedish budget deficits exceeding 10 percent of GDP. Zero tolerance drug policy reinforced

1986: P.M. Olof Palme assassinated; 24-year investigation yields no convictions

Late 1980s: Collapse of Soviet Union

Late 1980s–early 1990s: Swedish political party fragmentation

Early 1990s: Håkan Nesser and Åke Edwardson begin publishing crime novels

Early 1990s: World recession control

1992: Start of Glass Key Awards

1991–1993: Severe financial crisis due to rupture of real estate bubble, caused by lack of lending

1992: Run on Swedish currency causes interest rates to rise to 500 percent; government cuts spending.

1993: Kerstin Ekman's *Blackwater*

1993: Dane Peter Høeg publishes Smilla's Sense of Snow

January 1, 1995: Sweden joins European Union

1997: Henning Mankell's first Wallander novel, *Faceless Killers*; Liza Marklund begins *"femikrim" "new wave"*

1997–2007: Rise of organized crime activity in Sweden

1998: The Act on Violence against Women is introduced

1998: Liza Marklund wins first Polani Prize; Camilla Läckberg takes *Jury*-initiated writing course; Lars Gustafson's *The Tale of a Dog*; Helene Tursten's debut, *Detective Inspector Huss*; Karin Alvtegen's debut, *Skuld (Guilt)*

1998–2001: Poloni Prize awarded to women crime writers

2000: Mons Kallentoft's debut, *Pesetas*

2001: Terrorist attack on U.S. World Trade Center and Pentagon

2002: Astrid Lindgren dies at 94; parental leave increased to 480 days

2003: Camilla Läckberg publishes first novel, *The Ice Princess*; Mari Jungstedt's *Unseen*; Karin Alvtegen's *Missing*

2004: Malmö's mosque set afire; Amnesty International denounces Sweden's lack of prosecution of rapes

2005: Victimization survey indicates Sweden has above average crime rates compared to other EU countries; new anti-sexual crime laws enacted

2005–2008: Publication in Sweden of Stieg Larsson's Millennium Trilogy

2006: Jens Lapidus' debut, *Easy Money*; far-right Sweden Democrats win municipality seats

2007: Björn Ranelid, Ernst Brunner, and Leif G.W. Persson criticize women crime writers, setting off "war against the crime queens"

2008: Carin Gerhardsen begins Hammarby series

2008 and 2010: Anti-immigration riots in Malmö's city district

2008–2010: Publication of Stieg Larsson's Millennium Trilogy in English

2009: Lars Kepler's debut, *The Hypnotist*; the Discrimination Act replaces older anti-discrimination laws

2010: Camilla Ceder's debut, *Frozen Moment*; Mari Jungstedt's *The Killer's Art* Sweden Democrats enter Swedish parliament

2010: Sweden collects 45.8 percent of the Swedish GDP in taxes, almost double the U.S. rate

2010: Liza Marklund becomes second Swedish author to head *New York Times* bestseller list

2011: 27 percent of the Swedish population is foreign born. Kristina Ohlsson's debut, *Unwanted*; Leif G.W. Persson's *Between Summer's Longing and Winter's End*; anti-stalking laws enacted

2013: Anti-immigration riots in Stockholm; rightist Swedish Democrat party opposes immigration. Muslims in Sweden number approx. 500,000 of a population of approx. 9.5 million; riots in Sweden and elsewhere

Contemporary Swedish Authors
of Crime Fiction

An asterisk (*) indicates some or all of the author's work is available in English.

Kennet Ahl (pseudonym of Lasse Strömstedt and Christer Dahl)

Lasse Strömstedt: b. May 23, 1935, Gävle, Sweden; d. July 4, 2009, Gränna, Sweden; Residence: Gränna, Sweden; Occupations: laborer, actor, co-author

Christer Dahl: b. December 30, 1940, Solna, Sweden; Residence: Stockholm, Sweden; Occupations: theater director, scriptwriter, producer, journalist; co-author

After 1971, Lasse Strömstedt drew on his troubled youth, his drug abuse, and his frequent imprisonments as the basis for the seven crime novels he co-authored as "Kennet Ahl" with Christer Dahl. Their collaboration began in the early 1970s when Strömstedt had just been released from prison. He wanted to change his life, but he was having difficulties with his studies at the University of Umea and he was heavily in debt, so he accepted an offer to work in the theater at Gothenburg with director Christer Dahl. They brainstormed their first novel, *Grundbulten* ("The Linchpin," also called "The Cornerstone"), 1974, from Strömstedt's highly detailed prison experiences, specifically a true tale about a stoned prisoner who kept looking for the bolt that held the whole prison together; if he could find it, he reasoned, he could set himself free for life. "The Linchpin" is considered one of the most profound portrayals of prison life in Sweden, the Stockholm underworld, and even Sweden's famous criminal attorney Trygve Marin. Strömstedt and Dahl collaborated on another crime novel, *Lyflet* ("Initiative"), 1976, before they split up; Dahl then produced the next two Kennet Ahl novels before returning to work with Strömsted for *Mordvinnaren* ("Murder Winner"), 1987, and *Hämndemännen* ("Revenge Men"), 1991.

Besides the crime novels Strömstedt co-authored with Christer Dahl, he produced three volumes of his autobiography, "Go to Jail," 1981; "In Prison," 1981; and "Moment of Truth," 1984. His final Kennet Ahl novel, *Högriskbegravning* ("High Risk Burial"), 2006, returned to the main character of "The Linchpin," now an elderly man. All of Strömstedt's work displays black humor and scalding criticism of a government-dictated prison system which as he stingingly described in "Initiative," devotes vastly more resources to civil servants' salaries and their comparatively luxurious work environments than it does to the welfare and rehabilitation of prisoners (Müller). Strömstedt, who became a popular lecturer on his criminal background and his subsequent life, was working on the fourth volume of his autobiography at the time of his death in 2009.

Collaborative Crime Novels:

1974: *Grundbulten* ("The Cornerstone")
1976: *Lyftet* ("Initiative")
1987: *Mordvinnaren* ("Murder Winner")
1991: *Hämndemännen* ("Revenge Men")

By Christer Dahl as "Kennet Ahl":

1978: *Rävsaxen* ("Leghold Trap")
1980: *Slutstationen* ("End Station")

By Lasse Strömstedt as "Kennet Ahl":

2006: *Högriskbegravning* ("High Risk Burial")

Major Awards: N/A

Website for Christer Dahl: http://www.ne.se/christer-dahl

Mats Ahlstedt

b. 1949, Jämtland, Sweden; Residence: Gothenburg, Sweden; Occupations: journalist, author

As the son of a prison chaplain in Gothenburg, where he has lived since boyhood, Mats Ahlstedt grew up hearing tragic stories that inspired his series of crime novels involving sudden suspicious deaths. Set in Gothenburg, most of these novels feature young detective Fatima Wallinder whose ancestral roots are in Somalia, and county police superintendent Soren Hogstrom. Ahlstedt notes that his fears for his "two wonderful daughters" and his "two wonderful grandchildren" have inspired him to focus his fiction on women's vulnerability, "A kind of therapy if you will" (quoted on Ahlstedt's website).

Vulnerable women abound in Ahlsted's novels. His debut, *Dödsängeln* ("Angel of Death"), 2003, opens the series with the mysterious shooting of a Gothenburg dressage judge. Ahlsted's second novel, *Violinisten* ("Violinist"), 2006, deals with the disappearance and murder of a small girl and the stalking of Beatrice Larsdotter, a world-famous violinist. In *Den röda damcyklen* ("The Red Woman's Bicycle"), 2007, Fatima investigates a case involving silent victims, here young girls, of men's violence against women (sometimes referred to as "femicide"). *Mordet på Ragnhildsholmen* ("Murder at Ragnhildsholmen"), 2009, shows Superintendent Soren Hogstrom faced with a murder victim found in an old castle's ruins, while Fatima probes the deaths of an elderly couple whose daughter is now also in great danger. Currently Ahlsted is working on a trilogy featuring prison chaplain John Brobeck. Its first volume, *Trasdockorna* ("Trash"), 2013, presents the burgeoning problem of human trafficking in Scandinavia, where refugee women are increasingly being sold as sex slaves and subjected to violent abuse and even murder.

Crime Novels:

2003: *Dödsängeln* ("Angel of Death")
2006: *Violinisten* ("The Violinist")
2007: *Den röda damcykeln* ("The Red Woman's Bicycle")
2009: *Mordet på Ragnhildsholmen* ("Murder at Ragnhildsholmen")
2010: *Dömd för livet* ("Sentenced for Life")
2012: *Dockmakarens dotter* ("However Maker's Daughter")
2013: *Trasdockorna* ("Trash")
2014: *Ondskans spår* ("Evil Track")

Major Awards: N/A

Website: http://www.matsahlstedt.se

Hans Folke "Hasse" Alfredsson

b. June 28, 1931, Malmö, Sweden; Residence: Lidingö, Sweden; Occupations: actor, cinema director, comedian, author

Best known for his work with film as actor and director and his leftist opposition to nuclear power, pollution, and Nazism, Hans Alfredsson also produced detective fiction which served as the basis for two of his most notable films. His 1980 novel *En ond man* ("An Evil Man") grew into the highly praised 1982 film "The Simple-Minded Killer," set in 1930s Sweden, in which a boy with a harelip is tormented by the tyrannical landowner who employs him. One of the short stories in Alfredsson's 1982 collection *Lagens långa näsa* ("Law's Long Nose") inspired his 1985 thriller film "Fake as Water." Alfredsson's son Daniel directed the Swedish film version of Stieg Larsson's *The Girl with the Dragon Tattoo*.

Crime Fiction:

1980: *En ond man* ("An Evil Man"), basis for the 1982 film *A Simple-Minded Killer*
1983: *Lagens långa näsa* ("Law's Long Nose," a collection of 21 short stories)

Major Awards: N/A

Website: N/A

Karin Alfredsson

> b. 1953; Residence: Stockholm; Karin Alfredsson also has extensively traveled the world in support of women's issues; Occupations: journalist, editor, activist against violence toward women, author

Karin Alfredsson's crime novels powerfully support her lifelong campaign to stamp out violence against women worldwide. Margot Wallstrom, UN special representative on sexual violence, claims that some thirty years ago, Alfredsson almost singlehandedly persuaded Swedish government authorities to act more forcefully against domestic violence (quoted in Yerkey). Since then, Alfredsson has become one of the most prominent advocates of attempts to curb all violence directed against women; she claims that violence against women aged 15 to 44 "causes more deaths and injuries than cancer—more than traffic accidents, malaria and war combined" (quoted in Yerkey).

Alfredsson currently heads "Cause of Death: Woman," a nongovernmental project that has inspected ten countries to document worldwide violence against women and highlighted results of legislation and other initiatives attempting to curb it. The project's conclusions were presented in Washington, D.C., at a February 2012 conference organized by the U.S.–based National Network to End Domestic Violence. Its $390,000 funding was provided by the Swedish International Development Cooperation Agency, where Alfredsson has been a longtime participant as have the philanthropist Sigrid Rausing and the brother and father of Stieg Larsson, whose Millennium Trilogy powerfully denounced violence against women. "Cause of Death: Woman" also presents a virtual online photojournalism exhibit whose theme is summed up by a twenty-three-year-old survivor: "I asked him to forgive me for making him beat me" (quoted in the Cultural Curator interview with Alfredsson).

Alfredsson's crime novel series stars Swedish physician and midwife Ellen Elg, according to Alfredsson, a "strong and passionate person … [who] wants to change the world" ("Dutch interview," on Alfredsson's website). In each of these novels, Elg works in a different third-world country. Her award-winning 2006 debut, *80 grader från Varmvattnet* ("Beauty, Blessing and Hope") finds Elg faced with a fourteen-year-old girl bleeding to death in Zambia, while a Supreme Court Justice mysteriously dies in the United States and Swedish activists meet to learn about a catastrophe. Alfredsson insists that this novel proves that the economically or ideologically powerful—nearly always men—victimize the helpless—almost always women. Elg appears next in Vietnam in *Kvinnorna på 10.e våningen* ("The Women on the Tenth Floor"), 2008, working in a Hanoi maternity ward from which infants are mysteriously disappearing while a Swedish charity worker has plunged from the tenth floor of the Hotel Continental. Alfredsson came under the censure of the Roman Catholic Church for "9.37 p.m.," her novel set in Roman Catholic Poland, where abortion is forbidden, focusing on a desperate young girl with a life-threatening pregnancy who tries to abort the child and involving Ellen Elg, herself on maternity leave, who has joined the Dutch organization which performs abortions in international waters. *Den sjätte gudinnan* ("The Sixth Goddess"), 2010, set in India, revolves around Kali, a raped teenager trying to support her newborn baby by begging and her friend Amarita, horribly burned by her husband. Elg attempts to help them receive their day in court. In *Poyken i hiss 54* ("The Boy in Elevator 54"), 2011, set in Muslim Pakistan and Dubai, Muslim security forces kidnap Elg because she has probed too deeply into officially sanctioned torture and Muslim honor killings. All of Alfredsson's disturbing novels carry out her mission, which the Swedish journal *Damernas värld* describes as opening "our eyes to the inequities that affect women in the third world [which] ... touches you and makes you feel angry and involved" (quoted on Alfredsson's website).

Crime Novels:

2006: *80 grader från Varmvattnet* ("Beauty, Blessing and Hope")
2008: *Kvinnorna på 10.e våningen* ("The Women on the Tenth Floor")
2009: *Klocken 21:37* ("9.37 p.m.")
2010: *Den sjätte gudinnan* ("The Sixth Goddess")
2011: *Poyken i hiss 54* ("The Boy in Elevator 54")

Major Awards:

2006: The Swedish Crime Academy Debutant Award for *80 grader från Varmvattnet* ("Beauty, Blessing and Hope")

Website: http://www.karinalfredsson.se

Tove Alsterdal

> b. December 28, 1960, Malmö, Sweden; Residence: Alsterdal lived in Dubai for several years and now resides in Stockholm, with summers in Tornedalen, northern Sweden; Occupations: mental hospital aide, journalist, playwright; editor (of Liza Marklund's novels), author

In a 2010 interview in Los Angeles, Ingrid Landstrom concluded that Tove Alsterdal is breaking the unwritten rules for contemporary Swedish crime fiction, which Landstrom describes as "grisly murders committed in quaint towns" solved by a detective with "a messy private life" (Landstrom). After writing plays, children's books, and scripts for radio plays, films, and operas, Tove Alsterdal began writing novels with far-flung settings based closely on reality, beginning with *Kvinnorna på stranden* ("Women on the Beach"), 2009, a noir thriller rewritten from one of Alsterdal's movie scripts, set in five countries and several different and frightening venues and featuring three women who undergo brutal changes in their lives. Terese stumbles onto the body of an African man on a Spanish beach; Mary, smuggled into Spanish waters, tries to escape her captors; and Ally Cornwall, a New York stage designer, is searching for her missing husband Patrick, a journalist investigating human trafficking in Europe. Ally's hunt takes her into sleazy European human trafficking centers in five countries, told in "fast-paced, action-driven language" (Lundstrom) often compared to the styles of American thriller authors Dan Brown and John Grisham. Alsterdal says she didn't write that way intentionally, "It's just how I enjoy writing" (quoted in Landstrom).

Landstrom describes Alsterdal's novels as different from those of other Swedish *femikrim* authors, who usually immerse their women detectives in mundane women's chores, "picking up kids from day care, fighting with their spouses, making dinners, visiting in-laws and getting divorced" (Landstrom). Alsterdal claims, "I get enough everyday life in my, well, everyday life" (quoted in Landstrom). Because she says she is "easily bored," Alsterdal created a main character who can do almost anything: "All it takes is a big enough fury"—or desperation, as revealed in "Women on the Beach." Alsterdal believes that throughout history men have dealt with the big issues, "life and death and power and guilt," while women have had to cope with trivialities (quoted in Landstrom). She intends to make her female characters grapple with larger questions, like the obscene backdrop for "Women on the Beach," the 27 million women worldwide today held as slaves or who perish trying to escape their traffickers.

Alsterdal's second novel, *I tystnaden begravd* ("Tomb of Silence"), 2012, takes place in Kivikangas, a village on Sweden's far north border with Finland, an area where Alsterdal has family ties. In this novel, Lapp-Erik, a former cross country skier, is found beaten to death in a remote farmstead. Katrine, a Swedish journalist recently made redundant in London, goes north to uncover family secrets, where she becomes involved in the murder investigation, while she explores the bleak history of Sweden and the former Soviet Union. In 2012, *Dagens Nyhater* called "Tomb of Silence" "a brilliant detective intrigue, where the old north Sweden meet[s] the new, the old and new Russias collide, and a woman tries to find her family's history in a tangle of lies and helpless idealism" (quoted on Alsterdal's website). Alsterdal's literary representatives, the Grand Agency, indicate that an English draft translation of "Tomb of Silence" is available.

Alsterdal won the 2014 Best Swedish Crime Novel Award with *Låt mig ta din hand* ("Let Me Take Your Hand"), 2014, also nominated for the 2014 Glass Key Award. This novel opens on a freezing Walpurgis Eve, when drug addict Charlie Eriksson plunges to her death from the eleventh floor of her apartment block in a Stockholm suburb. Her death is initially assumed to be a suicide, but it soon sets off a homicide investigation that the Swedish Detective Academy praised as "a consummate and linguistically variegated tapestry of mystery and contemporary issues" (quoted on Alsterdal's website).

Alsterdal also participated in a 2008 collaborative novel, "A Place in the Sun," with several other Swedish authors, including Liza Marklund. Alsterdal has edited Marklund's novels since 1998, in the process coming close to her long time friend's thought and writing processes. Alsterdal has commented about the experience, "To have someone who is so involved in one's own book means everything" (quoted on Alsterdal's website).

Crime Novels:

   2009: *Kvinnorna på stranden* ("Women on the Beach")
   2012: *I tystnaden begravd* ("Tomb of Silence")
   2014: *Låt mig ta den hand* ("Let Me Take Your Hand")

Collaborative Novel:

   2008: "A Place in the Sun"

Major Awards:

   2014: The Best Swedish Crime Novel, for *Låt mig ta din hand* ("Let Me Take Your Hand")

Website: http://www.alsterdal.se

Karin Alvtegen

b. June 8, 1965, Huskvarna, Sweden; Residence: Stockholm, Sweden; Occupations: television scriptwriter, author

On a personal statement contained in her official website, Karin Alvtegen, a teleplay writer for a Swedish soap opera and one of Sweden's bestselling authors of psychological thrillers, attributes the beginning of her writing career to the death of her brother Magnus in a 1993 mountain climbing accident, when she was almost nine months pregnant with her second child. Hiding her grief at the shock of his death sent her into a three-year depression, a "self-consuming fear" that culminated in severe panic attacks, which she describes as "the soul's need to vomit," but one day she awakened with the germ of a story about one Peter Brolin, who has the courage to break through a similar affliction. Alvtegen says she phoned her husband and asked him how to turn on the computer, beginning her literary career with "the feeling of having reclaimed the urge, the belief in a future, the joy of living" (personal statement on website).

Karin Alvtegen praises her great-aunt Astrid Lindgren, one of Sweden's most revered, even adored, figures, as her "great human role model." Alvtegen observes that Lindgren, creator of the beloved Pippi Longstocking children's series, was not only one of the world's most translated authors, selling nearly 150 million books worldwide, but also a "fantastic" human being. Lindgren's less well known children's series about boy detective Kalle Blomkvist who becomes involved with some serious crimes probably also inspired Alvtegen's desire to explore dark human motivations in her own novels. In a 2009 interview, Alvtegen shared her personal reactions toward the powerful effects the psyche can have on human consciousness and behavior. She says she consistently puts herself into the mind of the character she writes about, and "at times that strongly affects me. However, since these books also aim to bring understanding into why my characters feel and act the way they do, I always end up feeling good afterwards," because each writing experience teaches her something important about human behavior (quoted in Zeringue).

Each of Alvtegen's novels reveals disturbing but vital insights into the dark side of human nature, connected with her own painful experiences. *Skuld* (*Guilt*), 1998, tr. 2007, finds its hero Peter Brolin mired in debt, devoid of job and hope, and subject to the shattering panic attacks Alvtegen herself had experienced. As he sits alone in a Stockholm café, a strange deranged woman mistakes him for someone else and insists he must deliver a package to her husband. The nightmarish consequences of Brolin's hunt for the woman's husband confront him with the worst fears from his own past. The idea for *Saknad* (*Missing*), 2000, tr. 2003, nominated for the Edgar Allan Poe Award in 2009, came to Alvtegen one morning in the subway when she saw a barefoot woman begging for money. Filled with profound respect for her and all those who refuse to give in to their frightening isolation, Alvtegen explored the lives of Stockholm's homeless through Sibylla Forsenström, fifteen years a bag lady, who becomes a prime suspect in a brutal murder case. In *Svek* (*Betrayal*), 2003, tr. 2005, Sweden's high divorce rate and consequent violent aftermaths spurred Alvtegan to write this novel, probing "the Limbic system," a portion of the brain which drives individuals, especially those stricken by the fear of abandonment, to defend themselves "exactly as the animals we are." Out of the emotional trauma following her own divorce, Alvtegen concluded in *Betrayal* that neither punishments nor rewards exist; "there are only consequences."

In *Skam* (*Shame*), 2005, tr. 2006, Alvtegen again addressed the power of fear, but this time she moved out of her own direct experience into an analysis of religious pietism, in a searing case where a rigidly reared girl is forced to deny her sexuality by parents she feels have never loved her. Bo Tao Michaelis observed that Alvtegen "writes Protestant crime novels with an existential thematic [position] ... very Swedish ... when compared [to] ... Strindberg, Bergman and Lars

Norén" (quoted from *Politiken* on Alvtegen's website). *Skugga* (*The Shadow*), 2007, tr. 2008, reflects Alvtegen's reverence for Astrid Lindgren in a mirror image: a fictional Nobel Prize winner, apparently highly respected, turns out to be at the root of a family's most dysfunctional secrets. Often called Alvtegen's darkest and most disturbing thriller, *The Shadow*, poses questions Alvtegen finds tormenting: How does the current media climate affect our children? Why do we numb our brains with drugs? Whom do we blame when everything goes wrong? And most pervasive of all in *Shadow*, "What is, in truth, genuine success?" (see Alvtegen's website).

After announcing that she was moving away from the crime fiction genre, Alvtegen undertook two psychological novels. The second of those, *Fjärilseffekten* ("The Butterfly Effect"), was released in April 2013 and immediately reached Sweden's top ten bestseller list. Its title refers to the scientific theory that even the smallest event can change the course of the entire universe forever. This novel explores the issues of power and powerlessness through Viktoria, a woman caught in a loveless marriage and facing a fatally debilitating disease, and Andreas, suffering from anxiety attacks so severe he becomes reclusive. Each character's struggles demonstrate Alvtegen's treatment of psychological damage due to a parent's refusal to love a child, one of the cruelest crimes of all. "The Butterfly Effect" has received critical praise for its "beautifully melancholic" tone in portraying an older woman reviewing her life as she faces death (*Tidningen VI*, quoted in Alvtegen's website), and its psychological acuity and insight, "in a language so melodious that you can almost hear it singing" (*Jonköpingsposten*, quoted in Alvtegen's website).

In a joint *Literature Portal* interview Alvtegan shared with Maj Sjöwall in 2004, Karin Alvtegen summed up the goals she set for her crime novels: "I write primarily for myself…. But I also … feel more and more responsibility … to my readers to [advance] empathy, respect for human beings…. I also use as little blood and violence as possible. Violence disgusts me…. I want to give people something to think about" (quoted in Hagenguth).

Crime Novels:

1998: *Skuld* (*Guilt*, tr. Anna Paterson, 2007)
2000: *Saknad* (*Missing*, tr. Anna Paterson, UK, 2003, U.S., 2009)
2003: *Svek* (*Betrayal*, tr. Steven T. Murray, 2005)
2005: *Skam* (*Shame*, tr. Steven T. Murray, 2006)
2007: *Skugga* (*The Shadow*, tr. Steven T. Murray, 2008)
2010: *En sannolik historia* ("A Probable Story")
2011: *Shame* was reissued in the UK under the title *Sacrifice*

Psychological Novel:

2013: *Fjärilseffekten* ("The Butterfly Effect")

Major Awards:

2001: The Glass Key Award, for *Saknad* (*Missing*)
2002: The Silver Pocket Award (outstanding paperback sales) for *Saknad* (*Missing*)
2004: The Gold Pocket Award (outstanding paperback sales) for *Svek* (*Betrayal*)
2006: The Platinum Pocket (*Platinapocket*) Award (outstanding paperback sales), for *Skam* (*Shame*)
2008: The Palle Rosenkrantz Award (Denmark) for *Skugga* (*The Shadow*)

Website: http://www.karinalvtegen.com/index_eng.htm

Kristina Appelqvist

b. September 17, 1968. Skar, Sweden; Residence: Lerdala, near Skövde, Sweden; Occupations: journalist, university head of communications and press officer, author

In "Kristina Appelqvist," an autobiographical statement issued by her publisher, Kristina Appelqvist cites as her literary inspirations English mystery authors Caroline Graham, whose small-town Inspector Barnaby stars in the popular UK television series *Midsummer Murders*, and Dorothy L. Sayers, the Golden Age creator of amateur sleuth Lord Peter Wimsey. Appelqvist feels a special kinship with Sayers because of Sayers' famous novel *Gaudy Night*, set amidst Oxford's "dreaming spires," an academic environment with which Appelqvist's professional work at the University of Skövde has made her familiar ("Kristina Appelqvist").

After more than a decade as the university's Head of Communications, Appelqvist concluded that academia provides an amazing detective environment which proves stable over the years and is consistent in its workings regardless of its geographical location. In Appelqvist's opinion, the university also fosters a "creative and dynamic atmosphere" that employs "power-hungry, intelligent and strong-willed people who are often in conflict with each other (quoted in "Kristina Appelqvist"). (Appelqvist may have been familiar with Dorothy L. Sayers' opinion, looking back on her miserable year teaching ungrateful undergraduates at Hull, that "For some reason, nearly all school murders are good ones—probably because it is so easy to believe that murder could be committed in such places" [Sayers, "Review"].) Accordingly, Appelqvist set her first four detective novels at the University of Skövde, with newly-named university rector Emma Lundgren and Detective Superintendent Philip Alexandersson as her sleuths. For her fifth novel, *Minns mig som en ängel* ("Remember Me Like an Angel"), 2013, with Emma and Philip who married in 2011's *Liv i överflöd* ("Life in Abundance"), Appelqvist later created a new heroine, researcher Helena Waller, finding it "exciting" to explore the complex academic world from a new and different perspective ("Kristina Appelqvist").

Crime Novels:

2009: *Den svarta löparen* ("The Black Slider")
2010: *Den som törstar* ("Whoever Is Thirsty")
2011: *Liv i överflöd* ("Life in Abundance")
2012: *De blå damerna* ("The Blue Ladies")
2013: *Minns mig som en ängel* ("Remember Me Like an Angel")

Major Awards: N/A

Website: N/A

Tomas Arvidsson

b. 1931, Älmhult, Småland, Sweden; Residence: Kalmar and Öland, Sweden; Occupations: teacher; program director, University of Kalmar; print and television journalist and manager; author

Having pursued careers in education, journalism, and television, Tomas Arvidsson has also produced ten crime novels. After retiring in 2000 to write full time, Arvidsson noted, "I want to tell a story that is exciting and hopefully funny. I want to try to show that the voltage [thriller] [does] not require violence and humor can include streaks of gravity for those who want to see them." If readers wish, he claims, they can see his tales as "a silent protest against the speculative entertainment violence" that he says has found "grotesque expression" in the crime fiction genre (see quoted material in http://www.bbb.se/books/forfattarportratt/tomas_arvidsson.htm). His first novel, *Enkelstöten* ("Why Me"), 1976, does not involve a murder, rather a 3.5 million *kronor* robbery of Stockholm Handelsbanken at Karlaplan, carried out by Kalmar citizens Jan Bertilsson, a Director of Studies at the university there, and Dr. Gunnar Stensson. Upon sensing arrest is imminent, the pair flees in the doctor's new Jaguar which has an exhaust pipe plated in a millimeter of gold. The criminal-minded Bertilsson figures in several, though not all, of Arvidsson's later novels.

Arvidsson's detectives John Lundén and FBI agent Par Eliasson appear in his first three books, and Arvidsson also uses some of the criminal characters from "Why Me" to link the novels through installments in a chain of villainy. In *Dubbelstöten* ("Double Impact"), Dr. Stensson and his beautiful blonde wife Violet set about conning the year's Nobel Prize winners out of their cash awards. Violet then laces Stensson's coffee with a psychotropic drug, after which he and the money burn up in a drug-induced car crash. In the third novel, the widowed Violet and her 62-year-old friend Elin rob an armored car and head for Switzerland hoping for a new life. To the great disgust of his friend Eliasson, Lundén lets the women go because he feels they are far less culpable than genuine criminals like drug dealers, money launderers, and corrupt politicians.

While maintaining a light humorous touch throughout his novels, often setting them in Kalmar, Arvidsson skewers Swedish governmental policies and figures, especially the *Skoloverstyrelsen* (the public works bureaucracy), but he consistently respects all levels of the Swedish police.

Swedish Television presented four of Arvidsson's novels in three popular series: *Dual Shocks, Double Fortune Cookie*, and *The Vice-Principal's Last Shock*, starring Björn Gustafson with screenplays by Arvidsson in collaboration with director Pelle Berglund.

Crime Novels:

    1976: *Enkelstöten* ("Single Impact" also "Why Me?")
    1976: *Dubbelstöten* ("Double Impact")
    1977: *Bakstöten* ("Former Impact")
    1979: *Tröskeln* ("Threshhold")
    1981: *Utanförskapet* ("Exclusion")
    1986: *Huset med de gamla damerna* ("The House with the Old Ladies")
    1991: *Trippelstöten* ("Triple Impact")
    1996: *För gammal vänskaps skull* ("For Old Times' Sake")
    2001: *Studierektorns byte* ("The Vice-Principal's Bytes")
    2004: *Studierektorns sista stöt* ("The Vice-Principal's Last Shock")
    2006: *Andras pengar* (Other People's Money")
    2008: *Farfar nu* ("Grandfather")
    2009: *Den poetiska hunden* ("The Poetic Dog")

Major Awards:

    1976: Debut Award, Swedish Crime Academy, for *Enkelstöten* ("Why Me")

Website: http://www.tomelius.se/deckare/arvidssonram.html

Bo Balderson (pseudonym for an unknown author or authors)

For a long time, the identity of "Bo Balderson," a detective fiction author of traditional puzzlers spiked with pointed humorous satire directed against high governmental officials, has been one of Sweden's best-guarded literary secrets, with guesses ranging from a single writer to a collective of less well-known writers with governmental contacts, to Swedish Prime Minister Olof Palme and famed children's author Astrid Lindgren. The novels' narrator is Vilhelm Persson, a high-minded humanist and teacher related to a member of the Council of State, allowing the author to comment on corruption in the political system. The name of the fictional Prime Minister is never given in the novels, where he is simply referred to as "the Government," but his relatives call him "Little Man."

Controversy continues about Bo Balderson's real identity. In an extensive textual analysis updated in 2014, freelance journalist Carin Stenstrom postulated that deceased author Ebbe Carlsson had authored the eleven wickedly satirical Balderson novels, claiming that the last published Balderson novel, *Statsrådet klarer krisen* ("The Government Manages the Crisis"), where the crisis ends the fictional Prime Minister's career and the bourgeois family idyll disintegrates (Stenstrom), was the self-created epitaph for both the series and for Carlsson himself, who died in 1993 of AIDS. On September 23, 2009, however, *Arbetarbladet* reported that Gavle City Libraries Manager Conny Persson had declared that 88-year-old SAF director Curt-Steffan Giesecke had written the Balderson novels, but Giesecke insisted that he was "completely innocent." Balderson's literary representative, the Nordin Agency, refuses to confirm or deny any of the many theories about Bo Balderson's identity, which thus remains a mystery.

Crime Novels:

> 1968: *Statsrådet och döden* ("Government and Death")
> 1969: *Harpsundsmordet* ("The Harpsundsvägen Murder")
> 1971: *Statsrådets fall* ("The Government's Case")
> 1973: *Statsrådets verk* ("The Government's Work")
> 1975: *Mord, herr talman* ("Murder, Mr. President")
> 1978: *Statsrådet sitter kvar* ("The Government Remains")
> 1980: *Statsrådet i tiden* ("The Government of the Time")
> 1982: *Partiledarn avgår med döden* ("Depart with Death")
> 1983: *Statsrådet och den utsträckta handen* ("The Government and the Outstretched Hand")
> 1986: *Statsrådets klipp* (The Government's Clip")
> 1990: *Statsrådet klarar krisen* ("The Government Ends the Crisis")

Major Awards: N/A

Website: N/A

Jenny Berthelius

> b. September 29, 1923, Stockholm, Sweden; Residence: Arles, France; Occupations: translator, children's books author, adult crime author

After her crime novel debut in 1968 with *Mördarens ansikte* ("The Killer's Face"), Jenny Berthelius produced twenty-eight children's books and twenty-four adult crime novels featuring Inspector Sanger and novelist Vera Kruse. Berthelius' first adult crime novels were traditional whodunits featuring the "fears and struggles of ordinary people" (Blom 24), but after 1972 she emphasized psychological motivations. *Mord, lilla mamma* ("Murders, Little Mama"), 1977, is a historical mystery set during World War II in Helsingborg, dealing with Nazi sympathizers among the Swedish citizens there.

Selected Crime Novels:

1968: *Mördarens ansikte* ("The Killer's Face")
1972: *Offret* ("The Victim")
1977: *Mord, lilla mamma* ("Murders, Little Mama")
1991: *Turturduvorna i Arles* ("Sweethearts in Arles")
2007: *Näckrosen* ("Näckrosen")

Major Awards:

1969: The Sherlock Award, for *Den heta sommaren* ("The Hot Summer")
2004: Grand Master Award, Swedish Crime Academy

Website: N/A

K. (Karl) Arne Blom (see also "Bo Lagevi")

b. January 22, 1946. Nassjo, Sweden; Residence: Lund, Sweden; Occupations: translator, editor, author

K. Arne Blom belongs to the generation of Swedish crime authors who began publishing just when the Sjöwall-Wahlöö Martin Beck series ended in 1975. They broke with the traditional "purportedly apolitical" kind of crime fiction that had previously been popular in Sweden and instead featured police collectives as the Beck series did, most of them incorporating "an underlying political agenda" into their crime novels (Lundstrom 11). Blom, a prolific author of nearly a hundred books ranging from formulaic detective stories almost all set in Lund to the nonfiction history of Lund's old brewery, also wrote detective fiction under the pseudonym "Per A. Ekblom." With several other Swedish crime novelists under the collective pseudonym "Bo Lagevi" Blom wrote for the "Crime Scene Sweden" series published between 1976 and 1978. Blom also contributed to the American periodical *The Mystery Fancier*, notably the 1983 article "The Crime Story in Sweden," which traces the genre from its Swedish beginnings in the 1830s to the late 1970s.

Blom's debut novel *Någon borde sörja* ("Somebody Ought to Mourn"), 1971, filmed for television in 1975, is representative of his crime fiction. Called by some reviewers the first realistic Swedish detective novel operating in a university student environment, it opened a series of five novels set at Lund University, heavily influenced by 1970s socialism (Eriksson). Blom himself indicated in 1983 that his books dealt with the "expectations and fears of modern people in a troubled society" (Blom 24). Blom received the Sherlock Award in 1974 for *Sanningens ögonblick* ("Moment of Truth"), 1974, which shows caring detectives perplexed by the violent social disorder around them. In the mid–1970s he opened his seven-volume "Heaven Holm" series, set in his birthplace of Nässjö and advancing socialist themes, like the condition of children growing up in a welfare state and the humane rehabilitation of criminals, as well as the sociological theme of how violence begets violence (Blom 24).

Blom later experimented with other detective figures, like the female journalist he named Margaret Turèll to honor the Danish thriller author Dan Turèll. Beginning with *Skuggan av en stövel* ("Shadow of a Boot") 1988, and continuing to *Ingenstans i Sverige* ("Nowhere in Sweden"), 1994, he produced anti–Nazi novels denouncing the cooperation of Sweden's General Security Service (the Swedish secret police organization) with the Nazi regime. He also described German-inspired experimentation on patients at Lund's St. Lars mental hospital, in novels representing two small World War II episodes of Sweden's "forgotten," or, some observers say, "hidden," history.

Blom then returned to police procedurals set in Lund, but after four installments in his Superintendent Dahl-Nielsen series, Blom announced that he would stop writing detective novels in favor of historical fiction set in the 1600s (Eriksson).

Selected Crime Novels:

> 1971: *Någon borde sörja* ("Someone Ought to Mourn")
> 1974: *Sanningens ögonblick* ("Moment of Truth")
> 1977: *Frihetssökarna* ("Freedom Seekers")
> 1994: *Ingenstans i Sverige* ("Nowhere in Sweden")
> 1995: *Offerlamm* ("Sacrificial Lamb")

Major Awards:

> 1974: The Sherlock Award, for "Moment of Truth"

Website: N/A

Stig O. Blomberg (pseudonyms *Olla Villner, Pam Hoogan*)

> b. October 10, 1922, Stockholm, Sweden; d. April 10, 1999, Nacka Parish, Stockholm County, Sweden; Residence: Stockholm area, Sweden; Occupations: journalist, translator, editor, author

After debuting in 1954 with a crime magazine short story, Stig O. Blomberg, an early twentieth century Swedish Golden Age crime writer, wrote a series of crime novels for a Swedish weekly newspaper under the pseudonym "Olla Villner" and one under the pseudonym "Pam Hoogan." Between 1967 and 1999 Blomberg produced a series of highly popular crime novels that made him one of Sweden's best selling authors in the 1960s and 1970s, most of them hardboiled private investigator novels in the mode of American author Mickey Spillane. Blomberg's son Anders O. Blomberg, an artist, provided the covers for several of his father's books.

Selected Crime Novels:

> 1954: *Mord i alla fall* ("Murder in All Cases") (debut novel by "Olla Villner")
> 1967: *Med döden på turné* ("With Death on Tour") (first novel by Stig O. Blomberg)
> 1999: *Brattsplats Bråviken* ("Bråviken Crime") (last crime novel)

Major Awards: N/A

Website: N/A

**Therese Bohman*

> b. 1978; Residence: N/A; Occupations: cultural journalist, editor, author

Therese Bohman was a literary critic for *Aftonbladet* between 2006 and 2009. She now writes on art and literature for *Aftonbladed expressen* and other Swedish cultural periodicals.

Her "chilling, atmospheric" debut novel (Death), *Den drunknade* (*The Drowned*), 2010, set one lovely summer in the beautiful Swedish countryside near Skåne, begins when twentyish Marina, burned out by her art history university studies, comes to visit her older sister Stella and Stella's older lover, Gabriel, a brooding author whose personality hints at violence. Stella is gone most of the time that summer, and Marina yields to the passion she feels for Gabriel, then leaves. She returns the next November after Stella has drowned, suspecting that Gabriel may have engineered the "accident," but the strong chemistry between Marina and Gabriel soon surges into an "increasingly bullying and humiliating" sexual relationship, with Marina finding she "even enjoys his sadism" (Death). Bohman gradually intensifies the foreboding atmosphere into sheer psychological terror, as she explores how human beings expose themselves as dangerously passive, a condition that *Reviewing the Evidence* critic Yvonne Klein describes as affecting twenty-somethings of Sweden "as much as it does those in New York" (Klein). An *Oprah* reviewer called Bohman's writing "lush enough to create a landscape painting with every scene. No shoot-outs, showdowns or explosions end this story, but be prepared to gasp all the same, not with fear, but with understanding" ("Pageturners").

Crime Novels:

2010: *Den drunknade* (*The Drowned*, tr. Marlaine Delargy, 2012)
2014: *Den andra kvinnan* ("The Other Woman")

Major Awards: N/A

Website: N/A

Jean Bolinder (pseudonyms *Elisabeth Schalin and Jesper Borghamn*) (*see also "Bo Lagevi"*)

> b. December 5, 1935, Linköping, Sweden; Residence: Skåne Bajärred, Sweden; Occupations: theater and film director, publisher, author

Between 1967 and 2011, the extremely prolific author Jean Bolinder, best known for his crime fiction, has published more than thirty detective novels and two detective morality plays, earning the Grand Master title from the Swedish Crime Writers Academy. His best known fictional sleuths are Joran and Marianne Bundin, who figure in several of his novels. Bolinder also has participated as one of the authors involved in the collective pseudonym "Bo Lagevi."

In a 2009 interview with Per Erik Tell, Bolinder claimed he was not especially good at writing detective stories, but his many readers and the Swedish Crime Academy disagree. He is also the descendant of the Jean Bolinder who with his brother Carl founded Bolinders Engineering Workshop in Stockholm, a firm originally producing steam engines. It eventually became Volvo BM. The author Jean Bolinder enjoyed a privileged and flaming youth and then a successful and notorious career as the Swedish national theater's director, but he settled down after he married, and he and his wife have been together over 40 years. He took up teaching, which he describes as the only thing he is really good at, but he was so appalled at his students' poor use of Swedish he undertook a traditional puzzle-style detective series inspired by his favorite author, William Faulkner, leading off with the novel *Skulle jeg sörja då* ("I Would Mourn Then"), 1967, which showcases a husband and wife detective team and garnered rave reviews. His later novels shifted away from whodunits and feature taxi driver Joran Bundin as one of the genre's first Swedish antiheroes and reflects Bolinder himself. These later novels gradually became "accounts of lost souls" (Blom 23). *Livet är långt* ("Life Is Long"), 1973, echoes the naturalistic theme of an August Strindberg play (Blom 23). Bolinder himself felt *Dödisgropen*, 1990, was probably his best novel. Subtitled "The Story of a Murder," it follows an anti-heroic figure who, under the influence of Linnaeus' book *Divine Vengeance* and tormented by the commandment "Thou shalt not kill" nevertheless plots revenge on the man responsible for the loss of his job and his wife's leaving him after twenty-nine years of marriage.

Bolinder believes that by writing his books he worked through his own psychological issues via first-person narratives told by killers coping with self-loathing, separation anxiety, and guilt (Tell). In his 2009 autobiography, "In the Shadow of Bolinder's Mechanical Workshop," Bolinder noted that while his readers cherish his books, he and his critics share a mutual distrust, so in his memoirs he would say exactly what he thinks, as a crime writer who claims the theater is his life and teaching is the only area where he excels.

Selected Crime Novels:

1967: *Skulle jeg sörja då…* ("I Would Mourn When…")
1985: *För älskarns och mördarns skull* ("For the Sake of the Lover and the Murderer")
1990: *Dödisgropen* (sometimes translated as "Kettle Holes")
2007: *Djävulen och egna köttet* ("The Devil and His Own Flesh")

As Elisabeth Schalin:

1977: *Picassofisken* ("Picasso Fish")
1978: *Stenskeppel* ("Stone Ship")

Major Awards:

1985: Best Swedish Crime Novel, for *For älskarns och mördardns skull* ("For the Sake of the Lover and the Murderer")
1990: Best Swedish Crime Novel, for *Dödisgropen*
2012: Grand Master title from the Swedish Crime Writers Academy

Website: http://www.jeanbolinder.se

Robert Boman (with Lars Lambert, collective pseudonym Bob Alman)

b. 15 February 1926, Lugnvik, Sweden; d. July 29, 2002, Uppsala, Sweden; Residence: Uppsala, Sweden; Occupations: professor of procedural law, Uppsala University; author

In collaboration with Lars Lambert, Robert Boman wrote two detective novels set at Uppsala, drawing on his training and experience in procedural law.

Crime Novels:

1965: *Den farliga kunskapen* ("The Dangerous Knowledge")
1966: *Mordsommarfesten* ("Summer Festival Murder")

Major Awards: N/A

Website: N/A

Jan Bondeson

b. December 17, 1962, Sweden; Residence: Cardiff, Wales; Occupations: senior lecturer and consultant rheumatologist, author

Though not a crime fiction author *per se*, Jan Bondeson, a distinguished Swedish-born medical researcher, senior lecturer and rheumatologist at the University of Cardiff, Wales, has also written in English about macabre real-life criminal cases involved with medical history. *The London*

Monster, 2000, recounts the career of a Welsh artificial flower maker who was convicted (or possibly framed) for stabbing fifty London women in the buttocks between 1788 and 1790. *Buried Alive*, 2002, is subtitled "The Terrifying History of Our Most Primal Fear." *Blood on the Snow: The Killing of Olof Palme*, 2005, explores the still-unsolved mystery of the assassination of Sweden's controversial Swedish Prime Minister. *Queen Victoria's Stalker*, 2010, deals with Edward "The Boy" Jones, a disturbed youth who stalked the youthful Queen Victoria and broke into Buckingham Palace, stealing her underclothes and spying on her in her dressing room. In 2013, Bondeson published both *The True History of Jack the Ripper* and *Amazing Dogs: A Cabinet of Canine Curiosities*, which contains a chapter on the Nazi experiments to create superdogs loyal to the Nazi "Master Race."

Nonfiction Crime Books:

1997: *A Cabinet of Medical Curiosities*
2000: *The London Monster: A Sanguinary Tale*
2002: *Buried Alive*
2005: *Blood on the Snow: The Killing of Olof Palme*
2010: *Queen Victoria's Stalker*
2013: *Amazing Dogs: A Cabinet of Canine Curiosities*
2013: *The True History of Jack the Ripper*

Major Awards: N/A

Website: N/A

Sören Bondeson

b. July 12, 1956, Dalarna, Sweden; Residence: Stockholm, Sweden; Occupations: teacher, author

After debuting in 1989 with a short story collection, *Sent på förmiddagen* ("After the Morning"), Sören Bondeson, who teaches creative writing at the Forsberg Advertising School in Stockholm and also works in publishing, has published six crime novels as well as a handbook on writing crime fiction in which he analyzes popular contemporary crime novels by Jens Lapidus, Åsa Larsson, and Tove Klackenberg. He advises young writers to familiarize themselves thoroughly with the techniques of their craft, warning that 90 percent of the novel manuscripts that publishers receive are simply not good enough to be published (Svensson).

Selected Crime Novels:

1994: *Lita inte på gryningen* ("Do Not Trust the Dawn")
1997: *I skuggan av mörkret* ("In the Shadow of Darkness")

Handbook on Writing Crime Novels:

2011: *Konsten att döda: så skriver du en kriminalroman* ("The Art of the Dead: How to Write Crime Novels")

Major Awards: N/A

Website: N/A

Rolf Börjlind and Cilla Börjlind

Rolf Börjlind: b. October 7, 1943, West Skravlinge, Sweden; Residence: Nacka, Sweden; Occupations: screenwriter, satirical humorist, author

Cilla Börjlind: b. March 8, 1961, N/A; Residence: Nacka, Sweden; Occupations: screenwriter, author

Rolf and Cilla Börjlind are two of Sweden's best-known movie and television scriptwriters, authors of scripts for twenty-six Martin Beck films as well as for Arne Dahl's A-Group television series and the Swedish Wallander series. Their two original crime series, the eight-part *Graven* ("The Grave") and the six-part *Morden* ("The Murders"), were aired by Swedish Television in 2004 and 2009 respectively. Prior to screenwriting, Rolf Börjlind, "perhaps Sweden's funniest and certainly most bitingly satirical humorist" (Holmberg 35), authored eighteen film scripts, for one of which, *Yrrol*, he received a Guldbagge Award.

After a successful career in scriptwriting for nearly fifty movies and numerous television productions, the Börjlind husband and wife team launched a three-book detective novel series in 2012 with *Springfloden* (*Spring Tide*, tr. 2014), sold to more than twenty countries. According to the Grand Agency, their literary representatives, the series portrays a Sweden full of social conflict. Its empathetic characters are leavened with the couple's trademark humor and surrealistic plot twists.

Spring Tide opens with the two-decades-old brutal murder of a pregnant young woman on the Swedish west coast, left buried in the sand of a Nordkostet beach with only her head above its surface, so that she drowned as the tide came in. Twenty-three years later, former police officer Tom Stilton and young police trainee Olivia Rönning probe this cold case, which Olivia's deceased father, a policeman, had earlier been investigating. The Börjlinds parallel this disturbing plot line by showing serial beatings of Stockholm's homeless and questionable mining practices carried out in Africa by a powerful multinational corporation, producing "an intricate tale of social delinquency and crimes in high places" (*Publishers Weekly* review July 28, 2014). Rapid cuts between these plots and intense atmospherics maintain the pace of this debut thriller, which was followed in 2013 by *Den tredje rösten* (*The Third Voice*, tr. 2015).

Crime Novels:

2012: *Springfloden* (*Spring Tide*, tr. Rod Bradbury, 2014)
2013: *Den tredje rösten* (*The Third Voice*, tr. Hilary Painfors, 2015)
2014: *Svart gryning* ("Black Dawn")

Major Awards: N/A

Website: N/A

*Kjell-Olof Bornemark

b. 1924, Sweden; d. 2006, Sweden; Residence: N/A; Occupations: sailor, journalist, Bible salesman, real estate agent, professional gambler, author

Kjell-Olof Bornemark made his literary debut at 56, encouraged by Hans Stertman, a member of the Swedish Crime Academy. Influenced by the fiction of John Le Carré, Bornemark's 1982 debut novel, *Legat till en trolös* (*The Messenger Must Die*, tr. 1986), is a Cold War psychological spy thriller featuring low-level intelligence agents in an international game of shifting rules and utter lack of surety about whom to trust (Wopenka). Several of Bornemark's other novels treat a similar theme. Bornemark's award-winning *Skyldig utan skuld* ("Guilty Without Guilt"), based on the assassination of Prime Minister Olof Palme, caused a sensation in Sweden. In 1994, Bornemark requested to resign from the Swedish Crime Academy, leaving behind novels "with fine psychological portrait[s] and believable portrayals of … international intelligence operations" (Wopenka).

Crime Novels:

1982: *Legat till en trolös* (*The Messenger Must Die*, tr. Laurie Thompson, 1986)
1983: *Skiljelinjen* (*The Dividing Line*, tr. Laurie Thompson, 1988)
1984: *Förgiftat område* ("Poisoned Area")
1986: *Handgången man* (*The Henchman*, tr. Laurie Thompson, U.S. 1990)
1989: *Skyldig utan skuld* ("Guilty Without Guilt")
1991: *De malätna* ("The Moth-eaten")
1992: *Kontrollören* ("The Verifier")
1994: *Spelaren* ("The Player")

Major Awards:

1982: The Swedish Crime Academy Debut Award for *Legat till en trolös* (*The Messenger Must Die*)
1982: The Sherlock Prize, for *Legat till en trolös* (*The Messenger Must Die*)
1989: Best Swedish Crime Novel, for *Skyldig utan skuld* ("Guilty Without Guilt")

Website: N/A

Annika Bryn

b. 1945; location N/A; Residence: Stockholm, Sweden; Occupations: freelance journalist, author

Annika Bryn's mother was Swedish and her father was a Norwegian who was active in his country's resistance against the Nazi occupation. When she was nine, Annika Bryn began to write, and since then she has published short fiction, magazine and newspaper journalism, and three crime novels featuring Crime Commissioner Margareta Davidsson, who investigates neo–Nazi activities in Sweden. In *Den sjätte natten* ("The Sixth Night"), Davidsson probes two cases: the serial killings of four Stockholm anti–Nazi activists and the kidnapping of a young father whose wife and daughter are on a camping trip in Norrland. Bryn links her first novel with her second, *Brottsplats Rosenbad* ("Crime Scene Rosenbad"), 2005, with three characters, who are not a police team but figures from entirely different backgrounds. In this novel, Bryn combines locked-room mystery elements with sociopolitical commentary about Swedish xenophobia and homophobia. Critics currently view Bryn's work as "average Sweden Crime in an interesting environment" (Reiss) but "miles away from the top of the Swedish crime writers" (Kümmel).

Crime Novels:

Margareta Davidsson Series:

2003: *Den sjätte natten* ("The Sixth Night")
2005: *Brottsplats Rosenbad* ("Crime Scene Rosenbad")
2006: *Morden i Buttle* ("Murders in Buttle")

Major Awards: N/A

Website: N/A

*Carina Burman

> b. 1960; location N/A; Residence: Uppsala, Sweden; Occupations: literary scholar, university professor, author

After receiving her doctorate in comparative literature from Uppsala University in 1988, Carina Burman has devoted most of her literary efforts to historical research and writing, but she has also published three historical detective novels set in the nineteenth century with writer and amateur detective Euthanasia Bondeson as her heroine, novels that depart radically from the contemporary social criticism–police procedurals being written by many of today's Swedish authors.

Opening in 1851 at London's Great Exhibition in the Crystal Palace, this novel begins when the novel's narrator Euthanasia Bondeson, a self-centered successful Swedish author, suddenly realizes her naive young niece and traveling companion Agnes has gone missing at the Crystal Palace. Euthanasia, given to much literary quotation and high-flown prose allows herself to read an English novel by "one of those Yorkshire sisters." She fears the worst has happened to Agnes, so she enlists the help of a handsome Scotland Yard inspector who happens to be one of her fans. They track Agnes into the sleazy depths of Victorian London, where "Burman's extraordinary feeling for history and eccentric wit make for a most unusual kind of crime caper" (Tomaszewski).

Crime Novels:

Euthanasia Bondeson Series:

2004: *Babylons gator: ett Londonmysterium* (*The Streets of Babylon: A London Mystery*, tr. Sarah Death, 2008)

2006: *Vit som marmor: ett romerskt mysterium* ("White as Marble: a Roman Mystery")

2008: *Hasten från porten: ett österländskt äventyr* ("The Horse from the Gate: An Eastern Adventure")

Major Awards: N/A

Website: N/A

Christoffer Carlsson

> b. 1986, Halmstad, Sweden; Residence: Stockholm, Sweden; Occupations: university graduate student, author

While studying for his doctorate in criminology at the University of Stockholm, Christoffer Carlsson produced three crime novels. Both his debut novel, *Fallet Vincent Franke* ("The Case of Vincent Granke"), 2010, an undergraduate *noir* work, and his second, *Den enögda kaninen* ("The One-eyed Bunny"), 2011, received critical praise in Sweden and were sold to several other European countries. Carlsson opened a crime series starring police detective Leo Junker with *Den osynlige mannen från Salem* ("The Invisible Man from Salem"), 2013, which received the Best Swedish Novel of the Year Award, cited by the Swedish Crime Writers Academy as "a strong *noir* novel of ... dense atmosphere of melancholy and resignation."

Crime Novels:

2010: *Fallet Vincent Franke* ("The Case of Vincent Franke")
2011: *Den enögda kaninen* ("The One-eyed Bunny")

The Detective Leo Junker Series:

2013: *Den osynlige mannen från Salem* (*The Invisible Man from Salem*, tr. n/a, 2015)
2014: *Den fallande detektiven* ("The Falling Detective")
2015: *Mästare, Väktare, Lögnare, Vän* ("Master, Security Guard, Liars, Friends")

Major Awards:

2013: Best Swedish Crime Novel of the Year for *Den osynlige mannen från Salem*

Website: http://christoffercarlsson.wordpress.com/ (author's blog)

Camilla Ceder

b. 1976; Residence: Goteborg, Sweden; Occupations: counselor and social worker, author

In an interview supplied by Wahlström & Widstrand, her literary representatives, Camilla Ceder, who has written since she was very young, notes that so many authors have inspired her that she cannot name them all. She says she does not do much research for her novels, instead visiting places for inspiration, drawing upon her own and others' emotions and moods, reading books, and sorting her thoughts through writing, which she always does "strictly for myself" (Wahlström & Widstrand interview). Her writing feels easiest when stories pop up quickly and she simply writes them down, but she finds it very difficult when "a big vacuum cleaner during the night [has] vacuumed up all the words," and often she says that she herself doesn't know how a story will develop, allowing her to be surprised as it unfolds (Wahlström & Widstrand interview).

Ceder's first novel, *Fruset ögonblick*, 2008 (*Frozen Moment*, tr. 2010), takes place in wintry rural Gothenberg, where life on antiquated farms and struggling small businesses is harsh. On his last day before retiring, Åke Melkersson discovers a dead body in a ramshackle garage and asks his young neighbor Seja Lundberg, a journalist, to stay with him while he calls the police. Inspector Christian Tell, struggling with his own emotional stresses, becomes romantically involved with Seja as they untangle old secrets and passions in this remote region. Critic Maxine Clarke found that this novel had "no surprises," but she praised Ceder's intention to portray the "region and its inhabitants and to look at cause and effect from many different perspectives" (Clarke). Ceder herself commented that she wanted to capture a feeling she had been experiencing for a long time, "the fading memory of a world that no longer exists…. I often think that the author's main purpose is to dream" (Ethan Jones Blog interview).

Ceder notes that Inspector Christian Tell, who also appears in *Babylon*, the 2010 sequel to *Frozen Moment*, is "pretty stuck in the [police] routines, a little square, but with a sensitivity (and an open-mindedness) that is not always as quick as his spontaneous reactions to change" (Ethan Jones Blog interview). Christian Tell and Seja Lundberg begin a relationship despite his fear of commitment and her continual attempts to smooth over their tensions, a relationship which reflects Ceder's professional concerns in counseling and social work. *Babylon* involves a double murder and a theft of artifacts stolen from an Iraqi museum, giving the novel an international flavor.

For her third novel in the series, Ceder intends to return to the rural Swedish setting of

Frozen Moment. Ceder believes that she avoids writing formulaic and commercial crime fiction by adhering to her own feeling for what is important and interesting, in her case the psychological and emotional tensions between her characters, probing deeply in their psyches to discover the motivations they hide from the outside world, the kind of selective repression she described in Seja's words: "'Memory is like a bloody sieve—you decide for yourself what you want to remember, depending on your self-image at the time'" (*Frozen Moment* 281). Since *Babylon,* Ceder has published *Djurfiket* ("Animal Diner"), 2014, the first installment of a humorous children's series.

Crime Novels:

Inspector Christian Tell Series:

2009: *Fruset ögonblick* (*Frozen Moment,* tr. Marlaine Delargy, 2010)
2010: *Babylon* (*Babylon,* tr. Marlaine Delargy, UK 2012)

Major Awards: N/A

Website: http://www.camillaceder.com

Marianne Cedervall

b. February 20, 1949, Hallandale Parish on Gotland, Sweden; Residence: Västerås, Sweden; Occupations: employers' consultant, author

After retiring from her work as an employers' consultant with the Swedish Church's employers' organization, Marianne Cedervall began her Miriam and Hervor cozy mystery series with *Svinhugg* ("Pork Chop"), 2009. Her heroines, two gently eccentric fifty-somethings in their first outing return to a picturesque village on the island of Gotland. Miriam, a physician, has retired after working for years in the remote north and Hervor, her longtime friend from Norrland, accompanies her to Gotland. The two are bent on avenging themselves on three men who defrauded Miriam of most of her property. For their second novel, *Svartvintern* ("Black Winter"), 2010, they travel to equally scenic Vittangigatan, returning to Gotland for *Spinnsidan* ("Spin Page"), 2010, and traveling to New York in *Stormsvala* ("Storm Petrel"), 2012. Cedervall's literary representative, the Grand Agency, lauds Cedervall's "unique and wonderful mix of saga, crime, and epic" as she comfortingly deals with "love, friendship, and revenge," but other commentators, less cozy-crime oriented, seem to feel that a beautiful summer in Gotland is not enough to raise her novels above the prosaic two dimensional plane (*SvD Kultur*).

Crime Novels:

Miriam and Hervor Series:

2009: *Svinhugg* ("Pork Chop")
2010: *Svartvintern* ("Black Winter")
2011: *Spinnsidan* ("Spin Page")
2013: *Stormsvala* ("Storm Petrel")
2014: *Solsvärta* ("Blackbird")

Major Awards: N/A

Website: N/A

*Arne Dahl (pseudonym of Jan Arnold)

b. January 11, 1963; Residence: unknown; Occupations: editor, literary critic, author

In an autobiographical statement on his website, Arne Dahl celebrates crime fiction as "the perfect tool to reach deep down into the contemporary human mind and society." Writing literary criticism and regular articles for Sweden's *Dagens Nyheter* under his own name, Jan Arnold, he uses the pseudonym "Arne Dahl" for his crime fiction, because, as he explained in a 2013 *Krimi-Couch* interview with Andreas Kurth, after five experimental mainstream novels as "Jan Arnald," he wanted "more body and more excitement and more readers," so in "a new birth" as a different person, he took the name "Arne Dahl" to write more about his environment (Kurth), and "to tell intriguing and captivating stories of a changing Sweden in a changing world" ("Interview with … Arne Dahl").

Arne Dahl also says he has no patience with boring literature. As a new father at thirty-five, he was planning his ten-book crime fiction series and influenced by the work of American crime author Ed McBain, he felt one protagonist would not suffice. Besides, he decided the field was overpopulated with characters he described as lonely drunken cops. His solution was the Intercrime series (called the "A-Team series" in Sweden), "a different dynamic between different police officers" on a highly specialized team whose members work simultaneously at different locations (Kurth). The series' initial novel, *Mysterioso*, 1999, which the author calls "the birth of Arne Dahl" ("Interview with … Arne Dahl") had a ten-month gestation. Dahl plans his work thoroughly, collecting ideas, plotting, researching, re-plotting—in this case, about five months for the pre-writing and another five for the actual writing, which he calls "pure pleasure," since he feels the police procedural ideally suits his purpose and personality ("Interview with … Arne Dahl").

The worldwide financial crisis of the mid 1990s sparked *Mysterioso*, where Dahl explores the multifaceted effects of the crisis on his characters' private lives. Detective Paul Hjelm is assigned to an elite task force, the Swedish equivalent of CSI, dedicated to apprehending a serial killer targeting powerful Swedish businessmen. To a rare illegal recording of Thelonius Monk's classic jazz recording "Mysterioso," the assassin breaks into each victim's home and kills him with two bullets to the head. In their pursuit of the killer, Hjelm, his young partner Jorge Chavez, and the rest of their team face not only the Russian mafia responsible for much of Sweden's current underworld activity but also a secret society of Sweden's wealthiest citizens. In addition, the team confronts the problems connected with the rapid influx of mostly Muslim immigrants that is exacerbating Swedish xenophobia.

Dahl's second novel in the Intercrime series, *Ont blod*, 1999 (*Bad Blood*, tr. 2013), sets Paul Hjelm's team to catch another serial killer, this one an American responsible for torturing a Swedish literary critic to death in a cleaning closet at Newark's International Airport. The killer then boarded a Stockholm flight with the victim's ticket and vanished. Hjelm and his assistant Kerstin Holm find that a torture method secretly developed during the Vietnam War was the trademark of the "Kentucky Killer," a homicidal sociopath thought to be dead. With more victims of the same *modus operandi* being found near Stockholm, Hjelm and Holm travel to New York to investigate the killer's background. Norway's *Aftenposten* commented that *Bad Blood* "expertly weaves together the American involvement in Vietnam with the current unfolding events in Iraq."

With Paul Hjelm at the forefront of the Intercrime cases, Dahl based them all on current changes in society. He made sure, too, that readers could read any book out of sequence as though it was a stand-alone novel. When he finished the ten novels he had originally intended, he had "some kind of anxiety about leaving them and wrote number eleven," *Elva* ("Eleven"), an unusual stand-alone book resembling both Agatha Christie's *Ten Little Indians* and the *Decameron.* In this genre-crossing adventure, Dahl brings the ten members of the Intercrime team together at a country house to compare notes, as they said they would at the end of *Himmelsöga* ("Eye in the Sky"), 2007. Their host turns out to be Arne Dahl himself, and they produce ten stories full of murders and writers, "realized fiction and fictionalized realities ... the barriers between life and death, literature and life, high and low, the original and the copied crumbling before our eyes" (see Arne Dahl's official website).

Arne Dahl still could not let his Intercrime characters go, so he launched the Opcop quartet, a new crime series using some figures from the Intercrime novels and addressing painful contemporary issues like amoral gene research and human trafficking. In considering the development of crime in Europe and the world today, Dahl had begun to find it odd that difficulties exist in cooperation between the police forces of the various European countries and that no international police force exists, so "why not try to create an operational European police unit?" He felt this was "not illogical" and "not unrealistic" because technology has changed police work dramatically (quoted in Kurth). So far four of the Opcop novels have been published. Dahl declared the series closed with the fourth novel, *Sista paret ut* ("Last Couple Out"), 2014.

Throughout his crimewriting career, which he calls the "loneliest job in the world," Dahl insists he relies on balancing his work with a functioning social and family life. He travels widely to absorb international atmosphere and meets as many people as he can when he is not writing, "Otherwise you'll probably get a little bit insane" (quoted in Jack). Dahl also maintains that balance is the crucial factor in creating effective detective fiction. "If one of the fundamental ingredients –plot, character, dialogue, environment, mystery, thrill, style—gets too dominant, that will hurt the whole story ... really good meals never stem from a strict recipe" (quoted in "Interview with ... Arne Dahl"). Dahl claims that his favorite writer is Shakespeare, because killing is life's most horrible crime, and "no one shows this better than the master himself ... every crime fiction writer should read *Macbeth* once a year" (quoted in "Interview with ... Arne Dahl"). For Dahl, the question behind his crime writing is always the same: "What is life really like? What is this short flash of light between two darknesses? How do we use this all too fleeting time in the most decent and enjoyable way? And why do we have such trouble doing it?" (quoted in Arne Dahl's official website).

Five of Dahl's Intercrime novels appeared in 2011 television adaptations, made by an international group of producers led by Filmlance, one of Sweden's largest independent television production companies, and the other five are currently in preparation for televising. The series was broadcast in Germany in November–December 2012 and on the UK's BBC Four from April to June 2013. It was broadcast in the United States through MHz Networks from November 2013 to January 2014. The television adaptation of Dahl's Stockholm novels replaces the unit's male leader Jan-Olav Hultin, with a female officer, Jenny Hultin. H.Z. Mason feels this gives the false impression that women detectives function equally as supervisors with male police authority figures, an impression that Dahl's original works does not support (Mason 16).

Crime Novels Written as Arne Dahl:

Intercrime Series, also known as the A-Team Series:

1998: *Mysterioso* (*Mysterioso*, tr. Tiina Nunnally, U.S. 2011; titled *The Blinded Man* in Nunnally's 2012 UK translation)

1999: *Ont blod* (*Bad Blood*, tr. Rachel Willson-Broyles, 2013)

2000: *Upp till toppen av berget* (*The Top of the Mountain*, tr. Alice Menzies, 2014)

2001: *Europa Blues* ("Europe Blues")

2002: *De största vatten* ("Many Waters")
2003: *En midsommarnattsdröm* ("A Midsummer Night's Dream")
2004: *Dödsmässa* ("Requiem")
2005: *Mörkertal* ("Hidden Numbers")
2006: *Efterskalv* ("Afterquake")
2007: *Himmelsöga* ("Eye in the Sky")

The Opcop Quartet:

2011: *Viskleken* ("Chinese Whispers")
2012: *Hela havet stormar* ("Musical Chairs")
2013: *Blindbock* (working title: "Blindfold")
2014: *Sista paret ut* ("Last Couple Out")

Stand-Alone Novel:

2008: *Elva* ("Eleven")

Major Awards:

2003: The Palle Rosenkrantz Prize (Denmark), for *Europa Blues* ("Europe Blues")
2005: *Deutscher Krimi Preis* (Germany), for *Upp till toppen av berget* (*To the Top of the Mountain*)
2006: *Deutscher Krimi Preis* (Germany), for *Europa Blues* ("Europe Blues")
2007: Special Award from the Swedish Crime Writers' Academy
2011: Best Swedish Crime Novel Award for *Viskleken* ("Chinese Whispers")

Website: http://english.arnedahl.net

Tim Davys (pseudonym)

b. ? ; Residence: New York, New York, USA; Occupation: author

"Tim Davys" is the pseudonym for a Swedish writer, possibly one who is already established in the field. *The Speculator*'s Paul Di Filippo conjectures Davys may be Swedish novelist Walter Moers, who also combines "whimsy, black humor, anthromorphicism and feralness" (Di Filippo). The tongue-in-cheek biographical statement from Davys' U.S. publisher, HarperCollins, indicates that he/she never read a book before the age of twenty, rather learning how to tell a story from comics, magazines, and movies. (References in the HarperCollins statement to "a wife" may or may not identify the writer's gender.) Davys has studied literature and psychology, and now sits in front of a computer too much, spends a lot of time traveling, and believes that "the idea going forward is to stay alive, write a lot more, and adapt to a life in New York City," but things never seem to turn out the way they were intended (HarperCollins statement).

Tim Davys has authored the Mollisan Town Quartet, where the titles of each novel refer to a quarter of Mollisan, a fictional city run by dark forces and populated by approximately a million plush stuffed animals who behave much as humans do, their good and evil exploits reflecting Davys' existential *noir* position: "Evil is impossible without goodness. Evil seeks balance ... I can be good on my own. But to manifest evil requires a counterpart" (quoted from *Amberville* in Thompson). *Amber Ville*, 2007 (*Amberville*, tr. 2009), introduces the hero Eric Bear and his old gang, who each carry a surname indicating his or her species: Eric's philosophizing brother Teddy Bear; Tom-Tom Crow; an enforcer, male prostitute and druggie Sam Gazelle; Emma Rabbit; and so on. Eric was a wild bear in his youth, but after marrying Emma Rabbit, his lifelong love, he has forsworn drugs and works for a famous advertising agency until his past mobster affiliations come back to haunt him. He rounds up his old friends to do battle with the Chauffeurs, who kidnap victims on a Death List late at night in an ominous red pickup.

The other novels of the group show equally tongue-in-cheek characters and situations. *Lanceheim*, 2008, named for the Teutonic district of Mollisan, contains both a stuffed-toy Moses figure who becomes the object of a messianic cult and a blasé hardboiled private eye named Philip Mouse, to comment on the ambiguous good-and-evil aspects of religious fervor. *Tourquai*, 2010, with its teeming urban setting, has police superintendent Larry Bloodhound hot on the trail of Oswald Vulture, a shady financier. *Yok*, 2012, set in the poorest, grungiest section of Mollisan, unites four disparate tales into one animal allegory of humanity's hope for overcoming wickedness and living a good moral life.

Individually and as a tetralogy Davys' works have received mixed reviews. Some critics find them slow-paced and feel that the concept of stuffed animals performing clearly impossible bodily functions like sweating stretch the suspension of disbelief too far, while others find Mollisan a satisfying, even thought-provoking, experience.

Crime Novels:

2007: *Amber Ville* (*Amberville*, tr. Paul Norlén, U.S. 2009)
2008: *Lanceheim* (*Lanceheim*, tr. Paul Norlén, U.S. 2010)
2010: *Torquai* (*Torquai*, tr. Paul Norlén, U.S. 2011)
2012: *Yok* ("*Yok*")

Major Awards: N/A

Website: N/A

*Anders de la Motte

> b. January 1, 1971, Sweden; Residence: Southern Sweden; Occupations: police officer, security director, international security consultant, author

Formerly a police officer and a security director for two large international IT firms, Anders de la Motte now writes witty, action-packed high-tech thrillers full of linguistic innovation which Denmark's *Literatursiden* called "pure entertainment." Prior to its full publication in English, de la Motte's [*geim*] (*sic*) (*Game*) trilogy had sold more than 200,000 copies in less than three years and was prepared as a full-length 2014 theater film.

Game, the award-winning first novel in de la Motte's high-tech Game Trilogy, released in English in 2013, features thirty-something Henrik ("H.P.") Pettersson, a small-time crook stalled emotionally at self-gratifying age 18. To balance his aimless anti-heroship, de la Motte created Detective Rebecca Normén of the Swedish Secret Service, whose controlling personality de la Motte thinks arose from his Swedish Lutheran background and his career in security ("Anders de la Motte Interviewed"). Henrik, sunk in marijuana and video games, becomes addicted to the thrill and rewards—the "Buzz"—of the large-scale "real" Alternate Reality Game, but he finally suspects that he is being watched continually both by the Game itself and by the police. Rebecca, too, feels stalked because enigmatic handwritten notes about her past keep appearing in her locker. Their worlds eventually mesh, and in *Buzz* and *Bubble*, Henrik and Rebecca collide with a huge organization that is using personal data to shape public opinion (Connolly). The trilogy thus poses one of today's most troubling dilemmas: how much information is too much to share?

Anders de la Motte believes that today's world has become fatally social media-obsessed. He compares the Facebook phenomenon, fueled, he says, by narcissism and desperation, with the credo of the Stasi, the fearsome East German secret police: "To be really safe, you need to know everything." To do this, the Stasi wanted half the population to be listening and reporting on the other half; "And look at us now –all this information that they were prepared to kill for, we provide ourselves" (quoted in Connolly).

Through Henrik, de la Motte's Game trilogy exposes the thirst for excitement coupled with the need for appreciation that de la Motte sees in Facebook addicts, providing a foundation of serious cultural commentary beneath a humorous surface of digital playfulness. De la Motte sees this unusual combination as an example of young Swedish crime authors' current success: "We are a small, slightly exotic country way up in the dark and cold north, sometimes seen as an ideal society. Mixing that with terrible crime or conspiracies creates a very interesting dynamic" ("Anders de la Motte Interviewed").

MemoRandom (*MemoRandom*), 2013, tr. 2014, first of a planned diptych, differs from its predecessors by being more *noir* with no real heroes. It revolves around David Sarac, a handler in the Intelligence Unit of the Stockholm Police Force who recruits informants and uses whatever means he can to deliver information to his superiors. He suffers a stroke and loses his memory, an enormous threat to his network of secret informers. The novel allows de la Motte to create another trenchant exploration of the impact that information technology is making upon today's society.

Crime Novels:

The Game Trilogy:

2010: *[geim]* (*Game*, tr. Neil Smith, 2013)
2011: *[buzz]* (*Buzz*, tr. Neil Smith, 2013)
2012: *[bubble]* (*Bubble*, tr. Neil Smith, 2013)

First Novel of a Planned Diptych:

2013: *MemoRandom* (*MemoRandom*, tr. Neil Smith, 2014)

Major Awards:

2010: Debut Crime Novel Award, the Swedish Crime Academy for *[geim]* (*Game*)

Website: N/A

Ulf Durling

b. 1940, Stockholm, Sweden; Residence: Sollentuna, Sweden; Occupations: psychiatrist, author

As a boy, Ulf Durling often listened to his father read classic literary mysteries by Agatha Christie and other Golden Age authors, and long afterwards, in the late 1960s, when Durling had become a psychiatrist and a clinical instructor in psychiatry, the notion of writing a whodunit detective novel struck him. *Gammal ost* ("The Old Cheese"), where three detective fans provide their theories about the same event, received the first Debut Prize awarded by the Swedish Crime Academy. Durling founded the Society of Forensic Authors in 1977, continuing to combine his psychiatric training with fiction to produce sixteen psychologically oriented crime novels and hundreds of short stories. Durling saw psychiatry as basing its understanding of problems in the human soul, when experiences cause emotional trauma, a worldview that closely approaches literature ("Presentation av Ulf Durling på *Foreningen Kriminalforfattare*").

Crime Novels:

1971: *Gammal ost* ("Old Cheese")
1972: *Hemsökelsen* ("Plague")
1975: *Säg PIP!* ("Say PEEP!")
1977: *Annars dör man* ("Otherwise You Die")
1980: *Min kära bortgångna* ("My Dear Departed")
1981: *Tack för lånet* ("Thanks for the Loan")
1983: *Lugnet efter stormen* ("The Calm After the Storm")
1985: *Aldrig i livet* ("Never in My Life")
1988: *In memoriam* ("In memoriam")
1990: *Synnerliga skäl* ("Specific Reasons")
1993: *Tills döden förenar oss* ("Until Death Unites Us")
1996: *Komma till skott* ("Getting the Shot")
1999: *Vilddjurets tal* ("Number of the Beast")
2001: *Domaredans* ("Judge's Dance")
2005: *Vägs ände* ("End of the Road")
2008: *Den svagaste länken* ("The Weakest Link")

Major Awards:

1971: Debut Crime Novel Award, for *Gammal ost* ("Old Cheese")
1983: Best Swedish Crime Novel, for *Lugnet efter stormen* ("The Calm After the Storm")
1983: The Sherlock Award, for *Lugnet efter stormen* ("The Calm After the Storm")

Website: N/A

Dagmar Edqvist

b. April 20, 1903, Visby, Sweden; d. January 21, 2000, Luleå, Sweden; Residence: Various; Occupation: author

According to *The History of Nordic Women's Literature*, between 1932 and 1985, Dagmar Edqvist authored more than twenty novels, most of them touching on problems relating to modern career women's attitudes toward men and love. Like other women writers of her generation, Edqvist, unlike those of feminists writing in the earlier decades of the Swedish women's movement, saw those problems as "private and marital rather than social and political" (Gustafson 528), a position particularly evident in Edqvist's novel *Kamrathustru* ("Companion Wife"), 1932. Her best known work is probably *Fallet Ingegerd Bremssen* ("The Case of Ingegerd Bremssen), 1937, an anti-racist novel "describing a rape from a psychoanalytical perspective" (Witt-Brattström) made into a 1942 film for which Edqvist wrote the screenplay.

Selected Crime Novel:

1937: *Fallet Ingegjerd Bremssen* ("The Case of Ingegjerd Bremssen")

Major Awards: N/A

Website: N/A

Carin Bartosch Edström

> b. 1965, Malmö, Sweden; Residence: Various, including Lund, Sweden; Occupation: composer, author

Carin Bartosch Edström, a composer with an international upbringing including time spent in the United States, graduated from Lund University's Malmö Academy of Music in 1999 and was elected to the Society of Swedish Composers in 2000. She wrote both the score and the libretto for a 1999 opera and the score for a 2005 one-act opera, *Huvudsaken* ("The Main Thing") with libretto by Kerstin Perski. Her only crime novel to date is *Furioso* ("Furioso"), 2011, a Christie-influenced whodunit that places four female *Furiosokvartetten* ("Furioso quartet") musicians on a secluded Swedish island to record the Swedish classic composer Stenhammar's final string quartet. When one of the group, Louise Armstahl, is injured and her close male friend, world famous violinist Raoul Liebekind, replaces her, old and new intrigues arise, and police commissioner Ebba Schroeder deals with the predictably consequent homicide.

Carin Bartosch Edstrom has observed that the "steaming passion of music" dominates her debut novel. Since chamber music drives the plot, she identifies each of her characters with the music closest to him or her. She points out one work in particular as most appropriate for a detective novel: Eugene Ysaye's second sonata, which quotes the medieval *Dies Irae*—the Day of Wrath (adlibris comments).

Crime Novel:

2011: *Furioso* ("Furioso")

Major Awards: N/A

Website: N/A

*Åke Edwardson

> b. March 10, 1953, Eksjö, Småland, Sweden; Residence: Gothenburg, Sweden; Occupations: journalist, press officer, educator, author

Åke Edwardson, a three-time winner of the Swedish Crime Writers Academy's Best Swedish Crime Novel of the Year Award, has drawn on his varied background as a journalist, United Nations press officer, and university professor for his ten-novel police procedural series featuring Gothenburg Inspector Erik Winter. Besides obvious resemblances to the Martin Beck series created by Sjöwall and Wahlöö and Henning Mankell's Wallander series, the Erik Winter series, Edwardson observes, was inspired by his admiration for the hard-boiled novels of Americans Ross Macdonald, Raymond Chandler, and in particular James Ellroy, whom Edwardson cites as the chief motivator for his crime fiction career ("Åke Edwardson," *Scandinavian Crime Fiction*).

Edwardson's sophisticated Erik Winter is as different from world-weary, Old Leftish Wallander as industrial Gothenburg is from Wallander's rural Ystad, but both detectives mourn the passing of traditional Swedish culture and the consequent decay of morals against which they stand, melancholy but unyielding ("Your Favorite Thrillers: Åke Edwardson"). Edwardson often juxtaposes Winter's past and present in the series, in some of the novels paralleling an old case from Winter's young days on the police force with one in his present time as a Chief Inspector, allowing Winter to observe changes in his city and himself. As Winter mused in *Rum nummer 10* (*Room No. 10*), seventh in the series, "the city had become a worse place to live during the nearly twenty years he had been a police officer here…. Like an ax to the skull on a mild spring evening" (*Room No. 10* 73). Interviewed in 2010 by Karin Fossum's translator K.E. Semmel, Edwardson also claimed he had decided to start with Winter as an insecure young man, good at police work but bad at everything else, especially relationships. Edwardson also intended that Winter be "someone on his way full throttle into the new millennium," letting him develop from being a snobbish couturier-dressed, hard to live with, and detached individual to being a husband and father. Winter originally wore his designer suits as a medieval knight wore his armor, and Edwardson said at first it didn't help much; Winter had to learn how to be a decent human being, and "It's a damn hard thing" (quoted in Semmel).

Edwardson's crime novels, about half of his literary output, often feature wayward teenagers or abducted children (Clarke), symptoms of the degradation of Swedish society that many of its crime writers today deplore. Although Winter and his crime team work out of Gothenburg, Edwardson also uses foreign settings based on his own travels. In *Rop från långt avstånd*, 1998 (*The Shadow Woman*, tr. 2010), Edwardson treats his character Helene Andersen as an orphaned and traumatized human casualty of crime, who therefore can never achieve intimacy with any other human being, a treatment of crime's emotional impact which Edwardson believes must balance with plot to produce effective crime fiction (Semmel). The sequel to this novel, *Sol och skugga*, 1999 (*Sun and Shadow*, tr. 2005), takes Winter to Costa del Sol, where his father is recovering from a heart attack. Expecting his first child, Winter finds his time in Spain allows him to reflect on his own life, while on his return to Gothenburg he faces a double murder whose perpetrator seems to be directing the investigation.

In *Låt det aldrig ta slut*, 2000 (*Never End*, tr. 2006), Edwardson shows Erik Winter troubled by the unsolved five-year-old rape and murder case of victim Beatrice Wagner, with Winter and his detectives Fredrik Halders and Swedish-African Aneta Djanali all interviewing another rape victim, assaulted in the same place as Wagner. That interview proves so fruitless that Winter begins to doubt if anyone can be trusted in a world where everyone is a victim. This methodical investigation also includes two other touchy issues. One is racism, because both Djanali and one victim are black, and the other is the romantic tension between Djanali and Halders, who is mourning his divorce and struggling to raise his two young children by himself. Both *New York Times* crime critic Marilyn Stasio and *Invisible Mentor* reviewer Avil Beckford felt *Never End* suffered from a draggy translation that kept the novel's pace "positively glacial" (Stasio) and "too North American" (Beckford). In the next Winter novel, *Himlen år en plats på jorden*, 2001 (*Frozen Tracks*, tr. 2007), Winter has to deal with two apparently unrelated cases, one involving nightly attacks on college students in Gothenburg's parks, and the other the strange daylight abductions and returns of youngsters from day care centers. As he discovers connections between the two crimes, the perpetrator gradually and frighteningly closes in on Winter's own family.

In a 2002 interview with Julia Buckley, Edwardson described the admiration he shares with other Scandinavian crime authors for Shakespeare's *Macbeth*. He used many allusions from the play in his 2002 novel *Segel av sten* (*Sail of Stone*, tr. 2012), where Erik Winter and his friend McDonald visit the site of Cawdor Castle while investigating the disappearance of a man whose daughter Winter was once romantically involved with. This novel also reveals Edwardson's existential focus, especially evident in Winter's recognition of his inherent restlessness, which Edwardson feels was both a result of Winter's being drawn to police work in the first place. Edwardson believes being a detective involves pressure and desperation that is "like a drug. The only other profession I can compare it with is writing." To stave off the depression he always experiences, Edwardson told Buckley, he laughs a lot and allows Winter, in contrast to the utterly *noir* figures in James Ellroy's fiction, to have hope, making him at the close of this novel ready to embrace "a new era" (quoted in Buckley).

Edwardson feels that the success of 2005's *Rum nummer 10* (*Room No. 10*, tr. 2013), considered his best Winter novel, is due to what a Swedish critic called his "intelligent procrastination of tension," since in two deliberately intertwined narratives he presents Erik Winter as a mature investigator and as a young man (quoted in Hagenguth). The dual perspective arises because when Winter is called to a decrepit Gothenburg hotel where a young woman has been found hanged, he realizes that he was in the same hotel room years before, on a similar case that has never been solved.

Edwardson had announced that the tenth Winter novel, *Den sista vintern* ("The Last Winter") in which he leaves his hero stricken with a cerebral hemorrhage, his fate uncertain, would close the series, but after two years. Erik Womter returned to service with his old associates Frederick Halder and Aneta Djanali in *Hus vid världens ände* ("The House at the End of the World"), 2012. His latest Winter novel, *Marconi Park*, 2013, is named for a residential area in Gothenburg where Winter faces puzzle-like serial murders. It has been widely hailed as one of Edwardson's best crime novels

As the Winter series progressed, Edwardson maintained that writing a good crime novel is almost the hardest thing a writer can do, because the challenge lies in the writer's attitude. "The overall 'truth' of my crime novels is that you can never escape the shadows of your past; they will track you down wherever you hide. And it's all about human behavior" (quoted in Semmel).

Crime Novels:

Chief Inspector Erik Winter Series:

1997: *Dans med en ängel* (*Death Angels*, tr. Ken Schubert, 2009)

1998: *Rop från långt avstånd* (*The Shadow Woman*, tr. Per Carlsson, 2010)

1999: *Sol och skugga* (*Sun and Shadow*, tr. Laurie Thompson, 2005)

2000: *Låt det aldrig ta slut* (*Never End*, tr. Laurie Thompson, 2006)

2001: *Himlen år en plats på jorden* (*Frozen Tracks*, tr. Laurie Thompson, 2007)

2002: *Segel av sten* (*Sail of Stone*, tr. Rachel Willson-Broyles, 2012)

2005: *Rum nummer 10* (*Room No. 10*, tr. Rachel Willson-Broyles, 2013)

2006: *Vänaste land* ("Vanaste Country")

2007: *Nästan död man* ("The Almost Dead Man")

2008: *Den sista vintern* ("The Last Winter")

2011: *Hus vid världens ände* ("The House at the End of the World")

2013: *Marconi Park* ("Marconi Park")

Stand-Alone Crime Novel (Debut):

1995: *Till allt som varit dött* ("To All Who Have Died")

Major Awards:

1995: Best Swedish Crime Novel, for *Till allt som varit dött* ("To All Who Have Died")

1997: Best Swedish Crime Novel, for *Dans med en ängel* (*Death Angels*)

2001: Best Swedish Crime Novel, for *Himlen är en plats på jorden* (*Frozen Tracks*)

Website: http://akeedwardson.com

Niklas Ekdal

b. May 6, 1961, Sävsjövägen, Sweden; Residence: Stockholm, Sweden; Occupations: journalist, political editor of *Dagens Nyheter* (Sweden's *Daily News*), 2001–2009; author

Niklas Ekdal served as a United Nations officer in Lebanon during the 1980s and in Saudi Arabia during 1961's Desert Storm conflict. He has also worked as a foreign policy analyst and his extensive experience in editing includes a specialization in politics. Since 2006 he has appeared as the host of *Studio Ekdalsvägen*, an award-winning alternative Swedish cultural and social television program. That year he was listed sixth in a listing of Sweden's most influential figures, after finishing tenth the previous year in *Elle* Magazine's list of Sweden's sexiest men.

Ekdal's 2008 historical political thriller *I döden dina män* ("The Death of Your Men") treats metaphysical issues in the Swedish soul. *Kvinnan utan egenskaper*, 2010 ("Woman Without Qualities"), involves power, medicine, and morality, welding two plots together to criticize aspects of recent Swedish history. Here a psychiatrist who is searching for her daughter, gone missing from her studies at Oxford, also had a patient who was recently murdered, possibly due to his denunciation of medical exploitation, especially the Swedish mid-twentieth century policy of forcibly institutionalizing and sterilizing the "feeble-minded." Critic Darcy Hurford found this long, detail-packed novel compelling, reflecting social change and social fears, though she also believed that "the minutiae of the characters' daily lives" indicated the journalist's ambition to document them more fully than perhaps is necessary (Hurford).

Thrillers:

2008: *I döden dina män* ("The Death of Your Men")
2010: *Kvinnan utan egenskaper* ("Woman Without Qualities")

Major Awards: N/A

Website: N/A

Jan-Olof Ekholm

b. October 20, 1931, Grytnäs, Sweden; Residence: Stockholm, Sweden; Occupations: journalist, author of children's, young adult, and adult crime fiction

After publishing eight children's books, Jan-Olof Ekholm turned to adult crime fiction with 1968's *Sista resan—Mord!* ("Last Trip—Murder!") starring anti-hero Goran Sandahl, a bumbling small town reporter with a penchant for not recognizing the truth until it is too late (Blom 23). Sandahl's environment was intimately familiar to Ekholm because he himself had worked for ten years for three rural Swedish newspapers. He subsequently wrote thirty-plus whodunits and contributed short stories to several short fiction anthologies. He was elected to the Swedish Crime Academy in 1974 and became a member of Stockholm's Society of Forensic Authors in 1977.

Selected Adult Crime Novels:

1968: *Sista resan—Mord!* ("Last Trip—Murder!")
1984: *Stark såsom döden* ("Strong as Death")

Major Awards:

1979: Best Swedish Crime Novel, for *Mälarmördaren* ("Malaren Murderer"), a documentary Ekholm co-authored with Sven Sperrlings

Website: N/A

*Kerstin Ekman

> b. August 27, 1933, Risinge, Sweden; Residence: Valsjoebyn, Sweden; Occupations: documentary filmmaker, teacher, author

As one of Sweden's most distinguished novelists, in 1978 Kerstin Ekman became the third woman (after Selma Lagerlöf and Elin Wagner) elected to the Swedish Academy, but she left the Academy in 1989 in protest at the Academy's tepid defense of author Salman Rushdie when he received death threats issued by Muslim clerics. The rules of the Academy specify that she will remain a member for life.

Ekman's literary career began with six conventional detective novels, set in the far north of Sweden, where she was born and still lives. In *De tre små mästarna*, 1961 ("The Three Little Masters"), Police Constable Torsson, a conventional policeman from southern Sweden, and David Malm, his amateur sleuth and friend, confront a suspicious death related to a young girl's suicide some time earlier, about which the Sami villagers maintain a conspiracy of silence. The novel's strength "lies primarily in the evocation of the landscape—desolate expanses of mountains, forest, and marshland hidden in months-long darkness or bathed in continual light—and in the insightful portrayal of collective village mentality" (Wright 67).

In the early 1990s, Ekman moved away from the straightforward crime story with its rational cause-and-effect structure to "the functions of myth, imagination and memory," in narratives that eschew crimes of commission for either obscure acts that "generate ripples of unforeseen consequences or, in the context of social injustice, 'crimes against humanity'" (Paterson), often in relation to Ekman's perseverant theme, the societal and psychological changes that modernization of society has forced upon the people of Sweden's far north. Between 1974 and 1983, she produced *Kvinnorna och stadien* ("Women and the City"), a quartet of novels dealing with the transformation of Katrineholm from a small town on a railroad main line into a modern industrialized city.

After moving to northern Sweden in the early 1980s, Ekman surprised herself by returning to the detective genre with the award-winning and best-selling *Håndelser vid vatten*, 1993 (*Blackwater*, tr. 1995). Set again in the far north, this novel shows that road-building, logging, and mining are changing the landscape forever and disrupting both Swedish and Sami residents, while in significant contrast, migrants from Sweden's southern industrial cities are arriving in hopes of living a peaceful life with nature. Tensions mount and two tourists are axe-murdered, their killings left unsolved, with painful reverberations in the small closed community; then eighteen years later, another homicide occurs and two separate murderers are identified, but "their punishment is grief and isolation; more we are not told" (Paterson).

Ekholm's most recent fiction is the *Vargskinnet* ("Wolfskin") trilogy written from 1999 to 2003, a powerful treatment of the effects on a rural village of the modern large-scale logging industry, told over two centuries and "showing how old practices have become crimes as the wilderness was tamed. One crime haunts the narrative and is a core element of the trilogy" (Clarke). Again, "as in so many of Ekman's novels, a crime infects the body of the story, but we are never quite sure what happened—let alone why" (Paterson).

Crime Novels:

1959: *30 meter mord* ("30 Meters Murder")
1960: *Han rör på sig* ("He Moves")
1960: *Kalla famnen* ("Cold Arms")
1961: *De tre små mästarna* (*Under the Snow*, tr. Joan Tate, 1998)
1962: *Den brinnande ugnen* ("The Fiery Furnace")

1963: *Dödsklockan* ("Death Clock") (made into a movie in 1999)
1993: *Händelser vid vatten* (*Blackwater*, tr. Joan Tate, 1995)

The Wolfskin Trilogy:

1999: *Guds barmhärtighet* (*God's Mercy*, tr. 2003 by Linda Schenk)
2002: *Sista rompan* ("Final Rump")
2003: *Skrapplotter* ("Scratch")

Major Awards:

1961: Sherlock Award for *De tre små mästarna* (*Under the Snow*)
1993: Best Swedish Crime Novel for *Händelser vid vatten* (*Blackwater*)
1994: Nordic Council Literary Prize for *Händelser vid vatten* (*Blackwater*)

Website: N/A

*Jan Ekström

> b. 1923, Falun, Sweden; d. February 8, 2014, Stockholm, Sweden; Residence: Stockholm, Sweden;
> Occupations: advertising executive, author

Often described as "the Swedish John Dickson Carr," Jan Ekström, a long-time member of the Swedish Crime Academy, was best known in Sweden for his intellectual whodunits starring red-haired opera devotee and detective Bertil Durell, who solved painstakingly constructed mysteries notable for their lack of bloody violence. Ekström debuted in 1962 with *Döden fyller år* ("Death's Birthday") and in 1967 published *Ålkistan* ("The Eel Chest"), one of Sweden's best examples of the locked-room mystery. Another locked-room story, Ekstrom's only novel to have been translated into English, *Ättestupan*, 1975, tr. 1983 as *The Ancestral Precipice* and also called *Deadly Reunion*, brings fifteen squabbling family members to the home of their wealthy relative Charlotte Lethander to help her celebrate her approaching ninetieth birthday. The abundant family secrets gradually unravel and soon two relatives are found dead in an apparent murder-suicide that turns out to involve a cleverly disguised homicide in a bedroom locked from the inside. Involved complications follow for some 400 pages in a brooding Lew Archer–type atmosphere until Durell achieves a clever solution. Swedish commentators find the novel a satisfying puzzler, though an American *Kirkus Review* critic compared its English version in 1983 to "an overgrown, thickened version of Christie's old-fashioned (but crisp) family-gathering mysteries." *The Ancestral Precipice* is, however, listed in Ed Gorman's *The World's Finest Mystery and Crime Stories* (2001).

Selected Crime Novels:

1962: *Döden fyller år* ("Death's Birthday")
1963: *Träfracken* ("The Wood Tuxedo")
1967: *Ålkistan* ("The Eel Chest")
1975: *Ättestupan* (*The Ancestral Precipice*, tr. Joan Tate, 1983, also titled *Deadly Reunion*)

Major Awards:

1963: The Sherlock Award, for *Döden fyller år* ("*Death's Birthday*")
1997: Grand Master Diploma of the Swedish Crime Writers Academy

Website: N/A

Ingrid Elfberg

> b. August 9, 1958, Östersun, Jämtland County, Sweden; Residence: Gothenburg, Sweden; Occu-
> pations: advertising and IT development, author

According to her website, Ingrid Elfberg's first novel, *Gud som hover* ("The God Who Loves"), 2009, a psychological thriller, sold 40,000 copies in Sweden and has been published in Norway and Germany as well. Set in Gothenburg with glimpses of Jämtland and Härjedalen, it deals with the abduction of a two-year-old boy by a pedophile. Elfberg says "life came between" her debut novel and her second, *Tills döden skiljer oss åt* ("Deceived"), 2013, which explores the ominous theme "A policeman does not beat his wife." Elfberg believes her writing, sensitive treatments of painful Swedish social issues, "is driven by my fascination with what we humans do to each other … jealousy, control needs, hatred, envy, greed, passion, love, survival" (from Elfberg's website).

Crime Novels:

2009: *Gud som hover* ("The God Who Loves")
2013: *Tills döden skiljer oss åt* ("Deceived")

Major Awards:

2004: The Ballograf Prize, awarded by the Ballograf Company and the newspaper *Espressen* for the year's best crime short story, for "The Tempest"; the judge was Håkan Nesser.

Website: http://www.ingridelfberg.se

Thomas Engström

> b. 1975; Residence: Skåne Söderslätt, Sweden; Occupations: journalist, translator, author

Thomas Engström holds a law degree from Lund University and writes about politics and culture for both Sweden's *Fokus*, a weekly newspaper, and the daily *Svenska Dagbladet*. He has also translated more than twenty works by Barack Obama, Mark Bowden, and others from English to Swedish. He began a series of international political thrillers with his third novel, *Väster om friheten*, 2013 ("West of Liberty"), featuring freelance investigator Ludwig Licht, a former up-and-coming Stasi (East German secret police) agent who was an invaluable informer for the CIA for many years. Licht, in 2011 a depressed freelancer, is severely indebted to a Moldavian criminal, but he is sent to Berlin to find a woman who called the American embassy there with information about three Americans who were found dead in Marrakech. *Söder om helvetet* ("South of Hell"), its sequel, set in rural Pennsylvania and Washington, D.C., during the 2012 U.S. presidential campaign, appeared in 2014.

Thrillers:

2003: *Mörker som gör gott* ("Darkness Does Good")
2006: *Dirty Dancer* ("Dirty Dancer")

Ludwig Licht Thrillers:

2013: *Väster om friheten* ("West of Freedom")
2013: *Söder om helvetet* ("South of Hell")

Major Awards:

2013: Best Swedish Debut Crime Novel, for *Väster om friheten* ("West of Freedom")

Website: N/A

Jerker Eriksson and Håkan Axlander Sundquist (pseudonym *Erik Axl Sund*)

Jerker Eriksson: b. 1974, Gävle, Sweden; Residence: Stockholm, Sweden; Occupations: music and film producer and editor, prison librarian, author

Håkan Axlander Sundquist: b. 1975, Linköping, Sweden; Residence: Stockholm, Sweden; Occupations: artist, imprisoned for "total refusal"; manual laborer

Partners Jerker Eriksson and Håkan Axlander Sundquist share a mutual interest in contemporary music. While Eriksson was producing performances for Sundquist's electropunk band "iloveyoubaby!" on a tour through eastern Europe, each began individually to write a first novel. Eventually marrying Eriksson's tightly organized style to what they call Sundquist's "ADHD-related verbiage," the pair has produced a crime trilogy called "*Victoria Bergmans svaghet* ("Victoria Bergman's Weakness"), with female central figures Detective Superintendent Jeanette Kihlberg and psychotherapist Sofia Zetterlund. In the first installment, *Kråkflickan* (*The Crow Girl*, tr. 2015), Sofia is treating both her middle-aged patient Victoria Bergman, traumatized in childhood, and a young boy from Sierra Leone exhibiting a multiple personality disorder when she and Jeanette, with whom Sofia is beginning a romantic relationship, are drawn into a murder investigation that forces them to confront the moral question of how much suffering a perpetrator can inflict before he or she ceases to become human. In *Hungerelden* ("Hunger Fire"), the second novel of the trilogy, the women face another brutal homicide while their relationship deepens, and in the third, *Pythians anvisningar* ("Pythia's Instructions"), Victoria undertakes self-therapy while Sofia assists Jeanette in her search for the men who injured the youthful Victoria and also Victoria's daughter Madelaine, against the backdrop of Babi Yar, the infamous Nazi killing field in Ukraine.

Regarding their literary partnership, Erikson and Sundquist comment on their joint website that their key issues are embodied in the questions, What creates a perpetrator? When does the victim become an abuser? When does crime become attributable to earlier abuse? "It's about psychology," they insist. "Jerker is the therapist and Håkan [the] patient. We are two people talking to each other. Analyzing each other. The writing is really psychotherapy" (quoted in "Eriksson/Axlander–Sundquist").

Crime Novels:

Victoria Bergman's Weakness Trilogy (also called The Melancholy Trilogy):

2010: *Kråkflickan* (*The Crow Girl*, tr. Neil Smith, 2015)
2011: *Hungerelden* ("Hunger Fire")
2012: *Pythians anvisningar* ("Pythia's Instructions")

Major Awards: N/A

Website: http://krakflickan.se/eas.html

*Kjell Eriksson

b. 1953, Uppsala, Sweden; Residence: Uppsala, Sweden, and Brazil; Occupations: union activist, horticulturist, author

Kjell Eriksson, who has cited American Dennis Lehane, Scottish authors Denise Mina and Ian Rankin, and fellow Swede Henning Mankell as his favorite crime authors (Strainchamps), describes the main purpose of his own crime novels as "to describe my home town, my society, the conflict between east and west" (quoted in Rozovsky). Elsewhere Eriksson has claimed, "I want to experience and deliver suspense…. I write about death, about the unexpected punch, the swing of a knife, the hands around the neck … the shot in the dark, and the deep, senseless fear. But most of all, I write about my life, my hometown, and the world surrounding it" (Eriksson, "Behind the Headlines" 47).

In Eriksson's debut novel, *Knäppgöken* ("The Weirdo"), 1993, he explored the plight of society's outcasts—dropouts, the unemployed, and those made redundant—that seems to grow as living conditions change, a theme that he continues to incorporate into his crime novels. He received the Swedish Trade Union's Ivar-Lo Prize for his work "where the mundane, the community, cohesion and solidarity are the main and prime incentives" (Leonardt & Høier). Eriksson's "unique achievement" has been described as crafting "a richly layered novel packed with sublime character detail out of which his murder puzzle seamlessly emerges" (*Kirkus Reviews* 2005).

Eriksson's crime novels have earned considerable recognition in Sweden. The first novel in Eriksson's Ann Lindell crime novel series, *Den upplyste stigen* ("The Illuminated Path"), 1999, received the Swedish Crime Writers Academy Debut Prize; Eriksson's next two novels, *Jorden må rämna* ("Earth Might Rend"), 2000, and *Stenkistan* ("The Stone Coffin"), 2001, were shortlisted for the Academy's Best Crime Novel Award; and the fourth, *Prinsessan av Burundi* (*The Princess of Burundi*), 2002, did receive that award.

As a novelist, Eriksson especially succeeds in his realistic depiction of characters. He bases them on residents of Uppsala with whom he feels a special kinship: "They are my neighbors" (quoted in Rozovsky, "Evening"). His protagonist Ann Lindell is a workaholic Detective Inspector in the Uppsala police Violent Crimes Division, a single mother of a little boy. In *The Princess of Burundi* Eriksson intertwines two plots, one the killing of an unemployed welder, the other the interplay of Uppsala police detectives, especially Ola Haver and Ann Lindell, who cope with each other's differences in order to right wrongs, "a conscious homage to Ed McBain's 87th Precinct novels" (Clarke). *Nattens grymma stjärnor* (*The Cruel Stars of the Night*), 2004, tr. 2007, has Ann tentatively reaching out to a new relationship with one of her colleagues while probing the disappearance of a local professor. Seventh in the series, *Mannen från bergen* (*The Demon of Dakar*), 2005, tr. 2008, sympathetically features impoverished Mexicans in Sweden who have been involved in drug smuggling, and *Den hand som skälver*, 2007 (*The Hand That Trembles*, tr. 2009), takes Ann into a cold case of a fatal beating being investigated by her boss. In *Svarta lögner, rött blod*, 2008 (*Black Lies, Red Blood*, tr. 2014), Ann has found love with Anders Brant, a warmhearted journalist quite different from all her failed earlier attachments, but after he disappears and becomes the prime suspect in another missing person case, Ann begins to experience tormenting doubts. *Öppen grav*, 2009 (*Open Grave*, tr. 2015), parallels events from Ann's past with nefarious actions taken against a winner of the Nobel Prize for Medicine.

Interviewed in 2012, Eriksson claimed he created his characters by mixing real and invented people, which he calls a freedom that is "pure happiness for a novelist." Another joy for him is writing about "the whole Sweden, not just the urban, chic areas, the cities … [but] ordinary, humble people" not seen in smart magazines or on television shows (Strainchamps). Eriksson's major achievement is creating "a believable universe of people … [who] are multifaceted and complex, and it's difficult to judge any of them too harshly—even the killer" (*Boston Bibliophile*).

Crime Fiction:

The Ann Lindell Series:

1999: *Den upplyste stigen* ("The Illuminated Path")
2000: *Jorden må rämna* ("Earth Might Rend ")

2001: *Stenkistan* ("The Stone Coffin")
2002: *Prinsessan av Burundi* (*The Princess of Burundi*, tr. Ebba Segerberg, 2006)
2003: *Nattskärran* ("The Nut Jar")
2004: *Nattens grymma stjärnor* (*The Cruel Stars of the Night*, tr. Ebba Segerberg, 2007)
2005: *Mannen från bergen* (*The Demon of Dakar*, tr. Ebba Segerberg, 2008)
2007: *Den hand som skälver* (*The Hand That Trembles*, tr. Ebba Segerberg, 2011)
2008: *Svarta lögner, rött blod* (*Black Lies, Red Blood*, tr. Paul Norlén, 2014)
2009: *Öppen grav* (*Open Grave*, tr. Paul Norlén, 2015)

Major Awards:

1999: Best First Novel, Swedish Crime Academy for *Den upplyste stigen* ("The Illuminated Path")
2002: Best Swedish Crime Novel for *Prinsessan av Burundi* (*The Princess of Burundi*)

Website: http://www.ordfront.se/Bocker/Varaforfattare/KjellEriksson.aspx

Bertil Falk

b. 1933; Residence: N/A; Occupations: journalist, editor, translator, lecturer, author

Bertil Falk, a veteran crime reporter for Sweden's *Kvällsposten* (*Evening Post*) principally wrote collections of short crime fiction often blended with fantasy or science fiction techniques, such as "Locked Rooms and Open Spaces and Crime—the Swedish Way." He translated his own work into English including fourteen mystery and science fiction novels, all published in Sweden. In 2009 he produced a notable short-story detective pastiche, "As in a Dream," featuring a figure he had often used earlier, a nameless detective working in Malmö. He is currently working on a comprehensive literary history of Swedish science fiction beginning in the 1600s.

Selected Fiction:

1996: *Mord på mäfä* (*Murder at Random*)
2009: *Liksom i en dröm* (*As in a Dream*)
2010: *Mind-Boggling Mysteries of a Missionary*

Nonfiction and Anthologies:

2008: *Crime—The Swedish Way*
2008: *Locked Rooms and Open Spaces*

Major Awards: N/A

Website: N/A

*Aris Fioretos

b. February 6, 1960, Gothenburg, Sweden; Residence: Berlin, Germany; Occupations: poet, literary critic, university professor, author

Literary scholar Aris Fioretos, Counselor for Culture at the Swedish Embassy in Berlin, studied in Stockholm, at Yale University, and with Jacques Derrida in Paris. Fioretos set his one crime novel *Sanningen om Sascha Knisch*, 2002 (*The Truth About Sascha Knisch*), tr. 2006, in 1928 Berlin, Weimar Germany's hotbed of decadence. His unreliable eponymous narrator, a cross-dresser, had a close relationship with Dora, an occasional prostitute who is apparently murdered by an unknown intruder, and becomes the prime suspect in her death. Fioretos' theme highlights the wide variety of dubious theories of sexuality at a time when the Nazi movement was rising, soon to attempt eradication of what it felt to be perverse anti–German activity. Fioretos conceived of this novel as second in a trilogy which would take a different bodily organ as a point of departure, the first, *Stockholm noir*, dealing with the brain; *The Truth About Sascha Knisch*, the testicles; and the third, as yet unwritten, to deal with emotion (Jarzebinski).

Crime Novel:

2002: *Sanningen om Sascha Knisch* (tr. by himself as *The Truth About Sascha Knisch*, 2006)

Major Awards:

2009: The Gleerups Literary Prize, for *Den sista greken* ("The Last Greek")
2013: The Grand Prize of the Nine Society literary academy "for a transnational authorship, marked by brilliance, humor and warmth"

Website: N/A

Ramona Fransson (Ramona Danlén, Ramona Danlén Fransson)

b. March 23, 1956. Borås, Sweden; Residence: Tjörn, Sweden; Occupations: school economist, publisher, author

In her author's statement for Anomar Publishers where she is a partner, Ramona Fransson says she writes books to shake off all of her frustration, anger, and imagination. Injustice angers her most, especially the lack of help from the Swedish government for people who are sick or debilitated, and so she wants her self-published novels to speak for them. Fransson's conventional police procedural series follows the investigations of Reconnaissance Chief Gregor Thulin and Detective Superintendent Catherine Engman, who work on the west coast of Sweden.

Crime Novels:

2006: *Iskall hämnd* ("Ice-Cold Revenge")
2007: *Mord i Skärhamn* ("Murder in Skärhamn)
2009: *Lyckohjulet* ("Wheel of Fortune")
2010: *Mord under Tjörn Runt* ("Murder in Tjörn Around")
2012: *Hämnaren från Tjörn* ("The Tjörn Eagle")
2013: *Mord på Stenungsbaden Yacht Club* ("Murder at the Stenungsbaden Yacht Club")
2014: *Korsfäst på Kladesholmen* ("Crucified on Kladesholmen")
2015: *Gift med djävulen* ("Married to the Devil")

Major Awards: N/A

Website: http://ramona-fransson.blogspot.com

Nils-Olof Franzén

b. August 23, 1916, Oxelösund, Sweden; d. February 24, 1997, Stockholm, Sweden; Residence: Stockholm, Sweden; Occupations: program director, Swedish Radio, 1956–1973; author of biographies and crime fiction

Nils-Olof Franzén wrote eleven popular young adult detective novels set in London, starring boy sleuth Agathon Sax and Scotland Yard Detective Inspector Lispington, originally intended for his son, from 1955 to 1978.

Selected Young Adult Mystery Novels (translators' names not available):

1955: *Agaton Sax klipper till* (*Agathon Sax and the Big Rig*, published 1976)

1959: *Agation Sax och de slipade diamanttjuvarna* (*Agathon Sax and the Diamond Thieves*, published 1965)

1978: *Agathon Sax och den mörklagda ljusmaskinen* (*Agathon Sax and Lispington's Grandfather Clock*, published 1978)

Major Awards: N/A

Website: N/A

Inger Frimansson

> b. November 14, 1944, Stockholm, Sweden; Residence: Bergviksgatan in Södertälje, Sweden; Occupations: journalist, poet, author of young people's and adult fiction

Inger Frimansson, the only woman to have twice won the Swedish Crime Writers Academy Award for Best Swedish Crime Novel of the Year, likes to switch between different genres. Her searing adult psychological novels push the limits of psychological thrillers, as seen in her breakthrough novel *God natt min älskade* (*Good Night, My Darling*), 1998, tr. 2007, which was inspired by a bullying incident Frimansson had witnessed as a child when boys shoved a girl's face into the snow, causing her to suffer a serious asthma attack. Much later, after she had become an author, Frimansson wondered, "I had to help her get revenge, but how? … I decided to send her out into the world so she could kill" (quoted in Rozovsky, "Evening"). Frimansson's heroine Justine Salvik, a well-to-do eccentric fortyish woman, still suffers from childhood abuse carried out by her archetypically wicked stepmother Flora. As Justine's thirst for revenge, which she thinks of as justice, mounts, the horrors around her begin to escalate in a novel that is not so much a whodunit but a "how-could she-do-it" which forces readers to look into the mind of a black soul. Seven years later, Frimansson followed *Good Night, My Darling* with *Skuggan i vattnet* (*The Shadow in the Water*, tr. 2008), which many commentators find even more disturbing than the first volume of this diptych, since Justine feels increasing pressures from the ramifications of her earlier actions, with a dogged policeman who has his own violent tendencies opening up the old cold cases Justine thought were buried forever.

Frimansson's other novels couple modern tragedies with chilling psychological insights. Her 2002 novel *De nakna kvinnornas ö* (*The Island of the Naked Women*, tr. 2009) again deals with guilt and innocence, life and death, in the context of a father-son conflict: young Tobias, a mystery writer, returns to his family's farm and falls in lust with his father's young wife Sabina, only to be observed by an ill-wishing neighbor, a situation rife with horrifying possibilities. Frimansson's most recent novel to appear in English, 2000's *Katten som inte dog* (*The Cat Did Not Die*, tr. 2013), builds on a brutal crime in rural Smaland, where Beth and Ulf, a middle-aged couple, have come to find peace after their premature twins died soon after birth. One evening after too much to drink, a panic-stricken Beth axe-murders a stalker who seems to have been haunting them. She and Ulf bury him behind the outhouse, but both actual and psychological recriminations inevitably ensue. The couple try to escape by taking a position in Tanzania, where catastrophe meets them in a near-unbearable climax.

Frimansson says she differs from most other crime authors because "I write from inside the mind (and heart) of the murderers, from inside the unhappy, mostly quite common persons who suddenly find themselves in a situation they can't extricate themselves from in ways other than by using violence" (Frimansson, "The Company I've Kept" 51). Having authored more than twenty novels, young adult books, and poetry collections, Inger Frimansson says that she has often been asked, "You look so nice and decent, how is that you write such horrific novels? ... And the answer is, I don't exactly choose to. I more or less was compelled to. The characters I meet up with in my fictions, they just seem to take over" (quoted in Clarke, "SinC25").

Selected Crime Novels/Psychological Thrillers:

1999: *Mannen med oxhjärtät* ("The Man with the Ox Heart")
2000: *Katten som inte dog* (*The Cat Did Not Die*, tr. Laura A. Wideburg, 2013)
2001: *Ett mycket bättre liv* ("A Much Better Life")
2002: *De nakna kvinnornas ö* (*The Island of the Naked Women*, tr. Laura A, Wideburg, 2009)
2003: *Mörkerspår* ("Hidden Tracks," "Night Song")
2009: *Råttfångerskan* ("The Rat Keeper")

Justine Dalvik Diptych:

1998: *God natt min älskade* (*Good Night, My Darling*, tr. Laura A. Wideburg, 2007)
2005: *Skuggan i vattnet* (*The Shadow in the Water*, tr. Laura A. Wideburg, 2008)

Major Awards:

1998: Best Swedish Crime Novel, for *God natt min älskade* (*Good Night, My Darling*)
2005: Best Swedish Crime Novel, for *Skuggan i vattnet* (*The Shadow in the Water*)

Website: http://www.frimansson.se

Eva Gabrielsson

b. November 17, 1953; Residence: Stockholm, Sweden; Occupations: translator, essayist, computer-aided designer, architectural author; writer, feminist activist

As Stieg Larsson's partner for three decades, feminist activist Eva Gabrielsson lived closely with his creation of the Millennium Trilogy. In her own right, she is a translator and an author of nonfiction works, including a book criticizing Swedish law regarding unmarried couples, which prevent her from inheriting any of the profits from his writing. For a long time Gabrielson has been preparing a large-scale study of the Stockholm architect and city planner Per Olof Hallman; Larsson used her research for that project in his famous novels: "all the good guys in the [Larsson's] books live in areas planned by Hallman" (Holmberg 96). Gabrielson's memoir "There Are Things I Want You to Know: About Stieg Larsson and Me," appeared in Swedish in 2011 and in English translation by Linda Coverdale, 2012.

Crime Fiction (Short Story):

2014: "Paul's Last Summer"

Major Awards: N/A

Website: N/A

Per Gahrton

b. February 2, 1943, Malmö, Sweden; Residence: Malmö, Sweden; Occupations: politician, author

Per Gahrton has served in the Swedish Parliament for most of his adult life, first as a Member of Parliament for the Liberal Party, and later for the Green Party. In the 1994 referendum, he opposed Sweden's membership in the European Union, to which Sweden now belongs. He is currently the president of the Swedish Association for Solidarity with Palestine.

Gahrton published a political thriller, *EU-politikerns död* ("Life and Death in the European Parliament"), 2004. Some members of the parliament accused him of committing near-plagiarism in this novel to cash in on Dan Brown's *The Da Vinci Code*, then leading Swedish bestseller lists. Gahrton subsequently decided to distribute his book himself through Books-on-demand.

Selected Thriller:

2004: *EU-politikerns död* ("Life and Death in the European Parliament")

Major Awards: N/A

Website: http://mo.se/pergahrton.asp

*Carin Gerhardsen

b. December 6, 1962, Katrineholm, Sweden; Residence: Östermalm, Stockholm, Sweden; Occupations: mathematician, IT consultant, author

Carin Gerhardsen made her literary debut in 1992 with a philosophical novel, *På flykt från tiden* ("Escape from Time"), but her love of mathematical problems and puzzles brought her to writing crime fiction. Since 2008 she has published seven police procedurals set in southern Stockholm, led by Detective Inspector Conny Sjöberg who heads a team of characters that Gerhardsen says she herself likes to explore. In a 2012 interview, Carin Gerhardsen cited the three most important things her crime writing must be: "thrilling, credible, and captivating." She energizes her novels through exciting parallel plots and rapid filmic cuts, and for credibility, she ensures the story "must work all the way to the end." So that her stories must also captivate both herself and her readers, "I step inside all my characters, minor as well as main characters, murderers or victims" (quoted in Rudolph).

Most of the crimes in Gerhardsen's Hammarby series are violent, even brutal, involving children and victimized women. They generally accompany traumatic stresses in the lives of Gerhardsen's detective team and reflect similar events in the author's own life. *Pepparkakshuset*, 2008 (*The Gingerbread House*, tr. 2012), for example, depicts bullying in schools; Gerhardsen says writing it came easily to her, because she had experienced such harassment herself as a child. The chief message of her novels clearly insists that everyone "should take responsibility for the well-being of the people around us" (quoted in Rudolph), and she created variations on that theme throughout the series. *Vyssan lull* ("Hush, Little Baby"), 2010, confronts the Hammarby team with the execution-style killing of a Filipino woman and her two small sons in their home. Despite individual personal problems DI Sjöberg and his team are facing—Jens Sanden is recovering from a heart attack, Petra Westman is seeking the identity of her rapist, and Sjöberg himself has learned one of his grandmothers he believed was dead, still lives—Sjöberg maintains a sensitive and conscientious investigation. In *Helgonet* ("The Saint"), 2011, set at Christmastime, the team, now joined by Odd Andersson, an amateur rock musician, and Hedvig Gerdin, the middle-aged widow of a diplomat, pursues the killer of a beloved philanthropist. In *Hennes iskalla ögon* ("Her Icy Eyes"), 2013, set in a frigid Stockholm winter, the team members each encounter ominous shadows from the past while they battle cases of physical and emotional abuse where often evil disguises itself as love and preys on the most vulnerable victims.

According to Carin Gerhardsen, "the best crime novels contain much more than the actual crime," so she made her detectives resemble most of the people she knows, "nice, friendly" and honest without any drinking problems (quoted in Rudolph). Accordingly, admirers of her work find that "her novels linger in the mind long after the finish" (Rudolph).

Crime Novels:

Hammarby Crime Series:

2008: *Pepparkakshuset* (*The Gingerbread House*, tr. Paul Norlén, 2012)
2009: *Mamma, pappa, barn* ("Mother, Father, Children" tr. Paul Norlén, 2013)
2010: *Vyssan lull* ("Hush, Little Baby")
2011: *Helgonet* ("The Saint")
2012: *Gideons ring* ("Gideon's Ring")
2013: *Hennes iskalla ögon* ("Her Icy Eyes")
2014: *Tjockare än vatten* ("Thicker Than Water")

Major Awards: N/A

Website: http://www4.hemsida.net/gildaojenny/hammarbyserien/cms

Malin Persson Giolito

b. 1969, Stockholm, Sweden; Residence: Brussels, Belgium; Occupations: lawyer, author

Malin Persson Giolito is the daughter of criminologist and crime author Leif G.W. Persson. She graduated from Uppsala University's law school in 1994 and originally envisioned a career in international law, specializing in human rights. At twenty-seven she received a position with the large law firm of Mannheimer Swartling, "a conservative bastion" whose unofficial motto was "Up or Out." After several hectic workaholic years trying to balance the demands of work and family, she learned she could not become a partner and thus had no future with that firm, so she turned her feelings of revenge into her debut crime novel, *Dubbla slag* ("Double Blow"), 2008. In a 2009 interview, she observed that similar women's problems "can be changed" by achieving a gender balance in management, matching capable women with the needs of organizations. She now works as a public employee for the European Union Commission in Brussels, and her husband, who is French, is beginning to assist with household responsibilities (Power).

Crime Novels:

2008: *Dubbla slag* ("Double Blow")
2010: *Bara ett barn* ("Only a Child")
2012: *Bortom varje rimligt tvivel* ("Beyond All Reasonable Doubt")

Major Awards: N/A

Website: http://malinsblogg.piratforlaget.se (author's blog)

Tage Giron

b. December 22, 1922, Karlskrona, Sweden; d. March 13, 2010, Stockholm, Sweden; Residence: Karlskrona, Sweden; Occupations: shipbroker, author

Tage Giron and eleven other crime fiction enthusiasts founded the Swedish Society of Crime Authors (FKIS), an organization which existed from 1982 to 2009 to promote fellowship among crime authors. He himself made his literary debut in 1963 with *Maskerad* ("Masquerade"), and continued a gently humorous police procedural series starring Commissioner Erik Holmberg for thirteen more books, in which Holmberg investigated old cold cases by probing situations in which individuals changed because of events they would rather forget (Noren).

Selected Crime Novels:

1963: *Maskerad* (*"Masquerade"*)
1966: *Gift in i döden* ("Married into Death")
1977: *Blodsvittnet* ("Blood Witness")
1981: *Ond cirkel* ("Vicious Circle")
1991: *Bankrånarna* ("Bank Robbers")

Major Awards:

1966: The Sherlock Award, for *Gift in i döden* ("Married into Death")

Website: http://www.keg.se/tg.html

Peter Gissy

b. April 21, 1947, Landskrona, Sweden; Residence: Gothenburg, Sweden; Occupations: translator, adult and children's crime author

Between 1996 and 2002 Peter Gissy wrote several well-received thrillers featuring sleuth Kent Land. Gissy then began the "Jill and Jonathan" series of children's detective books for which he is best known. He has also produced three "Diagnosis-sleuths" medical thrillers about emergency physician Robert Kruger, set in Sahlgrenska, Sweden.

Crime Novels:

1996: *Röd död* ("Red Death")
1997: *Vit sorg* ("White Grief")
1998: *Blå åtrå* ("Blue Lust")
2000: *Svart hämnd* ("Black Revenge")
2002: *Fallet Ewenius* ("The Ewenius Case")
2004: *Mam med kapuschong* ("Man with a Hood")
2006: *Diagnos: mördad* ("Diagnosis: Murder")
2007: *Diagnos: strypt* ("Diagnosis: Strangled")
2008: *Diagnos: gisslan* ("Diagnosis: Hostage")
2010: *Gul ondska* ("Yellow Gold")

Major Awards:

2002: Year's Best Mystery Short Story

Website: http://www.petergissy.se

*Camilla Grebe and Åsa Träff

Camilla Grebe: b. 1968; Residence: Stockholm, Sweden; Occupations: economist, publisher, author
Åsa Träff: b. 1970; Residence: Älvsjö, Sweden; Occupations: clinical psychologist, author

Sisters Camilla Grebe, who founded the audiobook publishing firm Story Side and now runs her own telecommunications consulting business, and Åsa Träff, a behavioral psychologist specializing in cognitive behavioral therapy, have united their professions and talents in their psychological thrillers starring Dr. Siri Bergman, a thirty-four-year-old psychologist who lives alone in a cottage outside Stockholm. In the sisters' first crime novel, *Någon sorts frid*, 2009 (*A Kind of Peace*, tr. 2012), Siri attempts to deal with a traumatic secret in her past by shutting herself off from most of her friends and drinking too much. She suspects she is being stalked when her young patient Sara Matteus, a victim of drugs and sexual abuse, is found dead, floating in the water near Siri's cottage. In the subsequent investigation, Markus, a sympathetic young policeman; Siri's professional mentor; and Aina, her best friend, help Siri profile the stalker, but her ability to distinguish past from present begins to disintegrate, leading to a shattering climax that fellow crime author Kristina Ohlsson found "utterly intriguing." The second novel in the series, *Bittrare än döden*, 2010 (*More Bitter Than Death*, tr. 2013), presents disturbing scenes of vicious domestic abuse; a five-year-old child witnesses her mother being kicked to death by a boyfriend with a history of violence, and Siri, now attempting to adjust to her own improved domestic situation, again finds her professional and personal lives becoming blurred. A *Crimepieces* reviewer finds the graphic depictions of the killings involved lend the novel "an air of unreality" that weakens it. The third novel in the series, *Innan du dog* ("Before You Die"), 2011, finds Siri and Markus settling into parenthood when a brutal crime provokes memories of her ex-husband, a suicide, that rise up to haunt her, causing her recollections of the late 1980s, when yuppies frantically pursued fate and fortune, to disrupt her equilibrium again.

Crime Novels:

Siri Bergman Series:

2009: *Någon sorts frid* (*A Kind of Peace*, tr. Paul Norlén, 2012)
2010: *Bittrare än döden* (*More Bitter Than Death*, tr. Paul Norlén, 2013)
2011: *Innan du dog* ("Before You Die")

Major Awards: N/A

Website: N/A

Jan Guillou

b. January 17, 1944, Södertälje, Sweden; Residence: Stockholm, Sweden; Occupations: journalist, publisher, author

As an investigative reporter in the early 1970s, Jan Guillou, then a member of the Maoist Communist Party of Sweden, sparked a major political scandal by uncovering a secret Swedish intelligence agency (*Informationsbyrån*, or "IB") gathering data on Swedish Communists and others considered by the government to be security risks. Beginning in 1967, Guillou had also been paid by the Soviet secret police (KGB) to write reports on Swedish politics. In 2009 the Swedish tabloid *Expressen* exposed Guillou's *sub rosa* activities, referring to him as a secret Soviet agent. Today Guillou describes himself as a far-left socialist. With author Liza Marklund and his wife

Ann-Marie Skarp, Guillou owns *Piratförlaget* (Pirate Publishing), one of Sweden's largest publishing houses. He writes a column for the Swedish tabloid *Aftonbladet,* where following the 2001 terrorist attack on the U.S. World Trade Center he called the U.S. "the great mass murderer of our time" and described the bombings as "an attack on U.S. imperialism" (*"Tre aldrig..."*).

From 1986 to 2008, Guillou produced a twelve-book series of thrillers featuring Swedish military spy Carl Hamilton, a fictional leftist character called *"Coq Rouge"* ("Red Rooster") who had trained as a U.S. Navy SEAL. Guillou based several characters in the series on real individuals, including himself as "Erik Ponti," the name he used in his 1981 autobiographical novel *Ondskan* ("The Evil"), which deals with boarding-school violence. "The Evil" was made into an award-winning Swedish film in 2003 which was nominated for an Academy Award in 2003, but Guillou, who is still listed by the United States as a terrorist, could not get a ticket to attend the Oscar ceremony. Several other films and four television adaptations of the *Coq Rouge* novels have been made. Guillou has also written the historical "Crusades Trilogy" about a fictional medieval Swedish character forced to become a Knight Templar.

Selected *Coq Rouge* Novels:

> 1986: *Coq Rouge* ("Red Rooster")
> 1990: *Den hedervärde mördaren* ("The Honorable Murderer")
> 1996: *Hamlon* ("Hamlon")
> 2006: *Madame Terror* ("Madame Terror")
> 2008: *Men inte om det gäller din dotter* ("But Not If It Concerns Your Daughter")

Major Awards:

> 1988: Best Swedish Crime Novel Award, for *I nationens intresse* ("In the Nation's Interest")

Website: N/A

Varg (Wolf) Gyllander

> b. 1964, Skåne, Sweden; Residence: Essingeöarna, Sweden; Occupation: crime reporter, chef, teacher, naval officer, police press officer, author

In 2009 Gyllander, currently Head of Press for Stockholm's National Police, opened his five-novel police procedural series featuring forensic scientist Ulf Holtz and Pia Levin. He described his crime novels in a 2012 interview as "low-key and bloodless," because he prefers to focus on people's lives and failings, not on violence. Gyllander feels an effective detective story should have engaging and complex characters, with a convincing plot. He also insists that all of his books are "hidden messages" about contemporary issues that affect the whole community, made up of people who struggle with their ordinary problems and personal failings. He further believes that the "insatiable" Swedish craving for detective fiction in his opinion seems a good thing, because competition forces all the genre's practitioners to be better writers (quoted in Hallberg).

Crime Novels:

Ulf Holtz and Pia Levin Series:

> 2009: *Somliga linor brister* ("Some Ropes Break")
> 2010: *Bara betydelsefulla dör* ("Only Important People Die")
> 2011: *Det som vilar på botten* ("What Rests on the Bottom")
> 2012: *Ingen jord den andra lik* ("No Land Is Ever the Same")
> 2014: *Min är hämnden* ("Vengeance Is Mine")

Major Awards: N/A

Website: http://www.varggyllander.se

Olle Häger

> b. September 19, 1935, Söderala, Sweden; d. November 1, 2014, Stockholm, Sweden; Residence: Stockholm, Sweden; Occupations: documentary filmmaker, historian, television producer, author

Olle Häger, well known for both documentary filmmaking and for historical writings, had a special interest in portraying human lives in the context of community development. His two detective novels are distinguished for their intrinsic humor, poking fun at Swedish institutions like professional hockey, which he treats in "The Bandy Player Who Disappeared in Gambia" as involving cheer chants that excite the home team to great efforts and provoke the audience to sacrifice substantial funds in sausages.

Crime Novels:

1991: *Bandyspelaren som försvann i Gambia* ("The Bandy Player Who Disappeared in Gambia")

1993: *Skratta får du göra i Sibirien* ("You Get to Laugh in Siberia")

Major Awards:

1991: Best Swedish Debut Crime Novel Award, for *Bandyspelaren som försvann i Gambia* ("The Bandy Player Who Disappeared in Gambia")

Website: N/A

Ingrid Hedström

> b. June 2, 1949, Söderhamns congregation, Hälsingland; Residence: N/A; Occupations: journalist, psychologist, author

Ingrid Hedström initially wrote for *Internationale*, the Communist Workers' Union journal, then started the women's magazine Q in 1981. From 1992 to 1997 she worked in Brussels as a correspondent for *Dagens Nyheter*. After attending a course in Wales on writing detective fiction conducted by British authors Denise Mina and Val McDermid, Hedström launched her award-winning feminist crime series in 2008, set in the fictional Belgian village of Villette and centered on examining magistrate Martine Poirot and her Swedish husband Thomas Heger. Hedström famously summed up her feminist perspective by insisting in a 2012 article that Christmas preparations, which her colleague Kerstin Hallert called "the Swedish woman's *burqa*," bombard women with images of "idealized femininity, just as seductive as ruthlessly demanding." Hedström urged that women today adopt the riotous pre–Christian "longest night" celebration, in which women abandoned their kitchens, dressed in animal masks and toured the countryside uninhibited: "Let us ... violate the norm, throwing [the] apron and skip[ping] the Christmas baking!" (quoted in Hedström, "Let's Embrace...") Her main character's surname refers to Agatha Christie's master sleuth Hercule Poirot.

In *Bortfall* ("Dropout"), 2014, Hedstrom opened a new detective series featuring Astrid Sammils, set in Dalarna, Sweden.

Crime Novels:

Martine Poirot Series:

2008: *Lärarinnan i Villette* ("The Teacher in Villette")
2009: *Flickorna i Villette* ("The Girls in Villette")
2010: *Under jorden i Villette* ("Underground in Villette")
2011: *Blodröd måne över Villette* ("Blood Red Moon Over Villette")
2012: *Svarta korpar över Villette* ("Black Ravens of Villette")

Astrid Sammils Series:

2014: *Bortfall* ("Dropout")
2015: *Måltavla* ("Target Plate")

Major Awards:

2008: Best Debut Crime Novel Award, for *Lärarinnan i Villette* ("The Teacher in Villette")

Website: N/A

Björn Hellberg

b. August 4, 1944, Borås, Sweden; Residence: Laholm, Sweden; Occupations: sports reporter, tennis authority, television personality, author

Since 1981, popular tennis authority Björn Hellberg has published more than sixty books of various kinds, including twenty-one light police procedurals originally set in a small fictional Swedish town resembling his home town of Laholm, featuring Superintendent Sten (Stone) Wall, whose cases address topical issues like bullying, racism, idolatry, Satanism, religious fanaticism, etc. According to Hellberg as cited on his Swedish Wikipedia page, when the voluptuous actress Jayne Mansfield gave a press conference in Kristianstad where Hellberg, then a 23-year-old journalist interested in "female geography," was then working, he was smitten by her "topographic perfect example—like an Italian switchback" and became inspired to start writing crime novels. After the Mansfield press conference he took his hero's name from the first person he met, one Lars-Göran Sten Wall, which Hellberg abbreviated to "Sten (Stone) Wall."

Hellberg still lives in his childhood home in Laholm, because he has a passion for the Swedish culture that animates such places, surviving what he calls "the 60 and 70s grating hysteria" (quoted in Rystad). Hellberg's mother often read two or three mysteries a week, which Hellberg feels was instrumental in keeping the genre close to his heart, and he seems never to have tired of writing about his hero Sten Wall. His native town seems never to have tired of Hellberg, either, for they have named both a street and a chocolate confection, the Hellbergare, after him. He was elected to the Swedish Tennis Hall of Fame in 2011.

Selected Crime Novels:

Superintendent Stone Wall Series:

1981: *Gråt i mörker* ("Crying in the Dark")
1996: *Dä dagboken dog* ("Then the Diary Died")
2001: *Den grå* ("The Grey")
2006: *Dödslängtan* ("Death Desire")
2013: *Skumrask* ("Shady")

Major Awards:

2006: Temmelburken Detective Prize

Website: N/A

Ann-Christin Hensher

b. 1948; Residence: Marbella, Spain; Occupations: lawyer, author

Former social law attorney Ann-Christin Hensher, now retired, says she finds her detective novels a joy to create. The first installment of her Ulrika Stäl series came to Hensher almost in its entirety when she was stuck in a rain-soaked Brussels traffic jam. Her protagonist Ulrika Stäl, a lawyer with a stay at home husband, seemed to choose Hensher, not the other way around, and after her first story, Hensher felt she had so much more to tell about Ulrika that she "continued to kill people so that she would be employed" (quoted in "Detective Focus" interview). Hensher drew facets of her heroine's personality from her female legal colleagues and friends, then seasoned Ulrika with "a pinch of male bad habits. How could I reasonably leave her aside?" (quoted in "Detective Focus" interview).

Crime Novels:

Ulrika Stäl Series:

2000: *Skulden till Daniel* ("The Debt to Daniel")
2002: *I orätta händer* ("In the Wrong Hands")
2004: *I lögnens spår* ("In the Lie Track")
2006: *Naken ängel* ("Naked Angel")
2007: *Kobrans öga* ("Cobra Eye")

Major Awards: N/A

Website: http://www.achensher.com

*Marie Hermanson

b. 1956, Sävedalen, Sweden; Residence: Gothenburg, Sweden; Occupations: journalist, author

Marie Hermanson briefly worked as an assistant in a Lillhagens mental hospital, an experience which influenced her later production of psychological thrillers. On her website, Hermanson describes her lengthy process of writing a novel, which typically takes her several years from the inception of an idea to the actual writing, usually one to two years more. She feels her stories are created "unconsciously in the brain, just like dreams," so that for her, her books are like waking dreams, "messy, illogical, and almost impossible to explain," and so she must consciously shape them into readable stories. Besides her early favorite authors, Ray Bradbury, Michel Tournier, and Italo Calvino, Hermanson cites several "sensible, English-speaking women" whose work she often reads: Anne Tyler, Ruth Rendell, P.D. James, Joyce Carol Oates, and others, reflecting Hermanson's interest and proficiency in depicting abnormal psychology. *Himmelsdalen,* 2011, her first novel to appear in English translation (*The Devil's Sanctuary,* tr. 2013), is a "twisted thriller" involving twin brothers in an exclusive Swiss psychiatric clinic. When one brother, Daniel, caught in financial difficulties, visits his brother Max at remote Himmelstal to seek help (they were raised separately), Max reveals he himself is in debt to the Mafia and suggests they exchange places so he can take care of the problem. After Max leaves, Daniel realizes that taking back his own identity will pose dangerous problems (*Publishers Weekly* review). Hermanson's 2014 novel *Skymningslandet* ("Receding") traces the entry of two twenty-somethings into an elderly woman's fantasy world, with dangerous results.

Crime Novels:

1990: *Snövit* ("Snow White")
1993: *Tvillingsystrarna* ("Twin Sisters")
1995: *Värddjuret* ("The Host Animal")
1998: *Musselstranden* ("Musselstranden")
2001: *Ett oskrivet blad* ("A Clean Sheet")
2004: *Hembiträdet* ("Maid")
2005: *Mannen under trappan* ("The Man Under the Stairs")
2007: *Svampkungens son* ("The Mushroom King's Son")
2011: *Himmelsdalen* (*The Devil's Sanctuary*, tr. Neil Smith, 2013)
2014: *Skymningslandet* ("Receding")

Major Awards:

2012: "Your Book—Our Choice" Award, the Swedish Bookstore Labourers' Association, for *Himmelsdalen* (*The Devil's Sanctuary*)

Website: http://www.mariehermanson.se

Michael Hjorth and Hans Rosenfeldt

Michael Hjorth: b. May 13, 1963, Visby, Sweden; Residence: N/A; Occupations: television and film writer and producer, advertising writer

Hans Rosenfeldt (born Hans Petersson): b. July 13, 1964, Borås, Sweden; Residence: Täby, Uppland, Sweden; Occupations: radio and television writer and host

After studying in New York, Michael Hjorth began work as a scriptwriter at Swedish Television, where he created the first successful Swedish sitcom, *Svensson, Svensson*, which earned the Golden Gate Award. He since co-founded Sweden's largest independent production company. With Hans Rosenfeldt, a screenwriter and radio and television personality who created the Danish-Swedish detective series *The Bridge*, an international hit, Hjorth has written three crime novels starring forensic psychologist and profiler Dr. Sebastian Bergman. In a reversal of the more usual development pattern of book-to-television series, *Det Fordölda* ("The Secret," titled in English *Dr. Sebastian Bergman*) had already been made as a television series when the pair turned it into a novel that became an international success even before it had been published in Sweden. Hjorth noted, "We have worked backwards this time. The stories in the books are becoming more complex than the TV version," because they can develop the concepts more, making the television series and the books completely different" (quoted in Creates).

The complex protagonist of the Hjorth Rosenfeldt crime novels is Sebastian Bergman, an "arrogant antihero" with a "mysterious past" that left him washed up in his profession as a criminal psychologist. Hjorth says that Bergman solves cases not with a gun (he does not own one), but with his head (Creates). Bergman's wife and child died in the 2004 Indian Ocean earthquake and tsunami, and after abusing drugs and alcohol, he developed a reputation as an arrogant sex addict, seducing fortyish women and abandoning them before the next morning. He is "a bastard," Hjorth says, "who makes it easy to hate him," but one with "a very brilliant mind" (quoted in Creates). Having departed on grounds of misbehavior from earlier police work, he returns to settle his mother's estate in Vasteras, his genteel home town, and through a chance meeting with a former police colleague, he becomes a consultant to the international police task force, "Unit One," on a serial homicide case involving a missing boy found murdered. In a shocking twist, he discovers that the young woman detective he finds objectionable is actually his illegitimate daughter from a relationship he had nearly forgotten. In his second case, Bergman experiences even more personal involvement, because each of the three female victims was one of his former lovers (Barkman). According to Rosenfeldt, "It's always more fun to play the villain as the hero" (quoted in Creates).

Feature-length stand-alone episodes of *The Condemned*, the British title of the television series featuring Dr. Sebastian Bergman and the Unit One Homicide Squad, were previously broadcast on Christmas Day and Boxing Day 2010 by BBC 1, with 1.1 million viewers each, nearly 35 percent of the viewing audience. Two new episodes were broadcast on December 25 and 26, 2011. A Swedish police procedural series based on the first two Hjorth-Rosenfeldt Sebastian Bergman novels opened with English subtitles in late 2014 on MNZ in rotation with other international mysteries.

Crime Novels:

Sebastian Bergman Series:

2010: *Det fördölda* (literally, "The Cursed One," *Sebastian Bergman*, tr. Marlaine Delargy, 2012)
2011: *Lärjungen* ("The Disciple")
2012: *Fjällgraven* ("The Mountain Tomb")
2014: *Untitled #4* ("Untitled #4")

Major Awards: N/A

Website: N/A

Olle Högstrand

> b. September 18, 1933, Arjang, Sweden; d. March 16, 1994, Johanneshov, Sweden; Residence: Sweden; Occupations: journalist, author

Olle Högstrand served as the press officer for the Swedish United Nations contingent during the 1960s Congo crisis and later worked for a prominent Swedish news agency. He is best known for his police procedural novel *Skulden* ("The Debt") which was made into a popular 1982 Swedish television series.

Selected Crime Novels:

1971: *Maskerat brott* ("The Masked Criminal")
1973: *Skulden* ("The Debt")
1979: *När hela socknen brann* ("When the Whole Parish Burned")

Major Awards:

1971: The Sherlock Award, for *Maskerat brott* ("The Masked Criminal")

Website: N/A

Bo R. Holmberg

> b. 1945, Ytterlännäs parish, Ångermanland, Sweden; Residence: Örnsköldsvik and Norrfällsviken, Sweden; Occupations: teacher, author

Bo R. Holmberg has published more than forty books, including children's and young people's novels, historical and contemporary mainstream fiction, graphic novels and crime novels, though he specializes in young people's literature. In crime fiction, he is best known for *Liemannen* ("The Grim Reaper"), 2002, a historical thriller, and in 2010 he published an adult crime novel, *Knivsliparen* ("The Knife Grinder").

Selected Crime Novels:

　2002: *Liemannen* ("The Grim Reaper")
　2010: *Knivsliparen* ("The Knife Grinder")

Major Awards:

　2002: The Flint Ax Award for Best Historical Thriller, for *Liemannen* ("The Grim Reaper")

Website: http://www.borhomberg.net

Hans Holmér

> b. December 28, 1930, Stockholm, Sweden; d. October 4, 2002, Alstad, Sweden; Residence: Stockholm, Sweden; Occupation: police official, author

Hans Holmér served as Chief of SÄPO, the Swedish National Security Service, from 1970 to 1976. In 1984 he became head of Stockholm County's Police, and during 1986–1987 he headed the special investigative unit working on the assassination of Prime Minister Olof Palme, which has never been solved. As a member of the Social Democrat party, Holmér was accused of favoring their positions, and his conduct of the Palme investigation, to which he had appointed himself as chief and in which he concentrated on trying to prove the guilt of the Kurdish liberation group PKK, caused his removal from the investigation and his resignation as County Police Chief in 1987. He spent the rest of his life writing moderately successful police procedural crime novels and has been the subject of many conspiracy theories surrounding the Palme affair.

Terroristerna (*The Terrorists*), 1975, the final novel in the Martin Beck series by Maj Sjöwall and Per Wahlöö, includes a Chief of the Secret Police character modeled on Holmér. In this fictional book, written a decade before the actual Palme assassination, Palme is killed by a totally inexperienced young woman protester.

Selected Crime Novels:

　1990: *Loppan* ("Flea")
　1996: *Cykeln* ("Cycle")
　2002: *Mardröm i midsommartid* ("Nightmare in Midsummer")

Major Awards: N/A

Website: N/A

Tord Hubert (Lindström)

b. 1933; Residence: Höganäs, Sweden; Occupations: human rights activist, photographer, author

Tord Hubert Lindström, who published as "Tord Hubert," wrote six crime novels between 1966 and 1982. In a 2009 tribute to Hubert, Christer Johansson found Hubert's political thrillers "magnificent" and "internationally recognized," and highly relevant today. They feature Peter Ross, Hubert's alter ego, whom Johansson compared to Modesty Blaise, a famous British comic strip heroine prone to hilarious adventures, unarmed combat, and the use of unusual weaponry. Johansson wondered why Hubert's work had been forgotten in only seventeen years and interviewed the author, who has been traveling extensively with his wife, engaging in Third World development activities and producing illustrated articles promoting human rights issues. Johansson concluded that Huber's fiction seems far ahead of its time in theme and development. Hubert himself indicated that he would write no more crime novels or thrillers because he feels that no appropriate publisher for his work would be available today (Johansson).

Crime Novels:

Peter Ross Series:

1966: *Fjällhöga mord* ("Mountain High Murder")
1967: *Mord och morske män* ("Murder and Morske Men")
1970: *Ett mord i vägen* ("A Murder in the Road")
1974: *Fällan* ("The Trap")
1976: *Den andres död* ("The Other's Death")
1982: *Den omänskliga faktorn* ("The Inhuman Factor")

Major Awards:

1970: The Sherlock Award, for *Ett mord i vägen* ("A Murder in the Road")
1976: The Sherlock Award, for *Den andres död* ("The Other's Death")

Website: N/A

Catharina Ingelman-Sundberg

b. 1948, unknown; Residence: Various; Occupations: diving archaeologist, journalist, author

Catharina Ingelman-Sundberg worked for fifteen years as a diving archaeologist, exploring all kinds of sunken wrecks, from Viking long ships to Dutch East Indiamen cargo ships. She has also sold more than 300,000 copies of her books in Sweden, including historical novels and non-fiction historical and archaeological texts. Her two cozy, "gently humorous and pleasantly daft" crime novels (Wilon) star septuagenarian "criminal mastermind-cum-philanthropist Martha Andersson and her League of Pensioners." In both 2012's *Kaffe med Rån* (*The Little Old Lady Who Broke All the Rules*, tr. 2013), and its 2014 sequel *Låna är silver, Råna är guld* (*The Little Old Lady Who Struck Lucky Again!*, tr. 2015) Martha and her crew carry out zany wealth-distributing schemes, even in the latter novel holding up a Las Vegas casino on motorized wheelchairs and taking on a local biker gang after they return to Stockholm (Wilson).

Crime Novels:

2012: *Kaffe med Rån* (*The Little Old Lady Who Broke All the Rules*, tr. Rod Bradbury, 2015)

2014: *Låna är silver, Råna är guld* (*The Little Old Lady Who Struck Lucky Again!* tr. Rod Bradbury, 2015)

Major Awards:

1999: Lars Widding Prize, for historical fiction

Website: http://www.catharinaingelman-sunberg.com

Inger Jalakas

b. December 15, 1951, Nässjö, Sweden; Residence: Gothenburg, Sweden; Occupations: journalist, lecturer, author

Inger Jalakas indicates on her website that she originally wanted to be a geologist "but went astray." Besides several nonfiction books, Jalakas has published two collections of short crime fiction and six detective novels centered on Margareta Nordin, Sweden's first fictional lesbian detective. Introduced in 2001's *Borde vetat bättre* ("Mind Without Guile"), Margaret Nordin of Gothenburg's county judicial police handles a case of a dead man found at the altar of a medieval church, in a narrative that Jalakas packs with fire and brimstone biblical quotations. In her subsequent novels she tackles contemporary social ills like human trafficking, the plight of Eastern European refugees, child pornography, and hate crimes, especially those directed toward homosexuals.

Lustmord ("Lust Killer"), 1999, five short crime stories Jalakas co-authored with Ulla Trenter, parodies the stock figure of many Swedish police procedurals. Their central figure, Superintendent Knut Welander, is "listless and disheartened," overweight and asthmatic, and battling not only crime but governmental cuts and the retrenching of his police organization. The stories' savage humor hits hard at "hard-boiled heroes" who rise up bloodied but unbowed from every vicious assault, "gloomy commissars" who brood over society's decline, and "righteous macho men" who flaunt their "antiquated sexist view of women." Jalakas intends her targeting of fictional male Swedish policemen to provoke smiles for Swedish crime fiction readers, because she believes the Swedish genre lacks the saving grace of humor (quoted in Jalakas' website).

Crime Novels:

Margareta Nordin Series:

2001: *Borde vetat bättre* ("Should Have Known Better")
2005: *Sinne utan svek* ("Mind Without Guile")
2006: *Den ryske mannen* ("The Russian Man")
2007: *Ur min aska* ("From My Ashes")
2009: *Hat* ("Hate")

Short Crime Fiction Collections:

1999: *Lustmord* ("Lust Killer"), with Ulla Trenter
2000: *Krokodilens leende* ("Crocodile Smile"), with Ulla Trenter

Major Awards: N/A

Website: http://www.jalakas.se

*Anna Jansson

b. February 13, 1958, Visby, Sweden; Residence: Vintrosa, near Örebro, Sweden; Occupations: nursing, adult and children's book author

Anna Jansson, one of Sweden's most popular crime writers, grew up in Visby, a medieval town on the island of Gotland. She trained as a nurse and still works part time at Örebro Hospital's lung clinic, where on her night shifts she often worked with terminal cancer patients who told her that they wished they had spent more time doing what they really loved. This inspired Jansson to write her crime novels and her children's books (Picker). Since her crime novel debut in 2000, Jansson has published one Maria Wern detective novel per year, but only two have been translated into English to date. The Maria Wern novels were adapted for Swedish television series airing between 2008 and 2013, and twelve are available as full-length films, all starring Swedish actress Eva Röse.

Jansson set her highly popular Maria Wern novels, which despite modern technology like cell phones and the Internet tend more toward the "cozy" category than to hard-boiled police procedural fiction, first on the Swedish mainland, but she later moved her heroine and her stories' locale to her native Swedish island of Gotland. Maria Wern, a young police detective and single mother with two children, struggles to balance her personal and professional lives. In her some-what dated Agatha Christie–type mysteries, Jansson's strongly drawn characters almost all deal with post-divorce problems.

Främmande fågel, 2006 (*Strange Bird*, tr. 2013), emerged from Jansson's own life, since her mother, also a nurse, had contracted near-fatal tuberculosis from the patients she cared for. Jansson herself wanted to explore responses people today might make to an epidemic, so in *Strange Bird*, she postulates that a pigeon brings a strain of avian flu to Gotland, nearly devastating the island. In her second Maria Wern novel to be translated into English, *Drömmen förde dig vilse*, 2010 (*Killer's Island*, tr. 2013), is also set on Gotland, based on the ancient Gotland myth of the White Sea lady, in which a bride drowns on her wedding night and returns as a ghost to lure men to their deaths in the sea. In *Killer's Island*, Maria sees a boy being beaten savagely by three men. She tries to help him and is so viciously assaulted herself that she has to spend several days in the Gotland hospital. According to crime critic Maxine Clarke, Jansson presents "engaging, pleasing account[s] in which everything is solved and tied up in a ribbon at the end" (Clarke). A television series based on the Maria Wern novels has been aired in fourteen countries, including the United States.

In 2010, Anna Jansson began a children's series paralleling her adult novels, featuring Maria Wern's eleven-year-old son Emil, who inspired by his mother's work sets up his own private detective agency.

Crime Novels:

Maria Wern Series:

2000: *Stum sitter guden* ("Dumb Sitting God")
2001: *Alla de stillsamma döda* ("All the Quiet Dead")
2002: *Må döden sova* ("May Death Sleep")
2003: *Silverkronan* ("Silver Crown")
2004: *Drömmar ur snö* ("Dreams from Snow")
2005: *Svart fjäril* ("Black Butterfly")
2006: *Främmande fågel* (*Strange Bird*, tr. Paul Norlén, 2013)
2007: *I stormen ska du dö* ("Boy Missing")
2008: *Inte ens det förflutna* ("Not Even the Past")

2009: *Först när givaren är död* ("Only When the Donor Is Dead")
2010: *Drömmen förde dig vilse* (*Killer's Island*, tr. Paul Norlén, 2012)
2011: *Alkeminse eviga ed* ("Eternal Flame")
2012: *När skönheten kom till Bro* ("When Beauty Came to Bro")
2013: *Dans på glödande kol* ("A Dance on Glowing Embers")
2014: *Skymningens barfotabarn* ("Child of the Shadows")
2014: *Ödesgudinnan på Salong d'Amour* ("The Goddess of Fate at Salon d'Amour")

Major Awards:

2007: Nomination for the Glass Key Award, for *Främmande fågel* (*Strange Bird*)

Website: http://www.thriller.se

Marianne Jeffmar

> b. 1935 in Grindnäset, Sweden; Residence: Uppsala, Sweden; Occupations: psychologist, translator, adult and children's books author

Marianne Jeffmar has written more than thirty books, including stand-alone psychological crime novels and the five-volume Suzanne Decker crime novel series, written between 1999 and 2002 and emphasizing relationships between parents and children, particularly focusing on children's vulnerability. Drawn from Jeffmar's eleven years in Brussels, Belgium, middle-aged Suzanne De Decker, sometimes called Jeffmar's alter ego, is a crime reporter for the Belgian newspaper *Le Soir*. For a story she's pursuing in the first installment of the series, she visits Sweden for the first time and experiences dramatic culture shock, while in her second novel, a diary dating from 1934 to 1947 introduces not only historical material but old tensions in Suzanne's family which contribute to a contemporary murder.

Selected Crime Novels:

1978: *Dödens ängel* ("The Angel of Death")
1979: *I enslig gård* ("The Lonely Garden")
1980: *Professorn och hans offer* ("The Professor and His Victim")

The Suzanne Decker Series:

1999: *I skuggan av en lögn* ("In the Shadow of a Lie")
1999: *Mördarens ankomst* ("Killer's Arrival")
2000: *Mannen som ville vara Simenon* ("The Man Who Wanted to Be Simenon")
2001: *Ikaros hämnd* ("Ikaros' Revenge")
2001: *Flickan i ljungen* ("The Girl in the Heather")
2002: *Det största brottet* ("The Biggest Crime")

Major Awards: N/A

Website: N/A

*Jonas Jonasson (Per Ola Jonasson)

> b. July 6, 1961, Växjö, Sweden; Residence: Gotland, Sweden; Occupations: journalist, media company founder, author

After several years as a journalist, Jonas Jonasson founded the OTW media company, eventually employing a hundred workers. Burned out in 2005 after two decades in the media business which he sold for about $20 million (Levin), he experienced various personal and marital difficulties, eventually settling in 2010 on the island of Gotland with his young son.

Jonasson's widely acclaimed 2009 comic debut, *Hundraåringen som klev ut genom fönstret och försvann* (titled in English *The Hundred-Year-Old Man Who Climbed Out of the Window and Disappeared*, tr. 2012), became a worldwide sensation, selling three million copies in two years. His amoral centenarian hero and his own alter ego Allan Karlsson escapes his 100th birthday celebration in a old people's home, steals a cash-filled suitcase belonging to a criminal gang who pursue him across Sweden while he gathers a peculiar mob of followers, including an elephant. Through flashbacks he relates his involvement with important world leaders, including some dictators whom he saved from assassination (Levin). His second novel, *Analfabeten som kunde räkna* (titled in English *The Girl Who Saved the King of Sweden*, tr. 2014), follows Norbeko, a Soweto slum girl who somehow educated herself and suddenly in 2007 finds herself confined in a potato truck with the king and the prime minister of Sweden, Written in a "light and frothy" style, both novels insist that nothing should be taken seriously (Martelli)—Jonasson's recipe, he declares, for happiness (Levin).

Comic "Crime" Novels:

2009: *Hundraåringen som klev ut genom fönstret och försvann* (*The Hundred-Year-Old Man Who Climbed Out of the Window and Disappeared*, tr. Rod Bradbury, 2012)

2013: *Analfabeten som kunde räkna* (*The Girl Who Saved the King of Sweden*, tr. Rod Bradbury, 2014)

Major Awards:

2010: Swedish Booksellers Prize, for *Hundraåringen...* (*The Hundred-Year-Old Man...*)

2011: The German Pioneer Prize (M-Pioneer Preis), for *Hundraåringen...* (*The Hundred-Year-Old Man...*)

2011: *The Danish Audiobook Award*, for *Hundraåringen....* (*The Hundred-Year-Old Man...*)

Website: http://www.jonasjonasson.com

*Mari Jungstedt

b. October 31, 1962; Residence: Stockholm; summers spent in Gotland; Occupations: television journalist, author

In a statement contributed to Barry Forshaw's *Death in a Cold Climate*, Mari Jungstedt declared that the island of Gotland is a perfect setting for her crime novels, because "It is a version of the 'locked room' scenario," with an "immensely evocative" environment of rocks and beaches, the medieval town of Visby, and the flat and wild landscape (Forshaw 53) with its famous light that inspired film director Ingmar Bergman to live on Gotland and shoot several of his films there. Jungstedt's meticulous research for her novels assures that "every house, path and gate in my books actually exists. You can travel around Gotland and see all the places I wrote about" (quoted in "Mari Jungstedt"). She also indicates that "the same themes recur in each novel," which focus on the relationships between parents and children. Her own painful childhood with an alcoholic father and an insecure mother who divorced when she was nine but remained antagonistic, and with her mother's cancer when Mari was fourteen, all formed her consciousness and convinced her that such suffering needs to be brought into the open (Forshaw 52).

While Jungstedt worked as a radio and television reporter and as a news anchor for Swedish public television, she dreamed of writing fiction. The method she developed for her writing depends on seeing her book as a film and its chapters as scenes ("Mari Jungstedt"). Since the debut of her Superintendent Anders Knutas series with *Den du inte ser*, 2004 (*Unseen*, tr. 2005), her books have been translated into twenty different languages and have sold over three million copies worldwide (see Jungstedt's home page). All her Knutas novels are set on Gotland and involve violent crimes played out and investigated in that dramatic environment. Six have been filmed for Swedish Television.

Superintendent Anders Knutas and his associate, investigative reporter Johan Berg, appear first in *Unseen* on the trail of a possible serial killer threatening Gotland's lucrative tourist trade. Each of their succeeding cases revolves around one or more brutal murders at various seasons of the year, each of which mirrors some significant aspect of the plot. In *Den inre kretsen*, 2006 (*The Inner Circle*, tr. 2008), a young woman is discovered naked and hanging in a tree with ritualistic markings on her body that suggest she has been killed according to the ancient Viking three-fold death. In *Den döende dandyn*, 2006 (*The Killer's Art*, tr. 2010), one of Jungstedt's most accomplished works, the corpse of art gallery owner Egon Wallin is found hanging from Visby's medieval wall, leading Knutas and Berg into one of their most challenging cases, one that exposes the corruption inherent in a society where cheating the system, including the government, has become the norm. *Den mörka ängeln*, 2008 (*Dark Angel*, tr. 2012), opens with a Christie-type ploy in which event planner Viktor Algård ingests cyanide at the grand opening of Gotland's new convention center. To solve this disturbing case, Detective Superintendent Kautas must discover the connection between Algård's murder and the agonizing self-examination of a seriously depressed character in Stockholm.

As in all her crime novels, Jungstedt provides keen insights into her main characters' private lives in *Dark Angel*. Knutas and his police deputy Karin Jacobssen find their collegial relationship deepens as each case proceeds, and Johan Berg's wife Emma makes an appearance toward the end of *Dark Angel*. By 2012's *Den sista akten* ("The Last Act"), the relationship between Knutas and Karin has begun to exceed friendship, while Berg struggles to hold himself together after the tragedy that struck him and his family in *Det fjärde offret* ("The Fourth Victim"), 2011.

Jungstedt's novels always involve the inescapable effect of childhood on adult life. She consistently wants her readers to come away from each of her books with something to dwell further on productively. With craftsmanship and solid psychological insights, she demonstrates how much she loves "the thought of having readers all over the world. People with different backgrounds, ways of life, cultures and histories—the thought of that is unreal and magical—almost as magical as the joy of writing itself!" (quoted in "Mari Jungstedt").

Crime Novels:

Detective Superintendent Anders Knutas Series:

2004: *Den du inte ser* (*Unseen*, tr. Tiina Nunnally, 2006)
2004: *I denna stilla natt* (*Unspoken*, tr. Tiina Nunnally, 2007)
2006: *Den inre kretsen* (*The Inner Circle*, also published as *Unknown* and *A Lonely Place*, tr. Tiina Nunnally, 2008)
2006: *Den döende dandyn* (*The Killer's Art*, tr. Tiina Nunnally, 2010)
2007: *I denna ljuva sommartid* (*The Dead of Summer*, tr. Tiina Nunnally, 2012)
2008: *Den mörka ängeln* (*Dark Angel*, tr. Tiina Nunnally, 2012)
2009: *Den dubbla tystnaden* (*The Double Silence*, tr. Tiina Nunnally, 2013)
2010: *Den farliga leken* (*The Dangerous Game*, tr. Tiina Nunnally, 2014)

2011: *Det fjärde offret* ("The Fourth Victim")
2012: *Den sista akten* ("The Last Act")
2013: *Du går inte ensam* ("You Are Not Alone")
2014: *Den man alskar* ("The Loved One")

Major Awards: N/A

Website: http://www.marijungstedt.se

*Mons Kallentoft

b. April 15, 1968, Ljungsbro, near Linköping, Sweden; Residence: Stockholm, Sweden; Occupations: journalist, author

According to the autobiographical statement in Mons Kallentoft's official website, he discovered literature at fourteen while convalescing from a severe sports injury. The novels of Kafka, Hemingway, George Orwell, and most of all Fitzgerald's *Great Gatsby* (Hasham) introduced him to "a whole new world," one that he himself has been exploring to considerable worldwide acclaim. After three mainstream novels published between 2000 and 2005, Kallentoft published his award-winning travelogue-cum-food book, *Food noir: mat, mord, och myter* ("Food Noir: Food, Murder and Myths") and then launched his Detective Malin Fors series with *Midvinterblod*, 2007 (*Midwinter Sacrifice*, tr. 2012), which immediately reached the top of bestseller charts and has sold over 300,000 copies in Sweden alone. The Malin Fors series re-establishes Kallentoft's boyhood connection to the Lynköping area, the setting for the series, "a place that the truly cosmopolitan Kallentoft has spent all his life running from," resulting in poignant and suspenseful crime novels (Kallentoft website) set in a locale in which one of Sweden's most advanced technological centers is surrounded by plains and forests "where time often seems to have stood still" (Kallentoft website). Kallentoft sees Linköping as a microcosm of Sweden, with a university and a hospital as well as IT firms, and with new millionaires on its streets and social differences as threatening as its problems with immigration and unemployment (Hasham).

Kallentoft's fellow Swedish crime author Camilla Läckberg praises his plotting and "his ability to create strongly realized female protagonists"—the best, Läckberg said, she'd read by a male writer (Forshaw 44). As a female police detective, Malin Fors, a divorced single mother of a teenage daughter, allows Kallentoft to portray a convincing Swedish police protagonist whose perspective differs from those of male detectives, although he insists that he doesn't necessarily see her as a woman, but as a working detective who also has to cope with parenthood and other personal stresses (Long). In *Midwinter Sacrifice*, Malin Fors and her colorful police partner Zeke Martinsson investigate the bizarre murder of 330-pound Bengt Andersson, found beaten and mutilated, hanging naked from an oak tree in the coldest Swedish February in recent memory, a parody of a Viking sacrifice. As the novel proceeds, Kallentoft develops Malin's complicated relationships with her Violent Crime Squad colleagues and her thirteen-year-old daughter, and the murder victim's spirit makes wry observations on the proceedings (*Publishers Weekly* review). In a 2012 interview, Kallentoft noted the "element of magic" he combines with "gruesome realism" by including the voices of the dead victims in all his books.

In *Sommardöden*, 2008 (*Summer Death*, tr. 2013), Kallentoft reveals that Malin Fors' mentor Sven Sjöman taught her to listen to those ghostly voices. This novel contains poignant messages from dead raped girls swirling through both Malin's police work and her personal life, becoming increasingly tense as she worries incessantly about her own daughter Tove and grieves the loss of the love she and her ex-husband Janne, married too young, seem to have thrown away. She concludes that the decay of her society springs from "mediatocracy," the elevation of the mediocre, indicts today's soul-consuming "celebrity culture." (*Publishers Weekly* review). Victims' voices pervade Kallentoft's succeeding novels, too, heartbreakingly in *Varlik*, 2010 (*Savage Spring*, tr. 2013), where children cry out for their father as a bomb explodes in the town square just as Malin is attending her mother's funeral. In *Den femte årstiden*, 2011 (*The Fifth Season*, tr. 2014), the voices of the female victims of a years-old cold rape-murder case and a similar contemporary one lead Malin into a brutal probe of torture and murder.

Kallentoft has declared, "For me it is all about the dark side of human nature … but I ask, who actually was the villain? … The abuser becomes the abused or actually do they? Who and what is it that causes things to go the way they do and the differing depths of human nature?" (quoted in Long).

Crime Novels:

Malin Fors Series:

2007: *Midvinterblod* (*Midwinter Sacrifice*, tr. Neil Smith, 2012)
2008: *Sommardöden* (*Summer Death*, tr. Neil Smith, 2013)
2009: *Höstoffer* (*Autumn Killing*, tr. Neil Smith, UK 2012, U.S. 2014)
2010: *Vårlik* (*Savage Spring*, tr. Neil Smith, 2013)
2011: *Den femte årstiden* (*The Fifth Season*, tr. Neil Smith, 2014)
2012: *Vattenänglar* (*Water Angels*, tr. Neil Smith, 2015)
2013: *Vindsjälar* ("Wind Souls")
2014: *Jordstrom* ("Jordstrom")

Notable Stand-Alone Works:

2004: *Food noir: mat, mord och myter* ("Food Noir: Food, Murder and Myths")
2013: *Food junkie* ("Food Junkie")

Major Awards:

2005: Gourmand World Cookbook Award

Website: http://www.monskallentoft.se

Theodor Kallifatides

> b. March 12, 1938. Molai, Greece; Residence: Stockholm, Sweden; Occupations: professor of philosophy, translator, editor, poet, novelist

As a young immigrant from his native Greece, Theodor Kallifatides washed dishes, read Strindberg's works to learn Swedish, and studied philosophy. He has since produced several volumes of poetry and more than a dozen distinguished mainstream novels in which he has both successfully depicted Greece's contemporary history in Swedish and analyzed the problematic situation of immigrants entering Swedish culture. He has also written three philosophical thrillers, basing the central figure, Inspector Kristina Vendel, on his own daughter and exploring touchy contemporary issues like the ethical ramifications of selling body organs for transplantation, the topic of *Den sjätte passageraren*, 2002 (*The Sixth Passenger*, tr. 2006).

Philosophical Crime Novels:

Inspector Kristina Vendel Series:

2000: *Ett enkelt brott* (*A Very Simple Crime*, tr. 2002; no translator's name given)

2002: *Den sjätte passageraren* (*The Sixth Passenger*, tr. 2006, no translator's name given)

2004: *I hennes blick* ("In Her Eyes")

Major Awards: N/A

Website: N/A

Johannes Källström

b. February 25, 1972, Örebro, Sweden; Residence: Stockholm, Sweden; Occupations: businessman, author

After publishing *Mörkersikt—annorlunda sago rom kaos* ("Night Vision: Different Tales of Chaos"), 2009, businessman Johannes Källström published *Offerrit—en annorlunda berättelse om besatthet* ("Sacrificial Rite: A Different Story About Obsession") in 2010, a horror novel about pathological obsession.

Horror Novel:

2010: *Offerrit—en annorlunda berättelse om besatthet* ("Sacrificial Rite: A Different Story About Obsession")

Major Awards: N/A

Website: http://www.afraidofthedark.se

Thomas Kanger

b. 1951, Stockholm, Sweden; Residences: Stockholm, Sweden, and Hanoi, Vietnam; Occupations: journalist, author

Veteran journalist Thomas Kanger published the book-length study, "The Assassination of Olof Palme" in 1987 and "Communist Hunters: the Social Democratic Political Espionage Against Swedish People," with Jonas Gummesson, 1990. Kanger is well known in Sweden for his three-part documentary about government-sanctioned orphanage abuse in Sweden from the 1950s through the 1970s, sparking a nationwide inquiry that grew into one of the world's largest such investigations, lasting until 2011 and eventually involving thousands of victims, to whom the Swedish government has offered compensation of 250,000 Swedish kronor each (Kanger's website). Kanger has also produced a series of police procedurals beginning in 2001, centering on Västerås Detective Inspector Elina Wiik, according to SIG-*Tidningen* "a spiritual relative of Stieg Larsson's Lisbeth Salander." *Dagens Nyheter* noted that Kanger knows how "to mirror world politics through his characters, so that the big events become sadly personal." *Söndagsmannen* ("Sunday Man"), 2004, and *Gränslandet* ("Borderland"), 2007, based on the tragic history of the former Yugoslavia, were both nominated for the Year's Best Crime Novel Award of the Swedish Crime Academy (quotations from Kanger website). In a review of *The Borderland*, France's *La Gazette* observed, "His [Kanger's] fairy tales are very cruel."

Crime Novels:

2001: *Första stenen* ("First Stone")
2002: *Sjung som en fågel* ("Sing Like a Bird")
2003: *Den döda vinkeln* ("The Blind Spot")
2004: *Söndagsmannen* ("Sunday Man")
2005: *Ockupanterna* ("Occupiers")
2007: *Gränslandet* ("Borderland")
2011: *Drakens år* ("Year of the Dragon")

Major Awards: N/A

Website: http://www.kanger.se

Robert Karjel

> b. 1965, Örebro, Sweden; Residence: Stockholm, Sweden; Occupations: military helicopter pilot, author

A lieutenant colonel in the Swedish Air Force and the only Swedish pilot trained by the U.S. Marine Corps, Robert Karjel served in the Gulf of Aden and the Indian Ocean, combatting Somali pirates as the helicopter division leader for the United Nations and the European Union. He led efforts there to avert over a hundred pirate attacks and to bring relief aid of food and medicine to the famine stricken Somalians. He also flew attack Black Hawk helicopters in Afghanistan in 2013. He draws on his military experiences for his lectures on organizational efficiency and for his suspense novels, which he researched in the Libyan Desert, in France, and in the Vatican Library.

Crime Novels:

1997: *Gå över gränsen* ("Go Over the Limit")
1999: *Skuggan av floden* ("Shadow of the River")
2005: *De hängdas evangelium* ("The Hanged Gospel")
2010: *De redan döda* ("The Already Dead")

Major Awards: N/A

Website: http://www.robertkarjel.se

Lars Kepler (pseudonym of *Alexander Ahndoril and Alexandra Coelho Ahndoril*)

> Alexander Ahndoril: b. January 20, 1967, Stockholm, Sweden; Residence: Stockholm, Sweden; Occupations: playwright, author
>
> Alexandra Coelho Ahndoril: b. March 2, 1966, Helsingborg, Sweden; Residence: Stockholm, Sweden; Occupations: literary critic, author

Before they teamed to write mystery fiction as "Lars Kepler," both Alexander Ahndoril and his wife Alexandra Coelho Ahndoril had authored successful novels. Alexander Ahndoril's bestselling novel *Regissören* (*The Director*, tr. 2008 by Sarah Death), about Swedish film director Ingmar Bergman, was nominated for the 2009 *Independent* Foreign Fiction Prize. Alexandra

Coehlo Ahndoril made her literary debut with *Stjarneborg*, 2003, a novel about the astronomer Tycho Brahe. Wishing to differentiate their collaborative crime novels from their individual work, they adopted the joint pseudonym "Lars Kepler," as a tribute to Stieg Larsson and the German astronomer Johannes Kepler. According to their official website, the pair originally intended to keep their identities secret, but the immediate success of *Hypnotisören*, 2009 (*The Hypnotist*, tr. 2011), ignited enormous media attention. Elements of the British press suggested "Lars Kepler" was a ploy by Henning Mankell to kill off his hero Kurt Wallander and start a new series, and the *New York Times* conjectured that "Lars Kepler" was "an author-bot engineered by the Swedes to further their takeover of the global publishing industry." The Ahndorils then revealed their identities (see Lars Kepler website).

Lars Kepler's unusual protagonist is Joona Linna, Chief Inspector with the Swedish National Police in Stockholm, a laconic, insightful, and respected Finnish-Swedish police detective with sea-grey eyes that see everything and a tortured past slowly being revealed through the series. The authors made him half Finnish because his status as "a bit of a stranger" in Sweden attracted them, "someone who is both inside and outside of the culture" (Foster). Joona Linna's personal woes impel him to seek justice, occasionally through unconventional means, in cases which resemble his own losses, particularly those involving families and children. His method of crime solution requires him to study the crime scene in intense detail, allowing him to enter the mind of the killer so thoroughly that it "opens like a book" to him, revealing not only the *modus operandi* but the emotional and psychological upheavals that caused the killer to commit his gruesome acts (Lars Kepler website). In a 2011 interview, the authors revealed that they "wouldn't dare to write about what scares us the most if we didn't have him [Joona Linna]" (quoted in Butki).

Because Lars Kepler believes that "extreme and horrible violence is one of humanity's contributions to the world" (quoted in Butki), the authors center each novel of the Joona Linna series on a near-unspeakable crime, treated in a filmic atmosphere. They plan at least eight books in the series (DuChateau), which also includes one of the very few women superior police officials in Swedish crime fiction, Detective Superintendent Lillemor Blom (Mason 17). *Hypnotisören*, 2009 (*The Hypnotist*, tr. 2011), in part based on the work of Alexander Ahndoril's brother, a professional hypnotist, uses a cinematic present tense throughout, and opens with the savage murder of a family. One son, a witness, is left so badly traumatized that he cannot speak about the killings until Dr. Erik Bark, a retired hypnotist, attempts to release the boy's memories of the crime. *Paganinikontraktet*, 2010 (*The Nightmare*, tr. 2012), treats Sweden's ranking as the world's largest exporter of arms per capita as the "nightmare" of "arms smuggling and dirty politicians." *Eldvittnet*, 2011 (*The Fire Witness*, tr. 2013), involves both Joona Linna's intense observation and his contacts with a medium in a brutal murder case that impacts the detective's own painful memories. *Sandmannen* 2012 (*The Sandman*, tr. 2014), starts one cold dark night with a half-frozen young man, officially dead for years, who proves to be the victim of a serial killer arrested by Joona Linna.

The authors believe that the source for all thrillers is the fear of darkness, so they conceive of their job as crime fiction writers as disarming that fear for a moment (DuChateau) and temporarily making the world understandable. They have found their collaborative work "the best thing we've ever done ... very satisfying and creative.... After a while we don't even know who wrote what in the first place. That's when Lars Kepler has taken over" (quoted in Foster).

Crime Novels:

The Joona Linna Series:

2009: *Hypnotisören* (*The Hypnotist*, tr. Anna Long, 2011)
2010: *Paganinikontraktet* (*The Nightmare*, tr. Laura A. Wideburg, 2012)

2011: *Eldvittnet* (*The Fire Witness*, tr. Laura A. Wideburg, 2013)
2012: *Sandmannen* (*The Sandman*, tr. Laura A. Wideburg, 2014)
2014: *Stalker* ("Stalker")

Major Awards:

2011: *The Hypnotist* named one of the year's ten best crime novels by the *Wall Street Journal*

Website: http://www.larskepler.com

Tove Klackenberg

b. 1956, Stockholm, Sweden; Residence: Värmland, Sweden; Occupations: lawyer, District Court Judge, author

Tove Klackenberg, formerly a prosecutor in Karlstad and now a District Court Judge of Värmland, bases the work of her heroine Svea Lundström Duval on her own experiences in Sweden's legal system. In her fourth novel, 2009's *Dömd på förhand* ("Doomed Beforehand"), she also features Monika Larsson, a secondary character in the earlier books. Before she began her novels, Klackenberg wondered why Sweden has produced very little crime fiction centered on the judicial process, so she decided to create legal thrillers, never citing actual case material in her books but using them as a source that she adapts for her fiction. She created Svea Lundström Duval as an antithesis to herself, "extreme, square and aloof," qualities she herself tries to avoid, preferring to be known as a human being inside a judge's robe (Lundberg).

Crime Novels:

Svea Lundström Duval Series:

2002: *Påtaglig risk att skada* ("Substantial Risk of Injury")
2004: *Självtäkt* ("Self Extraction")
2007: *Inlåst* ("Locked Up")
2009: *Dömd på förhand* ("Doomed Beforehand")

Major Awards:

2002: Best Swedish Debut Crime Novel Award, the Swedish Crime Academy, for *Påtaglig risk att skada* ("Substantial Risk of Injury")

Website: N/A

Hans Koppel (pseudonym of *Karl Petter Lidbeck*)

b. 1964, Helsingborg, Sweden; Residence: N/A; Occupations: children's book author, adult author (revealed in 2010)

After Petter Lidbeck had become the famous author of more than two dozen children's books including a detective series starring teenaged girl sleuths, he decided to write adult detective novels under the pseudonym "Hans Koppel," because he felt people didn't take children's authors seriously, and because he wanted to separate his works into the two genres. After his first adult book, a satirical novel, Koppel decided to write a trilogy of detective novels inspired by American crime writers Ed McBain, Harlan Coben, John Grisham, and Richard Brautigan. Koppel discovered that writing thrillers was easier than producing humorous books, because "what scares us is pretty universal—and everybody loves excitement" (quoted in O'Yeah). Koppel also feels that fellow Swedish crime writers Leif Persson and the team of Roslund and Hellström "share his own passionate concern for human decency" (Forshaw 93), a concern reflected in Koppel's adult detective novels, each presenting a different bizarre event in his home town of Helsingborg, with no central series protagonist.

In Koppel's first thriller, *Kommer aldrig mer igen*, 2008 (*Never Coming Back*, tr. 2012), he disrupts the lives of a middle class couple by having the wife kidnapped and held in appalling conditions, including torture and sexual debasement, in the house next door, with Koppel "bluntly and expertly" mining "very adult themes of male sexual insecurity and female victimization to page-turning but off-putting effect" (*Publishers Weekly* review), an assessment that seems to suit both of the later thrillers Koppel has produced "after incubating dark things" (Forshaw, *Independent* review).

Crime Novels:

The Collin Series:

2008: *Kommer aldrig mer igen* (*Never Coming Back*, tr. Kari Dickson, 2012)
2012: *Kom så ska vi tycka om varandra* ("Come, We Like Each Other")
2013: *Om döda ont* ("If the Dead Are Evil")

Major Awards: N/A

Website: N/A

Robert Kviby

b. 1976, Oxelösund, Sweden; Residence: Stockholm, Sweden; Occupations: software developer, author

Robert Kviby's debut novel, *De korrupta* ("The Corrupt"), 2012, a conspiracy thriller set in the late 1980s, shortly after the assassination of Prime Minister Olof Palme, involves the disappearance of investigative reporter Annie Lander after she visits an exclusive gentleman's club while she is working on a story about missing prostitutes. The theme of men's exploitation of women has been familiar in Swedish crime fiction since Stieg Larsson's Millennium Trilogy, but Kviby also involves a Yugoslavian mob family to deepen the *noir* element. *De korrupta* placed first on the Swedish bestseller list on April 11, 2012.

Crime Novels:

The Annie and Max Lander Series:

2012: *De korrupta* ("The Corrupt")
2013: *Listan* ("The List")
2014: Untitled #3

Major Awards: N/A

Website: N/A

Camilla Läckberg

> b. August 30, 1974, Fjällbacka, Sweden; Residence: Fjällbacka, Sweden; Occupations: marketing, author

Camilla Läckberg claims on her official website, "It's always been my life's dream to write detective novels," and in her crime novels to date she has turned that dream into fictional nightmares based on her profound interest in psychology: "just how 'horrible' people are capable of being!" (see Läckberg website). Her series takes place in Fjällbacka, a seaside village of about 1000 permanent residents north of Göteborg, where Läckberg herself still lives, insisting that Fjällbacka is the "red thread" that runs throughout her novels: "I love describing my hometown and its beautiful surroundings" (Cogdill March 28, 2014).

A few months after Stieg Larsson's *The Girl with the Dragon Tattoo* appeared in the United States, Pegasus Books gave Läckberg one of the highest advances they had ever paid and brought out her first novel, *Isprinsessan*, 2003 (*The Ice Princess*, tr. 2008) (Bosman). Läckberg has since become one of the most widely translated Swedish crime writers, selling in more than 20 countries worldwide. At home each of her crime novels has been number one on the Swedish bestseller lists. Läckberg has also published two cookbooks and several children's novels.

Läckberg describes herself as a very visual writer, assembling her stories from specific images and emphasizing motivation through alternating chapters that narrate the story with chapters about the killer: "To get inside the murderer's head is the best way," she claims (quoted in Wegener). In the process she reveals "a picture of modern society that is as penetrating and allusive as her narrative is involving" (Forshaw, *Death* 36). She closes each book with an "imaginary peripateia," "a reversal showing everything from a new perspective" (see http://www.dn.se).

In contrast to recent Nordic male detective protagonists who are flawed, middle aged, cynical, and nearly or completely alcoholic, Läckberg's Patrik Hedström is a young husband and father; Läckberg calls him "the guy next door as a hero" (quoted in Wegener). She develops her other main character, Erica Falck, a writer and his girlfriend, later wife, through the series. Sometimes Läckberg allows Patrik to take the lead, and sometimes she places Erika at the forefront of the investigation (Wegener). Läckberg thus creates "an intriguing interaction" between them, "both loving and fractious" (Forshaw, *Death* 38), which by the fourth novel in the series, *Olycksfågeln*, 2006 (*The Stranger*, tr. 2011), takes Erica into her mother's—and Sweden's—dark secrets from World War II, while Patrik deals with a case suggesting a potential serial killer. Barry Forshaw calls Patrik and Erica "two of the most fully rounded characters in contemporary crime fiction, with a warmth that cuts through the Nordic chill" (Forshaw, *Death* 39).

Even though Fjällbacka is a small village, Läckberg treats topics of national and even international significance, like religious fanaticism in *Predikanten*, 2004 (*The Preacher*, tr. 2009), postpartum depression in *Stenhuggaren*, 2005 (*The Stonecutter*, tr. 2010), and reality television in *Olycksfågeln*. In her eighth Patrik and Erica novel, *Änglamakerskan* (*Buried Angels*) Läckberg uses a particularly unsettling episode from Swedish history, the nineteenth century business of taking in unwanted babies for money, babies that were often killed—turned into "angels" (Forshaw, *Death* 41). Published in Sweden in September 2013, this novel immediately sold more than 300,000 copies, a 40 percent increase over the sales of the previous installment in the series.

New York Times crime critic Marilyn Stasio calls *Tyskungen*, 2007 (*The Hidden Child*, tr. 2014), Läckberg's 500-page "historical-biographical-romantic-domestic-police-procedural-crime-and-love saga" (Stasio, "Tell No One"). The Swedish maternity leave policy is generous and childcare benefits are universal, but "women characters in Swedish crime fiction often struggle to balance family duties with their jobs" (Suit 39). In *The Hidden Child*, Erica, now a young mother trying to get back into her crime writing, finds a Nazi medal among her dead mother's possessions; she consults Erik Frankel, a retired teacher and an expert on World War II, but two days later he is found dead, the victim of death by blunt instrument. As Erika compulsively pores over her mother's wartime diaries, Patrik, supposedly on paternity leave, can't resist getting back to police work, taking one-year-old Maja along and often meeting his ex-wife and her children for play dates, an arrangement that disturbs Erica and helps give this novel its highly complicated structure.

The neo–Nazi element in *The Hidden Child* is also one of Läckberg's major concerns, because she believes World War II "really marked" Swedes. This novel carries out her conviction that Swedes need to be constantly reminded of "the horrible consequences of human ignorance and extreme right-wing thoughts," because she sees neo–Nazism growing in Sweden "as well as all over Europe" (quoted in Cogdill). On the other hand, since Läckberg believes that very few people are completely evil, she consistently showcases both good and bad aspects of human personalities, a key to the success of the characterizations that keep her readers involved with her stories of Fjällbacka and its absorbing people and their pasts. "The only limit," Läckberg maintains, "is our own imagination" ("Murder, She Writes").

Läckberg wants to give her books, which she considers her children, to people who will take care of them well ("Tre Vänner"). Besides being in the hands of her growing readership, Läckberg's crime novels have been adapted as a popular Swedish television series, *Fjällbackamorden* ("Fjäll-backa Murders"), based on characters from Läckberg's novels but with new stories, which began airing in August 2011.

Crime Novels:

Erika Falck-Patrik Hedström Series:

2003: *Isprinsessan* (*The Ice Princess*, tr. Steven T. Murray, 2008)

2004: *Predikanten* (*The Preacher*, tr. Steven T. Murray, 2009)

2005: *Stenhuggaren* (*The Stone Cutter*, tr. Steven T. Murray, 2010)

2006: *Olycksfågeln* (*The Gallows Bird*, also published as *The Stranger*, tr. Steven T. Murray, 2011)

2008: *Tyskungen* (*The Hidden Child*, tr. Tiina Nunnally, 2011, U.S. 2014)

2008: *Sjöjungfrun* (*The Drowning*, tr. Tiina Nunnally, 2012)

2009: *Fyrvaktaren* (*The Lost Boy*, tr. Tiina Nunnally, 2013)

2011: *Änglamakerskan* (*Buried Angels*, tr. Marlaine Delargy, UK 2014)

2014: *Lejontämjaren* ("The Lion Tamer")

Short Fiction Collection:

The Scent of Almonds and Other Stories, tr. n/a, 2015

Major Awards:

2005: SKTF Prize for Author of the Year
2006: People's Literature Award

Website: http://www.camillalackberg.com

"Bo Lagevi" (pseudonym)

"Bo Lagevi" is the collective pseudonym including Swedish mystery authors Jenny Berthelius, K. Arne Blom, Jean Bolinder, Kjell E. Genberg, Sture Hammenskog, and Jan Moen. Between

1976 and 1978 thirteen "pulp" crime novels were published by these authors under the name "Bo Lagevi" in the "Crime Scene Sweden" series, which also included works by Tommy Schinkler and Bo Sehlberg.

*Maria Lang (Dagmar Maria Lange)

b. March 31, 1914, Västerås, Sweden; d. October 9, 1991, Nora, Sweden; Residence: Nora, Sweden; Occupations: teacher and school administrator, literary scholar, author

The prolific Maria Lang, Sweden's first female crime fiction writer and from the 1950s through the 1970s one of Sweden's most widely read authors, is now hailed as a lesbian feminist. She produced one historical mystery, *Tre små gummor* ("Three Little Old Ladies") set in 1929; four young adult crime novels; and 40 adult mysteries featuring Puck Ekstedt, a strong and independent woman, and Inspector Christer Wijk, sometimes compared to Dorothy L. Sayers' Lord Peter Wimsey. Her setting was Skoga, a thinly disguised portrait of her home town of Nora, and she based *Vem väntar på värdshuset?* ("Who Is Waiting at the Inn?"), 1975, on Nora's Kolback's Inn, where Lang herself lived for a long time. Lang's traditional cozy village mysteries were unusual for their time because of sexual elements seething beneath the surfaces of their small town settings, like the secret homosexual affair that appears in her first book, *Mördaren ljuger inte ensam* ("The Killer Does Not Lie Alone"), 1949. In the 1960s Lang also inserted the character of a female mystery writer into some of her novels, with the name "Almi Graan," an anagram of "Maria Lang."

In 1951, Maria Lang openly disagreed forcefully with the theme of Raymond Chandler's famous essay, *The Simple Art of Murder*. Lang refused to accept the concept of "a realistic detective novel." She felt the true detective story had to be artificial: "its job is not to present a realistic, poignant and harrowing depiction of murder, crimes and horrors," appealing "not to our emotions, but rather to our intellect. It shall solve a problem ... [the] main thing is that it is possible to resolve and that it prepares the solver reader a sufficient degree of excitement and intellectual satisfaction" (quoted in Ekstrom). This traditional theory of detective fiction probably explains why Lang's novels fell from critical favor in the late 1960s, when the Martin Beck novels presented a new concept of crime fiction as sociopolitical commentary. Though Lang continued to write her novels and readers continued to buy millions of them, she died virtually penniless, possibly from a combination of malnutrition and alcoholism (Ekstrom).

Lang was included in 1971 as one of the original thirteen members of the Swedish Crime Academy, but she left that group later after internal disagreements. Her home town erected a statue of Lang beside Lake Nora and the town's tourist office now offers "murder walks" in her favorite areas, guided by her nephew Ove Hoffner. Six of Lang's mysteries have been adapted for film, the first, *The Killer Does Not Lie Alone*, released in March 2013 and the others in DVD versions appearing on TV4 in 2014. In 2013, Borstedts Agency announced that three of Lang's classical whodunits were being re-launched: *The Killer Does Not Lie Alone*, *Harmful If Eaten*, and *No More Murders!*

Selected Crime Novels:

1949: *Mördaren ljuger inte ensam* (*The Killer Does Not Lie Alone*, tr. Joan Tate, reissued 2013)
1950: *Farligt att förtära* (*Harmful if Eaten*, tr. Joan Tate, reissued 2013)
1951: *Inte flera mord* (*No More Murders*, tr. Joan Tate, 1967, reissued 2013)
1955: *Se döden på dig väntar* (*Death Awaits Thee*, tr. Joan Tate, 1967)
1957: *Kung Liljekonvalje av dungen* (*A Wreath for the Bride*, tr. Joan Tate, 1966)

1963: *Tre små gummor* ("Three Little Old Ladies")

1972: *Vem väntar på värdshuset?* ("Who Is Waiting at the Inn?")

1990: *Se Skoga och sedan...* "See Skoga and Then..."

Memoir:

1985: *Vem ar du? Dagmar Lange eller Maria Lang* ("Who Are You? Dagmar Lange and Maria Lang")

Major Awards: N/A

Website: N/A

Jens Lapidus

> b. May 24, 1974, Hagersten, Sweden; Residence: Stockholm, Sweden; Occupations: criminal defense attorney, author

One of Sweden's most prominent defense attorneys, Jens Lapidus feels his roles of lawyer and author go hand in hand. Although Lapidus believes Sweden is still a comparatively safe place to live, his legal experience has shown him that the 1960s–1970s image of the country as harmonious and safe, 'bound by social democratic ideals," has become outdated: "Before, we didn't have gangs ... the Hells Angels, the Russians, the prison gangs, but now we do and they've been here 15, maybe 20 years" (quoted in Landes). Lapidus opened his hard-boiled *Stockholm Noir* trilogy, influenced by the work of James Ellroy, with *Snabba Cash*, 2006 (*Easy Money*, tr. 2012), a grungy tale of the Stockholm underworld told from the perspectives of mobsters and drug kingpins that deliberately turns the usual crime formula of "murder, investigation, solution" upside down. Inspired by an actual courtroom outburst by three young criminals who insisted that their judge knew nothing about their lives, Lapidus produced a "genre-defining novel detailing the struggles of a young Swede called 'JW' to be a successful social climber. JW, the escaped convict Jorge, and the Yugoslav mobster Mrado navigate a violent mix of drugs, blackmail, and deceit in their quest for 'easy money'" (quoted in Landes). Lapidus sees a "very Swedish" element perhaps hard for Americans to grasp in the Swedish "class-based society" he depicts, which considers anyone who tries to change his class as "fishy," a cynical viewpoint that dominates Lapidus' whole *Stockholm Noir* trilogy. A movie version of *Easy Money* directed by Daniel Espinosa premiered in 2010, with two sequels in 2012 and 2013 respectively. Warner Brothers holds the rights for a U.S. remake of *Easy Money*, to star Zac Efron and Robin Mylund.

Crime Novels:

Stockholm Noir *Trilogy:*

2006: *Snabba cash* (*Easy Money*, tr. Astri von Arbin Ahlander, 2012)

2008: *Aldrig fucka upp* (*Never Fuck Up*, also published as *Never Screw Up*, tr. Astri von Arbin Ahlander, 2013)

2011: *Livet deluxe* (*Life Deluxe*, tr. Astri von Arbin Ahlander, 2015)

Crime Short Story Collection:

2012: *Mamma försökte* ("Mama Tried")

Major Awards: N/A

Website: http://www.jenslapidus.se

*Åsa Larsson

b. June 28, 1966, Kiruna, Sweden; Residence: Mariefred, Sweden; Occupations: tax attorney, author

In 2012 Åsa Larsson stated that her goal was to become a "hysterically good storyteller." The reception and sales of her novels suggest that she is close to achieving it, with critics praising her ability to depict "the pathology of psychological and physical violence" and her "baleful and intense" writing (*Kirkus* 2006). A *Publishers Weekly* reviewer found *Svart stig*, 2007 (*The Black Path*, tr. 2008), "a superb, gut-wrenching police procedural ... [that] carries tremendous emotional heft" (*Publishers Weekly* June 23, 2008). Some commentators, however, have found Larsson's graphic scenes of cruelty inflicted on animals, especially dogs, objectionable (EuroCrime).

Larsson's harsh early life in Kiruna, 200 kilometers north of the Arctic Circle, marked her lifestyle and her personality. Not only the frigid climate but family tensions affected her as a youngster; her grandfather had become a preacher in a strict religious denomination, and her parents, rebelling against his views, became Communists and refused on principle to marry. Larsson herself for a while similarly rebelled against her father, who refused to let her read Nancy Drew stories. She also defied her mother by joining a free church, "happily embracing the halleluiah mumbo jumbo they were feeding us on. It all eventually ended badly, of course ... the kind of freaky childhood that makes you a writer" (quoted in Purcell).

In a letter to her readers contained in a 2008 Penguin newsletter, Larsson hoped they would like her 2003 novel *Solstorm* (*Sun Storm*, also *The Savage Altar*, tr. 2006): "the biting cold of midwinter, the austerity of the people, the dogs that are so important in all my books ... my police officers ... [and] my main character, Rebecka Martinsson, "a workaholic; "and I hope you'll like the violence. I have a weakness for shattered bones and bleeding internal organs" (quoted in *EuroCrime*). This novel focuses on the ritualistic murder of a youth who had performed religious healings. Lawyer Rebecka Martinsson and Inspector Anna-Maria Mellam, whose pregnancy affects her police work, join forces to solve the religion-related crime, a motif Larsson repeated in her second novel, *Det blod som spiltts*, 2004 (*The Blood Spilt*, tr. 2007), where controversial feminist pastor Mildred Nilsson is the victim, allowing Larsson to take aim at religious fanaticism as well as the Swedish judicial system. The traumatic events in that novel cause Rebekah to seek psychiatric care. Later in *The Black Path* she leaves her position with a large Stockholm law firm and returns to her home town of Kiruna to prosecute white-collar crimes, but she also becomes involved with the fatal stabbing and electrocution of a well-to-do businesswoman. This novel analyzes obsessive behavior and portrays one of the coldest-hearted killers in Larsson's work. World War II history pervades *Till dess din vrede upphör*, 2009 (*Until Thy Wrath Be Past*, tr. 2011), where the search for the wreckage of a Nazi transport airplane in a remote northern lake revives bitter memories of the war years which village residents would prefer to leave buried. Rebekah finds herself in mortal danger in *Till offer åt Molok*, 2011 (*The Second Deadly Sin*, tr. 2013), where the ice and the contents of a wild bear's stomach hide deadly secrets wrapped in warped religious fervor.

From her often gruesome novels, Larsson hopes readers will take away "a feeling for Northern Scandinavia. For the people living in this harsh climate. For our lifestyle, our rough humour [sic]" (quoted in Purcell)—and respect for a storyteller who can make it all seem so terribly convincing.

Crime Novels:

Rebecka Martinsson Series:

2003: *Solstorm* (*Sun Storm*, also published as *The Savage Altar*, tr. Marlaine Delargy, 2006)
2004: *Det blod som spiltts* (*The Blood Spilt*, tr. Marlaine Delargy, 2007)

2007: *Svart stig* (*The Black Path*, tr. Marlaine Delargy, 2008)
2009: *Till dess din vrede upphör* (*Until Thy Wrath Be Past*, tr. Laurie Thompson, 2011)
2011: *Till offer åt Molok* (*The Second Deadly Sin*, tr. Laurie Thompson, 2013)

Major Awards:

2003: Martin Beck Award, Swedish Crime Academy, for *Solstorm* (*The Savage Altar*)
2004: Best Swedish Crime Novel of the Year, for *Det blod som spillts* (*The Blood Spilt*)

Website: N/A

Stieg Larsson (Karl Stig-Erland Larsson)

> b. 1954, Västerbotten, Sweden; d. November 9, 2004, Stockholm, Sweden; Residence: Stockholm, Sweden; Occupations: investigative journalist, graphic designer, anti-racism activist, editor and publisher, author

An investigative reporter whose specialty was racism and right-wing extremism, Stieg Larsson died unexpectedly in 2004 shortly after delivering the manuscripts of his first three novels, since known as the *Millennium Trilogy*, to his Swedish publisher, Norstedt. In 2009, after English translations of the novels were published by Christopher Maclehose, head of Quercus, a small British publishing firm, and Alfred A. Knopf in the United States, Larsson became the overall best selling fiction writer in Europe, and by December 2012 the three novels of the *Millennium Trilogy* had sold 73 million copies (Hachman). As for the popularity of Larsson's novels in Sweden itself, Uppsala University professor Torsten Pettersson noted in 2009, "A very safe and idyllic nation like Sweden may feel it needs a jolt with some of these atrocities in the books" (quoted in Magnusson and Lindstrom). *Män som hatar kvinnor*, 2005 (lit. "Men Who Hate Women," *The Girl with the Dragon Tattoo*, tr. 2008), adapted first as a Swedish theater film, was followed by *Flickan som lekte med elden*, 2006 (*The Girl Who Played with Fire*, tr. 2009), and *Luftslottet som sprängdes*, 2007 (*The Girl Who Kicked the Hornet's Nest*, tr. 2009), adapted as a six-part Swedish television series starring Michael Nyqvist as Mikael Blomkvist and Noomi Rapace as Lisbeth Salander. The production company Nordisk Film set the cost of producing the first Swedish Larsson movie and six television episodes at about $11.3 million. Swedish theatrical films of *The Girl Who Played with Fire* and *The Girl Who Kicked the Hornet's Nest* starring Nyqvist and Rapace were released in September 2009 and November 2009 respectively. A U.S. movie version of *The Girl with the Dragon Tattoo* starring Daniel Craig as Mikael Blomkvist and Rooney Mara as Lisbeth Salander was released by Columbia Pictures in 2011. Sony Pictures has an adaptation ready for *The Girl Who Played with Fire*, possibly a merger of books two and three of the series, but due to rights issues and the replacement of Amy Pascal, a passionate backer of the project, as head of Sony Pictures, the project has not yet been finalized. Scottish crime fiction author Denise Mina has adapted *The Girl with the Dragon Tattoo* and *The Girl Who Played with Fire* as graphic novels, published in 2012 and 2013.

Larsson had planned not a trilogy but a ten-novel sequence, a structure possibly inspired by the ten-novel Martin Beck series. Two earlier experiences involving "men who hate women" inspired Larsson's enormous project. At fifteen, he had witnessed a girl being gang raped and ever afterward blamed himself for not attempting to help her. Later the murders of two Swedish women had revolted him: Melissa Nordell, a model, was slain by her lover, and the father of a Swedish-Kurdish woman, Fadima Sahindal, murdered her in an honor killing (Baski). Larsson's life partner Eva Gabrielson has observed that through his three novels, Larsson could "denounce everyone he loathed for their cowardice, their irresponsibility, and their opportunism: couch-potato activists, sunny-day warriors, fair-weather skippers, false friends who used him to advance their own careers; unscrupulous company heads and shareholders" (Gabrielson, *Things* 54).

Raised by his grandparents in a northern Swedish village, Larsson adopted the political positions of his leftist grandfather, jailed during World War II for his anti–Nazi views. As an adult, Larsson dedicated himself to anti-racism and opposition to Swedish right-wing extremism. He belonged to the Communist Workers League (*Kommunistiska Arbetareförbundet*) and edited a Trotskyist journal while working from 1977 to 1999 as a graphic designer for a Swedish news agency. He also co-founded *Expo*, a quarterly magazine which was dedicated to safeguarding "democracy and freedom of speech by ... documenting extremist and racist groups in society" (quoted in Acocella). Larsson became one of the world's foremost authorities on right-wing and extremist groups (Forshaw 64) and his attacks on neo–Nazis, an expanding force in Swedish culture and politics, often brought him death threats, the chief reason he did not marry Gabrielson and kept both their address and their relationship secret, to try to prevent attacks on her that he felt were inevitable if she were his wife (Cooke). *Expo* was the model for "*Millennium*," crusader journalist Mikael Blomkvist's home publication in Larsson's novels.

In writing novels that he sometimes referred to as a fun-filled hobby and sometimes as his retirement fund (Acocella), Larsson used middle-aged Mikael Blomkvist, a journalist who did prison time for libel and is now trying to redeem himself, as his fictional alter ego. Larsson also created one of the most unusual and fascinating female characters in contemporary crime literature. Lisbeth Salander, a twenty-four-year old computer genius, is a complex and unforgettable character, a severely traumatized, tattooed and pierced, bisexually voracious, vengeful and anarchistic individual. In *The Girl with the Dragon Tattoo*, each chapter bearing statistics about crimes against women, she and Blomkvist team up to solve the missing-person case of the forty-year-old niece of the head of the powerful Vanger industrial family. In the process of locating that woman, Blomkvist and Lisbeth begin a strange personal relationship while uncovering neo–Nazism and massive corruption in the highest echelons of the Swedish industrial world. In *The Girl Who Played with Fire*, Blomkvist publishes a story exposing a huge sex trafficking operation that has entered the Nordic countries from Eastern Europe with tentacles reaching into Swedish business and government. Lisbeth Salander becomes the prime suspect in the murder of the two reporters who had investigated and written this story, and Blomkvist, in trying to clear her, plunges them both into black secrets from their personal and Sweden's national past. In *The Girl Who Kicked the Hornet's Nest*, fortified with chapter epigraphs about history's famous women warriors like the Amazons, Salander, despite recuperating from a near-fatal bullet to the brain, with Blomkvist's help works out her revenge against the persons and the government institutions that have wronged her so brutally.

New Yorker critic Joan Acocella effectively refutes the common notion that Lisbeth Salander is a sociopath, even though Larsson once referred to her as such, because "the primary diagnostic feature" of a sociopath is callousness, whereas Lisbeth falls in love with Mikael and tenderly brings gifts to her hospitalized mother, the brain-damaged victim of Lisbeth's father's beatings (Acocella). A convincing refutation of identifying Lisbeth Salander as a sociopath also is that besides the personal and professional experiences of violence against women that helped to inspire Larsson's novels, Larsson himself once described Lisbeth Salander as an adult version of Astrid Lindgren's beloved children's story heroine, nine-year-old Pippi Longstocking, a "mighty force of inappropriate behavior powered by good intentions" (Schultz) who "had no mother and no father. And that was of course very nice because there was no one to tell her to go to bed" (quoted in Acocella). Pippi, with her unconventional red-orange stick-out-straight braids, her weird choices of clothing and diet, and her refusal to submit to any authority she feels is unjust or illogical or silly, often takes revenge she feels is appropriate on persons or institutions (like school) who she thinks treat her unfairly. She can even save other children—even boys—from torment by bullies. Pippi once easily and singlehandedly subdued and tied up two large adult male burglars, in much the same spirit Lisbeth assaulted her rapist Bjurman in *The Girl with the Dragon Tattoo* by tasering him into immobility and tattooing him with the slogan, "I AM A SADISTIC PIG, A PERVERT, AND A RAPIST." Larsson also made Lisbeth Salander refer to her apartment as "Villa Villakula," the name of Pippi's home. In addition to the analogies between Pippi Longstocking and Lisbeth Salander, Larsson in his male protagonist's name, Mikael Blomkvist, also alludes to Astrid Lindgren's *Mästerdetektiven Blomkvist* ("Master Detective Blomkvist") juvenile series which stars "Kalle Blomkvist" (an irritating nickname his colleagues toss at Mikael Blomkvist), a bumptious boy detective who is regularly outdone in his sleuthing by a girl.

Following Larsson's untimely death from a heart attack after climbing seven flights of stairs (probably brought on by years of cigarettes and hamburgers), it was discovered that his only will, made in 1977 and leaving everything to the Communist Party he had then belonged to, had never been witnessed and thus was invalid. No other will exists. At his death in 2004 Larsson left about three-fourths of a fourth novel and notes for a fifth on a computer in the possession of Eva Gabrielson, but because they never married, Swedish law mandates that only Larsson's father and brother can inherit his estate, leaving nothing to Gabrielson. This situation has sparked current criticism of the Swedish inheritance system, whose policies on such inheritance cases Gabrielson still is trying to change. On the Stieg Larsson website (see http://www.stieglarsson.com) Gabrielson is quoted as saying that she could finish the fourth manuscript that she and Larsson had been working on, which she refers to as "*Guds hämd*" ("God's Revenge"). Elsewhere Gabrielson has stated that she will never publish the material she has, the basis for one or two more novels in the series (McGrath). She protested the December 2013 announcement from Larsson's Swedish publisher Norstedt that the fourth installment of the *Millennium* series would be written by David Lagercrantz, whom they chose in cooperation with Larsson's father and brother, without the unpublished material Gabrielson possesses, to be published in English in the U.K. by Quercus Publishing (see http://www.marketwired.com/press-release). Larsson's brother and father have publicly offered Eva Gabrielson a considerable financial settlement which she has refused to accept.

The *Millennium* saga continues. On March 31, 2015, Sonny Mehta, editor in chief of the Alfred A. Knopf publishing company, unveiled the English title "The Girl in the Spider's Web" and the cover photo of Lisbeth Salander's tattoos and punk trousers for the fourth installment of the series, called in Swedish *Det som inte dödar oss* ("What Doesn't Kill You"). According to its Swedish publisher, Norstedt, this novel, said to open with an artificial intelligence intrigue involving an ultra-secret U.S. spy agency, has been created under "extreme security measures," with both the writing and the translating for English done by British publisher Maclehose Press, carried out on computers disconnected from the Internet to prevent hacking. David Lagercrantz, the co-author of Swedish football star Zlatan Ibrahimovic's autobiography, notes that "If you write about Lisbeth Salander its easy to get a little paranoid" (quoted in Tomlinson). *The Girl in the Spider's Web* was scheduled for publication in late August or early September 2015 by Norstedt in Sweden, Maclehose Press in the UK, and Alfred A. Knopf in the U.S. It is being translated into a total of thirty-eight languages. Christopher Maclehose told *The Guardian* that no pre-publication review copies will be issued: "...nobody will be in a position to beat the ring of steel around this book" (quoted in Tomlinson). Eva Gabrielson has observed that Larsson would have been "furious" about the production and release of *The Girl in the Spider's Web* (Tomlinson).

Controversy also persists regarding the editing of the first three *Millennium* novels, which some commentators feel contain too much extraneous detail. Eva Gedin of Norstedt insisted the first novel had had extensive revisions. Gabrielson, who others feel may have done considerable work on the books, maintains that the English version was "prissified" by Christopher Maclehose and that Kurdo Baksi, a fellow *Expo* journalist who published the memoir *My Friend Stieg Larsson* and insisted that Larsson's work had needed extensive editing, had written a "slanderous" opinion that should be withdrawn (Cooke). Joan Acocella finds that the *Millennium* novels contain "blatant violations of logic and consistency," dangling loose ends, "vast dumps of unnecessary detail," banal phrasing, and jokes "that aren't funny" (Acocella).

As well as generating enormous commercial success, Larsson's *Millennium Trilogy* is considered an important commentary on contemporary Sweden. *New York Times* crime critic Marilyn Stasio believes that Larsson's "horrific [fictional] acts of violence against women" become "his idiom for exposing the hypocrisy of a government that ignores the internal criminal abuses threatening its progressive social system" (Stasio, "Cold Cases"). Literary scholars Anna Stenport and Cecilia Alm have noted that besides being one of Sweden's largest international literary commercial successes, *The Girl with the Dragon Tattoo* "must also be viewed ... as a paragon for how twenty-first century Swedish culture construes itself in a global paradigm," reflecting gaps between Sweden's cultivated image as an apparently successful welfare state with significant economic development and gender equality and the actual practices of Swedish policy and public discourse: "the novel ... endorses a pragmatic acceptance of a neoliberal world order that is delocalized, dehumanized, and misogynistic" (Stenport and Alm 158). John-Henri Holmberg, Larsson's friend, has also enumerated specific contrasts between Sweden's vision of itself and Larsson's critique of his country's policies. While Swedes believe their nation is uniquely egalitarian, Larsson unveils huge differences between rich and poor; while Swedes believe Sweden is politically neutral, Larsson reveals a frightening Swedish far right-wing movement; while Swedes feel their health care system is the world's best, Larsson through Lisbeth Salander's treatment shows its inherent abuses; and while Swedes see their government as working for its citizens' benefit, Larsson shows it is "an instrument of violence," directed against individuals who threaten those who have managed to control governmental power (quoted in Acocella). Overall, Larsson describes Sweden's *Folkhemmet* welfare society that he and a significant of other Swedish crime writers have convincingly portrayed as "an empty promise" (Acocella).

The qualities of the *Millennium Trilogy* that play a significant role in its vast commercial success involve Larsson's main characters: "As private investigators, both independently employed, Blomkvist and Salander represent the novel's belief in the individual rather than in a collective." In addition, "Blomkvist insists on the separation between perception and 'actual' policy and business practices" (Stenport and Alm 172–3). Holmberg declares Salander is "the nightmare of all doctrines, all consensus thinkers, all moralists and all politicians" (quoted in Acocella). "In Larsson's Sweden, the country's well-polished façade belies a broken apparatus of government whose rusty flywheels are little more than the playthings of crooks.... These are Larsson's twin themes: the failure of the welfare state to do right by its people and the failure of men to do right by women ... [and] only when the story's out in the open can the crime even begin to be solved" (MacDougall).

Crime Novels:

The Millennium Trilogy:

2005: *Män som hatar kvinnor* (*The Girl with the Dragon Tattoo*, tr. Reg Keeland, 2008)
2006: *Flickan som lekte med elden* (*The Girl Who Played with Fire*, tr. Reg Keeland, 2009)
2007: *Luftslottet som sprängdes* (*The Girl Who Kicked the Hornet's Nest*, tr. Reg Keeland, 2009)
("Reg Keeland" is the pseudonym of translator Steve Murray)

Sequel to the Millennium Trilogy:

2015: *Det som inte dödar oss,* by David Lagercrantz ("What Doesn't Kill You"; published English title *The Girl in the Spider's Web,* translator's name not available)

Major Awards:

2006: Glass Key Award, for *Män som hatar kvinnor* (*The Girl with the Dragon Tattoo*)
2006: Best Swedish Crime Novel Award, for *Flickan som lekte med elden* (*The Girl Who Played with Fire*)
2008: Glass Key Award, for *Luftslottet som sprängdes* (*The Girl Who Kicked the Hornet's Nest*)
2008: ITV Crime Thriller Award, International Author of the Year, for *The Girl with the Dragon Tattoo*

Website: http://www.stieglarsson.com

Eva-Marie Liffner

b. September 26, 1957, Gothenburg, Sweden; Residence: Various; Occupations: journalist, author

Eva-Marie Liffner has specialized in combining historical fiction and mystery, winning awards in both genres for her richly detailed novels. Her debut novel, *Camera,* 2001 (tr. 2003), follows a female photographer who traces the life of her deceased relative Jacob Hall, eventually uncovering a pedophile network and an unsolved murder case. *Imago,* 2003 (tr. 2005), takes Esmé Olsen, an amateur historian who cleans at Copenhagen's Institute of Historical Studies and comes upon documents from the 1930s, into the story of a corpse discovered in a peat bog and the related disappearance of one of the men investigating that archaeological find. Praised for its exquisite diction and its "misty-damp, floor board-creaking, cellar vault suffocating ambience (*Kristianstadbladet*), *Drömmaren och sorgen, 2006* (*The Dreamer and the Sorrow,* tr. 2015), is a middle-aged architect's midsummer night's fairy tale about loss and love and death, again drifting its protagonist into the past. *Lacrimosa* ("Lacrimosa"), 2011, evokes Jean-Jacques Rousseau's 19th century theory of shaping human personality with a mystery involving radical Swedish thinker Carl Jonas Love Almqvist. None of Liffner's novels is a classic mystery, yet Liffner, like her character Esmé Olsen, wants to uncover history's secrets, "to see history in situ, to see the past walk round the corner with its collar turned up, to hear the sound of vanishing footsteps, to hear voices no one was capable of understanding" (quoted in Greenland), and she makes her readers thirst to do the same.

Crime Novels:

2001: *Camera* (*Camera,* tr. Anna Paterson, 2003)
2003: *Imago* (*Imago,* tr. Silvester Mazzarella, 2005)
2006: *Drömmaren och sorgen* (*The Dreamer and the Sorrow,* tr. 2015, translator n/a)
2011: *Lacrimosa* ("Lacrimosa")

Major Awards:

2001: Best Swedish Debut Crime Novel of the Year, Swedish Crime Academy, for *Camera* ("Camera")
2001: The Poloni Prize for *Camera* ("Camera")
2001: The Flint Ax Award for *Camera* ("Camera")

Website: N/A

Pontus Ljunghill

> b. 1971, Stockholm, Sweden; Residence: Stockholm, Sweden; Occupations: criminologist, journalist, author

Pontus Ljunghill made his literary debut in 2012 with the historical crime novel *En osynlig* ("An Invisible"), set in Stockholm in 1928 and 1953, with a cunning murderer constantly eluding his police pursuer, Johan Stierna, a once-idealistic young detective gradually worn down by the demands of his duties. Stierna becomes obsessed with the killing of eight-year-old Ingrid Bengtsson, found murdered at the closed shipyard on the island of Djurgården in Stockholm. When Stierna is put in charge of the investigation, the murder adversely affects his marriage in this melancholy personal tragedy that takes place in the scrupulously detailed and highly atmospheric environments of a bygone Stockholm (Gellerfelt).

Crime Novel:

2012: *En osynlig* ("An Invisible")

Major Awards: N/A

Website: N/A

Olle Lönnaeus

> b. January 17, 1957; Residence: Various; Occupations: investigative journalist, author

In his twenty years with the newspaper *Sydsvenska Dagbladet*, Olle Lönnaeus has won multiple awards for his investigative reporting on politics in Sweden, Europe, and the Mideast. His subjects have included political and religious extremism, human trafficking, and the exploitation of foreign workers. In his first novel, *Det som ska sonas* ("Atonement"), 2009, Lonnaeus' borderline alcoholic protagonist Konrad Jonsson, depressed over the murders of his adoptive parents, returns to the small town of Tomelilla in Skåne where he grew up. His biological mother Agnes, a Polish immigrant, had been an outcast there and had vanished when he was seven, and Konrad was never allowed to speak of her afterward. Since his adoptive parents died, racism has been again running rampant in Tomelilla, and two immigrant boys are linked to the case. Konrad, himself a prime suspect, must solve the murders to clear his name, uncovering unsavory realities about the deficiencies of the Swedish welfare state.

Crime is more tangential to Lönnaeus' later novels, which explore large cultural issues. *Mike Larssons rymliga hjärta* ("Mike Larsson's Spacious Heart"), 2010, involves a murder, but its real focus is the rehabilitation of Mike Larsson, a petty criminal who after his release from prison resolves to change his life and become a good father to his son Robin. *En enda sanning* ("One Single Truth"), 2012, a *noir* rural tale opens during a blizzard in the southern Swedish town of Österlen. Joel Lindgren, the long-estranged son of Mårten Lindgren, a failed local artist, finds Mårten hanged in his home with the Arabic phrase *Ghadeb Allah* ("the wrath of God") scrawled on the wall near him in red paint. To complicate the racially tense situation, Detective Inspector Fatima al Husseini is assigned to investigate the case, in which not one simple truth but several collide. *Jonny Liljas skuld* ("Jonny Lilja's Debt"), 2014, begins with Malmö narcotics detective Jonny Lilja hitting bottom: his wife has left him and he owes an enormous gambling debt to Yugoslav mafia boss Jokovic, one he can pay back only by betraying his vocation as a policeman. With police detective Eva Ström, Lilja works through the case of a dead girl that turns out to be not a suicide but a murder with dire connections to human trafficking.

Crime Novels:

2009: *Det som ska sonas* ("Atonement")
2010: *Mike Larssons rymliga hjärta* ("Mike Larsson's Spacious Heart")
2012: *En enda sanning* ("One Single Truth")
2014: *Jonny Liljas skuld* ("Jonny Lilja's Debt")

Major Awards:

2009: Best Swedish Crime Debut Crime Novel for *Det som ska sonas* ("Atonement")

Website: N/A

Kristian (also *Christian*) Lundberg (*Nils Kristian Lundberg*)

b. February 6, 1966, Malmö, Sweden; Residence: Malmö, Sweden; Occupations: literary critic, poet, author

Kristian Lundberg has published more than twenty books in various genres, including poetry, short fiction, autobiographical writings, and a few detective novels. After a period of youthful dissolution, he explored various Christian modes of belief, eventually settling into a liberal Christian position of service to humanity which often pervades his writings. His poem *Job* was nominated for the August Prize in 2005. He received considerable notoriety in December 2006 as a reviewer for *Helsingborgs Dagblad* when he wrote a critique of a detective novel by Britt-Marie Mattsson which had been announced in its publisher's catalog but which in fact did not exist. After being fired from the newspaper, Lundberg worked as a day laborer in the port of Malmö, which gave him the background for his widely praised working class novel *Yarden*, 2009, recently adapted for radio and stage theater.

Lundberg planned a series of five police procedural novels featuring forensic investigator Nils Forsberg, a depressed alcoholic in charge of the Malmö police Unit of Extraordinary Investigations. To date Lundberg has published only four, which have been collected in hardcover and audiobook versions called "Four × Forsberg." Swedish critic Lotta Olsson has observed that Lundberg's Forsberg novels can be read as a correlative of all bad-detective stories. In the first novel, Forsberg appears as a hopelessly, uselessly, helplessly dependent alcoholic, as capable of fumbling away a case as he is of solving it (Olsson). Despite attempts by an Alcoholics Anonymous buddy and a Catholic priest to help him, Forsberg blunders through this painful serial case involving murdered child prostitutes. Through the next three novels, Forsberg's world gradually slips away from him, his deadly fatigue mirroring his city's despair, shown reeling with both individual and collective despair in the third installment of the series, *Malmömannen* ("Malmö Man), where Forsberg leads inquiries into serial rape-killings of young immigrant girls that set off vicious racial unrest and rioting in the city, which has Sweden's highest immigrant population. Olsson describes the striking language Lundberg uses in these novels as "a steep granite staircase" stripped of everything unnecessary, and what is left is "cold and hard and necessary," and so beautiful you get tears in your eyes (Olsson).

Crime Novels:

Nils Forsberg Series:

2004: *Eldätaren* ("Eldätaren")
2005: *Grindväktaren* ("Gatekeeper")

2006: *Malmömannen* ("Malmö Man")
2008: *Grymhetens stad* ("Cruelty City")

Major Awards:

2011: *Sydsvenska Dagbladet* Culture Prize

Website: N/A

Lars Bill Lundholm

> b. September 15, 1948, Enskede, Sweden; Residence: Stockholm, Sweden; Occupations: script-writer, author

Since 1987, Lars Bill Lundholm, who describes himself as "author, player, farsa, vegetarian, and unsuccessful rock musician" ("Interview with Lars Bill Lundholm"), has written scripts for several award-winning television series, scripts for ten feature films, and seven detective novels, each of the most recent four set in a different part of Stockholm. In a telling 2010 interview, he disclosed that he has always read crime novels, and he said that before he came to detective fiction, he had already written scripts for crime-related television and films. Advised by the late Swedish film director Ingmar Bergman to "always stay provincial" in his fiction, Lundholm got "the idea that the anatomy of the murder should in some way correspond to the anatomy of a particular part of the town [Stockholm]" (Lundholm, "A Long Road").

Lundholm believes his Stockholm novels featuring police detective Axel Hake turned out well because for forty years after the Sjöwall-Wahlöö Martin Beck series no crime series was set in Stockholm, so it was "about time to let Stockholm be the scene again." He suggested that crime fiction is popular because it can include "everything"—"Love, violence, madness and everyday life," and he prefers that it can retain its low "gutter" status "and not [appear] on the cultural pages. There they are still too ignorant and flabby to be helpful ... it [crime fiction] requires knowledge and interest ... and they have not" (quoted in "Interview with Lars Bill Lundholm"). Lundholm's protagonist, Inspector Axel Hake, shows Lundholm's own interest: Hake "sees the unfortunates and the misfits day after day and tries to do something about it. Tries to honor the dead because no one else will" (Lundholm, "A Long Road" 56).

Lundholm especially admires Ruth Rendell's and Georges Simenon's mystery fiction (he owns all 75 Maigret novels). He is continuing to add to his *Stockholm Murder* series, and he has adapted *Skärgårdsdoktorn* as both a feature film and a new television series. "My novels," Lundholm believes, "are like an archaeological site, where layer after layer are removed to unearth the truth about the people and their lives. About right and wrong and about the way we live our lives under this sky of stones..." (Lundholm, "A Long Road" 56).

Crime Novel:

1987: *So long, Isabelle* ("So Long, Isabelle")

The Stockholm Murders Series (Inspector Axel Hake Series):

1998: *Skärgårdsdoktorn: den första sommaren* ("Skärgårdsdoktorn: the First Summer")
1999: *Skärgårdsdoktorn: kräftor och kvällsdopp* ("Skärgådsdoktoren: Crayfish and Evening Swim")
2002: *Östermalmsmorden* ("Östermalm Murders")
2003: *Södermalmsmorden* ("Södermalm Murders")

2005: *Kungsholmsmorden* ("Kungsholm Murders")

2009: *Gamla Stan-morden* ("Gamla Stan Murders")

Major Awards: N/A

Website: http://www.larsbill.com

Lennart Lundmark

> b. August 17, 1942, Arvidsjaur, Sweden; Residence: Umeå, Sweden; Occupations: historian, journalist, author

Historian Lennart Lundmark writes for Swedish newspapers, with a special interest in the relationship between the Sami people and the Swedish government. His one historical mystery novel, *Den motsträvige kommissarien* ("The Recalcitrant Commissioner"), 1997, nominated for the Glass Key Award, is set in the summer of 1793, shortly after the assassination of King Gustav III. Its major characters are seeking new religious goals while lawyer and poet Samuel Roos is investigating the murder of an army officer at a time when all manner of political intrigue is swirling around everyone.

Crime Novel:

1997: *Den motsträvige kommissarien* ("The Recalcitrant Commissioner")

Major Awards:

1997: The Best Debut Crime Novel of the Year, for *Den motsträvige kommissarien* ("The Recalcitrant Commissioner")

Website: N/A

*Henning Mankell

> b. February 3, 1948, Stockholm, Sweden; d. October 1, 2015, Gothenburg, Sweden; Residences: Skäne, Sweden; Maputo, Mozambique; vacation home in Antibes; Occupations: theater director, manager, and playwright, social activist, children's literature writer, author

One of the giants of Swedish crime literature (Holmberg 193), Henning Mankell has written over forty adult and juvenile fiction, thirty plays, many screenplays, and several significant non-fiction works (Moss). Mankell was deeply committed to Africa; around 2003 he set up a publishing firm to support African, Middle Eastern, and Asian novels, and for about half of each year he ran a theater in Mozambique. For Africa, Mankell claimed, he gave rather than took (quoted in Moss).

Despite living out his lifelong leftist philosophy in Africa, Mankell is best known worldwide for his Kurt Wallander police procedural series, which "jump-started what has developed into a nearly 20-year golden age" of Swedish crime literature (Ott). Mankell claimed that he worked "in an old tradition that goes back to the ancient Greeks. You hold a mirror to crime to see what's happening in society.... I always want to talk about certain things in society" (quoted in Thomson). The portrait of Swedish society that has emerged from Mankell's Wallander novels "is not a good advertisement for the success of the welfare state," showing cracks widening in Swedish society and Swedish family life, cracks turning into crevasses "riven by deep psychological traumas" (Forshaw 21).

Mankell summed up the debilitating changes he saw developing in Sweden through his leading character Kurt Wallander. Mankell said Wallander's work is so essential to him that if he did not do it, "he would leave a big black hole in himself…. I think he's of the Calvinist generation, in the sense that you are supposed to work and pray, which you are sweating. That is supposed to be your life" (quoted in Leavy 16). Mankell also said that Calvinism played a significant role in his own life, through his father's demanding Calvinist work ethic and "its damning vision of an unredeemed world" (quoted in Leavy 16).

In *Den vita lejoninnan*, 1993 (*The White Lioness*, tr. 1998), Wallander dismissed himself as a "pretty good policeman in a medium sized Swedish police district" (136). As he moves through the novels which followed, he battles aging, diabetes, incipient alcoholism, addiction to junk food, and issues with anger. His marriage disintegrated and he was unable to establish any other lasting romantic relationship. For a long time he was mostly estranged from his daughter Linda who tried to kill herself at fifteen, and he had severe disagreements with his late father, a victim of Alzheimer's Disease, which will also destroy Kurt Wallander himself. He loves opera and once intended to become an impresario, but the plan dissolved, one of the major disappointments in his life. Another is his police career; Wallander was once accused of police brutality and on another occasion he nearly resigned over killing a man in the fog, which drove him into a serious depression. He often questions his choice of profession, and his colleagues, though they generally acknowledge his intellect and intuition, often find his rough tactics and his professional manner as unpleasant as the "blustery vistas" of their Ystad environment: "Grey mud, grey trees, grey sky … greyest of all are the people" (*The Dogs of Riga*, quoted in Polito), all resonating with "metaphysical, even moral, desolation" (Polito).

Mankell told Robert Polito "without any hubris" that he, Polito, "would have difficulty finding novels that in a better way tried to give a description of what was going on in Europe during the 1990s (quoted in Polito). Ystad, probably "the Swedish town best known for murder and mayhem" (West 31), is located on the Baltic Sea near Latvia, Lithuania, and Poland. Ystad is also rife with what Mankell called "the new kind of criminality": organized crime operated by criminal and political elites from Eastern Europe and Russia due to the breakdown of the Soviet Union. These criminals exploit racism and the refugee problem through human trafficking for the prostitution of women and children, with "the use of accusations of organized crime to discredit national movements" (Polito). Each of the Wallander novels approaches one or more serious societal issues, usually in Ystad, accompanied by one of Wallander's personal crises. "Much as his [leftist] politics have responded to the real-time transformation of Europe, so his personal life has evolved in real time as well: divorce; a difficult, then dying, father; a strained kinship with Linda; clumsy or distant crushes on women; muddled angers; fatigue, messy isolation" (Polito).

In *Mördare utan ansikte*, 1991 (*Faceless Killers*, tr. 1997), Wallander's marriage has just unraveled when the Ystad police are called to investigate a violent assault on an elderly rural couple, setting off fierce xenophobia among the local residents. *Hundarna i Riga*, 1992 (*The Dogs of Riga*, tr. 2001) takes Wallander, tormented by self-doubts, to a largely lawless post–Soviet Union Latvia. *Den vita lejoninnan*, 1993 (*The White Lioness*, tr. 1998), involves Wallander with Africa, a country close to Mankell's heart, as the detective hunts a former KGB agent, now in Sweden, who had trained black South Africans to assassinate Nelson Mandela. *Mannen som log*, 1994 (*The Man Who Smiled*, tr. 2006) finds Wallander out sick and considering resigning from the police, but after a friend is killed Wallander returns to work, eventually exposing a tycoon who profits from unspeakable crimes. One of Mankell's most praised novels, *Villospår*, 1995 (*Sidetracked*, tr. 1999), disrupts Wallander's long overdue vacation with the axe-murder and scalping of Sweden's retired Minister of Justice. In *Den femte kvinnan*, 1996 (*The Fifth Woman*, tr. 2000), Wallander, increasingly emotionally frail and physically fragile, faces a sadistic torturer-killer, and as his own problems mount in his seventh novel, *Steget efter*, 1997 (*One Step Behind*, tr. 2003), he has to solve the murder of his enigmatic colleague Svedberg. Terrorism dominates *Brandvägg*, 1998 (*Firewall*, tr. 2002), while Wallander extricates himself from departmental politics. The Wallander short story collection *Pyramiden*, 1999 (*The Pyramid*, tr. 2008), ninth in the Wallander fiction series, takes place prior to the action of *Faceless Killers*, giving important insights into Wallander's early development. In 2002's *Innan frosten* (*Before the Frost*, tr. 2004), Mankell concentrates on Wallander's daughter Linda, now graduating from the police academy and, nearly as beset by doubts about her career as her father has been, she must deal with a fanatic religious cult predicting a fiery doomsday.

In 2009, Mankell provided "a poignant farewell" (Sexton) to Kurt Wallander in *Den orolige mannen* (*The Troubled Man*, tr. 2011), with a Cold War spy plot and Wallander at a sadly deteriorating sixty years old, facing both the loss of his memory and the death of Baiba, the woman he loves, from cancer. Meeting Kurt Wallander here affects readers "not least because it is a substantial investment of our own time and commitment to which we are bidding farewell" (Sexton). Despite the melancholy of Wallander's last years, "Mankell never lets his story become engulfed by darkness…. Wallander shows an intensity of emotion here, a last gasp of felt life that is both moving and oddly inspiring" (Ott). Marilyn Stasio of the *New York Times* declared, "Wallander saves our sanity by taking the weight of the world off our minds and onto his own shoulders—an honorable legacy for someone who thought all his friends were dead" (Stasio).

In a brief note at the back of *An Event in Autumn*, which covers the period of Wallder's life just before *A Troubled Man* and which he had written many years earlier and republished in 2013, Mankell described how the series began, how it finished, and the events between (*Event* 155–169). Significantly, he also revealed that while he wrote these novels, an inner voice reminded him, "You must make sure that you drop him at the right moment" (*Event* 166), so he declared, "There are no more stories about Kurt Wallander" (*Event* 152).

The popularity of Kurt Wallander, "so grumpy, always tired, never physically well, struggling on, so fundamentally decent" (Sexton), has burgeoned with film and television adaptations of Mankell's fiction. All the first nine of the Wallander books were made into feature length Swedish films between 1994 and 2007, starring Rolf Lassgård. Swedish Television aired thirteen new Wallander stories from 2005 to 2006, the first episode drawn from *Before the Frost* and the rest from original stories not based on any of the novels. Yellow Bird released a second series of new Swedish-language Wallander films, beginning in January 2009, when some 18 million viewers tuned in for the first episode, and continuing through 2010. All starred Swedish actor Krister Henriksson and were released on DVD.

With a budget of $12 million, Yellow Bird and Left Bank Pictures adapted Mankell's first nine Wallander books for the BBC, starring Kenneth Branagh and photographed during the summer of 2008 at Ystad, airing them later that fall. Their second Wallander series appeared in 2010. Branagh, also the series' executive producer, feels the Ystad setting provides "a physical space in which to reflect, in which you can be lost" (quoted in Keveney). The third Wallander series, shot in Ystad and Riga in 2011, was broadcast in July 2012, and the fourth and final series concluded with an adaptation of *The White Lioness* and two episodes adapted from *The Troubled Man*. Kenneth Branagh observed, "I enjoy the ingenuity of good plotting, and I like … searching character work. I felt Henning Mankell had broken through to a treatment of the middle-aged, rather bruised and battered detective, and produced in Wallander something pretty original … not simply … a morose man but [one] trying to be a better person … a man who wants to be happy" (quoted in Keveney).

Mankell believes he "learn[ed] more about the human condition with one foot in the snow and one foot in the sand" (quoted in Moss), referring to his long involvement with African issues, specifically the AIDS epidemic there and widespread African poverty. He maintained his "fierce instinct for social criticism" in his stand-alone crime novels (Bergman), several of which deal with problems related to Africa, where he spent part of his time. In *Danslärarens återkomst* (*Return of the Dancing Master*, tr. 2004), Mankell's detective hero Stefan Lindman, recently diagnosed with cancer, investigates a neo–Nazi network with frightening tentacles reaching into high levels of Sweden's society. In *Kennedys hjärna*, 2005 (*Kennedy's Heart*, tr. 2007), Mankell showed "how powerful Western pharmaceutical companies exploit poor black Africans by using them as guinea pigs in order to develop a cure for AIDS ... a parallel to the AIDS memory books from Uganda" (Bergman). In *Kinesen*, 2008 (*The Man from Beijing*, tr. 2010), Mankell echoed Ingmar Bergman's assessment that a "virulent, terrifying evil" exists within all humanity, asking, "Why does barbarism always wear a human face?" (Peed) through Judge Birgitta Roslin, on leave due to diagnosed fatigue, who probes the grisly discovery of nineteen dead disfigured bodies in a small Swedish town. Because Mankell's novels are also discourses on solidarity against such abuses, "they attempt to force readers to think through solidarity's ethical and political dimensions" (Nestingen 232). Mankell's *The Shadow Girls*, 2012, a foray into dark humor, blends Mankell's concern for Africa's problems with ironic commentary on Swedish crime writing. He based *Minnet av an smutsig ängel*, 2012 (*A Treacherous Paradise*, tr. 2013, also called "Memoirs of a Dirty Angel"), on the true account of Hanna Renstrom, a young Swedish woman who left Sweden during a famine because her family could no longer feed their children. In 1904, shortly after when she arrives in Mozambique, she becomes the operator of a brothel there, an opportunity for Mankell to exhibit his unique insights into "cold north versus hot south, Swedish temperament combining with African license" (Boyd), in this exposure of "the dark heart of colonialism" (Moss).

By both attempting to better the lives of Africans and through his Wallander novels exploring the "anxieties of modern Sweden" (Moss), Mankell sometimes felt "a little alone" (quoted in Moss), because he believed "too few writers accept they have a moral responsibility to take a stand" (quoted in Moss). Mankell, though, made his own position clear; his writing was his life (Moss). As the representation of contemporary Swedish society and the indictment of its welfare state that Mankell intended his Wallander series to be, these books as well as his stand alone crime novels shattered the popular façade of Sweden as "a pristine region, full of nice people, liberal to a fault" (Ott). With the Wallander novels, too, Henning Mankell, son-in-law of Swedish director Ingmar Bergman and himself a gifted theatrical director and playwright, also set the stage for the achievements of many Swedish crime authors who followed him. One of the most famous of them, Stieg Larsson, "may be an international publishing phenomenon, but without Mankell to set his Swedish table, he might have been just another talented author with a limited audience" (Ott).

Crime Novels:

The Kurt Wallander Series:

1991: *Mördare utan ansikte* (*Faceless Killers*, tr. Steven T. Murray, 1997)
1992: *Hundarna i Riga* (*The Dogs of Riga*, tr. Laurie Thompson, UK 2001, U.S. 2003)
1993: *Den vita lejoninnan* (*The White Lioness*, tr. Laurie Thompson, 1998)
1994: *Mannen som log* (*The Man Who Smiled*, tr. Laurie Thompson, 2006)
1995: *Villospår* (*Sidetracked*, tr. Steven T. Murray, U.S. 1999, UK 2000)
1996: *Den femte kvinnan* (*The Fifth Woman*, tr. Steven T. Murray, U.S. 2000, UK 2001)
1997: *Steget efter* (*One Step Behind*, tr. Ebba Segerberg, 2003)

1998: *Brandvägg* (*Firewall*, tr. Ebba Segerberg, UK 2003, U.S. 2002)

1999: *Pyramiden* (*The Pyramid*, tr. Ebba Segerberg, 2008)

2009: *Den orolige mannen* (*The Troubled Man*, tr. Laurie Thompson, 2011)

2013: *Handen* (*An Event in Autumn*, tr. Laurie Thompson, 2014, originally published in Dutch as *Het graf*, 2004)

The Linda Wallander Crime Novel:

2002: *Innan frosten* (*Before the Frost*, tr. Ebba Segerberg, UK 2004, U.S. 2005)

Selected Other Novels:

2000: *Danslärarens återkomst* (*Return of the Dancing Master*, tr. Laurie Thompson, U.S. 2004)

2005: *Kennedys hjärna* (*Kennedy's Brain*, tr. Laurie Thompson, 2007)

2008: *Kinesen* (*The Man from Beijing*, tr. Laurie Thompson, 2010)

2012: *Minnet av en smutsig ängel* (*A Treacherous Paradise*, tr. Laurie Thomson, 2013)

Humor Novel:

2001: *Tea bags* (*Tidens gåla*); (*The Shadow Girls*, tr. Ebba Segerberg, 2012)

Selected Nonfiction:

2003: *Jag dör, men minnet lever* (*I Die, but the Memory Lives On: A Personal Reflection on AIDS*, tr. Laurie Thompson, 2004)

Major Awards:

1991: The Glass Key Award, for *Mördare utan ansikte* (*Faceless Killers*)

1991: Best Swedish Crime Novel, for *Mördare utan ansikte* (*Faceless Killers*)

1995: Best Swedish Crime Novel, Swedish Crime Academy, for *Villospår* (*Sidetracked*)

1999: Golden Paperback Award, for *Villospår* (*Sidetracked*) and *Den femte kvinnan* (*The Fifth Woman*)

2001: Macallan Golden Dagger Award, British Crime Writers Association, for *Villospår* (*Sidetracked*)

2004: Gumshoe Award for Best European Crime Novel, Mystery Ink

Websites: http://www.inspector-wallander.org; http://www.branaghswallander.com; http://www.inspector-wallander.org; http://www.ystadsallehanda.se/allandersystadu

*Liza Marklund (Eva Elizabeth Marklund)

b. September 9, 1962, Pålmark, Sweden; Residence: Stockholm, Sweden, and Marbella, Spain; Occupations: journalist, UNICEF goodwill ambassador, co-owner of publishing company, *Expressen* columnist, author

Bestselling Liza Marklund's literary representative, the Salomonsson Agency, claims that she revolutionized the modern Swedish police procedural in the 1990s with her Annika Bengtzon novels, which have sold over 15 million copies in more than 30 languages. After Stieg Larsson, Marklund, a media star in Sweden experienced at promoting her books (Hindersmann 12), was the second Swedish author to reach the number one position on the *New York Times* bestseller list, which she accomplished with *The Postcard Killers*, a collaboration with American author James Patterson.

Marklund had been a working journalist for a decade when she left what she calls one of the greatest jobs in Sweden as the manager of news broadcasts at Sweden's TV4 to devote herself to writing crime fiction. In her website's autobiographical statement, she admits, "People thought I was crazy," but her decision proved solid; she parlayed it into highly successful careers as a crime fiction author and with fellow author Jan Guillou and his wife, as co-owner of *Piratförlaget*, now Sweden's third largest publishing house.

Marklund debuted in 1995 with *Gömda* (*Buried Alive*), which garnered several literary awards and sold a million copies as a paperback categorized as "biography/autobiography" dealing with a woman so badly abused by a boyfriend that she was forced into hiding because Sweden's welfare state could not protect her. After Marklund reworked it and reissued it in 2000 from *Piratförlaget* subtitled "a true story" she marketed it as "autobiography/biography" (*Vad för slags bok är Gömda?*). That reworked version made Marklund one of Sweden's best selling novelists of all time and the fourth most popular woman in Sweden in 2004 (O'Loughlin). *Gömda* also aroused controversy. Swedish journalist Monica Antonsson published a 2008 book criticizing the factual background of *Buried Alive*, and since then, Marklund and Guillou have publicly announced that "based on a true story" would have been a more accurate subtitle. "Maria Eriksson," the real woman represented by the abused main character was also listed as co-author of the first editions of the two novels in the "Maria Eriksson" series. She has written three more books about her experiences with domestic violence, all without any involvement from Liza Marklund. "Maria Eriksson" publicly confirmed her identity in 2009 and now lives in Arizona (Edblom). The controversy has also produced academic studies dealing with the nature of and the techniques involved with writing documentary novels. The second novel in this series, *Asyl* ("Asylum Granted"), deals with "Maria Eriksson"'s five-year struggle to obtain asylum in the United States as a victim of gender-based abuse and domestic violence.

Marklund, who admires the novels of Anne Holt, Henning Mankell, Karin Slaughter, and the Israeli author Amos Oz, gave her heroine Annika Bengtzon, a courageous and compassionate investigative reporter, "a dark and destructive streak" (Marklund website). Annika Bengtzon is a character that Marklund says she has known for her entire life (Marklund website). Marklund also gave this character her oldest daughter's first name and the family name of one of Marklund's favorite editors (Hindersmann 13). Marklund put Annika into a tough world Marklund herself knew intimately from first hand experience, with convincing results. Marklund's fellow Nordic *femikrim* author Anne Holt placed Annika Bengtzon sixth on Holt's list of top ten female detectives, calling her "the hardest-headed professional in Scandinavian literature today" (Holt).

Marklund had excelled as a tabloid journalist for ten years, with more front pages than any other female in the field. She then became an editor for one of the largest tabloids in northern Europe. She recreated strong elements of that demanding career in the Bengtzon series with such "vivid intensity" that another of her fellow authors, Karin Slaughter, has remarked that the Bengtzon novels make "the reader feel as if they are looking over Annika's shoulder" (quoted in O'Loughlin). In her first Bengtzon novel, *Sprängeren*, 1996 (*The Bomber*, tr. 2001), Marklund began with how Annika Bengtzon had become a television news manager and the troubles this caused (Marklund website). In the second novel, *Studio sex*, 1999 (*Studio 69*, tr. 2003) she moved backward to Bengtzon's early career, then worked her way to the present through the fifth Annika Bengtzon novel, *Den röda vargen*, 2003 (*The Red Wolf*, tr. 2010), set in the far north of Sweden where Marklund grew up. Professionally, from being "a gawky intern," Bengtzon develops into a "cynical editor" of a major newspaper's crime section, while personally she grows from an abuse victim to a married mother of two, then to a divorced single mother with all the tensions and problems that status involves (Marklund website).

Marklund believes that writing "keeps her going" and "keeps her sane" (Marklund website).

She told Vanessa O'Loughlin, "I want to keep it all in my head, and for that I need to concentrate, I write twelve hours a day—starting around 10 am and finishing at 10 p.m." She also says that the "key perspective" to her work is "media criticism and journalistic consequences" (quoted in Forshaw 90). She takes about four months to write a book, doing considerable research first, often turning raw material into dialogue, and planning each chapter in detail (Marklund website). The long interest in human rights she incorporates into her novels has taken her to every location she writes about, including Africa, where she has family interests in Kenya. Being a close friend of Swedish government minister Anna Lindh, a murder victim, intensified Marklund's campaign against domestic abuse: "I couldn't write for three years after Anna was killed. I think crime fiction is only read by people untouched by crime—if you experience it, you don't want to read or write about it." For Marklund in 2011, this explained "why Scandinavia is such a popular backdrop for crime novels. It is the most peaceful society on earth ... we like to think that the reason the rest of the world has problems is because they are not Swedish!" (quoted in O'Loughlin).

Marklund is, however, hardly oblivious to Sweden's current problems, like domestic abuse and alcoholism. Calling herself "a political writer" who uses her novels to "get a message across" (quoted in Forshaw 90), she insists that Sweden "is by no means heaven.... We're way up there in the suicide league.... We drink too much, and too many men beat their women on a daily basis ... all my books are really about power—what people are willing to do to get it and keep it" (quoted in Forshaw 91). Violence against women, gender issues, child abuse and media flaws "are Marklund's key topics" (Forshaw 91), though she has indicated that her long association with Annika Bengtzon may be coming to an end since she says she and Annika "need a break from each other." Even without Annika, Liza Marklund is not through with writing fiction: "the long and dark winters definitely have some kind of magic about them, what else is there to do than develop creativity?" (quoted in Krugly).

Marklund's Annika Bengtzon novels are being adapted for theater film and television. English director Colin Nutley filmed *The Bomber* and *Paradise* in Swedish, starring Helena Bergström and released in 2001 and 2002 respectively. Yellow Bird, a film and television production company that belongs to the trans–European group Zodiak Entertainment and produced film versions of Stieg Larsson's Millennium Trilogy and Henning Mankell's Wallander series, began airing six more of the Bengtzon novels for about 10 million euros, starting in 2012, hoping to make Annika Bengtzon and her creator Liza Marklund household names around the world.

Crime Novels:

Annika Bengtzon Series:

1996: *Sprängaren* (*The Bomber*, tr. Kajsa con Hofsten, 2001, retr. Neil Smith, U.S. 2011)

1999: *Studio sex* (*Studio Sex*, also published as *Studio 69* and *Exposed*, tr. Kajsa von Hofstem, 2003, retr. Neil Smith, 2011)

2000: *Paradiset* (*Paradise*, tr. Ingrid Eng-Rundlow, 2004)

2002: *Prime Time* (*Prime Time*, tr. Ingrid Eng-Rundlow, 2006)

2003: *Den röda vargen* (*The Red Wolf*, tr. Neil Smith, 2010)

2007: *Nobels testamente* (*Last Will*, tr. Neil Smith, 2012)

2007: *Livstid* (*Lifetime*, tr. Neil Smith, 2012)

2008: *En plats i solen* (*The Long Shadow*, tr. Neil Smith, 2013)

2011: *Du gamla, du fria* (*Borderline*, tr. Neil Smith, 2014)

2013: *Lyckliga gatan* ("Lucky Street," proposed English title "Nora's Book")

2015: *Järnblod* (*The Final Word*, tr. Neil Smith, scheduled for 2016)

Maria Eriksson Series:

1995: *Gömda* (*Buried Alive*, tr. N/A, first marketed as a "true story" in the "autobiography/biography" category; re-issued in 2000. It is in fact a novel based on a true story)

2004: *Asyl: den sanna fortsättningen på Gömda* (*Asylum Granted: A True Story*, tr. N/A)

Other Crime Novel:

2010: *The Postcard Killers*, with James Patterson (in English)

Major Awards:

1998: The Poloni Prize, for *Sprängaren* (*The Bomber*)
1998: Best Debut Crime Novel, for *Sprängaren* (*The Bomber*)
1999: Swedish Union's Award for Author of the Year, for *Studio Sex* (*Studio 69*)
2013: Petrona Award, for *Nobels testamente* (*Last Will*)

Website: http://www.lizamarklund.com

Jan Mårtenson

b. January 14, 1933; Residence: Ammeberg, Sweden; Occupations: diplomat, author

Jan Mårtenson, a distinguished Swedish diplomat, served as Deputy Secretary General of the United Nations and headed the United Nations' European offices in Geneva. Beginning in 1973, Mårtenson has published one popular cozy detective novel per year, almost all featuring amateur sleuths Johan Kristian Homan, an antique dealer who hates blood, and his blue point Siamese cat partner Cléo de Merode. Mårtenson set three of his crime novels in the late 18th century, with Homan's ancestor Johan Sebastian Homan as the detective, but in the contemporary novels, Homan and Cléo together solve gentle but exciting literary investigations into natural and supernatural murders involving refined culture and history, gourmet cuisine and exquisite red wines. Besides his crime fiction, Mårtenson has also written poetry, history and art studies, a cookbook combining his interests in murder and food, and his memoirs.

Selected Crime Novels:

Johan Kristian Homan Series:

1973: *Helgeandsmordet* ("Helgeand's Murder")
1987: *Den röda näckrosen* ("Red Water Lily")
1995: *Karons färja* ("Charon's Ferry")
2013: *Den grekiska hjälmen* ("The Greek Helmet")

Major Awards: N/A

Website: http://www.homansalskapet.se (The Homan Society's website)

Bertil Mårtensson

b. 1945, Malmö, Sweden; Residence: Rydebäck, Sweden; Occupations: philosopher, composer, author

Bertil Mårtensson has held academic positions in philosophy at Umeå University and Lund University and has published widely in the field. He has also composed music and written science fiction short stories and novels as well as four conventional crime fiction novels written in the late 1970s, all set in the Malmö area.

Selected Crime Novels:

1976: *Mah-jongmorden* ("Mah-jong Murders")
1977: *Växande hot* ("A Growing Threat")
1985: *Kontrakt med döden* ("Contracts with Death")

Major Awards:

1977: The Sherlock Prize for *Växande hot* ("A Growing Threat")

Website: http://www.flyingbird.se

Bodil Mårtensson

> b. 1952, Karlskrona, Sweden; Residence: Rydebeck, a suburb of Helsingborg, Sweden; Occupation: author

Bodil Mårtensson was married to famous Swedish philosopher Bertil Mårtensson from 1971 to 2005. She began writing adult hard-boiled police procedurals in 1999, featuring Commissioner Joakim Hill and his Helsingborg Police team, treating her themes with humor and a firm moral perspective. *En chans för mycket* ("One Chance Is Too Many"), the first novel of the series, was nominated for the Poloni Prize. Mårtensson's later procedurals include excursions to other Swedish areas, to Denmark, and to Florida in *Cuba Red*, 2005. In 2011 Mårtensson began a series of historical thrillers set in fourteenth century Helsingborg, the era of King Magnus Eriksson, with "Burkha's Daughter," followed by "Burkha's Son" and "Burkha's Cross."

Shortly after Bodil Mårtensson's *Brottskod 09* appeared in 2007, veteran Swedish crime author and critic Jean Bolinder used his review of that novel for *DAST Magazine* (founded in 1967 and online since 2007, it's Sweden's premier journal for popular fiction in the detective ["D"], secret agent ["A"], science fiction ["S"], and thriller ["T"] subgenres) as a springboard for pungent commentary on other Swedish crime authors and the dark secrets beneath contemporary Sweden's deceptively idyllic surface. Bolinder denounced the "cheap thrills" of "paper waste such as Lisa Marklund's books" and Henning Mankell's "repeated recipes," but he praised the psychological acuity and moral stance of Mårtensson's crime novels. In *Brottskod 09* Mårtensson exposes the human trafficking becoming rampant in Sweden, and Bolinder responded, "the slave traders are among us, and 'honest' Swedish family men pay to humiliate the poor young girls who have been duped into dreamland Sweden with false promises of well-paying jobs.... Bravo Bodil Mårtensson, this is one of the last decade's best Swedish crime novel[s]" (Bolinder).

Crime Novels:

The Commissioner Joakim Hill Series:

1999: *En chans för mycket* ("One Chance Is Too Many")
2000: *Beckmörker* ("Pitch Black")
2001: *Torpeden* ("The Hitman")
2002: *Konsten att dö* ("The Noble Art of Dying")
2004: *Jag vet att du är ensam* ("I Know You Are All Alone")
2005: *Cuba Red* ("Cuba Red")
2006: *Nattportierns historia* ("The Night Porter's Story")

2007: *Brottskod 09* ("Brottskod 09")

2008: *Rebeccas blod* ("Rebecca's Blood")

2009: *Greppet* ("The Grip")

2010: *Justine Raschans hämnd* ("Justine Raschan's Revenge")

Major Awards: N/A

Website: http://bodilmartensson.se/in_english.html

Magnus Montelius

> b. August 5, 1965, birthplace N/A; Residence: Stockholm, Sweden; Occupations: civil engineer and environmental consultant, author

Magnus Montelius has lived and worked extensively in Latin America, in Africa, and in the former Soviet-bloc and eastern European countries as a civil engineer specializing in water projects. He drew on his wide experience with Communist governments for his debut crime novel, *Mannen från Albanien* ("The Man from Albania"), 2011, a widely praised Cold War espionage/political thriller set in 1990 around the time of the collapse of the Soviet Iron Curtain domain. The novel opens with the apparent suicide of a man carrying an Albanian passport, though the Albanian authorities refuse to admit he even existed. Three persons arrive at the scene of the death, a hill overlooking Stockholm, each with an apparently simple reason: one is a policeman, another a woman journalist, and the third simply wants to get out of the weather, but their involvement soon uncovers frightening secrets dating from the radical 1960s student movement at Uppsala.

Crime Novel:

2011: *Mannen från Albanien* ("The Man from Albania")

Major Awards: N/A

Website: N/A

Michael Mortimer (pseudonym of Daniel Sjölin and Jerker Virdborg)

> Daniel Sjölin: b. 1977, Bälsta, Stockholm, Sweden; Residence: Stockholm, Sweden; Occupations: literary critic, television presenter, author
>
> Jerker Virdborg: b. 1971, Lindome, Sweden; Residence: Stockholm, Sweden; Occupation: author

Before joining authorial forces with Jerker Virdborg as "Michael Mortimer," Daniel Sjölin, a television presenter, had published several novels, including "The World's Last Novel," 2007, which was nominated for the prestigious August Prize. Jerker Virdborg had published five novels between 2002 and 2012, including "Black Crab," 2002, which received the *Tidningen litteraturpris*. Together they have produced *Jungfrustenen*, 2013 (*The Maidenstone*, tr. 2014), followed by *Fossil-drottningen* ("The Escape from Paradise") and *Blodssystrana* ("Blood Sisters"). The first three novels of a projected six-novel series.

The Maidenstone has received glowing reviews praising its historical background, which includes actual figures like Greta Garbo, Goethe, and Linnaeus, as heroine Ida Nordlund seeks to unravel the mystery of the artifact called the "Maidenstone" which she believes will help her understand her family history. According to the novel, in 1769 Carl von Linné's disciple Daniel Solander found that strange stone in New Zealand; it broke into four pieces, which over the centuries were held by such personages as Josef Stalin, Garbo, and Niels Bohr. These artifacts were sent to Ida by her grandmother but they were lost on their way to her and their couriers were murdered. Ida and her father are then pursued throughout Europe by a secret scientific organization bent on finding the mysterious artifacts. Critic Nichola Smalley feels that Mortimer's skillful shifts between past and present are "well-suited to the short attention spans of so many readers today." Smalley also feels that "Mortimer's deft characterization through voice ... the creepy comments and connivances of one character, combined with the neuroticism of his travelling companion, are spinetingling" (Smalley).

Crime Novels:

2013: *Jungfrustenen* (*The Maidenstone*, tr. Laura A. Wideburg, 2014)
2014: *Fossildrottningen* ("The Escape from Paradise")
2015: *Blodssystrana* ("Blood Sisters")

Major Awards: N/A

Website: N/A

Jonas Moström

> b. 1973, Bracke, Jämtland, Sweden; Residence: Stockholm, Sweden; Occupations: family physician, author

In a 2010 interview, family physician Jonas Moström observed that writing had became for him a way of coping with the difficulties a physician routinely encounters in his work: "life and death are tangible ingredients in both professions" (quoted in "Interview with Jonas Moström"). Moström's crime novels feature cardiologist Erik Jensen and Detective Lieutenant John Axbergsgränd of the Sundevall police. Moström cites Dennis Lehane, Åke Edwardson, and Karin Fossum as three of his favorite crime writers, and he also finds Karin Alvtegen's psychological problem formulations fascinating. Moström says he deals with his involved life—the demands of helping his wife raise small children while writing his novels and working 60 percent of fulltime practice as a physician—by setting priorities and often doing two things at once.

From that dualistic perspective, Moström maintains that the two major characters of his police procedurals will remain together in future books, because Johan, the policeman, is a lonely person who has difficulties with his relationships with women, and he needs Erik's friendship badly. Together they utilize historical analogues to present-day problems in cases involving thorny contemporary medical issues like euthanasia and alternative medicine. *Storsjöodjuret*, 2013, Moström's eighth procedural, shifts their setting to Jämtland, a picturesque Swedish rural county. As a physician-author, Moström feels that reading detective novels contributes to one's health, because it provides primitive adrenalin surges not usually possible in today's civilized environments ("Interview with Jonas Moström").

Crime Novels:

2004: *Dödens pendel* ("Death Pendulum")
2006: *Svart cirkel* ("Black Circle")
2008: *Hjärtats mörker* ("The Heart's Darkness")
2009: *Rymd utan stjärnor* ("Space Without Stars")

2010: *Mirakelmannen* ("Miracle Man")
2011: *Evig eld i* ("Eternal Flame")
2012: *Stryparen* ("Strangler")
2013: *Storsjöodjuret* ("Storsjoodjuret")
2014: *Himlen är alltid högre* ("The Sky Is Always Higher")
2015: *Dominodöden* ("Domino Death")

Major Awards: N/A

Website: http:www.jonasmostrom.se

Håkan Nesser

> b. February 21, 1950, Kumla, Sweden; Residence: Uppsala, Sweden (for most of his life); now Gotland, Sweden, and London, England; Occupations: teacher, author

One of Sweden's most honored crime fiction writers, Håkan Nesser has published two crime series and ten stand-alone novels. Nesser grew up in Kumla, Sweden's largest prison city, and worked as a high school teacher in Uppsala until he turned to writing full time in 1998. He has also lived in Greenwich Village, New York City, and London, where his wife practiced as a psychiatrist. He also knows Finland and Spain, and recently he and his wife are dividing their time between London and Gotland, Sweden. Nesser's cosmopolitan background is reflected in his most famous work, the popular ten-novel Detective Chief Inspector Van Veeteren series, written between 1993, when Nesser was 40, and 2003. The first five of these feature Van Veeteren as an active police detective, divorced and grouchy but also intuitive, warm, and funny, caring for a sick elderly dog. The last five show him running his antiquarian bookshop and helping his former colleagues with their cases. Van Veeteren had only one unsolved case in his career, which Nesser addressed in 2003's *Fallet G* (*The G File*, tr. 2014).

Because he feels a fictional setting allows him to create his own geography to fit his themes, Nesser set the Van Veeteren series in Maardam, a fictitious northern European city of about 300,000 in an unnamed country, amalgamating elements of Sweden, Poland, Germany, and the Netherlands (most of the names in these novels sound Dutch). Missing is the conviction many Scandinavian writers exhibit that their countries are plunging downhill because of their wrongheaded welfare state policies; "Nesser never openly grinds any sociological axes" (Forshaw 73). The Van Veeteren novels have been ably translated by Laurie Thompson, but they have appeared in English out of compositional order.

Nesser's other works include the Inspector Gunnar Barbarotti police procedural series begun in 2006 and as yet not translated into English, with a new protagonist, a Swedish police Inspector whose father was Italian. Gunnar Barbarotti works in Kymlinge, a fictitious Swedish town Nesser named after an abandoned Stockholm subway station. The series concludes with *Styckerskan från Lilla Burma* ("Styckerskan from Little Burma"), 2012, in which Barbarotti, attempting to deal with the sudden death of his wife, is assigned the cold case of Ellen Bjarnebo from a farm called "Little Burma," who has served eleven years for murdering and dismembering a man close to her.

Nesser's stand-alone novels range from his 1988 literary debut *Koreografen* ("Choreography"), a love story; a growing-up novel, *Och Piccadilly Circus ligger inte i Kumla* ("And Piccadilly Circus Is Not in Kumla"); *Kära Agnes!* 2002 ("Dear Agnes!"), an epistolary novel; the haunting 2014 novel *Levande och döda i Winsford* (*The Living and the Dead in Winsford*, tr. 2015), the untangling of a heinous crime, told in lonely Exmoor; and a short story collection, *Barins triangel*

("Barin's Triangle"), 1996. His Van Veeteren series has been translated into twenty-five languages and has been adapted as ten films and a Swedish television series of six ninety-minute episodes in which Van Veeteren's former police associates Moreno and Münster continue to consult him about their cases. Though Van Veeteren has now retired from the Maardam police, he often can't resist taking an active role with the investigations himself. He is also trying to rebuild his relationship with his estranged son Erich, whose troubled background with crime and drugs Van Veeteren blames at least partly on his own concentration on his police work. He also has a new romantic interest.

Interviewed in 2008 regarding *Det grovmaskiga nätet*, 1993 (*The Mind's Eye*, tr. 2008), his first Van Veeteren novel but the third to be published in English, Nesser remarked that he enjoyed the work of Dutch crime author Janwillem van de Wetering, for whom he named Van Veeteren, because "they sort of look in the wrong direction most of the time ... but perhaps Van Veeteren is different in this respect" (quoted in Rozovsky). He also noted that his books often empathize with characters who have been imprisoned or held in other kinds of institutions, because he feels "With different circumstances the good guy would have been the bad guy. It's important to understand the motive, and to not demonize the criminal" (quoted in Rozovsky). British crime author Ann Cleeves, who also interviewed Nesser in 2008, elicited a practical paternal response from him regarding criminals, whom he often treats sympathetically in his novels. "Nesser said that he had told his daughters that if they were ever being assaulted or raped to tell the perpetrator that 'my father will seek you out and kill you'" (quoted in Robinson).

Nesser feels "no way there is such thing as a Swedish way of writing a crime story. Because a book—every book—is a dialogue between two people. One writer, one reader ... people are people everywhere. And when it comes to important matters—e.g., good stories—we understand each other" (Nesser, "Portrait" 57). Nesser addressed the topic of his own "good stories" in 2012, in particular the human capacity for crime, observing, "Given the right circumstances, almost everybody could become a murderer.... I want for the reader as for myself to have an understanding of the criminal.... It gives a humanistic touch to it" (quoted in Diaz). Making such touches psychologically convincing required considerable effort by Nesser as a novelist. When he began writing his Van Veeteren novels, he was teaching half time, which he enjoyed, but he realized that it required a large commitment of energy. When he chose to write full time, he put enormous effort into his work, writing each first draft by hand and then revising thoroughly. In 2012, he thought he had two or three more books to publish, "and then I am done as a writer." He also declared that the type of story he writes is not important to him: "what is important is that it is a good story, a story that I would like to read myself" (quoted in Diaz). Nesser's many awards for his crime fiction support British crime critic Barry Forshaw's estimate of the impressive quality of Nesser's writing as "splendid stuff ... so rivetingly written it makes most contemporary crime fare—Scandinavian or otherwise—seem rather undernourished" (Forshaw 69).

Crime Novels:

The Van Veeteren Series:

1993: *Det grovmaskiga nätet* (*The Mind's Eye*, tr. Laurie Thompson, 2008)

1994: *Borkmanns punkt* (*Borkmann's Point*, tr. Laurie Thompson, 2008)

1995: *Återkomsten* (*The Return*, tr. Laurie Thompson, 2007)

1996: *Kvinna med födelsemärke* (*Woman with Birthmark*, tr. Laurie Thompson, 2009)

1997: *Kommissarien och tystnaden* (*The Inspector and Silence*, tr. Laurie Thompson, 2010)

1998: *Münsters fall* (*Munster's Case*, also published as *The Unlucky Lottery*, tr. Laurie Thompson, 2011)

1999: *Carambole* (*The Hour of the Wolf*, tr. Laurie Thompson, 2012)
2000: *Ewa Morenos fall* (*The Weeping Girl*, tr. Laurie Thompson, 2013)
2001: *Svalan, katten, rosen, döden* (*The Strangler's Honeymoon*, tr. Laurie Thompson, 2013)
2003: *Fallet G* (*The G File*, tr. Laurie Thompson, 2014)

The Inspector Barbarotti Series:

2006: *Människa utan hund* ("A Man Without a Dog")
2007: *En helt annan historia* ("A Completely Different Story")
2008: *Berättelse om herr Roos* ("A Tale of Mr. Roos")
2010: *De ensamma* ("They Alone")
2012: *Styckerskan från Lilla Burma* ("Styckerskan from Little Burma")

Selected Stand-Alone Fiction:

1988: *Koreografen* ("Choreography")
1996: *Barins triangel* (Barin's Triangle), short stories
1998: *Kim Novak badade aldrig i Genesarets sjö* ("Kim Novak Never Swam in Genesaret's Lake")
2002: *Och Piccadilly Circus ligger inte i Kumla* ("And Piccadilly Circus Is Not in Kumla")
2002: *Kära Agnes!* ("Dear Agnes!")
2009: *Maskarna på Carmine Street* ("The Worms on Carmine Street")
2011: *Himmel över London* ("Sky Over London")
2014: *Levande och döda i Winsford* (*The Living and the Dead in Winsford*, tr. n/a, 2015)

Major Awards:

1993: Best Swedish Debut Crime Novel Award for *Det grovmasloga nätet* (*The Mind's Eye*)
1994: Best Swedish Crime Novel Award for *Borkmanns punkt* (*Borkmann's Point*)
1996: Best Swedish Crime Novel Award for *Kvinna med födelsemärke* (*Woman with Birthmark*)
2000: The Glass Key Award for *Carambole* (*Carambole*)
2007: Best Swedish Crime Novel Award for *En helt annan historia* ("A Completely Different Story")
2014: Shortlisted for Petrona Award, Best Scandinavian Crime Novel of the Year, *The Weeping Girl*

Websites: http://www.nesser.se; http://www.hakannesser.com (fan site)

Åsa Nilsonne

b. January 25, 1949; birthplace N/A; Residence: Stockholm, Sweden; Occupations: psychiatrist, professor of medical psychology, translator, author

Åsa Nilsonne, a professor of medical psychology at Stockholm's Karolinska Institute, says that when her colleagues go sailing or play golf, she writes crime novels because, like England's P.D. James, she enjoys the challenges of the genre (Nilsonne website). As well as six nonfiction books dealing with her medical specialty, Nilsonne has published five novels about Monika Pedersen, whose work as a policewoman Nilsonne feels is vital to society, since she feels safety "is a crucial aspect of any society. Who protects us against those that want to take advantage of us? … in for instance Sweden, the police" (Nilsonne website). Nilsonne grew up in Sweden, Thailand, Lebanon, and Ethiopia, the setting she chose for her fourth and fifth novels.

As part of her research project "Science in the Crime Genre" for Lund University, 2009, Kristin Bergman examined Nilsonne's crime novels to discover to what extent the genre "depicts and mediates scientific theories and knowledge," concluding that crime fiction does "contribute to spreading knowledge about scientific reasoning and methods" (Bergman 193). Pedersen believes that while Nilsonne's earlier crime novels heavily emphasized the scientific ingredients in her novels, "this ambition has faded over time," and Nilsonne seems have turned to conveying "social criticism about Swedish health care and law enforcement" (Bergman 203).

Crime Novels:

Monika Pedersen Series:

1991: *Tunnare än blod* ("Thinner Than Blood")
1992: *I det tysta* ("In the Quiet")
2000: *Kyskhetsbältet* ("Chastity Belt")
2004: *Bakom ljuset* ("Hoodwinked")
2006: *Ett liv att dö för* ("A Life to Die For")

Major Awards:

2000: The Poloni Prize for *Kyskhetsbältet* ("Chastity Belt")

Website: http://www.nilsonne.se

Andreas Norman

> b. 23 October 1972, Farsta parish, Stockholm, Sweden; Residence: Various; Occupations: Swedish Foreign Ministry, author

Andreas Norman worked from 2003 to 2013 in various posts in the Swedish Foreign Ministry, including the counter-terrorism group, the Middle East—North Africa Department, the Baltics Department, and the Western Balkans Department. He worked in disaster management during the 2004 tsunami disaster in Thailand, the basis for his 2014 nonfiction book, *9,3 på Richterskalan* ("9.3 on the Richter Scale"), which was dramatized in 2014 and premiered in 2015 at the Malmö City Theatre. Norman's 2013 debut novel *En rasende eld* (*Into a Raging Blaze*, tr. 2014), a political thriller, involves counterterrorism, global surveillance, and the interplay between international intelligence services. *Into a Raging Blaze* has been filmed by Thrill Friends to premiere in the spring of 2016.

Thrillers:

2013: *En rasende eld* (*Into a Raging Blaze*, tr. Ian Giles, 2014)
2014: *9.3 på Richterskalan* ("9.3 on the Richter Scale")

Major Awards: N/A

Website: N/A

Hans-Olov Öberg

> b. June 21, 1964, Skultuna, Sweden; Residence: N/A; Occupations: financial analyst, musician, football columnist, publisher, author

After graduating from the Stockholm School of Economics, Hans-Olov Öberg, also a jazz and blues musician, founded Cold Bullets Publishing in 2001 and began to write formulaic thrillers which reflect his interests in sports, jazz, and finance. He describes his writing as "Tempo, presence, passion, evil and issues with authority" ("Interview with Hans-Olov Öberg").

Selected Thrillers:

Debut Novel:

2001: *En gunabenådad bullshitter* ("A Brilliant Bullshitter")

The Jazz, Blues & Beyond Series:

2002: *Svart stajl—en jazzthriller* ("Black Stajl: A Jazz Thriller")

The Jack Bohlander Series:

2005: *Döden går på lustgas* ("Death Goes on Laughing Gas")

The Micke Norell Series:

2007: *En jagad man* ("A Hunted Man")

The Benny Modigh Series:

2011: *Djävulens tonsteg* ("The Devil's Tone Steps")
2012: *Någon att lita på* ("Someone to Trust")
2015: *Kungarmördaren* ("The Royal Killer")

Major Awards: N/A

Website: http://kallakulor.com/portfolio-item/hans-olov-oberg

*Kristina Ohlsson

> b. March 2, 1979, Kristianstad, Sweden; Residences: Stockholm, Sweden; Vienna, Austria; Occupations: political scientist, intelligence analyst, security advisor, counterterrorism officer, adult and children's author

Like many other crime writers, Kristina Ohlsson had hoped to write fiction ever since she was a child. In her acknowledgements to her first adult novel, *Askungar*, 2009 (*Unwanted*, tr. 2012), she notes she had already spent twenty years amusing herself "writing endless tales and stories." She has worked in police organizations and is now a counterterrorism officer at the Organization for Security and Cooperation in Europe, with special interests in Middle East affairs and European Union policy. Ohlsson wrote the first draft of *Unwanted* between August 2007 and January 2008, launching her crime series featuring Fredrika Bergman, an investigative analyst. *Tusenskönor*, 2010 (*Silenced*, tr. 2012) and *Änglavakter*, 2011 (*The Disappeared*, tr. 2013), were both shortlisted for Swedish Crime Writers Academy Best Crime Novel of the Year Awards. Ohlsson has since also produced a highly regarded children's trilogy about three twelve-year-olds in a small Swedish town.

Ohlsson's adult novels interweave multiple story lines involving the personal lives of her investigators at the same time they are untangling complicated cases involving women and/or children victimized by deficiencies in Sweden's governmental system. In her first case, Fredrika Bergman assists Stockholm Police Inspector Alex Recht and his rough but talented police subordinate Peder Rydh with the abduction of a small girl from a crowded train in the Stockholm station after the child's mother had accidentally been left behind at a previous stop. At first the situation seems to be the result of a bitter custody dispute, but the child's body is then found in northern Sweden with the word "unwanted" inscribed on her forehead. Fredrika, a civilian criminologist who specializes in crimes against women and children, and the police team that initially resents her assignment to them must deal with an "implacable killer" (Forshaw 53), as well as "men's violence against women" then prevalent in Sweden, which revolts decent men like Alex Recht: "*Some* [italics in original] men hit women. A huge number of others did not. Unless that was the accepted starting point, the problem would never be properly addressed" (*Unwanted* 67).

In *Tusenskönor*, 2010 (*Silenced*, tr. 2012), Fredrika is late-stage pregnant and regretting the loss of her pre-pregnancy comfortable life, while Alex Recht is feeling insecure about his own marriage. This time their investigation involves an undocumented-immigrant case and a strange situation where the identity of a Swedish woman on a mission to Thailand is being gradually erased. These factors coalesce into Ohlsson's commentary on how human relationships are shaped by "greed, jealousy, or hope for a better life for one's family" (Review of *Silenced*). In *Änglavakter*, 2011 (*The Disappeared*, tr. 2013), Ohlsson addresses snuff films, the ultimate exploitation of women. *The Disappeared* also shows the team's personal lives becoming ruthlessly complicated: Fredrika is back from maternity leave too soon, her much older partner is being denounced by a vengeful student, and Alex Recht is recently widowed. This complex investigation also brings on a painful internal inquiry (Review of *The Disappeared*).

Ohlsson, who says she has been inspired by male American and British authors like Stephen King, Dennis Lehane, and Peter Robinson, does not consider herself part of the Scandinavian crime writers' "community" or feel herself duty-bound to teach her readers about her country or its region. An example of her far-reaching inspiration is the 2013 stand-alone novel *Davidsstjärnor* ("Stars of David"), developed from the Israeli urban legend of the "Paper Boy" serial killer. She considers her novels "fairytales for adults" (Forshaw 54), but if so, they resemble the old Scandinavian tales which came out of "fierce winters and incredibly long nights" and are "earthy, vital, and filled with contrasts of light and dark ... ghostly and terrible, joyous and lighthearted, realistic and sexy, poetic, comic and bizarre" (Booss xiii).

Crime Novels:

Frederika Bergman Series:

2009: *Askungar* (*Unwanted*, tr. Sarah Death, 2012; also called *Cinderellas*)
2010: *Tusenskönor* (*Silenced*, tr. Sarah Death, 2012, also called *The Daisy*)
2011: *Änglavakter* (*The Disappeared*, tr. Marlaine Delargy, 2015, also called *Guardian Angels*)
2012: *Paradisoffer* (*Hostage*, tr. Marlaine Delargy, 2014)

Martin Benner Series:

2014: *Lotus Blues* ("Lotus Blues")
2015: *Mios Blues* ("Mios Blues")

Stand-Alone Novel:

2013: *Davidsstjärnor* ("Stars of David")

Major Awards:

2010: Stabilo Prize for Best Crime Writer of Southern Sweden

Website: http://www.kristinaohlsson.net/blog.html

Dag Öhrlund and Dan Buthler

> Dag Öhrlund: b. October 30, 1957, Stockholm, Sweden; Residences: Stockholm, Sweden, and south-west Florida, USA; Occupations: journalist, photographer, co-author with Dan Buthler; Website: http://ohrlund.se
>
> Dan Buthler: b. 1965, Ronne, Denmark; Residence: Täby, Sweden; Occupations: internet developer, co-author with Dag Öhrlund

Veteran journalist and photographer Dag Öhrlund, who by himself has broad experience with documentary books, cookbooks, travel books, a book devoted to protecting children from the Internet, and *Crime in Sweden*, which discusses a dozen of Sweden's most infamous criminal cases, collaborates with Danish author Dan Buthler in a procedural series centered on Inspector Jacob Colt, joined in several cases by the psychopathic character Christopher Silferstrand Bielkegatan. The first novel in the series, 2007's *Mord.net* ("Murder Network"), treats a fictional world-wide Internet murder network, an idea from Buthler that Öhrlund found so brilliant that he felt it would have been a mistake to drop it (Malmaeus). Interviewed just after the publication of *Uppgörelsen* ("The Settlement"), 2013, Öhrlund indicated that "I can not think and Dan can not write. Therefore we develop the story together," with Dan providing "crazy ideas" and Dag doing the actual writing (quoted in Malmaeus).

Crime Novels:

> *Criminal Inspector Jacob Colt and Psychopathic Serial Killer*
> *Christopher Silferstrand Bielkegatan Series:*

2007: *Mord.net* ("mord.net" or "Murder Network")
2008: *En nästan vanlig man* ("An Almost Ordinary Man")
2009: *Förlåt min vrede* ("Forgive My Anger")
2010: *Ares Tecken* ("Ares' Characters")
2010: *Grannen* ("The Neighbor")
2011: *Jordens väktare* ("Earth Guardian")
2012: *Återvändaren* ("Return Comforter")
2013: *Uppgörelsen* ("The Settlement")
2014: *Erövaren* ("Conqueror")
2015: *Hämnaren* ("Avenger")

Major Awards: N/A

Joint website: http://www.butherohrlund.se

Fredrik T. Olsson

> b. November 1, 1969; near Gothenburg, Sweden; Residence: Stockholm, Sweden; Occupations: actor, screenwriter, author

Fredrik T. Olsson wanted a typewriter for his tenth birthday, which he says got his career as an author rolling. Originally he intended to become an actor and still does some standup comedy on the side, but he has mainly concentrated on play- and scriptwriting for film and television. He calls his 2013 debut novel, *Slutet på kedjan* (*Chain of Events*, tr. 2014), the story of a depressed, disgraced, and divorced military cryptologist hired by a super-secret organization to decode mysterious prophecies hidden in human DNA "the most fun" he's had in years ("Fredrik T. Olsson," *Partners in Stories*).

Techno-Thriller:

2013: *Slutet på kedjan* (*Chain of Events*, tr. Dominic Hinde, 2014)

Major Awards: N/A

Website: N/A

*Klas Östergren

b. February 20, 1955; birthplace N/A; Residence: Skåne, Sweden; Occupations: screenwriter, translator, author

Elected in 2014 as one of eighteen members of the prestigious Swedish Academy, Klas Östergren, a longtime member of Sweden's literary elite often hailed as a master storyteller, has authored twenty cross-genre novels and created the film and television scripts for important literary works including the 2013 television adaptation of Kerstin Ekman's award-winning novel *Blackwater.* He has also written children's suspense fiction. His breakthrough novel *Gentlemen*, 1980 (*Gentlemen*, tr. 2007), considered a landmark in Swedish fiction, its 2005 sequel *Gangsters* (*Gangsters*), and 2009's *Den sista cigarretten* ("The Last Cigarette") were cited by the jury of the Sixten Heyman Award as having revitalized the realistic tradition in Swedish literature by placing the individual's contradictory everyday existence in "a larger, almost mythical context. With humor and clear-sighted elegance, Östergren captures late modernity's conditions and consequences for art and for life" (quoted in the Salomonsson Agency's biographical statement on Östergren).

Gentlemen covers forty years in the lives of the Morgan Brothers. Henry, a boxer, jazz pianist, and an old fashioned gentleman, has a younger brother Leo, a drunk, a political activist, and a poet, who involves them with gangsters in an illegal-weapon scandal. "Klas Östergren" the narrator, is involved in the brothers' international plots, eventually becoming unable to distinguish between real and imagined events. Östergren wrote the screenplay for a movie version of *Gentlemen* that was released in 2014.

The dystopian *Orkanpartyt* (*The Hurricane Party*), written for the Myths series in which modern novelists reworked classic myths, has central figure Hanck Orn seeking the truth behind the death of his son Toby, a parallel to a Norse hero-god's mythic quest for his dead son from the top of the world-tree Yggdrasil to the depths of the underworld.

Controversy arose when the Albert Nonniers Forlag, publishers of Östergren's *Den sista cigaretten* ("The Last Cigarette"), written in 2009, hired attorneys to examine similarities between "The Last Cigarette" and Liza Marklund and James Patterson's collaborative novel *The Postcard Killers*, composed in 2009 and published in 2010, because both make indispensable references to the famous Swedish painting "The Dying Dandy." Marklund and her publishing firm *Piratenförlag* deny that any plagiarism was committed or exists.

Novels with Crime Elements:

1980: *Gentlemen* (*Gentlemen*, tr. Tiina Nunnally, 2007)
2005: *Gangsters* (*Gangsters*, tr. Tiina Nunnally, 2006)
2009: *Orkanpartyt* (*The Hurricane Party*, tr. Tiina Nunnally, 2007)
2009: *Den sista cigaretten* ("The Last Cigarette")
2014: *Twist* ("Twist")

Major Awards:

2005: Grand Prize of 250,000 Swedish *kronor* from *Samfundet De Nio*, Sweden's premier literary society

Website: N/A

Håkan Östlundh

b. December 1, 1962, Uppsala, Sweden; Residences: Gotland, Sweden (summer); Stockholm, Sweden (winter); Occupations: journalist, film and television scriptwriter, author

Because he feels it best for an author to stop while readers still enjoy his work, Håkan Östlundh intends to cease his popular Fredrik Broman procedural series with its seventh installment. He intends then to explore ecoterrorism in a new detective venture. He compares writing fiction to cooking, since each profession has an audience that must be satisfied (see Östlundh's website). *Blot*, 2008 (*The Viper*, tr. 2012), the only one of Östlundh's novels to appear in English thus far, follows the modern Swedish tradition of using crime stories to explore and attempt to explain social issues. The novel's precipitating double homicide is set in a deserted Gotland farmhouse, and Broman's subsequent investigation unearths more grisly secrets. *Män ur mörkret* ("Men from the Darkness"), 2014, the last case for ailing Fredrik Borman, now Acting Head of the Gotland police, involves the serial killings of influential Gotland citizens, assumed to be the work of militant activists opposing a new lime quarry on Gotland. Broman ignores his own ominous physical symptoms to track the most lethal killer he has ever faced. Here, as in all of his Fredric Broman novels, Östlundh plunges deeply into the reasons behind the human ability to carry out crimes of implacable evil.

Crime Novels:

Detective Fredrik Broman Series:

2004: *Släke* ("Seaweed")
2005: *Dykaren* ("Diver")
2006: *Terror* ("Terror")
2008: *Blot* (*The Viper*, tr. Per Carlsson, 2012)
2011: *Inkräktaren* ("Intruder")
2012: *Laglöst land* ("Lawless")
2014: *Män ur mörkret* ("Men from the Darkness")

Stand-Alone Novel:

2010: *Jag ska fånga en ängel* ("To Catch an Angel")

Major Awards: N/A

Website: http://www.hakanostlundh.se

Robert Påhlsson

b. 1956; birthplace N/A; Residence: Gothenburg, Sweden; Occupations: professor of tax law, author

Robert Påhlsson's career as a professor of tax law at the University of Gothenburg's School of Economics has been the source of most of his writing, which includes four textbooks on tax law and four related scientific studies. He has also authored two conventional thrillers, the most recent of which, *Sandlers samvete* ("Sandler's Conscience"), 2012, treats the ethical dilemma of a detective nearing retirement who investigates a case involving a ship lost under mysterious circumstances, while its equally mysterious cargo reaches its ominous destination.

Thrillers:

1991: *Den lyska länken* ("The German Connection")
2012: *Sandlers samvete* ("Sandler's Conscience")

Major Awards: N/A

Website: N/A

Uno Palmström

b. August 9, 1947, Vänersborg, Sweden; d. April 27, 2003, Stockholm, Sweden; Residence: Stockholm, Sweden; Occupations: journalist, translator, publisher, editor, author

One of the earliest members elected to the Swedish Crime Academy, Uno Palmström began writing crime novels with a journalist as amateur sleuth in 1976, but later Palmström's heavy workload as an editor and publisher made it impossible for him to continue writing his own fiction. His colleagues remembered him as always putting "a wealth of ideas" at their disposal, "which made him the multi-faceted cultural personality he was" (Svedelid). Palmström's novels express "fundamental doubts" about Swedish society, because he recognized an "unholy alliance" of politicians and financiers bilking the citizenry for the alliance members' own benefit (Holmberg 12).

Selected Crime Novels:

1976: *Kuppen* ("The Coup")
1983: *Slutstation Stockholm* ("Situation Stockholm")
1990: *Bara till graven* ("Just to the Grave")

Major Awards: N/A

Website: N/A

*Leif G.W. Persson

b. March 12, 1945. Stockholm, Sweden; Residence: Stockholm, Sweden; Occupations: criminologist, author

Notwithstanding his formidable body of acclaimed works, Leif G.W. Persson observed in a 2012 interview with *The Literary Magazine* that "It's fun to write books," but "Everything I have written so far can be much better" (quoted in Kreü). Persson also insists he always carries with him "That Great Novel which I haven't written yet ... no better companion on the journey of life" (quoted in Glansholm).

Persson's crime fiction career parallels his profession, criminology. From 1992 to 2012 he served as a professor of criminology at the Swedish National Police Board and appeared from 1999 to 2009 as an expert commentator in Swedish TV 3's *Efterlyst*. He presently appears with Camilla Kvartoft on the television show *Veckans Brott*, discussing unsolved Swedish crimes. Several of his own fictional works, including *Pröfitörerna* ("The Profiteers") were adapted for television in the 1980s. In February 2012 Persson announced that Twentieth Century–Fox had bought the rights to his Evert Backström novels for a proposed U.S. television series.

Among the authors Persson admires as "so good that I can't even begin to understand how they've done it" are the late nineteenth century Swedish writer August Strindberg and "the Hemingway who wrote 'Death in the Afternoon'" (quoted in Glansholm; original is without italics), authors whose work provides clues to two qualities that stand out in Persson's own work. Strindberg's novel *The Red Room* sharply denounces the moral turpitude and hypocrisy which Strindberg saw in 1890s Stockholm, and *Death in the Afternoon* celebrates *duende*, that Spanish concept of elegant excellence under the gravest of pressures, the negative and positive polarities resonating throughout Persson's own fiction.

In 1977 Persson himself encountered corruption and societal depravity in Swedish governmental circles. He turned that unhappy experience into the background for his debut crime novel, *Grisfesten*, 1978 ("Pig Party"). As an employee of the Swedish National Police Board, Persson had confirmed a classified memo sent by the National Police Commissioner to Prime Minister Olof Palme alleging that Minister for Justice Lennart Geijer had connections to a Stockholm prostitution ring. Persson's confirmation of that memo cost him dearly; his firing from the National Police Board sent him into a near-suicidal depression (Ekeroth 27). He recovered, became a lecturer at Stockholm University and wrote two more crime novels, *Profitörerna* ("The Profiteers"), 1979, and *Samhällsbärarna* ("The Pillars of Society"), 1982, the latter title echoing Ibsen's play of a very similar title that savagely unveils Norwegian governmental and societal fatal hypocrisy. Both of Persson's novels named above ferociously denounce Sweden's political and societal corruption. In 1992 Persson rejoined the National Police Board as a professor of criminology.

Persson is best known in the English-speaking world for his large-scale political thriller trilogy carrying on the strong realist tradition in Swedish literature. Its central event is the still-unsolved assassination of Swedish Prime Minister Olof Palme in February 1986. The first volume, *Mellan sommarens längtan och vinterns köld*, 2002 (*Between Summer's Longing and Winter's End*, tr. 2010), takes place immediately before and after Christmas 1985, exhibiting both similarities to and differences from the worlds Swedish *noir* novelists Sjöwall and Wahlöö and Stieg Larsson created. Like the Sjöwall-Wahlöö Martin Beck series, Persson's trilogy involves urban policemen, some cynical, some corrupt, some decent and disillusioned, all overworked and nearing burnout. Persson doesn't focus on one single police unit, rather showing individuals from both the Stockholm "regular" police and others from SÄPO, Sweden's secret police. Stieg Larsson also treated Sweden's secret police in his Millennium novels, and like Larsson, Persson unveils blatant Swedish misogyny as a major plot element, though his perspective differs sharply from Larsson's (Harper).

Unlike the relentless gravity that dominates much Swedish crime fiction, Persson's novels contain considerable humor, albeit such dark comedy, especially in scenes involving SÄPO ineptitude, that it verges on tears. Along with exerting his implacable power, Persson's fictional head of the national police is a butt of particular satire. The secret police, however comically bungling they appear, brutally affect the lives of both innocent and not-so-innocent citizens, all this supported by Persson's references to his own 1980s experience as a whistleblower who exposed governmental corruption. American readers may feel the Swedish view of the Cold War is skewed, because in Persson's novel, cooperation with the CIA is "no less damning" than cooperation with the Soviets, and ironically Persson's Swedish "secret police have to approach their American cousins through German intermediaries" (Harper).

Given the size and complexity of *Between Summer's Longing and Winter's End*, some critics have found it hard going: "The far-reaching back story" that eventually turns into Palme's assassination begins with a "shoddy police investigation" into the supposed suicide of an American student in Sweden to research his uncle's CIA work there in the 1940s (Stasio, "Cold Cases"). *New York Times* crime fiction critic Marilyn Stasio believes the police procedural format cannot support Persson's "elaborate plot mechanism ... to expose the layers of incompetence and venality" in Sweden's secret police, and she concludes that Persson's solution to the Palme mystery seems surprisingly dull" (Stasio, "Cold Cases"). Barry Forshaw, on the other hand, finds that Persson did create a convincing "state-of-the-nation novel" which uncovers "a truly malodorous can of worms, involving Olympian levels of corruption from the police to deeply compromised politicos" (Forshaw 55). Persson carries that purpose through in the second and third volumes of the trilogy.

Less well known outside Scandinavia than Persson's Palme trilogy, Persson's Evert Bäckström novels revolve around "the most obnoxious of creatures, the force of nature that is Evert Bäckström" ("Review: Leif G.W. Persson: *Linda, as in the Linda Murder*"), a lazy, self-serving minor detective from *En annan tid, ett annat liv* (*Another Time, Another Life*, tr. 2012). In the first Bäckström novel, *Linda—som i Lindamordet*, 2005 (*Linda, as in the Linda Murder*, tr. 2012), Bäckström is sent to Vaxjo, where a trainee named Linda in the police academy there has been discovered raped and murdered. Despite the sordidness of the crime and Bäckström's abhorrent personality, the novel and Bäckström strike many readers as "very, very funny" ("Review: Leif G.W. Persson: *Linda, as in the Linda Murder*"), due to the enormous incongruity between the leading character's repulsive qualities and his policeman's intuition necessary to solve the crime. The Backstory novels began appearing as a United States television series in 2014.

Den döende detektiven, 2010 (*The Dying Detective*, tr. 2014), Persson's most lauded novel, finds Lars Martin Johansson, formerly chief of Persson's fictional ex–National Crime Squad from the Palme Trilogy, debilitated by a stroke but personally involved with the cold case of the rape and murder of an Iranian child, Yasmine Ermegan. The case brings the detective into contact with "a culture of child abuse." Johansson's condition worsens as he doggedly pursues justice despite the 2010 change in Swedish law regarding unsolved crimes that means "cold case" killers apprehended after the law was enacted cannot be brought to justice (Hinde).

Persson based his long and demanding novels meticulously on his professional expertise as one of Sweden's leading criminologists and on his respect for his readers' intelligence, because he forces them to pay close attention to his dense narrations (Forshaw 56). The theme that anchors the Palme trilogy—that the murder of its Prime Minister forced Sweden to confront the death of its dream of a perfected society—pervades all of his work. Even without the "Great Novel" that Persson says he carries within him, he has brought that theme to fruition.

Crime Novels:

1978: *Grisfesten* ("Pig Party")
1979: *Profitörerna* ("The Profiteers")
1982: *Samhällsbärarna* ("The Pillars of Society")
2010: *Den döende detektiven* (*The Dying Detective*, tr. 2014)

The Evert Bäckström Series:

2005: *Linda—som i Lindamordet* (*Linda, as in the Linda Murder*, tr. Neil Smith, 2012)
2008: *Den som dödar draken* (*He Who Kills the Dragon*, tr. Neil Smith)
2013: *Den sanna historien om Pinocchios näsa* ("The True Story of Pinocchio's Nose")

The Palme Trilogy:

2002: *Mellan sommarens längtan och vinterns köld* (*Between Summer's Longing and Winter's End*, tr. Paul Norlén, 2010)

2003: *Annan tid, ett annat liv* (*Another Time, Another Life*, tr. Paul Norlén, 2012)
2007: *Faller fritt som i en dröm* (*Free Falling, as if in a Dream*, tr. Paul Norlén, 2014)

Autobiography/Memoir:

2011: *Gustavs grabb* ("Gustav's Boy")

Major Awards:

1982: Best Swedish Crime Fiction Novel, for *Samhällsbärarna* ("The Pillars of Society")
2003: Best Swedish Crime Fiction Novel, for *Annan tid, ett annan liv* (*Another Time, Another Life*)
2010: Best Swedish Crime Fiction Novel, for *Den döende detektiven* (*The Dying Detective*)
2011: The Finnish Whodunnit Society's Annual Award for Excellence in Foreign Crime Writing
2011: The Danish Academy of Crime Writers' Palle Rosenkrantz Prize
2011: Glass Key Award, for *Den döende detektiven* (*The Dying Detective*)
2014: The Petrona Award, for *Linda—som i Linda mördet* (*Linda, as in the Linda Murder*)

Website: http://www.leifgwpersson.se (Leif G.W. Persson's blog)

*Elisabet Peterzén

b. 1938, Stockholm, Sweden; Residence: Osmo, Sweden; Occupation: author

Elisabet Peterzén's career as a professional writer began when she moved to England and began publishing four of what she calls "the usual" autobiographical novels. In 1974, she won a competition for the best novel set in a developing county with *En mans liv* ("A Man's Life") under the pseudonym "Mustafa Sard." She claims to have read crime fiction her whole life, probably inspired by her father's collection of John Dickson Carr's crime novels. Peterzén used the pseudonym "Katrin & Erik Skafti" for her first crime story, *Sista sticket* ("Last Trick"), 1983, because she thought the times seemed to favor literary collaborations like the Sjöwall-Wahlöö team. She believed that the pen name also had "a feminist tinge" appropriate to "Last Trick," because the novel shows that men kill women more often than women kill men. Peterzén describes her second crime novel, *Sista ordet* ("The Last Word"), 1992, as "a satirical crime novel." She has not published a crime novel since, though in a 2009 *DAST Magazine* interview, she indicated that she had started on a third, somewhat sadly concluding, "crime seems to be the only artistic activity that the community supports" (all quotations from Fornaess, DAST interview).

Crime Novels (written under pseudonym "Katrin & Erik Skafte"):

1983: *Sista sticket* (*The Last Draw*, tr. Laura Desertrain)
1993: *Sista ordet* ("The Last Word")

Major Awards: N/A

Website: N/A

Lars Pettersson

b. N/A; Residences: Kautokeino, Lapland, Norway (winters); Stockholm, Sweden; Occupations: freelance filmmaker, author

Lars Pettersson himself spends winters in Kautokeino, a village in Finnmark, Norwegian Lapland, where the indigenous Sami people live by herding reindeer in one of the world's harshest climates. He wrote his award-winning *Kautokeino: en blodig kniv* ("Kautokeino: a Bloody Knife"), 2012, first as a screenplay, then converted it to novel form. The novel's protagonist, Anna Magnusson, a Stockholm deputy public prosecutor who has roots in Kautokeino, receives a call from her grandmother, begging Anna to come there to restore her family's honor by convincing Karen Margrethe, an unstable Kaitokeino woman, to withdraw her accusation of rape against Anna's cousin Nils Mattis. Almost immediately on Anna's arrival in Lapland, serious conflicts besiege her; the Sami, with their mafia-like code of silence, live by their own laws and their traditional system of justice, quite different from the laws of modern Sweden. On the personal level, too, the Sami suspect Anna because they blame her mother for leaving Kautokeino for Stockholm, abandoning the villagers' reindeer herding traditions (Scherman). After Karen Margrethe dies either of exposure or of a drug overdose, other suspicious deaths follow. Anna assists the local police with their investigation, but she constantly questions her own feelings about the villagers and the conflict they represent with the modern civilization whose values and far different morality the Oslo government is trying to impose on them.

Crime Novel:

2012: *Kautokeino, en blodig kniv* ("Kautokeino, a Bloody Knife")

Major Awards:

Best Debut Crime Novel of the Year, for *Kautokeino, en blodig kniv*

Website: N/A

Torsten Pettersson

b. July 9, 1955, Turku, Finland; Residence: Upssala, Sweden; Occupations: professor of comparative literature, author

After serving as a professor of comparative literature at the Universities of Oulu and Helsinki in Finland and later at the University of Uppsala in Sweden and producing several volumes of lyric poetry and literary studies of classical European authors, Torsten Pettersson, a Finnish-Swedish author, has produced two novels of a projected crime fiction trilogy set in a Swedish-speaking Finnish town, Forshälla, where his fictional Detective Superintendent Harald Lindmark and his team, including Sonja Alder, trained in the United States as a profiler of serial killers, are investigating three horrifying mutilation-killings that on the surface seem unrelated. The highly complex multi-narrator structure Pettersson uses, as well as his command of various narrative styles, highlight many current issues: "the psychological effect of fighting in Bosnia on a young man and its exacerbation by relentless police cross-examination; the dangers of nuclear energy; [and] the heartless exploitation of young girls forced into prostitution" make this "a manyfaceted and often gripping novel" (Scobbie).

In *Göm mig i dit hjärta* ("Hide Me in Your Heart"), Lindmark and the team again face three apparently unrelated crimes near Forshälla. Simpler in structure than its predecessor, this novel is narrated by Lindmark alone with a more realistic dénouement. It poses him an intense moral dilemma: would he break a solemn oath in order to bring a criminal to justice? (Scobbie), Torsten Pettersson commented in 2009 that fictional and filmic crime seem to appeal to a safe and apparently idyllic nation like Sweden because such countries have so little of the real thing (Magnusson);

but his own crime novels, like those of many Swedish crime fiction authors, insist that the "real thing," crime fostered by failures of their governmental system, lurks close beneath that idyllic surface.

Crime Novels:

> 2008: *Ge mig dina ögon* ("Give Me Your Eyes")
> 2010: *Göm mig i dit hjärta* ("Hide Me in Your Heart")

Major Awards:

> 2000: *Schückska priset*

Website: N/A

Lars Rambe

> b. September 19, 1968, Täby, Sweden; Residence: Nacka, Sweden; Occupations: lawyer, former athlete, author

Lars Rambe works as a lawyer for the pharmaceutical industry. Besides writing crime and horror novels, he also runs Hoi Publishers, which allows authors to invest in their own books (Berg). His two traditional crime novels feature co-sleuths Fredrik Gransjö, a journalist who leaves Stockholm to work for a local Strängnäs newspaper, and his friend Maria Carlsson. Rambe's most recent work, *Kvinnorna i sjön* ("Women in the Lake"), 2012, a horror novel, involves psychological theories of dreams. Visions of two women murdered in Lake Järlo haunt the protagonist Johan Åberg, suggesting he may know more about the crime than he consciously understands.

Crime Novels:

> 2007: *Spåren på bryggan* ("The Tracks on the Bridge")
> 2010: *Skuggans spel* ("Shadow Games")

Horror Novel:

> 2012: *Kvinnorna i sjön* ("Women in the Lake")

Major Awards: N/A

Website: http://www.larsrambe.se

*Anders Roslund and Börge Hellström ("Roslund and Hellström")

> Anders Roslund: b. 1961; Residence: N/A; Occupations: journalist, author
> Börge Hellström: b. 1957; Residence: N/A; Occupations: former criminal, rehabilitation counselor, author

Often considered the heirs of Stieg Larsson in Swedish *noir* crime thriller fiction, the writing team of Anders Roslund and Börge Hellström produce stomach-wrenching thrillers packed with grisly action and social criticism. In a 2011 interview (they answer questions jointly in the third person), they remarked that prior to 2000, it was extremely difficult for Swedish authors to obtain their share of the 5 percent of books in all other languages that are translated to English in the UK. Despite such difficulties, in 2003 they learned that their work was going to be translated into English, so that *Odjuret*, 2004 (*The Beast*, tr. 2006), appeared in English translation before Stieg

Larsson's Millennium Trilogy, though they also feel that Larsson "opened the door" for the translation of Swedish crime novels. They attribute the subsequent success of Swedish crime fiction to two factors, tradition and diversity. First, they believe that that success derives from the common tradition initiated by the Sjöwall-Wahlöö Martin Beck series, with its ten books serving as chapters in one long police procedural narrative criticizing failures in their society. Second, the pair feels that Swedish crime fiction writers utilize a broad range of styles and approaches, from whodunits to thrillers, almost all containing political opinions on the state of Swedish society and utilizing a broad range of perspectives. Roslund and Hellström feel that it took nearly 20 years for Swedish writers to learn to use the literary tools pioneered by the Martin Beck series ("An Interview with Anders Roslund and Börge Hellström").

In contrast to the writing method of Sjöwall and Wahlöö where each wrote a chapter imitating the other's style, Roslund and Hellström never reveal who does what in their fiction. It takes them about two years to produce a novel, about eight months on each phase: research, then story development, and finally the writing itself. They say they "fight a lot" but at the end of each day they part as friends (Foster). In their novels, where their characters Evert Grens and Sven Sundkvist investigate inflammatory social issues like the exploitation of women and the organized drug trade in Scandinavian prisons, they draw on Roslund's background as a investigative reporter and Hellström's experiences as a former convict who had been abused himself as a child. The pair then depicts shocking failures in Swedish governmental policies and practice in dealing with serious crimes.

The Roslund-Hellström collaboration continues to probe sensitive societal problems. *Tre sekunder*, 2009 (*Three Seconds*, 2010), the harrowing tale of an undercover prison assignment that goes horrifyingly wrong, was scheduled for filming in 2015 starring *The Hobbit*'s Luke Evans (McClintock). Their most recent novel, *Två soldater*, 2012 (*Two Soldiers*, tr. 2014), is set against the frightening world of juvenile gangs terrorizing a Stockholm suburb with drug sales, car thefts, arson, and bomb-making, a stinging indictment of the conditions which allow crime to be perpetuated from generation to generation. The special impact of Roslund and Hellström's collaborative fiction has been to blur the line between police and criminals, portraying "the enormous gray zone" between black and white: Is a criminal who was victimized himself good or evil? "Who is the perpetrator and who is the victim, or are they both?" (Foster).

Crime Novels:

Detective Superintendent Evert Grens and Sven Sundkvist Series:

2004: *Odjuret* (*The Beast*, tr. Anna Paterson, 2006)

2005: *Box 21* (no translator given; *Box 21*, also published in the UK as *The Vault*, 2008)

2006: *Edward Finnigans upprättelse* (*Cell 8*, no translator given, tr. 2011)

2007: *Flickan under gatan* ("The Girl Below the Street")

2009: *Tre sekunder* (*Three Seconds*, tr. Kari Dickson, 2010)

2012: *Två soldater* (*Two Soldiers*, tr. Kari Dickson, 2014)

Major Awards:

2005: The Glass Key Award, for *Odjuret* (*The Beast*)

2010: Best Swedish Crime Novel of the Year, for *Tre sekunder* (*Three Seconds*)

2010: The Great Readers Prize, for *Tre Sekunder* (*Three Seconds*)

2011: CWA International Dagger for Best International Crime Novel of the Year for *Tre sekunder* (*Three Seconds*)

Website: http://www.roslund-hellstrom.com

Ann Rosman

b. February 27, 1973; Residence: Marstrand, Sweden; Occupations: IT specialist, author

One day during her maternity leave in 2005, Ann Rosman looked out over Marstrand Fjord toward the Pater Noster lighthouse and wondered what might happen at such an inaccessible location—and what might be hidden there. That experience inspired her first detective novel, *Fyrmästarens dotter* ("The Lighthouse Keeper's Daughter"), 2009, starring Detective Karin Adler. Rosman says she struggled to organize her Post-it notes for her first novel to find a timeline for that story, and eventually promised herself she would work out a better writing process ("The Full Interview"). She believes that Sherlock Holmes's ingenious powers of observation fascinate her primarily because she feels something of his London's "shadowy alleys" can be found in Marstrand, the setting of all of her books, "where mist and twilight descend over the old wooden town" (*CrimeHouse* interview).

Rosman constructed her fourth novel, *Mercurium*, 2012, around an actual historical event, the story of Metta Rock Ridderbielke, accused in 1806 of a poisoning murder and incarcerated at Marstrand's Carlsten Fortress on a barren island in the fjord. In Rosman's novel, set in 2011, a locked room murder case for Karin Adler develops from a grand masquerade ball held at the fortress where two people die, one of the many episodes of Marstrand's "dark and colorful history" that Rosman intends to continue exploring in her crime fiction ("The Full Interview").

Crime Novels:

Karin Adler Series:

2009: *Fyrmästarens dotter* ("The Lighthouse Keeper's Daughter")
2010: *Själakistan* ("Soul Casket")
2011: *Porto Francos väktare* ("Porto Franco Guardian")
2012: *Mercurium* ("Mercurium")
2014: *Havskatten* ("The Catfish")

Major Awards:

2010: The Marstrand Prize

Website: http://annrosman.se

Denise Rudberg

b. June 19, 1971; Residence: Stockholm, Sweden; Occupation: author

In the 1990s, Denise Rudberg studied drama in New York City. She then returned to Sweden, where she published two trilogies of "chick lit" and several young adult books. In 2010, Rudberg, a friend of Camilla Läckberg, launched a popular police procedural series she calls "Elegant Crime," planned for nine novels, which one reviewer has dismissed as pedestrian chick lit with murder ("Stepping Out of Line").

Rudberg's protagonist is Marianne Jidhoff, a recently widowed middle-aged Prosecution Secretary who returns to work in the Stockholm Public Prosecution Office. She has personal wounds beyond widowhood, for her late husband, a State Prosecutor, was more faithful to his job than he was to her ("Stepping Out of Line") She solves high-profile crimes with Detective Chief Inspector Torsten Ehn and Detective Inspector Augustin Madrid. Rudberg's first novel of the series sold over 140,000 copies in Sweden, and it appeared for seven months on the national bestseller list (Norstedts Agency information).

Crime Novels:

Marianne Jidhoff Series:

2010: *Ett litet snedsprång* ("Stepping Over the Line")
2011: *Två gånger är en vana* ("Twice Is a Habit")
2012: *Bara tre kan leka så* ("Only Three Can Play That Game")

Major Awards: N/A

Website: http://www.deniserudberg.se

Elisabeth Schalin see "Jean Bolinder"

Ninni Schulman

b. August 2, 1972, Rämmen, Sweden; Residence: Stockholm, Sweden; Occupations: journalist, editor, author

Ninni Schulman survived birth-defect scoliosis so severe doctors predicted she would die as a child. Two surgeries and six months in the hospital, where she constantly listened to fairy tales, corrected the physical problem, but she is only 144 centimeters tall, making her an outcast at school and the target of unkind comments even today by strangers on the street: "As a parent. I think you afterwards can tell ... children that everyone is different and that it may not be as [much] fun to answer the same questions all the time" (quoted in Sjöblom). For her, coming to terms with her situation does not mean "looking on the bright side." Instead she tells others "how it can feel to be odd and stand out" ("Ninni Schulman"), not only in ordinary conversation but through her detective novels, which carry "a vein of melancholy and sadness" that has become her trademark (Glansholm). Her novels have sold more than 300,000 copies in Sweden.

Schulman was a journalist until her debut as a crime fiction author at age thirty-five. She wanted to write about life in a small town, which she feels can be both positive and negative. She believes that if a person is good at something, "it can be very encouraging to stay at a small place," but she feels it is also hard to get rid of "a stamp" the town has put on you (Glansholm). In Schulman's planned series co-sleuths journalist Magdalena Hansson and police detective Christer Berglund work in the small town of Hagfors, amid its symptoms of the growing malaise Schulman sees beneath Sweden's "happy" surface: demolished houses and abandoned parking lots with flowers sprouting in the cracks of their asphalt surfaces: "I think this does something to people ... many people probably feel that they are no longer counted and feel a bit forgotten," enduring the unemployment and hopelessness and growing xenophobia (quoted in Sjöblom) that Schulman compassionately portrays in her fiction.

Crime Novels:

Magdalena Hansson Series:

2010: *Flickan med snö i håret* ("The Girl with Snow in Her Hair")
2012: *Pojken som slutade gråta* ("The Boy Stopped Crying")
2013: *Svara om du hör mig* ("Reply if You Hear Me")
2015: *Vår egen lilla hemlighet* ("Our Own Little Secret")

Major Awards:

2011: Värmland Literature Debut Scholarship, for *Flickan med snö i håret* ("The Girl with Snow in Her Hair")

Website: http://blog.amedlia.se/ninnischulman

Bo Sehlberg

> b. February 19, 1944, Stockholm, Sweden; d. January 29, 2004, Upper Valsta Farm, Haninge, Sweden; Residence: Haninge, Sweden; Occupations: photographer, aviator, author

Bo Sehlberg, a well-known Swedish pilot and aviation consultant, wrote popular "pulp" crime novels for the B. Wahlström *Crime Scene Sweden*. B. Wahlström, founded in 1914, began by publishing young adult books, Sweden's analogue to the United States' Hardy Boys and Nancy Drew series. B. Wahlström also published adult Westerns, science fiction, and detective stories.

Major Awards: N/A

Website: N/A

Dan T. Sehlberg

> b. 1969; Residences: Stockholm, Sweden; and Sörmland, Sweden; Occupations: entrepreneur, author

Son of aviation consultant and popular pulp mystery author Bo Sehlberg, Dan T. Sehlberg has recently produced an unusual genre-crossing thriller diptych, *Mona*, 2013, and *Sinon*, 2014, novels which have been sold to more than twenty foreign countries. *Mona* is being adapted for the screen by Max Borenstein, screenwriter for the film *Godzilla*.

Mona, 2013, a near-future speculative novel, involves a chilling combination of cyber warfare and bioterrorism. Sehlberg's protagonist, Eric Soderqvist, a professor of computer science at Stockholm's Royal Institute of Technology, has invented a thought-controlled computer system that allows disabled individuals to browse the Internet. When his wife Hanna tests the system, she becomes comatose, and Eric believes she has been infected by "Mona," a computer virus, and to save her, he must find its terrorist creator. In *Sinon*, 2014, the Mona virus is spreading across northern Europe, and in desperation Soderqvist attempts to stop it by infecting himself.

In an autobiographical statement on his official website, Sehlberg declares that "In Sweden, storytelling is in the very soil of the land…. With its dynamic history and diverse scenery, Sweden has always represented a source of inspiration for artists, writers and entrepreneurs." He does most of his writing in Sörmland, which he calls "the perfect place to reflect as well as to uncover new ideas and narratives," but he also finds inspiration in two other favorite places, Stockholm, with its combination of 700-year-old history and bustling modernity, and a "very small cabin" in far northern Sweden where each summer he hunts and fishes and walks the land of the Sami.

Techno-Thriller Novels:

2013: *Mona* (*Mona*, tr. Rachel Willson-Broyles, 2014)
2014: *Sinon* ("Sinon")

Major Awards: N/A

Website: http://www.dantsehlberg.com

*Maj Sjöwall and Per Wahlöö

Maj Sjöwall: b. September 25, 1935, Stockholm, Sweden; Residence: Stockholm, Sweden; Occupations: translator, journalist, editor, scriptwriter, author

Per Wahlöö: b. August 5, 1926, Tölö, Sweden; d. June 22, 1975, Malmö, Sweden; Residence: Stockholm, Sweden; Occupations: translator, journalist, scriptwriter, author

"For thirty-five years, Maj Sjöwall and Per Wahlöö were the indisputably best known, most highly regarded, and most read of all Swedish crime novelists" (Holmberg 271). With their Martin Beck series, ten police procedurals written from 1965 to 1975 and called collectively "The Story of a Crime," they revolutionized the genre and laid the foundation for the Swedish Golden Age of detective fiction to follow a generation later. The Beck novels have sold approximately 10 million copies and have been translated throughout the world, currently being reissued by Vintage. All of them have been adapted as films at least once, with the U.S. version of *The Laughing Policeman* set in San Francisco and starring Walter Matthau. Several of the Beck film versions have appeared on international television, notably the 1993 Swedish *Martin Beck* serial featuring Gösta Ekman as Beck and the 1997 *Martin Beck* television films starring Peter Haber. Beginning in October 2012, BBC Radio 4 broadcast the first of five Martin Beck adaptations, followed by a second five adaptations, starting in July 2013 with Steven Mackintosh playing Martin Beck. The 1968 Martin Beck novel titled *Den skrattande polisen* (*The Laughing Policeman*, tr. 1970) was the first Swedish mystery novel to win the Edgar Award.

Prior to his literary debut in 1959, Per Wahlöö, a leftist political journalist, worked for newspapers, radio and television and took part in radical political causes. The eight novels he wrote by himself include two science fiction thrillers and *Generalerna* (*The Generals*), 1965, which aired his views on dictatorship. Wahlöö and Maj Sjöwall, then both Communist Party members, met in 1961 when they were working for magazines published by the same company. She once described her youth as "rather wild" (quoted in Liukkonen, "Maj Sjowall"). He was married and she was the twice-divorced single parent of a daughter. They fell in love, and though they never married, they were inseparable life partners and co-authors until his death in 1975.

In an appearance at the 2013 Edinburgh International Book Festival, Maj Sjöwall, now widely recognized as the "grandmother" of Swedish crime fiction, indicated their Communist philosophy and party activities had led to their writing the Martin Beck novels. Noting that when they began writing together, Swedish crime fiction offered "just Agatha Christie–type stories with amateur detectives," she said that they instead "wanted to present a view of our society and to describe an era and a time in Sweden" and "show how the social democrats were pushing the country in a more and more bourgeois and rightwing direction" (quoted in Higgins). Wahlöö put their purpose more pungently: to "use the crime novel as a scalpel cutting open the belly of the ideological pauperized and morally debatable so-called welfare state of the bourgeois type" (quoted in Liukkonen). British critic Julian Symons acknowledged that Wahlöö was "an extreme Left-winger" whose books "represent an attempt to bring his political feelings into a literary form with a wide appeal" (quoted in Liukkonen).

Sjöwall, who has left the Communist Party and now calls herself a socialist, described the working method she and Wahlöö established: "We were talking, talking, talking" about their characters as they discussed each story in detail before establishing a 20-chapter synopsis. Each night after her daughter and their two boys were in bed, one would write the first chapter, the other the second, both in longhand. The next night they would exchange their work, typing and editing each other's work (Higgins).

Fifty years ago, when the Martin Beck novels first appeared, Sjöwall says, "no one was interested in the authors," and because the Beck novels have never been out of print and the original contracts are still in effect, she herself has enjoyed very little financial profit from them. She now lives in a one-room Stockholm apartment and works as a translator, claiming she doesn't want to publish any more: "I don't want to be part of this circus" (quoted in Higgins). She regrets that because Wahlöö never adopted her daughter, her daughter cannot receive any revenue from any of the Beck novels or films.

Sjöwall believes that today's Swedish police procedural authors are too wrapped up in their film adaptations, and that their books "are not about police work and crime, but very much about love and relationships—like girls' books" (quoted in Higgins). The middle-aged, worn out, dyspeptic Martin Beck she and Wahlöö created is anything but obsessed by "love and relationships." At the outset his marriage is failing, due at least in part to his absorption in his methodical work with the Stockholm National Homicide Department, where he eventually becomes chief. He also becomes ambivalent about his work, fearing that he is contributing to the violence in Swedish society rather than preventing it (Liukkonen, "Maj Sjöwall"). He has an affair with Rhea Nilsen, openly a socialist and a good cook, but it does not result in a second marriage.

Recently Maj Sjöwall set off a Swedish literary debate by stating that the crime genre has been "dirtied by kissing" (quoted in Maxted). She feels that romance has no place in crime writing and is only inserted into procedurals to make them attractive to filmmakers. Anna Maxted took serious exception to Sjöwall's position: "Desire is why crime occurs—love or lust will rear its ugly head, as without passion, without the id, there would be no crime fiction" (Maxted).

Sjöwall and Wahlöö avoided passion in their fiction by surrounding Martin Beck with a highly varied group of policemen, each with his highly detailed and convincing background and personality, an ensemble cast where each plays a slightly different role in each of the novels, but all revolve around the "crime" that Sjöwall and Wahlöö had used for the metaphoric series title "The Story of a Crime": that "crime" is the welfare state's abandonment of its ideals for materialistic gains, bringing about an unstoppable torrent of violence that has engulfed the Western world. Toward the end of the series, an exhausted Beck hears from a colleague, "You can't stop or steer that avalanche on your own. It just increases. That's not your fault" (quoted in Weinman). In a thoroughgoing comparative analysis of the processes of crime solving in the Buffy the Vampire Slayer series and the Martin Beck series, Stephanie Buus cites Peter Brooks' contention that narrative makes sense of the traumas of life by "'going back over the ground, and thereby realizing the meaning of the cipher left by a life'" (Peter Brooks, *Reading for the Plot*, 1984, pp. 24–25, 34, quoted in Buus). Buus then observes, "It is interesting to note that the life that the Beck series frequently strives to make sense of is not only the victim's but also the perpetrator's" (Buus 409), thus concluding that the groundbreaking achievement of the Beck novels establishes "a new Swedish tradition of contemporaneous, realistically-oriented police novels" that shows criminality as "an extremely incomprehensible phenomenon from within one's own society and culture" (Buus 410).

At seventy-five, Maj Sjöwall looked back at how she and Wahlöö had birthed the modern Swedish police procedural: "Everybody wrote at the time that Sweden was so idyllic, but it was of course not true. Everything started to get more inhuman and capitalistic. But you don't change society by writing books. Maybe you could change individuals' thinking" (quoted in Kachka). As a testament to the power of the Martin Beck novels to change individuals' minds, the list of Swedish crime authors who have adopted the Sjöwall-Wahlöö criticism of the abuses of state power continues to grow: "Olov Svedelid, Kenneth Ahl, Leif G.W. Persson, K. Arne Blom, Henning Mankell, and Stieg Larsson. Also the Chinese mystery writer Qiu Xiaolong" (Liukkonen, "Maj Sjöwall").

Sjöwall herself has coauthored a bloodless detective novel, *Kvinnan som liknade Greta Garbo* ("The Woman Who Looked like Greta Garbo"), 1990, about a visiting governmental minister who sees his own daughter in a porn video that he watches at the Grand Hotel in Stockholm. Today Sjöwall confines herself to translation, principally the work of Robert B. Parker and rejects her publisher's frequent requests to write a memoir. Asked in 2009 whether the materialistic Swedish society she and Wahlöö feared has come to pass, she replied, "Yes. All of it … faster. People think of themselves not as human beings but consumers," and therefore she believes their purpose in creating "The Story of a Crime" has failed. In 2004, she told *Schwedenkrimi* interviewer Alexandra Hagenguth, "I am forgotten" (quoted in Hagenguth). She also ruefully conceded elsewhere, "The problem was that the people who read our books already thought the same of us. Nothing changed" (quoted in France). Of her life partner Wahlöö and the acclaim their work today enjoys, Maj Sjöwall sighed, "I always think of him when we get a prize…. I always think…. Per would have loved this" (quoted in France).

Crime Novels:

Martin Beck Series:

1965: *Roseanna* (*Roseanna*, tr. Lois Roth, 1967)

1966: *Mannen som gick upp i rök* (*The Man Who Went Up in Smoke*, tr. Joan Tate, 1969)

1967: *Mannen på balkongen* (*The Man on the Balcony*, tr. Alan Blair, 1968)

1968: *Den skrattande polisen* (*The Laughing Policeman*, also published as *Investigation of Murder*, tr. Alan Blair, 1970)

1969: *Brandbilen som försvann* (*The Fire Engine That Disappeared*, tr. Joan Tate, 1970)

1970: *Polis, polis, potatismos!* (*Murder at the Savoy*, tr. Joan Tate, 1970)

1972: *Det slutna rummet* (*The Locked Room*, tr. Paul Britten Austin, 1973)

1974: *Polismördaren* (*Cop Killer*, tr. Thomas Teal, 1975)

1975: *Terroristerna* (*The Terrorists*, tr. Joan Tate, 1976)

Crime Novel Co-Authored by Maj Sjöwall with Tomas Ross

1990: *Kvinnan som liknade Greta Garbo* ("The Woman Who Resembled Greta Garbo")

Sjöwall-Wahlöö Short Story Collection:

2007: *Sista resan och andra berättelser* ("The Last Trip and Other Stories"), including a previously unpublished story by Per Wahlöö

Selected Novels by Per Wahlöö Alone:

1959: *Himmelsgeten* ("Heaven's Gate")

1962: *Lastbilen* (*The Lorry*, tr. Joan Tate, UK 1968; also titled *A Necessary Action*, tr. Joan Tate, U.S. 1969); film: 1978

1963: *Uppdraget* (*The Assignment*, tr. Joan Tate, 1966); film: 1977

1964: *Mord på 31 våningen* (*The Thirty-First Floor*, tr. Joan Tate, 1967; also *Murder on the Thirty-First Floor*, tr. Joan Tate, 1982); films: 1980, 1982

1965: *Generalerna* (*The Generals*, tr. Joan Tate, 1974)

1970: *Stålsprånget* (*The Steel Spring*, tr. Joan Tate, 1970)

Major Awards:

1965: Swedish *Dagbladet Literature Prize*

1971: Edgar Allan Poe Award (for best crime novel published in the United States), for *Den skrattande polisen* (*The Laughing Policeman*)

2013: The Pepe Carvalho Prize given by the Barcelona Crime Festival, for Maj Sjöwall's literary career and the importance of the Martin Beck series in the crime novel genre

Website: N/A

Åke Smedberg

b. 1948 Hjässberget, Sweden; Residence: Uppsala, Sweden; Occupations: poet, author

After his literary debut with a 1976 poetry collection, Åke Smedberg has become one of Sweden's most honored mainstream novelists and short story authors, usually treating some facet of his lifelong theme of individuals excluded by their society. His prizewinning crime novel *Försvinnanden* ("Disappearances"), 2001, first of his crime novels featuring the quiet freelance journalist John Lean Nielsen, deals with the disappearance of a young woman near Bracke, Jamtland, an unsolved case until a stranger appears in the area where she vanished. Gradually Smedberg uncovers layers of psychological intensity.

Crime Novels:

The John Lean Nielsen Series:

2001: *Försvinnanden* ("Disappearances")
2003: *Den mörka floden* ("The Dark River")
2005: *Blod av mitt blod* ("Blood of My Blood")

Stand Alone Novel:

2008: *Jag är inte den du ser* ("I'm Not the One You See")

Short Fiction Collection:

2013: *Borges i Sundsvoll* ("Borges in Sundsvoll")

Major Awards:

2001: Best Swedish Debut Crime Novel, for *Försvinnanden* ("Disappearances")

Website: N/A

*Alexander Söderberg

b. 1970; Residence: Rural southern Sweden; Occupations: television scriptwriter, author

Alexander Söderberg, who has adapted novels by both Camilla Läckberg and Åke Edwardsson for television, originally conceived the plot of *Den Andalusiske vännen*, 2012 (*The Andalusian Friend*, tr. 2013) as a television script, but he says, "I soon realized that I wanted to expand the story ... to paint with more colors than were available for television ... it was great fun to spin out the narrative full blast ... allowing them [the characters] to live their own lives" (quoted in McCoubrey).

Rights for *Den Andalusiske vännen* have been sold in 33 countries and optioned for film. Its main character, Sophie Brinkmann, a nurse who falls in love with one of her patients, becomes entangled in a drug smuggling turf war between rival organizations of international mobsters, courtly sinister Spaniards battling "a callous German outfit with a backup crew of Russian muscle.... Soderberg ... writes with feeling about the crushing psychological stress felt by both cops and criminals" (Stasio, "Bodies"). Söderberg himself sees Sophie's story as a trilogy because he approaches it as the three-act structure familiar in writing a TV or film script: "Act one is the setup, the second act is action and act three is the outcome and resolution" (quoted in McCoubrey).

The second volume of the trilogy, *Den andre sonen*, 2014 (*The Other Son*, tr. 2015), explores the dire consequences of Sophie's joining Hector Guzman's crime empire. After the general praise for *Den Andalusiske vännen*, Söderberg feels "thrilled to be in the company of fellow Swedish writers" who he feels are contributing powerfully to the mystery category: "It's a fascinating moment for crime fiction right now ... the quality of genre fiction has been so elevated that I think we're in a bit of a Golden Age" (quoted in Danford).

Crime Novels:

The Sophie Brinkmann Trilogy:

2012: *Den Andalusiske vännen* (*The Andalusian Friend*, tr. Neil Smith, 2013)
2014: *Den andre sonen* (*The Other Son*, tr. Neil Smith, 2015)

Major Awards: N/A

Website: N/A

Sven Sörmark

b. April 27, 1923, Hörby, Skåne, Sweden; d. October 14, 1987, Solna, Sweden; Residence: Skåne, Sweden; Occupations: journalist, author

Swedish crime fiction historian K. Arne Blom called Sven Sörmark's 1968 psychological crime fiction debut *Väck inte Marie* ("Don't Wake Marie") "a brilliant study of a criminal's mind" that might remind readers of the works of fellow Europeans Georges Simenon and Friedrich Dürrenmatt (Blom 24). Besides his crime novels and thrillers, Sörmark wrote two volumes of short stories, including *Sherlock Holmes i Stockholm* ("Sherlock Holmes in Stockholm," 2001).

Selected Crime Novels:

1968: *Väck inte Marie* ("Don't Wake Marie")
1971: *Ett mord i solen* ("A Murder in the Sun," filmed in 1986 as *Den nervösa mannen* ["The Nervous Man"])
1981: *I morgon din fiende* ("Tomorrow Your Enemy")
1983: *En oscariansk skandal: ur doktor John H. Watsons efterlämnade anteckningar* ("A Oscarian Scandal: from Dr. John H. Watson's Posthumous Notes" [Sherlock Holmes pastiche])

Major Awards: N/A

Website: N/A

Bobi Sourander

b. 1928, Kemi, Finland, d. 2008; Residence: Various; Occupations: journalist, author

Bobi Sourander, a Finnish-Swedish journalist who worked from 1969 to 1974 as the Swedish newspaper *Dagens Nyheter*'s first Latin American correspondent, was imprisoned during the 1973 Chilean military coup, an experience which affected the rest of his life. He subsequently wrote five political crime novels, the last of which, *Förlorarna* ("The Losers"), 1995, dealt with the assassination of Prime Minister Olov Palme.

Crime Novels/Political Thrillers:

1984: *Ett kilo diamanter* ("A Kilo of Diamonds")
1985: *En hjältes liv* ("A Warrior Lives")
1988: *Bara action räknas* ("Just Action Counts")
1990: *Farväl Fidel* ("Farewell, Fidel")
1993: *Vinnarna* ("Vinnarna")
1995: *Förlorarna* ("The Losers")

Major Awards:

1984: Best Debut Crime Novel of the Year, for *Förlorarna* ("The Losers")

Website: N/A

Birgitta Stenberg

b. April 26, 1932, Stockholm, Sweden; Residence: Åstol, Sweden; Occupations: translator, illustrator, adult and children's author

One of Sweden's most prolific and respected female authors, Birgitta Stenberg has produced nine mainstream novels, five autobiographical novels, three collections of poetry, two collections of short fiction (one titled *Erotic Fiction*), twenty young people's books, a cookbook, and one crime novel, as well as over a dozen screenplays and radio and television scenarios. During the Cold War, she edited the journal *Culture*, funded by the CIA under the auspices of the Ford Foundation, and in the spring of 2009 she starred in Swedish Television's live program "Debate: 'Unleash the pot at the pharmacy.'"

Crime Novel:

1998: *Antligen av med liket* ("At Last, with the Corpse")

Major Awards:

2005: The Literature Prize, Selma Lagerlöf Foundation

Website: N/A

Jan-Jöran Stenhagen (pseudonym, possibly of Jan Freese)

Strong suspicion exists that "Jan-Jöran Stenhagen" was the pseudonym of Jan Freese, 1933–2007, who served as director general of the Swedish Data Inspection Board, as vice president of Swedish Industries, and director general of PTS, the Swedish telecommunications agency. He also founded and chaired Nordic Mobile Telephony Sweden. The satiric crime novels attributed to Jan-Jöran Stenhagen, all dealing with computer crime as it existed a quarter century ago, comment on both the Swedish government and the Swedish tax system. The novels may have been written in collaboration with Bengt Göran Wennersten, editor in chief of the magazine *Computer World*.

Crime Novels:

1982: *Datadyrkarna* ("Datadyrkarna")
1983: *Samkörarna* ("The Cross-Breakers")
1984: *Infomania* ("Info Mania")
1986: *Dubbeldyrkarna* ("Dubbeldyrkarna")
1989: *Lucy—i tangentens riktning* ("Lucy, in the Direction of the Tangent")
1996: *År 00* ("Year 00")

Major Awards: N/A

Website: N/A

Erik Axl Sund (joint pseudonym of *Jerker Eriksson and Håkan Sundquist*) see *Jerker Eriksson and Håkan Sundquist*

Vic Suneson (pseudonym of *Sune Lundquist*)

b. September 11, 1911, Stockholm, Sweden; d. September 5, 1975, Sundberg, Sweden; Residence: Stockholm County, Sweden; Occupations: civil engineer, author

Although almost all of Vic Suneson's crime fiction was produced in the 1950s and 1960s and it never received the recognition that the books of his crime fiction contemporaries Stieg Trenter and Maria Lang did, he was the first Swedish crime writer to feature a detective team in a series of novels, years before the appearance of the Martin Beck series by Maj Sjöwall and Per Wahlöö.

Suneson's first police detective, Commissioner Kjell Myrhman, initially appeared in *I dimma dold* ("The Fog Concealed"), 1951, later made into a popular feature film. Suneson's next novel, *Är jag mördaren?* ("Am I the Murderer?"). 1953, introduced another main character, the occasionally violent Sergeant P.O. (later O.P.) Nilsson, who was promoted to Inspector at the end of the novel and subsequently became the protagonist of the following novels in the series. Suneson sent Myrhman, who had a drinking problem, off on United Nations missions, not allowing him to reappear until *Tjuogett* ("Twenty-one"), 1968. Nilsson's team included a forensic assistant, a psychologist, and a "fact collector."

Suneson's O.P. Nilsson novels combined elements of the classic whodunit and the police procedural, but Suneson also experimented with the psychological crime novel in *Fäll inga tårar* ("Fold No Tears"). 1953, and with the Ellery Queen type of whodunit in *Ordet är mord* ("The Word Is Murder"), 1958. He also produced three young adult mysteries between 1974 and his death in 1975.

Selected Crime Novels:

1948: *Mord kring Maud* ("Murder Around Maud")
1951: *I dimma dold* ("The Fog Concealed")
1953: *Fäll inga tårar* ("Fold No Tears"); *Är jag mördarer?* ("Am I the Murderer?")
1968: *Tjuogett* ("Twenty-one")
1971: *Mord är mitt mål* ("Murder Is My Goal")

Major Awards:

1975: Grand Master Award, Swedish Academy of Crime Writers

Website: N/A

Olov Svedelid and Leif Silbersky

Olov Svedelid: b. August 26, 1932, Stockholm, Sweden; d. September 22, 2008, Stocksund, Sweden; Residence: Stocksundstorps, outside Stockholm, Sweden; Occupations: author, president of the Swedish Crime Authors Association

Leif Silbersky: b. March 8, 1938, Malmö, Sweden; Residence: Stockholm, Sweden; Occupations: defense attorney, author

One of Sweden's most popular and highly productive authors, Svedelid produced a popular police procedural series starring Detective Roland Hassel in two short story collections and twenty-seven novels, eleven of which were filmed between 1986 and 2000. He also authored over seventy other books, including historical novels, satires, biographies, and essays, both by himself and with several co-authors, and the 10-novel "Concrete Roses" young adult series. He also ran a senior citizens' theater. He once remarked, "I'll write books until I'm a hundred and then I'll learn to play golf."

Leif Silbersky is one of Sweden's most famous defense attorneys. He takes high-profile cases, most recently that of Wikileaks editor Julian Assange, accused of rape and molestation in 2010. Between 1974 and 2002, Silbersky and his close friend Olov Svedelid co-wrote twenty-five crime novels featuring elderly lawyer Samuel Rosenbaum.

Debut Crime Novel (Olov Svedelid):

1964: *Döden tystar mun* ("Death Silences the Mouth")

Selected Novels of Roland Hassel Series (Olov Svedelid):

1972: *Anmäld försvunnen* ("Reported Missing"), filmed in 1986
1989: *De giriga* ("The Greedy")
1994: *Förfalskarna* ("Counterfeiters")
2004: *Död i ruta ett* ("Death in a Box")

Major Awards (Olov Svedelid):

1972: The Sherlock Award, for *Anmäld försvunnen* ("Reported Missing")
1977: Best Young Adult Crime Novel Award, Swedish Crime Academy, for *Concrete Roses* and *False Keys*
1987: Best Swedish Crime Novel Award, for *Barnarov* ("Child Abduction")
2007: Grand Master Award, Swedish Crime Academy

Selected Novels of Samuel Rosenbaum Series (Leif Silberksy):

1977: *Sista vittnet* (*The Last Witness*, tr. 1979)
1988: *Narrspel* ("Applause for a Killer")
1989: *Sprängstoff* ("Black Mass for a Corpse")
1990: *En röst för döden* ("A Voice for Death")
2000: *Den sista lögnen* ("The Last Lie")
2006: *Hämnden är aldrig rättvis* ("Revenge Is Never Fair")

Major Award as Co-Authors: N/A

Website as Co-Authors: N/A

*Stefan Tegenfalk

> b. August 20, 1965, Stockholm, Sweden; Residence: Stockholm, Sweden; Occupations: founder of IT company, author

In a 2012 CrimeHouse interview, IT developer Stefan Tegenfalk revealed that until a few years previously he was as close as possible "to an illiterate when it came to fiction" and "even less interested in writing" (quoted in "Interview with Stefan Tegenfalk"). He changed his mind after receiving a writing course as a gift, and today he spends most of his time writing, up to a year per novel. His crime trilogy features Detective Chief Inspector Walter Gröhn and Jonna de Brugge of the Special Investigation Unit of Sweden's National Police Board. Its initial concept arose from a news article about a grandmother and her grandchildren all killed by a drunk driver, who then received only a brief sentence since driving drunk was considered a mitigating factor. Another article showed that an individual withholding half a million dollars in taxes received a much harsher sentence. The existential issue for Tegenfalk was what a human life is worth in Sweden today. Tegenfalk believes his novels, which involve the societal implications of the Swedish judicial system, science, extremism, terrorism, and homosexuality ("Interview with Stefan Tegenfalk"), should be read in the order they appeared. Swedish Television is adapting Tegenfalk's Walter Gröhn novels as films.

Crime Novels:

Detective Chief Inspector Walter Gröhn Trilogy:

2010: *Vredens tid* (*Anger Mode*, also called "Wrath Time," tr. David Evans, 2011)
2010: *Nirvanaprojektet* ("The Nirvana Project")
2011: *Den felande länken* ("The Missing Link")

Stand-Alone Continuation of the Gröhn Trilogy:

2012: *Pianostämmaren* ("The Piano Tuner")

Major Awards: N/A

Website: http://www.stefantegenfalk.com

*Johan Theorin

> b. 1963, Gothenburg, Sweden; Residences: Gothenburg, Sweden; Öland, Sweden (summers); Occupations: journalist, scriptwriter, author

Johan Theorin calls his fiction "dark mystery novels with some supernatural overtones" (quoted on official website), set on the Baltic island of Öland about three miles off Sweden's east coast, his mother's home where he spent summers as a child. He still visits there at least once a year. The island is a popular summer tourist venue, but in winter it is dark, stormy, and cold, a venue for many shipwrecks along its eastern coast. Öland has been settled since 8000 BC, with many ancient burial sites and other mysterious places (Holmberg 293). Theorin says he "can write about Öland anywhere.... I can just close my eyes and relocate to Öland in a second" (quoted in "Interview with Johan Theorin"). He describes his prizewinning crime novel quartet as "sort of a combination of dark crime stories and Scandinavian folklore and ghost stories," but he allows his readers to decide whether "such things as ghosts and premonitions" really exist (quoted in Flood).

Judges for the 2010 Crime Writers' Association International Dagger Award, in which Theorin's *Nattfåk,* 2008 (*The Darkest Room,* tr .2009) unexpectedly beat out the late Stieg Larsson's *The Girl Who Kicked the Hornet's Nest,* indicated that Theorin's novel, in which a family moves to an old reputedly haunted Öland manor house, built from timber from a ship sunk in 1846 on Eel Point, where the mother is found drowned a few days later, was "impossible to reduce to [a] ghost story, a police procedural or a gothic tale" (quoted in Flood), even though young policewoman Tilda Davidsson, related to a character from *Skumtimmen,* 2007 (*Echoes of the Dead,* tr. 2008) investigates the drowning, which also involves a gang of thieves raiding summer homes for antiques.

All Theorin's novels seem difficult to classify, since he says he enjoys mixing "a lot of ingredients" to see what happens in his fiction. His novels follow no traditional crime genre structure like police procedurals or whodunits, but each combines crime and mystery with supernatural elements. According to his website, he wrote one novel of the Öland quartet for each of the seasons, "where the weather and the mood of the landscape affect the characters in the story," and where when the tourists go home only the villagers and some few occasional visitors "with good ideas or evil plans remain on the island" (quoted from website): "The dead are our neighbours everywhere on the island, and you have to get used to it" (quoted on website from *The Darkest Room*).

Theorin says he loves most daydreaming of the stories he will write. He considers writing "a hobby and a passion" that he would have pursued even if his novels had never been published (quoted in "Interview with Johan Theorin"). In fusing reality with inspirations from his dreams, Theorin challenges his readers to ponder such disquieting questions as "How close can you get to the truth before you become the target?" (quoted on website from *The Quarry*). He plans to use a local expression, either *Alvargrimma* or *Sjömansvåd,* for the title of his next novel, to be set in Stenvik, a small fishing village on Öland (quoted on website).

Crime novels (the Öland Quartet):

2007: *Skumtimmen* (*Echoes from the Dead,* tr. Marlaine Delargy, 2008)
2008: *Nattfåk* (*The Darkest Room,* tr. Marlaine Delargy, 2009)
2010: *Blodläge* (*The Quarry,* tr. Marlaine Delargy, 2011)
2013: *Rörgast* ("The Mission")

Stand-Alone Crime Novel:

2011: *Sankta Psyko* (*The Asylum,* tr. Marlaine Delargy, 2013)

Major Awards:

2007: Best Debut Crime Novel, for *Skumtimmen* (*Echoes from the Dead*)
2008: Best Swedish Crime Novel, for *Nattfåk* (*The Darkest Room*)
2009: The Crime Writers' Association John Creasey Award (New Blood Dagger) for *Skumtimmen* (*Echoes from the Dead*)
2009: The Glass Key Award, for *Nattfåk* (*The Darkest Room*)
2010: The Crime Writers' Association International Dagger, for *Nattfåk* (*The Darkest Room*)

Website: http://www.johantheorin.co.uk

Mats Tormod

b. 1946, Luleå, Sweden; Residence: Sandnäset, Norrbotten, Sweden; Occupation: author

According to the autobiographical statement on his website, Mats Tormod was surprised to win the 1995 Swedish Crime Writers Academy Award for Best Debut Crime Novel for *Movie*, since he did not realize it was a detective novel. Since then he wrote *Skrivarens intrig* ("Printer's Scheme"), which he calls a "metathriller," three children's books, and his academic dissertation on the renowned early twentieth century Swedish modernist author Eyvind Johnson.

Selected Crime Novels:

1985: *Movie* ("Movie")
1999: *Skrivarens intrig* ("Printer Scheme," under pseudonym "Sean Fall")

Major Awards:

1985: Best Swedish Crime Novel Debut, for *Movie*

Website: http://www.matstormod.se

Laura Trenter

> b. May 29, 1961, Stockholm, Sweden; Residence: Mariefred in Södermanland, Sweden; Occupations: journalist, children's and adult fiction author

Laura Trenter, currently called Sweden's *Barnens deckardrottning* ("Children's Crime Fiction Queen") is the daughter of the famous Swedish detective authors Stieg and Ulla Trenter. By herself and with co-authors Laura Trenter has produced over twenty young adult crime novels, as well as guidebooks, picture books, and computer games. Her special interest in archaeology often appears in her books, which she generally plots completely before she begins the actual writing. She claims she has a "pretty black imagination," often taking ideas from news stories or television programs but keeping in mind that "Much blood and many murders [do] not automatically mean that the story gets exciting" (quoted in "Laura Trenter—Interview"). To see if her stories appeal to young people, she often submits portions of her manuscripts to her own two sons for their verdict.

Selected Young Adult Crime Novels:

2002: *Julian och Jim* ("Julian and Jim")
2004: *Puman* ("Cougar")

Major Awards:

2003: Gothenburg Book Fair Prize as best youth crime novelist

Website: http://www.lauratrenter.tiden.se

Stieg Trenter (Stig Ivar Johansson)

> b. August 14, 1914, Stockholm, Sweden; d. July 4, 1967, Stockholm, Sweden; Residence: Stockholm, Sweden; Occupations: journalist, author

The first Swedish crime author to set his stories in Sweden and also create "thoroughly Swedish detectives with unmistakably Swedish names" (Holmberg 7), Stig Johansson took the name "Trenter" for his crime novel pseudonym from Eric C. Bentley's crime novel *Trent's Last Case*. Stieg Trenter set all of his twenty-nine detective novels, published between 1943 and 1966, in Stockholm and based his primary characters, photographer Harry Friberg and Detective Superintendent Vesper Johnson, on Trenter's friends K.W. Gullers and the Stockholm editor Runar Karlströmer respectively. After Trenter's death in 1967, his wife Ulla Trenter continued to use Friberg and Johnson as lead characters, but with some adjustments for her own detective series. Four of Stieg Trenter's Harry Friberg novels were adapted as Swedish television series in 1987.

Selected Harry Friberg Novels:

> 1943: *Ingen kan hejda döden* ("No One Can Stop Death")
> 1955: *Tiga är silver* ("Silence Is Silver")
> 1956: *Narr på nocken* ("Fools on the Ridge")
> 1966: *Sjöjungfrun* ("Mermaid")

Major Awards:

> 1956: The Sherlock Award, for *Narr på nocken* ("Fools on the Ridge")

Website: N/A

Ulla Trenter

> b. December 18, 1936, Södermalm, Stockholm, Sweden; Residence: Mariefred, Sweden; Occupations: translator, author

Ulla Trenter says that she served her literary apprenticeship under her husband, crime author Stieg Trenter, from 1959 to 1967. Upon his death in 1967, she completed his novel *Rosenkavaljeren*. Since then she published over twenty detective novels of her own from 1968 to 2000, using Stieg Trenter's fictional amateur detective Harry Friberg but adapting his personality and the plots of his cases to her own literary purposes. Generally the plots of her novels have been considered weaker than his plots, and they "have little of his trademark depiction of Stockholm settings" (Holmberg 7). Her work adheres to the traditional Swedish detective genre, influenced by older Swedish crime authors like Vic Suneson and H.K. Rönblom, as well as her work with her husband.

Among her many other literary activities, Ulla Trenter has recently translated Swedish versions of the works of Peter Tremayne, whose crime novels feature Sister Fidelma, a seventh-century Irish nun; the legal crime novels of Italian author Carafiglio; and a biography of Agatha Christie. In a 2009 *Deckahuset.se* (*CrimeHouse Scandinavia*) interview, Ulla Trenter, who is a member of the Swedish Crime Writers' Academy, noted that one of her duties there is to chair the reading group responsible for choosing the best foreign detective novel for each year. She also recalled how her writing method has changed, from typing her husband's dictated stories to using her own computer some nine hours a day, following her chapter outlines. Chapters two through nineteen, she says, are mostly irrelevant discussions "and bam! resolution in chapter eighteen" (quoted in "Interview with Ulla Trenter"). Ulla Trenter also has actively participated in Centre Party cultural and religious activities since 1975.

Selected Crime Novels:

> 1970: *Odjuret* ("Small Ladybird")
> 1976: *Drakblodet* ("Blood of the Dragon," not a Harry Friberg novel)
> 1984: *Grodmuggen* ("The Cup Frog")
> 1991: *Sköna juveler* ("Rough Cut")
> 2006: *Varför dör grannarna?* ("Why Do Neighbors Die?")

Major Awards: N/A

Website: http://www.keg.se/fkis/ut.html

Aino Trosell

> b. May 22, 1949, Malung, Sweden; Residence: Gothenburg, Sweden; Occupations: playwright and author

With more then twenty adult books in various genres, short fiction, several children's books, plays, film scripts, and audiobooks, Aino Trosell is one of the most prolific contemporary Swedish authors. Early in her life she worked as a social worker and then became a welder. She found her calling as an author with her 1978 debut novel *Socialsvängen* ("Social Slew"). In the late 1990s, she published *Ytspänning* ("Surface Tension"), her first crime novel, as did Inger Frimansson, Liza Marklund, and Helene Tursten, women crime fiction authors breaking the virtual monopoly male Swedish authors had theretofore maintained in the genre. The protagonists of Aino Trosell's "largely proletarian realist novels" were "crime-solving female 'anti-heroes'" (Holmberg 15), the most well known of whom is named "Siv Dahlin."

Crime Fiction:

> 1998: *Ytspänning* ("Surface Tension") (also an audiobook)

Siv Dahlin Novels:

> 2000: *Om hjärtat ännu slår* ("If the Heart Still Beats")
> 2002: *Se dem inte i ögonen* ("See Them in the Eyes")
> 2012: *Krimineller* ("Criminals") (also an audiobook)
> 2013: *En egen strand* ("One's Own Beach")
> 2014: *Min grav är den* ("My Grave or Yours")

Major Awards:

> 1999: Poloni Prize for *Ytspänning* ("Surface Tension")
> 2000: Best Swedish Crime Novel Prize, for *Om hjärtat ännu slår* ("If the Heart Still Beats")

Website: http://www.ainotrosell.se

*Helene Tursten

> b. 1954, Gothenburg, Sweden; Residence: Sunne, Värmland, Sweden; Occupations: nurse, dentist, author

After a severe rheumatic disease forced Helene Tursten, a trained nurse as well as a dentist, to retire from her dental practice, she turned first to translating medical articles and then began to write crime novels, debuting in 1998, the same year as female Swedish crime authors Aino Trosell, Liza Marklund, and Inger Frimansson, breaking into that previously male-dominated field. Tursten drew on her husband's six years as a policeman for her female protagonist who is unlike the amateur female sleuths that Trosell, Marklund, and Frimansson created. Tursten's forty-ish Irene Huss is a middle-aged Detective Inspector in the Gothenburg Police Department's Violent Crimes Division, happily married to a successful chef, a capable mother of twin teenaged daughters, and a judo expert. Tursten feels "One could say that Irene Huss is so ordinary she becomes extraordinary" (Tursten, "A Crime Writer" 66). Swedish crime literature now often includes female characters in positions of responsibility, but "they still have had to struggle to get and keep their positions. Dealing with resentful colleagues is a thread running through nearly all the Swedish mysteries written by women" (Suit 39). Tursten's Irene Huss manages those professional tensions better than most of her fictional sister-investigators.

In 1999 after the publication of her first Irene Huss novel, Tursten insisted, "I did not write about a whiskey-drinking loner. I really do not like it when female heroes perform as well as their male predecessors in crime—boozing, cursing…" (quoted in Johansson). She later recalled that except for Maj Sjöwall who wrote with Per Wahlöö, "we didn't have any women to redress the balance [in perceiving Swedish society]. So I decided to write the kind of books that I wanted to read myself—books that reflected different viewpoints" (quoted in Forshaw 62–3).

Although her overarching topic is crime against children (Forshaw 63), Tursten's fiction, unlike that of many of her fellow Swedish crime writers, conveys a sense of hope, because she firmly believes that such brutal crimes as child and spousal abuse, human trafficking, and incest need to be forced "into the light" (quoted in Forshaw 63) so that the perpetrators can be brought to justice and future crimes prevented. In *Den krossade tanghästen*, 1998 (*Detective Inspector Huss*, tr. 2003), Tursten tackled a complex combination of social ills, not only murders which require plenty of routine police procedure, but also the biker gang problem, neo–Nazi skinhead violence, drug addiction, sexism among police officers, and the peculiar "interplay of mutual discomfort and curiosity that defines interactions between Finns and the rest of Scandinavia … [as an example, when] Finns are cops, [they are] respected but also mistrusted by their colleagues" (Cummins). Irene Huss's associates include Hannu Rauhala, a Finn of few words but professional competence; Huss's hypertensive boss, Detective Superintendent Sven Andersson; and officers Birgitta Moberg and Tommy Persson. To illustrate her alarm at the strength of Sweden's neo–Nazi movement, the largest in Europe (Rozovsky, "Evening"), Tursten had Irene Huss enlist Tommy Persson, some of whose Jewish family members had been victims of Nazism, to prove to her daughter Jenny that despite Jenny's skinhead boyfriend's neo–Nazi tirades, the Holocaust really happened.

Tursten develops her plots for months before writing, collecting inner pictures until she believes the story is complete: "It may seem as if I do nothing for months on end, but in reality I'm working intensely on the book in my mind" (quoted in "Helene Tursten," *Scandinavian Crime Fiction*). The Irene Huss novels that emerge from her detailed preliminary work carry a "fitful" sense of hope (Forshaw 62) often lacking in the *noir* novels of Sweden's male crime authors. "Tursten's Sweden may not be a rose-colored land, but neither is it a place of unrelenting gloom." To Irene Huss, "it's also a most worthwhile place to be" (Cummins).

The Irene Huss cases have enjoyed considerable filmic success both in Sweden and abroad. A Swedish-Danish-German cooperative effort produced film adaptations of the first six Irene Huss novels, released beginning in the fall of 2007. Another six Huss films were released beginning in 2010, with DVD versions available in 2011. Tursten wrote new stories for the 2010 releases, which she felt posed the biggest challenge in inventing new stories, because she needed to show each case as unique. She developed two of the film templates into books, 2010's *De som vakar i mörkret* ("The Watcher in the Dark") and 2012's *I skydd av skuggorna* ("Sitting in the Shade").

In 2014 Tursten felt she had to "reload her batteries" (quoted in Tursten, "My New Project" 40) and she created a new detective heroine, Embla Nystrom, an independent red-haired police officer, an experienced hunter, and a Nordic champion welterweight boxer, for *Jaktmark* ("Hunting Ground"), the opening novel of Tursten's second detective series. Tursten plans its next novel for 2016, though she insists that she and Irene Huss are just resting temporarily. Tursten also says the concept for the Embla Nystrom series has been on Tursten's mind since 2006. Embla works in the fictional Swedish police "Mobile Unit," allowing Tursten to explore various rural environments as well as analyze Embla's attachment to nature through hunting, which Tursten bases on the sport by which her sister and brother-in-law provide "boars, deer, seabirds" and moose— "antibiotic-free food" for their family's table—although Tursten herself has been a vegetarian for twenty years (Tursten, "My New Project" 41).

Despite the intense effort she puts into her writing, Tursten insists, "If I have the plot once in the head, then it is a joy to write down everything. I like the feeling" (quoted in "Interview with Helene Tursten," *Das Erste*).

Crime Novels:

Detective Inspector Irene Huss Series:

1998: *Den krossade tanghästen* (*Detective Inspector Huss*, tr. Steven T. Murray, 2003)
1999: *Nattrond* (*Night Rounds*, tr. Laura A. Wideburg, 2012)
1999: *Tatuerad torso* (*The Torso*, tr. Katarina E. Tucker, 2006)
2002: *Glasdjävulen* (*The Glass Devil*, tr. Katarina E. Tucker, 2007)
2004: *Guldkalven* (*The Golden Calf*, tr. Laura A. Wideburg, 2013)
2005: *Eldsdansen* (*The Fire Dancer*, tr. Laura A. Wideburg, 2014)
2007: *En man med litet ansikte* (*The Beige Man*, tr. Marlaine Delargy, 2015)
2008: *Det lömska nätet* ("The Fire House")
2010: *De som vakar i mörkret* ("The Watcher in the Dark")
2012: *I skydd av skuggorna* ("Under Cover of the Shadows")

Embla Nystrom Series:

2014: *Jaktmark* ("Hunting Ground")

Short Fiction:

2003: *Kvinnan i hissen: och andra hoist mystiska historier* ("The Woman in the Elevator and Other Mysterious Stories")

Major Awards: N/A

Websites: http://www.helenetursten.com; http://www.irenehuss.se

Carl-Johan Vallgren ("Lucifer")

b. July 26, 1964, Linköping, Sweden; Residence: Stockholm, Sweden; Occupations: musician, songwriter, author

Carl-Johan Vallgren has written in several genres, including *noir* thrillers, which he writes under the pen name "Lucifer." The first novel of his projected *noir* thriller series featuring Danny Katz, a military language specialist with a troubled past, 2013's *Skuggpojken* (*The Boy in the Shadows*, tr. 2014), deals with the 1970 disappearance of a young boy from a Stockholm subway station and the similar vanishing of the boy's brother many years later.

Noir Thrillers:

Danny Katz Series:

2013: *Skuggpojken* (*The Boy in the Shadows*, tr. Rachel Willson-Broyles, 2014)

Major Awards:

2002: The August Award for mainstream novel *The Horrific Sufferings of the Mind-Reading Monster Hercules Barefoot*

Website: http://www.carljohanvollgren.nu

Veronica von Schenck

b. 1971; Residence: Stockholm, Sweden; Occupations: live computer gamer and games reviewer, editor, recruitment consultant, children's books writer, author

After her two adult crime novels about profiler Althea Sang Min Molin, Veronica von Schenck, a business headhunter, has also been writing crime novels targeted at children 9 to 12 (the "sub-rosa" series). Whether writing for adults or young people, von Schenck, whose favorite character is Sherlock Holmes (Holmberg 313), has always loved detective stories and claims she writes primarily to entertain (author's website). In "Interview with Veronica von Schenck," *Crime-House,* she also noted that her central character Althea Sang Min Molin, whose mother was Korean, shares little with von Schenck herself, except for a keen talent for observation, fascination with people at large, an "inability to keep a pair of pantyhose whole for eight hours," and the constant consumption of lattes. Von Schenck begins her novels by researching, which she says she can do anywhere—"brainstorming on the bus, reading FBI reports in the bathtub." She also admits to liking any crime novel with "a core of humanity—not just brutality" ("Interview with Veronica von Schenck," *CrimeHouse*).

Crime Novels:

Profiler Althea Sang Min Molin Series:

2008: *Änglalik* ("Angelic")
2009: *Kretsen* ("The Circuit")

Major Awards: N/A

Website: http://veronicasverkstad.se

Helena von Zweigbergk

b. February 18, 1958, Stockholm, Sweden; Residence: Stockholm, Sweden; Occupations: journalist, film critic, author

After her three crime novels featuring women's prison chaplain Ingrid Carlberg, Helena von Zweigbergk has shifted her literary focus to mainstream romance novels. She has described all of her writing as "starting the magical process that makes my text start breathing and moving ... sometimes in ways beyond my control.... My passion is getting people to think about themselves and each other." She believes her books are about trying to find a balance between "total freedom" and "earth-shattering love," and the only question she asks herself when she writes is, "Is it alive?" (quoted from "Helena von Zweigbergk," *Partners in Stories*).

Crime Novels:

Ingrid Carlberg Series:

2001: *Det Gud inte såg* ("That God Did Not See")

2003: *Kärleken skär djupa spår* ("Love Cuts Deep Grooves")
2004: *Hon som bar skammen* ("She Who Bore the Shame")

Major Awards: N/A

Website: N/A

*Karin Wahlberg

b. 1950, Kalmar, Sweden; Residence: Lund, Sweden; Occupations: obstetrician, author

Karin Wahlberg made her literary debut at 51, "mature but happy" about her third career. She trained first as a teacher, then became a gynecologist-obstetrician and was working full time at Lund's University Hospital when the idea for her first novel came to her: "I walked briskly home and had killed a doctor and created ... [the] eventually married couple Veronika Lundborg [a doctor] and Claes Claesson [a Chief Inspector]" (quoted in "Karin Wahlberg," Wahlström & Widstrand statement). Her detective novels are traditional whodunits, often compared to Agatha Christie's carefully plotted fiction, with no politics but abundant detail about the characters' ordinary lives.

In addition to her medically-based crime fiction, Wahlberg published *Sigrids hemlighet* (*Sigrid's Secret*) in 2009, a historical novel set in the transitional eleventh century, when the old gods of the Viking Age were giving way to the Christian Middle Ages in Sweden. Wahlberg commented, "When it [this novel] finally came clear, it was like a bond developed between me and all the characters.... I am not a Middle Ages fanatic, but oh, how I like them all" (quoted in Grand Agency's *Grand News*, March 2009).

Currently working part time as a physician at a small clinic, Wahlberg bases her writing on her experiences in health care. Her most recent novel, a stand-alone mainstream book about the polio epidemic of 1953, opens Wahlberg's new series with crime or violence, when it does occur, clearly subsidiary to her depiction of Swedish small-town life centered on a hospital in the 1950s: "Pain, anxiety and death, but also joy and relief characterize the contents of all my books" (quoted in "Karin Wahlberg," Wahlstrom & Widstrand statement).

Crime Novels:

Chief Inspector Claes Claesson and Dr. Veronika Lundborg Series:

2001: *Sista jouren* ("Last Shelter")
2002: *Hon som tittade in* ("She Looked Into")
2003: *Ett fruset liv* ("A Frozen Life")
2006: *Blocket* ("Block")
2007: *Tröstaren* ("Comforter")
2009: *Matthandlare Olssons död* (*Death of a Carpet Dealer*, tr. Neil Betteridge, 2012)
2011: *Glasklart* ("Crystal Clear")
2012: *Rosa boken* ("Pink Paper")

Semi-Mainstream Series Set in the 1950s:

2013: *Än finns det hopp* ("Still There Is Hope")
2014: *Livet går vidare* ("Life Goes On")

Major Awards: N/A

Website: http:www.karinwahlberg.se

Jan Wallentin

> b. April 8, 1970, Linköping, Sweden; Residence: Stockholm, Sweden; Occupations: Journalist, author

Before its Swedish publication in 2010, the rights to *Strindbergs stjärna* (*Strindberg's Star*, tr. 2012) had been sold to sixteen countries. Like Dan Brown's highly popular 2003 thriller *The Da Vinci Code*, *Strindberg's Star* involves a hectic trans–Europe pursuit involving a secret society and a missing treasure, entangled by Wallentin with Egyptian and Norse myth, northern European history, the ill-fated 1897 Andree North Pole Expedition, and Third Reich conspiracies laced with Nazi mysticism. *Strindberg's Star* enjoyed impressive pre-publication publicity but received mixed reviews, some European critics finding the narrative boring and the characterizations unconvincingly contrived (Thente). Wallentin himself says he intended to create "an irresistible story of suspense … without a lot of violence and blood," switching genres unpredictably from a crime story to a traditional whodunit, to "a sort of Hitchcock thriller," then an adventure story, then "something completely different." Since 2012, when profits from *Strindberg's Star* allowed him to write full time, Wallentin has been working on "a new novel with a very different theme" (quoted from "Author Interview: Jan Wallentin," *Roof Beam Reader*).

Crime Novels:

2010: *Strindbergs stjärna* (*Strindberg's Star*, tr. Rachel Willson-Broyles, 2012)

Major Awards: N/A

Website: http://www.strindbergsstar.com

Katarina Wennstam

> b. August 9, 1973, Gothenburg, Sweden; Residence: Stockholm, Sweden; Occupations: journalist, lecturer, author

Katarina Wennstam's powerful commitment to women's rights has motivated all of her writing. Her 2002 documentary *Flickan och skulden* ("Girl and Debt") dealt with Swedish society's view of rape and questioned the media's role in reporting sex crimes. It was nominated for the prestigious August Prize and received the Swedish Bar Association's Prize for Journalism. The main characters of her novels are two women working in a violent man's world, Detective Inspector Charlotta Lugn and attorney Shirin Sundin. Beginning with *Smuts* ("Dirt"), 2007, Wennstam has addressed crimes against women and children: human trafficking, domestic violence among police officers and their spouses, violence in the sports world, and sexual abuse in the film industry. On her website, Wennstam defines the impulse which drives her work: "a combination of a deep-seated anger over the state of affairs together with a [conviction that it is] actually possible to change things" (author's website).

Crime Novels:

Detective Inspector Charlotta Lugn and Attorney Shirin Sundin Series:
2007: *Smuts* ("Dirt")
2008: *Dödergök* (Made-up word from a children's song)
2010: *Alfahannen* ("The Alpha Male")
2012: *Svikaren* ("The Betrayer")

2013: *Stenhjärtat* ("Stone Heart")
2014: *Skuggorna* ("Shadows")

Major Awards:

Nominated for August Award for *Smuts*

Website: http://www.katarinawennstam.se

Sven Westerberg

b. 1945, Vanersborg, Sweden; Residence: Partille, Sävedalen, near Gothenburg, Sweden; Occupation: author

Sven Westerberg, a member of the Swedish Crime Academy, first produced five thrillers with Lennart Brask, who works in Stockholm for a secret military intelligence group. Westerberg's sixth novel, *Det gåtfulla mordet i Partille* ("The Mysterious Murder at Partille"), 1998, addresses issues related to mental illness. Westerberg's subsequent novels feature Hanna Skogholm, a legal psychiatrist at Gothenburg.

Crime Novels:

Lennart Brask Series:

1987: *Onsalaaffären* ("The Onsala Transaction")
1989: *Pragincidenten* ("The Prague Incident")
1991: *Kabinettssekreteraren* ("The State Secretary")
1994: *Göteborgsmorden* ("The Gothenburg Murder")
1996: *Skuggan av Vasa högre allmänna läroverk* ("The Shadow of Vasa Grammar School")

Stand-Alone Crime Novel:

1998: *Det gåtfulla mordet i Partille* ("The Mysterious Murder at Partille")

The Hanna Skogholm Series:

1999: *Guds fruktansvärda frånvaro* ("God's Awful Absence")
2000: *Judinnans tystnad* ("Judinnan's Silence")
2002: *Abonnemanget har upphört* ("Your Subscription Has Expired")
2003: *Andras väg har rastplatser i solen* ("Andras Road Has Picnic Areas in the Sun")
2006: *Flugfiskaren* ("The Fly Fisherman")
2012: *Onsala, höstvinden och T.S. Eliot* ("Onsala, Autumn Wind and T.S. Eliot")

Major Awards:

1999: Best Swedish Crime Novel, for *Guds fruktansvärda frånvaro* ("God's Awful Absence")

Website: N/A

Steffan Westerlund

b. March 5, 1942; d. March 22, 2012; Residence: Uppsala, Sweden; Occupations: lawyer, naturalist, professor of environmental law, author

From a critic of Swedish governmental policies in the 1980s and 1990s, the common theme of Steffan Westerlund's crime novels is "the inhumanity of both big business and big government."

In his fiction he addressed the "meddling and callous outrages" Swedish authorities regularly committed, especially regarding environmental issues, as well as the "indifference towards individuals" that he believed profiteering medical, chemical, and energy corporations were displaying toward the Swedish people (Holmberg 12).

Selected Crime Novels:

> 1983: *Institutet* ("Institute")
> 1984: *Svärtornas år* (Svärtorna's Year")
> 1986: *Större än sanningen* ("Larger Than the Truth")
> 1994: *O-lösningen* ("Zero Solution")
> 2003: *Rörligt mål* ("Moving Target")

Major Awards:

> 1984: Best Swedish Crime Novel, for *Svärtornas år* ("Svärtorna's Year")
> 1986: Best Swedish Crime Novel, for *Större än sanningen* ("Larger Than the Truth")

Website: N/A

Liselott Willén (also *Lise Lott Willén*)

> b. June 12, 1972, Saltviksvägen, Aland Islands, Sweden; Residence: Örebro, Sweden; Occupations: physician, author

While working part time as a physician at Örebro University, Liselott Willén writes science-based crime novels of psychological suspense. Her 2011 *Ingenstans under himlen* ("Nowhere Under the Sky"), a scientific thriller, departs from the usual procedural pattern. It deals with the risks of developing a national DNA registry through her fictional politician, Christian Weber, a proponent of such a registry. When to publicize his cause he gives a saliva sample during a television appearance, his DNA is found to match evidence from a decade-old murder of a young girl. He disappears a day later, kidnapped by criminals who are friends of the dead girl's mother. Willén focuses on human responsibility and the consequences of human acts, as well as strongly exposing violence against women in Swedish society.

Crime Novels:

> 2001: *Sten för sten* ("Stone by Stone")
> 2003: *Eldsmärket* ("Eldsmärket")
> 2008: *Islekar* ("Islekar")
> 2011: *Ingenstans under himlen* ("Nowhere Under the Sky")
> 2013: *Jakthistorier* ("Hunting Stories")

Major Awards: N/A

Website: N/A

*Joakim Zander

> b. 1975, Stockholm, Sweden; Residence: Lund, Sweden; Occupations: lawyer, author

Attorney Joakim Zander, who has lived in Syria, Israel, and the United States, received his Ph.D. in Law from Maastricht University and has worked for the European Parliament and the

European Commission in Brussels, Belgium. In 2012 he published *Simmaren* (*The Swimmer*, tr. 2014), a complex espionage bestselling thriller highly praised in Europe. In it, an unnamed American spy who decades ago abandoned his newborn child in Damascus, now, smitten with guilt, embarks on a lifelong quest to forget that deed by seeking out the most dangerous places he can find, including Lebanon, Iraq, and Afghanistan. In the present day, too, Zander's protagonist Swedish EU Parliament employee Klara Waldéen and her former lover Mahmoud Shammosh begin a dangerous investigation into a cover-up of American black op sites for torturing captured terrorists. After he learns that Klara is his abandoned daughter, the unnamed spy works to save her from his CIA superior who heads a team hunting her and Mahmoud to destroy them.

Crime Novel:

Projected Klara Waldéen Series:

2013: *Simmaren* (*The Swimmer*, tr. Elizabeth Clark Wessel, 2014)

Major Awards:

2012: The Rabobank Prize, for his legal dissertation, *The Application of the Precautionary Principle in Practice*

Website: N/A

Anthology of Swedish Short Crime Fiction

Stockholm Noir, ed. Nathan Larson and Carl-Michael Edenborg, Akashic Books, 2016).

According to Akashic Books, this collection includes an introduction plus thirteen dark short stories by various authors, each written specifically for the anthology and set in a different neighborhood of Stockholm. They share the theme of the deterioration and corruption of the welfare state.

Selected Crime Fiction Set in Sweden
by Non-Swedish Authors

Torquil MacLeod

According to British author Torquil MacLeod who formerly has worked in advertising, his frequent visits to Sweden and his acquaintance with police detectives there have inspired his series of crime novels set in Malmö, which MacLeod finds a fascinating cosmopolitan city. They feature Inspector Anita Sundstrom, competent yet predictably plagued by boorish sexist male superiors. She is informally teamed with Ewan Stachan, a lazy but appealing nearly-unemployed journalist.

Crime Novels (all published as ebooks in 2015):

Meet me in Malmö
Murder in Malmö
Missing in Malmö
Midnight in Malmö

Olivier Nilsson-Julien

British television writer and translator Olivier Nilsson-Julien grew up in Sweden, the inspiration for his crime fiction. Nilsson-Julien feels all Nordic crime stories indirectly attempt to explain the reason Prime Minister Olaf Palme was assassinated, a crucial event that he feels destroyed the idealistic Swedish welfare model and forced Scandinavians to enter a new and darker world of corruption and lost ideals, one he began to explore in *The Ice Cage*, 2015, the first novel of his projected Baltic Trilogy.

WORKS CITED

Introduction

Edwardson, Åke. *Room No. 10*, Translated by Rachel Willson-Broyles. New York: Simon & Schuster, 2015. Print.

Forshaw, Barry. *Death in a Cold Climate*. New York: Palgrave Macmillan, 2012. Print.

Denmark

Acharekar, Jankavi. "Much Ado About Reading." *The Hindu*, n.d. Web. 1 September 2013. http://www.thehindu.com.

Ackerman, Peter, and Jack DuVall. *A Force More Powerful*. New York: St. Martin's Press, 2000. Print.

Adler-Olsen, Jussi. *The Alphabet House*, tr. Steve Schein. New York: Dutton, 2015. Print.

Albrechtsen, Rikke. "Knitwear in Prime Time." *Focus Denmark*, June 2012. Web. 26 November 2013. http://denmark.dk/en/lifestyle/film/knitwear-in-prime-time.

Amdrup, Erik. "To Write Crime Novels." *Pinkerton* 13 (1984). Web. 19 November 2013. http://www.sherlockiana.dk/ljemmesiden/amdrup.htm.

Andersen, Carsten. "Best-Selling Danish Writer: I Can't Be Bothered to Write Splatter." *Politiken*. Web. 27 November 2013. http://www.jussiadlerolsen/dk/?page+article_politiken.

Andreasen, Rebecca. "Crime Writer Steffen Jacobsen." 4 February 2013. Web. 27 December 2013. http://www.goodreads.com/author/show/4587812.

Arun, Neil. "Storming Denmark's Drugs Stronghold." *BBC News Online*, 19 March 2004. Web. 6 October 2013. http://news.bbc.co.uk/2/hi/europe/3524274/stm.

Baehr, Anne Klara. Review of "A Time to Die" by Morten Hesseldahl. *Litteratursiden* 2013. Web. 18 August 2013. http:.www.litteratursiden.dk.

Bartholdy, Birgitte. "'He sees through women.' Interview with Christian Jungersen On *The Exception*." October 2004. Web. 26 December 2013. http://www.christianjungersen.com/interviews/he-see-through-women; originally in http://www.altfordamerne.dk.

"Benni Bødker and Karen Vad Bruun." The Nordin Agency, n.d. Web. 1 April 2015. http://www.nordinagency.se/portfolio-item.

Bertel, Haarder. "*Nye Myter Om Samarbejdspolitikken*" ("New Myths About the Cooperation Policy"), 14 February 2–13. Web. 1 September 2013.

Blecher, George. "The Danish Welfare State Works." *New York Times* 5 May 2013. Web. 6 October 2013. http://www.nytimes.com/roomfordebate/2013/05/05.

Blundell, Graeme. *The Australian*, 15 May 2013. Web. 17 May 2013. http://www.theaustralian.com.au/arts/television.

Booss, Claire, ed. *Scandinavian Folk & Fairy Tales*. New York: Avenel Books, 1984. Print.

Boffey, Daniel. "Inside Denmark's 'Fixing Rooms,' Where Nurses Watch as Addicts Inject in Safety." *The Observer* 4 May 2013. Web. 6 October 2013. http://www.theguardian.com/society/2013/may/04/denmark-nurses-addicts-inject.

Bowlby, Chris. "Do Denmark's Immigration Laws Breach Human Rights?" BBC Radio 4. 9 February 2011. Web. 6 October 2013. http://www.bbc/co.uk/news/world-europe-12366676.

Bowman, Daniel, Jr. "Character, Plot, and Pastries: An Interview with Thom Satterlee." 20 February 2013. Web. 15 September 2013. http://english.taylor.edu?p=307.

Brandes, Georg. *Reminiscences of My Childhood and Youth*. n.p., 1906. Print.

Brown, Birgitta. Rosenkrantz Award Citation to Erik Amdrup, *Pinkerton* 32 (1990). Web. 19 November 2013. http://www.sherlockiana.dk/ljemmesiden/amdrup.htm.

Brunson Winton. "Goodbye, Denmark: An American Student's View on Politics, Religion, and Humor in Denmark." n.d. Web. 2 September 2013. http://studyindenmark.dk.news.

Bryld, Claus. "Occupied Denmark as Mirror: Danish Attitudes to War and Occupation 55 Years After the Event." Lecture presented at the Seminar on European Research on Nazism, Nazi Germany and the Holocaust. Stockholm, 14–16 March 2002. Manuscript dated June 2000. Print.

Buckser, Andrew. "Rescue and Cultural Context During the Holocaust: Grundtvigian Nationalism and the Rescue of the Danish Jews." *Shofar* 19.2 (2001). Print.

Chest, Andreas. Review of "The Mercedes-Benz Syndrome" by Gretelise Holm. *Litteratursiden*, 5 January 2002. Web. 25 December 2013. http://www.litteratursiden.dk.

Cogdill, Oline. "Review: 'Farewell to Freedom' by Sara Blaedel." *Sun Sentinel* 20 January 2013. Web. 20 January 2013. http://www.tulsaworld.com/scene/article.aspx.

Clark, Clare. "Comedy of Blunders." *The Sunday Book Review, New York Times*, 26 February 2009. Web. 2 January 2014. http://www.nytims.com/2009/03/01/books/review/Clark-t.html?_r=0.

Clarke, Maxine. Review of *The Dinosaur Feather. Euro-Crime*, June 2011. Web. 22 July 2012. http://www.eurocrime.co.uk/reviews/The_Dinosaur_Feather.html.

_____. Review of *The Woman from Bratislava. Eurocrime*, May 2010. Web. 30 April 2012. http://www.eurocrime.co.uk/revews/The_Woman_from_Bratislava.html.

Cornwell, Bob. Review of *The Snake in Sydney* by Michael Larsen. *Tangled Web UK*, September 2000. Web. 22 July 2012. http://www.twbooks.co.uk/reviews/bcornwell.thesnakepbkbc.html.

"Cover-Ups, Personal and Political." *New York Times*, 21 October 2011. Web. 3 January 2014. http://www.tv.nytimes.com/2011/10/21/arts/television.

Cremer, Justin. "The New Face of the Immigration Debate?" *The Copenhagen Post*, 21 August 2012. Web. 6 October 2013. http://cphpost.dk/new/making-cut-immigration-dk/new-face-immigration-debate.

"Crime Meeting: Ole Frøslev." *Krimifan* 19 March 2012. Web. 22 December 2013. http://www.krimifan.dkkrimier-ole-froslev.

Daley, Suzanne. "Danes Rethink a Welfare State Ample to a Fault." 21 April 2013. Web. 6 October 2013. http://www.nytimes.com/2013/04/21/world/europe.

Davidson, Hilda R. Ellis. *Gods and Myths of the Viking Age.* New York: Bell Publishing Company, 1964. Print.

"Denmark; Biker Gangs Raided by Murder Police." 2 May 2013. Web. 23 November 2013. http://news/sky.com/story/1086123.

"Denmark: Copenhagen Police Hemorrhaging from Having to Deal with Rampant Muslim Crime." 12 April 2012. Web. 23 November 2013. http://www.barenakenislam.com/2013/04/12.

"Denmark: Interpol Copenhagen in Action." 4 September 2013. Web. 23 November 2013. http://www.interpol.int/Member-countries/Europe/Denmark.

"Denmark's 'Lazy Robert' Fuels Welfare Criticism." n.d. Web. 6 October 2013. http://www.globalpost.com/dispatch/news/afp/131006.

"Denmark: Public Schools Facing Collapse Specifically Because of Muslim Immigration." *Bare Naked Islam.* 11 March 2012. Web. 6 October 2013. http://www.barenakedislam.com/2012/11/03.

"Denmark 2013 Crime and Safety Report." Web. 23 November 2013. https://www.osac.gov/pages/ContentReportDetails.aspx?cid.

"Denmark's Gang War." FLARE, 15 April 2010. Web. 23 November 2013. http://www.flarenetwork.org/learn/europe/article/denmarks_gang-war.htm.

"Don Bartlett: Interview of a Translator (Part 3)." *EuroCrime* , 5 November 2009. Web. 3 January 2014. http://eurocrime.blogspot.com/2009/11/don-bartlett-interview-of-translator_05.html.

Donelson, Linda G., and Marianne Stecher-Hansen.

"Karen Blixen (Isak Dinesen)" in *Dictionary of Literary Biography*, Vol. 214, *Twentieth Century Danish Writers*, Ed. Marianne Stecher-Hansen. Farmington Hills, MI: The Gale Group, 1999. Print.

"Drug Use Soars in Denmark." n.d. Web. 6 October 2013. http://www.eurad.net/en/news/consumption_data.

Eeg, Helle. "The Entire Portrait of Grete Lise Holm." *Dagbladet Information*, 2012. Web. 5 February 2013. http://www.dagbladet.com.dk.

"The Effect of Susan by Peter Hoeg": *Litteratursiden* 27 May 2014. Web. 20 January 2015. http://www.litteratursiden.dk/anmeldelser/effekten-af-susan-af-peter-hoeg.

Egesholm, Christian. "Peter Høeg." *Danish Literary Magazine*, Fall 2007. Web. 16 April 2012. http://www.danishliterature.info/fa20029/Action/002/fid/39/lang/eng.

Einhorn, Eric S. and John Logue. *Modern Welfare States.* 2nd ed. Westport, CT: Praeger, 2003. Print.

"Elite Kids Are Spoiled Rotten." *Politiken*, 23 February 2013. Web. 27 December 2013. http://www.politiken.dk.

Enker, Debi. "Stability Begets Great Danes." *The Age*, 2 May 2013. Web. 2 May 2013. http://www.theage.com.au/entertainment.

Ergang, Barry. "Kevin's Corner: Book Reviews and More." FFB Review: "The Murder Book" (1971) by Tage la Cour and Harald Mogensen. 28 December 2012. Web. 1 December 2013. http://kevintipplescorder.blogspot.com/2012/12/ffb-review.

Espersen, Jamila, and Maribel Vasquez. "Human (Re) Trafficking in Denmark: Looking for a Solution or Recycling a Problem?" Web. 6 October 2013. http://www.humanityinaction.org/knowledgebase/53.

"The Executioner." *Jyllenposten* interview with Jussi Adler-Olsen, 2009. Web. 27 November 2013. http://www.jussiadlerolsen.dk/?page=artikel_executioner.

Foote, Galen. "Youth, Family, and Values: The Culture of Alcohol in Denmark." Berkley Center for Religion, Peace & World Affairs. 14 October 2012. Web. 6 October 2013. http://berkleycenter.ceorgetown.edu/letters.

Forshaw, Barry. *Death in a Cold Climate.* New York: Palgrave Macmillan, 2012. Print.

Foster, Jordan. "The Copenhagen Connection." *Publishers Weekly*, 19 September 2011: 41. Print.

Fourouklas, Lakis. "Fresh Meat: *Only One Life* by Sara Blaedel." *Criminal Element* 30 June 2012. Web. 21 July 2012. http://www.criminalelement.com.

Garrison, Laura Turner. "Klovn [Sic] Your Enthusiasm: The Many Layers Of Discomfort in Danish Humor." 14 December 2011. Web. 2 September 2013. http://splitsider.com/2011/12.

"Get the Facts." DrugWarFacts.org. Web. 6 October 2013. http://www.drugwarfacrs.org/cms/?q=node/1165.

Glass Key Citation: Erik Otto Larsen, 1995. *Koch's Mysteries* 22 May 1995. Web. 29 December 2013. http://www.kochsmysteries.co.uk.

Gress, David. "Daily Life in the Danish Welfare State." *National Affairs* 69 (Fall 1982). Web. 10 October 2013. http://www.nationalaffairs.com.

Hæstrup, Jørgen. *Secret Alliance: A Study of the Danish Resistance Movement 1940–1945.* Odense: n.p., 1976. Print.

Hansen, Kim Toft. "The Devil Hides in the Detail," review of *The Morelli Method.* 17 October 2008. Web. 29 August 2013. http://www.kulturkapellet .dk.

_____. "When the Lights Are Switched on ..." Review of "Blackout," 1992 (television miniseries). *Kulturkapellet* 7 October 2008. Web. 15 December 2013. http://www.kulturkapellet.dk/filmanmeldelse.php?id=283.

Hansen, Stine Charlotte. "We Are Our Brains." Interview with Christian Jungersen on *You Disappear,* April 2013. Web. 26 December 2013. http://www.christian jungersen.com/interviews/we-are-our-brains, originally in http://www.fyens.dk.

Hedeboe, Jens et al. "Interpersonal Violence: Patterns in a Danish Community. *American Journal of Public Health* 75 (9 June 1985): 651–653. Print.

"A High-Tech Welfare State." *The Copenhagen Post.* 20 September 2013. Web. 6 October 2013. http://cpjpost.dk.national/high-tech-welfare-state.

Hoffgaard, Line. "*Svalen Graph of* Sissel-Jo Gazan." 27 August 2013. Web. 22 December 2013. http://www.litteratursiden.dk.

Hong, Howard V. and Edna Hong. *The Essential Kierkegaard.* Princeton: Princeton University Press, 2000. Print.

HopeNow. "Human Trafficking in Denmark." 2011. Web. 27 October 2013. http://hopenow.dk.en/about-human-trafficking/human-trafficking-in-denmark.

Hornbaek, Tonny [sic]. Review of "Driven" by Jonas Bruun. *Litteratursiden.Dk.* 10 April 2006. Web. 29 August 2013. http://www.litteratursiden.dk.

House, Christian. "Nordic Crime Writers: The Truth Behind Inspector Norse." *The Independent.* 30 September 2012. Web. 29 October 2012. http://www.indepedent.co.uk/arts-entertainment/books/features.

_____. "A Page in the Life: Peter Hoeg." *The Telegraph,* 10 October 2012. Web. 24 December 2013. http://www.telegraph.co.uk/culture/books/bookreviews/99587052.a-page-in-the-life-peter-hoeg.

Høyer. Michael. "Nordkraft of Jacob Ejersbo." *Litteratursiden* 11 November 2002. Web. 19 August 2013. http://www.litteratursiden.dk/anmeldels.

Hundahl, Anne Birgitte. "Juul, Pia-Murder of Halland"; review of "The Murder of Halland." 1 October 2010. *Litteratursiden,* 1 October 2010. Web. 28 December 2013. http://www.litteratursiden.dk.

Hunt, Arlene. "*Those Who Kill* Preview," *Crime Fiction Lover* 21 February 2012. Web. 21 December 2013. http://www.crimefictionlover.com/2012/02.

"Immigrants Are Good for the Economy, Report Says." *The Copenhagen Post,* 30 September 2013. Web. 6 October 2013. http://www.cppost.dk/national/immigrants-are-good-economy-report-says.

"In Love with Destiny." Review of *Isak Dinesen and Karen Blixen: The Mask and the Reality. Times Literary Supplement* 10 September 1971: 47. Print.

"International Cannabis and Weapons League." Danish Intelligence and Security Service. 2010. Web. 23 November 2013. https://www.pet/dk/English/Organised%20crime/International%20cannabis.aspx.

"Interview—Michael Katz Krefeld." *The CrimeHouse,*12 August 2010. Web. 18 August 2013. http://www.thecrimehouse.com/interview-michael-katz-krefeld.

"An Interview with Jussi Adler-Olsen." 26 May 2013, Once Upon a Crime Bookstore, Minneapolis, MN. Web. 26 November 2013. http://scandinaviancrime fiction.wordpress.com/category/denmark.

"An Interview with Mikkel Birkegaard by Transworld." 1 May 2009. Web. 21 July 2012. http://authorsplace.co.uk/mikkel-birkegaard/interviews/uk-interview/.

"Jussi Adler-Olsen to Amazon." Interview for Amazon.com. Web. 27 November 2013. http://www.jussiadler olsen.dk/?page=qanda_amazon.

"Jussi Adler-Olsen to Laura from *ShotsMag.*" Web. 27 November 2013. http://www.jussiadlerolsen.dk/?page=qanda_laura.

Kaaberbøl, Lena. "Will There Be Snow?" *Mystery Readers Journal* 30 (Winter 2014–2015): 27–29. Print.

Kachka, Boris. "No 1 with an Umlaut." *New York Magazine* 8 May 2011. Web 29 October 2012. http://nymag.com/arts/books/features/scandinavian-crime-fiction-guide-2011-5.

Kardel, Una. "Jesus, Money and Life of Grete Lise Holm." Review of *Jesus, Money and Life, by Grete Lise Holm.* 26 September 2012. Web. 25 December 2013. http://www litteratursiden.dk.

Kern, Soeren. "Converting Denmark into a Muslim Country." 21 November 2012. Web. 6 October 2013. http://www.gatestoneinstitute.org/3459/Denmark-muslim-country.

_____. "Muslim Gangs Terrorize Denmark." 14 March 2012. Web. 23 November 2013. http://www.gate stoneinstitute.org/2941/muslim-gangs-denmark.

Knudsen, Per. "Portrait: Morten Hesseldahl. *Dagbladene* 22 January 2010. Web. 18 August 2013. http://danskedagblade.dk/nyhed/portrait-morten-hessel dahl.

Kousgaard, Jakob Mikkelsen. "Sarvig, Ole—Sea Under My Window." *Litteratursiden,* 19 April 2006. Web. 2 January 2014. http://www.litteratursiden.dk.

Kubulus Alumni, Københavns Universitet. "Education Provides New Perspectives on The World. Education Services, University of Copenhagen. Web. 26 December 2013. http://www.alumni.ku.dk.

Lambert, Pam. "The Passion of Anna: PW Talks with Sissel-Jo Gazan." *Publishers Weekly* 30 August 2013. Web. 22 December 2013. http://www.publishers weekly.com/pw/by-topic/authors/interviews/article/58934.

_____. "Through the Looking Glass." *Publishers Weekly* 14 October 2013: 38. Print.

"Lars Kjaedegaard." *Litteratursiden.Dk* 14 November

2004. Web. 29 December 2013. http://www.litter
atursiden.dk/forfattere/lars-kjaedegaard.

Larsen, Arne. "*Derailed by* Michael Katz Krefelt." *Litteratursiden,* 26 August 2013. Web. 30 December 2013.
http:www.litteratursiden.dk.

_____. "The Seventh Child of Erik Valeur." *Litteratur-
siden* 12 September 2011. Web. 3 January 2014.
http://www.litteratursiden.dk.

Larsen, Lisbeth. "Flirt with the Crime Genre. Interview
with Christian Dorph" (translated title). *Litteratursiden* 1 May 2004, updated 4 January 2011.. Web. 20
November 2013. http://www.litteratursiden.dk/flirt-
med-krimigenren-interview_med_Christian_Dorph.

Lauridsen, Søren. "The Allerød Thriller." *Fredriksborg
Amts Avis,* 12 April 2003. Web. 27 November 2013.
http://www.jussiadlerolsen.dk/?page=artikel_f_
amtsavis.

Levring, Peter. "Scandinavia's Weakest Nation Finds
Welfare Habits Too Costly." 30 August 2013. Web. 6
October 2013. http://www.bloomberg.com.news/
2013-08-30.

Lidegaard, Kresten. "Anita Lillevang: 'The Stairs and
Fog' and 'Anger and Warmth' [sic]."*Jammerbugt Bib-
liotekerne,* n.d. Web. 3 September 2013. http://www.
jammerbugtbibliotekerne.dk.

"Lisbeth A. Bille." *Litteratursiden.* 2013. Web. 8 December
2013. http://www.literatursiden./lisbethabille.

"Lotte Petri." *Litteratursiden.Dk* 2014. Web. 20 January
2015. http://www.litteratursiden.dk/forfattere/lotte-
petri.

MacAllan, Susan. "Denmark and the Muslim Immigration Crisis. the Assyrian International News Agency.
18 July 2008. Web. 6 October 2013. http://www.aina.
org/news/20080718105208.htm.

"Mail Interview with Lotte Petri." *Krimisiden* 2014. Web.
20 January 2015. http://krimisiden.dk/content.
php?page=article+value=10073.

Majgaard, Lise Mortensen. "An Average Femina Crime."
Kulturkapellet 3 March 2013. Web. 4 December 2013.
http://www.kulturkapellet.com.

Mathiasen, Helle. "Marie Bregendahl," in *Dictionary of
Literary Biography,* vol. 214. *Twentieth Century Danish
Writers,* ed. Marianne Stecher-Hansen. Farmington
Hills, MI: The Gale Group, 1999. Print.

Maxted, Anna. "Sorry, Maj Sjöwall, the Best Crime Is
One of Passion." *The Telegraph.* 15 August 2013. Web.
23 August 2013. http://www.telegraph.co.uk/culture/
books/10245102.

"*Mercy, by* Jussi Adler-Olsen, Trans. Lisa Hartford." *The
Independent,* 13 May 2011. Web. 30 April 2012.
http://www.independent.co.uk/arts-entertainment/
books/reviews/mercy-by-jussi-adlerolsen.

Michaelis, Bo Tao. "The Author Kirsten Holst's Death."
Politiken, 23 September 2008. Web. 26 December
2013. http://www.politiken.dk.

_____. "Soft-Boiled Crime Fiction Delivers Cozy
Creepy." *Politiken,* 18 April 2011. Web. 17 November
2012. http://www.politiken.dr.

Mitchell, P.M. *A History of Danish Literature. 2nd Ed.*

New York: Kraus-Thomson Organization Ltd., 1971.
Print.

Neild, Barry. "9 Top Cities for 'Detective Travel.'" *CNN
International* 27 August 2013. Web. 15 September
2013. http://www.cnn.com/travels-detective-810836.

Nestingen, Andrew, and Paula Arvas. *Scandinavian
Crime Fiction.* Cardiff, Wales: University of Wales
Press, 2011. Print.

Nexø, Tue Andersen. "Death from Above," n.d. Web. 31
December 2013. http://www.kunst.dk.

Nielsen, Peter. "With a Penchant for Murder." *Information,* 16 April 2009. Web. 28 December 2013. http://
information.dk/.

O'Brien, Lauren. Review of *The Forgotten Girls. Mystery
Readers Journal* 30 (Winter 2014–2015): 47–48.

"Ole Frøslev." *Litteratursiden* 2012. Web. 22 December
2013. http://www.litteratursiden.dk/forfattere/ole-
froslev.

Olling, Anders. "Henning Mortensen." *Dagbladet Information. the Great Danish Encyclopedia,* 2011. Web. 31
December 2013. http://www.dagbladet.dk.

"Organised Crime in Denmark in 2005." A Report by
the Civil and Police Department, Copenhagen, 2005.
Web. 22 November 2013. http://www.polit.dk/NR.

Osborn, Andrew. "Denmark Urged to Reveal Long List
of Nazi Collaborators." *The Guardian* 27 August 2001.
Web. 11 September 2013. http://www.theguardian.
com/world/2002/aug/28/andrewosborn.

Østergaard, Flemming. "Dan Hilfing Petersen: 9 April
1940: *Hele Historien. Hvad Der Virkelig Skete* ('The
Whole History: What Really Happened") *Jyllands-
Posten* 19 March 2010. Web. 15 September 2013.
http://kpn.dk/boger/article2014662.ece.

Paterson, Anna. "Politics and Contemporary Danish
Fiction." *World Literature Today* 82 (January 2006):
46–49. Print.

Pew Research Center. "Region: Europe. Pew Research
Center's Religion & Public Life Project" 27 January
2011. Web. 7 March 2015. http://www.pewforum.
org/2011/01/27/future-of-the-global-muslim-popula
tion.

"The Poor Were Always [The] Bank." Interview with
Gretelise Holm. *Avisen* 8 February 2013. Web. 25 December 2013. http://www.avisen.dk.

Popper, Karl. *The Open Society and Its Enemies.* London:
Routledge, 2002. Print.

Poulsen, Henning. "Danish Opposition and German
Politics." *Jyske Historiker* 71 (1995). Print.

Powers, John. "Frustrating Heroine Stars in Fresh, Feminist 'Nightingale.'" NPR, 10 December 2013. Web.
28 December 2013. http://www.npr.org/2013/12/
10/249961216.

Ravn, Martin. *Dagbladet Information.* 2013. Web. 19 December 2013. http://www,forfatterweb.dk/oversigt/
zzola.oo/print_zzola.12.

"Reading Group Guide for A.J. Kazinski's the *Last Good
Man.*" Simon and Schuster. Web. 29 December 2013.
http://books.simonandschuster.com:80/Last-Good-
Man/A-J-Kazinski/ 9781451640762.

Reimann, Anna. "Putting a Price on Foreigners: Strict Immigration Laws 'Save Denmark Billions.'" *Spiegel Online International*, 29 April 2011. Web. 6 October 2013. http://www.spiegel.de/internationa/europe/putting-a-price-on-foreigners.

"Revealed: The Real Borgen." *The Radio Times*, 4 February 2012. Web. 3 January 2014. http://www..radio times/com/news/2012-02-04.

Review of *Baboon* by Naja Marie Aidt. *Publishers Weekly* 25 August 2014: 77. Print.

Review of *Doctor Death* by Lene Kaaberbøl. *Publishers Weekly* 15 December 2014: 50. Print.

Review of *From the Book of Dreams*. N.d. Web. 12 December 2013. http://www.andrewnurnberg.com/books/from-the-book-of-dreams.

Review of *The Absent One* by Jussi Adler-Olsen. *Publishers Weekly* 18 June 2012: 38. Print.

Review of *The Elephant Keeper's Children* by Peter Høeg. *Publishers Weekly* 13 August 2012: 40. Print.

Review of *The Forgotten Girls* by Sara Blaedel. *Publishers Weekly* 17 November 2014: 32. Print.

Review of *The King's Hounds* by Martin Jensen. *Publishers Weekly* 19 August 2013: 32. Print.

Rock, Lucy. "What Britain Could Learn from Denmark's Childcare Model." *The Observer* 18 February 2012. Web. 6 October 2013. http://www.theguardian.com/society/2012/feb/18.

Rossel, Sven H. "Crisis and Reemption: An Introduction to Danish Writer Ole Sarvig." *World Literature Today* 53:4 (Autumn, 1979): 606–609. Print.

Ryan, Hugh. "'The Boy in the Suitcase' by Lene Kaaberbøl and Agnete Friis: Interview." *The Daily Beast*, 4 January 2012. Web. 30 April 2012. http://www.thedailybeast.com/articles/2012/01/04.

"Sanne Udsen." *Djs Krimiblog*, 11 January 2010. Web. 3 January 2014. http://www.DJskrimiblog.blogspot.com/2010.

Seymour-Smith, Martin. *The New Guide to Modern World Literature*, 3rd ed. New York: Peter Bedrick Books, 1985. Print.

Smale, Alison. "Lashing Out in Verse." *New York Times* 3 April 2014. Web. 5 April 2014. http://www.nytimes.coom/20134/04/03/books/young-immigrant-in-denmark-lashes-out-in-verse.html

Steen, Vivi. Review of Dragons of Kabul by Morten Hesseldahl. *Litteratursiden*, 22 October 2007. Web. 27 December 2013. http://www.litteratursiden.dk.

"Steen Langstrup." (Contributed by Langstrup). *Litteratursiden* 16 March 2000, updated 3 October 2012. Web. 9 November 2013. http://www.lititeratursiden.dk.

Stougaard, Jakob. "Category Archives: Scandinavian Crime Fiction." 2 May 2013 and 9 June 2013. Web. 15 September 2013. http://scancrime.wordpress.com/category/scandinavian-crime-fiction.

Surgey, Sarah. "The Extraordinary Danish Crime Writer Jakob Melander." *Nordic Style Magazine* 20 January 2015. Web. 20 January 2015. http://www.nordic stylemag.com/2015.01/jakob-melander-danish-crime-writer.

_____. "Jesper Stein [sic]—Nordic Noir's Elite." *Nordic Style Magazine* 12 September 2014. Web. 15 September 2014. http://www.nordicstylemag.com/2014/09/jesper-stein-nordic-noirs-elite.

"Svalen Graph of Sissel-Jo Gazan." *Litteratursiden* 27 August 2013. Web. 22 December 2013. http://www.literatursiden.dk.

Syberg, Karen. "Breaker and Eye Opener." Review of *Jesus, Money and Life*, by Grete Lise Holm. 14 September 2012. Web. 27 October 2012. http://www.information.dk.

Szabo, Michael. "Danish Film Lifts Lid on 'Crime of the Century' Co2 Trading Scams." Reuters Point Carbon. 11 September 2013. Web. 23 November 2013. http://carboncrooks.tv/danish-film-lifts-lid.

Theroux, Marcel. "Cruel World." *The Sunday New York Times Book Review*, 22 July 2007. Web. 26 December 2013. http://www.nytimes.com/2007/07/22/books/review/Yheroux-t.html?_r=0.

Torfing, Jacob. "Workfare with Welfare: Recent Reforms of the Danish Welfare State." *Journal of European Social Policy* 9 (February 1999): 5–28. Print.

"The Twisted Danish Sense of Humor. 20 November 2007. Web. 2 September 2013. http://crankyflier.com/2007/11/20.

Vestergaard, Niels. "The Entire Portrait of Christian Dorph & [Sic] Simon Pasternak." *Dagbladet Information*, 2011. Print.

Vilhjálmsson, Vilhjálmur Orn. "The King and the Star," in *Denmark and the Holocaust*, Bastholm Jensen, Mette and Steven B. Jensen, eds. Institute for International Studies, Department for Holocaust and Genocide Studies 2003: 102–117. Print.

Vilhjálmsson, Vilhjálmur Orn, and Bent Blüdnikow. "Rescue, Expulsion, And Collaboration: Denmark's Difficulties with Its World War II Past." *Jewish Political Studies Review* 18.3–4 (Fall 2006). Web. 11 September 2013. http://www.jcpa.org/phas/phas-vilhjalmsson-f06.htm.

"*Vinterbergs Fiasko Fär Oprejsning*." 5 November 2010. Web. 17 December 2013. http://www.berlingske.dk.

Voorhis, Jerry. "Germany and Denmark: 1940–1945. *Scandinavian Studies* 44.2 (1972). Print.

Wegner, Nina. Interview with Sara Blaedel. *Krimimessen* 13 July 2004, Updated 20 December 2010. Web. 21 July 2012. http://www.litteratursiden.dk.

"The Welfare System in Denmark." Medicolink: Your International Recruitment Agency." N.d. Web. 6 October 2013. http://medicolink.dkwelfare-system-in-denmark.

Wenande, Christian. "New Immigration Laws Set to Kick in Next Month." *The Copenhagen Post*, 12 April 2012. Web. 6 October 2013. http://cphpost.dk/news/,aking-cut-immigration-dk.

The Western Literary Messenger 13 (1850). Print.

Westerso, Rikke Struck. "Denmark's New Success Author: So Abject Was My Childhood." Portraits Interview, *BT*, 29 March 2013. Web. http://www .BT.dk.

Westwood, Rich. Review of *Death Sentence* by Mikkel Birkegaard. October 2011. Web. 12 December 2013. http://www.eurocrime.co.uk/reviews/Death_Sentence.html.

Wilson, Emily. "Danish Writer Naja Marie Aidt on American English, Growing Up in Greenland, and Sentimentality." *SF Weekly* 23 December 2014. Web. 15 January 2015. http://www.sfweekly.com/exhibitionist/2014/09/23.

"Zero Tolerance to Violence Against Women and Girls." The Official Website of Denmark. Web. 25 November 2013. http://denmark.dk/en/society/government-and-politics.

Zohar—Man of La Book. "Q and a with Sara Blaedel." 19 July 2012. Web. 21 July 2012. http://manoflabook.com/wp/?p=6097.

Finland

Ahokas, Jaako. *A History of Finnish Literature*. Bloomington, IN: Indiana University Research Center for the Language Sciences, 1973. Print.

Alaja, Antti. "Social Democracy: The Finnish Progressive Movement and the Red Green Divide." *Social Europe* 15 April 2011. Web. http://www.social-europe.ed/2011/04.

_____. "True Finns and the Politics of Distrust and Insecurity in Finland." *Social Europe Journal* 29 December 2010. Web. 14 November 2014. http://www.social-europe.eu/2010/12.

Alasuutari, Pertti. *Desire and Craving: A Cultural Theory of Alcoholism*. Albany, NY: State University of New York Press, 1992. Print.

Allen, Inna. "Pekka Hiltunen—Creating Intelligent and Topical Crime Fiction." *Scan Magazine* 2013. Web. 28 April 2014. http://www/scanmagazine.co.uk/2013/09.

Al-Munajid, Shaykh Muhammad Saalih. "Islam Question and Answers." 21 November 2014. Web. 21 November 2014. http://islamqa.info/en/110455.

"Amman Reading Time." 15 February 2013. Web. 14 December 2014. http://wwww.ammanleirjablogi.blogspot.com.

Argon, Kemal. "Confronting Neo-Nazi and Skinhead Fanaticism in Northern Europe?" *The Huffington Post* 23 January 2012. Web. 27 April 2014. http://www.huffingtonpost.com.

Arvas, Paula. "Best Murder Rewarded." *Detective Shelf* 17 September 2011. Web. 28 December 2014. http://www.detectiveshelf.com/ Cited in text as Arvas, "Best Murder Rewarded."

_____. "Contemporary Finnish Crime Fiction: Cops, Criminals and Middle Men." *Mystery Readers Journal* 23 (Fall 2007): 4–8. Print. Cited in text as Arvas, "Contemporary Finnish Crime Fiction."

_____. "Next to the Final Frontier: Russians in Contemporary Finnish and Scandinavian Crime Fiction,"

in *Scandinavian Crime Fiction*, ed. Andrew Nestingen and Paula Arvas. Cardiff, Wales: University of Wales Press, 2011, 115–127. Print. Cited in Text as "Arvas."

Backman, Johan. "'The Wolf Has a Hundred Paths...': The Organized Crime of St. Petersburg in the Framework of the Russian Culture of Criminal Justice." National Criminal Justice Reference Service 2000. Web. 26 November 2014. http://www.ncjrs:gov/App/publications/abstract.aspx?ID=187756.

Bagge, Tapani. "Dancing with Myself." *Sea Minor* 28 April 2012. Web. 13 September 2014. http://nigelpbird.blogspot.com/2012/04/dancing-with-myself-tapani-bagge.html.

Bell, Bethany. "Violence Against Women." *BBC News World* 2014. Web. 27 April 2014. http://www.bbc,cim/news/world-26444655.

Benedek, M. "Kalavala as a Movie." *What's Up Finland?* 4 May 2012. Web. 4 March 2015. http://whatsupfinland.org/english/kalevala-as-a-movie.

"A Book a Month If Not Two." *Ruumiin Kulttuuri* 2/2010. Web. 10 January 2015. http://www.dekkariseura.fi/rk_210_en.html.

"Book Review: Raid and the Blackest Sheep" *Petrona* November 2010. Web. 28 April 2014. http://petrona.typepad.com/petrona/2010/11.

"Brick Bite." Review of *Enkelimies* ("Angel Man") by Marja-Liisa Heino. *WSOY* 2006. Web. 14 December 2014. http://www.kiitomato.net.

Bruno, Carla. "Finland and Domestic Violence: The Strong Nordic Woman Is in Trouble." *On the Issue Magazine* Fall 2012. Web. 27 April 2014. http://ontheissuemagazine.com/cafe2/article/273.

Bujalance, Pablo. "The Legend of 'Outsider.'" *Leisure and Arts* 29 August 2014. Web. 10 November 2014. http://www.malagahou.es.

Burstein, Nathan. "Finland's Jewish Answer to 'The Girl with the Dragon Tattoo.'" *The Times of Israel* 30 April 2012. Web. 28 April 2014. http://www/timesofisrael.com.

Burton, Fred, and Dan Burges. "Russian Organized Crime." *Security Weekly* 14 November 2007. Web. 26 November 2014. http://www.stratfor.com/weekly/russian_organized_crime.

Clarke, Maxine. "Book Review: Raid and the Blackest Sheep by Harri Nykanen." *Petrona* November 2010. Web. 28 April 2014. http://petrona.typepad.com/petrona/2010/11.

"CNN: Finland Tops List of Countries with Muslim Fighters in Syria." 9 February 2014. Web. 19 November 2014. http://yle.fi/uutiset/cnn.

"Controversial Cleric Urges Muslims to Be Active in Society." *YLE* 30 March 2014. Web. 27 April 2014. http://yle.fi/uutiset.

Cord, David J. "Finnish Blood Runs in Nordic Crime Novels." *This Is Finland: Arts and Culture*," February 2013. Web. 2 November 2014. http://finland.fi/public/default.aspx?contentid+270970.

Cornwell, Bob. "Bloody Foreigner." *Crime Scene, TW Books* 2006. Web. 28 April 2014. http://www.

twbooks.co.uk/crimescene/bloodyforeignerbob cornwell.htm.

"Country Studies," in "The Rise of Finnish Nationalism." Library of Congress. Web. 7 November 2013. http://countrystudies.us/finland/11.htm.

"The Crime Writer Harry Hiekikko." *Helsingen Sanomat* 20 July 2013. Web. 14 December 2014. http://wwww.helsingensanomat.com.

Demko, G.L. "Murder in the Land of the Midnight Sun: Mysteries in Finland." *G.L. Demko's Landscapes of Crime.* Web. 7 November 2014. http://www.dart mouth.edu/~gjdemko/Finland.htm.

"Detective Series Decided by Matti Rönkä." *Book Circuit* 25 October 2013. Web. 26 April 2014. http://www.avatv.fi/,inisaitit.shtml/kirjapiiri.

Dickens, Eric. "Review: Kjell Westö, *Lang.*" *Swedish Book Review* 2005:2. Web. 27 November 2012. http://www.swedishbookreview.com/show-review.php?i=130.

"Discrimination and Racism." *Infopankki.* Web. 19 November 2014. http://www.infopankki.fi/en/living-in-finland/problem-situations.

Duncan, J. N. "Helsinki Homicide: Darling by Jarkko Sipila." *The Big Thrill* September 2014. Web. 2 January 2015. http:www.thebigthrill.org/2014/09/Helsinki-homicide-darking-by-Jarkko-Sipila.

Dutton, Edward. "Violent Male Culture May Be at Root of Finnish School Massacre." *The Guardian* 23 September 2008. Web. 27 April 2014 http://www.theguardian.com/education/2008/sep/23/finland.school.shooting.comment.

Einhorn, Eric S., and John Logue. *Modern Welfare States,* 2nd ed. Westport, CT: Praeger, 2003. Print.

Elonheimo, Henrik, et al. "Generic and Crime Type Specific Correlates of Youth Crime." *Social Psychiatry & Psychiatric Epidemiology* 46 (September 2011): 903–914. Print.

"English Summary." *Ruumiin Kulttuuri* 3/2009. Web. 28 April 2014. http://www.dekkariseura.fi/rk_309_en.html.

"Euroskeptic [Sic] Finns Party Has 'Changed the Political Landscape.'" *Deutsche Welle* 17 May 2011. Web 13 November 2014. http://www/deutschewelle.de/.

"Finland Is Eu's Second Most Violent Country for Women." *YLE* 3 May 2014. Web. 27 April 2014. http://yle/fi/uutiset.

"Finland's New Gender Equality Plan." United Nations General Assembly WOM/1693. 9 July 2008, Presented by Arto Kosanen, Director of the Ministry for Foreign Affairs of Finland. Web. 27 April 2014. http://www.un.org.News/Press/docs/2008/wom1693.doc.htm.

"Finnish Muslims Want Police Hijab." *OnIslam* [sic] *& News Agencies.* 23 April 2014. Web. 21 November 2014. http://www/onislam.bet/english/news/europe/470939.

"Finnish Mystery Series." *Sequels.Com: An Online Guide to Series Fiction* 9 December 2012. Web. 10 November 2014. http://www.esequels.com/blog/?p=1461.

"Finns in Minnesota." *Scandinavian Crime Fiction in English Translation* 10 August 2014. Web. 4 January 2015. http://scandinaviancrimefiction.wordpress/com/tag/jari-tervo.

Forshaw, Barry. *Death in a Cold Climate.* New York: Palgrave Macmillan, 2012. Print.

Frazer, Jenni. "The Nordic Noir Detective You've Been Waiting For." *The Jewish Chronicle Online* 27 April 2012. Web. 28 April 2014. http://www.thejc.com/arts/arts-features/6698.

Fritzsche, Kerstin. "Meet the Germans: The Eloquent Jan Costin Wagner." *The Goethe Institute* October 2008. Web. 13 September 2014. http://www.goethe.de/ins/gb/lp/prj/mtg/men/wor/wag/enindex.htm.

Godwin, Richard. "Chin Wag at the Slaughterhouse: Interview with James Thompson." 14 April 2013. Web. 14 September 2014. http://www.richardgodwin.bet/author-interviews-extensive/chin-wag-at-the-slaughterhouse.

Grussner, Kaj. "The Bankrupt Finnish Welfare State. " *Mises Daily* 31 August 2010. Web. 24 February 2013. http://mises.org/daily/4655.

Gustafsson, Kimmo. "Reijo Mäki: Helsingen Sanomat, the Criticism Does Not Judge a Book by a Writer." *YLE Turku* 8 February 2013. Web. 26 April 2014. http://www.ylenews.com.

Hagenguth, Alexandra. "Interview with the Author Taavi Soininvaara." *Literature Portal* November 2005. Web. 29 April 2014. http://www.schwedenfrimi.de/taavi_soininvaara-interview.htm.

"Hannu Vuorio." *Dekkari Netti* 2012. Web. 7 January 2015. http://www.tornio.fi/index.php?p=Vuorio.

Hashi, Wali. "Opinion: High Time for Self-Scrutiny in Finland's Muslim Community." *YLE* 12 September 2014. Web. 19 November 2014. http://yle/fi/uutiset.

Hiekkapelto, Kati. *The Hummingbird,* tr. David Hackston. Chester Springs, PA: Dufour Editions, Inc., 2014. Print.

Hildenheimo, Silja. "New Worlds." *Books from Finland* 3/1998. Web. 28 April 2014. http://www.finlit.fi/booksfromfinland/bff/398/fagerholm.htm.

Holt, Karen. "A Helsinki Whodunit." *O Magazine* April 2010. Web. 28 April 2014. http://www.oprah.com/omagazine.

Hopkins, Valerie. "Finland's Paradox of Equality: Professional Excellence, Domestic Abuse." *Open Democracy* 27 December 2013. Web. 27 April 2014. http://www.opendemocracy.bnet/5050/valerie-hopkins/finland.

Huhtanen, Ann-Mari, and Aleksi Teivainen. "'Finland Is a Racist Country.'" *Helsingen Sanomat* 6 December 2013. Web. 19 November 2014.http://www.helsinki times.fi/finland/finland-news/domestic/8635.

Huuhtanen, Matti. "Epidemic of Domestic Violence Plagues Finland." *Los Angeles Times* 19 April 1998. Web. 27 April 2014. http://articles.latimes.com/1998/apr/19/news/mn-40777.

Ingström, Pia. "Food for Thought." *Books from Finland* 31 March 2006. Web. 8 December 2014. http://www.booksfromfinland.fi/?s=joensuu.

_____. "Food for Thought." *Books from Finland* 29 October 2012, Web. 26 April 2014. http://www.finlit. fi/booksfromfinland/bff/106/ingstrom.htm. Cited in text as Ingström 2012.

"Interview: Jarkko Sipilä." *FinPop: The Finnish Pop Culture Portal* 2006. Web. 29 April 2014. http://www. finpop.net/litterature/jarkko¬sipila.php.

"Interview with James Thompson, Author of *Lucifer's Tears*." *Scandinavian Crime Fiction* 8 March 2011. Web. 27 April 2014. http://scandinaviancrimefiction. wordpress.com/2011/02/08.

"Interview with Finnish Minister for International Development Pekka Haavisto." *UN Women* 19 December 2013. Web. 27 April 2014. http://www.unwomen. org/ru/news/stories/2013/12.

"Jaakko Piira." *Thrilling Detective Web Site* [sic] 2012. Web. 24 December 2014. http://www.thrillingdetec tive.come/etes/pira.html.

"Jari Järvelä: How the Girl and the Bomb Was Born." *Crime Time* 2014. Web. 1 January 2015. http://www/ crime.fi/2014/03/jari-jarvela-miten-tytto-ja-pommi-sai-alkunsa.

Järvinen, Matti. "Hannu Vuorio, Socially Critical Crime Novel." *Literary Homepage* 13 December 2011. Web. 7 January 2015. http://www.kirsampo.fi/fi/node315.

Jauhiainen, Jonna. "Reijo Mäki Improved Home Security." *Ilta-Sanomat* 11 July 2012. Web. 26 April 2014. http://www.iltasanomat.com.

"Juha Numminen." *Crime Time Writers* 2011. Web. 27 December 2014. http://www.crimetime.co.uk.

Kaariainen, Juha. "Why Do the Finns Trust the Police?" *Journal of Scandinavian Studies in Criminology And Crime Prevention* 9 (2008): 141–159. Print.

Kachka, Boris. "No. 1 with an Umlaut." *New York Magazine,* 8 May 2011. Web. 28 November 2011. http:// www.nymag.com/arts/books/features/scandinavian-crime-fiction-guide-2011.

Kaiser, Robert G. "In Finland's Footsteps." *The Washington Post* 25 August 2005. Web. 24 February 2013. http://www.sanders.senate.gov/newsroom/news.

Karlsson, Markus. "Alexander Stubb, Finnish Minister for European Affairs." *The Interview* 28 August 2012. Web. 14 November 2014. http://www.france24/eu/ 20120818.

Karvonen, Kyösti. "What's Up with the 'True Finns' Party?" *This Is Finland* May 2011. Web. 13 November 2014. http://finland.fi/public/default.aspx?contentid=220384.

Kern, Soeren. "Muslim Immigration Transforms Finland." *The Gatestone Institute* 28 April 2011. Web. 19 November 2014. http://www/gatestoneinstitute. org/2075/finland-muslim-immigration.

Kukkola, Timo. *Sherlock Holmes & Co. Suomen Dekkariseuran Julkaisuja* 1. Helsinki: Suomen dekkariseura, 1985. Print.

"Leena Lehtolainen—Finland's Queen of Murder." Ambassade van Finland, Brussels. 28 April 2004. Web. 13 September 2014. http://www.finalnde.be.

Lefran, Vincent. "Interview: Tapani Bagge." *FinPop*

2003. Web. 26 April 2014. http://www.finpop.bet/ litterature/tapani_bagge.php.

Lehtainen, Leena. "Dancing with Myself: Leena Lehtolainen Interviews Leena Lehtolainen." *Sea Minor* 28 February 2011. Web. 1 March 2011. http://nigelbired. blogspot.com/2011/02.

Lehtolainen, Leena. *My First Enemy*, tr Owen F. Witesman. Las Vegas, NV: Amazon Crossing, 2012. Print.

Leino, Marko. "My Life as a Crime Writer." Stilton Agency 7 April 2010. Web. 28 April 2014. http:// www.stilton.se/news/author/Marko_Leino. This site also includes "Clue of the Year to Marko Leino," 17 February 2010.

Lindroos, Veiko. "Journey into the Heart of Darkness." *Ruumiin Kulttuuri* 2/2010. Web. 10 January 2015. http://www.dekkariseura.fi/rk_210_en.html.

Liukkonen, Petri. "Mika Waltari." *Books and Writers.* Web. 8 November 2014. http://www.kirjasto.sci.fi/ mwaltari.htm.

Lykkegaard, Marie Hauge. "Fagerholm, Monika." *Forfatterweb, Dagbladet Information* 2013. Web. 5 December 2014. http://www.forfatterweb.dk/oversigt/ fagerholm-monika.

MacDougall, David. "U.S. Crime Author Has Dark Take on Finnish Society." *The Big Story* 21 December 2012. Web. 26 April 2014. http://bigstory.ap.org/article/ us-crime-author-has-dark-take-finnish-society.

Malmio, Kristina. "'He Strongly Envied Sherlock Holmes but He Decided Not to Take Him to His Model.'" *Scandinavian Studies* 80 (Winter 2008): 455–476. Print.

Mars, Carl. "The Rise of Right-Wing Populism in Finland: The True Finns." *Transform Network Journal* August 2011. Web. 13 November 2014. http://www. transform-network.net/journal/issue-082011/news/ detail/Journal.

"Matti Rönkä." *Crime Time Writers* 2011. Web. 26 April 2014. http://www.crime.fi/2011/11/matti-ronka

"Mauri Sariola." *Books and Writers.* Web. 8 November 2014. http://www.kirjasto.sci.fi/msariola.htm.

"Ministry Report Warns of Neo-Nazi and Religious Radicalisation" [sic]. *YLE* 21 January 2013. Web. 27 April 2014. http://yle.fi/uutiset.

"Moslems [sic] in Finland Demanding 4 Exclusive Paid Public Holidays Just for Themselves." *Tundra Tabloids* 3 September 2013. Web. 27 April 2014. http://tun dratabloids.com/2013/09.

Morten, Peter. "Newsweek: Finland Is Best in the World." August 2010. Web. 14 November 2014. http://finland. fi /Public/default.aspx?cotentid=198541.

Murphy, Bruce F. *The Encyclopedia of Murder and Mystery.* New York: St. Martin's Press, 1999. Print.

Nestingen, Andrew. "Unnecessary Officers: Realism, Melodrama and Scandinavian Crime Fiction in Transition," in *Scandinavian Crime Fiction*. Cardiff, Wales: University of Wales Press, 2011, 171–183. Print.

Nestingen, Andrew, and Paula Arvas. *Scandinavian Crime Fiction.* Cardiff, Wales: University of Wales Press, 2011. Print.

"New Crime Fiction to Try." *The Metro* 1 February 2013. Web. 1 February 2013. http://metro.co.uk/2013/02/01/new-crime-fiction-to-try.

Niemelä, Jari. "Salo Examines Hard Drug Story." *Tampere History* 2004. Web. 28 April 2014. http://www.tampereenhjistoria.fi/ihmisia/wexi-korhonen.

_____. "Wexi Korhonen: The Long-Awaited Salo-Detective Is Coming." *Tamperelainen* 29 October 2011. Web. 12 December 2014. http://www.tamperelainen.fi/77463-wexi-korhonen.

"Nordic Alcohol." *IceNews* 18 May 2009. Web. 27 April 2014. http://www.icenews.is/2009/05/18.

Novak, Nadia, and Seppo Puttonen. "*YLE Living Archive* 2013. Web. 31 December 2014. http://yle.fi/elevaarkisto/artikkelit/,arkku-ropponen.

Nummelin, Juri. "What Finnish Crime Writers Should Be Translated?" *Pulpetti* May 2013. Web. 14 December 2014. http://pulpetti.blogspot.com/2013/05.

Nykanen, Harri. *Nights of Awe*, tr. Kristian London. London: Bitter Lemon Press, 2012. Print.

"One Way to Solve the Muslim Immigration Problem: Pay Them to Leave!" *Bare Naked Islam* 14 March 2011. Web. 27 April 2014. http://www.barenakedislam.com/2011/03/14.

"Organized Crime in Finland." n.d. Web. 19 December 2014. http://people.exeter.ac.uk/watupman/undergrad/jaako.

"Outi Pakkonen." *Dekkari Netti* 2014. Web. 31 December 2014. http://www.dekkarinetti.com.

"Overview of Gender Equality Issues in Finland." The Finnish Institute of Occupational Heslth 2004. Web. 27 April 2014. http://www.gender-equality.webinfo.lt/results/finland/htm.

Paavolainen, Nina. "Matti Yrjana Joensuu: Harjunpaa Ja Rautahuone." *Books from Finland* 19 November 2010. Web. 8 December 2014. http://www.booksfromfinalnd.fi/?s=joensuu.

"Pan Macmillan Snaps Up the 'Finnish Miss Marple.'" *The Independent.* 25 November 2014. Web. 23 February 2015. http://www.independent.co.uk/arts-entertainment/books/news//pan-macmillan-snaps-up-the-finnish-miss-marple-9882903.html.

Papinniemi, Jarmo. "Keeping the Day Job." *Books from Finland* 2003. Web. 25 April 2014. http://www/finlit.fi/booksfromfinland/bff/303/papinniemi.html.

_____. "Jari Tervo: Layla" and "Jari Tervo: Kiljatti [Goliath]." *Books from Finland* 28 October 2011 and 23 October 2009. Web. 4 January 2014. http://www.booksfromfinland.fi/?s=jari+tervo.

_____. "Letter from Finland, Context No. 18." *Dalkey Archive Press.* Web. 30 April 2014. http://www.dalkeyarchive.com/letter-from-finland.

Pitt, Bob. "Finns Party Leadership Finally Takes Action Against Racist Islamophobe." *Islamophobia Watch* 5 October 2013. Web. 13 November 2014. http://www.islamophobiawatch.co.uk.

"The Priest of Evil, by Matti Joensuu." Review. *Scandinavian Books* 2003. Web. 1 March 2014. http://www.scandinavianbooks.com/crime-book/finnish-writer.html.

Pyrhönen, Heta. "Five-Finger Exercises: Mika Waltari's Detective Stories." *Orbis Litterarum* 59 (2004): 23–38. Print.

Rabe, Annina. "Severe Ystad Thrill Mystery of Fagerholm." SvD *Kultur* 1 February 2013. Web. 28 April. 2014. http://www.svd.se/kultur/litteratur/svarnystad-thrillergata-av-fagerholm.

"Readers Loved Eve Tenhunen." Web. 14 December 2014. http://www.savolinna.fi/lehtonet/tenhunen.html.

"Reijo Mäki." *Bazar Publishing* 2010. Web. 16 April 2014. http://www.bazarpublishing.com.

"Review of *Behind God's Back.*" *Publishers Weekly* 8 December 2014: 58. Print.

Review of *The Healer. Publishers Weekly* 25 March 2013: 43. Print.

Rytkonen, Annika. "Ilkka Remes—The Great Unknown." *Iltalehti.Fi*, 25 December 2012. Web. 26 April 2014. http://www.iltalehti.fi.

Saarikoski, Laura, and Saska Saarikoski. "Finland's Left Has Become a Victim of Its Own Success." *The Guardian* 2 February 2012. Web. 15 November 2014. http://www.theguardian.com/commentsisfree/2012/feb/02.

Sairanen, Petter. Interview in *The Review of Contemporary Fiction*, Summer 1996, excerpted in *Harper's Magazine* February 1997: 24. Print.

Salminen, Vaino W. and Vilko Tarinainen, "The Kalevala," in *Iso Tietosanakirja* ["The Great Encyclopedia"]. 2nd ed., vol. 5. (Helsinki 1933), contained in edited form in *The Kalevala*, Cambridge, MA: 1963: 350–361. Print.

Salvén, Kimmo. "The Author Marko Kilpi: How I Became a Detective Story Writer." Kantii.net 24 February 2012. Web. 28 April 2014. http://kantii.net/artikkeli/2012/02/kirjaili-mark0-kilpi.

Schoolfield, George C. *A History of Finland's Literature.* Omaha, ND: University of Nebraska Press, 1998. Print.

Sharkey, Betsy. "Toronto 2013: 'Heart of a Lion" a Neo-Nazi Family Dramedy?" *Los Angeles Times* 7 September 2013. Web. 27 April 2014. http://www.latimes.com/entertainment/envelope/moviesnow.

"Sharp Decline in Suicides Among Finnish Men." *Helsingen Sanomat* 27 April 2013. Web. 28 April 2014. http://www.hs.fi/english/article.

Sipilä, Jarkko. "Thus Was Born Takamäki." *Crime Time* 2014. Web. 2 January 2015. http://www.crimetime.com.

Smolej, Mirka, and Janne Kivivuori. "Crime News Trends in Finland." *Journal of Scandinavian Studies in Criminology and Crime Prevention* 9 (2008): 202–219. Print.

Söderling, Trygve. "Johanna Holmstrom: *Asfaltsänglar.*" *FILI* 2013. Web. 4 March 2015. http://www.finlit.fi/fili/en/authors/holmstrom-johanna.

Sorvali, Ritva. "Paul-Erik Haataja, a Finnish Man in a Graph." *Dekkarituotteet* 2 June 2001. Web. 28 April 2014. http://www.dekkaripavat.fi.

_____. "Tuula-Liina Varis, My Wife." *Dekkarituotteet* 26 May 2005. Web. 6 January 2015. http://www.dekkaripavat.fi.

"Success[Ful] Author. Ilkka Remes [Sic] and the Eu's 'Banking Mafia.'" *Verkolehti* 25 September 2013. Web. 26 April 2014. http://www.kansannutiset.fi/uutiset/kotimaa/3054400.

Szalavitz, Maia. "Why the Happiest States Have the Highest Suicide Rates." *Healthland* 25 April 2011. Web. 27 April 2014. http://healthland.time.com/2011/04/25.

Tanner, Arno. "Finland's Balancing Act: The Labor Market, Humanitarian Relief, and Immigrant Integration." *Migration Policy Institute* 31 January 2011. Web. 27 April 2014. http://www.migrationpolicy.org/article.

Thomas, D. "Report Suggests Drug Use Will Be More Common in Finland in 2020." *What's Up in Finland* 14 May 2012. Web. 27 April 2014. http://whatsupinfinland.org/english.

Thompson, James. "My Life Just Isn't Anybody Else's Business." *Book Reviews by Elizabeth A. White* 15 March 2011. Web. 27 April 2014. http://www/elizabethawhite.com/2011/03/15.

_____. *Snow Angels.* New York: Berkeley Publishing Group, 2009. Print.

Thompson, James, ed. *Helsinki Noir.* Brooklyn, NY: Akashic Books, 2015. Print.

Tormanen, Eve. "'Electricity Book [E Book] Is the Very Devil,' Says Reijo Mäki." *Talentum* 1 July 2014. Web. 26 April 2014. http://www.talentum.com.

Tuija, "Tuula-Linna Varis: A Woman's Best Friend." *Book Tips* 25 October 2014.Web. 6 January 2015. http://www.wsoy.fi.com.

"Vilho Helanen." *Books and Writers.* Web. 10 November 2014. http://www.kirjasto.sci.fi/helanen.htm.

Viuhko, Minne, and Anniina Jokinen. *Human Trafficking and Organized Crime Trafficking for Sexual Exploitation and Organized Procuring in Finland.* Helsinki: European Institute for Crime Prevention and Control, Series 62, 2009. Print.

Walkley, Ian. "Helsinki Homicide: Cold Trail by Jarkko Sipilä." *The Big Thrill* May 2013. Web. http://www.thebigthrill.org/2013/05/helsinki-homicide-cold-trail-by-jarkko-sipila.

Westö, Kjell. "Compelled to Write." *Books from Finland* 2/2000. Web. 30 April 2014. http://www.finlit.fi/booksfromfinland/bff/200/westo1.htm.

Yu-Juonikas, Jaakko."Mastermind of Detective Stories Reijo Mäki Reveals the True Financial Backers for the Vares Films." *Turku 2011—Magazine.* Web. 26 April 2014. http://www.turku2011.fi/en/Turku2011 magazine/reijo-maki_en.

Iceland

Allard, Joseph C. "Einar Már Guðmundsson," in *Icelandic Writers, Dictionary of Literary Biography*, Patrick J. Stevens, ed. Vol. 293: 50–54. Print.

Anderson, George K., tr. *The Saga of the Volsungs.* Newark: University of Delaware Press, 1982. Print.

Bachman, W. Bryant and Guðmundur Erlingsson, trs. *Swarfdale Saga and Other Tales.* New York: University Press of America, 1994. Print.

Barraclough, Eleanor Rosamund. "Inside Outlawry in *Grettis Saga Ásmundarsonar and Gísla Saga Súrssonar*: Landscape in the Outlaw Sagas." *Scandinavian Studies* 65 (1993): 365–388). Print.

Bates, Quentin. "Icelandic Noir." *International Crime Authors.* 18 February 2015. Web. 18 February 2015. http://www.internationalcrimeauthors.com/?3031.

_____. "An Interview with the Author of *Frozen Out/Frozen Assets.*" *Scandinavian Crime Fiction* 4 April 2011. Web. 7 January 2014. http://scandinaviancrimefiction.wordpress.com/2011/04/04.

_____. "Joining the Nordic Pretenders." *Mystery Readers Journal* 30 (Winter 2014–2015): 22–24. Print.

_____. "On Iceland's Crimewriting Legacy, Part 1." *Crime Time* 2013. Web. 16 January 2013. http://www.crimetime.co.uk/community/mag.php/showarticle/2543.

Bjðrnsdóttir, Ingibjórg Rósa. "Drug Abuse Not a Great Problem in Iceland." *The Reykjavik Grapevine*, 28 October 2013. Web. http:grapevine.is/home/read/article.

caite [sic]. "A Lovely Shore Breeze…" A Review of "The Hitman's Guide to House Cleaning." 2012. Web. 27 March 2013. http://caitesdayatthebeach.blogspot.com/2011/12.

Carr, David. "Media Deals and Novels from One Busy Mind," *New York Times* 5 March 2012. Web. 17 February 2015. http://www.nytimes.come/2012/-3/06/books/olaf-olafsson-restoration-author-and-time-warner.

Clark, Andrew. "Why Violent Crime Is So Rare in Iceland." *BBC News Magazine* 3 December 2013. Web. 17 January 2014. http://www.bbc.co.uk/newsmagazine-25201471.

"Crime and Society: Iceland." *A Comparative Criminology Tour of the World.* Web. 17 January 2014. http://www-rohan.sdsu.edu/faculty/rwinslow/europe/iceland.html.

Cochrane, Kira. "Is Iceland the Best Country for Women?" *The Guardian*, 3 October 2011. Web. 17 January 2014. http://www.theguardian.com/world/2011/oct/03.

Cornwell, Bob. "An Icelandic Agatha Christie?" *Crime Time* 2009. Web. 6 January 2014. http://www.crimetime.co.uk/mag/index/php/showarticle/1402.

Cummins, Anthony. "Burial Rites Author Hannah Kent: I Hate the Term 'Historical Novel.'" *Metro*, 4 September 2013. Web. 7 September 2013. http://metro.co.uk/2013/09/04.

Dagsdóttir, Úlfhildur. "Heroines in Distress." *literatur.is.* n.d. Web. 16 January 2014. http://www.literature.is.

_____. "The Mystery of Viktor Arnar Ingolfsson." n.d. Web. 28 January 2014. http://www.literature.is.

_____. "Stumbling Over a Clue: The Crime Ficiton of Aevar Örn Jósepsson. N.D. Web. 3 February 2013. http://www.literature.is.

_____. "The Writer Has Nine Lives: Þráinn Bertelsson." n.d. Web. 10 January 2014. http://www.literature.is.

Davidson, H.R. Ellis. *Gods and Myths of the Viking Age.* New York: Bell. 1964. Print.

Draghincescu, Rodica. "Olafur Gunnarsson" (Interview), tr. Howard Scott. *Levure Littéraire.* Web. 28 January 2014. http://levurelitteraire.com.

Edwards, Anna. "Police in Iceland Shoot a Criminal Dead for the First Time…" *Mail Online* 3 December 2013. Web. 17 January 2014. http://www.dailymail.co.uk/news/article-2517360.

Einhorn, Eric S. and John Logue. *Modern Welfare States: Scandinavian Politics and Policy In the Global Age,* 2nd ed. Westport, Connecticut: Praeger, 2003. Print.

"Euro but Not Trash." *Eurodrama.* 19 September 2012. Web. 3 February 2014. http://eurodrama.wordpress.com/2012/09/19/svartir-englar-black-angels.

Eydal, Guðny Björk, and Guðbjörg Ottósdóttir. "Immigration and the Economic Crisis: The Case of Iceland." (Working Paper 4. 4–6 May 2009). Reykjavik: Þjóðmástofnun Háskóla Íslands [University of Iceland]: 4–6 May 2009: 1–27. Print.

Fister, Barbara. "Crime Fiction with an Icelandic Accent—Arnaldur Indriðason." *Shots Crime And Thriller Ezine,* n.d. Web. 7 January 2014. http://www.shotsmag.co.uk.

Fontaine-Nikolov, Paul. "THE SHADOWS: Inside with the Unknowns of the Drug Culture." *The Reykjavik Grapevine* 7 August 2005. Web. 17 January 2014. http://www.grapevine.is/Features/Read/Article.

Forshaw, Barry. *Death in a Cold Climate.* New York: Palgrave Macmillan, 2012. Print.

_____. "*I Remember You,*" by Yrsa Sigurdardottir [Sic], Translated by Philip Roughton. *The Independent* 5 November 2012. Web. 6 November 2012. http://www.independent.co.uk.

Gislason,Theodor, A. Yngvadóttir, and B. Benediktsdóttir. "Alcohol Consumption, Smoking and Drug Abuse Among Icelandic Teenagers." *Drugs: Education, Prevention, and Policy* 2 (1995): 243–258. Print.

Guðmundsdóttir, Gunnþórunn. "Einar Kárason," in *Icelandic Writers, Dictionary of Literary Biography.* Patrick J. Stevens, ed. Vol. 293: 43–45. Print.

Guðmundsson, Hjörtur J. "Even Up There: Muslims Want Mosque in Reykjavik." *The Brussels Journal* 9 July 2006. Web. 17 January 2014. http://www/brusselsjournal.com/node/1311.

Hermann, Pernille. "Concepts of Memory and Approaches to the Past in Medieval Icelandic Literature." *Scandinavian Studies* 2009: 287–308). Print.

Holm, Ruurik. "The Mission of the Icelandic Left: Rescue the Welfare State." *Transform!* 2009. Web. 7 March 2013. http://transform,-network.net/journal/issue-042009/news/detail/Journal.

Human Rights Committee, 105th Session. "Review of Iceland." 27 July 2012. Web. 17 January 2014. http://www.youtube.com.

"I Hunt Translators." *Tag Archives: Icelandic Crime Fic tion.* 30 December 2008. Web. 5 January 2014. https://scandinaviancrimefiction.wordpress.com/tag/Icelandic-crime-fiction.

"Iceland Economy Profile 2012." Web. 7 March 2013. http://www.indexmundi.com/inceland/economyu_profile.html.

"Iceland Gives Local Muslims a Free Plot to Build Mega Mosque." *The Iconoclast* 27 September 2013. Web. 21 January 2014. http//www.newenglishreview.org.

"Iceland 2012 Crime and Safety Report." OSAC , Bureau of Diplomatic Security, U.S. Department of State. Web. 17 January 2013. http://www.psac.gov.

Indriðason, Arnaldur. *Jar City.* New York: Picador, 2006. Print.

"Interview with Sigurjón Pálsson." *Spotted by Normann Copenhagen* 26 September 2014. Web. 17 February 2015, http://spottedbynormanncopenhagen.com/tag/sigurjon-palsson.

"Interview: Yrsa Sigurdardottir, Writer." *The Scotsman,* 23 July 2010. Web. 18 April 2012. http://www.scotsman.com.

Jakobsson, Ármann. "The Fearless Vampire Killers: A Note About the Icelandic *Draugr* and Demonic Contamination in *Grettis Saga.*" *Folklore* 120 (December 2009): 307–316. Print.

Johnson, Janet Elise. "The Most Feminist Place in the World." *The Nation,* 3 February 2011. Web. 17 January 2014. http://www.thenation.com/article/158 279.

Jones, J. Sidney. "Taking on the Nordic Crime Waves: Michael Ridpath's Icelandic Crime Novels." *Scene of the Crime* 22 August 2011. Web. 7 January 2014. http://jsydneyjones.wordpress.com/2011/08/22.

Jonsson, Asgeir. "Iceland's Banks Come in from the Cold." *Wall Street Journal,* 16 June 2011. Web. 23 January 2012. http://online.wsj.com.

Jonsson, Gudmundur. "The Icelandic Welfare State in the Twentieth Century." *Scandinavian Journal of History* 26 (2000): 150–267. Print.

"Justice Undone by Thor Vilhjalmsson." In *Goodreads,* n.d. Web. 5 February 2014. http://www.goodreads.com/book/show/321935. Justice_Undone.

Kachka, Boris. "No. 1 with an Umlaut." *New York,* 8 May 2011. Web. 29 October 2011. http://nymag.com/arts/books/features/scandinavian-crime-fiction-guide-2011–5/8/2011.

Kennedy, Margrit. "An Update on the Iceland Financial Crisis." *Beyond Money* 23 September 2011. Web. 23 January 2012. http://beyondmoney.net/2011/1/20/06.

Kerridge, Jake. "Arnaldur Indridason Interview." *The Telegraph.* 3 September 2013. Web. 31 January 2014. http://www.telegraph.co.uk/culture/books/1028 3048.

Kerridge, Jake, "Meet Yrsa Sigurdardottir, Iceland's Answer to Stieg Larsson." *The Telegraph* 26 July 2010.

Web. 8 June 2012. http://www.telegraph.co.uk/culture/boks/bookreviews/7904288.

Klein, Naomi. "All of Them Must Go." *The Nation,* 23 February 2009: 10. Print.

Knútsdóttir, Hildur. "Stella Blomkvist're [Sic] Coming Out of the Closet." DV 19 September 2011. Web. 5 January 2014. http://www.dv.is/menning/2011/9/19.

"Krepponomics." *The Economist,* 9 October 2008. Web. 23 January 2012. http://www.economist.com/finance/displaystory/cfm?story_id+12382011.

Kress, Helga. "Halldór Laxness," in *Icelandic Writers, Dictionary of Literary Biography,* ed. Patrick J. Stevens. Vol. 293, ed. Patrick J. Stevens. Detroit, Michigan: Gale, 2004: 125–149. Print.

Lovgren, Stefan. "'Sagas' Portray Iceland's Viking History." *National Geographic News,* 7 May 2004. Web. 32 January 2012. http://news.nationalgeographic.com/news/2004/05/0507_040507_icelandsagas.html.

Mason, Rowena. "Iceland Banking Inquiry Finds Murky Geysers Run Deep." *The Telegraph,* 14 April 2009. Web. 23 January 2012. http://www.telegraph.co.uk/finance/finance topics/financial crisis.

Medley, Mark. "Iceland Reads." *The National Post* 11 July 2014. Web. 14 February 2015. http://arts.nationalpost.com/2014/07/11/iceland-reads.

Müller, Margrit and Tano Myllyntaus. *Pathbreakers; Small European Countries Responding to Globalisation and Deglobalisation.* Berne, Switzerland: Peter Lang Verlag, 2007. Print.

Neijmann, Daisy, ed. *A History of Icelandic Literature.* Lincoln, Nebraska: The University of Nebraska Press, 2006. Print.

Nestingen, Andrew, and Paula Arvas, eds. *Scandinavian Crime Fiction.* Cardiff, Wales: University of Wales Press, 2011. Print.

"Ólafur Gunnarsson Interview." *New American Press* 23 April 2014. Web. 13 February 2015. http://asitoughttobe.com/2014/-04/23/olafur-gunnarsson-interview.

Ólason, Vesteinn. "Old Icelandic Poetry." *A History of Icelandic Literature.* Ed. Daisy Neijmann. Lincoln, Nebraska: University of Nebraska Press, 2006. 1–63. Print.

Olsen, Lise Smed. "A Renewed Focus on Gender Equality in Iceland. *Nordregio News* Issue 2: 2013. Web. 17 January 2014. http://www.nordregio.se/en/metameny/nordregio-news/2013.

Quinn, Ben. "Iceland Financial Crisis: Voters Reject Debt Repayment Plan." *Christian Science Monitor,* 7 March 2010. Web. 23 January 2012. http://www.csmonitor.com/World/Europe/2010/0207.

_____. "Iceland Financial Crisis: Will Chill Deepen in Wake of Repayment Veto?" *The Christian Science Monitor,* 6 January 2010. Web. 23 January 2012. http://www.csmonitor.com/World/Europe/2010/0106.

Ramirez, Janina. "The Sagas of Iceland Creating Terra Nova." *History Today* 61 (May 2011): 10–16. Print.

Reiss, Sabine. Review of *Valkyries* by Thrainn Bertelsson. *Krimi-Couch,* December 2013. Web. 10 January 2014. http://www.krimi-couch.de.

"Report on Foreign Nationals and Immigrants in Iceland." *Vision Media: The Multicultural Voice in Iceland* 28 September 2013. Web. 17 January 2014. http://visionmedia.is.

Review: *Someone to Watch Over Me.* Publishers Weekly 1 December 2014: 36. Print.

Ruckh, Jürgen. "Interview with Arnaldur Indriðason." *Literature Portal* 2006. Web. 29 January 2014. http://schwedenkrimi.de.

_____. "Interview with the Author Stella Blomkvist." *Literature Portal* 2005. Web. 5 January 2014. http://schwedenkrimi.de.

_____. "Interview with the Author Stella Blomkvist." *Literature Portal* 2007. Web. 5 January 2014. http://schwedenlrimi.de.

_____. "Interview with the Translator Elena Teuffer." *Literature Portal* 2005. Web. 5 January 2014. http://schwedenkrimi.de.

Rushton, Katherine. "CWA Raises Concerns Over Bias." *The Bookseller,* 18 November 2005:8. Print.

"Sagafilm Readies New Drama Series." *Iceland Cinema Now.* 24 September 2013. Web. 4 February 2013. http://icelandcinemanow.com/2013/09/24.

Serafin, Tatiana. "Fixing Iceland." ForbesWoman in Forbeswww, 21 August 2009. Web. 7 March 2013. http://www.forbes.com/2009/08/21.

Sigfussdóttir, Inga, et al. "Substance Use Prevention for Adolescents: The Icelandic Model." *Health Promotion International* 24 (2009): 16–25. Web. 22 January 2014. http://heapro.oxfordjournals.org/content/24/1/16.full.

Sigfússon, Steingrímur J. "Iceland's Road to Recovery: What Lessons to Be Learned." Report by the Icelandic Ministry of Finance 26 May 2011. Print.

"Sigrun Davidsdottir-Reporter." *540 Floors,* 2012.Web. 27 January 2014. http://www.540floors.com.

Sigurðardóttir, Yrsa. "A Depressing Lack of Crime." *Mystery Readers Journal* 23 (Fall 2007): 61–63.

_____. "Murderous Greetings from Iceland." *Mystery Readers Journal* 30 (Winter 2014–2015): 35–37. Print.

Social Values, Science and Technology Analysis. European Commission Eurobarometer, June 2005. http://ec.europa.eu/public_opinion/archives/ebs/ebs_225-report_en.pdf.

Spencer-Fleming, Julia. "Julia Interviews Arnaldur Indriðason." 2013. Web. 31 January 2014. http://www.juliaspencerfleming.com.

Stasio, Marilyn. "Missing Persons." *New York Times Book Review,* 28 September 2008: 28. Print.

"Steinar Bragi Goes [Sic] Hard Words of Literary Criticism in Iceland." DV 1 May 2012. Web. 11 January 2011. http://www.dv.is/menning/2012/3/1.

"Steinar Bragi: My Faith in Ghosts Wide Open and Humble." *Vidskiptabladid* 23 November 2013. Web. 11 January 2013. http://www/vb.is/eftirvinnu/98749.

Stevens, Patrick J., ed. *Dictionary of Literary Biography.* Vol. 283 (*Icelandic Writers*). Detroit, Michigan: Gale, 2004.

Sullivan, Patrick. "Olafsson, Olaf: *Valentines*: Stories." *Library Journal* 132.1 (1 January 2007): 102. Print.

Svartir Englar (Black Angels): *Euro but Not Trash* 19 September 2012. Web. 3 February 2014. http://www.eurodrama.wordpress.com2012/09/19/svartir-englar-black-angels/.

Teicher, Jordan G. "Literary Iceland Revels in Its Annual Christmas Book Flood." *NPR News,* 25 December 2012. Web. 5 January 2013. http://www.npr.org/2012/12/25/167537939.

"Ten Minutes with Arnaldur Indridason." *Dead Good Newsletter,* n.d. Web. 31 January 2014. http://www.deadgoodbooks.co.uk/index.php.

Thomsen, Poul M. "How Iceland Recovered from Its Near-Death Experience." *IMF Direct—The IMF Blog.* 26 October 2011. Web. 7 March 2013. http://blog-imfdirect.imf.org/2011/10/26.

Toma, Toshiki. "Immigrants—Pandora's Box in Iceland." *The Reykjavik Grapevine,* 12 January 2006. Web. 17 January 2014. http://www.grapevine.is/Home/Read/Article/Immigrants.

"Two Crime Authors Feature Reykjavik Chess Duel." *Iceland Review-Online* 7 November 2011. Web. 31 January 2014. http://www.icelandreview/com.

Valdimarsdóttir, Thorunn. "Lines Drawn in Snow." Speech given at the Sylvia Kekkonen Symposium in Finland, 2010. Web. 29 January 2014. http://thorwvald.is/?page_id=80.

Valgardson, W.D. "Sigrun Davidsdottir: Combining Journalism and Fiction." 29 February 2012. Web. 27 January 2014. http://wdvalgardsonkaffihus.com.

_____. "Sigrun Davidsdottir: The Kreppa [Crash]." 2 March 2012. Web. 27 January 2014. http://wdvalgardsonkaffihus.com.

Vogler, Agnes. "Olafur Gunnarsson: Their Best Guardian." Web. 28 January 2014. http://www.literature.is.

Waugh, Robin. "Misogny, Women's Language, and Love-Language." *Scandinavian Studies* 70, (Summer 1998): 151–188.

Webb, Betty. "Iceland's Cannibal Serial Killers." *Mystery Readers Journal* 30 (Winter 2014–2015): 41–43. Print.

Weinman, Edward J. "A View to a Killer." *Huffington Post* 25 March 2013. Web. 27 March 2013. http://www.huffingtonpost.com.

"When the King Came." Interview with Helgi Ingólfsson. *Sagenhaftes Island* [Icelandic titles], n.d. Web. 30 January 2013. http://www.islit.is/promotion-and-translations.

Zakalwe, Cheradenine. "Another Bastion Falls: Iceland to Get Its First Mosque." *Islam Versus Europe,* 11 July 2013. Web. 21 January 2014. http://islamversuseurope.blogspot.com/2013/07.

Norway

Baehr, Anne Clare. "*The Girl with the Balloon* by Merete Junker." *Litteratursiden* 16 December 2008. Web. 6 Nov. 2012. http://www.litteratursiden.dk/anmelelser.

Baldwin, Rosecrans. "'Before I Burn' Uses Autobiography to Tell a Crime Story." *NPR* 2 January 2014. Web. 19 February 2014. http://www.npr.org/2014/01/02/259177525.

Beardsley, Eleanor. "Can the European Welfare State Survive?" *NPR* 14 July 2010. Web. 7 Mar. 2013. http://www.npr.org/templates.story/story.php?storyId=128485416.

Berglund, Nina. "Why Norway's Welfare State Works: Views and News from Norway." *News in English* 2 January 2012. Web. 12 Mar. 2013. http://www.newsinenglish.no/2011.01/02.

_____. "State Set to Allow Heroin Smoking: Views and News from Norway." *News in English* 1 May 2013. Web. 12 May. 2013. http://www.newsinenglish.no/2013/03/01.

Bevanger, Lars. "Norway's Formula for a Happy Life." Web. 25 Feb. 2013. *BBC News* 8 September 2008. http://www.bbc.co.uk/2/hi/programmes/from_our_own-correspondent/4223148.stm.

Beyer, Harald. *A History of Norwegian Literature,* ed. and tr. Einar Haugen. New York: New York University Press, 1979. Print.

Bjørnskau, Hilde and Ana Letitia Sigvartsen. "Author Jorn Lier Horst Wrote Last Year's Best Crime Novel, 'Hunting Dogs.'" *NRK Literature* 12 March 2013. Web. 2 August 2013.

"Book Awards: Dagbladet 25 Best Norwegian Crime Novels." *Library Thing* 2009. Web. 14 February 2013. http://www/librarything.com/bookaward/Dagbladet.

"Books of Redeeming Value." *Publishers Weekly* 25 March 2013: 45. Print.

Booss, Claire, ed. *Scandinavian Folk & Fairy Tales.* New York: Avenel Books, 1984. Print.

Botten, Grete, Kari Tove Elvbakken and Nanna Kildal, "The Norwegian Welfare State on the Threshold of a New Century." *Scandinavian Journal of Public Health* 31 (2003): 81–84. Print.

Brekke, Jørgen. *Dreamless,* tr. by Steven T. Murray. New York: Minotaur Books, 2015. Print.

The Browser. "Jo Nesbø on Norwegian Crime Writing." *The Browser* 10 May 2010. http://old.thebrowser.com/interviews/jo-nesb%C3%B8-on-norwegian-crimewriting. Web. 27 June 2013.

Christiansen, Anette Broteng. "The Norwegian 'Easter-Crime' Phenomena," *ThorNews: Norwegian News and Culture,* posted 7 April 2012. http://thornewes.com/2012/04/07/the-norwegian-easter-crime-phenomena. Web. 24 April 2012.

Clare, Nancie. "Author Jo Nesbø Talks New Novel, Being Courted by Hollywood." 4 June 2014. Web. 6 June 2014. http://www.hollywoodreporter.com/news.

Clarke, Maxine. Review of Frode Grytten's *The Shadow in the River.* 2012. http://www.eurocrime.co.uk/reviews/The_Shadow_in_the_River.html. Web. 15 Nov. 2012.

_____. Review of Gunnar Staalesen's *The Consorts of*

Death. Web. 11 Aug. 2013. http://www.eurocrime.co.uk/reviews/The-Consorts-of-Death.html.

_____. Review of Gunnar Staalesen's *Yours Until Death.* Web. 11 Aug. 2013. http://www.eurocrime.co.uk/reviews/Yours-Until-Death.html.

_____. Review of Pernille Rygg's *The Butterfly Effect. EuroCrime* 1 November 2009. http://www.eurocrime.co.uk/reviews/The_Butterfly_Effect.html. Web. 23 April 2012.

Crace, John. "Jo Nesbø: 'If Salman Rushdie Had Been Norwegian, He'd Have Written a Thriller.'" *The Guardian.* 28 October 2012. http://www.guardian.co.uk/books. Web. 29 Oct. 2012.

Creer. Anna. "No Love in a Cold Climate for Sophomore Scandinavians." *Sidney Morning Herald* 16 November 2012. Web. 20 November 2012. http://www.smh.com.au/entertainment/books.

Dahl, Willy. "*Rasisme i Massellitteraturen*," ["Racism in Popular Literature"] in Bjarte Birkeland et al., *Nazismen og Norsk Litteratur*, 2nd ed. Oslo: Universitetsforlaget, 1995. Print.

Davies, Hannah. "Scandi Sensation: Former Norwegian Minister of Justice Anne Holt Is Taking on the UK with an Agatha Christie–Style Thriller. Hannah Davies Talks to the Bestselling Crime Author." the *Bookseller* 5449, 2010: 23. Print.

DeMarco, Laura. "Norwegian Author Anne Holt's Heroine Hanne Wilhelmsen Is a Different Kind of Nordic Investigator." *Cleveland Plain Dealer*, 9 June 2012. http://www.cleveland.com/books.index.ssf./2012/06. Web. 22 July 2013.

Derbyshire, Jonathan. "Anne Holt" [interview]. *New Statesman* 13 December 2010: 49. Print.

"Drinking and Drug Safety Issues in Norway." 2013. Web. 12 March 2013. http://safety:worldnomads.com/Norway/75038.

"The Drug Situation in Norway 2011." Annual Report to the European Monitoring Centre for Drugs and Drug Addiction." http://www.sirus.no. Web. 12 Mar. 2013.

Dufour, Christian. "Review of Asbjørn Wahl's the *Rise and Fall of the Welfare State*," *Global Labour Journal* 4 (2013): 71–2. Print.

Edigheki, Omano. "Globalization and Evolving Local Governance in Norway." *Globalizations* 6 (June 2009): 207–223. Print.

Elphick, Nicole. "Jo Nesbø's 'The Son' Lives Up to the Scandinavian Crime Fiction Hype." *Daily Life* 14 April 2014. Web. 14 April 2014. http://www.dailylife.com.au/dl-people/dl-entiertainment.

Engelstad, Audun. "Dealing with Crime: Cyclic Changes in Norwegian Crime Films." *Journal of Scandinavian Cinema* 1 (2011): 205–221. Print.

Enger, Thomas. "How Did I Become an Author?" http://www.thomasenger.net/background. Web. 31 July 2012.

Ermolino, Louisa. "Jo Nesbø Is Not the Next…" *Publishers Weekly* 23 July 2012: 28. Print.

Finocchiaro, Peter. "Adam Lanza Motivated by Norway Massacre." Reuters, posted 18 February 2013. Web. 19 Feb. 2013. http://huffingtonpost.com/2013/02/18.

Fister, Barbara. "Reparations: World War II in Scandinavian Crime Fiction." *Mystery Readers Journal* 20 (Winter 2014–2015): 4–6. Print.

_____. "Scandinavian Crime Fiction," Web. 20 April 2012. http://barbarafister.com/norway.html.

Fjellberg, Anders. "Nygårdshaug Belongs in the 1700s." *Dagbladet* 1 March 2012. Web. 26 March 2012. http://www.dagbladet.no/2012.

Fleishman, Jeffrey. "Norway's Heroin Lows." *Los Angeles Times.* 29 November 2009. Web. 23 Mar. 2013. http://articles.latimes.com/2004/nov/29/world/fg-heroin29.

Forshaw, Barry. *Death in a Cold Climate: A Guide to Scandinavian Crime Fiction.* New York: Palgrave Macmillan, 2012. Print.

_____. "New Stars of Nordic Noir: Norway's Authors Discuss Their Country's Crime Wave." *The Independent* 8 July 2011. Web, 7/26/2013. http://www.independent.co.uk/arts-entertainment/books/features.

Foster, Jordan. "Norwegian Noir," *Publishers Weekly* 25 January 2010: 94. Print.

Franssen, Wolfgang. "*Blood Scripture:* Jørgen Jaeger." *Crime Coach* 2009. Print.

Fund, John. "Norway's Right Turn." *National Review* 9 August 2013. Web. 9 March 2015. http://www.nationalreview.com/article/355330/norways-right-turn-john-fund.

Gilyard, Burl. "U of M Press Finds Success with Norwegian Mystery." *Twin Cities Business.* 2 January 2014. Web. 1 July 2014. http://tcbmag.com/News/Recent-News/2014/January.

Greenfield, Daniel. "Norway Loses $713,000 on Every Muslim Immigrant." *Frontpage Magazine* 25 May 2013. Web. 7 March 2015. http://www.frontpagemag.com,/2013/dgreenfield/norway-loses…

Gulbransen, Kristin. "Global Financial Crises, Part II: Norway 1987." *The Big Picture*, 10 February 2008. Web. 9 Mar. 2013. http://bigpicture.typepad.com/comments/2008/02/global-financial.html.

Hagelund, Anniken. "Why It Is Bad to Be Kind. Educating Refugees to Life in the Welfare State: A Case Study from Norway." *Social Policy & Administration* 39 (December 2005): 669–683. Print.

Halla, Martin, Mario Lackner, and Johann Scharler. "Does the Welfare State Destroy The Family? Evidence from OECD Member Countries." Working Paper No. 1304, February 2013. Johannes Kepler University of Linz, Austria. Print.

Harperat, Glenn. "The Other Igi Heitman Novel." *International Noir* 20 March 2007. Web. 23 April 2012. http://internationalnoir.blogspot.com.

"Harvill Secker Announces Two New Books from Jo Nesbo" [sic]. 20 July 2013. Web. 20 July 2014. http://www.booktrade.info/index.php/showarticle/49997.

Haugen, Siv, and Else Lie. "Norwegian Welfare System Facing Major Challenges." the Research Council of

Norway. Web. 25 Feb. 2013. http://www/forskn
ingsradet.no/en/Newsarticle.

Henriksen, Petter, Ed. "Øyulv Gran." *Store Norske Leksikon*. Oslo: Kunnskapsforlagen, 2007. Print.

Hesse, Monika. "Jo Nesbø, the Next Stieg Larsson." the
Washington Post 3 May 2011. Web. 3 March 2015.
http://www.washingtonpost.com/life.

Hipp, Van. "Conservatives, If You Want to Win Look at
How Erna Solberg, Norway's 'Iron Lady' Did It." *Fox
News* 13 September 2013. Web. 7 March 2015. http://
www.foxnews.com/opinioons/2013/09/13/con
servatives-i…

Hodapp, Christopher. "Norwegian Terror Suspect's Masonic Membership." *Freemasons for Dummies* 23 July
2011. Web. 5 December 2012. http://freemasons
fordummies.blogspot.com/2011/07.

Hoge, Warren. "In Scenic Norway, a Death Scene of Addiction." *New York Times*. Web. 12 Mar. 2013. http:
www.nytimes.com/2002/08/08.

Holt, Anne. "Anne Holt's Top Ten Female Detectives."
The Guardian 8 December 2010. Web. 11 August
2013. http://www.theguardian.com/books/2010/
dec/08/anne-holt-top-10-female-detectives.

Hutchinson, Gunn Strand, and Wendy Weeks. "Living
Conditions of Women Who Experience Violence
from Their Partners: Norway and Australia Comparisons." *Australian Journal of Social Issues* 39 (4 November 2004): 393–407. Print.

"Inspector Norse." *The Economist* 394, 13 March 2010:
86. Print.

Kachka, Boris. "No. 1 with an Umlaut." *New York Magazine*, 8 May 2011. Web. 28 Nov. 2011. http://www.
nymag.com/arts/books/features/scandinavian-
crime-fiction-guide-2011.

_____. "One Long Winter: Landmark Moments in
Scandinavian Crime Fiction." *New York*, 16 May 2011.
Print.

Keslassy, Elsa. "Yellow Bird and Lionsgate TV Ready to
Headhunt for HBO," *Variety* 7 November 2013. Web.
12 November 2013. http://variety.com/2013/tv/news.

Krøger, Cathrine. "Too Cryptic Thriller." *Dagbladet* 4
November 2011. Web. 17 Nov. 2011. http://www.
dagbladet.com.

Kurzman, Dan. *Blood and Water: Sabotaging Hitler's
Bomb*. New York: Henry Holt, 1997. Print.

Ladegaard, Isak. "Norway's Problem with Immigration."
ScienceNordic 28 January 2013. Web. 21 January 2014.
http://sciencenordic.com/norways-problem-immi
gration.

_____. "The Welfare State Reduces Income Gap Be-
tween the Sexes." *ScienceNordic* 7 October 2012. Web.
25 February 2013. http://sciencenordic.com/wel
fare-state-reduces-income-gap-between-the-exes.

Lie, Øystein. "'Pimp-Frank' Attacks." *Dagbladet* 9 August
2013. Web. 31 July 2014. http://www.dagbladet.no.

Madslien, Jorn. "Norway's Far Right Not a Spent Force."
BBC News Europe, 23 July 2011. Web. 4 Dec. 2012.
http://www.bbc.co.uk/news/world-europe-14260
195.

Magson, Adrian. "Thomas Enger Debuts with *Burned*."
Shots n.d. Web. 31 July 2012. http://www.shotsmag.
co.uk/interview_view.aspx?interview_id=222.

"Martin Scorsese to Take on Jo Nesbo's [sic] the *Snowman*." *Words and Film* 2011. Web. 20 April 2012.
http://www.wordsandfilm.com.

Mason, Bobbie Ann. *The Girl Sleuth: A Feminist Guide*.
New York: Feminist Press, 1975. Print.

Matthews, Jeanne. "Trespassing on Scandinavian Turf."
Mystery Readers Journal 30 (Winter 2014–2015): 33–
35. Print.

Max Manus: Man of War (2008). *Rotten Tomatoes* 2010.
Web. 29 Feb. 2013. http:www.rottentomatoes.com/
m/max_manus_man_of_war.

McCabe, Alec D.B. "'Harry Hole's Creator Goes to Hollywood." *Bloomberg News* 17 May 2014. Web. 18 May
2014. http://www.bloomberg.com/news/2014-05-
17.

McNary, Dave. "Leonardo DiCaprio Books Jo Nesbo's
[sic] 'Blood on the Snow.'" *Variety* 21 October 2013.
Web. 20 July 2014. http://variety.com/2013/film/
news.

McWeeney, Myles. "Books: Jo Nesbø's Latest Thriller
Is Ice Cold in Norway." *The Independent* 6 April 2014.
Web. 6 April 2014l http://www.independent.ie/enter
tainment/books-arts.

Melia, Silje. "Schemer: Interview with Unni Lindell."
Bokklubben 6 August 2008. Web. 9 Nov. 2012. http://
www.bokklubben.no.

Mogk, Marja. Karin Fossum's Norway," *Mystery Readers
Journal* 23 (Fall 2007): 21–23. Print.

Moyer, Jessica E, "Nesbø, Jo. the Redbreast." *Library
Journal* 132.17 (2007): 61. Print.

Mulcahy, Orna. "Not So Ordinary Jo." *The Irish Times*,
10 November 2012. Web. 13 Nov. 2012. http://www.
irishtimes.com/newspaper/magazine/2012/1110/
1224326212456.html.

Murphy, Bruce F. *The Encyclopedia of Murder and Mystery*. New York: St. Martin's Minotaur, 1999. Print.

Nielsen, Bjarne, ed. and trans. *Scandinavia and Sherlock
Holmes*. London: The Baker Street Irregulars International Series, 2006. Print.

Nilsen, Sylvi I. "Immigration and the Welfare State in a
Norwegian Context: A Literature Review on the Debate on Immigration and the Welfare State Among
Scholars in Norway." Thesis Submitted for the Master['s] Degree in International Social Welfare and
Health Policy, Fall 2008, to the Faculty of Social Sciences, Oslo University College. Print.

Nixdorf, Franziska. "The Norway Killer: Neo-Nazi Massacres 77 People." *Cape Chameleon* 15 (2011). Web.
4 Dec. 2012. http://www/capechameleon.co.za.

Nordberg, Nils. "Murder in the Midnight Sun: Crime
Fiction in Norway 1825–2005." *CrimeTime* 10 April
2012. Web. 23 Apr. 2012. http://www.crimetime.co.
uk/mag/index.phpshowarticle/2746.

_____. "Murderers' Cheerful Siblings: Riverton Club
History," in *Riverton Library: The All-Time Best Crime
and Suspense Books*. Book Clubs, 1993. Print.

Norseng, Mary Kay. "Uprooting Old Values in New Norwegian: *Dollar Road by* Kjarten Fløgstad, Translated by Nadia M. Christensen." *Los Angeles Times.*19 November 1984. Web. 23 May 2012. http://articles. latimes.com/1989-11-19/books/bk-159_1_dollar-road.

North, Synnøve. "Minnesota Trilogy Completed: Vidar Sundstøl." *Kulturkompasset* 7 June 2011. Web. 6 Nov. 2012. http://www.kulturkompasset.com/2011/07/ minnesota-trilogien.

"Norway Deports Record Number of Immigrants." *The Local* 10 November 2014. Web. 10 March 2015. http://www/thelocal.no/20141110/norway-deports-record-number-of-immigrants.

"Norway's Islamic Extremism Problem." *The Daily Caller* 9 April 2014. Web. 5 March 2015. http://www. dailycaller.com/2014/09/04/norways-islamic-extremism-problem.

"Norwegian Collaborationist Forces During World War II." *Feldgrau* n.d. Web. 21 November. 2012. http:// www.feldgrau.com/a-norway.html. [*Feldgrau* is a nonpolitical research webpage on German military history which has supplied more than 10,000 pages of information since February 1996.]

"Norwegian Crime Author Roy Jacobsen in Singapore." 9 November 2013. Web. 11 Nov. 2012. http://www. scandasia.com/viewNews.php?coun_code=no& news_id=11451.

"The Norwegian 'Easter-Crime' Phenomena," *Thor News.* 7 April 2012.Web. 24 April 2012. http://www. thornews.com/2012/04/07.

O'Brien, Sean. "A Criminal Compass." *Times Literary Supplement* 21 June 2013: 19. Print.

"Oil Makes Norway Different." *The Economist.* 2 February 2013. Web. 9 March 2013. http://www. economist,com/news/special-report/21570842.

O'Kelly, Kevin. Review of *Don't Look Back. Boston Globe* 24 March 2004, F7. Print.

Øklund, Einar. "A New [Sic] Golden Age for Norway." *Times Literary Supplement* 9 October 1971: 1077–1078. Print.

Orskaug, Oliver. "Pimp-Frank Convicted of Abuse." *Dagbladet* 9 August 2013. Web. 31 July 2014. http:// www. dagbladet.no.

Page, Katherine Hall. Review of *Death in a Cold Climate* by Robert Barnard. *Mystery Reders Journal* 30 (Winter 2014–2015): 48–49. Print.

Pearson, Bob. "Norwegian Gold Bullion Snatch," in *Royal Navy Memories* 2009. Web. 27 Nov. 2012. http://royalnavymemories.co.uk/norwegian-gold-bullion-snatch.

Pew Research Center. "Pew Research Center's Religion & Public Life Project." 27 February 2011. Web. 7 March 2015. http://www. pewforum.org/2011/01/ 27/future-of-the-glbal-muslim-polulation....

Poggioli, Sylvia. "Crime Writers Expose Scandinavia's Dark Side." *NPR News* 27 July 2011. Web. 14 Feb. 2013. http://www.npr.org/2011/07/27/138756602/ crime-writers-expose-scandinavia's-dark-side.

Preston, John. "Jo Nesbø Talks About 'Phantom.'" *The Telegraph* 12 March 2012. Web. 20 Apr. 2012. http:// www.telegraph.co.uk/culture/books/author interviews/9130821.

"The Rescue That Really Worked." Reprint of Jerry Guo's interview with Jens Stoltenberg in *Newsweek,* 21 April 2010. Web. 9 Mar. 2013. http://www. thedailybeast.com/newsweek/2010/04/21/the-rescue-that-really-worked.html.

Research Council of Norway. "Rethinking Societal Security," *Norwegian-American Weekly* 13 (13 April 2012): 5. Print.

Review of *Modern Welfare States: Scandinavian Politics and Policy in the Global Age,* 2d ed. Eric S. Einhorn and John Logue. Westport, CT: Praeger, 2003. *Future Survey* 28 (8 August 2003): 11. Print.

Review of *Phantom,* by Jo Nesbo. *Publishers Weekly* 27 August 2012: 50. Print.

Rice, James Mahmud, Robert E. Goodin, and Antti Parpo, "The Temporal Welfare State: A Crossnational Comparison." *Journal of Public Policy* 26 (September-December 2006): 198. Print.

Ridgeway, James. "Andres Breivik, Stieg Larsson, and the Men with the Nazi Tattoos." Web. 4 Dec. 2012. http://www.motherjones.com/mojo/2011/07/ anders-breivik-stieg-larsson.

Ringen, Stein. "Wealth and Decay: Norway Funds a Massive Political Self-Examination—And Finds Trouble for All." *TLS* 13 February 2004: 3–5. Print.

Risker, Paul. "Special Features; America's Rape of Scandinavian Crime Drama." 28 December 2012. Web. 5 Jan. 2013. http://www.flickering myth.com/2012.

Riverton, Stein. *The Iron Chariot:* Originally published as *Jernvognen (Norsk-Engelsk Lesebok),* ed. and tr. James P. Jensen, ill. Sonja Can Guilder, Forword by J. Randolph Cox. Minneapolis, MN: Nelsbok Publishing, 2005. Print.

Root, Laura. Review of "Lethal Investments" by K.O. Dahl. Web. 31 July 2012. http://eurocrime.co.uk/ reviews/Lethal_Investments.html.

Rubin, Charlie. "Thrillers." *New York Times Book Review* 1 June 2014: 18–19. Print.

Saarinen, Risto. "The Surplus of Evil in Welfare Society: Contemporary Scandinavian Crime Fiction." *Dialog: A Journal of Theology* 42 (Summer 2003): 131–135. Print.

Sandberg, Sveinung. "Black Drug Dealers in a White Welfare State: Cannabis Dealing and Street Capital in Norway." *British Journal of Criminology* 48 (September 2008): 604–619. Print.

Siegel, Lee. "Pure Evil." *The New Yorker* 12 May 2014. Web. 3 March 2015. http://www.newyorker.com.

Simon, Juliet. "What Is It About Scandinavian Crime Series? Introducing Karin Fossum's Bad Intentions." *Everyday EBook* 19 October 2012. Web. 29 Oct. 2012. http://www.everydayebook.com/2012/10.

Singh, Anan, and Natalie Normann. "Against All Odds." *Mystery Readers Journal* 23 (Fall 2007): 63–66. Print.

_____, and Natalie Normann. "Crime at Easter." *Mystery Readers Journal* 23 (Fall 2007): 30–31. Print.

Skredderberger, Asle. "'Nuff Noir?" *Mystery Readers Journal* 20 (Winter 2014–2015): 37–38. Print.

Smith, Lindsey. "Financial Expert Believes Economic Crisis Will Reach Norway." *The Foreigner* 2 August 2010. Web. 9 Mar. 2013. http://theforeigner.no/pages/news.

Sorknes, Mailer. "Crime Author Merete Junker Knew Cruelty." *Dagbladet* 2 February 2012. Web. 6 Nov. 2012. http://www.dabladet.no/2012.

Søvik, Margrete. "The Norwegian Welfare State." *University of Bergen* n.d. Web. 4 March 2013. http://web.hist.uib.no/staben/solli/sas13/welfarestate.htm.

Spines, Christine. "Otherwise 'Occupied': Norwegian Crime Phenom Jo Nesbø Hits the Small Screen." *Words and Film* April 2013. Web. 30 April 2013. http://www.wordandfilm.com/2013/04.

Stasio, Marilyn. "Cold Case." *New York Times Book Review* (9 July 2006): 23. Print.

_____. "Killing by Numbers." *New York Times Book Review* (14 March 2010): 26. Print.

_____. "Missing Girl, Lost Boys." *New York Times Book Review* (27 July 2008): 25. Print.

Stenport, Anna Westerstahl. "The Mind and Nature of Locked Rooms: Tarjei Vesaas's Novel the *Ice Palace* and Metaphysical Crime Fiction." *Studies in the Novel* 42.3 (Fall 2010): 305*ff*. Web. 30 Nov. 2012. http://go.galegroup.com.

Stewart, Danny. "Big Interview—Arild Stavrum." *Sunday Post* 11 November 2013. Web. 31 July 2014. http://www.sundaypost.com/sport/football.

Stock, Jon. "Jo Nesbø to Retell Macbeth." *The Telegraph* 14 January 2014. Web. 14 January 2014. http://www/telegraph.co.uk/culture.books.booknews.10568820.

Strand, Harry. "*Han Som Elsker Amerika*." *Menninger Koemtaret* 3 November 2009. Web. 22 July 2013. http://www.adressa.no/meninger/article1406106.ece.

Sunder, M. "The Making of Giants in a Welfare State: The Norwegian Experience in The 20th Century." *Economics Humanities Biology* 1 (June 2003): 276. Print.

Sutterud, Tone. "Where the Blood Always Runs Cold." Review of *The Consorts of Death* by Gunnar Staalesen. *The Independent*, 19 October 2009. Web. 11 August 2013. http://www.independent.co.uk/arts-entertainment/books/reviews.

Swift, Camilla. "Crime Fiction at Easter? Look No Further than Our Scandinavian Neighbors." the *Spectator* 29 March 2013. Web. 31 Mar. 2013. http://blogs.spectator.co.uk/camilla-swift/2013/03.

Syltevik, Liv J. "Taking Control of One's Own Life? Norwegian Lone Mothers Experiencing the New Employment Strategy." *Community, Work, and Family* 9 (February 2006): 75–94. Print.

Syvertsen, Jan-Sverre. "This Is How I Work: Kjetil Try, Try Advertising Agency CEO, Oslo." 2 June 2012. Web. 6 Nov. 2012. http://blogg.telenor.no/jobbsmartere/2012/02/06.

Thomas, Landon Jr. "Thriving Norway Provides an Economics Lesson." *New York Times* 14 May 2009. Web. 9 Mar. 2013. http://www.nytimes.com/2009/05/14/business/global/24frugal.html>_r=0.

"Thomas Enger." *ScandiNoir* 30 June 2013. Web. 24 Nov. 2012. http://www.scandinoir.com/index.

Tookey, Chris. "*Max Manus: Man of War:* Dark World War II Drama with Real Heart." *Daily Mail Online*, 4 June 2009. Web. 19 Feb. 2013. http://www.dailymail.co.uk/tvshowbiz/reviews/article-1190960.

Tualla, Kris. "Why Norway?" *Mystery Readers Journal* 30 (Winter 2014–2015): 38–40. Print.

Turnbull, Sue. "Sun and Sin Down Under." 29 December 2012. Web. 5 Jan. 2013. http://www.smh.com.au/entertainment/books/sun-and-sin-down-under.

Turner, Barry. "Classic Crime." *The Daily Mail* 12 February 2015. Web. 13 February 2015. http://www.dailymail.co.uk/home/books/article-2951405/CLASSIC-CRIME.html.

Undset, Sigrid. "*Fortschritt, Rasse, Religion*," in *Die Gefahrdung des Christentums Durch Rassenwahn und Judenverfolgung* ["The Endangerment of Christianity Through Race-Insanity and Persecution of the Jews"]. Lucerne, Switzerland: Vita Nova Verlag, 1935. Print.

_____. *Return to the Future*. New York: Knopf, 1942. Print.

Vermeil, Edmond. *Hitler et Le Christianisme*. (London, 1944). Print.

Voksø, Per, ed. "*Hirden i Sammestøt*," in *Krigens Dagbok*. Oslo: Det Beste, 1984. Print.

Wengel, Lida. "Torkil Damhaug Talks About *Ildmannen*." *Krimimessen* 29 May 2002. Web. 6 Nov. 2012. https://www.bbfolk.horsens.dk.

Wilhelmsen, Ken Willy. "Focusing on Murder from NRK." NRK News Telemark n.d.. Web. 11 Nov. 2012. http://www.nrk.no/telemark.

Wilson, Laura. "The Best Recent Crime Novels—Review Roundup." *The Guardian* 12 February 2015. Web. 12 February 2015. http://www.theguardian.com/books/2015/feb/12/best-crime-recent-fiction-novels.

_____. "Laura Wilson's Crime Fiction Roundup—Reviews." Web, 22 March 2013. http://www.guardian.co.uk/books/2013/mar/22/crime-fiction-roundup-Reviews.

Wolff, Carlo. "'Phantom': Jo Nesbo's Ninth Novel of Norwegian Crime and Morality is Far More than a Procedural." *The Post-Gazette* 4 November 2012. Web. 4 Nov. 2012. http://www/post-gazette.com.

Zacharias, Lee. "Nancy Drew, Ballbuster." *Journal of Popular Culture* 9 (1976): 1027–1038. Print.

Sweden

Acacello, Joan. "Man of Mystery." *The New Yorker* 86 (10 January 2011): 70–74. Print.

"Åke Edwardson." *Scandinavian Crime Fiction* 2008. Web. 13 February 2014. http://www.scandinavian crimefiction.com/Ake_Edwardson.htm.

Alvarez, Lisette. "Sweden Faces Facts on Violence Against Women." *New York Times* 30 March 2005. Web. 16 April 2014. http://www.nytimes.com/2005/03/29/world/europe/29iht-letter-4909045.html.

"Anders De La Motte Interviewed." *Crime Fiction Lover* 28 November 2013. Web. 12 February 2014. http://www.crimefictionlover.com/2013/11/interview-with-anders-de-la-motte.

"Anders Roslund and Borge Hellström on Swedish Crime Writing." *The Browser* 2011. Web. 22 May 2012. http://thebrowser.com/interviews.

Armstrong, Stephen. "The Dark Side of Swedish Society." *The Telegraph* 13 March 2010. Web. 16 April 2014. http://www.telegraph.co.uk/culture/film/7430122.

"Åsa Larsson's Letter to Her Readers." *EuroCrime* 4 February 2008. Web. 14 March 2014. http://eurocrime.blogspot.com/2008/02.

"Author Interview: Jan Wallentin." *Roof Beam Reader* 29 April 2012. Web. 1 April 2014. http://roofbeamreader.com/2012/04/29.

Barkman, Clas. "New Swedish Television Detective Sales Success as Book." *DN.BOK.* 28 April 2010. Web. 10 March 2014. http://www.dn.bok.se.

Baski, Kurdo. "How a Brutal Rape and a Lifelong Burden of Guilt Fuelled Girl with the Dragon Tattoo Writer Stieg Larsson." *The Daily Mail.* Web. 17 March 2014. http://www.dailymail.co.uk/news/article-12992.

Beckford, Avril. "*Never End* by Åke Edwardson, Book Review." *The Invisible Mentor* 2000. Web. 13 February 2014. http://theinvisiblementor.com.

Bennhold, Katrin. "In Sweden, Men Can Have It All." *New York Times* 9 June 2010. Web. 16 April 2014. http://www.nytimes.com/2010/06/10/world/europe.

Berg, Karin. "Interviews Before the Book Fair—Lars Rambe." August 2012. Web. 24 March 2014. http://www.larsrambe.se.

Bergh, Andreas, and Magnus Henrekson. "Lessons from the Swedish Welfare State." *The Wall Street Journal* 10 July 2010. Web. 14 April 2014. http://online.wsj.com/news/articles.

Bergman, Kerstin. "Crime Fiction as Popular Science. the Case of Åsa Nilsonne." *Norlit 2009:* Codex and Code. Aesthetics, Language and Politics in an Age of Digital Media, a Conference of Linköping University, Stockholm, 6–9 August 2009: 193–2007. Print.

Bevanger, Lars. "Sweden Election: Left Turn as Far Right Soars." *BBC News Europe* 14 September 2014. Web. 23 January 2013. http://www.bbc.com/news/world-europe-29201660.

Bjurwald, Lisa. "From Boots to Suits: Sweden Democrats' Extreme Roots." *Euobserver* 11 March 2014. Web. 11 April 2014. http://euobserver.com/eu-elections/123316.

Blom, K. Arne. "The Crime Story in Sweden." *The Mystery Fancier* 7 (September-October 1983): 16–25. Print.

Bolinder, Jean. "BROTTSKOD 09 [Sic] by Bodil Mårtensson." *DAST Magazine* 1 February 2008. Web. 3 February 2015. http://www.dast.nu/recension/brottskod09.

Booss. Claire, ed. *Scandinavian Folk & Fairy Tales.* New York: Avenel Books, 1984. Print.

Bosman, Julie. "A Scandinavian Hit Sets Publishers Seeking More." *New York Times* 14 June 2010. Web. 9 February 2011. http://www.nytimes.com/2010/06/16/books/16noir.html.

Boyd, William. "On Their Own Terms: 'A Treacherous Paradise,' by Henning Mankell." *Sunday Book Review. New York Times.* 19 July 2013. Web. 2 February 2015. http://www.nytimes.com/2013/07/21/books/review/a-treacherous-paradise-by-henning-mankell.

Buckley, Julia. "Swedish Writer Åke Edwardson on Mystery, Melancholy, and Macbeth." *Mystery Musings,* April 2012. Web. 13 February 2014. http://juliabuckley.blogspot.com/2012/04.

Butki, Scott. "An Interview with Lars Kepler, Author of the *Hypnotist.*" *Seattle PI* 27 July 2011. Web. 13 March 2014. http://www.seattlepi.com/lifestyle.

Buus, Stephanie. "Hell on Earth: Threats, Citizens and the State from Buffy to Beck." *Cooperation and Conflict* 44 (2009): 400–419. Print.

"Camilla Ceder." Interview. Wahlstrom & Widstrand, 2009. Web. 12 February 2014. http://www.wwd.se/forfattere.

"Camilla Grebe and Åsa Träff—More Bitter than Death." *Crimepieces* 21 December 2013. Web. 13 February 2014. http://www.crimepieces/cp,/2013/12/21.

Clarke, Maxine. "Alphabet in Crime Fiction: Eriksson, Edwardson and Edwards." *Petrona,* 2 November 2009. Web. 13 February 2014. http://petrona.typepad.com/petrona/2009/11.

_____. "Book Review: Killer's Island by Anna Jansson." *Petrona* 2 August 2012. Web. 26 November 2012. http://petronatwo.wordpress.com.

_____. "Ceder, Camilla—"Frozen Moment." *EuroCrime* February 2011. Web. 13 February 2014. http://www.eurocrime.co.uk/reviews.

_____. "Crime Fiction Special on Kerstin Ekman." *Petrona* 7 May 2010. Web. 14 February 2014. http://petrona.typepad.com/petrona/2010/05.

_____. "Kjell Eriksson—'The Princess of Burundi.'" *EuroCrime* July 2007. Web. Htto://www.eurocrime.co.uk/reviews/The_Princess_of_Burundi.html.

_____. "Sinc25: Inger Frimansson, #6 Post of Expert Challenge." *Petrona* 10 January 2012. Web. 14 February 2014. http://petronatwo.wordpress.com/2012/01/10.

Cogdill, Oline H. "Sweden and WW II." *Publishers Weekly* 31 March 2014: 40. Print.

Cohen, Roger. "The (Not So) Neutrals of World War II." *New York Times* 26 January 1997). Web. 11 April 2014. http://www.nytimes.com/1997/01/26/week inreview.

Connolly, Paul. "Author Anders De La Motte: Facebook Is Fueled by Narcissism And Desperation." *Metro News* 27 November 2013. Web. 12 February 2014. http://metro.co.uk/2013/11/27.

Cooke, Rachel. "Stieg Larsson—By the Woman Who Shared His Life." *The Observer* 20 February 2010. Web. 10 March 2014. http://www.theguardian.com/books/2010/feb21.

Creates, Lars. "Interview with Michael Hjorth and Hans Rosenfeldt." *Krimi-Couch* 2012. Web. 24 January 2015. http://www.krimi-couch.de/krimis/interview-mit-michael-hjorth-und-hans-rosenfeldt.

Crouch, David. "The Rise of the Anti-Immigrant Sweden Democrats." *The Guardian* 14 December 2014. Web. 23 January 2015. http://www/theguardian.com/world/2014/dec/14.

Cummins, Caroline. "Northern Lights." [Review of *Detective Inspector Huss* by Helene Tursten.] *January Magazine* February 2003. Web. 31 March 2014. http://www.januarymagazine.com/crfiction/detinsphuss.html.

Danford, Natalie. "First Fiction 2013: Alexander Soderberg: Swedish Suspense." *Publishers Weekly* 1 February 2013. Web. 27 March 2014. http://www/publishersweekly.com/pw/by-topic/authors/profiles/article/55783.

Death, Sarah. "Review: Therese Bohman, *Den Drunknade* (Drowned)." *Swedish Book Review* 2011:1. Web. 3 March 2013. http://www.swedishbookreview.com/show-review.php?i=287.

Demko, G.J. "The Mystery in Sweden." N.d. Web. 10 February 2014. http://www.dartmouth.edu/~gjdemko/swedish/htm.

"Detective Focus: Ann-Christin Hensher." *Enannansida: En Bokdjavuls Liv Och Lustar.* 22 March 2006. Web. 10 March 2014. http://enannansidabok.blogspot.com.

Diaz, Antonio. "Interview with Swedish Writer Håkan Nesser." *Free! Magazine* 15 September 2012. Web. 21 March 2014. http://www.freemagazine.fi/interview-with-swedish-writer-Hakan-Nesser.

Dickson, Daniel, and Alistair Scrutton. "Swedes Tire of Tax Cuts as Welfare State Shows Strains." *Reuters* 17 March 2014. Web. 14 April 2014. http://www.reuters.com/article/2014/03/17.

Di Filippo, Paul. "*Yok, by* Tim Davys." *The Spectator* 17 September 2012. Web. 1 March 2014. http://bnreview.batnsandnobel.com.

DuChateau, Christian. "'The Hypnotist' Unleashes Terrifying Events." *CNN Living* 26 June 2011. Web. 13 March 2014. http://www.cnn.com/2011/LIVING/06/15/Lars.Kepler.interview.

Edblom, Kristina. "*Skräcken Finns Fortfarande Kvar.*" *Aftenbladet* 13 February 2013. Web. 25 February 2011. http://www.aftonbladet.se/nyheter/article4398864.ab.

Edwardson, Åke. *Room No. 10,* tr. Rachel Willson-Broyles. New York: Simon & Schuster, 2013. Print.

Einhorn, Eric S. and John Logue. *Modern Welfare States.* 2nd ed. Westport, CT: Praeger, 2003. Print.

Ekeroth, Daniel, Magnus Henriksson and Christine Lundberg. *Swedish Sensationsfilms: A Clandestine History of Sex, Thrillers, and Kicker Cinema.* Brooklyn, NY: Bazillion Points, 2011. Print.

Ekstam, Jane Mattisson. "The Other Side of Swedish Detective Fiction." *Mystery Readers Journal* 30 (Winter 2014–2015): 3–4. Print.

Ekstrom, Peter. "The Mystery of Mary Lang." *Kulturdelen* 26 February 2013. Web. 14 March 2014. http://www.kulturdelen.com.

Eriksson, Kjell. "Behind the Headlines, Behind the Dividing Lines." *Mystery Writers Journal* 23 (Fall 2007): 47–48. Print.

"Eriksson/Axlander-Sundquist." 2014. Web. 4 March 2014. http://:krakflickan.se/eas.html.

Erlingur, O. "Swedish Judge Slammed for Justifying Violence Against Women." *IceNews* 10 April 2012. Web. 16 April 2014. http://www.icenews.is/2012/04/10.

Fjellro, Ragnhild. "The Swedish Gender-Equal Man Is a Myth." *ScienceNordic* 10 September 2012. Web. 16 April 2014. http://sciencenordic.com.

Flood, Alison. "Johan Theorin Beats Stieg Larsson to Crime Writing Award." *The Guardian* 26 July 2010. Web. 30 March 2014. http://www.theguardian.com/books/2010/jul/26.

Fornaess, Jon Egil. "Elisabet [Sic] Peterzén: Author Sought Breadth by Writing Detective Fiction." [subtitle translated]. *DAST Magazine* 19 September 2009. Web. 23 March 2014. http://dastmagazine.com.

Forshaw, Barry. *Death in a Cold Climate.* New York: Palgrave Macmillan, 2012. Print.

_____. "She's Never Coming Back, by [sic] Hans Koppel." *The Independent* 10 January 2012. Web. 13 March 2014. http://www.independent.co.uk.

Foster, Jordan. "A Finn in a Strange Land." *Publishers Weekly* 21 May 2012: 35. Print.

_____. "The Perpetrator and the Victim." *Publishers Weekly* 3 January 2011: 31. Print.

France, Louise. "The Queen of Crime." *The Observer* 21 November 2009. Web. 29 March 2014. http://www.theguardian,.com/books/2009/nov/22.

"Fredrik T. Olsson." *Partners in Stories,* n.d. Web. 31 March 2015. http://partnersinstories.se/authors/fredrik-t-olsson.html.

Frimansson, Inger. "The Company I've Kept." *Mystery Writers Journal* 23 (Fall 2007)" 48–51. Print.

"The Full Interview with Ann Rosman." *Deckarhuset* [*CrimeHouse*] 11 May 2009. Web. 24 March 2014. http://www.deckarhuset.se.

"Furioso of Carin Bartosch Edstrom." Ad libris comments by Edstrom 2011. Web. 12 February 2014. http://www.adlibris.co.sebok/furioso.

Gabrielson, Eva. *There Are Things I Want You to Know.* New York: Seven Stories, 2011. Print.

Gellerfelt, Mats. "An Atmospheric Detective Debut." *SvD* 25 February 2014. Web. 14 March 2014. http://www.svd/kultur/litteratur.

Glansholm, Hanna Modigh. "Interview: Leif G.W. Persson Wants to Keep Developing as a Writer." *The Lit-*

erary Magazine 16 June 2012. Web. 23 March 2014. http://www.literarymagazine.com.leif-gw-persson/interview/five-questions.

_____. "Ninni Schulman Wants to Portray Exclusion in Rural Areas." *The Literary Magazine* 27 January 2012. Web. 27 March 2014. http://www.literarymagazine.com.

Golson, Eric B. "Did Swedish Ball Bearings Keep the Second World War Going? Re-Evaluating Neutral Sweden's Role." Paper delivered at various academic venues, including the Economic History Association, Evanston, IL, version 23 August 2011. Web. 12 April 2014 http://es.handels.gu.se/digitalAssets/1341/1341645_golson.pdf.

Greenland, Colin. "Digging Up the Peat." *The Guardian* 4 February 2005. Web. 16 March 2014. http://www.theguardian.com/books/2005/feb/05/features.

Gustafson, Alrik. *A History of Swedish Literature.* Minneapolis, MN: University of Minnesota Press, for the American-Scandinavian Foundation, 1961. Print.

Hachman, Mark. "Stieg Larsson Sells a Million Books on Amazon's Kindle." *PC Magazine* 28 July 2010. Web. 17 March 2014. http://www.pcmag.com.

Hagenguth, Alexandra. "Interview with the Author Åke Edwardson." *Literature Portal.* September 2006. Web. 23 March 2014. http://literatureportal.schwedenkrimi.de.

_____. "Interview with the Authors Karin Alvtegen and Maj Sjöwall." *Literature Portal*, May 2004. Web. 10 February 2014. http://literatureportal.schwedenkrimi.de.

Hall, Allan. "Revealed: How 'Neutral' Sweden Made Secret Loans to Nazi Germany During WW II." *Mail Online (The Daily Mail)* 16 February 2009. Web. 11 April 2014. http://www.dailymail.co.uk/news/article-1146462.

Hallberg, Sofia. "Sofia Interview: Varg Gyllander." 12 July 2012. Web. 10 March 2014. http://debutantbloggen.wordpress.com/2012/07/12.

Harper, Glenn. "Cold Swedish Noir: Leif G.W. Persson." *International Noir Fiction* 5 July 2010. Web. 14 February 2011. http://internationalnoir.blogspot.com/2-1-/07.

Harrell, Eben. "Behind Assange's Arrest: Sweden's Sex-Crime Problem." *Time* 16 December 2010. Web. 16 April 2014. http://content.time.com/time/world/article/0,8599,2037078,00.html.

Harvey, Lynn. "Review: Kallentoft, Mond—'Savage Spring.'" *EuroCrime* September 2013. Web. 13 March 2014. http://eurocrime.co.uk.

Hasham, Alyshah. "Mons Kallentoft on *Midwinter Blood.*" *The Star* 23 October 2012. Web. 17 January 2013. http://www.thestar.com/entertainment/books.

Hedstrom, Ingrid. "Let's Embrace Our Inner Lucia Bride." *DN.Se* 17 December 2012. Web. 10 March 2014. http://www.dn.se/nyheter/ingrid-hedstrom.

"Helena Von Zweigbergk." *Partners in Stories.* 2013. Web. 1 April 2014. http://partnersinstories.se/authors/helena-von-zweigbergk.html.

"Helene Tursten." *Scandinavian Crime Fiction.* Web. 31 March 2014. http://www.scandinaviancrimefiction.com/Helene_Tursten.htm.

Higgins, Andrew. "In Sweden, Riots Put an Identity in Question." *New York Times* 26 May 2013. Web. 15 April 2014. http://www/nytimes.com/2013/05/27/world/europe.

Higgins, Charlotte. "Sweden's Crime Writers Too Interested in Love, Says Maj Sjöwall." *The Guardian* 14 August 2013. Web. 29 March 2014. http://www.theguardian.com/books/2013/aug/14.

Hinde, Dominic. "Review: Leif G.W. Persson, *Den döende detektiven* [*The Dying Detective*]." *Swedish Book Review* 2011:1. Web. 23 March 2014. http://www.swedishbookreview.com/show-review.php?i=299.

Hindersmann, Jost. "Sweden's Queen of Crime: Liza Marklund's Novels." *Mystery Readers Journal* 23 (Fall 2007): 12–14. Print.

Holmberg, John-Henri, ed. and trans. *A Darker Side of Sweden.* New York: The Mysterious Press, 2014. Print.

Holt, Anne. "Anne Holt's Top 10 Female Detectives." *The Guardian* 8 December 2010. Web. 11 August 2013. http://www.theguardian.com/boks/2010/dec/08.

Hurford, Darcy. Review of Niklas Ekdal, *Kvinnan Utan Egenskaper* [*Woman Without Qualities*]. *Swedish Book Review* 2011. Web. 3 March 2014. http://www.swedishbookreview.com.

"In the Crime Fiction Shelf: K. Arne Blom." *Eriksson's Culture Pages.* 20 January 2013. Web. 21 February 2014. http://erikssonskultursidor.wordpress.com.

"An Interview with Anders Roslund and Börge Hellstrom." *Crimepieces* 22 May 2012. Web. 4 February 2015. http://www.fivebooks.com/interview/anders-roslund-and-n=borge-hellstrom.

"Interview with Hans-Olov Öberg." *CrimeHouse* 16 September 2011. Web. 20 March 2014. http://www.thecrimehouse.cominterview-with-hans-olov-oberg.

"Interview with Helene Tursten." *Das Erste* February 2012. Web. 31 March 2014. http://www.daserste.de/unterhaltung/film.

"Interview with Johan Theorin." *CrimeHouse* 17 June 2010. Web. 31 March 2014. http://www.thecrimehouse.com/interview-with-johan-theorin.

"Interview with Jonas Moström" *CrimeHouse* 25 October 2010. Web. 3 February 2015. http://www/thecrimehouse.com/interview-with-jonas-mostrom.

"Interview with Lars Bill Lundholm." *CrimeHouse* 5 April 2010. Web. 1 February 2015. http://wwwthecrimehouse.com/interview-with-lars-bill-lundholm.

"Interview with Stefan Tegenfalk." *CrimeHouse* 16 January 2012. Web. 26 November 2012. http://www.thecrimehouse.com/interview-with-stefan-tegenfalk.

"Interview with the Swedish Crime Novelist Arne Dahl." *Mystery Tribune*, 16 February 2012. Web. 12 February 2014. http://www.mysterytribune.com/2012/02/16.

"Interview with Ulla Trenter." *Deckarhuset* 9 November

2009. Web. 8 February 2015. http://www.deckar huset.se/intervju-med-ulla-trenter.

"Interview with Veronica Von Schenck." *CrimeHouse* 26 November 2010. Web. 1 April 2014. http://www.thecrimehouse.com.

Jack, Malcolm. "Arne Dahl Interview." *The Big Issue* 25 September 2013. Web. 12 February 2014. http://www.bigissue.com/features/interviews/3047/arne-dahl-interview.

Jarzebinski, Krzysztof. "Interview: Aris Fioretos." *Foreigner* 2010. Web. 14 February 2014. http://www.foreigner.de/interviews.

Johansson, Anne. *"Deckarna Föds På Boardwalks"* [Interview with Helene Tursten]. *Göteborgs-Posten* 19 September 1999:52. Print.

Johansson, Christer B. "Tord Hubert: Why Was This Fantastic Writer Suddenly So Coy?" *DAST Magazine* 15 September 2009. Web. 10 March 2014. http://www.dast.nu/artikel.

JTA [author identified only by initials]. "Kippa-Wearing Swedish Reporter Assaulted in Malmø." *The Times of Israel* 24 January 2015. Web. 17 February 2015, http://www.timesofisrael.com/ kippa-wearing...

Kachka, Boris. ""No. 1 with an Umlaut." *New York Magazine* 8 May 2011. Web. 29 October 2011. http://www.nymag.com/arts/books/features.

"Karin Wahlberg." [Autobiographical statement]. Wahlström & Widstrand Agency. 2013. Web. http:www.wahlstromandwidstrand.se.

Kellogg, Amy. "Sweden's Immigration Debate." *Fox News* 28 October 2011. Web. 15 April 2014. http://www.foxnews,com/world/2011/10/28.

Kendall, Ben. "Neo-Nazi Groups More Active in Sweden." *Göteborg Daily* 19 March 2014. Web. 11 April 2014. http://www.goteborgdaily.se/news.

Keveney, Bill. "'Wallander' Returns to Complex Life on PBS." *USA Today* 30 September 2010: Life 08b. Print.

"Kjell Eriksson." Leonhardt & Høier LiteraryAgency. 2014. Web. 13 February 2014. http://www.leonhardt-hoier.dk/authors/4.

Klein, Yvonne. Review of *Drowned* by Therese Bohman. *Reviewing the Evidence* May 2012. Web. 12 February 2012. http://www.reviewingtheevidence/review.

Koblik, Steven. *Sweden's Development from Poverty to Affluence 1750–1970.* Minneapolis, MN: University of Minnesota Press, 1975. Print.

Kreü, Emma. "Five Questions" and "Writer Portrait: Leif G.W. Persson." *The Literary Magazine* 18 October 2013. Web. 4 February 2015. http://www.theliterary magazine.se.

"Kristina Appelqvist." *Alfabeta Bokförlag* 5 December 2013. Web. 25 February 2014. http://www.piratfor laget.se.

Krugly, Emelie. "Liza Marklund—an Unstoppable Force in Swedish Crime Fiction." *Scan Magazine* November 2011. Web. 16 March 2014. http://www.scanmaga zine.co.uk/2010.11.

Kümmel, Peter. "The Sixth Night: Annika Bryn." *Krimi-*

Couch, 2003. Web. 27 February 2014. http://www.krimi-couch.ed.

Kurth, Andreas. "Interview with Arne Dahl." *Krimi-Couch*, April 2013. Web. 12 February 2014. http://www.krimi-couch.de/kromis.

Landes, David. *The Local* 13 April 2012. Web. 5 November 2012. http://www.thelocal.se.

Landstrom, Ingrid. "Mini-Profile: Swedish Crime Author Tove Alsterdal." 11 May 2010. Web. 20 February 2014. http://www.ilandstrom.com.

"Laura Trenter—Interview." *Barnens Bibliotek* 2010. Web. 20 March 2014. http://www.barnensbibliotek.se.

Lawson, B.V. "Nature and the Writings of Kerstin Lillemor Ekman." *Mystery Readers Journal* 30 (Winter 2014–2015): 13–14. Print.

Leavy, Barbara Fass. "Some Thoughts on Depressed Northern Detectives." *Mystery Readers Journal* 30 (Winter 2014–2015): 15–16. Print.

Levin, Angela. "Jonas Jonasson: My 100-Year-Old Hero, and the Secret of Happiness." *The Telegraph* 9 July 2009. Web. 15 March 2015. http://www.telegraph.co.uk/lifestyle/9386562/jonas-Jonasson...

Liukkonen, Petri. "Maj Sjöwall (1935-)." *Kuusankosken Kaupunginkirjasto* 2008. Web. 29 March 2014. http://www.kirjasto.sci.fi/sjowall.htm.

_____. "Per Wahlöö (1926–1975)." *Kuusankosken Kaupunginkirjasto* 2008. Web. 29 March 2014. http://www.kirjasto.sci.fi/wahloo.htm.

Long, Kirstie. "Mons Kallentoft Interview." *Shots* 2011. Web. 17 January 2013. http://www.shotsmag.co.uk

Lundberg, Stefan. *"Tove—domaren som skriver deckare."* *Ordförrådet Reportage* April 2008. Web. 13 March 2014. http: www.ord-forradet.se/page20.html.

Lundholm, Lars Bill. "A Long Road from Poetry to Mystery Writing." *Mystery Readers Journal* 23 (Fall 2007): 56–57. Print.

MacDougall, Ian. "The Man Who Blew Up the Welfare State." *N Plus One Magazine* 27 February 2010. Web. 7 February 2013. http://nplusonemag.com/man-who-blew-up-welfare-state.

Magnusson, Niklas and Jakob Lindstoem. "Swedish Small-Town Crime Hits Big Screen as Larsson Mania Grows." *Bloomberg News* 26 February 2009. Web. 23 March 2014. http://www.bloomberg.com/apps/news.

Malmaeus, Marc. "Hårdhudad [Tough] Globetrotter." *Lokaltidningen* 6 October 2013. Web. 20 March 2014. http://www.arkiv.mitti.se"4711/2012/2/22.

Mankell, Henning. *An Event in Autumn.* New York: Vintage Books, 2014. Print.

"Mari Jungstedt." *Partners in Stories.* Web. 12 March 2014. http://partnersinstories.se/authors.

Martelli, Sophia. "The Girl Who Saved the King of Sweden [,] Review." *The Guardian* 4 May 2014. Web. 15 March 2015. http://www.theguardian.com/books/2014/may/04/the girl...

Mason, H.Z. "Women Detectives in Recent Scandinavian Police Procedurals." *Mystery Readers Journal* 30 (Winter 2014–2015): 16–18. Print.

Matthews, Antonia. "Riots Erupt in Sweden: The Nordic Welfare Myth?" *CNBC* 22 May 2013. Web. 14 April 2014. http://www.cnbc.com/id/100757907.

Maxted, Anna. "Sorry Maj Sjöwall, the Best Crime Is One of Passion." *The Telegraph* 15 August 2013. Web. 12 August 2013. http://www.telegraph.co.uk/culture/books/10245102.

McClintock, Pamela. "Luke Evans Signs Up for 'Three Seconds.'" *The Hollywood Reporter* 4 February 2015. Web. 5 February 2015. http://www.hollywoodreporter.com.

McCoubrey, Joe. "Getting to Know New Swedish Author Alexander Soderberg." 16 May 2013. Web. 27 March 2014. http://www.writing.ie/interviews.

McGrath, Charles. "The Afterlife of Stieg Larsson." *New York Times Magazine* 23 May 2010. Web. 7 November 2012. http://nytimes.com/2010/05/23/magazine.

McLaughlin, Liam. "The Swedish Riots: What Really Happened?" *New Statesman* 14 June 2013. Web. 15 April 2014. http://www.newstatesman.com/economics/2013/06.

Megraw, Jeremy. "A Cold Night's Death: The Allure of Scandinavian Crime Fiction." A Presentation by the New York Public Library 14 January 2013. Web. 10 February 2014. http://www.nypl.oprg/blog/2013/02/14/scandinavian-crime-fiction.

Mezzofiore, Gianluce. "Europe's Dark Core: The Neo-Nazi Movements on the March." *Ibtimes* 9 January 2014. Web. 11 April 2014. http://www.ibtimes.co.uk.

"Modern Swedish Literature." *Sweden.Se* 2014. Web. 24 January 2015. https://sweden.se/culture-traditions/modern-swedish-literature.

"More for Less." *The Economist* 2 February 2013. Web. 14 April 2014. http://www.economist.com/news/special-report/21570831.

Moss, Stephen. "Henning Mankell: 'I Shall Not Miss Wallander.'" *The Guardian* 15 July 2013 Web. 2 February 2015. http://theguardian.com/books.2013.jul/15/henning-mankell-not-miss-wallander.

Moynihan, Michael. "Neo-Nazis Pour into Kiev." *The Daily Beast* 28 February 2014. Web. 11 April 2014. http://www.thedailybeast.com/articles/2014/04/11.

Müller, Kim. "RIP—Lasse Strömstedt and Kennet Ahl." 6 July 2009. Web. 23 February 2014. http://kimmuller.wordpress.com.

"Murder She Writes." Embassy of Sweden. 2014. Web. 31 January 2015. http://www.visitsweden.com.

Murphy, Bruce F. *The Encyclopedia of Murder and Mystery.* New York: St. Martin's Press/ 1999. Print.

"The Muslim Issue: The Living Hell for Swedish Women." 20 August 2012. Web. 16 April 2014. http://themuslimissue.wordpress.com/2012/08/20.

Nair, Roshni. "Partners in Crime." *Daily News and Analysis* [Mumbai, India] 18 January 2015. Web. 18 January 2015. http://www.dnindia.com/lifestyle/books-and-more-partners-in-crime-2053358.

Nesser, Håkan. "Portrait of the Artist as an Old Dog (Country Not Inportant)." *Mystery Readers Journal* 23 (Fall 2007): 57–58.

Nestingen, Andrew and Paula Arvas. *Scandinavan Crime Fiction.* Cardiff, Wales; University of Wales Press, 2011. Print.

"Ninni Schulman: Do Not Touch My Little Body." *Expressen* 21 March 2009. Web. 6 February 2015. http://www.expressen.se.

Nordstrom, Byron J. *Scandinavia Since 1500.* Minneapolis: University of Minnesota Press, 2000. Print.

Nordström, Ruth. "Why Sweden Leads the Way in Tackling Human Trafficking and the Sex Trade." *Human Rights Europe.* February 2014. Web. 19 April 2014. http://www.humanrightseurope.org/2014/02.

Norén, Johan. "Doyen of Swedish Crime Writers." *Foreningen I Kriminalförfattere.* 17 September 2009. Web. 5 March 2014. http://www.keg.se/tg.html.

"NTN: Anders De La Motte Interviewed." *Crime Fiction Lover* 28 November 2013. Web. 12 February 2014. http://www.crimefictionlover.com/2013/11.

Ohlsson, Kristina. *Unwanted.* New York: Atria, 2009. Print.

"Olof Palme and Swedish Crime Fiction." *Nordic Noir* 17 April 2010. Web. 10 February 2014. http://nordicnoir.wordpress.com/2010/04/17/olof-palme.

O'Loughlin, Vanessa. "Liza Marklund: Exposed." *Writing Magazine* 10 August 2011. Web. 19 March 2014. http://www.writing.ie/special-guests/liza-marklund-exposed.

Olsson, Lotta."Kristian Lundberg['s] "Cruelty City." *DN.BOK* 22 September 2007. Web. 1 February 2015. http://www.dn.se/dnbokrecenssioner/kristian-lundberg-gryndelens-stad.

Ott, Bill. "Wallander's Last Stand." *American Libraries* 42 (March-April 2011): 57. Print.

O'Yeah, Zac. "The Hans Koppel Mystery." *The Hindustan Times:* Leisure. 20 September 2012. Web. 13 March 2014. http://www.livemint.com/Leisure.

"Page Turners You'll Tear Through." *Oprah* May 2012, Web. 12 February 2014. http://www.oprah.com/book/drowned.

Paterson, Anna. "Bringing the Criminal to Justice." *Swedish Book Review* 2010:1. Web. 3 March 2014. http://www.swedishbookreview.com/article-2010-1-paterson.php.

Peed, Mike. "Murder Most Global." *New York Times Book Review* 28 February 2010: 32. Print.

Pew Research Center. "Region: Europe. the Pew Research Center's Religion & Public Life Project." 27 January 2011. Web. 7 March 2015. http://www.pewforum.org/2011/01/27/future-of-the-global-muslim-population.

Picker, Lenny. "Death Is the Thing with Feathers: PW Talks with Anna Jansson." *Publishers Weekly* 6 September 2013. Web. 11 March 2014. http://www.publishersweekly.com.

Polito, Robert. "Murder, My Swede: Henning Mankell's Scandinavian Noir." *Artforum International* 43 (April 2005): S36. Print.

Power, Andreas. "Malin's Struggle to Be a Lawyer and Mother." *DN.Livsstil* 23 April 2009. Web. 10 March 2014. http://www.dnlivstil.se.

Pred, Allan. *Even in Sweden: Racisms, Racialized Spaces, and the Popular Geographical Imagination.* Berkeley, CA: University of California Press, 2000. Print.

"Presentation Av Ulf Durling På Foreningen Kriminalforfattare." N.d. Web. 27 February 2014. http://www.keg.se/fkis/ud.html.

Purcell, John. "Åsa Larsson: Ten Terrifying Questions." *Booktopia* 28 August 2012. Web. 15 March 2014. http://blog.booktopia.com.au/2012/08/28.

Reiss, Sabine. "Motive Unknown: Annika Bryn." *Krimi-Couch*, 2005. Web. 27 February 2014. http://www.krimi-couch.de.

Review: "Kristina Ohlsson—The Disappeared." *Crimepieces* 19 January 2014. Web. 22 March 2014. http://crimepieces.com/2014/01/19.

Review: "Leif G.W. Persson—Linda, as in the Linda Murder." *Crimepieces* 5 March 2013. Web. 23 March 2014. http://www.crimepieces.com/2013/03/05.

Review of *The Black Path* by Åsa Larsson. *Kirkus Reviews* 23 June 2008. Web. 13 March 2014. http://www.kirkusreviews.com.

Review of *Deadly Reunion* by Jan Ekstrom. *Kirkus Reviews* 1 December 1982. Web. 3 March 2014. http://www.kirkusreviews.com.

Review of *Never Coming Back."* *Publishers Weekly* 22 October 2012: 41. Print.

Review of *Midwinter Blood.* *Publishers Weekly* 23 April 2013: 54. Print.

Review of *Silenced* by Kristina Ohlsson. *Scandinavian Crime Fiction.* March 2013. Web. 20 March 2014. http://scandinaviancrimefiction.wordpress.com/tag/kristina-ohlsson.

Review of *Spring Tide* by Cilla and Rolf Börjlund. *Publishers Weekly* 28 July 2014: 64. Print.

Review of *Summer Death.* *Publishers Weekly* 22 April 2013: 30. Print.

Review of *Sun Storm.* *Kirkus Reviews* 15 March 2006: 256. Print.

Review of *The Black Path* by Åsa Larsson. *Publishers Weekly* 23 June 2008: 48. Print.

Review of *The Demon of Dakar.* *Boston Bibliophile,* 1 August 2008. Web. 11 February 2011. http://www.bostonbibliophile.com.

Review of *The Devil's Sanctuary.* *Publishers Weekly* 15 August 2013: 51. Print.

Robinson, Uriah. "Håkan Nesser Interviewed by Ann Cleeves." *Crime Scraps* 26 May 2009 [material from a 2008 interview]. Web. 21 March 2014.

Rozovsky, Peter. "Crimefest Blogfest III; Interview with Håkan Nesser." *Detectives Beyond Borders* 6 May 2009 [material from a 2008 interview]. Web. 21 March 2014. http://detectivesbeyondborders.blogspot.com/2008/06.

_____. "An Evening with Inger Frimansson, Kjell Eriksson, Håkan Nesser and Helene Tursten, Part I." *Detectives Beyond Borders* 25 April 2007. Web. 14 February 2014. http://detectivesbeyondborders.blogspot.com/2007/04.

Rudolph, Janet. "Swedish Crime Queen: Carin Gerhard-

sen." *Mystery Fanfare* 5 June 2012. Web. 6 March 2014. http://mysteryreadersinc.blogspot.com/2012/06.

Ryan, Pat. "Pippi Longstocking, with Dragon Tattoo." *New York Times* 22 May 2010. Web. 24 August 2010. http://www.nytimes.com/2010/05/23/weekinreview/23ryan.html.

Rystad, Johan G. "Bjorn Hellberg: I Have Given the Name to Both a Street and a Praline." 12 May 2012. Web. 10 March 2014. http://www.journal.se.

Sawyer, Birgit, and Peter Sawyer. *Medieval Scandinavia: From Conversion to Reformation, Circa 800–1500.* Minneapolis, MN: University of Minnsota Press, 1993. Print.

Sayers, Dorothy L. "Review," *Sunday Times* 9 September 1934: 8. Print.

Schultz, Connie. "Three Cheers for Pippi!" *Parade* 24 February 2013: 12. Print.

Semmel, J.E. "Interview: Åke Edwardson, Author of the *Shadow Woman.*" 1 November 2010. Web. 13 February 2014. http://artandliterature.cordpress.co,/2010/11/01.

"Senaste Om Kristina Appelqvist." 5 December 2013. Web. 25 February 2014. http://www.piratforlaget.se.

Sexton, David. "A Poignant Farewell to One of the Greatest of Detectives." *Evening Standard* 17 March 2011: 36. Print.

Scherman, Nisse. "Kautokeino, a Bloody Knife." *DAST Magazine* 29 September 2012. Web. 23 March 2014. http://www.dastmagazine.com.

Scobbie, Irene. "Torsten Pettersson, *Ge Mig Dina Ögon* (Give Me Your Eyes) [Sic]. *Swedish Book Review* 2011:1. Web. 23 March 2014. http://www.swedishbookreview.com.

Shubert, Atika. "The Battle Against Sex Trafficking: Sweden Vs. Denmark." *CNN Freedom Project* 30 March 2011. Web. 19 April 2014. http://thecnnfreedomproject/blogs.cnn.com/2011/03/30.

Sjöblom, Johan. "The Author Ninni Schulman: 'It Happens More in Small Towns Than Many People Think.'" *Land* 2012. Web. 6 February 2015. http://www.tidningenland.se.

Sjöwall, Maj, and Per Wahlöö. "*Kriminalromanen Som Samhällsskildring* (1967), Norstedts Press Release Reprinted in *Brottslig Blandning* (Stockholm: Svenska Deckarakademin, 1978). Print. Quoted in Nestingen and Arvas 22, 32*n*5.

"Skandinaviens Juden Fühlen Sich Nicht Mehr Sicher" ("Scandinavian Jews No Longer Feel Secure"). Web. 15 April 2014. http://www.diepresse.come/home/politik/aissenpolitik/546769.

Smalley, Nichola. Review: Michael Mortimer, *Jungfrustenen* [*The Maidenstone*]. *Swedish Book Review* 2013. Web. 16 March 2014. http://www.swedishbookreview.com.

Somers, Maartje. "The Problem with Swedish Integration." *NRC Handelsblad Amsterdam* 12 August 2013. Web. 15 April 2014. http://www.presseurop.eu/en/content/article/4049791.

"Summer…. Gotland Is Not Enough for a Novel." *SvD*

Kultur, 5 February 2009. Web. 27 February 2014. http://www. SvD.se/kultur/litteratur.

Stasio, Marilyn. "Bodies for Hire." *New York Times Book Review* 10 March 2013: 28. Print.

_____. "Cold Cases." *New York Times Sunday Book Review* 17 September 2010. Web. 14 February 2011. http://www.nytimes.com/2010/09/19/books/review/Crime-t.html.

_____. "Mankell's Endgame." *New York Times Book Review* 27 March 2011: 23. Print.

_____. "Offbeat Cops." *New York Times Book Review,* 25 June 2006: 26. Print.

_____. "Tell No One." *New York Times Book Review,* 18 May 2014: 25.

Stenport, Anna Westerstähl, and Cecilia Ovesdotter Alm. "Corporations, Crime, and Gender Construction in Stieg Larsson's the *Girl with the Dragon Tattoo.*" *Scandinavian Studies* 81 (Summer 2009): 147–178. Print.

"Stepping Out of Line by Denise Rudberg." *CrimeHouse* 14 December 2010. Web. 25 March 2014. http://www.thecrimehouse.com.

Strainchamps, Bernard. "Interview of Kjell Eriksson." *Feedbooks* 17 September 2012. Web. 13 February 2014. http://www.feedbooks.com/interview/113.

Suit, Verna. "Swedish Mysteries Give Clues to the Old Country." *Mystery Readers Journal* 23 (Fall 2007): 38–40. Print.

Svedelid, Olov. "Uno Palmström Is Dead." *DAST Magazine* 12 September 2009.Web. 23 March 24, 2014. Web. 23 March 2014. http://www.dastmagazine.com.

Svensson, Kristina. "Advertiser Bondesongatan." 29 December 2012. Web. 26 February 2014. http://www.kristinasvensson.se.

"Sweden Drug Abuse." *Narconon International* 2008. Web. 16 April 2014. http://www.narconon.org/drug-information/Sweden-drug-abuse.html.

"Swedish Kids Invited to Neo-Nazi Summer Camp." *The Local, Sweden,* 14 June 2011. Web. 11 April 2014. http://www.culteducation.com/group/1071-neo-nazis/14958.

"Swedish Mafia: Fighting a Losing Battle." *The Local* 8 November 2007. Web. 16 April 2014. http://www.thelocal.se/200711108/9046.

Tell, Per Erik. "Interview with Jean Bolinder." 11 September 2009. Web. 20 February 2014.

Thente, Jonas. "Wallentin: 'Strindberg's Star.'" *DN.BOK* 1 April 2014. Web. 8 April 2014. http://www.dn.se.

Thompson, Robert. "*Amberville* by Tim Davys." *Fantasy Book Critic* 25 February 2009. Web. 1 March 2014. http://fantasybookcritic.blogspot.com/200902.

Thomson, Ian. "True Crime" Interview with Henning Mankell. *The Guardian* 1 November 2003. Print.

Tomaszewski, Tom. "The Streets of Babylon, by Carina Burman, Tr. Sarah Death." *The Independent* 35 February 2014. Web. 25 February 2014. http://www.independence.co.uk/arts-entertainment/books/reviews.

Tomlinson, Simon. "Extreme Security Measures Used to Keep Details of Forthcoming Girl With the Dragon Tattoo Sequel Secret Are Revealed." *The Daily Mail* 1 April 2015. Web. 1 April 2015. http://www.dailymail.co.uk/news/article-3020989/Extreme…

Traynor, Ian. "Sweden Joins Europe-Wide Backlash Against Immigration." *The Guardian* 24 September 2010. Web. 15 April 2014. http://www.theguardian.com/world/2010/sep/24.

"*Tre Vänner.*" Web. 14 March 2014. http://www/evri.com/media.

Tursten, Helene. "A Crime Writer—In Spite of Everything." *Mystery Readers Journal* 23 (Fall 2007): 66–67. Print.

_____. "My New Project." *Mystery Readers Journal* 30 (Winter 2014–2015): 40–41). Print.

"Ulla Trenter." *Deckarhuset* [*CrimeHouse Scandinavia*] 9 November 2009. Web. 30 March 2014. http://www.deckarhuset.so.

"*Vad För Slags Bok Är "Gömda?"*["What Kind of Book Is "Gömda"?]. *Sydsvenskan* 17 January 2009. Web. 25 February 2011. http://sydsvenskan.se/kultur/article406479.

"*Vi Blev Tvångs-Kommenderade Att Bli Amerikaner.*" *Aftonbladet* 6 March 2006. Web. 7 February 2013. http://www.aftonbladet.se/vss/nyheter/story.

Warme, Lars G., ed. *A History of Swedish Literature.* Lincoln, Nebraska: University of Nebraska Press, 1996. Print.

"A Waxing Crescent." *The Economist* 20 January 2011. Web. 13 April 2014. http://www.economist.com/node/18008022.

Wegener, Brenda. "Camilla Läckberg." Interview, *The Center for Fiction, 2009.* Web. 14 March 2014. http://centerforfiction.org.

Weinman, Sarah. "Before Stieg Larsson, There Was Maj Sjöwall & Per Wahlöö." *Confessions Of an Idiosyncratic Mind* 27 July 2010. Web. 29 March 2014. http://www.sarahweinman.com/confessions/2010/07.

Wente, Margaret. "Sweden's Immigration Consensus Is in Peril." *The Globe and Mail* 1 June 2013. Web. 15 April 2014. http://www.theglobeandmail.com/globe/debate.

West, Charlotte. "A Bookworm's Tour of Murder and Mayhem." *Mystery Readers Journal* 23 (Fall 2007): 31–33. Print.

Wilson, Laura. "The Best Recent Crime Novels—Review Roundup." *The Guardian* 12 February 2015. Web. 12 February 2015. http://www.theguardian.com/books/2015/feb/12/best-crime-recent-fiction-novels.

Witt-Brattström, Ebba. "Edqvist, Dagmar." *The History of Nordic Women's Literature.* Gothenburg: Kvinbo, 2012. Web. 12 February 2014. http://nordicwomens literature.net/writer/edqvist-dagmar.

Wright, Rochelle. "Kerstin Ekman." *Dictionary of Literary Biography* 257: 66–81. Detroit, MI: Gale Publishing, 2003. Print.

Wopenka, John. "Kjell-Olof Bornemark." [Obituary]. 9 November 2006. Web. 20 February 2014. http://deckarajademin.org.

Yerkey, Gary G. "Karin Alfredsson Travels the World to Help Stop Violence Against Women." *The Christian Science Monitor* 19 September 2011. Print.

"Your Favorite Thrillers by Åke Edwardson." *Krimi-Couch* 2013. Web. 13 February 2014. http://www.krimicouch.de/krimis/ake_edwardson.

Zerengue, Marshal. "Author Interviews: Karin Alvtegen." 25 March 2009. Web. 10 February 2014. http://writerinterviews.blogspot.com/2009/03/karin-alvtegen.html.

INDEX